2009 PASSPORT® to

25th Edition

TABLE OF CONTENTS

Global Focus

6 **World of World Band Radio**
Map pinpoints stations, time zones.

10 **Colombia: Bandits, Ballads and Broadcasts**
Radio serves many masters.

Getting Started

30 **Quick Start**
Four pages and you're ready.

32 **Quicker Start**
PASSPORT's three-minute kickoff.

34 **World Time: Setting Your Clock**
Global time avoids confusion.

36 **Best Times and Frequencies for 2009**
Where to tune, night or day.

40 **Ten of the Best: 2009's Top Shows**
Curious Orange to Zap Mama.

89 **Getting Past Airport Security**
Avoid the Dreaded Search.

346 **Worldly Words**
World band's ultimate glossary.

What to Choose: PASSPORT REPORTS—2009

54 **How to Choose a World Band Radio**
What to check for. What to avoid.

58 **Portables for Home and Away**
Workhorses of world band.

83 **Handheld Scanner**
High price, poor value.

102 **Recordable Portables**
Time shifting uses docked MP3 module.

105 **World Band on the Road**
Three Sony car stereos. No satellite fees.

106 **PASSPORT to Preparedness®**
Stay informed when life goes awry.

168

58

World Band Radio

TABLE OF CONTENTS

116 **Tabletop Receivers**
British legend gears up for change.

129 **Build Your Own**
Radio solders on.

130 **Professional Receivers**
Best buy from Dolly Parton's hometown.

142 **PC Receivers**
New Italian model wows.

161 **Index to Tested Radios**
A–Z by make and model.

66 **Hillbilly Skyhooks**
Better reception on the cheap.

162 **Wire Antennas**
Aerials do much, cost little.

168 **Active Antennas**
Indoors, outdoors or on the road.

183 **Compact Antenna**
Pole needs no juice.

192 **Index to Tested Antennas**
Wires, loops and telescopes.

40

10

When and Where: WorldScan®

194 **HOUR-BY-HOUR**
What's On Tonight?
Hundreds of shows in English. Daytime, too.

310 **COUNTRY-BY-COUNTRY**
Worldwide Broadcasts in English
Albania to Yemen.

328 **Voices from Home**
News and sports for expats. Music for all.

360 **CHANNEL-BY-CHANNEL**
The Blue Pages
Quick access to world band schedules.

Making Contact

246 **Addresses PLUS**
Webcasts, email, post, phone, fax, local time, who's who, souvenirs.

International Broadcasting Services, Ltd.

ISSN 0897-0157

OUR READER IS THE MOST IMPORTANT PERSON IN THE WORLD!

Editorial

Editor in Chief	Lawrence Magne
Editor	Tony Jones
Assistant Editor	Craig Tyson
Consulting Editor	John Campbell
Founder Emeritus	Don Jensen
Passport Reports	Lawrence Magne, Dave Zantow; along with George Heidelman, George Zeller
WorldScan® Contributors	David Crystal (Israel), Graeme Dixon (New Zealand), Nicolás Eramo (Argentina), Paulo Roberto e Souza (Brazil), Alokesh Gupta (India), Jose Jacob (India), Anatoly Klepov (Russia), Célio Romais (Brazil), David Walcutt (U.S.)
WorldScan® Software	Richard Mayell
Laboratory	J. Robert Sherwood
Artwork	Gahan Wilson, cover
Graphic Arts	Bad Cat Design; Mike Wright, layout
Printing	Transcontinental Printing

Administration

Publisher	Lawrence Magne
Associate Publisher	Jane Brinker
Offices	IBS North America, Box 300, Penn's Park PA 18943, USA; www.passband.com; Phone +1 (215) 598-9018; Fax +1 (215) 598 3794; mktg@passband.com
Advertising & Media Contact	Jock Elliott, IBS Ltd., Box 300, Penn's Park PA 18943, USA; Phone +1 (215) 598-9018; Fax +1 (215) 598 3794; mktg@passband.com

Bureaus

IBS Latin America	Tony Jones, Casilla 1844, Asunción, Paraguay
IBS Australia	Craig Tyson, Box 2145, Malaga WA 6062; mktg@passband.com
IBS Japan	Toshimichi Ohtake, 5-31-6 Tamanawa, Kamakura 247-0071; Fax +81 (467) 43 2167; ibsjapan@passband.com

Library of Congress Cataloging-in-Publication Data

Passport to World Band Radio.
1. Radio Stations, Shortwave—Directories. I. Magne, Lawrence
TK9956.P27 2008 384.54'5 08-22739
ISBN 978-0-914941-80-4

Opener photo credits: H. Klemetz (p. 10)

Printed in Canada

–1
0 WORLD TIME (UTC)
+1
+2
+3
+4
+5
+6
+7
+8
+9
+
Monchegorsk, Russia
Virrat, Finland
Riga, Latvia
Sitkunai, Lithuania
Kaliningrad, Russia
Hörby, Sweden
Arkhangel'sk, Russia
St. Petersburg, Russia
Yakutsk, Russia
Magadan, Russia
Berlin, Germany
Nauen, Germany
Skelton, England
Minsk, Belarus
Moscow, Russia
Krasnoyarsk, Russia
Novosibirsk, Russia
Irkutsk, Russia
Selenginsk, Russia
Chita, Russia
Komsomol'sk-na-Amure, Russia
Khabarovsk, Russia
Hailar, China
Jülich, Germany
Rampisham, England
Wavre, Belgium
Litomyšl, Czech Republic
Issoudun, France
Wertachtal, Germany
Moosbrunn, Austria
Jászberény, Hungary
Andrate, Italy
Deanovec, Croatia
Lisbon, Portugal
Noblejas, Spain
Nador, Morocco
Rimavská Sobota, Slovakia
Samara, Russia
Lviv, Ukraine
Kharkiv, Ukraine
Bucharest, Romania
Grigoriopol, Moldova
Mykolayiv, Ukraine
Armavir/Krasnodar, Russia
Sofia, Bulgaria
Cerrik/Shijak, Albania
Vatican City
Yerevan, Armenia
Ankara, Turkey
Baku, Azerbaijan
Ashgabat, Turkmenistan
Mashhad, Iran
Tehran, Iran
Athens, Greece
Cyprus
Amman, Jordan
Tel Aviv, Israel
Sfax, Tunisia
Ulaanbaatar, Mongolia
Almaty, Kazakstan
Urumqi, China
Sapporo, Japan
Vladivostok, Russia
Bishkek, Kyrgyzstan
Hohhot, China
Beijing, China
Kashi, China
Shijiazhuang, China
Pyongyang, North Kore
Dushanbe, Tajikistan
Lingshi, China
Tokyo, Japan
Geermu, China
Leh, Kashmir, India
Xi'an, China
Kabul, Afghanistan
Islamabad, Pakistan
Quetta, Pakistan
New Delhi, India
Lhasa, Tibet, China
Nanjing, China
Seoul, South Korea
Shanghai, China
Jinhua, China
Cairo, Egypt
Kuwait
Riyadh, Saudi Arabia
Kathmandu, Nepal
Thimpu, Bhutan
Karachi, Pakistan
Kunming, China
Fuzhou, China
Jiddah, Saudi Arabia
Dhabayya, UAE
Dhaka, Bangladesh
Nanning, China
Taipei, Taiwan
Asmara, Eritrea
Sib, Oman
Kolkata (Calcutta), India
Hanoi, Vietnam
Paochung, Taiwan
Nouakchott, Mauritania
Omdurman, Sudan
A'Seela, Oman
Vientiane, Laos
Ouagadougou, Burkina Faso
Jeypore, India
Thamarit, Oman
Udon Thani, Thailand
Saipan, Northern Mariana Islands
Niamey, Niger
N'Djamena, Chad
Mumbai (Bombay), India
Yangon, Myanmar
Palauig, Philippines
Panaji, Goa, India
Bangkok, Thailand
Manila, Philippines
Kaduna, Nigeria
San'a, Yemen
Hyderabad, India
Chennai (Madras), India
Tinian, Northern Mariana Islands
Bamako, Mali
Abuja, Nigeria
Guam
Conakry, Guinea
Addis Ababa, Ethiopia
Port Blair, Andaman Islands
Bangui, Central African Republic
Bengaluru (Bangalore), India
Palau
Monrovia, Liberia
Iranawila, Sri Lanka
Trincomalee, Sri Lanka
Rabaul, Papua New Guinea
Parakou, Benin
Colombo, Sri Lanka
Wewak, Papua New Guinea
Accra, Ghana
Buea, Cameroon
Narus, Sudan
Kuala Lumpur, Malaysia
Vanimo, Papua New Guinea
Ikorodu, Nigeria
Libreville, Gabon
Bunia, Congo (Dem Rep)
Singapore
Samarinda, Indonesia
Enugu, Nigeria
Kampala, Uganda
Padang, Indonesia
Biak, Indonesia
Kuching, Malaysia
Makassar, Indonesia
Ascension
Seychelles
Jakarta, Indonesia
Madang, Papua New Guinea
Brazzaville, Congo (Rep)
São Tomé e Príncipe
Kigali, Rwanda
Mendi, Papua New Guinea
Malabo, Equatorial Guinea
Zanzibar, Tanzania
Diego Garcia, British Indian Ocean Territory
Morobe, Papua New Guinea
Bata, Equatorial Guinea
Dar es Salaam, Tanzania
Port Moresby, Papua New Guinea
Luanda, Angola
Darwin, Australia
Humpty Doo, Australia
St. Helena
Kununurra, Australia
Lusaka, Zambia
Antananarivo, Madagascar
Katherine, Australia
Tennant Creek, Australia
Brandon, Australia
Gweru, Zimbabwe
Alice Springs, Australia
Selebi-Phikwe, Botswana
Manzini, Swaziland
Meyerton, South Africa
Shepparton, Australia
THE WORLD
OF WORLD BAND RADIO
WORLD TIME EXAMPLE: 1300 World Time is 7AM (–6 hours)
in Chicago. For more, see Addresses PLUS section.
WORLD TIME (GMT)
–1
0
+1
+2
+3
+4
+5
+6
+7
+8
+9
+1

+11
+12
–11
–10
–9
–8
–7
–6
–5
–4
–3
–2
Anchor Point, Alaska, USA
Petropavlovsk-Kamchatskiy, Russia
Calgary AB, Canada
Vancouver BC, Canada
Mississauga ON, Canada
Montréal PQ, Canada
Monticello ME, USA
Greenbush ME, USA
St. John's NF, Canada
Sackville NB, Canada
Bethel PA, USA
Red Lion PA, USA
Nashville TN, USA
Manchester TN, USA
Greenville NC, USA
Newport NC, USA
Cypress Creek SC, USA
Vandiver AL, USA
New Orleans LA, USA
Okeechobee FL, USA
Miami FL, USA
Saddlebunch Keys FL, USA
Havana, Cuba
Boulder CO, USA
Frisco TX, USA
Rancho Simi CA, USA
Mesquite NM, USA
Kekaha, Kauai Island, Hawai'i, USA
Pearl Harbor, Oahu Island, Hawai'i, USA
Naalehu, "Big Island," Hawai'i, USA
Santo Domingo, Dominican Republic
Anguilla
México City, Mexico
Chiquimula, Guatemala
Tegucigalpa, Honduras
Bonaire, Netherlands Antilles
Puerto Ayacucho, Venezuela
Georgetown, Guyana
Paramaribo, Surinam
Montsinéry, French Guiana
Cariari de Pococí, Costa Rica
Puerto Lleras, Colombia
San José del Guaviare, Colombia
Quito, Ecuador
Tena, Ecuador
Pohnpei, Micronesia
Manaus, Brazil
Belem, Brazil
Saraguro, Ecuador
Iquitos, Peru
Yurimaguas, Peru
Cajamarca, Peru
Porto Velho, Brazil
Guayaramerín, Bolivia
Cobija, Bolivia
Lima, Peru
Cusco, Peru
Arequipa, Peru
La Paz, Bolivia
Putre, Chile
Santa Cruz, Bolivia
Sucre, Bolivia
Honiara, Solomon Islands
Port-Vila, Vanuatu
Brasília, Brazil
Goiânia, Brazil
Belo Horizonte, Brazil
Rio de Janeiro, Brazil
São Paulo, Brazil
Curitiba, Brazil
Foz do Iguaçu, Brazil
Florianópolis, Brazil
Puerto Iguazú, Argentina
Porto Alegre, Brazil
Santiago, Chile
Montevideo, Uruguay
Buenos Aires, Argentina
Temuco, Chile
Rangitaiki, New Zealand
Levin, New Zealand
Base Esperanza, Antarctica (–3)

GRUNDIG
TIMELESS PERFORMANCE
LISTEN TO THE WORLD
G8 TRAVELER II DIGITAL
AM/FM-stereo/selectable Shortwave Bands
• Analog Tuner, Digital Readout, Clock, Alarm
G3 VOYAGER
AM/FM with RDS/Aircraft Band/LW/Continuous Shortwave with SSB and Sync Detector
• Line In/Out
Satellit 750
AM/FM-Stereo/Shortwave/Aircraft Band Radio with SSB
• AM, FM, Aircraft Band (118-137 MHz) and Shortwave (1711-30000 KHz)

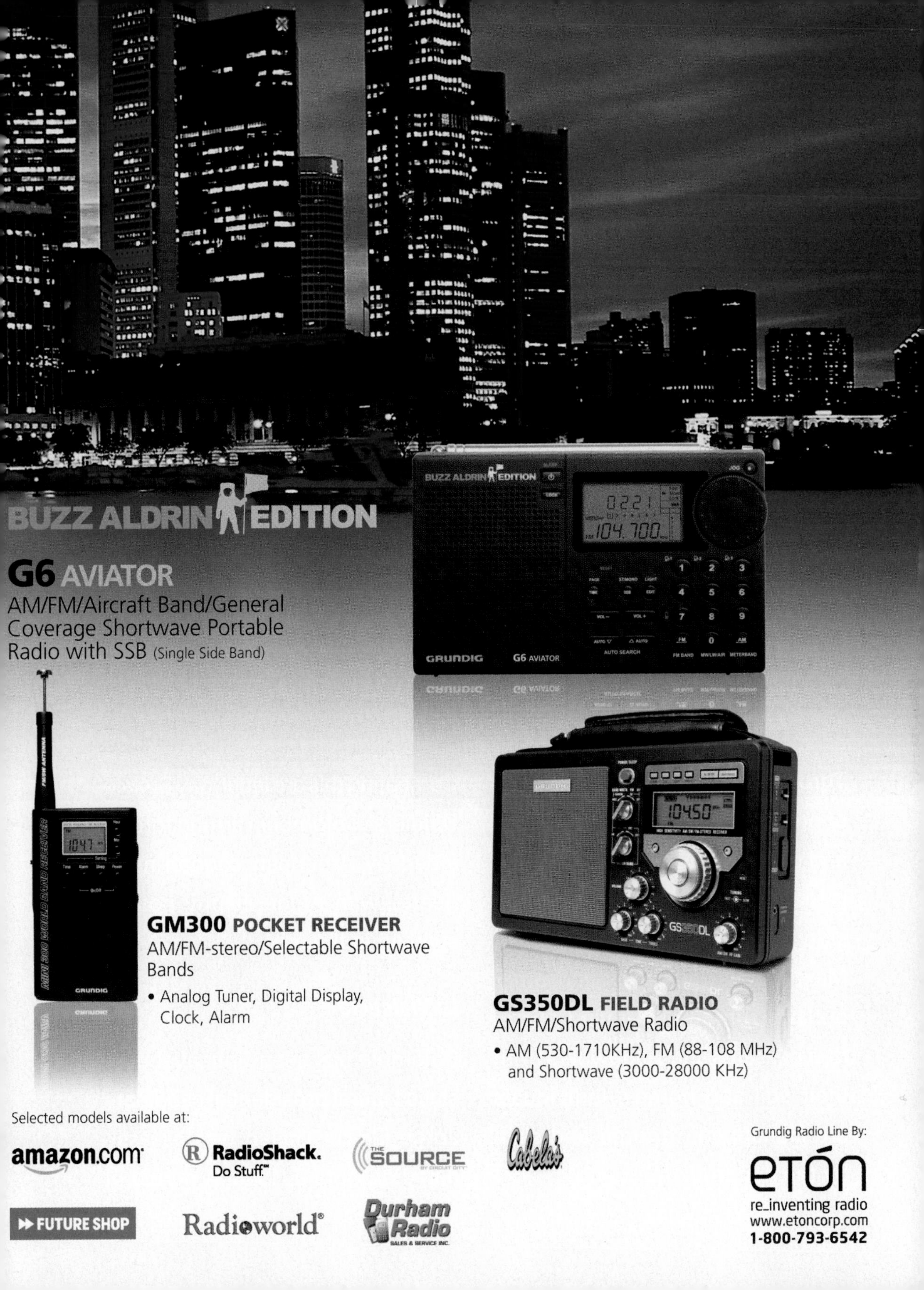

BUZZ ALDRIN EDITION
G6 AVIATOR
AM/FM/Aircraft Band/General Coverage Shortwave Portable Radio with SSB (Single Side Band)
GRUNDIG
G6 AVIATOR
GM300 POCKET RECEIVER
AM/FM-stereo/Selectable Shortwave Bands
• Analog Tuner, Digital Display, Clock, Alarm
GS350DL FIELD RADIO
AM/FM/Shortwave Radio
• AM (530-1710KHz), FM (88-108 MHz) and Shortwave (3000-28000 KHz)
Selected models available at:
amazon.com
RadioShack. Do Stuff.
THE SOURCE BY CIRCUIT CITY
Cabela's
FUTURE SHOP
Radioworld
Durham Radio SALES & SERVICE INC.
Grundig Radio Line By:
etón
re_inventing radio
www.etoncorp.com
1-800-793-6542

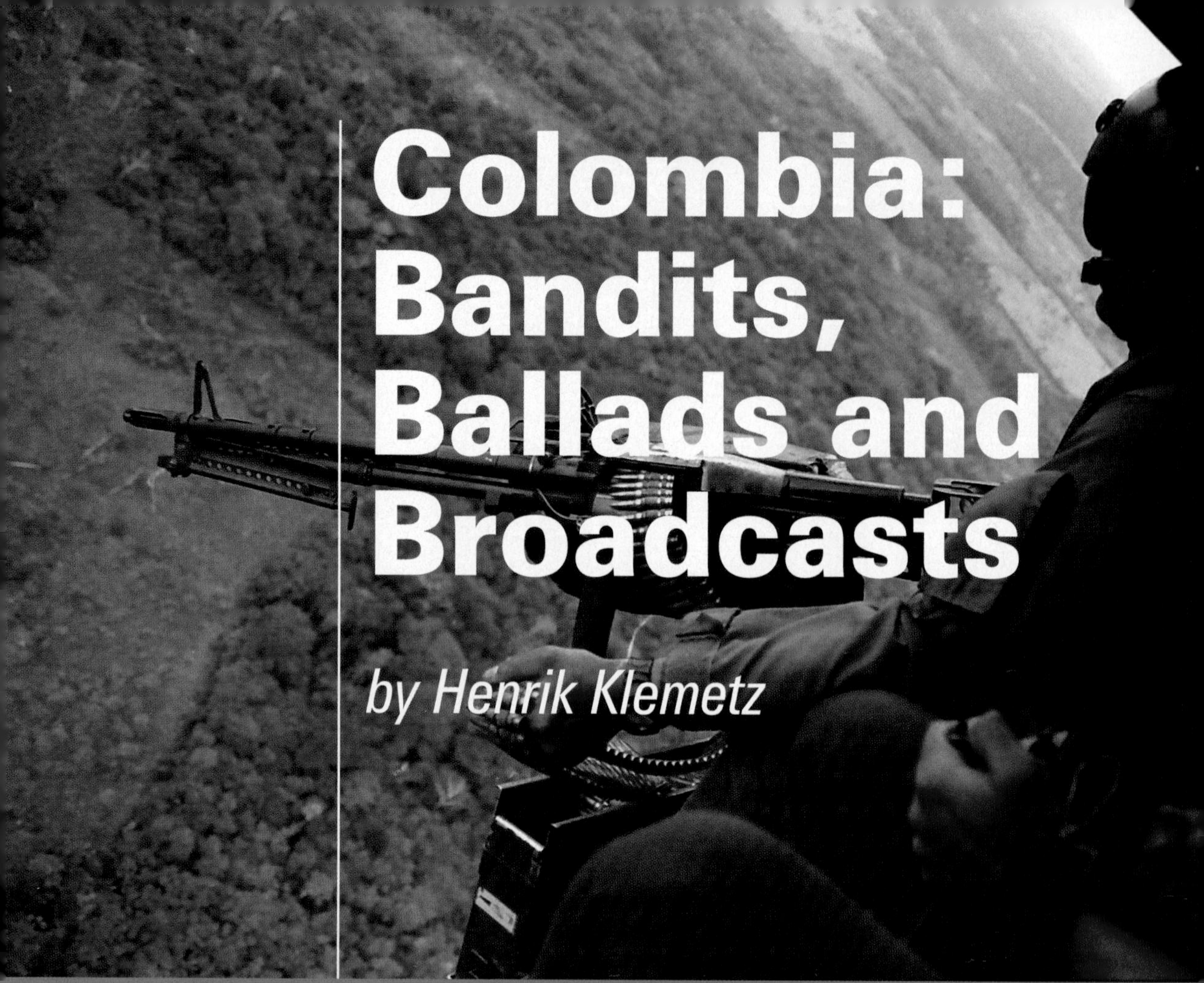

Colombia: Bandits, Ballads and Broadcasts

by Henrik Klemetz

Throughout Latin America, islands of prosperity are ringed by poverty and unrest. In Colombia this divide is magnified by swaths of countryside mirroring scenes from Mad Max. Marxist guerrillas and other outlaws run amok, driving terrorized peasants and landowners from their soil and homes. Individuals are kidnapped, tortured and slain by the hundred.

Combating this are latter-day Buffalo Soldiers: Colombian armed forces, aided by American counterinsurgents—with trigger-happy posses swirling in the mix.

La Violencia

Colombia has seen upheaval ever since Liberal presidential candidate Jorge Eliécer Gaitán was assassinated on April 9, 1948. A period of brutal civil war then ensued. Known as *La Violencia*, it wound down after a military takeover in the 1950s and a power-sharing accord between the Liberal and Conservative parties.

The National Liberation Front's (ELN) Father Camilo Torres was killed in 1966. El Espectador

Events thickened in the 1960s when breakaway *bandoleros* from the civil war began to thrive in the "independent state" of Marquetalia in central Colombia. There, rebels formed a Soviet-sponsored guerrilla force, the Revolutionary Armed Forces of Colombia (FARC).

About the same time, another group surfaced—the National Liberation Army (ELN). Espousing liberation theology, it saw wealth as an unforgivable sin. Unlike the FARC, essentially a band of armed peasants, the ELN contained defrocked clerics and self-styled intellectuals sympathetic to Moscow and Havana. One was former priest Camilo Torres, killed in fighting on February 15, 1966.

By 1969 the ELN had already started kidnapping people for ransom, a practice which gained force among guerilla movements of the day. Emboldened by this way of making money, the tiny but violent M-19 movement abducted a member of the Ochoa family, founders of the Medellín drug cartel.

World band radio and two-way shortwave both serve in Colombia's civil war.

The cartel's kingpins were not amused. They responded by founding a hit squad with the no-nonsense title of *Muerte a Secuestradores*—Death to Kidnappers, or MAS. Suitably chastened, the guerrillas turned instead to levying tribute on coca produce—*el gramaje*. Later, they became directly involved in the chain of production.

At the same time, wealthy landowners in several areas of the country organized to fend off guerrilla attacks. These vigilante groups were precursors of paramilitary "self-defense" organizations such as the AUC and ACCU. The majority eventually degenerated into drug gangs.

Today, most armed paramilitary bands have broken up, with various of their leaders either dead or extradited to the United States. However, new gangs—*Aguilas Negras*, or Black Eagles—have emerged. Just like

Police guide Col. Leonardo Gallego shows a captured cocaine laboratory to Swedish Minister of Justice Laila Frievalds. The operation is being torched by officials.

H. Klemetz

An *escalera* shuttles riders in Angostura, Antioquia. Sporting colorful paintings and ladders in the rear, these vehicles rumble throughout the countryside. They were initially imported as "C&C" trucks—cab and chassis only—so local craftsmen could adapt them to specific needs. H. Klemetz

their predecessors and the Marxist guerillas they oppose, they appear to be deeply involved in drug trafficking and smuggling.

Two-Way Shortwave Serves All

With high mountain *cordilleras* walling off the country into segments and with jungles in the southeast, guerrillas and drug traffickers began resorting to two-way shortwave communication. In part, this was because mountains block VHF signals. But, also, existing wired and cell phone systems didn't provide adequate coverage, while satellite phone signals could be easily blocked.

In the 1980s and 1990s, shortwave between 5 and 8 MHz was the usual playground for drug traffickers. Producers and dealers were widely monitored on single sideband using plain language, albeit riddled with coded words.

Shortwave has long been part of hybrid two-way communication, such as phone patches by hams. In Colombia, from a vehicle on the road or a jungle cocaine lab a call is made by shortwave to a communications center in a nearby town. The shortwave caller is then patched to the requested number using normal telephone circuits.

Two-way shortwave has also been used by the army, the police and various other official agencies and non-governmental organizations. One of these, the International Committee of the Red Cross, maintains a fleet of motor vehicles linked by shortwave to its base station in Bogotá.[1]

Two-way shortwave has also been used by kidnappers to negotiate the release of abductees. Captors have even asked victims' relatives to purchase a "757"—Yaesu FT-757 transceiver—so they could negotiate terms of release.[2]

ELN radio operators—*radistas*—often relied on alphanumerical codes to indicate verbs, activities, names and people.[3] Indeed, QAP, as in "*quedamos QAP*," has made it into common usage in Colombia thanks to a major television newscast.

In recent years rebels have added satellites to complement shortwave and other traditional means of delivering messages.

Sureshot and The Priest

The guerrillas, following Soviet practice, underlined their covert activities by using *noms de guerre*. Take Manuel Pérez Martínez, the defrocked Spanish-born priest who led the ELN until his death in 1998. To the public he was known as *el cura Pérez*—the priest Pérez—but among his confederates he was "Poliarco."

It could get complicated. FARC's founder, Pedro Antonio Marín, was widely known by the nickname of "Tirofijo"—Sureshot. But within his own organization he had yet another fake handle: "Manuel Marulanda Vélez." His deputy, "Raúl Reyes"—dead in an air strike on a FARC encampment in Ecuador on March 1, 2008—was actually Luis Edgar Devia Silva.

FARC's founder, Pedro Antonio Marín—better known as "Sureshot."

Getty Images

World Band Lifeline to Hostages

Unsurprisingly, given the advent of small portables, shortwave broadcasting—world band radio—has become a messaging venue for families and friends of abductees.

In 2002, Franco-Colombian presidential candidate Ingrid Betancourt was kidnapped by the FARC, then eventually rescued in a daring army operation on July 2, 2008. During this period Radio France Internationale (RFI) repeatedly aired messages to her from family members.

Betancourt minces no words: RFI's world band transmissions were a lifeline during her agonizing captivity.

Alejandro Valente, chief editor of RFI's Spanish department, explains, "For years, we have been trying to add new venues of broadcasting in Spanish towards Latin America. We now have local relays, satellite broadcasts and, more recently, streaming audio. But we also see that in extreme situations, and in very secluded areas, shortwave radio remains an important vector."[4]

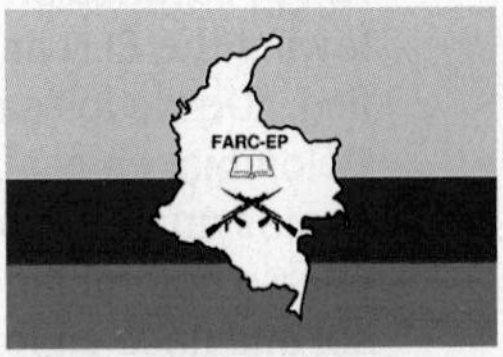

FARC's official flag.

Redresistencia

Many international broadcasters include personal messages when their citizens are in peril, but not so the VOA and BBC World Service. They cover kidnap cases only as news items.

Guerillas Take to Airwaves

World band radio has been a key propaganda medium for the two major left-wing guerrilla groups. In order to recruit new members and to boost morale among those already on board, guerrilla outlets have aired music, news and commentary over mobile transmitters operating in and around 49 meters.

In 1994, the broadcast schedule of the ELN's "Radio Patria Libre" was being scribbled onto the walls of the Bogotá's Universidad Nacional, a cradle for guerrilla sympathizers. But with low power, varying frequencies and irregular operation, clandestine guerrilla stations didn't achieve the broad listenership they desired. Also, "Radio Patria Libre" and the FARC's "Voz de la Resistencia" were intermittently jammed by the Colombian army.

GUERRILLERO
DE LAS FARC
No lo piense más, entréguese y recobre la libertad
EL EJÉRCITO LOS RECIBE.
Entréguese con su fusil y reciba los beneficios del plan de desmovilizados del Ministerio de Defensa Nacional

Poster offers friendly assistance to guerillas who turn themselves in to authorities.

Colombia Estéreo

"Radio Patria Libre"

The nation's first known guerrilla broadcaster, appearing in the 1980s, was reportedly "La Voz del M-19," the Voice of the M-19 movement. Some say the station identified as "Radio Macondo."[5]

Late in that decade two other rebel stations surfaced. "Radio Patria Libre" was run by the ELN's Carlos Alirio Buitrago Front from various

Grafitti on Universidad Nacional building in Bogotá shows Radio Patria Libre's 1994 broadcast schedule.

H. Klemetz

locations in eastern Antioquia department; and "Voz de la Resistencia" was the FARC's mouthpiece, operating from sites throughout the country.

On October 27, 1988, in the midst of a national strike, "Radio Patria Libre" made its appearance on 6760 kHz at 7:30 AM. Following the ELN anthem, the station identified, "Desde los campamentos de la Nueva Colombia, en el aire, 'Radio Patria Libre.' Somos una emisora rebelde al servicio del pueblo colombiano. 'Radio Patria Libre,' un sol que nace en los Andes."

Locals check out a truck set aflame by ELN guerillas between Medellín and Bogotá. Skanska

"RPL" stayed on the air for 51 days before the army struck. It returned from a new location in February 1989, but encountered jamming. It responded by jumping from one frequency to another, a novel but ineffective countermeasure. Eventually the Colombian army hit "RPL's" new shelter, but it was in vain. The rebels had been tipped off, and had spirited away most of the equipment to yet another site.

At the end of 1992, ELN commander "Francisco Galán" was captured in the town of Bucaramanga. The station's regular feature, "Rompiendo las cadenas"—Breaking the chains—was aired in his honor and that of his deputy, "Felipe Torres," who was captured and sent to prison two years later.

A report on "RPL's" first decade mentions a counterfeit station set up by the Colombian army "where they imitated the voices of our speakers to make our listeners confused."[6] This apparently refers to the government's "black" clandestine station "El Pueblo Responde," which to enhance the ruse operated near or atop "Radio Patria Libre's" frequency.

No verification card or letter is known to have been issued by "RPL." Despite this, the station was concerned about audience reaction, asking listeners to tell friends abroad and others about "lies and disinformation" exposed by the station. Indeed, during their ninth anniversary broadcast, monitored on October 27, 1997, the speaker was happy to report that the signal had been picked up "in the very heartland of the gringo empire," as

Guerrillas rehearsing a *vallenato*—a style of Colombian music—for their daily "cultural hour." They have composed a number of songs dealing with *"el imperio yanqui"*—the Yankee empire. A. Tellerías

confirmed on Radio Netherlands "by one of its stateside branches."[7]

"RPL" was now a *sistema radial*, a network consisting of four stations: "Radio Frontera Rebelde," which claimed to be in the northeast; "Radio Resistencia Caribe," nominally on the northern coast; "Radio 15 de Agosto," said to be in the south of Bolívar; and "Radio Rebelde," supposedly in northeastern Antioquia.[8]

One year later, two more stations had joined the net: "Oriente Rebelde," nominally in eastern Antioquia; and "Radio Serranía," supposedly in Magdalena Medio and lower Cauca. The outlet "on the northern coast" was now named "Radio Insurrección Caribeña."

Meanwhile, Colombian army strikes were producing casualties—several collaborators had died, others had defected. The crooners "Clodomiro y Filomeno," who used to ridicule the established order in music and rhymed lyrics, ceased to be heard.

"Voz de la Resistencia"

"RPL's" morning and afternoon programs were heard at fair level in Bogotá. Yet, "Voz de la Resistencia," run by fronts belonging to the Revolutionary Armed Forces of Colombia–People's Army (FARC–EP), was putting out a weak and distorted signal.

This station was first logged by the author on January 24, 1994, on the out-of-band frequency of 6626 kHz. The station later moved to the upper edge of the 49 meter band, where several commercial Colombian broadcasters were operating. Also nicknamed "la estación fariana," the station called on Colombian youth to join the guerrillas instead of "exposing themselves to the abuse" of the Colombian army.

"Voz de la Resistencia's" frequency was constantly on the move. 6259 kHz became 6231 kHz by the end of 1996, and later the station shifted to frequencies in the 6240 to 6330 kHz range.

On 6259.2 kHz a "black" clandestine station appeared on November 25, 1995, announcing as " 'La Voz del Pueblo,' desde las montañas de Colombia." Like "Voz de la Resistencia," this station was playing lots of vallenato music, albeit only instrumentals.

Jesús Santrich, director of the "Bloque Caribe" outlet of "Voz de la Resistencia," revealed that FM broadcasts were added in 1996. From an undisclosed location on the hillside of the Sierra Nevada, the "Resistencia Caribe" signal was easily picked up on 104.9 MHz—not only in Santa Marta, but

Voz de la Resistencia FM studio building in the demilitarized zone of San Vicente del Caguán. It remained in operation from 1999 to 2002.

El Espectador

also in Barranquilla and even as far away as Cartagena.[9]

According to Santrich, the station identified as, "Somos CRB—Cadena Radial Bolivariana—'Voz de la Resistencia,' transmitiendo desde la Cordillera de los Andes, rincón de lucha por la dignidad y libertad."[10]

For whatever reason, Santrich feels that direction finding an FM signal is not as easy as one on shortwave, so FM became of interest to the guerrillas. On the other hand, "on shortwave we are reaching many parts of Latin America and Europe. On Radio Netherlands, for instance, we had a reception report of our shortwave signal when we were airing our 'Viva Bolívar' program."[11]

In 1999 a large demilitarized zone was ceded by the government to the FARC as an incentive to peace talks; there, FM broadcasts were aired daily. In a prelude to planned peace talks, no less than the president of the New York Stock Exchange met that June with "Raúl Reyes" and other FARC representatives, inviting them to visit the NYSE "to get to know the market personally." The following year, top guerrilla leaders traveled to various European countries, and while in Sweden were offered a course in international economics.

A rebel broadcast schedule was picked up by Italian journalist Rocco Cotroneo while visiting Colombia in 1999. It showed that several guerrilla fronts were using world band frequencies in and near 49 meters, as well as FM.

Taking advantage of this period of apparent easing of tensions, the Finnish DXer Patrik Willför managed to obtain an e-mail verification from "Olga Lucía Marín" of the International Commission of the FARC-EP. She also replied by e-mail to Colombian DXer Yimber Gaviria and PASSPORT editor Tony Jones.

After 2002 when the FARC had to leave their haven, "CRB-Voz de la Resistencia" appears to have migrated to FM. It operated from various undisclosed sites in Colombia and abroad, reportedly including Manastara in the lofty Perijá mountains of Venezuela.[12] Indeed, in May 2008 the Colombian minister of communications, traveling to Arauca, reported hearing a FARC transmitter supposedly located on the Venezuelan side of the border on 93.5 MHz.[13]

The station is still on the air. In Sucumbíos and other Ecuadorian provinces bordering on Colombia, "Voz de la Resistencia" is audible on FM every day.[14]

Colombian cops croon over Bogotá's National Police Radio in 1998. After more than fifteen hours of improvised singing, they finally succeeded in beating the old Guinness record. H. Klemetz

Army Responds with Radio Networks

Roughly at the same time, the Colombian army started deploying several low-power mediumwave AM stations. This included La Voz de los Héroes, initially dubbed Colombia Mía, then Colombia Estéreo. It grew into a powerful satellite-linked network called La Emisora del Ejército, which now uses 36 FM outlets to cover most of the country. It airs brief news bulletins and musical segments that focus on love and reunification.

Shortwave? The Colombian army used it during the mid-1950s, during the Rojas Pinilla military government. They used world band again in 2000, but that was all.[15]

Much to the chagrin of the guerrilla leadership, La Emisora del Ejército has been hugely successful in inviting guerrillas to turn themselves in. A regular feature—"Revivir," or New Life—includes interviews with actual deserters. It also explains details of the reinsertion program which has lured thousands of guerrillas back to civilian life.

Back in the 1980s the patience of some citizens and landowners had begun to wear thin. In areas forlorn of national police and courts, paramilitary and vigilante groups were formed and began attacking guerrillas—all the while competing with them in the drug trade. These posses, long on violence and short on persuasion, do not seem to have been significantly involved in broadcasting. However, a station calling itself "Colombia Libre" reportedly was on FM from Hacienda El Cedrón, not far from Santa Fé de Ralito, where vigilante groups gathered in 1994 pending demobilization.

Oral Tradition's Powerful Impact

Broadcasting has high status in Colombia, as the spoken word reaches out to everyone—including those who don't usually read. "People listen to the radio at home, at work, when traveling, everywhere," Jesús Santrich of "Voz de la Resistencia" explains.

Personally flavored comment on political and economic issues in so-called *radio-periódicos* are traditional features on Colombian radio. However, in revealing corruption and untangling political misdemeanor, many talented speakers wind up exposing themselves to danger.

Santrich puts it like this, "The Colombian régime is built on lies. The media, the press, radio and TV are part of this. This we have to counter by educating, informing and entertaining. This explains why we refer to Marxism-Leninism and the Bolivarian thought."[9]

Persuasion extends to lyrics. FARC crooners, such as "Julián Conrado" and "Lucas Iguarán" have produced several clandestine CDs over the years. Most feature songs in the popular vallenato genre.

Guerrillas have also used violence to silence competing stations: Radio Cadena Nacional (RCN) and Caracol affiliates in towns such as Cúcuta, Bucaramanga, Armenia, Medellín and Cali; as well as Cadena Super in Villavicencio.

In Bucaramanga, RCN was silent only for a day or two, as Bogotá headquarters had a spare transmitter. In Armenia, bombs were deactivated in time, while in Medellín Caracol had to move its studios to new premises.

In 2003, according to Reporters Without Borders, five radio and television journalists were killed. Many more were kidnapped, threatened or physically attacked, while others were forced to flee their region or the country.[16] That same year, five more foreign journalists were kidnapped and released after only a few days in captivity.

An American man and a British woman on assignment for the *Los Angeles Times* were kidnapped by the ELN in the Arauca department next to the Venezuelan border. The ELN's "La Voz de la Libertad," apparently the former "Radio Frontera Rebelde," announced that they would be liberated in exchange for an interview to be published in the *Times*.

"Julián Conrado," one of the FARC's best-known singers. Several of his songs have been edited and distributed on vinyl and CDs. A. Tellerías

Radio Helps Abducted Foreigners

In captivity, hostages have discovered the comfort of world band radio, which keeps them in touch with the outside world and sometimes carries messages of hope.

Ulrich Künzel, a German aid official with GTZ, was heading for one of their development projects in Silvia, Cauca. He and his two assistants were stopped at a roadblock and captured at gunpoint by several guerillas.[17]

In the guerrilla camp, Künzel noticed that the leader had a world band portable. Wishing to listen to news from his home country, he asked to listen to the soccer results on Deutsche Welle.

Künzel's brother eventually managed to escape. In a briefing with German authorities, he revealed that they had begun listening to Deutsche Welle. "From that moment on we would notice embedded messages in the news, such as our families being alright, that the Embassy urged us not to try and escape because the negotiations for our release were going well, etc. This was excellent news which boosted our morale and gave us hope."[18]

Meanwhile, another German, Lothar Hintze, was held hostage for five years but received scant attention from German media. When released, he said he believed this was because he had emigrated from his native homeland, making his story potentially less popular.

However, Hintze could hear his wife's messages on local mediumwave AM station HJ Doble K in Neiva. As soon as he and the other hostages arrived at a new site—Hintze thinks they moved some 300 times over the years—they used to sling antenna wire onto surrounding trees. "The camps looked like a cobweb," he said.

Working with Wycliffe bible translators in Lomalinda, Meta, American radio technician Ray Rising was abducted on Maundy

GRUNDIG
TIMELESS PERFORMANCE
LISTEN TO THE WORLD
GRUNDIG

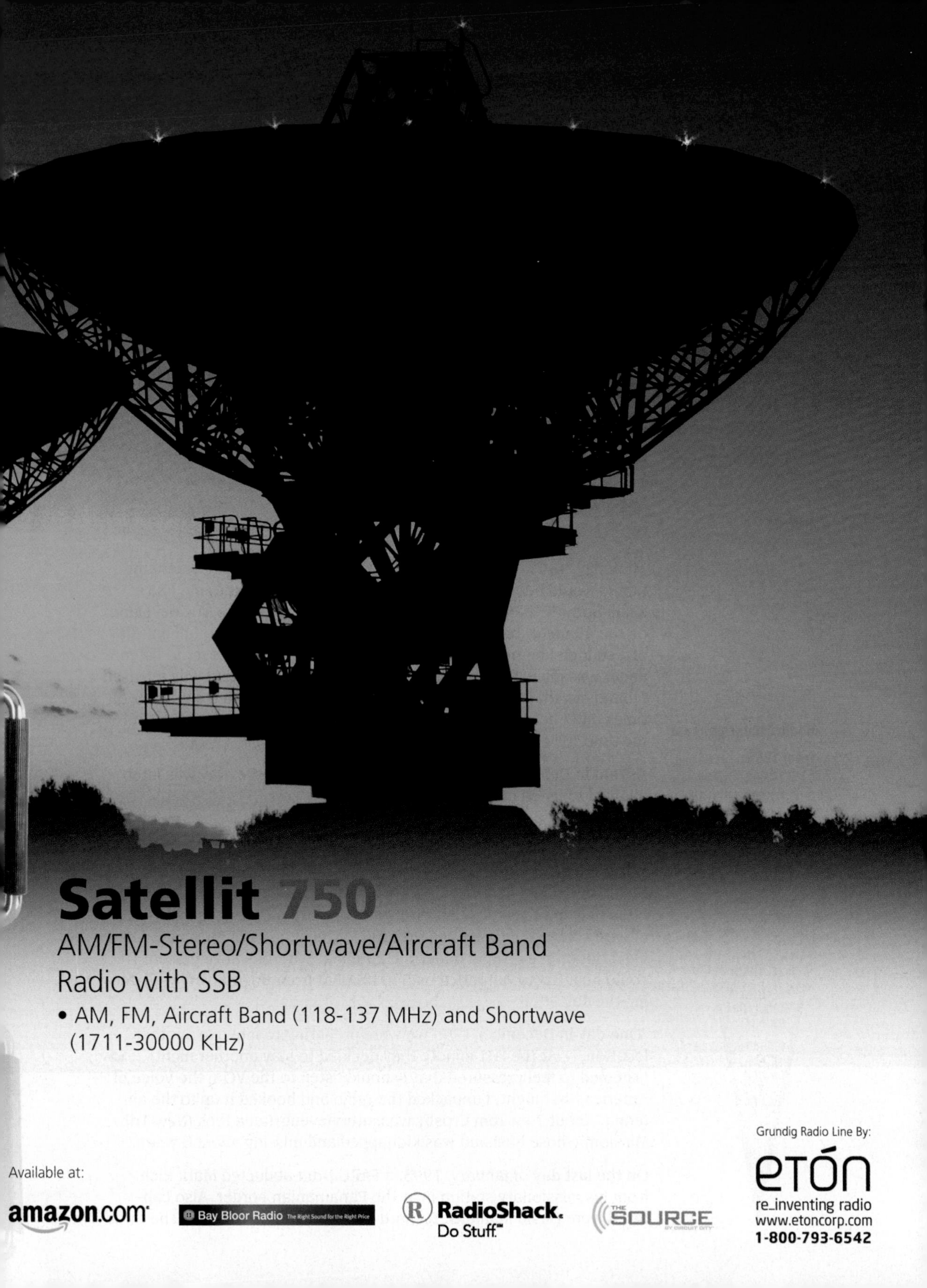
Satellit 750
AM/FM-Stereo/Shortwave/Aircraft Band
Radio with SSB
• AM, FM, Aircraft Band (118-137 MHz) and Shortwave (1711-30000 KHz)
Available at:
amazon.com
Bay Bloor Radio The Right Sound for the Right Price
RadioShack.
Do Stuff.
THE SOURCE
Grundig Radio Line By:
etón
re_inventing radio
www.etoncorp.com
1-800-793-6542

Former captive Ray Rising installs an audio processor for Radio Nuevo Continente in Medellín.

Rising collection

Thursday, 1994. "The day before Christmas I was thinking where my family would be. The guerrilla that had his shelter next to me had a small Sony 12-band analog radio. He was listening to La Voz del Llano on the 49 meter band. He left for a moment with the radio full on. All of a sudden I heard someone speaking English. So I ran over to listen and it was my wife Doris with a message for me. . . After I was released I found out that the same message had been broadcasted a number of times and I heard it the last time it was played. God is good to me all the time."[18]

Radio Militar pennant from 1956. H. Klemetz

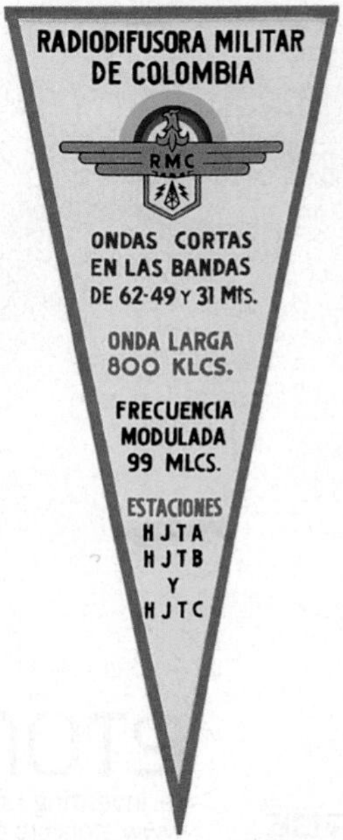

As told in Denise Marie Siino's book *Guerrilla Hostage*, Ray was later allowed to listen on his own radio.

"I had a Sony Walkman with AM/FM. Opening the radio I found where to connect a long wire antenna on the tuning capacitor. The antenna was a metal scouring pad used to wash pots and pans. The wire is kind of hooked in and carefully unhooking it produced about 80 feet of wire. I tied one end to a stick and threw it up in a tree. I used the same type of wire connected to the negative battery post as a counter-wire. This I laid out on the ground under the antenna. With this arrangement I could hear Radio Auténtica on 540 kHz AM from Bogotá very well during the day."[18,19]

"One day in December 1995 we were preparing to move to another location. . . At the last minute they decided to stay another night. . . So I seemed to feel pressured that I should listen to the VOA, the Voice of America, that night. I unpacked the radio and hooked it up to the antenna. About 7 PM Tom Crosby was interviewing Tania Rich (New Tribes Mission) whose husband was kidnapped and missing about 3 years."[18]

On the last day of January, 1993, a FARC front abducted Mark Rich from his missionary station near the Panamanian border. Also captured were David Mankins, Richard Tenenoff and their wives. The three women were sent back to the camp, but their husbands were forced to remain in the jungle.

An initial ransom demand for five million dollars was turned down by the New Tribes Mission. Spouses and children of the three captives returned to Colombia in 1996 in order to arouse public opinion, but nothing much could be done. Some time later, a guerrilla deserter said on Colombian TV that as a radio operator he had received a message for his boss, "comandante Víctor," demanding him to have the three missionaries executed.

Philip Halden was an avid British listener of HCJB World Radio. In 1996 he was driving to the Río Claro cement factory southeast of Medellín. Also with him were a Dane, Ulrik Schultz, along with a German and a Colombian national.

All were taken hostage by the ELN. The German was swiftly released, a result of special services rendered by Werner Mauss, a German double agent supposedly working for the ELN. The remaining three hostages had to endure six more months of jungle hardship.

It was thanks to the International Committee of the Red Cross that a backpack with clothes, medicine and a couple of world band radios made it to the captives. After his release, Halden sent an email to HCJB saying, "My hours of listening to HCJB on shortwave radio helped me more than I ever can explain. You at HCJB gave me hope and strength to bring me through."

Meanwhile, the Danish company F. L. Smidth was conducting secret negotiations with ELN agent Mauss. Radio Denmark wanted to convey helpful messages, yet not spoil these negotiations. So, in what was probably the only covert message it had aired since World War II, it started off with the Beatles' *Help!* as a cue. Then there was the message, "Torben Skipper and Auntie from Valby send their warmest greetings to friends and family in South America, hoping to see you soon again." Schultz later said that it took him a couple of days to realize that this message was actually meant for him, "Auntie from Valby" being a nickname for the firm he was working for.[20]

The Norwegian government was less vague when Stein Vatne was captured by the ELN. On a world band radio forwarded to him through the Red Cross, Vatne was soon to hear his mother sending him a long message on Radio Norway, NRK. "Her voice gave me comfort," he pointed out when celebrating his release at the Swedish Embassy in Bogotá.

Vatne was working for the Swedish contractor Skanska, which two years earlier had already had a couple of its engineers abducted; those had been held by the FARC for five months. Danny Applegate later said he felt great satisfaction when listening to Radio Sweden, where news related to their kidnap was a recurring item. His companion Tommy Tyrving said he was happy to learn that many people were working on their release.[21]

Hostage Ignored by VOA, BBC

American agricultural expert Tom R. Hargrove was in big trouble when stopped by guerrillas in a roadblock on September 23, 1994. His ID card said he was working for

Red Cross vehicles use two-way shortwave to keep in touch with their base station in Bogotá. H. Klemetz

Norwegian Stein Vatne happily celebrates his return to freedom after being held captive by guerillas. During captivity Vatne was comforted by his mother's voice over Radio Norway. H. Klemetz

CIAT, Spanish acronym for International Center for Tropical Agriculture.

To the guerrillas, this meant that Hargrove, a Vietnam veteran, was working for a branch of the CIA. During the ensuing 333-day ordeal, "worse than anything he had been through in Vietnam," Hargrove occasionally listened to news from the VOA and the BBC World Service without hearing a single mention of his case. Only on the semi-local Radio Palmira, 1050 kHz, and two or three of Colombia's nationwide networks did the American specialist hear his own situation being mentioned.

He was mighty pleased. In his diary, which was jotted down in a chequebook and on loose scraps of paper, he wrote, "Keep up the publicity, CIAT. Keep my name on the radio, so it will be embarrassing for FARC if I disappear."

After Hargrove's release, Hollywood made his saga into the gripping movie *Proof of Life*, starring Meg Ryan, Russell Crowe and David Morse. He now resides in a spacious historic home in Galveston, Texas with his wife Susan and two dogs.

Captive Audience

Herbin Hoyos Medina is the host of a weekly six-hour program, "Voces del secuestro"—Voices of the kidnapped—aired after midnight Sunday mornings on the nationwide Caracol network. Here, hostages can listen to messages from their loved ones.

While held in captivity by the FARC for 17 days in 1994, Hoyos had met a man chained to a tree with a transistor radio in one hand. Recalling that he had been hearing Hoyos' program "Amanecer en América" a few nights earlier, the man asked why there was no program for the kidnapped.

Hoyos agreed. Returning to civilian life, he started a program which has been on the air continuously since the end of 1994. "The program will go on for as long as there is one kidnapped person in this country," declares Hoyos of his award-winning program.[22]

A similar offering, "En busca de la libertad"—In search of liberty—was aired on the state-owned Radiodifusora Nacional for several years, but seems to have been discontinued. Its timing, in the late afternoon, was probably less suitable than at night.

Two other nationwide networks carry similar programs: Todelar's "Alas de libertad" (Wings of freedom) daily at 6 PM, and RCN's "La noche de la libertad" (Night of freedom) Monday from midnight to 3 AM. After her rescue, Ingrid Betancourt said that she regularly listened to both these programs, as well as to "Voces del secuestro."

According to País Libre, a private organization helping kidnap victims return to civilian life, one in four Colombian families has experienced kidnapping. Not all cases are made public, as kidnappers then might retaliate by increasing the ransom, so the precise number is unknown. Yet, around

700 are believed to be currently held by guerrillas and perhaps a thousand more by other groups.

Locally, despite menaces and threats, certain local broadcasters reach out to the kidnapped. In Valledupar, station Radio Guatapurí, 740 kHz, mixes personal messages to kidnap victims among their commercials. In the towns of Cali and Neiva, Radio Calidad, 1230 kHz, and HJ Doble K, 840 kHz, carry messages just before dawn when mediumwave propagation is at its best.

On Radio Calidad the service got off to a flying start in 1997 after a FARC attack on a military facility which was protecting antennas used by national broadcasting and television networks. Several soldiers were killed and 18 abducted. Worried relatives rushed to their phones to talk to loved ones on the popular morning show "La Carrilera de las 5," aired at five in the morning.

Inspirational programs can also prove uplifting. For example, J.C. Radio, 1520 kHz, specializes in contemporary Christian music. Ex-hostages have sent the station tokens of appreciation for its programs.

Missionary Radio Fosters Reconciliation

Strictly speaking, a guerrilla is a hostage, too. Like the Roach Motel, it is easy to get in but nearly impossible to leave. Indeed, parting from rebel ranks is equivalent to high treason and carries capital punishment.

Taken hostage by FARC guerrillas 25 years ago, American missionary Russell Martin Stendal believes that radio is excellent for reaching out to fighters on the battlefield—whether guerrillas, paramilitaries or just plain soldiers of the Colombian army. During his 123-day captivity he noticed that the guerrillas regularly listened to Radio Habana Cuba, as well as Salvadoran world band clandestine "Radio Venceremos."

Stendal was freed for the equivalent of 55 thousand dollars in ransom. His parents had sent him a backpack which concealed a homing device. In so doing, they were

Herbin Hoyos hosts "Voces del secuestro"—Voices of the kidnapped—from a Caracol studio in Bogotá. Heard nationwide, it airs messages from loved ones to those held hostage by guerillas. H. Klemetz

capable of locating him and eventually picking him up in an old Cessna 170 plane once the ransom was paid. "We are really letting you go for a bargain price," the commander told Stendal. "The going price for a ransom is many times what you are paying," he added.[23]

In the mid-1990s Stendal was offered a license for a community mediumwave AM station in Puerto Lleras, Meta. He accepted, and also obtained a license for shortwave and FM. He constructed the facilities on a ranch that had been vacated by the Wycliffe Bible Translators of Lomalinda, Meta, following a FARC bombing.

The new stations—La Voz de tu Conciencia and Marfil Estéreo—began by airing music and short messages. Initially on 6065 kHz, a frequency vacated by the Colmundo network, Stendal later had to move to 6010 kHz, cuddling Radio Habana Cuba on 6000 kHz. He added 5910 kHz as a complement to Marfil Estéreo's FM operation.

Former captive Russell Stendal now operates two radio stations on 49 meters. He is regarded with trust by guerillas and government officials, alike. Abel Parra

The idea was, as Stendal puts it, to air "healthy and soul-inspiring Colombian music to lure in the difficult audience and [to air] short gospel messages that would surprise them before they could change the dial."[24]

Stendal is highly regarded by all fighting parties, as he is perceived as nonpartisan and concerned only with reconciliation on a personal level. With the help of the support organization The Voice of the Martyrs, Stendal has distributed some 60,000 Galcom fixed-frequency solar powered receivers to listeners in the area. He is also free to distribute literature, a camouflage-covered Bible being among the most popular items.

Stendal also has a recording studio in Bogotá. As a longtime resident of Colombia he knows the impact music and lyrics have on the local audience. So he has invited Christian country musicians to Colombia to work on creating "good" lyrics for the kind of rhythms popular in the area: vallenato, joropo and ranchera. Although sweet and lovely to the ear, these types of songs can glorify war and drug trafficking. However, Stendal's similar-sounding songs with wholesome lyrics act as something of an antidote.

Stendal urges American lawmakers to include provisions in their Patriot Act for missionaries "to contact and relate to terrorists and terrorist organizations for the purpose of evangelizing them. If those whose hearts are hard and bitter are converted by the love of Jesus Christ, they will no longer participate in any terrorist activity."[24]

Who Triumphs?

The fight against guerilla violence and the drug trade continues to go well, and attacks by paramilitary goons on union organizers have also declined sharply. Confidence in the government continues to rise, and true democratic elections are on the horizon.

Anti-trade forces in the United States periodically threaten to penalize Colombia for not having improved enough. However, assuming these differences get resolved, there is good reason to hope that today's *violencia* will eventually be but a chapter in history where the good guys eventually triumph.

Henrik Klemetz arrived in Colombia on a one-year scholarship in 1966, when guerrilla priest Camilo Torres was killed. By the mid-1990s, from his vantage point in Bogotá, he was covering several kidnap cases for Scandinavian media, as well as broadcast industry news for Radio World. *He has been a DXer for 50 years.*

[1]Phone patch centers in Cali, Villavicencio and Ibagué have been noted on various frequencies between 5800 and 6300 kHz; ICRC is on 6994 kHz upper sideband. Bogotá HQ is identified as "691," although the full call is "5JG-691/CCIR." There were 15 substations in the various areas of conflict in 1996.

[2]Lia Posada, *Colombia's Kidnapping Industry*, Bogotá, 1998?, ISBN 958-33-0451-4.

[3]Villamarín Pulido, Luis Alberto: *El ELN por dentro. Historia de la cuadrilla Carlos Alirio Buitrago*, Bogotá 1995, ISBN 958-33-0257-0.

[4]In Spanish: www.youtube.com/watch?v=8Dl9j9myf qc&feature=related

In French: www.youtube.com/watch?v=CQoTJYXW_q8

[5]www.clandestineradio.com quoted by BBC Monitoring and published in www.angelfire.com/ok/worldofradio/dxld1110.txt

[6]In Correo del Magdalena, 116, Nov. 1999, at www.nodo50.org/eln-voces/webanterior/Documentos/CM

[7]"Supimos que esa voz que nace en los Andes fue noticia y que causó revuelo porque fue escuchada en la misma entraña del imperio gringo y el eco de la voz llegó hasta Europa a través de Radio Nederland, quien la escuchó [sic] en una de sus sucursales estadounidenses" [apparent reference to Glenn Hauser, who reported the item in Spanish on Radio Netherlands]. Taped and transcribed by author.

[8]"Radio Frontera Rebelde" has probably changed its name to "La Voz de la Libertad" (*see* www.nodo50.org/patrialibre/fgo/index.htm)

[9]www.lafogata.org/003latino/latino1/col_suenos.htm/1999/CM116.html

[10]lahaine.org/internacional/estamos_poder.htm explains how the FARC has leaped from being a peasants' self-defense group to becoming a "politico-military revolutionary organization guided by the principles of Marxism-Leninism and the thoughts of our Liberator Simón Bolívar and all the revolutionary thoughts of Latin America." Spanish newspaper *El País* reported on May 11, 2008, that the FARC controls an undercover organization, "Coordinadora Continental Bolivariana," involving legal and clandestine groups with ramifications in 17 countries. The 2nd Conference of the Coordinadora was held in Quito, Ecuador, at the end of February 2008, just one week before the Colombian army attacked a guerrilla camp on the Ecuadorean side of the border, killing, among others, FARC spokesman "Raúl Reyes."

[11]www.worldofradio.com/dxld4068.txt, www.worldofradio.com/mr0404.html. This signal was aired on 10.0 MHz, interfering with WWV and other time stations.

[12]According to Javier Armato, member of the legislative council of Zulia state, in the weekly publication *Versión Final*, Maracaibo, Feb 1, 2008. A report on www.noticierodigital.com tells about Venezuelan community stations openly supporting the FARC. One on them was operating on 94.6 MHz from the Caracas neighborhood 23 de Enero. Early 2007 this station was playing the FARC anthem "in broad daylight," with deejays saluting guerillas belonging to a local "Bolivarian front" identified with the FARC. "Nowadays, with the computer thing and the threat of [turning matters to the] International Court of Justice, they are a little more quiet," says "Noalco Munismo," nom de keyboard of the Venezuelan correspondent of *Cuba, Democracia y Vida*, May 30, 2008.

[13]www.cmi.com.co/Contenido/Noticia.asp?nota=15198&seccion=8

[14]www.hoy.com.ec/impnoticia.asp?row_id=271337

[15]Radiodifusora Militar was active in 1956 on 6155 kHz; in mid-2000 Colombia Mía, "la emisora de la Cadena radial del Ejército," was on 4895 kHz, a frequency ceded by La Voz del Río Arauca.

[16]www.rsf.org/article.php3?id_article=10198

[17]www.farc.de, Künzel's own website.

[18]In e-mails to author.

[19]Pastor Jorge Enrique Gómez was kidnapped by FARC guerrillas on Feb 14, 2001, tied to a pole for two months and finally released in August. No ransom was paid. Gómez is the founder of Centro Misionero Bethesda and the Cadena Radial Auténtica radio network, 540 kHz being the network's flagship station.

[20]Kyrø, Øjvind, *Gidsel for Fred*, Copenhagen, 1997, ISBN 87-7880-045-5. Includes pictures and background research provided by the author of this article.

[21]Researched by author on the spot.

[22]www.youtube.com/watch?v=bYoCPRw3acY is just one among several pieces on YouTube relating to Herbin Hoyos and "Voces del secuestro."

[23]Stendal, Russell, *Rescue the Captors*, 1984, ISBN 0-931221-01-3

Stendal, Chad & Pat, *The Guerrillas Have Taken Our Son*, ISBN 0-931221-02-1

[24]Stendal, Russell, *Rescue the Captors 2*, 2008, ISBN 0-931221-61-7

Wycliffe's American missionaries shut down operations and fled Colombia after guerillas laid waste to their ranch. Abel Parra

GRUNDIG
TIMELESS PERFORMANCE
LISTEN TO THE WORLD

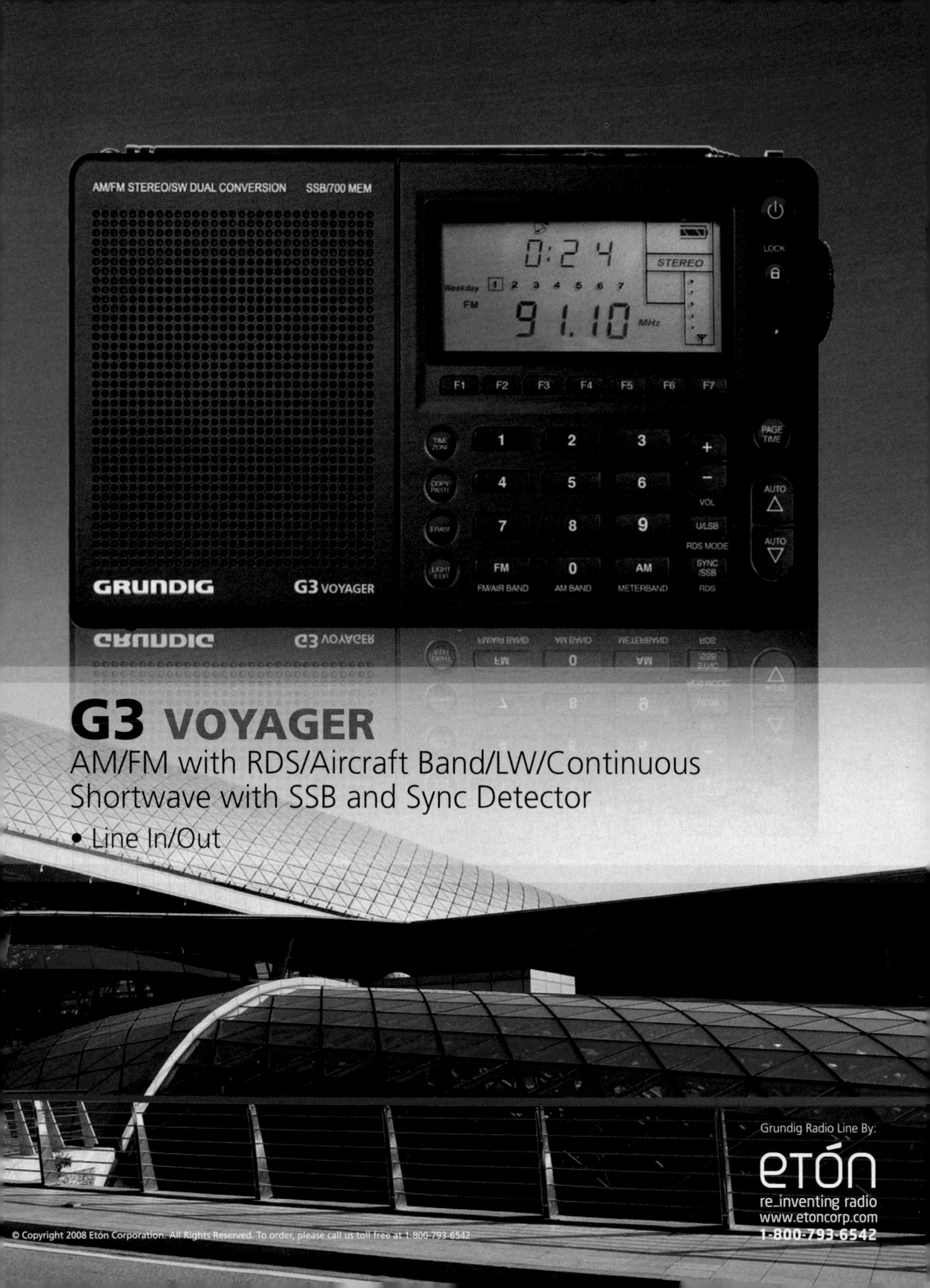
AM/FM STEREO/SW DUAL CONVERSION SSB/700 MEM
STEREO
FM
MHz
F1 F2 F3 F4 F5 F6 F7
LOCK
PAGE TIME
VOL
U/LSB
RDS MODE
SYNC /SSB
AUTO
FM/AIR BAND
AM BAND
METERBAND
RDS
GRUNDIG
G3 VOYAGER
G3 VOYAGER
AM/FM with RDS/Aircraft Band/LW/Continuous Shortwave with SSB and Sync Detector
• Line In/Out
Grundig Radio Line By:
etón
re_inventing radio
www.etoncorp.com
1-800-793-6542
© Copyright 2008 Etón Corporation. All Rights Reserved. To order, please call us toll free at 1-800-793-6542

Getting Started

World Band's Three Musts

World band isn't like everyday radio—it travels freely by skywave and needs special receivers. So here are three handy "musts" to get started.

Must #1: World Time and Day

World band uses a single time. World band is global, with programs aired around the clock from nearly every time zone. Imagine the chaos if each station's schedule were given in local time to listeners scattered all over the world.

Solution: World Time—one time zone for one planet.

World Time—officially Coordinated Universal Time (UTC)—has replaced the virtually identical Greenwich Mean Time (GMT) as the global standard. It's 24-hour format, so 2 PM is 14:00 ("fourteen hundred" or "fourteen hours").

Don't forget to "wind your calendar," because at midnight a new *World Day* arrives. This can trip up even experienced listeners—sometimes radio stations, too. So if it is 9:00 PM EST Wednesday in New York, it is 02:00 hours World Time *Thursday*.

Bottom line for clocks: Most decent radios have a 24-hour clock or you can buy a standalone clock or watch. See "World Time: Setting Your Clock."

Alarm clock with world time from L.L. Bean.

Must #2: Finding Stations

PASSPORT gives station schedules three ways: by country, time of day and frequency. "Worldwide Broadcasts in English" and "Voices from Home" are for tuning to a specific station. "What's On Tonight's" hour-by-hour format is like *TV Guide*, complete with program descriptions. Blue Pages' quick-access grids show what you might be hearing when dialing around.

World band frequencies are usually in kilohertz (kHz), but some stations and radios use Megahertz (MHz). The only difference is three decimal places so, say, 6170 kHz is the same as 6.17 MHz, while 6175 kHz equals 6.175 MHz.

News unfettered by corporate or civil overlordship.

FM and other stations are on the same frequency, day and night—webcast URLs rarely move, either. But world band is like a global bazaar where merchants come and go at various times of the day and night. So, where you once tuned to a French station, hours later you might find a Russian roosting on that same spot.

Or on a nearby perch. If you suddenly hear interference, it doesn't necessarily mean something is wrong with your radio—another station may have fired up on a nearby frequency. There are more stations than available space, so sometimes they rub elbows.

Shutterstock/Sebastian Knight

New York-based correspondent Margaret Besheer covers the UN for Voice of America. VoA

or the schedule. Shortwave transmitters are located on *terra firma*. Yet, because of the earth's curvature their signals eventually shoot off towards the sky, where they run into the ionosphere—a gaseous layer surrounding our planet. When the ionosphere is suitably energized, it deflects these signals down, after which they bounce off oceans or soil to sail once again up to the ionosphere for additional bounces.

This bouncing up and down like a basketball continues until the signal arrives at your radio. However, if the ionosphere at any one "bounce point" isn't in a bouncing mood—it varies daily and seasonally, like the weather—the signal passes through the ionosphere and sails off into space. That's the main reason a scheduled signal might be audible one hour, gone the next.

To cope with this, purchase a radio with superior adjacent-channel rejection—selectivity—and lean towards models with synchronous selectable sideband. PASSPORT REPORTS tells which models shine.

Because world band is full of surprises from one day to the next, experienced listeners like to scan the airwaves. Daytime, most stations are above 11500 kHz; at night, below 10000 kHz.

If a station can't be found or fades out, there is probably nothing wrong with your radio

Gatekeepers Begone

World band stations cope with the ionosphere's changeability by using different frequency ranges, depending on season and time of day as well as the 11-year sunspot cycle. The ionosphere is also why world band radio is free from regulation and snooping. Unlike on the Internet, nobody can keep tabs on what you're hearing.

The ionosphere also helps analog shortwave broadcasts to be heard even with skywave jamming. Deliberate jamming, detailed in the Blue Pages, is a staple of authoritarian regimes—Cuba, China and North Korea, for starters.

PASSPORT'S THREE-MINUTE KICKOFF

Owner's manual hopeless? Try this:

1. Night time is the right time, so start out evenings when signals are strongest. In a high rise put your radio by a window or on a balcony.
2. Make sure your radio is plugged in or has fresh or charged batteries. Extend its telescopic antenna fully and vertically. Set the DX/local switch, if there is one, to DX, but otherwise leave controls at default settings.
3. Fire up your radio after dark. Set it to 5900 kHz and begin tuning slowly toward 6200 kHz. You should hear stations from around the world.

Other times? Read "Best Times and Frequencies for 2009."

Even some democratic governments are secretly equipped to disrupt and manipulate communications during emergencies. Yet, foreign world band radio is largely beyond their control, so it tends to inform no matter what.

Must #3: The Right Radio

Choose carefully, but start affordably. If you just want to hear powerhouse stations, try one of the higher-rated affordable portables. If you want something better, today's top portables do surprisingly well with challenging signals and offer superior audio quality. Tabletop and PC supersets are more robust, but pricey for what they do.

Spring for a radio with digital frequency display—this makes digging out stations much easier. Virtually all radios in Passport Reports have this, but portables with analog (slide rule) display still abound. Some inexpensive hybrids mix analog tuning with digital frequency readout. However, most digital-display radios use synthesized tuning with such handy tuning aids as presets and keypads.

Ideally, get a radio that covers at least 4750–21850 kHz with no significant frequency gaps. Otherwise, as the Blue Pages detail, it may miss some interesting stations.

Nearly all portables are designed to work nicely, even optimally, with their built-in telescopic antennas. If you want to enhance a portable's weak-signal reception (sensitivity), simply clip several yards or meters of insulated wire onto that antenna, or use one of the portable active antennas that passes muster in Passport Reports.

Prepared by Jock Elliott, Tony Jones and Lawrence Magne.

WORLD TIME: SETTING YOUR CLOCK

PASSPORT's "Addresses PLUS" lets you figure out local time in other countries by adding or subtracting from World Time. Use it to ascertain local time in a country you are hearing.

Here, it's the opposite: what to add or subtract from your local time to get World Time. For example, if you live near Chicago and it's 7:00 AM winter, the list below shows World Time as six hours later, or 13:00. In the summer, with daylight-saving time, World Time is only five hours later—noon, or 12:00. That's because, unlike Chicago time, it doesn't change with the seasons. So, once you've set your clock for World Time you won't have to fool with it again.

Many major international broadcasters announce World Time at the hour. On the Internet, it is given at numerous sites, such as time5.nrc.ca/webclock_static_e.shtml. For North America and vicinity, it is announced over official stations WWV in Colorado, WWVH in Hawaii and CHU in Ottawa. WWV and WWVH use world band frequencies of 5000, 10000 and 15000 kHz, with WWV also being on 2500 and 20000 kHz. CHU ticks away on 3330, 7335 and 14670 kHz.

WHERE YOU ARE	*TO FIGURE WORLD TIME*
North America	
Newfoundland St. John's NF, St. Anthony NF	Add 3½ hours, 2½ summer
Atlantic St. John NB, Battle Harbour NF	Add 4 hours, 3 summer
Eastern New York, Miami, Toronto	Add 5 hours, 4 summer
Central Chicago, Mexico City, Nashville, Winnipeg	Add 6 hours, 5 summer
Mountain Denver, Salt Lake City, Calgary	Add 7 hours, 6 summer
Pacific San Francisco, Vancouver	Add 8 hours, 7 summer
Alaska	Add 9 hours, 8 summer
Hawaii	Add 10 hours
Central America & Caribbean	
Bermuda	Add 4 hours, 3 summer
Barbados, Puerto Rico, Virgin Islands	Add 4 hours
Bahamas	Add 5 hours, 4 summer
Cuba	Add 5 hours, 4 summer
Jamaica	Add 5 hours
Costa Rica	Add 6 hours

Europe	
United Kingdom, Ireland, Portugal	Same time as World Time winter, subtract 1 hour summer
Continental Western Europe; parts of Central and Eastern Continental Europe	Subtract 1 hour, 2 hours summer
Elsewhere in Continental Europe: Belarus, Bulgaria, Cyprus, Estonia, Finland, Greece, Latvia, Lithuania, Moldova, Romania, Russia (Kaliningradskaya Oblast), Turkey, Ukraine	Subtract 2 hours, 3 summer
Moscow	Subtract 3 hours, 4 summer
Mideast & Africa	
Côte d'Ivoire, Ghana, Guinea, Liberia, Mali, Senegal, Sierra Leone	World Time exactly
Angola, Benin, Chad, Congo, Nigeria	Subtract 1 hour
Tunisia	Subtract 1 hour, 2 summer
Egypt, Israel, Jordan, Lebanon, Syria	Subtract 2 hours, 3 summer
South Africa, Zambia, Zimbabwe	Subtract 2 hours
Ethiopia, Kenya, Kuwait, Saudi Arabia, Tanzania, Uganda	Subtract 3 hours
Iran	Subtract 3½ hours, 4½ summer
Asia & Australasia	
Pakistan	Subtract 5 hours (6 during energy crises)
India, Sri Lanka	Subtract 5½ hours
Bangladesh	Subtract 6 hours
Laos, Thailand, Vietnam	Subtract 7 hours
China (including Taiwan), Malaysia, Philippines, Singapore	Subtract 8 hours
Japan, Korea	Subtract 9 hours
Australia: ***Victoria, New South Wales, Tasmania***	Subtract 11 hours local summer, 10 local winter (midyear)
Australia: ***South Australia***	Subtract 10½ hours local summer, 9½ hours local winter (midyear)
Australia: ***Queensland***	Subtract 10 hours
Australia: ***Northern Territory***	Subtract 9½ hours
Australia: ***Western Australia***	Subtract 9 hours local summer, 8 hours local winter (midyear)
New Zealand	Subtract 13 hours local summer, 12 hours local winter (midyear)

BEST TIMES AND FREQUENCIES FOR 2009

Dialing the shortwave spectrum at random can get you dead air and weird noises. That's because world band stations usually operate within defined segments scattered within that spectrum. Some segments are alive and kicking by day, others at night. Time of year also counts.

World band is always active, but many signals are strongest evenings because they're aimed your way. Still, interesting stuff can be heard outside prime time when, thanks to shortwave's scattering properties, signals beamed elsewhere become audible.

Experienced station hunters especially enjoy the hour or two on either side of dawn, when you may hear parts of the world that are normally elusive. Try after lunch, too—especially towards sunset—and winters after midnight.

Bad wind rising? World band is but a click away.

Fine Print and Slippery Excuses: Treat this time and frequency guide like a good weather forecast: helpful, but not holy writ. Nature, as always, has a mind of its own, and world band is nature's radio.

This guide is most helpful if you're north of Africa and South America. Even then, what you hear will vary depending on your location, where the station transmits from, time of year and your radio hardware.

☞ There are fourteen official world band frequency segments, plus out-of-band operation that's allowed if it doesn't cause harmful interference to primary users.

☞ "Night" refers to your local hours of darkness, give or take.

Night—Rare Reception
Day—Local Reception

2 MHz (120 meters) **2300–2495 kHz**—used by very few domestic stations; plus 2496–2504 kHz for time stations only.

Night—Limited Reception
Day—Local Reception

3 MHz (90 meters) **3200–3400 kHz**—overwhelmingly domestic broadcasters, but also some international stations.

Day and Night—Good-to-Fair Eurasia except Summer Nights;
Elsewhere, Limited Reception Night

4 MHz (75 meters) **3900–4050 kHz**—international and domestic stations, primarily not in or beamed to the Americas; 3900–3950 kHz mainly Asian and Pacific transmitters; 3950–4000 kHz also includes European transmitters; 4001–4050 kHz currently out-of-band.

Night—Fair Reception
Day—Regional Reception

5 MHz (60 meters) **4750–4995 kHz** and **5005–5100 kHz**—mostly domestic stations; plus 4996–5004 kHz for time stations only; 5061–5100 kHz currently out-of-band.

Night—Excellent Reception
Day—Regional Reception

6 MHz (49 meters) **5730–6300 kHz**—5730–5899 kHz and 6201–6300 kHz currently out-of-band.

Night—Good Reception
Day—Mainly Regional Reception

7 MHz (41 meters) **6890–6990 kHz** and **7100–7600 kHz**—6890–6990 kHz and 7351–7600 kHz out-of-band until March 29, 2009; 7100–7300 kHz no American-based transmitters and few transmissions targeted to the Americas. ☞ 7100–7350 kHz outside the Americas officially shifts to 7200–7450 kHz on March 29, 2009; 7300–7350 kHz within the Americas officially shifts to 7300–7400 kHz on that same date.

Day—Fair Reception Winter; Regional Reception Summer
Night—Good Reception Summer

9 MHz (31 meters) **9250–9995 kHz**—9250–9399 kHz and 9901–9995 kHz currently out-of-band; plus 9996–10004 kHz exclusively for time stations.

Day—Good Reception
Night—Variable Reception Summer

11 MHz (25 meters) **11500–12200 kHz**—11500–11599 kHz and 12101–12200 kHz currently out-of-band.

13 MHz (22 meters) **13570–13870 kHz**

15 MHz (19 meters) **15005–15825 kHz**—15005–15099 kHz and 15801–15825 kHz currently out-of-band; plus 14996–15004 kHz exclusively for time stations.

Day—Good Reception
Night—Limited Reception Summer

17 MHz (16 meters) **17480–17900 kHz**

19 MHz (15 meters) **18900–19020 kHz**—few stations.

Day—Limited and Variable Reception
Night—Rare Reception

21 MHz (13 meters) **21450–21850 kHz**

Nobody can know what you're hearing.

Day—Rare, if Any, Reception
Night—No Reception

25 MHz (11 meters) **25670–26100 kHz**

POWER GENERATOR
WATER RESISTANT AM/FM/SW EMERGENCY RADIO
TUNING
VOLUME
etón
Radio
Light
Cell Phone Charger
FR-250
FR350
Self-Powered, Water Resistant AM/FM/Short-wave Radio with Flashlight, Siren, Hand Crank Power & Cell Phone Charger
FR250
Self-Powered AM/FM/Shortwave Radio with Flashlight, Siren, Hand Crank Power & Cell Phone Charger
Selected models available at:
KROMER
WHERE ENTERTAINMENT BEGINS • SINCE 1957
RadioShack.
Do Stuff.
THE SOURCE
BY CIRCUIT CITY
amazon.com
FUTURE SHOP
etón
re_inventing radio
www.etoncorp.com
1-800-793-6542

Ten of the Best: 2009's Top Shows

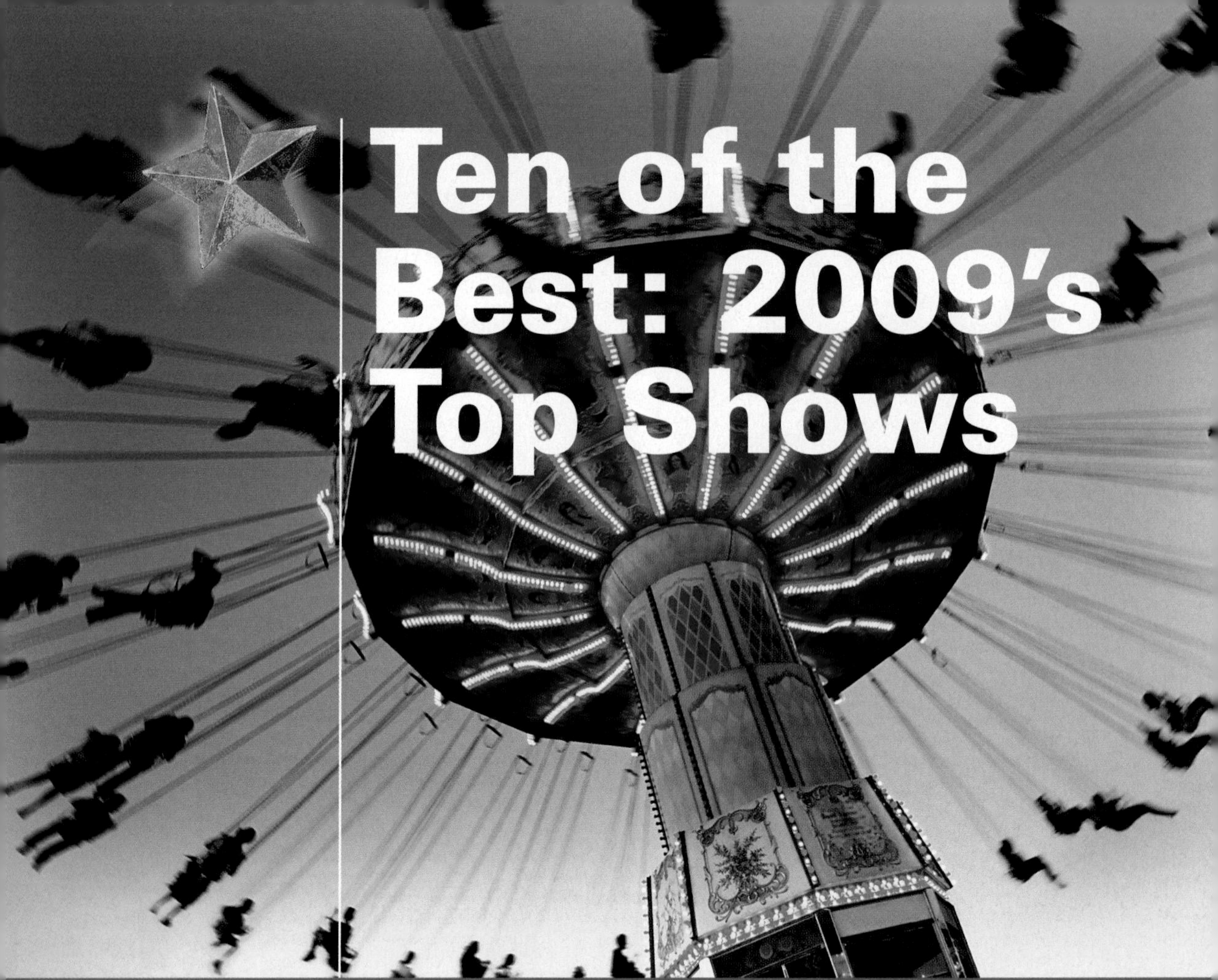

World band serves up aardvark to zarzuela, but some choices are boring or worse. Occasionally the truly awful makes for fun listening, like "news-ah" from Pyongyang. But the good stuff is what holds our attention, so here are ten solid winners that are widely audible.

Times and days are in World Time (UTC). "Winter" and "summer" refer to seasons in the Northern Hemisphere, where summer is in the middle of the calendar year.

"World in Progress"
Deutsche Welle

Most media gravitate to a cluster of established topics, but not Deutsche Welle. Its "World in Progress" goes below the radar to examine ignored problems and to get fresh takes on known issues—and what's being done about them.

Health, education, and social and political concerns are the show's red meat. Topics range from the relatively known, like human trafficking, to Islamic studies in Germany, violence against immigrants and the struggle of China's Uighurs to keep their identity.

Sturdy Teutonic fare, but the show does lighten up with the likes of a snappy one-on-one with Zap Mama. And why do German couples flock to Denmark to get married?

Deutsche Welle no longer beams to *North America*. No matter, frequencies aimed elsewhere can get through—especially east of the Rockies—thanks to the scattering properties of shortwave. The same applies to *Europe* and the *Mideast*, so try DW's off-beam frequencies in "What's On Tonight" and "Worldwide Broadcasts in English."

Southern Africa: 0430 Monday midyear on 12045 kHz; and 2030 the same day winter on 9735, 13780 and 15275 kHz; midyear on 11795, 11865 and 15205 kHz.

Asia: (*East*) 0030 Tuesday winter on 15595 kHz, and summer on 15595 and 17525 kHz; (*Southeast*) same slot, winter on 7265 and 9785 kHz, and summer on 9885 and 17525 kHz; also 1630 Monday winter on 9560 kHz, and summer on 9540 kHz; 1630 can also be heard in parts of *Australasia*, especially midyear.

Why do Germans flock to Denmark to get married?

"Jade Bells and Bamboo Pipes"
Radio Taipei International

"Jade Bells and Bamboo Pipes" is one of world band's longest running shows, going back decades. Today the jade bells and bamboo pipes of early programs have largely been replaced by stringed instruments, and the show is no longer just Taiwanese music. A sign of changing

Anke Rasper hosts Deutsche Welle's "World in Progress," which avoids the well-trodden story. Instead, it pounces on rarely covered issues.
DW

Carlson Wong hosts "Jade Bells and Bamboo Pipes" over Radio Taipei International. This show hails back many years, but has been tweaked to reflect evolving tastes in Chinese music. RTI

times is that traditional music from the mainland now shares some of the spotlight with its Taiwanese counterpart.

Even though "Jade Bells" is as exotic as it is enjoyable, it appeals to Western and Eastern ears, alike.

All are Wednesday, World Time.

North America: (*East* and *Central*) 0233 (Tuesday evening local date) on 5950 and 9680 kHz; (*West*) 0333 and 0733 on 5950 kHz. The 0333 airing is also available for *South America* on 15215 kHz. All transmissions are relayed via Family Radio in Okeechobee, Florida, so reception is usually pleasant.

Europe: 1833 and 2233 on 3965 kHz.

Asia: (*Southeast*) 0133 on 11875 kHz, 0333 on 15320 kHz, and 1133 on 7445 and 11715 kHz; (*South*) 1633 winter on 9785 or 11995 kHz, summer on 11600 or 15515 kHz, and year-round on 11550 kHz. Best for *Australasia* is 1133 on 11715 kHz.

Central and *Southern Africa:* 1733 winter on 11850 kHz, and summer on 15690 kHz.

"Frontline"
China Radio International

Perhaps something was lost in translation, but the title of China Radio International's Monday feature gives little indication of the content. "Frontline" is basically a weekly story from real life, where persistence is often a key factor. Many stories involve police investigation or legal proceedings, and often shed light on aspects of Chinese life largely unknown to people outside the country.

That China's official national broadcaster is coming to grips with once-taboo topics is a sign of how much things are evolving in the country. This openness is a far cry from the impression of heavy-handed official media control left during the 2008 Olympics.

North America: 0030 (Sunday evening local date) on 6020 and 9570 kHz, repeating 0130 on 6005 (winter), 6020, 6080 (winter), 9570, 9580 and (summer) 9790 kHz; 0330 on 9690 and 9790 kHz; 0430 winter on 6190 kHz, summer on 6020 and 6080 kHz; 0530 on 5960 (winter), 6020 (summer) and 6190 kHz; 0630 winter only on 6115 kHz; 1330 winter on 9570, 11885 and 15230 kHz, summer on 9570, 9650 and 15260 kHz; 1430 winter on 13675, 13740 and 15230 kHz, summer on 13740 kHz; and 1530 on 13740 kHz.

Europe: 0030 on 7130 or 7350 kHz; 0130 winter on 7130 or 7350 kHz, summer on 9470 kHz; 0830 on 11785 (winter), 13710 (summer) and 17490 kHz; 0930 on 15270, 17490 and 17570 kHz; 1230 on 13790 kHz; 1330 on 13610 and 13790 kHz; 1430 winter

on 9700 and 9795 kHz, summer on 13710 and 13790 kHz; 1530 winter on 9435 and 9525 kHz, summer on 11695 and 13640 kHz; 1630 winter on 7255, 9435 and 9525 kHz, summer on 11965 and 13760 kHz; 1730 winter on 6100, 7205, 7255 and 7335 kHz, summer on 6145, 7335, 9695 and 13760 kHz; 1830 winter on 6100 and 7110 kHz, and summer on 7120, 9600 and 13760 kHz; 2030 on 5960, 7190, 7285 and 9600 kHz; and 2130 on 5960, 6135, 7190, 7285 and 9600 kHz.

China Radio International's "Frontline" includes once-taboo topics.

Mideast: 0530 on 17505 kHz; 0630 winter on 11770 and 15145 kHz, summer on 11870 and 15140 kHz; 1630 summer only on 6180 and 9760 kHz; 1730 winter on 6180 and 9600 kHz, summer on 7265 and 7315 kHz; 1930 on 7295, (summer) 9435 and (winter) 9440 kHz; and 2030 on 7295 and 9440 kHz.

Southern Africa: 1430 on 13685 kHz; 1530 on 6100 and 13685 kHz; 1630 and 1730 on 6100 kHz; and 2030 on 13630 kHz.

East Asia: 0030 winter on 9425 kHz, summer on 13750 kHz; 0330 and 0430 winter on 9460, 13620 and 15120 kHz, summer on 13750, 15120 and 15785 kHz; 0830 and 0930 winter on 9415 kHz, summer on 11620 kHz; 1230, 1330, 1430 and 1530 on 5955 kHz.

Southeast Asia: 0030 on 11730, 11650 (winter), 11885 and (summer) 15125 kHz; 0130 winter on 11650 and 11885 kHz, summer on 15125 and 15785 kHz; 0630 and 0730 on 13645 (winter), 13660 (summer) and 17710 kHz; 1230 on 9600, 9645, 9730 and 11980 kHz; 1330 on 9730, 9870 and 11980 kHz; 1430 on 9870 kHz; and 1530 on 7325 kHz.

Australasia: 0930 on 15210 and 17690 kHz; and 1230 and 1330 on 9760 (midyear), 11760 and (winter) 11900 kHz.

Chinese police speak with one another as they attend "Police Open Day" March 2, 2008 in Shenzhen, China.

Shutterstock/Bartlomiej Magierowski

In June 2008, Radio Netherlands Worldwide's "Earthbeat" reported extensively from inside Burma on the aftermath of Cyclone Nargis. RNW

"Earthbeat"
Radio Netherlands Worldwide

Despite the suggestive title, "Earthbeat" is not world music. Rather, it looks at environmental issues and sustainable development. Climate changes, natural disasters, renewable energy and food production are characteristic of topics which fall within its remit. It's the kind of program Radio Netherlands Worldwide does with aplomb.

All are Thursday local date in the reception area.

North America: RNW's English transmissions no longer target North America, but the 1927 and 2027 airings to West Africa on 17810 kHz via Bonaire are well heard in parts of the United States.

Southern Africa: 1827 on 6020 kHz; 1927 winter on 7120 kHz, and summer on 7425 kHz.

East and *Southeast Asia:* 1000 winter on 6040, 9720, 9795 and 12065 kHz, and summer on 11895, 12065, 13820 and 15110 kHz. There is no specific broadcast for *Australasia*, but frequencies for Asia sometimes provide adequate reception.

South Asia: 1427 winter on 5825, 9345, 12080, 13615 and 15595 kHz, and summer on 5830 (or 9345), 9885 (or 9890) and 17550 kHz. Also audible in parts of *Southeast Asia*.

"Insight"
Deutsche Welle

Not only PASSPORT holds Deutsche Welle's "Insight" in high esteem; it has also been honored at a prestigious international festival. Whatever the subject—Britain's struggle against terrorism, the 1968 invasion of Prague or Vietnamese living in the Czech Republic—the focus is on people's everyday lives.

Although it doesn't receive the airtime and global coverage it deserves, there are fully two features within each 30-minute airing.

Southern Africa: 0430 Saturday midyear on 12045 kHz, but nothing in winter.

Asia: (*East*) 0930 Saturday winter on 17710 and 21840 kHz, and summer on 15340 and 17705 kHz; (*South*) 1630 Sunday winter on 5965 and 9560 kHz, and summer on 6170, 9540 and 15640 kHz; (*Southeast*) same slot, winter on 9560 kHz, and summer on 9540 and 15640 kHz. Frequencies for East and Southeast Asia are also heard in parts of *Australia*.

Zhou Jing, host and producer of "Voices from Other Lands" hoofs with locals while on African assignment for China Radio International. CRI

"Voices from Other Lands"
China Radio International

"Voices from Other Lands" is a series of one-on-one interviews with foreigners visiting or working in China. It is one of CRI's most popular shows.

Teachers, engineers, journalists, investors, retirees or just vacationers—they all have something to say, and it is nearly always interesting. Indeed, some observations and comments might otherwise not make airtime because of government sensitivity to certain topics.

Foreigners get to sound off about China.

"Voices from Other Lands" is on Thursday, World Time.

North America: 0030 (Wednesday evening local date) on 6020 and 9570 kHz; 0130 on 6005 (winter), 6020, 6080 (winter), 9570, 9580 and (summer) 9790 kHz; 0330 on 9690 and 9790 kHz; 0430 winter on 6190 kHz, summer on 6020 and 6080 kHz; 0530 on 5960 (winter), 6020 (summer) and 6190 kHz; 0630 winter only on 6115 kHz; 1330 winter on 9570, 11885 and 15230 kHz, summer on 9570, 9650 and 15260 kHz; 1430 winter on 13675, 13740 and 15230 kHz, summer on 13740 kHz; and 1530 on 13740 kHz.

Europe: 0030 on 7130 or 7350 kHz; 0130 winter on 7130 or 7350 kHz, summer on 9470 kHz; 0830 on 11785 (winter), 13710 (summer) and 17490 kHz; 0930 on 15270, 17490 and 17570 kHz; 1230 on 13790 kHz; 1330 on 13610 and 13790 kHz; 1430 winter on 9700 and 9795 kHz, summer on 13710 and 13790 kHz; 1530 winter on 9435 and 9525 kHz, summer on 11695 and 13640 kHz; 1630 winter on 7255, 9435 and 9525 kHz, summer on 11965 and 13760 kHz; 1730 winter on 6100, 7205, 7255 and 7335 kHz, summer on 6145, 7335, 9695 and 13760 kHz; 1830 winter on 6100 and 7110 kHz, and summer on 7120, 9600 and 13760 kHz; 2030 on 5960, 7190, 7285 and 9600 kHz; and 2130 on 5960, 6135, 7190, 7285 and 9600 kHz.

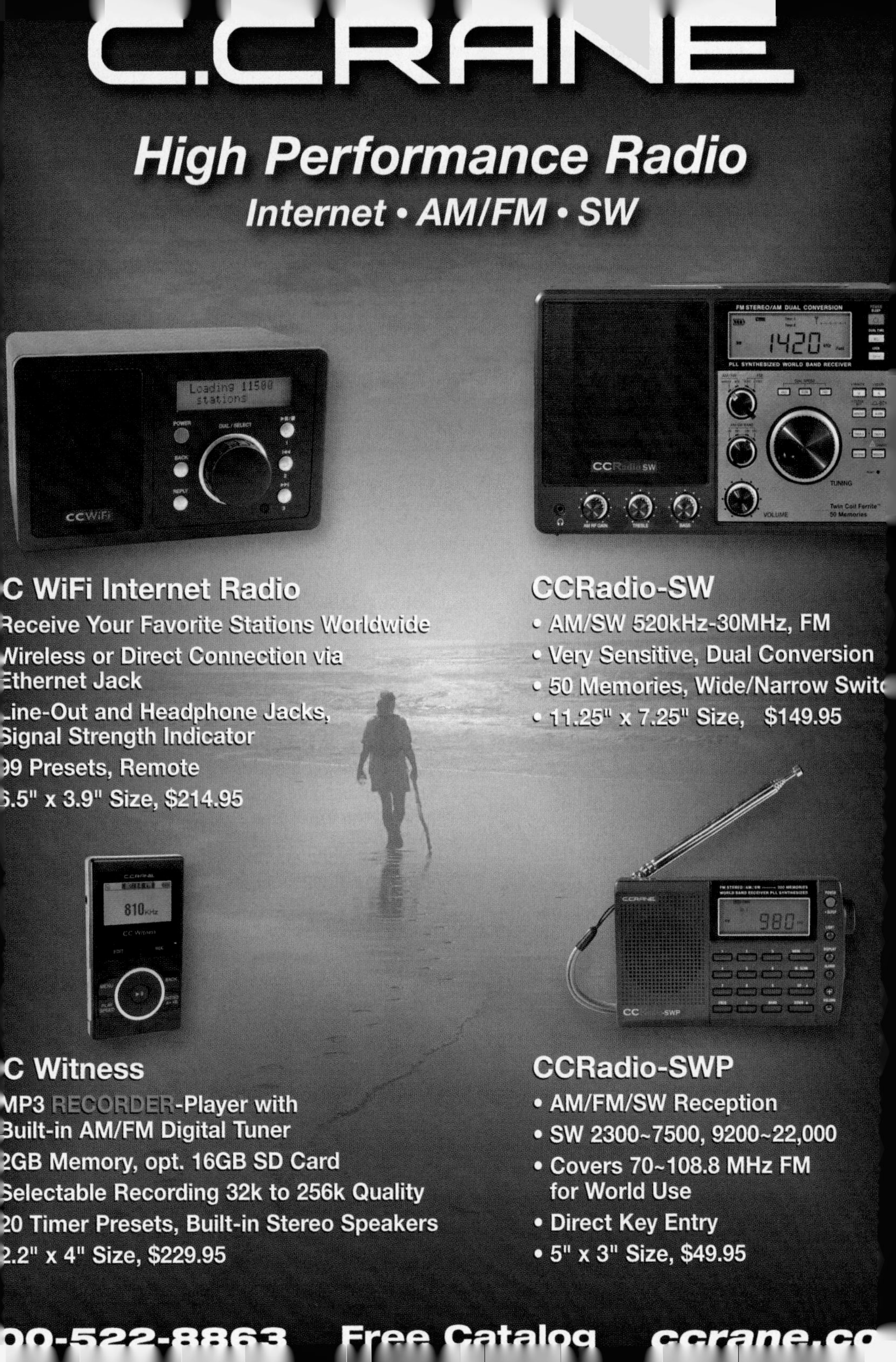
C.CRANE
High Performance Radio
Internet • AM/FM • SW
Loading 11580 stations
CCWiFi
FM STEREO/AM DUAL CONVERSION
1420
PLL SYNTHESIZED WORLD BAND RECEIVER
CCRadio SW
TUNING
VOLUME
Twin Coil Ferrite™
50 Memories
C WiFi Internet Radio
Receive Your Favorite Stations Worldwide
Vireless or Direct Connection via
Ethernet Jack
Line-Out and Headphone Jacks,
Signal Strength Indicator
99 Presets, Remote
5.5" x 3.9" Size, $214.95
CCRadio-SW
• AM/SW 520kHz-30MHz, FM
• Very Sensitive, Dual Conversion
• 50 Memories, Wide/Narrow Swit
• 11.25" x 7.25" Size, $149.95
C.CRANE
810KHz
CC Witness
CCRANE
980
CC -SWP
C Witness
MP3 RECORDER-Player with
Built-in AM/FM Digital Tuner
2GB Memory, opt. 16GB SD Card
Selectable Recording 32k to 256k Quality
20 Timer Presets, Built-in Stereo Speakers
2.2" x 4" Size, $229.95
CCRadio-SWP
• AM/FM/SW Reception
• SW 2300~7500, 9200~22,000
• Covers 70~108.8 MHz FM
for World Use
• Direct Key Entry
• 5" x 3" Size, $49.95
00-522-8863 Free Catalog ccrane.co

Kateri Jochum hosts Deutsche Welle's "Money Talks." Coverage includes financial issues relevant to ordinary consumers and investors. DW

Mideast: 0530 on 17505 kHz; 0630 winter on 11770 and 15145 kHz, summer on 11870 and 15140 kHz; 1630 summer only on 6180 and 9760 kHz; 1730 winter on 6180 and 9600 kHz, summer on 7265 and 7315 kHz; 1930 on 7295, (summer) 9435 and (winter) 9440 kHz; and 2030 on 7295 and 9440 kHz.

Southern Africa: 1430 on 13685 kHz; 1530 on 6100 and 13685 kHz; 1630 and 1730 on 6100 kHz; and 2030 on 13630 kHz.

East Asia: 0030 winter on 9425 kHz, summer on 13750 kHz; 0330 and 0430 winter on 9460, 13620 and 15120 kHz, summer on 13750, 15120 and 15785 kHz; 0830 and 0930 winter on 9415 kHz, summer on 11620 kHz; and 1230, 1330, 1430 and 1530 on 5955 kHz.

Southeast Asia: 0030 on 11730, 11650 (winter), 11885 and (summer) 15125 kHz; 0130 winter on 11650 and 11885 kHz, summer on 15125 and 15785 kHz; 0630 and 0730 on 13645 (winter), 13660 (summer) and 17710 kHz; 1230 on 9600, 9645, 9730 and 11980 kHz; 1330 on 9730, 9870 and 11980 kHz; 1430 on 9870 kHz; and 1530 on 7325 kHz.

Australasia: 0930 on 15210 and 17690 kHz; and 1230 and 1330 on 9760 (midyear), 11760 and (winter) 11900 kHz.

"Money Talks" Deutsche Welle

Deutsche Welle's "Money Talks" covers business and economic issues, including those faced by ordinary people: personal data protection, international energy deals, the tourist trade, convictions for graft, even a New York organic eatery—all get their moment in the ionosphere.

Deutsche Welle no longer targets *North America*, but frequencies beamed elsewhere are often heard there, especially in the eastern and southern United States. The same applies to *Europe* and the *Mideast*, so check DW's schedules in "What's On Tonight" and "Worldwide Broadcasts in English."

Southern Africa: 0430 Wednesday midyear on 12045 kHz; and 2030 the same day winter on 9735, 13780 and 15275 kHz; midyear on 11795, 11865 and 15205 kHz.

Asia: (*East*) 0030 Tuesday winter on 15595 kHz, and summer on 15595 and 17525 kHz; (*Southeast*) same slot, winter on 7265 and 9785 kHz, and summer on 9885 and 17525 kHz; also 1630 Monday winter on 9560 kHz, and summer on 9540 kHz; 1630 is also audible in parts of *Australasia*, especially midyear.

"Curious Orange"
Radio Netherlands Worldwide

RNW describes this show as a look at modern-day Holland, but some topics, like Chinese poetry competition, have a tenuous link. But no question, a Dutch Indonesian rock band performing "Rip It Up" in true 1950's style is modern, Dutch . . . and curious. "Orange" refers to The House of Orange, The Netherlands' royal family.

"Curious Orange" has an infectious informality about it, and succeeds where others fail. It is an experiment that comes off.

All are Monday local date in the reception area.

North America: RNW's English transmissions no longer target North America, but the 1927 and 2027 airings to West Africa on 17810 kHz via Bonaire are well heard in parts of the United States.

Southern Africa: 1827 on 6020 kHz; 1927 winter on 7120 kHz, and summer on 7425 kHz.

East and *Southeast Asia:* 1000 winter on 6040, 9720, 9795 and 12065 kHz, and summer on 11895, 12065, 13820 and 15110 kHz. There is no specific broadcast for *Australasia*, but frequencies for Asia sometimes provide adequate reception.

South Asia: 1427 winter on 5825, 9345, 12080, 13615 and 15595 kHz, and summer on 5830 (or 9345), 9885 (or 9890) and 17550 kHz. Also audible in parts of *Southeast Asia*.

"Music Calendar"
Voice of Russia

"Music Calendar" can pass unnoticed if you're not a regular Voice of Russia listener. The station's website calls it, "a program about musicians and musical events that have stood the test of time," but it's really an undiscovered gem. Wonderful music and historic recordings make it a melomanic must.

The bad news? It's only monthly, usually during the first week or ten days of the month.

North America: Winter, 0531 Tuesday (Monday evening local American date) on 7150, 7350, 9840, 9855 and 12040 kHz; and 0331 Friday on 6155, 6240, 7350, 12040 and 13735 kHz. In summer, one hour earlier, it's 0431 Tuesday on 5900 (or 9800), 9435, 9665, 9860, 13635 and 13775 kHz; and 0231 Friday on 9480, 9665, 9860, 13635 and 13775 kHz.

Winter times for *Europe* are 1631 Sunday, Monday, Tuesday and Thursday on 6130 and 7320 kHz; 2031 Wednesday on 6145, 7105 and 7330 kHz; and 2131 Friday on 6145, 7290 and 7330 kHz. Summer slots are 1531 Sunday, Monday, Tuesday and Thursday on 9810 (or 12040) kHz; 1931 Wednesday on 7195 (or 12070), 7310 and 9890 kHz; and 2031 Friday on 7195 (or 12070) and 9890 kHz.

There is little or nothing for the *Mideast* and *Southern Africa*, nor for *East* and *Southeast Asia*.

Canadian Ashleigh Elson and Dutchman Michel Walraven are the co-hosts of "Curious Orange" on Radio Netherlands Worldwide. RNW

Olga Fyodorova, music editor and author, and Elena Gashennikova, sound engineer, of the Voice of Russia's "Music Calendar." VoR

Australasia: Winter times are 0631 Tuesday and 0731 Wednesday and Thursday on 17665 and 17805 kHz, and 0931 Friday on 17495, 17665 and 17805 kHz. Midyear, one hour earlier, it's 0531 Tuesday and 0631 Wednesday and Thursday on 17635 and 21790 kHz, and 0831 Friday on 17495, 17635 and 21790 kHz.

"News and Reports" China Radio International

Much of the international broadcasting community has moved away from world band in favor of alternative delivery options. Yet, China Radio International has embraced both paths, retaining its ability to reach out to the one in ten among the world's population that listens to shortwave.

CRI's half-hour "News and Reports" is not only a major source of Chinese and other Asian news, it is the most frequent English-language newscast of any type on shortwave. Credibility may be the gold standard of newscasting, but the first step is to connect content with audience. Here, CRI excels where others lag.

There remains room for upgraded reporting on sensitive issues within China. Nevertheless, CRI's vast human, financial and physical resources make it the region's most accessible source for news and information.

North America: 0000 on 6020 and 9570 kHz; 0100 on 6005 (winter), 6020, 6080 (winter), 9570, 9580 and (summer) 9790 kHz; 0300 on 9690 and 9790 kHz; 0400 winter on 6190 kHz, summer on 6020 and 6080 kHz; 0500 on 5960 (winter), 6020 (summer) and 6190 kHz; 0600 winter only on 6115 kHz; 1300 winter on 9570, 11885 and 15230 kHz, summer on 9570, 9650 and 15260 kHz; 1400 winter on 13675, 13740 and 15230 kHz, summer on 13740 kHz; 1500 on 13740 kHz; 2300 winter on 6040 and 11970 kHz, and summer on 6145 and 11840 kHz (also to the Caribbean year-round on 5995 kHz).

Europe: 0000 on 7130 or 7350 kHz; 0100 winter on 7130 or 7350 kHz, summer on 9470 kHz; 0800 on 11785 (winter), 13710 (summer) and 17490 kHz; 0900 on 15270, 17490 and 17570 kHz; 1200 on 13790 kHz; 1300 on 13610 and 13790 kHz; 1400 winter on 9700 and 9795 kHz, summer on 13710 and 13790 kHz; 1500 winter on 9435 and 9525 kHz, summer on 11695 and 13640 kHz; 1600 winter on 7255, 9435 and 9525 kHz, summer on 11965 and 13760 kHz; 1700 winter on 6100, 7205, 7255 and 7335 kHz, summer on 6145, 7335, 9695 and 13760 kHz; 1800 winter on 6100 and 7110 kHz, and summer on 7120, 9600 and 13760 kHz; 2000 on 5960, 7190, 7285 and 9600 kHz; and 2100 on 5960, 6135, 7190, 7285 and 9600 kHz.

Mideast: 0500 on 17505 kHz; 0600 winter on 11770 and 15145 kHz, summer on 11870 and 15140 kHz; 1600 summer only on 6180 and 9760 kHz; 1700 winter on 6180 and 9600 kHz, summer on 7265 and 7315 kHz; 1900 on 7295, (summer) 9435 and (winter) 9440 kHz; and 2000 on 7295 and 9440 kHz.

Southern Africa: 1400 on 13685 kHz; 1500 on 6100 and 13685 kHz; 1600 and 1700 on 6100 kHz; and 2000 and 2100 on 13630 kHz.

One of Russia's best shows is all but hidden.

East Asia: 0000 winter on 9425 kHz, summer on 13750 kHz; 0300 and 0400 winter on 9460, 13620 and 15120 kHz, summer on 13750, 15120 and 15785 kHz; 0800 and 0900 winter on 9415 kHz, summer on 11620 kHz; 1200, 1300, 1400 and 1500 on 5955 kHz.

Southeast Asia: 0000 on 11730, 11650 (winter), 11885 and (summer) 15125 kHz; 0100 winter on 11650 and 11885 kHz, summer on 15125 and 15785 kHz; 0600 and 0700 on 13645 (winter), 13660 (summer) and 17710 kHz; 1200 on 9600, 9645, 9730 and 11980 kHz; 1300 on 9730, 9870 and 11980 kHz; 1400 on 9870 kHz; and 1500 on 7325 kHz.

Australasia: 0900 on 15210 and 17690 kHz; and 1200 and 1300 on 9760 (midyear), 11760 and (winter) 11900 kHz.

Prepared by the staff of PASSPORT TO WORLD BAND RADIO.

Deutsche Welle World's English Service staff include Monika Lindenberg, Mark Mattox, Breandain O'Shea, Kateri Jochum, Carla Gehrmann-Zellen, Angelika Ditscheid, Rick Fulker and Features Editor Irene Quaile. DW

GRUNDIG
TIMELESS PERFORMANCE
LISTEN TO THE WORLD
BUZZ ALDRIN EDITION
G6 AVIATOR
AM/FM/Aircraft Band/General Coverage Shortwave Portable Radio with SSB (Single Side Band)
G8 TRAVELER II DIGITAL
AM/FM-stereo/selectable Shortwave Bands
• Analog Tuner, Digital Readout, Clock, Alarm
G3 VOYAGER
AM/FM with RDS/Aircraft Band/LW/Continuous Shortwave with SSB and Sync Detector
• Line In/Out

GRUNDIG
POWER
TUNING

GRUNDIG
GS350DL

How to Choose a World Band Radio

Some electronic products are like bananas. Pick through the bunches with a little common sense and you can find pretty much what you want.

Not so with world band receivers, which can vary greatly from model to model. As usual money talks, but even that's fickle. Fortunately, many perform well and we rate them accordingly. Yet, even among models with similar star ratings it helps to read the pros and cons.

Tough Voyage

World band radio offers hundreds of channels, each crammed five kilohertz apart. That's much more crowded than FM and medium-wave AM.

Take a long flight and you'll arrive weary and rumpled. The same holds true for world band signals, where skywave treks result in fading and reduced strength. To cope, a world band radio has to perform electronic gymnastics. Some succeed, others don't.

This is why Passport Reports was created. At International Broadcasting Services we've independently tested hundreds of world band radios, antennas and accessories since 1977. Evaluations include hands-on use by listeners and specialized lab tests which are summarized in Passport Reports. Full-length internal reports on some receivers and antennas are published as Radio Database International White Papers®.

Four-Point Checkoff

Radios vary greatly from model to model.

✔ **Price.** Want to hear major stations, or do you prefer gentler voices from exotic lands? Powerful evening signals, or weaker stations by day? Decide, then choose a radio that slightly surpasses your needs—this helps ensure against disappointment without spending too much.

Bargain-basement radios are clumsy to tune, and can receive poorly and sound terrible. That's why we rarely cover analog-readout radios. Yet, even models with digital frequency readout can disappoint.

Most are satisfied with digital-readout portables selling for $50–160 in the United States or €50–130 in the United Kingdom, and having a rating of ✪¾ or more. If you're looking for elite performance, shoot for a costlier portable rated ✪✪✪✪ or better. If you want bragging rights, a five-star tabletop, professional or PC model is *número uno*.

✔ **Location.** Signals are usually strongest around Europe, North Africa and the Near East; they're almost as good evenings in eastern North America. Otherwise, elsewhere in the Americas—or in Hawaii, Australasia or the Middle East—spring for a receiver with superior sensitivity to weak signals; an accessory antenna helps, too.

✔ **Features.** Divide features between those for performance and those that impact operation (sidebars), but be wary. Radios with relatively few features sometimes outperform those tricked out with goodies.

PASSPORT'S STANDARDS

At International Broadcasting Services we have been analyzing shortwave equipment since 1977. Our reviewers, and no one else, write and edit everything in Passport Reports, and tests are performed by an independent laboratory recognized as the world's leader. (See the Radio Database International White Paper, *How to Interpret Receiver Lab Tests and Measurements*.)

The review process is separate from equipment advertising, which is not allowed within Passport Reports. Our team members may not accept review fees from manufacturers, nor may they "permanently borrow" radios. And International Broadcasting Services does not manufacture, sell or distribute world band radios or related hardware.

PERFORMANCE FEATURES

Whenever possible a signal should sound pleasant, not just be audible. To help, some radios have features to ward off unwanted sounds or improve audio quality. Of course, just because a feature exists doesn't mean it functions properly, but PASSPORT REPORTS' team checks this out.

What's Most Important

Full world band coverage from 2300–26100 kHz is best, but 3200–21850 kHz is plenty good—even 5730–21850 kHz is often okay. Less coverage? Look over PASSPORT's "Best Times and Frequencies for 2009" to see what's missed.

Synchronous selectable sideband helps knock out adjacent-channel interference and reduce fading distortion. This advanced feature is found on a few portables, along with many tabletop and professional models and PC receivers; there's an outboard accessory for this, too. PASSPORT REPORTS indicates which work well.

Especially if a receiver doesn't include properly performing synchronous selectable sideband, it benefits from having two or more *bandwidths* to reduce adjacent-channel interference. Some premium models have multiple bandwidths and effective synchronous selectable sideband—a killer combo.

Double (or dual or multiple) conversion, done properly, helps reject unwanted images, growls, whistles and dih-dah sounds. Few cheaper models have it.

Great Goodies

Tone controls are a plus, especially continuous bass and treble. Utility and "ham" signals require *single-sideband* (SSB), but for world band it's needed only for the American Forces Radio and Television Service.

Most tabletop and professional models, some PC models and elite portables are ideal for snaring tough signals. Look for a tunable or automatic *notch filter* to zap howls; *passband offset* (also called *passband tuning* and *IF shift*) for superior adjacent-channel rejection and audio contouring, especially in conjunction with synchronous selectable sideband; and multiple *AGC* decay rates. At electrically noisy locations a *noise blanker* is essential, although performance varies greatly.

Digital signal processing (DSP) is to enhance reception quality. Until recently it has been much smoke, little fire, but it has been improving—slowly.

Software Defined Radios (SDR) use computer-related software and hardware in place of discrete circuit components. This concept is not yet commonly applied, and still has a ways to go before fully realizing its potential. Yet, benefits are increasingly apparent. Eventually, most radios may be SDR, if only because they'll be cheaper.

Digital Radio Mondiale (DRM), a form of digital transmission, has good points (fidelity) and drawbacks (easily jammed, disrupts adjacent signals). Global DRM has yet to catch on, and so far there have been few models of DRM receivers. However, some regular receivers feed 12 kHz IF to a personal computer to process DRM signals.

An *AC adaptor* reduces portable operating costs and may improve weak-signal performance. Some cause hum or buzzing, but many are okay. With tabletop models an *inboard AC power supply* is preferable but not essential.

✔ **Where to buy?** World band radios don't test well in stores, so whether you buy there or from afar makes little difference. But what you can nail down in a store is ergonomics—user friendliness. Audio quality, too, by hearing mediumwave AM or muscular world band stations.

Internet purchases from foreign countries sometimes save money, but rarely provide enforceable warranties. There can also be uncollectible shipping damage, inappropriate AC voltages, no safety certification, and packets can be refused by customs.

CONVENIENCE FEATURES

To find stations quickly, look for *digital frequency readout*, found on virtually all models tested for PASSPORT REPORTS.

A number of handy features derive from *synthesized tuning*, found on most models with digital frequency readout. These include direct-access tuning by *keypad* and station *presets* ("memories"); and various combinations of a *tuning knob*, up/down *slewing controls* and/or *"signal-seek" scanning* to find stations. A few models have handy *one-touch presets* buttons, like a classic car radio, while others cluster multiple presets within *pages*. Quick access to *world band segments* (meter bands) is another time saver. ☞ Tuning knobs are a real plus, but as detailed in PASSPORT REPORTS we're now finding some to tune erratically over time.

Presets are important because world band stations change frequencies throughout the day. Being able to store these makes a station easier to find—especially if presets use alphanumeric *tags*. With sophisticated receivers, presets should be able to store not only frequency, but also such parameters as bandwidth, mode and AGC.

A *24-hour World Time clock*, built into many radios, lets you know when to tune in. The best allow time to be read while the frequency is being displayed. Seconds displayed numerically are also a nice touch so you can be alert for station IDs.

If your radio lacks a World Time clock, try a standalone 24-hour clock or watch. Most accurate are "atomic," synchronized to a time station like WWV/WWVH or CHU; surprisingly, virtually no world band radio offers this, just accessory timepieces.

On/off timers are best if they have multiple *events*. Also look for an *illuminated display* and a meaningful *signal-strength indicator*.

Travelers prefer portables with *travel power locks* or *recessed power buttons* so the radio won't go on by itself in luggage. ☞ Power locks on some Chinese-made portables don't disable display illumination.

If ergonomics stand out, bad or good, PASSPORT REPORTS says so. But fewer controls doesn't necessarily mean handier operation. Some receivers with many discrete controls are more user friendly than comparable receivers with few controls—especially if there are complex software choices.

Icom's IC-R9500.

D. Zantow

Portables for 2009

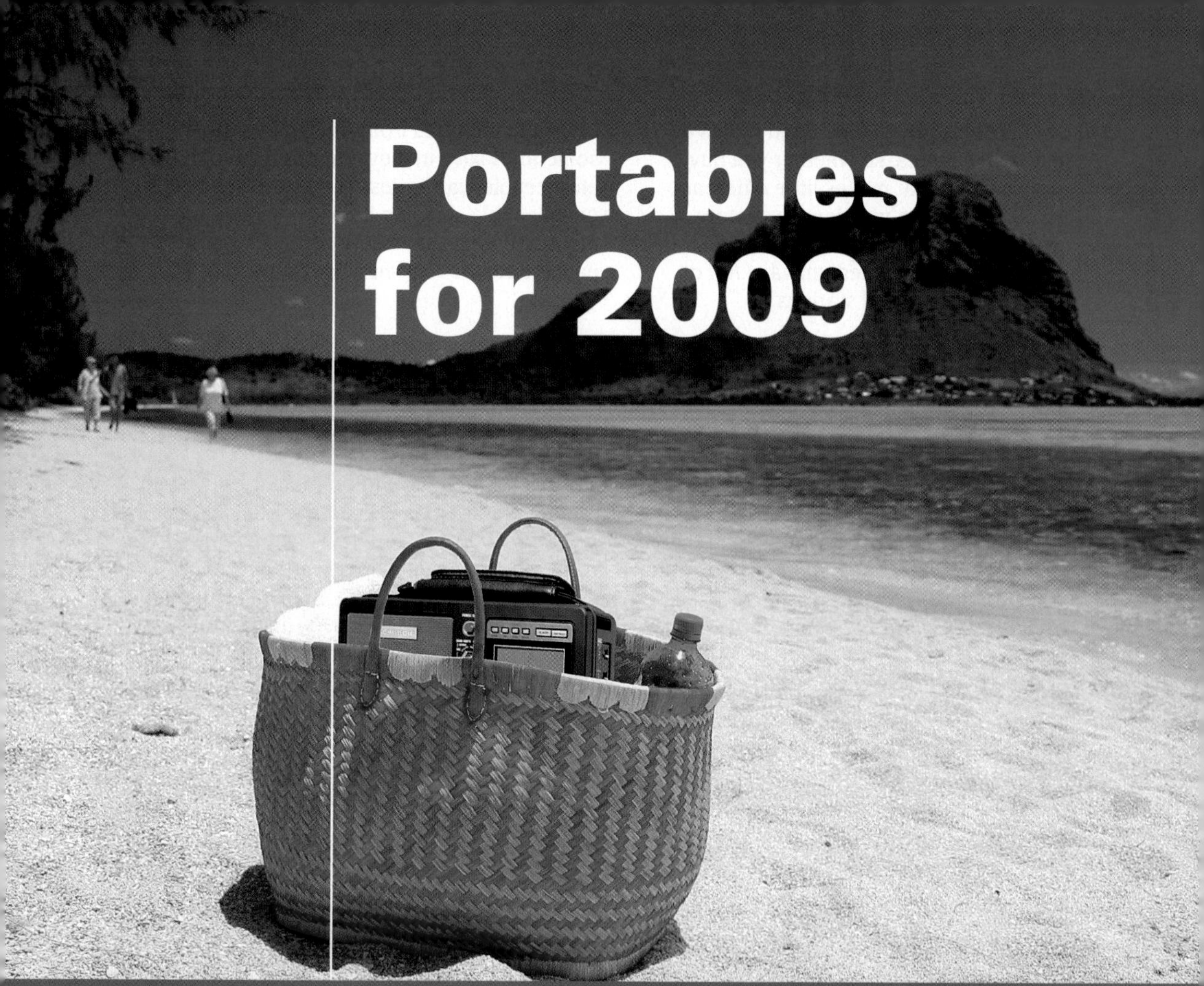

Portables used to be also-rans, but no more. Today's best now give tabletop models a run for their money.

Another change: More stations now tease their way into the afternoon and around sunrise, rather than at prime time. These weaker signals may not be beamed your way. Yet, thanks to shortwave's scattering properties they can be heard on a superior receiver, perhaps boosted by an accessory antenna as shown in PASSPORT REPORTS.

Digital Broadcasts for Alaska

Digital Radio Mondiale (DRM) broadcasts potentially offer superior audio quality at reduced power. However, success continues to elude because they disrupt adjacent signals, flip in and out during fades, are easy to jam and are relatively ineffective for multi-hop service.

Another roadblock is that there's still no viable market for DRM receivers, even after years of trying. Nonetheless, DRM may yet succeed, even if only with domestic shortwave broadcasts.

To this end, Digital Aurora Radio Technologies is constructing an experimental DRM facility in Alaska to test the feasability of domestic statewide broadcasts within world band segments below 10 MHz. Domestic broadcasts aren't jammed; are typically one-hop; and generally have differing propagational requirements and thus lower frequency usage than international broadcasts. Taken together, these characteristics point to a substantially greater potential for success than heretofore.

Three Flavors

Pocket portables aren't much bigger than everyday cellphones, while compacts are like Blackberrys but thicker. Top-rated lap portables might be more than you need, but probably not more than you want.

Unfriendly skies? Pocket models shine, and their thin speaker audio can be overcome with earpieces. Yet, compact models aren't much bigger, can suffice for home, usually perform better and tend to sell for less. It's no wonder these are the workhorses of world band radio.

Find major updates to the 2009 PASSPORT REPORTS at www.passband.com.

Longwave Band

Longwave is for Europe, North Africa and Russia. If you live or travel there in rural areas, great. Otherwise forget it.

Fix or Toss?

Portables aren't friends for life. The most robust models might serve for a decade or more, but don't count on it. Only the top handful of models are usually worth fixing outside warranty.

DOA? Get an immediate exchange without a restocking fee. If out-of-warranty service is important to you, consider a tabletop model or the Etón E1 portable that's serviced by R.L. Drake in Ohio.

Shelling Out

Street prices are quoted, including European VAT where applicable. Shortwave specialty outlets and electronics retailers may offer tempting prices, but airport duty-free is no bargain.

eBay is no different with radios than anything else. You might find the lowest price, and in time you'll probably receive what you ordered—indeed, eBay is the main global outlet for radios for the domestic Chinese market. Yet, if there's a problem, such as a damaged radio, you can usually forget making a successful claim even if you paid extra for insurance. eBay is also where hurt radios wind up being palmed off as

WHAT TO LOOK FOR

- **AC adaptor.** Those from the radio's manufacturer are usually best. Some are multivoltage and operate globally, but all should be free from significant hum and noise. Switching-type power supplies, legally required in some places, may disrupt radio signals.
- **Adjacent-channel rejection—I: *selectivity, bandwidth*.** World band stations are about twice as tightly packed together as ordinary mediumwave AM stations. So, they tend to slop over and interfere with each other—DRM broadcasts in particular. Radios with superior selectivity are better at rejecting interference, but at a Pricing: better selectivity also means less high-end (treble) audio response and muddier sound. But having more than one bandwidth allows you to choose between tighter selectivity when it is warranted, and more realistic audio when it isn't.

Portables used to be also-rans, but no more.

- **Adjacent-channel rejection—II: *synchronous selectable sideband*.** Synchronous selectable sideband minimizes selective-fading distortion and adjacent-channel interference. *Bonus:* It squashes fading distortion with fringe mediumwave AM stations at twilight and evenings.
- **Ergonomics.** Some radios are a snap to use because they don't have complicated features. Yet, even sophisticated models can be designed to operate intuitively. Choose accordingly—there's no reason to take the square root and cube it just to hear a station.
- **Single-sideband demodulation.** For non-broadcast shortwave signals—hams and utility stations—single-sideband circuitry is *de rigueur*. The popular low-powered American Forces Radio-Television Service also requires this. Not needed otherwise.
- **Speaker audio quality.** Unlike many tabletop models, few portables have pleasant speaker audio, but some are better than others. An audio line output can feed amplified speakers for pleasant home listening; FM micro-transmitters work, too.
- **Tuning features.** Models with digital frequency readout are so superior to analog that these are now the only radios normally tested by PASSPORT. Look for such handy tuning features as direct-frequency access via keypad, station presets (memories), up-down tuning by tuning knob and/or slewing keys, band/segment selection, and signal-seek or other (e.g., presets) scanning. These make a radio much easier to tune—no small point, given that dozens of channels may be audible at a time.
- **Weak-signal sensitivity.** Sensitivity especially counts if you live in a weak-signal location or tune exotic or daytime stations. Most portables have enough sensitivity for major stations during prime time if you're in the likes of Europe, North Africa or eastern North America.
- **World Time clock.** World Time is in 24-hour format, so a 24-hour clock is a must. You can buy one separately, but why bother when many radios have them built in? The best display time whether the radio is on or off, but many gain or lose time if not reset periodically. In North America and beyond, official shortwave time stations WWV on 2500, 5000, 10000, 15000 and 20000 kHz and CHU on 3330, 7335 and 14670 kHz are ideal for this; the Pacific is also served by WWVH in Hawaii on 2500, 5000, 10000 and 15000 kHz.

"new in box." If you get stuck, don't expect the manufacturer to bail you out.

Specialized terms can be useful but puzzling. But if you come across something unclear, *see* Worldly Words.

What PASSPORT's Ratings Mean

Star ratings: ✪✪✪✪✪ is best. Stars reflect overall performance and meaningful features, plus to some extent user-friendliness and perceived build quality. Price, appearance, country of manufacture and the like aren't taken into account. To facilitate comparison, portable rating standards are similar to those used for tabletops and other types reviewed in PASSPORT REPORTS.

A rating of ✪✪¾ is more than adequate for major stations during the evening. However, for casual use on trips nearly any small portable might do.

Passport's Choice. La crème de la crème. Our test team's personal picks of the litter—models we would buy or have bought for our personal use. Unlike star ratings, these choices are unapologetically subjective.

¢: A relative bargain, with decidedly more performance than the price would suggest.

Tips for Using This Section

Models are listed by size, and within that they're in order of suitability for world band with their built-in antennas. Street selling prices are given, including European VAT where applicable.

Unless otherwise indicated, each model features:

- Keypad tuning, up/down slewing keys, station presets and signal-seek tuning/scanning.
- Digital frequency readout to the nearest kilohertz or five kilohertz.
- Coverage of the shortwave spectrum, including world band, from at least 3200–26100 kHz.
- Coverage of the usual 87.5–108 MHz FM band, but not the Japanese and other FM bands below 87 MHz.
- Coverage of the mediumwave AM band in selectable 9 and 10 kHz channel steps from about 530–1705 kHz. No 153–279 kHz longwave coverage.
- Adequate image rejection, usually resulting from double-conversion circuitry.
- Telescopic antenna that swivels and rotates.

Unless otherwise indicated, each model lacks:

- Single-sideband and DRM demodulation.
- Synchronous selectable sideband. However, when it is present the unwanted sideband is rejected ≤25 dB by phase cancellation, not IF filtering.
- World Time clock, when included, does not show seconds numerically.

LAP PORTABLES

Pleasant for Home, Acceptable for Travel

A lap portable is mainly for use around the house and yard, highway trips, yachts and arguably on the occasional flight. They are large enough to potentially perform well, usually sound better than compact models, yet are not too big to fit into a carry-on. Most take 3–4 "D" (UM-1) or "C" (UM-2) cells, plus sometimes a couple of "AA" (UM-3) cells for memory backup.

These are typically just under a foot (30 cm) wide and weigh in around 3–5 pounds (1.4–2.3 kg).

New Version for 2009

✪✪✪✪⅜ *Passport's Choice*

Etón E1, Etón E1XM, E1 "Lextronix"

Pricing: *E1XM:* $419.95 in the United States. CAD$499.99 in Canada. *E1:* $399.95 in the United States. £399.95 in the United Kingdom. *E1 "Lextronix":* €598.00 in Germany. *AudioVox CNP2000 XM antenna with cable and required CNP2000H docking station:* $58.95 for both in the United States.

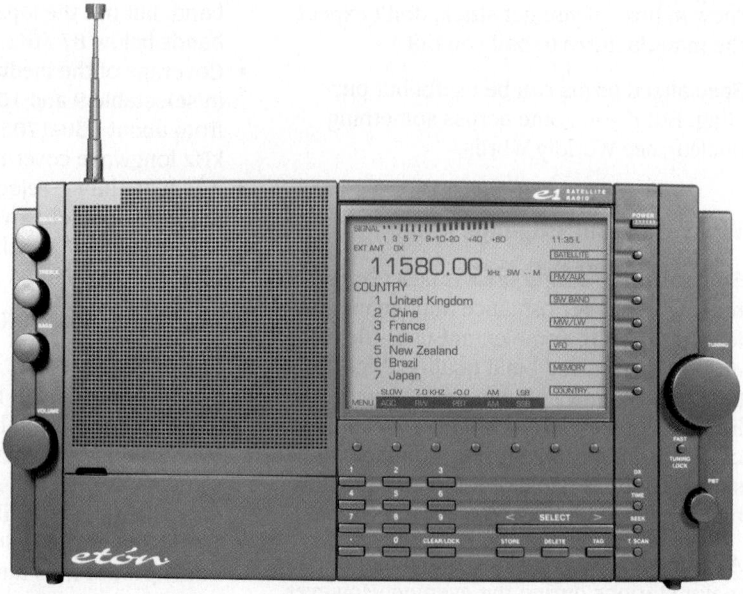

Etón's top-gun E1XM is a poster child for international teamwork. The concept originated at Grundig AG of Germany. Etón, headquartered in California by a onetime Iranian official, commissioned the legendary R.L. Drake Company of Ohio to engineer the circuitry. Finish engineering and production went to defense giant Bharat Electronics of India.

Terk XM-EXT50 50-foot extension cable for CNP-2000: $39.95 in the United States. *SO-239-to-KOK1 aftermarket antenna jack adaptor:* $14.95 in the United States. *E1/Satellit 1000: KOK1 aftermarket male connector (for raw antenna cable):* $5 or so in the United States. *Universal Radio CLEAR LRG Portable Stand:* $16.95 in the United States. *Tenba Port Air 1114 padded carrying case:* $139.95 in the United States.

Pros: Incorporates virtually every tuning method available, including frequency/presets scanning, up/down slewing, keypad frequency selection, quick access to world band segments and a tuning knob. Tuning knob (*see* Cons) features variable rate incremental tuning (VRIT); for many this makes bandscanning more convenient. 1,700 easy-to-use presets, non-volatile; 500 allow for user-written ID tags, while remainder have factory-created country ID tags. Keypad frequency may be entered in kHz or MHz. Pleasant audio quality, aided by separate bass and treble controls (*see* Cons). Overall receiver distortion unusually low (*see* Cons). Full three-watt (nominal) audio amplifier with AC adaptor; when batteries in use, amplifier output is automatically reduced so battery drain can be cut by half. Agreeable ergonomics, including keys with superior feel. Passband tuning (PBT, a/k/a IF shift), a first for a portable; performance excellent. Synchronous selectable sideband holds lock unusually well; adjacent-channel interference reduction and tonal response aided by passband tuning adjustment. Synchronous double sideband overcomes selective fading distortion and enhances fidelity during twilight and darkness (mixed skywave/groundwave) reception of fringe mediumwave AM stations "in the clear." Wide (20 kHz signal spacing) dynamic range good, IP3 excellent with preamp off, to the point that resistance to overloading, even with Beverage antennas, comparable to that of excellent tabletop supersets; wide DR/IP3 still tests as good with preamp on (*see* Cons). Blocking good. Phase noise good, although still intrudes beyond 80 dB down. Sensitivity/noise floor good-to- excellent with preamp off, excellent-to-superb with 10 dB preamp on. Three well-chosen voice/music bandwidths (2.5, 5 and 8 kHz) with skirt selectivity and ultimate rejection that are excellent or better. Image rejection approaches professional caliber. Excellent first IF rejection. Tuning and display in 10 Hz steps, exceptionally precise for a portable; 100 Hz and 1 kHz tuning steps also selectable. On our current unit, frequency display came from factory absolutely accurate after lengthy warmup (*see* Cons); frequency readout accuracy user-adjustable with a small flat-blade screwdriver through first vent slot just to right of "CE" sticker on back of cabinet. No chuffing or muting when tuning. Octave filters provide good front end selectivity by tabletop standards, which is exceptional for a portable. Single-sideband performance above average for a portable, aided by excellent frequency stability. Signal-strength indicator, with 21 bars, uncommonly accurate from S3 through 60 dB over S9 even by professional standards. Audio line output jack (stereo on E1XM's FM/XM, E1's FM) with proper level to feed external amplifier/ speaker system, recorder or FM/AM microtransmitter; also, external speaker jack and separate jack for headphones or earpieces. Audio line input jack allows radio to be used as amp/speaker for CD players and the like. Useful battery-strength indicator. Selectable slow/fast AGC decay adjustment; a third AGC option, "Auto," aids bandscanning by switching from slow to fast when radio tuned. Squelch. Telescopic antenna large and robust (*see* Cons). Switches for internal/ external antennas (if radio sounds "deaf," ensure these are in correct positions). Clock displays separately from frequency (*see* Cons). Two-event timer with selectable on/off times. Snooze and sleep delay. FM above average with excellent sensitivity, aided by switchable FM preamp (17 dB). 0.1–30 MHz tuning range includes longwave broadcast band. Japanese FM. Three-level LCD illumination (*see* Cons). Travel power lock. Elevation panel (*see* Cons) helps tilt radio to handy operating angle. Well-written printed owner's manual; also on CD-ROM along with quick-start guide. *E1XM, North America:* XM ready, easily implemented (*see* Cons). XM module easily removable for future uses or modes. *E1XM and E1, North America:* Excellent toll-free tech support. Atomic clock automatically kept accurate by world band WWV/WWVH (but not longwave WWVB in Colorado on 0.06 MHz) (*see* Cons).

Cons: No carrying handle or strap, nor provision for one to be user-affixed; remedied by pricey aftermarket Tenba carrying case. When 2.5 kHz bandwidth used with BFO (or certain PBT settings with wider bandwidths), audio suffers from harshness resulting from high-order distortion products. Muted-sounding audio comes off as somewhat lifeless; needs to be crisper to reach fidelity potential. Narrow (5 kHz signal spacing) dynamic range/IP3 poor, although IP3 improves to fair with preamp off. Preamp, used by default with the telescopic antenna, generates mixing products in stressful reception situations; ironically, a major external antenna without the preamp tends to remedy the problem. Tuning knob feels slightly "grizzly" when rotated and some units also have minor wobble. No rubber grip around tuning knob's circumference; no finger dimple, either (remediable, see fingerdimple.com). Front-mounted battery access door difficult to open. Telescopic antenna keels over when moved from full upright position. Dot-matrix LCD has limited useful viewing angle and lacks contrast in bright rooms or with illumination off; best contrast at angle provided by aftermarket tilt stand, although built-in elevation panel helps. Non-standard connector for world band external antennas, and no adaptor or plug included. Variable-rate incremental tuning (VRIT), which some don't care for, cannot be disabled. Mediumwave AM lacks directional reception, as it relies on the telescopic antenna in lieu of a customary horizontal ferrite-rod antenna. Included AC adaptor produces minor hum at headphone output. Lacks certain features, such as tunable notch and noise blanker, found on tabletop receivers. No PC interface. No attenuator or RF gain control, although neither needed. No dedicated keys for presets. Frequency readout drifts very slightly until full warmup; can be off by ~30 Hz at cold start before settling into full accuracy after two hours. Clock display lacks numeric seconds; local time option in 24-hour format only. Line input jack requires above-average audio level to perform properly. Elevation panel flimsy. Paint on knobs, keys and cabinet could eventually wear through. Four "D" cells not included. Like essentially all other world band portables, not designed to receive DRM, DAB or HD Radio digital broadcasts, nor is there a 12 kHz IF output to feed a DRM-configured PC. *E1:* Cannot receive XM satellite broadcasts. *E1XM:* XM reception requires purchase of separate outboard antenna and payment of monthly fee. XM reception not possible when traveling outside United States and Canada. Does not receive signals of former Sirius satellites. Significant current consumption when XM circuitry in use. *United States and Canada:* Warranty honored only if radio purchased from authorized dealer, listed under each product at www.etoncorp.com.

☞ Reader complaints of unreliability have disproportionately come from units—unusually refurbs—prior to s/n 5463 or units purchased on eBay. Units manufactured after early 2006 and purchased from authorized dealers appear to be holding up somewhat better.

Verdict: Etón's flagship receiver offers a killer combination of features and performance never before found in a portable. Indeed, it even outperforms a number of tabletop and PC-controlled models.

Although earlier E1XM units have had significant QA issues, and long-term robustness has yet to be established, overall this complex piece of hardware is the best portable we've ever tested.

New Version: A Grundig version planned for 2008 never materialized. Instead, Etón introduced the E1, which lacks satellite capability. Although intended mainly for the European market, it is sometimes sold alongside the classic E1XM in the United States.

An *RDI WHITE PAPER* is available.

NUMBERS: TOP PORTABLE

	Etón E1/E1XM
Max. Sensitivity/Noise Floor	0.15 µV Ⓢ/–132 dBm Ⓔ(1)
Blocking	123 dB Ⓖ
Bandwidths *(Shape Factors)*	8.0 *(1:1.45 Ⓢ)*, 5.0 *(1:1.6 Ⓔ)*, 2.5 (1.7, Ⓔ)
Ultimate Rejection	80 dB Ⓔ(2)
Front-End Selectivity	Ⓖ(3)
Image Rejection	>90 dB Ⓢ
First IF Rejection	75 dB Ⓔ
Dynamic Range/IP3 (5 kHz)	55 dB Ⓟ/–50 dBm Ⓟ(4)
Dynamic Range/IP3 (20 kHz)	87 dB Ⓖ/–2 dBm Ⓖ(5)
Phase Noise	113 dBc Ⓖ
AGC Threshold	0.3 µV Ⓖ(6)
Overall Distortion, sync	2.6% Ⓖ(7)

IBS Lab Ratings: Ⓢ Superb Ⓔ Excellent Ⓖ Good Ⓕ Fair Ⓟ Poor

(1) Preamp on; 0.28 µV Ⓔ/–126 Ⓖ with preamp off.
(2) Phase noise prevents accurate measurement beyond 80 dB.
(3) Octave filters, unusually good for a portable.
(4) Preamp on; 57 dB Ⓟ/–39 dBm Ⓕ with preamp off.
(5) Preamp on; 88 dB Ⓖ/+7 dBm Ⓔ with preamp off.
(6) Preamp on; 0.9 µV Ⓢ with preamp off.
(7) Harmonic distortion includes several high-order products.

The latest addition to Grundig's classic Satellit series is the 750. It includes a fully rotatable antenna for mediumwave AM reception and an assortment of handy tuning features.

New for 2009

✪✪✪⅛

Grundig Satellit 750

Pricing: $299.95 in the United States. CAD$299.99 in Canada.

Pros: Handy tuning features include keypad, up/down slewing, a thousand scannable station presets within various pages (*see* Cons), scan-pause-resume frequency scanning, lockable two-speed knob with spin dimple (*see* Cons), and quick access to world band segments. Keypad unusually easy to use; typically, just tap in a frequency and it's there. No muting when tuning (*see* Cons). Presets store bandwidth (*see* Cons). ATS (auto tuning storage) automatically stores active FM, mediumwave AM and longwave stations into presets. Superior audio with continuous bass and treble controls (*see* Cons). Superior dynamic range allows significant outdoor antenna to be used successfully. Two separate quick-connect low-impedance BNC external antenna jacks for FM and shortwave, plus high-impedance antenna terminals for shortwave; also, phone jack for mediumwave AM/longwave antenna. Switch to select internal/external antenna. Very good world band sensitivity. Dual bandwidths offer flexible selectivity, with "wide" allowing for quality audio (see Cons). Double conversion provides superior image rejection; also free from other spurious signals. Fully rotatable mediumwave AM/longwave ferrite-rod antenna helps enhance desired signal and/or potentially attenuate co-channel interference (*see* Cons). Decent ergonomics (*see* Cons). Illuminated analog signal-strength indicator-meter (*see* Cons). RF gain control. Two-step RF attenuator (10 dB, 20 dB), plus off; uses LCD icons. Stereo audio line output with proper level. Stereo audio line input on front panel for MP3 players and such. Useful carrying handle folds away. World Time clock displays separately from frequency. Clock radio/buzzer alarm with 10-minute snooze. Sleep timer, up to two hours. Japanese FM. Longwave. Aero band (*see* Cons). Adjustable squelch works on all bands. Microprocessor reset button (*see* Cons). Padded feet. Small rear compartment for earbuds. Four-bar battery indicator. Special menu setting for rechargeable batteries (not tested, *see* Cons). Large "D" cells reduce frequency of changing batteries (*see* Cons).

Cons: Wobbly tuning knob. On our unit, wide bandwidth for shortwave/longwave/mediumwave AM sounds "on frequency" only when detuning 5 kHz to either side of signal (narrow bandwidth okay). Wide bandwidth somewhat broad for most world band signals. Both bandwidths too wide for worthy single sideband; e.g., USB signals heard when LSB selected and *vice versa*. Although stability generally good, some single-sideband warble and audio "pumping" because AGC decay too fast. No synchronous selectable sideband; ECSS alternative unsatisfactory. Mediumwave AM, longwave and world band audio would profit from greater high-frequency response. Distortion on shortwave/longwave/mediumwave AM

UPGRADE YOUR PORTABLE'S "HEARING"

Regardless of which portable you use, weak-signal sensitivity can be enhanced on the cheap. How cheap? Nothing, for starters.

Experiment with "sweet spots" near windows, appliances, telephones, building I-beams and so on. If your portable has an AC adaptor, try that, then batteries, and go with what works better. Electrically noisy places to avoid include near computer hardware and appliances with microprocessors; also, light dimmers, non-incandescent lighting and cable television or telephone lines. Electrical wiring can be noisy, too.

Simple Outdoor Antenna

A portable usually doesn't need an outdoor antenna. Yet it might help, especially if there's not enough weak-signal sensitivity with the built-in telescopic antenna.

Bored? Create your own antenna!

Go simple, as highfalutin' antennas may cause overloading. Run several meters or yards of ordinary insulated wire to a tree, then attach one end to the set's telescopic antenna with an alligator or claw clip from someplace like RadioShack. It's fast, cheap and really cuts the mustard.

If you're in a weak-signal location—say, Australia or central/western North America—try an inverted-L ("longwire") antenna. They're at radio specialty outlets or can be put together from instructions in the RDI White Paper, *Passport Evaluation of Popular Outdoor Antennas*. Length isn't critical, but keep the lead-in wire reasonably short.

☞ Disconnect outdoor antennas during thunder and snow or sand storms. And don't touch a connected antenna during dry weather, as a spark from your body could damage the radio.

Hillbilly Skyhooks

Antennas flourish in the fresh outdoors, away from electrical noises. But if your outboard antenna must be indoors, run it along the middle of a window with Velcro, tape or suction cups. Even better for inside reinforced-concrete buildings, which absorb signals, is to affix a telescopic car antenna so it sticks outdoors like a wall flagpole.

Compact amplified ("active") antennas, reviewed in Passport Reports, can also be handy. Most are for tabletop models, but a few are for portables.

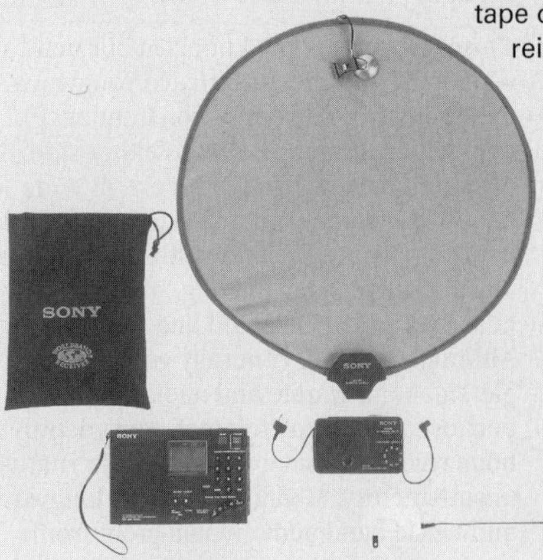

The Sony AN-LP1 is tops for travel. Get it while you can, as remaining supplies are nearly exhausted. J. Brinker

with exceptionally strong signals; decreasing RF gain helps. Directivity of rotatable mediumwave AM/longwave antenna altered by hand placement (avoided by touching only ends); can scrape atop cabinet if not turned carefully; and tuning detents wear quickly. Minor chuffing. Difficult to extend telescopic antenna without bending or breaking thinner segments; antenna can flop when extended. Keys, although okay, wobbly with spongy feel. Flimsy speaker grille. Non-tuning knobs small and slightly cramped. Dreadful aero band sensitivity. Marginal LCD contrast when viewed head-on. Signal indicator overreads and is dimly illuminated; excessively recessed, too, so unhandy to view. Presets have no alphanumeric tags. Microprocessor reset button easier than most to press by accident, an inconvenience. Tuning knob's rubberized paint might wear off. Illumination defaults away from "continuously on" selection when powering down. No travel power lock. Included 120V AC adaptor causes minor hum on shortwave except with outside antenna. Sensitivity barely average on FM and mediumwave AM; latter limits attraction of rotatable antenna. No elevation panel or rod. Includes menu setting for recharging batteries, but no inboard battery-recharging feature exists. Four "D" batteries not included. Skimpy owners manual's uses light gray ink, so hard to read.

☞ A variation, the Tecsun S-2000, could eventually materialize for the domestic Chinese market.

Verdict: The new Grundig Satellit 750, produced by Tecsun in China, seemingly was created without input from the R.L. Drake Company. It was Drake which largely engineered the top-rated Etón E1/E1XM and discontinued Grundig Satellit 800.

Drake's apparent absence shows: no synchronous selectable sideband, inferior single sideband and odd-performing wide bandwidth. Engineering aside, the '750's tuning knob is woefully wobbly.

Nevertheless, world band performance, including audio, is generally good. Dynamic range is especially noteworthy, as it allows a serious outdoor antenna to be used—a rarity among portables. There are also tuning aids aplenty, and mediumwave AM is made handier by a fully rotatable antenna.

Problem is how the '750 compares with its sibling E1/E1XM, which runs around $100 more. The E1 series is much superior except for the lack of a carrying handle or ferrite rod mediumwave AM antenna.

But if you can't justify the higher price or prefer something more straightforward to operate, the new Satellit 750 offers pleasant listening and superior audio.

Evaluation of New Model: The new Grundig Satellit 750 has more than its share of frequency coverage: longwave 100–519 kHz; mediumwave AM 520–1710 kHz; shortwave 1711–29999 kHz, including all world band segments; FM 76–108 MHz (Japan) or 87–108 MHz (elsewhere); and aero 118–137 MHz. At around six pounds and 14½ inches (37 cm) it is far from airplane friendly, but is handy for around the house and yard.

Tuning Features Aplenty

The '750 includes just about every tuning method available. The keypad is unusually handy; all you do in most cases is tap in the frequency and—poof!—the station appears. No fumbling with enter keys, decimals and other earmarks of clueless software.

One thousand presets store bandwidth, but have no alphanumeric tags. They are banked into two groups, with configuration depending on system code settings which, unfortunately, are not the easiest to enter or access: 10 pages, each with 50 presets; 20 pages, each with 25 presets; 25 pages, each with 20 presets; and 50 pages, each with 10 presets.

Every reception mode has two handy knob-tuning steps and two steps for slew tuning. Scanning—by frequency or presets—stops at each active channel for five seconds, then resumes. A handy feature is ATS (auto tuning storage), which stores active mediumwave AM, longwave and FM frequencies within page 0.

Mystery Compartment

The included 117V unregulated AC adaptor causes hum with world band signals, but is resolved by an outdoor antenna. It is UL listed.

This brings up a mysterious little rear-cabinet compartment, which hints that Tecsun may have had something else in mind for power. Look closely, and there's what seems like a line-cord notch in the compartment's cover. This suggests that the receiver may have been designed for an inboard power supply instead of an outboard AC adaptor—say, in a version for the domestic Chinese market.

User Friendly, Yet . . .

Ergonomics are decent, and there are handy touches. Yes, knobs are a bit small and congested for the radio's size, and presets aren't the easiest to program or access. But there's a nice carrying handle that folds out of the way—a vast improvement over the pricier E1/E1XM sibling with no handle whatsoever. There are even soft pads on the feet to keep the radio from sliding around and to prevent scratching, although there's no elevation panel or rod.

However, the microprocessor reset button has been foolishly placed near the tuning knob, where it is easily pressed by accident. Fortunately, it does not alter clock or presets entries, but you have to re-enter system code settings.

There are two low-impedance, quick-connect BNC external antenna connectors for, respectively, FM and shortwave, plus 500-ohm terminals for a high-impedance shortwave antenna. A switch selects between telescopic and external antennas. More on this later.

An eight-inch (20 cm) fully rotatable mediumwave AM/longwave antenna roosts atop the cabinet. This is potentially very handy, as it can be aimed for optimum reception quality without turning around the entire radio. But don't nudge it down during rotation or it might scrape the cabinet, and touch it only on the ends to avoid directionality-altering hand capacitance. Numerous clicky detents help steady the antenna, but these wear out with use.

The telescopic antenna, with a large plastic tip, is hard to pull out fully without damaging smaller elements. Once extended it has a tendency to keel over from its own weight.

The large tuning knob has a non-rotating dimple and spins nicely. So far, so good, but in a reprise of initial Grundig Satellit 800 production there is disappointing wobble. This gives the receiver a down-market feel—especially surprising, as Grundig should have learned this lesson the first time. The flimsy speaker grille doesn't enhance perceived quality, either.

A genuine analog mechanical meter displays signal strength. This should be cause for joy, but readings are too high, illumination is dim and it is recessed so far as to impede viewing.

LCD contrast is good from above, but mediocre head-on. Illumination is okay, and continuous operation can be chosen in lieu of the default three-second timed setting. A minor annoyance is that it reverts to default once the radio has been powered down.

The World Time clock displays separately from frequency, a nice touch. Its circuitry also controls sleep and snooze timers, along with two buzzer/clock-radio alarms.

Shines and Scuffs

The '750's dynamic range shines, which allows a serious outdoor antenna to be used without causing undue overloading. Obviously this tabletop-caliber performance was not incidental, as the radio also includes quick-connect jacks for outboard antennas and a switch to choose between these and inboard antennas.

Audio quality is commendable, thanks in part to a beefy speaker tweaked by separate bass and treble controls. Good as it sounds, though, non-FM audio would have benefitted from greater high-frequency response. Also, some distortion creeps in with very strong world band and mediumwave AM stations—seemingly because of AGC timing. (Reducing RF gain helps.)

Multiple bandwidths provide the flexibility to reduce adjacent-channel interference without unduly throttling audio fidelity; synchronous selectable sideband helps, too. The S750 includes two bandwidths and the LCD even displays the choice, but there's no synchronous selectable sideband. ECSS doesn't work well enough to act as a fallback, either.

The narrow bandwidth is appropriate for typical world band reception. However, "wide" is broad enough so heterodynes can be heard squealing, although it allows for superior audio when a signal isn't hemmed in. On our unit, that bandwidth sounds "on frequency" only when the radio is detuned 5 kHz to either side of the desired signal.

Both bandwidths are too wide for most single-sideband reception. For example, USB signals can be heard when LSB is selected and *vice versa*. Although stability is good, there is a degree of warble and audio "pumping" because the AGC decay is too fast.

Spurious noises and groans are virtually absent, thanks in large measure to superior image rejection. No annoying muting during bandscanning, either, and chuffing is minor.

World band sensitivity is commendable, and most will be satisfied using the built-in telescopic antenna. FM and mediumwave AM sensitivity are not quite in that lofty league, while the aero band is nigh deaf.

DRM = MIA

A 12 kHz output for DRM reception was listed in the manufacturer's preproduction advertising. Apparently this feature was dropped, as our unit doesn't have it.

In all, the new Grundig Satellit 750 sounds unusually pleasant, has plenty of tuning smarts, and boasts superior sensitivity and dynamic range—a mix that general listeners will appreciate. Nevertheless, if you're a DXer and willing to spend at this level, you'll probably wish to take a fresh look at the top-rated Etón E1/E1XM.

Not everybody wants a pricey superset or tiny travel portable. For them, the CCRadio-SW performs nicely, sounds great and is eminently affordable.

✪✪¾ ✪ *Passport's Choice*

CCRadio-SW, Kaito KA-2100, K-PO WR2100, Redsun RP2100

Pricing: *CCRadio:* $149.95 including shipping in the United States. *Kaito KA-2100:* $129.00 as available in the United States. *K-PO:* €79.95 in The Netherlands. *CCRadio-SW/CSWC protective carry case:* $29.95 in the United States.

Pros: Helpful tuning features include two-speed (1/5 kHz) mute-free knob tuning knob with speed dimple (*see* Cons); up/down slewing (*see* Cons); signal-seek frequency scanning that works well; 50 station presets (*see* Cons), of which 30 are for world band; and meter key for quick access to world band segments (*see* Cons). Worthy sensitivity to weak world band (*see* Cons) signals. Superior sensitivity to mediumwave AM signals, thanks in part to the inboard Twin Coil Ferrite™ antenna (confirmed on tested Redsun and CCRadio versions). Useful selectivity, with two well-chosen bandwidths. Unusually pleasant audio quality; includes separate and continuously variable bass and treble, beefy speaker magnet and superior audio electronics. Decent image rejection (*see* Cons). Virtually no frequency drift. Travel power lock. Large LCD with good contrast; LCD/keys illumination (*see* Cons) keys activated manually or when any knob turned or key pressed (*see* Cons). Five-bar signal-strength indicator (*see* Cons). One-step attenuator. Continuous RF gain control (*see* Cons). Internal-external antenna switch for shortwave and FM. Separate mediumwave AM external antenna connection (*see* Cons). 455 kHz IF output jack for ancillary devices. Excellent FM performance, in stereo through headphones and line-output jack. "Roger beep" when keys pressed; can be switched off. Robust telescopic antenna. Excellent carrying handle folds into cabinet. Three-bar battery indicator. Two clocks—World Time and local, 12 or 24 hour format (*see* Cons). Sleep delay, up to 90 minutes. Two clock-radio/alarm timers with handy snooze bar. NiMH cells (*see* Cons) can be recharged internally. May also be operated from—user's choice—four "D" or four "AA" batteries of any type. Aftermarket protective case available. *CCRadio:* Improved tuning knob speed dimple. Included AC adaptor UL approved. *CCRadio purchased at C. Crane:* 30-day money-back guarantee. *Kaito and Redsun:* Powered by shielded internal AC mains transformer instead of customary outboard AC adaptor (*see* Cons); nevertheless, may also be powered by an external 6–9V DC source, including AC adaptor. *Redsun (all versions):* Outboard passive reel accessory antenna aids slightly in weak-signal reception. *Redsun Export/English version:* Nominally includes stereo earphones, NiMH rechargeable cells, and line-out cable and adaptor.

Cons: No keypad, a major omission. Mediocre dynamic range ameliorated only slightly by attenuator or RF gain control. Poor front-end selectivity, so local mediumwave AM stations can "ghost" into shortwave spectrum and disrupt some world band reception. Although image rejection decent, smattering of weak images. LCD unevenly illuminated. Illumination shifts from fulltime-on to timed-off when tuning knob turned. Shortwave spectrum in three "bands," complicating world band tuning and allowing only ten presets per "band." Volatile memory, including presets. Quick-access meter key for world band segments does not store last tuned frequency, although bandswitch does. Signal-strength indicator overreads. Frequency display can be off by 1 kHz or so. Band-edge beep can't be turned off. Scanning and up/down slewing mute, hindering bandscanning. With stereo headphones, at lower volume the left ear may be slightly louder. Pressing keys usually requires that radio be held in place with other hand. No elevation panel. Clocks do not display independently of frequency readout. Sensitivity drops off above ~23 MHz. No single-sideband. Antenna and IF output jacks of type normally not found in much of world; however, two antenna plugs provided with radio to remedy this. Internal mediumwave AM antenna doesn't disconnect when outboard antenna connected, degrading outboard's directionality. *Kaito:* Lacks UL or CSA approval, although has CE approval for Europe. *Redsun:* No warranty or repair support outside China; our insured eBay unit arrived damaged, but "insurance" impossible to collect. Lacks UL or CSA approval. *Except Redsun export/English version:* Earpieces and required four "AA" or "D" batteries not included. NiMH rechargeable cells not included.

☞ CCRadio and Kaito 120V AC; others 220V.

Verdict: The North American CCRadio-SW and Kaito KA-2100, like their European and Asian stable mates, offer pleasant audio and decent overall world band performance. For hour-after-hour listening to news and entertainment, it is hard to beat, which accounts for its PASSPORT's Choice citation.

This receiver—at least the tested CCRadio and Redsun versions—also stands out because of superior long-distance FM and mediumwave AM. Nevertheless, it craves better front-end selectivity and dynamic range; synchronous selectable sideband, inboard single-sideband demodulation and a keypad, too.

✪✪½

Roadstar TRA-2350P

Pricing: €69.95 in Germany.

Identical to erstwhile Redsun RP2000. Also identical to existing Redsun RP2100, above, except 1) no station presets, 2) no signal-seek scanning, and 3) LCD and keys not automatically illuminated when knob turned or key pressed.

✪✪⅜

Etón S350DL, Grundig GS350DL, S350 Deluxe "Lextronix," Tecsun BCL-3000

Pricing: *Etón S350DL:* CAD$129.99 in Canada. £59.95 in the United Kingdom. *Grundig GS350DL:* $99.95 in the United States. *S350 Deluxe "Lextronix":* €98.00 in Germany. *PAL-to-F adaptor for external FM antenna:* $2.29 in the United States. *Franzus FR-22 120>220V AC transformer for BCL-3000:* $15–18 in the United States.

Pros: Speaker audio quality substantially above norm for world band portables. Separate bass and treble help shape audio frequency response. Reasonably powerful audio, helpful where ambient noise at least average. Two bandwidths, well-chosen, provide effective and flexible adjacent-channel rejection *vis-à-vis* audio fidelity. Sensitive to weak signals. No synthesizer, so exceptionally free from circuit noise ("hiss") and can't chuff. Relatively intuitive to operate, even for newcomers. World Time clock (*see* Cons) with alarm, clock radio and sleep delay; may also be set to 12-hour format. Four-level (four pair of bars) signal-strength indicator. Battery indicator (*see* Cons). Low battery consumption and four "D" cells greatly reduce battery replacement. Exceptionally comfortable carrying handle seconds as a shoulder strap. Easy-to-read LCD has large numbers, high contrast, visible from many angles and brightly illuminated. LCD illumination either fulltime or timed; also illuminates when tuning knob turned. FM reception slightly above average. FM in stereo through headphones. Sturdy, flexible telescopic antenna. Stereo line output for recording, home FM transmitters and outboard audio. Mediumwave AM better than most. Battery cavity holds four "AA" and/or four "D" cells; switchable between "AA" and "D." Available in various colors. *Except Tecsun:* Supplied outboard AC adaptor can be left behind on trips, making it lighter than BCL-3000. *North America:* Excellent toll-free tech support. *Tecsun:* Built-in 220V AC

The Grundig S350DL has superior audio and a snazzy appearance, but no keypad or presets.

power supply eliminates need for outboard AC adaptor.

Cons: Analog tuned with digital frequency counter, so tunable only by pair of concentric (fast/slow) knobs; consequently, it lacks such helpful tuning aids as station presets, keypad and scanning. Unhandy MW/SW1/SW2/SW3 switch complicates tuning; switch can be touchy, altering frequency readings. Analog tuning uses string-pulley-gearing hardware, causing tuning backlash and frequency drift; also, variable tuning capacitor uses thermally sensitive solid dielectric, further adding to frequency drift. Single-conversion, so poor image rejection. No single sideband. Power key activates 90-minute sleep delay; full-time "on" only when held down three seconds. Some user-correctable nighttime overloading in strong-signal parts of the world. Does not tune scarcely used 2 MHz (120 meter) tropical world band segment. Clock not displayed independent of frequency, but control allows time to replace frequency for three seconds. Nominal 30 MHz low-pass filter has such high apparent insertion loss as to be useless except as *de facto* attenuator. Battery-strength indicator gives little warning before radio dies. Batteries (4 × "D") not included. *Except Tecsun:* AC adaptor less handy than built-in power supply. *Etón and Grundig:* Warranty honored only if radio purchased from authorized dealer, listed under each product at www.etoncorp.com. *North America:* Minor hum from speaker, headphones and line output with supplied 120V AC adaptor.

Verdict: The S350DL—sold in China as the similar Tecsun BCL-3000—is full of welcome surprises as well as the other variety. The big plus is sound, but flaws include images, no single-sideband, a paucity of tuning aids and frequency drift.

For world band listening the S350DL sounds terrific, is value priced and has solid customer support within North America and Europe.

COMPACT PORTABLES

Nice for Travel, Okay for Home

Compacts are hugely popular, and no wonder. They offer a value mix of affordable price, worthy performance, manageable size and acceptable speaker audio. They tip in at one to two pounds, under a kilogram, and are typically sized less than 8 × 5 × 1.5 inches/20 × 13 × 4 cm. Like pocket models, they almost always feed off "AA" (UM-3 penlite) batteries—but, usually, more of them. They travel almost as well as pocket models, but sound better through their larger speakers. They may also suffice for home use.

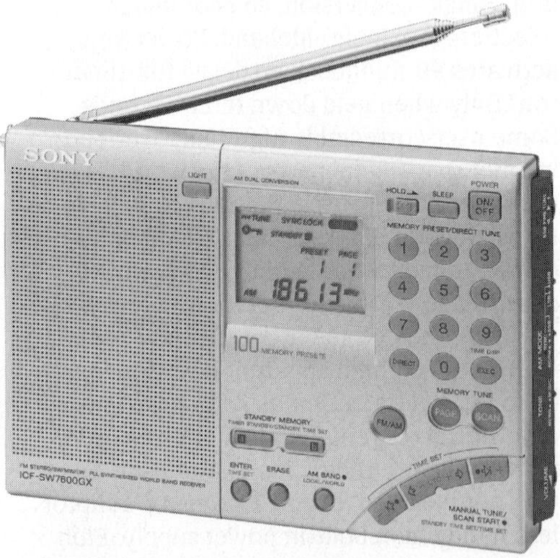

The Sony ICF-SW7600GR's synchronous selectable sideband puts it a notch above anything else on the sunny side of $400 or €600.

✪✪✪⅜ ✓ *Passport's Choice*

Sony ICF-SW7600GR

Pricing: *ICF-SW7600GR:* $149.95 in the United States. £124.00 in the United Kingdom. €169.00 in Germany. *Universal MW-41-680 120V regulated AC adaptor (aftermarket, see below):* $19.95 in the United States. *Radio Shack 273-025 120V adaptor with 273-1705 plug (aftermarket, see below):* $12.99 in the United States.

Pros: One of the great values in a meaningful world band radio. Least-costly model with high-tech synchronous selectable sideband; this generally performs well at reducing adjacent-channel interference and selective-fading distortion on world band, longwave and mediumwave AM (*see* Cons). Lone bandwidth provides suitable all-round selectivity. Robust, with superior quality of components and assembly. Numerous helpful tuning features, including keypad, two-speed up/down slewing, 100 non-volatile station presets and "signal-seek, then resume" tuning. Single-sideband performance among best of any portable; analog clarifier, combined with LSB/USB switch, allow single-sideband signals (AFRTS, utility, amateur) to be tuned with uncommon precision, which helps create natural-sounding audio. Dual-zone 24-hour clock with single-zone readout, easy to set. Outboard reel passive wire antenna accessory slightly boosts weak-signal reception. Simple timer with sleep delay. Illuminated LCD has high contrast when read head-on or from below. Travel power lock. Superior reception of difficult mediumwave AM stations. Superior FM capture ratio aids reception when band congested and helps separate co-channel stations. FM stereo through earpieces or headphones. Japanese FM (most versions) and longwave. Superior battery life. Weak-battery indicator. Stereo line output for recording, FM home transmitters and outboard audio. Hinged battery cover prevents loss. Automatic switching of optional AN-LP1 active antenna.

Cons: Lacks tonal quality for pleasant world band or mediumwave AM music reproduction, and speaker audio tiring for FM. Weak-signal sensitivity, although respectable, not equal to that of a few other well-rated portables; helped considerably by extra-cost Sony AN-LP1 active antenna reviewed in this edition. Three switches, including those for synchronous selectable sideband, located unhandily at side of cabinet. No tuning knob. Slow microprocessor lock time while slew tuning degrades bandscanning. No meaningful signal-strength indicator. Synchronous selectable sideband holds lock decently, but tends to lose lock if batteries weak. Synchronous selectable sideband alignment can vary with temperature, factory alignment and battery voltage, causing synchronous selectable sideband reception to be slightly more muffled in one sideband than the other. No AC adaptor included. Optional Sony AC-E60A 120V AC adaptor for North America causes serious interference to radio signals; much better are after-market options that fit the radio's unusual power jack: Universal Radio MW-41-680 and Radio Shack 273-025/273-1705 adaptor/plug combo. Reader reports indicate Sony's recommended 240V AC adaptor also causes serious radio interference. 1621–1705 kHz portion of American AM band and 1705–1735 kHz potential public-service segment are erroneously treated as shortwave, although this does not harm reception. Even though LCD is relatively large, same portion of display is for clock and frequency; so clock doesn't display when frequency is shown, but pressing EXE key replaces time with frequency for nine seconds. No earphones or earpieces. No batteries (four "AA" needed).

Verdict: The robust Sony ICF-SW7600GR provides exceptional bang for the buck, even though it is manufactured in high-cost Japan. Its advanced-tech synchronous selectable sideband is a valuable feature that most other portable manufacturers have yet to engineer properly—even some professional models costing thousands of dollars still haven't got it right. To find this useful operating feature operating properly at this price is breathtaking.

There's also top drawer single-sideband reception for a portable, along with superior tough-signal FM and mediumwave AM reception—even if musical audio quality through the speaker is only *ordinaire* at best.

✪✪✪ *Passport's Choice*

Etón E5, E5 "Lextronix," Grundig G5

Pricing: *G5:* $149.95 in the United States. CAD$149.99 in Canada. *E5:* £89.95 in the United Kingdom. €129.00 in Germany.

Pros: Much improved ergonomics over Degen/Kaito siblings, including dedicated volume controls and additional slewing keys; main keypad and slewing keys are nicely sized (*see* Cons) with pleasant feel. Worthy tuning knob does not mute (*see* Cons). Useful auto scanning that on shortwave offers two stop modes (scan, five-second pause, then resume scan; scan, then stop), with FM-only mode to auto-store presets. 700 non-volatile station presets store mode; each of 100 seven-presets pages can display a four-letter alphanumeric ID tag (*see* Cons). Two ways to quick-access individual world band segments; returns to last-tuned frequency within each segment. Two bandwidths, well chosen. Superior sensitivity, low circuit noise. Superior dynamic range for compact portable, so suitable with outdoor wire antennas. Above average single-sideband reception, aided by analog fine-tuning thumbwheel (*see* Cons) and little drift. Effective LED illumination (*see* Cons)

Etón got it right with the compact E5. Although it lacks the Sony ICF-7600GR's sync circuit, it includes a tuning knob, two bandwidths and 700 non-volatile presets.

stays on 15 seconds with battery, continuously with AC adaptor. Audio slightly above average for compact and powerful enough to drive some external speakers (*see* Cons). Clock displays separately from frequency (*see* Cons). Four-event alarm. Sleep delay; once the 99-minute default is changed (to something between one and 98 minutes), new setting is retained. Four-bar battery indicator. Useful five-bar signal-strength indicator (*see* Cons). NiMH batteries recharge inside radio (*see* Cons). Travel power lock (*see* Cons). Time not erased during battery charging or if batteries replaced quickly. Hinged battery cover prevents loss. Superior FM sensitivity. Excellent FM capture ratio aids when band congested, including to separate co-channel stations. FM in stereo through earbuds, included (*see* Cons). Simple tone control for FM (*see* Cons). Stereo line output with proper level for recording, home FM transmitters and outboard audio. Japanese FM. Longwave. Indoor wire antenna and single-voltage AC adaptor/charger (*see* ☞). Worthy vinyl carrying case (*see* Cons). *North America:* Excellent toll-free telephone support.

Cons: World band and mediumwave AM audio would profit from more crispness and a tone control (tone control works only on FM). Volume blasts when radio initially turned on, although there's a way around this. Some keys small. LCD a strain to read in low ambient light without using illumination. Minor chuffing. Single sideband uses fine-tuning thumbwheel instead of USB/LSB selector; thumbwheel lacks center detent. Touchy fine-tuning thumbwheel makes manual ECSS reception impractical. AGC too fast in single-sideband mode, causing distortion; too, AGC swamped by exceptionally strong signals unless single-level attenuator used. Tuning knob has only 1 kHz step, although slewing keys complement this nicely with 5 kHz step. Individual presets do not store bandwidth or ID tag. Signal-strength indicator does not work on FM. Bandwidth chosen by hard-to-select slide switch on side of cabinet. No standard or rechargeable batteries (four "AA" needed). Carrying case has creosote odor, needs airing. Warranty honored only if radio purchased from authorized dealer, listed under each product at www.etoncorp.com.

Verdict: The Chinese-made G5/E5 clears up the Degen DE1103's seriously flawed ergonomics by. On the other hand, the '1103 includes rechargeable batteries, while the pricier G5/E5 doesn't.

Overall, this is one of the best compact portables around, even if it lacks synchronous selectable sideband.

✪✪✪ ✐ *Passport's Choice*

Degen DE1102, Kaito KA1102, Scott RXP80, Thieking DE1102

Pricing: *Kaito:* $79.95 in the United States. CAD$89.00 in Canada. *Scott:* €39.95 in France. *Thieking:* €69.00 in Germany.

Pros: Unusually small and light for a sophisticated compact model; only a skosh larger and one ounce (28 grams) heavier than its simpler sibling '1101. Two bandwidths, both well chosen. A number of helpful tuning features, including keypad, up/down slewing (1 or 5 kHz steps for world band, 1 or 9/10 kHz for mediumwave AM), carousel selector for 49–16 meter segments, and signal-seek frequency scanning (*see* Cons) and memory scanning; also, ten 19-preset pages provide a total of 190 station presets, 133 usable for shortwave (*see* Cons). Auto-store function automatically stores presets; works on all bands. Tunable BFO allows for precise signal phasing for single-sideband (*see* Cons). No muting during manual shortwave bandscanning in 1 or 5 kHz steps, or mediumwave AM bandscanning in 1 kHz steps. PLL and BFO relatively free from drift for single-sideband (*see* Cons). Above-average weak-signal sensitivity and image rejection. Little circuit "hiss." Superior speaker audio quality, intelligibility and loudness for size. Four-LED signal-strength indicator for mediumwave AM and shortwave (*see* Cons); three-bar signal-strength indicator for FM (fourth LED becomes stereo indicator). World Time 24-hour clock displays seconds numerically when radio off; when on, time (sans seconds) flashes on briefly when key held down; can choose 12-hour format, instead. Unusually appropriate for use in the dark, as display and keypad illuminated which works only in dark (*see* Cons). Clicky keys have superior feel. Excellent LCD contrast when viewed from sides or below. Alarm with sleep delay (*see* Cons). Travel power lock. Rechargeable NiMH batteries (3 × "AA"), included, charge within radio; station presets and time not erased during charging. Switchable bass boost supplements high-low tone switch, significantly improves FM audio (*see* Cons). Low battery consumption except with FM bass boost. Battery-strength indicator. Hinged battery cover prevents loss. Superior FM weak-signal sensitivity. Excellent FM capture ratio aids reception when band congested, also helps separate co-channel stations. FM in stereo through earbuds, included (*see* Cons). Japanese FM. Includes short external wire antenna accessory, which in many locations is about the most that can be used without overloading. Available in black or aluminum. *Degen/Scott:* AC adaptor (220/230V). *Kaito:* AC adaptor (120V).

Cons: Speaker audio, except FM, lacks low-frequency audio as compared to larger models. Bass-boost circuit, which could relieve this on world band, works only on FM. Dynamic range, although typical for a compact portable, nowhere equal to that of sibling '1101; overloads easily with significant outdoor antenna, although much less often with the built-in antenna or short outboard antenna. Not as user friendly as some other portables; for example, single-sideband mode works only when presets "page 9" is selected (or SSB key is held in manually), even if no presets are to be chosen (in any event, presets don't store mode). Slight audio warble with ECSS; varies with power draw resulting from how many signal LEDs illuminated. Earphone volume sometimes inadequate with weak or undermodulated signals; variable-level earphone jack misleadingly described as "line out." Power key activates 99-minute sleep delay; to turn radio on fulltime, a second key must be pressed immediately afterwards. No tuning knob. No LSB/USB switch. Displays in nonstandard XX.XX/XX.XXx MHz format. Signal-strength indicator overreads. Little-used 2 MHz (120 meter) world band segment not covered. Clock doesn't display when frequency is shown, although key allows time to replace frequency briefly. Always-on LCD/keypad illumination with AC adaptor, as described in owner's manual, does not necessarily function. LCD/keypad illumination dim and uneven. FM IF produces images 21+ MHz down.

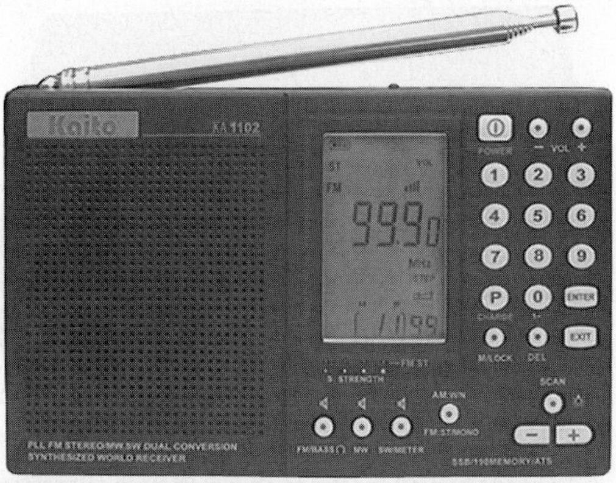

The Kaito KA1102 includes dual bandwidths and single sideband at a relatively lower price. Ergonomics are mixed, but reliability and overall performance are good.

Verdict: An exceptional price and performance winner from Degen—just don't expect much in the way of low-end audio.

✪✪⅞ (*see* ☞) ✆

Degen DE1103, Kaito KA1103, Thieking DE1103

Pricing: *Kaito:* $99.95 in the United States. CAD$99.00 in Canada. *Thieking:* €119.00 in Germany.

Pros: Two bandwidths, both well chosen (*see* Cons). Helpful tuning features include tuning knob (*see* Cons), keypad (*see* Cons), world band segment up/down carousel, signal-seek (pause, resume) frequency scanning and presets scanning; also, sixteen pages of 16 stations presets each provide 256 presets, plus another dozen to quick-access world band segments (pages can also be bypassed for quick-access tuning, reducing available presets to 100). Presets store mode (*see* Cons). Tuning knob not

The Thieking DE1103, sold in Germany, is available in North America as the Kaito KA1103. It performs unusually well for the price, albeit with operational peculiarities.

muted when tuned, facilitating bandscanning (*see* Cons). Scanner works better than most. Can return to last-tuned frequency within ten world band segments, as well as FM and mediumwave AM. Superior dynamic range for a compact portable—better than that of DE1102/KA1102, and approaching that of DE1101/KA1101. Tunable BFO (*see* Cons) allows for precise single-sideband phasing. Relatively free from drift during single-sideband. Above-average sensitivity aided by quiet circuitry. Has dual conversion, so image rejection above average (*see* Cons). Speaker audio, although limited, fairly good except for single-sideband (*see* Cons). Four-bar signal-strength indicator (*see* Cons). World Time clock (*see* Cons). Top-notch display and keypad illumination. During battery operation, illumination can be switched not to go on; otherwise, it is automatically activated by any of various controls, including those for tuning, and stays on 15 seconds. Clicky keys with superior feel (*see* Cons). Sleep delay. Two-event timer. NiMH batteries (4 × "AA"), included, slowly rechargeable within radio. Travel power lock. Station presets and time not erased during battery charging or if batteries replaced quickly. Battery-strength indicator. Hinged battery cover prevents loss. Superior FM sensitivity. Excellent FM capture ratio aids reception when band congested, including helping to separate co-channel stations. FM in stereo through earbuds, included (*see* Cons). Stereo audio line output with appropriate level for recording, home FM transmitters and outboard audio systems. Japanese FM. Longwave (*see* Cons) down to 100 kHz. Elevation panel tilts radio to handy operating angle. Includes short external wire antenna accessory. Available in black or aluminum colors. *Degen:* AC adaptor (220V). *Kaito:* AC adaptor (120V).

Cons: Hostile ergonomics include having to operate two controls to change volume; nonstandard single-row keypad; small keys; stiff slider controls; knob has only one poky tuning rate (1 kHz) for world band and mediumwave AM; and no center detent for BFO's fine-tuning thumbwheel. Pseudo-analog LCD "dial," a pointless gimmick that takes up space which could have been used to display useful information and provide proper keypad layout. No up/down slewing. No tone control except "news-music" switch only for FM. No LSB/USB selection, just SSB. Single-sideband has audible distortion, seemingly from AGC. Image rejection fairly good, but not all it could be for a model with enough dynamic range to handle some outboard antennas. Even though dynamic range superior, AGC seemingly swamped by exceptionally powerful signals, causing lowered volume; switching attenuator to "LO" brings volume to normal level. Signal-strength indicator overreads and does not function on FM. Clock doesn't display when frequency shown, although key allows time to replace frequency briefly. Presets do not store bandwidth. Longwave less convenient to access than other bands. Unobtrusive microprocessor noise when tuning knob turned.

☞ The '1103 merits three stars for performance, but only two for user friendliness.

☞ Unlike with siblings DE1101/KA1101 and DE1102/KA1102, the '1103's AC adaptor jack requires standard center-pin-positive polarity.

Verdict: Dreadful ergonomics and a wasted LCD make this a model to approach with caution. Yet, the Degen DE1103/Kaito KA1103 is a solid and versatile performer at a surprisingly low price. If you can endure its user unfriendliness, the '1103 offers excellent performance value.

✪✪⅞

Sangean ATS 909, Sangean ATS 909W, Roberts R861

Pricing: *ATS 909:* $249.95 in the United States. CAD$274.95 in Canada. £159.99 in the United Kingdom. *ATS 909W:* €165.00 in Germany. *R861:* £169.00 in the United Kingdom. *AC adaptor:* Free in the United Kingdom. €9.95 in Germany.

Pros: Exceptionally wide range of tuning facilities, including hundreds of world band station presets (one preset is single-touch) and tuning knob; uses 29 pages and alphanumeric station descriptors for world band. Two voice bandwidths. Handily tunes single-sideband in unusually precise 0.04 kHz steps without need for fine-tuning control (*see* Cons). Shortwave dynamic range slightly above portable average, so performs unusually well with outboard antennas (*see* Cons). Travel power lock. 24-hour clock always shows and can display local time in various worldwide cities (*see* Cons). Excellent ten-bar signal-strength indicator. Weak-battery indicator. Elevation panel tilts radio to handy operating angle (*see* Cons). Clock radio has three "on" times for three discrete frequencies. Sleep delay. FM sensitive to weak signals (*see* Cons) and performs well overall, has RDS, and is in stereo through included earpieces. Illuminated display. Superior ergonomics, including tuning knob with detents. Longwave. *ATS 909W:* Japanese FM. *ATS 909 (North American units) and Roberts:* Superb, but relatively heavy, multivoltage AC adaptor with North American and European plugs. ANT-60 outboard reel passive wire antenna accessory slightly aids weak-signal reception. Sangean service provided by Sangean America on models sold under its name. *ATS 909+mini-antenna (not tested):* includes accessory travel antenna.

Cons: Weak-signal sensitivity with built-in telescopic antenna not equal to that of comparable models; usually remediable with included ANT-60 accessory antenna or other suitable external antenna. Tuning knob mutes. For traveling, larger and heavier than most compact models. Signal-seek tuning, although flexible and sophisticated, stops on few active world band signals. Although scanner can operate outside world band segments, reverts to default segment parameters after one pass. When entering new page, an initial two-second wait between when preset keyed and station audible. Although synthesizer tunes in 0.04 kHz steps, frequency readout only in 1 kHz steps. Software oddities; e.g., under certain conditions, alphanumeric station descriptor may stay on fulltime. Speaker audio only fair, scarcely aided by three-level tone control. No carrying handle or strap. The 24-hour clock set up to display home time, not World Time, although easily overcome by not using world-cities-time feature or by creative setup of World/Home display to London/Home. Clock does not compensate for Daylight Saving (summer) Time in each displayed city. FM can overload in high-signal environments, and capture ratio only average. Heterodyne interference, possibly related to LCD, sometimes interferes with reception of strong mediumwave AM signals. Battery consumption well above average. No batteries (four "AA" required). Elevation panel flimsy.

The robust Sangean ATS 909 is the only world band portable engineered and built in Taiwan.

☞ Frequencies preprogrammed into pages vary by country of sale.

Verdict: Relatively high battery consumption and insufficient weak-signal sensitivity lower the '909's standing as a portable, and our star rating reflects this. Yet, when it is used as a *de facto* tabletop connected to household current and an outboard antenna, it performs more like three stars. In part, this is because its circuitry is more capable than those of most other compact portables in handling the increased signal load from an outboard antenna. As a result, this feature-laden model is most attractive when portability is not important.

Like the tabletop Icom IC-R75, the '909 is a favorite for tuning utility and ham signals, as it offers superior single-sideband at an attractive price. It is also the only Sangean model still made exclusively in Taiwan.

✪✪⅞

Sangean PT-80, Grundig Yacht Boy 80

Pricing: *PT-80:* $159.95 in the United States. CAD$159.00 in Canada. *Yacht Boy 80:* €96.00 in Germany.

Pros: Excellent world band selectivity (*see* Cons). Worthy sensitivity and image rejection. Numerous helpful tuning features, including disc-type tuning knob with raised dots (*see* Cons); nicely located up/down slewing-scan keys; 18 world band presets; 9 additional presets each for longwave, FM and mediumwave AM; "auto arrange" scanning of presets from low-to-high frequency; auto entry of presets (*see* Cons); meter-segment selector; and selectable 5 kHz/1 kHz tuning steps on shortwave. For size, generally pleasant speaker audio in all bands (*see* Cons). Single-sideband (*see* Cons), with precise analog +/– 1.5 kHz fine-tuning thumbwheel. Tuning disc does not mute. Attractively sheathed in flip-open tan leather case which protects nicely (*see* Cons); case affixed with snaps and magnetic catches, so nearly impossible to misplace. Frequency easy to read, with decent-sized digits and good contrast. Illuminated LCD (*see* Cons). Travel power lock (*see* Cons). Tuning-disc lock. Superior mediumwave AM performance. On FM, superior capture ratio and worthy sensitivity. Dual-zone clock in 12 or 24 hour format (*see* Cons). Alarm/clock radio with sleep delay. Rubber feet on bottom to prevent slipping. Stereo indicator (*see* Cons). Hinged battery cover prevents loss. Keys have good feel (*see* Cons). Weak-battery indicator. Outboard reel passive wire antenna accessory aids slightly with weak-signal reception. Longwave. Earbuds. *Sangean (North America):* 120V AC adaptor (*see* Cons).

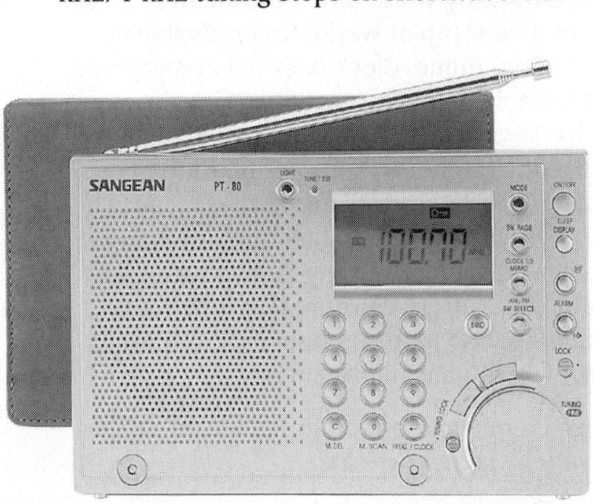

Sangean has moved most radio production to China, where the PT-80 is made. In Germany, it is sold as the Grundig Yacht Boy 80.

Cons: With single-sideband, circuit "pulling" during strong modulation peaks causes audio to warble. Just enough drift to prompt occasional tweaking with single-sideband. World band and mediumwave AM audio slightly muffled; becomes clearer when off-tuned by 1 kHz or so, which also can reduce adjacent-channel interference. Limited dynamic range; tends to overload with significant external antenna; attenuator helps, but also reduces signal considerably—better, yet, use the outboard reel antenna, letting out just enough wire for good reception. Birdies. Tuning disc has some "play," and raised dots can irritate finger. Long-stroke keys need to be depressed fully to make contact. No meaningful signal-strength indicator. IF rejection wanting; in rare circumstances this allows a utility signal to "ghost" throughout the entire shortwave spectrum. When radio on, displays either frequency or time, but not both simultaneously. FM stereo indicator worked at some locations, but not all. External antenna jack functions only on shortwave; however, this can also be a convenience. No audio line output for recording, home FM transmitters and outboard audio. Auto entry of presets does not function on world band. Leather case: 1) sags when used as an elevation panel; 2) has no holes for speaker on front, so audio muffled when case closed; and 3) does not protect receiver's sides or bottom. Travel power lock does not deactivate LCD illumination. No batteries (four "AA" required). *Sangean:* Country of origin, China, not shown on radio, manual or box. Instructions for setting clocks may confuse newcomers, as both clocks are referred to as being for "local time," not UTC, and the manual's mention of UTC mis-states it as "Universal Time Coordinated" instead of Coordinated Universal Time. *Sangean (North America):* 120V AC adaptor generates minor hum.

Verdict: This entry from Sangean is no barnburner, but is pleasant on world band and superior on mediumwave AM and FM.

✪✪⅞ ⊘ *Passport's Choice*

Degen DE1101, Kaito KA1101

Pricing: *Kaito:* $59.95 in the United States.

Pros: Exceptional dynamic range for compact portable. Unusually small and light for compact model. Two bandwidths, both well chosen. A number of helpful tuning features, including keypad, up/down slewing and signal-seek frequency scanning (*see* Cons); also, 50 station presets of which ten for 3,000–10,000 kHz and ten for 10,000–26,100 kHz; others are for FM, FML and mediumwave AM. Above-average weak-signal sensitivity and image rejection. Little circuit "hiss." Superior intelligibility and loudness for size. World Time clock displays seconds numerically when radio off; when on, time (sans seconds) flashes briefly when key held down. Illuminated display, works only in dark. Clicky keys have superior feel. LCD has excellent contrast when viewed from sides or below. Alarm with sleep delay (*see* Cons). AC adaptor (120V Kaito, 220V Degen). Rechargeable NiMH batteries (3 × "AA"), included, can be charged within radio; station presets and time not erased during charging. Low battery consumption. Battery-strength indicator. Hinged battery cover prevents loss. Travel power lock. Superior FM weak-signal sensitivity. Excellent

If you're watching your money, the Degen DE1101/Kaito KA1101 is a tough value to beat. D. Zantow

FM capture ratio aids reception when band congested, including helping separate co-channel stations. FM in stereo through earbuds, included. "FML" covers Japanese FM. Line output socket (separate from earphone socket) for recording, FM home transmitters and outboard audio. Available in gray or aluminum colors. *Kaito:* Mediumwave AM 9/10 channel steps selectable, tunes up to 1710 kHz.

Cons: Speaker audio quality lacks low-frequency audio as compared to larger models. Power key activates 99-minute sleep delay; to turn the radio on fulltime, another key must be pressed immediately afterwards. Station presets, slewing and scanning require pressing bandswitch carousel key up to four times when tuning from below 10 MHz to above 10 MHz and *vice versa*. No tuning knob. Tunes world band only in 5 kHz steps and displays in nonstandard XX.XX/ $XX.XX_5$ MHz format. Digital buzz under some circumstances, such as when antenna touched. Spurious signals can appear when hand is pressed over back cover. With our unit, microprocessor locked up when batteries removed for over a day; resolved by pressing tiny reset key. No signal-strength indicator (what appears to be an LED tuning indicator is actually an ambient-light sensor to disable LCD illumination except when it's dark). Clock doesn't display when frequency is shown, although key allows time to replace frequency briefly. Little-used

2 MHz (120 meter) world band segment not covered. *Degen:* Upper limit of mediumwave AM tuning is 1620 kHz, rather than the 1705 kHz band upper limit in the Americas, Australia and certain other zones. Medium-wave AM tunes in only 9 kHz steps, inappropriate for Americas.

☞ Kaito version comes with proper 120V AC adaptor for North America, whereas Degen comes with 220V AC adaptor for most other world zones. Both are safe when used "as is," or with a Franzus or other recognized 120V-to-220V or 220V-to-120V AC converter. However, according to unconfirmed reports, the Degen version ordered from a vendor in Hong Kong comes with a 220-to-120V AC converter that appears to pose a fire hazard.

Verdict: Sixty-Buck Chuck. Degen's DE1101, sold in North America as the Kaito KA1101, is a knockout bargain. Engineered and manufactured in China, it is one of the smallest compact models tested and has exceptional dynamic range. It comes with an enviable grab-bag of features and accessories, right down to inboard rechargeable batteries. But if you want music-quality audio, be prepared to use earpieces.

New for 2009

✪✪¾

Tecsun PL-450

Pricing (via stores.ebay.com/radio-component): *PL-450 with English markings:* $78.99 including worldwide (except Italy) air shipping from China. *120-to-220V AC converter:* add $7.90 when ordering.

Pros: Numerous handy tuning features include knob and up/down slewing with two speeds, signal-seek/presets scanning (five-second resume), 600 non-volatile station presets that store bandwidth (*see* Cons), ATS (auto-tuning storage) for FM and medium-wave AM, and quick access to world band segments. Various page/presets combinations:10 pages with 50 presets, 20 pages with 25 presets, 25 pages with 20 presets or 50 pages with 10 presets. Virtually no muting or chuffing when tuning. Worthy ergonomics, including keys with nice feel. Good sensitivity on all bands except FM with built-in or external antenna (*see* Cons, *With external antenna*). Pleasant audio for size (*see* Cons). Two well-chosen bandwidths. Superior dynamic range. Double conversion provides worthwhile image rejection (*see* Cons, *With external antenna*). Two-level attenuator (*see* Cons, *With external antenna*). FM stereo with earpieces. Single-event 1–90 minute radio/clock-radio timer. 1–120 minute sleep timer. Ten-minute snooze. Superior illuminated LCD (*see* Cons). Five-bar signal strength indicator overreads somewhat; nonetheless, performs reasonably well. Four-bar battery indicator. Control setting for operation with rechargeable batteries. Built-in timed battery recharger. Clock displays independently of frequency. Travel power lock. Reset button. Includes earbuds, external wire antenna (on open plastic reel), thin cloth carrying pouch, 220V regulated AC adaptor (*see* Cons, *North America*) and three 1000 mAh rechargeable NiMH batteries. Optional 120-to-220V AC converter (*see* Cons, *North America*). Japanese FM. Prompt shipment (*see* Cons).

Cons: Available outside Asia seemingly from only from one dealer, an eBay vendor in China. Shipped with minimal protective packing material. Packet wrapped in twine, discouraged by shippers as it can get caught in machinery. Vendor's shipping insurance and nominal 12-month warranty worthless, based on past experience. English-language owners manual promised online by vendor, but none received; may be because model very new when ordered. Audio lacks low-frequency (bass) response. No single sideband. Presets can't be alphanumerically tagged. Slight wobble in tuning knob. Dark LCD background profits from fulltime illumination, except in bright ambient light, for no-strain viewing. Attenuator, not commonly needed, excessively vigorous. FM sensitivity only so-so. Unusual FM fine tuning control complicates operation. Battery cover not hinged to protect from loss. Flimsy elevation panel. Thin plastic on speaker grill. No audio line output. *With external antenna:* Local mediumwave AM signals sometimes tax front-end selectivity and intrude into shortwave spectrum. Images occasionally peek through 910 kHz down. External antenna jack not for mediumwave AM or longwave. Carrying case has creosote odor, needs airing. *North America:* AC adaptor only 220V, but: 1) 220-to-120V converter costs extra and not UL listed; and 2) DC power jack has nonstandard negative tip and unusual size, complicating replacement with aftermarket 120V AC adaptor.

Verdict: Tecsun's compact PL-450 is a pleasure to operate. It performs nicely and sounds agreeable, but the one-shot buying experience is *caveat emptor*.

Evaluation of New Model: The PL-450 is awash with useful tuning features, including 600 nonvolatile station presets which store bandwidth. A real tuning knob, too, with virtually no chuffing or muting even though it wobbles slightly.

Ergonomics are generally commendable—even the keys have superior feel. Another nice touch is that the World Time clock is displayed separate from the frequency, even if it is done like musical chairs: When the radio is off, the frequency display becomes the clock, while what was the clock shows as the alarm setting. Numeric seconds aren't displayed at any time.

The only way to turn on the radio fulltime is to hold down the power button for a second (ditto to turn the radio off); otherwise, the sleep timer takes over. And although there is an FM fine tuning control, it complicates operation.

The LCD is substantial for the panel's size, and most icons are large enough to be readily visible. The five-bar signal strength meter overreads somewhat, but is still better than what's usually found on compact portables. However, the display's background is so dark that illumination is almost always needed to relieve eyestrain except in bright ambient light.

Performance Pluses

Selectivity profits from two well-chosen bandwidths. Unsurprisingly at this price, there is no synchronous selectable sideband

New for 2009 is the Tecsun PL-450. It's user friendly and awash in tuning features, but has no single sideband. Virtually unavailable outside China except from a solitary eBay vendor.

or even ECSS to further enhance adjacent-channel rejection.

Sensitivity on most bands is good, and for more kick an outboard accessory wire antenna is included. FM, however, is slightly less sensitive.

Superior dynamic range allows the '450 to handle much more than that modest accessory antenna. Indeed, the radio does yeoman's service even with a high-performance outdoor antenna—no small feat at this price. There is an attenuator should dynamic range be strained, but it comes down harder than it should.

Front-end selectivity and image rejection are fine for a portable of this type, but not up to the likes of premium models like the Etón E1. If you use a major outdoor antenna, mediumwave AM signals may ghost in to annoy world band reception. Also, images may poke through 910 kHz down.

Audio is pleasant, considering the radio's size, but lacks low-frequency (bass) response.

Complications

The radio comes with a regulated 220V AC adaptor suitable for many parts of the world, but not North America. The radio's adaptor jack has a nonstandard negative tip and unusual size, making it difficult for North Americans to mate it with an aftermarket 120V AC adaptor. The '450's Chinese vendor offers an optional 120-to-220V converter which, although not UL listed, seems to be the only practical alternative for Americans and Canadians.

Once the AC adaptor is connected, the radio can be powered not only directly, but also by recharging batteries internally—the needed three NiMH cells are included.

The Tecsun PL-450 appears to be available outside Asia from only one dealer, an eBay vendor in China. Shipment was prompt, but the promised English operating manual did not materialize, possibly because the model was relatively new when ordered. Although there was no damage en route, there was minimal protective packing. Also, twine was used—a practice discouraged by shippers as it can get caught in machinery.

When we tried to make a claim with this vendor on an earlier shipment that suffered damage, we wound up having to eat the loss—insurance and 12-month "warranty" notwithstanding.

✪✪¾

Sangean ATS 606AP, Sangean ATS 606S, Sangean ATS 606SP, Roberts R876

Pricing: *ATS 606AP:* $119.95 in the United States. CAD$169.00 in Canada. *ATS 606S:* €95.00 in Germany. *ATS 606SP:* 9.00 in Germany. *R876:* £129.99 in the United Kingdom.

The Sangean ATS 606AP sounds pleasant and is sized for travel. No real shortcomings, but lacks single sideband and is priced above similar models.

Pros: Relatively diminutive for a compact model. Single bandwidth reasonably effective. Speaker audio better than most for size (*see* Cons). Weak-signal sensitivity at least average. Various helpful tuning features, including keypad, 54 station presets, slewing, signal-seek tuning and meter band selection. Keys have superior feel. Easy to operate. Longwave. Dual-zone 24-hour clock. Illuminated LCD. Alarm. Sleep delay. Travel power lock (*see* Cons). Multi-bar battery strength indicator; also, weak-battery warning. Stereo FM through earphones or earbuds. Above-average FM weak-signal sensitivity and selectivity. Above-average capture ratio aids reception when band congested, including helping separate co-channel stations. Memory scan. Elevation panel tilts radio to handy operating angle; rubber feet reduce sliding while panel extended. *R876 and ATS 606AP:* UL-approved 120/230V AC adaptor, with American and European plugs, adjusts automatically to proper AC voltage. *ATS 606AP:* ANT-60 outboard reel passive wire antenna accessory aids slightly with weak-signal reception. In North America, service provided by Sangean America to models sold under its name.

Cons: No tuning knob. Speaker audio has limited low-frequency audio. No single sideband. Clock not readable while frequency displayed. No meaningful signal-strength indicator. Keypad not in telephone format. Travel power lock doesn't disable LCD illumination. No carrying strap or handle. No batteries (three "AA" needed). *ATS 606AP:* Country of manufacture (China) not specified on radio or box.

Verdict: This classic continues to soldier on in the face of lower-cost competition.

✪✪⅝

Sangean ATS 505P, Sangean ATS 505, Roberts R9914

Pricing: *ATS 505P:* $119.95 in the United States. CAD$149.00 in Canada. €89.00 in

ICOM'S IC-R20 HANDHELD

The popularity of handheld wideband scanners keeps marching on. Some even cover world band, but rarely well. And at US$520/£300 the 'R20 is costlier than a dedicated world band portable.

But there are advantages. Frequency coverage in the United States, where eavesdropping on cellular bands is *verboten*, is 150 kHz–822 MHz, 851–867 MHz and 896–3305 MHz. Elsewhere, or within the United States for government use, it's 150 kHz to 3305 MHz. And there's neat tuning-related feature called "dual watch," which like television's PIP allows users to monitor two signals simultaneously. The catch: It doesn't work on world band.

Affordable wideband coverage compromises world band performance.

The large LCD is uncomfortable to read except when illuminated. Keys have good feel; otherwise, ergonomics are only so-so because of limited real estate for controls. Tuning is by knob, keypad, up/down slewing and a thousand presets in steps of .01, .1, 5 , 6.25, 8.33, 9, 10, 12.5, 15, 20, 25, 30, 50 and 100 kHz.

The 'R20 has three bandwidths, each assigned by the received mode so none can be selected independent of mode. Unfortunately, the lone bandwidth for the AM mode, which includes world band, is a whopping 12 kHz. Single-sideband's bandwidth, around 3 kHz, comes to the rescue by allowing for worthy ECSS reception of world band and mediumwave AM stations. It's a tiresome procedure but does the trick.

Alas, sensitivity disappoints—only powerful signals are suitably audible with the telescopic antenna. Another letdown is that the antenna tends to keel over when fully extended. The 'R20's dynamic range is significantly limited, too, so a serious outboard antenna tends to introduce overloading. Tweaking the RF gain and 30 dB attenuator can help, but not always.

Stability, as well as image and spurious-signal rejection, are commendable. Speaker audio lacks punch, but otherwise is good considering the radio's size. There's also a built-in digital audio recorder. Its 65-minute "fine" setting is hardly high fidelity, but fares nicely for world band.

The Icom IC-R20 makes a tempting choice for scanning VHF and above, and offers built-in recording. For niche applications, like low-profile field surveillance, the radio's characteristics occasionally come together to make it a best-of-breed choice.

Icom's pricey IC-R20 handheld is a poor value for world band. However, if you're into portable scanning and world band is only secondary, this may be just the specialty model you've been looking for.

Icom's handheld IC-R20 is chiefly for scanner use.

The Sangean ATS 505P costs the same as sibling ATS 606AP, but has single sideband.

Germany. *ATS 505:* £79.95 in the United Kingdom. €85.00 in Germany. *AC adaptor for ATS 505:* £16.95 in the United Kingdom. *R9914:* £99.00 in the United Kingdom.

Pros: Numerous helpful tuning features, including two-speed tuning knob, keypad, station presets (*see* Cons), up/down slewing, meter-band carousel selector, signal-seek tuning and scanning of presets (*see* Cons). Automatic-sorting feature arranges station presets in frequency order. Analog clarifier with center detent and stable circuitry tunes single-sideband with uncommon precision, where it stays tuned and allows for superior audio phasing for a portable (*see* Cons). Illuminated LCD. Dual-zone 24/12-hour clock. Alarm with sleep delay. Modest battery consumption. Nine-bar battery- strength indicator. Travel power lock (*see* Cons). FM stereo through earbuds, included. Longwave. *ATS 505P and R9914:* AC adaptor. *ATS 505P:* Tape measure antenna.

Cons: Bandwidth slightly wider than appropriate for a single-bandwidth receiver. Large for a compact. Only 18 world band station presets in two pages. Tuning knob tends to mute, notably when step is set to fine (1 kHz). Keys respond slowly, needing to be held down momentarily rather than simply tapped. Stop-listen-resume scanning of station presets wastes time. Pedestrian overall single-sideband reception because of wide bandwidth and occasional distortion from AGC timing. Clock does not display independent of frequency. No meaningful signal-strength indicator. No carrying handle or strap. Country of manufacture (China) not specified on radio or box. Travel power lock does not deactivate LCD illumination. No batteries (four "AA" needed).

Verdict: An okay portable that demodulates single-sideband signals.

Now is closeout time for the Sony ICF-SW35. Attractively priced, but clunky to tune.

✪✪⅝

Sony ICF-SW35

Pricing (as available): $89.95 in the United States. €99.00 in Germany.

Pros: Superior reception quality, with excellent adjacent-channel rejection (selectivity) and image rejection. Fifty world band station presets, which can be scanned within five pages. Signal-seek-then-resume scanning works unusually well. Two-speed slewing. Illuminated display. Dual-zone 24-hour clock. Dual-time alarm. Sleep delay. Travel power lock. FM stereo through earpieces (*see* Cons). Weak-battery indicator. Japanese FM (most versions) and longwave.

Cons: Dwindling availability. No keypad or tuning knob. Muting while tuning and poky slewing degrade bandscanning. Speaker audio quality clear, but lacks low-frequency audio. Clock not displayed independent of frequency. LCD lacks contrast when viewed from above. No jacks for recording or outboard antenna. No AC adaptor, earpieces or batteries (three "AA" required).

Verdict: The Chinese-made Sony ICF-SW35, a poor seller, was discontinued in 2008. Yet, some retailers have enough stock to carry them into 2009.

The 'SW35 offers superior rejection of images, which are usually the bane of inexpensive models, but there's no keypad or tuning knob. Overall, a decent choice only for listening to a predictable roster of stations.

✪✪½

Degen DE1105

Pricing: *via stores.ebay.com/v-com-collections:* $68.99 including global air shipping from China.

Pros: One thousand non-volatile presets (*see* Cons) within ten pages (*see* Cons). Other handy tuning features include keypad, signal-seek frequency scanning, automatic tuning system (ATS) and up/down slewing. Also, knurled wheel with un-muted variable-rate tuning shifts from slow (1 kHz) to fast (5 kHz) steps when rotated quickly (*see* Cons). Worthy sensitivity and selectivity. Double conversion provides effective image rejection. Dynamic range resists overloading. Keys have excellent feel (*see* Cons). LCD and most keys illuminate when touched or tuning wheel turned. Ten-bar signal-strength indicator accurate and precise for price class. Internal automatic NiMH battery recharging virtually eliminates battery purchases. Three-bar battery-strength indicator seconds as battery-charging indicator. Radio shuts down if batteries too low. Clock selectable 12- or 24-hour formats; seconds displayed numerically (*see* Cons). Worthy FM sensitivity and selectivity. FM in stereo with earpieces. Bass boost, albeit only on FM with earpieces. Japanese FM. Three alarms with sleep delay. Travel power lock. Hinged battery cover prevents loss. Includes soft carrying case, two "AA" NiMH batteries, earbuds, accessory wire antenna and either

The Degen DE1105 can be unearthed outside China only on eBay. Nice, but not terribly user friendly and outclassed by similar models. D. Zantow

a 220V or a 110V AC adaptor (*see* Cons). Displays ambient (e.g., room) temperature (*see* Cons).

Cons: Not available outside China except via eBay with no warranty. Potentially confusing presets page system and user setup. Power key activates 99-minute sleep delay; radio turned on fulltime only by quickly pushing another key. World band coverage from 5800 to 26100 kHz misses lesser 2, 3, 4 and 5 MHz (120, 90, 75 and 60 meter) segments and 5730–5795 kHz end of important 6 MHz (49 meter) segment. Because only one (narrow) bandwidth provided, world band and mediumwave AM audio quality only fair with earpieces and internal speaker. Except for frequency/clock, LCD information small and hard to see. Keys undersized. Keypad not in standard telephone format. Tuning wheel operates only in slow (1 kHz) steps within many "out-of-segment" frequency zones. Clock shares display with frequency, so can't show both simultaneously. Clock setting volatile. Mediumwave AM sensitivity only fair. No external antenna or audio line-out jacks. Temperature only in Celsius. AC adaptor not UL approved.

Verdict: The Chinese-made Degen DE1105 is a solid performer within its price class.

Size and features make it especially welcome for use on trips, but for similar money there are better choices.

✪✪½

Etón E100, E100 "Lextronix," Grundig G100

Pricing (as available): *Grundig:* $99.95 in the United States. *Etón:* CAD$69.97 in Canada. £59.95 in the United Kingdom. *120V AC adaptor:* CAD$19.95 in Canada. *"Lextronix":* €79.00 in Germany.

Pros: Handy size for travel. Very good weak-signal sensitivity. Above-average dynamic range. Superior audio for size, aided by hi/lo tone switch. Several handy tuning features, including keypad; tuning knob in 1 kHz segments for world band/MW AM (*see* Cons); 200 station presets, with eight pages where user selects how many presets per page; world band segment selector; and slewing keys (5 kHz world band steps, 9/10 kHz MW AM steps). Illuminated LCD, easy to read. World Time clock (*see* Cons) with alarm, clock radio, snooze and sleep delay; may also be set to 12-hour format. Clock reads out separately from frequency. Signal-seek frequency scanning searches world band segments or preset channels (*see* Cons). Five-bar signal/battery strength indicator, works well. Keys have positive-action feel (*see* Cons). FM stereo with earbuds, included. Japanese FM. Travel power lock. Setting to allow for optimum performance from either regular or rechargeable batteries. Elevation panel tilts radio to handy operating angle. *Etón, Grundig:* Excellent hardside leather travel case. Stylish curved front panel (Etón in silver, Grundig in black). *Grundig:* Two "AA" alkaline batteries. *North America:* Excellent toll-free tech support. Owner's manual unusually helpful for newcomers.

If you find most compacts a tad large for travel. yet are unimpressed by pocket models, consider the Etón E100/Grundig G100.

Cons: Single-conversion IF circuitry results in mediocre image rejection. Signal-seek frequency scanning progresses slowly. Some muting when tuning by knob or slewing, slows down bandscanning. Tuning knob has no 5 kHz step. Power key activates 90-minute sleep delay; fulltime "on" only if held down for two seconds; also, three more seconds to boot up, so total is five seconds to turn on radio. World band frequencies on our units display 1 kHz high. Small, cramped keys. No jacks for line output or external antenna. AC adaptor optional. Warranty honored only if radio purchased from authorized dealer, listed under each product at www.etoncorp.com.

Verdict: A nicely sized offering for tuning major stations at home or away.

New for 2009

✪✪½

Tecsun PL-600

Pricing (via stores.ebay.com/radio-component): *PL-600 with English markings:* $94.95 including worldwide (except Italy) air shipping from China. *120-to-220V AC converter:* add $7.90 when ordering.

Pros: Numerous handy tuning features include knob and up/down slewing with two speeds, signal-seek/presets scanning (five-second resume), 600 non-volatile station presets that store bandwidth and mode (*see* Cons), ATS (auto-tuning storage) for FM and mediumwave AM, and quick access to world band segments. Various page/presets combinations: 10 pages with 50 presets, 20 pages with 25 presets, 25 pages with 20 presets or 50 pages with 10 presets.

Virtually no muting or chuffing when tuning. Worthy ergonomics. Good sensitivity on all bands with built-in or external antenna (*see* Cons, *With external antenna*). Overall very good audio quality on FM, with good bass response (*see* Cons). Two well-chosen bandwidths. Superior dynamic range. Double conversion provides worthwhile image rejection (*see* Cons, *With external antenna*). Two-level attenuator (*see* Cons, *With external antenna*). Single sideband mode's BFO knob for sideband selection has midpoint detent. FM stereo with earpieces. Two-event 1–90 minute radio/clock-radio timer. 1–120 minute sleep timer. Ten-minute snooze. Superior illuminated LCD (*see* Cons). Five-bar signal strength indicator overreads somewhat, but still performs reasonably well. Four-bar battery indicator. Control setting for operation with rechargeable batteries. Built-in timed battery recharger. Clock displays independently of frequency. Travel power lock. Reset button. Includes earbuds, external wire antenna (on open plastic reel), worthy carrying case (*see* Cons), English owner's manual, 220V regulated AC adaptor (*see* Cons, *North America*) and four 1000 mAh rechargeable NiMH batteries. Optional 120-to-220V AC converter (*see* Cons, *North America*). Japanese FM. Prompt shipment (*see* Cons).

Cons: Apparently available outside Asia only from one dealer, an eBay vendor in China. Shipped with minimal protective packaging material. Packet wrapped in twine, discouraged by shippers as it can get caught in machinery. Vendor's shipping insurance and nominal 12-month warranty worthless, based on past experience. Significant audio distortion in all bands except FM; if this results from a lapse in QA, then overall rating rises. Presets can't be alphanumerically tagged. Slight wobble in tuning knob. Single sideband has minor warble and lacks separate LSB/USB switching. ECSS not viable. Dark LCD background profits from full-time illumination, except in bright ambient light, for no-strain viewing. Attenuator, not commonly needed, excessively vigorous. FM sensitivity only fair. Battery cover not hinged to protect from loss. No audio line output. Carrying case has creosote odor,

Among newer "from China only" compacts is the Tecsun PL-600, offered on eBay. It has heaps of handy tuning features, along with mostly superior ergonomics and performance.

needs airing. *With external antenna:* Local mediumwave AM signals sometimes tax front-end selectivity and intrude into shortwave spectrum. Images occasionally peek through 910 kHz down. Telescopic antenna can't be fully vertical when elevation panel extended. External antenna jack not for mediumwave AM or longwave. *North America:* AC adaptor only 220V, but: 1) 220-to-120V converter costs extra and not UL listed; and 2) DC power jack has nonstandard negative tip and unusual size, complicating replacement with aftermarket 120V AC adaptor.

Verdict: Tecsun's PL-600 is among the larger compact models. Easy to use, it offers superior FM audio and passable single sideband. However, our unit sounds distorted in all bands but FM, diminishing an otherwise pleasant experience; if this arises from QA, then more satisfactory units would be rated higher. The '600 does not appear to be available outside Asia except via an eBay vendor with a mixed track record.

Evaluation of New Model: The PL-600 is nicely equipped with handy tuning features. These include 600 nonvolatile station presets which store bandwidth and mode, along with a tuning knob having some wobble but virtually no chuffing or muting.

User Friendly

Ergonomics are generally superior, including a World Time clock that's independently displayed from the frequency, and there's a bonus: When the radio is off, the frequency display becomes the clock, while what was the clock alternates between showing timer 1 and timer 2. Numeric seconds aren't displayed at any time.

Chinese manufacturers seem to have an obsession about timers, as many of their radios activate a sleep-delay timer when the power button is turned on. The '600 is no exception, so to turn on the radio fulltime you have to hold down the power button for one second (ditto to turn the radio off).

The LCD is fairly large, which allows most icons to be readily visible—the five-bar signal strength meter, too, although it overreads to a degree. However, the display's background is so dark that illumination is almost always needed except in bright ambient light.

Worthy Performance, Except . . .

Selectivity is above average for a compact, thanks to two well-chosen bandwidths. Unsurprisingly at this price, there is no synchronous selectable sideband to further enhance adjacent-channel rejection. ECSS isn't a fallback, either, as its performance is woeful.

Sensitivity is good and profits from the included outboard accessory wire antenna. Superior dynamic range allows the '600 to handle much more than that antenna, though—it works surprisingly well even with a high-performance outdoor antenna. There's an attenuator in case dynamic range starts to flag, but it reduces signal strength excessively.

Front-end selectivity and image rejection are pretty good for a portable of this type, but this is no DX superset. With a serious outdoor antenna, mediumwave AM signals can mix in with world band signals. Too, weak images may appear 910 kHz lower down in frequency.

Audio is pleasant on FM, right down to low-frequency (bass) response. However, at least on our unit, distortion reared its head on the other bands, diminishing the listening experience. Given the level of alleged quality control coming from Chinese electronics manufacturers, this may vary from sample to sample, but it was too late before going to press for us to obtain more units. If the distortion arises from a lapse in QA, then the radio's overall rating would rise accordingly. (A superb commentary on the dismal state of electronics quality control is at pcmag.com/article2/0,2817,2326330,00.asp.)

Single sideband performs adequately for casual use, although there is some audible warbling. LSB/USB selection is made by the rudimentary method of adjusting a BFO knob, which includes a center detent as a tactile aid.

Where's The Juice?

A regulated 220V AC adaptor is provided for most of the world outside North America. Yanks and Canadians trying to substitute that adaptor with one of 120V obtained locally bump up against incompatibilities: The radio's adaptor jack has a nonstandard negative tip, and its offbeat size doesn't mate with plugs found on aftermarket 120V AC adaptors. The radio's vendor offers an optional 120-to-220V converter, not UL listed, which seems to be the only ready solution for North Americans.

Once the AC adaptor is connected, the '600 can be powered directly or by recharging the supplied four NiMH cells internally.

In the spirit of Henry Ford, who famously boasted that you could have any color so long as it was black, the '600 is available from only one dealer: an eBay vendor in China. Shipment is quick enough—a one-week turnaround—and in this instance there was no shipping damage. However, our packet had minimal protective packing, and twine that's used can become ensnared in postal machinery.

We once tried to make a claim with this vendor when a shipment suffered damage. No details of insurance were provided; instead, we were told simply to complain to our local post office.

HAVE RADIO, WILL TRAVEL

Getting Past Security

Air travel with a world band radio is rarely a hassle if you take some common-sense steps. To minimize odds of a delay at airport security, remember that their job is to be paranoid about you, so it's prudent to be paranoid about them.

- Answer questions honestly, but don't volunteer information or joke around. Avoid rudeness and arguments.
- The nail that sticks out gets hammered first. Security focuses on the unusual, so be gray.
- Terrorists like big radios (they don't call them boom boxes for nothing). Take a pocket or compact portable.
- Stow your radio and batteries—especially if they are non-rechargeable lithium—in a carry-on bag, not in checked luggage or on your person. Don't stuff the radio at the bottom or wrapped in clothing, like you're trying to hide something. Equally, it's usually best not to place your portable outside your carry-on where it can be readily seen. However, if you decide to put a small radio into the manual inspection basket at the security portal, have it playing FM softly with earbuds attached, like a Walkman or iPod. Place world band accessories, extra batteries, guides and instruction books in checked luggage, or at least in a separate carry-on.
- Before going into the terminal, and certainly before entering security, preset the radio to a popular FM music station, then keep batteries inside the radio so you can demonstrate that it actually works. Unless you're asked, don't mention world band—and try not to use the word "shortwave," as they may think you have a transmitter.
- If asked why you're taking a world band radio, state the truth: It's for your own listening. If they persist, reply that you like to keep up with news and sports while away, and leave it at that. Don't volunteer information about alarm, snooze or other timer facilities, as timers can be components in bombs. If you're asked about stations, cite something that's usually safe, like the BBC in London, and avoid potentially "flagged" stations like Radio Pakistan or Radio Habana Cuba.
- If traveling in zones of war or civil unrest, or off the beaten path in parts of Africa or South America, take a pocket radio you can afford to lose.
- If traveling to Bahrain, avoid a radio which has "receiver" visible on its cabinet. Security personnel may think you're a spy.
- When traveling to Malaysia, Bahrain or Saudi Arabia, don't take a model with single-sideband capability—or, at the very least, take steps to disguise this capability so it is not visually apparent. If things get dicey, point out that you listen to news and sports from the popular American AFRTS station, which transmits only in the upper-sideband mode. (PASSPORT can be used to verify this.)

Theft? Radios, cameras, binoculars, laptops and other glitzy goodies are almost always stolen to be resold. The more worn the item looks—affixing scuffed stickers helps—the less likely it is to be confiscated by corrupt inspectors or stolen by thieves.

Finally, if you're not traveling solo have somebody watch your stuff when it's on the X-ray belt. If something is stolen there, it's all but guaranteed the security people will—or can—do little more than shrug.

Grundig has discontinued the YB 550PE, but it should still be on sale through early 2009.

✪✪⅜

Grundig YB 550PE

Pricing (as available): $59.98 in the United States.

Pros: Worthy selectivity and dynamic range. Several handy tuning features, including 200 station presets with eight pages and world band segment selector. Slewing tunes world band in 5 kHz steps; fine-tuning thumbwheel tunes world band and mediumwave AM in 1 kHz steps. Generally pleasant audio (*see* Cons). Illuminated LCD (*see* Cons). World Time clock (*see* Cons) with alarm, clock radio and sleep delay; may also be changed to 12-hour format. Clock readout separate from frequency display, shows whether radio on or off. Signal-seek frequency scanning searches world band segments or preset channels (*see* Cons). Accurate five-bar signal/battery strength indicator. FM stereo with earbuds, included. Japanese FM. Travel power lock. Stylish. Removable elevation panel (*see* Cons) tilts radio to handy operating angle. LCD easy to read. Three "AA" alkaline batteries. *North America:* Excellent toll-free tech support.

Cons: Weak-signal sensitivity only fair. Single-conversion IF circuitry results in mediocre image rejection. Signal-seek frequency scanning stops only on very strong signals. Power key activates 90-minute sleep delay; radio on fulltime only if key held down for two seconds; takes an additional five seconds to fully turn on. Small, cramped keys. FM audio not crisp through earpieces. Keypad's zero key oddly placed. Telescopic antenna placement on right side disallows tilting to left. Illumination dim. Snap-on elevation panel must be removed to replace batteries. Battery cover comes loose easily if elevation panel not attached. Frequency readout not always spot-on. No AC adaptor. Warranty honored only if radio purchased from authorized dealer, listed under each product at www.etoncorp.com.

Verdict: Discontinued and hard to find, but with closeout pricing.

The Sangean ATS 404 is similar to other models, but priced higher.

✪✪⅜

Sangean ATS 404, Sangean ATS 404P

Pricing: *ATS 404:* $79.95 in the United States. €59.00 in Germany. *ATS 404P:* €65.00 in Germany. *ADP-808 120V AC adaptor:* $12.95 in the United States.

Pros: Superior weak-signal sensitivity. Some handy tuning features (*see* Con). Stereo FM through earpieces, included. Dual-zone 24/12-hour clock displays seconds numerically. Alarm with sleep delay. Travel power lock (*see* Cons). Illuminated LCD. Battery-strength indicator. *ATS 404P:* Includes ANT 60 accessory antenna.

Cons: Single-conversion IF circuitry results in poor image rejection. No tuning knob. Overloading, controllable by shortening telescopic antenna on world band and collapsing it on mediumwave AM band. Some internal digital "buzz." Tunes only in 5 kHz steps. No signal-strength indicator. Frequency and time cannot be displayed simultaneously. Travel power lock does not disable LCD illumination. No handle or carrying strap. AC adaptor extra. Country of manufacture (China) not specified on radio or box. No batteries (four "AA" needed).

Verdict: Better values found elsewhere.

✪✪⅜ ¢

Grundig Yacht Boy 300PE

Pricing: $49.98 as available in the United States.

Pros: Sensitive to weak world band and FM signals. Various helpful tuning features. World Time 24-hour clock with alarm, clock radio and 10–90 minute sleep delay (*see* Cons). Illuminated LCD (*see* Cons). 120V AC adaptor and supplementary antenna. Travel power lock (*see* Cons). Stereo FM through earbuds, included. Excellent toll-free tech support.

Cons: Hard to find; seems to be sold only by Universal Radio. Single-conversion IF circuitry results in mediocre image rejection. No tuning knob. Few station presets; e.g., only six for 2300–7800 kHz. Tunes world band only in 5 kHz steps and displays in nonstandard XX.XX MHz/$XX.XX_5$ MHz format. If keypad entry is of an even channel and all digits keyed in (e.g., 6 - 1 - 9 - 0, Enter) tunes radio 5 kHz higher (e.g., 6195); remedied by not entering trailing zero (e.g., 6 - 1 - 9, Enter). Unhandy carouseling "MW/SW1/SW2/FM" control required for tuning within 2300–7800 kHz *vs.* 9100–26100 kHz range or *vice versa*. Clock not displayed independent of frequency; key alters which is visible. Nigh-useless signal-strength indicator. LCD illumination not disabled by travel power lock. No longwave. Does not tune unimportant 7805–9095 kHz range. Warranty honored only if radio purchased from

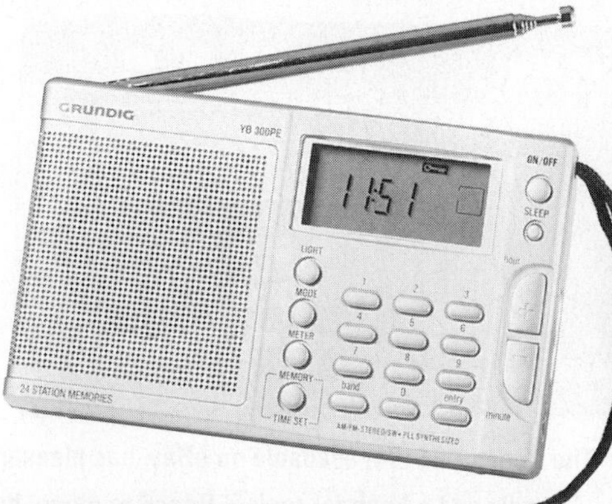

Revived From The Dead: The Grundig Yacht Boy 300PE was discontinued in 2004, then suddenly resurfaced three years later.

authorized dealer, listed under each product at www.etoncorp.com.

Verdict: This model was dropped from Grundig's lineup in 2004, then revived at a lower price for North America in the late summer of 2007—there's no indication whether this is new old stock or revived production. Except for LCD illumination being enabled when the travel power lock is used, this Chinese-made model is a genuine bargain and handy for air travel, especially where signals are weak.

✪✪

Degen DE1104

Pricing: *Export/English version via stores. ebay.com/radio-component:* $62.90 including global air shipping from China.

Pros: Generally excellent sensitivity (*see* Cons). Pleasant, punchy audio with no audible hiss. Tone control with healthy bass boost. Dual conversion provides worthy image rejection. LCD easy to read, with excellent orange illumination and large characters; illumination can be switched on fulltime, even with battery power (*see* Cons). Tuning knob (*see* Cons) smooth, with minimal play. Keys and switches have good feel. Electronic bandswitching for medium-

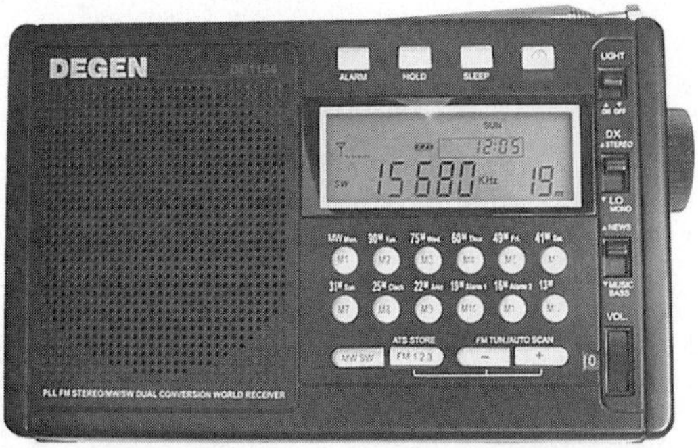

The Degen DE1104, available on eBay, has pleasant audio and a knob for tuning. Priced to move, but reception is impaired by inadequate dynamic range, broad selectivity and mixed sensitivity. D. Zantow

wave AM/world band avoids mechanical pitfalls. Antenna jack for world band and FM (*see* Cons). One-step attenuator (*see* Cons). Four-bar signal-strength indicator. Volume level shows in ten steps within little window. Travel power lock. Batteries recharge internally (*see* Cons). Hinged battery cover prevents loss. Clock, in 12-or 24-hour format, displays separately from frequency. Sleep feature, up to 90 minutes. Two clock-radio "on" times include setting for day of week. Three-bar battery indicator. Three pages with 12 FM presets each. ATS (auto store) for FM, especially handy on trips. Signal-seek scanning on FM. Japanese FM. AC adaptor (*see* Cons), thin cloth case, earbuds and indoor wire antenna (*see* Cons).

Cons: Not available outside China except via eBay with no warranty. World band and mediumwave AM analog tuned with digital frequency counter, so tunable only by knob. Poor dynamic range causes overloading, especially evenings within 6 and 7 MHz (49 and 41 meter) segments, even with telescopic antenna; attenuator helps only slightly. Antenna jack meaningless, as wire antenna causes serious overloading. Some spurious variable-pitch whistles (not images). Lone bandwidth relatively broad. Sensitivity rolls off over upper 100 kHz of each world band segment and above 1300 kHz mediumwave AM. Annoying AC adaptor hum with telescopic antenna or included indoor wire antenna. World band coverage not continuous, omitting little-used 2, 19 and 26 MHz (120, 15 and 11 meter) segments; also, 5730–5780, 7575–7600, 9250–9310, 9955–10000, 11500–11575, 15000–15030 and 15675–15825 kHz in other segments. Mediumwave AM tunes to roughly 1670 kHz, missing upper three channels in Americas and some other zones. Frequency readout not always spot-on. LCD illumination not timed when batteries in use. FM presets volatile, erase if more than one minute to change batteries. FM performance only fair. Tuning knob inoperative on FM. No line-audio output. Internal battery recharger has no timer. Required 4 × "AA" batteries not included.

Verdict: Worthy as a travel clock radio, although only FM has handy tuning features. World band sensitivity and audio are superior, particularly for daytime listening, but dynamic range disappoints.

✪⅞ ©

Etón E1100, Grundig G1100

Pricing: *Grundig:* $49.95 in the United States. CAD$49.95 in Canada. *Etón:* £34.95 in the United Kingdom. €49.95 in Germany.

Pros: Good world band and mediumwave AM sensitivity. Pleasant, vigorous audio (*see* Cons). Easy-to-read LCD has large digits and good contrast. Clever, effective LCD illumination turns on and off by rotating tuning knob or pushing key. Travel power lock (*see* Cons). Weak battery indicator. Elevation panel tilts radio to handy operating angle. World Time clock (*see* Cons) with alarm, clock radio and snooze; may be changed to 12-hour format. Sleep delay up to two hours. FM in stereo through included earbuds; FM stereo indicator. Two "AA" batteries included. Superior carrying case. *North America:* Excellent toll-free tech support.

Cons: Tunes, stiffly, only by knob. Single conversion IF circuitry results in poor image rejection Selectivity only okay. Analog tuning uses string and pulley configuration to turn variable capacitors; this results in play and makes it harder to zero in on stations. Lacks coverage of little-used 2 and 25 MHz (120 and 11 meter) world band segments; also misses relatively unimportant 3 MHz (90 meter) segment and 5.73–5.9 MHz portion of important 6 MHz (49 meter) segment. Unhandy bandswitch must be accessed often to tune mediumwave AM and within shortwave spectra. Hand on or near cabinet rear causes frequency drift of up to 5 kHz. Placing hand or finger on LCD generates buzzing on mediumwave AM and lower world band frequencies. Limited low-frequency audio. FM prone to overloading. Frequency reads out only in 5 kHz steps in $XX.XX/XX.XX_5$ MHz format. No signal-strength indicator. Clock shows only when radio off. Travel power lock does not disable LCD illumination. No AC adaptor. Battery cover not hinged to prevent loss. Warranty honored only if radio purchased from authorized dealer, listed under each product at www.etoncorp.com.

Verdict: The G1100 has more spit and polish and better daytime frequency coverage than most cheaper alternatives. It's also backed up by a solid warranty and, in North America, a free help line.

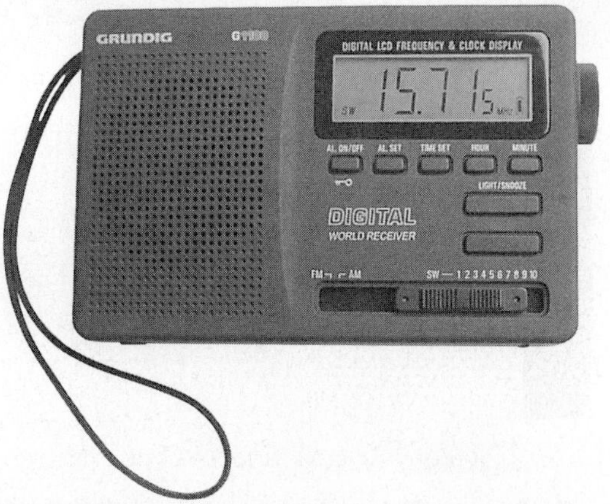

The Grundig G1100 is temptingly priced, with good sensitivity and pleasant audio. It is attractive for traveling, although tuning is strictly by knob. D. Zantow

✪¾

Tecsun DR-910

Pricing: $29.80 including air shipping from stores.ebay.com/v-com-collections in China.

Pros: Clock/timer with sleep delay (*see* Cons). Illuminated LCD has bigger digits than most models of this size. Elevation panel tilts radio to handy operating angle. FM in stereo with earbuds, included. Japanese FM. Two "AA" batteries included.

Cons: Not available outside China except via eBay with no warranty. Analog tuned with digital frequency counter, so tunable only by touchy thumbwheel. Does not tune relatively unimportant 2, 3, 4, 5, 19 and 25 MHz (120, 90, 75, 60, 15 and 11 meter) segments; misses a small amount of expanded coverage of important 41 and 31 meter segments. Single-conversion IF circuitry results in poor image rejection. Lacks low-frequency audio. Frequency drifts with changes in temperature. Clock in 12-hour format, shows only when radio off. Displays in nonstandard $XX.XX/XX.XX_5$ MHz format. Bandswitch play allows wiggling to slightly alter frequency readout. FM overloads. If finger placed over LCD display, buzzing audible on mediumwave AM and lower world band frequencies. No AC adaptor.

Verdict: More spit and polish, and better daytime frequency coverage, than truly cheaper alternatives.

The Tecsun DR-910 was once offered as the Grundig G1000A, but no more.

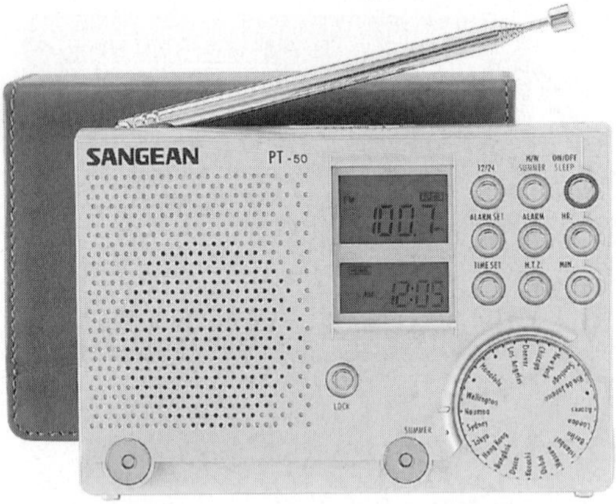

The Sangean PT-50 makes a great travel clock, but it doesn't inspire as a radio.

✪¾

Roberts 9968, Sangean PT-50

Pricing: *Sangean:* $79.95 in the United States. *Roberts:* £49.99 in the United Kingdom.

Pros: Flip-open tan leather case excellent at protecting much of cabinet (*see* Cons). Leather case affixed to receiver with snaps and magnetic catches, so nearly impossible to misplace. Two clocks, with separate display windows for home time and World Time. Changing home time to Daylight Savings (summer) Time setting does not alter World Time. Handy disc to select time in any of 24 world zones (*see* Cons). 24 or 12 hour clock format (*see* Cons). Illuminated display. Reasonably clean, pleasant speaker audio for size (*see* Cons). Travel power lock (*see* Cons). FM in stereo through earpieces (*see* Cons). Generally good mediumwave AM performance (*see* Cons). Weak-battery indicator. Stereo indicator (*see* Cons). Hinged battery cover prevents loss. Keys "clicky," with excellent feel. Alarm/clock radio with sleep delay and snooze. Rubber feet on bottom to prevent slipping.

Cons: Analog tuned with digital frequency counter, so tunable only by touchy thumbwheel. Bandswitch for changing world band segments complicates operation. World band coverage omits 5730–5795 kHz portion of 49 meters; 6890–6990 and 7535–7600 kHz portions of 41 meters; 9250–9305 kHz portion of 31 meters; and all of 120, 90, 75, 60, 15, 13 and 11 meters. Frequency display nonstandard, in Megahertz and only to nearest 10 kHz; thus, 6155 kHz shows as 6.15 and/or 6.16 MHz. Single-conversion IF circuitry results in poor image rejection. World band sensitivity and selectivity only fair. No external antenna socket. Weak low-frequency speaker audio. Audio amplifier lacks punch; stations with weak audio hard to hear or break into distortion. Frequency drift with changes in temperature. Time-format selection applies to World and home displays alike, so 24 hours can't be used for World Time and 12 hours for home. Small LCDs with thin characters. FM performance ordinaire, with mediocre capture ratio and potential overloading. FM stereo indicator worked at some test locations, but not all. Pedestrian spurious-signal rejection on mediumwave AM. No meaningful signal-strength indicator. Bandswitch designates world band segments 1–7 rather than MHz. No AC adaptor, batteries (two "AA" required) or earpieces. No audio line output for recording, home FM transmitters and outboard audio. Leather case: 1) collapses when used as elevation panel; 2) no perforations over speaker, so case has to be opened for listening; 3) does not protect receiver's sides or bottom; 4) when case closed, telescopic antenna can only be extended roughly horizontally, to the left; and 5) even when open, case blocks folded telescopic antenna and no cabinet detent for finger, so extending antenna is cumbersome. Travel power lock does not deactivate LCD illumination key. Country of origin, China, not shown on radio, manual or box.

Verdict: Great clock, so-so radio. Unusually handy as a multi-zone timepiece and a class-act eyeful. Yet, by today's yardstick its radio performance and features are inferior to various other models priced comparably or lower.

✪⅝

Anjan A-1004

Pricing: *via stores.ebay.com/v-com-collections:* $36.90 including global air shipping from China.

Pros: Appears to be solidly made; includes a beefy aluminum front panel in lieu of the customary plastic. Reasonable sensitivity for price class. LCD illumination, unusually effective (*see* Cons). Pleasant room-filling audio for size (*see* Cons). Clock/alarm function (*see* Cons). Insertable elevation tab tilts radio to handy operating angle.

Cons: Not available outside China except via eBay with no warranty. Analog tuned with digital frequency counter, so tunable only by touchy thumbwheel with backlash. Single-conversion IF circuitry results in poor image rejection. Audio lacks low-frequency audio. World band coverage omits the 2, 3, 4, 5 and 25 MHz (120, 90, 75, 60 and 11 meter) world band segments. Defaults to FM when first turned on. Frequency display in nonstandard Megahertz only to the nearest 10 kHz; thus, 6155 kHz shows as 6.15 and/or 6.16 MHz. Volume control touchy, especially on FM. Telescopic antenna doesn't rotate. Some batteries too snug. Battery cover not hinged to prevent loss. Clock only in 12-hour format. Does not 1640–1710 kHz mediumwave AM found in the Americas and other zones. Mediumwave AM sensitivity poor. FM sensitivity marginal. FM in mono only. No travel lock. Key must be kept depressed for LCD to be illuminated. Batteries (2 × "AA") and AC adaptor not included.

Verdict: Nicely assembled, but no breakthrough model. Image rejection and selectivity are lousy, there's overloading, tuning coverage isn't quite complete, frequency readout is imprecise and controls can be touchy. FM and mediumwave AM performance are both wanting, too.

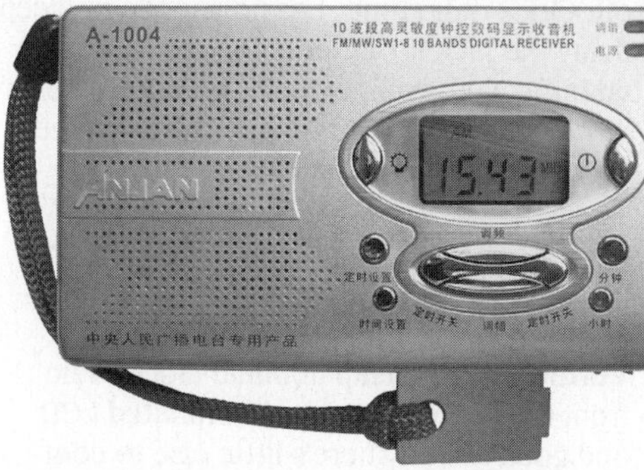

The Anjan A-1004 sounds as cheap as it costs, but it boasts retro-1950s styling. D. Zantow

✪½ ¢

Coby CX39, Roadstar TRA-2415/N, Tecsun R-333

Pricing: *Coby:* $11.99 in the United States. *Roadstar:* €28.24 in Germany.

Pros: Reasonable weak-signal sensitivity. Pleasant audio (*see* Cons). Large, easy-to-read LCD with good contrast and timed illumination. Superior carrying handle. Clock radio timer (*see* Cons). Batteries last (*see* Cons). Built-in AC power supply.

Cons: Analog tuned with digital frequency counter, so tunable only by hit-and-miss thumbwheel only partially improved by fine-tuning control; also, can require extra step of choosing shortwave "band." Does not tune 2, 3, 19, 21 and 25 MHz (120, 90, 15, 13 and 11 meter) world band segments and 1650–1705 kHz portion of mediumwave AM band in Americas and other world zones. Displays only to nearest 10 kHz and in nonstandard XX.XX MHz format. Poor selectivity. Single-conversion IF circuitry results in poor image rejection. Lacks low-frequency audio. FM mediocre and only in mono. Clock in 12-hour format, displays only when radio

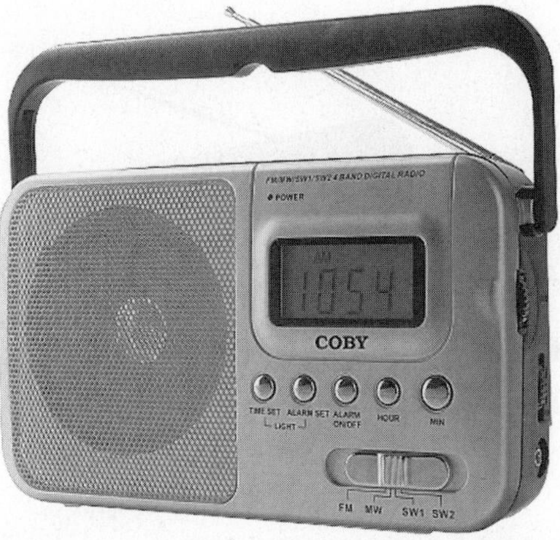

We've come across the Coby CX39 at Cave Shepherd in Barbados, so it appears to be widely sold. No wonder, at $11.99 a pop.

off. Clock radio timer has no snooze or sleep delay. No jack for AC adaptor, much less an adaptor. No travel power lock. Battery cover not hinged to prevent loss. Required three "D" batteries not included.

☞ The R-333 pushes the size envelope for a compact model—it's just over eight inches/21 cm wide.

Verdict: Ultra-cheap nominal clock radio from China with superior illuminated LCD and good audio. There's little else to commend it, not even for certain customary clock-radio functions, but at $12 Coby is hard to resist as a throwaway or youngster's gift.

✪½

SRX-50

Pricing: £24.95 in the United Kingdom.

Pros: Five world band station presets, plus ten station presets for mediumwave AM and FM. Relatively simple to operate. Illuminated display. Alarm/snooze. FM stereo via earpieces, included. World Time clock. Longwave.

Cons: Mediocre build quality. Does not tune important 5800–5895, 15505–15695, 17500–17900 and 21750–21850 kHz portions of 49, 19, 16 and 13 meters. No tuning knob; tunable only by presets and multi-speed up/down slewing/scanning in 5 kHz steps. Frequencies displayed in XX.XX/XX.XX$_5$ MHz format. Single conversion IF circuitry results in poor image rejection. Mediocre selectivity. Lacks low frequency audio. Does not receive 1605–1705 kHz portion of mediumwave AM found in Americas and some other world zones. No signal-strength indicator. No travel power lock. Clock not displayed independent of frequency. Mediumwave AM tuning step only 9 kHz, so inappropriate for Americas where 10 kHz spacing is used. Power switch shows no "off," although "auto radio" power-switch position performs comparable role.

Verdict: Although thoroughly outclassed by newer models, this "new old stock" is still sold in the U.K. by Waters & Stanton (wsplc.com) as the "SRX-50."

The Lowe SRX-50 appeared in the U.K. under several names in 1992, then vanished in 1999. It resurfaced years later simply as the SRX-50.

POCKET PORTABLES

Practical for Travel, Marginal for Home

Pocket portables weigh around half a pound/0.2 kg and are roughly the size of a cheap cellphone or slightly larger. They operate off two to four "AA" (UM-3 penlite) batteries.

They're intended for on-the-go use and are priced accordingly. If lost or stolen, no big deal, and they make great stocking stuffers for youngsters and Father's Day.

These are ideal to carry on your person, but their tiny speakers are a tough slog; to listen for long periods—especially to music—use headphones or earpieces. Alternatively, look over the smallest compact models, such as Grundig's G6, with a higher rating than any pocket radio.

New for 2009

✪✪⅞

Grundig G6 Aviator, Grundig G6 "Buzz Aldrin Edition"

Pricing: $99.95 in the United States. CAD$99.99 in Canada.

Pros: "Almost compact" that's nicely sized for travel, yet adequate for home. Handy tuning features include front-panel tuning wheel (*see* Cons), signal-seek scanning, and 700 non-volatile presets (*see* Cons) within 100 pages with four-character tags. ATS (auto tuning storage) automatically stores active FM stations into presets. Quick access to individual world band segments. Superior audio for size class; includes two-step tone control with healthy bass boost. Excellent sensitivity. Good selectivity (*see* Cons). Dual up-conversion for superior image rejection. Excellent stability and precise (20 Hz) tuning aid single sideband performance (*see* Cons). Superior AC adaptor generates no hum, buzzes or other artifacts. Built-in battery charger (*see* Cons).Three-level battery indicator. Travel power lock. Three-event 1–99 minute timers programmable by day(s) of week. Sleep timer, up to 99 minutes. Excellent LCD illumination timed with batteries, fulltime with AC adaptor. Five-bar signal-strength indicator (*see* Cons). Tuning wheel does not mute audio (*see* Cons). Overall ergonomics worthy (*see* Cons), including keys with good layout and feel (*see* Cons). World Time clock displays independent of frequency readout. External antenna jack for world band and FM (*see* Cons). Hinged battery cover. FM stereo with earbuds, included. Japanese FM. Longwave. Aero band. Travel case (*see* Cons).

Cons: Erratic tuning wheel encoder on our unit causes skipped frequencies. Lone bandwidth somewhat wide for single sideband. AGC too fast for single-sideband, so strong signals distort. Minor audio warble with single sideband. Signal-strength indicator inoperative in single-sideband mode. Presets can't store single-sideband mode. Rechargeable (2 × "AA") batteries not included. Some keys small. Icons tend to be tiny and hard to make out. Dynamic range and front-end selectivity fine with telescopic antenna, but not significant aftermarket antenna—and no attenuator. No line output for audio recording. Volume blasts at initial power-up. Only 30 seconds to change batteries before clock resets, and batteries cumbersome to remove. Travel case odoriferous until thoroughly aired out. Normal white noise between FM channels almost nonexistent with battery power, although present with AC adaptor; FM performance otherwise comparable, so more a curiosity than a drawback.

This year there's a worthwhile new pocket portable: the Grundig G6 Aviator. It pretty well hits all bases, yet is moderately priced.

Verdict: Seemingly manufactured for Grundig by Shenzhen Degen Electronics, the new G6 is unusually handy for travel, yet useful at home. It is a surprisingly pleasant set that hits nearly all bases except tuning-encoder quality and the lack of synchronous selectable sideband. Also available as the "Buzz Aldrin Edition"—identical except for cabinet marking and baseball-type collector's card.

Evaluation of New Model: Veteran world band listeners know that the same radio can't serve as both pocket portable and first-rate performer with pleasant audio. Grundig's new G6 is no exception, but it nudges the envelope at a surprisingly affordable price.

Size, Features and Ergonomics

Take size: Height and width are comparable to a 3 × 5 inch (76 × 127 mm) index card, so it's great for today's space-starved travelers. Yet, it is also nicely featured, including single sideband, longwave, Japanese FM and even the 117–136 MHz aero band. The only big batter absent from the lineup is synchronous selectable sideband.

Ergonomics are generally worthy, as well. All but three keys are nicely sized with good feel. Frequency, time and presets' page tags are easy to read, with good contrast and size, even if various icons are tiny. The LCD, nicely illuminated, includes a three-bar battery-life/charging indicator and five-bar signal-strength indicator.

There's a genuine tuning wheel that is smooth and free from play. However, after some use there was some frequency skipping: It momentarily tunes down or doesn't tune at all when being tuned up. Although we can't be entirely certain that Degen manufactures this model, we've found erratic frequency encoders in various Degen models.

Bandscanning—especially handy with the tuning wheel—is enhanced by a welcome lack of chuffing and muting. This is the way synthesized tuning should be, but often isn't.

Volume is electronically controlled, in 31 steps, by up/down slewing keys, although an ordinary knob would have been better. At initial power-up the volume defaults to earblaster level, so tweak it beforehand.

Most AC adaptors are poorly made and degrade radio performance. However, the G6's 117V AC adaptor shines, with nary a trace of hum or buzz.

Portable use calls for two "AA" batteries, and there's even an unusually flexible built-in recharger. However, no batteries are included, so figure on coughing up another six percent or so. Battery insertion is normal, but removal is hindered by a stiff spring—no big deal if you use rechargeables. The battery door is hinged to prevent loss.

There are 700 non-volatile presets, seven for each of 100 pages with alphanumeric tags. The clock, on the other hand, is volatile and takes only 30 juiceless seconds before it needs to be reset. Nevertheless, we once had to do a reset to get out of a lockup following a quick battery change.

The clock, which displays separately from frequency, shows not only World Time but also up to 24 preset time zones. The sophisticated three-event on/off "clock radio" timer allows day(s) of the week to be designated, but there's no audio line output for turnkey recording.

A tap of the AM key while in world band allows for quick access of individual world band segments. However, on our unit it had moods, occasionally allowing only three or four segments to be selected.

Tuning steps for regular world band listening are 5/1 kHz with the tuning wheel, 5 kHz with up/down slewing. For single-sideband—there's no LSB or USB, just SSB—tuning-wheel steps are 1 kHz and a surprisingly precise 20 Hz.

The signal-strength indicator—five bars, not nine as the labeling suggests—works acceptably, albeit with inflated readings. Oddly, in single-sideband mode it shows four bars no matter what.

Solid Performance

Most small radios are cursed with tinny audio, but not so the G6. It is loud and sounds pleasant, given its size, and there's no audible hiss. This is not only welcome on trips, it also helps the radio to pass muster at home.

Image rejection is excellent. Ditto sensitivity with the built-in telescopic antenna. Reception improves slightly with an outboard antenna of a few yards or meters, but any more can overwhelm circuitry.

There's only one bandwidth, well-chosen for general reception. For single-sideband, though, it's wide and there's a trace of warble, another earmark of Degen-made sets. AGC distorts with stronger signals and there's no synchronous selectable sideband.

All in all, the new G6 is a superior offering. It's sized for travel, priced to move, and is generally good enough for use in the house and garden.

✪✪⅜

CCRadio-SWP

Pricing: $49.95 including shipping in the United States. *120V AC adaptor:* $10.95 in the United States.

Pros: "Almost compact" that's nicely sized for travel, yet adequate for home. Good sensitivity on all bands, with no digital hash. Selectivity adequate. Handy tuning features include knob with mechanical encoder (*see*

Cons), keypad, up/down slewing, signal-seek scanning and presets scanning (*see* Cons). 200 non-volatile presets. Easy-to-read LCD with good contrast, proper (kHz) frequency format and ten-second illumination (*see* Cons). Single-step attenuator for shortwave and FM. Clock in either 12- or 24-hour format. Up to 90-minute sleep delay. Tone switch helps ameliorate any shrillness. Beep alarm or single-event radio timer. Travel power lock. Punchy audio (*see* Cons). Mediumwave AM performs nicely and tunes in 9 kHz or 10 kHz steps. FM stereo through earbuds, supplied. Japanese FM. Elevation panel. Battery indicator. Superior softside carrying case. *Purchased via C. Crane:* 30-day money-back guarantee.

Cons: Single conversion, so suboptimal image rejection. Keys, with only fair feel, sometimes sluggish to respond. Tuning knob's lone step, 1 kHz, sometimes ideal but can be annoyingly slow. Shortwave in two "bands," complicating tuning. Lacks low-frequency audio. Misses 7500–9200 kHz. Displays either frequency or time, but not both simultaneously. Tuning knob lacks feel and rubs on case. On one sample, when turned fast the mechanical tuning encoder skips over frequencies; problem hasn't improved with use. No meaningful signal-strength indicator. Volume controlled only by up/down keys, with earpiece volume being excessive; speaker volume too loud at low settings. Marginal LCD illumination from only one side. FM fine for nearby reception, but not long distance. Battery cover not hinged to prevent loss. No antenna jack. No audio line output. AC adaptor and two "AA" batteries not included. Some shortwave hum with optional AC adaptor.

Verdict: The diminutive CCRadio-SWP is exceptionally appropriate and attractively priced for travel. Manufactured for C. Crane by Redsun Electronics of China.

Grundig G6 exceeds your travel budget? The CCRadio-SWP costs half as much, partly because of lesser image rejection.

✪✪

Degen DE11, Kaito KA11

Pricing: *Kaito:* $49.95 in the United States.

Pros: Satisfactory world band sensitivity. Several handy tuning features, including 1,000 non-volatile station presets within ten pages of 100 presets each; keypad (1 kHz steps for world band and mediumwave AM); up/down slewing (5 kHz steps for world band, 9/10 kHz for mediumwave AM); scanning by-frequency and by-preset; quick access to world band segments; and ATS (*see* glossary). Keypad in standard telephone format. No muting or chuffing on world band and FM (*see* Cons). Above-average speaker audio and power for tiny radio. Keys have good feel. LCD has good contrast and excellent timed illumination. Clock displays independent of frequency. Excellent ten-bar signal-strength indicator. Four-bar battery indicator. Displays room temperature (*see* Cons). Three on/off clock radio events; also, single-on alarm. Sleep timer, up to 99

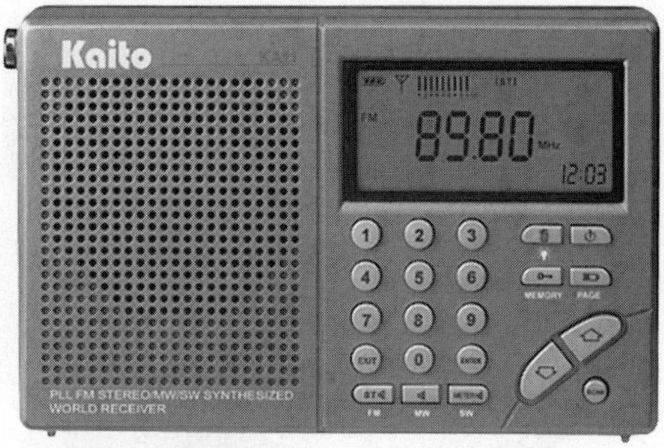

The Kaito KA11/Degen DE11 offers reasonable performance, user-friendly tuning and a clock that always shows—all at a travel-friendly price.

minutes (*see* Cons).Travel power lock also disables illumination. External antenna jack. Attenuator for world band and FM (*see* Cons). FM in stereo with included earpieces that offer worthy audio. Japanese FM. Elevation tab. Accessory wire antenna. Built-in recharging for two "AA" NiMH cells (*see* Cons). *Degen:* 220/230V AC adaptor (110V adaptor optional at some Chinese dealers). *Kaito*: 117V AC adaptor. Mediumwave AM coverage to 1710 kHz.

Cons: No world band coverage below 5800 kHz or above 18100 kHz, so misses 2, 3, 4, 5, 19, 21 and 25 MHz (120, 90, 75, 60, 15, 13 and 11 meter) world band segments and 5730–5795 kHz portion of 6 MHz (41 meter) segment. Power key activates 99-minute sleep delay; to turn radio on fulltime, a second ("exit") key must be pressed within two seconds. Single conversion, so poor image rejection. Poor selectivity from lone bandwidth. Microphonic or similar ringing with powerful world band signals. Modest dynamic range; attenuator little help. Volume control requires much rotation before any sound, then becomes unusually touchy. No tuning knob. No single sideband. LCD characters, other than for frequency, extremely small. Most keys undersized. Fair-to-poor overall FM performance. Telescopic antenna exits from side, limiting tilt angle for optimum FM reception. Frequency readout not always spot-on. Digital buzz makes mediumwave AM DX all but impossible. Half-second muting pauses when bandscanning mediumwave AM. No audio line output for recording. If AC adaptor unplugged then reinserted while radio on, microprocessor locks up; no reset control, but remediable by removing batteries for a minute or so. Required two "AA" batteries not included. No carrying case. Ambient temperature shown in Fahrenheit if clock in 12-hour format, but in Celsius if 24-hour (World Time) format. *Degen:* Mediumwave AM coverage to only 1620 kHz. *Kaito*: AC adaptor creates slight hum.

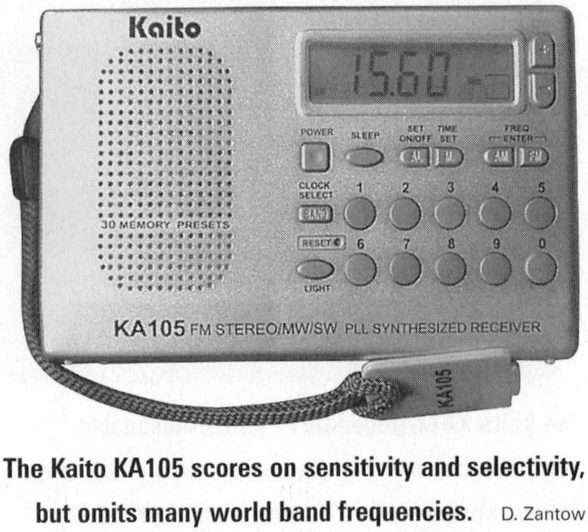

The Kaito KA105 scores on sensitivity and selectivity, but omits many world band frequencies. D. Zantow

☞ Don't confuse with very different Kaito KA011 emergency radio (*see* "Radios for Emergencies").

Verdict: The Degen DE11/Kaito KA11's world band coverage is limited, image rejection and selectivity are poor, and there are unwelcome buzzing and ringing sounds. Even turning on the radio is a clunky procedure.

The kindred but slightly larger Degen DE1101/Kaito KA1101 covers all world band frequencies. It is a vastly superior performer for not much more money.

✪✪ ✆

Kaito KA105

Pricing: $49.95 in the United States. CAD$49.00 in Canada.

Pros: Reasonably good selectivity from lone bandwidth. Good voice reproduction, with ample volume, for small speaker (*see* Cons). A number of helpful tuning features, including keypad (*see* Cons), up/down slewing (*see* Cons) and signal-seek frequency scanning; also, 30 station presets, of which ten are for world band with others divided between FM and mediumwave AM. Above-average weak-signal sensitivity. Dual-zone 24-hour clock (*see* Cons) with clock radio/alarm and sleep delay. Illuminated display via non-timed key. Clicky keys have superior feel. LCD has excellent contrast. Low battery consumption. Weak-battery indicator. Hinged battery cover prevents loss. Travel power lock (*see* Cons). FM in stereo through earbuds, included (*see* Cons). Insertable elevation tab tilts radio to handy operating angle. Includes short external wire antenna accessory. Tough, attractive matte aluminum alloy face plate. 120V AC adaptor (*see* Cons).

Cons: World band coverage of 5950–15600 kHz misses important 17 and 21 MHz (16 and 13 meter) segments, skips chunks of 6 and 15 MHz (49 and 19 meters), and omits lesser 2, 3, 4, 5, 19 and 25 MHz (120, 90, 75, 60, 15 and 11 meter) segments. Single-conversion IF circuitry results in poor image rejection. Speaker audio bereft of low-frequency response. No tuning knob. Keypad not in standard telephone format. Tunes world band only in 5 kHz steps and displays in nonstandard $XX.XX/XX.XX_5$ MHz format. Slow microprocessor lock time degrades bandscanning. No signal-strength indicator. Clock doesn't display when frequency shown. Mediumwave AM coverage omits 1625–1705 kHz used in Americas and some other world zones. Slight digital hash on mediumwave AM. FM has so-so sensitivity, mediocre capture ratio and some tendency to overload. FM audio distorted through earbuds. Audio through earbuds may be stronger in one channel at lower volume, whether in mono or stereo. Because telescopic antenna exits from side, it can't tilt to the right for optimum FM reception. Travel power lock does not disable LCD illumination. Two "AA" batteries not included. Minor hum with AC adaptor.

Verdict: Except for the lack of single-sideband, this Chinese travel portable is a thrifty choice. Still, the larger Degen/Kaito siblings DE1101/KA1101 and DE1102/KA1102 cover more frequencies, perform significantly better and cost little more.

✪5/8 ✆

Etón Mini 300PE, Grundig Mini 300PE, Mini 300 "Lextronix," Tecsun R-919

Pricing: *Etón:* £24.95 in the United Kingdom. *Grundig:* $29.95 in the United States. CAD$29.95 in Canada. *"Lextronix":* €29.00 in Germany.

Pros: Unusually small except for protruding antenna. Reasonable weak-signal sensitivity. Pleasant room-filling audio for size (*see* Cons). Clock/alarm-timer with sleep delay (*see* Cons). FM in stereo with earbuds, included. Low battery consumption. Available in up to seven colors. Soft carrying case affixes to belt or purse strap. Two "AA" batteries included. *North America:* Excellent toll-free tech support.

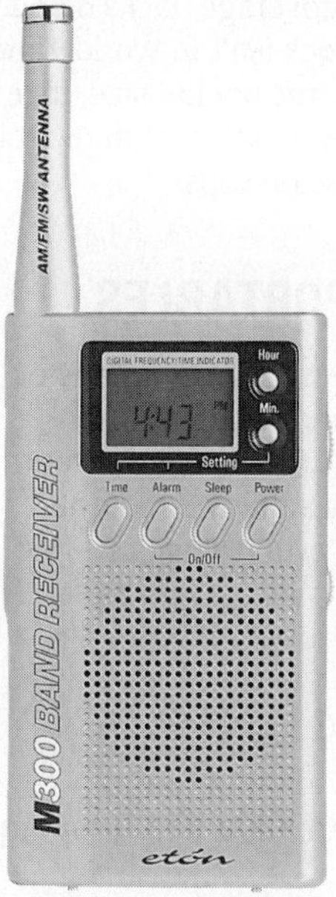

Etón's Mini 300PE is no radio Maserati, but it is tiny, sensitive and truly cheap.

Cons: Analog tuned with digital frequency counter, so tunable only by touchy thumbwheel. Does not tune 2, 3, 4, 5, 19, 21 and 25 MHz (120, 90, 75, 60, 15, 13 and 11 meter) segments; misses small bits of other world band segments. Single-conversion IF circuitry results in poor image rejection. Lacks low-frequency audio. Frequency drift with temperature changes. Telescopic antenna does not rotate or swivel. Antenna's plastic base protrudes even when antenna collapsed. Displays in nonstandard $XX.XX/XX.XX_5$ MHz format. Display not illuminated. Minor drift when hand grasps back of cabinet. Slight digital hash when finger placed over LCD during mediumwave AM reception. Some FM overloading. Clock in 12-hour format, displays only when radio off. No jack for AC adaptor, much less an adaptor. *Grundig:* Warranty honored only if radio purchased from authorized dealer, listed under each product at www.etoncorp.com.

Verdict: One of the smaller and better cheap portables for travel, even though it is lacking in daytime frequency coverage, lacks display illumination and its clock isn't in World Time format. But thanks to true pocket size, nice weak-signal sensitivity and decent audio it is tempting for casual use on trips.

RECORDABLE PORTABLES

What happens if a favorite show comes on when you're not around to listen, or are simply too busy? Why, record it, of course. You can do this with a separate recorder, but it's handier when everything is stuffed into one box.

Updated for 2009

✪✪⅞

Degen DE1121, Kaito KA1121, Thieking und Koch DE1121

Price: *Kaito:* $159.95 in the United States. CAD$139.95 in Canada. *Thieking und Koch:* €198.00 in Germany.

Pros: Docked MP3 recorder-player with large LCD that's "information central" for recorder and radio. Records direct from radio or detaches for standalone use, whereupon separated radio makes do with small secondary LCD (*see* Cons). Records MP3 in commendable fidelity (selectable settings of 128, 80 and 32 kbps), as well as WAV in low fidelity (32 kbps, 4 bit, 8 kHz IMA ADPCM format). Very good sensitivity. Dual conversion provides superior image rejection. Handy tuning methods include knob (*see* Cons) with 1/5 kHz world band steps—9/10 kHz for mediumwave AM, 50/100 kHz for FM, 1 kHz for longwave—with soft detent for each step; up/down slewing for world band in 5 kHz steps (9/10 kHz for mediumwave AM, 50 kHz for FM, 1 kHz for longwave); effective signal-seek scanning; keypad in customary telephone format; quick access to world band segments; 100 pages with up to four presets each for a total of 400 non-volatile presets, and each page can display an eight-character alphanumeric tag (*see* Cons). Little chuffing during bandscanning, and muting rarely intrudes (*see* Cons). Two well-chosen bandwidths (*see* Cons). Generally pleasant 27-step audio (*see* Cons) with punch, superior bass and no hiss. Decent single-sideband performance (*see* Cons) aided by good stability. Sleep timer, up to 60 minutes (*see* Cons). Automatic powering off after up to 120 minutes. Three-event on/off timer can also be used for unattended MP3 recordings (*see* Cons). Main LCD's (*see* Cons) worthy illumination can be timed or left on (*see* Cons). External antenna jack for world band and FM (*see* Cons). Mute key. Keys have good feel. Internal battery recharging with automatic shutoff for both radio and MP3 module, which charge separately. Clock, in 12- or 24-hour/World Time format (*see* Cons), displays separately from frequency. Non-presets data retained for one minute after batteries removed. MP3 playback has fast forward/reverse, repeat, shuffle, pause (*see* Cons) and six equalization (EQ) settings. Easy to program with computer, using standard text files; transferring MP3 or "memory" text files to and from computer via USB 2.0 also straightforward. Firmware can be updated. MP3 recorder's audio line input suitable for making MP3 recordings from other devices. Travel power lock and separate tuning-knob lock. Hinged battery cover (*see* Cons). Two-level attenuator. Good FM sensitivity and selectivity. Japanese FM. Longwave. No driver needed for XP and, apparently, Vista; Windows 98SE driver included on CD. Includes all needed NiMH rechargeable batteries: 3 × "AA" for receiver, DF-6 NiMH (*see* Cons) for MP3 module; also,

The Kaito KA1121 uses docking to create a new concept in recordable radios. Fairly priced for all it does.

thin cloth carrying bag, USB cable, line-input audio cable, indoor shortwave wire antenna, earbuds and AC adaptor. Robust elevation panel. *Degen and Kaito:* Timer recording, fixed at low (32 kbps) bitrate, stores around 17 hours. *Kaito:* Firmware backup. *Thieking und Koch:* Timer recording fixed at quality-fidelity 128 kbps (*see* Cons). Continuously tunes 50 kHz–29.999 MHz. Firmware can be updated, as available, by downloading. RoHS compliance signifies minimal use of undesirable substances during manufacture.

Cons: Hostile ergonomics, with menus and sub-menus poorly labeled and/or illogical; owner's manual offers little assistance. Nigh-useless pseudo-analog "dial" on dot-matrix LCD hogs panel space, forcing miniaturization and disallowing useful controls and displays; as a result, icons, some keys and sub-LCD are undersized—also, no signal-strength indicator. Mediocre dynamic range limits use of accessory antennas. Substandard front-end selectivity, so strong local mediumwave and FM stations can bleed into shortwave spectrum. No audio line output. No tone control for mediumwave AM and world band. AGC decay too fast for single sideband, with clipping and distortion especially on stronger signals. AC adaptor causes minor hum with indoor antenna. Audible buzz sometimes audible over headphones, whether radio powered by batteries or AC adaptor. No separate LSB/USB switching; instead, fine-tuning control with no center detent. Minor muting during mediumwave AM bandscanning with tuning knob and slewing. Limited skirt selectivity allows powerful world band signals to splatter widely. Mediumwave AM 9/10 kHz spacing, 12/24 hour clock format choices and page tagging doable only via computer. Tuning knob's digital encoder skips frequencies on some samples, not an uncommon issue with Degen portables. AC adaptor/DC input jack requires nonstandard negative tip. Sub-LCD's frequency readout uses nonstandard XX.XXx MHz layout, while main LCD displays in XX.XXX MHz format. Sub-LCD not illuminated. Illumination toggle for main LCD squirreled within menu tree. Memory (256 MB) in MP3 player not ungradable to 512 MB. No pause control during recording, just playback. When radio section turned on, volume sometimes blasts briefly until preset volume level recognized. Three-event timer only daily; can't choose given day(s) of week. Power key activates 60-minute sleep delay; stays on fulltime only after left-arrow key pressed (does not have to be repeated unless batteries removed). Hinged battery cover's foam can impede battery insertion/removal. MP3 module uses nonstandard DF-6 NiMH rechargeable battery. *Degen and Kaito:* Omits little-used 2 MHz (120 meter) world band segment. Longwave, unlike on Thieking und Koch version, starts at 140 kHz (Kaito)/150 kHz (Degen). *Thieking und Koch:* High bitrate limits recording time to around 4:20.

Verdict: The most exciting part of this receiver is its detachable MP3 recorder, which provides up to 17 hours of quality off-air recording. Although the '1121 suffers from hostile ergonomics and so-so receiver performance, for many the recorder is enough to seal the deal.

Update to Degen DE-1121: When the Degen DE1121's MP3 module is docked with the radio while its included 120V AC adaptor is connected, uploaded files may become corrupted and not playback correctly. This can result in a displayed HEAD ERROR message, with either no playback or playback that stops prematurely. Other earmarks of corruption are power resets, popping/buzzing or "raspberry" sounds accompanied by total lockup, and/or scrambled display. These symptoms may appear right away or during playback.

The culprit is the electrically noisy AC adaptor. To resolve this, with the internal battery charged, either remove the adaptor plug from the radio or undock the record module before starting an upload.

Better yet, substitute a quiet AC adaptor or outboard power supply. We could locate no ready replacement, but you can get a $6.95 Jameco #283573 AC adaptor, then snip off its connector and replace it with a size H power plug: 99-cent Universal Radio #0910, 95-cent Jameco #71192 or $2.99 Radio Shack #274-1532. Be sure to maintain correct polarity.

The Grundig G4, based on the Degen DE1121, was introduced and withdrawn in record time. No wonder, as it cost more but did less.

New, but Being Discontinued

✪✪⅝

Grundig G4 World Recorder

Pricing: $199.95 in the United States. CAD$199.95 in Canada.

☞ The G4 was introduced early in the summer of 2008. Although priced higher than the Degen DE1121 upon which it was based, its overall performance was inferior. Accordingly, in July 2008 the manufacturer notified us that the G4 was to be discontinued.

For those who may still be interested, our summer 2008 review of the G4 remains posted at www.passband.com.

The Sangean ATS-818ACS is a warhorse among recordable portables. It even uses audio cassettes.

✪✪½

Sangean ATS-818ACS, Sangean ATS-818ACS "Deluxe"

Pricing: *ATS-818:* $219.95 in the United States. €165.00 in Germany. *ATS-818 "Deluxe":* $249.95 in the United States.

Pros: Built-in cassette recorder. Superior overall world band performance. Numerous tuning features, including 18 world band station presets. Two bandwidths offer good fidelity/interference tradeoff. Analog clarifier with center detent and stable circuitry allows single-sideband signals to be tuned with uncommon precision, which results in superior audio phasing for a portable (*see* Cons). Illuminated display. Signal-strength indicator. Dual-zone 24-hour clock, with one zone displayed separately from frequency. Alarm/timer with sleep delay. Travel power lock. Stereo through earpieces. Longwave. Built-in condenser mic. AC adaptor. *ATS818ACS "Deluxe" from C. Crane:* Eliminates muting between stations when bandscanning; also, RCA instead of mini jack for external antenna.

Cons: No multiple recording events, just one "on" time (quits when tape runs out). Tends to mute when tuning knob turned quickly, making bandscanning difficult; remedied in "Deluxe" version. Wide bandwidth a bit broad for world band. Keypad not in telephone format. Touchy single-sideband clarifier. Recorder has no level indicator and no counter. Fast-forward and rewind controls installed facing backwards. No batteries, four "D" and three "AA" needed. Country of manufacture, China, not specified on radio or box.

Verdict: A warhorse that eschews complicated operation, but at a price: Recording is by ye olde cassette tape, is only single-event, and there's no timed "off."

The Passport *portable-radio review team: David Zantow and Lawrence Magne; also, Tony Jones, with laboratory measurements performed independently by J. Robert Sherwood. Additional feedback from David Crystal and David Walcutt, with a tip of the hat to Lawrence Bulk, Fotios Padazopulos and Ray Lalleu.*

WORLD BAND ON THE ROAD

World band is car stereo's redheaded stepchild. Years back, Philips thought otherwise and spent big for publicity from *Playboy* and others. The outcome was a flop, and others have fared little better.

Tough Challenges

It's no wonder, as in addition to public disinterest these radios have had a tough row to hoe. World-weary signals struggle against electrical noise from engine microprocessors, wiper motors and onboard digital gizmos—ignition pulses, too, except with diesels and electrics. Taken together, this produces more on-air snap, crackle and pop than a bowl of Rice Krispies.

Over the years we've found that all car radios with significant world band coverage otherwise perform decently. Outboard shortwave car tuners that work through a car's FM are another matter: consistently awful. A portable on your console or seat won't do, either—there's rarely enough volume, and a car's metal body keeps out signals.

Sony Shortwave

Sony's world band car stereos have comparable world band circuitry which covers 2940–7735 and 9500–18135 kHz—only daytime 13 and 15 meter segments and the important 9250–9495 kHz range are omitted. They offer worthy audio and perform well enough to snare major stations during prime time—just how well depends partly on vehicular electrical noise.

Professional installation is virtually a must, but don't use the window antenna. Instead, have them install a long telescopic antenna on a quarter panel or near the roof's aft.

These radios are harder to find than delicious coffee at Starbucks. However, there is one established dealer for the United States and Canada—Durham Radio (durhamradio.com), which offers two models:

- Sony CDX-GT370, 54 watts with CD and three audio codecs (CAD$269.95/US$259.00); and
- Sony CDX-GT470U, 54 watts, iPod ready with CD and several audio codecs (CAD$299.95/US$289.00).

There is also the Sony CDX-GT160S, 45 watts with CD, from thepowerhour.com ($249.00).

Elsewhere, forget it. They're scarcer than rabbis in Riyadh.

Sony's high-end world band car stereo is the CDX-GT470U. It's also iPod ready.

PASSPORT to Preparedness®

Stay Informed When Things Go Wrong

World band offers trusted information no matter what.

During crises, Internet sites become overloaded when they are most needed. Not so world band broadcasts, which perform equally well whether there are two hundred listeners or two million. World band is infinitely scalable, so it's always there when you need it.

Last Man Standing

World band radio is renowned as the last man standing for information. That's because it is nature's radio, soaring from faraway without cables, satellites or transmission towers that can go off or be manipulated. World band even resists deliberate jamming.

Act in Advance

If you don't already have a world band portable, consider getting one now—not after a crisis when dealers are sold out. Self-powered portables have obvious advantages, although they perform crudely as radios and aren't known for long-term reliability. Those that include shortwave coverage typically go for $35 to $80.

Only the Etón/ARC FR500, Etón FR550, Freeplay Summit, Kaito KA008 and KA011 meet PASSPORT's minimum requirements. However, we've bent the rules to include one analog-tuned series, as it has outsold all others combined and has significant emergency features.

World band is nature's radio, bobbing off oceans and sky.

A conventional world band portable (*see* Portables for 2009) usually outperforms a self-powered radio. Spare batteries are cheap, last for years and let any world band portable—even Palstar's R30A tabletop—serve in a crisis. Not enough? Then consider something like a Sun Star solar battery charger from C. Crane, Universal Radio and others.

Favor models that handle single-sideband signals, explained in "Worldly Words." These can eavesdrop on ham radio—invaluable during a crisis—and various aeronautical and other utility communications; under the right conditions, even the low-powered American Forces Radio and Television Service. Also, look for effectively illuminated LCDs, *de rigeur* for tuning in the dark—illuminated keypads help, too.

What to avoid? Battery hogs and, if possible, old-tech offerings lacking digital frequency readout.

Does It Work?

Your radio has to be ready the moment there's a crisis, so check it out now. Go outdoors and tune to foreign stations that are weak but intelligible, then head to your safe room. Compare how these same frequencies come in, and if reception is similar then you're ready.

Sun Star and others manufacture solar battery chargers. These allow conventional world band portables and Palstar's R30A tabletop to operate indefinitely without line power.

If not, you need to steer those signals into your safe room. Erect a simple outdoor inverted-L wire antenna—basically just a few yards or meters of insulated wire run well above the ground to something like a tree. Place the near end into your safe room without nicking the insulation, then snip off any excess and clip the wire to your radio's antenna. If yard availability is an issue, consider a compact antenna (*see* Compact Antennas for 2009); one model doesn't even require electricity.

Either way, keep a copy of PASSPORT nearby so you'll know what's on, when.

SELF-POWERED DIGITAL PORTABLES

New for 2009

✪3/8

American Red Cross ARC FR-500 Solarlink, Etón FR-500 Solarlink, Etón FR-550 Solarlink

Pricing: *Etón FR-500/ARC FR-500:* $79.95 in the United States. *Etón FR-500:* CAD$79.95 in Canada. *Etón FR-550 (not tested):* £59.95 in the United Kingdom.

The FR-500 is the latest in a series of emergency portables from Etón and Grundig. D. Zantow

Pros: Powered four ways—direct and by charging the internal rechargeable 600 mAh battery: 1) hand-cranked dynamo, 2) built-in solar panel (*see* Cons), 3) AC adaptor (*see* Cons), and 4) computer USB port (cable not included). Alternatively, powered by three standard "AA" cells (*see* Cons) that bypass the rechargeable battery. Crank and solar also lightly charge most cellphone batteries; cable included, and variety of phone plugs available free. Good world band sensitivity even though telescopic antenna unusually short. Digital frequency readout to nearest 5 kHz (*see* Cons). Large, easy-to-read LCD with high contrast. Visually superior three-second LCD illumination. Loud, punchy audio (*see* Cons). Clock (*see* Cons) with single-event clock radio. Five-minute snooze and 10/30/60/90-minute sleep timers. Useful four-LED flashlight. Flashing red "SOS" LED (*see* Cons). Emergency siren loud enough to attract rescuers. Three-color battery indicator. Audio input jack for MP3 devices and the like, requires connecting cable (*see* Cons). Build quality appears to be above average for a self-powered model. Superior product support. *FR-500:* All seven 162 MHz NOAA (U.S. only) weather channels with good sensitivity. Weather alert (*see* Cons). *FR-550:* Nominally covers world band from roughly 5.8 to 18.1 MHz in two tuning ranges; longwave, too.

Cons: Wide bandwidth, so poor selectivity. Poor image rejection. Significant knob play makes tuning touchy. Frequency display slightly inaccurate on our sample. World band reads out in nonstandard XX.XXx MHz. Clock in 12-hour format, no World Time (24-hour). Battery cover not hinged to prevent loss. Telescopic antenna does not rotate or swivel. FM mono-only through earpieces. "SOS" LED too weak to be meaningful. USB and audio connecting cables not included. AC adaptor not included; requires unusual 5V DC, positive tip. Three standard "AA" batteries not included. *FR-500:* Nominal weather "alert" not really an alert such as exists on conventional weather alert radios from RadioShack, Midland and so on. When weather "alert" activated, performance on regular bands (mediumwave AM, FM, world band) drops substantially. Weather band reception infeasible during direct solar-power operation. Available volume drops in all other bands during direct solar-power operation. *FR-500:* Limited world band coverage, all crammed into a single tuning range from roughly 5.7 to 12.4 MHz.

Verdict: Slightly better than other emergency offerings.

For Americans the FR-500 includes excellent NOAA VHF weather band reception in lieu of daytime world band reception. However, its related weather-alert feature disappoints. The FR-550, sold in Europe, logically omits NOAA coverage. Instead, it provides a welcome expansion of world band coverage, plus longwave.

Evaluation of New Model: The Etón FR-500/FR-550 emergency portable is powered by a built-in battery charged by crank-operated inboard dynamo, built-in solar panels, outboard AC adaptor, and the USB port of a laptop or other PC. A helpful indicator shows when batteries need charging, but no USB cable or AC adaptor is included. The radio also works off a trio of everyday alkaline or comparable batteries.

Wristathon

A hand-cranked dynamo is the radio's main selling point, but it calls for effort and patience: Cranking 120 times for one minute allows the radio to play for only around four minutes at low volume. Using the weather band or boosting volume reduces playtime.

Fully charging the internal battery nominally requires 120 turns per minute for fully three hours. That's 21,600 fast turns of the crank, a wristathon worthy of Popeye at his spinached best. We'll take their word for it.

The solar charger gives life to the batteries in about 12 to 15 hours of strong, direct sunlight—no clouds or haze, please. Big Orb's rays also power the radio directly, but this reduces volume and nixes weather-channel reception. Nonetheless, the '500/'550's solar charger is the one-eyed man in the land of the blind.

In a pinch the radio can also provide a mild charge to most cellphones—ten minutes or so of cranking gives enough juice for one or two brief calls, which could be a lifesaver. Direct solar does the trick, as well. A short connecting cable is included, along with a postcard for a free cellphone plug.

Two World Band Versions

The '500 tunes mediumwave AM, FM, world band from roughly 5.7 to 12.4 MHz and all seven NOAA (U.S.) weather frequencies. This is fine for local listening anytime and long-distance reception evenings, but forget hearing daytime world band segments between 13570–26100 kHz. These are MIA, which is unfortunate—emergencies take place around midday, too.

In Europe there are no NOAA weather channels, so the FR-550, which we didn't test, tunes world band from around 5.8–18.1 MHz—much better, indeed. Too, these frequencies are spread out within two tuning ranges, which in principle should make tuning less touchy. The '550 receives longwave broadcasts, too. However, neither handles single-sideband ham, utility or American Forces Radio signals.

Tuning is ye olde analog, so there aren't any of the handy station-finding features found on synthesized receivers: keypad, station presets, frequency slewing and so on. Significantly for an analog-tuned emergency radio, the '500/'550 incorporates digital frequency readout (XX.XXx MHz) borrowed from the digital clock's circuitry; however, our sample tends to read a channel or so high.

This analog underpinning limits tuning to a single-speed knob, which has excessive play that results in hit-or-miss tuning. Shoehorning the entire shortwave tuning range into one "band" doesn't help, either.

Sensitivity is good in all tuning ranges—pleasantly surprising, given that the telescopic antenna is short—it's even better if you add a couple of yards or meters of wire. However, selectivity and image rejection are mediocre; powerful mediumwave AM stations especially tend to bleed over onto nearby channels.

Audio is pleasant and robust except during direct solar operation. It's hardly Mark Levinson surround sound, but for a mono portable it is pretty decent.

An inboard siren shrieks loudly enough to attract rescuers if you're trapped during an emergency. The four-LED flashlight can also be a godsend, although the single flashing red LED is dim and useless. While non-emergency features are limited, there is an audio input jack to play an iPod or MP3 player through the radio's speaker—even if no connecting cable is included.

Build quality for self-powered portables tends to be pedestrian. However, the '500/'550's construction appears to be comparatively solid.

Weather "Alert": Heap Big Wind

The '500 performs well at receiving all seven official NOAA weather-prediction frequencies aired within the United States between 162.400 and 162.550 MHz. The radio nominally also includes a weather alert.

NOAA weather alert radios have been around for decades, so most folks are familiar with the concept: Most commonly, the radio remains silent while in standby mode. It then springs to life with a howling alarm when NOAA warns of an impending regional weather event by broadcasting a fuzzy alert tone that triggers the radio's alarm. Most models follow up this howling alarm with a NOAA voice announcement detailing the emergency, then the radio reverts to standby. It's neat, effective, notifies even when you're asleep, and is a proven lifesaver.

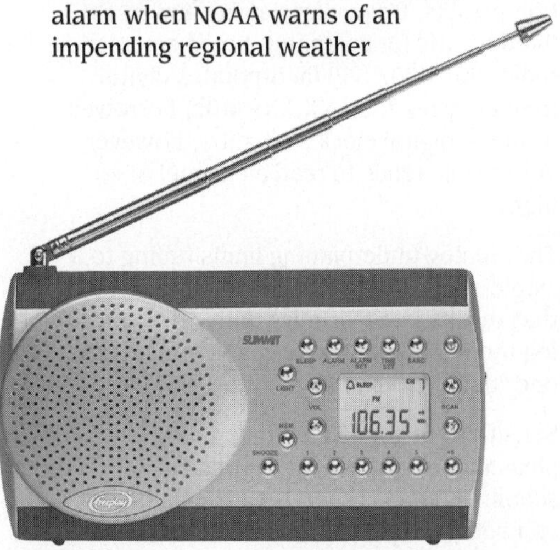

The Freeplay Summit offers something rare among emergency portables: presets to access favorite stations.

There's more. Better weather alert radios—available from Radio Shack, Midland and others—use programmable SAME technology to respond to local, rather than regional, warnings. This eliminates alerts for neighboring locales that don't relate to where you live. These radios are widely offered for $30 and up.

Yet, none of these established functions apply to this $80 portable's so-called weather "alert." For starters, there's no howling alarm—or any other alarm. Instead, the regular NOAA voice with predictions and such mixes in with the AM/FM/world band station you're trying to hear. If amidst this co-channel jumble you manage to hear the fuzzy tone NOAA emits to trigger alarms on genuine weather alert radios, you can manually tune to your local weather channel to hear the warning.

Additionally, when the "alert" mode is active, local and world band broadcasts come in at reduced level and with added distortion.

Etón has clearly overreached with its weather alert claim. Nevertheless, the FR-500 and FR-550 are welcome additions to the roster of available emergency radios. They are widely distributed, easily affordable and properly manufactured. Overall, they are as the best among today's emergency radios.

✪¼

Freeplay Summit

Pricing: $79.00 in the United States. CAD$99.95 in Canada. £49.99 in the United Kingdom. €99.95 in Germany.

Pros: Only emergency model with synthesized tuning. Five presets for world band, 25 more for other bands. Powered by rechargeable battery pack (*see* Cons) which, in turn, is juiced three ways: foolproof cranked alternator, solar energy and AC adaptor. NiMH battery pack replaceable, although radio nominally runs even if pack no longer takes charge. Reasonable audio. Timed LCD illumination (*see* Cons). Low-battery and crank-charge indicators. World Time or 12-hour clock with alarm and sleep functions. Accessory reel antenna and AC adaptor. Travel power lock. Mediumwave AM tunes in 9/10 kHz steps. FM includes NTSC (North American) channel 6 television audio (*see* Cons). Longwave. *Outside North America:* AC adaptor adjusts to line voltage (110–240V AC) anywhere in the world (*see* Cons). Three types of power plugs for different countries; also, carrying pouch. *North America:* 120V AC adaptor works well.

Cons: Full battery recharge requires 24 hours with AC adaptor, 40 hours using sunlight, or 40 full minutes of cranking. Poor sensitivity on world band using built-in undersized telescopic antenna; reel-in accessory antenna helps slightly. Lacks non-radio emergency features found on some other windup radios. Poor selectivity. Poor image rejection. Shortwave coverage of 5.95–15.6 MHz omits 2, 3, 4, 5, 17, 19, 21 and 25 MHz (120, 90, 75, 60, 16, 15, 13 and 11 meter) world band segments, along with lower end of 6 MHz (49 meters) and upper end of 15 MHz (19 meters). Inconvenient to tune, with no keypad, no tuning knob and "signal-seek" scanning that stops only at very powerful stations; this essentially leaves only single-speed (slow) up/down slewing and five world band presets to navigate the airwaves. No volume knob or slider; level adjustable only by up/down slew controls. Significant muting compromises bandscanning. No continuous frequency display—reverts to clock after ten seconds. Tunes world band only in 5 kHz steps and displays in nonstandard XX.XX MHz/XX.XX5 MHz. LCD hard to read in low light without illumination, which fades after only four seconds. FM overloads. Channel 6 NTSC audio disappears February 2009. One of the two units we purchased new was defective. No handle or carrying strap. *Outside North America:* Multivoltage AC adaptor disturbs reception with vigorous noise and hum.

Verdict: Yes, its world band performance is mediocre. And, yes, it is bereft of most tuning aids and non-radio emergency features. Still, the Chinese-made Freeplay Summit is one of the most acceptable emergency radio we have come across. It performs reasonably on FM and mediumwave AM, too.

✪⅛

Kaito KA008

Pricing: $34.95 in the United States. CAD$39.95 in Canada.

Pros: Three ways to power the radio directly, as well as indirectly by charging a battery pack: 1) hand crank, 2) solar cells and 3) AC adaptor. Can also conventionally be powered by three ordinary "AA" batteries (*see* Cons). Good world band sensitivity. Digital frequency readout (*see* Cons). Wide coverage of shortwave spectrum for self-powered model (*see* Cons). Clock (*see* Cons) with one-event alarm. Built in LED flashlight. LCD illuminated by LED (*see* Cons). Loud, punchy audio (*see* Cons). Telescopic antenna swivels and rotates. Unique LED battery status indicator. Includes 120V AC adaptor/charger, rechargeable battery pack, earbuds, short outboard wire antenna (*see* Cons) and waterproof carrying bag.

Cons: Extremely sloppy tuning. Poor image and ultimate rejection. Poor FM

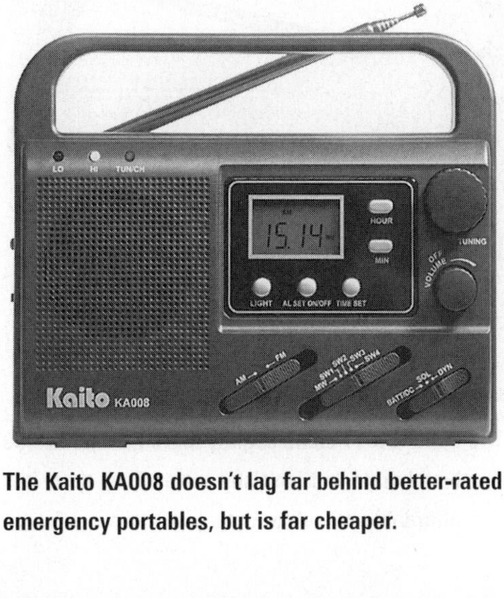

The Kaito KA008 doesn't lag far behind better-rated emergency portables, but is far cheaper.

performance. Frequency display/clock illumination too dim to be of any real use, a significant drawback for an emergency radio. Quality control appears below par. Analog-tuned with digital frequency counter, so lacks such digital tuning aids as station presets and keypad. Frequency display reads out only to nearest 10 kHz in XX.XX MHz format. Audio distorts at high volume. Battery cover not hinged to prevent loss. World band coverage, in four "bands"—4000–9200, 8910–14300, 13850–19400 and 18680–26500 kHz—misses relatively unimportant 2 and 3 MHz segments. Bandswitch must be adjusted when going from one world band segment range to another, complicating operation. Included wire antenna virtually worthless. FM in mono only. Clock 12-hour, no World Time. Three "AA" batteries not included for dry cell operation.

☞ The Kaito KA009 (around $45, not tested) is nominally similar, but adds coverage of the American weather band and VHF-TV audio.

Verdict: A marginal improvement over needle-and-dial emergency radios, the inexpensive Kaito KA008 offers flexible sources of power. Alas, performance is poor, tuning is extremely sloppy, quality control appears to be wanting, and dim LCD illumination makes tuning a shot in the dark.

The Kaito KA011 costs slightly more than its KA008 brand mate, but isn't any better. Even then, it is affordably priced for emergency use. D. Zantow

✪⅛

Kaito KA011

Pricing: $59.95 in the United States.

Pros: Three ways to power the radio directly, as well as indirectly by charging a battery pack: 1) hand crank, 2) solar cells and 3) AC adaptor. Can also be powered conventionally by three ordinary "AA" batteries (*see* Cons). Good world band sensitivity. Digital frequency readout (*see* Cons). Generally wide coverage of shortwave spectrum for self-powered radio (*see* Cons). Clock (*see* Cons) with one-event alarm. Built in LED flashlight. LCD illuminated by LED (*see* Cons). Loud, punchy audio (*see* Cons). Telescopic antenna swivels and rotates. Includes 120V AC adaptor/charger, rechargeable battery pack, earbuds and waterproof carrying bag.

Cons: Sloppy tuning. Poor image and ultimate rejection. Poor FM. Frequency display/clock illumination too dim to be of any real use, a significant drawback for an emergency radio. Quality control appears below par. Analog-tuned with digital frequency counter, so lacks such tuning aids as station presets and keypad. Frequency display reads out only to nearest 10 kHz in XX.XX MHz format; our sample reads slightly high. Audio distorts at high volume. Battery cover not hinged to prevent loss. World band coverage, in two "bands"—3.04–7.98 and 8.65–20.96 MHz— misses 21 MHz daytime segment and relatively unimportant 2 and 26 MHz segments. Bandswitch must be adjusted when going from one world band segment range to another. FM in mono only. Clock 12-hour, no World Time. Three "AA" batteries not included for dry cell operation.

☞ Do not confuse with the Kaito KA11, a conventional pocket portable (*see* Portables for 2009).

Verdict: Similar to the Kaito KA008, preceding, but more costly with minor drawbacks and little in the way of pluses.

POPULAR SELF-POWERED ANALOG PORTABLES

✪⅛

Grundig FR-200, Etón FR-200, Etón FR-250, FR-200 Lextronix, FR-250 Lextronix, Tecsun Green-88

Pricing: *Grundig FR-200:* $39.95 in the United States. *Etón FR-200:* £24.95 in the United Kingdom. *FR-200 Lextronix:* €37.95 in Germany. *Etón FR-250:* $49.95 in the United States. CAD$59.95 in Canada. £34.95 in the United Kingdom. *FR-250 Lextronix:* €49.00 in Germany. *AC adaptor (110–120V AC to 4.5V DC):* $9.95 in the United States. CAD$12.95 in Canada.

Standalone Dynamo

World band radios can be major sellers, but it takes understanding and focus that consumer electronics giants can rarely muster. For example, there have been millions of Grundig FR-200 and Etón FR-250 radios reportedly sold in North America in recent years. Also, a Tecsun version is offered in China and Etón now has a sales facility in Europe.

The '200/'250's sibling and related models succeed thanks to ubiquitous advertising, widespread availability and bargain pricing. They are powered not by ordinary batteries, but by a replaceable NiMH battery pack charged by crank-driven dynamo. Even if the battery pack dies the dynamo can power the radio.

Cellphone Charger

A key non-radio emergency feature of the '250 is a cellphone recharger. It includes a short cable and adaptor plugs for popular phones.

The front panel sports a bright flashlight that could be as important as the radio during a blackout. The '200 uses a bulb, while the '250 goes one better with long-life but none-too-bright LEDs that second as a flashing red light. For hiking, traveling or

The FR-250 is one of a number of similar analog emergency portables sold under Etón, Grundig, Tecsun, Lextronix and American Red Cross names.

bouncing around car trunks there's a rugged canvas bag with magnetic catch. The '250 also includes a siren loud enough to make neighborhood dogs bark.

Basic Radio

The '200 has two shortwave "bands" of 3.2–7.6 MHz and 9.2–22 MHz—nearly all world band segments.

Alas, the frequency readout crams hundreds of world band stations into a couple of inches—around five centimeters—of analog dial space, and the tuning knob has play. So global signals can be hunted down only by ear, and even then it's hard to tell whether you're hearing the station's real signal or its image 900 kHz or so down. However, there's a fine tuning control to make the process smoother.

Enter the FR-250. It has seven separate world band segments nicely spread out and augmented by a fine-tuning knob. Coverage omits the 3, 4, 5, 19 and 21 MHz (90, 75, 60, 15 and 13 meter) segments included on the '200, but it's a good tradeoff. As on the '200, the tuning knob has play.

Audio quality is pleasant with both models, but sensitivity to weak world band signals is marginal—ditto selectivity and image rejection. As to single-sideband signals, forget it.

FM, in mono only, includes NTSC (North American) channel 6 TV audio, scheduled to disappear in February 2009. FM overloads in strong-signal environments, but otherwise both it and mediumwave AM perform reasonably well.

The FR-200 and FR-250 don't send radio hearts aflutter. But they are eminently affordable, suffice for emergencies, are widely available and provide a number of non-radio emergency aids. Both come with a one-year warranty and superior product support.

✪⅛

American Red Cross ARC FR-350, Etón FR-350, FR-350 Lextronix

Pricing: *Etón/ARC FR-350:* $59.95 in the United States. CAD$61.00 in Canada. £39.95 in the United Kingdom. *FR-350 Lextronix:* €59.00 in Germany.

The new FR-350—no relation to the Etón S350—is the water resistant version of the FR-250. However, it's in a different package and has an additional daytime world band segment: 21 MHz.

The '350 tunes the important world band segments, skipping only 2, 3, 4 and 5 MHz used mainly by weak domestic stations in Latin America, Africa and Asia. The cabinet is slimmer than other FR models and includes a canvas carrying case and handy shoulder strap.

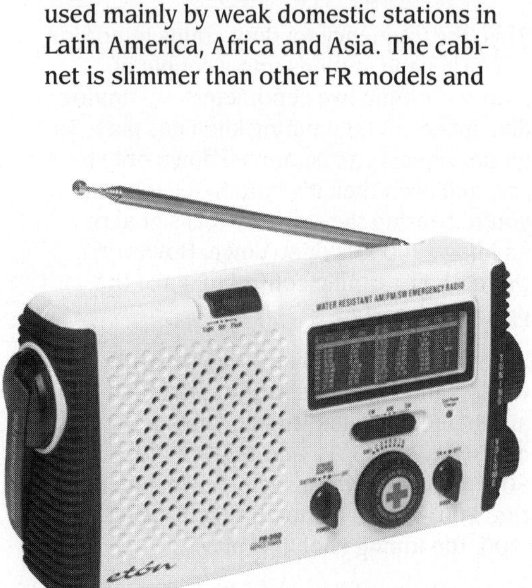

A portion of Etón's ARC FR-350 sales goes to the American Red Cross.

Rubber side panels and covered rear jacks help keep out water. We gave our '350 a vigorous dousing, and its innards emerged drier than a James Bond martini. This is an obvious plus not only for marine settings, but also for hurricanes, floods, tornadoes and tsunamis.

The power scheme is like what's on the larger, lower-cost '250. It comes with a replaceable NiMH battery pack that is charged internally by, among other things, a hand-cranked dynamo; an important backup is that the dynamo can also power the radio directly if the batteries are worn or missing. Three standard "AA" batteries (not included) can be used instead—say, if the dynamo fails—although it takes some doing to open the battery cavity.

An AC adaptor/battery charger is included, a convenience over the '250 and '200, as well as the newer FR-500 and FR-550. Although it reduces tiresome cranking and resulting dynamo wear, it also creates annoying hum at low volume.

Useful Gizmos

Like on the '250, the '350's dynamo can recharge cellphones. Anyone who has heard 9/11 recordings where conversations were cut short by dying cellphone batteries will appreciate this. A short cable and adapter plugs are included for most phones.

The '350, like the '250, includes a flashlight with two white LEDs for modest illumination, along with a switchable flashing red LED for visual warning. LEDs generally have a much longer life than conventional filament bulbs, so the flashlight might outlast the radio. Flashlights use more juice than little radios, so having dynamo power means reliable lighting no matter how long an outage lasts. Claustrophobics trapped in dark places may appreciate this more than the radio itself.

There's also a LOUD siren, and it's no toy. As hurricane Katrina showed, when people are stranded in attics or trapped under

Shutterstock/Norman Chan

rubble, an ear-blaster like this can make the difference between being overlooked and being rescued. Turn the crank occasionally and the siren wails nonstop.

No Digital Readout

The '350's frequency readout is analog, not digital, so finding a station is no stroll in the park: On our sample the dial is off by around 50 kHz, or fully ten world band channels. It spreads world band frequencies onto eight slide rule-type "bands," which allow for much easier fine tuning as opposed to the '200's "two 'bands' for everything."

On the '250 a concentric fine-tuning knob means you don't need safecracker's fingers. There is no such knob on the '350, although it is also is less needed because of the eight widely spread "bands." But the '350's string-and-pulley tuning has play, and on our unit the knob also rubs against the cabinet.

Same Performance, Different Features

The '350's world band performance and build quality are rudimentary and comparable to that of the '250 and '200: Single-conversion circuitry results in dismal image rejection. Too, sensitivity is marginal, selectivity isn't much better, and it doesn't handle single-sideband ham, utility or American Forces Radio signals. Audio, on the other hand, is surprisingly powerful and pleasant.

World band is fully scalable, so it's there when listenership spikes.

World band is uniquely resistant to censorship at national borders. Yet, any worthwhile emergency radio also needs to do yeoman's work with local and regional stations. Here, the '350 fares well. Its mediumwave AM band tunes to the Western Hemisphere/Pacific's upper frequency limit of 1705 kHz, while FM covers 87.5 to 108 MHz and outputs to mono earpieces. Both bands pull in stations nicely in urban and rural environments alike.

The PASSPORT *emergency radio review team: David Zantow, with Lawrence Magne.*

Tabletop Receivers for 2009

Tabletop receivers feast on tough signals. That's why they are prized by DXers—telegraph shorthand for "long distance listeners."

But money talks. This has put tabletop models under increasing competitive pressure from new-generation portables. One result: fewer tabletop offerings.

Superior Quality, Ready Repair

Most tabletop models are pricier than portables, but this buys superior quality control and durability. Tabletops are also easier to service and tend to be supported by knowledgeable repair facilities.

What you rarely find in a tabletop is reception of the everyday 87.5–108 MHz FM band. For this, look to a portable.

Rock Around The Clock

Like professional models and the very best portables, tabletops are ideally suited for where signals suffer from interference or tend to be weak—the North American Midwest and West, for example, or Australia and New Zealand.

Elsewhere, too, signals can weaken when they pass near the magnetic North Pole, which periodically erupts with geomagnetic fury. To check, place a string on a globe—a conventional map won't do—between your location and the station's transmitter as shown in the Blue Pages. If the string passes near or above latitude 60 degrees north, beware.

Tabletop receivers feast on tough long-haul signals—especially outside prime time.

Listening at dawn and in the afternoon is more relevant now, as a higher proportion of programs is found outside prime time. These signals are usually beamed elsewhere, but the scattering properties of shortwave allow them to be audible far beyond their intended targets, albeit at reduced strength. So superior hardware helps—better receivers and worthy antennas.

But not if reception is being disrupted by local electrical noise—nearby dimmers, digital devices and whatnot. A better receiver probably won't improve reception, as its superior circuitry boosts noise just as much as signals.

There's sometimes a way out. An active loop antenna (*see* Active Antennas for 2009) may improve the signal-to-noise ratio because it can be aimed away from noise sources. So, you may profit from a good tabletop model even when there's local electrical noise—provided you have the right antenna, properly aimed.

Antennas as Decisive as Receivers

A good antenna costs much less than a good receiver, but it's at least as important to successful reception. This is one reason most tabletops do well: They accept outboard antennas without the side effects these aerials often cause with portables.

Location, Location

If your antenna is inside a high-rise building, don't expect much—reinforced concrete soaks up radio signals. Too, in urban areas there can be intrusion from nearby broadcast, cellular and other transmitters.

Here, a good bet for tough signals is a superior receiver and antenna. Experiment with something like a homebrew insulated-wire antenna along, or just outside, a window or balcony. Or try an everyday telescopic car antenna angled out, like a wall flagpole, from a window or balcony ledge.

You can amplify that homebrew antenna with a good active preselector. Or look into ready-made amplified antennas with remote receiving elements, rated in PASSPORT REPORTS.

If you don't live in an apartment, consider a passive (unamplified) outdoor wire antenna. Performance details and installation steps are in

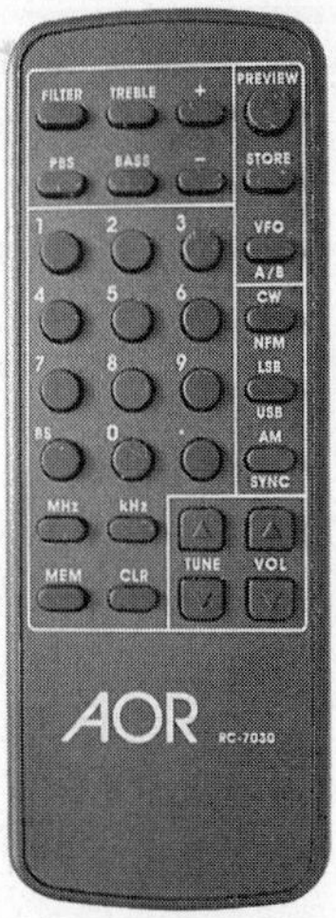

AOR's AR7030 uses a remote keypad. The forthcoming AR7030 is supposed to incorporate a keypad on its front panel.

D. Zantow

the Radio Database International White Paper, *Popular Outdoor Antennas*, and are also summarized in "Wire Antennas for 2009."

Shortwave's Hidden Signals

Some radio aficionados seek out shortwave utility and ham signals nestled between world band segments. These have reception challenges and rewards of their own and, unlike world band, don't need receivers with quality sound. This allows some receivers with uninspiring audio to work well with utilities: notably, Icom's IC-R75.

Of course, highly rated tabletop models with worthy audio perform solidly with world band, as well as utilities.

Complete Test Findings

Our unabridged laboratory and hands-on test results for each receiver are too exhaustive to reproduce here. However, they are available for selected current and classic models as PASSPORT's Radio Database International White Papers.

Tips for Using this Section

Receivers are listed in order of suitability for listening to difficult-to-hear world band stations; important secondary consideration is given to audio fidelity, ergonomics, perceived build quality and utility/ham reception. Street selling prices are cited, including British VAT where applicable. Prices vary, so take them as the general guide they are meant to be. Haggling is rarely successful.

Accessories listed are known to be readily available. Those not normally found in your country sometimes can be special-ordered at the time of receiver purchase.

Unless otherwise indicated, each model features:

- Digital frequency synthesis and display.
- Full coverage of at least the 155–29999 kHz longwave, mediumwave AM and shortwave spectra—including all world band frequencies—but no coverage of FM broadcasts (usually 87.5–108 MHz). Models designed for sale in certain countries have reduced shortwave tuning ranges; also, broadband models sold in the United States omit coverage of non-shortwave cellular frequencies.
- A wide variety of helpful tuning features.
- Synchronous selectable sideband via high-rejection IF filtering (not lower-rejection phasing), which when properly engineered greatly reduces adjacent-channel interference and fading distortion. On some models this is referred to as "SAM" (synchronous AM). ☞ **ECSS:** Professional models tune to the nearest 1 Hz, allowing the user to use the receiver's single-sideband circuitry to manually phase its BFO (internally generated carrier) with the station's transmitted carrier. Called "ECSS" (exalted-carrier, selectable-sideband) tuning, this can be used with AM-mode signals in lieu of synchronous selectable sideband. However, in addition to the relative inconvenience of this technique, unlike synchronous detection, which re-phases continually and essentially perfectly, ECSS is always slightly out of phase.
- Proper demodulation of modes used by utility and ham signals, although in a few non-Western countries this is outlawed. These modes include single sideband (LSB/USB) and CW ("Morse code"); also, with suitable ancillary devices, radioteletype (RTTY), frequency shift key (FSK) and radiofax (FAX).
- Meaningful signal-strength indication—either an analog meter or a digital indicator.
- Illuminated display.

What PASSPORT's Rating Symbols Mean

Star ratings: ✪✪✪✪✪ is best. Stars reflect overall performance and meaningful features, plus to some extent ergonomics and perceived build quality. Price, appearance, country of manufacture and the like are not taken into account. With tabletop models there is a slightly greater emphasis than on portables on the ability to flush out tough, hard-to-hear signals. Nevertheless, to facilitate comparison the tabletop rating standards are similar to those used for professional and portable models reviewed elsewhere in this PASSPORT REPORTS.

Passport's Choice. *La crème de la crème.* Our test team's personal picks of the litter—models we would buy or have bought for our personal use. Unlike star ratings, these choices are unapologetically subjective.

¢: A relative bargain, with decidedly more performance than the price suggests, but no tabletop receiver is really cheap.

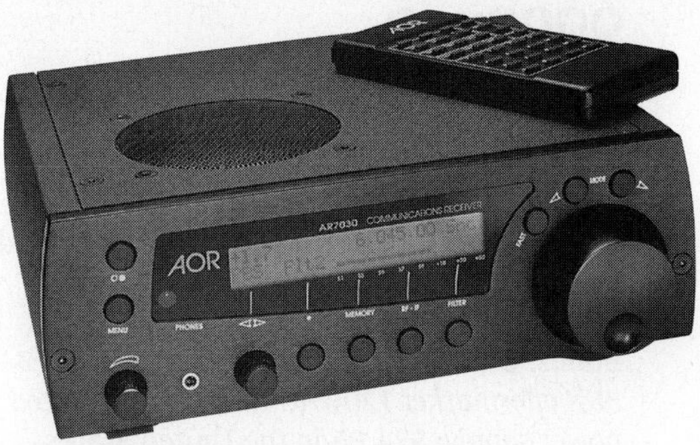

AOR-UK's AR7030 was the last of the great analog tabletop receivers with synthesized tuning. Its 2009 replacement reportedly will be DSP, so ears will be on the alert to see if the '7030's superb audio has been retained.

Replacement Scheduled for 2009

✪✪✪✪✪ 📄 *Passport's Choice*

AOR AR7030 PLUS, AOR AR7030

Pricing: *AR7030 PLUS:* $1,499.95 in the United States. N/A in the United Kingdom. €1,198.00 in Germany. *AR7030:* N/A in the United Kingdom. €1,039.00 in Germany.

Summary of Findings: Engineered by John Thorpe and manufactured in England, the AR7030 has been a smashing performer, with audio quality that can be a pleasure hour after hour. And it's even better and more robust in its PLUS incarnation.

But there is a catch. Like BMW's annoying iDrive, many functions are shoehorned into a tree-logic control scheme. The resulting ergonomics are uniquely hostile—especially in the PLUS version—even if operation ultimately is not that difficult to master. *Best bet:* Before buying, either lay hands on a '7030 or study the free online owner's manuals (www.aoruk.com/pdf/7030m.pdf and www.aoruk.com/pdf/fpu.pdf).

Ergonomics aside, for serious DXing the '7030 is a top performer, but there's more. With a suitable outboard speaker it is also one of the best sounding receivers at any price for hearing world band and mediumwave AM shows under a wide range of reception conditions.

Supplies of new AR7030 receivers almost certainly will have been exhausted in the United Kingdom and the United States by the time you read this, although almost-new units may represent good value.

☞ If you're hunting for a remaining new '7030, check out Ohio's Universal Radio at universal-radio.com and Germany's ThieCom at thiecom.de. For export, deduct the 19 percent VAT included in German prices, above.

Replacement Model for 2009: AOR-UK, in concert with engineering luminary John Thorpe, has been designing the AR7030's replacement, the AR7070, for some time. According to them, the '7070 would have immediately replaced the '7030 had it not been for certain key components becoming unavailable from suppliers just as the receiver was about to commence production. If this dog-chasing-tail doesn't recur, the '7070's likely ETA would be in early 2009. Otherwise, the date could slip by several months.

Not much is known about the forthcoming AR7070 except that its final stage is to be DSP based. The display is to be larger, as well, and the keypad will be inboard instead of outboard. We'll keep an eye on this saga at www.passband.com.

📄 An *RDI WHITE PAPER* is available for the AR7030 series.

✪✪✪✪⅜ ¢

Icom IC-R75

Pricing: *Receiver with UT-106 DSP accessory:* $599.95 in the United States. CAD$699.99 in Canada. *Icom Replacement FL-257 3.3 kHz Voice Bandwidth Filter:* $184.95 in the United States. CAD$310.00 in Canada. *SP-23 audio-shaping speaker:* $189.95 in the United States. CAD$260.00 in Canada. *Pyramid PS-3KX aftermarket 120V AC 13.8V DC regulated power supply:* $24.95 in the United States. *Sherwood SE-3 MK IV accessory:* $750.00 plus shipping worldwide.

Pros: Dual passband offset acts as variable bandwidth and a form of IF shift (*see* Cons). Reception of faint signals alongside powerful competitors aided by excellent ultimate selectivity and good blocking. Excellent front-end selectivity, with seven filters for the shortwave range and more for elsewhere. Two levels of preamplification, 10/20 dB, can be switched off. Excellent weak-signal sensitivity and good AGC threshold with 20 dB preamplification. Superior rejection of spurious signals, including images. Excellent stability, essential for unattended reception of RTTY and certain other utility transmissions. Excels in reception of utility and ham signals, as well as world band signals tuned via ECSS. Ten tuning steps, including ultra-precise 1 Hz (*see* Cons). Adjustable UT-106 DSP circuit with automatic variable notch filter helps to a degree in improving intelligibility, but not pleasantness, of some tough signals; also, it reduces heterodyne ("whistle") interference. Fairly good ergonomics, including smooth-turning weighted tuning knob with spinning finger dimple that doesn't spin very

NUMBERS: TOP TABLETOP

	Icom IC-R75
Max. Sensitivity/Noise Floor	0.35 μV (E)/–125 dBm (G)(1)
Blocking	>121 dB (G)
Shape Factors, voice BWs	1:1.6–1:1.9 (E)
Ultimate Rejection	80 dB (E)(2)
Front-End Selectivity	n/a
Image Rejection	>90 dB (S)
First IF Rejection	>80 dB (E)
Dynamic Range/IP3 (5 kHz)	69 dB (G)/–21 dBm (G)
Dynamic Range/IP3 (20 kHz)	n/a(2)
Phase Noise	107 dBc (F)
AGC Threshold	3.5 μV (F)
Overall Distortion, AM mode	0.1–8% (S)-(P)(3)
Overall Distortion, SSB mode	≤0.1% (S)
Stability	20 Hz (E)

IBS Lab Ratings: (S) Superb (E) Excellent (G) Good (F) Fair (P) Poor

(1) Preamplifier off. With 10 dB preamp: 0.14 μV (S)/–133 dBm (E). With 20 dB preamp: 0.1 μV (S)/136 dBm (E).

(2) Phase-noise limited.

(3) Usually <4.5% (S)-(F).

well. "Control Central" LCD easy to read and evenly illuminated by 24 LEDs with dimmer. Adjustable AGC—fast, slow, off. Tuning knob uses reliable optical encoder. Low overall distortion. Pleasant, hiss-free audio with suitable outboard speaker; audio-shaping Icom SP-23, although pricey, works well for a number of applications. 101 station presets. Two switchable antenna inputs. Digital signal-strength indicator unusually linear above S-9 and can hold peak reading briefly. Audio-out port for recording or micro-power FM transmitter. World Time clock, timer and sleep delay (*see* Cons). Tunes to 60 MHz, including 6 meter VHF ham band. Elevation rod (*see* Cons).

Cons: Dual passband offset usually has little impact on received world band signals. DSP's automatic variable notch usually doesn't work with AM-mode signals not received via "ECSS." Mediocre audio through internal speaker, and no tone control to offset slightly bassiness that originates prior to audio stage; audio improves to pleasant with appropriate external speaker, especially one that offsets bassiness. Suboptimal audio recovery with weak AM-mode signals having heavy fading; largely remediable by ECSS and switching off AGC. Display misreads up to 20 Hz, somewhat negating ultra-precise 1 Hz tuning. Keypad requires frequency entry in MHz with decimal or trailing zeroes, a pointless inconvenience. Some knobs small. Uses outboard AD-55 "floor brick" 120V AC adaptor in lieu of internal power supply; adaptor's emission field may cause minor hum on received signals (remediable by moving antenna or using shielded lead-in). AC adaptor over 17.5V while 'R75 designed for 13.8V, so receiver runs hot and thus its voltage regulator's reliability suffers; remedied by dropping input voltage to 13–14V, such as with Pyramid PS-3KX aftermarket regulated power supply. Can read clock or presets' IDs or frequency, but no more than one at the same time. RF/AGC control operates peculiarly. Elevation rod lacks rubber sheathing. Keyboard beep emits at audio line output. No schematic provided. Sold only in North America; lacks CE approval, so not available within EU even from American exporters.

The Icom IC-R75 excels at snaring tough utility and ham signals, but isn't quite as successful with world band audio. Attractively priced within North America.

Verdict: The Japanese-made Icom IC-R75 is a tempting value—provided you live in the United States or Canada, the only countries where it is now available. The 'R75 is first-rate for unearthing tough utility and ham signals, as well as world band signals received via ECSS. For these applications nothing else equals it on the sunny side of a kilobuck.

It is less of an unqualified success for world band listening. Sherwood's SE-3 Mk IV accessory brings the 'R75's fidelity to life by adding top-notch synchronous selectable sideband and audio, and some users have gone this route. But neat as it is, the accessory costs more than the receiver and adds operating steps.

✪✪✪✪

Icom IC-R8500A

Pricing: *ICF-8500A:* $1,799.95 (government use/export only) in the United States. CAD$2,099.00 in Canada. £1,199.00 in the United Kingdom. €1,898.00 in Germany. *CR-293 frequency stabilizer:* $299.95 in the United States. CAD$230.00 in Canada. £89.95 in the United Kingdom. €119.00 in Germany. *Aftermarket Sherwood SE-3 Mk IV:* $750.00 in the United States.

Pros: Wide-spectrum multimode coverage from 0.1–2000 MHz includes longwave, mediumwave AM, shortwave and scanner frequencies. Physically very rugged, with professional-grade cast-aluminum chassis and impressive computer-type innards. Gen-

Icom's wideband IC-R8500A is less costly than comparable models. Illegal for civilian sale within the United States, but it can be imported from Canada.

erally superior ergonomics, with generous front panel having large and well-spaced controls, plus outstanding tuning knob with numerous tuning steps. A thousand station presets and 100 auto-write presets have handy tag function. Superb weak-signal sensitivity. Pleasant, low-distortion audio aided by audio peak filter. Passband tuning ("IF shift"). Unusually readable LCD. Tunes and displays in precise 10 Hz increments. Three antenna connections. Clock-timer, combined with record output and recorder-activation jack, make for superior hands-off recording of favorite programs, as well as for feeding a low-power FM transmitter to hear world band around the house.

Cons: No longer legally available to the public in the United States, as it receives cellular frequencies—even though digital cellphone traffic is virtually impossible to decipher with a receiver like this. No synchronous selectable sideband. Bandwidth choices for world band and other AM-mode signals leap from a very narrow 2.7 kHz to a broad 7.1 kHz with nothing between, where something is needed; third bandwidth is 13.7 kHz, too wide for world band, and there's no provision for a fourth bandwidth filter. Only one single-sideband bandwidth. Unhandy carousel-style bandwidth selection with no permanent indication of which bandwidth is in use. Poor dynamic range, surprising at this price. Passband tuning ("IF shift") does not work in AM mode used by world band and mediumwave AM-band stations. No tunable notch filter. Built-in speaker mediocre. Outboard AC adaptor instead of inboard power supply.

☞ Also tested with Sherwood SE-3 aftermarket accessory, which proved to be outstanding at adding selectable synchronous sideband. This combo also provides passband tuning in the AM mode which is used by nearly all world band stations. Adding the SE-3 and replacing the widest bandwidth with a 4 to 5 kHz bandwidth filter markedly improves performance on shortwave, mediumwave AM and longwave.

Verdict: The large Icom IC-R8500 is a scanner that happens to cover world band, rather than *vice versa*. It is no longer available new in the Land of Legislation.

As a standalone world band radio, this Japanese-made wideband receiver makes little sense without a filter change and adding the Sherwood accessory. Yet, it is well worth considering if you want an all-in-one scanner that also serves as a shortwave receiver.

✪✪✪✪

AOR AR5000A+3

Pricing: *AR5000A+3 (cellular-blocked version) receiver:* $2,599.95 in the United States. *AR5000A+3 (full-coverage version) receiver:* $2,649.95 (government use/export only) in the United States. CAD$2,850.00 in Canada. £1,698.99 in the United Kingdom. *Collins MF60 6 kHz mechanical filter (recommended):* $99.95 in the United States. *SDU-5600 spectrum display unit:* $1,499.95 in the United States. CAD$1,899.00 in Canada. £975.00 in the United Kingdom.

Pros: Ultra-wideband multimode coverage from 0.01–3,000 MHz includes longwave, mediumwave AM, shortwave and scanner frequencies. Helpful tuning features include 2,000 station presets in 20 pages of 100 presets each. Narrow bandwidth filter and optional Collins wide filter both have superb skirt selectivity (standard wide filter's skirt selectivity unmeasurable because of limited ultimate rejection). Synchronous selectable and double sideband (*see* Cons). Front-end selectivity, image rejection, IF rejection, weak-signal sensitivity, AGC threshold and frequency stability all superior. Ultra-precise frequency readout to nearest Hertz.

Exceptionally accurate displayed frequency measurement. Superb circuit shielding, so virtually zero radiated digital buzzing. IF output (*see* Cons). Automatic Frequency Control (AFC) works on AM-mode, as well as FM-mode, signals. Unusually helpful owner's manual, important because of operating system.

Cons: Synchronous detector substandard on three counts: with selectable sideband, 1) loses lock easily and 2) substandard rejection of unwanted sideband; also, 3) overall distortion rises with synchronous detector (double sideband or selectable sideband). Ultimate rejection of narrow (2.7 kHz) bandwidth only 60 dB. Ultimate rejection of wide (7.6 kHz) bandwidth only 50 dB, mediocre, improves to uninspiring 60 dB when replaced with optional 6 kHz Collins mechanical filter. Installation of optional Collins bandwidth filter requires expertise, patience and special equipment. Poor dynamic range. Cumbersome ergonomics. No passband offset. No tunable notch filter. Needs good external speaker for worthy audio. World Time clock does not show when frequency displayed. IF output frequency 10.7 MHz instead of more-useful 455 kHz.

☞ Because of the unavailability of needed production parts, this model was discontinued in April, 2008. Nevertheless, as of presstime it continues to be stocked by certain vendors in North America and the United Kingdom. A replacement is scheduled for release at a later date.

Verdict: Unbeatable in some respects, woefully inferior in others—it comes down to what you want. The optional 6 kHz Collins filter is strongly recommended, but it should be installed by the dealer at the time of purchase. Although some AOR receivers are engineered and manufactured in the United Kingdom, this model is strictly Made in Japan.

✪✪✪✪

Palstar R30A/Sherwood

Pricing: *Sherwood SE-3 Mk IV:* $750.00 in the United States. *Palstar R30A:* See below.

Americans reluctant to import an Icom IC-R8500A can spring for the ultra-wideband AOR AR5000A+3. More money buys more coverage, but production stopped in 2008 so supplies are limited.

Pros: SE-3 provides nearly flawless synchronous selectable sideband, reducing adjacent-channel interference while enhancing audio fidelity. Foolproof installation; plugs right into the Palstar's existing IF output.

Cons: Buzz occasionally heard during weak-signal reception. SE-3 costs more than the receiver.

Verdict: If you're going to spend $750 to upgrade a $695 receiver, you may as well spring for another model.

Revised Version for 2009

✪✪✪⅞

Palstar R30A

Pricing: $695.00 in the United States. CAN$749.00 in Canada. £469.95 in the United Kingdom. €699.00 in Germany. *SP30 speaker:* $69.95 in the United States. €64.95 in Germany.

Pros: Generally good dynamic range. Overall distortion averages 0.5 percent, superb, in single-sideband mode (in AM mode, averages 2.9 percent, good, at 60% modulation and 4.4 percent, fair, at 95% modulation) (*see* Cons). Every other performance variable measures either good or excellent in PASSPORT's lab, and birdies are virtually absent. Excellent AGC performance with AM-mode and single-sideband signals. Robust physical construction of cabinet and related hardware. Microprocessor section

Palstar's receiver has come in several versions over the years. The current R30A is robust, but its tuning knob is unhandy. Universal Radio

well shielded to minimize radiation of digital buzzing. Includes selectable slow/fast AGC decay (*see* Cons), 20–100 Hz/100–500 Hz VRIT (slow/fast variable-rate incremental tuning) knob (*see* Cons), 0.5 MHz slewing and 455 kHz IF output. One hundred nonvolatile station presets, using a generally well-thought-out scheme (*see* Cons), that store frequency, bandwidth, mode, AGC and attenuator settings; also, presets displayed by channel number or frequency. Excellent illuminated analog signal meter reads in useful S1–9/+60 dB standard and is reasonably accurate (*see* Cons). LCD and signal-indicator illumination can be switched off. Also operates from ten firmly secured "AA" internal batteries (*see* Cons). Lightweight and small (*see* Cons). Good AM-mode sensitivity within longwave and mediumwave AM bands. Audio line output. Self-resetting circuit breaker for outboard power (e.g., AC adaptor); fuse used with internal batteries and comes with spare fuses. Elevation rod (*see* Cons). Optional AA30 active antenna, evaluated in PASSPORT REPORTS. Virtually superb skirt selectivity (1:1.4 wide and 1:1.5 narrow) and ultimate rejection (90 dB); bandwidths measure 6.3 kHz and 2.6 kHz, using Collins mechanical filters. Adjacent-channel 5 kHz heterodyne whistles largely absent with wide bandwidth. Audio quality pleasant with wide bandwidth (*see* Cons).

Cons: No keypad for direct frequency entry, not even as mouse-type outboard option; normally, only truly cheap portables lack a keypad. Recessed tuning knob difficult to grasp. No 5 kHz tuning step to aid in band-scanning. Lacks control to hop from one world band segment to another; instead, uses 0.5 MHz fast-slewing increments. No synchronous selectable sideband without pricey Sherwood SE-3 aftermarket accessory (see preceding review). ECSS tuning can be up to 10 Hz out of phase because of 20 Hz minimum tuning increment. Play in mechanical tuning encoder makes precise ECSS tuning more difficult. Lacks many features found in top-gun receivers, such as tunable notch filter, noise blanker, passband tuning and adjustable RF gain. Recovered audio fine with most signals, but with truly weak signals is not of the DX caliber found with top-gun receivers. No visual indication of which bandwidth in use. No tone controls. Identical front-panel keys, including "MEM" which, if accidentally pressed, can erase a preset. Presets could be more intuitive and easy to select; *e.g.*, lacks frequency information on existing presets during memory storage. No AGC off. No RF gain control. Uses AC adaptor instead of built-in power supply. High battery consumption. Batteries frustratingly difficult to install, requiring partial disassembly of receiver and care not to damage speaker connections or confuse polarities. Receiver's light weight and elevation rod's lack of rubber sheathing allow it to slide around; added weight of batteries helps slightly. Mono headphone jack produces output in only one ear of stereo 'phones; remedied by mono-to-stereo adaptor.

☞ Works best when grounded.

Verdict: Steak and potatoes radio—no sauce, no frills. Yet, what the Ohio-made Palstar R30A sets out to do, it tends to do to a high standard. If you can abide the convoluted battery installation procedure and don't mind having to add an outboard antenna, it can second as a field portable.

Revised Version for 2009: In the summer of 2008 the Palstar R30CC, which we've fully tested, was replaced by the R30A only because the original LCD became unavailable. According to the manufacturer, other changes are cosmetic (e.g., key sizes) or minor (e.g., LEDs in place of bulbs for illumination)—except that the tuning knob is now recessed and the U.S. price has been increased by fifty dollars.

The R30 series has traditionally been lacking in tuning and performance features. Yet, the new "A" version, rather than improving upon this, has made matters worse by recessing the tuning knob. Presumably creative minds will come up with an aftermarket solution before long.

✪✪✪⅝

Icom IC-R1500

Pricing: *IC-R1500 with control head and "black box" receiver:* $599.95 in the United States. CAD$499.00 in Canada. £389.00 in the United Kingdom. €625.00 in Germany. *UT-106 DSP unit:* $139.95 in the United States. CAD$140.00 in Canada. £79.95 in the United Kingdom. €99.00 in Germany. *OPC-1156 11 1/2-foot/3.5-meter controller extension cable:* $13.95 in the United States. CAD$25.00 in Canada. £24.95 in the United Kingdom. €16.95 in Germany. *OPC-441 16 1/2-foot/five-meter speaker extension cable:* $27.95 in the United States. £24.95 in the United Kingdom. €26.95 in Germany. *CP-12L 12V DC cigarette lighter power cable:* $29.95 in the United States. CAD$60.00 in Canada. £19.95 in the United Kingdom. €23.95 in Germany. *OPC-254L 12V DC fused power cord:* $12.95 in the United States. CAD$20.00 in Canada. £9.95 in the United Kingdom. €9.20 in Germany. *Aftermarket RF Systems DPX-30 antenna splitter for separate shortwave and scanner antennas:* $169.95 in the United States. €109.00 in Germany.

Pros: Generally excellent wired control head allows '1500 to be used as a standalone tabletop or, to a degree with the optional CP-12L power cord, a mobile receiver (*see* Cons)—as well as a PC-controlled model *à la* sibling PC-R1500 (*see* Receivers for PCs). Wideband frequency coverage in three versions: *(blocked U.S. version)* 0.01–810, 851–867, 896–1811, 1852–1868, 1897–2305.9, 2357–2812, 2853–2869, 2898–3109.8, 3136–3154.8, 3181–3300 MHz; *(blocked French version)* 0.01–30, 50.2–51.2, 87.5–108, 144–146, 430–440 and 1240–1300 MHz; *(unblocked version)* 0.01–3300 MHz (*see* Con). Very good shortwave sensitivity. Tunes and displays in ultra-precise 1 Hz increments. Vast number of user-selectable tuning steps. Useful ECSS (*see* Cons) aided by rock stability. Selectable fast/slow AGC decay (*see* Cons). Three different user screens when controlled by PC in lieu of control head. Excellent 'scope for up to a 1 MHz peek at radio spectrum in real time, 1–10 MHz in non-real time. Generally good IF shift (*see* Cons). Operating software works well and can be updated online. Fully 2600 station presets clustered into 26 pages of 100 channels each. Generally pleasant audio quality (*see* Cons). Audio available not only through the set's internal speaker (*see* Cons) or an external speaker, but also via USB through PC's audio system (*see* Cons). Can record audio in .wav format onto hard drive (*see* Cons). One-step (20 dB) attenuator (*see* Cons). Optional UT-106 AF-DSP unit (not tested) for noise reduction and AF notch filtering.

Cons: Poor dynamic range—no RF or IF gain control to reduce overloading, and attenua-

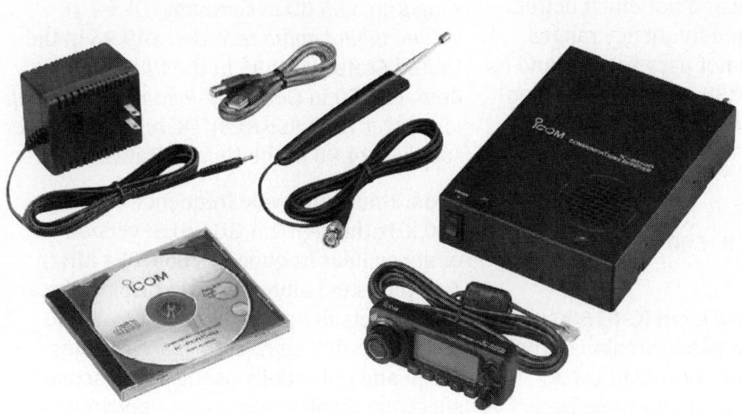

Cars aren't the only hybrids. The affordable Icom IC-R1500 is part tabletop, part mobile and part PC receiver.

A separate control module allows the Icom IC-R1500 to be operated without a PC. It then works as a tabletop or mobile receiver, but performance is still best when it is tethered to a PC. D. Zantow

tor only one-step. No synchronous selectable sideband; ECSS manual alternative slightly out of phase even with 1 Hz tuning step. Control head provides most, but not all, operating functions available via PC control; for example, no keypad or spectrum 'scope, and presets simultaneously display only one frequency or alphanumeric tag. Control head lacks stand or mounting bracket for desktop or mobile use, nor can it be attached to body of the "black box." At one test location, some distortion encountered with single-sideband signals through 3 kHz bandwidth. Slight hiss. Audio only fair through black box's built-in speaker. Audio slightly weak through computer's USB port. No AGC off. IF shift only for single-sideband and CW modes. Mediumwave sensitivity only fair. Poor longwave sensitivity. Marginal noise blanker. Specifications not guaranteed by Icom (all versions) from 0.01–0.5 and 3000–3300 MHz. No on/off multi-event timing for audio recording and such. Telescopic antenna and cable virtually useless on shortwave and not much better elsewhere within tuned frequency ranges. Software installation not user-friendly and is only via computer's USB port (no serial connection). No schematic or block diagrams.

☞ BFO (for single sideband and CW) operates up to 1300 MHz.

☞ Also, *see* Icom IC-R1500 within Receivers for PCs.

Verdict: The wideband Icom IC-R1500 is the more-or-less standalone version of the IC-PCR1500 computer-controlled black box receiver. It consists of the same basic box used by the 'PCR1500, along with an external wired control head that allows it to act independently as a real, if decidedly unusual, tabletop or, to a degree, a mobile receiver. Thus, the 'R1500 can be operated by PC or, using the control head, by itself—but not both at the same time. The control head includes an illuminated LCD, tuning knob, volume, squelch and other controls. Nevertheless, operation is more flexible using a PC, as it allows for keypad tuning and other capabilities not found with the control head.

Icom IC-R2500

The Icom IC-R2500 (not tested) is priced about half-again over the '1500. It uses the same platform as the '1500, but adds diversity reception to help reduce fading effects (two widely spaced antennas—or, outside the shortwave spectrum, one horizontally and one vertically polarized—are required).

Additional extras are multi-channel monitoring/display, P25 (public service digital) board, D-Star and similar features oriented to VHF/UHF/SHF scanning.

✪✪✪ ✐

Yaesu VR-5000

Pricing: *VR-5000 Receiver, including single-voltage AC adaptor:* $599.95 in the United States. £489.00 in the United Kingdom. €575.00 in Germany. *DSP-1 digital notch, bandpass and noise reduction unit:* $119.95 in the United States. £94.95 in the United Kingdom. €85.00 in Germany. *DVS-4 16-second digital audio recorder:* $49.95 in the United States. £29.95 in the United Kingdom. €28.50 in Germany. *Pyramid PS-3KX aftermarket 120V AC>13.8V DC regulated power supply:* $24.95 in the United States.

Pros: Unusually wide frequency coverage, 100 kHz through 2.6 GHz (U.S. version omits cellular frequencies 869–894 MHz). Two thousand alphanumeric-displayed station presets in up to 100 pages. Up to 50 programmable start/stop search ranges. Large and potentially useful "band scope" spectrum display (*see* Cons). Bandwidths have superb skirt selectivity, with shape factors between 1:1.3 and 1:1.4. Wide AM bandwidth (17.2 kHz) allows local mediumwave AM stations to be received with superior fidelity (*see* Cons). Flexible software provides considerable control over selected parameters. Sophisticated scanning choices (*see* Cons). Dual-receive function, with sub-receiver circuitry feeding "band scope" spectrum display; when display not in use, two signals may be monitored simultaneously if they are within 20 MHz of each other. Sensitivity excellent-to-superb within shortwave spectrum (*see* Cons). Above-average build quality. External spectrum display, fed by receiver's 10.7 MHz IF output, can perform very well for narrow-parameter scans (*see* Cons). Two 24-hour clocks, both shown except when spectrum display mode in use; one clock tied into elementary map display and database of time in many world cities. On-off timer, 48 events. Sleep-delay/alarm timers. Lightweight and compact. Multi-level display dimmer. Optional DSP unit includes adjustable notch filtering, bandpass feature and noise reduction (*see* Cons). Tone control. Built-in "CAT" computer control interface (*see* Cons). Control and memory backup/management software at www.g4hfq.co.uk.

Cons: Exceptionally poor dynamic range (49 dB at 5 kHz signal spacing, 64 dB at 20 kHz spacing) and IF/image rejection (as low as 30 dB); impacts shortwave reception in such high-signal parts of the world as Europe, North Africa and eastern North America unless a very modest antenna is used; VHF-UHF degradation depends, among other things, on whether powerful transmission(s) in receiver's vicinity. Sophisticated scanning choices of limited use, as stops on false signals caused by inadequate dynamic range. No synchronous selectable sideband. Only one single-sideband bandwidth, a too-wide 4.0 kHz. Wide AM bandwidth (17.2 kHz) too wide for shortwave. For world band, middle (8.7 kHz) AM bandwidth also too wide, lets through adjacent-channel 5 kHz heterodyne; narrow bandwidth (3.9 kHz, not SSB filter's 4.0 kHz) produces muffled audio. Audio distorts at higher volume. Limited low-frequency

The Yaesu VR-5000 is handsomely priced for a tabletop with substantial wideband tuning. Widely available, too, but there's a catch: Dynamic range is at least as low as the price.

audio. Audio hissy, especially with good outboard speaker. DSP-1 option a mediocre overall performer and adds distortion. Phase noise 94 dBc, poor. AGC threshold 11 microvolts, poor. No AGC decay adjustment, and single-sideband AGC decay too slow. Depending on sample and firmware version, tuning encoder may have rotational delay when changing directions. Mediocre tuning-knob feel. Signal-strength indicator has only five levels and overreads; an alternative software-selectable signal-strength indicator—not easy to access or exit—has no markings other than a single reference level. Built-in spectrum display's dynamic range only 20 dB (–80 to –100 dBm), with very slow scan rate. Single-sideband frequency readout after warmup can be off by up to 100 Hz. Long learning curve and unintuitive ergonomics: thirty buttons often densely spaced, lilliputian and multifunction; also, carouseling mode/tune-step selection and a menu-driven command scheme. Only one low-impedance antenna connector, inadequate for wideband device that needs multiple antennas. Longwave sensitivity mediocre. Clocks don't display seconds numerically. Marginal display contrast. LED illumination uneven. AC adaptor instead of built-in power supply; adaptor and receiver both tend to run warm. Repeated microprocessor lockups, sometimes displayed as "*ERROR* LOW VOLTAGE," even though the receiver includes a 7.2V NiCd battery pack to help prevent this; unplugging set for ten minutes resolves problem until it occurs again; also helpful is to replace provided

AC adaptor with properly bypassed and regulated non-switching power supply of at least one ampere that produces no less than 13.2–13.8V DC, such as Pyramid PS-3KX. Even with aforementioned battery, clock has to be reset if power fails. Squelch doesn't function through audio line output (for recording, etc.). Line output gain low. Sub-receiver doesn't feed line output. Computer interface lacks viable command structure, limiting usefulness. Tilt feet too short. Owner's manual omits some receiver functions, so user also has to learn by trial and error.

Verdict: With existing technology, so-called "DC-to-daylight" receivers that incorporate excellent shortwave performance are costly to produce and are priced accordingly.

The relatively affordable wideband Yaesu VR-5000 tries to overcome this. This Japanese-made model acts as a VHF/UHF scanner as well as a shortwave receiver, but falls woefully shy for world band in strong-signal parts of the world. Elsewhere, it fares better, especially if only a modest antenna is used.

✪✪✪

SI-TEX NAV-FAX 200

Pricing: $459.95 in the United States. *SI-TEX ACNF 120V AC adaptor:* $15.95 in the United States. *NASA AA30 (unrelated to Palstar AA30) antenna for NAV-FAX200:* €49.00 in Germany.

The SI-TEX NAV-FAX 200 is a paragon of simplicity with pleasant performance. Made in England.

Pros: Superior image rejection. Superior dynamic range. Superb ultimate rejection (*see* Con). Includes Mscan Meteo Pro Lite software for WEFAX, RTTY and NAVTEX reception using a PC with Windows XP or older Windows OS; may be upgraded to Vista at www.mscan.com. Wire antenna and audio patch cable. Two-year warranty at repair facility in Florida.

Cons: Lacks many handy tuning features; e.g., no keypad and only ten presets. Variable-rate tuning knob and volume control fussy to operate. Synthesizer tunes in relatively coarse 1 kHz increments, supplemented by analog fine-tuning "clarifier." Broad skirt selectivity. Single-sideband bandwidth relatively wide. Single sideband requires two tuning controls to be adjusted. No synchronous selectable sideband, notch filter or passband tuning. Frequency readout off by 2 kHz in single-sideband mode. Uses optional AC adaptor instead of built-in power supply. No clock, timer or sleep-delay feature. This British-made model available only through marine dealers in the United States and, to a degree, Canada.

Verdict: Pleasant world band performance, although numerous features are absent and operation can be frustrating. Its weather orientation and diminutive size make it handy for yachting and some other niche uses.

✪✪½

Realistic/Radio Shack DX-394

Price: £249.99 in the United Kingdom.

Pros: Advanced tuning features include 160 tunable presets (*see* Cons). Tunes in precise 10 Hz increments. Modest size, light weight and built-in telescopic antenna provide some portable capability. Bandwidths (*see* Cons) have superior shape factors and ultimate rejection. Two 24-hour clocks, one shown independent of frequency display. Five programmable timers. 30/60 minute snooze. Noise blanker.

Cons: Available only as new old stock at U.K. outlet www.haydon.info. What appears to be four bandwidths turns out to be virtually one that's too wide for optimum reception of many signals. Bandwidths, such as they are, not selectable independent of mode. No synchronous selectable sideband. Presets cumbersome to use. Poor dynamic range. Overall distortion higher than desirable.

Verdict: This uninspiring performer was discontinued years ago, but lives on within the bowels of a single store in Essex, England.

The PASSPORT *tabletop-model review team consists of Lawrence Magne and David Zantow. Also, David Crystal, George Heidelman, Chuck Rippel, David Walcutt and George Zeller. Laboratory measurements by J. Robert Sherwood.*

The 1996 Realistic/Radio Shack DX-394 was manufactured only briefly, but new old stock continues to be offered by a dealer in England. Its four "bandwidths" are actually only one.

RETRO RECEIVER

Shortwave receiver kits were popular during the Eisenhower era, but vanished decades ago. The few that have remained usually have been dubious novelties or regenerative models.

But hold on to your rabbit ears—there is an exception: Ten-Tec's 1254 world band radio at $195.00 or £169.00. Parts quality for this little superheterodyne is excellent, and assembly runs around 24 hours. That's just long enough to be a fun project without getting tiresome.

The 1254 includes 15 station presets, but otherwise is Zen-simple: no keypad, signal-strength indicator, synchronous selectable sideband, elevation rod, LSB/USB settings or adjustable AGC. Tuning increments are 500 Hz for single sideband and 5 kHz for AM mode, plus there's an analog clarifier for tweaking between increments. It includes a 120V AC adaptor—even when purchased from AOR-UK, Ten-Tec's EU vendor.

Phase noise, front-end selectivity, and longwave and mediumwave AM sensitivity are poor. Bandwidth is a respectable 5.6 kHz, and there is worthy ultimate rejection, image rejection, world band sensitivity, blocking, AGC threshold and frequency stability. Dynamic range and first IF rejection are fair, while overall distortion is good—with an external speaker, audio is pleasant. In short, this is a real receiver, not some toy.

The Ten-Tec 1254 brings back the solder smells of yesteryear, and is an accomplishment you can lay your hands on for years to come. And if you confuse a resistor with a capacitor, the manufacturer has an excellent record for patient hand-holding.

The Ten-Tec 1254 is the only world band receiver kit worth considering.

Professional Receivers for 2009

When Only The Best Will Do

Professional receivers are the *ne plus ultra* for conquering tough signals. Unsurprisingly, they also eavesdrop with aplomb on military, civilian and espionage utility signals—homeland security for the home.

Three Groupings

Professional receivers include models easy for direct human operation, "black boxes" with no direct human operation, and a third category: complex for direct human operation.

The first is for personnel, often military, with minimal radio training. As operational simplicity forces performance compromises, these aren't covered here.

Second are "black box" professional receivers with virtually no on-panel controls. They operate remotely or from computers, often at official surveillance facilities, and sell for stratospheric sums—provided they can be found: Some are so hush-hush that even manufacturers' names are aliases. However, consumer-grade black box receivers are evaluated in PASSPORT's "Receivers for PCs."

The final group incorporates all controls on receiver panels, along with top-end features and performance. Detailed in this section, these are the Maserati Quattroportes of receivers.

RX-340 for Digital Broadcasts

Alone among these, the Ten-Tec RX-340 is ready for DRM digital world band broadcasts. Actual DRM reception also requires interfacing with a PC having DRM software (www.drmrx.org).

Find major updates to the 2009 PASSPORT REPORTS at www.passband.com.

First-Rate Antenna Needed

A top-rated, properly erected antenna is a must for any professional receiver. Our test findings and installation tips for wire antennas are in the Radio Database International White Paper, *Evaluation of Popular Outdoor Antennas.* There are also active and passive antenna reviews in PASSPORT REPORTS.

If reception is already being disrupted by nearby electrical noise—even with a good antenna—a fancier receiver might be pointless. Before springing for a pricey new model, try eliminating the source of noise or reducing it by repositioning your antenna. If all else fails, consider a Wellbrook loop antenna—*see* "Active Antennas for 2009."

Static's Entry Points

Harmful static can lay low even the beefiest receiver. These zaps enter either through the power line or an outdoor antenna.

Shutterstock

Professional receivers typically include surge protection. Nevertheless, it helps to plug a serious receiver into an equally serious non-MOV surge arrestor, such as Zero-Surge (www.zerosurge.com) or Brick Wall (www.brickwall.com). We've used probably a dozen ZeroSurges over the past two decades with nary a hiccup or need for replacement.

An outdoor antenna should be fed through a static protector. This is especially so with the Watkins-Johnson WJ-8711A without the 8711/PRE option. Even better is to disconnect the antenna when thunder approaches.

Accessory Improves Audio

Most professional and a few consumer-grade receivers use DSP (digital signal processing) audio. In principle, there is no reason DSP audio quality can't equal that of analog audio, but in practice the tendency is for weak signals and static to sound harsh and tiring.

Helping offset this is recoverable audio, which with tough DX signals tends to be slightly better with DSP professional receivers. This is why these models are not strangers to "DXpeditions," where the most stubborn of radio signals are flushed out.

For world band, the Sherwood SE-3 fidelity-enhancing accessory has been exceptionally helpful with various current and discontinued professional receivers. While it doesn't fundamentally resolve the DSP audio issue, it helps significantly. It also provides exceptional-quality synchronous selectable sideband, a major plus.

Alas, it doesn't work with all receivers—notably the Icom IC-R9500. Other downsides are cost, operating complexity and a BFO that's less stable than those on most professional receivers. Nevertheless, with the WJ-8711A and RX-340 the SE-3 has become practically a must-have accessory.

What's Best?

Icom's pricey IC-R9500—German engineered, Japanese built—wins at stirring our collective juices. It's about as exciting as an F-16 and is priced accordingly, but has a couple of issues that should be dealt with.

Unless and until that happens, most will look to the other two. Among these, the Watkins-Johnson WA-8711A remains the valedictorian, although barely.

The remarkably similar Ten-Tec RX-340 costs less, is readily available, is DRM ready and is quickly serviced. It's the sensible choice in a field of champions.

Tips for Using this Section

Professional receivers are listed in order of suitability for listening to difficult-to-hear world band stations. Important secondary consideration is given to audio fidelity, ergonomics and reception of utility signals. Selling prices are as of when we go to press, and include European VAT where applicable.

Unless otherwise indicated, each model has the following characteristics:

- Digital signal processing, including digital frequency synthesis and display.
- Full coverage of at least the 5–29999 kHz VLF/LF/MF/HF portions of the radio spectrum, encompassing all the long-wave, mediumwave AM and shortwave portions—including all world band frequencies—but no coverage of the standard FM broadcast band (87.5–108 MHz).
- A wide variety of helpful tuning features, including tuning and frequency display in 1 Hz increments.
- Synchronous selectable sideband via high-rejection IF filtering (not lower-rejection phasing), which when properly engineered greatly reduces adjacent-channel interference and fading distortion. On some models this is referred to as "SAM" (synchronous AM). ☞ **ECSS:** Professional models tune to the nearest 1 Hz, allowing the user to use the receiver's single-sideband circuitry to manually phase its BFO (internally generated carrier) with the station's transmitted carrier. Called "ECSS" (exalted-carrier, selectable-sideband) tuning, this can be used with AM-mode signals in lieu of synchronous

selectable sideband. However, in addition to the relative inconvenience of this technique, unlike synchronous detection, which re-phases continually and essentially perfectly, ECSS is always slightly out of phase.

- Proper demodulation of modes used by non-world-band—utility and amateur—shortwave signals. These modes include single sideband (LSB/USB and sometimes ISB) and CW ("Morse code"); also, with suitable ancillary devices, radioteletype (RTTY), frequency shift key (FSK) and radiofax (FAX).
- Meaningful signal-strength indication.
- Illuminated display.
- Superior build quality, robustness and sample-to-sample consistency as compared to consumer-grade tabletop receivers.
- Audio output for recording and micropower (e.g., FM) retransmission.

What PASSPORT's Rating Symbols Mean

Star ratings: ✪✪✪✪✪ is best. Stars reflect overall performance and meaningful features, plus to some extent ergonomics and perceived build quality. Price, appearance, country of manufacture and the like are not taken into account. With professional models there is a strong emphasis on the ability to flush out tough, hard-to-hear signals, as this is usually the main reason these sets are chosen by world band enthusiasts. Nevertheless, to facilitate comparison professional receiver rating standards are similar to those used for tabletop and portable models reviewed elsewhere in PASSPORT REPORTS.

Passport's Choice. *La crème de la crème.* Our test team's personal picks of the litter—models we would buy or have bought for our personal use. Unlike star ratings, these choices are unapologetically subjective.

⊘: No professional model is a bargain or even close, but this indicates that it offers noticeably more performance than its price would suggest.

✪✪✪✪✪ *Passport's Choice*

Watkins-Johnson WJ-8711A

Price (receiver and factory options, FOB factory): *WJ-8711A:* $5,580.00 plus shipping worldwide. *871Y/SEU DSP Speech Enhancement Unit:* $1,200.00. *8711/PRE Sub-Octave Preselector:* $3,977.10. *871Y/DSO1 Digital Signal Output Unit:* $1,150.00. *8711/SPK Internal Speaker:* $171.00 in the United States.

Price (aftermarket options): *Hammond RCBS1900517BK1 steel cabinet/wraparound and 1421A mounting screws and cup washers (as available):* $131.17 in the United States from manufacturer (www.hammondmfg.com/rackrcbs.htm) or Newark Electronics (www.newark.com). *Sherwood SE-3 MK IV accessory:* $750.00 plus shipping worldwide.

Pros: BITE (built-in test equipment) diagnostics and physical layout allow technically qualified users to make most repairs on-site. Users can upgrade receiver performance over time by EPROM replacement. Exceptional overall performance. Unsurpassed reception of feeble world band DX signals, especially when mated to Sherwood SE-3 synchronous selectable sideband device and WJ-871Y/SEU noise-reduction unit (*see* Cons). Unusually effective "ECSS" reception, tuning AM-mode signals as though they were single sideband. Superb reception of non-AM mode "utility" stations. Generally superior audio quality when coupled to Sherwood SE-3 fidelity-enhancing accessory, the W-J speech enhancement unit and a worthy external speaker (*see* Cons). Unparalleled bandwidth flexibility, with no less than 66 outstandingly high-quality bandwidths. Trimmer on back panel allows frequency readout to be user-aligned against a known frequency standard, such as WWV/WWVH or a laboratory device. Extraordinary operational flexibility—virtually every receiver parameter is adjustable. One hundred station presets. Synchronous detection ("SAM," for synchronous AM) reduces selective-fading distortion with world band, mediumwave AM and longwave signals, and functions even on very narrow voice bandwidths (*see* Cons). Rock stable. Built-in preamplifier. Tunable notch filter.

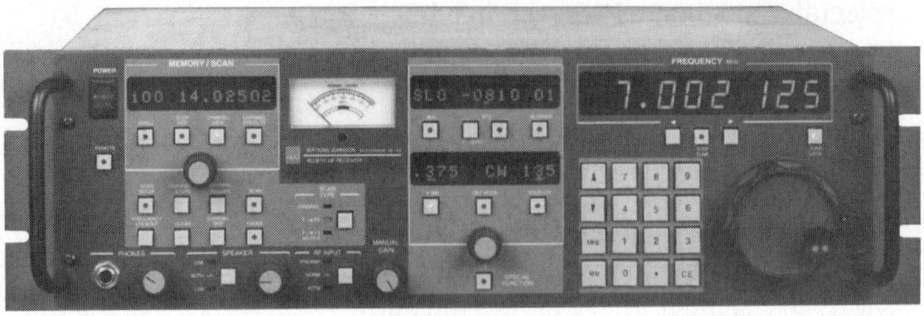

Watkins-Johnson's WJ-8711A is as good as it gets . . . and priced accordingly.

Effective noise blanking. Highly adjustable scanning of both frequency ranges and station presets. Easy-to-read displays. Large tuning knob. Unusually effective medium-wave AM performance. Can be fully and effectively computer and remote controlled. Passband shift (*see* Cons). Numerous outputs for data collection from received signals, as well as ancillary hardware; includes properly configured 455 kHz IF output, which facilitates installation of Sherwood SE-3 accessory, and balanced line outputs (connect to balanced hookup to minimize radiation of digital "buzz"). Remote control and dial-up data collection; Windows control software available from manufacturer. Among the most likely of all world band receivers tested to be able to be retrofitted for eventual reception of digital world band broadcasts. Inboard AC power supply, which runs unusually cool, senses incoming current and automatically adjusts 90–264 VAC, 47–440 Hz—a plus during brownouts or with line voltage or frequency swings. Superior-quality factory service (*see* Cons). Comprehensive and well-written operating manual, packed with technical information and schematic diagrams. Hammond aftermarket cabinet/wraparound exceptionally robust.

Cons: Static crashes and modulation-splash interference sound noticeably harsher than on analog receivers, although this has been improved in latest operating software. Synchronous detection not sideband-selectable, so it can't reduce adjacent-channel interference (remediable by Sherwood SE-3). Basic receiver has mediocre audio in straight AM mode; "ECSS" tuning or synchronous detection, especially with optional speech enhancement unit (W1 noise-reduction setting), alleviates this. Some clipping distortion in single-sideband mode. Complex to operate to full advantage. Circuitry puts out a high degree of digital buzz, relying for the most part on its own panels for electrical shielding; one consequence is that various versions emanate digital buzz through the nonstandard rear-panel audio terminals, as well as through the signal meter and front-panel headphone jack—problem lessened when Sherwood SE-3 used. Antennas with shielded (e.g., coaxial) feedlines less likely to pick up receiver-generated digital "buzz." Passband shift operates only in CW mode. Jekyll-and-Hyde ergonomics: sometimes wonderful, sometimes awful. Front-panel rack "ears" protrude, with the right one getting in the way of the tuning knob; fortunately, ears easily removed. Mediocre front-end selectivity, remediable by 8711/PRE option (with insignificant 1.2 dB insertion loss); e.g. for those living near medium-wave AM transmitters. 871Y/SEU option reduces audio gain and is extremely difficult to install; best to have all desired options factory-installed. Signal-strength indicator in dBm only. No DC power input. Keypad lettering wears off with use; replacement keys available at around $8 each, but minimum parts order is $100. Each receiver built on order (David Shane, 1-800/954-3577), so it can take up to four months for delivery. Factory service can take as much as two months. Cabinet/wraparound extra, available aftermarket from Hammond. Plastic feet have no front elevation and allow receiver to slide around. Available only through U.S. manufacturer, DRS Technologies (www.drs.com); receiver and factory options have been subjected to a number of price increases since 2000.

Verdict: The American-made WJ-8711A is, by a skosh, the ultimate machine for world band DXing when money is no object.

Had there not been digital "buzz," inexcusable at this price—and had there been better audio quality, a tone control, passband shift and synchronous selectable sideband—the '8711A would have been audibly better for program listening. Fortunately, the Sherwood SE-3 accessory remedies virtually all these problems and improves DX reception, to boot; W-J's optional 871Y/SEU complements, rather than competes with, the SE-3 for improving recovered audio.

Overall, the WJ-8711A DSP, properly configured, is as good as it gets. It is exceptionally well suited to demanding connoisseurs with the appropriate financial wherewithal—provided they seek an extreme degree of manual receiver control.

TOP TRIO: PROFESSIONAL RECEIVERS

	Watkins-Johnson WJ-8711A	Icom IC-R9500	Ten-Tec RX-340
Max. Sensitivity/ Noise Floor	0.13 µV Ⓢ/ –136 dBm Ⓔ	0.11 µV Ⓢ/ –136 dBm Ⓔ[1]	0.17 µV Ⓢ/ –130 dBm Ⓔ[8]
Blocking	123 dB Ⓖ	119 dB Ⓖ	109 dB Ⓕ
Shape Factors, voice BWs	1:1.21–1:1.26 Ⓢ	1:1.52–1:1.63 Ⓔ	1:1.15–1:1.33 Ⓢ
Ultimate Rejection	≥80 dB Ⓔ[5]	≥70–80 dB Ⓔ[5]	70 dB Ⓖ
Front-End Selectivity	F/Ⓔ[2]	Ⓔ	Ⓔ
Image Rejection	80 dB Ⓔ	>100 dB Ⓢ	>100 dB Ⓢ
First IF Rejection	—[3]	>100 dB Ⓢ	>100 dB Ⓢ
Dynamic Range/ IP3 (5 kHz)	74 dB Ⓖ/ –18 dBm Ⓔ	100 dB Ⓢ/ +23 dBm Ⓢ	55 dB Ⓟ/ –39 dBm Ⓕ
Dynamic Range/ IP3 (20 kHz)	99 dB Ⓢ/ +20 dBm Ⓢ	110 dB Ⓢ/ +38 dBm Ⓢ	86 dB Ⓖ/ +7 dBm Ⓔ
Phase Noise	115 dBc Ⓖ	134 dBc Ⓢ	113 dBc Ⓖ
AGC Threshold	0.1 µV Ⓟ[7]	0.16 µV Ⓟ[4,7]	0.3 µV Ⓖ[9]
Overall Distortion, sync	8.2% Ⓟ	0.4% Ⓢ	2.6% Ⓖ
Stability	5 Hz Ⓢ	1 Hz Ⓢ	5 Hz Ⓢ
Notch filter depth	58 dB Ⓢ	55 dB Ⓢ[6]	58 dB Ⓢ

IBS Lab Ratings: Ⓢ Superb Ⓔ Excellent Ⓖ Good Fair Ⓟ Poor

(1) Preamp 2 on. Preamp 1 on, 0.2 µV Ⓔ/–130 dBm Ⓔ. Preamp off, 0.7 µV, Ⓕ/–120 dBm, Ⓖ.

(2) Ⓕ standard/Ⓔ with optional preselector.

(3) Adequate, but could not measure precisely.

(4) Preamp 2 on. Preamp 1 on, 0.25 µV Ⓟ. Preamp off, 1.1 µV, Ⓔ.

(5) DSP measurements noise limited.

(6) Automatic notch (ANF). Manually tuned notches (two) 40–65 dB, Ⓔ–Ⓢ.

(7) Ⓟ here not significant relative to overall audible performance.

(8) Preamp on. With preamp off, 0.55 µV, Ⓖ/–122 dBm, Ⓖ.

(9) Preamp on. With preamp off, 1.3 µV, Ⓔ.

✪✪✪✪✪ *Passport's Choice*

Icom IC-R9500

Pricing: *IC-R9500 receiver:* $13,500.00 in the United States. CAD$13,999.00 in Canada. £7,999.95 in the United Kingdom. €11,900.00 in Germany. *UT-122 digital voice decoder:* $199.95 in the United States. CAD$300.00 in Canada. £149.95 in the United Kingdom. €215.00 in Germany. *SP-20 external speaker with four audio cutoff filters:* $249.95 in the United States. CAD$400.00 in Canada. £164.95 in the United Kingdom. €198.00 in Germany.

Pros: No-excuses 5 Hz–3.333 GHz broadband coverage on units sold outside the United States and France (*see* Cons). Large seven-inch (18 cm) TFT color LCD offers numerous screen options and displays—even a screen saver; can also feed an external computer monitor. Versatile spectrum scope (*see* Cons). Stellar dynamic range, image rejection and first-IF rejection—all as good as it gets. Preamplifier for below 30 MHz, plus a second preamp for all tuned frequencies. Exceptional dynamic range allows either preamplifier to be used virtually without introducing overloading (*see* Cons). Excellent sensitivity with either preamp engaged (*see* Cons). Excellent AGC threshold with both preamplifiers off (*see* Cons). Top-drawer DSP bandwidths include three user-selectable pushbutton bandwidths per mode and four roofing filter choices. Gain equalized among roofing filters, with only an unavoidable 3 dB increase in noise floor with the narrowest filter. Bandwidth shape factor adjustable for single-sideband and CW modes. Twin passband tuning (PBT) works in all modes. Worthy AGC includes three adjustable presets that can be further tweaked by a front-panel knob. Excellent front-end selectivity, with half-octave filtering. Automatic notch filter (ANF), simple to use, simultaneously eliminates or greatly reduces several heterodynes. Dual manually tunable notch filters, although scarcely necessary with ANF, act on up to two more heterodynes. Excellent recoverable audio, thanks in part to superb receiver phase noise. Generally excellent audio quality (*see* Cons), with very low overall distortion on all audio frequencies and in all modes; also, excellent built-in speaker, aided by separate bass and treble controls with contours that can be quasi-permanently optimized for each reception mode; also, low-pass audio filter selectable for each mode. Synchronous selectable sideband aids in reducing adjacent-channel interference; also has synchronous double sideband (*see* Cons). Tunes and displays in ultra-precise 1 Hz steps. Superior tuning knob includes moving spinner; also, "click" mode (*see* Cons) for tuning steps. Two built-in recorders; primary has five audio-quality settings (*see* Cons), using internal or external memory; secondary, with pleasant audio, useful for station IDs and addresses (*see* Cons). Over 1,000 presets with alphanumeric tagging for each preset and each bank of presets. Easy-to-program presets store many variables, including selected antenna. Ten VFOs. Excellent ergonomics, including logical menu. Keys have superior tactile response, with feedback "Roger beep" adjustable for volume and pitch. Gibraltar stability, as good as it gets. Fan cooled (*see* Cons). Superb signal-strength indicator reads out in "S" units, dBμ, dBμ (EMF) and dBm; readings, extremely accurate except low-"S", remain constant

Icom's IC-R9500 nudges the gold in price and performance. Yet, it needs software tweaks for its *ne plus ultra* hardware to reach full potential.

D. Zantow

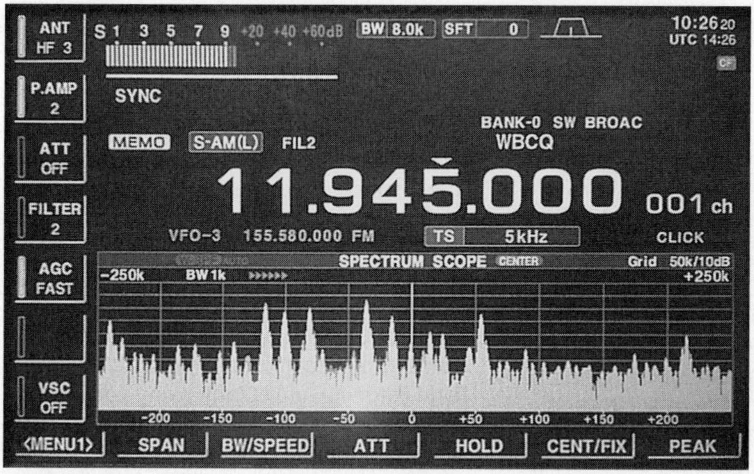

The Icom IC-R9500's sophisticated spectrum scope works well with most signals. But circuit noise produces "grass" along the bottom, which obscures weak signal pips. D. Zantow

regardless of changes in preamplification or attenuation; also, can output to an external analog signal meter. Separate discrimination indicator for FM and FM-wide. Five-step attenuator: 6, 12, 18, 24 and 30 dB. Speech synthesizer. FSK decoder. Ethernet for LAN and firmware updates. USB for external memory, keyboard and ancillary devices. Useful dual-mode noise blanker with adjustable depth and width. Three shortwave antenna inputs, front-panel selectable. Automatic center-tuning selectable for AM, SSB and CW signals; similarly, AFC selectable for FM and FM-wide. Dual clocks display discretely. Line output at appropriate level for audio recording; includes separate optical (TOSLINK) digital audio output (*see* Cons). Five-event on/off timer stores day of week to enhance unattended recording and other turnkey operations. Sleep timer. Excellent FM broadcast performance (*see* Cons). Owner's manual includes schematics and block diagrams (*see* Cons). *Outside United States:* Composite video can be fed to a television receiver.

Cons: Synchronous selectable/double sideband loses lock readily and is mediocre at reducing selective-fading distortion. Lack of suitable IF output, so Sherwood SE-3 device cannot be added to enhance synchronous selectable/double sideband performance. ECSS in lieu of synchronous selectable sideband results in significant audio dropouts. High power consumption by AC mains or DC power. Runs warm-to-hot, even with fan that noisily cycles on and off; in principle, this could result in premature component failure. Neither the noise blanker nor DSP noise reduction particularly helpful. Optical (TOSLINK) digital audio output has distortion in single-sideband modes. Slight rotational delay when tuning knob using "click" option. Some DSP audio harshness with weak signals (S1–S5); also with static and impulse noises. AGC threshold becomes overly sensitive if either preamplifier on, although audible impact not significant. Public versions sold in the United States and France have blocked segments that limit tuning above 30 MHz. Keyboard requires all frequencies to be entered in MHz, complete with decimal. Only three of primary recorder's five quality settings produce decent audio. Secondary recorder's 15-second limit too brief for most uses. Spectrum scope's circuit noise causes "grass" to appears along bottom of spectrum scope, covering up weak signal pips; this greatly diminishes scope's usefulness for DXing; remediable, if clunky, by having the 10.7 MHz IF output feed an external spectrum analyzer. At 44 pounds (20 kg), a challenge for one person to move and needs to be shipped carefully. No front elevation feet, which can make LCD hard to read; easily remediable by user or dealer. FM monaural only. Owner's manual lacks coverage of various operations, has no index and can be hard to follow.

☞ Once, after 12 hours of continuous operation, audio suddenly became "buzzy" and distorted in all modes. This was resolved by switching the set off then back on. It never occurred again.

☞ Firmware: v1.03; future upgrades could resolve some issues encountered during testing.

Verdict: The Icom IC-R9500, easily the costliest receiver tested to date, is in many ways the Mother of Supersets. For example, its dynamic range, image rejection, first IF rejection, stability and overall distortion are nearly off the charts—and most other indicators of performance are superior. Ergonomics are excellent for such a complex device, and robustness appears to be in the same league except for heat.

Yet, synchronous selectable sideband performance is mediocre, and there's not a suitable IF output for a Sherwood SE-3 to resolve it. Even ECSS—manually tuned selectable sideband—isn't an alternative, as that introduces audio dropouts. Were it not for this surprising triple whammy, along with scope limitations, the 'R9500 might well have ranked as PASSPORT's number one choice.

New Options for 2009
DRM Ready

✪✪✪✪✪ ❹ *Passport's Choice*

Ten-Tec RX-340

Pricing: *RX-340:* $4,250.00 in the United States. £2,999.00 in the United Kingdom. *Ten-Tec R9310 oak cabinet:* $259.00 in the United States. *Ten-Tec R9311 oak speaker:* $179.00 in the United States. *Sherwood SE-3 MK IV accessory:* $750.00 plus shipping worldwide.

Pros: BITE (built-in test equipment) diagnostics and physical layout allow technically qualified users to make most repairs on-site. Users can upgrade receiver performance over time by replacing up to three socketed EPROM chips. Superb overall performance, including unsurpassed readability of feeble world band DX signals, especially when mated to the Sherwood SE-3 device; in particular, superlative image and IF rejection, both >100 dB. Few birdies. Audio quality usually worthy when receiver coupled to Sherwood SE-3 accessory and a good external speaker. Average overall distortion in single-sideband mode a low 0.2 percent; in other modes, under 2.7 percent. Exceptional bandwidth flexibility, with no less than 57 outstanding-quality bandwidths having shape factors of 1:1.33 or better; bandwidth distribution exceptionally useful for world band listening and DXing, along with other activities (*see* Cons). Receives digital (DRM) world band broadcasts when connected to PC using DRM software. Tunes and displays accurately in ultra-precise 1 Hz increments. Extraordinary operational flexibility—virtually every receiver parameter is adjustable; e.g., the AGC's various time constants have 118 *million* possible combinations, plus pushbutton AGC "DUMP" to temporarily deactivate AGC (*see* Cons). Worthy front-panel ergonomics, valuable given exceptional degree of manual operation; includes easy-to-read displays (*see* Cons). Also, large, properly weighted rubber-track tuning knob with fixed dimple and Oak Grigsby optical encoder provide superior tuning feel and reliability; tuning knob tension user-adjustable for personalized feel. Attractive front panel. Two hundred station presets, 201 including scratchpad. Synchronous selectable sideband ("SAM," for synchronous AM), reduces selective-fading distortion; also, diminishes or eliminates adjacent-channel interference with world band, mediumwave AM and longwave signals (*see* Cons). Built-in half-octave preselector. Built-in preamplifier (*see* Cons). Adjustable noise blanker, works well in most situations (*see* Cons). Rock stable. Tunable DSP notch filter with exceptional depth of 58 dB (*see* Cons). Passband shift (passband tuning) works exceptionally well (*see* Cons). Unusually effective ECSS reception. Superb reception of "utility" (non-AM mode) stations using wide variety of modes and including fast filters for delay-critical digital modes. Highly adjustable scanning of both frequency ranges and station presets. Fully and effectively computer and remote controlled (*see* Cons). Numerous outputs for

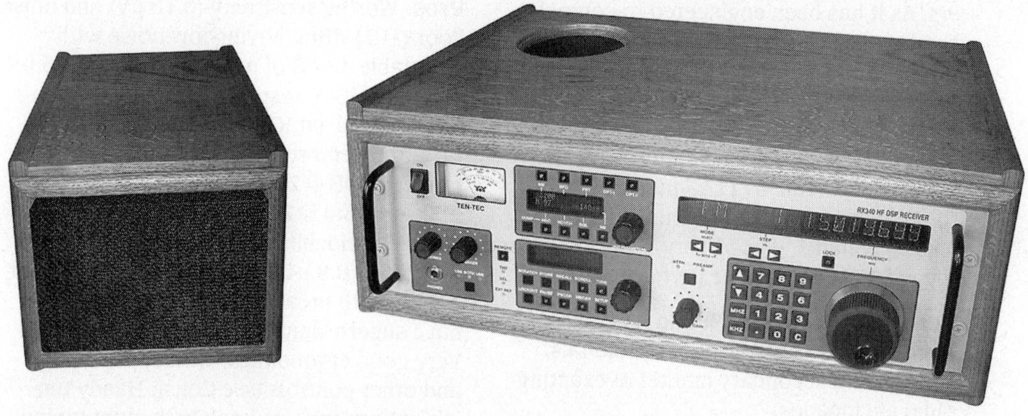

The value champ among professional models is the Ten-Tec RX-340, now in handsome Tennessee oak sheathing.

data collection and ancillary hardware, including properly configured 455 kHz IF output for hookup of Sherwood SE-3 accessory. Remote control and dial-up data collection. Superb analog signal-strength indicator (*see* Cons). Inboard AC power supply automatically adjusts from 90–264 VAC, 48–440 Hz. Superior control over fluorescent display dimming (*see* Cons). Unusually attractive optional oak cabinet and outboard speaker. Repair service at the Tennessee factory reasonably priced by professional standards; turnaround usually two weeks, sometimes up to five. Comprehensive and well-written operating manual, packed with technical information and schematic diagrams.

Cons: DSP microprocessor limitations result in poor dynamic range and fair IP3 at 5 kHz signal spacing. Blocking, phase noise and ultimate rejection fairly good but not professional-caliber. Complex to operate to full advantage. Static crashes sound harsher than on analog receivers. Not all bandwidths available in all modes. Spurious signals may appear around 6 MHz segment (49 meters). When 9–10 dB preamplifier turned on, AGC acts on noise unless IF gain reduced by 10 dB. Notch filter does not work in AM, synchronous selectable sideband or ISB modes. Synchronous selectable sideband loses lock easier than some other models; e.g., if listening to one sideband and there is a strong signal impacting the other sideband, lock can be momentarily lost; remediable by Sherwood SE-3 accessory. Passband shift tunes only plus or minus 2 kHz and does not work in ISB or synchronous selectable sideband modes; remediable with Sherwood SE-3. Audio quality not all it could be; profits from Sherwood SE-3 accessory and quality outboard speaker. Occasional "popping" in audio, notably when synchronous selectable sideband or ISB in use—may be from DSP overload. No AGC off except by holding down DUMP button. Noise blanker not effective at some test locations; for example, various other receivers work better at reducing certain noises. Audio power, especially through headphones, only adequate. With stereo headphones, one channel of headphone audio cuts out near full volume; also, at one position at lower volume. On our unit, occasional minor buzz from internal speaker. Keypad not in telephone format; rather, computer numeric-keypad layout. Some ergonomic clumsiness when going back and forth between station presets and VFO tuning; too, "Aux Parameter" and "Memory Scan" knobs touchy to adjust. Signal-strength indicator illuminated less than display. Digital "buzz" from fluorescent display emits from front of receiver, although not elsewhere. Standard serial cable does not work for computer control; instead, connector DB-25 pins have to be custom wired. No DC power input.

Verdict: The Ten-Tec RX-340 is the value choice among professional-grade receivers. As it has been engineered to compete head-to-head with the Watkins-Johnson WJ8711A, it's hardly surprising that these two models are almost fraternal twins. However, the '340 is less costly, DRM ready, more readily available and more quickly serviced than the '8711A—more attractive, too. When coupled to the Sherwood SE-3 fidelity-enhancing accessory, it is superb for rugged, no-compromise performance.

New Options for 2009: The RX-340, although aimed chiefly at professionals, appeals to a secondary market of exacting radio aficionados.

To date, these folks have had to content themselves with dreary aftermarket cabinets and bare-bones speaker housings. No more. Ten-Tec now offers an oak cabinet and an oak-sheathed outboard speaker as eye-catching options. This makes good sense, as another of Ten-Tec's traditional activities has been the manufacture of cabinets.

✪✪✪✪¼
Japan Radio Co. NRD-630

Pricing: *NRD-630 receiver:* $7,999.95 by special order in the United States. £6,999.95 in the United Kingdom; £5,957.40 plus shipping for export from the United Kingdom.

Japan Radio omitted its customary plug-in daughterboards with the NRD-630. Although this complicates repair, JRC models rarely act up. D. Zantow

Pros: Worthy sensitivity (0.16 µV) and noise floor (–131 dBm) having low noise with selectable 13 dB of preamplification (0.5 µV and –122 dBm, respectively, with preamp off). Dual 32-bit ICs. Excellent pseudo-octave front-end selectivity. Superior dynamic range (95 dB @ 20 kHz, 75 dB @ 5 kHz) and IP3 (+14 dBm @ 20 kHz, –16 dBm @ 5 kHz). Excellent blocking (129 dB). Superb AGC threshold (0.8 µV) with preamplifier on (fair, 3.6 µV, with preamp off). All bandwidths have superb shape factors (1:1.2 to 1:1.4). Very good ergonomics, with superior keys and other controls (*see* Cons). Handy tuning options include knob with eight tuning steps, keypad, up/down slewing with four steps, signal-seek scanning, and 300 tunable/scannable presets. Selectable pulse rate for tuning knob's encoder. Weighted tuning knob, among the best, has speed dimple. Tunes and displays in ultra-precise 1 Hz increments. Receiver Incremental Tuning (ΔF), tunes plus or minus 200 Hz. Helpful four-step display/panel dimmer. Stunning image rejection >110 dB. Superb first IF rejection (96 dB). Limited digital hash. Two selectable AGC decay settings, plus off, usually work well (*see* Cons). Passband tuning, performs nicely. Two-step (10/20 dB) attenuator. Two squelch modes. OCXO provides stability of <5 Hz. Superb overall distortion in single-sideband modes (≤0.5%) and in AM mode (≤1%) above 400 Hz AF (*see* Cons). Top-notch analog signal-strength indicator, also displays audio level (*see* Cons). Noise blanker, adequate for most situations. ISB mode. BITE (built-in test equipment) diagnostics. Cool operation, with quiet inboard switching power supply. Three balanced isolated audio line outputs (line, plus two for ISB). Button locks either tuning knob or all controls. Separate RS-232 and RS-423A computer ports. Can operate from 24V DC ship's power (*see* Cons). Automatic switchover from AC to/from DC. Instruction manual includes full schematics (*see* Cons).

Cons: Only six fixed DSP bandwidths, of which three—measuring 2.5, 3 and 6 kHz—are for voice. No provision for adding bandwidths. Ultimate rejection of 60 dB, although noise limited, uninspiring. Harsh audio quality, especially with static. Lacks

The NRD-630 is Japan Radio's latest DSP offering. Technologically advanced, it retains the ruggedness, superior ergonomics and silky feel that are JRC hallmarks.

D. Zantow

sophisticated adjustment of AGC attack, hang and decay times. AGC attack distortion with some single-sideband signals. No synchronous selectable sideband, although ECSS works well. Single-function noise blanker, no notch filtering, and generally deficient in DSP adjustment of audio and related variables. No motherboard or slide-in daughterboards, unlike past JRC premium models. No feet. No standard or optional cabinet. Touchy controls. PBT control lacks center detent. DSP overloading occasionally causes artifacts with strong signals. Overall distortion in AM mode degrades to 10% below 400 Hz AF. Keyboard occasionally intermittent. Poor internal speaker and no optional external speaker. Signal-strength indicator lacks illumination and proper markings. Nonstandard N-type antenna connector. Nonstandard AC and DC input jacks. Audio line outputs use DB-25 computer connector. No tension adjustment on tuning knob. Lacks UL, CE or CSA certification, which limits availability in some parts of the world. Does not operate from ~12V DC. Skimpy instruction manual lacks information on such relevant subjects as computer control and servicing.

Verdict: Superbly constructed and tank-tough, Japan Radio's new NRD-630 is claimed to be a "marine training radio," according to the manufacturer. It boasts the sort of first-rate ergonomics and feel that's long been associated with Japan Radio, even though it lacks the preferred motherboard/daughterboards configuration. It is a pleasure simply to sit down and manipulate its controls, which bespeak quality from another and more fastidious era.

Two professional models are almost identical—yet, one costs less.

Nearly all characteristics of its radio performance are top-notch, and its built-in scanner is unusually flexible. However, DSP receivers tend to have audio that is relatively abrasive and fatiguing, especially with static. Even though the '630's DSP is powerful and new, its audio is even more harsh and tiring than with some other DSP models. DSP artifacts and intrusive bugs further detract.

The NRD-630 reflects Japan Radio's legendary obsession with hardware quality. But even though the circuit design is relatively advanced, its firmware and software have yet to take full advantage of the hardware's considerable potential.

The PASSPORT *professional-model review team consists of David Zantow, with David Walcutt; also, Tony Jones, Lawrence Magne, Chuck Rippel and George Zeller. Laboratory measurements by J. Robert Sherwood.*

Receivers for PCs

Today's Best Is Italiano

Most folks prefer knobs and keys to flush out signals, but not all. Growing ranks of exacting radio enthusiasts prefer PC-controlled boxes, especially as tabletop choices diminish.

Each year sees real improvement, and 2009 is no exception. The Microtelecom Perseus is to some extent the best receiver of any sort we have ever tested, price be damned. If development continues as it has thus far, it has the potential to be a five-star champ. Even now, it's close.

Antenna Placement Crucial

Like a good marriage, mating a receiver with a PC adds new dimensions. For example, signals can be readily monitored from afar, using PC-controlled receivers in the field.

Yet, this synergy can be offset by drawbacks, such as hardware complications, software glitches and instability.

Signal disruption, too, by electrical noise from PC monitors, cables and so on. Solution: antenna location, with outdoor placement being best and proximate being worst.

This year PC receivers have finally come into their own.

Digital Broadcasts

Digital Radio Mondiale (DRM) has yet to catch on, but ongoing tests in Alaska may lead to success with domestic and regional shortwave broadcasts.

DRM ready receivers can process DRM broadcasts. These require separately purchased DRM software and, eventually, software updates. Slightly handier are radios with *DRM reception*, where you can hear DRM with no additional software or hardware—just an everyday PC.

Software Defined Receivers

PC receivers are increasingly software defined—SDR. There are a number of advantages to this, although pleasant audio isn't one.

Unlike conventional receivers, SDRs can be updated online with fresh software. Some manufacturers take this quite seriously and do frequent updates, while others are more conservative. But the capacity to update, usually for free, is a major plus.

Operating Systems

PASSPORT REPORTS' testing is done with Windows XP-Pro and XP-Home, as both are globally popular. New PC receivers now work with Windows Vista, but approach with caution unless drivers are certified for Windows Vista. If you're using Mac or Linux, check receiver manufacturers' websites for acceptable operating systems.

For long-term ownership keep in mind that once a receiver becomes discontinued, it eventually may not work to full advantage—or at all—with new or revised computer operating systems. This can be

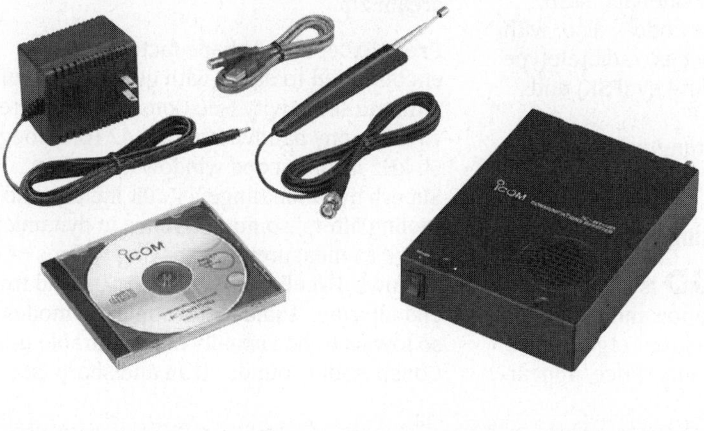

Icom's IC-PCR1500. Kindred IC-R1500 also doubles as a standalone receiver.

overcome by retaining a legacy OS; for example, on a dedicated disk partition or a veteran PC.

No matter how carefully a PC-controlled receiver is tested, its performance depends partly on your computer's configuration—even an operating system's service pack can alter outcomes. To avoid an unwelcome surprise, best bet is to purchase on a returnable basis.

Tips for Using This Section

Receivers are listed in order of suitability for listening to difficult-to-hear world band stations; important secondary consideration is given to audio fidelity, ergonomics and perceived build quality. Street selling prices are cited, including British VAT/GST where applicable. Prices vary, so take them as the general guide they are meant to be.

Unless otherwise stated, all PC-controlled models have the following characteristics. *See* Worldly Words for terminology.

- Digital frequency synthesis and display.
- Full coverage of at least the 155–29999 kHz longwave, mediumwave AM and shortwave spectra—including all world band frequencies—but no coverage of the dominant FM broadcast band (87.5–108 MHz). Models designed for sale in certain countries have reduced shortwave tuning ranges.
- A wide variety of helpful tuning features.
- No synchronous selectable sideband.
- Proper demodulation of modes used by non-world-band shortwave signals. These modes include single sideband (LSB/USB) and CW ("Morse code"); also, with suitable ancillary devices, radioteletype (RTTY), frequency shift key (FSK) and radiofax (FAX).
- Meaningful signal-strength indication.

What Passport's Rating Symbols Mean

Star ratings: ✪✪✪✪✪ is best. Stars reflect overall performance and meaningful features, plus to some extent ergonomics and perceived build quality. Price, appearance, country of manufacture and the like are not taken into account. To facilitate comparison, rating standards are similar to those used for tabletop, professional and portable models reviewed elsewhere in this Passport Reports. PC receivers as a class have inherent hassles and bonuses; we don't attempt to judge whether this makes them "better" or "worse" than comparable conventional tabletop or professional receivers, so merely the fact they are PC-controlled is not reflected in the star ratings.

Passport's Choice. *La crème de la crème.* Our test team's personal picks of the litter—models we would buy or have bought for our personal use. Unlike star ratings, these choices are unapologetically subjective.

¢: A relative bargain, with decidedly more performance than the price would suggest.

New for 2009 DRM Ready

✪✪✪✪¾ *Passport's Choice*

Microtelecom Perseus

Pricing: *Receiver:* $1,299.95 in the United States. £649.95 in the United Kingdom. €825.00 in Germany. *VHF, UHF and SHF converters:* TBA in 2009. *Aftermarket Griffin PowerMate tuning knob:* $45.00 in the United States. CAD$59.95 in Canada. £29.95 in the United Kingdom. €59.00 in Germany. *Virtual Audio Cable:* $20.00 in Russia, $30.00 elsewhere from software.muzychenko.net/eng/vac.html. *Dream software:* Free from pessoal.onda.com.br/rjamorim/dream.zip.

Pros: Exceptional shape factors—best encountered to date—with generally superb ultimate selectivity (*see* Cons). User creates virtually any bandwidth from 42 Hz through 50 kHz in sub-scope window (*see* Cons). Superb dynamic range; circuit includes no roofing filters, so no difference in dynamic range as measurement spacing widens or narrows. Excellent switchable 10-band front end filtering. Audio distortion in all modes so low as to be virtually unmeasurable (*see* Cons). Audio sounds clean and sharp (*see*

Cons). Superior recovered audio aids faint-signal intelligibility. No local oscillator, so no "birdies." No first-IF, so no intrusion of unwanted signals via first IF. Superb image rejection and phase noise. Excellent switchable front-end selectivity. Unlike some other computer-controlled DSP radios, AGC does not run on some wider IF bandwidth, so a very strong signal can be just outside the passband and not desensitize the receiver. Excellent blocking also minimizes desensitization. AGC has selectable fast, medium and slow decay times, plus off (*see* Cons). SpkRej reduces pulse noise by emulating the AGC behavior of an analog receiver; this reduces the digital AGC's reaction to very short, fast impulse noise spikes, a problem with most DSP radios since 2003; a secondary result is that DSP audio harshness is lessened. 10, 20, 30 dB attenuator. Software upgrade for 2009 should include user-adjustable AGC threshold to act much like reducing RF gain in an analog receiver. Excellent double-sideband synchronous detector (SAM) holds lock unusually well. Passband tuning (PBT), which adjusts in sub-spectrum display, upgrades synchronous detector into continuously tuned synchronous selectable sideband; superior ECSS, too. Excellent and narrow 70 dB manual and tunable notch filter (*see* Cons). Two continuously variable noise-attenuation features: AF noise reduction (NR), which performs very well, and noise blanker with two widths (*see* Cons). Frequency coverage 10 kHz to 30 MHz (useable at reduced specification to 40 MHz). Mouse wheel performs well as tuning thumbwheel; has several selectable tuning steps. Up/down slewing with many selectable steps via GUI. Displays and tunes in ultra-precise 1 Hz increments; calibrate function allows for spot-on accuracy of frequency display. Switchable dithering ameliorates intrusion from spurious signal (IMD); performs as designed at high signal levels as shown on the PC spectrum display when tested in the lab; however, unlike on analog receivers, IMD relatively constant regardless of signal level and generally below receiver noise level, so dithering impact difficult to perceive in real-world listening (*see* Cons). Superb, accurate spectrum scope of

The new Microtelecom Perseus raises the bar for software defined receivers. In some respects it outperforms any other receiver—regardless of type—tested to date. D. Zantow

professional lab quality; displays 100, 200, 400 or 800 kHz slices. Spectrum record function stores 5 or 10 minute blocks in real time to computer's hard drive (*see* Cons); with sufficient microprocessor power, wideband spectrum record/playback up to 2 MS/s with alias image rejection >110 dB in 1600 kHz bandwidth. Straightforward installation of USB driver and software. Switchable preamplifier (*see* Cons). Signal strength indicator of professional lab caliber; reads with nigh-perfect accuracy in dBm and "S" units, and displays either peak or RMS readings. Generally worthy ergonomics. Handy audio mute button. DRM ready (*see* Cons); DRM performs well. Squelch control. Three integrated broadcast station databases, including one created by user; any can appear on screen during bandscanning (*see* Cons). Solid, sensible construction. Doesn't overheat. Includes SO-239 to BNC adaptor. Multivoltage German AC adaptor (*see* Cons) includes a pair of power plugs for two-pin European and American wall sockets.

Pros (tuning knob): Aftermarket Griffin PowerMate allows for genuine hands-on knob tuning (*see* Cons). Includes selectable tuning rates and free online software upgrades. (Microsoft .NET Framework 2.0 required.)

Cons: Audio harsh and aurally fatiguing partly because, with such tight bandwidth shape factors, noise on edge of passband is exaggerated (*see* Pros); however, for 2009 manufacturer plans to add user control over shape factors to select between extreme selectivity and reduced audio harshness. Some brief audio dropouts, especially when spectrum scope in use; seems largely independent of PC's microprocessor rating. No tone/EQ controls. Sensitivity generally only fair (*see* first ☞). No conventional station presets; instead, relies on inboard station databases. No scanning. Calls for PC having 2.0 USB port and quad or at least dual core Pentium processor, especially if spectrum scope used at maximum (800 kHz) width; useable with lesser PC configurations, but *caveat emptor*. Some GUI icons small and hard to see; large, bright high-res PC display helps. Stability, although good, not fully equal to genre potential. AC adaptor's output plug readily comes loose from receiver. Power cannot be taken from PC's USB port. Only seven bandwidth presets. Preamplifier provides only 2 dB gain, virtually imperceptible (*see* first ☞). GUI frequency display in unusual XX.XXXxxx MHz format. Keyed frequency entry somewhat cumbersome. No clock or timer functions, so, *i.a.*, spectrum recorder cannot be timed to cycle on/off automatically. Spectrum recorder and DRM require Virtual Audio Cable software, not included; DRM also requires Dream freeware, not included. DRM Software Radio (drmrx.org) not supported. No built-in facility for audio recording of single program; requires separate computer software. No automatic notch filter, much less one that acts on multiple heterodynes—unusual omission for receiver of this type. Variable noise blanker only marginally effective. No quick access to world band segments. AGC threshold currently poor (*see* Pros). Occasional minor acoustic artifacts—thumps—on leading edge of an AGC attack, and at other times for reason(s) we were unable to nail down. AGC attack and hang times not adjustable. AGC decay rates not adjustable beyond three factory settings. Dithering of no practical use during hands-on testing, in part because receiver already has so little IMD (*see* Pros). Multivoltage AC adaptor uses switch mode that emits some hash; not an issue with outdoor antenna, but could be audible with proximate indoor antenna (replacement 5V DC ≥1A *regulated* adaptor should resolve this, but ensure polarity before connecting; 117V AC possibilities include $9.95 Jameco #1919220 or similar, but avoid 6V output or damage is likely). Skimpy PDF owners manual.

Cons (tuning knob): Some, but not all, of our Windows XP systems periodically did not recognize aftermarket Griffin PowerMate knob at bootup; remediable only by cumbersome software uninstall and reinstall. Knob has minor wobble and rotational play, and does not turn as smoothly as it could—all minor points. Possible alternatives, not tested, include Contour Designs Shuttle Xpress or 3D Connexion (Logitech) Space Navigator.

☞ Nominal inboard preamplifier provides only 2 dB gain, but it switches something in the A/D converter, not the front end. However, the front end has an amplifier of about 7 dB gain, plus a transformer with about 6 dB gain, bringing always-on true preamplification to about 13 dB. With high-performance antennas, this provides adequate sensitivity below around 16 MHz, but outboard preamplifier may be needed above 20 MHz and would be helpful above 24 MHz in an electrically quiet environment even with a great antenna. With a lesser antenna, preamplifier likely to be appreciated throughout the shortwave spectrum.

☞ Tested software v1.1b, then a later beta; firmware v1.0. Upgrades have been free thus far; however, manufacturer decided only at the last moment not to charge for a recent update, so who knows what future policy will be.

☞ Winrad (v1.31 tested) is open-source freeware that can replace Perseus' OEM software. Compared to what already comes with the Perseus, it omits a number of functions, is less user-friendly and its GUI layout is inferior. Stick with what Perseus provides.

Verdict: Microtelecom's new Perseus is the hands-down champ among today's software defined receivers. Its overall performance is most impressive and improves with each software revision. Bonuses include a superior spectrum display and DRM setup.

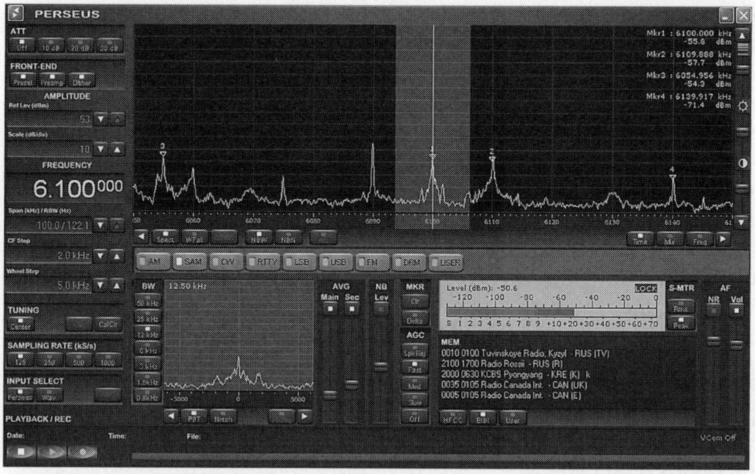

Perseus' screen acts as information central, but it is dark with smallish icons. Best is to use a large, bright display with high resolution. High refresh rate doesn't hurt, either. D. Zantow

Still, this radio freak's nitro burner needs more tweaking if it is to shine for commercial and high-end consumer applications. If and when that takes place, the Perseus will have become a historic benchmark in the evolving success of PC-controlled receivers.

Evaluation of New Model: The compact Microtelecom Perseus receiver is made in Italy by an independent firm that seems to have good rapport with AOR-Japan. Frequency coverage is 10 kHz through 30 MHz with reduced performance to 40 MHz, while converters are being engineered to extend this into the SHF spectrum.

Even though the receiver is automatically switched on and off by the PC—there's no separate power control—it cannot accept power from a PC's USB port. Instead, it relies on a German multivoltage AC adaptor that outputs 5V DC at one amp. The adaptor is switch mode, so it radiates some RF hash. This isn't picked up by an outdoor antenna, but a substitute adaptor may be appropriate with a proximate indoor antenna.

More Is Better

Minimum PC requirements are, in addition to Windows 2000, XP or Vista and a 2.0 USB port: 2 GHz Pentium 4 with 512 MB of memory for sampling rates of 125, 250, 500 KS/s; or 2.5 GHz Dual-Core with 512 MB of memory for 1000 KS/s sampling rate (100 kHz, 200 kHz, 400 kHz and 800 kHz spectrum slices). Some screen icons are small and dark, so a large, bright high-res display is also desirable.

Various test configurations indicate the obvious: The faster the processor and greater the memory, the better the receiver performs. Viewed at the other extreme, the Perseus sometimes functions passably with slightly substandard PCs, provided the spectrum scope's 800 kHz rate is not used.

All that having been said, there was the occasional freeze and performance quirk during testing with XP, and a couple of additional glitches have been reported with Vista; these should continue to diminish thanks to ongoing debugging. As always with software, the devil lies in the details, so it may help to regularly use proven pooper-scoopers like WinUtilities.

Yeoman Ergonomics

For setup, the first step is to install a USB driver from the included CD. Next comes Perseus software, which except for some setup data is not installed in Windows' registry but, rather, loads into a directory and runs from there.

Setup doesn't get any easier than this. However, if the USB port is changed, then Windows won't recognize Perseus and you'll have to reinstall.

Once fired up, Perseus' operation is generally ergonomic. The mouse wheel serves as a defacto tuning knob with selectable tuning steps of 1, 10 and 100 Hz, plus 1, 5, 9, 10, 12.5 and 25 KHz. For bandscanning this is supplemented by on-screen slewing with steps of 1, 2, 5, 10, 20, 25, 50, 100, 200, 400 and 500 KHz and 1 MHz. An outboard Griffin aftermarket tuning knob is even better, although it doesn't work on all Windows configurations that otherwise meet manufacturer's requirements.

Still, the Perseus misses a couple of beats. There is no scanning, and there are no normal station presets such as are found on most other world band radios with digital tuning. Instead, there are up to three on-screen station databases—one user-defined—that display active stations as the receiver is tuned. The databases are a welcome feature in their own right, but no substitute for easily accessed presets.

User friendliness also sags with direct keyboard entry. It calls for bringing up a sub-window, then clicking again to ensure the cursor is properly located. Only then can the keyboard or virtual keypad be used to enter a frequency, in kilohertz. Hopefully, software revisions will simplify this.

Generally Outstanding Performance

Seven user-defined bandwidths range from 42 Hz to 50 kHz. Skirt selectivity is razor sharp—more so than with any other receiver we've tested thus far—and ultimate selectivity is excellent-to-superb.

The first-rate synchronous detector almost never loses lock. Native, it is double sideband, which can profoundly reduce selective fading distortion with fringe mediumwave AM stations around and after dusk. More important for world band, when the sync is used in conjunction with passband tuning (PBT) it morphs into synchronous selectable sideband. Another plus: PBT is continuously tunable for the best mix of audio response and adjacent-channel rejection. And if all that is not enough, "stick shift" ECSS performs unusually well as a fallback.

Taken together, the Perseus' extreme selectivity and exceptional synchronous selectable sideband offer the best-yet arsenal against adjacent interference. Configured and operated properly, these two characteristics can turn some woefully hammered signals into useful listening, like resurrection from the dead.

Audio is akin to the class valedictorian who throws spitballs. On one hand, it is clean and distortion-free—more so, in fact, than any other model we've tested to date. And, to warm the heart of any faint-signal DXer, recovered audio is superior.

But audio is also in the DSP tradition—harsh and fatiguing for long listening sessions—compounded by aural artifacts from the extreme skirt selectivity. This isn't improved by the lack of any sort of tone control or EQ.

However, SpkRej helps by reducing pulse noise through emulating the AGC behavior of an analog receiver. This keeps the digital AGC from reacting to very short, fast impulse noise spikes. A fringe benefit is that SpkRej also reduces DSP audio harshness, but there's a downside: less audio sharpness.

Even though measured sensitivity is only okay, with a high-performance outdoor antenna even weak signals chug in nicely below around 20 MHz. Above that a preamp of, say, 9–12 dB would have been helpful, but the Perseus' preamp boosts by only a pitiful 2 dB.

Image rejection is superb. Thanks in part to DSP design, dynamic range also is superb and does not vary with signal spacing. Again thanks to that design, there are no birdies, and IMD spurious signals are so weak as to be meaningless—plus there is dithering that's effective in attenuating whatever IMD might be encountered. And because there is no first IF, there isn't and cannot be a problem with intrusion of unwanted signals via first IF.

Unlike many other SDR receivers, the Perseus boasts real half-octave front-end selectivity. This is about as good as it gets to minimize the possibility of superpower

NUMBERS: TOP PC RECEIVERS

	Microtelecom Perseus	**WiNRADiO G303i (G313i)**	**Ten-Tec RX-320D**
Sensitivity, World Band	0.7–0.9 μV Ⓕ	0.21 μV Ⓔ (0.3 μV Ⓔ)	0.31–0.7 μV Ⓔ-Ⓕ[10]
Noise Floor, World Band	–118 to –121 dBm Ⓕ-Ⓖ	–130 dBm Ⓔ (–126 dBm Ⓖ)	–126 to –119 dBm Ⓖ-Ⓕ[11]
Blocking	125 dB Ⓔ	120 dB Ⓖ (116 dB Ⓖ)	>146 dB Ⓢ
Shape Factors, voice BWs	1:1.1–1:1.2 Ⓢ	1:1.6 Ⓔ–1:2.4 Ⓖ (1:1.7 Ⓔ–1:2.4 Ⓖ)	n/a[12]
Ultimate Rejection	85–90 dB Ⓔ-Ⓢ[1]	70 dB Ⓖ (75 dB Ⓔ)	60 dB Ⓖ
Front-End Selectivity	Ⓔ	Ⓖ (Ⓕ)	Ⓕ
Image Rejection	90 dB Ⓢ	85 dB Ⓔ (75 dB Ⓔ)	60 dB Ⓖ
First IF Rejection	n/a[2]	52 dB Ⓕ (51 dB Ⓕ)	60 dB Ⓖ
Dynamic Range/ IP3 (5 kHz)	99 dB Ⓢ[3] ([4])	45 dB Ⓟ/–62 dBm Ⓟ (45 dB Ⓟ/–62 dBm Ⓟ)	n/a[12]
Dynamic Range/ IP3 (20 kHz)	99 dB Ⓢ[3] ([4])	90 dB Ⓔ/+5 dBm Ⓔ (85 dB Ⓖ/+2 dBm Ⓔ)	n/a[12]
Phase Noise	147 dBc Ⓢ	124 dBc Ⓔ[7] (120 dBc Ⓔ)	106 dBc Ⓕ
AGC Threshold	0.10 μV Ⓟ[5]	2.7–8.0 μV Ⓖ-Ⓟ (18 μV Ⓟ[8])	4.0 μV Ⓕ
Overall Distortion, voice	<0.1% Ⓢ[6]	<1.0% Ⓢ (<1.0% Ⓢ[9])	<1% Ⓢ
Stability	75 Hz Ⓖ	5 Hz, Ⓢ (10 Hz Ⓔ)	80 Hz, Ⓖ
Notch filter depth	70 dB Ⓢ	n/a (30 dB Ⓖ)	n/a

IBS Lab Ratings: Ⓢ Superb Ⓔ Excellent Ⓖ Good Ⓕ Fair Ⓟ Poor

(1) Close-in measurement noise limited.

(2) Receiver has no first IF.

(3) Because of its DSP design, DR does not change with signal spacing.

(4) IP3 is a figure of merit for a device like an amplifier or a mixer, and an analog receiver generally has distortion characteristics similar to those of an amplifier. When a radio is mostly DSP with little analog gain, there is no correlation between signal level and distortion, so an intercept point is meaningless.

(5) Preamp on. With preamp off 0.15 Ⓟ. Forthcoming software upgrade nominally to include adjustable AGC threshold.

(6) Distortion extremely low, actually measuring distortion of test equipment.

(7) Worse at close-in measurement.

(8) 0.3 μV Ⓖ with AVC enabled at –3 dB.

(9) See writeup, Cons: DSP audio.

(10) Excellent 60 meters (5 MHz) and up.

(11) Good 60 meters (5 MHz) and up.

(12) Could not measure accurately because of synthesizer noise and spurious signals, but appears very good.

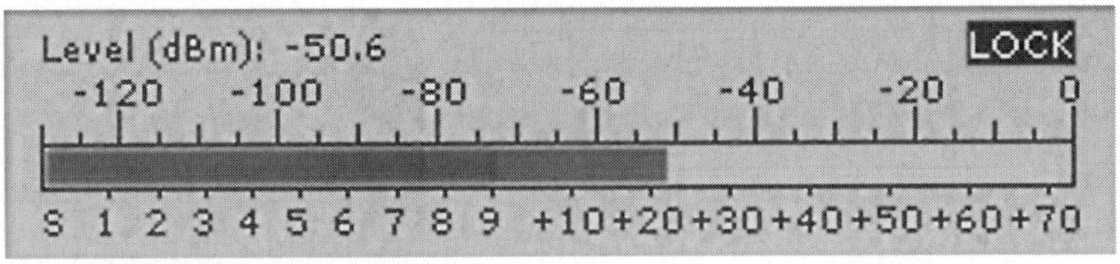

The Perseus signal strength indicator is the best we've seen.

D. Zantow

signals intruding in other parts of the radio spectrum; for example, local mediumwave AM signals "ghosting" into the shortwave spectrum.

AGC user control is consumer, rather than professional, grade. Decay timing can be set to slow, medium, fast or off, but there's no way to change any of these factory-defined times. There's no control over attack or hang times, either, although Perseus is implementing user-selectable AGC threshold—a plus, given that the existing fixed threshold measures as poor in our lab.

AGC performance nonetheless is good except for occasional minor acoustic artifacts—thumps—on the leading edge of an AGC attack.

Local electrical noises are an increasing problem worldwide, what with less interest by regulatory agencies combined with exponential increases in electrically noisy devices. This puts the coping onus on the receiver and antenna, and indeed the Perseus has not one but fully two distinct methods to reduce local electrical noise. Both are continuously adjustable.

Noise reduction (NR) doesn't disappoint, sometimes improving audio recovery by leaps and bounds even when signals are awash in local noise. However, the piper must be paid: NR adds a wooshy hollow "tube" sound that becomes wearisome. Alas, the other noise feature, a blanker (NB), is of marginal utility.

The signal-strength indicator is worthy of an award. It has a horizontal bar with dBm and "S" unit readings, and displays either as RMS or peak. Accuracy is nigh perfect, the best we've ever laid eyes on.

Also top drawer is the manually variable notch filter, which is sharp and very deep. However, this sort of post-2000 receiver should also have automatic notching of multiple heterodynes—it doesn't.

Superior DRM

Digital Radio Mondiale (DRM) may not yet have caught on, but it might ultimately work out for domestic and regional shortwave broadcasts.

The Perseus is unusually well prepared. It includes inboard DRM reception—once the user obtains and installs Dream freeware and Virtual Audio Cable software; DRM Software Radio (drmrx.org), however, is not supported. Driver qt-mt230nc.dll (prdownloads.sourceforge.net/netclipboard/qt-mt230nc.dll?download) is then added to Dream's program directory.

Of course, it would have been less of a hassle had Perseus included all necessary software on a CD that could be autoloaded. Although Dream offers no way to adjust input volume or metering, the end result is that DRM performance is as good as we've encountered.

Superb Recording Spectrum Display

The FFT (fast Fourier transform) spectrum display borders on perfection—fully equal to professional standalone spectrum analyzers used in laboratories—and is manifestly useful. It boasts spectrum slices of 100, 200, 400 or 800 kHz, and there are options and adjustments aplenty.

However, the larger the spectrum slice, the greater the CPU horsepower that's required. Too, periodic real-time adjustment of the amount of averaging helps smooth the display and reduce broadband noise on weak signals.

The Perseus can record up to 800 kHz of visually displayed radio spectrum activity for later playback in real time. Listening to the playback is like tuning around live: The receiver's mode, bandwidth and other variables can be changed exactly—just as if you were in some Twilight Zone time warp.

Playback performance is excellent once Virtual Audio Cable software has been installed, but it does eat up hard drive space like a goat. Alas, there is no event timer for the spectrum recorder or anything else, so turnkey operation is out of the question. Indeed, the Perseus has no clock or timer of any sort—a puzzling omission, especially with this sort of technology. There's also no way to record a single broadcast except by installing aftermarket software onto the PC.

The Microtelecom Perseus, warts and all, is the best SDR receiver we've tested and is sometimes brilliant. As the receiver is software defined, there may yet be improvements that could transform it into a benchmark receiver.

DRM Ready

✪✪✪✪¼

WiNRADiO G303i, WiNRADiO G303i-PD/P, WiNRADiO G303e, WiNRADiO G303e-PD/P

Pricing: *G303i:* $449.95 in the United States. £319.95 in the United Kingdom. €698.00 in Germany. *G303i-PD/P:* $549.95 in the United States. CAD$678.97 in Canada. £369.95 in the United Kingdom. €698.00 in Germany. *G303e (external, not tested):* $549.95 in the United States. £379.95 in the United Kingdom. €659.00 in Germany *G303e-PD/P (external, not tested):* $699.95 in the United States. £439.95 in the United Kingdom. €759.00 in Germany. *DRM software:* $49.95 worldwide from www.winradio.com/home/download-drm.htm.

Pros: Plug and play aids setup. Once receiver is installed, the included software loads without problem; software uses open-source code, which allows for development of third-party software. With optional software, receives digital (DRM) world band and other broadcasts; DRM software

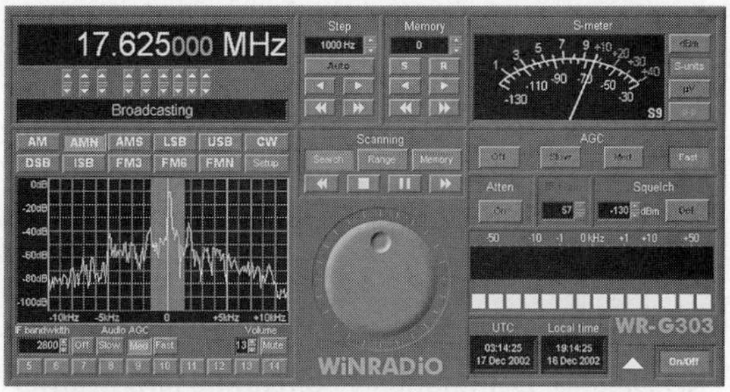

WiNRADiO G303's performance isn't much behind best-rated models, but it is priced considerably lower.

distributed by WiNRADiO, so odds are good for successful installation and performance. Superb stability. Tunes and displays in ultra-precise 1 Hz increments. A thousand station presets, which can be clustered into any of 16 groups (*see* Cons—Other). Excellent shape factors (1:1.6, 1:1.8) for 5.0 kHz and 3.2 kHz bandwidths aid selectivity/adjacent-channel rejection; 1.8 kHz bandwidth measures with good shape factor (1:2.3); many additional bandwidths available in the PD/P version, and perform similarly. Excellent shortwave sensitivity (0.21 µV)/noise floor (–130 dBm), good mediumwave AM and longwave sensitivity (0.4 µV)/noise floor (–125 dBm). Potentially excellent audio quality (see below). Excellent dynamic range (90 dB) and third-order intercept point (+5 dBm) at 20 kHz signal spacing (*see* Cons—AGC/AVC). Phase noise excellent (*see* Cons—AGC/AVC). Image rejection excellent. Spurious signals essentially absent. Screen, and operation in general, unusually pleasant and intuitive. Single-sideband performance generally excellent with strong signals (*see* Cons—AGC/AVC). AGC fast, medium, slow and off. Spectrum display shows real-time signal activity, performs commendably and in particular provides signal strength readings to within plus or minus 3 dB. Spectrum scope sweeps between two user-chosen frequencies, displays the output while receiver mutes, then a mouse click can select a desired "peak"; it works quickly and well, and when the step size is small (e.g., 1 kHz) resolution is excellent and quite useful, resolving signals having as little as 350 Hz separation. Large signal-strength indicator highly accurate, as good as we've ever tested; displays both as digitally and as a digitized "analog meter"; reads out in "S" units, dBm or microvolts. Two easy-to-read on-screen clocks for World Time and local time, display seconds numerically, as well as date. Superior, timely and free factory assistance via email, seemingly throughout the week. *G303i-PD/P (professional demodulation):* Continuously adjustable bandwidths from 1Hz to 15 kHz (single sideband/ECSS 1 Hz to 7.5 kHz), with bandwidth presets, aid greatly in providing optimum tradeoff between audio fidelity and adjacent-channel interference rejection. AVC settings, limited to "on-off" in standard version, allow for control over decay and attack times. Improved audio quality in some test configurations. Demodulates ISB signals used by a small proportion of utility stations. SINAD and THD distortion indicators. AF squelch for FM mode. Operating software can be updated online, albeit with minor complication under limited circumstances.

Pro/Con—Sound: Outstanding freedom from distortion aids in providing good audio quality with appropriate sound cards/chips and speakers; sound quality and level can run the gamut from excellent to awful, depending on the PC's sound card or chipset, which needs to be full duplex. Sound Blaster 16 cards are recommended by manufacturer, but not all models work. During our tests the $130 Sound Blaster Audigy 2 performed with considerable distortion—it doesn't offer full duplex operation for the line input—whereas the $43 Sound Blaster PCI 512 worked splendidly. (ISA sound cards perform terribly; quite sensibly, these are not recommended by the manufacturer.) All input settings for the audio card need to be carefully set to match the settings within the receiver's software. If wrong, there may be no audio or it may be grossly distorted. Indeed, a sound card isn't always necessary, as some sound chipsets commonly found within PCs produce excellent audio with the G303i. Another reason the chipset may be preferable is that Sound Blaster manuals recommend that if there is an audio chipset on the motherboard, it first be disabled in the BIOS and all related software uninstalled—potentially a Maalox Moment. However, even with a suitable board or chipset installed, the user must carefully set the AGC and AVC (automatic volume control, termed "Audio AGC" on the G303i) for distortion-free audio. Powerful amplified speakers provide room-filling sound and allow the AVC to be kept off, thus reducing band noise that can be intrusive when it is on during weak-signal reception.

Con—AGC/AVC: Weak-signal reception can be compromised by the AGC, which "sees" 10–15 kHz of spectrum within the IF upon which to act. So, if an adjacent world band channel signal is 20 dB or more stronger than a desired weak signal, the AGC's action tends to cause the adjacent signal to mask the desired signal. Inadequate gain with the AVC ("Audio AGC") off, but the aggressive AVC adds listening strain with single-sideband signals, as it tends to increase band noise between words or other modulation peaks. Powerful outboard amplified speakers help reduce the need for the additional audio gain brought about by the AVC and thus are desirable, but be prepared for jumps in volume when you tune to strong stations. Reception sometimes further improves if the AGC is switched off and IF gain is manually decreased, but the operator then has to "ride" the volume control to smooth out major fluctuations. Manual ECSS tuning frequently helps, too. During moments of transient overload, the AVC can contribute to the creation of leading-edge "pops" with powerful signals (slightly more noticeable in the PD/P version). Single-sideband performance, particularly within crowded amateur bands, can be even more audibly compromised by the aforementioned out-of-passband AGC action. Dynamic range/IP3 at 5 kHz signal spacing couldn't be measured with AGC on, as test signals trigger the AGC and keep the receiver from going into overload; measurement with the AGC off resulted in exceptionally poor numbers (45 db/–62 dBm). Phase noise poor when measured close-in (5 kHz signal spacing) for the same reason.

Con—Other: No synchronous selectable sideband, and double-sideband "AMS" mode loses lock easily. First IF rejection only fair. Front-end selectivity, although adequate for most uses, could be better. Station presets ("memory channels") store only frequency and mode, not bandwidth, AGC or attenuation settings. No passband offset or tunable notch filter. Emits a "pop-screech" sound when first brought up or when switching from standard to professional demodulator. Uses only SMA antenna connection, typically found on handheld devices rather than tabletop receivers; an SMA-to-BNC adapter is included, but for the many shortwave antennas with neither type of plug a second adaptor or changed plug is needed. On our sample, country of manufacture not found on receiver, box or enclosed printed matter; however, website indicates manufacturing facility is in Melbourne, Australia. Erratum sheet suggests that a discone antenna be used; this is fine for reception above roughly 25 MHz; however, in our tests we confirmed that conventional shortwave antennas provide much broader frequency coverage with the G303i, just as they do with other shortwave receivers.

☞ Minimum of 1 GHz Pentium recommended by manufacturer, although in the process of checking this out we obtained acceptable results using vintage 400 MHz and 500 MHz Pentium II processors with Windows 2000. However, if your PC is multitasking, then 2 GHz or more helps keep the PC from bogging down. Primary testing was done using various desktop Pentium IV PCs at 1.5–2.4 GHz, 256–512 MHz RAM and Windows 2000, XP-Home and XP-Pro operating systems; Vista, 98, ME and 2000 also supported. WiNRADiO operating software used during tests were v1.07, v1.14, v1.25 and v1.26.

Verdict: For the money the G303 is hard to beat, especially in the preferred Professional Demodulator version. It can also be configured for reception of DRM digital broadcast signals and is a pleasure to operate.

The G303 provides laboratory-quality spectrum displays and signal-strength indication. These spectrum-data functions are impressive, regardless of price or type of receiver, and that's just the beginning of things done well. The few significant warts: AGC/AVC behavior, possible audio hassles during installation, and the absence of synchronous selectable sideband.

Nevertheless, WiNRADiO's G303 is a great value. Although its costlier G313 sibling has certain advantages, for most the G303 is at least its equal for world band reception.

DRM Ready

WiNRADiO G313i, WiNRADiO G313e

Pricing: *G313i:* $949.95 in the United States and worldwide. CAD$1,299.00 in Canada. £619.95 in the United Kingdom. €1,049.00 in Germany. *G313e (external, not tested):* $1,149.95 in the United States and worldwide. CAD$1,599.00 in Canada by special order. £749.95 in the United Kingdom. €1,198.00 in Germany. *DRM software:* $49.95 worldwide from www.winradio.com/home/download-drm.htm. *Mini-Circuits BLP-30 BNC-to-BNC 30 MHz low-pass filter:* $32.95 in the United States.

Pros: Unlimited bandwidths—DSP bandwidths continuously variable in one Hertz increments from 1 Hz through 15 kHz (LSB/USB through 7.5 kHz). Bandwidth "presets" enhance ergonomics. Spectrum display either wideband (*see* Cons) or narrowband; narrow allows for first- rate test and measurement of audio-frequency response

Money talks, but not always. The WiNRADiO G313 is less desirable for world band than its G303 sibling that costs half as much.

of AM or single-sideband mode signals, spectra of data transmissions, frequency accuracy, amplitude modulation depth, frequency deviation, THD (total harmonic distortion) and SINAD (signal plus noise plus distortion to noise plus distortion ratio). Unlimited station presets—one thousand per file, each of which can be clustered into any of 16 groups; number of files limited only by hard disk capacity, so virtually no limit to presets. Station presets store frequency, IF shift, bandwidth and mode (*see* Cons). Four VFOs. Large signal-strength indicator as linear as any other tested to date; displays both digitally and as a digitized "analog meter." Signal-strength indicator reads out in "S" units, dBm or microvolts. Manufacturer's website, unusually helpful, includes downloadable calibration utility for signal-strength indicator. Open source code allows for third-party development of software. Includes DSP electronics for audio, so sound card acts only as an optional audio amplifier (*see* Cons) (*cf.* WiNRADiO G303), or 313's audio output can feed outboard audio system. Superb level of overall distortion (*see* Cons: DSP audio). Notch filter, tunable 0–7500 Hz, has good (30 dB) rejection (*see* Cons). Synchronous double sideband to help overcome selective fading distortion and enhance fidelity during twilight and darkness (mixed skywave/groundwave) reception of fringe mediumwave AM stations (*see* Cons). Integrated audio recorder, a convenience for those without ReplayRadio or similar. Integrated IF recorder stores spectrum slice for subsequent analysis of received signals, and to "re-receive" the same swath of signals over and again experimenting with, for example, IF bandwidth, notch filter and noise blanker settings (*see* Cons). Plug and play receiver software installed with no problems with XP Pro and XP Home. Does not overuse computer resources even while multitasking. Excellent shape factors at wider voice bandwidths (*see* Cons). Excellent ultimate rejection. Excellent image rejection. Excellent phase noise as measured in lab (*see* Cons). Spurious signals essentially nil. Screen, and operation in general, unusually pleasant and intuitive (*see* Cons). Automatic frequency control (AFC) with FM and AM mode signals. With optional software, receives digital (DRM) world band and other broadcasts; DRM software distributed by WiNRADiO, so odds are good for successful installation and performance. Demodulates ISB signals used by some utility stations. Single-step (18 dB) attenuator. Receiver incremental tuning (RIT) aids with transceiving. Two easy-to-read clocks displayed on screen for World Time; also, second clock for local time (*see* Cons); both show seconds numerically, as well as day and date. FM mode squelch. FM broadcasts receivable with extra-cost option. Specified for elder Windows 98, ME and 2000, as well as XP and Vista. Operating software can be updated online. Excellent owner's manual. Superior, timely and free factory assistance via email, seemingly throughout the week.

Cons: DSP audio causes static crashes and local noise to sound unusually harsh, potentially increasing listening fatigue. Synchronous detector lacks meaningful selectable sideband, IF shift notwithstanding. Poor AGC threshold contributes to reduced audibility of weak signals; improved by enabling switchable AVC at a low level, although this also increases pumping with single-sideband signals. AGC gain determined by all signals within the 15 kHz first IF filter, so background noise and audio can change in concert with on/off (e.g., CW) activity from adjacent carriers within the 15 kHz filter window; this can be an issue with utility and ham monitoring, but only rarely disturbs world band signals. Mediocre front-end selectivity, largely remediable by adding a Mini-Circuits BLP-30 or other outboard ~30 MHz low-pass filter. Poor close-in (5 kHz signal spacing) dynamic range/IP3. Bandwidth shape factors slip from excellent at wider bandwidths (e.g., 6 kHz) to fair at narrower voice bandwidths (e.g., 1.9 kHz). Phase noise or a kind of local oscillator noise keeps CW bandwidths (e.g., 0.5 kHz) from being measurable at –60 dB; consequently, CW shape factors also not measurable. Significant audible distortion if computer-screen volume turned up high; remediable if level not adjusted beyond "6"; sound card or outboard audio amplifier can provide additional volume if needed. Cyclical background sound, which doesn't vary with carrier-BFO phasing, in manual ECSS mode. Mixed ergonomics—some functions a pleasure, others not. Tuning-steps in 5 kHz increments (world band channel spacing) impractical with mouse scroll wheel, as three keys have to be held down simultaneously; instead, up/down screen slewing arrows can be used. Some screen icons small for typical PC displays/video cards. Real-time (always active) spectrum analyzer coverage width limited to 20 kHz (+/– 10 kHz), a pity given the exceptional resolution and analytical capabilities. IF recorder bandwidth also limited to 20 kHz. Tunable notch filter includes adjustable notch breadth, a creative but marginal option that complicates notch use. Notch filter takes unusually long to adjust properly using keypad, and small indicators make it prone to operating errors with GUI. First IF rejection only fair. Wideband spectrum analyzer not in real time, has disappointing resolution and thus of minor utility. SMA antenna connection; SMA-to-BNC adapter included, but for the many shortwave antennas with neither type of plug a second adaptor or changed plug is needed. Station presets don't store AGC or attenuator values. Noise blanker only marginally effective. Local-time (secondary) clock displays only in 24-hour format—no AM/PM.

☞ Also available with 9 kHz–180 MHz coverage in lieu of regular 9 kHz–30 MHz.

Verdict: With audio processing independent of the host PC—and heaps of additional goodies—the Australian WiNRADiO G313 is in many ways a solid improvement over the lower-cost WiNRADiO G303.

Alas, there's a hefty price to be paid for not using the PC sound card for audio processing: DSP harshness that aggravates static crashes and more. This limits its appeal, especially for tropical band and mediumwave AM DXing, but how much depends on your hearing and listening preferences.

The G313 is tempting for DRM, and it has excellent synchronous detection for alleviating selective fading distortion—a serious issue with dusk-to-dawn fringe analog mediumwave AM reception. But its selectable sideband capability is effectively nonexistent, and the "IF shift" doesn't help. This is a huge drawback in a kilobuck receiver, given that effective synchronous selectable sideband can be found on a $160 portable.

So, the G313's price/performance ratio is uninspiring for listening to broadcasts or monitoring utility/ham signals. But it excels with signal analysis and storage, thanks to a high-resolution spectrum analyzer with excellent test, measurement and recording capabilities. Add to that a highly linear and adjustable signal-strength indicator, and you can see why this model has been successful with certain professional/surveillance applications. This also explains the kilobuck price, downright cheap by professional standards.

DRM Ready

✪✪✪⅞ ✆

Ten-Tec RX-320D

Pricing: *RX-320D:* $369.00 plus shipping worldwide. *DRM software:* $49.95 worldwide from www.winradio.com/home/download-drm.htm. *Third-party control software:* Varies from free to $99 worldwide.

The Ten-Tec RX-320D shines when price and factory support are paramount. It has become something of a classic, but technology marches on.

Pros: Specified for elder Windows 3.1, 95 and 98, as well as XP (*see* Cons). "D" version's 12 kHz IF output allows the receiver to receive digital (DRM) world band and other broadcasts by using DRM software purchased separately. Superior dynamic range. Apparently superb bandwidth shape factors (*see* Cons). In addition to the supplied factory control software, third-party software is available, often for free, and may improve operation. Up to 34 bandwidths with third-party software. Tunes in extremely precise 1 Hz increments (10 Hz with tested factory software); displays to the nearest Hertz, and frequency readout is easily user-aligned. Large, easy-to-read digital frequency display and faux-analog frequency bar. For PCs with sound cards, outstanding freedom from distortion aids in providing good audio quality with most but not all cards and speakers. Fairly good audio, although with limited treble, available via line output jack and speaker jack to feed PCs and/or an external speaker. Superb blocking performance helps maintain consistently good world band sensitivity. Passband offset (*see* Cons). Spectrum display with wide variety of useful sweep widths (*see* Cons). World Time on-screen clock (*see* Cons). Adjustable AGC decay. Thousands of station presets, with first-rate memory configuration, access and sorting—including by station name and frequency. Only PC-controlled model tested which returns to last tuned frequency when PC turned off. Includes serial port-to-USB adaptor cable and related drivers. Operating software can be updated online. Superior owner's manual. Generally superior factory help and repair support.

Cons: Not specified for Windows 2000 or Vista. No synchronous selectable sideband, although third-party software nominally automates retuning of drifty AM-mode signals received as ECSS. Some characteristic DSP roughness in the audio under certain reception conditions. Synthesizer phase noise measures only fair; among the consequences are that bandwidth shape factors cannot be measured exactly. Some tuning ergonomics only fair as compared with certain standalone receivers. No tunable notch filter. Passband offset doesn't function in AM mode. Signal-strength indicator, calibrated 0–80, too sensitive, reading 20 with no antenna connected and 30 with only band noise being received. Mediocre front-end selectivity can allow powerful mediumwave AM stations to "ghost" into the shortwave spectrum, thus degrading reception of world band stations. Uses AC adaptor instead of built-in power supply. Spectrum display does not function with some third-party software and is only a so-so performer. Mediumwave AM reception below 1 MHz suffers from reduced sensitivity, and longwave sensitivity is atrocious. No internal speaker on outboard receiver module. World Time clock tied into computer's clock, which may not be accurate without periodic adjustment. Almost no retail sources outside the United States.

Verdict: The American-made Ten-Tec RX-320D is value priced and robust. It performs nicely, and its hardware is commendably supported by the manufacturer.

Icom IC-PCR2500, Icom IC-R2500

The $720 (€730) Icom IC-PCR2500 and $880 (€840) Icom IC-R2500 (both not tested) use the same platform as the '1500 series evaluated below. However, they add diversity reception to help reduce fading effects (accomplished with two widely spaced antennas—or, outside the shortwave spectrum, one horizontally and one vertically polarized). Synchronous selectable sideband also reduces the effects of AM-mode fading, but is unavailable on the '2500.

Additional extras are multi-channel monitoring/display, P25 (public service digital) board, D-Star (but not Icom's digital audio standard for PMR446) and other features oriented to VHF/UHF/SHF scanning.

✪✪✪⅝

Icom IC-PCR1500, Icom IC-R1500

Pricing: *IC-PCR1500 "black box" receiver:* $479.95 in the United States. CAD$499.00 in Canada. £345.00 in the United Kingdom. €529.00 in Germany. *IC-R1500 with control head and "black box" receiver:* $599.95 in the United States. CAD$599.00 in Canada. £389.00 in the United Kingdom. €625.00 in Germany. *UT-106 DSP unit:* $139.95 in the United States. CAD$140.00 in Canada. £79.95 in the United Kingdom. €99.00 in Germany. *OPC-1156 11½-foot/3.5-meter controller extension cable:* $13.95 in the United States. CAD$25.00 in Canada. £14.95 in the United Kingdom. €16.95 in Germany. *OPC-441 16½-foot/five meter speaker extension cable:* $27.95 in the United States. £14.95 in the United Kingdom. €26.95 in Germany. *CP-12L 12V DC cigarette lighter power cable:* $29.95 in the United States. CAD$60.00 in Canada. £19.95 in the United Kingdom. €23.95 in Germany. *OPC-254L 12V DC fused power cord:* $12.95 in the United States. CAD$20.00 in Canada. £9.95 in the United Kingdom. €9.20 in Germany. *Aftermarket RF Systems DPX-30 antenna combiner (to 2000 MHz) for separate shortwave and scanner antennas:* $169.95 in the United States. €109.00 in Germany. *Aftermarket Diamond CX-210N two-position antenna switch (to 3000 MHz):* $69.95 in the United States. £56.95 in the United Kingdom. €69.95 in Germany. *Aftermarket Daiwa CS-201 GII two-position antenna switch (to 1300 MHz):* $44.95 in the United States. *Aftermarket (sold under various names and no brand name) CX-201N two-position antenna switch (to 500 MHz):* $30.00 in the United States. €18.95 in Germany. *Aftermarket Alpha Delta 4B/N four-position antenna switch (to 1300 MHz):* $94.95 in the United States.

Pros: Specified for elder Windows ME and 98SE, as well as 2000 and XP (*see* Cons). Wideband frequency coverage in three versions: *(blocked U.S. version)* 0.01–810, 851–867, 896–1811, 1852–1868, 1897–2305.9, 2357–2812, 2853–2869, 2898–3109.8, 3136–3154.8, 3181–3300 MHz; *(blocked French version)* 0.01–30, 50.2–51.2, 87.5–108, 144–146, 430–440 and 1240–1300 MHz; *(unblocked version)* 0.01–3300 MHz; with all versions, specifications not guaranteed 0.01–0.5 and 3000–3300 MHz; BFO operation (single sideband and CW) up to 1300 MHz; includes FM broadcast reception. Fully 2600 station presets clustered into 26 pages of 100 channels each. Tunes and displays in unusually precise 1 Hz increments. Vast

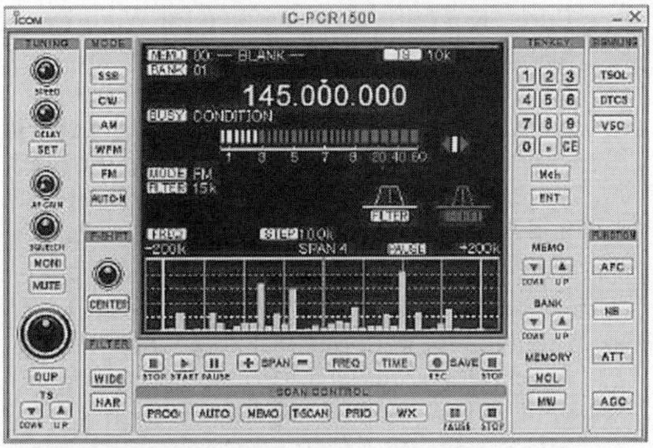

The Icom IC-PCR1500 has become popular worldwide. It is relatively affordable for a broadband model, even if performance isn't top-drawer.

number of user-selectable tuning steps. Useful manual ECSS operation (*see* Cons) aided by Gibraltar-class stability. Very good shortwave sensitivity. Selectable fast/slow AGC decay (*see* Cons). Generally good IF shift (*see* Cons). Operating software and firmware work well and can be updated online at www.icom.co.jp/world/download/index.htm. Plenty of IF gain and AGC acts in the final bandwidth, which help provide single-sideband performance that's significantly above average among PC-controlled models (*see* Cons). Generally pleasant audio quality (*see* Cons). Audio available not only through the set's internal speaker (*see* Cons) or an external speaker, but also via USB through the PC's audio system (*see* Cons). Can record audio in .wav format onto hard drive (*see* Cons). One-step (20 dB) attenuator (*see* Cons). Optional UT-106 AF-DSP unit (not tested). *IC-PCR1500 and IC-R1500 via PC:* Three different PC user screens. Excellent 'scope for up to a 1 MHz peek at radio spectrum in real time, 1–10 MHz in non-real time (*see Cons*). Keypad tuning. Up to 22 alphanumeric tags and frequencies for presets display simultaneously. *IC-R1500:* Generally excellent wired control head so '1500 can also be used as a standalone tabletop receiver or, to a degree with the optional CP-12L power cord, a mobile receiver (*see* Cons), as well as a PC-controlled model *à la* the IC-PCR1500.

Cons: Not currently specified for Windows Vista. Few bandwidth choices. Poor dynamic range at 5 and 20 kHz separation points, although this improves considerably at wider spacing. No RF or IF gain control to help alleviate overloading, and attenuator has only one step. No synchronous selectable sideband; manual ECSS alternative sounds slightly out of phase even with 1 Hz tuning step. With one PC configuration, but not others, some distortion encountered with single-sideband signals through 3 kHz bandwidth. Slight hiss. Audio only fair through black box's built-in speaker. Audio a bit weak through computer's USB port. No AGC off. IF shift operates only in single-sideband and CW modes. Mediumwave sensitivity only fair. Poor longwave sensitivity. Marginal noise blanker. No on/off multi-event timing for audio recording. Telescopic antenna and cable virtually useless on shortwave and not much better elsewhere within tuned frequency ranges. Software installation not always easy. No schematic or block diagrams. *IC-R1500:* Control head provides most, but not all, operating functions available from PC control; for example, there's no keypad or spectrum 'scope, and presets simultaneously display only one frequency or alphanumeric tag. Control head has no stand or mounting bracket for desktop or mobile use, nor can it be attached to the body of the "black box."

Verdict: Icom's '1500 series' frequency coverage is vast, with performance that is generally worthwhile by broadband standards. Even though it suffers from poor dynamic range at 5 and 20 kHz separation points, this improves dramatically at wider separation. However, a paucity of bandwidth choices and the lack of synchronous selectable sideband are clear drawbacks. Also, the otherwise-excellent recording facility would have profited from multi-event timing.

Icom's '1500 series receivers are better than most other PC models for single-sideband reception of utility and amateur signals. Ergonomics are top drawer, too, reflecting user-friendly software that's about as good as it gets. And—important for a PC receiver—audio is pleasant.

DRM Reception

✪✪✪½

ELAD FDM77

Pricing: *FDM77, including DRM software:* £399.95 in the United Kingdom. €598.00 in Germany.

Pros: Receives world band and other DRM transmissions immediately after connection to a PC. Commendable ergonomics (*see* Cons), with superior graphic interface and large icons. Handy tuning features include numeric selection directly above each digit, using keyboard arrows; MHz or kHz keypad entry, using PC keyboard or on-screen virtual keypad; up/down slewing, using on-screen or keyboard arrows; knob tuning, using mouse wheel or on-screen virtual tuning knob; 200 station presets per page, with as many page files as PC's hard disk can hold; two VFOs; and auto bandscanning with real-time graphic spectrum display (*see* Cons). 1 Hz frequency resolution (*see* Cons) and tuning step. Large, accurate signal-strength indicator uses screen graphics that make it look like an analog "S" meter. Nineteen DSP bandwidths with shape factors that improve from good (1:2.1) to superb (1:1.4) as bandwidth narrows. Two variable notch filters with superb (50 dB) heterodyne (whistle) rejection. IF shift to aid in adjacent-channel interference rejection. Very good audio that includes a six-band graphic equalizer that can be bypassed by "flat" selection. Good sensitivity (0.5 µV) and noise floor (–125 dBm) with preamplifier on (*see* Cons). Good image rejection (74 dB) and paucity of other spurious signals. AGC threshold good (3 µV) with preamplifier on (*see* Cons). Overall distortion excellent-to-superb (2.2% to 0.1%), especially in single-sideband mode. Front-end selectivity good, thanks to octave filtering. Superb first IF rejection (93 dB). Drift under 100 Hz from near-cold start. Graphically displays 20 kHz of radio-spectrum, audio spectrum and oscilloscope. Selectable 10 dB preamp. Two antenna connectors: SO-239 for significant antennas; and BNC with an additional 20 dB of preamplification for use with whip and other short antennas. 15 dB attenuator. WAV recorder, with single-event timer, stores onto hard drive. World Time and local clocks (*see* Cons). Operating software and firmware can be updated online from manufacturer's sometimes-poky server. Convenient mute key.

Cons: No synchronous selectable sideband. Ergonomics, although usually superior, are compromised because bandwidth selection requires unnecessary screen shifting and the main screen doesn't show which bandwidth is in use; also, installation sometimes unforgiving (e.g., high-pitched audio can mix with received output if directions on CD and in owner's manual not followed precisely). Graphic equalizer can degrade audio quality in certain situations, requiring that the flat setting be substituted. AGC controlled by 455 kHz intermediate bandwidth of 7.5 kHz that's usually much wider than the PC sound card's DSP bandwidth; so, for example, when listening to a weak single-sideband signal and there's a stronger signal 5 kHz or less away on the opposite sideband, the weak signal can made impossible to copy because the AGC is controlled by the undesired signal. Phase noise (98 dBc) poor; prevents accurate assessment of blocking performance, which because of this measures as poor—even though it may actually be much better. AGC threshold drops to poor (8 µV) with preamplifier off. Sensitivity drops to only fair with preamplifier off. Measured dynamic range of 63 dB consistent at 50, 20 and 5 kHz separation points (translates to fair at 5 kHz separation, poor at 20 kHz separation); nevertheless, resisted overloading effectively during hands-on testing. Radio spectrum display shows only narrow 20 kHz slice—i.e., plus or minus 10 kHz on either side of the received signal. No noise blanker. Most front-panel LEDs are blue and excessively bright. Station presets store only frequency and mode, not such other variables as bandwidth. No external speaker jack, so audio must run through computer's sound card. Frequency display on our unit misreads by around 45 Hz. Runs warm; plastic end caps affixed with double-stick tape that loses stickiness as cabinet heats up. Manual states USB 2.0 required; our tests underscore that this, as opposed

Another PC receiver from Italy is the ELAD FDM77. Its high card is ready-to-go DRM reception at an attractive price.

to USB 1.0, is necessary to avoid jerky responses and locking up. Clock shows local time only in 24-hour format; although only 24-hour format shown, LCD inappropriately displays AM and PM. Owner's manual, although recently improved, not all it could be. No longer sold within North America.

☞ Tested with v1.06 firmware and v1.15 and v3.06 operating software; all comments refer to results with the latter software.

Verdict: The Italian-made Elad FDM77 gets high marks for pioneering hassle-free DRM reception. It is also user friendly and performs nicely with conventional analog signals—even though it lacks synchronous selectable sideband.

DRM Ready

✪✪✪3/8

RFSPACE SDR-14

Pricing: *RFSPACE SDR-14:* $1,099.95 in the United States. *Comet HS-10 SMA-to-SO-239 antenna adaptor cable:* $16.95 in the United States. *DRM software:* $49.95 worldwide from www.winradio.com/home/download-drm.htm.

Pros: Excellent spectrum display shows, with audio ("demodulation"), up to a 150 kHz slice of radio spectrum; this can also be recorded to disk and played back in any mode or bandwidth (*see* Cons). Worthy sensitivity. DSP bandwidth filtering feels razor

The RFSPACE SDR-14 is mainly for specialized applications. Okay for world band, but better can be had for less.

sharp and performs beautifully. Relatively free from overloading. Stable. Tunes and displays down to 1 Hz increments. Passband tuning (*see* Cons). Three-level attenuator, labeled as RF gain control. Adjustable AGC decay and hang times. Good quality, flexible USB cable. Receives 30–260 MHz minus front end filtering or amplification (*see* Cons). Third-party software development supported. SpectraVue software nominally has Linux server support (not tested), in addition to Windows 2000/XP/Vista. With optional software, receives digital (DRM) world band and other broadcasts. World Time (UTC) clock shows date and day of the week. Operating software can be updated online from www.moetronix.com/spectravue.htm. Build quality appears solid. One year warranty. Fifteen day return privilege when ordered from the manufacturer. Helpful PDF operating manual (*see* Cons).

Cons: Switch mode AC adaptor emits noise that disrupts reception even with outdoor antenna and shielded lead-in. Initial installation not always successful, necessitating troubleshooting with or without the assistance of the manufacturer; however, manufacturer's phone number and street address aren't published. SMA antenna connector, with no adaptor included for non-SMA antenna plugs; for most shortwave antennas an adaptor or new antenna plug is required. No synchronous selectable or double sideband, tunable notch filter, presets or scanning. Passband tuning operates only in LSB and USB modes and is complex to use. Noise blanker performs marginally, and no DSP noise reduction offered. Inadequate front end filtering, so mediumwave AM stations may bleed through slightly to impact world band listening. With demodulation, spectrum display limited to 150 kHz maximum bandwidth. Marginally useful 30–260 MHz reception, with an abundance of spurious signals that not even maximum attenuation can overcome. Requires a speedy computer with large disk capacity to use to full benefit; even then, heavy resource drain may impact multitasking. Harsh audio quality in AM mode. About a half-second lag when operating controls and when listening. No power switch, even though manufacturer recommends receiver be powered down when not in use. Operation manual, only on CD, not printed as a book.

☞ The included switch mode AC adaptor is electrically noisy and should be replaced with something quieter. Requirements are 12V DC output, one ampere minimum rating, center (tip) positive.

☞ Tested: software .014, SpectraVue 1.30.

Verdict: The RFSPACE SDR-14 is a niche device that does one thing very well: recording a slice of spectrum for later playback and analysis. However, this requires a speedy processor and substantial disk space—especially in a multitasking environment.

However appropriate the SDR-14 is for spectrum analysis, it is a dismal choice for world band listening and DXing.

Robert Sherwood and David Zantow, with Lawrence Magne; also, Greg Burnett and Pete Gaddie.

WHERE TO FIND IT: INDEX TO TESTED RADIOS

PASSPORT REPORTS evaluates nearly every receiver on the market with digital frequency readout. Here is where each review is found, with those that are new, forthcoming, revised, rebranded or retested for 2009 in **bold**.

Comprehensive Radio Database International White Papers® are available for a number of popular new and classic premium receivers. Each RDI White Paper®—$6.95 in North America, $9.95 airmail elsewhere, including shipping—contains virtually all our panel's findings and comments during hands-on testing, as well as laboratory measurements and what these mean to you. These unabridged reports are available from key world band dealers, or order 24/7 from www.passband.com, autovoice +1 215/598-9018 or fax +1 215/598 3794—or write PASSPORT RDI White Papers, Box 300, Penn's Park, PA 18943 USA.

Receiver	*Page*
American Red Cross ARC FR-350	114
American Red Cross ARC FR-500 Solarlink	**108**
Anjan A-1004	94
AOR AR5000A+3	122
📄 AOR AR7030	119
📄 AOR AR7030 PLUS	119
AOR AR7070 (info)	**119**
CCRadio-SW	69
CCRadio-SWP	98
Coby CX39	95
Degen DE11	99
Degen DE1101	79
Degen DE1102	74
Degen DE1103	75
Degen DE1104	91
Degen DE1105	85
Degen DE1121	**102**
Elad FDM77 (PC)	158
📄 **Etón E1**	**61**
📄 Etón E1XM	61
Etón E5	73
Etón E100	86
Etón E1100	**92**
Etón FR-200	**113**
Etón FR-250	113
Etón FR-350	114
Etón FR-500 Solarlink	**108**
Etón FR-550 Solarlink	**108**
Etón Mini 300PE	101
Etón S350DL	71
Freeplay Summit	110
Grundig FR-200	113
Grundig G4 World Recorder (info)	**104**
Grundig G5	73
Grundig G6 Aviator	**96**
Grundig G6 "Buzz Aldrin Edition"	**96**
Grundig G100	**86**
Grundig G1100	92
Grundig GS350DL	**71**
Grundig Mini 300PE	101
Grundig Satellit 750	**65**
Grundig Yacht Boy 80	78
Grundig Yacht Boy 300PE	91
Grundig YB 550PE	90
Icom IC-PCR1500 (PC)	156
Icom IC-PCR2500 (PC, info)	156
Icom IC-R20	83
Icom IC-R75	120
Icom IC-R1500	125
Icom IC-R2500 (info)	126
Icom IC-R8500A	121
Icom IC-R9500	136
Japan Radio NRD-630	140
Kaito KA008	111
Kaito KA011	112
Kaito KA11	99
Kaito KA105	100
Kaito KA1101	79
Kaito KA1102	74
Kaito KA1103	75
Kaito KA-1121	**102**
Kaito KA-2100	69
K-PO WR2100	**69**
"Lextronix" E1	61
"Lextronix" E5	73
"Lextronix" E100	86
"Lextronix" FR-200	**113**
"Lextronix" FR-250	**113**
"Lextronix" FR-350	**114**
"Lextronix" Mini 300	**101**
"Lextronix" S350 Deluxe	71
Microtelecom Perseus (PC)	**144**
Palstar R30A	**123**
Palstar R30A/Sherwood	**123**
Realistic/Radio Shack DX-394	128
Redsun RP2100	69
RFSPACE SDR-14 (PC)	159
Roadstar TRA-2350P	70
Roadstar TRA-2415/N	95
Roberts R861	77
Roberts R876	82
Roberts R9914	82
Roberts R9968	**94**
Sangean ATS 404	90
Sangean ATS 404P	90
Sangean ATS 505	82
Sangean ATS 505P	82
Sangean ATS 606AP	82
Sangean ATS 606S	82
Sangean ATS 606SP	82
Sangean ATS-818ACS	104
Sangean ATS-818ACS "Deluxe"	104
Sangean ATS 909	77
Sangean ATS 909W	77
Sangean PT-50	94
Sangean PT-80	78
Scott RXP80	**74**
SI-TEX NAV-FAX 200	128
Sony CDX-GT160S (car, info)	**105**
Sony CDX-GT370 (car, info)	**105**
Sony CDX-GT470U (car, info)	**105**
Sony ICF-SW35	84
Sony ICF-SW7600GR	72
SRX-50	96
Tecsun BCL-3000	71
Tecsun DR-910	93
Tecsun Green-88	113
Tecsun PL-450	**80**
Tecsun PL-600	**86**
Tecsun R-333	95
Tecsun R-919	101
Ten-Tec 1254 (kit)	129
Ten-Tec RX-320D (PC)	155
Ten-Tec RX-340	138
Thieking DE1102	74
Thieking DE1103	75
Thieking und Koch DE1121	**102**
Watkins-Johnson WJ-8711A	133
WiNRADiO G303e (PC)	151
WiNRADiO G303e-PD/P (PC)	151
WiNRADiO G303i (PC)	151
WiNRADiO G303i-PD/P (PC)	151
WiNRADiO G313e (PC)	153
WiNRADiO G313i (PC)	153
Yaesu VR-5000	126

📄 *Radio Database International White Paper®* available.

Wire Antennas for 2009

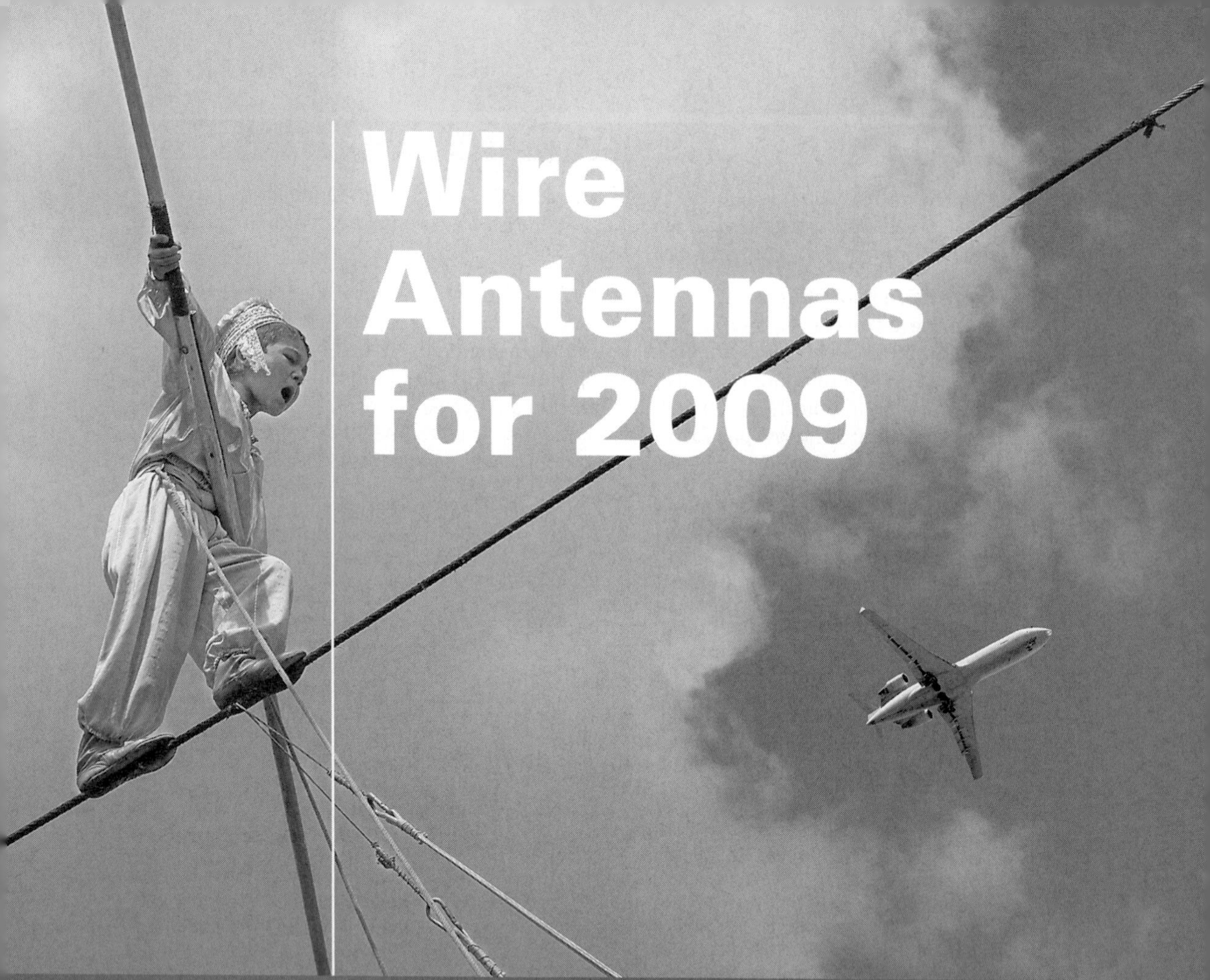

Everyday portables work nicely off built-in antennas. But tabletop models and premium portables are different. For them, outboard antennas are needed for best performance.

The basics:

• *Apples and oranges.* The better the receiver, the more important the antenna. Simple antennas for simple portables, sophisticated antennas for fancy models.

• *Location.* Wire antennas are usually best, but should be erected outdoors. If you can't do this, consider a compact antenna (*see* Active Antennas for 2009). Erect safely and for best performance.

• *Signal-to-noise:* Just boosting signals isn't enough. They need to be enhanced relative to local electrical noise and receiver circuit noise, and the best way to do this is to place the antenna outdoors. The result—more signal, proportionately less noise—is decisive, as it upgrades the signal-to-noise ratio.

Objective: more signal, less noise.

When Wire Antennas Help

No surprise—signals already booming in aren't going to profit from an El Supremo antenna. Your receiver's signal-strength indicator may read higher than Lindsay Lohan, but its automatic-gain control (AGC) ensures that what you hear isn't going to sound much different than before. In fact, it might sound slightly worse.

With all portables except premium models, forget sophisticated antennas—outdoor or in, passive or active. Make do with the radio's built-in telescopic antenna, or for more oomph use a short inverted-L "Volksantenne" (below) or one of the simpler active antennas.

At the other extreme, a first-rate outdoor antenna is essential to elite receivers, which is why these rarely have built-in antennas.

Volksantenne

An inverted-L is the Volksantenne of antennas: simple, flexible and inexpensive. Inconspicuous, too, with no unsightly traps and, being end-fed, their feedlines are easily placed next to the house rather than dangling out in the open. For most radios they provide excellent results, and are even reasonable for omnidirectional mediumwave AM reception.

World band and specialty outlets stock inverted-L antennas or parts to make your own—add-ons like baluns and antenna tuners, too. Some are basic and inexpensive, while others are made from superior materials and priced accordingly; for example, the Watson SWL-DX1 is £25.95 in the United Kingdom. Vendors also offer a rich variety of end-fed variants of the classic inverted-L.

Preassembled inverted-L antennas are too long for many portables, causing overloading from hefty signals. Experiment, but usually the cheaper the portable, the shorter the inverted-L. Unlike most other antennas, the inverted-L performs decently when snipped to avoid stressing the receiver or to fit into a yard.

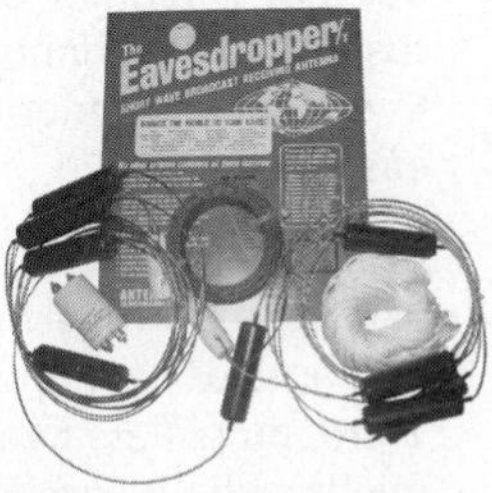

The Eavesdropper Model T comes with static protection and fully assembled.

Longwire Reduces Fading

Acres aplenty?

Lengthy inverted-L antennas, detailed in an RDI White Paper on outdoor antennas, can be over 200 feet/60 meters. These homebrew skyhooks are readily cobbled together from parts found at world band and amateur radio outlets and flea markets.

They qualify as genuine longwire antennas, thanks to their having one or more wavelengths. This helps reduce fading—something shorter antennas can't do—while improving the all important signal-to-noise ratio.

Lightning Protection

Nearby lightning generates inductive charges that can come in through the antenna and seriously damage your receiver. So a good static protector is essential for an antenna during nearby thunderstorms, as well as windy snow and sand storms. Some of the best are made by Alpha Delta Communications, but even these won't help against a direct lightning strike—for that, you need to disconnect the antenna and toss its feedline well outdoors.

Antennas aren't the only entry point. Utility poles are magnets for lightning which can enter your radio through AC mains wiring. Best protection is a powerline surge arrestor like the advanced ZeroSurge 2R7.5W, $129.

An emergency power plant, such as one of top performers from Kohler or Onan, is especially helpful. With the right transfer switch it can be manually activated to decouple from utility power so surges can't even enter your home.

Pitfalls

Most folks don't encounter legal prohibitions on erecting world band antennas. However, covenants and deed restrictions can limit options in gated and other communities.

Most wire antennas are robustly constructed to withstand ice buildup during storms, but copper tends to stretch. Bungee straps or pulley counterweights help overcome this.

Outdoors Good, Indoors Bad

Digital devices create so much RF pollution—electrical noise—that antenna location has become crucial. Indoors is usually the worst place.

You don't bathe in dirty water, so don't put your antenna where it is electrically "dirty." Instead, place it away from your house, power lines, cables and other potential sources of local electrical noise. Once your antenna is hanging free in the breeze, you're likely to hear less "stuff" bothering stations.

IS BIGGER BETTER?

Accessory antennas come in two flavors: unamplified or "passive," usually outdoor; and amplified or "active," which depending on the model can be indoor or outdoor. Unamplified antennas use a wire or rod receiving element to feed radio signals straight to the receiver. All wire antennas we've tested are unamplified and fairly long.

Amplified or active antennas are electronically boosted, like Viagra, to make up for their relatively short receiving elements. A few sought-after models even outperform big outdoor antennas, at least with staticky signals below 5 MHz. As backyards shrink and restrictive covenants grow, limited-space amplified antennas have become more popular. Even landed homeowners sometimes prefer them because most are inconspicuous and easy to set up.

But bigger still tends to be better because amplified antennas have drawbacks. First, their usually short receiving elements usually don't provide the signal-to-noise enhancement of lengthier elements. Second, antenna amplifiers can generate circuit noise of their own. Third, amplifiers can overload, with results like when a receiver overloads: a mumbling mishmash up and down the dial. Indeed, if antenna amplification is excessive it can overload the receiver, too.

Finally, active antennas often have mediocre front-end selectivity. This can allow mediumwave AM supersignals to become commingled with world band signals.

Crispy The Cadaver Says . . .

Safety is Rule One during installation. Avoid falls or making contact with potentially lethal electrical lines. If you want to be fried, get a sunburn.

There's more to this than can be covered here, but safety tips and a step-by-step erection guide are in the RADIO DATABASE INTERNATIONAL report, *Evaluation of Popular Outdoor Antennas*. Safety tips are also at www.universal-radio.com/catalog/sw_ant/safeswl.html.

Which Is Best?

That RDI White Paper also includes test results for various popular outdoor wire antennas, three of which are touched on here. All are dipoles which rely on traps for frequency resonance, but a variety of mounting layouts are used:

- End-fed sloper, with the antenna about 30 degrees from horizontal.
- Center-fed tapered wing, with a tall (about 20 feet/6 meters) mounting midway, plus two lower mountings.
- Center-fed horizontal, hung between two points of comparable height.

PASSPORT's star ratings mean the same thing regardless of whether an antenna is active or passive, big or little, indoor or out. Nevertheless, passive antennas are more tricky than actives to evaluate, as their performance is partly dependent on such local variables as soil composition, moisture and bedrock formation.

Create, Experiment, Enjoy

Lots of once-fun candidates for hands-on experimentation are now the inscrutable domain of no-touch technology. Not so world band antennas, especially passive wire aerials.

So don't hold back from "rolling your own" or buying something that, tests be damned, you think might do well at your location. There are countless designs on the market and in how-to publications, and most wire antennas are frugal and forgiving.

✪✪✪✪¾ *Passport's Choice*

Alpha Delta DX-Ultra

Pricing: $160.00 in the United States; coaxial cable $15–30 extra. CAD$180.00 in Canada; coaxial cable CAD$12–29 extra. €114.00 plus coaxial cable in the Netherlands (rys.nl).

Pros: Best overall performer. Little variation in performance from one world band segment to another. Rugged construction. Built-in static protection. Wing design appropriate for certain yard layouts. Covers mediumwave AM.

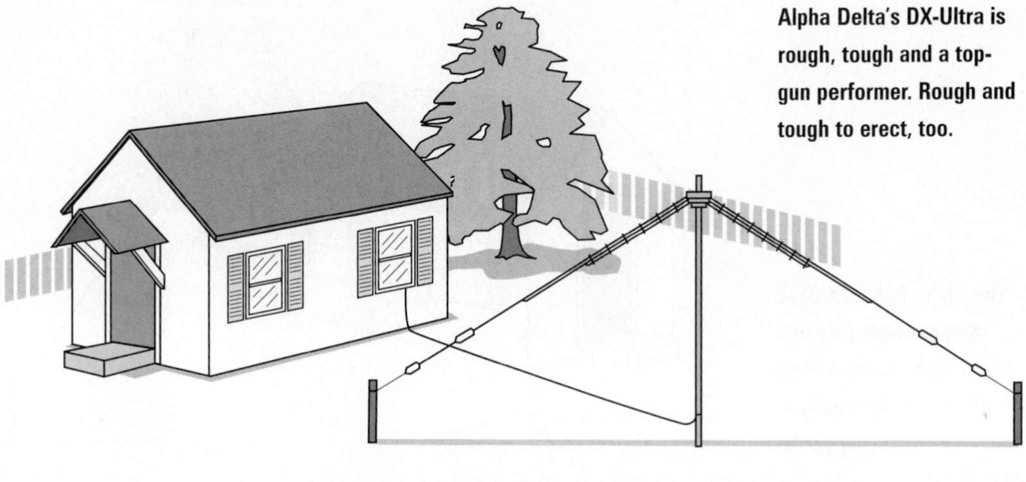

Alpha Delta's DX-Ultra is rough, tough and a top-gun performer. Rough and tough to erect, too.

Cons: Assembly a major undertaking, with stiff wire having to be bent and fed through spacer holes, then affixed. Unusually lengthy, 80 feet/25 meters. Coaxial cable lead-in not included. Relatively heavy, adding to erection effort. Warranty only six months.

Verdict: The Alpha Delta DX-Ultra rewards sweat equity—it is really more of a kit than a ready-to-go product. First, you have to purchase the needed lead-in cable and other hardware bits, then assemble, bend and stretch the many stiff wires, section by section.

Because the wire used should outlast the Pyramids, assembly is a trying and unforgiving exercise. Each wire needs to be rigorously and properly affixed, lest it slip loose and the erected antenna comes tumbling down, as it did at one of our test sites.

While all outdoor antennas require yard space, the Ultra is the longest manufactured antenna tested. It is also relatively heavy, making installation even more challenging. In ice-prone climates, ensure any trees or poles attached to the antenna are sturdy, and don't even think about using a chimney unless your cousin is a mason.

But if you have yard space and don't object to assembly and erection hurdles, you are rewarded with a mighty robust performer. Properly mounted, is outmatched only by the longest of inverted-L aerials and costly professional-grade antennas.

✪✪✪✪½ *Passport's Choice*

Alpha Delta DX-SWL Sloper

Pricing: $120.00 in the United States; coaxial cable $15–30 extra, Transi-Trap static protector $29.95 extra. CAD$140.00 in Canada; coaxial cable CAD$12–29 extra, Transi-Trap static protector CAD$65 extra. €125.00 plus coaxial cable and static protector in the Netherlands (rys.nl).

Pros: Rugged construction. Sloper design uses traps to keep length down to 60 feet/18 meters, ideal for smaller yards. Covers mediumwave AM.

Cons: Requires assembly, a significant exercise. Does not include static protection or coaxial cable lead-in. Warranty only six months.

☞ A greatly shortened version of the Ultra, the 40-foot/12-meter DX-SWL-S (not tested), is available for the same price, with coaxial cable and static protector extra. Its nominal coverage is 3.2–22 MHz, omitting the little-used 2 MHz (120 meter) world band segment.

☞ Although both Sloper versions nominally don't cover the virtually unused 25 MHz (11 meter) segment, our measurements of the full-length Sloper show excellent results at 25650–26100 kHz.

Verdict: A popular and robust performer for where space is limited. A chore to assemble, but less so than the DX-Ultra.

The Alpha Delta DX-SWL Sloper needs only one high mount, not two. This allows it to fit readily in many yards.

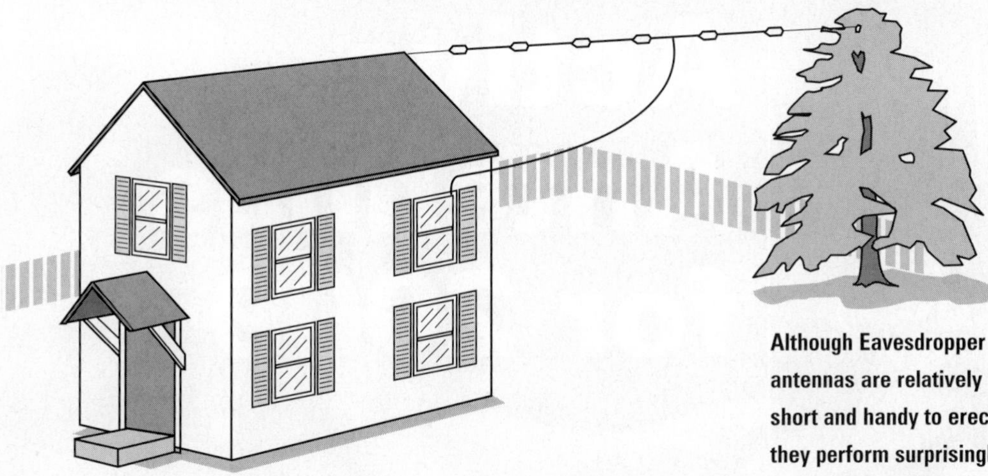

Although Eavesdropper antennas are relatively short and handy to erect, they perform surprisingly well.

✪✪✪✪⅛ *Passport's Choice*

Eavesdropper Model T, Eavesdropper Model C

Pricing: *Model T:* $99.95, complete, in the United States. CAD$129.00 in Canada. *Model C:* $99.95 in the United States; coaxial cable $15–30 extra. CAD$98.95 in Canada; coaxial cable CAD$12–29 extra.

Pros: Unusually compact at 43 feet/13 meters, it fits into many yards. Comes with built-in static protection. Attractively priced. One-year warranty, after which repairs made "at nominal cost." *Model T:* Easiest to install of any Passport's Choice antenna—unpack, and it's ready to hang. Comes with ribbon lead-in wire, which tends to have less signal loss than coaxial cable. *Model C:* Easier than most to install, with virtually everything included and assembled except the coaxial cable lead-in.

Cons: Some performance drop within the 2 MHz (120 meter) and 3 MHz (90 meter) tropical world band segments. *Model C:* Coaxial cable lead-in not included.

☞ Eavesdropper also makes the Sloper antenna (not tested), similar to Alpha Delta's DX-SWL Sloper and priced like the Eavesdropper Model C. It comes with static arrestor, but no coaxial cable lead-in.

Verdict: If your teeth gnash when you see "Some Assembly Required," take heart. The Eavesdropper T, unlike Alpha Delta alternatives, comes ready to go and is straightforward to erect. At most, you might want to get a set of bungee straps to provide flexibility at the ends.

The size is user-friendly, too—the result of a compromise. There's no getting around the rule that the longer the antenna, the more likely it is to do well at low frequencies. Eavesdropper's designer, the late Jim Meadow, once told Passport that he found few folks tuning below 4.7 MHz, but many with limited yard space. So, he shrunk the Eavesdropper by focusing on performance above 4.7 MHz, yet allowed it to function decently lower down.

Our tests confirm this. The Eavesdropper horizontal trap dipoles perform quite nicely above 4.7 MHz, with a notch less gain than Alpha-Delta models in the 2 MHz and 3 MHz tropical world band segments.

In practice the ribbon lead-in wire used by the T version works surprisingly well, using phasing to help cancel out electrical noise. Too, it stands up to the elements and usually has less signal loss than coaxial cable used by its C sibling.

Prepared by Stephen Bohac, Jock Elliott, Tony Jones, Lawrence Magne, David Walcutt and George Zeller.

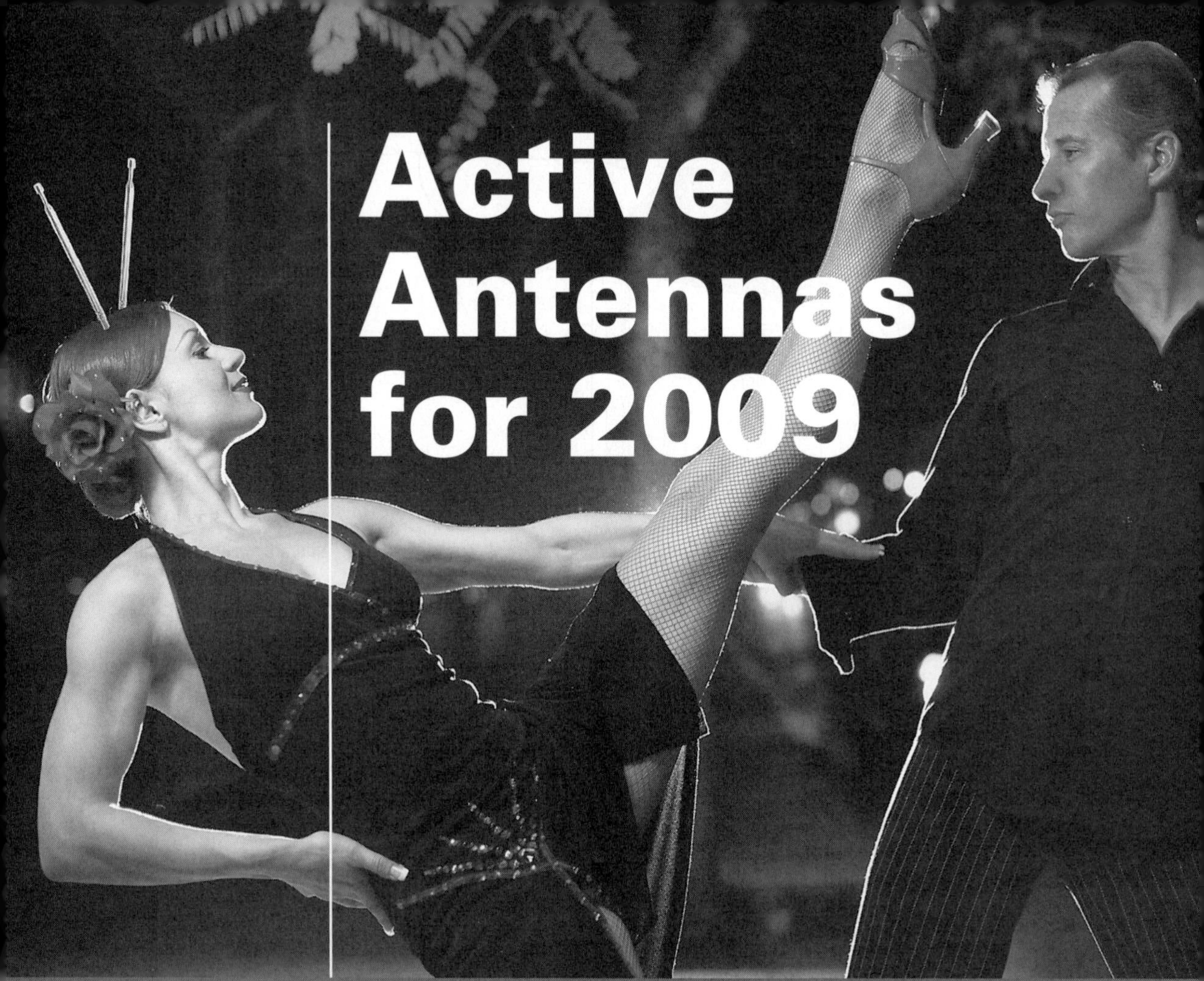

Active Antennas for 2009

Juicy programs aren't aired only in the evening, when scripts can be tailored for your region. Increasingly, "off beam" signals are being heard by day—particularly afternoons and at twilight.

Thanks to the scattering properties of shortwave, you can eavesdrop on these to hear what's being said to other parts of the world, often in English. Variations in what's being told to different audiences can reveal much about a country's real intentions.

Most daytime signals are not strong, but a high-performance antenna can help open up these new worlds. The gold standard is an outdoor wire antenna that is unamplified—*passive*. Trouble is, these are lengthy, a pain to erect (think "big trees") and require turf.

So if you lack acreage, face community restrictions or are allergic to high-wire gymnastics, consider an active antenna.

Loop antennas can turn noise and static into intelligibility.

Amplification Boost

Actives use a loop, rod (telescopic or fixed) or short wire receiving element to grab signals. These typically don't provide much oomph, so an amplifier is added to make up the difference—the antenna then becomes *active*. Most are ideal for townhouses, apartments and travel. Some detached homes, too, as lawns shrink while houses balloon. Too, if you erect a wire aerial, neighbors may grouse that it looks like a clothesline.

Early actives were the Rodney Dangerfields of antennas. They tended to be noisy, overloaded easily, generated harmonic "false" signals and deteriorated outdoors. They quickly earned a reputation for failing to deliver.

Now, for 2009, there are plenty of solid choices. While these rarely equal the performance of their outdoor wire cousins, the gap has narrowed considerably. Indeed, some occasionally outperform passive wire antennas on lower frequencies during high-static periods.

Best: Remote Element

Active antennas are either proximate or remote. A *proximate* model has its receiving element on or near an amplifier box by the receiver. A *remote* antenna, whether active or passive, allows the element to be mounted farther away—either indoors or, with some models, outdoors where reception tends to be audibly superior.

A remote model is the way to go. Its receiving element can be put where electrical noise is weakest, yet radio signals are relatively strong. Proximate models offer no such choice unless the receiver itself is where reception is best.

Most electrical noise comes from within your house or neighborhood, but not always. For example, some receivers emit electrical noise,

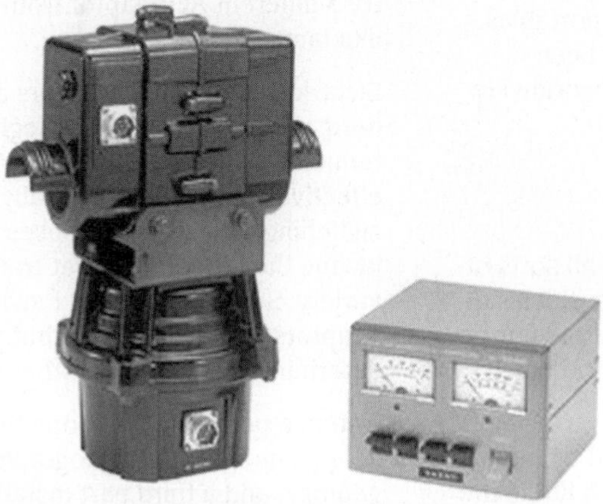

Yaesu's pricey G-5500 rotor is the *ne plus ultra* for Wellbrook's ALA 1530 antenna. It not only turns 360 degrees, it also yaws—ideal for fastidious mediumwave AM DXing.

usually from the front panel's digital display. With these, a proximate antenna should be placed towards the back or off to one side.

Loops Reduce Noise

Cognoscenti gravitate to loop antennas because they tend to offer signals less disturbed by static and other noise. Too, they are relatively directional, so they can be pointed away from local electrical noise. All this improves the signal-to-noise ratio—especially within lower frequency segments. Loops are antennas of choice for mediumwave AM and longwave DXing, as well.

Some government monitoring agencies even use costly banks of passive phased-array loops mounted near ground level. These outclass even massive rotatable beams, as they provide signals eerily devoid of noise.

Wellbrook loops stand out among affordable models, as they use a balanced loop receiving element, properly uncoupled from the unbalanced feedline, and can roost outdoors. During high-static months their superior signal-to-noise ratios can make the difference between hearing static and understanding what's being said. The catch: They tend to be larger and more conspicuous than the alternatives.

Most active antennas are designed for tabletop models, but not all. Degen's DE31, also sold as the Kaito KA33 and with variations under the Thieking brand, is a low-cost option for casual portable use. Kaito's KA35, too.

Sony's AN-LP1 is *el supremo* for portables. Although it almost certainly has been discontinued, it is still available worldwide from a proven vendor.

Preselection *vs.* Broadband

Broadband amplifiers can cause all sorts of mischief. Some add noise and spurious signals, such as "ghosting" from the mediumwave AM band. Yet others have too much gain and overload receiver circuitry.

These shortcomings are palliated by tunable or switchable preselection, which limits the band of frequencies getting full amplification. Problem is, outboard preselectors almost always have controls that need manual tweaking.

There is a middle ground: High-pass and band-rejection filters from Kiwa Electronics and Par Electronics needs less operator intervention than a preselector. For example, a ~2 MHz high-pass filter will usually squash mediumwave AM "ghosts."

How Much Gain?

One way to judge an active antenna is simply by how much gain it provides. But that's like judging a car only by its horsepower.

An active antenna should provide signal levels comparable to those from a good passive wire antenna. Any less, and receiver circuit noise may intrude. Too much, and the receiver's circuitry—maybe the antenna's, too—might overload.

Like Smucker's, it needs to be just right.

How You Can Help

Buying an antenna is only step one. Following that are things you can do to ensure the antenna reaches its full potential:

- Active antennas work best off batteries, which avoid hum and buzz caused by AC mains power. But if your antenna uses an AC adaptor, keep it and electrical cords away from the receiving element and feedline. If there's hum or buzz anyway, try a different AC adaptor from someplace like Jameco.com.

  Electrically quiet AC adaptors are getting hard to come by, thanks to legislation reducing power consumption. These rules effectively mandate potentially noisy switching-type power supplies by outlawing the inherently quiet transformer variety. Some of the newer switching adaptors emit less "hash," but you can determine this only by firsthand testing.

- Antenna performance is one third technology, another third geography and geology, and a third part installation.

PASSPORT reports on the first and gives tips on the third. Yet, much depends on the second: local conditions.

You can boost the odds by seeing how the receiving element performs at different spots—sometimes just moving it a few yards or meters can make a real difference. Jerry-rig the antenna until you're satisfied the best spot has been found, then mount it properly.

- Finally, if your radio has multiple antenna inputs, try each to see which works best.

What PASSPORT's Ratings Mean

Star ratings: ✪✪✪✪✪ is best. To help in deciding, star ratings for active antennas can be compared directly against those for passive wire antennas in PASSPORT REPORTS. Stars reflect overall world band performance and meaningful features, plus to a lesser extent ergonomics and build quality. Price, appearance, country of manufacture and the like are not taken into account.

Passport's Choice. La crème de la crème. Our test team's personal picks of the litter—what we would buy or have for our personal use. Unlike star ratings, these choices are unapologetically subjective.

¢: A relative bargain, with decidedly more performance than the price would suggest. Listed in descending order of merit. Unless otherwise indicated each has a one-year warranty.

Retested for 2009

✪✪✪✪½ *Passport's Choice*

Wellbrook ALA 100

Head amp and control unit; requires exceptionally large homemade outdoor loop. Active, remote, broadband, 0.05–30 MHz

Pricing: £139.00 plus £5.00 shipping in the United Kingdom and Eire. £139.00 plus £15.00 shipping elsewhere.

Wellbrook ALA 100 customers have to construct their own receiving elements. Originally we made ours square, but its bottom drooped. Now it's a sag-free octagon.

J.R. Sherwood

Pros: Exceptionally quiet on four counts: 1) very large 40-foot/12.2-meter circumference loop receiving element and relatively low-gain amplifier combine to produce the best signal-to-noise ratio, notably above 10 MHz, of any active model tested; 2) unusually low pickup of thunderstorm static, especially below 8 MHz during and near local summer; 3) balanced loop design inherently helps reduce pickup of local electrical noise; and 4) pronounced directional pickup pattern allows for superior nulling of local electrical noise and co-channel interference on mediumwave AM and to a lesser extent throughout the shortwave spectrum, thanks to receiving element's exceptional size (*see* Cons). Forty-foot/12.2 meter loop places resonant frequency at 23 MHz, where there is little activity, which reduces stress on antenna's amplifier and results in exceptional pickup level. Overall shortwave performance, especially quietness, makes it unusually complementary to passive outdoor wire antennas. Superior build quality. Supplied Stancor STA-300R 117V AC adaptor among best tested for freedom from hum or buzzing (220V adaptor not tested). Although any large loop inherently susceptible to inductive pickup of local thunderstorm static, our antenna's amplifier has not suffered static damage from storms; even nearby one kilowatt shortwave transmissions cause no harm. Protected circuitry, using easily replaced 315 mA fuse. Superior factory support. Easier to ship and less costly than most other tested Wellbrook loops.

Cons: Significant undertaking to install, as quasi-kit ALA 100 requires construction of 26–59 foot/8–18 meter homemade loop receiving element. For decent results, receiving element should be mounted outdoors, another installation burden; too, if element's framework made from white PVC it can be an eyesore (gray PVC electrical conduit, although less robust, could be substituted). Only moderate gain for reception within such modest-signal areas as Western Hemisphere, Asia and Australasia—a drawback only with receivers having relatively noisy circuitry. Loop size makes rotation exceptionally difficult, so benefits of high directivity are a challenge to fully realize. BNC connector at the receiving element's base is open to weather, needing to be user-sealed with Coax Seal, electrical putty or similar. Encapsulated amplifier makes repair impossible. Manufacturer cautions against allowing sunlight to damage head amplifier's plastic housing; yet, after years of intense exposure at our high-UV main test site, Wellbrook's plastic seems no worse for wear than any other outdoor antenna's plastic. Coaxial cable not supplied. Available for purchase or export only two ways: from the Welsh manufacturer (www.wellbrook.uk.com), using a pounds or dollars cheque or International Money Order; or with credit card via an English dealer's unsecured email address (sales@shortwave.co.uk).

☞ Star rating and evaluation applies to loop receiving element of around 40 feet/12 meters in circumference; at this size, directive pattern is 90 degrees different above 20 MHz. Performance drops with noticeably smaller receiving elements, but then that's why the ALA 100M (below) was created.

Verdict for 2009: The more we use this unusual antenna, the more we covet it. Quietness is its hallmark, with all manner of atmospheric, amplifier and local electrical noises diminishing to *sotto voce* so weak stations can stand out and be heard.

Size matters, and this quasi-kit can get seriously big by active antenna standards. Indeed, it almost occupies a "neither" world between compact active antennas and lengthy passive wire antennas. This makes it a major slog to construct and install. It also makes it relatively susceptible to damage from extreme weather events.

WIRY ART OF DECEPTION

Listeners facing antenna restrictions have concocted a dog's breakfast of camouflaged and low-visibility outdoor wire antennas. Some, hidden in the open, look like clotheslines or are woven into volleyball nets. Yet others are tucked underneath awnings or canopies. Spooks-at-heart play to urban apathy by hanging varnished thin-wire antennas, then waiting to see what happens.

Modest passive stealth antennas can perform surprisingly well when mated to the $100 MFJ-1020C/Vectronics AT-100. Just remove its telescopic antenna and—*voilà*—it becomes a tunable active preselector that outperforms comparably priced nominal preselectors.

Even regular active antennas can sometimes pass muster. One creative Australian went so far as to tell a curious neighbor that his loop antenna was "art sculpture"—it worked!

Deep pockets? If you want something James Bondish, the SGC Stealth Antenna Kit (not tested) from wsplc.com is £299.95 in the United Kingdom, $495.24 plus shipping overseas. Stirred, of course, not shaken.

Greater size impacts performance, too. The loop receiving element's length that we chose provides full-wave resonance around 20–30 MHz, which is why it has better pickup than the ALA-100M except below 5 MHz. This resonance also alters the directive pattern by 90 degrees above 20 MHz.

For 2009 we replaced the ALA 100's original square loop receiving element with one that is octagonal (we also used octagonal with the ALA 100M). Reception results are unchanged, but pipe bending from weight has been all but eliminated; too, in principle this should make it more resistant to wind and ice.

If installation, size, appearance and purchase hurdles don't deter you, you won't find a better active model than the British-made Wellbrook ALA 100. If you already use a passive outdoor wire antenna, this model's unique receiving characteristics should be deliciously complementary.

An octagon shape is nigh ideal for the Wellbrook ALA 100M's receiving element. J.R. Sherwood

New for 2009

✪✪✪✪½ *Passport's Choice*

Wellbrook ALA 100M

Head amp and control unit; requires large homemade outdoor loop. Active, remote, broadband, 0.05–30 MHz

Pricing: £139.00 plus £5.00 shipping in the United Kingdom and Eire. £139.00 plus £15.00 shipping elsewhere.

Pros: Unusually quiet because: 1) large 20-foot/6.1-meter circumference loop (receiving element) and relatively low-gain amplifier result in superior signal-to-noise ratio for an active model; 2) unusually low pickup of thunderstorm static, especially below 8 MHz during and near local summer; 3) balanced loop design inherently helps reduce pickup of local electrical noise; and 4) relatively directional pickup pattern allows for nulling local electrical noise and co-channel interference on mediumwave AM—also, world band stations can be directionally peaked and attenuated even within higher reaches of shortwave spectrum (*see* Cons). Gain similar to ALA 100 in roughly the lower third of shortwave spectrum and within 3 dB below 5 MHz (*see* Con). Overall shortwave performance, especially quietness, makes it unusually complementary to passive outdoor wire antennas. Performance virtually identical to ALA 100 within mediumwave AM band, except "M" model's smaller loop makes rotation less difficult. Superior build quality. Supplied Stancor STA-300R 117V AC adaptor among best tested for freedom from hum or buzzing (220V adaptor not tested). Although any large loop inherently susceptible to inductive pickup of local thunderstorm static, our antenna's amplifier has not suffered static damage from storms; even nearby one kilowatt shortwave transmissions cause no harm. Also can be used to some extent on trips by taking along 10–20 feet (3–6 meters) of wire, forming it into a makeshift triangular receiving element, then hanging it from a tree or balcony. Protected circuitry, using easily replaced 315 mA fuse. Superior factory support. Easier to ship and less costly than most other tested Wellbrook loops.

Cons: Lower gain than ALA 100 within shortwave spectrum above 5 MHz or so; differences range from 3–6 dB below 12 MHz to as much as 20 dB above 20 MHz. Significant undertaking to install, as quasi-kit ALA 100M requires construction of 10–33 foot/3–10 meter homemade loop receiving element. For decent results, receiving element should be mounted outdoors, another installation burden; too, if element's framework made from white PVC it can be an eyesore (gray PVC electrical conduit, although less robust, could be substituted). Only moderate gain for reception within such modest-signal areas as Western Hemisphere, Asia and Australasia—a drawback only with receivers having relatively noisy circuitry. Loop size makes rotation difficult, so benefits of directivity are not easy to fully realize. BNC connector at the receiving element's base open to weather, needing to be user-sealed with Coax Seal, electrical putty or similar. Encapsulated amplifier makes repair impossible. Manufacturer cautions against allowing sunlight to damage head amplifier's plastic housing; yet, our tests indicate that Wellbrook's plastic seems no worse for wear than any other outdoor antenna's plastic. Coaxial cable not supplied. Available for purchase or export only two ways: from the Welsh manufacturer (www.wellbrook.uk.com), using a pounds or dollars cheque or International Money Order; or with credit card via an English dealer's unsecured email address (sales@shortwave.co.uk).

☞ Star rating and evaluation applies to loop receiving element of around 20 feet/12 meters in circumference. Performance should vary to some extent at different lengths.

Verdict: A winner, and can even be configured for use on trips.

This unusually quiet active antenna is eclipsed only slightly by its yet-larger ALA 100 sibling with varying degrees of higher gain. However, the ALA 100M is easier to construct and less susceptible to damage from wind and ice. Too, it has less visual impact than its larger '100 sibling.

Evaluation of New Model: For last year's tests the primary loop was formed into a square using half-inch (13 mm) PVC. However, this year the PVC was cut into shorter lengths and formed into an octagon with five-foot (1.5 meter) sides and 45-degree elbows. Fourteen-gauge (1.9 mm) insulated copper wire was used again, as it has very low electrical resistance yet is pliable enough to be bent inside the PVC—a better long-term solution than dressing the wire outside with zip/twist ties, in part to avoid deterioration from UV rays. A "T" in the middle of the loop's bottom allows the wires to egress and connect to the head amplifier.

Best is to dress the antenna wire while you assemble the loop, as it is nearly impossible to pull wire around so many bends.

To facilitate repair, PVC fittings can be held together with self-tapping stainless screws rather than glue (file the screw tips smooth so they can't puncture the wire insulation). This was underscored when a 20-hour 70 mph (112 kph) wind brought our new loop crashing to the ground, breaking an elbow. Repair was cheap and relatively quick.

The ALA 100M also works as a triangle loop on certain types of trips, if you're determined enough. Take along a roll of wire—perhaps also four or five dowels and PVC sleeves for the triangle's bottom leg if you want to be fancy, duct tape or string if you don't—then form it into a 10–20 foot (3–6 meter) hillbilly receiving element. Hang it from a convenient tree or balcony—point or flat-side up makes little difference in reception, so go with what's easier to hang. Not quite plug-and-play, but the results more than make up for the effort.

The ALA 100M performs admirably for a single basic reason: Amplification is moderate, while the passive capture area of the loop receiving element is quite large. The result is that it mixes much of the virtue of a passive wire antenna with the quietness and directionality of a loop design.

It is unusually quiet, making it an excellent singleton antenna for tuning weak signals. Even better, if circumstances permit, is to have it as a second antenna to complement a first-rate passive wire antenna such as the Alpha-Delta DX-Ultra.

✪✪✪✪ *Passport's Choice*

Wellbrook ALA 330S

Outdoor-indoor loop. Active, remote, broadband, 2.3–30 MHz

Pricing: *ALA 330S:* £199.00 plus £10.00 shipping in the United Kingdom and Eire. £199.00 plus £33.00 shipping elsewhere. *TV or ham single-axis aftermarket rotor:* $70 and up in the United States (*see* ☞).

Pros: Among the best signal-to-noise ratios, including at times reduced pickup of thunderstorm static, on all shortwave frequencies, of any active model tested; low-noise/low-static pickup characteristics most noticeable below 8 MHz, especially during local summer, when it sometimes outperforms sophisticated outdoor wire antennas. Higher shortwave gain (above 3 MHz) than sibling '1530/'1530+, which helps get signals into a better AGC range on most receivers. Balanced loop design inherently reduces pickup of local electrical noise; additionally, aluminum loop receiving element can be affixed to a low-cost TV or ham aftermarket rotor to improve reception by directionally nulling local electrical noise and, to a lesser degree, static. Rotatability also can slightly reduce co-channel shortwave interference below 4 or 5 MHz and to even at times on higher frequencies. Superior build quality, including rigorous weatherproofing (*see* Cons). Supplied 117V AC adaptor (Stancor STA-300R) among best tested for freedom from hum or buzzing (*see* Cons). Although any large loop is inherently susceptible to inductive pickup of local thunderstorm static, during our tests of the prior and current versions the antenna's amplifier has never suffered static damage during storms; indeed, even nearby one kilowatt shortwave transmissions have not damaged it. Protected circuitry, using an easily replaced 315 mA fuse. Superior factory support.

Cons: Only moderate gain for reception within such modest-signal areas as Western Hemisphere, Asia and Australasia—a drawback only with receivers having relatively noisy circuitry. Slightly less gain than ALA 1530 within little-used 2.3–2.5 MHz (120 meter) tropical world band segment, a drawback only with receivers having relatively noisy circuitry. Mediumwave AM gain significantly inferior to that of the '1530. Flange for loop receiving element has metric pipe threading; U.S. users may need to re-thread. Loop receiving element, about one meter across, is large and cumbersome to ship. Mounting mast and optional aftermarket rotor add to cost and complexity (*see* ☞). BNC connector at the receiving element's base is open to the weather, thus needs to be user-sealed with Coax Seal, electrical putty or similar. Encapsulated amplifier makes repair impossible. Manufacturer cautions against allowing high winds to stress mounting flange; however, one of our units survived 90+ mph (145+ km/h)

Wellbrook's ALA 330S targets world band performance. It needs less space than an ALA 100M, too.

J.R. Sherwood

winds until the locally procured pipe coupling to which we had attached the antenna snapped. Manufacturer cautions against allowing sunlight to damage head amplifier's plastic housing; yet, after years of intense exposure at a high-UV PASSPORT test site, Wellbrook's plastic seems no worse for the wear than any other outdoor antenna's plastic. Adaptor supplied for 117V AC runs very warm after being plugged in for a few hours, while amplifier tends to run slightly warm; nonetheless, after years of use at PASSPORT test facility, neither has acted up. No coaxial cable supplied. Available for purchase or export only two ways: from the Welsh manufacturer (www.wellbrook.uk.com), using a pounds or dollars cheque or International Money Order; or with credit card via an English dealer's unsecured email address (sales@shortwave.co.uk).

☞ The standard mast size for a Channel Master or other television rotor in the United States is at least one inch, about twice that of the Wellbrook. Some kind of glued PVC or other improvised couplings or sleeves are needed to make the conversion.

Verdict: This excellent active antenna shines when it comes to reducing the impact of static and noise on weak signals below 8 MHz.

For limited-space situations, and even to complement passive wire antennas on large properties, the '330S is hard to equal. However, if your receiver tends to sound "hissy" with weak signals, then it probably needs an antenna which gives even more gain so it can overcome internal receiver noise. Of course, with top-rated receivers this should not be an issue.

For best reception the antenna should be mounted outdoors, away from the house and affixed to a rotor. However, this is more important with the ALA 1530 (below) when used for longwave and mediumwave AM reception.

WHERE TO PLACE A REMOTE ANTENNA

When a remote active antenna is installed properly it can perform very well. The bad news is that if you have space outdoors to mount it properly, you may also have room for a passive wire antenna that will perform better, yet. Maybe cheaper, too.

Here are three tips on placing remote models, but creativity rules:

- Outdoors, put the receiving element in the clear, away from objects. Metal degrades performance, so especially keep it away from metal and, if possible, use a nonconductive mast or capped PVC pipe. Optimum height from ground is usually around 10–25 feet/3–8 meters. Here, "ground" refers to the electrical ground—not only *terra firma*, but also buildings and the like.

  If a mast is impractical try a tree. Although sap is electrically conductive, this is a reasonable fallback, especially with hardwood deciduous varieties other than sugar maple. You may have to do some trimming to keep leaves or needles away from the receiving element.

- If yard placement is impractical, put the receiving element outdoors as far as you dare. In a high rise consider using a balcony or someplace just outside a window. For example, if the receiving element is a telescopic or fixed rod, point it away from the building 70 degrees or so, like a wall flagpole. If you reside on the top floor, the roof may also be a good bet.

  If outdoor placement is out of the question, try the attic if the roof isn't foil-insulated or metal. With larger models this beats having it hog an entire room.

- If all else fails affix the receiving element against the inside-center of a large window. Radio signals, like light, sail right through glass.

What's not to like? An ordering procedure that's inconvenient and démodé. There are no dealers outside the United Kingdom, and there is still no secure way for those elsewhere to order by credit card on the Internet.

Overall, the '330S isn't in the same league as top-rated outdoor wire antennas. However, it can outperform even those antennas with some static-prone signals or when local electrical noise is a problem—provided it is erected properly.

✪✪✪⅞ *Passport's Choice*
Wellbrook ALA 1530+, Wellbrook ALA 1530, Wellbrook ALA 1530P

Outdoor-indoor loop. Active, remote, broadband, 0.15–30 MHz

Pricing: *ALA 1530+/ALA 1530+P:* £180.00 plus £10.00 shipping in the United Kingdom and Eire, £33.00 shipping elsewhere. *ALA 1530/ALA 1530P:* £159.00 plus £10.00 shipping in the United Kingdom and Eire, £33.00 shipping elsewhere. *Yaesu G-5500/G-5500B twin-axis aftermarket rotor:* $639.95 in the United States. CAD$739.00 in Canada. £449.95 in the United Kingdom. €549.00 in Germany. *TV or ham single-axis aftermarket rotor:* $70 and up in the United States (*see* third ☞).

Pros: At comparable levels of performance, covers not only shortwave but also mediumwave AM and longwave (*see* Cons). Superb mediumwave AM and longwave when coupled to a Yaesu G-5500/G-5500B aftermarket rotor with twin-axis directionality, and almost as good with single-axis TV or ham rotor; also, any rotor can slightly reduce co-channel shortwave interference below 4 or 5 MHz and even occasionally on higher frequencies. Very nearly the best signal-to-noise ratio among active models tested, including reduced pickup of thunderstorm static. Balanced loop design inherently helps reduce pickup of local electrical noise. Low-noise/low-static pickup characteristic most noticeable below 8 MHz during summer, when it sometimes outperforms sophisticated outdoor wire antennas.

The Wellbrook ALA 1530+ is an excellent mediumwave AM performer. World band, too, if local signals aren't too strong. D. Walcutt

Slightly more gain than sibling ALA 330S within little-used 2.3–2.5 MHz (120 meter) tropical world band segment. Superior build quality, including rigorous weatherproofing (*see* Cons). Supplied AC adaptor, properly bypassed and regulated, is among the best tested for freedom from hum or buzzing (*see* Cons). Although any large loop's amplifier is inherently susceptible to inductive pickup of local thunderstorm static, during our tests the antenna's amp never suffered static damage during storms; indeed, even nearby one kilowatt shortwave transmissions did no damage to the antenna amplifier. Protected circuitry, using an easily replaced 315 mA fuse. Superior factory support. *ALA 1530+:* Nominal full-spec operating frequency range of 50 kHz to 100 MHz. Nominal mediumwave AM IP3 improvement resulting from nominal faint drop in mediumwave AM gain. *ALA 1530:* Nominal full-spec operating frequency range of 150 kHz (30 kHz with reduced sensitivity) to 30 MHz.

Cons: Extended frequency range, as compared to sibling '330S, can result in mediumwave AM signals surfacing within the shortwave spectrum, degrading reception—usually a more significant issue in urban and suburban North America than elsewhere (even a simple rotor can help by turning the antenna perpendicular to an offending mediumwave AM signal's axis); this tends to be less of a problem at night because of reduced local transmitting powers. Prone to overloading some receivers in locations rich with strong mediumwave AM signals; this also tends to be less of a problem at night because of reduced local transmitting powers. Only moderate gain, slightly less than sibling ALA 330S, for reception within such modest-signal areas as Western Hemisphere, Asia and Australasia. Balanced loop receiving element, about one meter across, not easy to mount and is large and cumbersome to ship. Mounting mast and optional aftermarket rotor add to cost and complexity of erection (*see* third ☞). Flange for loop receiving element has metric pipe threading; U.S. users may need to re-thread. BNC connector at the receiving element's base is open to the weather, thus needs to be user-sealed with Coax Seal, electrical putty or similar. Encapsulated amplifier makes repair impossible. Manufacturer cautions against allowing high winds to stress mounting flange; however, after years of wind and sun at our location nothing untoward has materialized. Manufacturer cautions against allowing sunlight to damage head amplifier's plastic housing; yet, after years of intense exposure at a high-UV PASSPORT test site, Wellbrook's plastic seems no worse for the wear than any other outdoor antenna's plastic. Adaptor supplied for 117V AC runs warm after being plugged in for a few hours; additionally, amplifier tends to run slightly warm; nonetheless, after years of use neither has acted up. No coaxial cable supplied. Available for purchase or export only two ways: from the Welsh manufacturer (www.wellbrook.uk.com), using a pounds or dollars cheque or International Money Order; or with credit card via an English dealer's unsecured email address (sales@shortwave.co.uk).

☞ An antenna tuner complicates operation, but at times may improve signal level by as much as 6 dB.

☞ Mediumwave AM and longwave performance directionality may suffer if the '1530 is not mounted well away from other antennas.

☞ The standard mast size for a Channel Master or other television rotor in the United States is at least one inch, about twice that of the Wellbrook. Some kind of glued PVC or other improvised couplings or sleeves are needed to make the conversion.

☞ "P" version, not tested, uses a semi-rigid plastic loop rather than aluminum and is for indoor use.

Verdict: Interested in distant broadcast goodies below the shortwave spectrum, as well as world band? If so, the Wellbrook ALA 1530+ and ALA 1530 are hard to beat—so long as you don't live near local mediumwave AM transmitters. A rotor is *de rigeur* for nulling co-channel interference below 1.7 MHz, and may help a skosh with tropical world band stations. As with all other Wellbrook loop antennas the '1530+ and '1530 excel at rejecting noise and static, particularly below 8 MHz.

For multiband coverage, including mediumwave AM and longwave, the '1530+ and '1530 are both top-drawer choices. Both are comparably solid performers for world band, although not always quite equal to siblings ALA 100 and ALA 330S.

✪✪✪½ *Passport's Choice*

RF Systems DX-One Professional Mark II

Outdoor-indoor "eggbeater." Active, remote, broadband, 0.02–60 MHz.

Pricing: *DX-One Pro antenna:* $799.95 in the United States. £399.99 in the United Kingdom. €498.00 in Germany. €550.00 plus shipping worldwide from the Netherlands.

Pros: Outstanding dynamic range. Very low noise. Outputs for two receivers. Comes with switchable band rejection filter to reduce odds of mediumwave AM signals ghosting into shortwave spectrum. Receiving element has outstanding build quality. Coaxial connector at head amplifier is completely shielded from weather by clever mechanical design. Superior low noise, high gain performance on mediumwave AM.

Cons: Unbalanced design makes antenna susceptible to importing buzz at some locations; this is especially noticeable because of otherwise-excellent performance. AC power supply not optimally bypassed, causing slight hum on some signals. More likely than most antennas to exacerbate fading, even though design nominally reduces fading effects. No coaxial cable supplied. Output position for 10 dB gain measures +6 dB. Warranty only six months.

Verdict: The pricey RF Systems DX-One Professional Mark II is a superior performer that's popular in certain professional circles. As with any antenna having a small capture area and an unbalanced design, at some locations it is prone to picking up local electrical noise. Manufactured in the Netherlands.

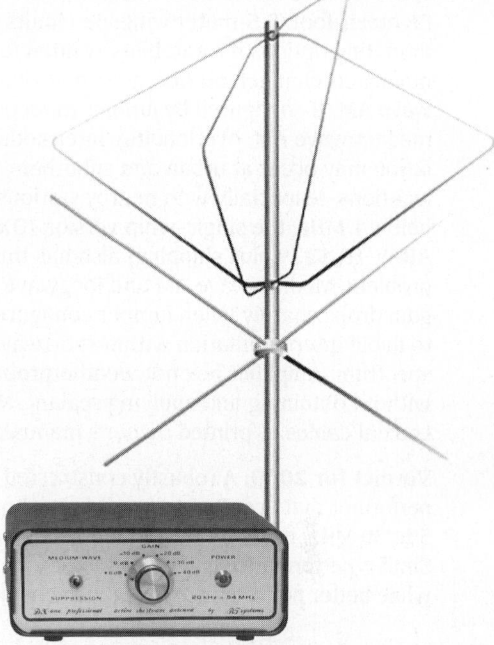

RF Systems DX-One Professional Mark II is costly, but it's on the short list of various government agencies. J.R. Sherwood

Retested for 2009

✪✪✪½

DX Engineering DXE-ARAH2-1P

Outdoor-indoor dipole. Active, remote, broadband 0.06–30 MHz.

Pricing: *DXE-ARAH2-1P:* $289.00 in the United States. *Aftermarket coaxial cable and plugs (required):* Usually $15–45 in the United States.

Pros: Unusual capture length helps produce superior signal-to-noise ratio. Worthy gain above about 9 MHz, rising to peak at 27 MHz. Excellent freedom from mediumwave AM "ghosting" when internal jumper configured to roll off below 3 MHz. Very good mediumwave AM and longwave performance when 1) internal jumper configured for flat response, and 2) antenna located in relatively rural setting with no nearby mediumwave AM stations. Excellent build quality. Circuit board not potted, facilitating repair.

Cons: Not widely available; when ordered from manufacturer, shipping charges not indicated until order nearly completed. Uses two nine-foot/2.75-meter CB whips for pickup element, so takes up much more

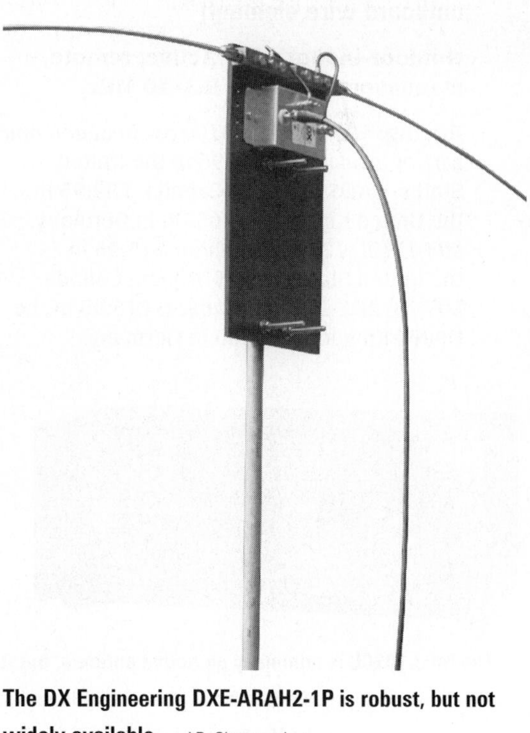

The DX Engineering DXE-ARAH2-1P is robust, but not widely available. J.R. Sherwood

space than usual for an active antenna. Eighteen-foot/5.5-meter wingspan limits mounting options if rotatability wanted for nulling co-channel interference on mediumwave AM. If configured by jumper to receive mediumwave AM, overloading/intermodulation may occur at urban and suburban locations—especially with nearby stations below 1 MHz; the single-whip version (DXE-ARAV-1P, $229 plus shipping) also has this problem. Mediumwave AM and longwave gain drops sharply when jumper configured to avoid intermodulation within shortwave spectrum. Amplifier box not weatherproof without obtaining and applying sealant. No coaxial cables or printed owner's manual.

Verdict for 2009: A robustly constructed performer that acquits itself well from about 5 to 30 MHz, but is prone to overloading. Similar performance can be had for less, while better performance isn't much costlier.

Revised for 2009

✪✪✪ *Passport's Choice*

MFJ-1020C, Vectronics AT-100 (with outboard wire element)

Outdoor-indoor wire. Active, remote, manual preselection, 0.3–40 MHz.

Pricing: *MFJ-1020C/AT-100 (without antenna wire or insulators):* $99.95 in the United States. CAD$109.00 in Canada. £89.95 in the United Kingdom. €105.00 in Germany. *MFJ-1312D 120V AC adaptor:* $15.95 in the United States. CAD$19.95 in Canada. *MFJ-1312DX 240V AC adaptor:* £15.95 in the United Kingdom. €19.00 in Germany.

The MFJ-1020C is nominally an active antenna, but it really shines as a preselector. Now also available under the Vectronics label. J.R. Sherwood

Pros: Superior dynamic range, so functions effectively with outboard wire receiving element, preferably mounted outdoors, in lieu of built-in telescopic receiving element. Sharp preselector peak unusually effective in preventing overloading. Works best off battery (*see* Cons). Choice of PL-259 or RCA connections. Suitable for travel. 30-day money-back guarantee if purchased from manufacturer (MFJ).

Cons: Preselector complicates operation; tune control needs adjustment even with modest frequency changes, especially within the mediumwave AM band. Knobs small and touchy to adjust. High current draw (measures 30 mA), so battery runs down quickly. Removing sheet- metal screws often to change battery should eventually result in stripping unless great care is taken. MFJ's AC adaptor, optional, causes significant hum on many received signals.

☞ The 1020C/AT-100 serves little or no useful purpose as a tunable preselector for reasonably long inverted-L antennas (anything above around 50–75 feet/15–20 meters) or resonant outdoor wire antennas. Additionally, the amplifier circuit is always present, so it cannot be used as an unamplified preselector targeted to improve front-end selectivity with significant wire antennas. Simply reducing amplification gain to improve front-end selectivity may or may not help, but won't improve signal-to-noise ratio or dynamic range, as the gain potentiometer is merely an output pad (measured range of 40 dB).

Verdict: The 1020C/AT-100 has a little secret: It's only okay the way the manufacturer sells it as a proximate active antenna, but as a preselector with an outdoor random-length wire antenna it is a worthy low-cost performer—better, in fact, than MFJ's designated shortwave preselector. Simply collapse (or, better, remove) the built-in telescopic element, then connect an outboard wire receiving element to the 1020C/AT-100's external antenna input.

Alas, MFJ's optional AC adaptor introduces hum much of the time, battery drain is considerable, and changing the built-in battery is inconvenient and relies on wear-prone sheet-metal screws. Best bet, unless you're into experimenting with power supplies: Skip the adaptor and use a large outboard rechargeable battery.

Peso for peso, the MFJ-1020C/Vectronics AT-100 fed by a remote wire receiving element is the best buy among active antennas. The rub is that the use of several yards or meters of wire, preferably outdoors, makes it something of a hybrid requiring more space than other active antennas. But for many row houses, townhouses, ground-floor and rooftop apartments with a patch of outdoor space it can be a godsend. If visibility is an issue, use ultra-thin wire for the receiving element.

Revised for 2009: The former Vectronics AT-100 once was nearly identical to the Palstar AA30/AA30P, but some months back it was changed to become a brand-only variation of the MFJ 1020C. The result is improved performance at the same price.

The Dressler ARA 60 S is one tough cookie, but not at its best near powerful local transmitters. J.R. Sherwood

✪✪✪

Dressler ARA 60 S

Outdoor-indoor fixed rod. Active, remote, broadband, 0.04–60/100 MHz.

Pricing: $349.95 in the United States. €219.00 in Germany.

Pros: Superior build quality, with fiberglass whip and foam-encapsulated head amplifier to resist weather (*see* Cons). Very good and consistent gain, even above 20 MHz. AC adaptor with properly bypassed and regulated DC output, better than most. Suitable for packing diagonally in wide suitcase.

Cons: Prone to overloading at locations rich with strong mediumwave AM signals or low-band VHF-TV stations, although less likely if antenna mounted close to ground; overloading seems exacerbated by pickup from coaxial lead-in, which appears not to be properly decoupled from antenna. Encapsulated design makes most repairs impossible. RG-58 coaxial cable permanently attached on antenna end, making user replacement impossible. Gain control cumbersome to adjust; fortunately, in practice it is rarely needed.

Verdict: The robust Dressler ARA 60 S, made in Germany, is an excellent low-noise antenna for locations not in proximity to one or more powerful mediumwave AM or low-band VHF-TV transmitters.

✪✪⅞

AOR LA380

Indoor loop. Active, essentially proximate, manual preselection 3–40 MHz/ broadband 0.01–3 MHz & 40–500 MHz

Pricing: *LA380:* $369.95 in the United States. *BNC female-to-PL259 adaptor:* $4.95 in the United States.

Pros: Above-average gain. High-Q tunable preselector reduces the possibility of overload between 3 and 40 MHz (*see* Cons). Rotatability reduces local electrical noise and static below 10 MHz, to a lesser extent up to about 18 MHz. Rotatability can sometimes also slightly reduce co-channel short-

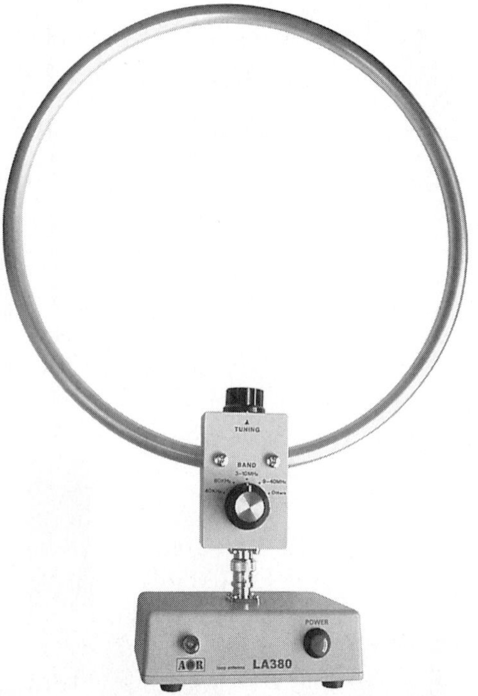

Loop antennas have real advantages, but the best are large. The AOR LA380 is much smaller, fitting easily atop a desk. D. Zantow

wave interference; as is the norm with loop antennas, this modest nulling of co-channel skywave interference is best at frequencies below 5 MHz. Outstanding and handy reception of time signals on 40 and 60 kHz, thanks to fixed preselector tuning. Broadband, 10 kHz–500 MHz (*see* Cons). Very easy to rotate and tune, with large knobs. Loop receiving element can be remotely mounted up to 16 feet/five meters away (*see* Cons). Hum-free AC adaptor complemented by built-in voltage regulator in base unit. Knobs use set screws. Very solid metal lower box that has beefy non-stick-on rubber feet; uses machined, not self-tapping, cabinet/loop and BNC-connector screws. Three-foot/90-cm male-to-male BNC cable. Small footprint. Loop of one foot/30 cm and small base module make antenna suitable for travel.

Cons: Quasi-proximate model with preselector controls on receiving element; however, to be practical that element needs to be within user's grasp to adjust 3–40 MHz tunable preselector. High-"Q" preselection requires frequent tweaking when frequencies changed between 3–40 MHz. Tunable preselection limited to 3–40 MHz, 40 kHz and 60 kHz; other frequencies broadband. Mediocre mediumwave AM. Male BNC connector on receiving element not snug, rocks slightly. Tuned by inexpensive plastic-cased tuning capacitor. Receiving element in plastic box; cover merely snaps on. Lacks 16-foot/five-meter male BNC/BNC cable needed for remote mounting of receiving element. Lacks BNC female-to-PL259 adaptor for connection to many models of tabletop receivers.

Verdict: The nicely sized AOR LA380 is a decent performer—free from spurious signals, overloading and hum. Yet, its tunable preselector is part of the receiving element and needs frequent tweaking, so remote mounting isn't practical.

Where local electrical noise doesn't intrude, the '380's superior gain, handy size and ease of rotation make it an effective choice for indoor use. Made in Japan, generally well constructed and priced accordingly.

✪✪¾ ¢ *Passport's Choice*

Sony AN-LP1

Indoor-portable loop. Active, remote, manual preselection, 3.9–4.3/4.7–25 MHz.

Price (as available): $106.00 via stores. ebay.com/buyfromjapan; includes prompt express air shipping from Japan to the United States.

Pros: Excellent for use with many portables, even those with no antenna input jack (*see* Cons).. Very good overall performance, including generally superior gain (*see* Cons), especially within world band segments—yet, surprisingly free from side effects. Battery operation, so no internally caused hum or noise (*see* Cons). Clever compact folding design for travel. Plug-in filter to reduce local electrical noise (*see* Cons). Low battery consumption (*see* Cons).

COMPACT, YET UNAMPLIFIED

Sometimes an antenna needs to be fairly small, yet can't be active. Applications vary from rural intelligence gathering to crisis survival, but for these the Dutch firm of RF Systems offers a high-caliber solution: the GMDSS-1.

The same company's similar MTA-1, not tested, nominally operates to full specification from 0.5–30 MHz.

Remote models are the way to go. More signal, less noise.

✪✪⅞

RF Systems GMDSS-1

Outdoor vertical fixed rod. Passive, remote, broadband, 0.1–25 MHz.

Pricing: *Antenna:* $259.95 in the United States. €165.00 plus shipping worldwide from the Netherlands. *AK-1 mounting bracket kit:* $54.95 in the United States. €32.00 in the Netherlands. *AK-2 mounting bracket kit:* €42.00 in the Netherlands.

Pros: Superior signal-to-noise ratio for an active antenna except within 21 MHz segment. Superior rejection of local electrical noise. Passive (unamplified) design avoids potential hum, buzz and other shortcomings inherent with active antennas (*see* Cons). No amplification required; yet, from about 9–12 MHz this short antenna (6.5 feet/2 m) produces signals almost comparable to those from a lengthy outdoor wire antenna (*see* Cons). Passive design allows it to function in emergency situations where electricity is not assured. Vertical configuration appropriate for some secreted locations; can be camouflaged with non-metallic paint. Superior build quality, using stainless steel and heavy UV resistant PVC; also, internal helical receiving element rigorously sealed. No radials required, unusual for a vertical antenna. Worthy mediumwave AM reception for a nondirectional antenna.

Cons: Except for about 9–12 MHz, weak-signal performance varies from fair to poor, depending on tuned frequency. Extra-cost mounting kit required; AK-1 mounting bracket kit not stainless. Connecting cable between antenna and radio not included.

Verdict: Although unamplified and scarcely taller than most men, the RF Systems GMDSS-1 vertical performs surprisingly well. However, pedestrian signal oomph in many world band segments limits its attraction except with a high-sensitivity receiver or boosted by an active preselector. Some portables also benefit from the modest signal input.

Made in the Netherlands, it is constructed like a tank. Between this and its complete independence from electricity, it is unusually appropriate for emergencies, civil disorders, hideaways and hostile climates.

No Batteries Needed: The RF Systems GMDSS-1 is small, yet unamplified. It occupies a niche between small active antennas and large passive aerials.

D. Zantow

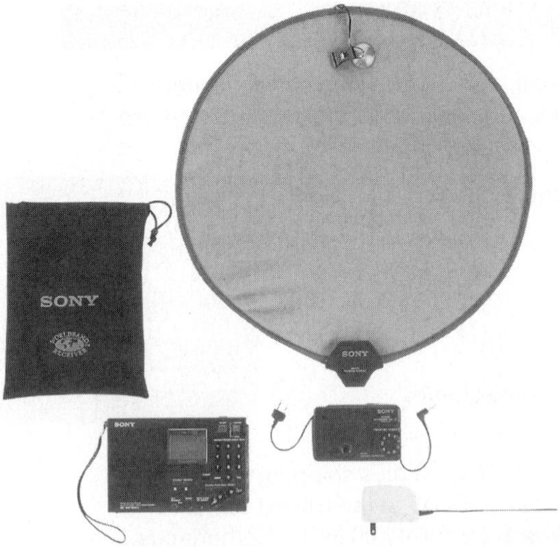

No other active antenna equals the Sony AN-LP1 for use on trips. Suitable for home, too, but get it while you can—remaining units are being snapped up.

J.R. Sherwood

Cons: Seemingly discontinued, but in any event available now only in and via Japan. Indoors only—can't be mounted outdoors during inclement weather. Functions acceptably on shortwave only 3.9–4.3 MHz and 4.7–25 MHz, with no mediumwave AM or longwave coverage. Gain varies markedly throughout the shortwave spectrum, in large part because the preselector's step-tuned resonances lack variable peaking. Preselector bandswitching complicates operation slightly. Operates only from batteries (two "AA," not included)—no AC adaptor, not even a socket for one. Consumer-grade plastic construction with no shielding. When clipped onto a telescopic receiving element instead of fed through an antenna jack, the lack of a ground connection reduces performance. Plug-in noise filter unit reduces signal strength by several decibels.

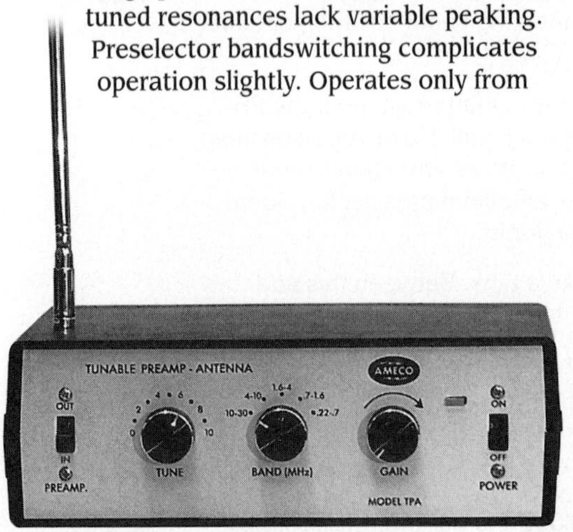

The Ameco TPA is a solid choice in a proximate antenna. Just don't connect it to an outboard receiving element, as it may overload. J.R. Sherwood

☞ Sony recommends that the AN-LP1 not be used with the discontinued Sony ICF-SW77 receiver. However, our tests indicate that so long as the control box and loop receiving element are kept as far as possible from the 'SW77, the antenna performs well.

☞ The discontinued Sony ICF-SW07 compact portable came with an AN-LP2 antenna. This is virtually identical in concept and performance to the AN-LP1, except that it is designed solely for the 'SW07 so it has automatic preselection. The AN-LP2 cannot be used with other models.

Verdict: This is the handiest model for travelers wanting superior world band reception on portables—and it is truly portable. This Japanese-made device has generally excellent gain, low noise and few side effects.

There is slightly limited frequency coverage—90/120 meter DXers should look elsewhere—and the loop receiving element cannot be mounted permanently outdoors. Too, the lack of variable preselector peaking causes gain to vary greatly by frequency.

The AN-LP1, seemingly discontinued in the first half of 2006, continues to be available from a reliable Japanese exporter.

✪✪½ ¢

Ameco TPA

Indoor telescopic rod. Active, proximate, manual preselection, 0.22–30 MHz.

Pricing: *TPA:* $76.95 in the United States. CAD$98.00 in Canada.

Pros: High signal recovery. Long receiving element. Superior ergonomics (*see* Cons), including easy-to-read front panel with good-sized metal knobs. Superior gain below 10 MHz. Suitable for travel.

Cons: Proximate model, so receiving element has to be placed near receiver. Above 15 MHz gain slips to slightly below average. Overloads with external antenna; because gain potentiometer is in the first stage, decreasing gain may actually increase overloading as current drops through the FET. Preselector complicates operation. No rubber feet, so slides around in use—user-remediable. Consumer-grade plastic construction with no shielding. Comes with no printed information on warranty; however, manufacturer states by telephone that it is the customary one year.

Verdict: Back in the heyday of Hammarlund, Hallicrafters and National, there also was Ameco with such offerings as CW learning kits. While most other American radio firms were crushed by the advance of technology, Ameco stayed light on its feet and survived. Well, sort of. Since 2004 Ameco has been associated with a new firm, Milestone Technologies of Colorado.

Ameco's TPA active antenna remains one of the best proximate models tested for bringing in usable signals with a telescopic receiving element, and signal recovery is excellent. However, when connected to an external antenna it overloads badly, and reducing gain doesn't help.

✪✪½

McKay Dymek DA100E

Indoor-outdoor telescopic rod. Active, remote, broadband, 0.05–30 MHz.

McKay Dymek DA100EM

Outdoor-marine fixed rod. Active, remote, broadband, 0.05–30 MHz.

Pricing: *DA100E:* $199.95 in the United States. *DA100EM (marine version):* $229.95 in the United States.

Pros: Respectable gain and noise. Generally good build quality (*see* Cons), with worthy coaxial cable and an effectively sealed receiving element; marine version appears to be even better yet for resisting weather. Jack for second antenna when turned off. Minor gain rolloff at higher shortwave frequencies.

The late George McKay introduced the Dymek DA100 34 years ago. Improved time and again, it is now in its fifth incarnation. The EM version holds up substantially better outdoors than the ordinary DA100E. J.R. Sherwood

Marginally suitable for travel. *DA100EM:* Weather-resistant fiberglass whip and brass fittings, designed to withstand salt and sea, help ensure optimum outdoor performance.

Cons: Not widely available. Slightly higher noise floor compared to other models. Some controls may confuse initially. Dynamic range mediocre; not usually an issue in the Americas except near local transmitters, but in Europe and other strong-signal parts of the world it's best to purchase on returnable basis. *DA100E:* When outdoors, telescopic receiving element can allow moisture and avian waste into gaps between segments and at base, and base's setscrews can rust; any of these can cause gradual resistance and/or spurious signals, so gaps, base area and screw heads should be sealed with Coax Seal, electrical putty or similar. Outdoor thermal heaving reportedly can cause receiving element to separate from slip fitting on base. Warranty only 30 days.

Verdict: The DA100E is a proven "out of the box" choice. Yet, because its dynamic range is relatively modest it is more prone than some other models to overload, especially in an urban environment or other high-signal-strength location.

The "E" version's receiving element can develop problems when permanently outdoors. To avoid this, the extra cost for the weatherproofed EM version should be money well spent.

✪✪¼

MFJ-1024

Indoor-outdoor telescopic rod. Active, remote, broadband, 0.05–30 MHz.

Pricing: $159.95 in the United States. CAD$159.00 in Canada. £139.95 in the United Kingdom. €159.00 in Germany. *MFJ-1312D 120V AC adaptor:* $15.95 in the United States. CAD$19.95 in Canada. *MFJ-1312DX 240V AC adaptor:* £15.95 in the United Kingdom. €19.00 in Germany.

Pros: Overall good gain and low noise. A/B selector for quick connection to another receiver. "Aux" input for passive antenna. Marginally suitable for travel. 30-day money-back guarantee if purchased from manufacturer (*see* Cons).

Cons: Significant hum with supplied AC adaptor; remedied with suitable aftermarket adaptor, although nonstandard power jack complicates adaptor substitution. Small sparks when live plug inserted into power jack. Dynamic range mediocre; not usually an issue in the Americas except near local transmitters, but in Europe and other strong-signal parts of the world it's bevst to purchase on returnable basis. Noise floor only okay. Telescopic receiving element allows moisture and avian waste penetration between segments, which can lead to potential resistance and/or spurious signals; gaps should be sealed with Coax Seal, electrical putty or similar. Control box/amplifier has no external weather sealing to protect from moisture, although printed circuit board nominally has water-resistant coating. Coaxial cable to receiver not provided. Mediocre coaxial cable provided between control box and receiving element. On our unit, a coaxial connector came poorly soldered from the factory.

Verdict: The MFJ-1024, made in America, performs almost identically to the McKay Dymek DA100E, but sells for less. However, that gap lessens after factoring in the cost of a worthy AC adaptor—assuming you can find or alter one to fit the unusual power jack—and the quality of the 1024's coaxial cable is not in Dymek's league.

A lower-cost alternative to McKay Dymek's offering is the MFJ-1024. Performs similarly, but there are hum, quality and other issues. J.R. Sherwood

New for 2009

✪✪¼ (performance), ✪✪✪✪✪ (build quality)

Apex Radio 700DTA

Indoor telescopic rod. Active, proximate, manual preselection, 0.5–30 MHz.

Pricing: $179.95 in the United States.

Pros: Exceptional-quality components throughout, including die-cast metal case with best-of-Japan construction; knobs even have dual set screws and rubber feet attached by screws, not glue. Very good gain below 17 MHz, with best performance around 11–16 MHz and throughout medium-wave AM band (*see* Cons). Superior dynamic range and freedom from spurious signals, thanks in large measure to high-"Q" preselector (*see* Cons). High quality three-meter (9 foot, 10 inch) micro coax cable. Generally worthy ergonomics and exceptional operating feel (*see* Cons). Small footprint, yet weighty construction minimizes sliding around during use. Low battery consumption (*see* Cons); green LED prompts to turn off (*see* Cons). Battery (9V) included.

Cons: Signal-to-noise ratio begins to deteriorate above 17 MHz, with gain tumbling by 26 MHz. Proximate antenna, so receiving element must be located near receiver. Indoor only. No gain control. Sharp preselection adjustment complicates operation. Included BNC cable may require aftermarket adaptor for receiver. Battery only, no DC jack or AC adaptor; when left on fulltime, which happens sooner or later, battery dies in less than a week.

☞ The original unit tested—purchased in the United States—had excessive gain. As a result, there was intrusive circuit noise, a high propensity to overload and countless spurious signals. In May 2008 we approached Apex Radio with our findings. They confirmed these, then halted sales until an improved version could be devised. In August 2008 the manufacturer recalled all units in dealer inventory so they could be upgraded. This review thus is based on two samples of that improved version.

Verdict: The Apex Radio 700DTA is engineered and manufactured in high-cost Japan, with markedly superior parts and rugged construction right down to its tank-tough case. No other active antenna we've laid hands on comes close to the 700DTA's professional-grade build quality.

Performance, however, is not better than what's found on some cheaper models. Too, there's no way to operate it except by inboard battery, so be prepared to use rechargeable cells.

Evaluation of New Model: What initially hits you with the 700DTA is its soup-to-nuts robustness, starting with a beefy die-cast metal enclosure. No corners are cut—it even eschews the usual snap-on battery cover in favor of one with machined screws.

Ditto other parts. There's an excellent bandswitch with positive soft clicks, a rugged

New for 2009 is the Apex Radio 700DTA. It is easily the best constructed of any active antenna. Universal Radio

power switch and superior BNC connectors. Even the humble 9V battery connector is a cut above.

It doesn't end there. The removable 23-inch (585 mm) telescopic receiving element is also top-drawer, as are both front-panel knobs—each with fully *two* setscrews. A Japanese-made "Alps" potentiometer controls the built-in preselector.

Even the ten-foot (three-meter) BNC connecting cable is borderline perfection. It uses Japanese micro coax (Kansai 1.5D–2V, or RG-174 equivalent) with heat-shrink tubing at each connector end. Nevertheless, you'll probably need an aftermarket adaptor to connect it to a receiver.

Operates from Battery Only

There is no jack for an AC adaptor or outboard battery, so as a practical matter the 700DTA operates only from an inboard 9V battery. This rules out the possibility of stray AC fields or inadequate filtering causing hum.

A battery is provided that's likely to take the better part of a week before going belly-up.

A green LED reminds you to turn off the power, but you'll probably spring for a rechargeable cell if you use the antenna often.

Revision Rescues Performance

The original version of the 700DTA, which featured astonishingly high gain, performed abysmally. We contacted Apex, which confirmed our findings. They then withdrew the product from distribution, then went back to the drawing board.

We tested two of the resulting upgrades, which thankfully showed around 20 dB less gain. Performance was indeed much improved, so from July 2008 sales were resumed and in August all units in dealer inventory were recalled.

How Is It Now?

The 700DTA has an unusually small footprint, a plus for crowded desks and the occasional trip. It is straightforward to use, although the preselector knob requires careful tweaking.

Gain is considerable but no longer excessive, so signals get a healthy boost. Dynamic range and freedom from spurious signals are all good. Yet, the signal-to-noise ratio becomes unexceptional above around 17–18 MHz, and by 26 MHz is woefully inadequate. This should not be an issue for most world band applications, but it is a deal-killer for, say, 27 MHz CB monitoring.

In all, the Apex 700DTA mixes toughness and precision in a single box—Muhammad Ali meets Henry Royce. That's what you pay for, and there is nothing else quite like it.

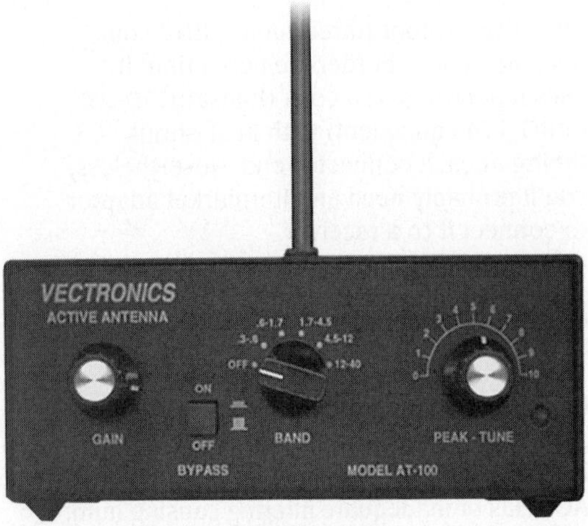

Today's Vectronics AT-100 is a clone of the MFJ-1020C. Before, it was completely different. J.R. Sherwood

Revised for 2009

✪✪¼

MFJ-1020C, Vectronics AT-100

Indoor telescopic rod. Active, proximate, manual preselection, 0.3–40 MHz.

Pricing: *MFJ-1020C/AT-100:* $99.95 in the United States. CAD$109.00 in Canada. £89.95 in the United Kingdom. €105.00 in Germany. *MFJ-1312D 120V AC adaptor:* $15.95 in the United States. CAD$19.95 in Canada. *MFJ-1312DX 240V AC adaptor:* £15.95 in the United Kingdom. €19.00 in Germany.

Pros: Superior dynamic range, and high-"Q" preselector unusually effective in preventing overloading. Performance best off battery (*see* Cons). Choice of PL-259 or RCA connections. Suitable for travel. 30-day money-back guarantee if purchased from manufacturer (MFJ).

Cons: Proximate model, so receiving element has to be placed near receiver (can be converted, *see* ☞, below). Preselector complicates operation; needs adjustment even with modest frequency changes, especially within mediumwave AM band. Knobs small and touchy to adjust. High current draw, so battery runs down quickly. Removing sheet-metal screws often to change battery can eventually result in stripping unless great care is taken. MFJ's optional AC adaptor causes significant hum on many received signals.

☞ Rating rises to three stars if converted from proximate to remote model by connecting wire receiving element to external antenna input; see separate review on earlier page.

Verdict: The MFJ-1020C/Vectronics AT-100, manufactured in Mississippi by MFJ, is okay as a proximate antenna with its own telescopic receiving element. However, it performs much better when coupled to a random-length wire in lieu of the built-in telescopic receiving element.

Alas, MFJ's optional AC adaptor introduces hum much of the time, battery drain is considerable, and changing the built-in battery is inconvenient and relies on wear-prone sheet-metal screws. Best bet, unless you're into experimenting with power supplies: Skip the adaptor and use an outboard rechargeable battery.

Revised for 2009: The former Vectronics AT-100 was nearly identical to the Palstar AA30/AA30P, but some months back it was changed to become a brand-only variation of the MFJ 1020C. The result is improved performance at the same price as before.

New for 2009 is the Kaito KA35, designed for use on trips or at home. It is preferable to the similar "TG35," as it can be conveniently recharged from an AC adaptor.

New Version for 2009

✪✪¼ (performance) ✪ (practicality) ⓒ

Kaito KA35, TG35

Indoor-portable loop (ferrite rod)/ telescopic rod receiving elements. Active, remote, broadband .03–3 MHz (ferrite)/3–30 MHz (telescopic).

Pricing: *Kaito:* $89.95 in the United States. CAD$79.95 in Canada.

Pros: Powered exclusively by rechargeable NiMH battery, so no internally caused hum or noise (*see* Cons). Worthy gain and low noise across full tuning range. Reasonably good dynamic range. Not prone to generate spurious signals. Long cable allows receiving element to be remotely mounted up to 16 feet/five meters away. Wide 0.3–30 MHz frequency coverage using two separate plugin receiving elements: ferrite rod for mediumwave AM and 120 meters, telescopic for 3–30 MHz. Handy inductive coupler allows antenna to operate with receivers lacking external antenna jack. Suitable for travel. Mediumwave AM receiving element rotates to null co-channel interference and help reduce local noise pickup (*see* Cons). Telescopic receiving element swivels and rotates. Rechargeable by PC USB port (*see* Cons). Rechargeable by solar panels, provided (*see* Cons); panels can offset battery depletion when idle over time. LED "on" indicator. *Kaito:* Also handily rechargeable by 120V AC adaptor, supplied (*see* Cons).

Cons: Battery, soldered into place, unusually difficult to replace. Charging battery by included solar cells for three days in sunlight yields merely 2.5 hours of operation. Charging battery via PC USB port for 20 hours yields only 7.5 hours of operation; however, manufacturer warns not to charge this way for more than 12 hours. PC can charge battery only when computer not in hibernation or standby. Indoors only—can't be permanently mounted outdoors. Mediocre build quality. Ferrite rod's small size—5½ inch/140 mm—limits potential to null co-channel mediumwave AM interference; placement some distance from receiver also makes rotation inconvenient. No antenna adaptors included for receivers with PL-259 or BNC connection. *Kaito:* Manufacturer warns not to charge with AC adaptor for over 12 hours. *TG35:* No AC adaptor, so battery unhandy to charge.

Verdict: This travel-friendly unit performs nicely with world band and mediumwave AM signals, alike. It is affordable and reasonably portable, with fairly good performance.

Difference with New Version: This novel antenna was originally made by Degen for eBay's "Radio and Component" outlet also located in China. This version bears no brand name whatsoever, just "TG35," and its battery is slow and unhandy to charge.

The TG35 continues to be offered, but an upgraded version, the Kaito KA35, is now available in North America. Unlike the TG35, the Kaito is readily charged by AC adaptor—a huge improvement—although charge time is supposed to be kept under 12 hours.

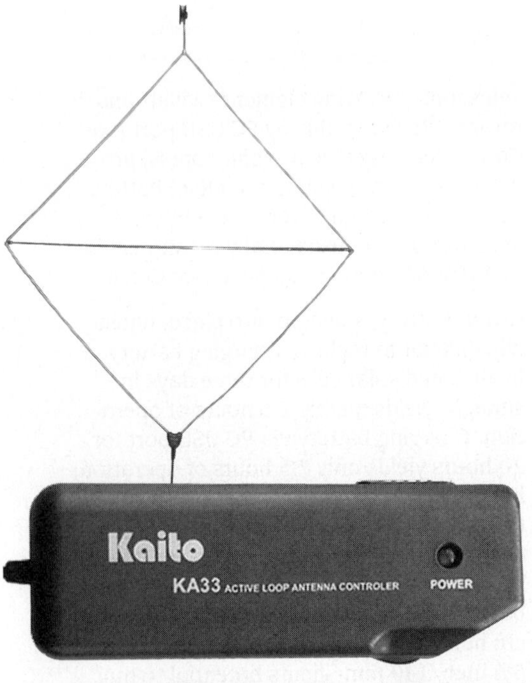

The Kaito KA33 offers travelers a handy, low-cost solution. D. Zantow

Degen DE31, Degen DE31MS, Kaito KA33, Thieking DE31-A, Thieking DE31-LM

Indoor-portable loop. Active, remote, manual preselection, 3.9–22 MHz

Pricing: *Kaito KA33:* $36.95 in the United States. CAD$39.95 in Canada. *Thieking DE31:* €59.99 in Germany. *Thieking DE31A:* €72.50 in Germany. *Thieking DE31-LM:* €69.00 in Germany.

Pros: Appropriate for portables. Meaningful gain, especially above 9 MHz. Very good dynamic range. Low noise and absence of spurious signals. Battery operation, so no internally caused hum or noise (*see* Cons). Compact collapsible design handy for airline and other travel. Long cable (*see* Cons) allows loop to be placed relatively far from radio. Adaptor sometimes allows for connection to a receiver lacking ⅛-inch/4-mm antenna jack (*see* Cons). Fairly low current draw (*see* Cons). *DE31MS and KA33:* Also covers mediumwave AM 531–1602 kHz. *DE31-LM:* Also covers longwave and 531–1602 kHz mediumwave AM. *DE31A:* 1.8–22 MHz coverage includes all tropical world band segments.

Cons: Receiving element not weatherproof, so can't be permanently mounted outdoors. Touchy preselector tuning. Operates only from small batteries (two "AAA," not included) and no AC adaptor or socket. Battery consumption, though low, nearly twice manufacturer's specification. Consumer-grade plastic construction with no shielding. When clipped onto radio's telescopic antenna instead of fed through antenna jack, the lack of a radio ground connection greatly reduces performance. Rotation for local-noise reduction impeded by limp-rope design. Small suction cup fails if it and glass surface not exceptionally clean; yet, when properly affixed, suction cup stubborn to remove. No carrying pouch to keep the various bits together. No reel to keep main cable from being tangled. *DE31, KA33 and DE31-LM:* Tunes shortwave only 3.9–22 MHz, so misses 2.3–2.5 and 3.2–3.4 MHz (120 and 90 meter) tropical world band segments.

Verdict: Respectable performance, minimal investment.

✪¾

Palstar AA30/AA30P

Indoor telescopic rod. Active, proximate, manual preselection, 0.3–30 MHz.

Pricing: $99.95 in the United States. £79.95 in the United Kingdom. €96.50 in Germany.

Pros: Moderate-to-good gain. Preselector tuning easily peaked. Can be powered directly by Palstar R30A tabletop receiver, internal battery or AC adaptor. Suitable for travel.

Cons: Spurious oscillation throughout 14–30 MHz range. Overloads with external antenna. Proximate model, so receiving element has to be placed near receiver. Preselector complicates operation. No AC adaptor.

Verdict: Oscillation makes this a dubious choice except for reception below 14 MHz. Manufactured in the United States.

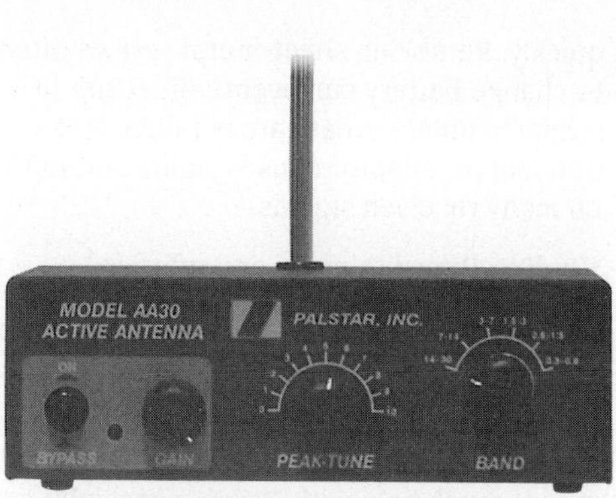

Palstar's AA30/AA30P has good gain, but is compromised by spurious oscillation above 14 MHz.

J.R. Sherwood

✪¾ ✆

MFJ-1022

Indoor telescopic rod. Active, proximate, broadband, 0.3–200 MHz.

Pricing: *MFJ-1022:* $69.95 in the United States. CAD$74.95 in Canada. £59.95 in the United Kingdom. €69.00 in Germany. *MFJ-1312D 120V AC adaptor:* $15.95 in the United States. CAD$19.95 in Canada. *MFJ-1312DX 240V AC adaptor:* £15.95 in the United Kingdom. €19.00 in Germany.

Pros: Unusually broadband coverage reaches well into VHF spectrum. Considerable gain, peaking at 22.5 MHz, audibly helps signals that do not suffer from intermodulation. Idiot-proof to operate. Works best off battery (*see* Cons). Suitable for travel. 30-day money-back guarantee if purchased from manufacturer.

Cons: Proximate model, so receiving element has to be placed near receiver. Broadband design results in local mediumwave AM stations ghosting up to 2.7 MHz, and to a lesser degree up through the 3 MHz (90 meter) tropical world band segment at many locations; this often drops at night because of reduced local transmitting powers. Broadband design and high gain tends to produce intermodulation products/spurious signals and hiss between reasonable-level signals and sometimes mixing with weaker signals. Within tropical world band segments, modest-level static from nearby thunderstorms, when coupled with overloading from local mediumwave AM signals, sometimes cause odd background sounds. High current draw, so battery runs down

The MFJ-1022 is affordable and easy to use, but its performance brings up the rear. J.R. Sherwood

quickly. Removing sheet-metal screws often to change battery can eventually result in stripping unless great care is taken. MFJ's optional AC adaptor causes significant hum on many received signals.

Verdict: Priced to move and offering broadband coverage, this compact antenna couldn't be simpler to operate—one button, that's it. It works nicely to help improve the listening quality of modest-strength international broadcasting signals. But don't expect much help with DXing, especially within tropical world band segments, unless you live far from mediumwave AM stations and maybe not even then.

Alas, MFJ's optional AC adaptor introduces hum much of the time, battery drain is considerable, and changing the built-in battery is inconvenient and relies on wear-prone sheet-metal screws. Best bet, unless you're into experimenting with power supplies: Skip the adaptor and use an outboard rechargeable battery.

Prepared by J. Robert Sherwood and David Zantow, with Lawrence Magne; also, a tip of the hat to George Heidelman, Tom Rauch, Chuck Rippel and David Walcutt, as well as to Lawrence Bulk.

WHERE TO FIND IT: INDEX TO TESTED ANTENNAS

PASSPORT REPORTS evaluates the most relevant indoor and outdoor antennas on the market. Here's where to find each review, with models that are new, revised or retested for 2009 shown in **bold**. Passive—unamplified—antennas are in *italics*.

A comprehensive Radio Database International White Paper®, *PASSPORT® Evaluation of Popular Outdoor Antennas*, is available for $6.95 in North America, $9.95 airmail elsewhere, including shipping. It encompasses virtually all our panel's findings and comments during testing of passive wire antennas. Also included are details for proper and safe installation, along with instructions for inverted-L construction. This unabridged report is available from primary world band dealers, or order 24/7 from www.passband.com, autovoice +1 215/598-9018 or fax +1 215/598 3794—or write PASSPORT RDI White Papers, Box 300, Penn's Park, PA 18943 USA.

Antenna	Page
🗎 *Alpha Delta DX-SWL Sloper*	*166*
🗎 *Alpha Delta DX-Ultra*	*165*
Ameco TPA	184
AOR LA380	181
Apex Radio 700DTA	**186**
Degen DE31	190
Degen DE31MS	190
Dressler ARA 60 S	181
DX Engineering DXE-ARAH	**179**
🗎 *Eavesdropper Model C*	*167*
🗎 *Eavesdropper Model T*	*167*
Homebrew antennas	66, 172
Inverted-L, long (info)	*163*
Kaito KA33	190
Kaito KA35	**189**
McKay Dymek DA100E	185
McKay Dymek DA100EM	185
MFJ-1020C/proximate	188
MFJ-1020C/remote (preselector)	180
MFJ-1022	191
MFJ-1024	186
Palstar AA30/AA30P	191
RF Systems DX-One Pro Mk II	178
RF Systems GMDSS-1	*183*
SGC Stealth Antenna (kit, info)	*172*
Sony AN-LP1	182
TG35	189
Thieking DE31-A	190
Thieking DE31-LM	190
Vectronics AT-100/proximate	**188**
Vectronics AT-100/remote (preselector)	**180**
Watson SWL-DX1 (info)	*163*
Wellbrook ALA 100 (quasi-kit)	**171**
Wellbrook ALA 100M (quasi-kit)	**173**
Wellbrook ALA 330S	175
Wellbrook ALA 1530	177
Wellbrook ALA 1530+	177
Wellbrook ALA 1530P	177
Yaesu G5500 rotor (info)	169

🗎 *Radio Database International White Paper®* available.

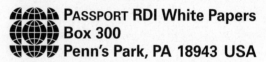

What's On Tonight?

PASSPORT's Hour-by-Hour Guide to World Band Shows

World band offers what is rarely found elsewhere, and it's unimpeded by gatekeepers and homegrown media nabobs. This section explains which of these shows are in English, with icons for the best:

- ■ Station superior, with several excellent shows
- ● Specific show worth hearing

Some stations provide schedules, others don't. Yet, even official online schedules aren't always credible or complete. To resolve this, PASSPORT monitors stations around the world, firsthand, to detail and confirm schedule activity throughout the year. Additionally, to be as useful as possible, PASSPORT's schedules consist not just of observed activity, but also that which we have creatively opined will appear well into the year ahead. This predictive material is based on decades of experience and is original from us. Although this is inherently less exact than confirmed real-time data, it has proven to be most useful.

Primary frequencies are shown for North America, western Europe, East Asia and Australasia, plus the Middle East, southern Africa and Southeast Asia. For secondary and seasonal channels, or frequencies for other parts of the world, check out "Worldwide Broadcasts in English" and the Blue Pages.

To eliminate confusion, World Time and World Day are used—both explained in "Getting Started" and "Worldly Words." Seasons are for the Northern Hemisphere (summer around July, winter around January).

The late Koji Yamada was central to Japan's "shortwave boom" of the 1970s. T. Ohtake

0000–0559
North America—Evening Prime Time
Europe & Mideast—Early Morning
Australasia & East Asia—Midday and Afternoon

00:00

■**Deutsche Welle,** Germany. Starts with five minutes of *News*, then ●*Newslink*—commentary, interviews, background reports and analysis. On the half-hour there's *Sports Report* and *Radio D*, a German language course (Monday), ●*World in Progress* (Tuesday), ●*Spectrum* (science and technology, Wednesday), ●*Money Talks* (Thursday), *Living Planet* (Friday) and ●*Inside Europe* (Saturday). Sunday features are *Sports Report* and *Inspired Minds*. An hour to East Asia winter on 15595 kHz, summer on 15595 and 17525 kHz. Also to Southeast Asia winter on 7265 and 9785 kHz, summer on 9885 and 17525 kHz.

Radio Bulgaria. Winter only at this time. Tuesday through Saturday (weekday evenings in North America), *News* is followed by *Events and Developments*, replaced Sunday and Monday by *Views Behind the News*. The remaining time is taken up by regular programs such as *Keyword Bulgaria* and ●*Time Out for Music*, and weekly features like ●*Folk Studio* (Monday), *Sports* (Tuesday), *Magazine Economy* (Wednesday), *The Way We Live* (Thursday), *History Club* (Friday), *DX Programme* (Saturday) and *Answering Your Letters*, a listener-response show, on Sunday. An hour to eastern North America and Central America on 5900 and 7400 kHz. One hour earlier in summer.

Radio Romania International. Summer only at this time; see 0100 for specifics. Fifty-five minutes to eastern North America on 9775 and 11790 kHz. One hour later in winter.

Radio Canada International. Tuesday through Saturday, it's *The Link*, replaced Sunday by *Blink* (*Behind The Link*) and Monday by *Maple Leaf Mailbag*. One hour to Southeast Asia winter on 9880 kHz, summer on 11700 kHz; and winter (one hour earlier in summer) to the central United States on 9755 kHz (starts at 0005). *The Link* is also aired Tuesday through Saturday summer at the same time on 6100 kHz, but weekend broadcasts are in other languages.

Radio Japan. Tuesday through Saturday (weekday evenings in North America),

00:00–01:00

there's *What's Up Japan* (current events, Japanese language lessons, and a listener-response segment Thursday). This is replaced Sunday by *World Interactive* or (the last Sunday of the month) *Listening Library*, readings from masterpieces of Japanese literature. Monday's feature is *Pop Up Japan*, a selection of Japanese pop music. Twenty minutes to Europe winter on 5920 kHz, summer on 5960 kHz; to eastern North America on 6145 kHz; and to Southeast Asia on 13650 and 17810 kHz.

Radio Exterior de España ("Spanish National Radio"). Tuesday through Saturday (local weekday evenings in the Americas), there's Spanish and international *news*, commentary, Spanish pop music, a review of the Spanish press, and a general interest feature. Weekends, it's all features, including rebroadcasts of some weekday programs. An hour to eastern North America on 6055 kHz. Popular with many listeners.

China Radio International. *News* and reports fill the first half-hour, followed by a daily feature: ●*Frontline* (Monday), *Biz China* (Tuesday), *In the Spotlight*(Wednesday), ●*Voices from Other Lands* (Thursday), *Life in China* (Friday), *Listeners' Garden* (Saturday) and *China Horizons* (Sunday). To Europe on 7130 (or 7350) kHz; to North America on 6020 and 9570 kHz; to East Asia winter on 9425 kHz, summer on 13750 kHz; and to Southeast Asia winter on 11650 and 11885 kHz, summer on 11885 and 15125 kHz. These days are World Time, so locally in North America it will be the previous evening.

Radio Ukraine International. Summer only at this time. A potpourri of things Ukrainian, with the Monday (Sunday evening in the Americas) broadcast often featuring some excellent music. Ample and interesting coverage of local issues, including news, sports, politics and culture. An hour to eastern North America on 7440 kHz. One hour later in winter.

Voice of Greece. Monday and winter only at this time, and starts at 0005. Approximately 60 minutes of music in *Greek in Style*. To North America on 7475 and 9420 kHz; and to Central and South America on 12105 kHz. One hour earlier in summer. ☞ Monday World Time is Sunday evening in the Americas.

Radio Australia. Part of a 24-hour service to Asia and the Pacific. Begins with *World News*, the Monday through Friday it's *The Breakfast Club*, a mix of talk and music for listeners in Asia and the Pacific. Winter Saturdays, there's *Asia Review*, *Asia Pacific Business* and *Talking Point*; and Sunday's feature is *The Spirit of Things*. In summer, Saturday features are *In the Loop (Rewind)* and *Australian Express*, replaced Sunday by *Background Briefing* (investigative journalism). On 9660, 12080, 13690, 15240, 15415 (from 0030), 17715, 17750, 17775 and 17795 kHz. In North America (best during summer) try 17715 and 17795 kHz. In East Asia tune to 13690 kHz; for Southeast Asia there's 15415, 17750 and 17775 kHz.

Radio Prague, Czech Republic. Summer only at this time. *News*, then Tuesday through Saturday (weekday evenings in the Americas) there's *Current Affairs* and one or more features: *One on One* (interviews, Tuesday); *Talking Point* (Wednesday); *Czechs in History*, *Czechs Today* or *Spotlight* (Thursday); *Panorama* and *From the Archives* (Friday); and *Business News* and *The Arts* on Saturday. Sunday lineup is *Magazine*, *Sound Czech* and *One on One*; replaced Monday by *Mailbox* and *Letter from Prague* followed by *Music Profile*, *Magic Carpet* (Czech world music) or *Czech Books*. Thirty minutes to North America and the Caribbean on 7345 and 9440 kHz. One hour later in winter.

Radio Thailand. *Newshour*. Thirty minutes to eastern and southern Africa. Winter on 9680 kHz, summer on 9570 kHz.

International Radio Serbia. Monday through Saturday (Sunday through Friday evenings in the Americas) and summer only at this hour. A half-hour news broadcast to central North America on 6190 kHz. One hour later in winter.

All India Radio. The final 45 minutes of a much larger block of programming targeted at East and Southeast Asia, and heard well beyond. To East Asia on 9950, 11620, 11645 and 13605 kHz; and to Southeast Asia on 9705, 11620 and 13605 kHz.

Radio Cairo, Egypt. The final half-hour of a 90-minute broadcast to eastern North America. *Arabic by Radio* can be heard on the hour, and there's a daily *news* bulletin at 0015. See 2300 for more specifics. Winter on 6850 kHz, summer on 9280 kHz. Interesting programs, but often suffers from poor audio quality.

Radio New Zealand International. A friendly package of *news* and features sometimes replaced by live sports commentary. Part of a 24-hour broadcast for the South Pacific, but also heard in parts of North America (especially during summer). On 15720 or 17675 kHz.

Radio PMR, Moldova. Monday through Friday (Sunday through Thursday evenings in North America), and winter only at this time. Fifteen minutes of newsy fare from the separatist, pro-Russian, "Pridnestrovian Moldavian Republic." May air 15 minutes earlier. To eastern North America on 6240 kHz. One hour earlier in summer.

AFRTS Shortwave, USA. Network news, live sports, music and features in the *upper-sideband* mode from the American Forces Radio & Television Service. Transmitted from modestly powered U.S. Navy stations around the globe, so usually a tough catch. Try 4319, 5446.5, 5765, 6350, 7811, 10320, 12133.5, 12579 and 13362 kHz.

00:30

Radio Vilnius, Lithuania. Thirty minutes of news and background reports, mainly about Lithuania. Of broader appeal is *Mailbag*, aired every other Sunday (Saturday evening in North America). For some Lithuanian music, try the next evening, towards the end of the broadcast. To eastern North America winter on 9875 kHz and summer on 11690 kHz.

Radio Tirana, Albania. Tuesday through Sunday (Monday through Saturday evenings in North America) and summer only at this time. Approximately 15 minutes of *news* and press review or commentary. To eastern North America on 9390 kHz. One hour later in winter.

Radio Thailand. *Newshour*. Thirty minutes to central and eastern North America winter on 12095 kHz, summer on 12120 kHz.

01:00

Radio Prague, Czech Republic. *News*, then Tuesday through Saturday (weekday evenings in the Americas) there's the in-depth *Current Affairs* and a feature or two: *One on One* (interviews, Tuesday), *Talking Point* (Wednesday), *Czechs in History*, *Czechs Today* or *Spotlight* (Thursday), *Panorama* and *From the Archives* (Friday), and *Business News* and *The Arts* on Saturday. Sunday news is followed by *Magazine*, *Sound Czech* and a repeat of Tuesday's *One on One*; and Monday's lineup is *Mailbox* and *Letter from Prague* followed by *Music Profile*, *Magic Carpet* (Czech world music) or *Czech Books*. Thirty minutes to eastern and central North America and the Caribbean on 6200 and 7345 kHz.

Radio Slovakia International. Tuesday through Sunday, there's *news* followed by features on Slovak life and culture. Monday (Sunday evening in North America), it's *Sunday Newsreel* and a listener-response program. Half an hour to eastern North America winter on 7230 kHz, summer on 5930 kHz. Also year-round to South America on 9440 kHz.

Radio Romania International. Winter only at this time. Starts with *Radio Newsreel*, a combination of news, commentary and press review. Features on Romania complete the broadcast. Regular spots include Tuesday's *Pro Memoria*, *Romanian Hits* and *Sports Roundup*; Wednesday's *Business Club* and ●*The Skylark* (Romanian folk music); Thursday's *Society Today* and *Romanian Musicians*; and Friday's *Europa Express*. Saturday fare includes ●*The Folk Music Box* and *Sports Weekend*; and Sunday there's

01:00–01:00

The Week and *World of Culture*. Monday's broadcast includes *Focus*. Fifty-five minutes to eastern North America on 6145 and 9515 kHz. These days are World Time, so locally in western North America it will be the previous evening. One hour earlier in summer.

International Radio Serbia. Monday through Saturday (Sunday through Friday evenings in the Americas) during winter; daily in summer. A half-hour news broadcast to central North America winter on 7115 kHz, and to western North America summer on 6190 kHz. The transmission to central North America is one hour earlier in summer, and for western parts it's one hour later in winter.

China Radio International. Repeat of the 0000 broadcast, but with news updates. One hour to North America on 6005 (winter), 6020, 6080 (winter), 9570, 9580 and (summer) 9790 kHz, via CRI's Albanian, Cuban and Canadian relays. Also to Europe winter on 7130 (or 7350) kHz, summer on 9470 kHz; and to Southeast Asia winter on 11650 and 11885 kHz, summer on 15125 and 15785 kHz (also on 11730 kHz year-round from 0130). The broadcast to North America on 6020 and 9570 kHz sometimes carries the weekday *China Drive* (replaced weekends by ●*News and Reports*, *CRI Roundup* (Saturday), *Reports from Developing Countries* (Sunday) and *China Beat*) in place of the mainstream programming.

Voice of Vietnam. A relay via the facilities of Radio Canada International. Begins with *News*, then Tuesday though Saturday (weekday evenings in North America) there's *Current Affairs*. These are followed Tuesday by *Vietnam, Land and People*; Wednesday, *Society* and *Business*; Thursday, *Letterbox* (listener response); Friday, *Vietnam Economy* and *Talk of the Week*; and Saturday, *Rural Vietnam* and *Culture*. Sunday has *Weekly Review* and *Weekend Music*, and Monday there's *Culture*, *Sports Roundup* and *Sunday Show*. A half-hour to eastern North America, with reception better to the south. On 6175 kHz. Repeated at 0230 and 0330 on the same channel.

Voice of Russia World Service. Summer only at this hour, and the start of a four-hour block of programming for North America. *News*, then Tuesday through Saturday (weekday evenings in North America), there's more news programming. This is replaced Sunday and Monday by *Moscow Mailbag*. Features fill the second half-hour: *Timelines* (Monday), *Kaleidoscope* (Tuesday and Friday), *Russian by Radio* (Wednesday), *The VOR Treasure Store* (Thursday), the evocative ●*Christian Message from Moscow* (Saturday) and *Moscow Yesterday and Today* on Sunday. Best for eastern North America are 7250 and 9665 kHz. Farther west, use 13775 kHz.

Radio Habana Cuba. The start of a two-hour cyclical broadcast to North America. Tuesday through Sunday (Monday through Saturday evenings in North America), the first half-hour consists of international and Cuban *news* followed by *RHC's Viewpoint*. The next 30 minutes consist of a *news* bulletin and the sports-oriented *Time Out* (five minutes each) plus a feature: *Caribbean Outlook* (Tuesday and Friday), *DXers Unlimited* (Wednesday and Sunday), the *Mailbag Show* (Thursday) and *Weekly Review* (Saturday). Monday, the hour is split between *Weekly Review* and *Mailbag Show*. To eastern and central North America on 6000 and 6140 (or 6180) kHz.

Voice of Korea, North Korea. Mind-numbing programs on themes such as the application of socialist thinking to steel production are basic fare for this world band curiosity. Worth the occasional listen just to hear how bad it is. One hour to East Asia on 3560, 7140, 9345 and 9730 kHz; and to Central America on 11735, 13760 and 15180 kHz.

Radio Taiwan International. Ten minutes of *News*, followed by features: *Time Traveler*, *Chinese to Go* (language lessons) and *Asia Review* (Monday); *People* and *We've Got Mail* (Tuesday); *Health Beats*, *Women Making Waves* and ●*Jade Bells and Bamboo Pipes* (Wednesday); *Strait Talk*, *Breakfast Club*, *Instant Noodles* and *Chinese to Go* (Thursday); *Ilha Formosa*, *Taiwan Indie* and *Taiwan*

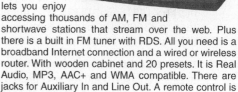

01:00–02:00

Outlook (Friday); *News Talk* and *Groove Zone* (Saturday); and *The Occidental Tourist, Spotlight* and *On the Line* (Sunday). One hour to the Philippines on 11875 kHz, and also heard in parts of Australasia.

Radio Australia. Part of a 24-hour service to Asia and the Pacific, but which can also be heard at this time in parts of North America (better to the west). Begins with *World News*, then Monday through Friday it's the final hour of *The Breakfast Club*. Winter weekends, there's live sport in *Grandstand*. In summer, this is replaced by Saturday's *Pacific Review* and *Asia Pacific Business*, and Sunday's *The Spirit of Things*. On 9660, 12080, 13690, 15240, 15415, 17715, 17750, 17775 (till 0130) and 17795 kHz. In North America (best during summer) try 17715 and 17795 kHz. In East Asia tune to 13690 kHz, and for Southeast Asia there's 15415, 17750 and 17775 kHz.

Radio Ukraine International. Winter only at this time; see 0000 for specifics. An hour of news and features targeted at eastern North America on 7440 kHz. One hour earlier in summer.

Radio New Zealand International. Continues with *news* and features sometimes replaced by live sports commentary. Continuous to the South Pacific, and also heard in parts of North America (especially during summer). On 15720 or 17675 kHz.

AFRTS Shortwave, USA. Network news, live sports, music and features in the *upper-sideband* mode from the American Forces Radio & Television Service. Transmitted from modestly powered U.S. Navy stations around the globe, so usually a tough catch. Try 4319, 5446.5, 5765, 6350, 7811, 10320, 12133.5, 12579 and 13362 kHz.

01:30

Radio Sweden. Summer only at this time. Tuesday through Saturday (weekday evenings in North America), there's *news* and features about Sweden. Sunday, it's a review of the main news stories of the previous week; and Monday, *Network Europe*. Thirty minutes to South Asia on 11550 kHz, and to eastern North America on 6010 kHz. One hour later in winter.

Radio Tirana, Albania. Tuesday through Sunday (Monday through Saturday evenings in North America) and winter only at this time. Approximately 15 minutes of *news* and press review or commentary. To eastern North America on 7425 kHz. One hour earlier in summer.

Voice of the Islamic Republic of Iran. Unlike the broadcasts to other parts of the world, the programs at this hour are from the separate "Voice of Justice" service, specially tailored to an American audience. One hour to North America winter on 6120 and 7160 kHz, summer on 7235 and 9495 kHz.

01:45

Radio Tirana, Albania. Tuesday through Sunday (Monday through Saturday evenings in North America) and summer only at this time. Repeat of the 0030 broadcast; see there for specifics. Fifteen minutes to eastern North America on 9390 kHz, one hour later in winter.

02:00

Radio Cairo, Egypt. The first hour of a 90-minute broadcast. A ten-minute *news* bulletin is aired at 0215, with the remaining time taken up by short features on Egypt, the Middle East and Islam. For the intellectual listener there's *Literary Readings* at 0245 Monday, and *Modern Arabic Poetry* at the same time Friday. More general fare is available in *Listener's Mail* at 0225 Thursday and Saturday. To North America winter on 7535 kHz, summer on 7270 kHz. Interesting programs, but often suffers from poor audio quality.

Radio Argentina al Exterior—RAE. Tuesday through Saturday only (local weekday evenings in the Americas). A freewheeling presentation of news, press review, short features and local Argentinean music. Not the easiest station to tune, but popular with many of those who can hear it. Fifty-five minutes nominally to North America on 11710 kHz, but tends to be best heard in the southern U.S. and the Caribbean. Sometimes pre-empted by live soccer commentary in Spanish.

Radio Bulgaria. Summer only at this time. Starts with *News*, then Tuesday through Saturday (weekday evenings in North America) there's *Events and Developments*, replaced Sunday and Monday by *Views Behind the News*. The remaining time is split between regular programs such as *Keyword Bulgaria* and ●*Time Out for Music*, and weekly features like ●*Folk Studio* (Monday), *Sports* (Tuesday), *Magazine Economy* (Wednesday), *The Way We Live* (Thursday), *History Club* (Friday), *DX Programme* (for radio enthusiasts, Saturday) and *Answering Your Letters*, a listener-response show, on Sunday. An hour to eastern North America and Central America on 9700 and 11700 kHz. One hour later in winter.

Voice of Croatia. Summer only at this time. Nominally 15 minutes of news, reports and interviews, but actual length varies. To Europe on 3985 kHz, and to North and South America on 9925 kHz. May also use 7285 kHz when necessary. One hour later in winter.

Radio Prague, Czech Republic. Winter only at this time. *News*, then Tuesday through Saturday (weekday evenings in the Americas) it's a combination of *Current Affairs* and one or more features: *One on One* (interviews, Tuesday), *Talking Point* (Wednesday), *Czechs in History*, *Czechs Today* or *Spotlight* (Thursday), *Panorama* and *From the Archives* (Friday), and *Business News* and *The Arts* on Saturday. Sunday lineup is *Magazine*, *Sound Czech* and a repeat of Tuesday's *One on One*; replaced Monday by *Mailbox* and *Letter from Prague* followed by *Music Profile*, *Magic Carpet* (Czech world music) or *Czech Books*. A half-hour to North America on 6200 and 7345 kHz. One hour earlier in summer.

Voice of Russia World Service. Winter, the start of a four-hour block of programming to North America; summer, it's the beginning of the second hour. *News*, features and music to suit all tastes. Winter fare includes *Russia and the World* (0211 Tuesday through Saturday), replaced Sunday and Monday by *Moscow Mailbag*. Features fill the second half-hour: *Timelines* (Monday), *Kaleidoscope* (Tuesday and Friday), *Russian by Radio* (Wednesday), *The VOR Treasure Store* (Thursday), ●*Christian Message from Moscow* (Saturday) and *Moscow Yesterday and Today* on Sunday. In summer, *News and Views* replaces *Russia and the World* and Sunday's *Moscow Mailbag*, with *Sunday Panorama* filling the Monday slot. There's a news summary on the half-hour, then *Russian by Radio* (Monday), ●*Folk Box* (Tuesday), *A Stroll Around the Kremlin* (or *Legends of Russian Sports*) and *Musical Tales* (Wednesday and Saturday), *Moscow Yesterday and Today* (Thursday), ●*Music Calendar*, *Hits in Russia* or ●*Jazz Show* (Friday), and *A Stroll Around the Kremlin* (or *Legends of Russian Sports*) and ●*Songs from Russia* (or ●*Russia–1000 Years of Music*) on Sunday. These days are World Time, so locally in North America it will be the previous

Meybod roosts within Iran's desert province of Yazd. The city is home to adobe castles and other ancient structures, many decaying because of neglect by authorities. L Rydén

02:00–03:00

evening. For eastern North America winter, tune to 6240 and 7250 kHz; summer, it's 9665 and 9860 kHz. Listeners in western states should go for 12040 and 13735 kHz in winter; and 9480, 13635 and 13775 kHz in summer.

International Radio Serbia. Winter only at this time. A newsy half-hour to western North America on 7115 kHz. One hour earlier in summer.

Radio Habana Cuba. The second half of a two-hour broadcast to eastern and central North America. Tuesday through Sunday (Monday through Saturday evenings in North America), opens with 10 minutes of international *news*. Next comes *Spotlight on the Americas* (Tuesday through Saturday) or Sunday's *The World of Stamps*. The final 30 minutes consists of news-oriented programming. Monday slots are *From Havana* and ●*The Jazz Place* or *Breakthrough* (science). On 6000 and 6140 (or 6180) kHz.

Radio Thailand. *News Magazine*. Thirty minutes to western North America on 15275 kHz.

KBS World Radio, South Korea. Opens with 10 minutes of *news*, then Tuesday through Saturday (weekday evenings in the Americas) there's a commentary and 30 minutes of *Seoul Calling* followed by a 15-minute feature: *Faces of Korea*, *Business Watch*, *Culture on the Move*, *Korea Today and Tomorrow* and *Seoul Report*, respectively. Sunday, the news is followed by *Worldwide Friendship* (a listener-response program), and Monday by *Korean Pop Interactive*. One hour to South America on 15575 kHz, and often heard in Japan, especially during summer. In North America, a shortened version of this broadcast can be heard at 0230; see there for specifics.

Radio Taiwan International. Ten minutes of *News*, followed by features: *Time Traveler*, *Chinese to Go* (language lessons) and *Asia Review* (Monday); *People* and *We've Got Mail* (Tuesday); *Health Beats*, *Women Making Waves* and ●*Jade Bells and Bamboo Pipes* (Wednesday); *Strait Talk*, *Breakfast Club*, *Instant Noodles* and *Chinese to Go* (Thursday); *Ilha Formosa*, *Taiwan Indie* and *Taiwan Outlook* (Friday); *News Talk* and *Groove Zone* (Saturday); and *The Occidental Tourist*, *Spotlight* and *On the Line* (Sunday). These days are World Time, so locally in North America it will be the previous evening. One hour to eastern and central North America on 5950 and 9680 kHz.

Radio Australia. Continuous programming to Asia and the Pacific, but well heard in parts of North America (especially to the west). Begins with *World News*, then Monday through Friday it's *The World Today* (comprehensive coverage of world events). Winter weekends and summer Sundays, it's all sport in *Grandstand*. Summer Saturdays bring *Total Rugby* and *The Sports Factor* (Asia) or ●*Rear Vision* (Pacific). On 9660, 12080, 13690, 15240, 15415, 15515, 17750 and 21725 kHz. Best heard in North America (especially during summer) on 15515 kHz; in East Asia on 13690 and 21725 kHz (programming for the Pacific); and in Southeast Asia on 15415 and 17750 kHz.

Voice of Korea, North Korea. Repeat of the 0100 broadcast. One hour to South East Asia on 13650 and 15100 kHz. Also audible in parts of East Asia on 4405 kHz.

AFRTS Shortwave, USA. Network news, live sports, music and features in the *upper-sideband* mode from the American Forces Radio & Television Service. Transmitted from modestly powered U.S. Navy stations around the globe, so usually a tough catch. Try 4319, 5446.5, 5765, 6350, 7811, 10320, 12133.5, 12579 and 13362 kHz.

02:30

Radio Sweden. Tuesday through Saturday (weekday evenings in North America), it's a smorgasbord of *news* and features about Sweden. Sunday's program is a review of the main news stories of the previous week; and Monday there's *Network Europe*. Thirty minutes to eastern North America winter and western North America summer on 6010 kHz, and to South Asia winter on

11550 kHz. For eastern North America and South Asia it is one hour earlier in summer, and for western North America it's one hour later in winter.

Radio Tirana, Albania. Tuesday through Sunday (Monday through Saturday evenings in North America) and summer only at this time. See 0330 for specifics. Thirty minutes to eastern North America on 7425 kHz, one hour later during winter.

Voice of Vietnam. Repeat of the 0100 broadcast; see there for specifics. A relay to eastern North America via the facilities of Radio Canada International on 6175 kHz. Reception is better to the south.

KBS World Radio, South Korea. Opens with 10 minutes of *news*, then Tuesday through Saturday (weekday evenings in North America) there's a commentary followed by a 15-minute feature: *Faces of Korea*, *Business Watch*, *Culture on the Move*, *Korea Today and Tomorrow* and *Seoul Report*, respectively. Sunday, the news is followed by *Worldwide Friendship* (a listener-response program), and Monday by *Korean Pop Interactive*. Thirty minutes to North America on 9560 kHz.

02:45

Radio Tirana, Albania. Tuesday through Sunday (Monday through Saturday evenings in the Americas) and winter only at this time. Approximately 15 minutes of *news* and press review or commentary. To eastern North America on 6100 kHz, one hour earlier in summer.

Vatican Radio. Starts at 0250. Concentrates heavily, but not exclusively, on issues affecting Catholics around the world. Thirty minutes to eastern North America on 6040 or 6100 (summer), 6100 (winter) and 7305 kHz.

03:00

Radio Taiwan International. Repeat of the 0200 broadcast; see there for specifics. One hour to western North America on 5950 kHz, to South America on 15215 kHz, and to Southeast Asia on 15320 kHz.

China Radio International. *News* and reports fill the first half-hour, and are followed by a daily feature: ●*Frontline* (Monday), *Biz China* (Tuesday), *In the Spotlight* (Wednesday), ●*Voices from Other Lands* (Thursday), *Life in China* (Friday), *Listeners' Garden* (Saturday) and *China Horizons* (Sunday). One hour to North America on 9690 and 9790 kHz. Also available to East Asia winter on 9460, 13620 and 15120 kHz; and summer on 13750, 15120 and 15785 kHz. These days are World Time, so locally in North America it will be the previous evening.

Radio Ukraine International. Summer only at this time, and a repeat of the 0000 broadcast; see there for specifics. An hour to eastern North America on 7440 kHz. One hour later in winter.

Voice of Russia World Service. Continuous programming to North America at this hour. *News*, then winter it's *News and Views*—except Monday (Sunday evening in North America) when *Sunday Panorama* is aired instead. Features during the second half-hour include *News and Views* replaces *Russia and the World* and Sunday's *Moscow Mailbag*, with *Sunday Panorama* filling the Monday slot. There's a news summary on the half-hour, then *Russian by Radio* (Monday), ●*Folk Box* (Tuesday), *A Stroll Around the Kremlin* (or *Legends of Russian Sports*) and *Musical Tales* (Wednesday and Saturday), *Moscow Yesterday and Today* (Thursday), ●*Music Calendar*, *Hits in Russia* or ●*Jazz Show* (Friday), and *A Stroll Around the Kremlin* (or *Legends of Russian Sports*) and ●*Songs from Russia* (or ●*Russia–1000 Years of Music*) on Sunday. In summer, the news is followed by a feature: *This is Russia* (Monday), *Encyclopedia "All Russia"* (Tuesday and Friday), *Moscow Mailbag* (Wednesday and Saturday), and *Science Plus* (Thursday). More features follow a brief news summary on the half-hour and include *Moscow Yesterday and Today* (Monday), *Guest Speaker* (Tuesday through Saturday), and *Spiritual Flowerbed* (Tuesday and Thursday). Pride of place at this hour goes to Sunday's 47-min-

03:00–03:30

ute ●*Music and Musicians* (classical music). In eastern North America, choose between 6155, 6240 and 7350 kHz in winter, and 9480, 9665, 9860 and 9880 (or 5900) kHz in summer. For western North America, there's 12040 and 13735 kHz in winter; and 9435, 12065, 13635 and 13775 kHz in summer.

■**Deutsche Welle,** Germany. *News*, then Tuesday though Saturday it's ●*Newslink Plus*—commentary, interviews, background reports and analysis. Sunday, there's *In-Box*, *Mission Europe* (German language lessons), *Sports Report* and *Inspired Minds*; and Monday, ●*Newslink* is followed by *Sports Report* and *Radio D* (German language lessons). An hour to South Asia winter on 9800 and 13810 kHz; and summer on 13770 and 15595 kHz. The latter frequency is also audible in Southeast Asia.

Radio Australia. *World News*, then Monday through Friday there's *Regional Sport* followed by *In the Loop* (Pacific) or *Connect Asia* (Asia). Weekends, for all areas, there's live sports coverage in *Grandstand*. Continuous to Asia and the Pacific on 9660, 12080, 13690, 15240, 15415, 15515, 17750 and 21725 kHz. Also heard in North America (best in summer) on 15515 kHz. In East Asia, tune to 13690 and 21725 kHz, although these frequencies carry programming for the Pacific. For Southeast Asia, there's 15415 and 17750 kHz.

Radio Habana Cuba. Repeat of the 0100 broadcast. To eastern and central North America on 6000 and 6140 (or 6180) kHz.

Voice of Croatia. Winter only at this time. Nominally 15 minutes of news, reports and interviews, but actual length varies. To Europe on 3985 kHz, and to North and South America on 7285 (or 7375) kHz. One hour earlier in summer.

Radio Prague, Czech Republic. Summer only at this hour; see 0400 for program specifics. A half-hour to North America on 7345 and 9870 kHz. This is by far the best opportunity for listeners in western states. One hour later in winter.

Radio Cairo, Egypt. The final half-hour of a 90-minute broadcast to North America. See 0200 for specifics. Winter on 7535 kHz, summer on 7270 kHz.

Radio Bulgaria. Winter only at this time, and a repeat of the 0000 broadcast; see there for specifics. A distinctly Bulgarian potpourri of news, commentary, features and music. Not to be missed is Monday's ●*Folk Studio* (Sunday evening in the Americas). An hour to eastern North America and Central America on 5900 and 7400 kHz. One hour earlier in summer.

Radio Romania International. Summer only at this time; see 0400 for specifics. Fifty-five minutes to western North America on 6150 and 9645 kHz, and to South Asia on 11895 and 15220 kHz. One hour later in winter.

Radio New Zealand International. Continues with *news* and features targeted at a regional audience. Part of a 24-hour transmission for the South Pacific, but also heard in parts of North America (especially during summer). On 15720 or 17675 kHz. Often carries commentaries of local sporting events. Popular with many listeners.

Voice of Korea, North Korea. Abysmal programs from the last of the old-style communist stations. Worth a listen just to hear how bad they are. One hour to East Asia on 3560, 7140, 9345 and 9730 kHz.

Voice of Turkey. Summer only at this time. *News*, followed by *Review of the Turkish Press* and features (some exotic and unusual). Selections of Turkish popular and classical music complete the broadcast. Fifty minutes to Europe and North America on 5975 and 7325 kHz, and to the Mideast on 7265 kHz. The broadcast on 7325 kHz is a relay via the facilities of Radio Canada International. One hour later during winter.

Voice of America. The start of four hours of continuous programming to Africa. Monday through Friday, *Daybreak Africa* fills the first half-hour, and is followed by *World News Now*. Weekends, 30 minutes of news are followed by Saturday's *Press Confer-*

One of the hundreds of islands near Stockholm, Sweden. L. Rydén

ence USA or Sunday's *Issues in the News*. On 4930, 6035 (winter), 6080, 7340 (till 0330), 9885 and (summer) 12080 and 15580 kHz. Best for southern Africa are 4930 and 9885 kHz.

AFRTS Shortwave, USA. Network news, live sports, music and features in the *upper-sideband* mode from the American Forces Radio & Television Service. Transmitted from modestly powered U.S. Navy stations around the globe, so usually a tough catch. Try 4319, 5446.5, 5765, 6350, 7811, 10320, 12133.5, 12579 and 13362 kHz.

03:30

Radio Sweden. Tuesday through Saturday (weekday evenings in North America), there's *news* and features about Sweden. Sunday, it's a review of the main news stories of the previous week; and Monday, *Network Europe*. Thirty minutes to western North America on 6010 kHz, one hour earlier in summer.

Radio Prague, Czech Republic. Summer only at this time. See the 0400 winter broadcast for North America for program specifics. A half-hour to western North America on 6080 kHz, and to the Mideast and South Asia on 9445 and 11600 kHz. The broadcast to North America is 30 minutes later in winter, and for the Mideast and South Asia it's one hour later.

Voice of Vietnam. A relay via the facilities of Radio Canada International. Begins with *News*, then Tuesday though Saturday (weekday evenings in North America) there's *Current Affairs*. These are followed Tuesday by *Vietnam, Land and People*; Wednesday, *Society* and *Business*; Thursday, *Letterbox* (listener response); Friday, *Vietnam Economy* and *Talk of the Week*; and Saturday, *Rural Vietnam* and *Culture*. Sunday has *Weekly Review* and *Weekend Music*, and Monday there's *Culture*, *Sports Roundup* and *Sunday Show*. Half an hour to eastern North America on 6175 kHz.

Radio Tirana, Albania. Tuesday through Sunday (Monday through Saturday evenings in North America). *News*, press review and features. Tuesday there's *The Week in Albania*, *Cultural Review* and *Sports Roundup*; Wednesday, a short topical report and *Mailbox* (listener response); Thursday, a short feature followed by Albanian music; Friday, *Focus on Albania*; Saturday, a talk on Albanian history (or *Foreigners on Albania*) followed by *Outstanding Personalities Profile*; and Sunday, *Mosaic of the Week* and *Folk Music*. Thirty minutes to North America winter on 6110 kHz, summer on 7425 kHz.

04:00–04:30

Gudrun Heise, host of Deutsche Welle's "Insight." Another of her shows was awarded the Silver WorldMedal at the 2004 New York Festival. DW

04:00

Radio Habana Cuba. Repeat of the 0200 broadcast. To eastern and central North America on 6000 and 6140 (or 6180) kHz.

Radio Prague, Czech Republic. Winter only at this time. *News*, then Tuesday through Saturday (weekday evenings in the Americas) there's the in-depth *Current Affairs* and a feature or two: *One on One* (interviews, Tuesday), *Talking Point* (Wednesday), *Czechs in History*, *Czechs Today* or *Spotlight* (Thursday), *Panorama* and *From the Archives* (Friday), and *Business News* and *The Arts* on Saturday. Sunday news is followed by *Magazine*, *Sound Czech* and a repeat of Tuesday's *One on One*; and Monday's lineup is *Mailbox* and *Letter from Prague* followed by *Music Profile*, *Magic Carpet* (Czech world music) or *Czech Books*. Thirty minutes to North America on 6080, 6200 and 7345 kHz. By far the best opportunity for western states. One hour earlier in summer.

■**Radio France Internationale.** Weekdays only at this time. Starts with a bulletin of African *news* and an international newsflash. Next, there's a review of the French dailies, an in-depth look at events in Africa, the main news event of the day in France, and sports. Thirty information-packed minutes to East Africa on 7315 (winter), 9805 and (summer) 11995 kHz. Heard well beyond the intended target area.

Radio Ukraine International. Winter only at this time, and a repeat of the 0100 broadcast. Ample coverage of local issues, including news, sports, politics and culture. Well worth a listen is ●*Music from Ukraine*, which fills most of the Monday (Sunday evening in the Americas) broadcast. An hour to eastern North America on 7440 kHz. One hour earlier in summer.

Radio Australia. *World News*, then Monday through Friday, it's the final hour of *In the Loop* for listeners in the Pacific. Asia gets one or more features: *National Interest* (Monday), *Counterpoint* (Tuesday), ●*Rear Vision* and *Innovations* (Wednesday), *Background Briefing* (investigative journalism, Thursday), and ●*The Science Show* on Friday. Weekends, it's live sport in *Grandstand*. Continuous to Asia and the Pacific on 9660, 12080, 13690, 15240, 15415 (from 0430), 15515, 17750 and 21725 kHz. Should also be audible in parts of North America (best during summer) on 15515 kHz. In East Asia, tune to 13690 or 21725 kHz, although these frequencies carry programming for the Pacific. For Southeast Asia there's 15415 and 17750 kHz.

■**Deutsche Welle,** Germany. *News*, followed Tuesday through Saturday by ●*NewsLink*—commentary, interviews, background reports and analysis. On the half-hour there's ●*Spectrum* (science and technology, Tuesday), ●*Money Talks* (Wednesday), *Living Planet* (Thursday), ●*Inside Europe* (Friday) and ●*Insight* (Saturday). Sunday, the news is followed by *In-Box*, *Mission Europe* (a German language course), *Sports Report* and *Inspired Minds*; and Monday by a 10-minute edition of *Newslink*, *Sports Report* and ●*World in Progress*. An hour to Africa winter on 5905, 5945, 6180 and 15600 kHz; and summer on 7225, 7245, 12045 and 15445 kHz. Audible in southern Africa winter on 15600 kHz, midyear on 12045 kHz.

04:00–04:30

Radio Romania International. Winter only at this time. Starts with *Radio Newsreel*, a combination of news, commentary and press review. Features on Romania complete the broadcast. Regular spots include Tuesday's *Pro Memoria*, *Romanian Hits* and *Sports Roundup*; Wednesday's *Business Club* and ●*The Skylark* (Romanian folk music); Thursday's *Society Today* and *Romanian Musicians*; and Friday's *Europa Express*. Saturday fare includes ●*The Folk Music Box* and *Sports Weekend*; and Sunday there's *The Week* and *World of Culture*. Monday's broadcast includes *Focus*. Fifty-five minutes to western North America on 6115 and 9515 kHz, and to South Asia on 9690 and 11895 kHz. These days are World Time, so locally in western North America it will be the previous evening. One hour earlier in summer.

Voice of Turkey. Winter only at this time. See 0300 for specifics. Fifty minutes to Europe and North America on 6010 and 6020 kHz, and to the Mideast on 7240 kHz. The broadcast on 6010 kHz is a relay via the facilities of Radio Canada International. One hour earlier in summer.

China Radio International. Repeat of the 0300 broadcast (see there for specifics); one hour to North America winter on 6190 kHz, summer on 6020 and 6080 kHz. Also to East Asia winter on 9460, 13620 and 15120 kHz; and summer on 13750, 15120 and 15785 kHz; and Central Asia on 17725 (winter), 17730 (summer) and 17855 kHz.

Radio New Zealand International. Continuous programming for the South Pacific. Part of a much longer broadcast, which is also heard in parts of North America (especially during summer). On 15720 or 17675 kHz. Sometimes carries commentaries of local sports events.

Voice of Russia World Service. Continues to North America at this hour. Opens with *News*, then a feature. Winter, there's *This is Russia* (Monday), *Encyclopedia "All Russia"* (Tuesday and Friday), *Moscow Mailbag* (Wednesday and Saturday), and *Science Plus* (Thursday). More features follow a brief news summary on the half-hour and include *Moscow Yesterday and Today* (Monday), *Guest Speaker* (Tuesday through Saturday), and *Spiritual Flowerbed* (Tuesday and Thursday). Pride of place at this hour goes to Sunday's 47-minute ●*Music and Musicians* (classical music). The summer schedule has plenty of variety, and includes *Encyclopedia "All Russia"* and *The VOR Treasure Store* (Monday), *Moscow Mailbag* and ●*Music Calendar*, *Russian Hits* or ●*Jazz Show* (Tuesday), *Science Plus* and *Moscow, Yesterday and Today* (Wednesday), the excellent ●*Music and Musicians* (Thursday), *Moscow Mailbag* and *The VOR Treasure Store* (Friday), *This is Russia* and *Timelines* (Saturday), and *Encyclopedia "All Russia"* and *Kaleidoscope* (Sunday). These days are World Time, so locally in North America it will be the previous evening. In eastern North America, choose from 6155, 6240, 7150 and 7350 kHz in winter, and 9665, 9860 and 9880 (or 5900) kHz in summer. Best winter bets for the West Coast are 9840, 12010, 12030 and 12040 kHz; and summer there's 9435, 13635 and 13775 kHz.

Voice of America. Continuous programming to Africa. Monday through Friday, *Daybreak Africa* fills the first half-hour, followed by *World News Now*. Weekends, 30 minutes of news are followed by *On the Line*. On 4930, 4960, 6080 and 9575 kHz; also winter on 9775 kHz, summer on 11835, 12080 and 15580 kHz. Best for southern Africa is 4930 kHz; and heard in North America on 9575 kHz.

AFRTS Shortwave, USA. Network news, live sports, music and features in the *upper-sideband* mode from the American Forces Radio & Television Service. Transmitted from modestly powered U.S. Navy stations around the globe, so usually a tough catch. Try 4319, 5446.5, 5765, 6350, 7811, 10320, 12133.5, 12579 and 13362 kHz.

04:30

Radio Prague, Czech Republic. Winter only at this time. See the 0400 broadcast to North America for program specifics. Thirty minutes to the Mideast and South Asia on 9855 kHz. One hour earlier in summer.

Radio Tirana, Albania. Tuesday through Sunday (Monday through Saturday evenings in the Americas) and winter only at this time. See 0330 for specifics. Thirty minutes to eastern North America on 6100 kHz, and one hour earlier in summer.

05:00

■**Deutsche Welle,** Germany. *News*, then Tuesday through Saturday it's ●*Newslink*—commentary, interviews, background reports and analysis. This is replaced Sunday by *Network Europe*, and Monday by a 10-minute edition of *Newslink* followed by *Sports Report*. Thirty minutes to Africa, winter on 6180, 7285, 9755, 12045 and 15600 kHz; and summer on 9700 and 9825 kHz. Best for southern Africa are 12045 and 15600 kHz in winter (summer in the Southern Hemisphere) and 9700 and 9825 kHz midyear.

■**Radio France Internationale.** Monday through Friday only at this time. Similar to the 0400 broadcast, but without the international newsflash. Thirty minutes to East Africa (and heard well beyond) on any two channels from 9805, 11995 and 13680 kHz.

Vatican Radio. Summer only at this time. Thirty minutes of programming oriented to Catholics. To Europe on 4005 and 7250 kHz. One hour later in winter.

Radio Ukraine International. Summer only at this time; see 0600 for specifics. A potpourri of things Ukrainian, with the Sunday broadcast often featuring some excellent music. An hour to western Europe on 9945 kHz. One hour later in winter.

Radio Japan. Ten minutes of *news*, then a feature. Monday through Friday there's *What's Up Japan* (current events, Japanese language lessons, and a listener-response segment Wednesday). This is replaced Saturday by *World Interactive* or (the last Saturday of the month) *Listening Library*, readings from masterpieces of Japanese literature. Sunday's feature is *Pop Up Japan*, a selection of Japanese pop music. Thirty minutes to Europe on 5975 kHz; to western North America on 6110 kHz; to Southeast Asia on 17810 kHz; to South Asia on 15325 kHz; and to southern Africa winter on 9770 kHz and midyear on 11970 kHz.

China Radio International. *News* and reports fill the first half-hour, and are followed by a daily feature: ●*Frontline* (Monday), *Biz China* (Tuesday), *In the Spotlight* (Wednesday), ●*Voices from Other Lands* (Thursday), *Life in China* (Friday), *Listeners' Garden* (Saturday) and *China Horizons* (Sunday). One hour to central and western North America on 5960 (winter), 6020 (summer) and 6190 kHz via CRI's Canadian relay. Also available to the Mideast and West Asia on 17505 kHz; and to Central Asia on 17725 (winter), 17730 (summer) and 17855 kHz. These days are World Time, so locally in North America it will be the previous evening.

Radio Habana Cuba. The start of a two-hour broadcast for North, Central and South America. Tuesday through Sunday (Monday through Saturday evenings in the Americas), the first half-hour consists of international and Cuban news followed by *RHC's Viewpoint*. The next 30 minutes consist of a news bulletin and the sports-oriented *Time Out* (five minutes each) plus a feature: *Caribbean Outlook* (Tuesday and Friday), *DXers Unlimited* (Wednesday and Sunday), the *Mailbag Show* (Thursday) and *Weekly Review* (Saturday). Monday, the hour is split between *Weekly Review* and *Mailbag Show*. On 6000, 6060, 6140 (or 6180), 9550 and 11760 kHz.

Radio New Zealand International. Continues with regional programming for the South Pacific. Part of a 24-hour broadcast, which is also heard in parts of North America (especially during summer). On 9615 or 15720 kHz.

Radio Australia. *World News*, then Monday through Friday, continues with current events: *The World Today* for Asia, and *Pacific Beat* (including *On the Mat* and a sports bulletin) for listeners in the Pacific. Weekends,

04:30–05:30

Zhou Jing, host and producer of "Voices from Other Lands." China Radio International is taking up much of the listenership slack left by fading broadcasting heavyweights in the West. CRI

it's live sport in *Grandstand*. Continuous to Asia and the Pacific on 9660, 12080, 13690, 15160, 15240, 15415 (from 0530), 15515 and 17750 kHz. In North America (best during summer) try 15160 and 15515 kHz. In East Asia, tune to 13690 kHz, although it carries programming for the Pacific. For Southeast Asia there's 15415 and 17750 kHz.

Voice of Russia World Service. Winter, the final 60 minutes of a four-hour block of programming to North America; summer, the first of four hours to Australasia. Opens with *News*, followed winter by features: *Encyclopedia "All Russia"* and *The VOR Treasure Store* (Monday), *Moscow Mailbag* and ●*Music Calendar*, *Russian Hits* or ●*Jazz Show* (Tuesday), *Science Plus* and *Moscow, Yesterday and Today* (Wednesday), the excellent ●*Music and Musicians* (Thursday), *Moscow Mailbag* and *The VOR Treasure Store* (Friday), *This is Russia* and *Timelines* (Saturday), and *Encyclopedia "All Russia"* and *Kaleidoscope* (Sunday). These days are World Time, so locally in North America it will be the previous evening. Tuesday through Saturday summer, there's *Focus on Asia and the Pacific*, replaced Sunday by *This is Russia* and Monday by *Moscow Mailbag*. On the half-hour, look for *Russian by Radio* (Monday and Wednesday), *Kaleidoscope* (Tuesday), *Moscow Yesterday and Today* (Thursday), ●*Music Calendar*, *Russian Hits* or ●*Jazz Show* (Friday), ●*Christian Message from Moscow* (Saturday) and *The VOR Treasure Store* on Sunday. Winter only to eastern North America on 7150 and 7350 kHz, and to western parts on 9840, 9855 and12040 kHz. Summer (winter in the Southern Hemisphere) to Australasia on 17635 and 21790 kHz.

AFRTS Shortwave, USA. Network news, live sports, music and features in the *upper-sideband* mode from the American Forces Radio & Television Service. Transmitted from modestly powered U.S. Navy stations around the globe, so usually a tough catch. Try 4319, 5446.5, 5765, 6350, 7811, 10320, 12133.5, 12579 and 13362 kHz.

05:30

Radio Thailand. Thirty minutes of *news* and short features relayed from one of the station's domestic services. To Europe winter on 11730 kHz, summer on 17655 kHz.

Radio Romania International. Summer only at this time. *News* and commentary followed by short features on Romania. Twenty-five minutes to western Europe on 9655 and 11830 kHz. Also available to Australasia on 15435 and 17770 kHz. One hour later in winter.

0600–1159
Australasia & East Asia—Evening Prime Time
Western North America—Late Evening
Europe & Mideast—Morning and Midday

06:00

■**Deutsche Welle,** Germany. *News*, then Tuesday through Saturday it's ●*Newslink*—commentary, interviews, background reports and analysis. This is replaced Sunday by *In-Box* and *Mission Europe* (German language lessons), and Monday by a 10-minute edition of *Newslink* followed by *Sports Report*. Thirty minutes to West and Central Africa and heard well beyond. Winter on 5945, 7240 and 12045 kHz; and summer on 7310 and 15275 kHz.

Radio Habana Cuba. The second half of a two-hour broadcast. Tuesday through Sunday (Monday through Saturday evenings in the Americas), opens with 10 minutes of international news. Next comes *Spotlight on the Americas* (Tuesday through Saturday) or Sunday's *The World of Stamps*. The final 30 minutes consists of news-oriented programming. Monday slots are *From Havana* and ●*The Jazz Place* or *Breakthrough* (science). To North, Central and South America on 6000, 6060, 6140 (or 6180), 9550 and 11760 kHz.

China Radio International. Winter only at this time, and a repeat of the 0500 broadcast (see there for specifics). One hour to western North America on 6115 kHz, to the Mideast and West Asia winter on 11770 and 15145 kHz, summer on 11870 and 15140 kHz, and year-round on 17505 kHz; and to Southeast Asia on 13645 (winter), 13660 (summer) and 17710 kHz.

Radio Ukraine International. Winter only at this time. News, commentary, reports and interviews, providing ample coverage of Ukrainian life. Recommended listening is ●*Music from Ukraine*, which fills most of the Sunday broadcast. An hour to western Europe on 7440 kHz. One hour earlier in summer.

■**Radio France Internationale.** Weekdays only at this time. Similar to the 0400 broadcast (see there for specifics), but includes a report on the day's main international story. Thirty minutes to East and West Africa winter on 7315 (or 9765), 11995 (or 15160) and 13680 kHz; and summer on 11725 (or 9765), 15160 and 17800 kHz. Heard well beyond the intended target area.

Radio Australia. Begins with *World News*, then Monday through Friday there's *Regional Sports* and *Talking Point*. Listeners in the Pacific then get a relay of Radio New Zealand International's *Dateline Pacific*. For Asia there's *Health Report* (Monday), *Law Report* (Tuesday), *Religion Report* (Wednesday), *Media Report* (Thursday), and *The Sports Factor* on Friday. These are replaced weekends by live sports coverage in *Grandstand*. Continuous to Asia and the Pacific on 9660, 12080, 13690, 15160, 15240, 15415, 15515 and 17750 kHz. Listeners in North America should try 15160 and 15515 kHz. In East Asia, tune to 13690 kHz, although the programming is for the Pacific. Southeast Asia has 15415 (from 0630 Monday through Friday) and 17750 kHz.

Radio New Zealand International. Continues with regional programming for the South Pacific, which is also heard in parts of North America (especially during summer). On 9615, 9765 or 9870 kHz.

Voice of Russia World Service. *News*, then Tuesday through Saturday winter, there's *Focus on Asia and the Pacific*, replaced Sunday by *This is Russia* and Monday by *Moscow Mailbag*. On the half-hour, look for *Russian by Radio* (Monday and Wednesday), *Kaleidoscope* (Tuesday), *Moscow Yesterday and Today* (Thursday), ●*Music Calendar*, *Russian Hits* or ●*Jazz Show* (Friday), ●*Christian Message from Moscow* (Saturday) and *The VOR Treasure Store* on Sunday. In summer, the news is followed by *Science Plus* (Monday), *This is Russia* (Tuesday and Friday), *Encyclopedia "All Russia"* (Wednesday and Saturday) and *Moscow Mailbag* on the remaining days. The second half-hour offers plenty of variety: *Kaleidoscope* (Monday and Friday), *Russian by Radio* (Tuesday), ●*Music Calendar*, *Russian Hits* or ●*Jazz Show* (Wednesday and Thursday), *Kaleidoscope* (Friday), ●*Folk Box* (Saturday) and *Timelines* on Sunday. Continuous programming to Australasia winter (local summer) on 17665 and 17805 kHz, midyear on 17635 and 21790 kHz.

Vatican Radio. Winter only at this time. Thirty minutes with a heavy Catholic slant. To Europe on 4005 and 7250 kHz. One hour earlier in summer.

Voice of Malaysia. *News*, followed Monday, Wednesday, Friday and Sunday by a two-minute Malayan language lesson (replaced by a local pop hit on Tuesday). The next 33 minutes are given over to *Hits All the Way*. Saturday, it's the 35-minute *Mailbag*. The hour is rounded off with a feature: *New Horizon* (Monday), *ASEAN Focus* (Tuesday), *Malaysia in Perspective* (Wednesday), *Personality* (Thursday), *News and Views* (Friday), and *Weekly Roundup* and *Current Affairs* on the weekend. The first hour of a 150-minute broadcast to Southeast Asia and Australasia on 6175, 9750 and 15295 kHz.

AFRTS Shortwave, USA. Network news, live sports, music and features in the *upper-sideband* mode from the American Forces Radio & Television Service. Transmitted from modestly powered U.S. Navy stations around the globe, so usually a tough catch. Try 4319, 5446.5, 5765, 6350, 7811, 10320, 12133.5, 12579 and 13362 kHz.

06:30

Radio Bulgaria. Summer only at this time. *News*, followed by *Answering Your Letters* (Monday), ●*Folk Studio* (Tuesday) and *DX Programme* (Sunday). Most of the remaining airtime is taken up by ●*Time Out for Music*. Thirty minutes to Europe on 7200 and 9400 kHz. One hour later in winter.

Radio Romania International. Winter only at this time. *News* and commentary followed by short features on Romania. Twenty-five minutes to western Europe on 7180 and 9690 kHz. Also available to Australasia on 15135 and 17780 kHz. One hour earlier in summer.

07:00

Radio Prague, Czech Republic. Summer only at this time. See 0800 for specifics. Thirty minutes to Europe on 9880 and 11600 kHz. One hour later in winter.

Radio Slovakia International. Monday through Saturday, there's *news* followed by features on Slovak life and culture. Sunday, it's *Sunday Newsreel* and a listener-response program. Half an hour to Australasia winter on 13715 and 15460 kHz, midyear on 9440 and 11650 kHz.

China Radio International. Weekdays, *News* is followed by *China Drive*, an upbeat "drive-time" show. Weekends there's *News and Reports*, *CRI Roundup* (Saturday), *Reports from Developing Countries* (Sunday) and *China Beat* (music). One hour to Europe on 11785 (winter), 13710 (summer) and 17490 kHz; and to Southeast Asia on 13645 (winter), 13660 (summer) and 17710 kHz.

■**Radio France Internationale.** Weekdays only at this time. Starts with a bulletin of African *news*. Next, there's a review of the French dailies, an in-depth look at events in Africa, the main news event of the day in France, and sports. Thirty information-packed minutes to West and Central Africa winter on 11725 kHz, summer on 13675 kHz. Audible in southern Africa midyear.

Radio Australia. *World News*, then Monday through Friday, listeners in the Pacific get a repeat of *Pacific Beat*. For Asia there's *Life Matters*. Winter weekends, there's a roundup of the latest sports action in *Grandstand Wrap*, then Saturday's *Rural Reporter* or Sunday's *Innovations*. These are replaced summer by the final hour of *Grandstand*

07:00–08:00

(live sport). Continuous to Asia and the Pacific on 9475, 9660, 9710, 11945, 12080, 13630, 15160, 15240, 15415 and 17750 kHz. Listeners in North America can try 13630 kHz (West Coast) or 15160 kHz (best during summer). For East Asia there's 9715 kHz, but with programs for the Pacific. Southeast Asia has 9745, 11945, 15415 and 17750 kHz.

Voice of Malaysia. Starts weekdays with 45 minutes of *Fascinating Malaysia*, replaced Saturday by *Malaysia Rama* and *Malaysia in Perspective*, and Sunday by *ASEAN Melody* and *Destination Malaysia*. Not much doubt about where the broadcast originates! The hour ends with a 15-minute feature. Continuous to Southeast Asia and Australasia on 6175, 9750 and 15295 kHz.

Voice of Russia World Service. Continuous programming to Australasia. Winter, opens with *News*, then features: *Science Plus* (Monday), *This is Russia* (Tuesday and Friday), *Encyclopedia "All Russia"* (Wednesday and Saturday) and *Moscow Mailbag* on the remaining days. The second half-hour offers plenty of variety: *Kaleidoscope* (Monday and Friday), *Russian by Radio* (Tuesday), ●*Music Calendar*, *Russian Hits* or ●*Jazz Show* (Wednesday and Thursday), *Kaleidoscope* (Friday), ●*Folk Box* (Saturday) and *Timelines* on Sunday. Summer, the news is followed by the informative *Russia and the World* on Tuesday, Thursday and Saturday. Other offerings include *This is Russia* (Wednesday), *Moscow Mailbag* (Friday) and *Science Plus* (Sunday). Class act of the week is Monday's masterpiece, ●*Music and Musicians*. On the half-hour there's a summary of the latest news, then more features: ●*Folk Box* (Tuesday), *A Stroll Around the Kremlin* (or *Legends of Russian Sports*) and *Musical Tales* (Wednesday), *The VOR Treasure Store* (Thursday), *Moscow, Yesterday and Today* (Friday), *Kaleidoscope* (Saturday) and *A Stroll Around the Kremlin* (or *Legends of Russian Sports*) and ●*Songs from Russia* (or ●*Russia–1000 Years of Music*) on Sunday. Winter (local summer) there's 17665 and 17805 kHz; and midyear, 17495, 17635 and 21790 kHz.

Radio New Zealand International. Continues with regional programming for the South Pacific, which is also heard in parts of North America (especially during summer). On 6095, 9765 or 9870 kHz.

Radio Taiwan International. Ten minutes of *News*, followed by features: *Time Traveler*, *Chinese to Go* (language lessons) and *Asia Review* (Monday); *People* and *We've Got Mail* (Tuesday); *Health Beats*, *Women Making Waves* and ●*Jade Bells and Bamboo Pipes* (Wednesday); *Strait Talk*, *Breakfast Club*, *Instant Noodles* and *Chinese to Go* (Thursday); *Ilha Formosa*, *Taiwan Indie* and *Taiwan Outlook* (Friday); *News Talk* and *Groove Zone* (Saturday); and *The Occidental Tourist*, *Spotlight* and *On the Line* (Sunday). These days are World Time, so locally in North America it will be the previous evening. One hour to western North America on 5950 kHz.

AFRTS Shortwave, USA. Network news, live sports, music and features in the *upper-sideband* mode from the American Forces Radio & Television Service. Transmitted from modestly powered U.S. Navy stations around the globe, so usually a tough catch. Try 4319, 5446.5, 5765, 6350, 7811, 10320, 12133.5, 12579 and 13362 kHz.

07:30

Radio Bulgaria. This time winter only. *News*, followed by *Answering Your Letters* (Monday), ●*Folk Studio* (Tuesday) and *DX Programme* (Sunday). Most of the remaining airtime is taken up by ●*Time Out for Music*. Thirty minutes to Europe on 5900 and 7400 kHz, and one hour earlier in summer.

08:00

Voice of Malaysia. *News* and commentary, then *Golden Oldies*. The final half-hour of a much longer transmission targeted at Southeast Asia and Australasia on 6175, 9750 and 15295 kHz.

Radio Prague, Czech Republic. Winter only at this time. *News*, then Monday through Friday it's the in-depth *Current Affairs* and one or more features: *One on One* (Monday), *Talking Point* (Tuesday), *Czechs in History*, *Czechs Today* or *Spotlight* (Wednesday), *Panorama* and *From the Archives* (Thursday), and *Business News* and *The Arts* (Friday). Weekends, the news is followed by Saturday's *Insight Central Europe* (or *Magazine*, *Sound Czech* and *One on One*), and Sunday's *Mailbox* and *Letter from Prague* followed by *Music Profile*, *Magic Carpet* (Czech world music) or *Czech Books*. Thirty minutes to Europe on 7345 and 9860 kHz. One hour earlier in summer.

Radio Australia. Part of a 24-hour service to Asia and the Pacific, but which can also be heard at this time throughout much of North America. Begins with a bulletin of *World News*, then Monday through Friday there's an in-depth look at current events in *PM*. Winter weekends, there's *Asia Pacific Review* and *Jazz Notes* (Saturday), and *Correspondents Report* and ●*Rear Vision* (Sunday). These are replaced summer by *Grandstand Wrap* followed by Saturday's *Total Rugby* or Sunday's *Innovations*. On 5995, 9580, 9590, 9475, 9710, 11945, 12080, 13630, 15415 and 17750 kHz. Audible in parts of North America on 9580, 9590 and 13630 kHz. Best for East Asia is 9710 kHz, with 11945, 15415 and 17750 kHz the channels for Southeast Asia.

Voice of Russia World Service. Continuous programming to Australasia. Winter, *News* is followed by the informative *Russia and the World* on Tuesday, Thursday and Saturday. Other offerings include *This is Russia* (Wednesday), *Moscow Mailbag* (Friday) and *Science Plus* (Sunday). Pick of the week is Monday's masterpiece, ●*Music and Musicians*. On the half-hour there's a summary of the latest news, then more features: ●*Folk Box* (Tuesday), *A Stroll Around the Kremlin* (or *Legends of Russian Sports*) and *Musical Tales* (Wednesday), *The VOR Treasure Store* (Thursday), *Moscow, Yesterday and Today* (Friday), *Kaleidoscope* (Saturday) and *A Stroll Around the Kremlin* (or *Legends of Russian Sports*) and ●*Songs*

08:00–09:00

Trakai Castle resisted every attack following its construction nearly 800 years ago. It then crumbled into ruin, but was eventually restored when Lithuania was under communist rule.
Shutterstock

from Russia (or ●*Russia–1000 Years of Music*) on Sunday. In summer, the news is followed Tuesday through Saturday by *News and Views*, and Sunday and Monday by *This is Russia*. On the half-hour there's a summary of the latest news and a feature: *A Stroll Around the Kremlin* (or *Legends of Russian Sport*) and *Musical Tales* (Monday), *Kaleidoscope* (Tuesday), *The VOR Treasure Store* (Wednesday), ●*Folk Box* (Thursday), ●*Music Calendar*, Russian Hits or ●*Jazz Show* (Friday), ●*Christian Message from Moscow* (Saturday) and *Timelines* on Sunday. Winter (local summer) there's 17665, 17805 and 17495 kHz; and midyear, 17495, 17635 and 21790 kHz.

Radio New Zealand International. Continues with regional programming for the South Pacific. Part of a 24-hour broadcast which is also heard in parts of North America (especially during summer). On 6095, 9765 or 9870 kHz.

China Radio International. *News* and reports fill the first half-hour, and are followed by a daily feature: ●*Frontline* (Monday), *Biz China* (Tuesday), *In the Spotlight* (Wednesday), ●*Voices from Other Lands* (Thursday), *Life in China* (Friday), *Listeners' Garden* (Saturday) and *China Horizons* (Sunday). One hour to Europe on 11785 (winter), 13710 (summer) and 17490 kHz; and to East Asia winter on 9415 kHz, summer on 11620 kHz.

KBS World Radio, South Korea. Opens with 10 minutes of *news*, then Monday through Friday, a commentary. This is followed by 30 minutes of *Seoul Calling* and a 15-minute feature: *Faces of Korea*, *Business Watch*, *Culture on the Move*, *Korea Today and Tomorrow* and *Seoul Report*, respectively. Saturday's news is followed by *Worldwide Friendship* (a listener-response show), and Sunday by *Korean Pop Interactive*. An hour to Southeast Asia on 9570 kHz.

AFRTS Shortwave, USA. Network news, live sports, music and features in the *upper-sideband* mode from the American Forces Radio & Television Service. Transmitted from modestly powered U.S. Navy stations around the globe, so usually a tough catch. Try 4319, 5446.5, 5765, 6350, 7811, 10320, 12133.5, 12579 and 13362 kHz.

08:30

Radio Vilnius, Lithuania. Summer only at this time; see 0930 for specifics. To western Europe on 9710 kHz. One hour later in winter.

09:00

■**Deutsche Welle,** Germany. *News*, then Monday through Friday it's ●*Newslink*—commentary, interviews, background reports and analysis. The second half-hour features *EuroVox* (Monday), *Hits in Germany* (Tuesday), ●*Arts on the Air* (Wednesday), *Cool* (a well produced youth show, Thursday) and *Dialogue* on Friday. Weekends, the news is followed by Saturday's *Network Europe* and ●*Insight*, and Sunday's *In-Box*, *Mission Europe* (German language lessons) and ●*World in Progress*. An hour to East Asia winter on 17710 and 21840 kHz, summer on 15340 and 17705 kHz. Also heard in parts of Southeast Asia.

China Radio International. *News* and reports fill the first half-hour, and are followed by a daily feature: ●*Frontline* (Monday), *Biz China* (Tuesday), *In the Spotlight* (Wednesday), ●*Voices from Other Lands* (Thursday), *Life in China* (Friday), *Listeners' Garden* (Saturday) and *China Horizons* (Sunday). One hour to Europe on 17490 kHz; to Australasia on 15210 and 17690 kHz; and to East Asia winter on 9415 kHz, summer on 11620 kHz.

Voice of Greece. Sunday and summer only at this time, and starts at 0905. Fifty-five minutes of music in *Greek in Style*. To Europe on 9420 and 15605 (or 15630) kHz. Two hours later in winter.

Radio Japan. Ten minutes of *news*, then a feature. Monday through Friday there's *What's Up Japan* (current events, Japanese language lessons, and a listener-response segment Wednesday). This is replaced Saturday by *World Interactive* or (the last Saturday of the month) *Listening Library*, readings from masterpieces of Japanese literature. Sunday's feature is *Pop Up Japan*, a selection of Japanese pop music. Thirty minutes to Hawaii and South America on 9825 kHz; to South Asia on 15590 kHz; to Southeast Asia on 11815 kHz; and to Australasia on 9625 kHz.

Radio New Zealand International. Continuous programming for the islands of the South Pacific on 6095 or 9765 kHz. Audible in much of North America, especially in summer.

Voice of Russia World Service. Winter only at this time, and the last of four hours for Australasia. Tuesday through Sunday, *News* is followed by *News and Views*, replaced Sunday and Monday by *This is Russia*. On the half-hour there's a news summary and a feature: *A Stroll Around the Kremlin* (or *Legends of Russian Sport*) and *Musical Tales* (Monday), *Kaleidoscope* (Tuesday), *The VOR Treasure Store* (Wednesday), ●*Folk Box* (Thursday), ●*Music Calendar*, Russian Hits or ●*Jazz Show* (Friday), ●*Christian Message from Moscow* (Saturday) and *Timelines* on Sunday. On 17495 and 17665 kHz.

Radio Prague, Czech Republic. Summer only at this time. See 1000 for program specifics. Thirty minutes to Europe on 9880 kHz, and to South Asia on 21745 kHz. One hour later in winter.

Radio Ukraine International. Summer only at this time. Interesting coverage of local issues, including news, sports, politics and culture. A popular feature is ●*Music from Ukraine*, which fills most of the Sunday broadcast. An hour to western Europe on 11550 kHz. One hour later in winter.

Radio Australia. *World News*, then Monday through Friday it's *Australia Talks* (a call-in show). Winter Saturdays there's *Margaret Throsby*, replaced summer by *Asia Review* and *Jazz Notes*. Sunday, it's *The Music Show Part I*. Continuous to Asia and the Pacific on 9475, 9580, 9590, 11945 and 15415 kHz; and heard in North America on 9580 and 9590 kHz. For Southeast Asia there's 11945 and 15415 kHz.

AFRTS Shortwave, USA. Network news, live sports, music and features in the *upper-sideband* mode from the American Forces Radio & Television Service. Transmitted from modestly powered U.S. Navy stations around the globe, so usually a tough catch. Try 4319, 5446.5, 5765, 6350, 7811, 10320, 12133.5, 12579 and 13362 kHz.

09:30–11:00

09:30

Radio Vilnius, Lithuania. Winter only at this time. Thirty minutes of mostly *news* and background reports about events in Lithuania. A listener-response program, *Mailbag*, is aired every other Sunday. For a little Lithuanian music, try the second half of Monday's broadcast. To western Europe on 9710 kHz. One hour earlier in summer.

10:00

Radio Netherlands Worldwide. Monday through Friday, opens with a short bulletin of *news*, which is then followed by one or more features: ●*Curious Orange* and ●*Earthbeat* (Monday), *The State We're In - Midweek Edition* and *Bridges with Africa* (Tuesday), *Radio Books* and ●*Curious Orange* (Wednesday), ●*Earthbeat* (environmental and development issues) and *Network Europe Extra* (Thursday), and *Bridges with Africa* and *Radio Books* (Friday). Weekends, the news is followed by Saturday's *The State We're In* or Sunday's *Network Europe Extra* and *Reloaded* (highlights of the previous week's shows). Fifty-seven minutes to East and Southeast Asia winter on 6040, 9720, 9795 and 12065 kHz; and summer on 11895, 12065, and 15110 kHz. Also heard in parts of Australasia.

Radio Australia. Monday through Friday, there's *World News*, *Asia Pacific* (regional current events) and a feature: *Health Report* (Monday), *Law Report* (Tuesday), *Religious Report* (Wednesday), *Media Report* (Thursday) and *Sports Factor* (Friday). Saturday slots are taken by *Asia Pacific Business*, *Talking Point* and *Verbatim*; Sunday, it's the second part of *The Music Show*. Continuous to Asia and the Pacific on 9475, 9580, 9590, 11945 and 15415 kHz; and heard in North America on 9580 and 9590 kHz. Listeners in Southeast Asia have 9475, 11945 and 15415 kHz.

Radio Prague, Czech Republic. Winter only at this time. *News*, then Monday through Friday there's *Current Affairs* and a feature or two: *One on One* (interviews, Monday), *Talking Point* (Tuesday), *Czechs in History*, *Czechs Today* or *Spotlight* (Wednesday), *Panorama* and *From the Archives* (Thursday), and *Business News* and *The Arts* (Friday). On Saturday the news is followed by *Magazine*, *Sound Czech* and a repeat of Monday's *One on One*. Sunday's lineup is *Mailbox* and *Letter from Prague* followed by *Music Profile*, *Magic Carpet* (Czech world music) or *Czech Books*. Thirty minutes to South and Southeast Asia on 15700 kHz, and to West Africa on 21745 kHz. Audible well beyond. To Asia one hour earlier in summer, but the broadcast to Africa moves to 2100.

Radio Ukraine International. Winter only at this time. Ample coverage of local issues, and some good music on Sunday. An hour to western Europe on 9950 kHz. One hour earlier in summer.

China Radio International. Weekdays, *News* is followed by *China Drive*, an upbeat "drive-time" show. Weekends there's *News and Reports*, *CRI Roundup* (Saturday), *Reports from Developing Countries* (Sunday) and *China Beat*. Although mostly Chinese popular music, *China Beat* can sometimes surprise with jazz or Chinese versions of American folk and urban blues. One hour to Europe on 17490 kHz; to Australasia on 15210 and 17690 kHz; to eastern North America summer on 6040 kHz; to Southeast Asia on 13590 and 13720 kHz; and to East Asia winter on 5955, 7135 and 7215 kHz; and summer on 11610, 11635 and 13620 kHz.

All India Radio. *News*, then a composite program of commentary, press review and features, interspersed with exotic Indian music. Look for a listener-response segment, *Faithfully Yours*, at 1030 Monday. One hour to East Asia on 13710 (or 13695), 15020, 15235 (or 15410) and 17800 kHz, and to Australasia on 13710 (or 13695), 17510 and 17895 kHz. Also beamed to Sri Lanka on 15260 kHz.

Voice of Korea, North Korea. The dinosaur of world band and the last of the old-style communist stations. Mind-numbing programs on themes such as the application of socialist thinking to steel production are basic fare for this world band curiosity. Worth the occasional listen just to hear how bad it is. One hour to Central America on 6285 (or 15180) and 9325 (or 11710) kHz; and to Southeast Asia on 6185 (or 11735) and 9850 (or 13650) kHz. Also audible in parts of East Asia on 3560 kHz.

Voice of Vietnam. Begins with *News*, then Monday though Friday there's *Current Affairs*. These are followed Monday by *Vietnam, Land and People*; Tuesday, *Society* and *Business*; Wednesday, *Letterbox* (listener response); Thursday, *Vietnam Economy* and *Talk of the Week*; and Friday, *Rural Vietnam* and *Culture*. Saturday has *Weekly Review* and *Weekend Music*, and Sunday there's *Culture*, *Sports Roundup* and *Sunday Show*. Half an hour to Southeast Asia on 9840 and 12020 kHz.

AFRTS Shortwave, USA. Network news, live sports, music and features in the *upper-sideband* mode from the American Forces Radio & Television Service. Transmitted from modestly powered U.S. Navy stations around the globe, so usually a tough catch. Try 4319, 5446.5, 5765, 6350, 7811, 10320, 12133.5, 12579 and 13362 kHz.

10:30

Radio Prague, Czech Republic. Summer only at this hour; see 1130 for program specifics. Thirty minutes to northern Europe on 9880 and 11665 kHz. One hour later during winter.

Voice of the Islamic Republic of Iran. News, commentary and features, and a little Iranian music. Strongly reflects an Islamic point of view. One hour to South Asia, and widely heard elsewhere. On 15460 (winter), 15600 (summer) and 17660 kHz.

Voice of Mongolia. Original programming is aired on Monday, Wednesday and Friday, and is repeated on the following day. Starts with *News*, and then it's either a listener-response program (Monday) or reports and interviews. The entire Sunday broadcast is devoted to exotic Mongolian music. Thirty minutes to Southeast Asia and Australasia on 12085 kHz. Often heard in parts of the United States during March and September.

Dutch electronic junk finds its way to Ghana as secondhand goods. However, a large proportion of these don't work, so they end up in toxic scrapheaps. "Earthbeat" exposed this scandal over Radio Netherlands Worldwide in August 2008. RNW

11:00

China Radio International. Repeat of the 1000 broadcast, but with updated news. One hour to East Asia on 5955 kHz; to Southeast Asia on 13590 and 13720 kHz; to Europe on 13650 (summer), 13665 (winter) and 17490 kHz; and to North America winter on 5960 kHz, summer on 6040 and 11750 kHz.

Radio Taiwan International. Ten minutes of *News*, followed by features: *People*, *Chinese to Go* (language lessons) and *Asia Review* (Monday); *Health Beats* and *We've Got Mail* (Tuesday); *Strait Talk*, *Women Making Waves* and ●*Jade Bells and Bamboo Pipes* (Wednesday); *Ilha Formosa*, *Breakfast Club*, *Instant Noodles* and *Chinese to Go* (Thursday); *News Talk*, *Taiwan Indie* and *Taiwan Outlook* (Friday); *The Occidental Tourist* and *Groove Zone* (Saturday); and *Time Traveler*, *Spotlight* and *On the Line* (Sunday). An hour to Southeast Asia on 7445 and 11715 kHz, and also heard in parts of Australasia.

11:00–12:00

Radio Australia. *World News*, followed Monday through Friday by a bulletin of the latest sports news and *PM* (current events). Weekends, there's Saturday's *Asia Review* and *All in the Mind*, replaced Sunday by *Sunday Profile* and *Speaking Out*. Continuous to East Asia and the Pacific on 5995, 6020, 9475, 9560, 9580, 9590, 11945 and 12080 kHz; and heard in much of North America on 6020, 9580 and 9590 kHz. Listeners in Southeast Asia should tune to 9475 and 11945 kHz. For East Asia there's 9560 kHz.

Radio Ukraine International. Summer only at this time. An hour of just about all things Ukrainian, including news, sports, politics and culture. A popular feature is ●*Music from Ukraine*, which fills most of the Sunday broadcast. To western Europe on 11550 kHz. One hour later in winter.

Voice of Greece. Sunday and winter only at this time, and starts at 1105. Fifty-five minutes of music in *Greek in Style*. To Europe on 9420 kHz, and to Australasia on 15650 kHz. For Europe it's two hours earlier in summer, and for Australasia it moves to 2305 Sunday.

Voice of Vietnam. Repeat of the 1000 broadcast; see there for specifics. Half an hour to Southeast Asia on 7285 kHz.

Cholon, now part of Ho Chi Minh City (Saigon), was a thriving ethnic Chinese enclave until 1978. Socialist policies then dampened the business climate.

Shutterstock/Muellek

AFRTS Shortwave, USA. Network news, live sports, music and features in the *upper-sideband* mode from the American Forces Radio & Television Service. Transmitted from modestly powered U.S. Navy stations around the globe, so usually a tough catch. Try 4319, 5446.5, 5765, 6350, 7811, 10320, 12133.5, 12579 and 13362 kHz.

11:30

Radio Bulgaria. Summer only at this time. *News*, followed by *DX Programme* (for radio enthusiasts, Sunday), *Answering Your Letters* (a listener-response show, Monday), and ●*Folk Studio* (Bulgarian folk music, Tuesday). Most of the remaining airtime is taken up by ●*Time Out for Music*. Thirty minutes to Europe on 11700 and 15700 kHz, one hour later in winter.

Radio Prague, Czech Republic. Winter only at this time. *News*, then Monday through Friday it's *Current Affairs* plus one or more features: *One on One* (Monday), *Talking Point* (Tuesday), *Czechs in History*, *Czechs Today* or *Spotlight* (Wednesday), *Panorama* and *From the Archives* (Thursday), and *Business News* and *The Arts* on Friday. Saturday news is followed by *Magazine*, *Sound Czech* and a repeat of Tuesday's *One on One*. Sunday's lineup is *Mailbox* and *Letter from Prague* followed by *Music Profile*, *Magic Carpet* (Czech world music) or *Czech Books*. Thirty minutes to northern Europe on 11640 kHz, and to eastern and southern Africa on 17545 kHz. The European broadcast is one hour earlier in summer, but for Africa it moves to 1600.

Voice of Vietnam. Begins with *News*, then Monday though Friday there's *Current Affairs*. These are followed Monday by *Vietnam, Land and People*; Tuesday, *Society* and *Business*; Wednesday, *Letterbox* (listener response); Thursday, *Vietnam Economy* and *Talk of the Week*; and Friday, *Rural Vietnam* and *Culture*. Saturday has *Weekly Review* and *Weekend Music*, and Sunday there's *Culture*, *Sports Roundup* and *Sunday Show*. A half-hour to East Asia on 9840 and 12020 kHz.

1200–1759
Western Australia & East Asia—Evening Prime Time
North America—Morning and Lunchtime
Europe & Mideast—Afternoon and Early Evening

12:00

China Radio International. *News* and reports fill the first half-hour, and are followed by a daily feature: ●*Frontline* (Monday), *Biz China* (Tuesday), *In the Spotlight* (Wednesday), ●*Voices from Other Lands* (Thursday), *Life in China* (Friday), *Listeners' Garden* (Saturday) and *China Horizons* (Sunday). One hour to Europe on 13650 (summer), 13665 (winter), 13790 and 17490 kHz; to East Asia on 5955 kHz; to Southeast Asia on 9600, 9645, 9730 and 11980 kHz, and to Australasia on 9760 (or 11900) and 11760 kHz.

Radio Japan. Ten minutes of *news*, then a feature. Monday through Friday there's *What's Up Japan* (current events, Japanese language lessons, and a listener-response segment Wednesday). This is replaced Saturday by *World Interactive* or (the last Saturday of the month) *Listening Library*, readings from masterpieces of Japanese literature. Sunday's feature is *Pop Up Japan*, a selection of Japanese pop music. Thirty minutes to Europe on 17585 kHz; to eastern North America on 6120 kHz; to Southeast Asia on 9695 kHz; and to Australasia on 9625 kHz.

KBS World Radio, South Korea. Opens with 10 minutes of *news*, then Monday through Friday, a commentary. This is followed by 30 minutes of *Seoul Calling* and a 15-minute feature: *Faces of Korea*, *Business Watch*, *Culture on the Move*, *Korea Today and Tomorrow* and *Seoul Report*, respectively. Saturday's news is followed by *Worldwide Friendship* (a listener-response show), and Sunday by *Korean Pop Interactive*. An hour to eastern North America on 9650 kHz via their Canadian relay.

■**Radio France Internationale.** Opens with a *news* bulletin, then there's a 25-minute feature—*French Lesson*, *Crossroads*, *Voices*, *Rendez-Vous*, *World Tracks*, *Weekend* or *Club 9516* (a listener-response program). Thirty minutes to East Africa on 21620 (or 17800) kHz, and heard far beyond.

Polish Radio External Service. This time summer only. An hour of news, commentary, features and music—all with a Polish accent. Weekdays, starts with *News from Poland*—a potpourri of news, reports, interviews and press review. This is followed Monday by *Focus* (an arts program) and *Talking Jazz* or *Chat and Serious*. Tuesday's *A Day in the Life* (interviews) alternates with *The Krakow Panoptikon* and is followed by *The Biz*; Wednesday there's *Around Poland* and the live *Studio 15*; Thursday, a repeat of Monday's features; and Friday has *Weekly Commentary*, *Business Week* and *Offside*. Saturday broadcast begins with a bulletin of *news*, and is followed by *Insight Central Europe* (a joint-production with other stations of the region) or an alternative feature, *A Look at the Weeklies*, and *Chart Show* (Polish pop music). Sunday lineup includes *Europe East* (correspondents' reports) and *In Touch*. To northern Europe on 7330 (or 11850) and 9525 kHz. One hour later in winter. 9525 kHz is sometimes heard in eastern North America.

Radio Romania International. Summer only at this time; see 1300 for specifics. Fifty-five minutes to Europe on 11875 and 15220 kHz. One hour later in winter.

Radio Australia. *World News*, then Monday through Thursday it's *Late Night Live* (round-table discussion). On the remaining days there's *Classic Late Night Live* (Friday), ●*Saturday Night Country*, and *Sunday Night*. Continuous to Asia and the Pacific on 5995, 6020, 9475, 9560, 9580, 9590 and 11945 kHz; and well heard in much of North America on 6020, 9580 and 9590 kHz. Listeners

12:00–13:00

in East Asia can tune to 9460 kHz; and in Southeast Asia to 9475 and 11945 kHz.

Radio Ukraine International. Winter only at this time. News, commentary, reports and interviews, providing wide coverage of Ukrainian life. A listener-response program is aired Saturday, and most of Sunday's broadcast is a showcase for Ukrainian music. An hour to Europe on 9950 kHz. One hour earlier in summer.

Voice of America. *East Asia News Now*. Weekends, the second half-hour consists of Saturday's *Press Conference USA*, and Sunday's *Issues in the News*. The first hour of continuous programming to East and Southeast Asia; winter on 9640, 9760, 11705 and 11730 kHz; and summer on 6140, 9645, 9760 and 11860 kHz. For Australasia there's 9640/9645 kHz.

AFRTS Shortwave, USA. Network news, live sports, music and features in the *upper-sideband* mode from the American Forces Radio & Television Service. Transmitted from modestly powered U.S. Navy stations around the globe, so usually a tough catch. Try 4319, 5446.5, 5765, 6350, 7811, 10320, 12133.5, 12579 and 13362 kHz.

12:15

Radio Cairo, Egypt. The start of a 75-minute package of news, religion, culture and entertainment, much of it devoted to Arab and Islamic themes. The initial quarter-hour consists of virtually anything, from quizzes to Islamic religious talks, then there's *news* and commentary, followed by political and cultural items. To South and Southeast Asia on 17835 kHz.

12:30

Radio Bulgaria. Winter only at this time. *News*, then *DX Programme* (for radio enthusiasts, Sunday), *Answering Your Letters* (a listener-response show, Monday), and ●*Folk Studio* (Bulgarian folk music, Tuesday). Most of the remaining airtime is taken up by ●*Time Out for Music*. Thirty minutes to Europe on 11700 and 15700 kHz and one hour earlier in summer.

Bangladesh Betar. Opens with *News*, then *Views* and features. These include *Press Comments*, (Sunday), *Prism* (general interest, Monday), *Sports Review* (Wednesday), *Panorama* (Thursday), a listener-response program or interview (Friday), and *Economic Review* on Saturday. Ends with enjoyable Bengali music when time allows. Thirty minutes to Southeast Asia, sometimes heard in Europe, on 7250 kHz.

Voice of Vietnam. Repeat of the 1100 transmission; see there for specifics. Half an hour to Southeast Asia on 9840 and 12020 kHz. Frequencies may vary slightly.

Radio Thailand. Thirty minutes of *news* and short features to Southeast Asia and Australasia, winter on 9810 kHz and summer on 9835 kHz.

Voice of Turkey. This time summer only. Fifty-five minutes of *news*, features and Turkish music. To Europe on 15450 kHz, and to Southeast Asia and Australasia on 13685 kHz. One hour later in winter.

13:00

China Radio International. Repeat of the 1200 broadcast; see there for specifics. One hour to Europe on 13610 and 13790 kHz; to North America winter on 9570, 11885 and 15230 kHz, and summer on 9570, 9650 and 15260 kHz; to East Asia on 5955 kHz; to Southeast Asia on 9730, 9870 and 11980 kHz; and to Australasia on 9760 (or 11900) and 11760 kHz.

Polish Radio External Service. This time winter only. *News*, commentary, music and a variety of features. See 1200 for specifics. An hour to Europe on 7325 and 9450 kHz. One hour earlier in summer.

Radio Prague, Czech Republic. Summer only at this hour. *News*, then Monday through Friday it's *Current Affairs* plus one or more features: *One on One* (interviews, Monday), *Talking Point* (Tuesday), *Czechs in History*, *Czechs Today* or *Spotlight* (Wednesday), *Panorama* and *From the Archives* (Thursday), and *Business News* and *The Arts* on Friday. Saturday news is followed by *Insight Central Europe* (or *Magazine*, *Sound Czech* and a repeat of Monday's *One on One*) and Sunday's lineup is *Mailbox* and *Letter from Prague* followed by *Music Profile*, *Magic Carpet* (Czech world music) or *Czech Books*. Thirty minutes to northern Europe on 13580 kHz, and to South Asia on 17540 kHz.

International Radio Serbia. Summer only at this time. A newsy half-hour to Europe on 7200 kHz. One hour later in winter.

Radio Romania International. Winter only at this time. Starts with *Radio Newsreel*, a combination of news, commentary and press review. Features on Romania complete the broadcast. Regular spots include Monday's *Pro Memoria*, *Romanian Hits* and *Sports Roundup*; Tuesday's *Business Club* and ●*The Skylark* (Romanian folk music); Wednesday's *Society Today* and *Romanian Musicians*; Thursday's *Europa Express*; and Friday's ●*The Folk Music Box* and *Sports Weekend*. Saturday there's *The Week* and *World of Culture*, and Sunday's broadcast includes *Focus*. Fifty-five minutes to Europe on 15105 and 17745 kHz. One hour earlier in summer.

KBS World Radio, South Korea. Opens with 10 minutes of *news*, then Monday through Friday, a commentary. This is followed by 30 minutes of *Seoul Calling* and a 15-minute feature: *Faces of Korea*, *Business Culture on the Move*, *Korea Today and Tomorrow* and *Seoul Report*, respectively. Saturday's news is followed by *Worldwide Friendship* (a listener-response show), and Sunday by *Korean Pop Interactive*. An hour to Southeast Asia on 9570 and 9770 kHz.

Radio Cairo, Egypt. The final half-hour of the 1215 broadcast, consisting of listener participation programs, Arabic language lessons and a summary of the latest news. To South and Southeast Asia on 17835 kHz.

Radio Australia. Monday through Friday, *News* is followed by *Asia Pacific* and a feature: *Innovations* (Monday), *Australian Express* (Tuesday), *Rural Reporter* (Wednes-

13:00–14:00

All India Radio maintains its own hostel for Delhi area trainees. A. Gupta

day), ●*Rear Vision* (Thursday) and *All in the Mind* (Friday). Weekends, it's the second hour of ●*Saturday Night Country* and *Sunday Night*. Continuous programming to Asia and the Pacific on 5995, 6020, 9560, 9580 and 9590 kHz; and easily audible in much of North America on 6020 (West Coast), 9580 and 9590 kHz. In East Asia, try 9560 kHz.

Voice of Korea, North Korea. Abysmal programs from the last of the old-time communist stations. Socialist thinking shares airtime with choral tributes to the Great Leader. One hour to Europe on 7570 (or 13760) and 12015 (or 15245) kHz; and to North America on 9335 and 11710 kHz. Also heard in parts of East Asia on 4405 kHz.

Voice of America. Continuous programming to East and Southeast Asia. The weekday *East Asia News Now* is replaced weekends by *Jazz America*. Continuous programming to East and Southeast Asia winter on 9640, 9760 and 11705 kHz; and summer on 9645 and 9760 kHz. In Australasia tune to 9640/9645 kHz.

AFRTS Shortwave, USA. Network news, live sports, music and features in the *upper-sideband* mode from the American Forces Radio & Television Service. Transmitted from modestly powered U.S. Navy stations around the globe, so usually a tough catch. Try 4319, 5446.5, 5765, 6350, 7811, 10320, 12133.5, 12579 and 13362 kHz.

13:10

Radio Japan. Ten minutes of *news*, then a feature. Weekdays, it's *What's Up Japan* (current events, Japanese language lessons, and a listener-response segment Wednesday). Saturday, there's *World Interactive* or (the last Saturday of the month) *Listening Library*, readings from masterpieces of Japanese literature. Sunday's *Pop Up Japan* is a selection of Japanese pop music. Thirty minutes to South Asia winter on 9875 kHz, summer on 11985 kHz, and heard well beyond.

13:30

Voice of Turkey. This time winter only. *News*, then *Review of the Turkish Press* and some unusual features with a strong local flavor. Selections of Turkish popular and classical music complete the program. Fifty-five minutes to Europe on 12035 kHz, and to South and Southeast Asia and Australasia on 11735 kHz. One hour earlier in summer.

Voice of Vietnam. Starts with *News*, then Monday though Friday there's *Current Affairs*. These are followed Monday by *Vietnam, Land and People*; Tuesday, *Society* and *Business*; Wednesday, *Letterbox* (listener response); Thursday, *Vietnam Economy* and *Talk of the Week*; and Friday, *Rural Vietnam* and *Culture*. Saturday has *Weekly Review* and *Weekend Music*, and Sunday there's *Culture*, *Sports Roundup* and *Sunday Show*. A half-hour to East Asia on 9840 and 12020 kHz.

All India Radio. The first half-hour of a 90-minute block of regional and international *news*, commentary, exotic Indian music, and a variety of talks and features of general interest. To Southeast Asia and beyond on 9690, 11620 and 13710 kHz.

14:00

Radio Japan. Ten minutes of *news*, then a feature. Monday through Friday there's *What's Up Japan* (current events, Japanese language lessons, and a listener-response segment Wednesday). This is replaced Saturday by *World Interactive* or (the last Saturday of the month) *Listening Library*, readings from masterpieces of Japanese literature. Sunday's feature is *Pop Up Japan*, a selection of Japanese pop music. Thirty minutes to northern Europe winter on 11780 kHz, summer on 13630 kHz; to eastern North America and Central America on 11705 kHz; to Central Africa on 21560 kHz; to South Asia winter on 9875 kHz, summer on 11985 kHz; and to Southeast Asia on 11705 kHz.

Voice of Russia World Service. Summer only at this time. Eleven minutes of *News*, followed Monday through Saturday by much of the same in *News and Views*. Completing the lineup are *Sunday Panorama* and *A Stroll Around the Kremlin* (or *Legends of Russian Sport*). A short summary of news on the half-hour is followed by features: *Moscow Yesterday and Today* (Monday and Friday), ●*Kaleidoscope* (Tuesday), *Russian by Radio* (Wednesday), *The VOR Treasure Store* (Thursday), *Timelines* (Saturday) and ●*Folk Box* on Sunday. To Southeast Asia on 6045, 7165, 15605 and 15660 kHz. One hour later in winter.

Radio Netherlands Worldwide. The first 60 minutes of an approximately two-hour broadcast targeted at South Asia. Monday through Friday, ●*Newsline* (current events) is followed by a 30-minute feature. Monday's ●*Curious Orange* is replaced Tuesday by the midweek edition of *The State We're In*, Wednesday by *Radio Books*, Thursday by ●*Earthbeat* (environmental and development issues) and Friday by *Bridges with Africa*. Weekends, a short news bulletin is followed by Saturday's *The State We're In* or Sunday's *Network Europe Extra* and *Reloaded* (highlights of the previous week's shows). Winter on 5825, 9345, 12080, 13615 and 15595 kHz; and summer on 5830, 9345, 9885 and 11835 kHz. Heard well beyond the target area, especially in Southeast Asia.

Radio Australia. Weekdays, *World News* is followed by one or two features: *Big Ideas* (Monday), *Awaye* (Tuesday), *All in the Mind* and *Philosopher's Stone* (Wednesday), *Hindsight* (Thursday), and *Movietime* and *Arts on RA* on Friday. Weekends, it's the third hour of ●*Saturday Night Country* and *Sunday Night*. Continuous to Asia and the Pacific on 5995, 6080, 7240, 9475 (from 1430), 9590 and (from 1430) 11660 kHz (5995, 7240 and 9590 kHz are audible in North America, especially to the west). In Southeast Asia, use 6080, 9475 and 11660 kHz.

Radio Prague, Czech Republic. Winter only at this time. *News*, then Monday through Friday it's *Current Affairs* plus one or more features: *One on One* (Monday), *Talking Point* (Tuesday), *Czechs in History*, *Czechs Today* or *Spotlight* (Wednesday), *Panorama* and *Czech Science* (Thursday), and *Business News* and *The Arts* on Friday. Saturday news is followed by *Insight Central Europe* (or *Magazine*, *Sound Czech* and *One on One*), and Sunday's lineup is *Mailbox* and *Letter from Prague* followed by *Encore* (classical music), *Magic Carpet* (Czech world music) or *Czech Books*. A friendly half-hour to eastern North America on 13580 kHz, and to South Asia on 11600 kHz.

14:00–15:30

China Radio International. *News* and reports fill the first half-hour, and are followed by a daily feature: ●*Frontline* (Monday), *Biz China* (Tuesday), *In the Spotlight* (Wednesday), ●*Voices from Other Lands* (Thursday), *Life in China* (Friday), *Listeners' Garden* (Saturday) and *China Horizons* (Sunday). One hour to Europe winter on 9700 and 9795 kHz, summer on 13710 and 13790 kHz; to North America winter on 13675, 13740 and 15230 kHz; and summer on 13740 kHz; to East Asia on 5955 kHz; to Southeast Asia on 9870 kHz; and to eastern and southern Africa on 13685 and 17630 kHz.

Voice of Africa, Libya. The first 60 minutes of a two-hour broadcast. Includes some lively African music. Look for a bulletin of *news* near the half-hour, and readings from "The Green Book" a little later. To Central and East Africa on 17725 and 21695 kHz. Sometimes heard in North America, especially in summer.

International Radio Serbia. Winter only at this time. A half-hour news broadcast to Europe on 7240 kHz. One hour earlier in summer.

Radio PMR, Moldova. Monday through Friday, and summer only at this time. Fifteen minutes of news-based programming from the self-denominated "Pridnestrovian Moldavian Republic." One of the curiosities of world band radio. To Europe on 12135 kHz, one hour later in winter.

All India Radio. The final hour of a 90-minute composite program of commentary, press review, features and exotic Indian music. To Southeast Asia and beyond on 9690, 11620 and 13710 kHz.

Radio Thailand. Thirty minutes of tourist features for Southeast Asia and Australasia. Winter on 9725 kHz, summer on 9805 kHz.

AFRTS Shortwave, USA. Network news, live sports, music and features in the *upper-sideband* mode from the American Forces Radio & Television Service. Transmitted from modestly powered U.S. Navy stations around the globe, so usually a tough catch. Try 4319, 5446.5, 5765, 6350, 7811, 10320, 12133.5, 12579 and 13362 kHz.

14:30

Radio Tirana, Albania. Monday through Saturday, and summer only at this hour. See 1530 for specifics. Thirty minutes to eastern North America on 13640 kHz. One hour later in winter.

Radio Sweden. Monday through Friday, it's a smorgasbord of *news* and features about Sweden. Saturday, there's a review of the week's main news stories; and Sunday it's *Network Europe*. Thirty minutes to South and Southeast Asia winter on 9400 kHz; and summer on 13820 (or 13840) kHz.

14:45

Radio PMR, Moldova. Monday through Friday, and summer only at this time. Repeat of the 1400 broadcast. Fifteen minutes to Europe on 12135 kHz. One hour later in winter.

15:00

China Radio International. See 1400 for program details. One hour to Europe winter on 9435 and 9525 kHz, summer on 11965 and 13640 kHz; to western North America on 13740 kHz; to East Asia on 5955 kHz; to Southeast Asia on 7325 and 9870 kHz; and to eastern and southern Africa on 6100, 13685 and 17630 kHz.

Radio Netherlands Worldwide. The final 57 minutes of an approximately two-hour broadcast targeted at South Asia. Monday through Friday, starts with *Network Europe* and ends with ●*Newsline* (current events). These are replaced weekends by Saturday's *Network Europe Week* and ●*Curious Orange*, and Sunday's *Network Europe Extra* and *Reloaded* (highlights of the previous week's shows). Winter on 5825, 9345, 12080, 13615 and 15595 kHz; and summer on 5830, 9345, 9885 and 11835 kHz. Heard well beyond the target area, especially in Southeast Asia.

Radio Australia. *World News*, then weekdays there's *Asia Pacific* and a feature on the half-hour: *Health Report* (Monday), *Law Re-*

port (Tuesday), *Religion Report* (Wednesday), *Media Report* (Thursday) and *The Sports Factor* on Friday. These are replaced weekends by the final hour of ●*Saturday Night Country* and *Sunday Night*. Continuous programming to the Pacific (and well heard in western North America) on 5995, 7240 and 9590 kHz. Additionally available to Southeast Asia on 6080, 9475 and 11660 kHz.

Voice of Africa, Libya. The final 60 minutes of a two-hour broadcast. Look for a bulletin of *news* near the half-hour. To Central and East Africa on 17725 and 21695 kHz. Sometimes heard in North America, especially in summer.

Voice of America. Continuous programming for East and Southeast Asia. The weekday lineup is five minutes of *news* followed by 55 minutes of music in *Border Crossings*. Weekends, there's Half an hour of news fare followed by Saturday's *Our World* or Sunday's *On the Line*, and an editorial. Winter on 13735 and 15460 kHz; and summer on 9760 and 15185 kHz. For Australasia, there's 15460 kHz in winter, 15185 kHz midyear.

Radio Canada International. Monday through Friday, it's *The Link*, replaced Saturday by *Blink* (*Behind The Link*) and Sunday by *Maple Leaf Mailbag*. An hour to South Asia winter on 9635 and 11975 kHz; and summer on 11675 and 17720 kHz. Heard well beyond the intended target area, especially to the west. Also summer to the northeastern United States (starts at 1505), on 9515 kHz. This transmission is one hour later in winter.

Voice of Russia World Service. Winter, *News* is followed Monday through Saturday by much of the same in *News and Views*. Completing the lineup are *Sunday Panorama* and *A Stroll Around the Kremlin* (or *Legends of Russian Sport*). A short summary of news on the half-hour is followed by features: *Moscow Yesterday and Today* (Monday and Friday), ●*Kaleidoscope* (Tuesday), *Russian by Radio* (Wednesday), *The VOR Treasure Store* (Thursday), *Timelines* (Saturday) and ●*Folk Box* on Sunday. Summer weekdays, the news is followed by *Focus on Asia and the Pacific*, replaced Saturday by *This is Russia* and Sunday by *Moscow Mailbag*. The features that follow include some of the station's best: ●*Music Calendar*, *Russian Hits* or ●*Jazz Show* (Sunday, Monday, Tuesday and Thursday), ●*Folk Box* (Wednesday), and ●*Christian Message from Moscow* on Saturday. To Southeast Asia winter on 7260 and 9660 kHz; and summer on 9660 kHz. Also available summer to Europe on 12040 (or 9810) kHz; and to the Mideast on 11985 kHz.

Radio PMR, Moldova. Monday through Friday, and winter only at this time. Fifteen minutes of newsy fare from the separatist, pro-Russian, "Pridnestrovian Moldavian Republic." To Europe on 7370 kHz, one hour earlier in summer.

Voice of Korea, North Korea. Repeat of the 1300 broadcast. One hour to Europe on 7570 (or 13760) and 12015 (or 15245) kHz; and to North America on 9335 and 11710 kHz. Also heard in parts of East Asia on 4405 kHz.

Voice of Vietnam. Repeat of the 1100 transmission; see there for specifics. Half an hour to Southeast Asia on 7285, 9840 and 12020 kHz. Frequencies may vary slightly.

AFRTS Shortwave, USA. Network news, live sports, music and features in the *upper-sideband* mode from the American Forces Radio & Television Service. Transmitted from modestly powered U.S. Navy stations around the globe, so usually a tough catch. Try 4319, 5446.5, 5765, 6350, 7811, 10320, 12133.5, 12579 and 13362 kHz.

15:30

Radio Tirana, Albania. Monday through Saturday, and winter only at this hour. *News*, press review and features. Monday there's *The Week in Albania*, *Cultural Review* and *Sports Roundup*; Tuesday, a short topical report and *Mailbox* (listener response); Wednesday, a short feature followed by Albanian music; Thursday, *Focus on Albania*; Friday, a talk on Albanian history (or *Foreigners on Albania*) followed by *Outstanding*

Personalities Profile; and Saturday, *Mosaic of the Week* and *Folk Music*.

Voice of the Islamic Republic of Iran. News, commentary and features, strongly reflecting an Islamic point of view. One hour to South and Southeast Asia (also heard in parts of Australasia), winter on 6160 and 7330 kHz, and summer on 7375 and 9600 kHz.

Radio PMR, Moldova. Monday through Friday, and summer only at this time. Repeat of the 1400 broadcast. Fifteen minutes to Europe on 12135 kHz. One hour later in winter.

Voice of Mongolia. Original programming is aired on Monday, Wednesday and Friday, and is repeated on the following day. Starts with *News*, and then it's either a listener-response program (Monday) or reports and interviews. The entire Sunday broadcast is devoted to exotic Mongolian music. Thirty minutes to East Asia on 12085 kHz. Sometimes heard in Europe, especially during summer.

15:45

Radio PMR, Moldova. Monday through Friday, and winter only at this time. Repeat of the 1500 broadcast. May start at 1600. Fifteen minutes to Europe on 7370 kHz. One hour earlier in summer.

16:00

■**Radio France Internationale.** *News* and reports from across Africa, international newsflashes and news about France. Next is a 25-minute feature—*French Lesson, Crossroads, Voices, Rendez-Vous, World Tracks, Weekend* or *Club 9516* (a listener-response program). A fast-moving hour to Africa winter on 11615 kHz (15605 and 17605 kHz during March); and summer on 15605 and 17605 kHz. Sometimes heard in parts of North America.

Radio Canada International. Winter, starts at 1505. The first 55 minutes of a two-hour broadcast to the northeastern United States. Summer, it's the final 65 minutes (ends at 1705) Monday through Friday, there's *The Link*, replaced Saturday by *Blink* (*Behind The Link*) and Sunday by *Maple Leaf Mailbag*. Winter on 9610 kHz, summer on 9515 kHz.

■**Deutsche Welle,** Germany. *News*, then the daily ●*Newslink*—commentary, interviews, background reports and analysis. The final 30 minutes consist of ●*World in Progress* (Monday), ● *Spectrum* (science and technology, Tuesday), ●*Money Talks* (Wednesday), *Living Planet* (Thursday), ●*Inside Europe* (Friday), *Dialogue* (Saturday), and ●*Insight* on Sunday. An hour to South Asia winter on 5965 and 9560 kHz, and summer on 6170, 9540 and 15640 kHz; and to Southeast Asia winter on 9560 kHz, and summer on 9540 and 15640 kHz. Listeners in Australia should try the frequencies for Southeast Asia.

KBS World Radio, South Korea. Opens with 10 minutes of *news*, then Monday through Friday, a commentary. This is followed by 30 minutes of *Seoul Calling* and a 15-minute feature: *Faces of Korea, Business Watch, Culture on the Move, Korea Today and Tomorrow* and *Seoul Report*, respectively. Saturday's news is followed by *Worldwide Friendship* (a listener-response show), and Sunday by *Korean Pop Interactive*. One hour to Europe on 9515 kHz.

Radio Taiwan International. Ten minutes of *News*, followed by features: *People, Chinese to Go* (language lessons) and *Asia Review* (Monday); *Health Beats* and *We've Got Mail* (Tuesday); *Strait Talk, Women Making Waves* and ●*Jade Bells and Bamboo Pipes* (Wednesday); *Ilha Formosa, Breakfast Club, Instant Noodles* and *Chinese to Go* (Thursday); *News Talk, Taiwan Indie* and *Taiwan Outlook* (Friday); *The Occidental Tourist* and *Groove Zone* (Saturday); and *Time Traveler, Spotlight* and *On the Line* (Sunday). An hour to South Asia and southern China on 11550 kHz; and to South and Southeast Asia winter on 9785 or 11995 kHz, summer on 11600 or 15515 kHz.

Voice of Korea, North Korea. Not quite the old-time communist station it was, but the

"Beloved Leader" and "Unrivaled Great Man" continue to feature prominently, as does socialist thinking. One hour to the Mideast and Africa on 9990 and 11545 kHz. Also audible in parts of East Asia on 3560 kHz.

Radio Prague, Czech Republic. Summer only at this time. *News*, then Monday through Friday it's *Current Affairs* plus one or more features: *One on One* (interviews, Monday), *Talking Point* (Tuesday), *Czechs in History*, *Czechs Today* or *Spotlight* (Wednesday), *Panorama* and *From the archives* (Thursday), and *Business News* and *The Arts* on Friday. Saturday news is followed by *Magazine*, *Sound Czech* and a repeat of Tuesday's *One on One*. Sunday's lineup is *Mailbox* and *Letter from Prague* followed by *Music Profile*, *Magic Carpet* (Czech world music) or *Czech Books*. Half an hour to Europe on 5930 kHz, and to East Africa on 17485 kHz. The transmission for Europe is one hour later in winter, but the one for East Africa moves to 1130.

Voice of Vietnam. Starts with *News*, then Monday though Friday there's *Current Affairs*. These are followed Monday by *Vietnam, Land and People*; Tuesday, *Society* and *Business*; Wednesday, *Letterbox* (listener response); Thursday, *Vietnam Economy* and *Talk of the Week*; and Friday, *Rural Vietnam* and *Culture*. Saturday has *Weekly Review* and *Weekend Music*, and Sunday there's *Culture*, *Sports Roundup* and *Sunday Show*. A half-hour to Europe on 7280 and 9730 kHz. Also available to West and Central Africa on 7220 and 9550 kHz.

Radio Australia. Continuous programming to Asia and the Pacific. Monday through Friday, *World News* is followed by *Australia Talks*, and weekends by *Margaret Throsby* (Saturday) and ●*The Science Show* (Sunday). Beamed to the Pacific on 5995, 7240 and 9710 kHz; and to Southeast Asia on 6080, 9475 and 11660 kHz. Also well heard in western North America on 5995 and 7240 kHz.

Radio Ethiopia. An hour-long broadcast divided into two parts by the 1630 *news* bulletin. Regular weekday features include *Kaleidoscope* and *Women's Forum* (Monday), *Press Review* and *Africa in Focus* (Tuesday), *Guest of the Week* and *Ethiopia Today* (Wednesday), *Ethiopian Music* and *Spotlight* (Thursday) and *Press Review* and *Introducing Ethiopia* on Friday. For weekend listening, there's *Contact* and *Ethiopia This Week* (Saturday), or Sunday's *Listeners' Choice* and *Commentary*. Best heard in parts of Africa and the Mideast, but sometimes audible in Europe. On 7165 and 9560 kHz.

Taipei 101 has been the world's tallest building since 2004. Shutterstock/K.P. Tan

Voice of Russia World Service. Continuous programming to Europe and beyond. *News*, then very much a mixed bag, depending on the day and season. Winter weekdays, the news is followed by *Focus on Asia and the Pacific*, replaced Saturday by *This is Russia* and Sunday by *Moscow Mailbag*. The features that follow include some of the station's best: ●*Music Calendar*, *Russian Hits* or ●*Jazz Show* (Sunday,

Monday, Tuesday and Thursday), ●*Folk Box* (Wednesday), and ●*Christian Message from Moscow* on Saturday. Summer, the news is followed by *Science Plus* (Monday and Wednesday), *Moscow Mailbag* (Tuesday and Friday), *Encyclopedia "All Russia"* (Saturday) and *This is Russia* on Sunday and Thursday. More features follow a news summary on the half-hour, including *Spiritual Flowerbed* (Monday and Wednesday), *Guest Speaker* (Monday through Friday), *The VOR Treasure Store* (Saturday) and *Timelines* on Sunday. To Europe winter on 6130 and 7320 kHz, summer on 9890 kHz; and to the Mideast winter on 9470 kHz, summer on 11985 kHz.

China Radio International. *News* and reports fill the first half-hour, and are followed by a daily feature: ●*Frontline* (Monday), *Biz China* (Tuesday), *In the Spotlight* (Wednesday), ●*Voices from Other Lands* (Thursday), *Life in China* (Friday), *Listeners' Garden* (Saturday) and *China Horizons* (Sunday). One hour to Europe winter on 7255, 9435 and 9525 kHz; and summer on 11965 and 13760 kHz; to eastern and southern Africa on 6100, 7150 (winter), 9570 and (midyear) 11900 kHz; and summer only to the Mideast on 6180 and 9760 kHz.

Radio Cairo, Egypt. The first 60 minutes of a two-hour broadcast of Arab music and features on Egyptian and Islamic themes, with *news*, commentary, quizzes, mailbag shows, and answers to listeners' questions. To southern Africa on 12170 kHz.

AFRTS Shortwave, USA. Network news, live sports, music and features in the *upper-sideband* mode from the American Forces Radio & Television Service. Transmitted from modestly powered U.S. Navy stations around the globe, so usually a tough catch. Try 4319, 5446.5, 5765, 6350, 7811, 10320, 12133.5, 12579 and 13362 kHz.

16:15

Radio PMR, Moldova. Monday through Friday, and summer only at this time. Fifteen minutes of news-based programming from the self-denominated "Pridnestrovian Moldavian Republic." The final broadcast to Europe on 12135 kHz. One hour later in winter.

16:30

Radio Slovakia International. Summer only at this time. Monday through Saturday, there's *news* followed by features on Slovak life and culture. Sunday fare includes *Sunday Newsreel* and a listener-response program. Half an hour to western Europe on 5920 and 6055 kHz. One hour later in winter.

Radio PMR, Moldova. Monday through Friday, and winter only at this time. Repeat of the 1500 broadcast. Fifteen minutes to Europe on 7370 kHz. One hour earlier in summer.

Xizang [Tibet] People's Broadcasting Station, China. Starts at 1635. *Holy Tibet*, a 30-minute package of information and local (mostly popular) music. Sometimes acknowledges listeners' reception reports during the program. Good reception in East Asia, and sometimes fair in Europe. On 4905, 4920, 5240, 6110, 6130 and 7385 kHz.

17:00

Radio Canada International. Winter only at this hour. The final 65 minutes (ends at 1805) of a two-hour broadcast to the northeastern United States. Monday through Friday, it's *The Link*, replaced Saturday by *Blink* (*Behind The Link*) and Sunday by *Maple Leaf Mailbag*. On 9610 kHz.

Radio Prague, Czech Republic. See 1800 for program specifics. Thirty minutes winter to West and Central Africa on 15710 kHz, summer on 17485 kHz. Also year round to Europe on 5930 kHz. Listeners in southern Africa should try 15710 kHz.

Radio Australia. Continuous programming to Asia and the Pacific. Starts with *World News*, then a feature: *Innovations* (Monday), *Australian Express* (Tuesday), *Rural Reporter* (Wednesday), ●*Rear Vision* (Thursday), and *Big Ideas* on Friday. Monday through

American missionary and former FARC hostage Russell Stendal operates two stations from Puerto Lleras in Colombia. Feeder lines are for the shortwave channels of 6010 and 5910 kHz.

Rafael Rodríguez

Thursday, *In the Loop (Rewind)* completes the hour. *Classic Late Night Live* fills the Saturday slot, and Sunday there's *In the Loop (Rewind)* and winter's *The Sports Factor* or summer's *Total Rugby*. Beamed to the Pacific on 5995, 9580, 9710 and 11880 kHz; and to Southeast Asia on 6080 and 9475 kHz. Also audible in parts of western North America on 5995 and 11880 kHz.

Polish Radio External Service. This time summer only. Monday through Friday, opens with *News from Poland*—a compendium of news, reports and interviews. A couple of features complete the broadcast. Monday's combo is *Around Poland* and *Talking Jazz* or *Chat and Serious*; Tuesday, it's *Letter from Poland* and *The Biz*; Wednesday, *A Day in the Life* (interviews) or *The Krakow Panoptikon*, followed by *Multimedia Show*; Thursday, *Focus* (the arts in Poland) and *High Note*; and Friday, *Business Week* and *In Touch*, a listener-response show. Saturday broadcast begins with *Europe East* (correspondents' reports), and is followed by *A Look at the Weeklies* and *Open Air*. Sundays, it's five minutes of *news* followed by *Insight Central Europe* (a joint-production with other stations of the region) or an alternative feature, *The Kids* and *Chart Show* (Polish pop music). An hour to northern Europe on 7140 and 7265 kHz. One hour later in winter.

Radio Romania International. Summer only at this time; see 1800 for specifics. Fifty-five minutes to Europe on 9535 and 11735 kHz. One hour later in winter.

Voice of Russia World Service. Continuous programming to Europe and beyond. Winter, *News* is followed by *Science Plus* (Monday and Wednesday), *Moscow Mailbag* (Tuesday and Friday), *Encyclopedia "All Russia"* (Saturday) and *This is Russia* on Sunday and Thursday. More features follow a news summary on the half-hour, including *Spiritual Flowerbed* (Monday and Wednesday), *Guest Speaker* (Monday through Friday), *The VOR Treasure Store* (Saturday) and *Timelines* on Sunday. In summer, the news is followed by *Moscow Mailbag* (Monday and Thursday), and *This is Russia* (Wednesday and Friday). Weekends (also Tuesday), it's the excellent ●*Music and Musicians*. On the half-hour, the lineup includes *Kaleidoscope* (Monday), *A Stroll Around the Kremlin* (or *Legends of Russian Sport*) and *Musical Tales* (Wednesday), *Moscow Yesterday and Today* (Thursday) and ●*Folk Box* on Friday. To Europe winter on 7320 kHz, summer on 9890 and (weekends) 9820 and 11675 (or 7320) kHz. For the Mideast, tune to 7270 or 9470 kHz in winter, 11985 kHz in summer. In Southern Africa, try 11510 kHz midyear.

Radio Taiwan International. Ten minutes of *News*, followed by features: *People*,

17:00–18:00

Chinese to Go (language lessons) and *Asia Review* (Monday); *Health Beats* and *We've Got Mail* (Tuesday); *Strait Talk*, *Women Making Waves* and ●*Jade Bells and Bamboo Pipes* (Wednesday); *Ilha Formosa*, *Breakfast Club*, *Instant Noodles* and *Chinese to Go* (Thursday); *News Talk*, *Taiwan Indie* and *Taiwan Outlook* (Friday); *The Occidental Tourist* and *Groove Zone* (Saturday); and *Time Traveler*, *Spotlight* and *On the Line* (Sunday). An hour to central and southern Africa winter on 11850 kHz, summer on 15690 kHz.

China Radio International. Weekdays, *News* is followed by *China Drive*, an upbeat "drive-time" show. Weekends there's *News and Reports*, *CRI Roundup* (Saturday), *Reports from Developing Countries* (Sunday) and *China Beat* (music). One hour to Europe winter on 6100, 7205, 7255 and 7335 kHz; and summer on 6145, 7335, 9695 and 13760 kHz; to the Mideast winter on 6180 and 9600 kHz, summer on 7265 and 7315 kHz; and to eastern and southern Africa on 6100, 7150 (winter), 9570 and (midyear) 11900 kHz.

Voice of Vietnam. Summer only at this time. Thirty minutes to western Europe via an Austrian relay on 9725 kHz. See 1800 for specifics. One hour later in winter.

Seasoned Australian DXer, writer and broadcaster Bob Padula searches for rare catches at the electrically quiet Valley Picnic Ground. R. Padula

Radio Cairo, Egypt. See 1600 for specifics. Continues with a broadcast to southern Africa on 12170 kHz.

AFRTS Shortwave, USA. Network news, live sports, music and features in the *upper-sideband* mode from the American Forces Radio & Television Service. Transmitted from modestly powered U.S. Navy stations around the globe, so usually a tough catch. Try 4319, 5446.5, 5765, 6350, 7811, 10320, 12133.5, 12579 and 13362 kHz.

17:15

Radio PMR, Moldova. Monday through Friday, and winter only at this time. Fifteen minutes of newsy fare from the separatist, pro-Russian, "Pridnestrovian Moldavian Republic." The final broadcast to Europe on 7370 kHz. One hour earlier in summer.

17:30

Radio Bulgaria. Summer only at this time. *News*, followed weekdays by *Events and Developments*, and Saturday and Sunday by *Views Behind the News*. Thirty minutes to Europe on 7200 and 9400 kHz, and one hour later in winter.

Radio Slovakia International. Winter only at this time; see 1630 for specifics. Half an hour to western Europe on 5915 and 6055 kHz. One hour earlier during summer.

17:45

All India Radio. The first 15 minutes of a two-hour broadcast to Europe, Africa and the Mideast, consisting of regional and international *news*, commentary, a variety of talks and features, press review and exotic Indian music. Continuous till 1945. To Europe on 7410, 9950 and 11620 kHz; to West Africa on 9445, 13605 and 15155 kHz; and to East Africa on 11935, 15075 and 17670 kHz.

Bangladesh Betar. *Voice of Islam*, a 30-minute broadcast of recitations from the Quran and Islamic themes. To Europe on 7250 kHz.

1800–2359
Europe & Mideast—Evening Prime Time
East Asia—Early Morning
Australasia—Morning
Eastern North America—Afternoon and Suppertime
Western North America—Midday

18:00

Radio Netherlands Worldwide. The first 60 minutes of three hours targeted at Africa. See 1900 for program specifics. Winter on 6020, 11655 and 12045 kHz; and summer on 6020 and 15535 kHz. Best for southern Africa is 6020 kHz, via the station's Madagascar relay.

Voice of Vietnam. Begins with *News*, then Monday though Friday there's *Current Affairs*. These are followed Monday by *Vietnam, Land and People*; Tuesday, *Society* and *Business*; Wednesday, *Letterbox* (listener response); Thursday, *Vietnam Economy* and *Talk of the Week*; and Friday, *Rural Vietnam* and *Culture*. Saturday has *Weekly Review* and *Weekend Music*, and Sunday there's *Culture*, *Sports Roundup* and *Sunday Show*. A half-hour to Europe on 5955 kHz. Via an Austrian relay, and should provide good reception. One hour earlier in summer.

All India Radio. Continuation of the transmission to Europe, Africa and the Mideast (see 1745). *News* and commentary, followed by programming of a more general nature. Look for a listener-response segment, *Faithfully Yours*, at 1830 Monday. To Europe on 7410, 9950 and 11620 kHz; to West Africa on 9445, 13605 and 15155 kHz; and to East Africa on 11935, 15075 and 17670 kHz.

Voice of Korea, North Korea. The dinosaur of world band and the last of the old-style communist stations. One hour to Europe on 7570 (or 13760) and 12015 (or 15245) kHz. Heard in parts of East Asia on 4405 kHz.

Radio Prague, Czech Republic. Winter only at this time. *News*, then Monday through Friday there's *Current Affairs* and one or more features: *One on One* (Monday), *Talking Point* (Tuesday), *Czechs in History*, *Czechs Today* or *Spotlight* (Wednesday), *Panorama* and *From the Archives* (Thursday), and *Business News* and *The Arts* (Friday). On Saturday the news is followed by *Insight Central Europe* (or *Magazine*, *Sound Czech* and *One on One*) and Sunday fare is *Mailbox* and *Letter from Prague* followed by *Music Profile*, *Magic Carpet* (Czech world music) or *Czech Books*. Thirty minutes to Europe on 5930 kHz, and to Australasia on 9400 kHz. Europe's broadcast is one hour earlier in summer, but for Australasia it's two hours later.

Radio Kuwait. The first 60 minutes of a three-hour partial relay of the station's domestic broadcasts. At this hour it's a mix of western pop music and features on Islam and Kuwait. A news summary is aired on the half-hour. To western Europe and eastern North America on 11990 kHz.

Radio Romania International. Winter only at this time. Starts with *Radio Newsreel*, a combination of news, commentary and press review. Features on Romania complete the broadcast. Regular spots include Monday's *Pro Memoria*, *Romanian Hits* and *Sports Roundup*; Tuesday's *Business Club* and ●*The Skylark* (Romanian folk music); Wednesday's *Society Today* and *Romanian Musicians*; Thursday's *Europa Express*; and Friday's ●*The Folk Music Box* and *Sports Weekend*. Saturday there's *The Week* and *World of Culture*, and Sunday's broadcast includes *Focus*. Fifty-five minutes to Europe on 7215 and 9640 kHz. One hour earlier in summer.

KBS World Radio, South Korea. Opens with 10 minutes of *news*, then Monday

18:00–18:30

through Friday, a commentary. This is followed by 30 minutes of *Seoul Calling* and a 15-minute feature: *Faces of Korea*, *Business Watch*, *Culture on the Move*, *Korea Today and Tomorrow* and *Seoul Report*, respectively. Saturday's news is followed by *Worldwide Friendship* (a listener-response show), and Sunday by *Korean Pop Interactive*. One hour to Europe on 7275 kHz.

Radio Australia. Sunday through Thursday, *World News* is followed by *Pacific Beat* (news and current events). Friday slots are *Pacific Review* and *Australian Express*. Winter Saturdays there's *Correspondents Report* and the first half-hour of *Australia All Over*, replaced summer by *In the Loop (Rewind)* and ●*Australian Country Style*. Part of a continuous 24-hour service, and at this hour beamed to the Pacific on 6080, 7240, 9580, 9710 and 11880 kHz. Heard in East Asia on 6080 kHz. In western North America, try 11880 kHz. Sunday through Thursday there's separate programming for Southeast Asia on 9475 kHz: *The Music Show* (Sunday), *Big Ideas* (Monday), *Awaye* (Tuesday), *All in the Mind* and *Philosopher's Stone* (Wednesday), and *Hindsight* on Thursday. Friday and Saturday, the programming is the same as that for the Pacific.

Polish Radio External Service. This time winter only. See 1700 for program specifics. *News*, features and music reflecting Polish life and culture. An hour to western Europe on 6015 and 7345 kHz. One hour earlier in summer. 6015 kHz is sometimes heard in eastern North America.

Voice of Russia World Service. Continuous programming to Europe and beyond. Predominantly news-related fare during the initial half-hour in summer, but the winter schedule offers a more varied diet. Winter, *News* is followed by *Moscow Mailbag* (Monday and Thursday), and *This is Russia* (Wednesday and Friday). Weekends (also Tuesday), it's the excellent ●*Music and Musicians*. On the half-hour, the lineup includes *Kaleidoscope* (Monday), *A Stroll Around the Kremlin* (or *Legends of Russian Sport*) and *Musical Tales* (Wednesday), *Moscow Yesterday and Today* (Thursday) and ●*Folk Box* on Friday. Summer weekdays, the first half-hour consists of *news* followed by *Russia and the World*. Saturday slot is filled by *This is Russia*, replaced Sunday by *Encyclopedia "All Russia."* More features complete the hour, and include *Spiritual Flowerbed* (Monday and Wednesday), *Guest Speaker* (Monday through Friday), *Kaleidoscope* (Saturday) and ●*Christian Message from Moscow* on Sunday. To Europe winter on 7105, 7320 and (weekends) 6055 and 6175 kHz; and summer on 9890 and 11630 (or 9480) kHz. Also available winter only to the Mideast on 7270 kHz. In southern Africa, tune to 11510 and (midyear) 9850 kHz.

Radio Argentina al Exterior—R.A.E. Monday through Friday only. *News*, press review and short features on Argentina, plus folk music and tangos. Fifty-five minutes to Europe on 15345 kHz. May also use 9690 kHz.

Voice of America. Continuous programming to Africa. Monday through Friday, there's *Africa News Tonight* (shortened on Wednesday, when there's *Straight Talk Africa*). Weekends, it's *Nightline Africa*. Winter on 4930 (from 1830), 11975, 13710, 15580 and 17895 kHz; and summer on 4930 (from 1830), 6080, 15410, 15580 and 17895 kHz. Best for southern Africa is 4930 kHz.

China Radio International. *News* and reports fill the first half-hour, and are followed by a daily feature: ●*Frontline* (Monday), *Biz China* (Tuesday), *In the Spotlight* (Wednesday), ●*Voices from Other Lands* (Thursday), *Life in China* (Friday), *Listeners' Garden* (Saturday) and *China Horizons* (Sunday). To Europe winter on 6100 and 7110 kHz; and summer on 7120, 9600 and 13760 kHz.

Radio Taiwan International. Ten minutes of *News*, followed by features: *People*, *Chinese to Go* (language lessons) and *Asia Review* (Monday); *Health Beats* and *We've Got Mail* (Tuesday); *Strait Talk*, *Women Making Waves* and ●*Jade Bells and Bamboo Pipes* (Wednesday); *Ilha Formosa*, *Breakfast Club*, *Instant Noodles* and *Chinese to Go* (Thursday); *News Talk*, *Taiwan Indie* and *Taiwan Outlook* (Friday); *The Occidental Tourist* and *Groove Zone* (Saturday); and *Time Traveler*,

Spotlight and *On the Line* (Sunday). One hour to western Europe on 3965 kHz.

Radio Canada International. Monday through Friday, it's *The Link*, replaced Saturday by *Blink* (*Behind The Link*) and Sunday by *Maple Leaf Mailbag*. One hour to Africa winter on 7185, 11875, 13650, 15365 (or 15325) and 17790 kHz, and summer on 9530, 11765, 15235 and 17810 kHz. Best for southern Africa are 15365 and 17790 kHz in winter (summer in the Southern Hemisphere), 17810 kHz midyear. Heard well beyond the African continent.

AFRTS Shortwave, USA. Network news, live sports, music and features in the *upper-sideband* mode from the American Forces Radio & Television Service. Transmitted from modestly powered U.S. Navy stations around the globe, so usually a tough catch. Try 4319, 5446.5, 5765, 6350, 7811, 10320, 12133.5, 12579 and 13362 kHz.

18:15

Bangladesh Betar. Opens with *News*, then *Views* and features. These include *Press Comments*, (Sunday), *Prism* (general interest, Monday), *Sports Review* (Wednesday), *Panorama* (Thursday), a listener-response program or interview (Friday), and *Economic Review* on Saturday. Ends with enjoyable Bengali music when time allows. Thirty minutes to Europe on 7250 kHz.

18:30

Radio Bulgaria. This time winter only. *News*, then *Events and Developments* (weekdays) or *Views Behind the News* (Saturday and Sunday). Thirty minutes to Europe on 6200 and 7400 kHz, and one hour earlier in summer.

International Radio Serbia. Summer only at this time. A newsy half-hour to Europe on 6100 and 7200 kHz. One hour later in winter.

Radio Slovakia International. Summer only at this time; see 1930 for specifics. A half-hour look at Slovaks and Slovakia. To western Europe on 5920 and 6055 kHz. One hour later in winter.

Voice of Turkey. This time summer only. See 1930 for program details. Unusual features and friendly presentation make for entertaining listening. Fifty minutes to western Europe on 9785 kHz. One hour later in winter.

18:45

Radio Tirana, Albania. Monday through Saturday, and summer only at this time. Approximately 15 minutes of *news* and press review or commentary. To Europe on 7430 and 13640 kHz. One hour later in winter.

19:00

Radio Netherlands Worldwide. Monday through Friday, ●*Newsline* (current events) is followed by a 30-minute feature: ●*Curious Orange* (Monday), *The State We're In - Midweek Edition* (Tuesday), *Radio Books* (Wednesday), ●*Earthbeat* (environmental and development issues, Thursday) and *Bridges with Africa* (Friday). Weekends, a short news bulletin is followed by Saturday's *The State We're In* or Sunday's *Network Europe Extra* and *Reloaded* (highlights of the previous week's shows). Winter on 7120, 11655, 12045 and 17810 kHz; and summer on 5905, 7425, 11660, 15335 and 17810 kHz. In southern Africa, tune to 7120 or 7425 kHz, depending on the season. Listeners in the United States should try 17810 kHz, which is via the station's Bonaire relay.

Radio Australia. Begins with *World News*, then Sunday through Thursday it's the second hour of *Pacific Beat* (in-depth reporting on the region). Friday's slots go to *Asia Review* and ●*Rural Reporter*. Winter Saturdays, it's a continuation of *Australia All Over*; in summer, there's *Correspondents Report* and the first half-hour of *Australia All Over*. Part of a continuous 24-hour service, and at this hour beamed to the Pacific on 6080, 7240, 9500, 9580, 9710 and 11880 kHz. Listeners in western North America should try 11880 kHz, and best for East Asia is 6080 kHz. Sunday through Thursday there's separate programming for Southeast Asia on 9500 kHz: Sunday, it's the second hour of *The Music Show*, and Monday through Thursday there's *Asia Pacific* and a feature. Monday has *Health Report*, replaced Tuesday by *Law Report*, Wednesday by *Religion Report* and Thursday by *Media Report*. Friday and Saturday, the programming is the same as that for the Pacific.

All India Radio. The final 45 minutes of a two-hour broadcast to Europe, Africa and the Mideast (see 1745). Starts with *news*, then continues with a mixed bag of features and Indian music. To Europe on 7410, 9950 and 11620 kHz; to West Africa on 9445, 13605 and 15155 kHz; and to East Africa on 11935, 15075 and 17670 kHz.

Radio Kuwait. The second of three hours of a partial relay of the station's domestic broadcasts. At this hour it's a mix of western pop music and features on Kuwait. To western Europe and eastern North America on 11990 kHz.

■**Deutsche Welle,** Germany. *News*, then the daily ●*Newslink*—commentary, interviews, background reports and analysis. Thirty minutes to Central, East and southern Africa winter on 9735, 11690, 13780 and 15275 kHz; and summer on 9565, 11795 and 17860 kHz. Best for southern Africa are 13780 and 15275 kHz in winter, 9565 and 11795 kHz midyear.

Voice of Russia World Service. Continuous programming to Europe at this hour. Winter weekdays, the first half-hour consists of *news* followed by *Russia and the World*. Saturday slot is filled by *This is Russia*, replaced Sunday by *Encyclopedia "All Russia."* More features complete the hour, and include *Spiritual Flowerbed* (Monday and Wednesday), *Guest Speaker* (Monday through Friday), *Kaleidoscope* (Saturday) and ●*Christian Message from Moscow* on Sunday. Monday through Saturday summer, it's *News and Views*, with *Sunday Panorama* and *A Stroll Around the Kremlin* (or *Legends of Russian Sport*) on the remaining day. On the half-hour, a news summary is followed by features: *Moscow Yesterday and Today* (Sunday and Monday), *Russian by Radio* (Tuesday), ●*Music Calendar*, *Russian Hits* or ●*Jazz Show* (Wednesday), *VOR Treasure Store* (Thursday), *A Stroll Around the Kremlin* (or *Legends of Russian Sport*) and *Musical Tales* (Friday) and ●*Christian Message from Moscow* on Saturday. On 6175, 7105 and 7290 kHz in winter; and 7310, 9890 and 12070 (or 7195) kHz in summer.

China Radio International. *News* and reports fill the first half-hour, and are followed by a daily feature: ●*Frontline* (Monday), *Biz China* (Tuesday), *In the Spotlight* (Wednesday), ●*Voices from Other Lands* (Thursday), *Life in China* (Friday), *Listeners' Garden* (Saturday) and *China Horizons* (Sunday). One hour to the Mideast and North Africa on 7295 and 9435 (or 9440) kHz.

Radio Station Belarus. Summer only at this time. The first 60 minutes of a two-hour broadcast. Starts with 20 minutes of *News*, then a couple of features: *International Review* and *Civil Society* (Monday), *Made in Belarus* and *Higher Education in Belarus* (Tuesday), *Event* (analysis of the main political and economic event of the week) and *Nature Unlimited* (Wednesday), *Belarus in the World Community* and *What Belarus Offers* (Thursday), *Opinions* and *Cultural Palette of Belarus* (Friday), *Sports and Health* and *Intellectual Factor* (Saturday), and *Problems of Security* (or *Military Review*) and *Magic Box* (Sunday) To Europe on 7105, 7360 and 7390 kHz. One hour later in winter.

Radio Ukraine International. Summer only at this time; see 2000 for specifics. A potpourri of things Ukrainian, with the Sunday broadcast often featuring some excellent music. An hour to western Europe on 7490 kHz. One hour later in winter.

Radio Thailand. A 60-minute package of *news*, features and (if you're lucky) enjoyable Thai music. To Northern Europe winter on 9805 kHz, summer on 7155 kHz.

Voice of Korea, North Korea. For now, of curiosity value only. An hour of old-style communist programming to the Mideast on 9975 and 11535 kHz; and to southern Africa on 7100 and 11910 kHz. Also heard in parts of East Asia on 4405 kHz.

Voice of Vietnam. Repeat of the 1800 transmission (see there for specifics). Half an hour to Europe on 7280 and 9730 kHz.

Voice of America. Continuous programming for Africa. Opens with 30 minutes of news, with programs in Special (slow speed) English completing the hour. Winter on 4930, 4940, 11975, 13710, 15580 and 17895 kHz; and summer on 4930, 4940, 6080, 15410, 15445, 15580 and 17895 kHz. Best for southern Africa is 4930 kHz. In North America, try 11975 kHz in winter and 15445 kHz in summer.

AFRTS Shortwave, USA. Network news, live sports, music and features in the *upper-sideband* mode from the American Forces Radio & Television Service. Transmitted from modestly powered U.S. Navy stations around the globe, so usually a tough catch. Try 4319, 5446.5, 5765, 6350, 7811, 10320, 12133.5, 12579 and 13362 kHz.

19:30

Voice of Turkey. Winter only at this time. *News*, then *Review of the Turkish Press* followed by features on Turkish history, culture and international relations. Some enjoyable Turkish music, too. Fifty minutes to western Europe on 6050 kHz. One hour earlier in summer.

Radio Slovakia International. Winter only at this time. Monday through Saturday, there's *news* followed by features on Slovak life and culture. Sunday fare includes *Sunday Newsreel* and a listener-response program. Half an hour to western Europe on 5915 and 6055 kHz. One hour earlier in summer.

International Radio Serbia. Winter only at this time. A half-hour news broadcast to

19:30–20:00

CBC Radio Canada's "exploding pizza" logo has greeted visitors to La Maison de Radio-Canada in Montréal since 1973. For years Ian McFarland's "Shortwave Listeners' Digest" was prepared here, each month featuring PASSPORT's Lawrence Magne. M. Wright

Europe on 6100 and 7240 kHz. One hour earlier in summer.

Voice of the Islamic Republic of Iran. A one-hour broadcast of news, commentary and features reflecting Islamic values. To Europe winter on 6010, 6025 and 7320 kHz; and summer on 6205, 7205 and 7260 kHz. Also available to southern Africa winter on 9855 and 11695 kHz, midyear on 9800 and 9925 kHz.

19:45

Radio Tirana, Albania. Monday through Saturday, and winter only at this time. Approximately 15 minutes of *news* and press review or commentary. To Europe on 7465 and 11645 kHz. The latter frequency is heard in parts of eastern North America. One hour earlier in summer.

Vatican Radio. Summer only at this time, and starts at 1950. Thirty minutes of programming oriented to Catholics. To Europe on 4005, 5885 and 7250 kHz. One hour later in winter.

20:00

■**Deutsche Welle,** Germany. *News*, then the in-depth ●*Newslink*. The second half-hour consists of features: ●*World in Progress* (Monday), ●*Spectrum* (science and technology, Tuesday), ●*Money Talks* (Wednesday), *Living Planet* (Thursday), ●*Inside Europe* (Friday), *Dialogue* (Saturday) and *Cool* (a youth show) on Sunday. One hour to East, Central and southern Africa, winter on 9545, 9735, 13780 and 15275 kHz; midyear on 6150, 11795, 11865 and 15205 kHz. Best for southern Africa are 13780 and 15275 kHz in winter, and 6150, 11795, 11865 and 15205 kHz midyear.

Radio Canada International. Summer only at this time. Monday through Friday, it's *The Link*, replaced Saturday by *Blink* (*Behind The Link*) and Sunday by *Maple Leaf Mailbag*. An hour to Europe, North Africa and the Mideast on 11765, 13650, 15235 and 17735 kHz. One hour later during winter.

Radio Netherlands Worldwide. The final 57 minutes of approximately three hours targeted at Africa, and a repeat of the 1900 broadcast (see there for specifics). Winter on 7120, 11655 and 17810 kHz; and summer on 5905, 7425 and 17810 kHz. Best for southern Africa is 7120 or 7425 kHz, depending on the season. Listeners in the United States can try 17810 kHz, which is via the station's Bonaire relay.

Radio Kuwait. The final 60 minutes of a three-hour partial relay of the station's domestic broadcasts. At this hour it's mostly western pop music, with a short bulletin of news at 2050. To western Europe and eastern North America on 11990 kHz.

Radio Ukraine International. Winter only at this time. Ample coverage of local issues, including news, sports, politics and culture. A listener-response program is aired Saturday, and most of Sunday's broadcast is a showcase for Ukrainian music. An hour to western Europe on 5840 kHz.

Radio Damascus, Syria. Starts at 2005. *News*, a daily press review, and different features for each day of the week. These can be heard at approximately 2030 and 2045, and include a mix of political commentary, Islamic philosophy and Arab and Syrian culture. Most of the transmission, however, is given over to Syrian and some western popular music. One hour to Europe, occasionally audible in eastern North America, on 9330 and/or 12085 kHz. Low audio level is often a problem.

Radio Australia. Starts with *World News*, then Sunday through Thursday it's the final hour of *Pacific Beat* (in-depth reporting). Winter, the Friday slots are *Saturday AM* and *Saturday Extra*; and summer, *Pacific Review* and ●*Australian Country Style*. Saturday, it's a continuation of *Australia All Over* (a popular show from the domestic ABC Local Radio network). Continuous programming to the Pacific on 6080 and 7240 (Friday and Saturday only), 9580, 11650, 11660, 11880 and 12080 kHz. In western North America, try 11650, 11660 and 11880 kHz. Sunday through Thursday there's separate programming for Southeast Asia on 9500 kHz: ●*The Science Show* (Sunday), and a feature followed by *In the Loop (Rewind)* on the remaining days. Monday's *Innovations* is replaced Tuesday by *Australian Express*, Wednesday by *Rural Reporter*, and Thursday by ●*Rear Vision*. Friday and Saturday, the programming is the same as that for the Pacific.

Voice of Russia World Service. Continuous programming to Europe at this hour. Starts with *News*, then Monday through Saturday winter, it's *News and Views*, with *Sunday Panorama* and *A Stroll Around the Kremlin* (or *Legends of Russian Sport*) on the remaining day. On the half-hour, a news summary is followed by features: *Moscow Yesterday and Today* (Sunday and Monday), *Russian by Radio* (Tuesday), ●*Music Calendar*, *Russian Hits* or ●*Jazz Show* (Wednesday), *VOR Treasure Store* (Thursday), *A Stroll Around the Kremlin* (or *Legends of Russian Sport*) and *Musical Tales* (Friday) and ●*Christian Message from Moscow* on Saturday. Monday through Friday summer, *News* is followed by *Focus on Asia and the Pacific*, and *Encyclopedia "All Russia"* on Saturday. There's a summary of news on the half-hour, then features: *A Stroll Around the Kremlin* (Monday and Wednesday), ●*Songs from Russia* or ●*Russia–1000 Years of Music* (Monday), *Kaleidoscope* (Tuesday), *Musical Tales* (Wednesday), ●*Folk Box* (Thursday), ●*Music Calendar*, *Russian Hits* or ●*Jazz Show* (Friday) and *Russian by Radio* on Saturday. Highlight of the week is ●*Music and Musicians* which follows the news on Sunday. Winter on 6145, 7105 and 7330 kHz; and summer on 9890 and 12070 (or 7195) kHz. Some channels are audible in eastern North America.

Radio Exterior de España ("Spanish National Radio"). Weekdays only at this time. Spanish and international *news*, commentary, Spanish pop music, a review of the Spanish press, and a general interest feature. An hour to Europe winter on 9690 (or 9700) kHz, summer on 9665 kHz; and to West and Central Africa winter on 9605 kHz, summer on 11620 kHz.

China Radio International. *News* and reports fill the first half-hour, and are followed by a daily feature: ●*Frontline* (Monday), *Biz China* (Tuesday), *In the Spotlight* (Wednesday), ●*Voices from Other Lands* (Thursday), *Life in China* (Friday), *Listeners' Garden* (Saturday) and *China Horizons* (Sunday). One hour to Europe on 5960, 7190, 7285 and 9600 kHz; to the Mideast and North Africa on 7295 and 9440 kHz; and to eastern and southern Africa on 5985 and 13630 kHz.

Radio Tirana, Albania. Monday through Saturday, and summer only at this time. See 2100 for specifics. *News*, short features and Albanian music (especially Saturday). Thirty minutes to Europe on 7460 or 7465 kHz, and to eastern North America on 13600 kHz. One hour later in winter.

Radio Station Belarus. Winter, the start of a two-hour broadcast; summer, the final 60 minutes. Starts with 20 minutes of *News*, then it's a potpourri of local issues, including news, sports, politics and culture, depending on the season and day of the week. The winter lineup is *International Review* and *Civil Society* (Monday), *Made in Belarus* and *Higher Education in Belarus* (Tuesday),

20:00–21:00

Event (analysis of the main political and economic event of the week) and *Nature Unlimited* (Wednesday), *Belarus in the World Community* and *What Belarus Offers* (Thursday), *Opinions* and *Cultural Palette of Belarus* (Friday), *Sports and Health* and *Intellectual Factor* (Saturday), and *Problems of Security* (or *Military Review*) and *Magic Box* (Sunday). Summer, there's *Heritage* and *Musical Gallery* (Monday), *Of Roots Slavonic* and ●*Best Songs of Slavonic Bazaar in Vitebsk* (Tuesday), *Popular Diplomacy* and *Music Store* (Wednesday), *Postcard from Belarus* and *At the Crossroads of Europe* (Thursday), *Youth Mode* and a repeat of *At the Crossroads of Europe* (Friday), *Our Letters* and *Music for All* (Saturday), and *In the Depth of the Country* and *Voices of the Century* (Sunday). To Europe on 7100 (winter), 7105 (summer), 7360 and 7390 kHz. Sometimes heard in eastern North America.

Radio Prague, Czech Republic. Summer only at this time. *News*, then Monday through Friday it's *Current Affairs* plus one or more features: *One on One* (interviews, Monday), *Talking Point* (Tuesday), *Czechs in History*, *Czechs Today* or *Spotlight* (Wednesday), *Panorama* and *From the Archives* (Thursday) and *Business News* and *The Arts* on Friday. Saturday news is followed by *Magazine*, *Sound Czech* and a repeat of Monday's *One on One*. Sunday's lineup is *Mailbox* and *Letter from Prague* followed by *Music Profile*, *Magic Carpet* (Czech world music) or *Czech Books*. Thirty minutes to western Europe on 5930 kHz, and to Australasia on 11600 kHz. The broadcast for Europe is one hour later in winter, and the one to Australasia two hours earlier.

Voice of America. Continuous programming for Africa. Monday through Friday, it's *Africa Beat* (modern African music, guest DJ spots, interviews), replaced weekends by ●*Music Time in Africa*. On 4930, 4940, 11975 (winter), 13710 (winter), 15445 (summer) and 15580 kHz. Best for southern Africa is 4930 kHz.

AFRTS Shortwave, USA. Network news, live sports, music and features in the *upper-sideband* mode from the American Forces Radio & Television Service. Transmitted from modestly powered U.S. Navy stations around the globe, so usually a tough catch. Try 4319, 5446.5, 5765, 6350, 7811, 10320, 12133.5, 12579 and 13362 kHz.

20:30

Radio Sweden. Monday through Friday, it's *news* and features about Sweden. Saturday, there's a review of the week's main news stories, and Sunday has *Network Europe*. Thirty minutes to East Africa winter on 9895 kHz, summer on 7420 kHz, via the Radio Netherlands relay in Madagascar, and heard well beyond the target area.

Radio Thailand. Fifteen minutes of *news* targeted at Europe. Winter on 9535 kHz, summer on 9680 kHz.

Radio Romania International. Summer only at this time. *News* and commentary followed by short features on Romania. Twenty-five minutes to Europe on 9515 and 11810 kHz, and to eastern North America on 11940 and 15465 kHz. One hour later in winter.

Voice of Turkey. This time summer only. *News*, followed by *Review of the Turkish Press* and features with a strong local flavor. Selections of Turkish popular and classical music complete the program. Fifty minutes to Southeast Asia and Australasia on 7170 kHz. One hour later during winter.

Radio Habana Cuba. The first half of a 60-minute broadcast. Monday through Saturday, there is international and Cuban news followed by *RHC's Viewpoint*. This is replaced Sunday by *Weekly Review*. To the Caribbean on 9505 kHz, and to eastern North America on 11760 kHz.

Voice of Vietnam. Starts with *News*, then Monday though Friday there's *Current Affairs*. These are followed Monday by *Vietnam, Land and People*; Tuesday, *Society* and *Business*; Wednesday, *Letterbox* (listener response); Thursday, *Vietnam Economy* and *Talk of the Week*; and Friday, *Rural Vietnam* and *Culture*. Saturday has *Weekly Review* and *Weekend Music*, and Sunday there's

Culture, *Sports Roundup* and *Sunday Show*. A half-hour to Europe on 7280 and 9730 kHz, and to West and Central Africa on 7220 and 9550 kHz.

20:45

All India Radio. The first 15 minutes of a much longer broadcast, consisting of a press review, Indian music, regional and international *news*, commentary, and a variety of talks and features of general interest. Continuous till 2230. To Western Europe on 7410, 9445, 9950 and 11620 kHz; and to Australasia on 9910, 11620 and 11715 kHz. Early risers in Southeast Asia can try the channels for Australasia.

Vatican Radio. Winter only at this time, and starts at 2050. Twenty minutes of predominantly Catholic fare. To Europe on 4005, 5885 and 7250 kHz. One hour earlier in summer.

21:00

Radio Exterior de España ("Spanish National Radio"). Summer weekends only at this time. Features, including rebroadcasts of programs aired earlier in the week. One hour to Europe on 9790 kHz, and to West and Central Africa on 11625 kHz. Sometimes pre-empted by live sports in Spanish, and may start around 2135, or not at all. One hour later in winter.

Radio Ukraine International. Summer only at this time. *News*, commentary, reports and interviews, providing ample coverage of Ukrainian life. Well worth a listen is ●*Music from Ukraine*, which fills most of the Sunday broadcast. An hour to western Europe on 7510 kHz. One hour later in winter.

Radio Canada International. Winter only at this time. See 2000 for program specifics. An hour to western Europe and North Africa on 9770 kHz. One hour earlier in summer.

Radio Prague, Czech Republic. Winter only at this time. See 2000 for program details. *News* and features on Czech life and culture. Half an hour to western Europe (and easily audible in parts of eastern North America) on 5930 kHz, and to Australasia on 9430 kHz. One hour earlier in summer.

Radio Bulgaria. This time summer only. Starts with *News*, then Monday through Friday there's *Events and Developments*, replaced weekends by *Views Behind the News*. The remaining time is taken up by regular programs such as *Keyword Bulgaria* and ●*Time Out for Music*, and weekly features like *Sports* (Monday), *Magazine Economy* (Tuesday), *The Way We Live* (Wednesday), *History Club* (Thursday), *DX Programme* (for radio enthusiasts, Friday) and *Answering Your Letters* (a listener-response show, Saturday). The week's highlight is Sunday's ●*Folk Studio* (Bulgarian folk music). An hour to Europe on 5900 and 9700 kHz. One hour later during winter.

Radio Station Belarus. Winter only at this time, and the final 60 minutes of a two-hour broadcast. Starts with 20 minutes of *News*, then two features: *Heritage* and *Musical Gallery* (Monday), *Of Roots Slavonic* and ●*Best Songs of Slavonic Bazaar in Vitebsk* (Tuesday), *Popular Diplomacy* and *Music Store* (Wednesday), *Postcard from Belarus* and *At the Crossroads of Europe* (Thursday), *Youth Mode* and a repeat of *At the Crossroads of Europe* (Friday), *Our Letters* and *Music for All* (Saturday), and *In the Depth of the Country* and *Voices of the Century* (Sunday). To Europe on 7100, 7360 and 7390 kHz.

China Radio International. Repeat of the 2000 transmission; see there for specifics. One hour to Europe on 5960, 6135, 7190, 7285 and 9600 kHz. A 30-minute shortened version is also available for eastern and southern Africa on 7325 and 13630 kHz.

Voice of Russia World Service. Winter only at this time. Monday through Friday, *News* is followed by *Focus on Asia and the Pacific*, and *Encyclopedia "All Russia"* on Saturday. There's a summary of news on the half-hour, then features: *A Stroll Around the Kremlin* (Monday and Wednesday), ●*Songs from Russia* or ●*Russia–1000 Years of Music* (Monday), *Kaleidoscope* (Tuesday), *Musical*

21:00–22:00

Tales (Wednesday), ●*Folk Box* (Thursday), ●*Music Calendar*, *Russian Hits* or ●*Jazz Show* (Friday) and *Russian by Radio* on Saturday. Highlight of the week is ●*Music and Musicians* which follows the news on Sunday One hour earlier in summer. To Europe on 6145, 7290 and 7330 kHz. Also audible in parts of eastern North America.

Voice of America. The final 60 minutes of seven hours of continuous programming for Africa. Opens with *news*, then it's music: *American Gold* (Monday), *Roots and Branches* (Tuesday), *Classic Rock* (Wednesday), *Top Twenty* (Thursday), *Hip Hop Connection* (Friday and Saturday), and *Fusion* (jazz) on Sunday. On 6080 and 15580 kHz.

Radio Australia. *World News*, then Sunday through Thursday there's a look at current events in *AM*, followed by *The Breakfast Club*. Winter Fridays, it's the final hour of *Saturday Extra*; summer, there's *Saturday AM* and the first half-hour of *Saturday Extra*. On the remaining day, it's Saturday's *Australia All Over*. Continuous to the Pacific on 9660, 11650, 11660, 12080, 13630 and 15515 kHz; and to Southeast Asia on 9500 and 11695 kHz. Listeners in western North America should try 11650 and 11660 kHz.

■**Deutsche Welle,** Germany. *News*, and then the daily ●*Newslink*—commentary, interviews, background reports and analysis. On the half-hour the weekday lineup is *EuroVox* (Monday), *Hits in Germany* (Tuesday), ●*Arts on the Air* (Wednesday), *Cool* (a youth show, Thursday), and *Dialogue* on Friday. Weekends, *Sports Report* is followed by *Radio D* (German language lessons, Saturday) and *Inspired Minds* (Sunday). One hour to West Africa, and audible in eastern and southern North America and the Caribbean. Winter on 7280, 9545 and 11690 kHz; and summer on 9735, 11865 and 15205 kHz. In North America, try 11690 kHz in winter, 11865 and 15205 kHz in summer.

KBS World Radio, South Korea. Summer only at this time. Opens with 10 minutes of *news*, then Monday through Friday, a commentary. This is followed by a 15-minute feature: *Faces of Korea*, *Business Watch*, *Culture on the Move*, *Korea Today and Tomorrow* and *Seoul Report*, respectively. Saturday's news is followed by *Worldwide Friendship* (a listener-response show), and Sunday by *Korean Pop Interactive*. Thirty minutes to Europe on 3955 kHz. One hour later in winter.

Radio Tirana, Albania. Monday through Saturday, and winter only at this hour. *News*, press review and features. Monday there's *The Week in Albania*, *Cultural Review* and *Sports Roundup*; Tuesday, a short topical report and *Mailbox* (listener response); Wednesday, a short feature followed by Albanian music; Thursday, *Focus on Albania*; Friday, a talk on Albanian history (or *Foreigners on Albania*) followed by *Outstanding Personalities Profile*; and Saturday, *Mosaic of the Week* and *Folk Music*. Thirty minutes to Europe on 7510 and/or 7530 kHz, and to eastern North America on 9345 kHz. One hour earlier in summer.

International Radio Serbia. Summer only at this time. A half-hour news broadcast to Europe on 6100 and 7200 kHz. One hour later in winter.

Voice of Korea, North Korea. Repeat of the 1800 broadcast. The last of the old-time communist stations. One hour to Europe on 7570 (or 13760) and 12015 (or 15245) kHz. Also heard in parts of East Asia on 4405 kHz.

Radio Habana Cuba. The final 30 minutes of a one-hour broadcast. Monday through Saturday, there's a *news* bulletin and the sports-oriented *Time Out* (five minutes each), then a feature: *Caribbean Outlook* (Monday and Thursday), *DXers Unlimited* (Tuesday and Saturday), the *Mailbag Show* (Wednesday) and *Weekly Review* (Friday). These are replaced Sunday by a longer edition of *Mailbag Show*. To the Caribbean on 9505 kHz, and to eastern North America on 11760 kHz.

All India Radio. Continues to Western Europe on 7410, 9445, 9950 and 11620 kHz; and to Australasia on 9910, 11620 and 11715 kHz. Look for a listener-response segment, *Faithfully Yours*, at 2120 Monday.

European frequencies are audible in parts of eastern North America, while those for Australasia are also heard in Southeast Asia.

21:15

Radio Damascus, Syria. Starts at 2110. *News*, a daily press review, and different features for each day of the week. These include a mix of political commentary, Islamic themes and Arab and Syrian culture. The transmission also contains Syrian and some western popular music. An hour to North America and Australasia on 9330 and/or 12085 kHz. Audio level is often very low.

Radio Cairo, Egypt. The start of a 90-minute broadcast focusing on Arab and Egyptian themes. The initial quarter-hour of general programming is followed by *news*, commentary and political items. This in turn is followed by a cultural program until 2215, when the station again reverts to more general fare. A big signal to Europe, but often with poor audio. Winter on 6250 kHz, summer on 11550 kHz.

AFRTS Shortwave, USA. Network news, live sports, music and features in the *upper-sideband* mode from the American Forces Radio & Television Service. Transmitted from modestly powered U.S. Navy stations around the globe, so usually a tough catch. Try 4319, 5446.5, 5765, 6350, 7811, 10320, 12133.5, 12579 and 13362 kHz.

21:30

Radio Romania International. Winter only at this time. *News* and commentary followed by short features on Romania. Twenty-five minutes to Europe on 6050 and 7145 kHz, and to eastern North America on 6115 and 9755 kHz. One hour earlier in summer.

Radio Prague, Czech Republic. Summer only at this time; see 2230 for program specifics. Thirty minutes to eastern North America on 11600 kHz, and to West Africa on 9410 kHz. One hour later in winter.

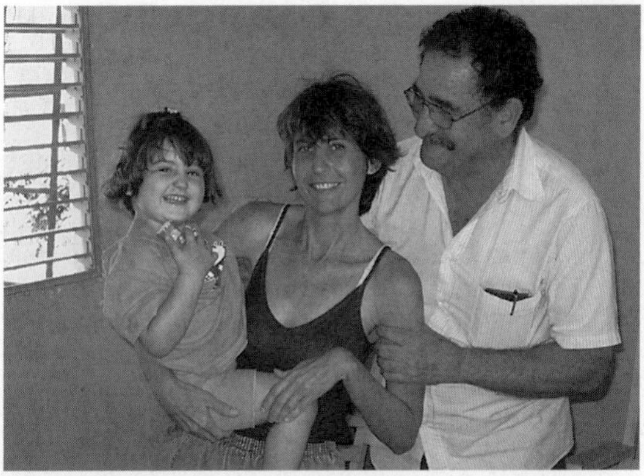

Radio Habana Cuba's Arnie Coro with wife Roxana Marquez and baby daughter Claudia. Arnie's "DXers Unlimited" is hugely popular with listeners throughout the political spectrum. RHC

Voice of Turkey. This time winter only. *News*, followed by *Review of the Turkish Press* and features, some unusual. Exotic Turkish music, too. Fifty minutes to South and Southeast Asia and Australasia on 7180 kHz. One hour earlier in summer.

Radio Sweden. Monday through Friday there's *news* and features about Sweden. Saturday has a review of the week's main news stories; and Sunday, *Network Europe*. To Europe summer (one hour later in winter) on 6065 kHz, and to Central Africa winter on 7420 kHz.

22:00

Radio Bulgaria. This time winter only. See 2100 for specifics. News and features from the Balkans—don't miss Sunday's ●*Folk Studio* (Bulgarian folk music). An hour to Europe, also heard in parts of eastern North America, on 6200 and 7400 kHz. One hour earlier in summer.

Radio Romania International. Summer only at this time; see 2300 for specifics. Fifty-five minutes to western Europe on 7185 and 9675 kHz, and to eastern North America on 9790 and 11940 kHz. One hour later in winter.

Voice of Turkey. Summer only at this time. *News*, then *Review of the Turkish Press* and

22:00–23:00

features on Turkish history and culture. Selections of Turkish popular and classical music complete the broadcast. Fifty minutes to western Europe and eastern North America on 6195 kHz. One hour later during winter.

Radio Cairo, Egypt. The second half of a 90-minute broadcast to Europe; see 2115 for program details. Winter on 6250 kHz, summer on 11550 kHz.

Radio Exterior de España ("Spanish National Radio"). Winter weekends only at this time. Features, including repeats of programs aired earlier in the week. One hour to Europe on 6125 kHz, and to West and Central Africa on 11625 kHz. Sometimes pre-empted by live sports in Spanish, and may start around 2235, or not at all. One hour earlier in summer.

China Radio International. Weekdays, *News* is followed by *China Drive*, an upbeat "drive-time" show. Weekends there's *News and Reports*, *CRI Roundup* (Saturday), *Reports from Developing Countries* (Sunday) and *China Beat* (music). One hour to Europe winter on 7170 kHz, summer on 7175 kHz, via CRI's Moscow relay; and to East Asia winter on 5915 kHz, replaced summer by 9590 kHz.

KBS World Radio, South Korea. Winter only at this time. Opens with 10 minutes of *news*, then Monday through Friday, a commentary. This is followed by a 15-minute feature: *Faces of Korea*, *Business Watch*, *Culture on the Move*, *Korea Today and Tomorrow* and *Seoul Report*, respectively. Saturday's news is followed by *Worldwide Friendship* (a listener-response show), and Sunday by *Korean Pop Interactive*. Thirty minutes to Europe on 3955 kHz. One hour earlier in summer.

Voice of America. The first of two hours to East and Southeast Asia and the Pacific. Predominantly news fare at this hour. To East and Southeast Asia winter on 7120, 9490 and 11725 kHz; and summer on 7120, 9415, 11725 and 15185 kHz. For Australasia there's 9490 and 11725 kHz in winter, 9415 kHz midyear.

Radio Australia. *News*, followed Sunday through Thursday by *AM* (current events) and, from 2240, *The Breakfast Club*. Winter Fridays, there's *In the Loop (Rewind)* and *Talking Point*, replaced summer by the final hour of *Saturday Extra*. Saturday, winter's *Correspondents Report* and *Innovations* are replaced summer by the final segment of *Australia All Over*. Continuous programming to the Pacific on 13630, 15230, 15515 and 17785 kHz; and to Southeast Asia on 15240 kHz. In North America, try 17785 kHz, especially during summer.

Radio Japan. Monday through Friday there's *What's Up Japan* (current events, Japanese language lessons, and a listener-response segment Wednesday). This is replaced Saturday by *World Interactive* or (the last Saturday of the month) *Listening Library*, readings from masterpieces of Japanese literature. Sunday's feature is *Pop Up Japan*, a selection of Japanese pop music. Twenty minutes to Australasia on 13640 kHz.

Radio Taiwan International. Ten minutes of *News*, followed by features: *People*, *Chinese to Go* (language lessons) and *Asia Review* (Monday); *Health Beats* and *We've Got Mail* (Tuesday); *Strait Talk*, *Women Making Waves* and ●*Jade Bells and Bamboo Pipes* (Wednesday); *Ilha Formosa*, *Breakfast Club*, *Instant Noodles* and *Chinese to Go* (Thursday); *News Talk*, *Taiwan Indie* and *Taiwan Outlook* (Friday); *The Occidental Tourist* and *Groove Zone* (Saturday); and *Time Traveler*, *Spotlight* and *On the Line* (Sunday). One hour to western Europe on 3965 kHz.

Radio Ukraine International. Winter only at this time. A potpourri of things Ukrainian, with the Sunday broadcast often featuring some excellent music. An hour to Europe and beyond on 5830 kHz. One hour earlier in summer.

International Radio Serbia. Winter only at this time. A newsy half-hour to Europe on 6100 kHz. One hour earlier in summer.

All India Radio. The final half-hour of a transmission to Western Europe and Australasia, consisting mainly of news-related fare. To Western Europe on 7410, 9445, 9950 and 11620 kHz; and to Australasia on 9910, 11620 and 11715 kHz. Frequencies for Europe are audible in parts of eastern North America, while those for Australasia are also heard in Southeast Asia.

AFRTS Shortwave, USA. Network news, live sports, music and features in the *upper-sideband* mode from the American Forces Radio & Television Service. Transmitted from modestly powered U.S. Navy stations around the globe, so usually a tough catch. Try 4319, 5446.5, 5765, 6350, 7811, 10320, 12133.5, 12579 and 13362 kHz.

22:15

Voice of Croatia. Summer only at this time. Nominally 15 minutes of news, reports and interviews, but actual length varies. To Europe on 3965 and/or 6165 kHz, and to eastern North America and South America on 9925 kHz. May also use 7285 kHz when necessary. One hour later in winter.

Radio PMR, Moldova. Sunday through Thursday, and summer only at this time. Fifteen minutes of newsy programming from the self-denominated "Pridnestrovian Moldavian Republic." One of the curiosities of world band radio. To eastern North America on 6040 kHz, and one hour later in winter.

22:30

Radio Sweden. Winter only at this time. Weekdays, it's a smorgasbord of *news* and features about Sweden. Saturday, there is a review of the week's main news stories; and Sunday it's *Network Europe*. Thirty minutes to Europe on 5850 and/or 6065 kHz, and one hour earlier in summer.

Radio Prague, Czech Republic. *News*, then Monday through Friday it's the in-depth *Current Affairs* and one or more features: *One on One* (Monday), *Talking Point* (Tuesday), *Czechs in History*, *Czechs Today* or *Spotlight* (Wednesday), *Panorama* and *From the Archives* (Thursday), and *Business News* and *The Arts* (Friday). Weekends, the news is followed by Saturday's *Insight Central Europe* (or *Magazine*, *Sound Czech* and *One on One*), and Sunday's *Mailbox* and *Letter from Prague* followed by *Music Profile*, *Magic Carpet* (Czech world music) or *Czech Books*. Half an hour to eastern North America winter on 5930 kHz, summer on 7345 and 9415 kHz; also to West and Central Africa winter on 9435 kHz.

22:45

All India Radio. The first 15 minutes of a much longer broadcast, consisting of Indian music, regional and international *news*, commentary, and a variety of talks and features of general interest. Continuous till 0045. To East Asia on 9950, 11620, 11645 and 13605 kHz; and to Southeast Asia on 9705, 11620 and 13605 kHz.

23:00

Radio Canada International. Summer only at this time, and starts at 2305. Monday through Friday, it's *The Link*, replaced Saturday by *Blink* (*Behind The Link*) and Sunday by *Maple Leaf Mailbag*. To the central United States on 6100 kHz, and one hour later in winter.

Voice of Turkey. Winter only at this hour. *News*, then *Review of the Turkish Press* and some unusual features with a strong local flavor. Selections of Turkish popular and classical music complete the program. Fifty minutes to western Europe and eastern North America on 5960 kHz. One hour earlier in summer.

Radio Habana Cuba. Monday through Saturday, there is international and Cuban news followed by *RHC's Viewpoint*. On the half-hour there's a *news* bulletin and the sports-oriented *Time Out* (five minutes each), then a feature: *Caribbean Outlook* (Monday and Thursday), *DXers Unlimited* (Tuesday and Saturday), the *Mailbag Show* (Wednesday) and *Weekly Review* (Friday). Sunday fare includes *Weekly Review* and a longer edition of *Mailbag Show*. One hour to

23:00–23:30

Bucharest's unfinished Palace of the Parliament is reportedly the world's largest civilian administrative building. Like many projects of the Ceausescu period it resulted in wholesale eradication of venerable historic centers.
Shutterstock/Remus

South America on 9550 kHz, and also heard in parts of the United States.

Radio Australia. *World News*, followed Sunday through Thursday by *Connect Asia* (news, commentary and analysis), and Friday by *Asia Review* and *Talking Point.* Winter Saturdays, there's *Background Briefing* and *Perspective*, replaced summer by *Correspondents Report* and *Innovations.* Continuous to the Pacific on 9660, 12080, 13690, 15230, 17785 and 17795 kHz; and to Southeast Asia on 15240 (till 2330), 15415 and 17750 kHz. Listeners in North America should try 17785 and 17795 kHz, especially during summer.

China Radio International. *News* and reports fill the first half-hour, and are followed by a daily feature: ●*Frontline* (Sunday), *Biz China* (Monday), *In the Spotlight* (Tuesday), ●*Voices from Other Lands* (Wednesday), *Life in China* (Thursday), *Listeners' Garden* (Friday) and *China Horizons* (Saturday). One hour to the United States and Caribbean via CRI's Cuban and Canadian relays, winter on 5990, 6040 and 11970 kHz; and summer on 5990, 6145 and 11840 kHz. Also available to East Asia winter on 5915 kHz, summer on 11690 kHz.

Voice of Greece. Sunday and summer only at this time. Starts at 2305. Approximately 60 minutes of music in *Greek in Style*. To North America on 7475 and 9420 kHz; and to Australasia on 15650 kHz. For North America it's one hour later in winter, and for Australasia it moves to 1105 Sunday.

☞ Monday World Time is Sunday evening in North America.

Radio Cairo, Egypt. The first hour of a 90-minute broadcast to eastern North America. A ten-minute *news* bulletin is aired at 2315, with the remaining time taken up by short features on Egypt, the Middle East and Islam. For the intellectual listener there's *Literary Readings* at 2345 Monday, and *Modern Arabic Poetry* at the same time Friday. More general fare is available in *Listener's Mail* at 2325 Thursday and Saturday. Winter on 6850 kHz, summer on 9280 kHz.

Radio Romania International. Winter only at this time. Starts with *Radio Newsreel*, a combination of news, commentary and press review. Features on Romania complete the broadcast. Regular spots include Monday's *Pro Memoria*, *Romanian Hits* and *Sports Roundup*; Tuesday's *Business Club* and ●*The Skylark* (Romanian folk music); Wednesday's *Society Today* and *Romanian Musicians*; Thursday's *Europa Express*; and Friday's ●*The Folk Music Box* and *Sports Weekend*. Saturday there's *The Week* and *World of Culture*, and Sunday's broadcast includes *Focus*. Fifty-five minutes to western Europe on 6015 and 7105 kHz, and to eastern North America on 6115 and 9610 kHz. One hour earlier in summer.

Radio Bulgaria. Summer only at this time. Starts with *News*, then Monday through Friday there's *Events and Developments*, replaced weekends by *Views Behind the News*.

The remaining time is taken up by regular programs such as *Keyword Bulgaria* and ●*Time Out for Music*, and weekly features like *Sports* (Monday), *Magazine Economy* (Tuesday), *The Way We Live* (Wednesday), *History Club* (Thursday), *DX Programme* (for radio enthusiasts, Friday) and *Answering Your Letters* (a listener-response show, Saturday). The week's highlight is Sunday's ●*Folk Studio* (Bulgarian folk music). An hour to eastern North America on 9700 and 11700 kHz. One hour later during winter.

All India Radio. Continuous programming to East and Southeast Asia. A potpourri of *news*, commentary, features and exotic Indian music. To East Asia on 9950, 11620, 11645 and 13605 kHz; and to Southeast Asia on 9705, 11620 and 13605 kHz.

Voice of America. The second and final hour of news-oriented programming to East and Southeast Asia and the Pacific. To East and Southeast Asia winter on 7120, 9490, 11725 and 15185 kHz; and summer on 7120, 9415, 11725 and 15185 kHz. For Australasia there's 9490 and 11705 kHz in winter, 9415 kHz midyear.

Radio PMR, Moldova. Summer only at this time. Repeat of the 2215 broadcast; see there for specifics. Fifteen minutes Sunday through Thursday to eastern North America on 6040 kHz, and one hour later in winter.

AFRTS Shortwave, USA. Network news, live sports, music and features in the *upper-sideband* mode from the American Forces Radio & Television Service. Transmitted from modestly powered U.S. Navy stations around the globe, so usually a tough catch. Try 4319, 5446.5, 5765, 6350, 7811, 10320, 12133.5, 12579 and 13362 kHz.

23:15

Voice of Croatia. Winter only at this time. Nominally 15 minutes of news, reports and interviews, but actual length varies. To Europe on 3985 and/or 6165 kHz, and to eastern North America and South America on 7285 (or 7375) kHz. One hour earlier in summer.

Radio PMR, Moldova. Sunday through Thursday, and winter only at this time. Fifteen minutes of newsy fare from the separatist, pro-Russian, "Pridnestrovian Moldavian Republic." May air 15 minutes earlier. To eastern North America on 6240 kHz. One hour earlier in summer.

23:30

Radio Prague, Czech Republic. Winter only at this time. *News*, then Monday through Friday there's *Current Affairs* and one or more features: *One on One* (Monday), *Talking Point* (Tuesday), *Czechs in History*, *Czechs Today* or *Spotlight* (Wednesday), *Panorama* and *From the Archives* (Thursday), and *Business News* and *The Arts* (Friday). On Saturday the news is followed by *Insight Central Europe* (or *Magazine*, *Sound Czech* and *One on One*), and Sunday's lineup is *Mailbox* and *Letter from Prague* followed by *Music Profile*, *Magic Carpet* (Czech world music) or *Czech Books*. Thirty minutes to eastern North America on 5930 and 7345 kHz, and one hour earlier in summer.

Radio Vilnius, Lithuania. Thirty minutes of mostly *news* and background reports about events in Lithuania. Of broader appeal is *Mailbag*, aired every other Saturday. For some Lithuanian music, try the second half of Sunday's broadcast. To eastern North America winter on 7325 kHz, summer on 9875 kHz.

Voice of Vietnam. Begins with *News*, then Monday though Friday there's *Current Affairs*. These are followed Monday by *Vietnam, Land and People*; Tuesday, *Society* and *Business*; Wednesday, *Letterbox* (listener response); Thursday, *Vietnam Economy* and *Talk of the Week*; and Friday, *Rural Vietnam* and *Culture*. Saturday has *Weekly Review* and *Weekend Music*, and Sunday there's *Culture*, *Sports Roundup* and *Sunday Show*. Half an hour to Southeast Asia on 9840 and 12020 kHz. Frequencies may vary slightly.

Prepared by Tony Jones and the staff of PASSPORT TO WORLD BAND RADIO.

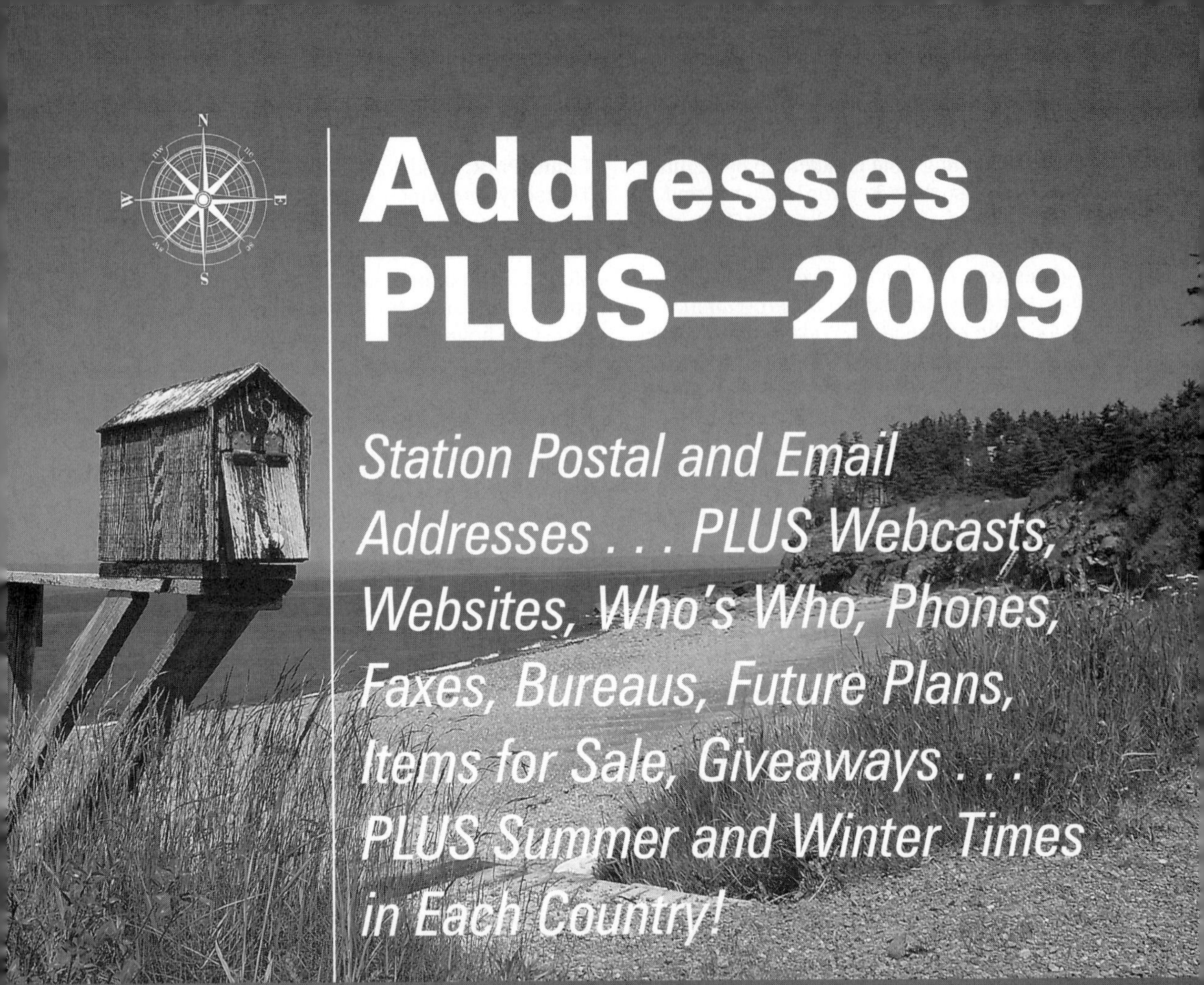

Addresses PLUS—2009

Station Postal and Email Addresses . . . PLUS Webcasts, Websites, Who's Who, Phones, Faxes, Bureaus, Future Plans, Items for Sale, Giveaways . . . PLUS Summer and Winter Times in Each Country!

PASSPORT usually shows how stations reach out to you, but Addresses PLUS also explains how you can reach out to stations. Here you'll find details, country by country, about how broadcasters go beyond world band radio to keep in touch, inform and entertain.

Making Contact

When broadcasting was in its infancy, listeners sent in "applause" cards to let stations how well they were being received. Stations would reply with a letter or illustrated card verifying ("QSLing" in Morse code) that the station the listener heard was, in fact, theirs. While they were at it, some stations threw in a free souvenir—station calendar, magazine, pennant or sticker.

The tradition continues, although obtaining QSLs is now more challenging—look under "Verification" in PASSPORT's "Worldly Words." Some stations also sell small items, while others air letters over audience feedback programs.

Postal Reimbursement

Stations go beyond world band radio to keep in touch, inform and entertain.

Most broadcasters reply to listener correspondence—even email—through the postal system. That way, they can send out printed schedules, verification cards and other "hands-on" souvenirs. Major stations usually do this for free, but smaller operations may seek postage reimbursement.

Best with Latin American and Indonesian stations is to enclose unused (mint) stamps from the station's country. These are available from two excellent sources: Plum's Airmail Postage, 12 Glenn Road, Flemington NJ 08822-3322 USA, plumdx@msn.com, phone +1 (908) 788-1020, fax +1 (908) 782 2612; as well as James E. Mackey, P.O. Box 270569, West Hartford CT 06127-0569 USA, phone +1 (860) 521-7254, http://users.net1plus.com/ryoung/OrderForm.htm. One way to help ensure your stamps are used to reply to you is to stick them onto a pre-addressed return airmail envelope—making it a self-addressed stamped envelope, or SASE.

You can also prompt reluctant stations by donating a U.S. dollar or two—or a euro or some loose unused stamps from their country—preferably hidden from prying eyes by something like a piece of reflective-lined plastic film from old packaging. Registration often helps, as items of value tend to get stolen. In some countries, though, registered mail attracts dishonest postal employees, especially in parts of Latin America.

Once popular but increasingly impractical are International Reply Coupons (IRCs), which recipients may exchange locally for air or surface stamps. These are available at a number of post offices worldwide, particularly in large cities; in the United States, this is explained at pe.usps.com/text/pub51/pub51txt_021.htm. Thing is, they're increasingly hard to find, relatively costly, not terribly effective, and aren't accepted by postal authorities in some countries.

Stamp Out Crime

Mail theft is still a problem in some countries, although the overall situation is improving. Addresses PLUS identifies problem areas and offers countermeasures, but start by using common sense. For example, some postal employees are stamp collectors and steal mail with unusual stamps, so use everyday stamps. Other options: a post office's postal meter, PC-generated postage or, where available, an aerogram.

¿Que Hora Es?

World Time, explained in "Setting Your World Time Clock," is essential if you want to find out when your favorite station is on. But if you want to know what time it is in any given country, World Time and "Addresses PLUS" come together to provide the answer.

Here's how. So that you don't have to wrestle with seasonal changes in your own time, "Addresses PLUS" gives local times for each country in terms of hours' difference from World Time (it stays constant year-round). For example, if you look below under "Albania," you'll see that country is World Time +1; that is, one hour ahead of World Time. So, if World Time is 12:00, the local time in Albania is 13:00 (1:00 PM). On the other hand, México City is World Time -6; that is, six hours behind World Time. If World Time is 12:00, in México City it's 6:00 AM.

Local times shown in parentheses are for the middle of the calendar year—roughly April-October; specific seasonal changeover dates for individual countries are at timeanddate.com/worldclock.

Spotted Something New?

Something changed since we went to press? Please let us know! Your update information, especially copies of material received from stations, is highly valued. Contact the IBS Editorial Office, Box 300, Penn's Park, PA 18943 USA, fax +1 (215) 598 3794, mktg@passband.com.

Muchas gracias to the kindly folks and helpful organizations mentioned at the end of this chapter for their tireless cooperation in the preparation of this section. Without you, none of this would have been possible.

Using PASSPORT's Addresses PLUS Section

Stations included: All stations are listed if known to reply, however erratically. Also, new stations which possibly may reply to future correspondence from listeners.

Leased-time programs: Private organizations/NGOs that lease program time, but which possess no world band transmitters of their own, are normally not listed. However, they can usually be reached via the stations over which they are heard.

Postal addresses are given. These sometimes differ from transmitter locations in the Blue Pages.

Phone and fax numbers. To help avoid confusion, telephone numbers have hyphens, fax numbers don't. All are configured for international dialing once you add your country's International access code (011 in the United States and Canada, 010 in the United Kingdom, and so on). For domestic dialing within countries outside the United States, Canada and most of the Caribbean, replace the country code (1–3 digits preceded by a "+") by a zero.

Giveaways. If you want free goodies, say so politely in your correspondence. These are usually available until supplies run out.

Web simulcasting. World band stations which use streaming audio to simulcast and/or offer archived programming over the Internet are indicated by ■.

Unless otherwise indicated, stations:

- Reply regularly within six months or so to most listeners' correspondence in English.
- Provide, upon request, free station schedules and verification ("QSL") postcards or letters (*see* Verification in "Worldly Words"). When other items are available for free or for purchase, it is specified.
- Do not require payment for postage to reply to you. Where compensation is appropriate, details are provided.

Local times. These are given in difference from World Time. For example, "World Time -5" means that if you subtract five hours from World Time, you'll get the local time in that country. So, if it were 11:00 World Time, it would be 06:00 local time in that country. Times in (parentheses) are for the middle of the year—roughly April–October. For exact changeover dates, see the explanatory paragraph, above, under "¿Que Hora Es?"

AFGHANISTAN World Time +4:30

Radio Afghanistan (when activated), Afghan Radio & TV, P.O. Box 544, Ansari Wat, Kabul, Afghanistan. Contact: Foreign Relations Department.

ALBANIA World Time +1 (+2 midyear)

Radio Tirana, External Service, Rruga Ismail Qemali Nr. 11, Tirana, Albania. Phone: +355 (4) 222-4705; (Drita Çiço) +355 (4) 222-2277. Phone/Fax: (technical directorate) +355 (4) 222 3650. Email: (general) radiotirana@rtsh.al; (English Section) radiotirana-english@hotmail.com; (reception reports) dcico@abcom-al.com. Web: www.rtsh.al (external service is "Program III"). Contact: Ms. Mira Bregu, Director of External Services; Adriana Bislea, English Department; Clara Ruci, Journalist/Translator/Broadcaster; Marjeta Thoma; Pandi Skaka, Producer; Diana Koci; (technical directorate), Agron Aranitasi, Technical Director ARTV; (frequency management) Mrs. Drita Çiço, Head of RTV Monitoring Center. May send free stickers and postcards. Email reports welcome.

ALGERIA World Time +1

Radio Algérienne (ENRS), 21 Boulevard des Martyrs, Algiers, Algeria. Phone: (Direction Générale) +213 (2) 148-3790. Fax: (Direction Générale) +213 (2) 123 0823. Email: (Direction Générale) dg@algerian-radio.dz; (International Relations) relex@algerian-radio.dz; (Direction Technique) technique@algerian-radio.dz. Web: (includes on-demand and streaming audio) www.algerian-radio.dz. Replies iregularly. French or Arabic preferred, but English accepted. Return postage helpful. Formerly transmitted direct from Algeria, but currently via transmitters in the United Kingdom.

ANGOLA World Time +1

Rádio Nacional de Angola, Caixa Postal 1329, Luanda, Angola. Phone: +244 (2) 321-258, +244 (2) 321-018; (Canal Internacional - External Service) +244 (2) 320-788. Fax: +244 (2) 323 956, +244 (2) 324 123. Email: (administration) dgeral@rna.ao; (Fernandes) alefernandes@rna.ao; (Diatezwa) fdiatezwa@rna.ao; (reception reports only) departamento133@hotmail.com. Web: www.rna.ao. Contact: Dr. Júlio Mendonça, Director do Departamento de Intercâmbio e Opinião Pública; Dr. Eduardo Magalhães, Director Geral; (technical) Alé Fernandes, Director Técnico; Eng. Filipe Diatezwa, Director de Rede Emissores. Replies irregularly. Best is to correspond in Portuguese and include $1, return postage or 2 IRCs.

ANGUILLA World Time –4

Caribbean Beacon, Box 690, Anguilla, British West Indies. Phone: +1 (264) 497- 4340. Fax: +1 (264) 497 4311. Email: beacon@anguillanet.com. Contact: Monsell Hazell, Chief Engineer; Doris Lussington. $2 or return postage helpful. Relays University Network—*see* USA.

ANTARCTICA World Time –3 (+2 midyear) Base Antárctica Esperanza

Radio Nacional Arcángel San Gabriel—LRA36, Base Esperanza, V9411XAD Antártida Argentina, Argentina. Phone/Fax: +54 (2964) 421-519. Email: lra36esperanza@yahoo.com.ar; lra36@infovia.com.ar. Web: www.ejercito.mil.ar/antartico/lra36.htm. Return postage required. Replies to correspondence in Spanish, and sometimes to correspondence in English or French, depending on who is at the station (the staff changes each year, usually around February).

ARGENTINA World Time –3 (+2 midyear)

Radio Baluarte (when operating), Casilla de Correo 45, 3370 Puerto Iguazú, Provincia de Misiones, Argentina. Phone: +54 (3737) 422-557. Email: contatoarmoniafm@hotmail.com. Contact: Pastor Paulo Lima. Free tourist literature. Return postage helpful. The same programs are aired on 100.7 MHz (Radio Armonia), and both outlets are believed to be unlicensed. However, given the current radio licensing situation in the country, this is not unusual.

Radiodifusión Argentina al Exterior—RAE, Casilla de Correos 555, C1000WAF Buenos Aires, Argentina. Phone/Fax: +54 (11) 4325-6368; (technical) +54 (11) 4325-5270. Email: (general) rae@radionacional.gov.ar; (German Section) raedeutsch@yahoo.com.ar; (Barrera) barrera@arg.sicoar.com. Web: (includes streaming audio) www.radionacional.gov.ar (click on appropriate icons/links for schedule and streaming audio). Contact: (general) John Anthony Middleton, Head of English Team; María Dolores López, Spanish Team; Sra. Rayen Braun, German Team; (administration) Lic. Susana Cuestas; (technical) Gabriel Iván Barrera, DX Editor. Return postage (3 IRCs) appreciated. The station asks listeners not to send currency notes, as it's a breach of local postal regulations. Reports covering at least 20-30 minutes of reception are appreciated.

Radio Nacional Buenos Aires, Maipú 555, C1006ACE Buenos Aires, Argentina. Phone: +54 (11) 4325-9100. Fax: (management—Gerencia General) +54 (11) 4325 9433; (director) +54 (11) 4325-4590, +54 (11) 4322-4313. Email: (director) direccionrna@radionacional.gov.ar. Web: (includes streaming audio) www.radionacional.gov.ar. Contact: Eduardo García Caffi, Director. Return postage (3 IRCs) helpful. Prefers correspondence in Spanish, and usually replies via RAE (*see*, above).

ARMENIA World Time +4 (+5 midyear)

Public Radio of Armenia/Voice of Armenia, Radio Agency, Alex Manoukyan Street 5, 375025 Yerevan, Armenia. Phone: +374 1055-1143. Fax: +374 1055 4600. Email: (general director) president@mediaconcern.am; (Amiryan) aa@arradio.am; (foreign broadcasts department, reception reports and comments on programs) pr@armradio.am. Contact: Armen Amiryan, Executive Director. Web: (includes on-demand and streaming audio) www.armradio.am. Free postcards and stamps. Requests 2 IRCs for postal reply. Replies slowly.

ASCENSION World Time exactly

BBC World Service—Atlantic Relay Station, English Bay, Ascension (South Atlantic Ocean). Fax: +247 6117. Contact: (technical) Mrs. Nicola Nicholls, Transmitter Engineer. Nontechnical correspondence should be sent to the BBC World Service in London (*see*).

AUSTRALIA World Time +11 (+10 midyear) Victoria (VIC), New South Wales (NSW), Australian Capital Territory (ACT) and Tasmania (TAS); +10:30 (+9:30 midyear) South Australia (SA); +10 Queensland (QLD); +9:30 Northern Territory (NT); +9 (+8 midyear) Western Australia (WA)

Australian Broadcasting Corporation Northern Territory HF Service—ABC Radio 8DDD Darwin, Administrative Center for the Northern Territory Shortwave Service, ABC, Box 9994, GPO Darwin NT 0801, Australia; (street address) 1 Cavenagh Street, Darwin NT 0800, Australia. Phone: +61 (8) 8943-3222; (engineering) +61 (8) 8943-3209. Fax: +61 (8) 8943 3235, +61 (8) 8943 3208. Contact: (general) Tony Bowden, Branch Manager; (administration) Theresa Regan, Administration Officer; Kathryn Ainsworth, Administration Officer, Business Service; (technical) Peter Camilleri; Yvonne Corby. Free stickers and postcards. "Traveller's Guide to ABC Radio" for $1. T-shirts US$20. Three IRCs or return postage helpful.

BBC World Service via Radio Australia—For verification direct from the Australian transmitters, contact John Westland, Director of English Programs at Radio Australia (*see*). Nontechnical correspondence should be sent to the BBC World Service in London (*see*).

Community Development Radio Service—CDRS (when operating), ARDS, Box 1671, Nhulunbuy NT 0881, Australia; (street address) 19 Pera Circuit, Nhulunbuy NT 0880, Australia. Phone: +61 (8) 8987-3910. Fax: +61 (8) 8987 3912. Email: (general) nhulun@ards.com.au; mediaservices@ards.com.au; (technical) dale@ards.com.au. Web: (includes on-demand audio) www.ards.com.au/broadcast.htm. Contact: Dale Chesson, Radio Service Manager. Free station literature. Verifies reception reports. Currently off the air but may return in the future.

Christian Vision Communications (CVC), P.O. Box 6361, Maroochydore, QLD 4558, Australia. Phone: + 61-7-5477-1555. Fax: + 61-7-5477-1727. Email: (technical and nontechnical) enquiry@cvc.tv; (reception reports) dxer@cvc.tv; ("Mailbag" program) mailbag@cvc.tv. Web: (includes on-demand and streaming audio, and online reception report form) www.cvc.tv. Contact: (general) Mike Edmiston, Director; Raymond Moti, Station Manager; Richard Daniel, Corporate Relations Manager. May send T-shirt, baseball cap, key ring or other small gifts. Formerly Voice International Limited, and before that, Christian Voice International Australia.

HONG KONG ADDRESS (CHINESE SERVICE): Liu Sheng, Flat 1b, 67 Ha Heung Road, Kowloon, Hong Kong, China.

INDIA ADDRESS (ENGLISH SERVICE): CVC, P.O. Box 3453, Koramangala PO, Bangalore 560034 India.

INDIA ADDRESS (HINDI SERVICE): CVC, P.O. Box 1, Kangra, Himachal Pradesh 176001, India; or CVC, P.O. Box 2, Ludhiana, Punjab 141008 India. Email: mail@thevoiceasia.com. Web: (streaming audio only) www.thevoiceasia.com.

INDONESIA ADDRESS (INDONESIAN SERVICE): CVC, P.O. Box 2634, Jakarta Pusat, 10026 Indonesia. Phone: +62 (21) 390-0039.

INTERNATIONAL TOLL-FREE NUMBERS: (Indonesia only) 001-803-61-555; (India only) 000-800-610-1019.

SOUTH AFRICA ADDRESS: One Africa, P.O. Box 3933, Tyger Valley 7536, South Africa. Fax: +27 (21) 914 9261. Email: 1africa@cvc.tv. Web: www.1africa.tv.

TRANSMITTER SITE: CVC, PMB 5777, Darwin NT 0801, Australia. Phone: (general) +61 (8) 8981-6591, (operations manager) +61 (8) 8981-8822. Fax: +61 (8) 8981 2846. Contact: Mrs. Lorna Manning, Site Administrator; Robert Egoroff, Operations Manager.

CVC—*see* Christian Vision Communications, above.

EDXP News Report, 404 Mont Albert Road, Mont Albert, Victoria 3127, Australia. Phone/Fax: +61 (3) 9898-2906. Email: info@edxp.org. Web: http://edxp.org. Contact: Bob Padula. " EDXP News Report" is compiled by the "Electronic DX Press" and airs over several world band stations. Focuses on shortwave broadcasters beaming to, or located in Asia and the Pacific. Currently heard on Adventist World Radio, HCJB-Australia, WINB, WWCR, and World Harvest Radio. Verifies postal reports with full-detail "EDXP" QSL cards showing Australian fauna, flora, and scenery. Return postage required; four 50c stamps within Australia, and one IRC or US dollar elsewhere. Email reports welcome, and are confirmed with animated Web-delivered QSLs. Does not verify reports on Internet broadcasts.

HCJB Australia, P.O. Box 291, Kilsyth VIC 3137, Australia. Phone: +61 (3) 9761-4844. Fax: +61 (3) 9761 4061. Email: office@hcjb.org.au. Web: (includes online email form) www.hcjb.org.au. Contact: Derek Kickbush, Director of Broadcasting; Dennis Adams; Ken Lingwood, Frequency Manager.

VERIFICATION OF RECEPTION REPORTS: Voice of the Great Southland, GPO Box 691, Melbourne VIC 3001, Australia. Email: english@hcjb.org.au. One IRC required for postal reply. Listeners to the Japanese broadcasts can send their reception reports to: HCJB Section, Yodobashi Church, Hyakunincho 1-17-8, Shinjuku-ku, Tokyo 169-0073, Japan. Return postage (stamps) required within Japan.

NEW DELHI OFFICE: Radio GMTA, P.O. Box 4960, New Delhi 110 029 India.

Radio Australia, GPO Box 428G, Melbourne VIC 3001, Australia. Phone: ("Openline" voice mail for listeners' messages and requests) +61 (3) 9626-1825; (switchboard) +61 (3) 9626-1800; (English programs) +61 (3) 9626-1922; (marketing manager) +61 (3) 9626 1723. Fax: (general) +61 (3) 9626 1899. Email: (general) english@ra.abc.net.au; (marketing manager) marketing@radioaustralia.net.au. Web: (includes on-demand and streaming audio) www.radioaustralia.net.au. Contact: (general) Brendon Telfer, Head of English Language Programming; Mark Hemetsberger, Marketing & Communications Manager; Hanh Tran, Chief Executive; (technical) Nigel Holmes, Chief Engineer, Transmission Management Unit. All reception reports received by Radio Australia are forwarded to the Australian Radio DX Club for assessment and checking. ARDXC will for-

ward completed QSLs to Radio Australia for mailing. For further information, contact Brendon Telfer, Director of English Programs at Radio Australia (Email: telfer.brendon@abc.net.au).
SAN FRANCISCO OFFICE, SCHEDULES: 2654 17th Avenue, San Francisco CA 94116 USA. Phone: +1 (415) 564-9968. Email: GPoppin@aol.com. Contact: George Poppin. This address, a volunteer office, only provides Radio Australia schedules to listeners (return postage not required). All other correspondence should be sent directly to the main office in Melbourne.
Radio Symban (when operating), 825 New Canterbury Road, Hurlstone Park NSW 2193, Sydney, Australia. Phone: +61 (2) 9554-6060. Fax: +61 (2) 9558 0556. Email: symban@radiosymban.co.au. Web: (includes streaming audio) www.radiosymban.com.au.
Yolngu Radio—*see* Community Development Radio Service, above.

AUSTRIA World Time +1 (+2 midyear)

Radio Austria International, Listener Service, Argentinierstrasse 30a, A-1040 Vienna, Austria. Phone: +43 (1) 5017-0371. Fax: +43 (1) 50101 18595. Email: (frequency schedules, comments, reception reports) roi.service@orf.at. Web: (includes online reception report form) http://oe1.orf.at/service/international_en; (on-demand and streaming audio from Ö1, which makes up most of Radio Austria International's European service) http://oe1.orf.at/inforadio/?filter=1. Contact: Listener Service.
FREQUENCY MANAGEMENT: ORS Austrian Broadcasting Services, Attn. Ernst Vranka, Würzburggasse 30, A-1136 Vienna, Austria. Phone: +43 (1) 87040-12629. Fax: +43 (1) 87040 12773. Email: ernst.vranka@ors.at. Contact: Ernst Vranka, Frequency Manager.
Trans World Radio—*see* USA.

AZERBAIJAN World Time +4 (+5 midyear)

Voice of Azerbaijan, Medhi Hüseyin küçäsi 1, AZ 1011 Baku, Azerbaijan. Phone: +994 12 492-7851. Fax: +994 (12) 439 8505. Free postcards, and occasionally, books. $1 or return postage helpful. Replies irregularly to correspondence in English.
AZERBAIJAN TV AND RADIO BROADCASTING (PARENT ORGANIZATION): Same address as Voice of Azerbaijan, above. Phone: +994 (12) 492-3807. Fax: +994 (12) 497 2020. Email: webmaster@aztv.az. Web: www.aztv.az.

BAHRAIN World Time +3

Coalition Maritime Forces (CMF) Radio One—*see* INTERNATIONAL WATERS.
Radio Bahrain, Broadcasting and Television, Ministry of Information, P.O. Box 194, Al Manãmah, Bahrain (if this fails, try P.O. Box 1075). Phone: (general) +973 1768-6000; (Arabic Service) +973 1778-1888; (English Service) +973 1762-9085. Fax: (Arabic Service) +973 1768 1544; (English Service) +973 1778 0911. Email: brtcnews@batelco.com.bh. Web: (English Service) www.radiobahrain.fm; (English Service, streaming audio only) www.radiobahrain.net. Contact: A. Suliman (for Director of Broadcasting). $1 or IRC required. Replies irregularly.

BANGLADESH World Time +6

Bangladesh Betar
NONTECHNICAL: (postal address, external service) External Services, Bangladesh Betar, Shah Bagh Post Box No. 2204, Dhaka-1000, Bangladesh; (street address, all services) 121 Kazi Nazrul Islam Avenue, Shah Bagh, Dhaka-1000, Bangladesh. Phone: (director general) +880 (2) 861-5294; (external service) +880 (2) 861-8119. Fax: (director general) +880 (2) 861 2021. Email: (director general) dgbetar@bd.drik.net; dgbetar@bttb.net.bd. Web: (includes on-demand audio) www.betar.org.bd. Contact: Setub Uddin Ahmed, Director - External Services.
TECHNICAL: Research and Receiving Centre, National Broadcasting Authority, 121 Kazi Nazrul Islam Avenue, Shah Bagh, Dhaka-1000, Bangladesh. Phone: +880 (2) 862-5538, +880 (2) 862-5904. Fax: +880 (2) 861 2021. Email: rrc@dhaka.net. Contact: Mahesh Chandra Roy, Senior Engineer. Sometimes verifies reception reports.

BELARUS World Time +2 (+3 midyear)

Belarusian Radio, 4 Krasnaya St., Minsk 220807, Belarus. Phone: +375 (17) 284-8424. Fax: +375 (17) 290 6242. Email: radio1@tvr.by. Web: (includes streaming audio) www.tvr.by. Reception reports are best sent to Radio Station Belarus (*see*, below).
Radio Grodno, ul. Gorkogo 85, Grodno 230015, Belarus. Phone/Fax: +375 (152) 438-310. Email: (general) radio@tvr.grodno.by; (technical) radiotech@tvr.grodno.by. Web: www.tvr.grodno.by/radio. Correspondence should be addressed to the attention of Mr. Alexander Bakurskiy. Verifies reception reports in Russian, Belarusian or English.
Radio Mogilev, Mogilev (Mahiliou) 212030, Belarus. Email: radiomogilev@tut.by. Contact: Yury Kurpatin. Verifies reception reports in Russian or Belarusian. May also respond to reports in English or German. Return postage helpful.
Radio Station Belarus, 4 Krasnaya St., Minsk 220807, Belarus. Phone: (director) +375 (17) 284-4277; (foreign languages department) +375 (17) 284-6910. Email: radiominsk@tvr.by. Web: (includes on-demand and streaming audio) www.radiobelarus.tvr.by. Contact: Naum Galperovich, Director; Viacheslav Laktjushin, Head of Foreign Languages Service; Elena Khoroshevich, German Service; Larisa Suarez, Listener Correspondence. Free stickers, Belarusian stamps and other small souvenirs.

BELGIUM World Time +1 (+2 midyear)

RTBF-International, Bd. Auguste Reyers 52, boîte 16, B-1044 Brussels, Belgium. Phone: +32 (2) 737-4014. Fax: +32 (2) 737 3032. Email: rtbfi@rtbf.be. Web: (includes on-demand audio and online reception report form in French) www.rtbfi.be; (streaming audio) www.rtbf.be. Contact: Philippe Caufriez, Directeur des Relations Internationales (or "Head, International Service" if writing in English). Broadcasts are essentially a relay of programs from the domestic services "La Première" and "VivaCité" of RTBF (Radio-Télévision Belge de la Communauté Française) via a transmitter in Wavre. Also airs two specific programs on Africa: "Afri K'hebdo" (African news) and "Afri K'danse" (African culture and music). Return postage not required. Accepts email reception reports.

Radio Traumland, P.O. Box 15, B-4730 Raeren, Belgium. Phone: +31 87 301-722. Email: radiotraumland@skynet.be. Email reports can only be confirmed with electronic QSLs; for a postal reply include 1 IRC, $1, 1 Euro or mint Belgian/German stamps. Transmits via T-Systems International facilities in Germany (see).

Radio Vlaanderen Internationaal (RVI), B-1043 Brussels, Belgium; (street address) Auguste Reyerslaan 52, B-1043 Brussels, Belgium. Phone: +32 (2) 741-5611, +32 (2) 741-3806/7, +32 (2) 741-3802. Fax: +32 (2) 741-4689. Email: info@rvi.be. Web: (includes on-demand and streaming audio) www.rvi.be. Contact: (station manager) Wim Jansen.

Transmitter Documentation Project (TDP), P.O. Box 1, B-2310 Rijkevorsel, Belgium. Phone: +32 (3) 314-7800. Fax: +32 (3) 314 1212. Email: info@transmitter.org. Web: www.broadcast.be; (shortwave schedule) www.airtime.be/schedule.html. Contact: Ludo Maes, Managing Director. A free online publication by Belgian Dxer Ludo Maes. TDP lists current and past shortwave transmitters used worldwide in country order with station name, transmitter site & geographical coordinates, transmitter type, power and year of installation etc. Also brokers leased airtime over world band transmitters.

BENIN World Time +1

Office de Radiodiffusion et Télévision du Benin (if reactivated), Boîte Postale 366, Cotonou, Benin. Phone/Fax: +229 2130-2184. Email: ortb@intnet.bj. Web: (includes on-demand audio) www.ortb.bj. Contact: (technical) Anastase Adjoko, Chef du Service Technique. Return postage, $2 or 2 IRCs required. Replies irregularly and slowly to correspondence in French.

PARAKOU REGIONAL STATION: ORTB-Parakou, Boîte Postale 128, Parakou, Benin. Phone: +229 2361-1096. Fax: +229 2361 0881. Web: (on-demand audio) www.ortb.bj. Contact: Eric Biokou, Ingénieur Chef. Return postage required. Replies tend to be extremely irregular, and a safer option is to send correspondence to the Cotonou address.

BHUTAN World Time +6

Bhutan Broadcasting Service, Department of Information and Broadcasting, Ministry of Communications, P.O. Box 101, Thimphu, Bhutan. Phone: +975 (2) 323-071/72. Fax: +975 (2) 323 073. Email: thiny@druknet.bt (email service is irregular and messages may bounce). Web: (includes streaming audio and on-demand songs) www.bbs.com.bt. Contact: (general) [Ms.] Pema Choden, Managing Director; (technical) Dorji Thinley, Station Engineer. Three IRCs, return postage or $2 required. Replies irregularly.

BOLIVIA World Time -4

NOTE ON STATION IDENTIFICATIONS: Many Bolivian stations listed as "Radio . . ." may also announce as "Radio Emisora . . ." or "Radiodifusora . . ."

Paitití Radiodifusión—*see* Radio Paitití, below.

Radio Amor de Dios (when operating), Iglesia Evangélica Amor de Dios, Calle Noaviri 2105, El Alto, La Paz, Bolivia.

Radio Camargo—*see* Radio Emisoras Camargo, below.

Radio Chicha, Tocla, Provincia Nor-Chichas, Departamento de Potosí, Bolivia.

Radio Eco

MAIN ADDRESS: Correo Central, Reyes, Ballivián, Beni, Bolivia. Contact: Gonzalo Espinoza Cortés, Director. Free station literature. $1 or return postage required. Replies to correspondence in Spanish.

ALTERNATIVE ADDRESS: Rolmán Medina Méndez, Correo Central, Reyes, Ballivián, Beni, Bolivia.

Radio Emisoras Ballivián (when operating), Correo Central, San Borja, Beni, Bolivia. Replies to correspondence in Spanish, and sometimes sends pennant.

Radio Emisoras Camargo, Casilla Postal 9, Camargo, Provincia Nor-Cinti, Chuquisaca, Bolivia. Email: jlgarpas@hotmail.com. Contact: Pablo García B., Gerente Propietario; José Luís García. Return postage or $1 required. Replies slowly to correspondence in Spanish.

Radio Estacion Frontera (when operating), Casilla de Correo 179, Cobija, Departamento de Pando, Bolivia.

Radio Estambul (when operating), Avenida Primero de Mayo esq. Loreto, Guayaramerín, Beni, Bolivia. Phone: +591 (3) 855-4145. Email: ninafelima@hotmail.com. Contact: Sra. Felima Bruno de Yamal, Propietaria, who welcomes postcards, pennants or small flags from foreign listeners.

Radio Fides, Casilla 9143, La Paz, Bolivia. Phone: +591 (2) 240-6363. Fax: +591 (2) 240 6632. Email: online form. Web: (includes streaming audio) www.radiofides.com. Contact: R.P. Eduardo Pérez Iribarne, S.J., Director. Replies occasionally to correspondence in Spanish.

Radio Guanay (when operating), calle Boston de Guanay 123, Guanay, La Paz, Bolivia; or Casilla de Correo 15012, La Paz, Bolivia. Replies irregularly to correspondence in Spanish.

Radio Illimani, Av. Camacho 1485 - 6to Piso, La Paz, Bolivia. Phone: +591 (2) 220-0473, +591 (2) 220-0282. Fax: +591 (2) 220-0390. Email: illimani@comunica.gov.bo. Web: (includes streaming audio) www.patrianueva.bo. Contact: Iván Maldonado, Director. $1 required, and registered mail recommended. Replies irregularly to friendly correspondence in Spanish. Key station of Patria Nueva network, and also identifies as Radio Patria Nueva.

Radio Juan XXIII [Veintitrés], Avenida Santa Cruz al frente de la plaza principal, San Ignacio de Velasco, Santa Cruz, Bolivia. Phone: +591 (3962) 2087. Phone/Fax: +591 (3962) 2188. Contact: Pbro. Elías Cortezón, Director; María Elffy Gutiérrez Méndez, Encargada de la Discoteca. Return postage or $1 required. Replies occasionally to correspondence in Spanish.

Radio La Voz del Campesino (when operating), Sipe Sipe, Provincia de Quillacollo, Departamento de Cochabamba, Bolivia. No known replies, but try using the good offices of DXer Rogildo Fontenelle Aragão: rogfara@yahoo.com.br; rogfara@bolivia.com (correspond in Spanish or Portuguese).

Radio Logos

U.S. BRANCH OFFICE: LATCOM, 1218 Croton Avenue, New Castle PA 16101 USA. Phone: +1 (412) 652-0101. Fax: +1 (412) 652 4654. Contact: Hope Cummins.

Radio Loyola, Calle Ayacucho 161, Zona Central, Sucre, Bolivia. Phone: +591 (4) 644-2555. Email: (general) loyola@radiofides.com; (Martínez Muñoz) renan_marti@hotmail.com. Web: (includes streaming audio and online email form) http://radioloyola.com. Contact: José Renan Martínez Muñoz, Responsable Radio Loyola.

Radio Mallku, Casilla No. 16, Uyuni, Provincia Antonio Quijarro, Departamento de Potosí, Bolivia. Phone: +591 (2693) 2145. Email: (Olazo) max_nelson_t@hotmail.com; (FRUTCAS parent organization) frutcas@hotmail.es. Contact: Max Nelson Olazo. Spanish preferred. Return postage in the form of two U.S. dollars appreciated, as the station depends on donations for its existence. Station owned by La Federación Unica de Trabajadores Campesinos del Altiplano Sud (FRUTCAS) and formerly known as Radio A.N.D.E.S.

Radio Minería—*see* Radiodifusoras Minería

Radio Mosoj Chaski, Casilla 4493, Cochabamba, Bolivia; (street address) Calle Abaroa 254, Cochabamba, Bolivia. Phone: +591 (4) 422-0641, +591 (4) 422-0644. Fax: +591 (4) 425 1041. Email: chaski@bo.net; phayo12@hotmail.com. Contact: Lic. P. Víctor Campos B., Director. Replies to correspondence in Spanish or English. Return postage helpful.

NORTH AMERICAN OFFICE: Quechuan Radio, c/o SIM USA, P.O. Box 7900, Charlotte NC 28241 USA.

Radio Norteña (when operating), Caranavi, Departamento de La Paz, Bolivia.

Radio Nacional de Huanuni (when operating), Casilla 681, Oruro, Bolivia. Phone: +591 (2552) 0421. Email: fstmb@hotmail.com. Web: http://es.geocities.com/primeradelpais. Contact: Rafael Lineo Morales, Director General. Return postage or $1 required. Replies irregularly to correspondence in Spanish.

Radio Paitití, Casilla 172, Guayaramerín, Beni, Bolivia. Contact: Armando Mollinedo Bacarreza, Director; Luis Carlos Santa Cruz Cuéllar, Director Gerente; Ancir Vaca Cuéllar, Gerente-Propietario. Free pennants. Return postage or $3 required. Replies irregularly to correspondence in Spanish.

Radio Panamericana, Av. 16 de Julio, Edif. 16 de Julio, Of. 902, El Prado, La Paz, Bolivia. Phone: +591 (2) 231-2644, +591 (2) 231-1383, +591 (2) 231-3980. Phone/Fax: +591 (2) 233-4271. Email: pana@panamericana.bo. Web: (includes streaming audio) www.panamericana-bolivia.com; www.panamericana.bo. Contact: Daniel Sánchez Rocha, Director. Replies irregularly, with correspondence in Spanish preferred. $1 or 2 IRCs helpful.

Radio Patria Nueva—*see* Radio Illimani.

Radio Perla del Acre (if reactivated), Casilla 7, Cobija, Departamento de Pando, Bolivia. Return postage or $1 required. Replies irregularly to correspondence in Spanish.

Radio Pío XII [Doce], Casilla 434, Oruro, Bolivia. Phone: +591 (258) 20-250, +591 (258) 20-747. Fax: +591 (258) 20 554. Email: rpiodoce@entelnet.bo. Web: www.radiopio12.org. Contact: Pbro. Roberto Durette, OMI, Director General; José Blanco Villanueva. Return postage necessary.

Radio San Gabriel, Casilla 4792, La Paz, Bolivia. Phone: +591 (2) 241-4371. Phone/Fax: +591 (2) 241-1174. Email: rsg@fundayni.rds.org.bo; (technical, including reception reports) remoc@entelnet.bo. Contact: (general) Hno. [Brother] José Canut Saurat, Director General; Sra. Martha Portugal, Dpto. de Publicidad; (technical) Rómulo Copaja Alcón, Director Técnico. $1 or return postage helpful. Free book on station, Aymara calendars and *La Voz del Pueblo Aymara* magazine. Replies fairly regularly to correspondence in Spanish. Station of the Hermanos de la Salle Catholic religious order.

Ray Rising tweaks antenna components at the Radio Logos transmitter site. The station operates on 6165 kHz from Santa Cruz, Bolivia, with a power of 5 kW. R. Rising

Radio San Miguel, Casilla 102, Riberalta, Beni, Bolivia. Phone: +591 (385) 8268, +591 (385) 8363. Fax: +591 (385) 8268. Email: radiosanmiguel_riberalta@yahoo.es, radiosanmiguel_riberalta@hotmail.com. Contact: David Terrazas Irina, Director. Free stickers and pennants; has a different pennant each year. Return postage or $2 required. Replies irregularly to correspondence in Spanish.

Radio Santa Ana, Calle Sucre No. 250, Santa Ana de Yacuma, Beni, Bolivia. Contact: Mario Roberto Suárez, Director; Mariano Verdugo. Return postage or $2 required. Replies irregularly to correspondence in Spanish.

Radio Santa Cruz, Emisora del Instituto Radiofónico Fé y Alegría (IRFA), Casilla 672, Santa Cruz, Bolivia; (street address) Calle Mario Flores esq. Guendá N° 20, Santa Cruz de la Sierra, Bolivia. Phone: +591 (3) 353-1817. Fax: +591 (3) 353 2257. Email: irfacruz@entelnet.bo. Contact: José Velasco, Director; Srta. María Yolanda Marcó Escobar, Secretaria de Dirección. Free pamphlets, stickers and pennants. Welcomes correspondence in English, French and Spanish, but return postage required for a reply.

Radio Tacana, Tumupasa, Provincia Iturralde, Departamento de La Paz, Bolivia. Contact: Roberto Carlos Chávez, Director.

Radio Universitaria (when operating), Campus Universitario, Av. Las Palmas, Cobija, Pando, Bolivia. Phone: +591 (384) 22-141. Email: radiouap@hotmail.com.

Radio Virgen de los Remedios, Casilla 198, Tupiza, Departamento de Potosí, Bolivia; (street address) Parroquia Nuestra Señora de la Candelaria, Tupiza, Departamento de Potosí, Bolivia. Phone: +591 (269) 44-662. Email: radiovirgenderemedios@hotmail.com. Contact: Padre Kazimierz Strzepek, Director General.

Radio Yura (La Voz de los Ayllus), Casilla 326, Yura, Provincia Quijarro, Departamento de Potosí, Bolivia; (street address) Calle Sucre 86 entre Bolívar y Omiste, Municipio Tomave-Ayllu, Yura, Provincia Quijarro, Departamento de Potosí, Bolivia. Phone: +591 (281) 36-216. Email: radioyura@hotmail.com; canal18@cedro.pts.entelnet.bo. Contact: Omar Flores. Free pennant, Bolivian stamps and stickers. Replies slowly to correspondence in Spanish.

Radiodifusoras Minería (if reactivated), Casilla de Correo 247, Oruro, Bolivia. Phone: +591 (252) 77-736. Contact: Dr. José Carlos Gómez Espinoza, Gerente Propietario. Free pennants. Replies to correspondence in Spanish.

Radiodifusoras Trópico, Casilla 60, Trinidad, Beni, Bolivia. Contact: Eduardo Avila Alberdi, Director. Replies slowly to correspondence in Spanish. Return postage required for reply.

BOTSWANA World Time +2

IBB Botswana Transmitting Station

TRANSMITTER SITE: International Broadcasting Bureau, Botswana Relay Station, Moepeng Hill, Selebi-Phikwe, Botswana; (postal address) International Broadcasting Bureau, Botswana Transmitting Station, Private Bag 0038, Selebi-Phikwe, Botswana. Phone: +267 810-932. Fax: +267 261 0185. Email: manager_botswana@bot.ibb.gov. Contact: Station Manager or Transmitting Plant Supervisor. This address for specialized technical correspondence only, although reception reports may occasionally be verified. All other correspondence should be directed to the regular VOA or IBB addresses (*see* USA).

BRAZIL World Time –1 (–2 midyear) Atlantic Islands; –2 (–3 midyear) Eastern, including Brasília and Rio de Janeiro; –3 (–4 midyear) Western; –4 Northwestern. There are often slight variations from one year to the next. Information regarding Daylight Saving Time can be found at http://pcdsh01.on.br.

NOTE: Postal authorities recommend that, because of the level of theft in the Brazilian postal system, correspondence to Brazil be sent only via registered mail.

CBN Anhanguera—*see* Rádio Anhanguera (Goiânia).

Rádio 9 de Julho, Rua Manoel de Arzão 85, 02730-030 São Paulo SP, Brazil. Email: radio9dejulho@terra.com.br. Web: (includes streaming audio) http://arquidiocesedesaopaulo.org.br/radio9dejulho/inicio.htm.

Rádio Alvorada (Londrina), Rua Dom Bosco 145, Jardim Dom Bosco, 86060-340 Londrina PR, Brazil. Phone: +55 (43) 3347-0606; (studio) +55 (43) 3347-0404. Fax: +55 (43) 3347 0303. Email: alvorada@radioalvorada.am.br; (Buranello) alburanello@sercomtel.com.br. Web: (includes streaming audio) www.radioalvorada.am.br. Contact: Padre Silvio Andrei, Diretor; Alcindo Buranello, Gerente Administrativo. $1 or return postage helpful. Replies to correspondence in Portuguese.

Rádio Alvorada (Parintins), Rua Governador Leopoldo Neves 516, 69151-460 Parintins AM, Brazil. Phone: +55 (92) 3533-2002, +55 (92) 3533-3097. Fax: +55 (92) 3533 2004. Email: radio-alvorada@uol.com.br; sistemaalvorada@jurupari.com.br. Contact: Raimunda Ribeiro da Silva, Diretora. Return postage required. Replies occasionally to correspondence in Portuguese.

Rádio Alvorada (Rio Branco), Avenida Ceará 2150, Jardim Nazle, 69900-460 Rio Branco AC, Brazil. Phone: +55 (68) 3226-2301. Email: seve@jornalatribuna.com.br. Contact: José Severiano, Diretor. Occasionally replies to correspondence in Portuguese.

Rádio Araguaia—FM sister-station to Rádio Anhanguera (*see* next entry) and sometimes relayed via the latter's shortwave outlet. Usually identifies as "Araguaia FM."

Rádio Anhanguera (Araguaína), BR-157 Km. 1103, Zona Rural, 77804-970 Araguaína TO, Brazil. Return postage required. Occasionally replies to correspondence in Portuguese. Sometimes airs programming from sister-station Rádio Araguaia, 97.1 FM (*see* previous item).

Rádio Anhanguera (Goiânia), Rua Thomas Edison, Quadra 7, Setor Serrinha, 74835-130 Goiânia GO, Brazil; or Caixa Postal 13, 74823-000 Goiânia GO, Brazil. Email: anhanguera@radioexecutiva.com.br. Contact: Fábio de Campos Roriz, Diretor; Eng. Domingo Vicente Tinoco. Return postage required. Replies to correspondence in Portuguese, often slowly. Although—like its namesake in Araguaína (*see*, above)—a member of the Sistema de Rádio da Organização Jaime Câmara, this station is also an affiliate of the CBN network and often identifies as "CBN Anhanguera," especially when airing news programming.

Rádio Aparecida, Avenida Getúlio Vargas 185, Centro, 12570-000 Aparecida SP, Brazil; or Caixa Postal 02, 12570-970 Aparecida SP, Brazil. Phone: +55 (12) 3104-4400. Fax: +55 (12) 3104-4427. Email: online form; (Macedo) cassianomac@yahoo.com. Web: (includes streaming audio) www.radioaparecida.com.br. Contact: Padre Inácio Medeiros, Diretor; Savio Trevisan, Departamento Técnico; José Moura; Cassiano Alves Macedo, Producer, "Encontro DX" (aired 2200 Saturday; one hour earlier when Brazil on DST). Return postage or $1 required. Replies to correspondence in Portuguese.

Rádio Bandeirantes, Rua Radiantes 13, Bairro Morumbi, 05699-900 São Paulo SP, Brazil. Phone: +55 (11) 3745-7552; (listener feedback) +55 (11) 3743-8040. Fax: +55 (11) 3745 8065. Email: (general) online form; (Huertas) ahuertas@band.com.br. Web: (includes streaming audio) www.radiobandeirantes.com.br. Contact: Augusto Huertas, Técnico Rádios. Free stickers, pennants and canceled Brazilian stamps. $1 or return postage required.

Rádio Boa Vontade, Av. São Paulo 722 - 3º andar, Bairro São Geraldo, 90230-160 Porto Alegre RS, Brazil. Phone: +55 (51) 3325-7019, +55 (51) 3374-0203. Email:

rbv1300@yahoo.com.br, rbv1300am@hotmail.com. Contact: José Joaquim Martins Rodrigues, Gerente da Rádio; (technical) Arnaldo Infanti Júnior, Engenheiro. Replies to correspondence in Portuguese.

Rádio Brasil, Av. Benjamin Constant, 1214 - 5º andar, Centro, 13010-141 Campinas SP, Brazil. Phone: (listener feedback) +55 (19) 3231-7860. Phone/Fax: +55 (19) 3231-5322. Email: radio@brasilcampinas.com. Web: (includes streaming audio) www.brasilcampinas.com. Contact: Adilson Gasparini, Diretor Comercial e Artístico. Email reports accepted. Free stickers. Replies to correspondence in Portuguese.

Rádio Brasil Central, Caixa Postal 330, 74001-970 Goiânia GO, Brazil; (street address) Rua SC-1 No. 299, Parque Santa Cruz, 74860-270 Goiânia GO, Brazil. Phone: +55 (62) 3201-7600; (Cozac) +55 (62) 3201-7675. Email: (Cozac) fernandocozacam@yahoo.com.br. Web: (includes streaming audio) www.agecom.go.gov.br/RBCAM.php. Contact: Fernando Cozac, Gerente. Free stickers. $1 or return postage required. Replies to correspondence in Portuguese, and sometimes to correspondence in English.

Rádio Cacique (if reactivated), Rua Saldanha da Gama 184, Centro, 18035-040, Sorocaba SP, Brazil. Phone: (Dpto. Comercial) +55 (15) 3234-3444; (listener feedback) +55 (15) 3232-2822. Email: contato@radiocacique.com.br. Web: www.radiocacique.com.br. Contact: Edir Correa.

TIPS FOR WINNING CORRESPONDENCE

Golden Rule: Write unto others as you would have them write unto you. The milk of human kindness is mighty skim, so a considerate message stands out.

Be interesting and helpful from the recipient's point of view, yet friendly without being chummy. Comments on specific programs are almost always appreciated, even if you are sending what is basically a technical report.

Incorporate language courtesies. Using the broadcaster's tongue is always best—Addresses PLUS indicates when it is a requirement—but English is usually the next-best bet. When writing in any language to Spanish-speaking countries, remember that what Anglos think of as the "last name" is actually written as the penultimate name. Thus, Juan Antonio Vargas García, which can also be written as Juan Antonio Vargas G., refers to Sr. Vargas; so your salutation should read, *Estimado Sr. Vargas*.

What's that "García" doing there, then? That's *mamita's* father's family name. Latinos more or less solved the problem of gender fairness in names long ago.

But, wait—what about Portuguese, used by all those stations in Brazil? Same concept, but in reverse. *Mamá's* father's family name is penultimate, and the "real" last name is where English-speakers are used to it, at the end.

In Chinese, the "last" name comes first. However, when writing in English, Chinese names are often reversed for the benefit of *weiguoren*—foreigners. For example, "Li" is a common Chinese last name, so if you see "Li Dan," it's "Mr. Li." But if it's "Dan Li"—and certainly if it's been Westernized into "Dan Lee"—he's already a step or two ahead of you, and it's still "Mr. Li" (or Lee). Less widely known is that the same can also occur in Hungarian. For example, "Bartók Béla" for Béla Bartók.

If in doubt, fall back on the ever-safe "Dear Sir" or "Dear Madam"—"Hi" is by now becoming fairly accepted, although "Hello" is a safer bet. Or use email, where salutations are not expected but "Hi" is largely accepted. Avoid first names, too, especially for recipients outside the United States. However, if you know the recipient is an amateur radio operator ("ham")—and especially if you're a fellow ham—you can use the first name if you also include ham call letters in the address; e.g. Norman Gorman, WA3CRN, Station Engineer.

Be patient, as replies by post take weeks, sometimes months. Slow responders, those that tend to take many months to reply, are cited in Addresses PLUS. Erratic repliers, too.

Rádio Caiari, Rua das Crianças 4646, Bairro Areal da Floresta, 78912-210 Porto Velho RO, Brazil. Phone: (studio) +55 (69) 3227-2277, +55 (69) 3216-0707; Phone/Fax: (Commercial Dept.) +55 (69) 3210-3621. Email: comercialcaiari@gmail.com; or online form. Web: www.radiocaiari.com.br. Contact: Fábio Hecktheuer, Diretor Geral; José Maria Llamazares, Diretor Administrativo. Free stickers. Return postage helpful. Replies irregularly to correspondence in Portuguese.

Rádio Canção Nova, Caixa Postal 57, 12630-000 Cachoeira Paulista SP, Brazil; (street address) Fundação João Paulo II s/n, Alto da Bela Vista, 12630-000 Cachoeira Paulista SP, Brazil. Phone: (studio) +55 (12) 3186-2046. Fax: (general) +55 (12) 3186 2022. Email: (general) radio@cancaonova.com; (reception reports) dx@cancaonova.com. Web: (includes streaming audio) www.cancaonova.com/portal/canais/radio. Free stickers, pennants and station brochure sometimes sent on request. May send magazines. $1 helpful.

Rádio Capixaba, Caixa Postal 509, 29000-000 Vitória ES, Brazil; (street address) Av. Santo Antônio 366, 29025-000 Vitória ES, Brazil. Email: radiocap@terra.com.br. Web: (includes streaming audio) www.radiocapixaba.com.br Contact: Jairo Gouvea Maia, Diretor; Sr. Sardinha, Técnico. Replies occasionally to correspondence in Portuguese.

Rádio Clube do Pará, Av. Almirante Barroso 2190 - 3° andar, Marco, 66095-020 Belém PA, Brazil. Phone/Fax: +55 (91) 3084-0100/111/112. Email: clubedamanha@radioclubedopara.com.br. Web: (includes on-demand and streaming audio) www.radioclubedopara.com.br. Contact: Geraldo Camilo Centeno, Diretor. Replies to correspondence in Portuguese or English, and verifies reception reports. Free stickers, postcards and occasional T-shirt.

Radio Clube Paranaense, Rua Rockefeller 1311, Rebouças, 80230-130 Curitiba PR, Brazil; (alternative address) Rua Amauri Lange Silvério 300, Pilarzinho, Curitiba PR, Brazil. Phone: +55 (41) 3271-4700. Email: online form. Web: (streaming audio and online email form only) www.clubeb2.com.br. Contact: Toni Casagrande, Diretor; Vicente Mickosz, Superintendente.

Rádio Congonhas, Praça da Basílica 130, 36404-000 Congonhas MG, Brazil. Phone: +55 (31) 3731-9000. Replies to correspondence in Portuguese. Free stickers.

Rádio Cultura Araraquara, Avenida Bento de Abreu 789, Bairro Fonte Luminosa, 14802-396 Araraquara SP, Brazil. Phone: +55 (16) 3303-7799. Fax: +55 (16) 3303 7792. Email: (administration) cultura@radiocultura.net; (listener feedback) ouvintes@radiocultura.net; (Wagner Luiz) wagner@radiocultura.net. Web: (includes streaming audio and online email form) www.radiocultura.net. Contact: Wagner Luiz, Diretor Artístico. Return postage required. Replies slowly to correspondence in Portuguese.

Rádio Cultura Filadélfia, Avenida Brasil 531, Sala 74, 85851-000 Foz do Iguaçu PR, Brazil. Phone/Fax: +55 (45) 3572-2410. Email: radioculturamorenafiladelfia@gmail.com. Web: (includes streaming audio) www.radiofiladelfia.com.br. Contact: Francisco Pires dos Santos, Diretor Administrativo; Julia Beatriz Som, Coordenadora de Programação; Davi Campos, Locutor. Replies irregularly to correspondence in Portuguese.

Rádio Cultura Ondas Tropicais, Rua Barcelos s/n, Praça 14 de Janeiro, 69020-200 ManausAM, Brazil. Phone: +55 (92) 2101-4967, +55 (92) 2101-4953. Fax: +55 (92) 2101 4950. Email: radiocultura@hotmail.com. Contact: Maria Jerusalem dos Santos (also known as Jerusa Santos), Diretora. Replies to correspondence in Portuguese. Return postage appreciated. Station is part of the FUNTEC (Fundação Televisão e Rádio Cultura do Amazonas) network.

Rádio Cultura São Paulo, Rua Vladimir Herzog 75, Água Branca, 05036-900 São Paulo SP, Brazil; or Caixa Postal 11544, 05049-970 São Paulo SP, Brazil. Phone: (general) +55 (11) 3874-3122; (Cultura AM) +55 (11) 3874-3081; (Cultura FM) +55 (11) 3874-3092. Fax: +55 (11) 3611 2014. Email: (Cultura AM, relayed on 9615 and 17815 kHz) falecom@radiocultura.am.br; (Cultura FM, relayed on 6170 kHz) falecom@radioculturasp.fm.br. Web: (includes streaming audio) www.tvcultura.com.br. Contact: Eduardo Weber, Coordenador de Produção Cultura AM; (technical) José Chaves Felippe de Oliveira, Diretor de Engenharia. $1 or return postage required. Replies slowly to postal correspondence in Portuguese.

Rádio Difusora Acreana, Rua Benjamin Constant 1232, Centro, 69900-161 Rio Branco AC, Brazil. Phone: +55 (68) 3223-9696. Fax: +55 (68) 3223 8610. Email: comercialdifusora@ac.gov.br; producao.difusora@ac.gov.br. Web: (streaming audio only) www.ac.gov.br/difusora.htm. Contact: Jorge Henrique Queiroz, Diretor. Replies irregularly to correspondence in Portuguese.

Rádio Difusora Cáceres, Rua Tiradentes 979, Centro, 78200-000 Cáceres MT, Brazil. Phone: +55 (65) 3223-3830, +55 (65) 3223-3820, +55 (65) 3223-5984. Phone/Fax: +55 (65) 3223-5986. Web: (includes streaming audio) www.difusoracaceres.com.br. Contact: Sra. Maridalva Amaral Vignard. $1 or return postage required. Replies occasionally to correspondence in Portuguese.

Rádio Difusora de Londrina, Caixa Postal 916, 86000-000 Londrina PR, Brazil; (street address) Rua Sergipe, 843 – Sala 05, 86010-360 Londrina PR, Brazil. Phone: +55 (43) 3322-1105; Phone/fax: +55 (43) 3324-7369. Email: online form. Web: (includes streaming audio) www.radiodifusoradelondrina.com.br. Contact: Oscar Simões, Diretor. Free tourist brochure, which sometimes seconds as a verification. $1 or return postage helpful. Replies irregularly to correspondence in Portuguese.

Rádio Difusora de Macapá, Rua Cândido Mendes 525, Centro, 68900-100 Macapá AP, Brazil. Phone: +55 (96) 3212-1123. Fax: +55 (96) 3212 1111. Email: difusoramcp@yahoo.com.br; jornalismo@rdm.ap.gov.br. Contact: Carlos Luiz Pereira Marques, Diretor. $1 or return postage required. Replies irregularly to correspondence in Portuguese or English. Sometimes sends stickers, key rings and—on rare occasions—T-shirts.

Rádio Difusora do Amazonas, Av. Eduardo Ribeiro 639 - 20° andar, Centro, 69010-001 Manaus AM, Brazil. Phone: +55 (92) 3633-1001. Fax: +55 (92) 3234 3750. Email: fesinha@uol.com.br; difusora@internext.com.br. Web: (includes streaming audio) www.difusoramanaus.com.br. Contact: Josué Filho, Diretor. Replies to correspondence in Portuguese. $1 or return postage helpful.

Rádio Difusora Roraima, Avenida Capitão Ene Garcez 888, São Francisco, 69301-160 Boa Vista RR, Brazil.

Phone/Fax: +55 (95) 3623-2259, +55 (95) 3623-2131, +55 (95) 3624-1700. Email: direcao@radiororaima.com.br. Web: (includes on-demand and streaming audio) www.radiororaima.com.br. Contact: Barbosa Júnior, Diretor. Return postage required. Replies occasionally to correspondence in Portuguese.

Rádio Difusora Taubaté (if reactivated), Rua Dr. Sousa Alves 960, 12020-030 Taubaté SP, Brazil. Contact: Emilio Amadei Beringhs Neto, Diretor Superintendente. May send free stickers, pens, keychains and T-shirts. Return postage or $1 helpful.

Rádio Educação Rural de Coari, Praça São Sebastião 228, 69460-000 Coari AM, Brazil. Phone: +55 (97) 3561-2474. Email: radiocoari@hotmail.com. Contact: João Batista de Almeida. $1 or return postage helpful. Replies irregularly to correspondence in Portuguese.

Rádio Educação Rural de Tefé, Caixa Postal 21, 69470-000 Tefé AM, Brazil. Phone: +55 (97) 3343-3017. Fax: +55 (97) 3343-2663. Email: rert@osite.com.br. Contact: Thomas Schwamborn, Diretor Administrativo. Verifies reception reports.

Rádio Educadora 6 de Agosto, Rua Coronel Brandão 1665, Bairro Aeroporto, 69930-000 Xapuri AC, Brazil. Phone: +55 (68) 3542-2830, +55 (68) 3542-3256. Email: raimari.cardoso@hotmail.com; educadora-xp@hotmail.com. Contact: Raimari Sombra Cardoso, Coordenador. Replies to correspondence in Portuguese.

Rádio Educativa 6 de Agosto—*see* Rádio Educadora 6 de Agosto, above.

Rádio Educadora (Bragança), Praça das Bandeiras s/n, 68600-000 Bragança PA, Brazil. Phone: +55 (91) 3425-1429. Email: fec@fundacaoeducadora.com.br. Web: (includes streaming audio) www.fundacaoeducadora.com.br. Contact: Pe. Maurício Soares de Souza, Presidente. $1 or return postage required. Replies to correspondence in Portuguese.

Rádio Educadora (Guajará Mirim), Praça Mário Corrêa No.90, 78957-000 Guajará Mirim RO, Brazil. Phone: Phone/Fax: +55 (69) 3541-6333. Email: radio.educadora@uol.com.br; radio-educadora@gm-net.com.br. Web: www.brasilcatolico.com.br/cursos/radiohome2.htm. Contact: José Hélio, Diretor. Return postage helpful. Replies to correspondence in Portuguese.

Rádio Educadora (Limeira), Rua Profesora Maria Aparecida Martinelli Faveri 988, Jardim Elisa Fumagalli, 13485-316 Limeira SP, Brazil. Phone: (listener feedback) +55 (19) 3441-3710. Email: (general) radio@educadoraam.com.br; (Bortolan) bab@zaz.com.br. Web: (includes streaming audio) www.educadoraam.com.br. Contact: Bruno Arcaro Bortolan, Gerente; Rosemary Ap. Giratto, Secretária Administrativa. Free stickers.

Rádio Gaúcha, Avenida Ipiranga 1075 - 3° andar, Bairro Azenha, 90169-900 Porto Alegre RS, Brazil. Phone: +55 (51) 3218-6600. Fax: +55 (51) 3218 6680. Email: (listener feedback) reportagem@rdgaucha.com.br; online form; (technical) gaucha@rdgaucha.com.br; (Klein) caio.klein@rdgaucha.com.br. Web: (includes streaming audio) www.rdgaucha.com.br. Contact: Caio Klein, Gerente Técnico. Replies irregularly to correspondence, preferably in Portuguese. Reception reports should be sent to the attention of "Eng. Caio Klein" at the station address above.

Rádio Gazeta, Avenida Paulista 900 -3° andar, Bairro Bela Vista, 01310-940 São Paulo SP, Brazil. Phone/Fax: +55 (11) 3170-5828. Email: fuba@radiogazeta.com.br; comercial@radiogazeta.com.br. Web: (includes streaming audio) www.radiogazeta.com.br. Contact: Benedito Leite da Costa, Supervisor de Operações. Free stickers. $1 or return postage necessary. Replies to correspondence in Portuguese.

Rádio Globo (Rio de Janeiro), Rua do Russel 434, Glória, 22210-210 Rio de Janeiro RJ, Brazil. Phone: +55 (21) 2555-8282. Fax: +55 (21) 2558 6385. Email: online form; (administration) gerenciaamrio@radioglobo.com.br; (technical, Küssler) gilberto.kussler@sgr.com.br. Web: (includes on-demand and streaming audio) http://radioclick.globo.com/globobrasil. Contact: Gilberto Küssler, Gerente Técnico. Rarely replies to correspondence, but try sending reception reports, in Portuguese, to Gilberto Küssler. Return postage helpful.

Rádio Globo (São Paulo), Rua das Palmeiras 315, Santa Cecilia, 01226-901 São Paulo SP, Brazil. Phone: +55 (11) 3824-3217. Fax: +55 (11) 3824 3210. Web: (includes streaming audio) http://radioclick.globo.com/globobrasil. Contact: (nontechnical) Paulo Novis, Diretor Geral; (technical) Roberto Cidade, Gerente Técnico. Replies occasionally to correspondence in Portuguese.

Rádio Globo Manaus, Av. Tefé 3025, Japiim, 69078-000 Manaus AM, Brazil. Phone: +55 (92) 2101-5541, +55 (92)

2101-5544. Phone/Fax: +55 (92) 2101-5543. Email: kandrade@radioglobomanaus.com.br; katia0392@hotmail.com. Web: www.radioglobomanaus.com.br (or www.radiobare.com.br). Contact: Kátia Cilene. Replies to correspondence in Portuguese. Formerly known as Rádio Baré.

Rádio Globo Santos, Rua José Vaz Porto 175, Vila Santa Rosa, 11431-190 Guarujá SP, Brazil. Phone: (Departamento Comercial) +55 (13) 3269-1010; (listener feedback) +55 (13) 3261-4100. Web: www.radioguarujaam.com.br. Formerly Rádio Guarujá Paulista.

Rádio Guaíba, Rua Caldas Júnior 219 - 2° Andar, 90019-900 Porto Alegre RS, Brazil. Phone: +55 (51) 3215-6222. Email: (Departamento Comercial) comerciais@radioguaiba.com.br; (technical) centraltecnica@radioguaiba.com.br; (Nagel) nagel@radioguaiba.com.br. Web: (includes streaming audio) www.radioguaiba.com.br. Contact: Ademar J. Dallanora, Gerente Administrativo; Luciano Nagel, Produtor Executivo. Reception reports are best sent to the attention of Luciano Nagel. Return postage helpful. Free stickers.

Rádio Guarujá, Rua Nunes Machado 94 -Ed. Tiradentes - 8° e 10° andar, Centro, 88010-460 Florianópolis SC, Brazil. Phone/Fax: +55 (48) 2108-5555. Email: online form. Web: (includes streaming audio) www.radioguaruja.com.br. Contact: Mario Silva, Diretor; Carlos Alberto Silva, Exec. de Contas. Return postage required. Replies irregularly to correspondence in Portuguese.

Rádio Imaculada Conceição, Avenida Mato Grosso 530, Centro, 79002-906 Campo Grande MS, Brazil. Phone: +55 (67) 3384-3164, +55 (67) 3382-2238, +55 (67) 3384-3345. E-mail: 580am@miliciadaimaculada.org.br. Web: (includes streaming audio from key network station in São Bernardo do Campo and which is mostly relayed by the Campo Grande station) www.miliciadaimaculada.org.br/v2/Rural580.asp. $1 or return postage required. Replies to correspondence in Portuguese.

Rádio Inconfidência, Avenida Raja Gabáglia 1666, Santa Lúcia, 30350-540 Belo Horizonte MG, Brazil. Phone: +55 (31) 3297-7344, +55 (31) 3297-5803; (transmitter site) +55 (31) 3394-1388. Fax: +55 (31) 3298 3400. Email: (general) faleconosco@inconfidencia.com.br; (technical) engenharia@inconfidencia.com.br; (reception reports) diretoriatecnica@inconfidencia.com.br. Web: (includes streaming audio) www.inconfidencia.com.br. Contact: Isaias Lansky, Diretor; Manuel Emilio de Lima Torres, Diretor Superintendente; Jairo Antolio Lima, Diretor Artístico; Eugenio Silva; (technical) Mário Veras Júnior, Diretor Técnico. Free stickers and postcards. May send CD of Brazilian music. $1 or return postage helpful.

Rádio Integração (if reactivated), Rua de Alagoas 270, Colégio, 69980-000 Cruzeiro do Sul AC, Brazil. Phone: +55 (68) 3322-4637. Fax: +55 (68) 3322 6511. Contact: Francisco Melo, Diretor. Return postage helpful.

Rádio Itatiaia, Rua Itatiaia 117, Bonfim, 31210-170 Belo Horizonte MG, Brazil. Phone: +55 (31) 2105 3588. Fax: +55 (31) 2105 3613. Email: itatiaia@itatiaia.com.br. Web: (includes on-demand and streaming audio) www.itatiaia.com.br. Contact: Lúcia Araújo Bessa, Assistente da Diretória; Claudio Carneiro.

Rádio Jornal "A Crítica" (if reactivated), Av. André Araujo 1024A, Aleixo, 69060-001 Manaus AM, Brazil. Phone: +55 (92) 2123-1039. Email: walteryallas@acritica.com.br. Contact: Walter Yallas.

Rádio Marumby, Avenida Paraná 1885, 82510-000 Curitiba PR, Brazil. Phone: +55 (41) 3257-2410. Phone/Fax: +55 (41) 3257-4109. Email: radio@radioevangelismo.com. Web: (includes on-demand and streaming audio) www.radiomarumby.com.br. Contact: João Falavinha Ienzen, Gerente. $1 or return postage required. Replies irregularly to correspondence in Portuguese. Formerly known as Rádio Novas de Paz.

Rádio Meteorologia Paulista, Rua Capitão João Marques 89, Jardim Centenário, 14940-000 Ibitinga, São Paulo SP, Brazil; or Caixa Postal 91, 14940-000 Ibitinga SP, Brazil. Phone: +55 (16) 3341-9900, +55 (16) 3341-9909. Email: radio.ibitinga@ibinet.com.br. Web: (includes streaming audio) www.radioibitinga.com.br. Contact: Roque de Rosa, Diretor. Replies to correspondence in Portuguese. $1 or return postage required.

Rádio Missões da Amazônia, Travessa Dr. Lauro Sodré 299, 68250-000 Óbidos PA, Brazil. Phone/Fax: +55 (93) 3547-1699. Web: www.kaleb.hpg.ig.com.br. Return postage required. Replies occasionally to correspondence in Portuguese.

Rádio Mundial, Av. Paulista 2198-Térreo, Cerqueira César, 01310-300 São Paulo SP, Brazil. Phone: +55 (11) 3016 5999. Email: (general) online form; radiomundial@radiomundial.com.br; (Departamento Comercial) comercial@radiomundial.com.br. Web: (includes on-demand and streaming audio) www.radiomundial.com.br. Contact: (nontechnical) Luci Rothschild de Abreu, Diretora Geral; Mirian Morato, Diretora Comercial. *REDE MUNDIAL DE COMUNICAÇÃO PARENT ORGANIZATION:* Av. Paulista, 2200 - 14° andar, Cerqueira César, 01310-300 São Paulo SP, Brazil. Phone: +55 (11) 3016 5999. Fax: +55 (11) 3016 5980. Email: comercial@mundialcomunicacao.com.br. Web: www.mundialcomunicacao.com.br.

Rádio Municipal, Avenida Álvaro Maia s/n, 69750-000 São Gabriel da Cachoeira AM, Brazil. Phone/Fax: +55 (97) 3471-1768. Email: rmunicipalsgc@yahoo.com.br. Contact: Rosane da Conceição Rodrigues Neto, Diretora. Return postage necessary. Replies to correspondence in Portuguese. Formerly Rádio Nacional de São Gabriel da Cachoeira, prior to the station's transfer from Radiobrás to the local municipality.

Rádio Nacional da Amazônia, SCRN 702/703 - Bloco B, Edif. Radiobrás, 70323-900 Brasília-DF, Brazil. Phone: +55 (61) 3327-4380, +55 (61) 3327-4300. Email: faleconosco@radiobras.gov.br; (listener feedback) centraldoouvinte@radiobras.gov.br. Web: (includes streaming audio) www.radiobras.gov.br/estatico/radio_nacional_amazonia.htm (if that fails, go to www.radiobras.gov.br and click on "Rádio Nacional da Amazônia"). Contact: (technical) Taís Ladeira de Madeiros, Chefe da Divisão de Ondas Curtas da Radiobrás. Free stickers. Will sometimes verify reception reports if a prepared card is included.

Rádio Novas de Paz—*see* Rádio Marumby, above.

Rádio Novo Tempo, Rua Amando de Oliveira 135, Bairro Amambaí, 79005-380 Campo Grande MS, Brazil. Phone: +55 (67) 3325-0630. Fax: +55 (67) 3324 8577. Email: (general) online form; (Saraiva) ivan.saraiva@ucob.org.br. Web: (includes streaming audio) www.radionovotempo.org.br (if it doesn't work, go to www.asm.org.br and click on "Rádio Novo Tempo"). Contact: Pr. Iván Saraiva, Diretor Geral. Return postage required. Replies to correspondence in Portuguese and verifies reception reports. Free stickers. A station of the Seventh Day Adventists.

Rádio Pioneira de Teresina, Rua 24 de Janeiro 150 sul, 64001-230 Teresina PI, Brazil. Phone: +55 (86) 2107-8121. Fax: +55 (86) 2107 8122. Email: rosemiro@radiopioneira.am.br. Web: (includes streaming audio) www.radiopioneira.am.br. Contact: Rosemiro Robinson da Costa. $1 or return postage required. Replies slowly to correspondence in Portuguese.

Rádio Record, Rua da Várzea 240, 01140-080 São Paulo SP, Brazil. Phone: (listener feedback) +55 (11) 3661-6727, +55 (11) 3661-6737. Fax: (listener feedback) +55 (11) 2184-4971. Email: online form; radiorecord@rederecord.com.br. Web: (includes on-demand and streaming audio) www.radiorecord.com.br. Contact: Mário Luíz Catto, Diretor Geral; Antonio Carlos Miranda. Free stickers. Return postage or $1 required. Replies occasionally to correspondence in Portuguese.

Rádio Relógio, Rua Paramopama 131, Ribeira, Ilha do Governador, 21930-110 Rio de Janeiro RJ, Brazil. Phone: +55 (21) 2467-0201. Fax: +55 (21) 2467 4656. Email: radiorelogio@ig.com.br. Contact: Olindo Coutinho, Diretor Geral; Renato Castro. Replies occasionally to correspondence in Portuguese.

Rádio Rio Mar, Rua José Clemente 500, Centro, 69010-070 Manaus AM, Brazil. Phone: +55 (92) 3633-2295. Fax: +55 (92) 3232 7763. Email: decom@click21.com.br. Web: (includes streaming audio) www.riomaronline.com.br. Contact: Martin James Lauman, Superintendente. Replies to correspondence in Portuguese. $1 or return postage helpful.

Rádio Roraima—*see* Rádio Difusora Roraima.

Rádio Rural (Petrolina) (if reactivated), Caixa Postal 8, 56300-000 Petrolina PE, Brazil. Phone: +55 (87) 3861-2874, +55 (87) 3862-1522. Email: emissoraruraI@silcons.com.br. Contact: Padre Bianchi, Gerente; Maria Letecia de Andrade Nunes. Return postage necessary. Replies to correspondence in Portuguese.

Rádio Rural (Santarém), Avenida São Sebastião 622 - Bloco A, 68005-090 Santarém PA, Brazil. Phone: +55 (93) 3523-1006. Phone/Fax: +55 (93) 3523-2685. Email: edilrural@gmail.com; rural@radioruraldesantarem.com.br. Web: (includes streaming audio) www.radioruraldesantarem.com.br; (under construction) http://radiorural.v10.com.br. Contact: Edilberto Moura Sena, Coordenador Geral. Replies slowly to correspondence in Portuguese. Free stickers. Return postage or $1 required.

Rádio Senado, Praça dos Três Poderes, Anexo II - Bloco B - Térreo, 70165-900 Brasília DF, Brazil. Phone: (general) +55 (61) 3311-1237; (administration) +55 (61) 3311-4691; (director) +55 (61) 3311-1236; (technical) +55 (61) 3311-1285; (shortwave department) +55 (61) 3311-1277. Fax: (general) +55 (61) 3311 4238. Email: (general) radio@senado.gov.br; (Radio Senado Shortwave) ondascurtas@senado.gov.br; (Fabiano) max@senado.gov.br. Web: (includes streaming audio from FM Service, partly relayed on shortwave) www.senado.gov.br/radio/ondascurtas.asp. Contact: Max Fabiano, Diretor; (technical) José Carlos Sigmaringa Seixas, Coordenador do Núcleo de Ondas Curtas.

Rádio Trans Mundial, Caixa Postal 18300, 04626-970 São Paulo SP, Brazil; (street address) Rua Épiro 110, 04635-030 São Paulo SP, Brazil. Phone/Fax: +55 (11) 5031-3533. Email: (general) rtm@transmundial.com.br; (technical) tecnica@transmundial.com.br; ("Amigos do Rádio" DX-program) amigosdoradio@transmundial.com.br. Web: (includes on-demand and streaming audio) www.transmundial.com.br. Contact: José Carlos de Santos, Diretor; Samuel Matos, Diretor Técnico; Rudolf Grimm, programa "Amigos do Rádio." Free stickers, postcards, bookmarkers or other small gifts. Sells religious books and CDs of religious music (from hymns to bossa nova). Prices, in local currency, can be found at the Website (click on "Publicações"). Programming comes from São Paulo, but transmitter site is located in Santa Maria, Rio Grande do Sul.

Rádio Tupi, Rua João Negrão 595, Centro, 80010-200, Curitiba PR, Brazil. Phone: +55 (41) 3323-1353. Contact: (technical) Eng. Latuf Aurani (who is based in São Paulo). Relays "Voz de Libertação" (*see*). Rarely replies, and only to correspondence in Portuguese.

Rádio Vale do Xingu, Rua 1° de Janeiro 1359, Catedral, 68371-020 Altamira PA, Brazil. Phone/Fax: +55 (93) 3515-1182, +55 (93) 3515-4899, +55 (93) 3515-4411. Email: producao@valedoxingu.com.br. Contact: Ana Claudia Barros, Diretora.

Rádio Verdes Florestas, Fundação Verdes Florestas, Travessa Mário Lobão 81, 69980-000 Cruzeiro do Sul AC, Brazil; (transmitter location) Estrado do Aeroporto, km 02, Bairro Nossa Senhora das Graças, Cruzeiro do Sul AC, Brazil. Phone/Fax: +55 (68) 3322-3309, +55 (68) 3322-2634. Email: verdesflorestas@yahoo.com.br. Contact: José Graci Soares Rezende. Return postage required. Replies occasionally to correspondence in Portuguese.

Rádio Voz do Coração Imaculado (when operating), Rua Barão de Cotegipe s/n, Centro, 75001-970 Anápolis GO, Brazil. Contact: Padre Domingos M. Esposito. Operation tends to be irregular, as the station is funded entirely from religious donations.

RádioVoz Missionária, Caixa Postal 2004, 88340-000 Camboriú SC, Brazil. Phone: +55 (47) 3261-3209, +55 (47) 3261-3207. Email:programavozmissionaria@hotmail.com. Web: (streaming audio only) www.gideoes.com/aovivo/radioaovivo.htm. $1 or return postage required. Free diploma and stickers. Replies to correspondence in Portuguese.

GMUH MISSIONARY PARENT ORGANIZATION: Gideões Missionários da Última Hora—GMUH, Rua Joaquim Nunes 244, 88340-000 Camboriú SC, Brazil; (postal address) Caixa Postal 2004, 88340-000 Camboriú SC, Brazil. Phone: +55 (47) 3261-3232. Email: gmuh@gmuh.com.br; bete@gmuh.com.br. Web: www.gmuh.com.br.

Super Rádio Alvorada —*see* Rádio Alvorada (Rio Branco).

Voz de Libertação. Ubiquitous programming originating from the "Deus é Amor" Pentecostal church's Rádio Universo (1300 kHz) in São Bernardo do Campo, São Paulo, and aired over several shortwave stations, especially Rádio Tupi, Curitiba (*see*). Streaming audio is available at the "Deus é Amor" Website, www.ipda.org.br.

Voz do Coração Imaculado—*see* Rádio Voz do Coração Imaculado.

Voz Missionária—*see* RádioVoz Missionária.

BRITISH INDIAN OCEAN TERRITORY World Time +6

AFRTS-American Forces Radio and Television Service (Shortwave), Naval Media Center, PSC 466 Box 14, FPO AP 96595-0014 USA. Phone: +246 370-3680. Fax: +246 370 3681. Replies irregularly.

BULGARIA World Time +2 (+3 midyear)

Radio Bulgaria
NONTECHNICAL AND TECHNICAL: P.O. Box 900, 1000 Sofia, Bulgaria; or (street address) 4 Dragan Tsankov Blvd., 1040 Sofia, Bulgaria. Phone: (general) +359 (2) 933-6633; (English Service) +359 (2) 933-6505, +359 (2) 933-6661, +359 (2) 933-6663, +359 (2) 933-6257; (French Service) +359 (2) 933-6662; (German Service) +359 (2) 933-6660; (Spanish Service) +359 (2) 933-6678, +359 (2) 933-6397; (Nedyalkov) +359 (2) 933 6733. Fax: +359 (2) 865 0560. Email: (English program and schedule information) english@bnr.bg (same format for other languages, e.g. french@ . . .; spanish@ . . .); (Nedyalkov) nedyalkov@bnr.bg. Web: (includes online reception report form, on-demand audio, plus streaming audio from domestice services not aired on shortwave) www.bnr.bg. Contact: (general) Mrs. Iva Delcheva, English Section; Svilen Stoicheff, Head of English Section; Ludmila Petra, Spanish Section; (administration and technical) Angel H. Nedyalkov, Director. Replies regularly, but sometimes slowly. Return postage helpful but IRCs may no longer be accepted. Verifies email reports with QSL cards. For concerns about frequency usage, contact Mr. Nedyalkov of Radio Bulgaria.
TRANSMISSION COMPANY: Bulgarian Telecommunications Company (BTC), Ltd., 8 Totleben Blvd., 1606 Sofia, Bulgaria. Phone: +359 (2) 949-4444, +359 (2) 951-5066. Fax: +359 (2) 954 9780. Contact: Roumen Petkov, Frequency Manager; Mrs. Margarita Krasteva, Radio Regulatory Department.
Radio Varna, 22 Primorski blvd, 9000 Varna, Bulgaria. Phone: +359 (52) 602-802. Fax: +359 (52) 664 411. Email: bnr@radiovarna.com. Web: (includes on-demand and streaming audio from the domestic service, not aired on shortwave) www.radiovarna.com. Contact: (technical) Kostadin Kovachev, Chief Engineer.

BURKINA FASO World Time exactly

Radiodiffusion du Burkina, 03 BP 7029, Ouagadougou 03, Burkina Faso. Phone: +226 5032-4302/03, +226 5032-4398. Fax: +226 5031 0441. Email: radio@rtb.bf; (Goba) nadowo2002@yahoo.fr. Web: (includes streaming audio) www.radio.bf. Contact: Pascal Goba, Chef des Programmes. Replies to correspondence in French. IRC or return postage helpful.

BURMA—*see* MYANMAR.

CAMEROON World Time +1

Cameroon Radio Television Corporation (CRTV)—Buea (when operating), P.M.B. Buea (Sud-Ouest), Cameroon. Phone: +237 3332-2525, +237 3332-2615. Email: crtvsudouest@crtv.cm.

Voice of the Gospel, Sawtu Linjila Radio Ministry, B.P. 02, Ngaoundéré, Cameroon. Airs via facilities of Germany's Media Broadcast (*see*).
ADDRESS FOR RECEPTION REPORTS: Lutheran World Federation, 150, route de Ferney, [or P.O. Box 2100], CH-1211 Geneva 2, Switzerland. Phone: +41 (22) 791-6111. Fax: +41 (22) 791 6630. Email: info@lutheranworld.org. Web: www. lutheranworld.org. Contact: Jukka Latva-Hakuni, Media Consultant. Email reports are verified by postal mail.

CANADA World Time -3:30 (-2:30 midyear) Newfoundland; -4 (-3 midyear) Atlantic; -5 (-4 midyear) Eastern, including Québec and Ontario; -6 (-5 midyear) Central; except Saskatchewan; -6 Saskatchewan; -7 (-6 midyear) Mountain; -8 (-7 midyear) Pacific, including Yukon.

Canadian Broadcasting Corporation (CBC)—English Programs, P.O. Box 500, Station A, Toronto, Ontario, M5W 1E6, Canada. Phone: (toll-free, Canada only) +1 (866) 306-4636; (Audience Relations) +1 (416) 205-3700. Email: cbcinput@toronto.cbc.ca. Web: (includes on-demand and streaming audio) www.radio.cbc.ca.
LONDON NEWS BUREAU: CBC, 43-51 Great Titchfield Street, London W1P 8DD, United Kingdom. Phone: +44 (20) 7412-9200. Fax: +44 (20) 7631 3095.
PARIS NEWS BUREAU: CBC, 17 avenue Matignon, F-75008 Paris, France. Phone: +33 (1) 4421-1515. Fax: +33 (1) 4421 1514.
WASHINGTON NEWS BUREAU: CBC, National Press Building, Suite 500, 529 14th Street NW, Washington DC 20045 USA. Phone: +1 (202) 383-2900.
Canadian Broadcasting Corporation (CBC)—French Programs, Société Radio-Canada, C.P. 6000, succ. centre-ville, Montréal, Québec, H3C 3A8, Canada. Phone: (Audience Relations) +1 (514) 597-6000. Web: (includes on-demand and streaming audio) www.radio-canada.ca. Welcomes correspondence, but may not reply due to shortage of staff.
CBC Northern Québec Shortwave Service—*see* Radio Canada International, below.
CFRX-CFRB
MAIN ADDRESS: 2 St. Clair Avenue West, Toronto, Ontario, M4V 1L6, Canada. Phone:(main switchboard) +1 (416) 924-5711; (talk shows switchboard) +1 (416) 872-1010; (news centre) +1 (416) 924-6717. Fax: (main fax line) +1 (416) 872 8683; (CFRB news fax line) +1 (416) 323 6816. Email: (comments on programs) cfrbcomments@cfrb.com; (general, nontechnical) info@cfrb.com; opsmngr@cfrb.com. Web: (includes on-demand and streaming audio) www.cfrb.com. Contact: (nontechnical) Pat Holliday, General Manager; Carlo Massaro, Information Officer; Steve Kowch, Operations Manager; (technical) Ian Sharp, Engineer. Reception reports should be sent to the verification address, below.
VERIFICATION ADDRESS: Ontario DX Association, 155 Main St. N., Apt. 313, Newmarket, Ontario, L3Y 8C2, Canada. Email: odxa@rogers.com; (Canney) Steve.Canney@cfrb.com. Web: www.odxa.on.ca. Contact: Steve Canney, VA3SC.
CFVP-CKMX, Classic Country AM 1060, 1110 Centre St. NE, Calgary, Alberta, T2E 2R2, Canada. Phone: (general) +1 (403) 240-5800; (news) +1 (403) 240-5844;

(technical) +1 (403) 240-5867. Fax: (general and technical) +1 (403) 240 5801; (news) +1 (403) 246 7099. Email: (Peacock) tpeacock@radio.astral.com; (Rigel) kennyr@classiccountry.com. Web: (includes streaming audio) www.classiccountryam1060.com. Contact: (general) Tom Peacock, General Manager; Ken Rigel, Program Director; (technical) Ken Pasolli, Technical Director; Richard Luddick, Broadcast Engineer.

CHU. Radio Station CHU, National Research Council of Canada, Bldg M-36, Room 1026, 1200 Montreal Road, Ottawa, Ontario, K1A 0R6, Canada. Phone: +1 (613) 993-3430. Fax: +1 (613) 952 1394. Email: radio.chu@nrc.ca, radiochu@nrc-cnrc.gc.ca, radio.chu.inms@nrc-cnrc.gc.ca; (Pelletier) raymond.pelletier@nrc.cnrc.gc.ca. Web: http://inms-ienm.nrc-cnrc.gc.ca/time_services/shortwave_broadcasts_e.html. Contact: Dr. Rob Douglas; Dr. Jean-Simon Boulanger, Group Leader; Raymond Pelletier, Technical Officer. Official standard frequency and World Time station for Canada on 3330, 7335 and 14670 kHz. Brochure available upon request. Those with a personal computer, Bell 103 compatible modem and appropriate software can get the exact time, from CHU's cesium clock, via the telephone; details available upon request, or direct from the Website. Verifies reception reports (including those sent via email) with a QSL card.

CKZN, CBC Newfoundland and Labrador, P.O. Box 12010, Station 'A', St. John's, Newfoundland, A1B 3T8, Canada. Phone: +1 (709) 576-5155. Fax: +1 (709) 576 5099. Email: (engineer) keith_durnford@cbc.ca. Web: (streaming audio) www.cbc.ca/listen/index.html# (click on "St. John's"). Contact: (general) Heather Elliott, Communications Officer; (technical) Shawn R. Williams, Manager, Transmission and Distribution; Keith Durnford, Supervisor, Transmission Operations; Terry Brett, Transmitter Department; Rosemary Sampson. Free CBC sticker and verification card with the history of Newfoundland included. Don't enclose money, stamps or IRCs with correspondence, as they will only have to be returned. Relays CBN (St. John's, 640 kHz) except at 1000-1330 World Time (one hour earlier in summer) when programming comes from CFGB Goose Bay.

CFGB ADDRESS: CBC Radio, Box 1029 Station C, Happy Valley, Goose Bay, Labrador, Newfoundland A0P 1C0, Canada. Email: (program relayed via CKZN) labmorns@cbc.ca.

CKZU-CBU, CBC, P.O. Box 4600, Vancouver, British Columbia, V6B 4A2, Canada—for verification of reception reports, mark the envelope, "Attention: Engineering." Phone: (general) +1 (604) 662-6000; (toll-free, U.S. and Canada only) 1-800-961-6161; (engineering) +1 (604) 662-6060. Fax: +1 (604) 662 6350. Email: (general) webmaster@vancouver.cbc.ca; (Newbury) newburyd@vancouver.cbc.ca. Web: (streaming audio) www.cbc.ca/bc (click on "690 AM Vancouver"); or www.cbc.ca/listen/index.html# (click on "Vancouver"). Contact: (general) Public Relations; (technical) Dave Newbury, Transmission Engineer.

Église du Christ, C.P. 2026, Jonquière, Québec, G7X 7X6, Canada. Phone: +1 (514) 387-6163, +1 (418) 695-3192. Fax: +1 (514) 387-1153. E-mail: egliseduchrist@videotron.ca; egliseduchrist@qc.aira.com. Contact: Jean Grenier. Broadcasts via a transmitter in the United Kingdom.

High Adventure Gospel Communication Ministries—*see* Bible Voice Broadcasting, United Kingdom.

Radio Canada International

NOTE: (CBC Northern Québec Service) The following P. O Box 6000 postal address and street address are also valid for the Northern Québec Service, provided that you mention the name of the service and "17th Floor" on the envelope. RCI does not issue technical verifications for Northern Québec Service transmissions. Contact: Nathalie Chamberland.

MAIN OFFICE: P.O. Box 6000, Montréal, Québec, H3C 3A8, Canada; or (street address) 1400 boulevard René-Lévesque Est, Montréal, Québec, H2L 2M2, Canada. Phone: (general) +1 (514) 597-7500; (Audience Relations, Bill Westenhaver) +1 (514) 597-5899; (Listener Response phone number, English/French) +1 (514) 528-8821 (collect calls not accepted). Fax: (Audience Relations) +1 (514) 597 7760. Email: info@rcinet.ca. Web: (includes online reception report form and on-demand and streaming audio) www.rcinet.ca. Contact: (general and technical verifications) Bill Westenhaver, Audience Relations; (administration) Jean Larin, Director. Free stickers, antenna booklet and lapel pins on request. May send other small gifts.

TRANSMISSION OFFICE, INTERNATIONAL SERVICES, CBC TRANSMISSION: Room B52-70, 1400 boulevard René-Lévesque Est, Montréal, Québec, H2L 2M2, Canada. Phone: +1 (514) 597-7618/19. Fax: +1 (514) 284 2052. Email: master_control@moncton.radio-canada.ca; (Théorêt) gerald_theoret@radio-canada.ca; (Bouliane) jacques_bouliane@radio-canada.ca. Contact: (general) Gérald Théorêt, Frequency Manager, CBC Transmission Management; Jacques Bouliane, Senior Manager, International Services. This office only for informing about transmitter-related problems (interference, modulation quality, etc.), especially by fax or email. Verifications are not given out at this office; requests for verification should be sent to the main office, above.

TRANSMITTER SITE: CBC, P.O. Box 6131, Sackville New Brunswick, E4L 1G6, Canada. Phone: +1 (506) 536-2690/1. Fax: +1 (506) 536 2342. Contact: Raymond Bristol, Sackville Plant Manager, CBC Transmission; Suzanne Gaudet, Sackville Master Control. All correspondence not concerned with transmitting equipment should be directed to the appropriate address in Montréal, above. Free tours given during normal working hours.

MONITORING STATION: P.O. Box 460, Station Main Stittsville, Ontario, K2S 1A6, Canada. Phone: +1 (613) 831-4802. Fax: +1 (613) 831 0343. Email: derek.williams@cbc.ca. Contact: Derek Williams, Manager of Monitoring.

Shortwave Classroom, R. Tait McKenzie Public School, 175 Paterson Street, Almonte, Ontario, K0A 1A0, Canada. Phone: +1 (613) 256-8248. Fax: +1 (613) 256 4791. Contact: Neil Carleton, VE3NCE, Editor & Publisher. *The Shortwave Classroom* newsletter was published three times per year as a nonprofit volunteer project for teachers around the world that use shortwave listening in the classroom, or as a club activity, to teach about global perspectives, media studies, world geography, languages, social studies and other subjects. Although no longer published, a set of back issues with articles and classroom tips from teachers around the globe is available for $10.

CENTRAL AFRICAN REPUBLIC World Time +1

Radio Centrafrique, Radiodiffusion-Télévision Centrafricaine, B.P. 940, Bangui, Central African Republic. Contact: (technical) Directeur des Services Techniques. Replies on rare occasions to correspondence in French. Return postage required.

Radio ICDI, B.P 362, Bangui, Central African Republic. Phone: +236 508 622. Email: info@icdinternational.org; radioicdi@gmail.com; (Mbami) jmbami@icdinternational.org. Web: www.icdinternational.org/radio.html. Contact: Josue Mbami, Directeur. Station is run by Integrated Community Development International (ICDI).

ICDI HEAD OFFICE: ICDI, 3792 N. Oakwood Dr., Warsaw IN 46582 USA. Phone: +1 (574) 527-8920. Fax: +1 (360) 248 2990. Email: (Hocking) jimhocking@icdinternational.org. Contact: Jim Hocking, General Director.

CHAD World Time +1

Radiodiffusion Nationale Tchadienne—N'djamena, B.P. 892, N'Djamena, Chad. Contact: Djimadoum Ngoka Kilamian; Ousmane Mahamat. Two IRCs or return postage required. Replies slowly to correspondence in French.

CHILE World Time –3 (–4 midyear)

CVC A Sua Voz—Portuguese Service of CVC La Voz—*see* next item.

CVC La Voz (formerly Radio Voz Cristiana)

TRANSMISSION FACILITIES: Casilla 395, Talagante, Santiago, Chile. Phone: (engineering) +56 (2) 855-7046. Fax: +56 (2) 855 7053. Email: ondacorta@cvclavoz.cl; (project engineer) antonio@cvclavoz.cl; (operations manager) gisela@cvclavoz.cl. Web: (includes streaming audio) www.cvclavoz.cl. Contact: Antonio Reyes B., Project Engineer; Mathias Svensson, Transmission Engineer; Ms. Gisela Vergara, Operations Manager. Free program and frequency schedules. Sometimes verifies reception reports.

PROGRAM PRODUCTION: P.O. Box 2889, Miami FL 33144 USA; (street address) 15485 Eagle Nest Lane, Suite 220, Miami Lakes FL 33014 USA. Phone: +1 (305) 231-7704; (Portuguese Service) +1 (305) 231-7742. Fax: +1 (305) 231 7447. Email: (Gallardo) jmarkgallardo@vozcristiana.com; (listener feedback) comentarios@cvc.tv. Web: www.vozcristiana.com. Contact: (administration) Juan Mark Gallardo, Director; Valeria Almeida, Gerente de Programación.

ENGINEERING DEPARTMENT: The Pavilion, Manor Drive, Coleshill, West Midlands B46 1DL, United Kingdom. Phone: +44 (1675) 435-500; (Flynn) +44 (1675) 435-502. Fax: +44 (1675) 435 501. Email: (Flynn) andrewflynn@christianvision.com. Contact: Andrew Flynn, Director of International Broadcasting.

VERIFICATIONS, PORTUGUESE DX PROGRAM: "Rádio DX," Caixa Postal 51, 90001-970 Porto Alegre RS, Brazil. Email: radiodx@radiocvc.com. Contact: Célio Romais.

Radio Esperanza (when operating), Calle Luis Durand 3057, Temuco, Chile; or Casilla 830, Temuco, Chile. Phone: +56 (45) 367-071. Phone/Fax: +56 (45) 367 070 [+56 (45) 213-790 may also work]. Contact: Rodolfo Campos, Gerente General. Free pennants, stickers, bookmarks and tourist information. Two IRCs, $1 or 2 U.S. stamps appreciated. Replies, often slowly, to correspondence in Spanish or English.

Radio Parinacota (when operating), Casilla 82, Arica, Chile. Phone: +56 (58) 245-889. Phone/Fax: +56 (58) 245 986. Email: rparinacota@latinmail.com; prensaputre@hotmail.com. Contact: Tomislav Simunovich Gran, Director.

CHINA World Time +8; still nominally +6 ("Urümqi Time") in the Xinjiang Uighur Autonomous Region, but in practice +8 is observed there, as well.

NOTE: If a Chinese regional station does not respond to your correspondence within four months, send your reception reports to China Radio International (*see*) which will verify them. CRI apparently no longer forwards correspondence to regional stations, as it sometimes did in the past.

Central People's Broadcasting Station (CPBS)—China National Radio (Zhongyang Renmin Guangbo Diantai), P.O. Box 4501, Beijing 100866, China. Phone: +86 (10) 8609-2610. Email: cn@cnr.cn; (services for Taiwan) cnrtw@cnrtw.com. Web: (includes on-demand and streaming audio) www.cnr.cn; (services for Taiwan) www.nihaotw.com. Contact: Wang Changquan, Audience Department, China National Radio. Free stickers, pennants and other small souvenirs. Return postage helpful. Responds regularly to correspondence in English or Standard Chinese (Mandarin). Although in recent years this station has officially been called "China National Radio" in English-language documents, all on-air identifications in Standard Chinese continue to be "Zhongyang Renmin Guangbo Dientai" (Central People's Broadcasting Station). To quote from the Website of China's State Administration of Radio, Film and TV: "The station moved to Beijing on March 25, 1949. It was renamed the Central People's Broadcasting Station (it [sic] English name was changed to China National Radio later on) . . ."

China Business Radio. The Second Program of Central People's Broadcasting Station—China National Radio (*see*).

China Huayi Broadcasting Corporation, P.O. Box 251, Fuzhou, Fujian 350001, China. Email: (station) hanyu@chbcnews.com. (Yuan Jia) chrisyuanjia@sohu.com; Web: (includes streaming audio) www.chbcnews.com. Contact: Lin Hai Chun, Announcer; Yuan Jia, Program Manager. Replies to correspondence in English or Chinese.

VERIFICATION OF RECEPTION REPORTS: Although verifications are sometimes received direct from the station, reception reports are best sent to the QSL Manager: Qiao Xiaoli, Fen Jin Xing Cun 3-4-304, Changshu, Jiangsu 215500, China. Email: 2883752@163.com. Recordings accepted, and return postage required for postal reply (IRC or $2US for a QSL card, 2 IRCs or $3US for a QSL folder).

China National Radio—*see* Central People's Broadcasting Station (CPBS), above.

China Radio International, 16A Shijingshan Street, Beijing 100040, China; (English Service) P.O. Box 4216, CRI-2, Beijing 100040 China (other language sections also use this address, but with a different CRI number;

for example, it's CRI-38 for the Spanish Service and CRI-39 for the Portuguese Service). Phone: (Director's office) +86 (10) 6889-1625; (Audience Relations.) +86 (10) 6889-1617, +86 (10) 6889-1652; (English Service) +86 (10) 6889-1465; (English newsroom/current affairs) +86 (10) 6889-1619; (Technical Director) +86 (10) 6609-2577. Fax: (Director's office) +86 (10) 6889 1582; (English Service) +86 (10) 6889 1378, +86 (10) 6889 1379, +86 (10) 6889 1599; (audience relations) +86 (10) 6889 3175; (administration) +86 (10) 6851 3174; (German Service) +86 (10) 6889 2053; (Spanish Service) +86 (10) 6889 1909. Email: (English) crieng@cri.com.cn, yinglian@cri.com.cn, garden@cri.com.cn; (Listener's Liason) gaohuiying@crifm.com; (English, technical, including reception reports) crieng@crifm.com; (Chinese) chn@cri.com.cn; (French) crifra@cri.com.cn; (German) ger@cri.com.cn (*see* also the entry for the Berlin Bureau, below); (Japanese) jap@cri.com.cn; (Portuguese) cripor@cri.com.cn; (Spanish) spa@cri.com.cn. Web: (includes on-demand and streaming audio) www.chinabroadcast.cn. Contact: Yang Lei, Director, English Service; Peichun Li, Deputy Director, English Service; Ms. Wang Anjing, Director of Audience Relations, English Service; Ying Lian, English Service; Gao Huiying, Editor, Listener's Liason; Shang Chunyan, "Listener's Garden"; Yu Meng, Editor; (administration) Li Dan, President, China Radio International; Xia Jixuan, Vice President; Wang Gengnian Director General; Xia Jixuan, Chen Minyi, Chao Tieqi and Wang Dongmei, Deputy Directors, China Radio International; Xin Liancai, Director International Relations, China Radio International. Pennants, stickers, desk calendars, pins, handmade papercuts and free bi-monthly *Messenger* newsletter for loyal listeners. Every year, China Radio International holds contests and quizzes, with the overall winner getting a free trip to China. CRI is also relayed via shortwave transmitters in Albania, Bonaire, Canada, Chile, Cuba, Mali, Russia, South Africa and Spain.

SAN FRANCISCO OFFICE, SCHEDULES: 2654 17th Avenue, San Francisco CA 94116 USA. Phone: +1 (415) 564-9968. Email: GPoppin@aol.com. Contact: George Poppin. This address, a volunteer office, only provides CRI schedules to listeners (return postage not required). All other correspondence should be sent directly to the main office in Beijing.

Fujian People's Broadcasting Station, 2 Gutian Lu, Fuzhou, Fujian 350001, China. $1 or IRC helpful. Contact: Audience Relations Section. Replies irregularly and usually slowly. Prefers correspondence in Chinese.

Gannan People's Broadcasting Station, 49 Renmin Xije, Hezuo Zhen, Xiahe, Gian Su 747000, China. Verifies reception reports written in Chinese or English. Return postage not required.

Guangxi Foreign Broadcasting Station, 75 Min Zu Dadao, Nanning, Guangxi 530022, China. Phone: +86 (771) 585-4181, +86 (771) 585-4352. Email: service@gxradio.com. Web: (includes on-demand and streaming audio) www.gxradio.com/foreignradio/index.asp. Free stickers and handmade papercuts. IRC helpful. Replies irregularly. Broadcasts in Vietnamese and Cantonese to listeners in Vietnam.

Hulunbuir People's Broadcasting Station, 11 Shengli Dajie, Hailar, Hulun Buir, Nei Menggu 021008, China. Phone: +86 (825) 6100-2065. Fax: +86 (825) 6100 2054. Replies in Chinese to correspondence in Chinese or English, and verifies reception reports.

Hunan People's Broadcasting Station, 167 Yuhua Lu, Changsha, Hunan 410007, China. Phone: +86 (731) 554-7202. Fax: +86 (731) 554 7220. Email: hnradio@163.com. Web: (includes on-demand and streaming audio) www.hnradio.com. Rarely replies.

Nei Menggu (Inner Mongolia) People's Broadcasting Station, 19 Xinhua Dajie, Hohhot, Nei Menggu 010058, China. Email: nmrb@nmrb.com.cn. Web: (includes streaming audio) www.nmrb.cn. Replies irregularly, mainly to correspondence in Chinese.

Qinghai People's Broadcasting Station, 96 Kunlun Lu, Xining, Qinghai 810001, China. Email: qhradio@sina.com. Web: (includes streaming audio) www.qhradio.com. Contact: Technical Department. Verifies reception reports in Chinese or English. $1 helpful.

Radio Television Hong Kong, C.P.O Box 70200, Kowloon, Hong Kong, China. Provides weather reports for the South China Sea Yacht Race (*see* www.rhkyc.org.hk./chinacoastraceweek.htm) on 3940 kHz.

CAPE D'AGUILAR HF STATION: P.O. Box 9896, GPO Hong Kong, China. Phone: +852 2888-1128; (station manager) +852 2888-1122; (assistant engineer) +852 2888-1130. Fax: +852 2809 2434. Contact: K.C. Liu, Station Manager; (technical) Lam Chi Keung, Assistant Engineer. Provides transmission facilities for weather reports to the South China Sea Yacht Race (*see*, above).

Shaanxi People's Broadcasting Station, 336 Chang'an Nanlu, Xi'an, Shaanxi 710061, China. Web: (includes streaming audio) www.sxradio.com.cn. Replies irregularly to correspondence in Chinese.

Sichuan People's Broadcasting Station, 119-1 Hongxing Zhonglu, Chengdu, Sichuan 610017, China. Replies occasionally.

Voice of China (Zhonghua zhi Sheng). The First Program of Central People's Broadcasting Station—China National Radio (*see*).

Voice of Jinling (Jinling zhi Sheng), P.O. Box 268, Nanjing, Jiangsu 210002, China; (street address) 8 Si Tze-Tang Lane, Nanjing, Jiangsu 210002, China. Phone: +86 (25) 8465-2900, +86 (25) 8465-2905. Fax: +86 (25) 8441 3235. Email: vojradio@163.com; (Liu) liuruoyi@hotmail.com. Web: www.vojradio.com; (streaming audio) mms://vod.jsgd.com.cn/audio0. Contact: [Ms.] Ruoyi Liu, Announcer/Reporter. Free stickers and calendars, plus Chinese-language color station brochure. Replies to correspondence in Chinese or English. Voice of Jinling is the Taiwan Service of Jiangsu People's Broadcasting Station.

Voice of Pujiang (Pujiang zhi Sheng), Shanghai Media Group, 1376 Hongquiao Road, Shanghai 200051, China. Phone: +86 (21) 6278-8177. Fax: +86 (21) 6208 2847. Web: (Shanghai Media Group parent organization, includes streaming audio from domestic radio) www.china-cbn.com. Replies irregularly to correspondence in Chinese or English.

Voice of the Strait (Haixia zhi Sheng), P.O. Box 187, Fuzhou, Fujian 350012, China. Web: (includes on-demand and streaming audio) www.vos.com.cn. Replies irregularly to correspondence in Chinese or English.

Xinjiang People's Broadcasting Station, 84 Tuanjie Lu, Urümqi, Xinjiang 830044, China. Phone: +86 (991)

256-0089, +86 (991) 257-8492. Email: mw738@21cn.com. Web: (includes on-demand and streaming audio) www.xjbs.com.cn. Contact: Editorial Office. Free tourist booklet, postcards and used Chinese stamps. Replies in Chinese to correspondence in Chinese or English. Verifies reception reports. $1 or 1 IRC helpful.

Xizang People's Broadcasting Station, 180 Beijing Zhonglu, Lhasa, Xizang 850000, China. Phone: (director) +86 (891) 681-9516; (technical division) +86 (891) 681-9521; (technical manager) +86 (891) 681-9525; (chief engineer) +86 (891) 681-9529. Phone/Fax: (general) +86 (891) 682-7910. Email: xzzbs2003@yahoo.com.cn; zbs@chinabroadcast.cn. Web: www.tibetradio.cn. Contact: Mo Shu-ji, Director; (technical) Tuo Baoshen, Technical Manager; Wang Yong (Chief Engineer). Chinese or Tibetan preferred, since correspondence in English is processed by freelance translators hired only when accumulated mail reaches a critical mass. Return postage required. Sometimes announces itself in English as "China Tibet Broadcasting Company" or "Tibet China Broadcasting Station."

"HOLY TIBET" ENGLISH PROGRAM: Foreign Affairs Office, China Tibet People's Broadcasting Company, 41 Beijing Middle Road, Lhasa, Xizang 850000, China. Phone: +86 (891) 681-9541. Contact: Ms.Tse Ring Dekye, Producer/Announcer. Two IRCs requested. Verifies reception reports.

Yunnan People's Broadcasting Station, 73 Renmin Xilu, Central Building of Broadcasting and TV, Kunming, 650031 Yunnan, China. Phone: +86 (871) 531-0270. Fax: +86 (871) 531 0360. Contact: Sheng Hongpeng or F.K. Fan. Free Chinese-language brochure on Yunnan Province, but no QSL cards. $1 or return postage helpful. Replies irregularly to correspondence in Chinese, and sometimes English.

CHINA (TAIWAN) World Time +8

China Radio, 53 Min Chuan West Road 9th Floor, Taipei 10418, Taiwan, Republic of China. Phone: +886 (2) 2598-1009. Fax: +886 (2) 2598 8348. Email: (Adams) readams@usa.net. Contact: Richard E. Adams, Station Director. Verifies reception reports. A religious broadcaster, sometimes referred to as "True Light Station," transmitting via leased facilities in Petropavlovsk-Kamchatskiy, Russia.

Fu Hsing Broadcasting Station, 5 Lane 280, Section 5, Chungshan North Road, Taipei 111, Taiwan, Republic of China. Email: fushinge@ms63.hinet.net. Contact: Xieyi Zhao, Station Manager. Free key rings and other small souvenirs. Replies to correspondence in Chinese or English and verifies reception reports. Return postage not required.

Radio Taiwan International (RTI), P.O. Box 123-199, Taipei 11 199, Taiwan, Republic of China; (street address) 55 Pei-An Road, Taipei 104, Taiwan, Republic of China (include in the address the laguage section you are contacting). Phone: +886 (2) 2885-6168, X-752 or 753; (English) X-385 or 387; (French) X-386; (German) X-382; (Japanese) X-328; (Spanish) X-384. Fax: +886 (2) 2885 0023; (European languages) +886 (2) 2886 7088; (Japanese) +886 (2) 2885 2254. Email: (general) rti@rti.org.tw; (English) prog@rti.org.tw; (French) fren@rti.org.tw; (German) deutsch@rti.org.tw; (Japanese) jpn@rti.org.tw. Web: (includes on-demand and streaming audio, and online reception report form) www.rti.org.tw. Contact: (general) Wayne Wang Tao-Fang, Chief of International Affairs Section; (administration) Lin Feng-Jeng, Chairman; (technical) Peter Lee, Manager, Engineering Department. Free stickers. May send publications and an occasional surprise gift. Broadcasts to the Americas are relayed via WYFR's Okeechobee site in the USA. Also uses relay facilities in France, Germany and the United Kingdom.

BERLIN ADDRESS (FOR CORRESPONDENCE IN FRENCH AND GERMAN): Postfach 309243, D-10760 Berlin, Germany.

MOSCOW ADDRESS: 24/2 Tverskaya St., Korpus 1, gate 4, 3rd Fl, 103050 Moscow, Russia.

NEW DELHI ADDRESS: P.O. Box 4914, P.O. Safdarjung Enclave, New Delhi, 110 029 India.

Trans World Broadcasting Ministry (when operating), 467 Chih Sien 1st Road 7/F, Kaohsiung 800, Taiwan, Republic of China. Phone: +886 (7) 235-9223. Fax: +886 (7) 235 9220. Email: letter@twbm.org.tw. Web: (includes on-demand audio) www.twbm.org.tw. Contact: Naishang Kuo, Manager; Daosheng Yao, Recording Engineer. Broadcasts via facilities of Radio Taiwan International (*see*).

NORTH AMERICAN OFFICE: 1 Spruce Street, Millbrae CA 94030 USA. Phone: +1 (925) 283-0210; (toll-free outside San Francisco Bay area) 1-866-235-224. Fax: +1 (650) 794 0172. Email: contact@twbm.com.

Voice of Han, B Building 5F, 3 Hsin-Yi Road, Sec.1, Taipei, Taiwan, Republic of China. Phone: +886 (2) 2321-5191, +886 (2) 2321-5400. Fax: +886 (2) 2341 4882. Email: (Tu) tony257@ms55.hinet.net. Web: (includes streaming audio) www.voh.com.tw. Contact: Tony Tu.

CLANDESTINE

Clandestine broadcasts are often subject to abrupt change or termination. Being operated by anti-establishment political and/or military organizations, these groups tend to be suspicious of outsiders' motives. Thus, they are more likely to reply to contacts from those who communicate in the station's native tongue, and who are perceived to be at least somewhat favorably disposed to their cause. Most will provide, upon request, printed matter on their cause, though not necessarily in English. For detailed information on clandestine stations, refer to one of the following Internet sites:

ClandestineRadio.com (www.ClandestineRadio.com) specializes in background information on these stations and is organized by region and target country.

Clandestine Radio Watch (www.schoechi.de) contains clandestine radio information plus a twice monthly report on the latest news and developments affecting the study of clandestine radio.

"Addis Dimts Radio," P.O. Box 21745, Washington DC 20009 USA. Phone: +1 (240) 472-4439. Email: abelewd@yahoo.com. Web: (includes on-demand audio) www.addisdimts.com. Opposes the current Ethiopian government. Also airs Sundays on 1390 kHz mediumwave/AM in Washington DC.

"Coalition Maritime Forces (CMF) Radio One"—*see* INTERNATIONAL WATERS.

"Degar Radio," Montagnard Foundation, Inc., P.O. Box 171114, Spartanburg SC 29301 USA. Phone: +1 (864) 576-0698. Fax: +1 (864) 595 1940. Email: ksorpo@yahoo.com. Web: (Montagnard Foundation parent organization) www.montagnard-foundation.org. Contact: Kok Sor, President, Montagnard Foundation. Mint stamps or $1 helpful.

"Democratic Voice of Burma" ("Democratic Myanmar a-Than"), P.O. Box 6720, St. Olavs Plass, N-0130 Oslo, Norway. Phone: (Executive Director/Chief Editor) +47 (22) 868-486; (Deputy Executive Director/Deputy Chief Editor) +47 (22) 868-472. Fax: +47 (22) 868 471. Email: (general) comment@dvb.no; (Director) director@dvb.no. Web: (includes on-demand audio) www.dvb.no. Contact: Aye Chan Naing, Executive Director/Chief Editor; Khin Maung Win, Deputy Executive Director/Deputy Chief Editor. Programs produced by Burmese democratic movements, as well as professional and independent radio journalists, to provide informational and educational services for the democracy movement inside and outside Burma. Opposes the current Myanmar government. Transmitted originally via facilities in Norway, but more recently has broadcast from sites in Germany, Madagascar and west or central Asia.

"EOTC Radio," EOTC Holy Synod, 4127 Redwood, Oakland CA 94610 USA. Email: eotcholysynod@eotcholysynod.org; online form. Web: (EOTC Holy Synod parent organization, includes on-demand audio from EOTC Radio) www.eotcholysynod.org. Broadcast of the Holy Synod of the Ethiopian Orthodox Tewahedo Church (EOTC) in Exile. Formerly known as Zena Tewahedo.

"Freedom Broadcast for North Korea"—*see* Radio Free North Korea.

"Furusato no Kaze"—*see* JAPAN.

"Ginbot 7 Dimts Radio," P.O. Box 4916, 2003 EX Haarlem, The Netherlands. Email: info@ginbot7.org. Web: (includes on-demand audio) www.ginbot7.org. Opposes the current Ethiopian government.

"Hmong Lao Radio" *see* USA.

"Information Radio" (when operating), 193rd Special Operations Wing, 81 Constellation Court, Middletown PA 17057 USA. Email: (Public Affairs Officer) pa.193sow@paharr.ang.af.mil. Web: (193rd Special Operation Wing parent organization) www.paharr.ang.af.mil. Contact: Public Affairs Officer. Psy-ops station operated by the 193rd Special Operations Wing of the Pennsylvania Air National Guard.

"Minghui Radio." Web: (includes on-demand audio) www.mhradio.org. Via leased facilities in Taiwan, and supports the Falun Dafa organization.

"Moj Them Radio" (Hmoob Moj Them), P.O. Box 75666, Saint Paul MN 55175-0666 USA. Phone: +1 (651) 230-2422. Email: hmoob@mojthem.com, info@mojthem.com. Web: (includes on-demand audio) www.mojthem.com. Via a leased transmitter in Taiwan.

"National Radio of the Democratic Saharan Arab Republic"—*see* Radio Nacional de la República Arabe Saharaui Democrática, Western Sahara.

"Nihon no Kaze"—*see* JAPAN.

"North Korea Reform Radio," Samsung-dong, Kangnam-gu, Seoul 135-090, Republic of Korea. Phone: +82 (2) 2242-6512. Fax: +82 (2) 6442-6512. Email: nkreform@naver.net; nkreform@naver.com. Web: (includes on-demand audio) www.nkreform.net.

"Quê Huong Radio"—*see* USA.

"Open Radio for North Korea," ("Yollin Pukhan Pangsong"), P.O. Box 158, Mapo, Seoul 121-600, Republic of Korea. Phone: +82 (505) 470-7470, +82 (10) 7151-2785. Fax: +82 (505) 471 7470. Email: nkradio@nkradio.com. Web: (includes on-demand audio) www.nkradio.com. Contact: Tae Keung Ha, Executive Director; Young Howard. Replies to correspondence in English, and sometimes verifies reception reports.

NORTH AMERICAN OFFICE: 3901 Fair Ridge Drive, Fairfax VA 22033 USA. Phone: +1 (202) 246-2571.

"Radio Anternacional," BM Box 1499, London WC1N 3XX, United Kingdom. Phone: +44 (20) 8962-2707. Fax: +44 (20) 8346 2203. Email: radio7520@yahoo.com; (Majedi) azarmajedi@yahoo.com. Web: (includes on-demand audio) www.radio-international.org. Contact: Ms. Azar Majedi. Broadcasts via a transmitter in Moldova. Has ties to the Worker-Communist Party of Iran.

"Radio Democracy Shorayee." Email: info@radioshora.org. Web: (includes on-demand audio) www.radioshora.org. Verifies reception reports. Opposes the government of Iran.

"Radio Free Afghanistan"—*see* USA.

"Radio Free Chosun." Web: (includes archived audio of most recent broadcast) http://rfchosun.org, (English) http://rfchosun.org/eng. Contact: Kim Yuntae, Director.

"Radio Free North Korea" ("Jayu Pukhan Pangsong"), Room 502, Sinjeong Building, Sinjeong 7 dong 210-16, Yengcheong-gu, Seoul, Republic of Korea. Phone: +82 (2) 2699-0977. Fax: +82 (2) 2699 0978. Web: www.freenk.net.

"Radio Freedom, Voice of the Ogadeni People"—*see* "Radio Xoriyo."

"Radio Insurgente." Email: online form. Web: (includes on-demand audio) www.radioinsurgente.org. Station of the Mexican "Ejército Zapatista de Liberación National."

"Radio International"—*see* "Radio Anternacional."

"Radio Nacional de la República Arabe Saharaui Democrática"—*see* WESTERN SAHARA

"Radio Payam-e Dost," P.O. Box 765, Great Falls VA 22066 USA. Phone: +1 (703) 671-8888. Fax: +1 (301) 292 6947. Email: payam@bahairadio.org. Web: (includes on-demand audio) www.bahairadio.org. Does not verify reception reports.

"Radio Racja"—*see* POLAND.

"Radio República," P.O. Box 110235, Hialeah FL 33011 USA. Email: info@radiorepublica.org. Web: (includes streaming audio) www.radiorepublica.org. Broadcasts are produced by the Florida-based "Directorio Democrático Cubano," and are partly funded by the U.S. government. Via WRMI (*see*, USA) and transmitters in the United Kingdom.

"Radio Voice of the People"—*see* ZIMBABWE.

"Radio VOP"—*see* ZIMBABWE.

"Radio Xoriyo" ("Halkani wa Radio Xoriyo, Codkii Ummadda Odageniya"). Email: raadioxoriyo@yahoo.com; ogaden@yahoo.com (some verifications received from this address). If these fail, try webmaster@ogaden.com. Web: www.ogaden.com (click on "Radio Xoriyo"). Broadcasts are supportive of the Ogadenia National Liberation Front, and hostile to the Ethiopian government. Via Germany's Media Broadcast (*see*).

"Radio Xoriyo Ogadenia"
Email: info@radioxoriyo.com. Web: www.radioxoriyo.com. Broadcasts via a transmitter in western Russia.

"Shiokaze"—*see* JAPAN.

"Sound of Hope"
TAIWAN OFFICE: Sound of Hope Radio Network, 42 Xingda Road, South District, Taichung 402, Taiwan, Republic of China. Contact: Yue Chen, Listeners' Service Department.
NORTH AMERICAN OFFICE: Sound of Hope Radio Network, 2520 Wyandotte Street - Suite A, Mountain View CA 94043 USA. Phone: +1 (866) 432-7764. Fax: +1 (415) 276 5861. Email: contact@soundofhope.org. Web: (includes on-demand audio) www.soundofhope.org.
Via leased facilities in Taiwan, and supports the Falun Dafa organization.

"Sudan Radio Service"—*see* USA.

"SW Radio Africa," P.O. Box 243, Borehamwood, Herts., WD6 4WA, United Kingdom. Phone: +44 (20) 8387-1406. Fax: +44 (20) 8387 1416 Email: (technical, including reception reports) tech@swradioafrica.com; (Jackson) gerry@swradioafrica.com; (Mommsen) les@swradioafrica.com. Web: (includes on-demand and streaming audio) www.swradioafrica.com. Contact: [Ms.] Gerry Jackson, Station Manager; (technical) Les Mommsen, Technical Manager. Run by exiled Zimbabweans in the United Kingdom.

"Voice of Biafra International," 1629 K Street NW, Suite 300, Washington DC 20036 USA. Phone: +1 (202) 508-3795. Fax: +1 (202) 508 3759. Email: biafrafoundation@yahoo.com; (Nkwocha) oguchi@mbay.net. Web: (includes on-demand audio) www.biafraland.com/vobi.htm. Contact: Oguchi Nkwocha, M.D. A project of the Biafra Foundation and the Biafra Actualization Forum. Formerly via South Africa's Sentech facilities, but in summer 2007 switched to a transmitter of World Harvest Radio (*see*) in the United States.

"Voice of China" ("Zhongguo zhi Yin"), P.O. Box 273538, Concord CA 94527 USA; or (street address) 2261 Morello Avenue - Suite A, Pleasant Hill, California 94523 USA. Web: www.china21century.org/default.asp?menu=xu (click on "VOC"). Financial support from the Foundation for China in the 21st Century. Transmits via facilities in Taiwan.
SPONSORING ORGANIZATION: Foundation for China in the 21st Century, P.O. Box 11696, Berkeley CA 94701 USA. Email: info@china21century.org.

"Voice of Democratic Eritrea International" ("Sawt Eritrea al-Dimuqratiya-Sawtu Jabhat al-Tahrir al-Eritrea"), c/o Eritreisches Zentrum, 2. Stock, Neue Mainzer Str. 24, D-60311 Frankfurt, Germany. Phone: +49 (69) 2424-8583. Phone/Fax: +49 (69) 2424-8637. Web: (on-demand audio) www.nharnet.com/Radio/radiopage.htm. Contact: Neguse Tseggai. Station of the Eritrean Liberation Front-Revolutionary Council, hostile to the government of Eritrea. Via Media Broadcast (*see*), in Germany.

"Voice of Ethiopian Unity"—*see* "Voice of the Democratic Path of Ethiopian Unity."

"Voice of Iranian Kurdistan"—*see* "Voice of Kurdistan."

"Voice of Iraqi Kurdistan"—*see* IRAQ.

"Voice of Jammu Kashmir Freedom" ("Sadai Hurriyati Jammu Kashmir"), P.O. Box 102, Muzaffarabad, Azad Kashmir, via Pakistan. Contact: Programme Manager. Pro-Moslem and favors Azad Kashmiri independence from India. Believed to transmit via facilities of Radio Pakistan. Return postage not required, and replies to correspondence in English.

"Voice of Komala" (when operating), c/o Representation of Komala Abroad, Postfach 800272, D-51002 Köln, Germany; Phone/Fax: (North America) +1 (561) 760 5814. Email: komala_radio@hotmail.com. Web: (includes on-demand audio) http://radio.komala.org. Replies to correspondence in English.

"Voice of Kurdistan" (formerly "Voice of Iranian Kurdistan"). Fax: +1 (717) 326 7615. Email: info@radiokurdistan.net. Web: (includes on-demand audio) www.radiokurdistan.net. For further contact, try one of the PDKI (Democratic Party of Iranian Kurdistan parent organization) offices, below.
PDKI INTERNATIONAL BUREAU: AFK, Boîte Postale 102, F-75623 Paris Cedex 13, France. Phone: +33 (1) 4585-6431. Fax: +33 (1) 4585 2093. Email: pdkiran@club-internet.fr. Web: www.pdk-iran.org. Contact: Khosrow Abdollahi. Replies to correspondence in English.
PDKI CANADA BUREAU: P.O. Box 29010, London, Ontario N6K 4L9, Canada. Phone/Fax: +1 (519) 680-7784. Email: pdkicanada@pdki.org. Web: www.pdki.org.

"Voice of Meselna Delina" ("Dimtsi Meselna Delina"), Tesfa Delina Foundation, Inc., 17326 Edwards Road, Suite A-230, Cerritos CA 90703 USA. Email: info@delina.org. Web: (on-demand audio) www.asmarino.com (if this fails, try www.asmarino.org). Opposed to the current Eritrean government. Currently via the facilities of World Harvest Radio (*see*, USA).

"Voice of Mesopotamia" ("Dengê Mezopotamya") Phone: +32 (53) 648-827/29. Fax: +32 (53) 680 779. Email: info@denge-mezopotamya.com. Web: (includes streaming audio) www.denge-mezopotamya.com. Contact: Ahmed Dicle, Director.
KURDISTAN WORKERS PARTY (PKK, also known as Kongra-Gel, KGK) SPONSORING ORGANIZATION: Web: www.kongra-gel.com.

"Voice of Oromia Independence"
Email: rswo2006@gmail.com; online form. Web: (includes on-demand audio) www.awofio.com/Radio-rswo.htm. Broadcast of the Front for Independence of Oromia (Adda Walabummaa Oromiyaa) via a transmitter in western Russia.

"Voice of Oromo Liberation" ("Sagalee Bilisummaa Oromoo"), SBO (VOL), Postfach 510610, D-13366 Berlin, Germany; (street address) SBO, Prinzenallee 81, D-13357 Berlin, Germany. Phone/Fax: +49 (30) 494 3372. Email: sbo13366@aol.com. Web: (includes on-demand audio) www.oromoliberationfront.org/sbo.html. Occasionally replies to correspondence in English or German. Return postage required. Station of the Oromo Liberation Front of Ethiopia, an Oromo nationalist organization. Via Germany's Media Broadcast (*see*).

"Voice of the Communist Party of Iran" ("Seda-ye Hezb-e Komunist-e Iran")
COMMUNIST PARTY OF IRAN SPONSORING ORGANIZATION: C.D.C.R.I., Box 704 45, S-107 25 Stockholm, Sweden. Phone/Fax: +46 (8) 786-8054. Email: cpi@cpiran.org. Web: www.cpiran.org.

"Voice of the Democratic Alliance"—Airs via facilities of Radio Ethiopia (*see*), so try sending correspondence c/o that station. Opposes the Eritrean government.

Radio Santa Fé in Bogotá, Colombia, was on 4965 kHz from late 1960 to 1989, when the old 2.5 kW homebrew transmitter was damaged by flooding. This is the present-day staff of the station, which now operates only on mediumwave AM. In a roundabout way, Radio Santa Fé wound up being partly responsible for the creation of PASSPORT.

Radio Santa Fé

"Voice of the Democratic Path of Ethiopian Unity," Finote Democracy, P.O. Box 73337, Washington DC 20056 USA. Fax: +1 (202) 291 7645. Email: efdpu@aol.com. Web: (includes on-demand audio) www.finote.org. Via Germany's Media Broadcast (*see*).

"Voice of the Iranian Revolution"—same contact details as "Voice of the Communist Party of Iran" (*see*).

"Voice of the Worker" ("Seda-ye Kargar") (when operating)

WORKER-COMMUNIST PARTY OF IRAN (WPI) PARENT ORGANIZATION: Web: www.wpiran.org.

WPI INTERNATIONAL OFFICE: WPI, Office of International Relations, Suite 730, 28 Old Brompton Road, South Kensington, London SW7 3SS, United Kingdom. Phone: +44 (77) 7989-8968. Fax: +44 (87) 0136 2182. Email: wpi.international.office@ukonline.co.uk, markazi@ukonline.co.uk.

"Voice of Tibet"

ADMINISTRATIVE OFFICE: Voice of Tibet Foundation, St. Olavsgate 24, N-0166 Oslo, Norway. Phone: +47 2211-1209. Email: voti@online.no. Contact: Øystein Alme, Director.

MAIN EDITORIAL OFFICE: Voice of Tibet, Narthang Building, Gangchen Kyishong, Dharamsala-176 215 H.P., India. Phone: +91 (1892) 228-179, +91 (1892) 222-384. Fax: +91 (1892) 224 913, +91 (1892) 224 957. Email: editor@vot.org; info@vot.org; (Karma Yeshi) kyeshi@vot.org; (Tenzin Peldon) tpeldon@vot.org; (Dekyi Methok) dekyi@vot.org. Web: (includes on-demand audio) www.vot.org. Contact: Karma Yeshi, Editor-in-Chief; Tenzin Peldon, Editor - Tibetan section; Dekyi Methok, Editor - Chinese section.

A joint venture of the Norwegian Human Rights House, Norwegian Tibet Committee and World-View International. Programs focus on Tibetan culture, education, human rights and news from Tibet. Opposed to Chinese control of Tibet. A colorful QSL card is issued from the office in Dharamsala. Return postage helpful. Broadcasts via transmitters in Madagascar, Tajikistan and United Arab Emirates.

"Voice of Wilderness"—*see* KOREA (REPUBLIC).

"Zena Tewahedo"—*see* "EOTC Radio," above.

COLOMBIA World Time –5

NOTE: Colombia, the country, is always spelled with two o's. It should never be written as "Columbia."

La Voz de Tu Conciencia, a/c Colombia para Cristo, Calle 44 No. 13-67, Bogotá, D.C., Colombia. Phone: +57 (1) 338-4716. Email: contacto@fuerzadepaz.com, libreria@fuerzadepaz.com; (Stendal, specialized technical correspondence only) martinstendal@etb.net.co. Contact: Russel Martín Stendal, Administrador; Rafael Rodríguez R., QSL Manager. Station is actually located in Puerto Lleras, in the guerrilla "combat zone." Replies to correspondence in English or Spanish. Return postage helpful. Free stickers and paper pennant.

La Voz del Guaviare, Carrera 22 con Calle 9, San José del Guaviare, Colombia. Phone: +57 (986) 840-153/4. Fax: +57 (986) 840 102. Email: mercorio@col3.telecom.com.co. Contact: Luis Fernando Román Robayo, Director General. Replies slowly to correspondence in Spanish.

Marfil Estéreo—*see* sister-station La Voz de Tu Conciencia, above, for details.

Radio Líder (if reactivated), Calle 45 No. 13-70, Bogotá, Colombia. Phone: +57 (1) 323-1500. Fax: +57 (1) 288 4020. Email: radiolider@cadenamelodia.com. Web: www.cadenamelodia.com. Rarely replies. A station of the Cadena Melodía network.

CONGO (DEMOCRATIC REPUBLIC) World Time +1 Western, including Kinshasa; +2 Eastern

Radio CANDIP, B.P. 373, Bunia, Democratic Republic of Congo. Letters should preferably be sent via registered mail. $2 or return postage required. Correspondence in French preferred.

Radio Kahuzi. Email: radiokahuzi@kivu-online.com. Web: www.besi.org. Contact: Richard & Kathy McDonald. Verifies reception reports by email.

HOME OFFICE: Believers Express Service, Inc. (BESI), P.O. Box 115, San Marcos CA 92079 USA. Phone/Fax: +1 (760) 598-1190. Email: radiokahuzi@sbcglobal.net. Contact: Harold Smith, President; Barbara Smith, Home Office Secretary. Verifies reception reports.

Radio Okapi, 12 Av. des Aviateurs, Kinshasa, Gombe, Democratic Republic of the Congo. Email: online form. Web: (includes on-demand and streaming audio) www.radiookapi.net. A joint project involving the United Nations Mission in the Democratic Republic of the Congo (MONUC) and the Swiss-based Fondation Hirondelle.

MONUC:

(USA) P.O. Box 4653, Grand Central Station, New York NY 10163-4653 USA. Phone: +1 (212) 963-0103. Fax: +1 (212) 963 0205. Email: info@monuc.org. Web: www.monuc.org. Verifies reception reports.

(Congo) 12 Av. des Aviateurs, Kinshasa - Gombe, Democratic Republic of the Congo; or B.P. 8811, Kinshasa 1, Democratic Republic of the Congo. Phone: +243 (81) 890-6000. Fax: +243 890 56208. Contact: Georges Schleger, VE2EK, Communications Officer & Head of Technical Services.

FONDATION HIRONDELLE: Avenue du Temple 19c, CH 1012-Lausanne, Switzerland. Phone: +41 (21) 654-2020. Fax: +41 (21) 654 2021. Email: info@hirondelle.org. Web: www.hirondelle.org. Contact: Dennis Roshier, Administrator. Verifies reception reports.

CONGO (REPUBLIC) World Time +1

Radio Congo—*see* Radiodiffusion Nationale Congolaise, below.

Radiodiffusion Nationale Congolaise (if reactivated), Tèlèdiffusion du Congo, B.P. 2912, Brazzaville, Congo. Contact: Félix Lossombo, Le Directeur Administratif et Financier; Gaspard Bemba, Le Directeur de l'Inspection Technique des Réseaux et de la Qualité des Services; Jean Médard Bokatola. Return postage required, but smallest denomination currency notes (e.g. $1US or 1 euro) reportedly cannot be changed into local currency. Replies irregularly to letters in French (and sometimes, English) sent via registered mail.

COSTA RICA World Time -6

Faro del Caribe—TIFC (if reactivated), Apartado 2710, 1000 San José, Costa Rica. Phone: +506 226-4358, +506 227-5048, +506 286-1755. Fax: +506 227-1725. Email: radio@farodelcaribe.org, 1080@farodelcaribe.org; (technical) tecnico@farodelcaribe.org. Web: (includes streaming audio) www.farodelcaribe.org. Contact: Lic. Ronald Ortiz R., Administrador; (technical) Salvador López, Ingeniero. Free stickers, pennants, books and bibles. $1 or IRCs helpful. Verifies reception reports in Spanish or English.

U.S. OFFICE, NONTECHNICAL: Misión Latinoamericana, P.O. Box 620485, Orlando FL 32862 USA.

Radio Exterior de España—Cariari Relay Station, Cariari de Pococí, Costa Rica. Phone: +506 767-7308, +506 767-7311. Fax: +506 225 2938.

Radio Universidad de Costa Rica (if reactivated), Ciudad Universitaria Rodrigo Facio, San Pedro de Montes de Oca, San José, Costa Rica. Phone: +506 207-4727. Fax: +506 207 4832. Email: online form. Web: (includes on-demand and streaming audio) www.radiouniversidad.ucr.ac.cr/static/index.htm. Contact: Nora Garita B., Directora. Free postcards, station brochure and stickers. Replies slowly to correspondence in Spanish or English. $1 or return postage required.

University Network—*see* USA.

CROATIA World Time +1 (+2 midyear)

Glas Hrvatske (Voice of Croatia), Prisavlje 3, HR-10000 Zagreb, Croatia. Phone: +385 (1) 634-2601; (Editor-in-Chief) +385 (1) 634-2602. Email: (Croatian) glas.hrvatske@hrt.hr; (English) voiceofcroatia@hrt.hr; (Spanish) vozdecroacia@hrt.hr; (Zlatko Kuretić) zlatko.kuretic@hrt.hr. Web: www4.hrt.hr/hr/glashrvatske/gh.php; (program schedule) http://raspored.hrt.hr (click on "HR: Radio emitiranje" and then on "Glas Hrvatske"); (streaming audio) www.hrt.hr/streams; (on-demand audio in Croatian, English and Spanish) www.hrt.hr (click on "emisije na zahtjev") [http://rnz.hrt.hr/index.php may also work] and choose "Glas Hrvatske" from the "Mreža" dropdown menu). Contact: Zlatko Kuretić, Editor-in-Chief. Glas Hrvatske is the external service of Croatian Radio.

TRANSMISSION COMPANY: Odašiljači i Veze d.o.o. (Transmitters & Communications Ltd.), Ulica grada Vukovara 269d, HR-10000 Zagreb, Croatia. Phone: +385 (1) 618-6000. Fax: +385 (1) 618 6100. Email: nikola.percin@oiv.hr; (shortwave coordination) mladen.golubic@oiv.hr. Web: www.oiv.hr. Contact: Nikola Perčin, Managing Director; Mladen Golubić, Shortwave Coordination. An independent state-owned company which replaced the former Transmitters and Communications Department of Hrvatska Radio-Televizija (HRT).

TRANSMITTING STATION DEANOVEC: P.O. Box 3, HR-10313 Graberje Ivanićko, Croatia. Phone: +385 (1) 2830-533. Fax: +385 (1) 2830 534. Email: dane.pavlic@oiv.hr. Contact: Dane Pavlić, Head of Station. Glas Hrvatske transmits from Deanovec shortwave station for listeners in Europe and the Mediterranean; and via Germany's Media Broadcast (see) to Australasia and the Americas.

CUBA World Time -5 (-4 midyear)

Radio Habana Cuba, Apartado Postal 6240, 10600 La Habana, Cuba. Phone: (general) +53 (7) 878-4954; (English Department) +53 (7) 877-6628. Fax: +53 (7) 870 5810. Email: radiohc@enet.cu; (Arnie Coro) arnie@rhc.cu, coro@enet.cu. Web: (includes on-demand and streaming audio) www.radiohc.cu; (streaming audio) http://multimedia-radio.cubasi.cu. Contact: (general) Lourdes López, Head of Correspondence Department; Isabel García, Director of English Department; (administration) Isidro Betancourt, General Director; (technical) Arnaldo Coro Antich, ("Arnie Coro"), Producer, "DXers Unlimited"; René Martínez, Head of Technical Department; Luis Pruna Amer, Senior Engineering Consultant. Free pennants, stickers, keychains, pins and other small souvenirs when available. DX Listeners' Club. Free sample *Granma*

International newspaper. Contests with various prizes, including trips to Cuba.

Radio Rebelde, Departamento de Relaciones Públicas, Apartado Postal 6277, 10600 La Habana 6, Cuba; (street address) Calle 23 nº 258 entre L y M, El Vedado, 10600 La Habana, Cuba. For technical correspondence (including reception reports), substitute "Servicio de Onda Corta" in place of "Departamento de Relaciones Públicas." Reception reports can also be emailed to Radio Habana Cuba's Arnie Coro (arnie@radiohc.cu) for forwarding to Radio Rebelde. Phone: +53 (7) 831-3514. Fax: +53 (7) 334 270. Web (includes on-demand and streaming audio): www.radiorebelde.com.cu; (streaming audio) http://multimedia-radio.cubasi.cu. Contact: Jorge Luis Martín Cuevas, Jefe de Relaciones Públicas. Replies slowly, with correspondence in Spanish preferred.

CYPRUS World Time +2 (+3 midyear)

Bayrak Radio International, BRTK Sitesi, Dr. Fazil Küçük Boulevard, Lefkoşa, TRNC, Via Mersin 10, Turkey. Phone: +90 (392) 225-5555. Fax: +90 (392) 225 4581. Email: online form. Web: (includes streaming audio) www.brtk.cc. Contact: Mustafa Tosun, Head of Transmission Department.

BBC World Service—East Mediterranean Relay Station, P.O. Box 209, Limassol, Cyprus. Contact: Steve Welch. This address for technical matters only. Other correspondence should be sent to the BBC World Service in London (*see*).

Cyprus Broadcasting Corporation, Broadcasting House, P.O. Box 4824, Nicosia 1397, Cyprus; (street address) RIK Street, Athalassa, Nicosia 2120, Cyprus. Phone: +357 (2) 286-2000. Fax: +357 (2) 231 4050. Web: (includes on-demand and streaming audio from domestic services, and on-demand audio from shortwave broadcasts) www.kypros.org/CYBC. Free stickers. Replies irregularly, sometimes slowly. IRC or $1 helpful.

CZECH REPUBLIC World Time +1 (+2 midyear)

Radio Prague, Czech Radio, Vinohradská 12, 12099 Prague 2, Czech Republic. Phone: +420 (2) 2155-2900; (Czech Department) +420 (2) 2155-2922; (English Department) +420 (2) 2155-2930; (German Department) +420 (2) 2155-2941; (French Department) +420 (2) 2155-2911; (Spanish Department) +420 (2) 2155-2950; (Russian Department) +420 (2) 2155-2964. Phone/Fax: (Oldrich Cip, technical) +420 (2) 2271-5005. Fax: (all languages) +420 (2) 2155 2903. Email: (general) cr@radio.cz; (English Department) english@radio.cz; (German Department) deutsch@radio.cz; (French Department) francais@radio.cz; (Spanish Department) espanol@radio.cz; (Russian Department) rusky@radio.cz; (Program Director) Gerald.Schubert@radio.cz; (Internet Department) cr@radio.cz; (free news texts) robot@radio.cz, writing "Subscribe English" (or other desired language) within the subject line; (technical, chief engineer) cip@radio.cz. Web: (includes on-demand and streaming audio) www.radio.cz. Contact: (general) Marie Pittnerová; Gerald Schubert, Editor-in-Chief; (administration) Miroslav Krupička, Director; (technical) Oldrich Čip, Chief Engineer. Free stickers; also key chains, pens, bookmarks, mouse pads and other souvenirs when available.

RFE/RL—*see* USA.

DIEGO GARCIA—*see* BRITISH INDIAN OCEAN TERRITORY

DJIBOUTI World Time +3

Radio Télévision de Djibouti, Boîte Postale 97, Djibouti, Djibouti; (street address) Avenue Saint Laurent du Var, Djibouti, Djibouti. Phone: +253 352-294, +253 350-484. Fax: +253 356 502. Email: (general) rtd@intnet.dj; (technical) rtdtech@intnet.dj. Web: (includes on-demand audio) www.rtd.dj. Contact: (general) Abdi Atteyeh Abdi, Directeur Général; (technical) Yahya Moussed, Chef du Service Technique. Verifies reception reports. Transmission facilities are located at Dorale, about 10 km west of Djibouti City.

DOMINICAN REPUBLIC World Time –4

Radio Amanecer Internacional (if reactivated), Apartado Postal 1500, Santo Domingo, Dominican Republic; (street address) Juan Sánchez Ramírez #40, Santo Domingo, Dominican Republic. Phone: +1 (809) 688-5600, +1 (809) 688-8067. Fax: +1 (809) 227 1869. Email: cabina@radioamanecer.org; online form. Web: (includes streaming audio) www.radioamanecer.org. Contact: (general) Lic. Germán Lorenzo, Director; (technical) Ing. Sócrates Domínguez. $1 or return postage required. Replies slowly to correspondence in Spanish.

Radio Cristal Internacional (when operating), Apartado Postal 894, Santo Domingo, Dominican Republic; or (street address) Calle Pepillo Salcedo No. 18, Altos, Santo Domingo, Dominican Republic. Phone: +1 (809) 565-1460, +1 (809) 566-5411. Fax: +1 (809) 567 9107. Contact: (general) Fernando Hermón Gross, Director de Programas; Margarita Reyes, Secretaria; (administration) Darío Badía, Director General; or Héctor Badía, Director de Administración. Seeks reception reports. Return postage of $2 appreciated.

ECUADOR World Time –5 (–4 sometimes, in times of drought); –6 Galapagos

NOTE: IRCs are exchangeable only in the cities of Quito and Guayaquil, so enclosing $2 for return postage may be helpful when writing to stations in other locations.

HCJB Global Voice, The Voice of the Andes

STATION: Casilla 17-17-691, Quito, Ecuador. Phone: (general) +593 (2) 226-6808; (frequency management) +593 (2) 226-6808 (X-4627). Fax: (general) +593 (2) 226 7263; +593 (2) 226 4765; (frequency manager) +593 (2) 226 3267. Email: (general) info@hcjb.org.ec; (Rosiak) hrosiak@hcjb.org.ec; (frequency management) irops@hcjb.org.ec; (language sections) format is language@hcjb.org.ec; so to reach, say, the Spanish Department, it would be spanish@hcjb.org.ec. Web: (English, includes on-demand audio and online reception report form) www.hcjbglobal.org; (Spanish, includes on-demand and streaming audio) www.radiohcjb.org. Contact: (general) Spanish [or other language] Department; (administration) Jim Estes, HCJB Regional Director;

Doug Weber, Radio Director; Horst Rosiak, Frequency Manager. Free religious brochures, calendars, stickers and pennants. IRC or $1 required.

INTERNATIONAL HEADQUARTERS: HCJB Global, P.O. Box 39800, Colorado Springs CO 80949-9800 USA; (street address) 1065 Garden of the Gods Rd., Colorado Springs CO 80907 USA. Phone: +1 (719) 590-9800. Fax: +1 (719) 590 9801. Email: info@hcjbglobal.org; (Hirst) jhirst@hcjbglobal.org. Web: www.hcjbglobal.org. Contact: Jon Hirst, Communications Director; Andrew Braio, Public Information; (administration) Richard D. Jacquin, Director, International Operations. Various items sold via U.S. address—catalog available. This address is not a mail drop, so listeners' correspondence, except those concerned with purchasing HCJB items, should be directed to the usual Quito address.

ENGINEERING CENTER: HCJB Global Technology Center, 2830 South 17th Street, Elkhart IN 46517-4008 USA. Phone: +1 (574) 970 4252. Fax: +1 (574) 293 9910. Email: info@hcjbtech.org. Web: www.hcjbtech.org. Contact: Dave Pasechnik, Project Manager; Bob Moore, Engineering. This address only for those professionally concerned with the design and manufacture of transmitter and antenna equipment. Listeners' correspondence should be directed to the usual Quito address.

REGIONAL OFFICES: Although HCJB has over 20 regional offices throughout the world, the station wishes that all listener correspondence be directed to the station in Quito, as the regional offices do not serve as mail drops for the station.

HD2IOA, Instituto Oceanográfico de la Armada (INOCAR), Avenida 25 de Julio, Vía Puerto Marítimo, Código Postal 5940, Guayaquil, Ecuador. HD2IOA is a time signal station operated by Ecuador's Naval Oceanographic Institute. Replies to correspondence in Spanish (and sometimes, English) and verifies reception reports.

INSTITUTO OCEANOGRÁFICO DE LA ARMADA PARENT ORGANIZATION:
Phone: +593 (4) 248-1300. Fax: +593 (4) 248 5166. Email: inocar@inocar.mil.ec. Web: www.inocar.mil.ec.

La Voz de Saquisilí—Radio Libertador (when operating), Calle 24 de Mayo, Saquisilí, Cotopaxi, Ecuador. Phone: +593 (3) 721-035. Contact: Arturo Mena Herrera, Gerente-Propietario. Reception reports actively solicited. Return postage, in the form of $2 or mint Ecuadorian stamps, appreciated; IRCs difficult to exchange. Spanish strongly preferred.

La Voz del Napo, Misión Josefina, Juan Montalvo s/n, Tena, Napo, Ecuador. Phone: +593 (6) 886-356. Email: coljav20@yahoo.es, lavozdelnapo@yahoo.es. Contact: Padre Humberto Dorigatti, Director. Free pennants and stickers. $2 or return postage required. Replies irregularly to correspondence in Spanish or Italian.

La Voz del Upano (when operating)

STATION: Vicariato Apostólico de Méndez, Misión Salesiana, 10 de Agosto s/n, Macas, Provincia de Morona Santiago, Ecuador. Phone: +593 (7) 505-247. Email: radioupano@easynet.net.ec. Contact: Sra. Leonor Guzmán, Directora. Free pennants and calendars. On one occasion, not necessarily to be repeated, sent tape of Ecuadorian folk music for $2. Otherwise, $2 required. Replies to correspondence in Spanish.

QUITO OFFICE: Procura Salesiana, Equinoccio 623 y Queseras del Medio, Quito, Ecuador. Phone: +593 (2) 255-1012.

Radio Buen Pastor—*see* Radio El Buen Pastor

Radio C R I, Centro Radiofónico de Imbabura, Calle Salinas 623 y Oviedo, Ibarra, Provincia de Imbabura, Ecuador. Phone: +593 (62) 612-720. Contact: Ing. Luis Adriano Calero, Director. Broadcasts sporadically, usually for just a few days at a time.

Radio Chaskis del Norte, Jirón Roldos Aguilera y Panamericana Norte, Otavalo, Imbabura, Ecuador; (office) Calle Bolívar 805 y Juan Montalvo, Otavalo, Imbabura, Ecuador. Phone: +593 (62) 920-922, +593 (62) 920-256. Email: radiochaskis@hotmail.com. Contact: Luis Enrique Cachiguango Cotacachi, Propietario. Welcomes correspondence in Spanish, but replies are irregular because of limited resources. Correspondence is best sent to the office address.

Radiodifusora Cultural Católica La Voz del Upano—*see* La Voz del Upano, above.

Radiodifusora Cultural, La Voz del Napo—*see* La Voz del Napo, above.

Radio El Buen Pastor, Asociación Cristiana de Indígenas Saraguros (ACIS), Reino de Quito y Azuay, Correo Central, Saraguro, Loja, Ecuador. Email: online form; (Quille) bpradio931@hotmail.com. Web: www.saraguros.com/radio.php. Contact: José Quille. $2 or return postage in the form of mint Ecuadorian stamps required, as IRCs are difficult to exchange in Ecuador. Station is keen to receive reception reports; may respond to English, but correspondence in Spanish preferred. $10 required for QSL card and pennant.

Radio Federación Shuar (when operating), Casilla 17-01-1422, Quito, Ecuador. Phone:+593 (2) 250-8301. Fax: +593 (2) 250-4264. Contact: Manuel Jesús Vinza Chacucuy, Director; Yurank Tsapak Rubén Gerardo, Director; Prof. Albino M. Utitiaj P., Director de Medios. Return postage or $2 required. Replies irregularly to correspondence in Spanish.

Radio María, Baquerizo Moreno 281 y Leonidas Plaza, Quito, Ecuador. Phone: +593 (2) 256-4714. Web: (includes streaming audio) www.radiomariaecuador.org. A Catholic radio network currently leasing airtime over La Voz del Napo (*see*), but which is looking into the possiblity of setting up its own shortwave station.

Radio Oriental (when operating), Casilla 260, Tena, Napo, Ecuador. Phone: +593 (6) 886-033, +593 (6) 886-388. Contact: Luis Enrique Espín Espinosa, Gerente General. $2 or return postage helpful. Reception reports welcome.

Radio Quito (when operating), Casilla 17-21-1971, Quito, Ecuador. Phone: +593 (2) 250 8301. Email: radioquito@ecuadoradio.com. Web: (streaming audio) www.elcomercio.com (click on "Radios"). Contact: Xavier Almeida, Gerente General; José Almeida, Subgerente. Free stickers. Return postage normally required, but occasionally verifies email reports. Replies slowly, but regularly.

EGYPT World Time +2 (+3 midyear)

WARNING: MAIL THEFT. Feedback from PASSPORT readership indicates that money is sometimes stolen from envelopes sent to Radio Cairo.

Egyptian Radio, P.O. Box 1186, 11511 Cairo, Egypt. Email: ertu@ertu.gov.eg. Web: (under construction) www.ertu.gov.eg; (streaming audio) http://live.sis.gov.eg/live. For additional details, *see* Radio Cairo, below.

Radio Cairo

NONTECHNICAL: P.O. Box 566, Cairo 11511, Egypt. Phone: +20 (2) 677-8945. Fax: +20 (2) 575 9553. Email: (English Service) egyptianoverseas_english@hotmail.com; (Spanish Service) radioelcairoespa@yahoo.com; (Brazilian Service) brazilian_prog@egyptradio.tv. Web: (English Service) www.freewebs.com/overseas-radio; (French Service) http://listen.to/overseas-radio-fra; (Russian Service) http://listen.to/overseas-radio-russia. Contact: Mrs. Amal Badr, Head of English Programme; Mrs. Sahar Kalil, Director of English Service to North America and Producer, "Questions and Answers"; Marwan Khattab; Mrs. Magda Hamman, Secretary; Amal El Disuky, Brazilian Department (Portuguese Service). Free stickers, postcards, stamps, maps, papyrus souvenirs and calendars. Avoid enclosing money (*see WARNING*, above). Replies irregularly.

TECHNICAL: Egyptian Radio and Television Union, Broadcast Engineering Sector, Maspero TV Building, P.O. Box 1186, 11511 Cairo, Egypt. Phone: (Lawrence) +20 (2) 347-6521. Fax: (Lawrence) +20 (2) 574 6840. Email: (general) freqmeg@yahoo.com; (Lawrence) niveenl@hotmail.com. Contact: Mrs. Niveen W. Lawrence, Director of Shortwave Department.

ENGLAND—*see* UNITED KINGDOM

EQUATORIAL GUINEA World Time +1

Radio Africa, P.O. Box 851, Malabo, Equatorial Guinea. Email: radioafrica@myway.com.

U.S. ADDRESS FOR CORRESPONDENCE AND VERIFICATIONS — see Pan American Broadcasting, USA.

Radio East Africa—same details as Radio Africa, above.

Radio Nacional de Guinea Ecuatorial—Bata ("Radio Bata"), Apartado 749, Bata, Río Muni, Equatorial Guinea. Phone: +240 (8) 2592. Fax: +240 (8) 2093. Contact: José Mba Obama, Director; Julián Esono Ela, Programa "Cartas del Oyente". Free tourist brochures. Replies irregularly to correspondence in Spanish.

Radio Nacional de Guinea Ecuatorial—Malabo ("Radio Malabo"), Apartado 195, Malabo, Isla Bioko, Equatorial Guinea. Phone: +240 (9) 2260. Fax: (general) +240 (9) 2097; (technical) +240 (9) 3122. Contact: (general) Román Manuel Mané-Abaga, Jefe de Programación; Ciprano Somon Suakin; Manuel Sobede, Inspector de Servicios de Radio y TV; (technical) Hermenegildo Moliko Chele, Jefe Servicios Técnicos de Radio y Televisión. $1 or return postage required. Replies irregularly to correspondence in Spanish.

ERITREA World Time +3

Radio Bana, Adult Education and Media, Ministry of Education, P.O.Box 609, Asmara, Eritrea. Phone: +291 (1) 125-546. Contact: Saada Ahmedin, English Panel; Donald Britten. Verifies reception reports.

Voice of the Broad Masses of Eritrea (Dimtsi Hafash), Ministry of Information, Radio Division, P.O. Box 872, Asmara, Eritrea; or Ministry of Information, Technical Branch, P.O. Box 242, Asmara, Eritrea. Phone: +291 (1) 116-084, +291 (1) 120-497. Fax: +291 (1) 126 747. Email: nesredin@tse.com.er. Web: (on-demand audio) www.shabait.com/articles/publish/cat_index_10.html. Contact: Ghebreab Ghebremedhin; Berhane Gerzgiher, Director, Engineering Division. Return postage or $1 helpful. Free information on history of the station and about Eritrea.

ETHIOPIA World Time +3

Radio Ethiopia: (external service) P.O. Box 654; (domestic service) P.O. Box 1020—both in Addis Ababa, Ethiopia (address your correspondence to "Audience Relations"). Phone: +251 (1) 1551-6977. Contact: Ms. Woinshet Woldeyes, Secretary, Audience Relations; Ms. Ellene Mocria, Head of Audience Relations; Melesse Edea Beyi, Head of English Programs; (administration) Kasa Miloko, Station Manager. Free stickers and tourist brochures. Poor replier.

ETHIOPIAN RADIO AND TELEVISION AGENCY (PARENT ORGANIZATION): P.O. Box 1020 [or 5544], Addis Ababa, Ethiopia. Phone: +251 (1) 1550-5483, +251 (1) 1553-6566, +251 (1) 1550-5483. Fax: +251 (1) 1550 5174. Email: ertv2@ethionet.et. Web: www.erta.et.

Radio Fana, P.O. Box 30702, Addis Ababa, Ethiopia. Phone: +251 (1) 516-777. Fax: +251 (1) 515 039. Email: rfana@ethionet.et; online form in English. Web: (includes on-demand audio) www.radiofana.com. Contact: Woldu Yemessel, General Manager; Mesfin Alemayehu, Head, External Relations; Girma Lema, Head, Planning and Research Department. Verifies reception reports. Station is autonomous and receives its income from non-governmental educational sponsorship.

Radio Oromia, P.O. Box 2919, Adama, Ethiopia.

Voice of the Tigray Revolution (Dimtsi Woyane Tigray), P.O. Box 450, Mekelle, Tigray, Ethiopia. Phone: +251 (34) 441-0545, +251 (34) 441-0544. Email: vort@ethionet.et; online form in English. Web: (includes on-demand audio) www.dimtsiwoyane.com. Contact: Abera Tesfay, Director. $1 helpful.

FINLAND World Time +2 (+3 midyear)

Scandinavian Weekend Radio, P.O. Box 99, FI-34801, Virrat, Finland. Phone: (live when on air, and includes SMS service) +358 (400) 995-559. Email: (general) info@swradio.net; (technical) esa.saunamaki@swradio.net; (reception reports) online report form. Web: www.swradio.net. Contact: Alpo Heinonen; Esa Saunamäki, Chief Editor; Teemu Lehtimäki, QSL Manager. Two IRCs, $2 or 2 euros required for verification via postal mail. Web reports verified via the Internet. Free stickers.

FRANCE World Time +1 (+2 midyear)

Radio France Internationale (RFI)

MAIN OFFICE: B.P. 9516, F-75016 Paris Cedex 16, France; (street address) 116, avenue du président Kennedy, F-75016 Paris, France. Phone: (general) +33 (1) 5640-1212; (International Affairs and Program Placement) +33 (1)

Mrs. Sini Salmirinne of YLE—Yleisradio Oy—interviews lifelong radio enthusiast Prof. Simo Soininen during a local fair in Kajaani, Finland.

S. Soininen

4430-8932, +33 (1) 4430-8949; (Service de la communication) +33 (1) 4230-2951; (Audience Relations) +33 (1) 4430-8969/70/71; (Media Relations) +33 (1) 4230-2985; (Développement et de la communication) +33 (1) 4430-8921; (*Fréquence Monde*) +33 (1) 4230-1086; (English Service) +33 (1) 5640-3062; (Spanish Department) +33 (1) 4230-3048. Fax: (general) +33 (1) 5640 4759; (International Affairs and Program Placement) +33 (1) 4430 8920; (Audience Relations) +33 (1) 4430 8999; (other nontechnical) +33 (1) 4230 4481; (English Service) +33 (1) 5640 2674; (Spanish Department) +33 (1) 4230 4669. Email: (Audience Relations) courrier.auditeurs@rfi.fr; (English Service) english.service@rfi.fr; (Maguire) john.maguire@rfi.fr; (Spanish Service) america.latina@rfi.fr. Web: (includes on-demand and streaming audio) www.rfi.fr. Contact: John Maguire, Editor, English Language Service; J.P. Charbonnier, Producer, "Lettres des Auditeurs"; Joël Amar, International Affairs/Program Placement Department; Arnaud Littardi, Directeur du développement et de la communication; Nicolas Levkov, Rédactions en Langues Etrangères; Daniel Franco, Rédaction en français; Mme. Anne Toulouse, Rédacteur en chef du Service Mondiale en français; Christine Berbudeau, Rédacteur en chef, *Fréquence* **Monde**; Marc Verney, Attaché de Presse; (administration) Jean-Paul Cluzel, Président-Directeur Général; Alain de Pouzilhac, CEO; (technical) M. Raymond Pincon, Producer, "Le Courrier Technique." Free *Fréquence* **Monde** bi-monthly magazine in French upon request. Free souvenir keychains, pins, lighters, pencils, T-shirts and stickers have been received by some—especially when visiting the headquarters at 116 avenue du Président Kennedy, in the 16th Arrondissement. Can provide supplementary materials for "Dites-moi tout" French-language course; write to the attention of Mme. Chantal de Grandpre, "Dites-moi tout." "Le Club des Auditeurs" French-language listener's club ("Club 9516" for English-language listeners); applicants must provide name, address and two passport-type photos, whereupon they will receive a membership card and the club bulletin. RFI exists primarily to defend and promote Francophone culture, but also provides meaningful information and cultural perspectives in non-French languages.

TRANSMISSION OFFICE, TECHNICAL: TéléDiffusion de France, Direction de la Production et des Méthodes, Service ondes courtes, 10 rue d'Oradour sur Glane, 75732 Paris Cedex 15, France. Phone: (Gruson) +33 (1) 5595-1553; (Meunier) +33 (1) 5595-1161. Fax: +33 (1) 5595 2137. Email: (Gruson) jacques.gruson@tdf.fr; (Penneroux) michel.penneroux@tdf.fr. Contact: Jacques Gruson; Alain Meunier; Michel Penneroux, Business Development Manager AM-HF; Mme Annick Daronian or Mme Sylvie Greuillet (short wave service). This office is for informing about transmitter-related problems (interference, modulation quality), and also for reception reports and verifications.

UNITED STATES PROMOTIONAL, SCHOOL LIAISON, PROGRAM PLACEMENT AND CULTURAL EXCHANGE OFFICES:

NEW ORLEANS: Services Culturels, Suite 2105, Ambassade de France, 300 Poydras Street, New Orleans LA 70130 USA. Phone: +1 (504) 523-5394. Phone/Fax: +1 (504) 529-7502. Contact: Adam-Anthony Steg, Attaché Audiovisuel. This office promotes RFI, especially to language teachers and others in the educational community within the southern United States, and arranges for bi-national cultural exchanges. It also sets up RFI feeds to local radio stations within the southern United States.

NEW YORK: Audiovisual Bureau, Radio France Internationale, 972 Fifth Avenue, New York NY 10021 USA. Phone: +1 (212) 439-1452. Fax: +1 (212) 439 1455. Contact: Gérard Blondel or Julien Vin. This office promotes RFI, especially to language teachers and others within the educational community outside the southern United States, and arranges for bi-national cultural exchanges. It also sets up RFI feeds to local radio stations within much of the United States.

NEW YORK NEWS BUREAU: 1290 Avenue of the Americas, New York NY 10019 USA. Phone: +1 (212) 581-1771. Fax: +1 (212) 541 4309. Contact: Ms. Auberi Edler, Reporter; Bruno Albin, Reporter.

WASHINGTON NEWS BUREAU: 529 14th Street NW, Suite 1126, Washington DC 20045 USA. Phone: +1 (202) 879-6706. Contact: Pierre J. Cayrol.

SAN FRANCISCO OFFICE, SCHEDULES: 2654 17th Avenue, San Francisco CA 94116 USA. Phone: +1 (415) 564-9968. Email: GPoppin@aol.com. Contact: George Poppin. This address, a volunteer office, only provides RFI schedules to listeners (return postage not required). All other correspondence should be sent directly to the main office in Paris.

Voice of Orthodoxy—*see* Voix de l'Orthodoxie, below.

Voix de l'Orthodoxie, B.P. 416-08, F-75366 Paris Cedex 08, France. Phone: +33 (1) 4977-0366. Fax: +33 (1) 4353 4066. Email: voix.orthodoxie@wanadoo.fr. Web: www.russie.net/orthodoxie/vo. Contact: Michel Solovieff, General Secretary. Broadcasts religious programming to Russia via a shortwave transmitter in Kazakstan. Verifies reception reports, including those written in English.

ADDRESS IN RUSSIA: Golos Pravoslavia, 39 Nab. Leyt. Schmidta, 199034 St. Petersburg, Russia. Phone/Fax: +7 (812) 323-2867.

FRENCH GUIANA World Time –3

TéléDiffusion de France (TDF) Guyane Transmitting Station, Télédiffusion de France S.A., Délégation Territoriale de Guyane, B.P. 7024, 97307 Cayenne Cedex, French Guiana. Phone: +594 350-550. Fax: +594 350 555. Contact: (technical) Le Responsable pour Groupe Maintenance. Can consider replies only to technical correspondence. French preferred, but may also respond to correspondence in English, depending on who is at the station. Sometimes verifies reception reports. Relays Radio France Internationale (RFI), Polish Radio External Service and BBC World Service, among others.

GABON World Time +1

Afrique Numéro Un, B.P. 1, Libreville, Gabon. Phone: +241 761-152/3. Fax: +241 742 133. Email: online form. Web: (includes on-demand and streaming audio) www.africa1.com. Contact: Hermann Madiba. Free calendars and bumper stickers. $1, 2 IRCs or return postage helpful. Replies very slowly.

RTV Gabonaise (when operating), B.P. 10150, Libreville, Gabon. Contact: André Ranaud-Renombo, Le Directeur Technique, Adjoint Radio. Free stickers. $1 required. Replies occasionally, but slowly, to correspondence in French.

GEORGIA World Time +4

Apsua Radio—*see* Abkhaz Radio, below.

Abkhaz Radio, (street address) Abkhaz State Radio and TV Co., Aidghylar St. 34, Soxum 384900, Abkhazia, Georgia. Currently there is no mail delivery to Abkhazia, so try the following address: National Library of Abkhazia, Krasnodar District, P.O. Box 964, 354000 Sochi, Russia. Phone: +995 (122) 24-867, +995 (122) 25-321. Fax: +995 (122) 21 144. Email: apsuaradio1@mail.ru. Contact: Zurab Argun, Director. Replies to correspondence in Russian, and verifies reception reports. A 1992 uprising in northwestern Georgia drove the majority of ethnic Georgians from the region. This area remains virtually autonomous from Georgia.

GERMANY World Time +1 (+2 midyear)

Christian Vision—*see* United Kingdom.

Christlichen Wissenschaft—*see* Der Herold der Christlichen Wissenschaft, below.

Der Herold der Christlichen Wissenschaft, Michael Seek, Chefredakteur, Postfach 370427,
D-14134 Berlin, Germany. Email: redaktion@csherold.de. Replies to correspondence in German. Return postage helpful. Via Media Broadcast (*see*).

ALTERNATIVE ADDRESSES:

Radiosendungen CW, Postfach 7330, D-22832 Norderstedt, Germany. Contact: Ms. Erika Bethmann (reception reports, etc.).

Radiosendungen CW, Steindamm 97, D-20099 Hamburg, Germany.

SCHEDULES AND RELIGIOUS PUBLICATIONS: Der Herold der Christlichen Wissenschaft,
210 Massachusetts Avenue, P03-30, Boston MA 02115-3195 USA. Email: herold@csps.com. Web: www.heroldcw.com/herold/radio.jhtml.

Deutsche Welle

MAIN OFFICE: Kurt-Schumacher-Str. 3, D-53113 Bonn, Germany; or (postal address) Deutsche Welle, D-53110 Bonn, Germany. Phone: (English Service) +49 (228) 429-164142. Fax: +49 (228) 429 154000. Email: info@dw-world.de; (English Service) english@dw-world.de. To reach specific individuals by email at Deutsche Welle the format is: firstname.lastname@dw-world.de. For language courses: bildung@dw-world.de. Web: (includes on-demand and streaming audio) www.dw-world.de. Contact: Erik Bettermann, Director General; Marco Vollmar, Head of English and German Services. Broadcasts via transmitters in Ascension, Kazakhstan, Netherlands Antilles, Portugal, Russia, Rwanda, Singapore, South Africa, Sri Lanka, United Arab Emirates and United Kingdom.

CUSTOMER SERVICE: Phone: +49 (228) 429-4000. Fax: +49 (228) 429 154000. Email: info@dw-world.de. All technical mail and reception reports should be sent to the Customer Service.

Deutschlandfunk, Raderberggürtel 40, D-50968 Köln, Germany. Phone: +49 (221) 345-0. Fax: +49 (221) 345 4802. Email: hoererservice@dradio.de. Web: (includes on-demand and streaming audio) www.dradio.de/dlf. Verifies reception reports in German or English.

Hamburger Lokalradio

STUDIO ADDRESS: Kulturzentrum Lola, Lohbrügger Landstrasse 8, D-21031 Hamburg, Germany. Phone: +49 (40) 7269-2422. Fax: +49 (40) 7269 2423. Web: www.hamburger-lokalradio.de, www.hhlr.de.

EDITORIAL ADDRESS: Michael Kittner, Hamburger Lokalradio, Max-Eichholz-Ring 18, D-21031 Hamburg, Germany. Phone/Fax: +49 (40) 738-2417. Email: m.kittner@freenet.de. Contact: Michael Kittner.

Broadcasts regularly on FM and cable, and intermittently on world band via Media Broadcast (*see*) and a Latvian transmitter. Replies to correspondence in German or English. Return postage required for postal reply.

Media Broadcast GmbH, OMB Köln, Bastionstrasse 11-19, D-52428 Jülich, Germany. Phone: (Behling) +49 (2461) 937-166; (Brodowsky) +49 (2461) 937-164; (frequency management) +49 (2461) 340-451. Fax: (sales office) +49 (2461) 937 165; (frequency management) +49 (2461) 340 452. Email: (reception reports) qsl-shortwave@media-broadcast.com. To contact individuals, the format is firstname.lastname@media-broadcast.com; so to reach, say, Walter Brodowsky, it would be walter.brodowsky@media-broadcast.com. Web: www.media-broadcast.com; (shortwave, including the latest schedule) www.media-broadcast.com/hoerfunk/kurzwelle.htm. Contact: Volker Behling, Account Manager Shortwave; Walter Brodowsky, Account & Product Manager Shortwave Broadcasting; Horst Tobias, Frequency Manager; Michael Puetz; Sabine Gawol. Email reports preferred. Media Broadcast operates transmitters at Jülich, Nauen and Wertachtal, which are leased to various international world band stations.

NOTE: Despite the sale of the Jülich transmitting site to CVC, media arm of the United Kingdom's Christian Vision (*see*), the contract allows Media Broadcast to continue using the site for its customers. Correspondence concerning Christian Vision broadcasts should be sent to the United Kingdom address.

Missionswerk Friedensstimme, Postfach 100638, D-51606 Gummersbach, Germany; (street address) Gimborner Str. 20, D-51709 Marienheide, Germany. Phone: +49 (2261) 24717. Fax: +49 (2261) 60170. Contact. N. Berg. Replies to correspondence and verifies reception reports in German or Russian. Broadcasts to Russia via Media Broadcast (*see*).

MV Baltic Radio, R&R Medienservice, Roland Rohde, Seestrasse 17, D-19089 Göhren, Germany. Phone: +49 (3861) 301-380, (mobile) +49 (178) 895-3872. Fax: +49 (3861) 302 9720. Email: info@mvbalticradio.de. Web: www.mvbalticradio.de. Contact: Roland Rohde. Replies to correspondence in German or English, and verifies reception reports. IRC or $1 required for postal reply. Sells small souvenirs. A monthly broadcast produced in Göhren, Mecklenburg-Vorpommern, and aired via facilities of Media Broadcast (*see*).

Radio 700, Funkhaus Euskirchen, Kuchenheimer Strasse 155, D-53881 Euskirchen, Germany. Phone: +49 (2251) 921300. Fax: +49 (2251) 921303. Email: kurzwelle@funkhaus-euskirchen.de; (Milling) christian@radio700.de. Web: (includes streaming audio) www.radio700.de. Contact: Christian Milling; Bernd Frinken, Chief Editor.

Radio Gloria International, Postfach 460143, D-01246 Dresden, Germany Email: radiogloria@aol.com. Verifies email reports via the Internet; $2 or 2 euros required for verification by postal mail. Broadcasts irregularly via Media Broadcast (*see*).

Radio Santec, Marienstrasse 1, D-97070 Würzburg, Germany. Phone: (0800-1600 Central European Time, Monday through Friday) +49 (931) 3903-264. Fax: +49 (931) 3903 195. Email: info@radio-santec.com. Web: (includes on-demand and streaming audio) www.radio-santec.com. Contact: Janett Wood. Reception reports verified with QSL cards only if requested. Radio Santec is the radio branch of Universelles Leben (Universal Life).

Stimme des Evangeliums, Evangelische Missions-Gemeinden, Jahnstrasse 9, D-89182 Bernstadt, Germany. Phone: +49 (7348) 948-026. Fax: +49 (7348) 948-027. Contact: Pastor Albert Giessler. Verifies reception reports in German or English. A broadcast of the Evangelical Missions Congregations in Germany, and aired via Media Broadcast (*see*).

GHANA World Time exactly

WARNING—CONFIDENCE ARTISTS: Attempted correspondence with Radio Ghana may result in requests, perhaps resulting from mail theft, from skilled confidence artists for money, free electronic or other products, publications or immigration sponsorship. To help avoid this, correspondence to Radio Ghana should be sent via registered mail.

Ghana Broadcasting Corporation—Radio Ghana (when operating), P.O. Box 1633, Accra, Ghana; (street address) Broadcasting House, Ring Road Central, Kanda, Accra, Ghana. Phone/Fax: +233 (21) 768-975, +233 (21) 221-161, +233 (21) 786-561. Email: online form. Web: www.gbcghana.com. Contact: (general) Director of Corporate Affairs; (administration) Director of Radio; (technical) Director of Engineering, or Propagation Department. Replies tend to be erratic, and reception reports are best sent to the attention of the Propagation Engineer, GBC Monitoring Station. Enclosing an IRC, return postage or $1 and registering your letter should improve the chances of a reply.

GREECE World Time +2 (+3 midyear)

Foni tis Helladas (Voice of Greece)

NONTECHNICAL: ERA-5, The Voice of Greece, 432 Messogeion, Aghia Paraskevi, 15342 Athens, Greece. Phone: +30 210-606-6310. Fax: +30 210 606 6309. Email: era5@ert.gr. Web: (includes streaming audio) www.voiceofgreece.gr. Contact: Angeliki Barka, Head of Programmes; Gina Vogiatzoglou, Managing Director. Free tourist literature.

TECHNICAL: ERA-5, General Technical Directorate, Messogeion 432, 15342 Athens, Greece. Phone: (Charalambopoulos) +30 210-606-6257. Fax: +30 210 606 6264, +30 210 606 6414, +30 210 606 6243. Email: (reception reports) era5@ert.gr; apodimos_era5@ert.gr; (technical information, schedules, Charalambopoulos) bcharalabopoulos@ert.gr. Contact: Babis Charalambopoulos, Planning Engineer. Technical reception reports may be sent via mail, fax or email.

Radiophonikos Stathmos Makedonias, Angelaki 2, 54636 Thessaloniki, Greece. Phone: +30 2310-299-400. Fax: +30 2310 299 550. Email: eupro@ert3.gr. Web: (includes streaming audio) www.ert3.gr. Contact: (general) Mrs. Tatiana Tsioli, Program Director; Lefty Kongalides, Head of International Relations; (technical) Dimitrios Keramidas, Engineer. Free booklets, stickers and other small souvenirs.

GUAM World Time +10

Adventist World Radio—KSDA

OPERATIONS AND ENGINEERING: P.O. Box 8990, Agat, GU 96928 USA. Phone: +1 (671) 565-2000, +1 (671) 565-2289. Fax: +1 (671) 565 2983. Email: brook@awr.org. Contact: Brook Powers. This address for specialized technical correspondence only. For further information, see AWR listing under USA.

Trans World Radio—KTWR

MAIN OFFICE, ENGINEERING INQUIRIES & FREQUENCY COORDINATION ONLY: P.O. Box 8780, Agat, GU 96928 USA. Phone: +1 (671) 828-8637. Fax: +1 (671) 828 8636. Email: (Ross) ktwrfcd@guam.twr.org. Contact: George Ross, Frequency Coordination Manager. This office will also verify email reports with a QSL card. Requests reports covering 15-30 minutes of programming. All English listener mail of a nontechnical nature should be sent to the Australian office (*see* next entry). Addresses for listener mail in other languages are given in the broadcasts. Also, *see* Trans World Radio, USA.

ENGLISH LISTENER MAIL, NONTECHNICAL: Trans World Radio, P.O. Box 390, Box Hill, Victoria 3128, Australia. Phone: +61 (3) 9899 3800. Fax: +61 (3) 9899 3900. Email: infoaus@twr.org. Web: http://twraustralia.org. Contact: John Reeder, National Director.

CHINESE WEBSITE, NONTECHNICAL: www.ktwr.net.

GUATEMALA World Time –6

Radio Buenas Nuevas, San Sebastián 13020, Huehuetenango, Guatemala. Contact: Israel G. Rodas Mérida,

Gerente. $1 or return postage helpful. Free religious and station information in Spanish. Sometimes includes a small pennant. Replies to correspondence in Spanish.

Radio Coatán—*see* Radio Cultural Coatán

Radio Cultural Coatán—TGCT, San Sebastián Coátan 13035, Huehuetenango, Guatemala. Phone: +502 7758-3491, +502 7758-5494. Email: radiocoatan@hotmail.com. Contact: Sebastián Pablo, Director. $1 or return postage required. Often announces as just "Radio Coatán."

Radio Verdad, Apartado Postal 5, Chiquimula, Guatemala. Phone: +502 7942-5689. Phone/Fax: +502 7942-0362. Email: radioverdad@intelnett.com; radioverdad5@yahoo.com. Web: (includes streaming audio) www.radioverdad.org. Contact: Dr. Édgar Amílcar Madrid Morales, Gerente. May send free pennants or calendars. Replies to correspondence in Spanish or English. Return postage appreciated. An evangelical and educational station.

GUINEA World Time exactly

Radiodiffusion-Télévision Guinéenne, B.P. 391, Conakry, Guinea. If no reply is forthcoming from this address, try sending your letter to: D.G.R./P.T.T., B.P. 3322, Conakry, Guinea. Phone/Fax: +224 451-408. Email: (Issa Conde, Directeur) issaconde@yahoo.fr. Contact: (general) Yaoussou Diaby, Journaliste Sportif; Boubacar Yacine Diallo, Directeur Général/ORTG; Issa Conde, Directeur; Seny Camara; (administration) Momo Toure, Chef Services Administratifs; (technical, studio) Mbaye Gagne, Chef de Studio; (technical, overall) Direction des Services Techniques. Return postage or $1 required. Replies very irregularly to correspondence in French.

GUYANA World Time –3

Voice of Guyana (when operating), Homestretch Avenue, Georgetown, Guyana. Phone: +592 223- 5162. Fax: +592 223 5163. Email: vog560am@homeviewguyana.com. Contact: (general) Mrs. Jasminee Sahoye, Programme Manager; (technical) Roy Marshall, Senior Technician; Shiroxley Goodman, Chief Engineer. $1 or IRC helpful. Sending a spare sticker from another station helps assure a reply. Note that when the station's mediumwave/AM transmitter is down because of a component fault, parts of the shortwave unit are sometimes 'borrowed' until spares become available. As a result, the station is sometimes off shortwave for weeks or months at a time.

HOLLAND—*see* NETHERLANDS

HONDURAS World Time –6

La Voz Evangélica—HRVC (if reactivated)

MAIN OFFICE: Apartado Postal 3252, Tegucigalpa, M.D.C., Honduras. Phone: +504 234-3468/69/70. Fax: +504 233 3933. Email: programas@hrvc.org. Web (includes streaming audio): www.hrvc.org. Contact: (general) Srta. Orfa Esther Durón Mendoza, Secretaria; Tereso Ramos, Director de Programación; Alan Maradiaga; Modesto Palma, Jefe, Depto. Tráfico; (technical) Carlos Paguada, Director del Dpto. Técnico; (administration) Venancio Mejía, Gerente; Nelson Perdomo, Director. Free calendars. Three IRCs or $1 required. Replies to correspondence in English, Spanish, Portuguese or German.

REGIONAL OFFICE, SAN PEDRO SULA: Apartado 2336, San Pedro Sula, Honduras. Phone: +504 557-5030. Contact: Hernán Miranda, Director.

REGIONAL OFFICE, LA CEIBA: Apartado 164, La Ceiba, Honduras. Phone: +504 443-2390. Contact: José Banegas, Director.

Radio HRMI, Radio Misiones Internacionales

STATION: Apartado Postal 20583, Comayagüela, M.D.C., Honduras. Phone: +504 233-9029, +504 238-4933. Contact: Wayne Downs, Director. $1 or return postage helpful.

U.S. OFFICE: IMF World Missions, P.O. Box 6321, San Bernardino CA 92412, USA. Phone +1 (909) 466-5793. Fax: +1 (909) 370 4862. Email: jkpimf@msn.com. Contact: Dr. James K. Planck, President; Gustavo Roa, Coordinator.

Radio Luz y Vida—HRPC, Apartado 303, San Pedro Sula, Honduras; (reception reports in English) HRPC Radio, P. O. Box 303, San Pedro Sula, Honduras. Phone: +504 654-1221. Fax: +504 557 0394. Email: efmhonduras@globalnet.hn. Contact: Donald R. Moore, Station Director; or, to have your letter read over the air, "English Friendship Program." Return postage or $1 appreciated.

HUNGARY World Time +1 (+2 midyear)

Hungarian Radio (Magyar Rádió), International Relations Department, Bródy Sándor utca 5-7, H-1800 Budapest, Hungary. Phone: +36 (1) 328-8108. Fax: +36 (1) 328 7004. Email: nki@radio.hu. Does not verify reception reports.

INDIA World Time +5:30

WARNING—MAIL THEFT: PASSPORT readers report that letters to India containing IRCs and other valuables have disappeared en route when not registered. Best is either to register your letter or to send correspondence in an unsealed envelope, and without enclosures.

VERIFICATION OF REGIONAL STATIONS: All Indian regional stations can be verified via New Delhi (see All India Radio—External Services Division for contact details), but some listeners prefer contacting each station individually, in the hope of receiving a direct QSL. Well-known Indian DXer Jose Jacob, VU2JOS, makes the following suggestions: address your report to the station engineer of the respective station; specify the time of reception in both World Time (UTC) and Indian Standard Time (IST); instead of using the SINPO code, write a brief summary of reception quality; and if possible, report on local programs rather than relays of national programming from New Delhi. Jose adds that reports should be written in English, and return postage is not required. Enclosing currency notes is against the law.

Akashvani—All India Radio

ADMINISTRATION/ENGINEERING: Directorate General of All India Radio, Akashvani Bhawan, 1 Sansad Marg, New Delhi-110 001, India. Phone: (Director General) +91 (11) 2371-0300 Ext. 102; (Engineer-in-Chief) +91 (11)

2342-1058; (Phone/Fax) +91 (11) 2342-1459; (Director, Spectrum Management) +91 (11) 2342-1062, +91 (11) 2342-1145. Fax: (Director General) +91 (11) 2342 1956. Email: airlive@air.org.in; (Director General) dgair@air.org.in; (Engineer-in-Chief) einc@air.org.in; (Director, Spectrum Management) spectrum-manager@air.org.in; (H.R. Singh, Engineer-in-Chief) hrsingh@air.org.in. Web: www.allindiaradio.gov.in. Contact: G. Jayalal, Acting Director General; (technical) H.R. Singh, Engineer-in-Chief; V.P. Singh, Director, Spectrum Management & Synergy; B.K Obrai, Deputy Director, Spectrum Management & Synergy.

AUDIENCE RESEARCH: Audience Research Unit, All India Radio, Press Trust of India Building, 2nd floor, Sansad Marg, New Delhi-110 001, India. Phone: (Director) +91 (11) 2342-1022, +91 (11) 2342-1006 X-422. Contact: M.N. Jha, Director in charge.

CENTRAL MONITORING STATION: All India Radio, Ayanagar, New Delhi-110 047, India. Phone: +91 (11) 2650-2955, +91 (11) 2650 1763.

INTERNATIONAL MONITORING STATION—MAIN OFFICE: International Monitoring Station, All India Radio, Dr. K.S. Krishnan Road, Todapur, New Delhi-110 097, India. Phone: +91 (11) 2584-2939. Contact: B.L. Kasturiya, Deputy Director; D.P. Chhabra or R.K. Malviya, Assistant Research Engineers—Frequency Planning.

NATIONAL CHANNEL: AIR, Gate 22, Jawaharlal Nehru Stadium, Lodhi Road, New Delhi-110 003. Phone: +91 (11) 2584-3825; (station engineer) +91 (11) 2584-3207. Email: (station engineer) sechair@yahoo.com. Contact: J.K. Das, Director; Pradeep Mehra, Station Engineer.

NEWS SERVICE DIVISION: News Service Division, Broadcasting House, 1 Sansad Marg, New Delhi-110 001, India. Phone: (general, newsroom) +91 (11) 2342-1100, +91 (11) 2342-1101; (Special Director General—News) +91 (11) 2342-1218; (News on phone in English) +91 (11) 2332-4343/1259; (News on phone in Hindi) +91 (11) 2332-4242/1258. Fax: +91 (11) 2371 1196. Email: (general, newsroom) nbhnews@air.org.in; (Director General) dgn@air.org.in. Web: (includes on-demand audio) www.newsonair.com. Contact: P.K. Bandopadhyay, Director General—News.

PROGRAMMING: New Broadcasting House, 27 Mahadev Road, New Delhi-110 001 India. Phone: +91 (11) 2342-1218.

RESEARCH AND DEVELOPMENT: Office of the Chief Engineer R&D, All India Radio, 14-B Ring Road, Indraprastha Estate, New Delhi-110 002, India. Phone: (general) +91 (11) 2337-8211/12; (chief engineer) +91 (11) 2337 9255, +91 (11) 2337-9329. Fax: +91 (11) 2337 9329, +91 (11) 2337 9674. Email: rdair@nda.vsnl.net.in; cerd.rdair.res.in. Contact: A.K. Bhatnagar, Chief Engineer.

TRANSCRIPTION AND PROGRAM EXCHANGE SERVICES: Akashvani Bhawan, 1 Sansad Marg, New Delhi-110 001, India. Phone: (Director, Transcription & Program Exchange Services) +91 (11) 2342-1927. Contact: D.P. Jadav, Director.

All India Radio—External Services Division

MAIN ADDRESS: Broadcasting House, 1 Sansad Marg, P.O. Box 500, Parliament Street, New Delhi-110 001, India. Fax: +91 (11) 2371 0057; (Deputy Director) +91 (11) 2371 0057. Contact: (general) H.K.Pani, Deputy Director of External Services; S.C. Panda, Audience Relations Officer; "Faithfully Yours" program. Email: esd@air.org.in. Web: (includes online reception report form) www.allindiaradio.gov.in. Replies can be somewhat erratic from External Services Division.

VERIFICATION ADDRESS: Director, Spectrum Management & Synergy, All India Radio, Room 204, Akashwani Bhavan, Sansad Marg, New Delhi-110 001, India. Phone/Fax: +91 (11) 2342- 1062, +91 (11) 2342-1145. Email: spectrum-manager@air.org.in; online form (www.allindiaradio.gov.in/recepfdk.html). Contact: V. P. Singh, Director, Spectrum Management & Synergy. Audio files accepted.

All India Radio—Aizawl, Radio Tila, Tuikhuahtlang, Aizawl-796 001, Mizoram, India. Phone: (engineering) +91 (389) 2322-415. Fax: +91 (389) 2322 114. Email: aizawl@air.org.in.

All India Radio—Aligarh Shortwave Transmitting Centre

EXTERNAL SERVICES: see All India Radio—External Services Division, above.

DOMESTIC PROGRAMS FROM NEW DELHI: see All India Radio—New Delhi.

All India Radio—Bengaluru [Bangalore] Shortwave Transmitting Centre

EXTERNAL SERVICES: see All India Radio—External Services Division, above.

VIVIDH BHARATI: see All India Radio—Mumbai.

AIR OFFICE NEAR TRANSMITTERS: Superintending Engineer, Super Power Transmitters, All India Radio, Yelahanka New Town, Bengaluru-560 064, Karnataka, India. Phone: +91 (80) 2846-0354. Fax: +91 (80) 2846-0379. Email: sptairynk@vsnl.net. Contact: (technical) L.M. Ambhast, Superintending Engineer; T. Rajendiran, Station Engineer.

All India Radio—Bhopal, Akashvani Bhawan, Shyamla Hills, Bhopal-462 002, Madhya Pradesh, India. Phone: (engineering) +91 (755) 2661-241. Email: bhopal@air.org.in; (station engineer) se_airbpl@datone.in. Contact: (technical) Ravindra Goyel, Station Engineer.

All India Radio—Chennai

EXTERNAL SERVICES: see All India Radio—External Services Division.

DOMESTIC SERVICE: S.M. Nagar P.O., Avadi, Chennai-600 062, Tamil Nadu, India. Phone: (engineering) +91 (44) 2638-3204. Email: chennai.avadi@air.org.in. Contact: B. Geetha Lakshmi, Station Engineer.

All India Radio—Gangtok, Old M.L.A. Hostel, Gangtok-737 101, Sikkim, India. Phone: (engineering) +91 (3592) 202-636. Email: gangtok@air.org.in; (station engineer) seairgtk@yahoo.co.in. Contact: (general) Swapna Mondal, Station Director; (technical) Sandeep Singh, Station Engineer.

All India Radio—Gorakhpur

EXTERNAL SERVICES: see All India Radio—External Services Division, above.

DOMESTIC PROGRAMS FROM NEW DELHI: see All India Radio—New Delhi.

All India Radio—Guwahati

EXTERNAL SERVICES: see All India Radio—External Services Division.

DOMESTIC SERVICE: P.O. Box 28, Chandmari, Guwahati-781 003, Assam, India. Phone: (engineering) +91 (361) 2660-235. Email: guwahati@air.org.in. Contact:

This may look like a Texas oilman's dream, but it's actually world band antenna towers at Khampur—one of All India Radio's "Delhi sites."

A. Gupta

(technical) P.C. Sanghi, Superintending Engineer; S.N. Basak, Station Engineer.

All India Radio—Hyderabad, Rocklands, Saifabad, Hyderabad-500 004, Andhra Pradesh, India. Phone: (engineering) +91 (40) 2323-4904. Fax: +91 (40) 2323 2239, +91 (40) 2323 4282. Email: hyderabad@air.org.in; airhyderabad@rediffmail.com. Contact: (technical) S.S. Reddy, Superintending Engineer; P.S. Nagabhushanam, Station Engineer.

All India Radio—Imphal, Palace Compound, Imphal-795 001, Manipur, India. Phone: (engineering) +91 (385) 2220-534. Phone/Fax: (general) +91 (385) 2220 248. Email: imphal@air.org.in; airimfal@sancharnet.in. Web: http://cicmanipur.nic.in/html/air_imp.htm. Contact: (technical) M. Jayaraman, Superintending Engineer.

All India Radio—Itanagar, Naharlagun, Itanagar-791 111, Arunachal Pradesh, India. Phone: (engineering) +91 (360) 2212-881. Fax: +91 (360) 2213 008, +91 (360) 2212 933. Email: itanagar@air.org.in. Contact: J.T. Jirdoh, Station Director; P.K. Bez Baruah, Assistant Station Engineer; P. Sanghi, Superintending Engineer. Verifications direct from station are difficult, as engineering is done by staff visiting from the Regional Engineering Headquarters at AIR—Guwahati (*see*); that address might be worth contacting if all else fails.

All India Radio—Jaipur, 5 Park House, Mirza Ismail Road, Jaipur-302 001, Rajasthan, India. Phone: +91 (141) 2366-263. Fax: +91 (141) 2363 196. Email: jaipur@air.org.in. Contact: (technical) S.C. Sharma, Station Engineer; C.L. Goel, Assistant Station Engineer.

All India Radio—Jammu—*see* Radio Kashmir—Jammu.

All India Radio—Jeypore, Jeypore-764 005, Orissa, India. Phone: (engineering) +91 (6854) 232-524. Email: jeypore@air.org.in; airjeypore@rediffmail.com. Contact: R. Harsha Latha, Station Engineer.

All India Radio—Kohima (when operating), P.O. Box 42, Kohima-797 001, Nagaland, India. Phone: (engineering) +91 (370) 2245-556. Email: kohima@air.org.in. Contact: (technical) M. Tyagi, Superintending Engineer; K.K Jose, Assistant Engineer; K. Morang, Assistant Station Engineer. Return postage, $1 or IRC helpful. Transmissions tend to be irregular.

All India Radio—Kolkata, Eden Garden, G.P.O. Box 696, Kolkata—700 001, West Bengal, India. Phone: (engineering) +91 (33) 2248-1705. Email: (superintending engineer) sgeairkolkata@rediffmail.com. Web: (unofficial) www.freewebs.com/airkolkata. Contact: (technical) S.K. Pal, Superintending Engineer.

All India Radio—Kurseong, Mehta Club Building, Kurseong-734 203, Darjeeling District, West Bengal, India. Phone: (engineering) +91 (354) 2344-350. Email: kurseong@air.org.in. Contact: (general) George Kuruvilla, Assistant Director; (technical) R.K. Sinha, Chief Engineer; B.K. Behara, Station Engineer.

All India Radio—Leh, Leh-194 101, Ladakh District, Jammu and Kashmir, India. Phone: (engineering) +91 (1982) 252-063. Email: leh@air.org.in; (station engineer) seairleh@rediffmail.com. Contact: (technical) Yogendra Trihan, Station Engineer.

All India Radio—Lucknow, 18 Vidhan Sabha Marg, Lucknow-226 001, Uttar Pradesh, India. Phone: (engineering) +91 (522) 2237-601. Email: lucknow@air.org.in. Contact: Dr. S.M. Pradhan, Superintending Engineer. This station now appears to be replying via the External Services Division, New Delhi.

All India Radio—Mumbai

EXTERNAL SERVICES: see All India Radio—External Services Division.

COMMERCIAL SERVICE (VIVIDH BHARATI): All India Radio, Gorai Road, Borivli West, Mumbai-400 091, Maharashtra, India. Phone: (director) +91 (22) 2869-2698; (station engineer) +91 (22) 2868-2699. Email: vbsmumbai@gmail.com. Web: www.vividhbharatimumbai.co.cc; www.freewebs.com/vividhbharati. Contact: Mahendra Modi, Acting Station Director.

DOMESTIC SERVICE: Broadcasting House, Backbay Reclamation, Mumbai-400 020, Maharashtra, India. Phone: (engineering) +91 (22) 2202-9853. Email: mumbai.malad@air.org.in; bhairmumbai@yahoo.com. Contact: R.B. Gupta, Suptg. Engingeer.

All India Radio—New Delhi, Broadcasting House, New Delhi-110 011, India. Phone: (engineering) +91 (11) 2371 0113. Email: delhi.bh@air.org.in. Contact: (technical) V. Chaudhry, Superintending Engineer.

EXTERNAL SERVICES: see All India Radio—External Services Division, above.

HIGH POWER TRANSMITTERS (250 kW), KHAMPUR: New Delhi-110036, India. Phone: +91 (11) 2720-2158; (Station Engineer) +91 (11) 2720-3560. Email: delhi.khampur@air.org.in. Contact: V.K. Baleja, Station Engineer.

HIGH POWER TRANSMITTERS (50 & 100 kW), KINGSWAY: New Delhi-110009, India. Phone: +91 (11) 2743-6661. Email: hptkingsway@yahoo.com.

All India Radio—Panaji Shortwave Transmitting Centre

HEADQUARTERS: see All India Radio—External Services Division, above.

HIGH POWER TRANSMITTERS, AIR: Goa University PO, Goa-403206, India. Phone: (engineering) +91 (832) 2230-696. Email: panaji.spt@air.org.in; airtrgoa@sancharnet.in.

All India Radio—Port Blair, Haddo Post, Dilanipur, Port Blair-744 102, South Andaman, Andaman and Nicobar Islands, Union Territory, India. Phone: (engineering) +91 (3192) 230-682. Fax: +91 (3192) 230 260. Email: pblairpb@sancharnet.in; airportblair@rediffmail.com. Contact: P.P. Baby, Suptg. Engineer. Registering letters appears to be useful.

All India Radio—Ranchi (when operating), 6 Ratu Road, Ranchi-834 001, Jharkhand, India. Phone: (engineering) +91 (651) 2283-310. Email: ranchi@air.org.in. Contact: (technical) H.K. Sinha, Superintending Engineer.

All India Radio—Shillong, North Eastern Service, P.O. Box 14, Shillong-793 001, Meghalaya, India. Phone: (engineering) +91 (364) 2222-272. Email: shillong.nes@air.org.in. Contact: (general) C. Lalsaronga, Director NEIS; (technical) H. Diengdoh, Station Engineer. Free booklet on station's history. Replies tend to be rare, due to a shortage of staff.

All India Radio—Shimla, Choura Maidan, Shimla-171 004, Himachal Pradesh, India. Phone: (engineering) +91 (177) 2811-355. Email: shimla@air.org.in; airshimla@yahoo.com. Contact: (technical) V.K. Upadhayay, Superintending Engineer; Krishna Murari, Assistant Engineer. Return postage helpful.

All India Radio—Srinagar—*see* Radio Kashmir—Srinagar.

All India Radio—Thiruvananthapuram, P.O. Box 403, Bhakti Vilas, Vazuthacaud, Thiruvananthapuram-695 014, Kerala, India. Phone: (engineering) +91 (471) 2325-009. Phone/Fax: (station director) +91 (471) 2324-406. Email: thiruvananthapuram@air.org.in; (comments on programs) pm@airtvm.com; (comments on reception} mail@airtvm.com. Web: www.airtvm.com. Contact: K.A. Muraleedharan, Station Director; (technical) K.V. Ramachandran, Station Engineer.

Radio Kashmir—Jammu (when operating), Palace Road, Jammu-188 001, Jammu and Kashmir, India. Phone: (engineering) +91 (191) 2544-411. Email: jammu@air.org.in.

Radio Kashmir—Srinagar, Sherwani Road, Srinagar-190 001, Jammu and Kashmir, India. Phone: (engineering) +91 (194) 2452-287/177. Email: srinagar@air.org.in. Contact: G.H. Zia, Station Director; Ayaz A. Malik, Station Engineer.

Trans World Radio India—*see* Trans World Radio, USA.

INDONESIA

World Time +7 Western: Waktu Indonesia Bagian Barat (Jawa, Sumatera); +8 Central: Waktu Indonesia Bagian Tengal (Bali, Kalimantan, Sulawesi, Nusa Tenggara); +9 Eastern: Waktu Indonesia Bagian Timur (Papua, Maluku)

NOTE: Except where otherwise indicated, Indonesian stations, especially those of the Radio Republik Indonesia (RRI) network, will reply to at least some correspondence in English. However, correspondence in Indonesian is more likely to ensure a reply.

Kang Guru Radio English, Indonesia Australia Language Foundation, P.O. Box 3095, Denpasar 80030, Bali, Indonesia. Phone: +62 (361) 225-243. Fax: +62 (361) 263 509. Email: online form; kangguru@ialf.edu. Web: www.kangguru.org. Contact: Kevin Dalton, Kang Guru Project Manager; Sue Rodger, ELT Media and Training Coordinator; Ms. Ogi Yutarini, Project Coordinating Officer. Free "Kang Guru" magazine. This program is aired over various RRI outlets, including Jakarta and Sorong.

Radio Pemerintah Daerah Kabupaten TK II—RPDK Manggarai, Ruteng, Flores, Nusa Tenggara Timur, Indonesia. Contact: Simon Saleh, B.A. Return postage required.

Radio Pemerintah Daerah Kabupaten Daerah TK II—RSPK Ngada, Jalan Soekarno-Hatta, Bjawa, Flores, Nusa Tenggara Tengah, Indonesia. Phone: +62 (384) 21-142. Contact: Drs. Petrus Tena, Kepala Studio.

Radio Republik Indonesia—RRI Biak (when operating), Kotak Pos 505, Biak 98117, Papua, Indonesia. Phone: +62 (981) 21-211, +62 (981) 21-197. Fax: +62 (981) 21 905. Contact: Butje Latuperissa, Kepala Seksi Siaran; Drs. D.A. Siahainenia, Kepala Stasiun. Correspondence in Indonesian preferred.

Radio Republik Indonesia—RRI Bukittinggi (when operating), Stasiun Regional 1 Bukittinggi, Jalan Prof. Muhammad Yamin 199, Aurkuning, Bukittinggi 26131, Propinsi Sumatera Barat, Indonesia. Phone: +62 (752) 21-319, +62 (752) 21-320. Fax: +62 (752) 367 132. Contact: Mr. Effendi, Sekretaris; Zul Arifin Mukhtar, SH; Samirwan Sarjana Hukum, Producer, "Phone in Program." Replies to correspondence in Indonesian or English. Return postage helpful.

Radio Republik Indonesia—RRI Fak Fak, Jalan Kapten P. Tendean, Kotak Pos 54, Fak-Fak 98612, Papua, Indonesia. Phone: +62 (956) 22-519, +62 (956) 22-521. Contact: Bahrun Siregar, Kepala Stasiun; Aloys Ngotra, Kepala Seksi Siaran; Drs. Tukiran Erlantoko; Richart Tan, Kepala Sub Seksi Siaran Kata. Station plans to upgrade its transmitting facilities with the help of the Japanese government. Return postage required. Replies occasionally.

Radio Republik Indonesia—RRI Gorontalo, Jalan Jendral Sudirman 30, Gorontalo 96115, Sulawesi Utara, Indonesia. Fax: +62 (435) 821 590/91. Contact: Drs.

Bagus Edi Asmoro; Drs. Muhammad. Assad, Kepala Stasiun; Saleh S. Thalib, Technical Manager. Return postage helpful. Replies occasionally, preferably to correspondence in Indonesian.

Radio Republik Indonesia—RRI Jakarta
STATION: Stasiun Nasional Jakarta, Kotak Pos 356, Jakarta 10110, Daerah Khusus Jakarta Raya, Indonesia; or (street address) Jalan Medan Merdeka Barat 4-5, Jakarta 10110, Indonesia. Phone: +62 (21) 345-9091, +62 (21) 384-6817. Fax: +62 (21) 345 7132, +62 (21) 345 7134. Email: info@rri.co.id. Web: (includes streaming audio) www.rri.co.id. Contact: Drs. Beni Koesbani, Kepala Stasiun; Drs. Nuryudi, MM. Return postage helpful. Replies irregularly.
TRANSMITTERS DIVISION: Jalan Merdeka Barat 4-5, Jakarta 10110 Indonesia. Phone/Fax: +62 (21) 385-7831. Email: sruslan@yahoo.com, sruslan@msn.com. Contact: Sunarya Ruslan, Head of Transmitters Division.

Radio Republik Indonesia—RRI Jambi (when operating), Jalan Jendral A. Yani 5, Telanaipura, Jambi 36122, Propinsi Jambi, Indonesia. Contact: Kepala Siaran; H. Asmuni Lubis, BA. Return postage helpful.

Radio Republik Indonesia—RRI Kendari, Kotak Pos 7, Kendari 93111, Sulawesi Tenggara, Indonesia. Phone: +62 (401) 21-464. Fax: +62 (401) 21 730. Contact: Drs. M. Hazir Kasrah, Manajer Seksi Siaran. Return postage required. Replies slowly to correspondence in Indonesian.

Radio Republik Indonesia—RRI Makassar, Jalan Riburane 3, Makassar, 90111, Sulawesi Selatan, Indonesia. Phone: +62 (411) 321-853. Contact: H. La Sirama, S. Sos., Senior Manager of Broadcasting Division. Replies irregularly to correspondence in Indonesian or English. Return postage, $1 or IRCs helpful.

Radio Republik Indonesia—RRI Manokwari (when operating), Regional II, Jalan Merdeka 68, Manokwari 98311, Papua, Indonesia. Phone: +62 (962) 21-343. Contact: Eddy Kusbandi, Manager; Nurdin Mokogintu. Return postage helpful.

Radio Republik Indonesia—RRI Nabire, Kotak Pos 110, Jalan Merdeka 74 Nabire 98811, Papua, Indonesia. Phone: +62 (984) 21-013. Contact: Muchtar Yushaputra, Kepala Stasiun. Free stickers and occasional free picture postcards. Return postage or IRCs helpful.

Radio Republik Indonesia—RRI Palangkaraya (when operating), Jalan M. Husni Thamrin 1, Palangkaraya 73111, Kalimantan Tengah, Indonesia. Phone: +62 (536) 21-779. Fax: +62 (536) 21 778. Contact: Andy Sunandar; Drs.Amiruddin; S. Polin; A.F. Herry Purwanto; Meyiwati SH; Supardal Djojosubrojo, Sarjana Hukum; Dr. S. Parlin Tobing, Station Manager; Murniaty Oesin, Transmission Department Engineer; Gumer Kamis; Ricky D. Wader, Kepala Stasiun. Return postage helpful. Will respond to correspondence in Indonesian or English.

Radio Republik Indonesia—RRI Palu, Jalan R.A. Kartini 39, Palu 94112, Sulawesi Tengah, Indonesia. Phone: +62 (451) 21-621, +62 (451) 94-112. Contact: Akson Boole; Nyonyah Netty Ch. Soriton, Kepala Seksi Siaran; Gugun Santoso; Untung Santoso, Kepala Seksi Teknik; M. Hasjim, Head of Programming. Return postage required. Replies slowly to correspondence in Indonesian.

Radio Republik Indonesia—RRI Pontianak, Kotak Pos 1005, Pontianak 78117, Kalimantan Barat, Indonesia. Phone: +62 (561) 734-987. Fax: +62 (561) 734 659. Contact: Sudiman Bonavarte, Kepala Stasiun. Return postage or $1 helpful. Replies irregularly to correspondence in Indonesian (preferred) or English.

Radio Republik Indonesia—RRI Serui, Jalan Pattimura Kotak Pos 19, Serui 98213, Papua, Indonesia. Phone: +62 (983) 31-150, +62 (983) 31-121. Contact: M. Yawandare, Manager Siaran. Replies occasionally to correspondence in Indonesian, although Mr. Yawandare also understands English. IRC or return postage helpful.

Radio Republik Indonesia—RRI Ternate (when operating), Jalan Sultan Khairun, Kedaton, Ternate 97720 (Ternate), Maluku Utara, Indonesia. Phone: +62 (921) 21-582, +62 (921) 21-762, +62 (921) 25-525. Contact: (general) Abd. Latief Kamarudin, Kepala Stasiun; (technical) Rusdy Bachmid, Head of Engineering; Abubakar Alhadar. Return postage helpful.

Radio Republik Indonesia—RRI Wamena (when operating), RRI Regional II, Kotak Pos 10, Wamena, Papua 99511, Indonesia. Phone: +62 (969) 31-380. Fax: +62 (969) 31 299. Contact: Yoswa Kumurawak, Penjab Subseksi Pemancar. Return postage helpful.

Voice of Indonesia, Kotak Pos 1157, Jakarta 10001, Daerah Khusus Jakarta Raya, Indonesia; (street address) Jalan Medan Merdeka Barat No. 4-5, 4th Floor, Jakarta 10110, Indonesia. Phone: +62 (21) 345-6811. Fax: +62 (21) 350 0990. Email: english@voi.co.id. Web: (includes streaming audio) www.voi.co.id. Contact: Anastasia Yasmine, Head of Foreign Affairs Section; Amy Aisha, Presenter, "Listeners Mailbag." Free stickers and calendars. Correspondence is best addressed to the individual language sections. Be careful when addressing your letters to the station as mail sent to the Voice of Indonesia, Japanese Section, has sometimes been incorrectly delivered to NHK's Jakarta Bureau. Very slow in replying but enclosing 4 IRCs may help speed things up.

INTERNATIONAL WATERS

Coalition Maritime Forces (CMF) Radio One (when operating), MARLO Bahrain, PSC 451 Box 330, FPO AE 09834-2800, USA. Email: (including reception reports) marlo.bahrain@marlobahrain.org. Web: (MARLO Bahrain parent organization) www.marlobahrain.org. Station of the Maritime Liaison Office (MARLO) of the United States Navy. Broadcasts via low power transmitters on ships in the Persian Gulf and nearby waters. Verifies reception reports.

IRAN World Time +3:30 (+4:30 midyear)

Voice of the Islamic Republic of Iran
MAIN OFFICE: IRIB External Services, P.O. Box 19395-6767, Tehran, Iran. Phone: +98 (21) 2204-2808; (English Service) +98 (21) 2201-3720, +98 (21) 2216-2895, +98 (21) 2216-2734. Fax: +98 (21) 2205 1635, +98 (21) 2204 1097; (English Service) +98 (21) 2201 3770. Email: (English Service) englishradio@irib.ir (same format for German, Spanish and Italian, e.g. spanishradio@irib.ir); (French Service) radio_fr@irib.ir. Web: (includes streaming audio) www.irib.ir/worldservice. Contact: Mohammad B. Khoshnevisan, IRIB English Radio. Free books on Islam, magazines, calendars, bookmarkers, tourist

literature and postcards. Return postage appreciated. Is currently asking listeners to send their telephone numbers so that they can be called by the station. You can send your phone number to the postal address above, or fax it to: + 98 (21) 2205 1635.
FREQUENCY MANAGEMENT: Islamic Republic of Iran Broadcasting, P.O. Box 1935-3333, Tehran, Iran. Phone: +98 (21) 2216-9215. Fax: +98 (21) 2201 3649. Email: sw@irib.ir. Contact: Saeed Alavivafa, Head of Shortwave Frequency Management.
SIRJAN TRANSMITTING STATION: P.O. Box 369, Sirjan, Iran. Contact: Aliasghar Shakoori Moghaddam, Head of Sirjan Station.
Mashhad Regional Radio, P.O. Box 555, Mashhad Center, Jomhoriye Eslame, Iran. Contact: J. Ghanbari, General Director.

IRAQ World Time +3 (sometimes +4 midyear)

Voice of Iraqi Kurdistan ("Aira dangi Kurdestana Iraqiyah") (when operating). Web: (includes streaming audio) http://kdp.nu (click on "KDP's Media," then on "KDP info"). Station of the Kurdistan Democratic Party-Iraq (KDP), led by Masoud Barzani. Broadcasts from its own transmitting facilities, located in the Kurdish section of Iraq. To contact the station or to obtain verification of reception reports, try going via one of the following KDP offices:
KDP INTERNATIONAL RELATIONS BUREAU (U.K.): Phone: +44 (207) 498-2664. Fax: +44 (207) 498 2531.
KDP REPRESENTATION IN WASHINGTON: 17115 Leesburg Pike #110, Falls Church VA 22043 USA. Phone: +1 (703) 533-5882. Fax: +1 (703) 599 5886. Email: pdk7usa@aol.com.
KDP-SWEDEN OFFICE: Email: party@kdp.se. Web: (includes streaming audio) www.kdp.se. Contact: Alex Atroushi. Reception reports to this address have sometimes been verified by email.

IRELAND World Time exactly (+1 midyear)

Radio Telefís Éireann (when operating on shortwave), Donnybrook, Dublin 4, Ireland. Phone: +353 (1) 208-3111. Fax: +353 (1) 208 3080. Email: (Pope) bernie.pope@rte.ie. Web: (includes on-demand and streaming audio) www.rte.ie/radio. Contact: Mrs. Bernie Pope, Network Support, who will verify reception reports, including those sent by email. Broadcasts irregularly, mainly for sports or election coverage.

ISRAEL World Time +2 (+3 midyear)

Bezeq—Israel Telecommunication Corp. Ltd., Engineering and Planning Division, Radio and T.V. Broadcasting Section, P.O. Box 62081, Tel-Aviv 61620, Israel. Phone: +972 (3) 955-4120. Fax: +972 (3) 941 0909. Email: (Oren) mosheor@bezeq.com. Web: www.bezeq.co.il. Contact: Moshe Oren, Frequency Manager. Bezeq is responsible for transmitting the programs of the Israel Broadcasting Authority (IBA), which *inter alia* parents Kol Israel. This address only for pointing out transmitter-related problems (interference, modulation quality, network mixups, etc.), especially by fax, of transmitters based in Israel. Does not verify reception reports.
Galei Zahal (Israel Defence Forces Radio), Zahal, Military Mail No. 01005, Israel. Phone: +972 (3) 512-6714. Fax: +972 (3) 512 6666. Email: glz@galatz.co.il. Web: (includes on-demand and streaming audio) www.glz.msn.co.il.
Kol Israel, P.O. Box 1082, Heleni Hamalka 21, Jerusalem 91010, Israel. Phone: (general) +972 (3) 693-6444; (Engineering Dept.) +972 (2) 501-3453. Email: (correspondence relating to reception problems, only) engineering@israelradio.org. Web: (includes on-demand and streaming audio) www.israelradio.org; (on-demand and streaming audio) www.iba.org.il. Contact: Edmond Sehayeq, Head of Programming, Persian broadcasts; (administration) Yonni Ben-Menachem, Director of External Broadcasting; (technical, frequency management) Raphael Kochanowski, Director of Liaison and Coordination, Engineering Dept. No verifications or freebies, due to limited budget. Shortwave broadcasts continue in Persian only and are likely to cease at the end of 2009.

ITALY World Time +1 (+2 midyear)

Italian Radio Relay Service, IRRS-Shortwave, Nexus-IBA, P.O. Box 11028, 20110 Milano, Italy; (reception reports) P.O. Box 10980, 20110 Milano, Italy. Phone: +39 (02) 266-6971. Fax: +39 (02) 7063 8151. Email: (general) info@nexus.org; (reception reports) reports@nexus.org; (Cotroneo) alfredo@nexus.org; (Norton) ron@nexus.org. Web: www.nexus.org/radio.htm; (streaming audio) http://mp3.nexus.org; (International Public Access Radio) www.nexus.org/IPAR; (European Gospel Radio) www.egradio.org. Contact: (general) Vanessa Dickinson; Anna S. Boschetti, President; Alfredo E. Cotroneo, CEO; (technical) Ron Norton, Verification Manager. Correspondence and reception reports by email are answered promptly and at no charge, but for budget reasons the station may be unable to reply to all postal correspondence. Two IRCs or $1 helpful.
Radio Maria, Via Mazzini 15, 21020 Casciago, Verona, Italy. Web: (includes streaming audio) www.radiomaria.org. Contact: Claudio Re, Radio Maria World Family Network Director.
VERIFICATION OF RECEPTION REPORTS: Radio Maria, c/o Giampiero Bernardini, via Tertulliano 35, 20137 Milano, Italy. Email: qsl@radiomaria.org. Return postage, IRC or $1 requested for postal reply.

JAPAN World Time +9

Furusato no Kaze (Wind of the Homeland), Headquarters for the Abduction Issue, 1-6-1 Nagata-cho, Chiyoda-ku, Tokyo 100-8968, Japan. Phone: +81 (3) 3522-2300. Email: info@rachi.go.jp. Web: (includes on-demand audio) www.rachi.go.jp/jp/shisei/radio/index.html. Contact: Sunouchi Tomoyuki. Replies to correspondence in Japanese or English, and occasionally verifies reception reports.
PROGRAM PRODUCTION: Japan Center for Intercultural Communications, 2-7-7 Hirakawa-cho, Chiyoda-ku, Tokyo 102-0093, Japan. Web: http://home.jcic.or.jp.
Nihon no Kaze (Ilbone Baram, Wind of Japan). Korean-language sister-station to Furusato no Kaze (*see*), with same contact details. Web: (includes on-demand audio) www.rachi.go.jp/jp/shisei/radio/radio_k.html.

Radio Japan/NHK World
MAIN OFFICE: NHK World, Nippon Hoso Kyokai, Tokyo 150-8001, Japan. Phone: +81 (3) 3465-1111. Fax: +81 (3) 3481 1350. Email: (general) nhkworld@nhk.jp; (Spanish Section) rj-espa@intl.nhk.or.jp. Web: (English, includes on-demand and streaming audio) www.nhk.or.jp/nhkworld; (Japanese, includes on-demand and streaming audio) www.nhk.or.jp/nhkworld/japanese. Contact: (administration) Saburo Eguchi, Deputy Director General; Shuichiro Sunohara, Deputy Director International Planning & Programming; Tadao Sakomizu, Director, English Service; Ms. Kyoko Hirotani, Planning & Programming Division; T. Sato, Verifications.
ENGINEERING ADMINISTRATION DEPARTMENT: Nippon Hoso Kyokai, Tokyo 150-8001, Japan. Phone: +81 (3) 5455-5395, +81 (3) 5455-5384, +81 (3) 5455-5376, +81 (3) 5455-2288. Fax: +81 (3) 3485 0952, + 81 (3) 3481 4985. Email: (general) rj-freq@eng.nhk.or.jp; yoshimi@eng.nhk.or.jp, kurasima@eng.nhk.or.jp. Contact: Fujimoto Hiroki, Frequency Manager; Akira Mizuguchi, Transmissions Manager; Tetsuya Itsuk; Toshiki Kurashima.
MONITORING DIVISION: NHK World/Radio Japan. Fax: +81 (3) 3481 1877. Email: info@intl.nhk.or.jp.
HONG KONG BUREAU: Phone: +852 2509-0238.
EUROPEAN (LONDON) BUREAU: Phone: +44 (20) 7393-8100.
LOS ANGELES OFFICE: Phone: +1 (310) 586-1600.
USA (NEW YORK) BUREAU: Phone: +1 (212) 704-9898.
Radio Nikkei, Nikkei Radio Broadcasting Corporation, 9-15 Akasaka 1-chome, Minato-ku, Tokyo 107-8373, Japan. Fax: +81 (3) 3583 9062. Web: (includes on-demand and streaming audio) www.radionikkei.jp. Contact: H. Nagao, Public Relations; M. Teshima; Ms. Terumi Onoda; H. Ono. Sending a reception report may help with a reply. Free stickers and Japanese stamps. $1 or 2 IRCs helpful.
Shiokaze (Sea Breeze), 3-8-401 Koraku 2-chome, Bunkyo-ku, Tokyo 112-0004, Japan. Phone: +81 (3) 5684-5058. Fax: +81 (3) 5684 5059. Email: chosakai@circus.ocn.ne.jp. Web: www.chosa-kai.jp. Broadcast of the Investigation Commission on Missing Japanese Probably Related to North Korea (COMJAM). Verifies reception reports with a QSL card, including those sent by email. Return postage not required.

JORDAN World Time +2 (+3 midyear)

Radio Jordan, P.O. Box 909, Amman, Jordan; or P.O. Box 1041, Amman, Jordan. Phone: (general) +962 (6) 477-4111; (International Relations) +962 (6) 477-8578; (English Service) +962 (6) 475-7410, +962 (6) 477-3111; (Arabic Service) +962 (6) 463-6454; (Saleh) +962 (6) 474-8048; (Al-Arini) +962 (6) 474-9161. Fax: (general) +962 (6) 478 8115; (English Service) +962 (6) 420 7862; (Al-Arini) +962 (6) 474 9190. Email: rj@jrtv.gov.jo; (Director of Radio TV Engineering) arini@jrtv.gov.jo. Web: (includes streaming audio) www.jrtv.jo/jrtv/index.php. At publishing deadline, this site was still partly under construction; and the former site, www.jrtv.jo/rj, under maintenance. Contact: (general) Jawad Zada, Director of Foreign Service; Mrs. Firyal Zamakhshari, Director of Arabic Programs; Qasral Mushatta; (administrative) Abdul Hamid Al Majali, Director of Radio; Mrs. Fatima Massri, Director of International

South Korean Kim Dong-sun actively financed his stepdaughter's spying for North Korea. A simple analog world band portable was used to receive instructions, although field agents usually prefer digital models, such as the Sony ICF-SW100.
Seoul Prosecutor's Ofc. via K.A. Elliott

Relations; Muwaffaq al-Rahayifah, Director of Shortwave Services; (technical) Youssef Al-Arini, Director of Radio TV Engineering. Free stickers. Replies irregularly and slowly. Enclosing $1 helps.

KOREA (DPR) World Time +9

Korean Central Broadcasting Station, Chongsungdong, Moranbong District, Pyongyang, Democratic People's Republic of Korea. If you don't speak Korean, try sending your correspondence via the Voice of Korea (*see*).
Regional KCBS stations—Not known to reply, but a longshot possibility is to try corresponding in Korean to the Pyongyang address, above.
Pyongyang Broadcasting Station—Correspondence should be sent to the Voice of Korea (*see* next item), which sometimes verifies reception reports on PBS broadcasts.

Voice of Korea, External Service, Radio-Television Broadcasting Committee of the DPRK, Pyongyang, Democratic People's Republic of Korea (*not* "North Korea"). Phone: +850 (2) 381-6035. Fax: +850 (2) 381 4416. Phone and fax numbers valid only in those countries with direct telephone service to North Korea. Free publications, pennants, calendars, newspapers, artistic prints and pins. Do not include dutiable items in your envelope. Replies can sometimes be irregular, especially to countries not having diplomatic relations with North Korea. Mail from these countries is sent via circuitous routes and apparently does not always arrive. One way around the problem is to add "VIA BEIJING, CHINA" to the address, but replies via this route tend to be slow in coming. An alternative route is to send your letters via the English Section of China Radio International. Place your correspondence in a separate envelope addressed to the Voice of Korea, and ask CRI to forward your letter to Pyongyang. Explain the mail situation to the people in Beijing and you may have success. Another gambit is to send your correspondence to an associate in a country—such as China, Ukraine or India—having reasonable relations with North Korea, and ask that it be forwarded. Send correspondence in a sealed envelope without any address on the back. That should be sent inside another envelope. Include 3 IRCs to cover the cost of forwarding.

KOREA (REPUBLIC) World Time +9.

KBS World Radio

MAIN OFFICE, INTERNATIONAL BROADCASTING DEPARTMENT: KBS World Radio, Global Center, Korean Broadcasting System, Yoido-dong 18, Youngdeungpo-gu, Seoul, Republic of Korea 150-790. Phone: (general) +82 (2) 781-3650/60/70; (English Section) +82 (2) 781-3674/5/6; (Korean Section) +82 (2) 781-3669/71/72/73; (German Section) +82 (2) 781-3682/3/9; (Japanese Section) +82 (2) 781-3654/5/6 (Spanish Section) +82 (2) 781-3679/81/97. Fax: (general) +82 (2) 781 3694/5/6. Email: (English) english@kbs.co.kr; (German) german@kbs.co.kr; (Japanese) japanese@kbs.co.kr; (Spanish) spanish@kbs.co.kr; (other language sections use the same format, except for Vietnamese: vietnam@kbs.co.kr); (Executive Director) hheejoo@kbs.co.kr. Web: (includes streaming audio) http://world.kbs.co.kr. (*NOTE:* in order to listen to the KBS World Radio audio stream, it may be necessary to first register and then download the KONG software to your computer.) Contact: Ms. Hee Joo Han, Executive Director, KBS World-External Radio & TV; Park Youngseok, Chief; (administration) Sang Myung Kim; (English Section) Chae Hong-Pyo, Manager; Ms. Seung Joo ("Sophia") Hong, Producer; Mr. Chun Hye-Jin, DX Editor, *Seoul Calling*; (Korean Section) Hae Ok Lee, Producer; (Japanese Section) Ms. Hye Young Kim, Producer; (Spanish Section) Ms. Sujin Cho, Producer; (German Section) Chung Soon Wan, Manager; Lee Bum Suk, Producer; Sabastian Ratzer, Journalist. Free stickers, calendars, *Let's Learn Korean* book and a wide variety of other small souvenirs. *History of Korea* is available on CD-ROM (upon request) and via the station's Website.

ADDRESS IN ARGENTINA: KBS World Radio, Casilla de Correo 950, S2000WAJ Rosario, Argentina.

ENGINEERING DEPARTMENT: IBC, Center, Korean Broadcasting System, Yoido-dong 18, Youngdeungpo-Gu, Seoul, Republic of Korea 150-790. Phone: (general) +82 (2) 781-5141/5137; (Radio Transmission Division) +82 (2) 781-5663. Fax: +82 (2) 781 5159. Email: (Radio Transmission Division) poeto@hanmail.net; (Frequency Manager) kdhy@kbs.co.kr; (Planning Engineer) pulo5@kbs.co.kr. Contact: Mr. Oh Daesik, Radio Transmission Division; Mr. Dae-hyun Kim, Frequency Manager; Mr. Chun-soo Lee, Planning Engineer.

Korean Broadcasting System (KBS), 18 Yoido-dong, Youngdeungpo-gu, Seoul, Republic of Korea 150-790. Phone: +82 (2) 781-1000; (duty officer) +82 (2) 781-1711/1792; (news desk) +82 (2) 781-4444; (overseas assistance) +82 (2) 781-1473/1497. Fax: +82 (2) 781 1698, +82 (2) 781 2399. Web: (includes streaming audio) http://kbs.co.kr.

Voice of Wilderness, P.O. Box 8, Seoul 135-660, Republic of Korea. Phone: +82 (2) 796-8846. Fax: +82 (2) 792 7567. Email: main@cornerstone.or.kr; (Hosea) dirhq@hanmail.net. Web: www.cornerstone.or.kr. Contact: Hosea, Program Director. Formerly known as North Korea Mission Radio.

NORTH AMERICAN OFFICE: Cornerstone Ministries International, P.O. Box 4002, Tustin CA 92781 USA. Phone: +1 (714) 569-0042. Fax: +1 (714) 569-0043. Email: info@cornerstoneusa.org. Web: (under construction) www.cornerstoneusa.org. Contact: Michael Jeter. Verifies reception reports.

KUWAIT World Time +3

IBB Kuwait Transmitting Station, c/o American Embassy-Bayan, P.O.Box 77, Safat, 13001 Kuwait, Kuwait. Contact: Transmitter Plant Supervisor. This address for specialized technical correspondence only, although reception reports may occasionally be verified. All other correspondence should be directed to the regular VOA or IBB addresses (*see* USA).

Radio Kuwait, P.O. Box 397, 13004 Safat, Kuwait. Phone: (general) +965 242-3774; (technical) +965 241-5301. Fax: (general) +965 245 6660; (technical) +965 241 5946. Email: info@media.gov.kw. Web: (streaming audio, when operating) www.media.gov.kw. Contact: (general) Manager, External Service; (technical) Wessam Najaf. Sometimes gives away stickers, desk calendars, pens or key chains.

TRANSMISSION AND FREQUENCY MANAGEMENT OFFICE: Ministry of Information, P.O. Box 967, 13010 Safat, Kuwait. Phone: +965 241-3590, +965 243-6193. Fax: +965 241 7830. Email: kwtfreq@media.gov.kw. Contact: Ahmed J. Alawdhi, Head of Frequency Section. Replies to correspondence in English, and occasionally verifies reception reports. Free postcards and calendars.

KYRGYZSTAN World Time +6

Kyrgyz National Radio, Kyrgyz TV and Radio Center, 59 Jash Gvardiya Boulevard, 720010 Bishkek, Kyrgyzstan. Phone: (general) +996 (312) 253-404, +996 (312) 255-741; (Director) +996 (312) 255-700, +996 (312) 255-709; (Assemov) +996 (312) 650-7341, +996 (312) 255-703; (technical) +996 (312) 257-771. Fax: +996 (312) 257 952. Contact: (administration) Myrsakul Mambetaliev, Direc-

tor; (general) Talant Assemov, Editor - Kyrgyz/Russian/German news; Gulnara Abdulaeva, Announcer - Kyrgyz/Russian/German news; (technical) Mirbek Uursabekov, Technical Director. Kyrgyz and Russian preferred, but correspondence in English or German can also be processed. For quick processing of reception reports, use email in German to Talant Assemov.
TRANSMISSION FACILITIES: Ministry of Transport and Communications, 42 Issanova Street, 720000 Bishkek, Kyrgyzstan. Phone: +996 (312) 216-672. Fax: +996 (312) 213 667. Contact: Jantoro Satybaldiyev, Minister. The shortwave transmitting station is located at Krasnaya-Rechka (Red River), a military encampment in the Issk-Ata region, about 40 km south of Bishkek.
Radio Maranatha, Kulatov Street 8/1, Room 411, Bishkek, Kyrgyzstan. Phone: +996 (312) 273-845.
Hit Shortwave—music programming aired over Radio Maranatha (*see*, above).

LAO PEOPLE'S DEMOCRATIC REPUBLIC World Time +7

NOTE: Although universally known as Laos, the official name of the country is "Lao People's Democratic Republic." English has now replaced French as the preferred foreign language.
Houa Phanh Provincial Radio Station, Sam Neua, Houa Phanh Province, Lao P.D.R. Phone: +856 (64) 312-008. Fax: +856 (21) 312 017. Contact: Mr. Veeyang, Hmong Announcer, and the only person who speaks English at the station; Ms. Nouan Thong, Lao Announcer; Mr. Vilaphone Bounsouvanh, Director; Mr. Khong Kam, Engineer.
Lao National Radio
PROGRAM OFFICE AND NATIONAL STUDIOS: Lao National Radio, Phaynam Road, Vientiane, Lao P.D.R; (postal address) P.O. Box 310, Vientiane, Lao P.D.R. Phone: +856 (21) 212-468; +856 (21) 243-250; (Head of External Relations) +856 (21) 252-863. Fax: +856 (21) 212 430. Email: laonradio@lnr.org.la. (Head of External Relations) inpanhs@hotmail.com. Web: www.lnr.org.la. Contact: Mr. Bounthan Inthaxay, Director General; Mr. Inpanh Satchaphansy, Head of External Relations; Mr. Vorasak Pravongviengkham, Head of French Service; Ms. Mativarn Simanithone, Deputy Head, English Section; Ms Chanthery Vichitsavanh, Announcer, English Section. Sometimes includes a program schedule and Laotian stamps when replying.
HF TRANSMITTER SITE: Transmitting Station KM6, Phone Tong Road, Ban Chommany Neuk, Vientiane Province, Lao P.D.R. Phone: +856 (21) 710-181. Contact: Mr. Sysamone Phommaxay, Station Engineer.
TECHNICAL OFFICE: Mass Media Department, Ministry of Information & Culture, 01000 Thanon Setthathirath, Vientiane, Lao P.D.R; or P.O. Box 122, Vientiane, Lao P.D.R. Phone/Fax: +856 (21) 212-424. Contact: Mr. Dy Sisombath, Deputy Director General & Manager, Technical Network Expansion Planning.

LATVIA World Time +2 (+3 midyear)

RNI Radio, c/o Raimonds Kreicbergs, P.O. Box 371, LV-1010 Riga, Latvia. Phone: +371 2922-4105. Email: kreicbergs@parks.lv. A shortwave relay service.

LEBANON World Time +2 (+3 midyear)

Radio Voice of Charity, B.P. 850, Jounieh, Lebanon; (street address), Rue Fouad Chéhab, Jounieh, Lebanon; or. Phone: +961 (9) 918-090, +961 (9) 917-917, +961 (9) 636-344. Fax: +961 (9) 930 272. Email: mahaba@radiocharity.org. Web: (includes streaming audio from domestic services) www.radiocharity.org. Contact: Father Fadi Tabet, General Director. Operates domestically on FM, and airs a daily 30-minute Arabic broadcast via the shortwave facilities of Vatican Radio. Replies to correspondence in English, French or Arabic, and verifies reception reports. Return postage helpful.

LESOTHO World Time +2

Radio Lesotho (if reactivated), P.O. Box 552, Maseru 100, Lesotho. Phone/Fax: +266 323-371. Email: online form. Web: (includes streaming audio) www.radioles.co.ls. Contact: (administration) Ms. Mpine Tente, Principal Secretary, Ministry of Information and Broadcasting; (technical) Motlatsi Monyane, Chief Engineer. Return postage necessary, but do not include currency notes—local currency exchange laws are very strict.

LIBERIA World Time exactly

Radio ELWA, Box 192, Monrovia, Liberia. Phone: +231 (6) 515-511. Email: radio.staff@elwaministries.org; (Nyantee) moses.nyantee@elwaministries.org. Web: www.elwaministries.org (click on "Radio Station"). Contact: Moses T. Nyantee, Station Manager.
Radio Veritas (when operating), P.O. Box 3569, Monrovia, Liberia. Phone: +231 221-658. Email: radioveritas@hotmail.com. Contact: Ledgerhood Rennie, Station Manager.
Star Radio, P.O. Box 3081, 1000 Monrovia 10, Liberia; (street address) 12 Broad Street, Snapper Hill, Monrovia, Liberia. Phone: +231 (77) 104-411. Email: online form; starradio_liberia@yahoo.com. Web: (includes on-demand audio from domestic FM service) www.starradio.org.lr. Contact: James K. Morlu, Station Manager. An independent station supported by the Swiss-based Fondation Hirondelle. Transmits round the clock on 104 FM in Monrovia, and airs a morning broadcast on world band via a leased transmitter operated by VT Communications (*see* United Kingdom).
FONDATION HIRONDELLE: Avenue du Temple 19c, CH 1012-Lausanne, Switzerland. Phone: +41 (21) 654-2020. Fax: +41 (21) 654 2021. Email: info@hirondelle.org. Web: www.hirondelle.org. Contact: Darcy Christen, Star Radio Program Officer. Verifies reception reports.

LIBYA World Time +2

Voice of Africa, P.O. Box 4677, Soug al Jama, Tripoli, Libya (P.O.B. 2009 and P.O.B. 4396 should also work). Phone: +218 (21) 444-0112, +218 (21) 444-9106. Fax: +218 (21) 444 9875. Email: (English) info@en.ljbc.net, info@voiceofafrica.com.ly. Web: www.voiceofafrica.com.ly. The external service of the Libyan Jamahiriyah Broadcasting Corporation. Replies slowly and irregularly.

LITHUANIA World Time +2 (+3 midyear)

Radio Vilnius, Lietuvos Radijas, Konarskio 49, LT-2600 Vilnius, Lithuania. Phone: +370 (5) 236-3079. Email: radiovilnius@lrt.lt. Web: (includes on-demand audio) www.lrt.lt (click on "English"). Contact: Ms. Ilona Rūkienė, Head of English Department. Free stickers, Lithuanian stamps and other souvenirs.

MADAGASCAR World Time +3

Radio Feon'ny Filazantsara, 165 Route Circulaire, Ankorahotra, Madagascar. Phone: +261 2022-30364. Email: info@filazantsara.org, mm.flm@wanadoo.mg. Web: www.filazantsara.org. A broadcast produced by the Lutheran Church of Madagascar (Fiangonana Loterana Malagasy) and aired via the Madagascar relay of Radio Nederland (*see*).

LUTHERAN CHURCH OF MADAGASCAR PARENT ORGANIZATION: Fiangonana Loterana Malagasy. P.O. Box 741, 101 Antananarivo, Madagascar. Phone: +261 321-2107, +261 2022-21001. Fax: +261 2022 33767. Email: flm@wanadoo.mg.

Radio Madagasikara, Anosy, Antananarivo, Madagascar 00101. Phone: +261 2022-21745. Fax: +261 2022 32715. Contact: Alain Rajaona, Directeur; Madame Rakotoma Soa Herimanitia; (technical) Chef de Service Technique. $1 required, and enclosing used stamps from various countries may help. Replies slowly and somewhat irregularly, usually to correspondence in French.

Radio Nederland Wereldomroep—Madagascar Relay, B.P. 404, Antananarivo, Madagascar. Contact: (technical) Rahamefy Eddy, Technische Dienst; J.A. Ratobimiarana, Chief Engineer.Verifies reception reports. Nontechnical correspondence should be sent to Radio Nederland Wereldomroep in the Netherlands (*see*).

MALAYSIA World Time +8

Asia-Pacific Broadcasting Union (ABU), P.O. Box 1164, Lorong Maarof, 59000 Kuala Lumpur, Malaysia. Phone: (general) +60 (3) 2282-3592; (Secretary-General) +60 (3) 2282-2480, +60 (3) 2284-4382; (Programme Department)+60 (3) 2282-2480; (Technical Department) +60 (3) 2282-3108. Fax: +60 (3) 2282 4606. Email: (general) info@abu.org.my; (Secretary-General) david.astley@abu.org.my; (Programme Department) prog@abu.org.my; (Technical Department) sharad.s@abu.org.my. Web: www.abu.org.my. Contact: (administration) David Astley, Secretary-General; (technical) Sharad Sadhu, Director, Technical Department.

Radio Malaysia, Kuala Lumpur

MAIN OFFICE: RTM, Angkasapuri, Bukit Putra, 50614 Kuala Lumpur, Malaysia; (postal address) RTM, P.O. Box 11272, 50740 Kuala Lumpur, Malaysia. Phone: +60 (3) 2282-5333, +60 (3) 2282-4976. Email: (programs) programradio@rtm.gov.my; (technical) teknikalradio@rtm.gov.my. Web: (includes streaming audio) www.rtm.gov.my (click on "Radio"). Contact: (general) Madzhi Johari, Director of Radio; (technical) Ms. Aminah Din, Deputy Director Engineering (Radio); Abdullah Bin Shahadan, Engineer, Transmission and Monitoring; Ong Poh, Chief Engineer. May sell T-shirts and key chains. Return postage required.

ENGINEERING DIVISION: 3rd Floor, Angkasapum, 50616 Kuala Lumpur, Malaysia. Phone: +60 (3) 2285-7544. Fax: +60 (3) 2283 2446. Email: zulrahim@rtm.gov.my. Contact: Zulkifli Ab Rahim.

KAJANG TRANSMITTING STATION: Batu 13, Jln. Cheras, 43009 Kajang, Selangor Darul Ehsan, Malaysia. Phone: +60 (3) 8736-1530. Fax: +60 (3) 8736 1227. Email: rtmkjg@rtm.gov.my; (Controller) abwahid@rtm.gov.my. Contact: Ab Wahid Bin ab Hamid, Controller of Engineering.

Radio Malaysia Sarawak (Kuching), RTM Sarawak, Bangunan Penyiaran, Jalan Tan Sri P. Ramlee, 93614 Kuching, Sarawak, Malaysia. Phone: +60 (82) 248-422. Fax: +60 (82) 241 914. Email: rtmkuc@rtm.gov.my. Web: www2.rtm.gov.my/rtmsarawak/default.htm; (streaming audio, Wai FM and other vernacular stations) www.radiokitai.com/portal. Contact: (general) Yusof Ally, Director of Broadcasting; Mohd. Hulman Abdollah; Wilson Eddie Gaong, Head of Secretariat for Director of Broadcasting; (technical, but also nontechnical) Colin A. Minoi, Technical Correspondence; (technical) Kho Kwang Khoon, Deputy Director of Engineering. Return postage helpful.

Radio Malaysia Sarawak (Miri), RTM Miri, Bangunan Penyiaran, 98000 Miri, Sarawak, Malaysia. Phone: +60 (85) 423-645. Fax: +60 (85) 411 430. Email: rtmmiri@rtm.gov.my. $1 or return postage helpful.

Radio Malaysia Sarawak (Sibu), RTM Sibu, Bangunan Penyiaran, 96009 Sibu, Sarawak, Malaysia. Phone: +60 (84) 323-566. Fax: +60 (84) 321 717. Email: rtmsibu@rtm.gov.my. $1 or return postage required. Replies irregularly and slowly.

Traxx FM, 2nd Floor, Wisma Radio, Angkasapuri, 50740 Kuala Lumpur, Malaysia. Phone: +60 (3) 2288-7663, +60 (3) 2288-7285. Fax: +60 (3) 2284 5750. Email: online form. Web: (includes on-demand and streaming audio) www.traxxfm.net. Traxx FM is the English Service of Radio Malaysia, Kuala Lumpur.

Voice of Islam—Program of the Voice of Malaysia (*see*, below).

Voice of Malaysia (Suara Malaysia), Wisma Radio Angkasapuri, P.O. Box 11272, 50740 Kuala Lumpur, Malaysia. Phone: (general) +60 (3) 2288-7824; (English Service) +60 (3) 2282-7826. Fax: +60 (3) 2284 7594. Email: vom@rtm.gov.my; (Albert Ng) albertng3@gmail.com. Web: http://202.190.233.9/vom/utama.htm; (streaming audio) www.rtm.gov.my (click on "Radio"). Contact: (general) Vasantha Vivekananda, Director, Voice of Malaysia; Albert Ng, English Service; (technical) Lin Chew, Director of Engineering; (Kajang transmitter site) Kok Yoon Yeen, Technical Assistant. Free calendars, stickers or other small souvenirs. Two IRCs or return postage helpful. Replies slowly and irregularly.

MALI World Time exactly

Office de Radiodiffusion Télévision du Mali, B.P. 171, Bamako, Mali. Phone: +223 212-019, +223 212-474. Fax: +223 214 205. Email: (general) ortm@ortm.ml; (Traore) cotraore@sotelma.ml; (Seriba) seriba43@yahoo.fr. Web: (includes streaming audio from Chaine 2, not on shortwave) www.ortm.ml. Contact: Karamoko Issiaka Daman, Directeur des Programmes; (administration) Abdoulaye Sidibe, Directeur General; (technical) Nouhoum Traore; Seriba Coulibaly, Chief Maintenance Engineer, Kati Transmitting Station. $1 or IRC helpful. Replies slowly and irregularly to correspondence in French (preferred) or English.

MAURITANIA World Time exactly

Radio Mauritanie, B.P. 200, Nouakchott, Mauritania; (street address) Av. Gamal Abdel Nasser 387, Nouakchott, Mauritania. Phone: +222 525-2820, +222 525-2101. Fax: +222 525 1264. Web: (streaming audio) http://wm-live.abacast.com/radio_mauritania-wm-32?.wma. Contact: Madame Amir Feu; Lemrabott Boukhary; Madame Fatimetou Fall Dite Ami, Secretaire de Direction; Mr. El Hadj Diagne; Mr. Hane Abou. Return postage or $1 required. Rarely replies.

MEXICO World Time –6 (–5 midyear) Central, South and Eastern, including D.F.; –7 (–6 midyear) Mountain; –7 Sonora; –8 (–7 midyear) Pacific

Radio Educación Onda Corta—XEPPM, Angel Urraza No. 622, Col. del Valle, 03100- México, D.F., Mexico; ("Sintonía Libre" communications program) Apartado Postal 44-227, 03100- México, D.F., Mexico. Phone: (switchboard) +52 (55) 4155-1050; (director's office) +52 (55) 4155-1051; (studios) +52 (55) 4155-1060; (engineering department) +52 (55) 4155-1087; (transmission plant) +52 (55) 5745-7282. Fax: (general) +52 (55) 4155 1097. Email: (general) rmoreno@radioeducacion.edu.mx; (Virginia Bello) direccion@radioeducacion.edu.mx; (Jesús Alvarez) ingenieria@radioeducacion.edu.mx; (Nicolás Hernández) nhem@radioeducacion.edu.mx; ("Sintonía Libre" communications program) radioeducacion@yahoo.com; ondacorta@ radioeducacion.edu.mx. Web: (includes on-demand and streaming audio from domestic service, part of which is carried on shortwave) www.radioeducacion.edu.mx. Contact: (administration) Virginia Bello Méndez, Directora General; (technical) Ing. Jesús Alvarez Tapia, Jefe Técnico; Nicolás Hernández Menchaca, Jefe del Departamento de Planta Transmisora. Free stickers, calendars and station photo. Return postage or $1 required. Replies, sometimes slowly, to correspondence in English, Spanish, Italian or French.

Radio Mil Onda Corta—XEOI, Prolongación Paseo de la Reforma No. 115, Col. Paseo de las Lomas, 01330-México, D.F., Mexico; or Apartado Postal 21-1000, 04021-México, D.F., Mexico (this address for reception reports and listeners' correspondence on the station's shortwave broadcasts, and mark the envelope to the attention of Dr. Julián Santiago Díez de Bonilla). Phone: (switchboard) +52 (55) 5258-1200; (toll-free within Mexico) 01-800-730-4566; (toll-free outside Mexico) +52 (86) 6737- 6553. Fax: +52 (55) 4155 1097. Email: online form; (reception reports) ingenieria@nrm.com.mx. Web: (includes on-demand and streaming audio) www.radiomil.com.mx. Contact: (administration) Lic. Gustavo Alvite Martínez, Director de Radio Mil; Edilberto Huesca P., Vicepresidente Ejecutivo de NRM Comunicaciones; (technical) Juan Iturria, Ingeniero Jefe; (shortwave service) Dr. Julián Santiago Díez de Bonilla. Free stickers. $1 or return postage required.

Radio Transcontinental de América—XERTA, Gabriel Guerra 13, Col. Zona Escolar Oriente, 07239-México 75, D.F., Mexico. Phone: +52 (55) 5306-4668, +52 (55) 5323-4060. Email: info_xerta@yahoo.com.mx; (Carrillo) davidcar230@yahoo.com.mx. Contact: Rubén Castañeda Espíndola, Director General; David R. Carrillo Blanco.

Radio UNAM [Universidad Nacional Autónoma de México]—XEYU (when operating), Adolfo Prieto 133, Colonia del Valle, 03100-México, D.F., Mexico. Phone: (general) +52 (55) 5536-8989; (Director General) +52 (55) 5623-3250/51; (voicemail) +52 (55) 5623-3281; (Huerta) +52 (55) 5623-3270. Fax: (Director General) +52 (55) 5687 3989. Email: (general) contacto@radiounam.unam.mx; (Huerta) teohm@unam.mx. Web: (includes on-demand and streaming audio) www.radiounam.unam.mx. Contact: Fernando Chamizo Guerrero, Director General; (technical) Lic. Teófilo Huerta Moreno, Jefe de Planeación. Free tourist literature and stickers. $1 or return postage required. Replies irregularly to correspondence in Spanish.

Radio Universidad—XEXQ Onda Corta, Apartado Postal 456, 78001-San Luis Potosí, SLP, Mexico; (street address) Gral. Mariano Arista 245, Colonia Centro, 78000-San Luis Potosí, SLP, Mexico. Phone: +52 (444) 826-1347/8, +52 (444) 826-1484. Fax: +52 (444) 826 1388. Contact: Lic. Leticia Zavala Pérez, Coordinadora; (technical) Ing. Francisco Moreno, Encargado Técnico de XEXQ.

RASA Onda Corta—XEQM (when operating), Apartado Postal 217, 97001-Mérida, YUC, Mexico; (street address) Edificio Publicentro, Calle 62, No. 508 Altos, 97000-Mérida, YUC, Mexico. Phone: +52 (999) 923-6155. Fax: +52 (999) 928 0680. Contact: Bernardo Laris Rodríguez, Director General del Grupo RASA Mérida.

MICRONESIA World Time +11

Pacific Missionary Aviation (PMA) Radio Station—The Cross (when operating), P.O. Box 517, Pohnpei FM 96941, Federated States of Micronesia. Phone: +1 (691) 320-1122, +1 (691) 320-2496. Fax: +1 (691) 320 2592. Email: radio@pmapacific.org. Web: www.radio.pmapacific.org. Contact: Roland Weibel, Station Manager.

PMA GUAM HEADQUARTERS: P.O. Box 3209, Hagatna, GU 96932 USA. Email: guam@pmapacific.org. Forwards station mail to Pohnpei, which can result in a quicker reply.

MOLDOVA World Time +2 (+3 midyear)

Radio PMR, ul. Rozy Lyuksemburg 10, MD-3300 Tiraspol, Moldova. Email: (general) radiopmr@inbox.ru; (English Service) irpmr@mail.ru. Contact: Ms. Antonina N. Voronkova, Head; Vlad Butuk, Engineer, Technical Service. Replies to correspondence in English. Return postage helpful. Broadcasts from the separatist, pro-Russian, "Pridnestrovian Moldavian Republic" (also known as "Trans-Dniester Moldavian Republic").

MONGOLIA World Time +8

Mongolian Radio—same postal and email addresses as Voice of Mongolia, below. Phone: (administration) +976 (11) 323-520, +976 (11) 328-978; (editorial) +976 (11)

Ulaanbaatar, like all of Mongolia, may seem hidden from foreign eyes. But it's not hidden from foreign ears, thanks to the Voice of Mongolia.

Shutterstock/Christopher Meder

329-766; (MRTV parent organization) +976 (11) 326-663. Fax: +976 (11) 327 234. Contact: A. Buidakhmet, Director.

Voice of Mongolia, C.P.O. Box 365, Ulaanbaatar 13, Mongolia. Phone: +976 (1) 321-624; (English Section) +976 (11) 327-900. Fax: +976 (11) 323 096; (English Section) +976 (11) 327 234. Email: mr@mongol.net; (Densmaa) densmaa9@yahoo.com. Contact: (general) Mrs. Narantuya, Chief of Foreign Service; Mrs. Zorigt Densmaa, Mail Editor; Mrs. Oyunchimeg Alagsai, Head of English Department; Ms. Tsegmid Burmaa, Japanese Department; (administration) Ch. Surenjav, Director; (technical) Ing. Ganhuu, Chief of Technical Department. Correpondence should be directed to the relevant language section and 2 IRCs or 1$ appreciated. Sometimes very slow in replying. Accepts reception reports with recordings, preferably containing five-minute excerpts of the broadcast(s) reported, but cassettes or CDs cannot be returned. Free pennants, postcards, newspapers, Mongolian stamps, and occasionally, CDs of Mongolian music.

TECHNICAL DEPARTMENT: C.P.O Box 1126, Ulaanbaatar Mongolia. Phone: +976 (11) 363-584. Fax: +976 (11) 327 900. Contact: Mr. Tumurbaatar Gantumur, Director of Technical Department; Ms. Buyanbaatar Unur, Engineer, Technical Center of Transmission System.

MOROCCO World Time exactly

NOTE: Morocco introduced Daylight Saving Time for a trial period of four months in June 2008, but future use of DST is uncertain.

Radio Medi Un

MAIN OFFICE: 3, rue Emsallah, 90000 Tanger, Morocco. Phone: +212 (39) 936-363. Fax: +212 (39) 935 755. Email: (general) medi1@medi1.com; (technical) technique@medi1.com; or multi-contact online form. Web: (includes on-demand and streaming audio) www.medi1.com. Contact: (technical) J. Dryk, Responsable Haute Fréquence. Two IRCs helpful. Free stickers. Correspondence in French preferred.

PARIS BUREAU, NONTECHNICAL: 78 Avenue Raymond Poincaré, F-75016 Paris, France. Phone: +33 (1) 45-01-53-30. Correspondence in French preferred.

Radio Mediterranée Internationale—*see* Radio Medi Un, above.

Radiodiffusion-Télévision Marocaine, 1 rue El Brihi, Rabat, Morocco; or B.P. 1042, Rabat, Morocco. Phone: (general) +212 (3) 776-6880; (technical) +212 (3) 770-1740, +212 (3) 720-1404. Fax: (general) +212 (3) 776 6888; (technical) +212 (3) 770 3208. Email: (general) rtm@rtm.gov.ma; online form; (technical) hammouda@rtm.gov.ma. Web: www.snrt.ma (click on "Radios"). Contact: (administration) Mme. Latifa Akharbach, Dir. de la Radio Marocaine; (technical) Mohammed Hammouda, Ingénieur. Correspondence welcomed in English, French, Arabic or Berber, but rarely replies.

MYANMAR (BURMA) World Time +6:30

Defense Forces Broadcasting Unit, Taunggi, Shan State, Myanmar. Email: sny@mandalay.net.mm. Occasionally replies to correspondence in English.

Myanma Radio, Ministry of Information, Nay Pyi Taw, Myanmar. Web: (includes streaming audio) www.myanmar.com/RADIO_TV.HTM.

Radio Myanmar—the English service of Myanma Radio (*see*, above).

NAGORNO-KARABAGH World Time +4 (+5 midyear)

Voice of Justice, Tigranmetz Street 23a, Stepanakert, Nagorno-Karabagh. Contact: Mikael Hajyan, Station Manager. Replies to correspondence in Armenian, Azeri, Russian or German.

NEPAL World Time +5:45

Radio Nepal (when operating), G.P.O. Box 634, Singha Durbar, Kathmandu, Nepal. Phone: (general) +977 (1) 421-1769, +977 (1) 421-1951; (executive director) +977 (1) 421-1910; (program division) +977 (1) 421-1582; (engineering) +977 (1) 421-1705; (chief engineer) +977 (1) 421-1667. Fax: (executive director) +977 (1) 421 1952; (news division) +977 (1) 421 1652. Email: (director) radio@rne.wlink.com.np; (program division) radioprogram@wlink.com.np; (news division) news@radionepal.org; (technical) radio@engg.wlink.com.np. Web: (includes on-demand and streaming audio) www.radionepal.org. Contact: (general) Er. Ram Sharan Karki, Executive Director; Rajendra Prasad Sharma, Deputy Executive Director; Dhanendra Bimal Chetri, Director of Programme Division; Khagendra Khatri, Chief, News Division; (technical) Er. Ramesh Jung Kharkee, Chief Engineer - Transmission. Three IRCs necessary, but station urges that neither mint stamps nor cash be enclosed, as this invites theft by Nepalese postal employees. Replies irregularly.

KHUMALTAR SHORTWAVE STATION: Email: radio@txs.wlink.com.np. Contact: Padma Jyoti Dhakhwa, Chief Technical Officer; Madhu Sudan Thapa, Deputy Chief Technical Officer.

NETHERLANDS World Time +1 (+2 midyear)

KBC Radio, Argonstraat 6, 6718 WT Ede, Netherlands. Phone: +31 (318) 552-491. Fax: +31 (318) 437 801. Email: kbc@planet.nl, info@k-po.com. Web: www.kbcradio.eu. Contact: Tom de Wit. Verifies reception reports (including those sent by email) with a QSL card. A former pirate broadcaster now legally airing via transmitters in Lithuania.

Radio Nederland Wereldomroep (Radio Netherlands Worldwide)

MAIN OFFICE: P.O. Box 222, 1200 JG Hilversum, Netherlands. Phone: (general) +31 (35) 672-4211; (English Language Service) +31 (35) 672-4242; (24-hour listener Answerline) +31 (35) 672-4222. Fax: (general) +31 (35) 672 4207, but indicate destination department on fax cover sheet; (English Language Service) +31 (35) 672 4239. Email: (English Service) letters@rnw.nl; (Spanish Service): cartas@rnw.nl; ("Media Network") medianetwork@rnw.nl. Web: (includes on-demand and streaming audio) www.radionetherlands.nl. Contact: (management) Jan Hoek, Director-General; Rik Rensen, Editor-in-Chief; Andy Clark, Head of English Language Service. The Radio Netherlands Music Department produces concerts heard on many NPR stations in North America, as well as a line of CDs, mainly of classical, jazz, world music and the Euro Hit 40. Most of the productions are only for rebroadcasting on other stations, but recordings on the NM Classics label are for sale. More details available at www.rnmusic.nl. Visitors welcome, but must call in advance.

PROGRAMME DISTRIBUTION, NETWORK AND FREQUENCY PLANNING: P.O. Box 222, 1200 JG Hilversum, The Netherlands. Phone: +31 (35) 672-4422. Fax: +31 (35) 672 4429. Contact: Leo van der Woude, Frequency Manager; Jan Willem Drexhage, Head of Programme Distribution.

NETHERLANDS ANTILLES World Time -4

Radio Nederland Wereldomroep—Bonaire Relay, P.O. Box 45, Kralendijk, Netherlands Antilles. This address for specialized technical correspondence only. All other correspondence should be sent to Radio Nederland Wereldomroep in the Netherlands (*see*).

NEW ZEALAND World Time +13 (+12 midyear)

Radio New Zealand International (Te Reo Irirangi O Aotearoa, O Te Moana-nui-a-kiwa), P.O. Box 123, Wellington, New Zealand. Phone: +64 (4) 474-1437. Fax: +64 (4) 474 1433. Email: info@rnzi.com. Web: (includes on-demand and streaming audio, and online reception report form) www.rnzi.com. Contact: Florence de Ruiter, Listener Mail; Myra Oh, Producer, "Mailbox"; (administration) Ms. Linden Clark, Manager; (technical) Adrian Sainsbury, Technical Manager. Free stickers, schedule/flyer about station, map of New Zealand and tourist literature available. English/Maori T-shirts for US$20; sweatshirts $40; interesting variety of CDs, as well as music cassettes and spoken programs, in Domestic "Replay Radio" catalog (VISA/MC). Two IRCs or $2 for QSL card, one IRC for schedule/catalog. Email reports verified by email only.

Radio Reading Service—ZLXA, P.O. Box 360, Levin 5500, New Zealand. Phone: +64 (6) 368-2229. Fax: +64 (6) 368 7290. Email: (general, including reception reports) info@radioreading.org. Web: (includes streaming audio) www.radioreading.org. Contact: (general) Ash Bell, Manager/Station Director; (technical, including reception reports) Kelvin Brayshaw. Operated by volunteers 24 hours a day, seven days a week. Station is owned by the "New Zealand Radio for the Print Disabled Inc." Free brochure, postcards, fridge magnets, information on New Zealand and stickers. $1, return postage or 3 IRCs appreciated.

NIGER World Time +1

La Voix du Sahel, O.R.T.N., B.P. 361, Niamey, Niger. Phone: (director) +227 7022-2208, +227 9697-9241; (technical director) +227 2072-2747, +227 9392-8014.

Signals from Trans World Radio's relay facility at Bonaire, Netherlands Antilles, have reached out to audiences for decades. TWR

Fax: +227 2072 2548. Email: (director) maigaric@yahoo.fr; (technical director) maraka_laouali@yahoo.fr. Web: (includes on-demand audio) www.ortn.ne. Contact: (administration) Mahaman Chamsou Maïgari, Directeur; (technical) Laouali Maraka, Directeur technique ORTN. $1 helpful. Correspondence in French preferred.

NIGERIA World Time +1

WARNING—MAIL THEFT: For the time being, correspondence from abroad to Nigerian addresses has a relatively high probability of being stolen.
WARNING—CONFIDENCE ARTISTS: For years, now, correspondence with Nigerian stations has sometimes resulted in letters from highly skilled "pen pal" confidence artists. These typically offer to send you large sums of money, if you will provide details of your bank account or similar information (after which they clean out your account). Other scams are disguised as tempting business proposals; or requests for money, free electronic or other products, publications or immigration sponsorship. Persons thus approached should contact their country's diplomatic offices. For example, Americans should contact the Diplomatic Security Section of the Department of State [phone +1 (202) 647-4000], or an American embassy or consulate.
Borno Radio (if reactivated), Borno Radio Television (BRTV), P.M.B. 1020, Maiduguri, Borno State, Nigeria. Contact: Alhaji Babakura Abba Jato, General Manager.
Radio Nigeria—Abuja, Broadcasting House, P.M.B. 71, Gark1, Abuja, Federal Capital Territory, Nigeria. Phone: +234 (9) 882-1065. Fax: +234 (9) 882 1341. Contact: Ben Obeta. Two IRCs, return postage or $1 required. Replies slowly.
Radio Nigeria—Enugu, P.M.B. 1051, Enugu, Enugu State, Nigeria. Phone: +234 (42) 254-400. Fax: +234 (42) 254 173. Two IRCs, return postage or $1 required. Replies slowly.
Radio Nigeria—Kaduna, P.O. Box 250, Kaduna, Kaduna State, Nigeria. Email: (Madugu) balamadugu@yahoo.com. Contact: Shehu Muhammad, Chief Technical Officer; Bala Madugu, P.T.O. Studios. $1 or return postage required. Replies slowly.
Voice of Nigeria
ABUJA OFFICE (CORPORATE HEADQUARTERS): 6th Floor, Radio House Herbert Macaulay, Garki, Abuja, Federal Capital Territory, Nigeria. Phone: +234 (9) 234-6973, +234 (9) 234-4017. Fax: +234 (9) 234 6970. Email: (general) von-online@voiceofnigeria.org; (Idowu) tidowu@yahoo.com. Web: (includes on-demand and streaming audio) www.voiceofnigeria.org. Contact: Ayodele Suleiman, Director of Programming; Tope Idowu, Editor "*Voice Of Nigeria Airwaves*" program magazine & Special Assistant to the Director General.
LAGOS OFFICE (BROADCASTING HOUSE): P.M.B. 40003, Falomo, Lagos, Nigeria. Phone: +234 (1) 269-3075, +234 (1) 269-3078. Fax: +234 (1) 269 3078, +234 (9) 269 1944. Email: vonlagos@nigol.net.ng; (English Service) englishvon@yahoo.com. Contact: Frank Iloye, Station Manager; (technical) Timothy Gyang, Deputy Director, Engineering.
Replies from the station tend to be erratic, but continue to generate unsolicited correspondence from supposed "pen pals" (*see WARNING—CONFIDENCE ARTISTS*, above); faxes, which are much less likely to be intercepted, may be more fruitful. Two IRCs or return postage helpful.

NORTHERN MARIANA ISLANDS World Time +10

Far East Broadcasting Company—Radio Station KFBS, P.O. Box 500209, Saipan, Mariana Islands MP 96950 USA. Phone: +1 (670) 322-9088. Fax: +1 (670) 322 3060. Email: saipan@febc.org; kfbsadmin@febc.org; (programs) kfbsprog@febc.org. Web: www.febcintl.org. Contact: Robert Springer, Director; Irene Gabbie, FEBC Programming. Replies sometimes take months. Also, *see* FEBC Radio International, USA.

OMAN World Time +4

BBC World Service—A'Seela Relay Station, Resident Engineer, VT Communications, BBC Relay Station, P.O. Box 40, Al Ashkarah, Post Code 422, Oman. Email: rebers@omantel.net.com. Contact: Dave Battey, Resident Engineer; Afrah Al Orimi. Nontechnical correspondence should be sent to the BBC World Service in London (*see*).
Radio Sultanate of Oman, Ministry of Information, P.O. Box 600, Muscat, Post Code 113, Sultanate of Oman. Phone: +968 2460-2127, +968 2460-4577, +968 2460-3222, +968 2460-3888; (frequency managment) +968 2460-2494; (engineering) +968 2460-1538. Fax: (general) +968 2469 3770; (frequency management) +968 2460 4629, +968 2460 7239. Email: feedback@oman-radio.gov.om. Web: (includes streaming audio) www.oman-tv.gov.om. Contact: (Directorate General of Technical Affairs) Mohamed Al Marhoubi, Director General of Engineering; Salim Al-Nomani, Director of Frequency Management. Sometimes verifies reception reports. $1, mint stamps or 3 IRCs helpful.

PAKISTAN World Time +5 (+6 during energy crises)

Pakistan Broadcasting Corporation (PBC)—same details as Radio Pakistan, below.
Radio Pakistan, P.O. Box 1393, Islamabad 44000, Pakistan; (street address) Broadcasting House, Constitution Avenue, Islamabad 44000, Pakistan. Phone: +2 (51) 921-6942, +92 (51) 921-7321. Fax: +92 (51) 920 1861, +92 (51) 920 1118, +92 (51) 922 3877. Email: (general) online form; info@radio.gov.pk; (Director General PBC) pbcdg@comsats.net.pk; (News Department) cnoradio@isb.comsats.net.pk. Web: (includes on-demand and streaming audio) www.radio.gov.pk. Contact: S. Waheed. Replies irregularly to postal correspondence; better is to use email if you can. Free stickers, pennants and *Pakistan Calling* magazine.
VERIFICATION OF RECEPTION REPORTS: Frequency Management Cell, Pakistan Broadcasting Corporation, 303 Peshawar Road, Rawalpindi, Pakistan. Email: cfmpbc@isb.comsats.net.pk (cfmpbchq@isb.comsats.net.pk may also work). Contact: Iftikhar Hussain Malik, Engineering Manager, Frequency Management Cell. Broadcast schedules available on request.

PALAU World Time +9

Radio Station T8WH—all correspondence, including reception reports, should be directed to World Harvest Radio (*see*, USA).

PAPUA NEW GUINEA World Time +10

NOTE: Regional stations are sometimes off the air due to financial or technical problems which can take weeks or months to resolve. IRCs are reportedly not exchangeable in the country, and some provincial stations prefer mint stamps to US currency notes.

National Broadcasting Corporation of Papua New Guinea, P.O. Box 1359, Boroko 111, NCD, Papua New Guinea. Phone: +675 325-5233. Fax: +675 325 6296. Email: info@nbc.com.pg. Web: www.nbc.com.pg. Contact: (general) Joseph Ealedona, Managing Director; Ephraim Tammy, Director, Radio Services; (technical) Bob Kabewa, Sr. Technical Officer; F. Maredey, Chief Engineer. Return postage helpful. Replies irregularly.

NBC Bougainville, P.O. Box 35, Buka, ARB, Papua New Guinea. Phone: +675 973-9911. Fax +675 973 9912. Contact: Ivo Tsika, Station Manager; Aloysius Rumina, Provincial Programme Manager; Ms. Christine Talei, Assistant Provincial Manager; Aloysius Laukai, Senior Programme Officer. Replies irregularly.

NBC Buka—*see* NBC Bougainville, above.

NBC Central, P.O. Box 1359, Boroko, NCD, Papua New Guinea. Phone: +675 321-7155. Fax: +675 321 7110. Contact: Steven Gamini, Station Manager; Lahui Lovai, Provincial Programme Manager; Amos Langit, Technician. Return postage (mint stamps) helpful. Replies irregularly.

NBC East New Britain, P.O. Box 393, Rabaul, ENBP, Papua New Guinea. Phone: +675 982-8966/67/68/69/70. Fax: +675 982 8971. Contact: Esekia Mael, Station Manager; Oemas Kumaina, Provincial Program Manager. Return postage required. Replies slowly.

NBC East Sepik, P.O. Box 65, Wewak, ESP, Papua New Guinea. Phone: +675 856-2316, +675 856-2398. Fax: +675 856 2405. Contact: Elias Albert, Assistant Provincial Program Manager; Luke Umbo, Station Manager.

NBC Eastern Highlands, P.O. Box 311, Goroka, EHP, Papua New Guinea. Phone: +675 732-1618, +675 732-1733, +675 732-1607. Fax: +675 732 1533. Contact: Tony Mill, Station Manager; Tonko Nonao, Program Manager; Ignas Yanam, Technical Officer; Kiri Nige, Engineering Division. $1 or return postage required. Replies irregularly.

NBC Enga (if reactivated), P.O. Box 300, Wabag, Enga Province, Papua New Guinea. Phone: +675 547-1013. Fax: +675 547 1069. Contact: (general) John Lyein Kur, Station Manager; Robert Papuvo, (technical) Gabriel Paiao, Station Technician.

NBC Gulf, P.O. Box 36, Kerema, Gulf, Papua New Guinea. Phone: +675 648-1076. Fax: +675 648 1003. Contact: Tmothy Akia, Station Manager.

NBC Madang, P.O. Box 2036, Jomba, Madang, Papua New Guinea. Phone: +675 852-2415, +675 852-2301. Fax: +675 852 2360. Email: (Gedabing) geo@daltron.com.pg. Contact: Geo Gedabing, Provincial Programme Manager; Michael Samuga, Acting Assistant Manager. Return postage helpful.

NBC Manus, P.O. Box 505, Lorengau, Manus, Papua New Guinea. Phone/Fax: +675 470-9079. Contact: (technical and nontechnical) John P. Mandrakamu, Provincial Program Manager. Replies regularly. Return postage appreciated.

NBC Milne Bay, P.O. Box 111, Alotau, Milne Bay, Papua New Guinea. Phone: +675 641-1334. Phone/Fax: +675 641-1028. Contact: (general) Trevor Webumo, Assistant Manager; Simon Muraga, Station Manager; Raka Petuely, Program Officer; (technical) Philip Maik, Technician. Return postage in the form of mint stamps helpful.

NBC Morobe, P.O. Box 1262, Lae, Morobe, Papua New Guinea. Phone: +675 472-1311, +675 472-7520, +675 472-4209. Fax: +675 472 6423. Contact: Henry Tamarus, Provincial Director; Ken L. Tropu, Assistant Program Manager; Peter W. Manua, Program Manager; Aloysius R. Nase, Station Manager.

NBC New Ireland, P.O. Box 477, Kavieng, New Ireland, Papua New Guinea. Phone: +675 984-2077. Fax: +675 984 2191. Contact:Tonko Nanao, Provincial Director; Otto A. Malatana, Station Manager; Ruben Bale, Provincial Program Manager. Return postage or $1 helpful. Replies slowly.

NBC Northern, P.O. Box 137, Popondetta, Oro, Papua New Guinea. Phone: +675 329-7037/8. Fax: +675 329 7362. Contact: Roma Tererembo, Assistant Provincial Programme Manager; Misael Pendaia, Station Manager. Return postage required.

NBC Simbu, P.O. Box 228, Kundiawa, Chimbu, Papua New Guinea. Phone/Fax: +675 735-1012. Contact: Jack Wera, Manager; Tony Mill Waine, Provincial Programme Manager.

NBC Southern Highlands, P.O. Box 104, Mendi, SHP, Papua New Guinea. Phone: +675 549-1020. Phone/Fax: +675 549-1017. Contact: (general) Andrew Meles, Director Provincial Radio; (technical) Ronald Helori, Station Technician. $1 or return postage helpful.

NBC West New Britain, P.O. Box 412, Kimbe, WNBP, Papua New Guinea. Phone: +675 983-5185, +675 983-5010. Phone/Fax: +675 983 5600. Contact: Valuka Lowa, Provincial Station Manager; Darius Gilime, Provincial Program Manager. Return postage required.

NBC West Sepik, P.O. Box 37, Vanimo, Sandaun Province, Papua New Guinea. Phone: +675 857-1144, +675 857-1149. Fax: +675 857 1305. Contact: (nontechnical) Gabriel Deckwalen, Station Manager; Celina Korei, Station Journalist; Elias Rathley, Provincial Programme Manager; Mrs. Maria Nauot, Secretary; (technical) Paia Ottawa, Technician. $1 helpful. Formerly known as Radio Sandaun.

NBC Western, P.O. Box 23, Daru, Western Province, Papua New Guinea. Phone: +675 645-9234, +675 645-9151. Fax: +675 645 9319. Contact: Robin Wainetti, Manager; (technical) Samson Tobel, Technician. $1 or return postage required. Replies irregularly.

NBC Western Highlands, P.O. Box 311, Mount Hagen, WHP, Papua New Guinea. Phone: +675 542-1000. Fax: +675 542-1001. Contact: (general) Anna Pundia, Station Manager; (technical) Esau Okole, Technician. $1 or return postage helpful. Replies occasionally. Often off the air because of theft, armed robbery or inadequate security for the station's staff.

Radio Sandaun—*see* NBC West Sepik, above.

Radio St. Gabriel (if reactivated), P.O. Box 7671, Boroko, NCD, Papua New Guinea. Email: (Fr. Zdzislaw Mlak) zdzislw@online.net.pg. Contact: Fr. Zdzislaw Mlak, Station Manager. Replies irregularly. Formerly known as Catholic Radio Network.

Wantok Radio Light, P.O. Box 1273, Port Moresby, NCD, Papua New Guinea. Fax: +675 321 4465. Email: online form; admin@wantokradio.net; (Olson, technical) david@heart-to-serve.com; (reception reports) qsl@wantokradio.net. Web: www.wantokradio.net. Contact: (general) Sarah Good; (technical) David Olson, Chief Engineer. Email reports verified by email only. Return postage or $2 required for postal reply. Wantok Radio Light is the shortwave station of the PNG Christian Broadcasting Network, and is a joint project involving Life Radio Ministries, HCJB Global Radio and others.

PARAGUAY World Time –3 (–4 midyear)

Radio Nacional del Paraguay (if reactivated), Blas Garay 241 entre Yegros e Iturbe, Asunción, Paraguay. Phone: +595 (21) 390-375. Fax: +595 (21) 390 376. Email: info@rnpy.com. Web: www.rnpy.com. $1 or return postage required. Replies, sometimes slowly, to correspondence in Spanish. Currently off the air, as the transmitter needs a new component costing several thousand dollars.

PERU World Time–5

NOTE: Obtaining replies from Peruvian stations calls for creativity, tact, patience—and the proper use of Spanish, not form letters and the like.

Radio Bethel Arequipa, Avenida Unión 225, Miraflores, Arequipa, Peru. Contact: Josué Ascarruz Pacheco. Usually announces as "Radio Bethel" and belongs to the "Movimiento Misionero Mundial" evengelistic organization.

RADIO BETHEL PARENT STATION IN LIMA: Avenida 28 de Julio 1781, La Victoria, Lima, Peru. Phone: +51 (1) 613-1701. Fax: +51 (1) 613 1726. Email: bethelradio@bethelradio.fm. Web: (includes on-demand and streaming audio) www.bethelradio.fm. Provides some of the programming for its namesake in Arequipa.

Frecuencia Líder (Radio Bambamarca), Jirón Jorge Chávez 416, Bambamarca, Hualgayoc, Cajamarca, Peru. Phone: (office) +51 (74) 713-260; (studio) +51 (74) 713-249. Contact: (general) Valentín Peralta Díaz, Gerente; Irma Peralta Rojas; Carlos Antonio Peralta Rojas; (technical) Oscar Lino Peralta Rojas. Replies occasionally to correspondence in Spanish.

Frecuencia San Ignacio (if reactivated), Jirón Villanueva Pinillos 330, San Ignacio, Cajamarca, Peru. Contact: Franklin R. Hoyos Cóndor, Director Gerente; Ignacio Gómez Torres, Técnico de Sonido. Replies to correspondence in Spanish. $1 or return postage necessary.

Frecuencia VH—*see* Radio Frecuencia VH

La Voz de la Selva—*see* Radio La Voz de la Selva

Ondas del Suroriente—*see* Radio Ondas del Suroriente

Radio Altura, Plazuela Gamaniel Blanco 127, Cerro de Pasco, Pasco, Peru. Phone: +51 (63) 422-398. Email: online form. Web: (includes streaming audio) www.radiotvaltura.com. Contact: Oswaldo de la Cruz Vásquez, Gerente General. Replies to correspondence in Spanish.

Radio Ancash (when operating), Casilla de Correo 221, Huaraz, Ancash, Peru; (street address) Jr. Francisco Araos 114 independencia, Huaraz, Ancash, Peru. Phone: +51 (43) 421-359, +51 (43) 421-381. Fax: +51 (43) 422 992. Contact: Armando Moreno Romero, Gerente General. Replies to correspondence in Spanish.

Radio Atlántida (when operating), Jirón Arica 441, Iquitos, Loreto, Peru. Phone: +51 (94) 234-452, +51 (94) 234-962. Contact: Pablo Rojas Bardales. $1 or return postage required. Replies irregularly to correspondence in Spanish.

Radio Bambamarca—*see* Frecuencia Líder, above.

Radio Chota, Jirón Anaximandro Vega 690, Apartado Postal 3, Chota, Cajamarca, Peru. Phone: +51 (76) 351-240. Contact: Aladino Gavidia Huamán, Administrador. $1 or return postage required. Replies slowly to correspondence in Spanish.

Radio Cultural Amauta, Apartado Postal 24, Huanta, Ayacucho, Peru; (street address) Jr. Cahuide 278, Huanta, Ayacucho, Peru. Phone/Fax: +51 (66) 322-153. Email: radioamauta@hotmail.com; radioamauta60@yahoo.es. Web: (includes streaming audio) www.rca.es.vg. Contact: Pelagio Ñaupa Gálvez, Administrador.

Radio Cusco, Apartado Postal 251, Cusco, Peru. Phone: (general)+51 (84) 225-851; (management) +51 (84) 232-457. Fax: +51 (84) 223 308. Contact: Sra. Juana Huamán Yépez, Administradora; Raúl Siú Almonte, Gerente General; (technical) Benjamín Yábar Alvarez. Free pennants, postcards and key rings. Audio cassettes of Peruvian music $10 plus postage. $1 or return postage required. Replies irregularly to correspondence in Spanish or English. Station is looking for folk music recordings from around the world to use in their programs.

Radio del Pacífico, Av. Guzmán Blanco 465 - 7° piso, Lima, Peru. Phone: +51 (1) 433-7879. Fax: +51 (1) 433 3276. Email: informes@grupopacifico.org. Web: (includes streaming audio) www.grupopacifico.org/radio.html. Contact: Doris Manco Flores. $1 or return postage required. Replies occasionally to correspondence in Spanish.

Radio El Sol de los Andes (when operating), Jirón 2 de Mayo 257, Juliaca, Peru. Phone: +51 (54) 321-115. Fax: +51 (54) 322 981. Contact: Armando Alarcón Velarde.

Radio Frecuencia VH ("La Voz de Celendín"), Jirón Arica, cuadra 5, Celendín, Cajamarca, Peru. Contact: Eleuterio Vásquez Castro, Director Gerente.

Radio Frecuencia San Ignacio—*see* Frecuencia San Ignacio

Radio Horizonte, Apartado Postal 69, Chachapoyas, Amazonas, Peru; (street address) Jirón Amazonas, 1177, Chachapoyas, Amazonas, Peru. Phone: +51 (41) 477-793. Web: (includes on-demand and streaming audio) www.horizonteperu.com. Contact: Sra. Rocío García Rubio, Ing. Electrónico, Directora; Percy Chuquizuta Alvarado, Locutor; María Montaldo Echaiz, Locutora; Marcelo Mozambite Chavarry, Locutor; Ing. María Dolores Gutiérrez Atienza, Administradora; Juan Nancy Ruíz de Valdez, Secretaria; Yoel Toro Morales, Técnico de Transmisión; María Soledad Sánchez Castro, Administradora. Replies to correspondence in English, French, German and Spanish. $1 required.

Radio Huanta 2000, Jirón Gervacio Santillana 455, Huanta, Peru. Phone/Fax: +51 (66) 332-105. Contact: Ronaldo Sapaico Maravi, Departmento Técnico; or Sra. Lucila Orellana de Paz, Administradora. Free photo of staff. Return postage or $1 appreciated. Replies to correspondence in Spanish.

Radio La Hora, Av. Garcilaso 180, Cusco, Peru. Phone: +51 (84) 225-615, +51 (84) 231-371. Contact: (general) Edmundo Montesinos Gallo, Gerente General; (reception reports) Carlos Gamarra Moscoso, who is also a DXer. Free stickers, pins, pennants and postcards of Cusco. Return postage required. Replies to correspondence in Spanish. Reception reports are best sent direct to Carlos Gamarra's home address: Av. Garcilaso 411, Wanchaq, Cusco, Peru.

Radio La Voz, Andahuaylas, Apurímac, Peru. Contact: Lucio Fuentes, Director Gerente.

Radio La Voz de Bolívar, Jirón Cáceres s/n, Bolívar, Provincia de Bolívar, Departamento de La Libertad, Peru. Phone: +51 4423-0277 Contact: Julio Dávila Echevarría, Gerente. May send free pennant. Return postage helpful.

Radio La Voz de la Selva, Jirón Abtao 255, Iquitos, Loreto, Peru. Phone: +51 (65) 265-244. Fax: +51 (65) 264 531. Email: lavozdelaselva@xploratelmex.com.pe (lvsradio@terra.com.pe may also work). Web: (includes streaming audio from the station's FM outlet) http://radiolvs.cnr.org.pe. Contact: Oraldo Reátegui, Director; Pedro Sandoval Guzmán, Announcer; Mery Blas Rojas. Replies to correspondence in Spanish.

Radio La Voz de las Huarinjas, Barrio El Altillo s/n, Huancabamba, Piura, Peru. Phone: +51 (74) 473-126, +51 (74) 473-259. Contact: Alfonso García Silva, Gerente Director (also the owner of the station); Bill Yeltsin, Administrador. Replies to correspondence in Spanish.

Radio Libertad de Junín, Cerro de Pasco 528, Apartado Postal 2, Junín, Peru. Phone: +51 (64) 344-026. Web: (includes streaming audio) www.rlibertadjunin.com. Contact: Mauro Chaccha G., Director Gerente. Replies slowly to correspondence in Spanish. Return postage necessary.

Radio Luz y Sonido, Apartado Postal 280, Huánuco, Peru; or (street address) Jirón Dos de Mayo 1286, Oficina 205, Huánuco, Peru. Phone: +51 (62) 512-394, +51 (62) 518-500. Fax: +51 (62) 511 985. Contact: (technical) Jorge Benavides Moreno; (nontechnical) Luis Condezo, Director. Return postage or $2 required. Replies to correspondence in Spanish, Italian and Portuguese. Sells video cassettes of local folk dances and religious and tourist themes.

Radio Madre de Dios, Apartado Postal 37, Puerto Maldonado, Madre de Dios, Peru; (street address) Daniel Alcides Carrión 385, Puerto Maldonado, Madre de Dios, Peru. Phone: +51 (82) 571-050. Fax: +51 (82) 571 018, +51 (82) 573 542. Contact: (administration) Padre Rufino Lobo Alonso, Director; (general) Alcides Arguedas Márquez, Director del programa "Un Festival de Música Internacional," heard Mondays 0100 to 0200 World Time. Sr. Arguedas is interested in feedback for this letterbox program. Replies to correspondence in Spanish. $1 or return postage appreciated.

Radio Manantial, a/c Templo La Hermosa, Jirón Santa Cecilia 107, Chilca, Huancayo, Peru. Email: manantialradio960am@hotmail.com; (music requests and webmaster) somosmanantial@hotmail.com; (Pastor Leoncio Paco) leonciopacoministro@hotmail.com. Web: (includes on-demand and streaming audio) www.somosmanantial.com. Contact: Pastor Leóncio Paco Conce, Gerente Administrativo.

Radio Marañón, Apartado Postal 50, Jaén, vía Chiclayo, Peru; or (street address) Francisco de Orellana 343, Jaén, vía Chiclayo, Peru. Phone: +51 (76) 431-147, +51 (76) 432-168. Fax: +51 (44) 732 580. Email: (general) correo@radiomaranon.org.pe; (director) pmaguiro@radiomaranon.org.pe. Web: www.radiomaranon.org.pe. Contact: Francisco Muguiro Ibarra S.J., Director. Return postage necessary. May send free pennant. Replies slowly to correspondence in Spanish and (sometimes) English.

Radio Melodía, San Camilo 501-A, Cercado, Arequipa, Peru. Phone: +51 (54) 205-811, +51 (54) 223-661. Fax: +51 (54) 204 420. Contact: Elba Alvarez Delgado, Gerente. Replies to correspondence in Spanish.

Radio Municipal, Jirón Tacna 385, Panao, Pachitea, Huánuco, Peru. Email: dalsmop1@hotmail.com. Contact: Pablo Alfredo Albornoz Rojas, Gerente Técnico, who collects station stickers and pennants. Replies to correspondence in Spanish.

Radio Ondas del Huallaga, Jirón Leoncio Prado 723, Apartado Postal 343, Huánuco, Peru. Phone: +51 (62) 511-525, +51 (62) 512-428. Contact: Flaviano Llanos Malpartida, Gerente. $1 or return postage required. Replies to correspondence in Spanish. Free stickers.

Radio Ondas del Suroriente, Jirón Ricardo Palma 510, Quillabamba, La Convención, Cusco, Peru. Replies irregularly and slowly to correspondence in Spanish

Radio Oriente (when operating), Vicariato Apostólico, Calle Progreso 112-114, Yurimaguas, Alta Amazonas, Loreto, Peru. Phone: +51 (65) 352-156, +51 (65) 351-611. Fax: +51 (94) 352 128. Email: (general) info@radiooriente.org; (director) rovay@qnet.co.pe, geovanni@radiooriente.org. Contact: (general) Sra. Elisa Cancino Hidalgo; Juan Antonio López-Manzanares M., Director; (technical) Pedro Capo Moragues, Gerente Técnico. $1 or return postage required. Replies occasionally to correspondence in English, French, Spanish and Catalan.

Radio Paucartambo, Plaza de Armas 124, Paucartambo, Departamento de Cusco, Peru. Contact: Roberto Villasante, Administrador.

Radio Quillabamba, Jirón Ricardo Palma 442, Apartado Postal 76, Quillabamba, La Convención, Cusco, Peru. Phone: +51 (84) 281-002. Fax: +51 (84) 281 771. Email: cpmaldonado@caritas.org.pe. Contact: Javier Cabrera, Administrador. Replies very irregularly to correspondence in Spanish.

Radio Reina de la Selva, Jirón Ayacucho 944, Plaza de Armas, Chachapoyas, Región Nor Oriental del Marañón, Peru. Phone: +51 (74) 757-203. Contact: José David Reina Noriega, Gerente General; Jorge Oscar Reina Noriega, Director General. Replies irregularly to correspondence in Spanish. Return postage necessary.

Radio San Antonio (Callalli), Parroquia San Antonio de Padua, Plaza Principal s/n, Callalli, Departamento de Arequipa, Peru. Contact: Hermano [Brother] Rolando.

Radio San Antonio (Villa Atalaya), Jirón Iquitos s/n, Villa Atalaya, Departamento de Ucayali, Peru. Email: (Zerdin) zerdin@terra.com.pe. Contact: Gerardo Zerdin.

Radio San Juan Bautista (when operating), Jirón Arica 105, San Juan Bautista, Ayacucho, Departamento de Huamanga, Peru.

Radio San Nicolás, Pasaje Hilario López 111 - entrada del "Hotel Grández", San Nicolás, Rodríguez de Mendoza, Peru. Contact: Abrahán Valcazar Grández. Return postage necessary.

Radio Santa Rosa, Convento Santo Domingo, Jirón Camaná 170, Lima 01, Peru. Phone: +51 (1) 427-7488. Fax: +51 (1) 426 9219. Email: radiosantarosa@terra.com.pe. Web: (includes on- demand and streaming audio) www.radiosantarosa.com.pe. Contact: Padre Juan Sokolich Alvarado, Director; Lucy Palma Barreda. Free stickers and pennants. $1 or return postage necessary. Replies to correspondence in Spanish or English.

Radio Sicuani, Jirón 2 de Mayo 212, Sicuani, Canchis, Cusco, Peru; or Apartado Postal 45, Sicuani, Peru. Phone: +51 (84) 351-136, +51 (84) 351-698. Fax: +51 (84) 351 697. Email: cecosda@mail.cosapidata.com.pe. Web: (includes on-demand and streaming audio) www.radiosicuani.org.pe. Contact: Doris Ochoa Vargas, Directora.

Radio Tawantinsuyo, Av. Sol Nº 806, Cusco, Peru. Phone: +51 (84) 226-955, +51 (84) 228-411. Contact: Iván Montesinos, Gerente; Teresa López, Administradora. Replies occasionally to correspondence in Spanish. If no reply is forthcoming, try using the good offices of Carlos Gamarra Moscoso of Radio La Hora (*see*). Return postage required.

Radio Tarma, Jirón Molino del Amo 167, Tarma, Departamento de Junín, Peru. Phone/Fax: +51 (64) 321-167, +51 (64) 321-510. Contact: Mario Monteverde Pomareda, Gerente General. Free stickers. $1 or return postage required. Replies irregularly to correspondence in Spanish.

Radio Unión, Av. José Pardo 138 - Oficina 1501, Lima 41, Peru. Phone: +51 (1) 712-0145. Email: informes@unionlaradio.com; online form. Web: (includes streaming audio) www.unionlaradio.com. Contact: Raúl Rubbeck Jiménez, Director Gerente; Juan Zubiaga Santiváñez, Gerente; Natividad Albizuri Salinas, Secretaria; Juan Carlos Sologuren, Dpto. de Administración, who collects stamps. Free satin pennants and stickers. IRC required, and enclosing used or new stamps from various countries is especially appreciated. Replies irregularly to correspondence and tape recordings, with Spanish preferred.

Radio Victoria, Jr.Reynel 320, Mirones Bajo, Lima 1, Peru. Phone: +51 (1) 336-5448. Fax: +51 (1) 427 1195. Email: (Ramos) silvioramos777@hotmail.com. Web: (streaming audio) www.ipda.com.pe. Contact: Henrique Silvio Ramos, Administrador. Replies to correspondence in Spanish. Free stickers. Station owned by the Brazilian-run Pentecostal Church "Dios Es Amor," with local headquarters at Av. Arica 248, Lima; Phone: +51 (1) 330-8023. Their program "La Voz de la Liberación" is produced locally and aired over numerous Peruvian shortwave stations.

Radio Virgen del Carmen ("RVC"), Plaza Bolognesi Nº 142, Cercado, Huancavelica, Peru. Fax: +51 (67) 451-257. Email: (López Alvarado) jlopez_alvarado@hotmail.com. Web: (includes sreaming audio) www.radiovirgendelcarmen.com.pe. Contact: José Santos López Alvarado, Director General. Replies irregularly to correspondence in Spanish. Return postage helpful.

Radio Visión, Jr. Juan Fanning, Urbanización San Juan, Chiclayo, Departamento de Lambayeque, Peru. Phone: +51 (74) 239-889. Email: informes@visionradioperu.com; online form; (Pastor Córdova) iplacosecha13@yahoo.es. Web: (includes streaming audio) www.visionradioperu.com. Contact: Jorge Tessen; Pastor Francisco Córdova Rodríguez. Replies to correspondence in Spanish. Return postage helpful for postal reply. Station owned by Iglesia Pentecostal "La Cosecha."

Radiodifusora La Voz del Rondero, Calle Unión 409, Huancabamba, Piura, Peru. Phone: +51 (74) 473-233. Contact: Federico Ibáñez Maticorena, Director.

PHILIPPINES World Time +8

Far East Broadcasting Company—FEBC Radio International (External Service)

MAIN OFFICE: P.O. Box 1, Valenzuela, Metro Manila, Philippines 0560. Phone: (general) +63 (2) 292-5603, +63 (2) 292-9403, +63 (2) 292-5790; (International Broadcast

Manager) +63 (2) 292-5603 ext. 158. Fax: +63 (2) 292 9430, +63 (2) 292-5603, +63 (2) 291 4982; (International Broadcast Manager) +63 (2) 292 9724, but lacks funds to fax replies. Email: info@febcintl.org; info@febc.org.ph (reception reports to this address are sometimes verified with a QSL card); (Peter McIntyre) pm@febc.jfm.org.ph. Web: www.febcintl.org. Contact: (general) Peter McIntyre, Manager, International Operations Division; (administration) Carlos Peña, Managing Director; (engineering) Ing. Renato Valentin, Frequency Manager; Larry Podmore, IBG Chief Engineer; (listener correspondence) Menchie Marcos. Free stickers and calendar cards. Three IRCs appreciated for airmail reply. Plans to add a new 100 kW shortwave transmitter.
INTERNATIONAL SCHEDULING OFFICE: FEBC International, 291 Serangoon Road, #04-00 Serangoon Building, Singapore 218107, Singapore. Phone: +65 6392-3154. Fax: +65 6392 3156. Email: freqmgr@febcintl.org. Contact: Chris Cooper, Information Systems Manager.

IBB Philippines Transmitting Station
MAIN ADDRESS: International Broadcasting Bureau, Philippines Transmitting Station, c/o US Embassy, 1201 Roxas Boulevard, Ermita 1000, Manila, Philippines.
ALTERNATIVE ADDRESS: IBB/PTS, PSC 500 Box 28, FPO AP 96515-1000.
These addresses for specialized technical correspondence only, although reception reports may occasionally be verified. All other correspondence should be directed to the regular VOA or IBB addresses (*see* USA).

Philippine Broadcasting Service—DUR2 (when operating), Bureau of Broadcasting Services, Media Center, Bohol Avenue, Quezon City, Philippines. Relays DZRB Radio ng Bayan and DZRM Radio Manila. Web: (Radio ng Bayan streaming audio) www.pbs.gov.ph.

Radyo Pilipinas, the Voice of the Philippines, Philippine Broadcasting Service, 4th Floor, PIA Building, Visayas Avenue, Quezon City 1100, Metro Manila, Philippines. Phone: (general) +63 (2) 924-2620, +63 (2) 920-3963, +63 (2) 924-2548; (engineering, Phone/Fax) +63 (2) 924-2268. Fax: +63 (2) 926 3926. Email: (general) radyo_pilipinas_overseas@yahoo.com (if this fails, try: pbs.pao@pbs.gov.ph). Contact: (nontechnical) Evelyn Salvador Agato, Station Manager; (technical) Miguelito ("Mike") Pangilinan, Chief Engineer. Free postcards and stickers. Verifies reception reports.

Radio Veritas Asia
STUDIOS AND ADMINISTRATIVE HEADQUARTERS: P.O. Box 2642, Quezon City, 1166 Philippines. Phone: +63 (2) 939-0011 to 14; (technical director) +63 (2) 938-1940. Fax: (general) +63 (2) 938 1940; (frequency manager) +63 (2) 939 7556. Email: (general) online form; transmitter@rveritas-asia.org; (program department) rvaprogram@rveritas-asia.org; (audience research) rvaars@rveritas-asia.org; (technical) technical@rveritas-asia.org. Web: (includes on-demand and streaming audio) www.rveritas-asia.org. Contact: (administration) Ms. Erlinda G. So, Manager; (general) Ms. Cleofe R. Labindao, Audience Relations Officer; Ms. Shiela Hermida, Audience Relations Section; Mrs. Regie de Juan Galindez; Msgr. Pietro Nguyen Van Tai, Program Director; (technical) Alex M. Movilla, Assistant Technical Director; Alfonso L. Macaranas, Frequency and Monitoring. Free caps, T-shirts, stickers, pennants, rulers, pens, postcards and calendars. Free bi-monthly newsletter *UPLINK*. Return postage appreciated.
TRANSMITTER SITE: Radio Veritas Asia, Palauig, Zambales, Philippines. Contact: Fr. Hugo Delbaere, CICM, Technical Consultant.
BRUSSELS BUREAUS AND MAIL DROPS: Catholic Radio and Television Network, 32-34 Rue de l' Association, B-1000 Brussels, Belgium; or UNDA, 12 Rue de l'Orme, B-1040 Brussels, Belgium.

PIRATE

Pirate radio stations are usually one-person operations airing home-brew entertainment and/or iconoclastic viewpoints. In order to avoid detection by the authorities, they tend to appear irregularly, with little concern for the niceties of conventional program scheduling. Most are found in Europe chiefly on weekends and holidays, often just above 6200 and 7375 kHz; and in North America mainly during evenings, just below 7000 kHz (usually 6925 plus or minus 10 kHz) or around 6855 kHz. These *sub rosa* stations and their addresses are subject to unusually abrupt change or termination, sometimes as a result of forays by radio authorities.
A popular Internet source of information is the Free Radio Network (www.frn.net). Too, the Website of The Association of Clandestine Radio Enthusiasts (www.theaceonline.com) archives the excellent "Free Radio Weekly" pirate newsletter. For Europirate DX news, try:
Swedish Report Service: SRS, Ostra Porten 29, SE-442 54 Ytterby, Sweden. Web: www.srs.pp.se.
Free Radio Service Holland: FRSH, P.O. Box 2727, NL-6049 ZG Herten, Netherlands. Email: freak55@gironet.nl, peter.verbruggen@tip.nl. Web: www.frsholland.nl.
FRC-Finland, P.O. Box 82, FIN-40101 Jyvaskyla, Finland.
A good list of pirate links can be found at: www.alfalima.net/links-links.htm.
For up-to-date listener discussions and other pirate-radio information on the Internet, the usenet URLs are: alt.radio.pirate and rec.radio.pirate.

POLAND World Time +1 (+2 midyear)

Polish Radio External Service (Polskie Radio dla Zagranicy), P.O. Box 46, PL-00-977 Warsaw, Poland; (street address) al. Niepodległości 77/85, 00-977 Warsaw, Poland. Phone: (general) +48 (22) 645-9305; (English Section) +48 (22) 645-9262; (German Section) +48 (22) 645-9333. Fax: +48 (22) 645 3952. Email: (Polish Section) polska@polskieradio.pl; (English Section) gb@polskieradio.pl; (German Section) deutsche.redaktion@polskieradio.pl. Web: (includes on-demand and streaming audio) www.polskieradio.pl/zagranica. Contact: Aleksander Kropiwnicki, Editor, English Service. On-air Polish language course with free printed material. Free stickers, pens, key rings, stamps and sometimes T-shirts, depending on resources.

Radio Racja, ul. Ciapla 1/7, PL-15-472 Bialystok, Poland. Phone: +48 (85) 654-5193. Email: info@racyja.com. Web: (includes on-demand audio) www.racyja.com. Broadcasts in Belarusian and is opposed to President Lukashenko.

PORTUGAL

World Time exactly (+1 midyear); Azores World Time –1 (World Time midyear)

Deutsche Welle—Relay Station Sines, Pro-Funk GmbH, Monte Mudo, P-7520-065 Sines, Portugal. Phone: +351 (269) 870-280. Fax: +351 (269) 870 290. Email: profunk@mail.telepac.pt. This address for specialised technical correspondence only. All other correspondence (including reception reports) should be directed to the main offices in Bonn, Germany *(see)*. Also used by RDP Internacional (*see* next entry).

RDP Internacional—Rádio Portugal, Av. Marechal Gomes da Costa 37, 1849-030 Lisboa, Portugal. Phone: (general) +351 (21) 382-0000. Fax: (general) +351 (21) 382 0165. Email: (general) rdp.internacional@rtp.pt; (Saraiva, listener correspondence) isabel.venes@rtp.pt; (Haupt) christiane.haupt@rtp.pt. Web: (includes on-demand and streaming audio, and bilingual English-Portuguese online reception report form) http://programas.rtp.pt/EPG/radio. Contact: Isabel Saraiva, Listeners' Service Department; Christiane Haupt. Verifies reception reports. Return postage not required. Free stickers and other small gifts. May also send literature from the Portuguese National Tourist Office.

ENGINEERING (INCLUDING FREQUENCY MANAGEMENT): Direcção Engenharia e Tecnologias, Rádio e Televisão de Portugal, Av. Marechal Gomes da Costa 37, Bloco B-2°, 1849-030 Lisboa, Portugal. Phone: +351 (21) 382-0228. Fax: +351 (21) 794 7670. Email: gabinete.tecnologias@rtp.pt; (Abreu) teresa.abreu@rtp.pt. Contact: Mrs. Teresa Beatriz Abreu, Chefe do Gabinete de Tecnologiasde Transmissão e Difusão.

ROMANIA

World Time +2 (+3 midyear)

Radio România International, 60-62 General Berthelot St., RO-70747 Bucharest, Romania; or P.O. Box 111, RO-70756 Bucharest, Romania. Phone: (general) +40 (21) 222-2556, +40 (21) 303-1172, +40 (21) 303-1488, +40 (21) 312-3645; (English Department) +40 (21) 303-1357, +40 (21) 303-1465; (engineering) +40 (21) 303-1193. Fax: +40 (21) 319 0562. Email: (general) rri@rri.ro; (English Service) engl@rri.ro; (Spanish Service) span@rri.ro; (Ianculescu) rianculescu@rri.ro. Web: (includes streaming audio and online reception report form) www.rri.ro; (on-demand audio) www.wrn.org/listeners/stations/station.php?StationID=106. Contact: Ioana Masariu, Head of the English Service; Daniel Bilt, Editor "DX Mailbag;" Victoria Sepciu, Spanish Service; (technical) Radu Ianculescu, HF Planning Engineer. Replies slowly.

TRANSMISSION AND FREQUENCY MANAGEMENT: National Radiocommunications Company, Blvd Libertatii 14-16, RO-70060 Bucharest, Romania. Phone: +40 (21) 307-3016/7. Fax: +40 (21) 307 3650. Email: (Strambeanu) a.strambeanu@radiocom.ro. Contact: Adrian Strambeanu, Broadcasting Manager.

RUSSIA

(Times given for republics, oblasts and krays):

- World Time +2 (+3 midyear) Kaliningradskaya;
- World Time +3 (+4 midyear) Adygeya, Arkhangelskaya, Astrakhanskaya, Belgorodskaya, Bryanskaya, Chechnya, Chuvashiya, Dagestan, Ingushetiya, Kabardino-Balkariya, Kalmykiya, Kaluzhskaya, Karachayevo-Cherkesiya, Ivanovskaya, Karelia, Kirovskaya, Komi, Kostromskaya, Krasnodarskiy, Kurskaya, Leningradskaya (including St. Petersburg), Lipetskaya, Mariy-El, Mordoviya, Moskovskaya (including the capital, Moscow), Murmanskaya, Nenetskiy, Nizhegorodskaya, Novgorodskaya, Severnaya Osetiya, Orlovskaya, Penzenskaya, Pskovskaya, Rostovskaya, Ryazanskaya, Saratovskaya, Smolenskaya, Stavropolskiy, Tambovskaya, Tatarstan, Tulskaya, Tverskaya, Ulyanovskaya, Vladimirskaya, Volgogradskaya, Vologodskaya, Voronezhskaya, Yaroslavskaya;
- World Time +4 (+5 midyear) Samarskaya, Udmurtiya;
- World Time +5 (+6 midyear) Bashkortostan, Chelyabinskaya, Khanty-Mansiyskiy, Komi-Permyatskiy, Kurganskaya, Orenburgskaya, Permskaya, Sverdlovskaya, Tyumenskaya, Yamalo-Nenetskiy;
- World Time +6 (+7 midyear) Altayskiy, Novosibirskaya, Omskaya, Tomskaya;
- World Time +7 (+8 midyear) Evenkiyskiy, Kemerovskaya, Khakasiya, Krasnoyarskiy, Taymyrskiy, Tyva;
- World Time +8 (+9 midyear) Buryatiya, Irkutskaya, Ust-Ordynskiy;
- World Time +9 (+10 midyear) Aginskiy-Buryatskiy, Amurskaya, Chitinskaya, Sakha;
- World Time +10 (+11 midyear) Khabarovskiy, Primorskiy, Yevreyskaya;
- World Time +11 (+12 midyear) Magadanskaya, Sakhalinskaya;
- World Time +12 (+13 midyear) Chukotskiy, Kamchatskaya, Koryakskiy.

VERIFICATION OF STATIONS USING TRANSMITTERS IN ST. PETERSBURG: Transmissions of certain world band stations—such as Radio Vlaanderen International or China Radio International—when emanating from transmitters in St. Petersburg, may be verified directly from: Mikhail Timofeyev, SPbRC Technical Department, St. Petersburg Regional Center, ul. Akademika Pavlova 3, 197022 St. Petersburg, Russia. The current schedule can be viewed (in Russian) at http://spb.rtrn.ru/info.asp?view=1553. Free stickers and paper pennants. $1 or IRC required.

Adygey Radio—*see* Maykop Radio

Arkhangel'sk Radio, GTRK "Pomorye", ul. Popova 2, 163061 Arkhangel'sk, Arkhangel'skaya Oblast, Russia; or U1PR, Valentin G. Kalasnikov, ul. Suvorov 2, kv. 16, Arkhangel'sk, Arkhangel'skaya Oblast, Russia. Replies irregularly to correspondence in Russian.

Buryat Radio—*see* Ulan-Ude Radio

Kabardino-Balkar Radio—*see* Nalchik Radio

Krasnoyarsk Radio, Krasnoyarskaya GTRK "Tsentr Rossii", ul. Mechnikova 44A, 660028 Krasnoyarsk, Krasnoyarsky Kray, Russia. Email: postmaster@telegid.krasnoyarsk.su. Contact: Valeriy Korotchenko; Anatoliy A. Potehin, RAØAKE. Free local information booklets in English/Russian. Replies in Russian to correspondence in Russian or English. Return postage helpful.

Kyzyl Radio, GTRK "Tyva", ul. Gornaya 31, 667003 Kyzyl, Respublika Tyva, Russia. Email: tv@tuva.ru. Replies to correspondence in Russian.

Magadan Radio, GTRK "Magadan", ul. Kommuny 8/12, 685024 Magadan, Magadanskaya Oblast, Russia. Phone: +7 (4132) 622-935. Fax: +7 (4132) 624 977. Email: center@magtrk.ru. Web: www.magtrk.ru/index.

Russian Mass Media head Boris Boyarskov, host of the B08 HFCC/ ASBU Frequency Coordination Conference at the Radisson SAS Slavyanskaya in Moscow. He confers with HFCC Chairman Oldrich Čip (glasses) of Czech Radio. HFCC

phtml?a=gn. Contact: Viktor Loktionov, V.G. Kuznetsov. Return postage helpful. Occasionally replies to correspondence in Russian.

Maykop Radio, GTRK "Adygeya", ul. Zhukovskogo 24, 385000 Maykop, Republic of Adygeya, Russia. Contact: A.T. Kerashev, Chairman. English accepted but Russian preferred. Return postage helpful.

Murmansk Radio, GTRK "Murman", per. Rusanova 7, 183032 Murmansk, Murmanskaya Oblast, Russia. Phone: +7 (8152) 472-327. Email: radio@tvmurman.com. Web: http://sampo.ru/~tvmurman/index_ie.html. Contact: D. Perederi (chairman).

Nalchik Radio, GTRK "Kabbalk Teleradio", pr. Lenina 3, 360000 Nalchik, Republic of Kabardino-Balkariya, Russia. Contact: Kamal Makitov, Vice-Chairman. Replies to correspondence in Russian.

Perm Radio, Permskaya GTRK "T-7", ul. Tekhnicheskaya 7, 614070 Perm, Permskaya Oblast, Russia. Contact: M. Levin, Senior Editor; A. Losev, Acting Chief Editor.

Petropavlovsk-Kamchatskiy Radio, GTRK "Kamchatka", ul. Sovetskaya 62, 683000 Petropavlovsk-Kamchatskiy, Kamchatskaya Oblast, Russia. Contact: A.F. Borodin, Head of GTRK "Kamchatka." Email: gtrkbuh@mail.iks.ru. $1 required for postal reply. Replies in Russian to correspondence in Russian or English. Verifies reception reports. Free stickers.

Radio Nalchik—*see* Nalchik Radio, above.

Radio Radonezh—*see* Radiostantsiya Radonezh

Radio Rossii (Russia's Radio), GRK "Radio Rossii", Yamskogo Polya 5-YA ul. 19/21, 125040 Moscow, Russia. Phone: +7 (495) 213-1054, +7 (495) 250-0511, +7 (495) 251-4050. Fax: +7 (495) 250 0105, +7 (495) 233 6449, +7 (495) 214 4767. Email: webmaster@radiorus.ru. Web: (includes on-demand and streaming audio) www.radiorus.ru. Contact: Sergei Yerofeyev, Director of International Operations [sic]; Sergei Davidov, Director. Free English-language information sheet.

Radiostantsiya Radonezh (when operating), ul. Pyatnitskaya 25, Moscow 115326, Russia. Phone/Fax: +7 (495) 950-6356. Email: radonezh@radonezh.ru. Web: (includes on-demand and streaming audio) www.radonezh.ru/radio. Replies to correspondence in Russian or English. Operates intermittently on shortwave.

Russian International Radio (Russkoye Mezhdunarodnoye Radio)—a service of the Voice of Russia (*see*) in cooperation with the domestic Russkoye Radio. Email: rir@ruvr.ru.

Tatarstan Wave ("Tatarstan Dulkynda"), GTRK "Tatarstan", ul. Gor'kogo 15, 420015 Kazan, Tatarstan, Russia. Phone: (general) +7 (8432) 384-846; (editorial) +7 (8432) 367-493. Fax: +7 (8432) 361 283. Contact: Hania Hazipovna Galinova. Formerly known as Voice of Tatarstan.

ADDRESS FOR RECEPTION REPORTS: QSL Manager, P.O. Box 134, 420136 Kazan, Tatarstan, Russia. Contact: Ildus Ibatullin, QSL Manager. Offers an honorary diploma in return for 12 correct reports in a given year. The diploma costs 2 IRCs for Russia and 4 IRCs elsewhere. Accepts reports in Russian or English. Return postage helpful.

Ulan-Ude Radio, Buryatskaya GTRK, ul. Erbanova 7, 670000 Ulan-Ude, Republic of Buryatia, Russia. Contact: Z.A. Telin; Mrs. M.V. Urbaeva, 1st Vice-Chairman; L.S. Shikhanova.

Voice of Russia, FGU RGRK "Golos Rossii", ul. Pyatnitskaya 25, 115326 Moscow, Russia. Phone: (Chairman) +7 (495) 950-6331; (International Relations Department) +7 (495) 950-6440; (Technical Department) +7 (495) 950-6115. Fax: (Chairman) +7 (495) 251 2017; (Letters Department, World Service in English & Zhamkin, Editor-in-Chief) +7 (495) 951 9552. Email: (Letters Department, World Service in English) world@ruvr.ru; (for all language services) letters@ruvr.ru; (Spanish) post_es@ruvr.ru; (German) post-de@ruvr.ru. Web: (includes on-demand and streaming audio, and online reception report form) www.ruvr.ru. Contact: (Letters Department, World Service in English) Elena Osipova or Yevdokiya Tolkacheva; (Chairman) Armen Oganesyan; (International Relations Department) Eduard Kroustkaln, Director; (Technical Department) Mrs. Rachel Staviskaya, Director; (World Service in English) Vladimir L. Zhamkin, Editor-in-Chief. For language services other than English contact the International Relations Department.

SAN FRANCISCO OFFICE, SCHEDULES: 2654 17th Avenue, San Francisco CA 94116 USA. Phone: +1 (415) 564-9968. Email: GPoppin@aol.com. Contact: George Poppin. This address, a volunteer office, only provides Voice of Russia schedules to listeners (return postage not required). All other correspondence should be directed to the Voice of Russia in Moscow.

Yakutsk Radio, NVK "Sakha", ul. Ordzhonikidze 48, 677007 Yakutsk, Respublika Sakha, Russia. Contact: (general) Alexandra Borisova; Lia Sharoborina, Advertising Editor; Albina Danilova, Producer, "Your Letters"; (technical) Sergei Bobnev, Technical Director. Russian books $15; audio cassettes $10. Free station stickers and original Yakutian souvenirs. Replies to correspondence in English.

RWANDA World Time +2

Deutsche Welle—Relay Station Kigali. Correspondence should be directed to the main offices in Bonn, Germany *(see)*.

Radio Rwanda, B.P. 83, Kigali, Rwanda. Phone: +250 76180. Fax: +250 76185. Email: radiorwanda@yahoo.com. Web: (streaming audio only) www.orinfor.gov.rw/radiorwanda.eng.html. Contact: Marcel Singirankabo. $1 required. Occasionally replies, with correspondence in French preferred.

SAO TOME E PRINCIPE World Time exactly

IBB São Tomé Transmitting Station, P.O. Box 522, São Tomé, São Tomé e Príncipe. Contact: Transmitting Station Manager. This address for specialized technical correspondence only, although some reception reports may be verified, depending on who is at the site. All other correspondence, including reception reports, should be sent to the usual VOA or IBB addresses in Washington (*see* USA).

SAUDI ARABIA World Time +3

Broadcasting Service of the Kingdom of Saudi Arabia, P.O. Box 61718, Riyadh-11575, Saudi Arabia. Phone: (general) +966 (1) 404-2795; (administration) +966 (1) 442-5493; (engineering) +966 (1) 442-5170; (frequency management) +966 (1) 442-5127. Fax: (general) +966 (1) 402 8177; (engineering and frequency management) +966 (1) 404 1692. Email: (Al-Samnan) alsamnan@yahoo.com. Web: (includes streaming audio) www.saudiradio.net. Contact: (general) Mutlaq A. Albegami; (technical) Suleiman Al-Samnan, Director of Engineering; Youssef Dhim, Frequency Management. Free travel information and book on Saudi history.

SERBIA World Time +1 (+2 midyear)

International Radio Serbia, Hilendarska 2, 11000 Beograd, Serbia. Phone: +381 (11) 324-4455. Fax: +381 (11) 323 2014. Email: radioju@sbb.co.rs. Web: (includes on-demand audio) www.glassrbije.org. Contact: Milena Jokić, Director; Predrag Graovac, Technical Director. Replies irregularly. $1 helpful.

SEYCHELLES World Time +4

BBC World Service—Indian Ocean Relay Station, P.O. Box 448, Victoria, Mahé, Seychelles. Phone: +248 78-496. Fax: +248 78 500. Contact: (technical) Albert Quatre, Senior Engineer. Nontechnical correspondence should be sent to the BBC World Service in London (*see*).

SIERRA LEONE World Time exactly

Cotton Tree News (CTN), Fourah Bay College, Mass Communication Department, Mount Aureol, Freetown, Sierra Leone. Phone: (Bennett) +232 (76) 536-394. Email: (general) online form; (Bennett) abennett@hirondelle.org. Web: (includes on-demand audio from the domestic FM service) www.cottontreenews.org. Contact: Anne Bennett, Project Coordinator in Sierra Leone. Reception reports can be emailed to Anne Bennett for verification. Cotton Tree News is an independent radio production directed by Fondation Hirondelle and funded by DFID, the European Commission, Irish Aid and the Swiss Agency for Development and Cooperation. Transmits on 107.3 MHz FM in Freetown, and airs a morning broadcast on world band via a leased transmitter operated by VT Communications (*see* UNITED KINGDOM).

FONDATION HIRONDELLE: Avenue du Temple 19c, CH 1012-Lausanne, Switzerland. Phone: +41 (21) 654-2020. Fax: +41 (21) 654 2021. Email: info@hirondelle.org. Web: www.hirondelle.org. Verifies reception reports.

SINGAPORE World Time +8

BBC World Service—Far Eastern Relay Station, VT Communications, 51 Turut Track, Singapore 718930, Singapore. Phone: + 65 6793-7511/3. Fax: +65 6793 7834. Email: (Wui Pin Yong) wuipin@singnet.com.sg. Contact: (technical) Mr. Wui Pin Yong, Operations Manager; or Far East Resident Engineer. Nontechnical correspondence should be sent to the BBC World Service in London (*see*).

SLOVAKIA World Time +1 (+2 midyear)

Radio Slovakia International, M_tna 1, P.O. Box 55, 817 55 Bratislava 15, Slovakia. Phone: +421 (2) 5727-3734, +421 (2) 5727-3731; (Editor-in-Chief) +421 (2) 5727-3730; (English Service) +421 (2) 5727-3736 or +421 (2) 5727-2737; (technical) +421 (2) 5727-3251. Fax: +421 (2) 5249 6282 or +421 (2) 5249 8247; (technical) +421 (2) 5249 7659. Email: (general) valocka@rozhlas.sk; (English Section) englishsection@rozhlas.sk; for other language sections, the format is language@rozhlas.sk, where the language is written in English (e.g. german@rozhlas.sk). To contact individuals, the format is firstname.lastname@rozhlas.sk; so to reach, say, Anca Dragu, it would be anca.dragu@rozhlas.sk. Web: (includes on-demand audio) www.slovakradio.sk/inetportal/rsi/index.php (www.rsi.sk may also work). Contact: Andra Dragu; Michael Groch; Ivan Bašnák; George Christopher (all members of the English Section).

SOLOMON ISLANDS World Time +11

Solomon Islands Broadcasting Corporation (Radio Happy Isles), P.O. Box 654, Honiara, Solomon Islands. Phone: +677 20051. Fax: +677 23159, +677 25652. Web: www.sibconline.com.sb. Contact: (general) David Palapu, Manager Broadcast Operations; Julian Maka'a, Producer,

"Listeners From Far Away"; Walter Nalangu, News & Current Affairs; Rachel Rahi'i, Commercial/Advertising; Bart Basi, Programmes; (administration) Grace Ngatulu; (technical) Cornelius Rathamana, Chief Engineer. IRC or $1 helpful. Problems with the domestic mail system may cause delays.

SOMALIA World Time +3

Radio Galkayo (when operating), 2 Griffith Avenue, Roseville NSW 2069, Australia. Phone/Fax: +61 (2) 9417-1066. Email: svoron@hotmail.com. Contact: Sam Voron, VK2BVS, 6O0A, Australian Director. Replies to email correspondence at no charge, but $5, AUS$5 or 5 IRCs required for postal replies. A community radio station in the Mudug region, Puntland State, northern Somalia and supported by local and overseas volunteers. Seeks volunteers, donations of radio equipment and airline tickets, and is setting up a Radio Galkayo Amateur Radio Club station.

Radio Hargeysa—*see* SOMALILAND.

SOMALILAND World Time +3

NOTE: "Somaliland," claimed as an independent nation, is diplomatically recognized only as part of Somalia.

Radio Hargeysa, P.O. Box 14, Hargeysa, Somaliland, Somalia. Email: radiohargeysa@yahoo.com. Contact: Muhammad Said Muhummad, Manager.

ADDRESS IN GERMANY: c/o Konsularische Vertretung Somaliland, Baldur Drobnica, Zedernweg 6, D-50127 Bergheim, Germany. Contact: Baldur Drobnica. Verifies reception reports (including those in English). Return postage required ($1 for Europe, $3 elsewhere). Baldur Drobnica is a radio amateur, call-sign DJ6SI.

SOUTH AFRICA World Time +2

BBC World Service via South Africa—For verification direct from the South African transmitters, contact Sentech (*see*, below). Nontechnical correspondence should be sent to the BBC World Service in London (*see*).

Channel Africa, P.O. Box 91313, Auckland Park 2006, South Africa. Phone: (general manager) +27 (11) 714-4145; (technical) +27 (11) 714-2537. Fax: + 27 (11) 714 2072. Email: (general) africancan@channelafrica.org; online form; (Moloto) molotod@sabc.co.za; (Mate, technical) matemm@channelafrica.org. Web: (includes on-demand and streaming audio) www.channelafrica.org. Contact: (nontechnical) David Moloto, General Manager; (technical) Maurice M. Mate, Web & Technical Senior Manager. Reception reports are best directed to Sentech (*see*), which operates the transmission facilities.

CVC One Africa—*see* Christian Vision Communications (CVC), Australia.

Radiosondergrense (Radio Without Boundaries), P.O. Box 91312, Auckland Park 2006, South Africa. Phone: +27 (11) 714-2702. Fax: +27 (11) 714 3472; (Olivier) +27 (11) 714-6445. Email: info@rsg.co.za; (Olivier) amanda@rsg.co.za. Web: (includes on-demand and streaming audio) www.rsg.co.za. Contact: Amanda Olivier. Reception reports are best directed to Sentech (*see*, below), which operates the shortwave transmission facilities. The shortwave operation is scheduled to be eventually replaced by a satellite and FM network.

Sentech Ltd., Transmission Planning, Private Bag X06, Honeydew 2040, South Africa. Phone: (general) +27 (11) 471-4400, +27 (11) 691-7000; (shortwave) +27 (11) 471-4658. Fax: (shortwave) +27 (11) 471 4754. Email: (Kathy Otto) ottok@sentech.co.za. Web: (schedules & frequencies) www.sentech.co.za. Contact: Kathy Otto, HF Coverage Planner. Sentech verifies reception reports on transmissions from the Meyerton shortwave facilities.

South African Radio League—Amateur Radio Mirror International, P.O. Box 90438, Garsfontein 0042, South Africa. Email: armi@sarl.org.za. Web: www.sarl.org.za/public/ARMI/ARMI.asp; (on-demand and streaming audio) www.amsatsa.org.za. Contact: Hans van deGroenedaal. Accepts email reception reports. Amateur Radio Mirror International is a weekly broadcast aired via Sentech's Meyerton facilities.

Trans World Radio Africa

NONTECHNICAL CORRESPONDENCE: Trans World Radio Africa, P.O. Box 4232, Kempton Park 1620, South Africa. Phone: +27 (11) 974-2885. Fax: +27 (11) 974 9960. Email: online form. Web: (includes streaming audio) www.twrafrica.org.

TECHNICAL CORRESPONDENCE: Reception reports and other technical correspondence are best directed to Sentech (*see*, above) or to the TWR office in Swaziland (*see*). Also, *see* USA.

SPAIN World Time +1 (+2 midyear)

Radio Exterior de España (Spanish National Radio, World Service)

MAIN OFFICE: Apartado de Correos 156.202, E-28080 Madrid, Spain. Phone: (general) +34 (91) 346-1081/1083; (audience relations) +34 (91) 346-1149. Fax: +34 (91) 346 1815. Email: (audience relations) audiencia@rtve.es; (director) dir_ree.rne@rtve.es; (English Service) english@rtve.es; ("Amigos de la Onda Corta" communications program) amigosdx@rtve.es. Web: (includes on-demand and streaming audio) www.ree.rne.es. Contact: Pilar Salvador M., Relaciones con la Audiencia. No verification of reception reports due to "staffing and budget constraints." Listeners are requested not to send cash or IRCs, since the limited services which still exist are free. An alternative, for those who understand Spanish, is to send a reception report on the program "Españoles en la Mar" which is produced in the Canary Islands by Mary Cortés. Times and frequencies can be found at the REE Website. Reports should be sent to: Programa "Españoles en la Mar," Apartado Postal 1233, Santa Cruz de Tenerife, Islas Canarias, Spain. Magazines and small souvenirs are sometimes included with verifications from this address. Correspondence in Spanish preferred, but English also accepted.

HF FREQUENCY PLANNING OFFICE: Prado del Rey, Pozuelo de Alarcon, E-28223 Madrid, Spain. Phone: (Almarza) +34 (91) 346-1639. Fax: +34 (91) 346 1275. Email: (Almarza) planif_red2.rne@rtve.es; (Huerta & Arlanzón) plan_red.rne@rtve.es. Contact: Fernando Almarza, HF Frequency Manager.

NOBLEJAS TRANSMITTER SITE: Centro Emisor de RNE en Onda Corta, Ctra. Dos Barrios s/n, E-45350 Noblejas-Toledo, Spain.

COSTA RICA RELAY FACILITY—see Costa Rica.

SRI LANKA World Time +5:30

Deutsche Welle—Relay Station Sri Lanka, 92/1 D.S. Senanayake Mawatha, Colombo 08, Sri Lanka. Phone: +94 (11) 2464-483. Fax: +94 (11) 2699 450. Contact: R. Groschkus, Resident Engineer. This address for specialized technical correspondence only. All other correspondence should be sent to Deutsche Welle in Germany (*see*).

Sri Lanka Broadcasting Corporation (also announces as "Radio Sri Lanka" in the external service), P.O. Box 574, Independence Square, Colombo 7, Sri Lanka. Phone: +94 (11) 269-7491/2/3/4/5. Fax: (general) +94 (11) 269 1568; (Director General) +94 (11) 269 7150. Email: (Director General) dg@slbc.sk. Web: (includes streaming audio) www.slbc.lk.

IBB Iranawila Transmitting Station.

ADDRESS: Station Manager, IBB Sri Lanka Transmitting Station, c/o U.S. Embassy, 210 Galle Road, Colombo 3, Sri Lanka. Contact: Station Manager. This address for specialized technical correspondence only, although some reception reports may be verified, depending on who is at the site. All other correspondence should be directed to the regular VOA or IBB addresses (*see* USA).

ST. HELENA World Time exactly

Radio St. Helena (when operating), P.O. Box 93, Jamestown, St. Helena STHL 1ZZ, South Atlantic Ocean. Phone/Fax: +290 4542. Email: station.manager@helanta.sh or radio.sthelena@helanta.sh. Contact: Gary Walters, Acting Station Manager. Verifies reception reports if 3 IRCs included. Does not verify email reports. Aired on world band once each year—usually late October or early November, but may test irregularly at other times.

SUDAN World Time +3

Miraya Sudan—*see* Radio Miraya, below.

Radio Miraya, P.O. Box 69, Khartoum, Sudan. Phone: +249 (1) 8708-7777. Fax: +249 (1) 8708 9465. Email: mirayasudan@mirayafm.org; online form. Web (includes on-demand and streaming audio from the domestic Miraya FM) www.mirayafm.org. Monday through Friday, airs specially prepared programs; weekends, relays Miraya FM. A joint project involving the United Nations Mission in Sudan (UNMIS) and the Swiss-based Fondation Hirondelle.

UNMIS:

(USA) P.O. Box 5013, Grand Central Station, New York NY 10163-5013 USA. Fax: +1 (917) 367 3523. Email: ecomment-pio@un.org. Web: www.unmis.org.

(Sudan) UNMIS Headquarters, Ebeid Khatim Street, P.O. Box 69, Khartoum 11111, Sudan. Phone: (general) +249 (187) 086-000; (Hersh) +249 (187) 087-562. Email: (Hersh) hersh@un.org; (Mester) mesterk@un.org. Contact: Nanci Hersh, Broadcast Technology Officer; Katalin Mester.

FONDATION HIRONDELLE: Avenue du Temple 19c, CH 1012-Lausanne, Switzerland. Phone: +41 (21) 654-2020. Fax: +41 (21) 654 2021. Email: info@hirondelle.org. Web: www.hirondelle.org. Contact: Jean-Luc Mootoosamy, Project Manager. Verifies reception reports.

Radio Omdurman—*see* Sudan Radio and TV Corporation, below.

Radio Peace

ADDRESS FOR RECEPTION REPORTS: pete@edmedia.org. Contact: Peter Stover, who requests that audio attachments not be sent with reception reports.

Sudan Radio and TV Corporation (SRTC), P.O.Box 1094, Mulazmin, Omdurman, Sudan. Phone: +249 (187) 572-956, +249 (187) 574-187. Fax:: +249 (187) 556 006, +249 (187) 572 956. Replies irregularly. Return postage necessary.

SURINAME World Time –3

Radio Apintie, Postbus 595, Paramaribo, Suriname; (street address) verl. Gemenelandsweg 37, Paramaribo, Suriname. Phone: (studio) +597 400-500, (office) +597 400-450. Fax: +597 400 684. Email: apintie@sr.net. Web: (includes streaming audio) www.apintie.sr. Contact: Charles E. Vervuurt, Director. Free pennant. Return postage or $1 required. Email reception reports preferred, since local mail service is unreliable.

SWAZILAND World Time +2

Trans World Radio, P.O. Box 64, Manzini, Swaziland. Phone: +268 505-2781/2/3. Fax: +268 505 5333. Email: (Chief Engineer) sstavrop@twr.org.sz; (Mrs. Stavropoulos) lstavrop@twr.org.sz. Web: (transmission schedule) www.twrafrica.org/programmes/index.asp. Contact: (general) J.M Blosser, Station Director; (technical) Mrs. L. Stavropoulos, DX Secretary. Free stickers, postcards and calendars. A free Bible Study course is available. May swap canceled stamps. $1, return postage or 3 IRCs appreciated. Also, *see* USA.

SWEDEN World Time +1 (+2 midyear)

IBRA Radio, SE-141 99 Stockholm, Sweden. Phone: +46 (8) 608-9600. Fax: +46 (8) 608 9650. Email: ibra@ibra.se. Web: (Swedish) www.ibra.se; (English) www.ibra.org. Contact: Hans Olofsson, Director; Gösta Åkerlund, International Coordinator; Eva Skog, Public Relations. Free pennants and stickers. IBRA Radio's programs are aired over various world band stations, including Trans World Radio and FEBA Radio; and also broadcast independently via transmitters in Germany and Russia. Accepts email reception reports.

Radio Sweden, SE-105 10 Stockholm, Sweden. Phone: (general) +46 (8) 784-7288 or +46 (8) 784-7207; (listener voice mail) +46 (8) 784-7238; (technical department) +46 (8) 784-7282/6. Fax: (general) +46 (8) 667 6283; (listener service) +46 8 660 2990. Email: (general) radiosweden@sr.se; (English Service) mark.cummins@sr.se; george.wood@sr.se; (PR & Information) victoria.padin@sr.se, frida.sjolander@sr.se; (technical) anders.backlin@sr.se. Web: (includes on-demand and streaming audio) www.sr.se/rs or (shortcut to the English web page) www.radiosweden.org. Contact: (administration) Ingemar Löfgren, Director General, SR International; Gundula Adolfsson, Head of Radio Sweden; (English Service) Gaby Katz, Head of English Service; Bill Schiller, Producer; George Wood, Webmaster; (public relations

Attendees at the 2007 EDXC Conference in Lugano, Switzerland, held in early November, 2007.
T. Ohtake

and information) Victoria Padi; (technical department) Anders Bäcklin.
TRANSMISSION SERVICE COMPANY: TERACOM, AB, P.O. Box 13666, SE-172 27 Sundbyberg, Sweden. Phone: (switchboard) +46 (8) 555-420-00. Fax: (general) +46 (8) 555 420 01. Web: www.teracom.se. Contact: (HF Broadcasting Matters via the switchboard) Mr. Ingemar Larsson, Head of HF Frequency Planning. Seeks monitoring feedback.

SWITZERLAND World Time +1 (+2 midyear)

European Broadcasting Union, L'Ancienne-Route 17A, CH-1218 Grand-Saconnex, Geneva, Switzerland. Phone: +41 (22) 717-2111. Fax: +41 (22) 747 4000. Email: ebu@ebu.ch. Web: www.ebu.ch. Contact: Mr. Jean Réveillon, Secretary-General. Umbrella organization for broadcasters in European and Mediterranean countries.
International Telecommunication Union, Place des Nations, CH-1211 Geneva 20, Switzerland. Phone: (switchboard) +41 (22) 730-5111; (radiocommunication bureau) +41 (22) 730-5560. Fax: (general) +41 (22) 733 7256; (radiocommunication bureau) +41 (22) 730 5785. Email: (general) itumail@itu.int; (radiocommunication bureau) brmail@itu.int. Web: www.itu.int. The ITU is the world's official regulatory body for all telecommunication activities, including world band radio. Offers a wide range of official multilingual telecommunication publications in print and/or digital formats.
Radio Réveil, Paroles, Les Chapons 4, CH-2022 Bevaix, Switzerland. Phone: +41 (32) 846-1655. Fax: +41 (32) 846 2547. Email: contact@paroles.ch. Web (includes on-demand audio): www.paroles.ch. An evangelical radio ministry, part of the larger Radio Réveil Paroles de Vie organization, which apart from broadcasting to much of Europe on longwave, mediumwave/AM and FM, also targets an African audience via the shortwave facilities of Germany's Media Broadcast (*see*). Replies to correspondence in French or English, and verifies reception reports.
Stimme des Trostes, Missions-und Erholungshaus Arche, Rosenbüelstrasse 48, CH-9642 Ebnat-Kappel, Switzerland. Phone: +41 (71) 992-2500. Fax: +41 (71) 992 2555. Email: info@missionswerk-arche.ch. Web: www.missionswerk-arche.ch. Contact: Herbert Skutzik, Secretary. Replies to correspondence in German or English, and verifies reception reports. Return postage helpful. Via Germany's Media Broadcast (*see*).

SYRIA World Time +2 (+3 midyear)

Radio Damascus, Syrian Radio and Television, P.O. Box 4702, Damascus, Syria. Fax: +963 (11) 223 4336. Email: (English Section) mmhrez@shuf.com; (Riad Sharaf Al-Din, Spanish Section) riadsharafaldin@yahoo.com; (Marian Galindo, comments and reception reports in Spanish) radiodamasco@yahoo.com. Web: (Spanish Department) http://cobaq10.iespana.es/damasco. Contact: Adnan Salhab; Farid Shalash; Mohamed Hamida; (Spanish Section) Riad Sharaf Al-Din, Supervisor de Programas; Marian Galindo, Locutora; (technical) Mazen Al-Achhab, Head of Frequency Department. Free stickers, pennants and occasionally books and newspapers. Replies can be highly erratic, and sometimes slow. Members of the Spanish Section have suggested listeners use email, because of letters going astray.

TAIWAN—*see* CHINA (TAIWAN)

TAJIKISTAN World Time +5

Radio Tajikistan, kuchai Chapaeva 31, 734025 Dushanbe, Tajikistan.
Radio Voice of Tajik (Radio Ovozi Tajik), Chapaev Street 31, 734025 Dushanbe, Tajikistan. Phone: +992 (37) 227-7417. Fax: +992 (37) 221 1198. Return postage (IRCs) helpful.

TANZANIA World Time +3

TBC (Tanzania Broadcasting Corporation) (when operating), Nyerere Road, P.O. Box 9191, Dar es Salaam, Tanzania. Phone: +255 (51) 860-760. Fax: +255 (51) 865 577. Email: radiotanzania@raha.com; (reception reports) nyamwocha@yahoo.com. Contact: (general) Abdul Ngarawa, Director of Broadcasting; Mrs. Edda Sanga, Controller of Programs; Ndaro Nyamwocha; Ms. Penzi Nyamungumi, Head of English Service and International Relations Unit; (technical) Taha Usi, Chief Engineer; Emmanuel Mangula, Deputy Chief Engineer. Replies to correspondence in English. Reports should go directly to Mr. Nyamwocha listed above. $1 return postage helpful. Formerly known as Radio Tanzania.

Voice of Tanzania—Zanzibar, Department of Broadcasting, Radio Tanzania Zanzibar, P.O. Box 1178, Zanzibar, Tanzania—if this address brings no reply, try P.O. Box 2503. Phone: +255 (54) 231-088. Fax: + 255 (54) 257 207. Contact: Yusuf Omar Sunda, Director-General. $1 return postage helpful.

THAILAND World Time +7

BBC World Service—Asia Relay Station, P.O. Box 20, Muang, Nakhon Sawan 60000, Thailand; (physical address) Mu 1, Tambon Ban Kaeng, Muang District, Nakhon Sawan 6000, Thailand. Phone: +66 5622-7275/6. Fax: +66 (56) 227 277. Contact: Ms. Jaruwan Meesaurtong, Executive Secretary; Ms. Sukontha Saisaengthong, Senior Engineer. Nontechnical correspondence should be sent to the BBC World Service in London (*see* UNITED KINGDOM).

IBB Thailand Transmitting Station, P.O. Box 99, Ampur Muang, Udon Thani 41000, Thailand. Email: thai@voa.gov. This address for specialized technical correspondence only, although some reception reports may be verified. All other correspondence should be directed to the regular VOA or IBB addresses (*see* USA).

Radio Thailand World Service, 236 Vibhavadi Rangsit Road, Huai Khwang, Bangkok 10320, Thailand. Phone: + 66 (2) 277-4022. Fax: +66 (2) 274 9298/9, +66 (2) 277 1840. Web: (includes streaming audio) www.hsk9.com. Contact: Mrs. Chantima Choeysanguan, Executive Director; Ms. Porntip Utogapach, Director; Ms. Suweraya Lohavicharn, Producer; (technical) Mr. Boontharm Ratanasang, Director; Mr. Weerasac Cherngchow, Assistant Director. Free pennants. Replies irregularly, especially to those who persist.

TUNISIA World Time +1 (+2 midyear)

Arab States Broadcasting Union, 6, rue des Entrepreneurs, Z.I. Ariana Cedex, TN-1080 Tunis, Tunisia. Phone: +216 (70) 838-855. Fax: +216 (70) 838 531, +216 (70) 838 203. Email: a.suleiman@asbu.intl.tn. Contact: Abdelrahim Suleiman, Director, Technical Department; Bassil Ahmad Zoubi, Head of Transmission Department.

Radiodiffusion Télévision Tunisienne, 71 Avenue de la Liberté, TN-1070 Tunis, Tunisia. Phone: +216 (71) 801-177. Fax: +216 (71) 781 927. Email: info@radiotunis.com. Web: (includes on-demand and streaming audio) www.radiotunis.com/news.html. Contact: Mongai Caffai, Director General; Mohamed Abdelkafi, Director; Kamel Cherif, Directeur; Masmoudi Mahmoud; Mr. Bechir Betteib, Director of Operations; Smaoui Sadok, Le Sous-Directeur Technique. Replies irregularly and slowly to correspondence in French or Arabic. $1 helpful. For reception reports try: Le Chef de Service du Controle de la Récepcion de l'Office National de la Télediffusion, O.N.T, Cité Ennassim I, Bourjel, 1002 Tunis, Tunisia; or B.P. 399, 1080 Tunis, Tunisia. Phone: +216 (71) 801-177. Fax: +216 (71) 781 927. Email: ont.@ati.tn. Contact: Abdesselem Slim.

TURKEY World Time +2 (+3 midyear)

Voice of Turkey (Turkish Radio-Television Corporation External Service)

MAIN OFFICE, NONTECHNICAL: TRT External Services Department, TRT Sitesi, Turan Güne_ Blv., Or-An Çankaya, 06450 Ankara, Turkey; or P.K. 333, Yenisehir, 06443 Ankara, Turkey. Phone: (general) +90 (312) 490-9800/9801; (English desk) +90 (312) 490-9842. Fax: (English desk) +90 (312) 490 9846. Email: (English desk) englishdesk@trt.net.tr; (French Service) francais@trt,net,tr; (German Service) deutsch@trt.net.tr; (Spanish Service) espanol@trt.net.tr. Web: (includes streaming audio) www.trt.net.tr. Contact: (English and non-technical) Mr. Osman Erkan, Chief, English desk. Technical correspondence, such as on reception quality should be directed to: Ms. Sedef Somaltin (*see* next entry below). On-air language courses offered in Arabic and German, but no printed course material. Free pennants, and tourist literature.

MAIN OFFICE, TECHNICAL (FOR EMIRLER AND ÇAKIRLAR TRANSMITTER SITES AND FOR FREQUENCY MANAGEMENT): TRT Teknik Yardimcilik, TRT Sitesi, C Blok No:525, ORAN, 06109 Ankara, Turkey. Phone: +90 (312) 490-1732. Fax: +90 (312) 490 1733. Email: sedef.somaltin@trt.net.tr, kiymet.erdal@trt.net.tr. Contact: Mr. Alaettin Korkmaz, TRT Acting Deputy Director General (Head of Engineering); Ms. Sedef Somaltin, Engineer & Frequency Manager; Ms. Kiymet Erdal, Engineer & Frequency Manager. The HFBC seasonal schedules can be reached directly from: www.trt.net.tr/wwwtrt/frekanstsr.aspx and www.tr/voiceofturkey/high.htm.

SAN FRANCISCO OFFICE, SCHEDULES: 2654 17th Avenue, San Francisco CA 94116 USA. Phone: +1 (415) 564-9968. Email: GPoppin@aol.com. Contact: George Poppin. This address, a volunteer office, only provides TRT schedules to listeners (return postage not required). All other correspondence should be sent directly to Ankara.

TURKMENISTAN World Time +5

Turkmen Radio, Magtymguly köçesi 89, 744000 Ashgabat, Turkmenistan. Phone: +993 (12) 351-515. Fax: +993 (12) 394 470. English correspondence is best directed to "News Editor, English Programs," even though the English broadcasts are currently on FM only.

UGANDA World Time +3

Dunamis Shortwave, High Adventure Gospel Communications Ministries (HAGCM), P.O. Box 425, Station E, Toronto, Ontario M6H 4E3, Canada. Email: (reception reports) dunamis4.750@hotmail.com.

Radio Uganda—*see* UBC Radio, below.
UBC Radio (formerly Radio Uganda)
GENERAL OFFICE: P.O. Box 7142, Kampala, Uganda. Phone: +256 (41) 257-256. Fax: +256 (41) 257 252. Email: news@ubconline.co.ug. Web: www.ubconline.co.ug. Contact: (general) Richard Lubagasira, Administrative Officer. $1 or return postage required. Replies infrequently and slowly. Correspondence to this address has sometimes been returned with the annotation "storage period overdue"—presumably because the mail is not collected on a regular basis.
ENGINEERING DIVISION: P.O. Box 2038, Kampala, Uganda. Phone: +256 (41) 256-647. Contact: Rachel Nakibuuka, Secretary. Four IRCs or $2 required. Enclosing a self addressed envelope may also help to get a reply.

UKRAINE World Time +2 (+3 midyear)

Radio Ukraine International, Kreshchatyk Str. 26, 01001 Kyiv, Ukraine. Phone: (Ukrainian Service) +380 (44) 279-1757; (English Service) + 380 (44) 279-5484; +380 (44) 279-1883; (German Service) +380 (44) 279-3134. Fax: (English Service) +380 (44) 278 2534; (Ukrainian Service) +380 (44) 279 7894; (Technical Department) +380 (44) 279 4179. Email: (Ukrainian Service) marinenko@nrcu.gov.ua; (English Service) vsru@nrcu.gov.ua; (German Service) rui@nrcu.gov.ua; (technical, including reception reports) egorov@nrcu.gov.ua. Web: (includes on- demand and streaming audio) www.nrcu.gov.ua. Contact: Olexander Dykyi, Director; Zhanna Mescherska, Deputy Director; Mykola Marynenko, Editor-in-Chief, Ukrainian Section; Volodymyr Perepadia, Editor-in-Chief, German Section; Tetiana Stechak, Editor-in-Chief, English Section; (technical) Alexander Egorov, Head of Technical Department. Free stickers, calendars and Ukrainian stamps.
Ukrainian Radio, National Radio Company of Ukraine, ul. Kreshchatik 26, 01001 Kiyv, Ukraine (reception reports should be sent to the Monitoring Department). Phone: (International Relations Department) +380 (44) 279-4258. Fax: (International Relations Department) +380 (44) 278 7914. Email: (International Relations Department) euroradiodep@nrcu.gov.ua; (Monitoring Department, reception reports) egorov@nrcu.gov.ua. Web: (includes on-demand and streaming audio) www.nrcu.gov.ua. Contact: Valeriy Krutouz, Head of International Relations Department; (technical) Alexander Egorov, Chief Engineer, Monitoring Department.

UNITED KINGDOM World Time exactly (+1 midyear)

BBC Monitoring, Caversham Park, Reading, Berkshire RG4 8TZ, United Kingdom. Phone: (Commercial) +44 (118) 948-6289. Fax: (Commercial) +44 (118) 946 3823. Email: marketing@mon.bbc.co.uk. Web: www.monitor.bbc.co.uk. BBC Monitoring focuses on providing hard news including international affairs, major domestic and regional developments, political and military conflict, disasters and crime. As well as reporting news from the media, BBC Monitoring has a team of media specialists which reports news about the media in individual countries as well as trends in the media industry, regionally and globally. Reports can be delivered by email or retrieved from a database. Contact the Commercial Department for subscription prices and information on their other products.
BBC World Service
MAIN OFFICE, NONTECHNICAL: Bush House, Strand, London WC2B 4PH, United Kingdom. Phone: (general) +44 (20) 7240-3456; (Press Office) +44 (20) 7557-2947/1; (International Marketing) +44 (20) 7557-1143. Fax: (Audience Relations) +44 (20) 7557 1258; ("Write On" listeners' letters program) +44 (20) 7436 2800; (Audience and Market Research) +44 (20) 7557 1254; (International Marketing) +44 (20) 7557 1254. Email: (general listener correspondence) worldservice@bbc.co.uk; ("Write On") writeon@bbc.co.uk. Web: (includes on-demand and streaming audio) www.bbc.co.uk/worldservice. Also, *see* Ascension, Oman, Seychelles, Singapore and Thailand. Does not verify reception reports due to budget limitations.
SAN FRANCISCO OFFICE, SCHEDULES: 2654 17th Avenue, San Francisco CA 94116 USA. Phone: +1 (415) 564-9968. Email: GPoppin@aol.com. Contact: George Poppin. This address, a volunteer office, only provides BBC World Service schedules to listeners (return postage not required). All other correspondence should be sent directly to the main office in London.
TECHNICAL: see VT Communications.
BFBS—British Forces Broadcasting Service (when operating), Services Sound and Vision, Chalfont Grove, Narcot Lane, Chalfont St. Peter, Gerrards Cross, Buckinghamshire SL9 8TN, United Kingdom; or BFBS Worldwide, P.O. Box 903, Gerrards Cross, Buckinghamshire SL9 8TN, United Kingdom. Email: (general) adminofficer@bfbs.com. Web: (includes on-demand and streaming audio) www.ssvc.com/bfbs. Normally only on satellite and FM, but hires additional shortwave facilities when British troops are fighting overseas.
Bible Voice Broadcasting
EUROPEAN OFFICE: P. O. Box 220, Leeds LS26 0WW, United Kingdom. Phone: +44 (1900) 827-355. Email: online form; mail@biblevoice.org; (schedules) reception@biblevoice.org. Web: (includes on-demand audio) www.biblevoice.org. Contact: Martin and Liz Thompson.
NORTH AMERICAN OFFICE: High Adventure Gospel Communication Ministries, P.O. Box 425, Station E, Toronto, Ontario M6H 4E3, Canada. Phone: +1 (905) 898-5447; (toll-free, U.S. and Canada only) 1-800-550-4670. Email: highadventure@sympatico.ca. Contact: Mrs. Marty McLaughlin.
Bible Voice Broadcasting is a partnership between Bible Voice (U.K.) and High Adventure Gospel Communication Ministries (Canada).
Christian Vision, P.O. Box 3040, West Bromwich, West Midlands, B70 0EJ, United Kingdom; (street address) The Pavilion, Manor Drive, Coleshill, West Midlands B46 1DL, United Kingdom. Phone: +44 (1675) 435-500; (Flynn) +44 (1675) 435-502. Fax: +44 (1675) 435 501. Email: (Watson) gemmawatson@christianvision.com; (Flynn) andrewflynn@christianvision.com. Web: www.christianvision.com. Contact: (nontechnical) Gemma Watson; (technical) Andrew Flynn, Director of International Broadcasting.

Commonwealth Broadcasting Association, CBA Secretariat, 17 Fleet Street, London EC4Y 1AA, United Kingdom. Phone: +44 (20) 7583-5550. Fax: +44 (20) 7583 5549. Email: cba@cba.org.uk. Web: www.cba.org.uk. Publishes the annual *Commonwealth Broadcaster Directory* and the quarterly *Commonwealth Broadcaster* (online subscription form available).

European Music Radio, c/o A. Taylor, 32 Shearing Drive, Carshalton, Surrey, SM5 1BL, United Kingdom. Phone: +44 (77) 4315-2908. Email: studio@emr.org.uk. Web (includes streaming audio) www.emr.org.uk. An Internet station which also airs intermittently on world band via Germany's Media Broadcast (*see*) and a transmitter in Latvia.

FEBA Radio, Ivy Arch Road, Worthing, West Sussex BN14 8BX, United Kingdom. Phone: +44 (1903) 237-281. Fax: +44 (1903) 205 294. Email: (general) info@feba.org.uk; (Whittington) rwhittington@feba.org.uk. Web: www.feba.org.uk. Contact: (nontechnical) Angela Brooke, Supporter Relations; (technical) Richard Whittington, Schedule Engineer. Does not verify reception reports. Try sending reports to individual program producers (addresses are usually given over the air).

IBC-Tamil, 3 College Fields, Prince George's Road, Colliers Wood, London SW19 2PT, United Kingdom. Phone: +44 (20) 8100-0012. Fax: +44 (20) 8100 0003. Email: radio@ibctamil.co.uk. Web: (includes on-demand and streaming audio) www.ibctamil.co.uk. Contact: A.C. Tarcisius, Managing Director; S. Shivaranjith, Manager; K. Pillai; or Public Relations Officer. Replies irregularly.

VT Communications Ltd, Blue Fin Building, 110 Southwark Street, London SE1 0TA, United Kingdom. Phone: +44 (20) 7969-0000; (Ayris) +44 7515-333-142. Fax: +44 (20) 7396 6221/3. Email: (Head of Marketing & Communications) laura.luckett@vtplc.com; (Ayris) tim.ayris@vtplc.com. Web: www.vtplc.com/communications. Contact: Fiona Lowry, Chief Executive; Rory Maclachlan, Director of International Communications & Digital Services; Ciaran Fitzgerald, Head of Engineering & Operations; Richard Hurd, Head of Transmission Sales; Laura Luckett, Head of Marketing and Communications; Laura Jelf, Marketing Manager; Kirsty Love, Marketing Coordinator; Tim Ayris, Business Development Manager for Broadcast. Formerly known as Merlin Communications International. Does not verify reception reports.

WRN (formerly World Radio Network), P.O. Box 1212, London SW8 2ZF, United Kingdom. Phone: (general) +44 (20) 7896-9000; (Sales and Marketing Department) +44 (20) 7896-4082. Fax: +44 (20) 7896 9007. Email: (general) contactus@wrn.org; (Sales and Marketing) sales@wrn.org; (Wilson) sophie.wilson@wrn.org. Web: (includes on-demand and streaming audio) www.wrn.org. Contact: Sophie Wilson, Business Development Manager. Provides Webcasts and program placements for international broadcasters in both the radio and TV sectors.

UNITED NATIONS World Time –5 (–4 midyear)

IRIN Radio

Email: feedback@irinnews.org; online form; (Tunbridge) louise@irinnews.org. Web: (includes on-demand audio) www.irinnews.org/radio.aspx. Contact: Louise Tunbridge, IRIN Radio Coordinator, Nairobi, Kenya. IRIN (Integrated Regional Information Networks) is part of the United Nations Office for the Coordination of Humanitarian affairs, but its services are editorially independent.

URUGUAY World Time –2 (–3 midyear)

Emisora Ciudad de Montevideo (when operating), Arenal Grande 2093, 11800 Montevideo, Uruguay. Phone: +598 (2) 924-1312. Email: online form. Web: (includes streaming audio) www.emisoraciudaddemontevideo.com.uy. Contact: Aramazd Yizmeyian, Director General. Free stickers. Return postage helpful.

Radiodifusion Nacional—*see* SODRE

Radio Universo (if activated on shortwave), Ferrer 1265, 27000 Castillos, Dpto. de Rocha, Uruguay. Email: am1480@adinet.com.uy. Web: (includes streaming audio) www.universoam.com. Contact: Juan Héber Brañas, Propietario. Currently only on 1480 kHz mediumwave/AM, but has been granted a license to operate on shortwave.

SODRE (if reactivated), Radiodifusión Nacional, Casilla 1412, 11000 Montevideo, Uruguay. Phone: +598 (2) 916-1933; (technical) +598 (2) 915-7865. Email: (director) direccionradios@sodre.gub.uy; (technical) organizacion@sodre.gub.uy. Web: (includes streaming audio) www.sodre.gub.uy. Contact: (management) Sergio Sacomani, Director de Radiodifusión Nacional; (technical) José Cuello, División Técnica Radio; Pedro Ramela, Jefe Dpto. Plantas.

USA World Time –4 Atlantic, including Puerto Rico and Virgin Islands; –5 (–4 midyear) Eastern, –6 (–5 midyear) Central, including northwest and southwest Indiana; –7 (–6 midyear) Mountain, except Arizona; –7 Arizona; –8 (–7 midyear) Pacific; –9 (–8 midyear) Alaska, except Aleutian Islands; –10 (–9 midyear) Aleutian Islands; –10 Hawaii; –11 Samoa

Adventist World Radio

HEADQUARTERS: 12501 Old Columbia Pike, Silver Spring MD 20904-6600 USA. Phone: +1 (301) 680-6304; (toll-free, U.S. only) 1-800-337-4297. Fax: +1 (301) 680 6303. Email: info@awr.org. Web: (includes on-demand and streaming audio) www.awr.org.

NONTECHNICAL LISTENER CORRESPONDENCE: E-mail: letters@awr.org.

RECEPTION REPORTS AND LISTENER QUERIES (BY REGION):

AFRICA, AMERICAS AND EUROPE: P.O. Box 29235, Indianapolis IN 46229 USA. Phone/Fax: +1 (317) 891-8540. Email: adrian@awr.org. Contact: Dr. Adrian M. Peterson, International Relations Coordinator. Provides technical information, processes reception reports and issues verifications.

ASIA AND THE PACIFIC: Listener Relations, Adventist World Radio—Asia/Pacific, 798 Thompson Road, Singapore 298186, Singapore. Email: radio@awr.org. Contact: Rhoen Catolico, Asst. Program Director/Listener Relations and Host/Presenter AWR Wavescan.

AWR FREQUENCY MANAGEMENT AND MONITORING OFFICE: Sandwiesenstr. 35, D-64665 Alsbach, Germany. Phone: +49 (6257) 944-0969. Fax: +49 (6257) 944 0985.

Email: (Dedio) dedio@awr.org; (Cirillo) pino@awr.org. Contact: Claudius Dedio, Frequency Manager; Giuseppe Cirillo, Associate Frequency Engineer/Monitoring Engineer.

Also, *see* GUAM.

AFRTS-American Forces Radio and Television Service (Shortwave), Naval Media Center, NDW Anacostia Annex, 2713 Mitscher Road SW, Washington DC 20373-5819 USA. Web:http://myafn.dodmedia.osd.mil/ShortWave.aspx; (AFRTS parent organization) www.afrts.osd.mil; (2-minute on-demand audio news clips): www.defenselink.mil/news/radio; (Naval Media Center) www.mediacen.navy.mil. The Naval Media Center is responsible for all AFRTS broadcasts aired on shortwave.

VERIFICATION OF RECEPTION REPORTS: Department of Defense, Naval Media Center Detachment, AFRTS-DMC, 23755 Z Street, Bldg. 2730, Riverside CA 92518-2017 USA (mark the envelope, "Attn: Officer in Charge"). Email: qsl@dodmedia.osd.mil. Replies irregularly.

FLORIDA ADDRESS: NCTS-Jacksonville-Detachment Key West, Building A 1004, Naval Air Station Boca Chica, Key West, FL 33040 USA.

Also, *see* BRITISH INDIAN OCEAN AUTHORITY.

Broadcasting Board of Governors (BBG), 330 Independence Avenue SW, Room 3360, Washington DC 20237 USA. Phone: +1 (202) 619-2538. Fax: +1 (202) 619 1241. Email: pubaff@ibb.gov. Web: www.bbg.gov. Contact: Kathleen Harrington, Public Relations. The BBG, created in 1994 and headed by nine members nominated by the President, is the overseeing agency for all official non-military United States international broadcasting operations, including the VOA, RFE/RL, Radio Martí and Radio Free Asia.

Eternal Good News, International Radio Broadcasts, Wilshire Church of Christ, Oklahoma City OK USA. Phone: +1 (405) 359-1235, +1 (405) 340-0877. Email: eternalgoodnews@sbcglobal.net. Web: (includes on-demand audio) www.oldpaths.net/Works/Radio/Wilshire/index.html. Contact: Germaine Charles Lockwood, Evangelist; Sandra Lockwood, Secretary; George Bryan. Programs are aired via world band transmitters in Germany, Russia and United Arab Emirates, as well as U.S. station World Harvest Radio.

Family Radio Worldwide

NONTECHNICAL: Family Stations, Inc., 290 Hegenberger Road, Oakland CA 94621-1436 USA. Phone: (general) +1 (510) 568-6200; (toll-free, U.S. only) 1-800-543-1495; (engineering) +1 (510) 568-6200 ext. 242. Fax: (main office) +1 (510) 568 6200. Email: (international department, shortwave program schedules) international@familyradio.com. Web: (includes streaming audio) www.familyradio.com. Contact: (general) Harold Camping, General Manager; David Hoff, Manager of International Department. Free gospel tracts (50 languages), books, booklets, quarterly *Family Radio News* magazine and frequency schedule. Free CD containing domestic and international program schedules plus audio lessons in MP 3 format and bible study materials. 2 IRCs helpful.

TECHNICAL: WYFR—Family Radio, 10400 NW 240th Street, Okeechobee FL 34972 USA. Phone: +1 (863) 763-0281. Fax: +1 (863) 763 8867. Email: (technical) fsiyfr@okeechobee.com; (frequency schedule) wyfr@okeechobee.com. Contact: Dan Elyea, Engineering Manager; Edward F. Dearborn, Chief Operator; (frequency schedule) Evelyn Marcy.

FEBC Radio International

INTERNATIONAL HEADQUARTERS: Far East Broadcasting Company, Inc., P.O. Box 1, La Mirada CA 90637 USA. Phone: +1 (310) 947-4651. Fax: +1 (310) 943 0160. Email: febc@febc.org. Web: www.febi.org. Operates world band stations in the Philippines and Northern Mariana Islands (*see*). Does not verify reception reports from this address.

Federal Communications Commission, 445 12th Street SW, Washington DC 20554 USA. Phone: +1 (202) 418-0190; (toll-free, U.S. only) 1-888-225-5322. Fax: +1 (202) 418 0232. Email: tpolzin@fcc.gov. Web: (general) www.fcc.gov; (high frequency operating schedules) www.fcc.gov/ib/sand/neg/hf_web/seasons.html. Contact: (International Bureau, technical) Thomas E. Polzin.

Fundamental Broadcasting Network, Grace Missionary Baptist Church, 520 Roberts Road, Newport NC 28570 USA. Phone: +1 (252) 223-4600. Email: fbn@fbnradio.com. Web: (includes streaming audio) www.fbnradio.com. Contact: Pastor Clyde Eborn; A. Robinson; (technical) David Gernoske, Chief Engineer. Verifies reception reports. IRC or (within the USA) SASE appreciated. Accepts email reports. Free stickers. A religious and educational non-commercial broadcasting network which operates sister stations WBOH and WTJC.

Gospel for Asia, 1800 Golden Trail Court, Carrollton TX 75010 USA. Phone: +1 (972) 300-7777; (toll-free, U.S. only) 1-800-946-2742. Email: info@gfa.org. Web: www.gfa.org. Contact: Michele Alexander, Radio Department. Verifies email reports with QSL cards. Transmits via facilities in Germany and U.A.E.

Haiv Hmoob Radio, 1300 Godward Avenue, Suite 6900, Minneapolis MN 55413 USA. Phone: +1 (651) 808-4647. Web: (includes on-demand audio) www.haivhmoobradio.com. Contact: Gymbay Moua. A broadcast of the Congress of World Hmong People, via leased facilities in Taiwan.

Hmong Lao Radio, P.O. Box 6426, St. Paul MN 55106 USA. Phone: +1 (651) 292-0774. Fax: +1 (651) 292-0795. Email: hmonglaoradioofficeusa@yahoo.com. Web: (includes on-demand audio) www.h-lr.com. Contact: Tong Yia Lor, President; Tou Pao Khang, Secretary. To Southeast Asia via a transmitter in Taiwan, and to North America via the facilities of World Harvest Radio (*see*).

Hmong World Christian Radio, P.O. Box 600427, St. Paul MN 55106 USA. Phone: +1 (651) 303-4386. Email: giatoulee@comcast.net. Web: (includes on-demand audio) www.hwcr.us. Contact: Rev. Gia Tou; May Bo Lee. Via leased facilities in Taiwan.

IBB—*see* International Broadcasting Bureau (IBB), below.

IBB Greenville Transmitting Station, P.O. Box 1826, Greenville NC 27834 USA. Phone: (site A) +1 (252) 752-7115 or (site B) +1 (252) 752-7181. Fax: (site A) +1 (252) 758 8742 or (site B) +1 (252) 752 5959. Contact: (technical) Bruce Hunter, Manager; Glenn Ruckleson. Nontechnical correspondence should be sent to the VOA address in Washington.

International Broadcasting Bureau (IBB)—Reports to the Broadcasting Board of Governors (*see*), and includes, among others, the Voice of America, RFE/RL, Radio Martí and Radio Free Asia. IBB Engineering (Office of Engineering and Technical Operations) provides broadcast services for these stations. Contact: (administration) Brian Conniff, Director; Joseph O'Connell, Director of External Affairs. Web: www.ibb.gov/ibbpage.html.

FREQUENCY AND MONITORING OFFICE, TECHNICAL: IBB/EOF: Spectrum Management Division, International Broadcasting Bureau (IBB), Room 4611 Cohen Bldg., 330 Independence Avenue SW, Washington DC 20237 USA. Phone: +1 (202) 619-1669. Fax: +1 (202) 619 1680. Email: (scheduling) dferguson@ibb.gov; (monitoring) bw@his.com. Web: (general) http://monitor.ibb.gov; (email reception report form) http://monitor.ibb.gov/now_you_try_it.html. Contact: Bill Whitacre (bw@his.com).

KAIJ (if reactivated)

STUDIOS AND ADMINISTRATION OFFICE: 1784 W. Northfield Blvd. - Suite 305, Murfreesboro TN 37129-1702 USA. Phone: +1 (615) 469-0702. Email: studio@kaij.us. Web: www.kaij.us.

TRANSMITTER SITE: RR#3 Box 120, Frisco TX 75034 USA; or Highway 380 West, Prosper TX 75078 USA (physical location: Highway 380, 3.6 miles west of State Rt. 289, near Denton TX; transmitters and antennas located on Belt Line Road along the lake in Coppell TX). Phone: +1 (972) 346-2758.

KJES—King Jesus Eternal Savior

STATION: The Lord's Ranch, 230 High Valley Road, Vado NM 88072-7221 USA. Phone: +1 (505) 233-2090. Fax: +1 (505) 233 3019. Email: kjes@family.net. Contact: Michael Reuter, Manager. $1 or return postage appreciated.

SPONSORING ORGANIZATION: Our Lady's Youth Center, P.O. Box 1422, El Paso TX 79948 USA. Phone: +1 (915) 533-9122.

KNLS—New Life Station

OPERATIONS CENTER: World Christian Broadcasting, 605 Bradley Ct., Franklin TN 37067 USA (letters sent to the Alaska transmitter site are usually forwarded to Franklin). Phone: +1 (615) 371-8707 ext.140. Fax: +1 (615) 371 8791. Email: knls@aol.com. Web: (includes on-demand audio of sample programs) www.knls.org. Contact: (general) Dale R. Ward, Executive Producer; L. Wesley Jones, Director of Follow-Up Teaching; Rob Scobey, Senior Producer, English Language Service; (technical) F.M. Perry, Frequency Coordinator. Free *Alaska Calling!* newsletter and station pennants. Free spiritual literature and bibles in Russian, Mandarin or English. Free Alaska books, tapes, postcards and cloth patches. Two free DX books for beginners. Special, individually numbered, limited edition, verification cards issued for each new transmission period to the first 200 listeners providing confirmed reception reports. Stamp and postcard exchange. Return postage appreciated.

TRANSMITTER SITE: P.O. Box 473, Anchor Point AK 99556 USA. Phone: +1 (907) 235-8262. Fax: +1 (907) 235 2326. Contact: (technical) Kevin Chambers, Chief Engineer.

KTMI—Transformation Media International (under construction), 240 2nd Avenue SW, Albany OR 97321 USA. Phone: +1 (541) 259-5900. Fax: +1 (541) 812 7611. Email: (Brosnan) mbrosnan03@yahoo.com; (Lund) bob@lund.com. Contact: Ms. Michele Brosnan, Director of Operations; Robert Lund, Chief Engineer.

KVOH—La Voz de Restauración, P.O. Box 8120, Los Angeles CA 90008 USA; (street address) 4409 W. Adams Blvd., Los Angeles CA 90016 USA. Phone: (general) +1 (323) 766-2454; (radio) +1 (323) 766-2428. Fax: +1 (323) 766-2458. Email: kvoh@restauracion.com. Web: (includes streaming audio) www.restauracion.com/main_pages/radio.htm (if this fails, go to www.restauracion.com, and click on "Radio").

KWHR-World Harvest Radio:

ADMINISTRATION OFFICE: see World Harvest Radio.

TRANSMITTER: Although located 6 1/2 miles southwest of Naalehu, 8 miles north of South Cape, and 2000 feet west of South Point (Ka La) Road (the antennas are easily visible from this road) on Big Island, Hawaii, the operators of this rural transmitter site maintain no post office box in or near Naalehu, and their telephone number is unlisted, Best bet is to contact them via their administration office (*see* World Harvest Radio), or to drive in unannounced (it's just off South Point Road) the next time you vacation on Big Island.

Leinwoll (Stanley)—Telecommunication Consultant, 305 E. 86th Street, Suite 21S-W, New York NY 10028 USA. Phone: +1 (212) 987-0456. Fax: +1 (212) 987 3532. Email: stanl00011@aol.com. Contact: Stanley Leinwoll, President. This firm provides frequency management and other engineering services for some private U.S. world band stations, but does not correspond with the general public.

Little Saigon Radio, 15781 Brookhurst St. - Suite 101, Westminster CA 92683 USA. Phone: +1 (714) 918-4444. Fax: +1 (714) 918-4445/6. Email: online form. Web: (includes on-demand and streaming audio from domestic broadcasts, and on-demand audio from shortwave service) www.littlesaigonradio.com. Contact: Joe Dinh, Technical Director. A Californian mediumwave/AM station which airs a special broadcast for Vietnam via leased facilities in Taiwan.

National Association of Shortwave Broadcasters, 10400 NW 240th Street, Okeechobee, FL 34972 USA. Phone: +1 (863) 763-0281. Fax: +1 (863) 763 8867. Email: nasbmem@rocketmail.com. Web: www.shortwave.org. Contact: Dan Elyea, Secretary-Treasurer. Association of most private U.S. world band stations, as well as a group of other international broadcasters, equipment manufacturers and organizations related to shortwave broadcasting. Includes committees on various subjects, such as digital shortwave radio. Interfaces with the Federal Communications Commission's International Bureau and other broadcasting-related organizations to advance the interests of its members. Publishes *NASB Newsletter* for members and associates and is available for free via their website. Annual one-day convention held early each spring; non-members wishing to attend should contact the Secretary-Treasurer in advance; convention fee typically $50 per person.

Overcomer Ministry ("Voice of the Last Day Prophet of God"), P.O. Box 691, Walterboro SC 29488 USA. Phone: (voicemail) +1 (843) 538-6689. Fax: +1 (843) 538 6689. Email: brotherstair@overcomerministry.org; (technical) brothermark@overcomerministry.org. Web: (includes on-demand and streaming audio) www.overcomerministry.org. Contact: Brother R.G. Stair. Sample "Overcomer" newsletter and various pamphlets free upon request. Via Germany's Media Broadcast (*see*) and various U.S. stations.

Pan American Broadcasting, 7011 Koll Center Pkwy, Suite 250, Pleasanton CA 94566-3253 USA. Phone: +1 (925) 462-9800; (toll-free, U.S. only) 1-800-726-2620. Fax: +1 (925) 462 9808. Email: online form; info@panambc.com; (Bernald) gbernald@panambc.com; (Jung) cjung@panambc.com. Web: www.radiopanam.com. Contact: (listener correspondence) Elizabeth Dubach; (general) Carmen Jung, Office and Sales Administration; Eugene Bernald, President. $1, mint U.S. stamps or 2 IRCs required for a reply. Operates transmitters in Equatorial Guinea (*see*) and hires airtime over a number of world band stations, plus Media Broadcast facilities in Germany (*see*).

Quê Huong Radio, 2670 South White Road, Suite 165, San Jose CA 95148 USA. Phone: +1 (408) 223-3130. Fax: +1 (408) 223 3131. Email: qhradio@aol.com. Web: (includes on-demand audio) www.quehuongmedia.com. Contact: Nguyen Khoi, Manager. A Californian Vietnamese station operating on mediumwave/AM, and which broadcasts to Vietnam via a transmitter in Central Asia.

Radio Farda, 7600 Boston Boulevard, Springfield VA 22153 USA. Email: info@radiofarda.com. Web: (includes on-demand and streaming audio) www.radiofarda.com. A joint venture between Radio Free Europe-Radio Liberty (*see*) and the Voice of America (*see*). Broadcasts a mix of news, information and popular Iranian and western music to younger audiences in Iran. Reception reports are best sent to Radio Free Europe-Radio Liberty.

Radio Free Afghanistan—the Afghan service of Radio Free Europe-Radio Liberty (*see*). Web: (includes on-demand and streaming audio) www.azadiradio.org.

Radio Free Asia, Suite 300, 2025 M Street NW, Washington DC 20036 USA (for reports on reception, add "Reception Reports" before "Radio Free Asia"). You can also submit reception reports at: www.techweb.rfa.org (click on the QSL REPORTS link) or send them via email to: QSL@rfa.org. Phone: (general) +1 (202) 530-4900; (president) +1 (202) 457-4902;(vice president of editorial) +1 (202) 530-4907; (vice-president of administration) +1 (202) 530-4906); (chief technology officer) +1 (202) 530-4958; (director of production support) +1 (202) 530-4943. Fax: +1 (202) 721 7468. Email: (individuals) the format is lastnameinitial@rfa.org; so to reach, say the CTO, David Baden, it would be badend@rfa.org; (language sections) the format is language@rfa.org; so to contact, say, the Vietnamese section, address your message to vietnamese@rfa.org; (general) communications@rfa.org; (reception reports) qsl@rfa.org. Web: (includes on-demand audio) www.rfa.org; (automated reception report system) www.techweb.rfa.org. Contact: (administration) Libby Liu, President; Daniel Southerland, Vice President of Editorial; (technical) David M. Baden, Chief Technology Officer; A. J. Janitschek, Director of Production Support; Sam Stevens, Director of Technical Support. RFA, originally created in 1996 as the Asia Pacific Network, is funded as a private nonprofit U.S. corporation by a grant from the US Congress to the Broadcasting Board of Governors (*see*).

HONG KONG OFFICE: Room 904, Mass Mutal Tower, 38 Gloucester Road, Wanchai, Hong Kong, China.

THAILAND OFFICE: Maxim House, 112 Witthayu Road, Pathomwan, Bangkok 10330, Thailand.

Radio Free Europe/Radio Liberty (RFE/RL)

PRAGUE HEADQUARTERS: Vinohradská 1, 110 00 Prague 1, Czech Republic. Phone: (main switchboard) +420 (22) 112-1111; (Deputy Director of Communications) +420 (22) 112-2074. Fax: +420 (22) 112 3010. Email: the format is lastnameinitial@rferl.org; so to reach, say, Luke Springer, it would be springerl@rferl.org; (reception reports) zvanersm@rferl.org. Web: (includes on-demand and streaming audio) www.rferl.org. Contact: Julian Knapp, Deputy Director of Communications; Luke Springer, Director of Technology.

WASHINGTON OFFICE: 1201 Connecticut Avenue NW, Washington DC 20036 USA. Phone: +1 (202) 457-6900; (Communications) +1 (202) 457-6948. Fax: +1 (202) 457 6992; (Communications) +1 (202) 457 6992. Email: *see*, above. Web: *see*, above. Contact: Martins Zvaners, Associate Director of Communications.

A private non-profit corporation funded by a grant from the Broadcasting Board of Governors (*see*), RFE/RL broadcasts from transmission facilities now part of the International Broadcasting Bureau (IBB), *see*.

Radio Martí, Office of Cuba Broadcasting, 4201 N.W. 77th Avenue, Miami FL 33166 USA. Phone: +1 (305) 437-7000; (Director) +1 (305) 437-7117; (Technical Operations) +1 (305) 437-7051. Fax: +1 (305) 437 7016. Email: infomarti@ocb.ibb.gov; (Ray de Arenas) mraydearenas @ ocb.ibb.gov. Web: (includes on-demand and streaming audio) www.martinoticias.com/radio.asp. Contact: (technical) Michael Pallone, Director, Engineering and Technical Operations; Tom Warden, Chief of Radio Operations; Margaret Ray de Arenas, Assistant to the Director, Engineering and Technical Operations.

Smyrna Radio International (projected), c/o Smyrna Baptist Church, 7000 Pensacola Blvd., Pensacola FL 32505 USA. Phone: +1 (850) 477-0998.

Somali Interactive Radio Instruction Program (SIRIP) (when operating)—*see* Sudan Radio Service, below, for EDC address and other information. Email: (Houssein) ahoussein@edc.org. Web: http://ies.edc.org/ourwork/project.php?id=3734&country=445. Contact: Abdoul Houssein. A project of International Education Systems (IES), a division of Education Development Center (EDC), funded by the U.S. Agency for International Development (USAID), and targeted at Somali-speaking children in East Africa. Broadcasts via the United Arab Emirates, and sometimes elsewhere. Off the air during school holidays.

Southern Sudan Interactive Radio Instruction (SSIRI) (when operating)—*see* Sudan Radio Service, below, for EDC address and other information. Email: (Tilson) ttilson@edc.org. Web: http://ies.edc.org/ourwork/project.php?id=3487&country=452. Contact: Tom Tilson. A project of the Education Development Center (EDC) funded by the U.S. Agency for International Development (USAID). Broadcasts are via transmitters brokered by VT Communications (*see* United Kingdom). Off the air during school holidays in southern Sudan.

PRODUCTION STUDIOS, KENYA: 28 Mugumo Road, P.O. Box 25010, 00603 Lavington, Nairobi, Kenya.

Suab Xaa Moo Zoo, Hmong District, 12287 Pennsylvania Street, Thornton CO 80241-3113 USA. Phone: +1 (303) 252-1793; (toll-free, U.S. only) +1 (877) 521-7814. Fax: +1 (303) 252 7911. Email: hkm@hmongdistrict.org;

Elder Jacob O. Meyer of the Assemblies of Yahweh in Bethel, Pennsylvania. He is heard six days a week over WMLK Radio on 9265 kHz. Sacred Name Broadcast

(Media Department) suabxaamoozoo@yahoo.com. Web: (includes on-demand audio) www.hmongdistrict.org/communication.htm. Sells CDs of Hmong music.

ALTERNATIVE ADDRESS: Christian and Missionary Alliance, P.O. Box 35000, Colorado Springs CO 80935-3500 USA. Phone: +1 (719) 599-5999. Email: webmaster@cmalliance.org.

A Hmong religious broadcast to Southeast Asia via leased facilities in Taiwan.

Sudan Radio Service, EDC, 1000 Potomac Street NW, Suite 350, Washington DC 20007 USA. Phone: +1 (202) 572-3700. Fax: +1 (202) 223 4059. Email: (Groce) jgroce@edc.org. Web: http://ies.edc.org/ourwork/project.php?id=3367&country=452. Contact: Jeremy Groce. A project of International Education Systems (IES), a division of Education Development Center (EDC), funded by the U.S. Agency for International Development (USAID).

SRS OFFICES & STUDIOS, KENYA: c/o EDC, P.O. Box 4392, 00100 Nairobi, Kenya. Phone: +254 (20) 387-0906, +254 (20) 387-2269. Fax: +254 (20) 387 6520. Email: news@sudanradio.org; (Renzi) mtamburo@sudanradio.org. Web: (includes on-demand audio) www.sudanradio.org. Contact: Tamburo Michael Renzi, SRS Marketing Coordinator.

Trans World Radio

INTERNATIONAL HEADQUARTERS: P.O. Box 8700, Cary NC 27512 USA. Phone: +1 (919) 460-3700; (toll-free, U.S. only) 1-800-456-7897. Fax: +1 (919) 460 3702. Email: online form. Web: (includes on-demand audio) www.twr.org. Contact: (general) Jon Vaught, Public Relations; Richard Greene, Director, Public Relations; Joe Fort, Director, Broadcaster Relations; Bill Danick; (technical) Glenn W. Sink, Assistant Vice President, International Operations. Free "Towers to Eternity" publication for those living in the U.S. This address for nontechnical correspondence only.

TRANS WORLD RADIO EUROPE (TECHNICAL): Trans World Radio, Postfach 141, A-1235 Vienna, Austria. Phone: +43 (1) 863-120. Fax: +43 (1) 863 1220, +43 (1) 862 1257. Email: (Schraut) bschraut@twr.org. Contact: Rudolf Baertschi, Technical Director; Bernhard Schraut, Deputy Technical Director; Jeremy Mullin, Frequency Coordinator. Verifies reception reports.

TRANS WORLD RADIO EUROPE (NONTECHNICAL): Trans World Radio Europe, Communications Department, P.O. Box 12, 820 02 Bratislava 22, Slovakia. Fax: +421 (2) 4329 3729. Web: www.twreurope.org.

TRANS WORLD RADIO INDIA: 15 Green Park, New Delhi - 110 016, India. Phone: +91 (11) 4603-4300. Email: info@twr.in; (Devadoss) ddevadoss@in.twrsa.org. Web: (includes on-demand and streaming audio) www.radio882.com. Verifies reception reports by email. Contact: E. Daniel Devadoss; Shakti Verma, Technical Director. Also, *see* GUAM, SOUTH AFRICA and SWAZILAND.

University Network, P.O. Box 1, Los Angeles CA 90053 USA. Phone: +1 (818) 240-8151; (toll-free, U.S. and Canada only) 1-800-338-3030. Web: (includes streaming audio) www.drgenescott.com. Transmits over WWCR (USA); Caribbean Beacon (Anguilla, West Indies) and the former AWR facilities in Cahuita, Costa Rica. Does not verify reception reports.

Voice of America—All Transmitter Locations

(Main Office) 330 Independence Avenue SW, Washington DC 20237 USA; (listener feedback) Voice of America, Audience Mail, Room 4409, 330 Independence Ave SW,Washington DC 20237 USA. If contacting the VOA directly is impractical, write c/o the American Embassy in your country. Phone: +1 (202) 203-4000; (Public Affairs) +1 (202) 203-4959. Fax: (listener feedback) +1 (202) 382 5417; (Public Affairs) +1 (202) 203 4960. Email: (general business) publicaffairs@voa.gov; (reception reports and schedule requests) letters@voa.gov; (listener feedback) letters@voanews.com; (VOA Special English) special@voanews.com. Web: (includes on-demand and streaming audio) www.voa.gov. Contact: Mrs. Betty Lacy Thompson, Chief, Audience Mail Division, B/K. G759A Cohen; Larry James, Director, English Programs Division; Joe O'Connell, Director, Office of Public Affairs; (reception reports) QSL Desk, Audience Mail Division, Room G-759-C. Free calendars and program schedules. Also, *see* Botswana, Philippines, São Tomé e Príncipe, Sri Lanka and Thailand.

WBCQ—"The Planet," 274 Britton Road, Monticello ME 04760 USA. Phone: (during normal business hours) +1 (207) 538-9180. Email: wbcq@wbcq.com. Web: (includes streaming audio) www.wbcq.com. Contact: Allan H. Weiner, Owner; Elayne Star, Assistant Manager. Verifies reception reports if 1 IRC or (within USA) an SASE is included. Does not verify email reports.

WBOH—*see* Fundamental Broadcasting Network

WEWN—EWTN Global Catholic Radio, 5817 Old Leeds Rd., Birmingham AL 35210 USA. Phone: +1 (205) 271-2900. Fax: +1 (205) 271 2926. Email: (general)

radio@ewtn.com; (Spanish) rcm@ewtn.com. To contact individuals, the format is initiallastname@ewtn.com; so to reach, say, Thom Price, it would be tprice@ewtn.com. Web: (includes on-demand and streaming audio, and online reception report form) www.ewtn.com/radio. Contact: (general) Thom Price, Director of English Programming; Doug Archer, Director of Spanish Programming; (marketing) John Pepe, Radio Marketing Manager; (administration) Michael Warsaw, President; Doug Keck, Sr. Vice-President, Programming & Production; Frank Leurck, Station Manager; (technical) Terry Borders, Vice President Engineering; Glen Tapley, Frequency Manager. Listener correspondence welcome. IRC or return postage appreciated for correspondence. Although a Catholic entity, WEWN is not an official station of the Vatican, which operates its own Vatican Radio (*see*).

WHRA-World Harvest Radio:
ADMINISTRATION OFFICE: see World Harvest Radio.
TRANSMITTERS: Located in Greenbush, Maine. Technical and other correspondence should be sent to the main office of World Harvest Radio (*see*).

WHRI-World Harvest Radio:
ADMINISTRATION OFFICE: see World Harvest Radio.
TRANSMITTERS: Located in Cypress Creek, South Carolina. Technical and other correspondence should be sent to the main office of World Harvest Radio (*see*).

WINB—World International Broadcasters, 2900 Windsor Road, P.O. Box 88, Red Lion PA 17356 USA. Phone: +1 (717) 244-5360. Fax: +1 (717) 246 0363. Email: (general) info@winb.com; (reception reports) winb40th@yahoo.com. Web: www.winb.com. Contact: (general) Mrs. Sally Spyker, Manager; (Sales & Frequency Manager) Hans Johnson; (technical) Fred W. Wise, Technical Director; John H. Norris, Owner. Return postage helpful outside United States. No giveaways or items for sale.

WMLK—Assemblies of Yahweh, 190 Frantz Road, P.O. Box C, Bethel PA 19507 USA. Phone: +1 (717) 933-4518, +1 (717) 933-4880; (toll-free, U.S. only) 1-800-523-3827. Email: (general) aoy@wmlkradio.net; (technical) technician@wmlkradio.net; (Elder Meyer) jacobmeyer@wmlkradio.net; (McAvin) garymcavin@wmlkradio.net. Web: (includes streaming audio) www.wmlkradio.net. Contact: (general) Elder Jacob O. Meyer, Manager and Producer of "The Open Door to the Living World"; (technical) Gary McAvin, Operating Engineer. Free stickers, *The Sacred Name Broadcaster* monthly magazine, and other religious material. Bibles, audio and video (VHS) tapes and religious paperback books offered. Enclosing return postage ($1 or IRCs) helps speed things up.

World Harvest Radio, P.O. Box 12, South Bend IN 46624 USA; (street address) LeSEA Broadcasting, 61300 Ironwood Road, South Bend IN 46614 USA. Phone: +1 (574) 291-8200. Fax: +1 (574) 291 9043. Email: whr@lesea.com. Web: (includes streaming audio and online reception report form) www.whr.org; (LeSEA Broadcasting parent organization, includes streaming audio) www.lesea.com. World Harvest Radio T-shirts available. Return postage appreciated.
ENGINEERING DEPARTMENT: LeSEA Broadcasting, 1030 Shortwave Lane, Pineland SC 29934 USA. Contact: Larry Vehorn, Director of Engineering.

WRMI—Radio Miami International, 175 Fontainebleau Blvd., Suite 1N4, Miami FL 33172 USA. Phone: +1 (305) 559-9764. Fax: +1 (305) 559 8186. Email: info@wrmi.net. Web: (includes streaming audio) www.wrmi.net. Contact: (technical and nontechnical) Jeff White, General Manager/Sales Manager. Free station stickers and tourist brochures. Sells "public access" airtime to nearly anyone to say virtually anything for $1 per minute.

WRNO Worldwide, c/o Good News World Outreach, P.O. Box 895, Fort Worth TX 76101 USA. Phone: +1 (817) 850-9990. Fax: +1 (817) 850 9994. Email: wrnoradio@mailup.net. Web:www.wrnoworldwide.org. Contact: Dr. Robert Mawire; Janet Mawire; (technical) Larry Thom, Chief Engineer.
TRANSMITTER SITE: 4539 I-10 Service Road North, Metairie LA 70006 USA.

WTJC—*see* Fundamental Broadcasting Network.

WWCR—World Wide Christian Radio, F.W. Robbert Broadcasting Co., 1300 WWCR Avenue, Nashville TN 37218 USA. Phone: (general) +1 (615) 255-1300, +1 (615) 255-1377; (engineering) +1 (615) 255-0444. Fax: +1 (615) 255 1311. Email: wwcr@wwcr.com. Web: (includes streaming audio) www.wwcr.com. Contact: (nontechnical) Eric Westenberger, General Manager; Cathy Soares, Program Director; (technical) Brad Murray, Operations Manager. Free program guides, updated monthly. Return postage helpful. For items sold on the air and tapes of programs, contact the producers of the programs, and *not* WWCR. Replies as time permits. Carries programs from various political organizations, which may be contacted directly.

WWRB—World Wide Religious Broadcasters, (listeners) Airline Transport Communications Inc., Listener Services, Box 7, Manchester TN 37349 USA; (broadcasters) Airline Transport Communications Inc., Broadcast Services Group, 6755 Shady Grove Road, Morrison TN 37355 USA. Phone: (8:00 PM - 2:00 AM Eastern Time) +1 (931) 728-6087. Email: (general) online form; (Dave Frantz) dfrantz@tennessee.com. Web: www.wwrb.org. Contact: Dave Frantz, Chief Engineer; Angela Frantz. Verifies reception reports with a large certificate and automatic membership of the WWRB Shortwave Listener's Club. Does not accept email reports.

WWV/WWVB (official time and frequency stations): NIST Radio Station WWV, 2000 East County Road #58, Ft. Collins CO 80524 USA. Phone: +1 (303) 497-3914; (streaming audio, two minutes maximum) +1 (303) 499-7111. Fax: +1 (303) 497 4063. Email: (general) nist.radio@boulder.nist.gov; (Deutch) deutch@boulder.nist.gov. Web: http://tf.nist.gov/timefreq/stations/wwv.html. Contact: Matthew J. ("Matt") Deutch, Engineer-in-Charge. Along with branch sister station WWVH in Hawaii (*see*, below), WWV and WWVB are the official time and frequency stations of the United States, operating over longwave (WWVB) on 60 kHz, and over shortwave (WWV) on 2500, 5000, 10000, 15000 and 20000 kHz.
PARENT ORGANIZATION: National Institute of Standards and Technology, Time and Frequency Division, 325 Broadway, Boulder CO 80305-3328 USA. Phone: +1 (303) 497-3295. Fax: +1 303-497-6461. Email: lombardi@boulder.nist.gov.

WWVH (official time and frequency station): NIST Radio Station WWVH, P.O. Box #417, Kekaha, Kauai HI 96752 USA. Phone: +1 (808) 335-4361; (streaming audio, two minutes maximum) +1 (808) 335-4363. Fax: +1 (808) 335 4747. Email: (general) wwvh@boulder.nist.gov; (Okayama) dean.okayama@boulder.nist.gov. Web: www.tf.nist.gov/stations/wwvh.htm. Contact: Dean Okayama, Engineer-in-Charge; Adelamae Ochinang, Secretary. Along with sister stations WWV and WWVB (*see* preceding), WWVH is the official time and frequency station of the United States, operating on 2500, 5000, 10000 and 15000 kHz.

WYFR—Family Radio—*see* Family Radio Worldwide

VANUATU World Time +11

Radio Vanuatu, Information and Public Relations, Private Mail Bag 049, Port Vila, Vanuatu. Phone: +678 22999, +678 23026. Fax: +678 22026. Contact: Jean-Gabriel Manguy, Head; Maxwell E. Maltok, General Manager; Ambong Thompson, Head of Programmes; (technical) K.J. Page, Principal Engineer; Willie Daniel, Technician.

VATICAN CITY STATE World Time +1 (+2 midyear)

Radio Vaticana (Vatican Radio)

MAIN AND PROMOTION OFFICES: 00120 Città del Vaticano, Vatican City State. Phone: (general) +39 (06) 6988-3551; (Director General) +39 (06) 6988-3945; (Programme Director) +39 (06) 6988-3996; (Publicity and Promotion Department) +39 (06) 6988-3045; (technical, general) +39 (06) 6988-4897; (frequency management) +39 (06) 6988-5258. Fax: (general) +39 (06) 6988 4565; (frequency management) +39 (06) 6988 5062. Email: sedoc@vatiradio.va; (Director General) dirgen@vatiradio.va; (frequency management) gestfreq@vatiradio.va (sometimes verifies reception reports); (technical direction, general) sectec@vatiradio.va; (Programme Director) dirpro@vatiradio.va; (Publicity and Promotion Department) promo@vatiradio.va; (French Section) magfra@vatiradio.va; (German Section) deutsch@vatiradio.va. Web: (includes on-demand and streaming audio) www.vatican.va/news_services/radio; (includes on-demand and streaming audio) www.vaticanradio.org. Contact: (general) Elisabetta Vitalini Sacconi, Promotion Office and schedules; Carol Ganbardella, Secretary, English Service; Eileen O'Neill, Head of Program Development, English Service; Fr. Lech Rynkiewicz S.J., Head of Promotion Office; Fr. Andrzej Koprowski S.J., Program Director; Dr. Giacomo Ghisani, Head of International Relations; Sean Patrick Lovett, Head of English Service; Veronica Scarisbrick, Producer, "On the Air;" (administration) Fr. Federico Lombardi S.J., Director General; (technical) Sergio Salvatori, Frequency Manager, Direzione Tecnica; Dr. Alberto Gasbarri, Technical Director; Giovanni Serra, Frequency Management Department. Correspondence sought on religious and programming matters, rather than the technical minutiae of radio, but does verify reception reports. Free station stickers and paper pennants.

INDIA OFFICE: Loyola College, P.B. No 3301, Chennai-600 03, India. Fax: +91 (44) 2825 7340. Email: (Tamil) tamil@vatiradio.va; (Hindi) hindi@vatiradio.va; (English) india@vatiradio.va.

REGIONAL OFFICE, INDIA: Pastoral Orientation Centre, P.B. No 2251, Palarivattom, India. Fax: +91 (484) 2336 227. Email: (Malayalam) malayalam@vatiradio.va.

JAPAN OFFICE: 2-10-10 Shiomi, Koto-ku, Tokyo 135, Japan. Fax: +81 (3) 5632 4457.

VENEZUELA World Time -4:30

Observatorio Cagigal—YVTO, Apartado 6745, Armada 84-DHN, Caracas 103, Venezuela. Phone: +58 (212) 481-2266. Email: armdhn@ven.net; shlv@dhn.mil.ve. Contact: Luis Ojeda Pérez, Director; Jesús Alberto Escalona, Director Técnico. $1 or return postage helpful.

Radio Amazonas (when operating), Av. Simón Bolívar 4, Puerto Ayacucho 7101, Amazonas, Venezuela. Contact: Angel María Pérez, Propietario.

ADDRESS FOR RECEPTION REPORTS: Sr. Jorge García Rangel, Radio Amazonas QSL Manager, Calle Roma, Qta: Costa Rica No. A-16, Urbanización Alto Barinas, Barinas 5201, Venezuela. Two IRC's or $2 required.

Radio Nacional de Venezuela - Antena Internacional, Final Calle Las Marías, entre Chapellín y Country Club La Florida, 1050 Caracas, Venezuela. Phone: +58 (212) 730-6022, +58 (212) 730-6666. Fax: +58 (212) 731 1457 Email: canalinternacionalrnv@gmail.com; ondacortavenezuela@hotmail.com. Web: (includes streaming audio from domestic services not on shortwave) www.rnv.gov.ve. Contact: Ali Méndez Martínez, periodista y representativo de onda corta; Freddy R. Santos. Currently broadcasts via the transmission facilities of Radio Habana Cuba. "Antena Internacional" is also aired at 0600-0700 World Time (subject to change) on mediumwave/AM via Radio Nacional's domestic "Canal Informativo," available in streaming audio at the RNV Website.

VIETNAM World Time +7

NOTE: Reception reports on Vietnamese regional stations should be sent to the Voice of Vietnam Overseas Service (*see*).

Voice of Vietnam—Domestic Service (Đài Tiêng Nói Viêt Nam, TNVN)—Addresses and contact numbers as for all sections of Voice of Vietnam—Overseas Service, below. Contact: Phan Quang, Director General.

Voice of Vietnam—Overseas Service

MAIN ADDRESS FOR NONTECHNICAL CORRESPONDENCE AND GENERAL VERIFICATIONS: 58 Quán Sú Street, Hànôi, Vietnam. Phone: +84 (4) 934-4231. Fax: +84 (4) 934 4230. Email: (Vietnamese) vovnews@hn.vnn.vn; (English) english@vovnews.vn. Web: (includes on-demand and streaming audio) www.vov.org.vn. Contact: Ms. Hoang Minh Nguyet, Director of International Relations.

STUDIOS (NONTECHNICAL CORRESPONDENCE AND GENERAL VERIFICATIONS): 45 Ba Trieu Street, Hànôi, Vietnam. Phone: (director) +84 (4) 825-7870; (English Service) +84 (4) 934-2456, +84 (4) 825-4482; (Spanish Service) +84 (4) 934-2894; (newsroom) +84 (4) 825-5761, +84 (4) 825-5862. Fax: (English Service) +84 (4) 826 6707; (Spanish Service) +84 (4) 826 5875. Email: btdn.vov@hn.vnn.vn; (English) englishsection@vov.org.vn (Spanish) tiengnoi_vietnam2004@yahoo.es. Contact: Ms. Nguyen Thi Hue, Director, Overseas Service.

TECHNICAL CORRESPONDENCE: Office of Radio Reception Quality, Central Department of Radio and Television

Broadcast Engineering, Vietnam General Corporation of Posts and Telecommunications, Hànôi, Vietnam.

WESTERN SAHARA World Time exactly

Radio Nacional de la República Arabe Saharaui Democrática (when operating). Email: rasdradio@yahoo.es. Web: (streaming audio) http://web.jet.es/rasd/radionacional.htm. Pro-Polisario Front, and supported by the Algerian government. Operates from Rabuni, near Tindouf, on the Algerian side of the border with Western Sahara.

YEMEN World Time +3

Republic of Yemen Radio, Technical Department, P. O. Box 2371, Sana'a, Yemen. Phone: +967 (1) 282-060. Fax: +967 (1) 282 053. Email: (Altashy) ali_tashy@yahoo.com. Web: (includes on-demand audio): www.yradio.gov.ye. Contact: Eng. Ali Ahmed Altashy, Technical Director. Verifies reception reports. Return postage appreciated.

ZAMBIA World Time +2

The Voice Africa

STATION: Radio Christian Voice, Private Bag E606, Lusaka, Zambia. Phone: +260 (1) 273-191. Fax: +260 (1) 279 183. Email: (general) voicefm@zamnet.zm; (Sinyangwe) mwiza@zamnet.zm: (Phiri) edward@zamnet.zm. Web: (includes streaming audio) www.voiceafrica.net. Contact: Mwiza Sinyangwe, Acting Station Manager; Gibbs Mweemba, Programme Manager; (technical) Edward Phiri, Head of Transmission; John Kawele, Tecnical Services Manager; Precious Mweemba, Secretary, Technical. Free calendars and stickers. $1 or 2 IRCs appreciated for reply. Verifies reception reports. Broadcasts Christian teachings and music, as well as news and programs on farming, sport, education, health, business and children's affairs. Formerly known as Radio Christian Voice.

Radio Zambia, Mass Media Complex, Alick Nkhata Road, P.O. Box 50015, Lusaka 10101, Zambia. Phone: (general) +260 (1) 253-301, +260 (1) 252-005; (engineering) +260 (1) 250-380. Fax: +260 (1) 254 013. Web: www.znbc.co.zm; (streaming audio) www.coppernet.zm. Contact: (general) Keith M. Nalumango, Director of Programmes; Lawson Chishimba, Public Relations Manager; (administration) Duncan H. Mbazima, Director-General; (technical) James M. Phiri, Director of Engineering. Free *Zamwaves* newsletter. Sometimes gives away stickers, postcards and small publications. $1 required, and postal correspondence should be sent via registered mail. Tours of the station given Tuesdays to Fridays between 9:00 AM and noon local time; inquire in advance. Used to reply slowly and irregularly, but seems to be better now.

ZIMBABWE World Time +2

Radio Voice of the People, P.O. Box 5750, Harare, Zimbabwe. Phone: +263 (4) 707-123. Email: voxpopzim@yahoo.co.uk; voxpop@ecoweb.co.zw. Web: www.vopradio.co.zw. Contact: John Masuku, Executive Director. Airs via Radio Nederland Wereldomroep facilities in Madagascar.

Radio VOP—*see* Radio Voice of the People, above.

Zimbabwe Broadcasting Corporation, Broadcasting Center, Pockets Hill, P.O. Box HG444, Highlands, Harare, Zimbabwe. Phone: +263 (4) 498-610, +263 (4) 498-630; (Guinea Fowl Shortwave Transmitting Station) +263 (54) 22-104. Fax: +263 (4) 498 613. Email: zbc@zbc.co.zw; (general enquiries) pr@zbc.co.zw; (engineering) hbt@zbc.co.zw. Contact: (general) Rugare Sangomoyo; Lydia Muzenda; (administration) Alum Mpofu, Chief Executive Officer; (news details) Munyaradzi Hwengwere; (Broadcasting Technology, Engineering) Craig Matambo. $1 helpful.

Voice of Zimbabwe, 24 Seven Street, Gweru, Zimbabwe. Phone: +263 (54) 230-640, +263 (54) 230-108/9. Email: voiceof_zimbabwe@yahoo.com. Contact: Shadreck Mupeni, Station Manager.

Prepared by Craig Tyson (Australia), editor, with Tony Jones (Paraguay). Special thanks to David Crystal (Israel), Graeme Dixon (New Zealand), Alokesh Gupta (India), Jose Jacob (India), Fotios Padazopulos (USA), George Poppin (USA), Paulo Roberto e Souza (Brazil) and George Zeller (USA); also, the following organizations for their support and cooperation: Conexión Digital *and* RUS-DX/ *Anatoly Klepov (Russia).*

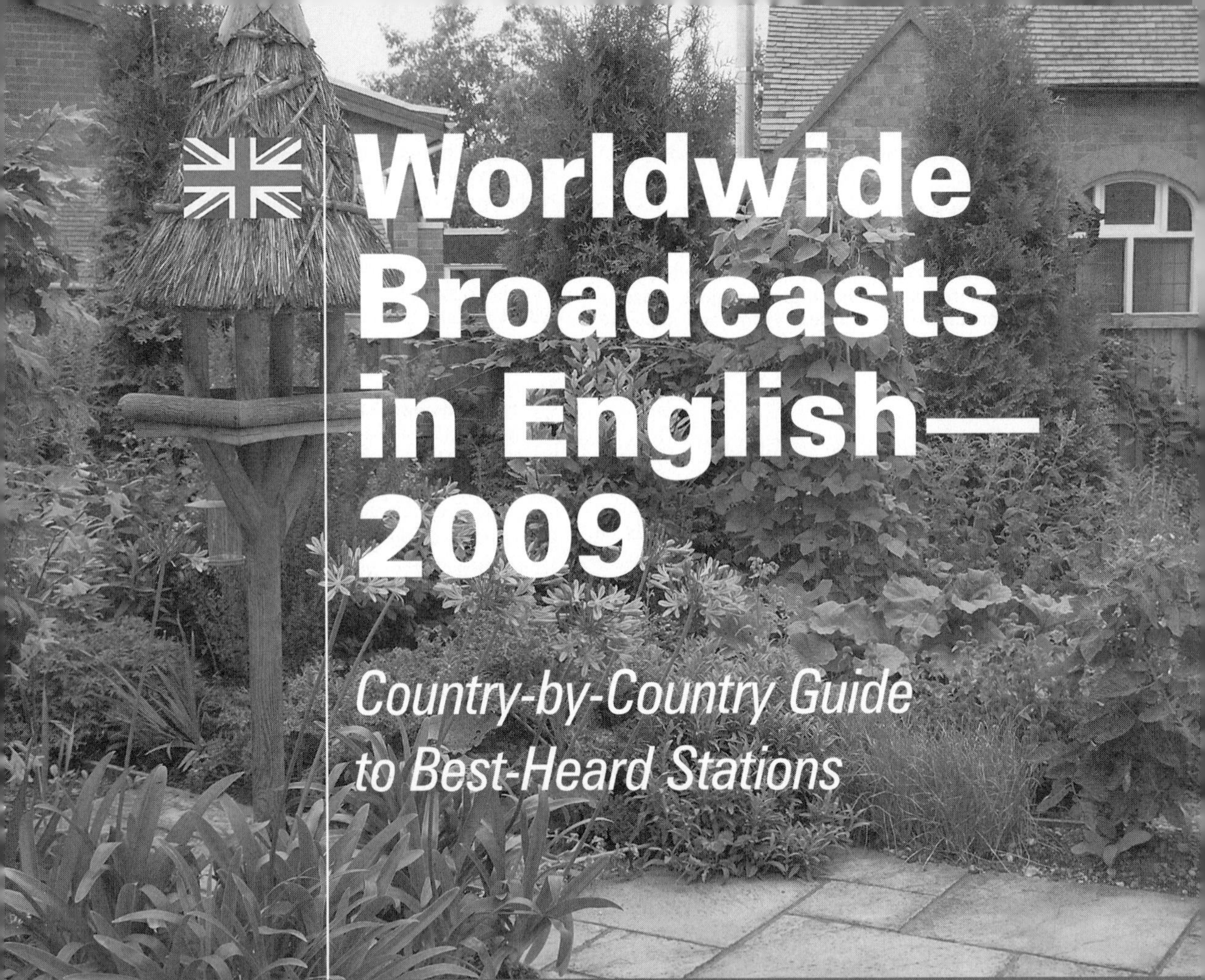

Worldwide Broadcasts in English—2009

Country-by-Country Guide to Best-Heard Stations

Dozens of countries reach out in English, and this is where you'll find their times and frequencies. For what shows are on, hour-by-hour, see "What's On Tonight."

• **Top Times:** "Best Times and Frequencies," earlier in PASSPORT, pinpoints where each world band segment is found and offers helpful tuning tips. Focus on late afternoon and evening, when most programs are beamed your way—although around dawn and early afternoon can be productive, as well.

☞ Dusk and evening, tune segments between 5730 and 10000 kHz in winter, 5730 and 15800 kHz in summer. Daytime it's 9250–21850 kHz winter, 11500–21850 kHz summer. Around dawn explore 5730–17900 kHz year-round for fewer but intriguing catches.

Times and days of the week are in World Time (UTC), explained in "Setting Your World Time Clock" and "Worldly Words"; for local times in each country see "Addresses PLUS." Midyear, typically April through October, some stations are an hour earlier (⬅) or later (➡) because of Daylight Saving/Summer Time. Stations may also extend their hours for holidays, emergencies or sports events.

Frequencies used only seasonally are labeled **S** for summer (midyear) and **W** for winter.

• **Strongest frequencies:** Frequencies in *italics* tend to be best, as they are from relay transmitters that may be near you. Some signals not beamed your way may also be heard, especially when targeted to nearby parts of the world. Frequencies with no target zones are typically for domestic coverage, so they're unlikely to be heard unless you're in or near that country.

English is available 24/7, but is strongest afternoons and evenings.

Indigenous Music

Programs not in English? Turn to "Voices from Home" or the Blue Pages. Stations for diaspora sometimes carry delightful native music that's enjoyable listening, regardless of language.

Schedules for Entire Year

To be as useful as possible over the months to come, PASSPORT's schedules consist not just of observed activity, but also that which we have creatively opined will take place during the forthcoming year. This predictive material is based on decades of experience and is original from us. Although inherently not as exact as real-time data, over the years it's been of tangible value to PASSPORT readers.

Shutterstock/Eric Isselée

The art deco William Jolly Bridge traverses the Brisbane River in Australia.

Shutterstock/Holger Mette

ALBANIA

RADIO TIRANA

0030-0045 & 0145-0200	**S** Tu-Su 9390 (E North Am)
0230-0300	**S** Tu-Su 7425 (E North Am)
0245-0300	**W** Tu-Su 6100 (E North Am)
0330-0400	**W** Tu-Su 6100 & **S** Tu-Su 7425 (E North Am)
0430-0500	**W** Tu-Su 6100 (E North Am)
1300-1330	**S** Tu-Su 13750 (E North Am)
1530-1600 ⇦	M-Sa 13640 (E North Am)
1845-1900	**S** M-Sa 7430 (W Europe), **S** M-Sa 13640 (E North Am)
1945-2000	**W** M-Sa 7465 (Europe), **W** M-Sa 11645 (E North Am)
2000-2030	**S** M-Sa 7465 (Europe), **S** M-Sa 13600 & **S** Tu-Su 13720 (E North Am)
2100-2130	**W** M-Sa 7510 & **W** M-Sa 9345 (W Europe)

AUSTRALIA

RADIO AUSTRALIA

0000-0130	17775 (SE Asia)
0000-0200	17715 (Pacific & N America), 17795 (Pacific & W North Am)
0000-0700	13690 (Pacific & E Asia), 17750 (SE Asia)
0000-0800	9660 & 15240 (Pacific)
0000-0900	12080 (S Pacific)
0030-0400	15415 (SE Asia)
0200-0500	21725 (E Asia)
0200-0700	15515 (Pacific & N America)
0430-0500	15415 (SE Asia)
0500-0800	15160 (Pacific & N America)
0530-0600	15415 (SE Asia)
0600-0630	Sa/Su 15180, Sa/Su *15290* & Sa/Su 15415 (SE Asia)
0630-1100	15415 (SE Asia)
0700-0900	9710 (Pacific), 13630 (Pacific & W North Am)
0700-1300	9475 & 11945 (SE Asia)
0800-0900	5995 (Pacific)
0800-1400	9580 (Pacific & N America)
0800-1600	9590 (Pacific & W North Am)
1100-1200	12080 (S Pacific)
1100-1400	5995 (Pacific), 6020 (Pacific & W North Am), 9560 (E Asia & Pacific)
1400-1700	7240 (Pacific & W North Am)
1400-1800	5995 (Pacific & W North Am), 6080 (SE Asia)
1430-1700	11660 (SE Asia)
1430-1900	9475 (SE Asia)
1600-2000	9710 (Pacific & W North Am)
1700-2000	9580 (Pacific)
1700-2100	11880 (Pacific & W North Am)

1800-2000	6080 (Pacific & E Asia), 7240 (Pacific)
1900-2200	9500 (SE Asia)
2000-2100	F/Sa 6080 & F/Sa 7240 (Pacific), F/Sa 12080 (S Pacific)
2000-2200	11650 & 11660 (Pacific)
2100-2200	9660 (Pacific), 11695 (SE Asia), 12080 (S Pacific)
2100-2300	13630 & 15515 (Pacific)
2200-2330	*15240* (SE Asia)
2200-2400	[W] 11840 (SE Asia), 15230 (Pacific), 17785/15560 (Pacific & N America)
2300-2400	9660 (Pacific), 12080 (S Pacific), 13690 (Pacific & E Asia), 17795 (Pacific & W North Am)
2330-2400	15415 & 17750 (SE Asia)

BANGLADESH

BANGLADESH BETAR

1230-1300	7250 (SE Asia)
1745-1900	7250 (Europe)

BELARUS

RADIO STATION BELARUS—(Europe)

2000-2200	[S] 7105
2100-2300 [⇦]	7360 & 7390
2100-2300	[W] 7100

BULGARIA

RADIO BULGARIA

0000-0100	[W] 5900 & [W] 7400 (E North Am)
0200-0300	[S] 9700 & [S] 11700 (E North Am)
0300-0400	[W] 5900 & [W] 7400 (E North Am)
0630-0700	[S] 7200 & [S] 9400 (W Europe)
0730-0800	[W] 5900 & [W] 7400 (W Europe)
1230-1300 [⇦]	11700 & 15700 (W Europe)
1730-1800	[S] 7200 & [S] 9400 (W Europe)
1830-1900	[W] 6200 & [W] 7400 (W Europe)
2100-2200	[S] 5900 & [S] 9700 (W Europe)
2200-2300	[W] 6200 & [W] 7400 (W Europe)
2300-2400	[S] 9700 & [S] 11700 (E North Am)

CANADA

CANADIAN BROADCASTING CORP—(E North Am)

0000-0300 [⇦]	Su 9625
0200-0300 [⇦]	Tu-Sa 9625
0300-0310 & 0330-0609 [⇦]	M 9625
0400-0609 [⇦]	Su 9625
0500-0609 [⇦]	Tu-Sa 9625
1200-1255 [⇦]	M-F 9625
1200-1505 [⇦]	Sa 9625
1200-1700 [⇦]	Su 9625
1600-1615 & 1700-1805 [⇦]	Sa 9625
1800-2400 [⇦]	Su 9625
1945-2015, 2200-2225 & 2240-2330 [⇦]	M-F 9625

CFRX-CFRB—(E North Am)

24 Hr	6070

CKZN—(E North Am)

24 Hr	6160

CKZU-CBU—(W North Am)

24 Hr	6160

RADIO CANADA INTERNATIONAL

0000-0005	[S] 6100 (N America)
0000-0100	[W] *9880* & [S] *11700* (SE Asia)
0005-0105	[S] Tu-Sa 6100 & [W] 9755 (N America)
0100-0200	[W] *5840*, [W] *6165* & [W] *7255* (S Asia)
0105-0205	[W] Tu-Sa 9755 (N America)
0300-0400	[S] 7325 (N America)
1500-1600	[W] *9635*, [S] *11675*, [W] *11975* & [S] *17720* (S Asia)
1505-1705	[S] 9515 (N America)
1605-1805	[W] 9610 (N America)
1800-1900	[W] *7185* & [S] *9530* (E Africa), [S] *11765* (C Africa), [W] *11875* (C Africa & E Africa), [W] 13650 (N Africa & W Africa), [W] 15365 (W Africa & C Africa), [S] 17735 (W Africa), [W] 17790 & [S] *17810* (W Africa & C Africa)

Retired teacher and football coach George Poppin with wife Dottie at their San Francisco home. For decades George has assisted world band stations by monitoring frequencies and aiding with listener relations. G. Poppin

2000-2100	[S] *11765* (Mideast & E Africa), [S] *13650* (N Africa & W Africa), [S] 15235 & [S] 17735 (W Africa)
2100-2200	[W] 9770 (W Europe)
2305-2400	[S] 6100 (N America)

CHINA

CHINA RADIO INTERNATIONAL

0000-0100	6075 & 7180 (S Asia), 7350/7130 (Europe), [W] 9425 (E Asia), 11885 (SE Asia), [S] 13750 (E Asia)
0000-0200	*6020* & *9570* (N America), [W] 11650 & [S] 15125 (SE Asia)
0100-0200	[W] *6005* (N America), [W] 6075 (S Asia), [W] *6080* (E North Am), [W] 7180 (S Asia), [W] 7350 & [S] 9470 (Europe), [S] 9535 (S Asia), *9580* (E North Am), [S] *9790* (W North Am), [S] *9800* (E North Am), [S] 11870 (S Asia), [W] 11885 & [S] 15785 (SE Asia)
0200-0300	13640 (S Asia)
0200-0400	11770 (S Asia)
0300-0400	*9690* (N America & C America), *9790* (W North Am), 15110 (S Asia)
0300-0500	[W] 9460, [W] 13620 & [S] 13750 (E Asia), 15120 (C Asia & E Asia), [S] 15785 (E Asia)
0400-0500	[S] *6080* (N America), [W] *6190* (W North Am)
0400-0600	[S] *6020* (W North Am), 17725/17730 & 17855 (C Asia)
0500-0600	[W] *5960* (N America), *6190* (W North Am), [W] *7220* (N Africa)
0500-0700	[S] *11710* (N Africa), 17505 (N Africa & W Africa)
0500-0900	11880, 15465 & 17540 (S Asia)
0500-1100	15350 (S Asia)
0600-0700	[W] *6115* (W North Am), [W] *11750* (N Africa), [W] 11770 (Mideast), [S] 11870 (Mideast & W Asia), 15145 (Mideast)
0600-0800	[W] 13645, [S] 13660 & 17710 (SE Asia)
0700-0900	[W] *11785* & *13710* (W Europe)
0700-1300	17490 (Europe)
0800-1000	[W] 9415 & [S] 11620 (E Asia)
0900-1000	17750 (S Asia)
0900-1100	15210 & 17690 (Australasia)
1000-1100	[W] 5955 (E Asia), [W] 7135, [W] 7215, [S] 11610 & [S] 11635 (C Asia & E Asia), [S] 13620 (E Asia), 15190 (S Asia)
1000-1200	[S] *6040* (E North Am), 13590 & 13720 (SE Asia)
1100-1200	[W] *5960* (E North Am), [W] 9570 (S Asia), [S] *11750* (W North Am), 11795 & 13645 (S Asia)
1100-1300	11650 (S Asia), [S] *13650* & [W] *13665* (W Europe)
1100-1400	[S] 11660 (S Asia)
1100-1500	5955 (E Asia)
1200-1300	[W] 7250 & 9460 (S Asia), 9760 (Australasia), 11690 (C Asia), [W] 12080, [S] 13610 & [S] 13645 (S Asia)
1200-1400	9730 (SE Asia), 11760 (Australasia), 11980 (SE Asia), 13790 (Europe)

1300-1400	*9570* (E North Am), [S] *9650* (E North Am & C America), [S] 9760 (Australasia), [W] *11885* (W North Am), [W] 11900 (Australasia), 13610 (Europe), [S] 13755 (S Asia), [S] *15260* (W North Am), [W] *15540* & [S] *17625* (S America)
1300-1500	[W] 7300 (S Asia), 9765 (C Asia), [W] *15230* (E North Am & C America)
1300-1600	9870 (SE Asia)
1400-1500	[W] 9460 (S Asia), [W] 9700 & [W] 9795 (Europe), 11675 & [S] 11765 (S Asia), [W] *13675* (W North Am), [S] 13710 & [S] 13790 (Europe)
1400-1600	*13685* (E Africa), *13740* (W North Am), *17630* (C Africa)
1500-1600	5955 (E Asia), 7160 (S Asia), 7325 (SE Asia), [W] 9785 & [S] 9800 (S Asia), [S] 13640 (Europe)
1500-1700	[W] 9435, [W] 9525 & [S] 11965 (Europe)
1500-1800	*6100* (S Africa)
1600-1800	[W] 7150 (E Africa & S Africa), [W] 7255 (Europe), [S] 9570 (E Africa & S Africa), [S] 11900 (S Africa), [S] 11940 (Europe)
1600-1900	[S] 13760 (Europe)
1700-1800	[W] 6100 & [S] 9695 (Europe)
1800-1900	[W] 6100 & [W] 7110 (Europe)
1900-2000	9440/9435 (Mideast, W Africa & C Africa)
1900-2100	7295 (Mideast & N Africa)
2000-2100	9440 (Mideast, W Africa & C Africa)
2000-2130	*11640* (E Africa & S Africa), *13630* (E Africa)
2000-2200	*5960* (W Europe), 7190 (Europe), *7285* (W Europe), 9600 (Europe)
2200-2300	[W] 5915 (E Asia), [W] *7170* & [S] *7175* (N Europe), [S] 9590 (E Asia)
2300-2400	[S] 5915 (S Asia), *5990* (C America), [W] *6040* (E North Am), [W] 6145 (E Asia), [S] *6145* (E North Am), 7180 (S Asia), [S] 11685 (E Asia), [S] *11840* & [W] *11970* (W North Am)

CHINA (TAIWAN)

RADIO TAIWAN INTERNATIONAL

0100-0200	11875 (SE Asia)
0200-0300	*5950* (E North Am), *9680* (N America)
0300-0400	*5950* (W North Am), *15215* (S America), 15320 (SE Asia)
0700-0800	*5950* (W North Am)
1100-1200	7445 (SE Asia), 11715 (SE Asia & Australasia)
1600-1700	[W] *9785/11995* (SE Asia), 11550 (E Asia & S Asia), [S] *15515/11600* (S Asia & SE Asia)
1700-1800	[W] *11850* & [S] *15690* (C Africa & S Africa)
1800-1900	*3965* (W Europe)
2200-2300	[S] *3965* & [W] *9355* (W Europe)

CROATIA

VOICE OF CROATIA

0200-0215	[S] *9925* (N America & S America)
0300-0315	[W] *7285* (N America & S America)
0300-0315 ⇦	3980 (Europe)

Dubrovnik's old town was completed in the 13th century and remains essentially unchanged. This Croatian town is considered to be the jewel of the Adriatic. Shutterstock/Plotnikoff

2215-2230	S 6165 (Europe), S *9925* (S America)
2315-2330	W 3980 (Europe), W *7285* (S America)

CUBA

RADIO HABANA CUBA

0100-0500	6000 (E North Am)
0100-0700	6140 (N America)
0500-0700	6000 (E North Am), 6060 (E North Am), 9550 (W North Am), 11760 (Americas)
2030-2130	11760 (E North America)
2300-2400	9550 (S America)

CZECH REPUBLIC

RADIO PRAGUE

0000-0030	S 7345 (E North Am & C America), S 9440 (N America & C America)
0100-0130	6200 & 7345 (N America & C America)
0200-0230	W 6200 & W 7345 (N America & C America)
0300-0330	S 7345 (N America & C America), S 9870 (W North Am & C America)
0330-0400	S 9445 (Mideast & E Africa), S 11600 (Mideast & S Asia)
0400-0430 ⇦	*6080* (Irr) (W North Am)
0400-0430	W 6200 (W North Am & C America), W 7345 (N America & C America)
0430-0500	W 9855 (Mideast, E Africa & S Asia)
0700-0730	S 9880 & S 11600 (W Europe)
0800-0830	W 7345 & W 9860 (W Europe)
0900-0930	S 9880 (W Europe), S 21745 (S Asia)
1000-1030	W 15700 (S Asia), W 21745 (W Africa)
1030-1100	S 9880 & S 11665 (N Europe)
1130-1200	W 11640 (N Europe), W 17545 (C Africa & E Africa)
1300-1330	S 13580 (W Europe), S 17540 (S Asia)
1400-1430	W 11600 (S Asia), W 13580 (N America)
1600-1630	S 17485 (E Africa)
1700-1730 ⇦	5930 (W Europe)
1700-1730	W 15710 (W Africa & C Africa), S 17485 (C Africa)
1800-1830 ⇦	5930 (W Europe)
1800-1830	W 9400 (Asia & Australasia)
2000-2030	S 11600 (SE Asia & Australasia)
2100-2130 ⇦	5930 (W Europe)
2100-2130	W 9430 (SE Asia & Australasia)
2130-2200	S 9410 (W Africa & C Africa), S 11600 (N America)
2230-2300	W 5930 (N America), S 7345 (E North Am & C America), S 9415 (N America), W 9435 (W Africa & C Africa)
2330-2400	W 5930 (N America), W 7345 (N America & C America)

EGYPT

RADIO CAIRO

0000-0030	W 6850 & S 9280 (E North Am)
0200-0330	7270/7535 (N America)
1215-1330	17835 (S Asia & SE Asia)
1600-1800	12170 (C Africa & S Africa)
1900-2030	S 9300 & W 9310 (W Africa & C Africa)
2115-2245	W 6255 & S 11550 (Europe)
2330-2400	W 6850 & S 9280 (E North Am)

FRANCE

RADIO FRANCE INTERNATIONALE

0400-0430	W 7315 & M-F 9805 (E Africa)
0500-0530	W M-F 9805/13680, W M-F 11995, S M-F 13680 & S M-F 15160/11995 (E Africa)
0600-0630	W M-F 7315 & S M-F 11725/9765 (W Africa & C Africa), W M-F

11995/15160, [W] M-F 13680, [S] M-F 15160 & [S] M-F 17800 (E Africa)
0700-0730 [W] 11725/15605 & [S] 13675 (W Africa & C Africa)
1200-1230 [S] 17800/21620 & [W] 21620 (E Africa)
1600-1700 [W] 11615/15605 (C Africa & E Africa), *15160* (W Africa & C Africa), [S] 15605 (C Africa & S Africa), [S] 17605 (E Africa)

GERMANY

DEUTSCHE WELLE

0000-0100 [S] *7245*, [W] *7265*, [W] *9785* & [S] *9885* (SE Asia), 15595 (E Asia), [S] *17525* (E Asia & SE Asia)
0100-0200 [W] *9850* (S Asia)
0300-0400 [W] *9800*, [W] *13810* & [S] *15595* (S Asia)
0400-0500 [W] *5905* (W Africa), [W] *5945* (W Africa & C Africa), [W] *6180* (C Africa & E Africa), [S] *7225* (W Africa), [S] *7245* (W Africa & C Africa), [S] *12045* (E Africa & S Africa), [S] *15445* (C Africa & E Africa), [W] *15600* (C Africa & S Africa)
0500-0530 [W] *6180* (C Africa & E Africa), [W] *7285* (W Africa), [S] *9700* (C Africa & S Africa), [W] *9755* (W Africa), [W] *12045* (S Africa), [W] *15410* & [W] *15600* (E Africa, C Africa & S Africa)
0600-0630 [W] *5945* & [S] *7310* (W Africa), [W] *12045* & [S] *15275* (W Africa & C Africa)
0900-1000 [S] *15340*, [S] *17705* & [W] *17710* (E Asia), [W] *21840* (E Asia & SE Asia)
1600-1700 [W] *5965* & [S] *6170* (S Asia), [S] *9540*, [W] *9560* & [S] *15640* (S Asia & SE Asia)
1900-1930 [S] *9565* & [W] *9735* (E Africa & S Africa), [W] *11690* (C Africa & E Africa), [S] *11795* (S Africa), [W] *13780* (E Africa & S Africa), [W] *15275* (C Africa, E Africa & S Africa), [S] *17860* (W Africa & C Africa)
2000-2100 [S] *6150* (S Africa), [W] *9545* (W Africa & C Africa), [W] *9735* (C Africa, E Africa & S Africa), [S] *11795* (E Africa & S Africa), [S] *11865* (C Africa & S Africa), [W] *13780* (W Africa, C Africa & S Africa), [S] 15205 (C Africa, E Africa & S Africa), [W] *15275* (C Africa & S Africa)
2100-2200 [W] *7280* (W Africa), [W] *9545* (W Africa & C Africa), [S] *9735* (C Africa & E Africa), [W] *11690* & [S] *11865* (W Africa), [W] *13780* (W Africa & C Africa), [S] *15205* (W Africa)

INDIA

ALL INDIA RADIO

0000-0045 9705 (E Asia & SE Asia), 9950 (E Asia), 11620 (SE Asia), 11645 (E Asia), 13605 (E Asia & SE Asia)
1000-1100 13695/13710 (E Asia & Australasia), 15020 (E Asia), 15260 (S Asia), 15410/15135 (E Asia), 17510 (Australasia), 17800 (E Asia), 17895 (Australasia)
1330-1500 9690, 11620 & 13710 (SE Asia)
1745-1945 7410 (Europe), 9445 (W Africa), 9950 & 11620 (Europe), 11935 (E Africa), 13605 (W Africa), 15075 (E Africa), 15155 (W Africa), 17670 (E Africa)
2045-2230 7410 & 9445 (Europe), 9910 (Australasia), 9950 (Europe), 11620 & 11715 (Australasia)
2245-2400 9705 (E Asia & SE Asia), 9950 (E Asia), 11620 (SE Asia), 11645 (E Asia), 13605 (E Asia & SE Asia)

The Tokyo Ham Fair also attracts world band enthusiasts, including from the Japan Short Wave Club. PASSPORT's Toshimichi Ohtake stands second from left in the back row. T. Ohtake

IRAN

VOICE OF THE ISLAMIC REPUBLIC

0130-0230 [W] 6120, [W] 7160, [S] 7235 & [S] 9495 (N America)
1030-1130 [W] 15460, [S] 15600 & 17660 (S Asia)
1530-1630 [W] 6160, [W] 7330, [S] 7375 & [S] 9600 (S Asia & SE Asia)
1930-2030 [W] 6010, [S] 6205 & [S] 7205 (Europe), *7260* (W Europe), [W] 7320 (Europe), [S] 9800, [W] 9855, [S] 9925 & [W] 11695 (S Africa)

JAPAN

RADIO JAPAN

0000-0020 [W] *5920* & [S] *5960* (W Europe), *6145* (E North Am & C America), 13650 & 17810 (SE Asia)
0500-0530 *5975* (W Europe), *6110* (W North Am), [W] *9770* & [S] *11970* (S Africa), 15325 (S Asia), 17810 (SE Asia)
0900-0930 9625 (Australasia), 9825 (Pacific & S America), 11815 (SE Asia), 15590 (S Asia)
1200-1230 *6120* (E North Am & C America), 9625 (Australasia), [S] 9695 & [W] 13660/9695 (SE Asia), *17585* (Europe)
1310-1340 [W] 9875 & [S] 11985 (S Asia)
1400-1430 [W] 9875 (S Asia), 11705 (SE Asia), *11705* (E North Am), [W] *11780* (N Europe), [S] 11985 (S Asia), [S] *13630* (N Europe), *21560* (C Africa & E Africa)
2200-2220 13640 (Australasia)

KOREA (DPR)

VOICE OF KOREA

0100-0200 3560, 7140, 9345 & 9730 (E Asia), 11735, 13760 & 15180 (C America)
0200-0300 4405 (E Asia), 13650 & 15100 (SE Asia)
0300-0400 3560, 7140, 9345 & 9730 (E Asia)
1000-1100 3560 (E Asia), [W] 6185 (SE Asia), [W] 6285 & [W] 9335 (C America), [W] 9850 (SE Asia), [S] 11710 (C America), [S] 11735 & [S] 13650 (SE Asia), [S] 15180 (C America)
1300-1400 & 1500-1600 4405 (E Asia), [W] 7570 (W Europe), 9335 & 11710 (N America), [W] 12015, [S] 13760 & [S] 15245 (W Europe)
1600-1700 3560 (E Asia), 9990 & 11545 (Mideast & N Africa)

1800-1900	4405 (E Asia), [W] 7570, [W] 12015, [S] 13760 & [S] 15245 (W Europe)
1900-2000	3560 (E Asia), 7100 (S Africa), 9975 (Mideast & N Africa), 11910 (S Africa)
2100-2200	4405 (E Asia), [W] 7570, [W] 12015, [S] 13760 & [S] 15245 (W Europe)

KOREA (REPUBLIC)

KBS WORLD RADIO

0200-0300	15575 (S America)
0230-0300	*9560* (W North Am)
0800-0900	9570 (SE Asia)
1200-1300	*9650* (N America)
1300-1400	9570 & 9770 (SE Asia)
1600-1700	9515 (Europe)
1800-1900	7275 (Europe)
2200-2230 ⇦	*3955* (W Europe)

KUWAIT

RADIO KUWAIT

0500-0800	15110 (S Asia)
1800-2100	11990 (Europe & E North Am)

LITHUANIA

RADIO VILNIUS

0030-0100 ⇦	9875 (E North Am)
0030-0100	[S] 11690 (E North Am)
0930-1000 ⇦	9710 (W Europe)
2330-2400	[W] 7325 (E North Am)

MOLDOVA

RADIO PMR

0000-0015	[W] M-F 6240 (E North Am)
1400-1415 & 1445-1500	[S] M-F 12135 (Europe)
1500-1515	[W] M-F 7370 (Europe)
1530-1545	[S] M-F 12135 (Europe)
1545-1600	[W] M-F 7370 (Europe)
1615-1630	[S] M-F 12135 (Europe)
1630-1645 & 1715-1730	[W] M-F 7370 (Europe)
2215-2230 & 2300-2315	[S] Su-Th 6040 (E North Am)
2315-2330	[W] Su-Th 6240 (E North Am)

MONGOLIA

VOICE OF MONGOLIA

1030-1100	12085 (E Asia, SE Asia & Australasia)
1530-1600	12085 (E Asia)

NETHERLANDS

RADIO NETHERLANDS WORLDWIDE

1000-1100	[W] *6040* (E Asia & SE Asia), [W] *9720* (E Asia), [W] *9795* (E Asia & SE Asia), [S] *11895* (SE Asia), [S] *12065* (E Asia & Australasia), [W] *12065* (SE Asia), [S] *13820* & [S] *15110* (E Asia & SE Asia)
1400-1600	[W] *5825*, [S] *5830*, [W] *9345*, [S] *9885*, [S] *11835*, [W] *12080*, [W] *13615* & [W] *15595* (S Asia)
1800-1900	*6020* (S Africa)
1800-2000	[W] *11655* (C Africa & E Africa), [W] *12045* & [S] *15535* (E Africa)
1900-2000	[S] *11660* (W Africa), [W] *11805* (E Africa), [S] *15335* (W Africa)
1900-2100	[S] *5905* (E Africa), [W] *7120* & [S] *7425* (C Africa & S Africa), *17810* (W Africa)
2000-2100	[W] *11655* (W Africa & C Africa)

The Dutch practice environmental friendliness in a variety of creative ways. Here, an Amsterdam houseboat sports a genuine sod roof. M. Wright

OMAN

RADIO SULTANATE OF OMAN

0300-0400	15355 (E Africa)
1400-1500	15140 (Europe & Mideast)

POLAND

POLISH RADIO EXTERNAL SERVICE

1200-1300	[S] *7330* (N Europe), [S] *9525* (W Europe)
1300-1400	[W] *7325* (N Europe), [W] *9450* (W Europe)
1700-1800	[S] *7140* (N Europe), [S] *7265* (W Europe)
1800-1900	[W] *6015* (W Europe), [W] *7345* (N Europe)

ROMANIA

RADIO ROMANIA INTERNATIONAL

0000-0100	[S] 9775 & [S] 11790 (E North Am)
0100-0200	[W] 6145 & [W] 9515 (E North Am)
0300-0400	[S] 6150 & [S] 9645 (W North Am), [S] 9735 (S Asia)
0400-0500 ⇦	11895 (S Asia)
0400-0500	[W] 6115 & [W] 9515 (W North Am), [W] 9690 (S Asia)
0530-0600	[S] 9655 & [S] 11830 (W Europe), [S] 15435 & [S] 17770 (Australasia)
0630-0700	[W] 7180 & [W] 9690 (W Europe), [W] 15135 & [W] 17780 (Australasia)
1200-1300	[S] 11875 & [S] 15220 (W Europe)
1300-1400	[W] 15105 & [W] 17745 (W Europe)
1700-1800	[S] 9535 & [S] 11735 (W Europe)
1800-1900	[W] 7215 & [W] 9640 (W Europe)
2030-2100	[S] 9515 & [S] 11810 (W Europe), [S] 11940 & [S] 15465 (E North Am)
2130-2200	[W] 6050 (W Europe), [W] 6115 (E North Am), [W] 7145 (W Europe), [W] 9755 (E North Am)
2200-2300	[S] 7185 & [S] 9675 (W Europe), [S] 9790 & [S] 11940 (E North Am)
2300-2400	[W] 6015 (W Europe), [W] 6115 (E North Am), [W] 7105 (W Europe), [W] 9610 (E North Am)

RUSSIA

VOICE OF RUSSIA

0100-0400	[S] *9665* (E North Am)
0100-0500	[S] 13775 (W North Am)
0200-0300 ⇦	*7250* (E North Am)
0200-0400	[W] *6240* (E North Am), [W] 15425 (W North Am)
0200-0500	[S] *9860* (E North Am), [S] 13635 (W North Am)
0200-0600	[W] 12040 & [W] 13735 (W North Am)
0300-0400	[S] 12065 (W North Am)
0300-0500	[W] *6155* (E North Am), [S] 9435 (W North Am), [S] *9515* & [S] 9880/5900 (E North Am)
0300-0600	[W] *7350* (E North Am)
0400-0500	[W] 12010 & [W] 12030 (W North Am)
0400-0600	[W] 7150 (E North Am), [W] 9840 (W North Am)
0500-0900	[S] 17635 & [S] 21790 (Australasia)
0600-0900	[W] 17805 (Australasia)
0600-1000	[W] 17665 (Australasia)
0800-1000 ⇦	*17495* (SE Asia & Australasia)
0800-1000	[W] 15195 (S Asia)
1400-1500	[S] 6045 & [S] 7165 (E Asia & SE Asia), [S] 9745, [S] *11755* & [S] 15605 (S Asia), [S] 15660 (SE Asia)
1500-1600	[S] 9625 (S Asia), *9660* (SE Asia), [S] 12040/9810 (Europe)
1500-1700	[W] 7260 (E Asia & SE Asia)
1500-1800	[S] 11985 (Mideast & E Africa)
1600-1700 ⇦	*4965* & *4975* (W Asia & S Asia)
1600-1700	[S] 6070 (S Asia), [W] 6130 (Europe), [W] 7305 (S Asia), [S] 12055 (W Asia & S Asia), [S] *12115* (S Asia), [S] 15540 (Mideast)
1600-1800	[S] 7350 (S Asia & SE Asia), [S] 9405 (S Asia), [W] 9470 (Mideast & E Africa)

1600-1900	W 7320 (Europe)
1600-2100	S 9890 (Europe)
1700-1800	S Sa/Su 9820 & S Sa/Su 11675/7320 (N Europe)
1700-1900	W 5910 (S Asia), W 7125 (SE Asia), W 7270 (Mideast)
1800-1900	W Sa/Su 6055 & W Sa/Su 6175 (N Europe), W 7295 (E Africa & S Africa), S 9850 (E Africa), S 11630/9480 (N Europe)
1800-2000 ⇦	*11510* (E Africa & S Africa)
1800-2100	W 7105 (N Europe)
1900-2000	W 6175 & W 7290 (N Europe), S 7310 (Europe), W 7335 (E Africa & S Africa)
1900-2100	S 12070/7195 (Europe, N Africa & W Africa)
2000-2100	W 6145 (Europe)
2000-2200	W 7330 (Europe)
2100-2200	W 7290 (N Europe)
2200-2400	W 5955 (E Asia)

Russia's rich musical traditions reach the world's ears over the Voice of Russia. Some of its music offerings have been cited as top shows. Shutterstock/Eugene Zhulkov

SAUDI ARABIA

BROADCASTING SERVICE OF THE KINGDOM—(W Africa & C Africa)

1000-1230	15250

SERBIA

INTERNATIONAL RADIO SERBIA

0000-0030	S M-Sa *6190* (E North Am)
0100-0130	S *6190* (W North Am), W M-Sa *7115* (N America)
0200-0230	W *7115* (W North Am)
1300-1330	S 7200 (Europe)
1400-1430	W 7240 (Europe)
1830-1900	S 7200 (Europe)
1930-2000 ⇦	*6100* (W Europe)
1930-2000	W 7240 (Europe)
2100-2130	S 7200 (Europe)
2200-2230 ⇦	*6100* (W Europe)
2200-2230	W 7240 (Europe)

SLOVAKIA

RADIO SLOVAKIA INTERNATIONAL

0100-0130	S 5930 & W 7230 (N America), 9440 (S America)
0700-0730	S 9440, S 11650, W 13715 & W 15460 (Australasia)
1630-1700	S 5920 (W Europe)
1730-1800 ⇦	6055 (W Europe)
1730-1800	W 5915 (W Europe)
1830-1900	S 5920 & S 6055 (W Europe)
1930-2000	W 5915 & W 7345 (W Europe)

SOUTH AFRICA

CHANNEL AFRICA

0300-0355	S 6135 & W 7390 (E Africa)
0300-0400	3345 (S Africa)
0400-0500	S 3345 & W 7230 (S Africa)
0500-0555	W 9550/9745 & S 9735 (W Africa & C Africa)
0500-0700	W 7230 (S Africa)
0600-0655	15255 (W Africa & C Africa)
0700-0800	S 7230 & W 9625 (S Africa)
1000-1200 & 1400-1600	9625 (S Africa)
1500-1555	S 15215 & W 17770 (E Africa)
1700-1755	15235 (W Africa & C Africa)
2000-2200	3345 (S Africa)

Radio Sweden maintains its long tradition of adding thought and perspective to current events.

L. Rydén

SWEDEN

RADIO SWEDEN

0230-0300 ←	*6010* (E North Am)
0230-0300	*11550* (S Asia)
0330-0400 ←	*6010* (W North Am)
1330-1400	[W] 7420 (E Asia)
1430-1500	[W] 9400 (SE Asia), [S] 13820 (S Asia)
1530-1600	[W] 9360 & [S] 11595 (Mideast)
2030-2100	[S] *7395* & [W] *9895* (E Africa)
2130-2200	[W] *7395* (C Africa)
2230-2300 ←	6065 (Europe & N Africa)

SYRIA

RADIO DAMASCUS

2005-2105	9330 (Europe), 12085 (W Europe)
2110-2210	9330 & 12085 (N America & Australasia)

THAILAND

RADIO THAILAND

0000-0030	[S] 9570 & [W] 9680 (E Africa & S Africa)
0030-0100	[W] 12095 & [S] 12120 (E North Am)
0200-0230	15275 (W North Am)
0530-0600	[W] 11730 & [S] 17655 (Europe)
1230-1300	[W] 9810 & [S] 9835 (SE Asia & Australasia)
1400-1430	[W] 9725 & [S] 9805 (SE Asia & Australasia)
1900-2000	[S] 7155 & [W] 9805 (N Europe)
2030-2045	[W] 9535 & [S] 9680 (Europe)

TURKEY

VOICE OF TURKEY

0100-0150	[S] 9620 (S Asia)
0300-0350	[S] 5975 (Europe & N America), [S] 7265 (Mideast)
0400-0450	[W] *6010* (W North Am), [W] 6020 (Europe & N America), [W] 7240 (Mideast), [S] *7325* (W North Am)
1230-1325	[S] 13685 (S Asia, SE Asia & Australasia), [S] 15450 (W Europe)
1330-1425	[W] 11735 (S Asia, SE Asia & Australasia), [W] 12035 (W Europe)
1830-1920	[S] 9785 (W Europe)
1930-2030	[W] 6050 (W Europe)
2030-2120	[S] 7170 (S Asia, SE Asia & Australasia)
2130-2220	[W] 7180 (S Asia, SE Asia & Australasia)
2200-2250	[S] 6195 (W Europe & E North Am)
2300-2350	[W] 5960 (W Europe & E North Am)

UKRAINE

RADIO UKRAINE INTERNATIONAL

0100-0200 & 0400-0500 [←]	7440 (E North Am)
0500-0600	[S] 9945/7420 (W Europe)
0600-0700	[W] 7440 (W Europe)
1100-1200	[S] 11550 (W Europe)
1200-1300	[W] 9950 (W Europe)
1900-2000	[S] 7490 (W Europe)
2000-2100	[W] 5840 (W Europe)
2100-2200	[S] 7510 (W Europe)
2200-2300	[W] 5830 (W Europe)

UNITED KINGDOM

BBC WORLD SERVICE

0000-0030	*5970* (S Asia & E Asia)
0000-0100	*6195* (SE Asia), *7105*, *9410* & [S] *11955* (S Asia), *17615* (E Asia)
0000-0200	*9740* & *15335* (SE Asia), *15360* (E Asia)
0030-0100	*5970* (E Asia)
0100-0200	[W] *5940* (W Asia), [W] *5970* (S Asia), [S] *7320* (W Asia), 9410 (S Asia), *11750* (S Asia & SE Asia), *11955* & 15310 (S Asia), *17615* (SE Asia)
0200-0300	[W] *6005* & [S] *6035* (E Africa), [W] *7410* (Mideast), [S] *9410* (E Europe), [W] *9410*, [S] *11955* & *15310* (S Asia)
0200-0400	*6195* (W Asia)
0300-0400	[S] *6005* (W Africa), [W] *6005* & [S] *6145* (S Africa), [W] *6145* (W Africa), [W] 7375 (E Africa), 9410 (E Europe), 9750 (E Africa), [W] 11760 (C Asia), [S] 12035 (E Africa), [S] *15360* (C Asia)
0300-0600	*3255* (S Africa), [S] *7160* & [W] *7255* (W Africa & C Africa), *15310* (S Asia)
0300-0700	*17790* (S Asia)
0300-2200	*6190* (S Africa)
0330-0600	*11945* (E Africa)
0400-0500	[W] *9650* (W Africa), 12035 (E Africa)
0400-0600	[S] *7120* (W Africa), [S] 9410 (E Europe), [W] *9410* (W Asia), *15360* (C Asia), [S] *15565* (E Europe)
0400-0700	[S] *12095* (W Asia)
0400-0708	*6005* (W Africa)
0500-0530	[W] Su-F *15420* (E Africa)
0500-0600	[W] *11765* (W Africa)
0500-0700	[W] 5875 & [W] *12095* (E Europe), *17640* (E Africa)
0530-0600	[W] M-F *15420* (E Africa)
0600-0700	[W] 7255 & [W] 9410 (N Africa), [W] *11760* (W Asia), *11765* (W Africa), [S] 13820 & [S] 15400 (N Africa)
0600-0800	[W] Sa/Su *15420* (E Africa)
0600-1400	*9860* (S Africa), *15310* (S Asia)
0700-0730	*15575* (W Asia)
0700-0800	[S] *11765* & [S] *13820* (N Africa), [S] *17830* (W Africa)
0700-1000	*15400* (W Africa)
0700-1300	*17790* (S Asia)
0700-1400	*11760* (Mideast)
0730-0900	Sa/Su *15575* (W Asia)
0800-1000	*17830* (W Africa & C Africa)
0800-1300	*21470* (S Africa)
0800-1400	[W] *17640* (E Africa)
0900-1000	*17760* (SE Asia)
0900-1100	6195 (SE Asia), [S] *21660* (E Asia)
0900-1200	[W] *11895* (E Asia)
0900-1400	*15575* (W Asia)
0900-1600	*9740* (SE Asia & Australasia)
1000-1100	Sa/Su *15400* (W Africa), Sa/Su *17830* (W Africa & C Africa)
1000-1200	[S] *17760* (E Asia)
1000-1300	[W] *9605* (E Asia)
1100-1130	*15400* (W Africa)
1100-1200	[S] *15340* (SE Asia)
1100-1600	*6195* (SE Asia)
1100-2100	*17830* (W Africa & C Africa)
1200-1400	[S] *11750* (E Asia)
1200-1500	[W] *5975* (E Asia)
1300-1400	*15420* (E Africa), [S] *17790* (S Asia)
1300-1500	[W] *9410* (S Asia)
1300-1700	*21470* (S Africa)
1400-1500	[W] *5960* (S Asia), [W] *11760* (W Asia), [W] *11915* (S Asia), [S] *12095* (W Asia)
1400-1600	[S] *5980* (E Asia), [S] *7230* & [W] *9860* (S Africa), [S] *15310* (S Asia)

1400-1700	S *11920* (S Asia), W *15420* & S *17640* (E Africa)
1500-1530	S *7380*, *11860*, W *15105* & S *15420* (E Africa)
1500-1600	5975 (S Asia), W *6040* (SE Asia), W *9410* & W *11915* (S Asia)
1500-1700	12095 (E Europe)
1500-2300	*15400* (W Africa)
1530-1615	S Sa *7380* & W Sa *9410* (E Africa)
1600-1800	*5975*, W *7270*, S *9625* & W *9740* (S Asia), W 11665 (N Africa)
1600-2000	S 17795 (N Africa)
1600-2200	*3255* (S Africa)
1615-1630	W Sa/Su *9410*, Su *11860* & S Sa/Su *15420* (E Africa)
1615-1700	S Sa/Su *7380*, W Sa/Su *15105* & W Sa/Su *17640* (E Africa)
1630-1700	W *9410*, Sa/Su *11860* & S *15420* (E Africa)
1700-1745	S *6005* & *9410* (E Africa)
1700-1800	S *7325* (S Asia)
1700-1900	S *6195* (E Europe), S *7380* (E Africa), S 13675 (E Europe & W Asia), W *15420* (E Africa)
1700-2100	*12095* (E Africa)
1800-1830	S *5975*, S *6015*, W 7260 & W *9740* (S Asia)
1800-2000	W 5875 (E Europe), W *5945* (W Asia), W *5955* & S *5995* (C Asia), W *7390* (E Europe)
1800-2100	W 9630 (N Africa)
1830-2000	S *9485* (W Asia)
1830-2100	*6005* & *9410* (E Africa)
2000-2100	S 13820 (N Africa)
2100-2200	*3915* (SE Asia), S *5905* & W *5975* (E Asia), *6005* (S Africa), *6195* (SE Asia), S *7120* & W *7445* (W Africa)
2100-2300	W 6110 & S 9670 (N Africa)
2100-2400	*5965* (E Asia)
2200-2300	S 5905 & W 5955 (E Asia & SE Asia), S *6005* (W Africa), S *6135* (E Asia), W *6155* (W Africa), S *9440* (E Asia), *9660* (SE Asia), *12080* (S Pacific)
2200-2400	*6195* & *9740* (SE Asia)
2300-2400	*3915* (SE Asia), W *6000*, W *9570* & S *9885* (E Asia), S *11850* & *11955* (SE Asia), S *12010* (E Asia)
2330-2400	W *6170* & S *9580* (E Asia)

USA

AFRTS-AMERICAN FORCES RADIO & TV SERVICE

24 Hr	*4319/12579* USB (S Asia), 5447 USB (C America), *5765/13362* USB & 6350/10320 USB (Pacific), 7811 USB & 12134 USB (Americas)

FAMILY RADIO

0000-0045	W 6085 & S 6985 (E North Am), S 17805 (S America)
0000-0100	W 11720 (S America)
0000-0200	5950 (E North Am), 15440 (W North Am)
0000-0445	9505 (N America)
0100-0200	*15195* (S Asia)
0100-0445	W 7455 (E North Am)
0200-0245	S 11835 (W North Am)
0200-0300	5985 (C America), W 9525 (W North Am), 11855 (C America)
0300-0400	W 9985 (S America), S 11740 & W 13615 (C America), S 15255 (S America)
0400-0500	S 7730 (Europe)
0400-0600	5950 (W North Am), 6915 (E North Am)
0400-0700	9680 (N America)
0500-0600	S 9355 (Europe)
0600-0700	S 5850 & W 6000 (C America), S 11530 (C Africa & S Africa), W 11530 & S 11580 (Europe), W 11580 (W Africa)
0600-0745	W 5745 & S 7520 (Europe)
0700-0800	W 9495 & S 9505 (C America), 9715 (W North Am)
0700-0845	S 9930 & W 9985 (W Africa)
0700-1100	6915 (E North Am)
0700-1245	S 5985 (N America)
0700-1345	W 7455 (N America)

0800-0845	5950 (W North Am)
0845-1145	[W] 5950 (W North Am)
0900-1100	*9450* (E Asia)
0900-1145	[S] 9755 (W North Am)
1000-1245	[S] 5950 & [W] 6890 (E North Am)
1100-1145	[W] 6000 & [S] 9550 (S America)
1100-1200	[S] 7730 (C America), [S] 9625 (S America), [W] 11725 (C America), [W] 11830 (S America)
1200-1300	[W] 11530 & [S] 17555 (S America)
1200-1345	[W] 11970 (W North Am)
1200-2145	[S] 17795 (W North Am)
1300-1400	[W] *7240* (SE Asia), 11830 & [S] 11865 (N America), [S] *11895* (SE Asia)
1300-1500	[W] *7155*, [S] *9415* & *11560* (S Asia)
1300-1600	[W] 11855 & [S] 11910 (E North Am)
1400-1500	[W] *7535* & [S] *11640* (E Asia), 13695 (E North Am)
1400-1600	[S] 11830 (N America)
1400-1645	[W] 11565 (N America), [W] 17760 (W North Am)
1500-1545	[W] 15210 & [S] 15770 (S America)
1500-1600	*6280* & [W] *12015* (S Asia), [W] *13660* (E Africa), [S] *15520* (S Asia), [S] *15750* (E Africa)
1600-1645	11830 & [S] 11865 (N America)
1600-1700	6085 (C America), [S] *11850* & [W] *12010* (S Asia), 13695 (E North Am), [W] 17690 (W Africa), [S] 21525 (C Africa & S Africa)
1600-1800	21455 (Europe)
1600-1945	18980 (Europe)
1700-1800 ➡	*3955* (W Europe)
1700-1800	*21680* (E Africa)
1700-2000	[S] 13690 & [W] 13695 (E North Am)
1700-2145	[W] 17555 (W North Am)
1800-1900	[S] *7240* (Mideast), [W] *7240* (W Europe), [W] *7345* (Mideast), [S] *9845* & [W] *9895* (S Africa), [W] *13660* (E Africa), [S] *13780* (Mideast), [S] *15750* (E Africa)
1800-2000	*7395* (E Africa)
1800-2145	[S] 13615 & [W] 17535 (N America)
1800-2200	[W] 15115 & [S] 17845 (W Africa)
1900-1945	6085 (C America), [W] 15565 (Europe)
1900-2000	[W] *7160*, [S] *11875* & [S] 18930 (Europe)
1900-2100	*3230* (S Africa), *6020* (E Africa)
1945-2145	[S] 18980 (Europe)
2000-2045	[W] 5745 & [S] 17750 (Europe)
2000-2100	[W] 17575 & [S] 17725 (S America)
2000-2145	[W] 6915 (Europe)
2000-2200	[S] *7360* (W Europe), *15195* (C Africa)
2100-2145	[S] 13690 (E North Am)
2100-2200	[W] 5950 (E North Am), [S] 11565 (Europe)
2115-2315	*11875* (C Africa)
2200-2245	[S] 15770 (C Africa & S Africa), [W] 17690 (W Africa)
2200-2345	11740 (N America)
2200-2400	5950 (E North Am), 15440 (W North Am)
2300-2400	[W] 9430, [S] 15255, [W] 15400 & [S] 17750 (S America)

PASSPORT editor Lawrence Magne enjoys lunch on July 4th before returning to work. J. Porcelet

Saint Peter's as viewed from the Vatican garden. Nearby Vatican Radio creates programs in a kaleidoscope of languages. These are followed, even when jammed, in every nook of the planet.

Shutterstock/Perov Stanislav

KJES

0200-0300 ← 7555 (W North Am)
0300-0330 ← 7555 (N America)
1400-1500 ← 11715 (E North Am)
1500-1600 ← 11715 (W North Am)
1900-2000 ← 15385 (Australasia)

KNLS-NEW LIFE STATION—(E Asia)

0800-0900 S 7355 & W 9615
1000-1100 W 6150 & S 6890
1200-1300 W 6150, W 6915, S 7355 & S 9780
1400-1500 W 6150 & S 7355

WEWN

0000-0300 W 11520 (W Asia & S Asia)
0000-0600 S 11520 (Mideast)
0300-0900 W 9455 (W Africa & C Africa)
0600-0800 S 7570 (Europe)
0800-1100 S 9355 (E Asia)
0900-1200 W 9390 (E Asia)
1100-1400 S 11560 (E Asia)
1200-1700 W 17510 (W Asia & S Asia)
1400-1900 S 15855 (W Asia & S Asia)
1700-2000 W 15610 (Mideast)
1900-2200 S 17595 (W Africa & C Africa)
2000-2400 W 11520 (Mideast)
2200-2400 S 15665 (W Africa & C Africa)

WINB-WORLD INTERNATIONAL BROADCASTERS—(C America & W North Am)

0000-0300 9265
0300-0400 W 9265
1130-1500 13570
1500-1600 W 13570
2100-2300 13570
2300-2400 9265

WMLK—(Europe & N America)

1600-2100 Su-F 9265

WWCR

0000-0100 S 3210/7465 & W 3210 (E North Am)
0000-0200 5935/13845 & W 7465 (E North Am)
0000-1200 5070 (E North Am)
0100-0300 5765/7465 (E North Am)
0100-0900 3210 (E North Am)
0200-1200 5935 (E North Am)
0300-1100 5765/5890 (E North Am)
0900-1000 3210/9985 (E North Am)
1000-1100 W 9985 & S Su-F 15825 (E North Am)
1100-1130 S Sa/Su 15825 (E North Am)
1100-1200 W Su-F 15825 (E North Am)
1100-1400 5765/7465 (E North Am)
1130-1200 S 15825 (E North Am)

1200-1230	[S] 15825 & [W] Sa/Su 15825 (E North Am)
1200-1300	[W] 5070 (E North Am)
1200-1400	5935/13845 (E North Am)
1230-2100	15825 (E North Am)
1400-1600	7465/9985 (E North Am), 12160 (Irr) (E North Am & Europe)
1400-2400	13845 (E North Am)
1600-1800	9985 (E North Am)
1600-2200	12160 (E North Am & Europe)
1800-1900	[S] 9975 & [W] 9985 (E North Am)
1900-2200	9975 (E North Am)
2100-2145	[S] Sa/Su 15825 (E North Am)
2100-2200	[W] 15825/7465 (Irr) (E North Am)
2145-2200	[S] 15825 (E North Am)
2200-2245	[W] Sa/Su 9985 (E North Am)
2200-2400	5070/12160 (E North Am & Europe), [W] 7465 (E North Am)
2300-2400	[W] 3210/9985 (E North Am)

VATICAN STATE

VATICAN RADIO

0140-0200	[W] 5915, [W] 7335, [W] 9650 & [S] 12055/7335 (S Asia)
0250-0320	[S] *6100* & [W] *6100/6040* (E North Am & C America), 7305 (E North Am)
0300-0330	[W] 7360 (E Africa), [S] 9660 (C Africa & E Africa), [W] *12070* & [S] *15560* (S Asia)
0500-0530	[W] 7360, 9660 & 11625 (C Africa & S Africa), [S] 13765 (E Africa)
0600-0630 ⬅	4005 (Europe), 7250 (W Europe)
0630-0645	[S] M-Sa 6185 (W Europe), [S] M-Sa 9645 (Europe)
0630-0700	[W] 7360, [W] 9660 & [S] 11625 (W Africa), [W] 11625 (C Africa & S Africa), [S] 13765 (W Africa), [S] 15570 (C Africa & S Africa)
0730-0745 ⬅	M-Sa 4005 (Europe), M-Sa 7250 (W Europe), M-Sa 11740 (W Europe & N Africa), M-Sa 15595 (Mideast)
0730-0745	[W] M-Sa 6185 (E Europe), [W] M-Sa 9645 (N Africa)
1130-1200	F 15595, [S] F 17515 & [W] F 17765 (Mideast)
1530-1600	[W] *9310*, [W] 11850, [S] *12065*, 13765 & [S] 15235 (S Asia)
1615-1630	[S] 15595 (Mideast)
1715-1730 ⬅	4005 (Europe), 7250 & 9645 (W Europe)
1715-1730	[W] 9635 (Mideast)
1730-1800	[W] 9755 & 11625 (E Africa), 13765 & [S] 15570 (C Africa & S Africa)
1950-2020	[S] 9645 (W Europe)
2000-2030	[W] 7365, [W] 9755 & [S] 11625 (W Africa), [W] 11625 (C Africa & S Africa), [S] 13765 (W Africa)
2050-2120 ⬅	4005 & 5885 (Europe), 7250 (W Europe)

VIETNAM

VOICE OF VIETNAM

0100-0130, 0230-0300 & 0330-0400	*6175* (E North Am & C America)
1000-1030	9840 & 12019 (SE Asia)
1100-1130	7285 (SE Asia)
1130-1200	9840 & 12019 (E Asia)
1230-1300	9840 & 12019 (SE Asia)
1330-1400	9840 & 12019 (E Asia)
1500-1530	7285, 9840 & 12019 (SE Asia)
1600-1630	7220 (Mideast), 7280 (Europe), 9550 (Mideast), 9730 (Europe)
1700-1730	[S] *9725* (W Europe)
1800-1830	[W] *5955* (W Europe)
1900-1930	7280 & 9730 (Europe)
2030-2100	7220 (Mideast), 7280 (Europe), 9550 (Mideast), 9730 (Europe)
2330-2400	9840 & 12019 (SE Asia)

YEMEN

REPUBLIC OF YEMEN RADIO—(Mideast)

1800-1900	9780

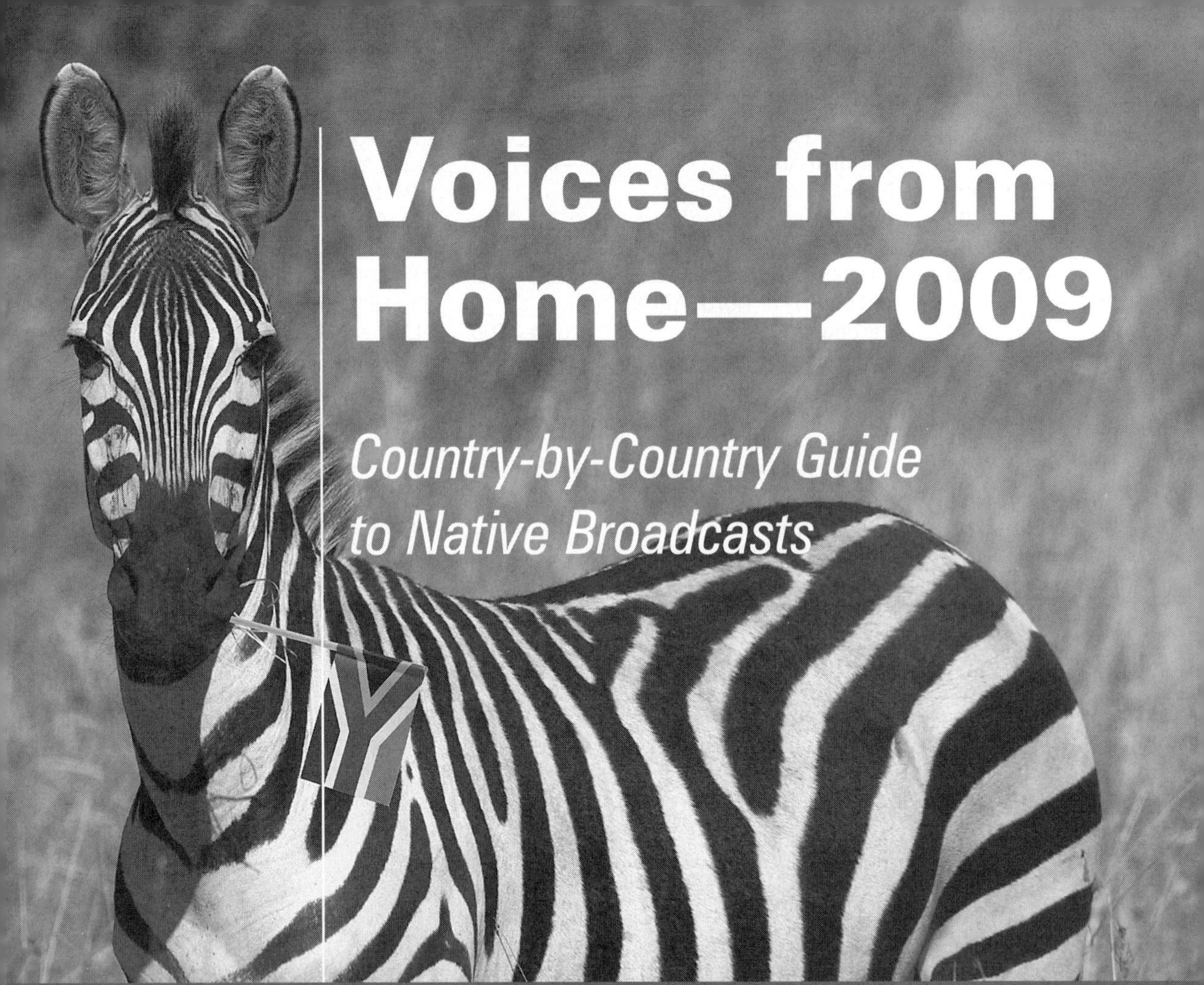

Voices from Home—2009

Country-by-Country Guide to Native Broadcasts

For some, English offerings are merely icing on the cake. Their real interest is in eavesdropping on broadcasts for *nativos*—the home folks. These can be enjoyable regardless of language, especially when they offer traditional music.

Some you'll hear, many you won't, sometimes because they're gone for political or economic reasons. Keep in mind that most native-language broadcasts are weaker than those in English, so you'll need patience, an electrically quiet location and superior hardware. PASSPORT REPORTS shows which radios and antennas work best.

When to Listen

Some broadcasts come in daytime between 9300 and 21850 kHz. However, signals from Latin America and sub-Saharan Africa peek through near twilight or during darkness, especially from 4700 to 5100 kHz. See "Best Times and Frequencies" for specifics.

Times and days of the week are in World Time (UTC), explained in "Setting Your World Time Clock" and "Worldly Words"; for local times in each country see "Addresses PLUS." Midyear, typically April through October, some stations are an hour earlier (⬅) or later (➡) because of Daylight Saving/Summer Time. Stations may also extend their hours for holidays, emergencies or sports events.

Travelers, expats and the merely curious eavesdrop on home broadcasts.

Frequencies used only seasonally are labeled **S** for summer (midyear) and **W** for winter. Frequencies in *italics* may be best, as they come from relay transmitters that may be near you. Signals not aimed your way may also be heard, especially when beamed to nearby regions. Frequencies with no target zones are usually for domestic coverage, so they're unlikely to be heard unless you're in or near that country.

Schedules for Entire Year

To be as useful as possible over the months to come, PASSPORT's schedules consist not just of observed activity, but also that which we have creatively opined will take place during the forthcoming year. This predictive material is based on decades of experience and is original from us. Although inherently not as exact as real-time data, over the years it's been of tangible value to PASSPORT readers.

For deluxe DXing, it's hard to beat these comfy cabins surrounded by water on Pangkor Island in Malaysia. Shutterstock

ALBANIA—Albanian

RADIO TIRANA

0000-0030		S 9345 (E North Am)
0000-0130	⬅	7425 (E North Am)
0000-0130		W 6110 (E North Am)
0730-1000	⬅	7105/7330 (Europe)
2030-2200		S 9390 & S 9395 (Europe)
2130-2300	⬅	6005 (Europe)
2130-2300		W 7485 & W 9345 (W Europe)
2300-2400		S 9345 (E North Am)

AUSTRIA—German

RADIO AUSTRIA INTERNATIONAL

0000-0030		W 7325 (C America)
0030-0100		W 7325 (E North Am)
0100-0130		S 9870 (C America)
0130-0200		S 9870 (E North Am)
0500-2200	⬅	6155 (Europe)
0600-0700	⬅	17870 (Mideast)
0600-1800	⬅	13730 (Europe)
1200-1300		S 17715 (SE Asia & Australasia)
1300-1400		W 17855 (SE Asia & Australasia)
1500-1600		S *13775* (W North Am)
1600-1700		W *13675* (W North Am)
2330-2400	➡	9870 (S America)

BANGLADESH—Bangla

BANGLADESH BETAR

1630-1730	7250 (Mideast)
1915-2000	7250 (Europe)

BELGIUM—Dutch

RADIO VLAANDEREN INTERNATIONAAL—(S Europe & N Africa)

0600-0700	S *13685*
0700-0800	S *9590* & W *13685*
0800-0900	W *9790*
1700-1800	S *13685*
1800-1900	W *5960* & S *9590*
1900-2000	W *6040*

BULGARIA—Bulgarian

RADIO BULGARIA

0000-0100		S 7400 & S 9400 (S America), S 9700 & S 11700 (E North Am)
0100-0200		W 5900 (E North Am), W 7200 & W 7300 (S America), W 7400 (E North Am)
0400-0430		S Sa/Su 7200 (Europe), S Sa/Su 7400 (S Europe), S Sa/Su 9400 (Europe)
0430-0500		S 7200 (Europe), S 7400 (S Europe), S 9400 (Europe), S 9800 (Mideast)
0500-0530		W Sa/Su 5900 (Europe), W Sa/Su 6000 (S Europe), W Sa/Su 7400 (Europe)
0530-0600		W 5900 (Europe), W 6000 (S Europe), W 6100 & W 7300 (Mideast), W 7400 (Europe)
1000-1030		S 7400 (S Europe)
1100-1130	⬅	11600 (E Europe), 11700 (W Europe), 13600 (E Europe), 15700 (W Europe)
1100-1130		W 6000 (S Europe)
1300-1500	⬅	11700 & 15700 (W Europe)
1300-1500		W 6000 (S Europe)
1500-1600		S 7400 (S Europe), S 9400 (E Europe), S 13800 (Mideast)
1600-1700	⬅	7200 (E Europe), 15700 (S Africa)
1600-1700		W 5900 (E Europe, N Africa & Mideast), W 5900 (N Africa & Mideast), W 7400 (Europe)
1800-1900		S 7400 (S Europe)
1800-2000		S 11800 (W Europe)
1800-2100		S 9800 (Mideast)
1900-2200		W 5900 (W Europe & N Africa), W 6000 (Mideast)

RADIO VARNA—(Europe)

0000-0400	⬅	M 6000
2230-2400	⬅	Su 6000

CANADA—French

CANADIAN BROADCASTING CORP—(E North Am)

0100-0300	⬅	M 9625
0300-0400	⬅	Su 9625 & Tu-Sa 9625
1300-1310 & 1500-1555	⬅	M-F 9625
1700-1715	⬅	Su 9625
1900-1945	⬅	M-F 9625
1900-2310	⬅	Sa 9625

The Wellbrook ALA 100M is large for an active antenna, but is dwarfed by the most serious of passive aerials.
J.R. Sherwood

RADIO CANADA INTERNATIONAL

1705-1905	[S] 9515 (N America)
1805-2005	[W] 9610 (N America)
1900-2000	[W] *9670* (C Africa), [W] *9770* & [S] *11765* (E Africa), [W] *11845* (N Africa & W Africa), [S] *11980* (C Africa, E Africa & S Africa), [W] 13650 (N Africa & W Africa), [S] *13730* (C Africa & E Africa), [S] 15235 (W Africa), [S] *15320* (N Africa & W Africa), [W] 15365 (W Africa & C Africa), [S] 17735 (W Africa), [W] 17790 (W Africa & C Africa)
2005-2105	[S] 9515 (N America)
2100-2200	[W] *7235* & [S] *7370* (N Africa), [S] *9690* (W Africa), [W] *9805* & [W] 11845 (N Africa), [S] *13650* (N Africa & W Africa), [S] 15330 (N Africa), [S] 17735 (W Africa)
2105-2205	[W] 6100 (N America)
2300-2330	[W] *6160* (E Asia), [S] *9525* (E Asia & SE Asia)

CHINA

CENTRAL PEOPLE'S BROADCASTING STATION

Chinese

0000-0005	5925, 7620, 9665
0000-0030	[W] 6040, [W] 7275, 7335, 11710, [S] 11800, [S] 11835, [S] 15380
0000-0100	[W] 4460, 5945, [W] 6080, 6090, 6125, 7150, [W] 7245, 7315, 9480, [S] 9620, [S] 9630, [S] 9645, [W] 9820, 9830, 9845, 11740, [S] 11845
0000-0105	6165, 9170
0000-0130	[W] 7290, [S] 17890
0000-0200	[W] 6155, 9755, 9775, [W] 11925, [S] 15500, [S] 17580
0000-0400	9530, 11685
0000-0600	4750, 4800, 6030, 7140, 7230, 9500, 9675, 9720, 11610, 11670, 11720, 11750, 11760, 11835, 11960, 12045, 13610, 15550, 17625
0030-0130	[W] 11710, [S] 17605
0030-0600	11800, 11915, 15380
0055-0613	9685, 11620, 11935
0100-0300	[W] 6090, [S] 9570
0100-0400	15570
0100-0600	9620, 9630, 9645, 9810, 11660, 11845, 15370, 15480, 15540, 17550, 17565, 17595
0130-0600	17605, 17890
0200-0500	11630, 12055, 13700, 15390
0200-0600	12080, 15270, 15500,

	17580
0300-0600	9570
0355-0900	11905
0355-1100	15710
0500-0600	9530, 11685, 15570
0600-0730	W-M 17565, W-M 17595
0600-0800	Th-Tu 9530, Th-Tu 11685, W-M 11750, Th-Tu 11845, W-M 15550, Th-Tu 15570
0600-0830	W-M 9645
0600-0850	W-M 4750, W-M 4800, W-M 6030, W-M 7230, W-M 9500, W-M 9630, W-M 9675, W-M 11720, W-M 11760, W-M 11960, W-M 12045, W-M 13610, W-M 15370, W-M 15380, W-M 15480, W-M 17550, W-M 17580, W-M 17605, W-M 17890
0600-0855	Th-Tu 17625
0600-0900	Th-Tu 7140, Th-Tu 9570, Th-Tu 9620, Th-Tu 9720, Th-Tu 9810, Th-Tu 11610, Th-M 11660, Th-Tu 11670, Th-Tu 11800, Th-Tu 11835, Th-Tu 11915, Th-Tu 12080, Th-Tu 15270, Th-Tu 15500, Th-Tu 15540
0600-1100	11835
0700-0850	W-M 11630, W-M 12055, W-M 13700, W-M 15390
0730-0850	W-M 9830, [S] W-M 17595, [W] W-M 17845
0800-0850	[W] W-M 7305, [W] W-M 7345, [S] W-M 11750, [S] W-M 15550
0800-0900	[W] Th-Tu 9820, [S] Th-Tu 11845
0830-0850	[W] W-M 4460, [S] W-M 9645
0850-0900	11630, 11960, 12055, 13700, 15390
0850-1000	[W] 7305, 9675, [S] 11750, 15480, 17580, 17605, [W] 17845, 17890
0850-1030	17550
0850-1100	[W] 4460, [W] 7345, [S] 9645, 11720, 12045, 15370, 15380, [S] 15550, [S] 17595
0850-1200	9630, 11760
0850-1300	13610
0850-1733	4750, W-M 4800, 6030, 7230, 9500, 9830
0855-1000	17625
0900-1000	9570, 9720, 11915, 12080, 15500
0900-1030	9530, 11800
0900-1100	[W] 7315, [W] 9820, 11610, [S] 11660, [S] 11845, 15540
0900-1200	[W] 6165, 11670, [S] 11905
0900-1230	9810
0900-1300	[W] 3985, [S] 7140, [W] 7245, [W] 7350, 9480, [S] 9620, [S] 11685
0900-1601	9775
0900-1733	6175

Beijing's old Summer Palace (Yuanming Yuan) in winter.

Shutterstock/Lim Yong Hian

0955-2200	9410
0955-2400	5925, 7620
1000-1100	[W] 6125, 11630, 12055, 13700, 15390
1000-1200	[W] 9515, [W] 11925, [S] 17580, [S] 17625, [S] 17890
1000-1300	[W] 5945, [W] 7335, [S] 11915, [S] 15480
1000-1601	6090, 6155, 9755
1000-1733	5030, 7305, 11710
1030-1200	[W] 7375, [S] 11800
1030-1300	[W] 6010, [S] 9530
1030-1733	9845
1100-1200	[W] 9860, [S] 12045
1100-1300	[W] 7130, [W] 7140, [S] 11610, [S] 11835
1100-1601	7315, 9820, 11740
1100-1733	4460, 6125, 7275, 7345, 9710
1100-1804	9170
1200-1400	[W] 6180, 9420, 9630, [W] 9890, [S] 11630, [S] 13700
1200-1601	6065, 7375, 9515
1200-1733	6080, 7110, 7290, 9860, 11925
1200-1804	6165
1230-1601	7150
1300-1601	3985, 7130, 7140, 7245, 7335
1300-1733	5945, 9810
1400-1601	6010, 7350, 9480
2000-2200	7305
2000-2300	5030, 6080, 7275, 9810, 9890, 9900
2000-2330	4460, 9710, 11925
2000-2400	4750, 4800, 5945, 6030, 6125, 6175, [W] 6180, 6950/7215, 7230, 7290, 7345, 9455, 9500, 9655, 9830, 9845, [S] 11630, 11710
2055-2400	6165, 9170
2100-2200	6040
2100-2300	6010, 6155, 6190, 7140, 7245, 7360, 9480, 9820
2100-2330	6065, 7130
2100-2400	6090, 7150, 7315, 7335, 9515, 9755, 9775, 11740
2200-2400	[W] 6040, 9665, 11750, [S] 11800
2300-2400	[W] 6080, [W] 6155, [W] 6190, [S] 7140, [W] 7140, [W] 7245, [W] 7275, [S] 9620, [S] 9630, 9675, [W] 9820, [W] 9890, [W] 9900, [S] 11610, [S] 11845, [S] 12045, 13610, [S] 13700, [S] 15380, [S] 15500
2330-2400	[W] 4460, [W] 7130, [S] 9645, 11670, 11720, [S] 11835, [W] 11925, [S] 17580

CHINA RADIO INTERNATIONAL
Chinese

0000-0100	[S] *5960* (E North Am), [W] *6005* (N America), [W] *6040* (E North Am), 11780 (E Asia), [W] 11845 (SE Asia), 11900 (E Asia), [S] *11930* (W North Am), [S] 12035 & 13580 (SE Asia)
0000-0300	13655 (E Asia)
0100-0200	[W] 7250, [W] 7300 & [S] 11640 (S Asia), [W] 11640 (SE Asia), [S] 11650 (S Asia), 13580 & [S] 15140 (SE Asia)
0100-0400	15160 (E Asia)
0200-0300	[W] 7330 (S America), *9580* (E North Am), *9690* (N America & C America), [S] 9815 (Mideast, N Africa & S America), 11695 (S America)
0200-0400	*6020* & *9570* (N America)
0300-0400	9450 (S Asia), [W] 13655 (E Asia), [S] 13690 (Europe), [S] 15230 (E Asia), 17540 (S Asia)
0300-0600	15130 (E Asia)
0400-0500	13640 & 15170 (S Asia)
0500-0700	[W] 13620 & [W] 13655 (E Asia), 15120 (C Asia & E Asia), 15170, [S] 15230 & [S] 15785 (E Asia)
0600-0800	[W] 13750, [S] 17615 & 17740 (SE Asia)
0600-0900	17650 (Europe)
0700-0900	[S] *11785* & [W] *11855* (W Europe)
0800-0900	[W] 7180, 11640, [W] 13610 & [S] 15230 (E Asia)
0800-1000	15565 & 17560 (W Asia & C Asia)
0800-1100	[S] 9880 (E Asia)

0900-1000	7190, **W** 9440 & **S** 13620 (E Asia), **W** 13850 (SE Asia), 15440 (Australasia), 17500 (S Asia), **S** 17540 (SE Asia), 17670 (Australasia)
0900-1100	**W** 5965 (E Asia), 11980, 15250 & **W** 15340 (SE Asia), 15525 (S Asia), **S** 17530 (SE Asia)
1000-1100	**W** 6020 (C Asia), **W** 7255 & **S** 9890 (C Asia & E Asia), 13850 (SE Asia), **S** 17540 (C Asia & E Asia)
1000-1200	17650 (Europe)
1100-1200	7160 & **W** 7200 (E Asia), **W** 11620 (Australasia), **S** 11750 (E Asia), **W** 11980 (S Asia), **W** 15440 & **S** 15460 (Australasia)
1100-1300	**S** 13755 (S Asia)
1200-1300	**W** 7205 (S Asia), *9570* (E North Am), 15110 (Mideast), **W** *15540* & **S** *17625* (S America)
1200-1400	7160 & 9855 (SE Asia)
1300-1400	7205 (E Asia), 13650 (Mideast)
1400-1500	7210 (E Asia), **S** 9730 (S Asia)
1400-1600	**S** *15220* (W North Am)
1500-1600	5910 (SE Asia), 7150 (E Asia), 7265 & 9560 (S Asia), **W** 9700 & **W** 9740 (Europe), **W** *13675* (W North Am), **S** 13680 & **S** 13710 (Europe)
1600-1700	**W** *17735* (W North Am)
1730-1830	**W** 7120 (Europe), 7160, 7315, **W** 9695 & **S** 9745 (Mideast), **S** 11660 (Europe)
1800-1900	*6100* (S Africa)
2000-2100	7120 (Europe), 7245 (Mideast & N Africa), 7335 (Europe), 9865 (Mideast)
2200-2300	5975 (Mideast), **W** 6100, 6140 & **W** 7125 (SE Asia), 7190 (E Africa & S Africa), **S** 7215 & **W** 7220 (SE Asia), 7265 (Mideast & W Asia), **W** 7305 (E Asia), 7325, **S** 9460 & **S** 9470 (SE Asia), **W** 9555 & **S** 9675 (E Asia)
2230-2300	*15505* (W Africa, C Africa & E Africa)
2230-2400	*11975* (N Africa)
2300-2400	*7170* (W Africa), **S** 11900 (E Asia)

Cantonese

0000-0100	11820 & 17495 (SE Asia)
0400-0500	*9790* (W North Am), **W** 13655, 15160 & **S** 15230 (E Asia)
0700-0800	11640, **W** 13610 & **S** 15230 (E Asia)
1000-1100	15440 & 17670 (Australasia)
1100-1200	9540 (Australasia), 9590 & 9645 (SE Asia), 13580 (Australasia)
1200-1300	**W** *9560* & **S** *11855* (E North Am & C America)
1700-1800	**W** 7220 (E Africa & S Africa), **S** 9435 (E Africa)
1900-2000	**S** 7140, **W** 7215, **W** 9770 & **S** 11895 (Europe)
2300-2400	6140, 7325, **W** 9425, 9460, **S** 11650, 11945/11935 & **S** 15100 (SE Asia)

CHINA (TAIWAN)

RADIO TAIWAN INTERNATIONAL

Amoy

0000-0100	11875 (SE Asia)
1000-1100	15465 (SE Asia)
1200-1300	11715 (SE Asia)
1300-1400	11635 (SE Asia)

Chinese

0000-0300	9660 (E Asia)
0000-0400	15245 (E Asia)
0000-0500	11640 & 11885 (E Asia)
0200-0500	15290 (SE Asia)
0900-1400	6150 (E Asia)
0900-1500	6085 (E Asia)
0900-1600	11665 (E Asia)
0900-1800	7185 (E Asia)
1000-1400	9780 (E Asia)
1100-1300	11710 (E Asia)
1100-1800	9680 (E Asia)
1400-1800	6145 & 7130 (E Asia)
1600-1800	7365 (E Asia)
2200-2400	6105 & 6150 (E Asia), 11635 (SE Asia), 11710 & 11885 (E Asia)
2300-2400	9660 & 15245 (E Asia)

Cantonese

0100-0130	15290 (SE Asia)
0200-0230	*15440* (W North Am), 15610 (SE Asia)
0500-0530	15320 (SE Asia)
0500-0600	*9680* (N America)
1000-1030	11635 & 15270 (SE Asia)
1200-1230	6105 (E Asia), 11915 (SE Asia)
1500-1530	11550 (SE Asia)

VOICE OF HAN—(E Asia)

Chinese

0755-0105	9745

CYPRUS—Greek

CYPRUS BROADCASTING CORP—(Europe)

2215-2245	[S] F-Su 5930, [W] F-Su 6180, F-Su 7210 & F-Su 9760

CZECH REPUBLIC—Czech

RADIO PRAGUE

0030-0100	[W] 5930 (S America), [W] 7345 (N America & C America)
0130-0200	[S] 6200 (N America & C America), [S] 7345 (S America)
0230-0300	[W] 6200 & [S] 7345 (N America & C America), [W] 7345 (S America), [S] 9870 (W North Am & C America)
0330-0400	[W] 6200 (W North Am & C America), [W] 7345 (N America & C America)
0830-0900	[S] 15710 (E Africa & Mideast)
0930-1000 ⇐	11600 (W Europe)
0930-1000	[S] 9880 (W Europe), [S] 21745 (S Asia), [W] 21745 (C Africa & E Africa)
1030-1100	[W] 15700 (S Asia), [W] 21745 (W Africa)
1100-1130	[S] 11665 (N Europe), [S] 15710 (S Asia)
1200-1230	[W] 11640 (N Europe), [W] 17545 (S Asia, SE Asia & Australasia)
1330-1400 ⇐	6055 (Europe), 7345 (W Europe)
1530-1600	[S] 17485 (E Africa)
1630-1700 ⇐	5930 (W Europe)
1630-1700	[W] 15710 (W Africa & C Africa)
1730-1800	[S] 5930 (E Europe & Asia), [S] 17485 (C Africa)
1830-1900	[W] 5930 (W Europe), [W] 9400 (Asia & Australasia)
1930-2000	[S] 11600 (SE Asia & Australasia)
2030-2100 ⇐	5930 (W Europe)
2030-2100	[W] 9430 (SE Asia & Australasia)
2100-2130	[S] 9410 (W Africa & C Africa), [S] 11600 (W Europe)
2200-2230	[W] 5930 (W Europe), [W] 9435 (W Europe & S America)
2330-2400	[S] 7345 (S America), [S] 9440 (N America & C America)

EGYPT—Arabic

EGYPTIAN RADIO

0000-0030	[W] 11540 (E Africa)
0000-0300	[S] 12050 (Europe & E North Am)
0000-0700 ⇐	6290 (Europe & E North Am)
0600-1000	[S] 15115 (W Africa)
0700-1100	[W] 15710 (W Africa)
1700-2300 ⇐	9250 (C Africa & E Africa)
1800-2330	[S] 9960 (E Africa)
1900-2400 ⇐	6290 (Europe & E North Am)
1900-2400	[W] 11540 (E Africa)
2300-2400	[S] 12050 (Europe & E North Am)

RADIO CAIRO

0000-0045	[W] 9250, 9360 & [S] 9735 (S America)
0030-0430	[W] 6850 & [S] 9280 (E North Am)
1015-1215	15170 (Mideast)
1300-1600	15080 (W Africa & C Africa)
2000-2200	6860 (Australasia)
2330-2400	[W] 9250, 9360 & [S] 9735 (S America)

Aminata Ouédraogo is interviewed by Radio France Internationale in Bama, Burkina Faso. RFI

FRANCE—French

RADIO FRANCE INTERNATIONALE

0400-0430	Sa/Su 9805 (E Africa)
0400-0500	[W] 5925 & 7135 (C Africa), [W] 9780/11995 (E Africa), [S] 9790 (C Africa & S Africa)
0500-0530	[W] Sa/Su 9805/13680, [W] Sa/Su 11995, [S] Sa/Su 13680 & [S] Sa/Su 15160/11995 (E Africa)
0500-0600 ◄	11700 (E Africa)
0500-0600	[W] 5925 (N Africa & W Africa), [W] 7135 & [S] 9790 (W Africa), [W] 9790 (C Africa & S Africa), [S] 11700/7135 (N Africa & W Africa), [S] 15300 (C Africa & S Africa)
0500-0700	[W] 7135 (N Africa & W Africa)
0600-0630	[W] Sa/Su 7315 & [S] Sa/Su 9765/11725 (W Africa & C Africa), [W] Sa/Su 11995/15160, [W] Sa/Su 13680, [S] Sa/Su 15160 & [S] Sa/Su 17800 (E Africa)
0600-0700 ◄	11700 (C Africa & S Africa)
0600-0700	[W] 5925 (W Africa), [S] 7135/13695, 9790 & [S] 11700 (N Africa & W Africa), 13695 & [S] 15300 (C Africa & S Africa)
0700-0800	[W] 9790, 11700 & 13695 (N Africa & W Africa), [W] 13695 (C Africa & S Africa), *15170* (C Africa), 15300 (W Africa, C Africa & S Africa)
0700-0900	17850 (C Africa & S Africa)
0800-0830	Sa/Su *11830* (C Africa)
0800-1000	13675 & 17620 (W Africa)
0800-1600	15300 (N Africa & W Africa)
0900-1400	[S] 17850 (C Africa & S Africa)
1000-1500	[W] 13675 (W Africa)
1100-1130	[S] 15365/17800 (C America)
1100-1200	*17525* (C Africa)
1130-1200	6175 (W Europe & Atlantic), *13640* & [W] 17610 (C America)
1200-1400	*15160* (C Africa), 17620 (W Africa), [W] 21580 (C Africa & S Africa)
1200-1500	[W] 21685 (W Africa)
1230-1300	[W] 21620 (E Africa)
1500-1600	[W] 17620 (W Africa)
1500-1700	13675 (W Africa)
1600-1700	[S] 15300 (W Africa), [W] 15300 (Africa), 17620 (W Africa), 17850 (C Africa & S Africa)
1700-1800	[W] 11705 (C Africa & S Africa), [S] 13695 (N Africa & W Africa), [W] 13695 (Africa), [S] 17850 (C Africa & S Africa)
1700-1900	[S] 15300 (Africa)
1700-2000	11995 (W Africa)
1800-1900	[W] 9790 (E Africa, C Africa & S Africa)
1800-2000	[S] 11705 (C Africa & S Africa), 13695 (N Africa & W Africa)
1900-2000	[W] 6175 & [W] 7315 (W Africa), 9790 (W Africa, C Africa & S Africa), [S] 15300 (W Africa)
2000-2100	[W] 9790 & [S] 11995 (W Africa), [S] 13695 (N Africa & W Africa)
2000-2200	[W] 6175 (W Africa), *7160* (C Africa), 7315 (N Africa & W Africa)

GABON—French

AFRIQUE NUMERO UN

0500-2315	9580 (C Africa)
0700-0800	17630 (Irr) (W Africa)
0800-1600	17630 (W Africa)
1600-1900	15475 (W Africa & E North Am)

GERMANY—German

DEUTSCHE WELLE

0000-0200	[W] *7120* (S Asia), [W] *7285* (C Asia), [S] *9430* (C America), [S] *9545* (S America), [W] *9545*, [S] *9640* & [W] *9655* (C America), [W] *11690* (S America)
24 Hr	6075 (Europe)
0200-0400	[W] *6075* & [S] *7310* (Mideast), [S] *9825* (Mideast & W Asia)
0400-0600	[S] *9480* (C Africa & E Africa), [S] *9620* (S Africa), [W] *9735* (C Africa & E Africa), [W] *13780* (E Africa), [S] *15605* (C Africa & E Africa), [W] *17800* (E Africa & S Africa)
0600-0800	[W] *11865* (Mideast), [W] *12005* (S Africa), [W] *12025* (E Europe & W Asia), [S] *12045* (S Africa), [S] *13780* (Mideast), [W] *15410* (W Africa & C Africa), [S] *15605* (C Africa & S Africa), [S] *17860* (W Africa)
0600-1000	[S] *9480* (N Europe)
0600-1800	[W] *9545* (S Europe & Atlantic)
0700-0800	[S] *15275* (W Africa & S Africa)
0800-1000	[W] *9785* & [S] *9855* (Australasia), [S] *15605* & [W] *17520* (SE Asia & Australasia)
0800-1600	13780 (Mideast)
1000-1100	[W] *9865* (S America)
1000-1200	*5905* (C America), [S] *9900* (SE Asia & Australasia), [W] *15430* (SE Asia), [S] *15595* (S America), [W] *15610* (SE Asia & Australasia), [S] *17635* & [S] *17845* (E Asia & SE Asia), [S] *21840* (S America)
1100-1200	[W] *17770* (S America)
1200-1400	[S] *9565* (C Asia), [W] *15610* (S Asia & C Asia), [W] *17630* & [S] *17845* (S Asia & SE Asia)
1400-1600	[S] *9655* & *15275* (Mideast), [W] *15335* (S Europe, Mideast & W Asia)
1600-1800	[W] *12055* (C Africa & E Africa), [W] *12070* (Mideast), [S] *13780* (E Africa), [W] *13780*, [S] *15275* & [S] *17650* (C Africa & E Africa)
1600-2000	[S] *6150* (C Africa & E Africa)
1800-1900	[W] *13780* (N Africa)
1800-2000	[S] *9735* (N Africa), [W] *11725* (W Africa), [W] *12070* (C Africa & S Africa), [S] *15275* (W Africa), [W] *15440* (S Africa), [S] *17610* (C Africa & S Africa)
1800-2200	[S] *9545* (Europe)
2000-2100	[W] *9510* (Australasia), [W] *9545* (S Europe & Atlantic), [W] *11935* (Australasia)

Deutsche Welle was headquartered near here in Cologne until after the reunification of Germany. Now, it resides in Bonn. Shutterstock/S. Volker

The ancient Zojoji Temple in Tokyo squares off against the neighboring "Eiffel Tower" antenna.

L. Rydén

2000-2200	**S** *7330* (Australasia), **S** *9545* (Atlantic & S America), **S** *9875* (Australasia)
2100-2200	**W** *11935* (Australasia)
2200-2400	9545 (S America), **S** *9775* (C America & S America), **W** *11690* & *11865* (S America), **S** *11965* (SE Asia)
2300-2400	**S** *5955* & **W** *6050* (SE Asia)

GREECE—Greek

FONI TIS HELLADAS

0000-0005	**W** 7475 (Europe), **W** 12105 (W Africa, Atlantic & S America), **S** M-Sa 15650 (Mideast & Australasia)
0000-0200	**S** 15650 (Mideast & Australasia)
0005-0105 ←	Tu-Su 7475 & Tu-Su 9420 (Europe & N America)
0005-0105	**W** Tu-Su 12105 (W Africa, Atlantic & S America)
0105-0300 ←	7475 (Europe & N America), 9420 (Europe & Americas)
0105-0300	**W** 12105 (W Africa, Atlantic & S America)
0200-0300	**S** M-Sa 15650 (Mideast & Australasia)
0300-0355	**S** 15650 (Mideast & Australasia)
0300-0400 ←	M-Sa 7475 (Europe & N America)
0300-0400	**W** M-Sa 9420 (Europe & N America), **W** M-Sa 12105 (W Africa, Atlantic & S America)
0400-0555 ←	7475 (Europe & N America)
0400-0600 ←	9420 (Europe & N America)
0400-0700	**W** 12105 (W Africa, Atlantic & S America)
0600-1000 ←	9420 (Europe)
0700-1000	**W** 12105 (W Africa)
0905-1000	**S** M-Sa 9420 (Europe)
1100-1200	**W** M-Sa 9420 (Europe), **W** M-Sa 17525 (Mideast & Australasia)
1100-1300	**S** 15630 (W Europe & Atlantic)
1200-1400 ←	9420 (Europe)
1200-1400	**W** 17525 (Mideast & Australasia)
1300-1400	**S** Su-F 15630 (W Europe & Atlantic)
1400-1500 ←	Su-F 9420 (Europe)
1400-1500	**S** 15630 (W Europe & Atlantic), **W** Su-F 17525 (Mideast & Australasia)
1500-1555	**W** 17525 (Mideast & Australasia)
1500-2400 ←	9420 (Europe)

1600-2000 ⇦ 15630 (W Europe & Atlantic)
1900-2255 S 15630 (W Europe, Atlantic & N America)
2000-2400 W 7475 (Europe)
2300-2400 W 12105 (W Africa, Atlantic & S America), S M-Sa 15650 (Mideast & Australasia)
2305-2400 S 15650 (Mideast & Australasia)

RS MAKEDONIAS—(Europe)
1100-1655 9935
1700-2255 7450

JAPAN—Japanese

RADIO JAPAN
0200-0300 S *11780* & W *11860* (SE Asia)
0200-0400 *11935* (S America)
0200-0500 *5960* (E North Am & C America), 15195 (E Asia), 15325 (S Asia), S 17560 & W 17560/15230 (Mideast), 17810 (SE Asia)
0700-0800 6145, 6165 & 15195 (E Asia)
0800-0900 9825 (Pacific & S America)
0800-1000 *11740* (SE Asia), S *15290* & W *17875* (W Africa)
0800-1700 9750 (E Asia)
0900-1000 *9795* (S America)
1000-1700 11815 (SE Asia)
1500-1700 9535 (W North Am & C America), *12045* (S Asia), *17735* (C Africa & E Africa)
1700-1900 6035 (E Asia), 7225 (SE Asia), W *9575* (Mideast & N Africa), 9835 (Pacific & S America), *11945* (S Africa), S *13740* (Mideast & N Africa)
1900-2200 S 9560 & W 9670 (Mideast)
2000-2100 9625 & W 13640 (Australasia)
2000-2200 W 6085 (E Asia)
2000-2400 11910 (E Asia)
2100-2200 W 7225 & S 11665 (SE Asia), 13640 (Australasia)
2200-2300 W *7115/7225* & S *9650* (Mideast)
2200-2400 W 11665 & S 13680 (SE Asia), S *15265* & W *17605* (S America)

RADIO NIKKEI
0000-0730 3945, 6115, 9760
0000-0800 3925
0000-1200 6055, 9595
0730-0800 Sa/Su 3945, Sa/Su 6115, Sa/Su 9760
0800-0900 Sa/Su 3945 (Irr), Sa/Su 6115 (Irr), Sa/Su 9760 (Irr)
0800-1200 3925
1200-1330 M-Sa 3925, M-Sa 6055, M-Sa 9595
1330-1500 M-Sa 3925 (Irr), M-Sa 6055 (Irr), M-Sa 9595 (Irr)
2045-2300 3925
2045-2400 6055, 9595
2300-2400 3925, 3945, 6115, 9760

KOREA (DPR)—Korean

KOREAN CENTRAL BROADCASTING STATION
0000-0630 6100
0000-1800 2850, 9665, 11680
0900-0950 4405, 7140 & 9345 (E Asia)
1200-1250 3560 (E Asia), W 6185 (SE Asia), W 6285 & W 9335 (C America), W 9850 (SE Asia), S 11710 (C America), S 11735, S 13650 & S 15180 (SE Asia)

Voice of Russia staff huddles during a visit with guest George Poppin. G. Poppin

Transmission towers take many forms, but Stockholm's Kaknäs Tower is easily one of the most unusual.

L. Rydén

1330-1800	6100
1400-1450	3560 (E Asia), W 6185, W 9850, S 11735 & S 13650 (SE Asia)
1700-1750	4405 (E Asia), W 7570 (W Europe), 9335 & 11710 (N America), W 12015, S 13760 & S 15245 (W Europe)
2000-2050	3560 (E Asia), W 6285 (Europe), 7100 (S Africa), 9325 (Europe), 9975 & 11535 (Mideast & N Africa), 11910 (S Africa), S 12015 (Europe)
2000-2400	2850, 6100, 9665, 11680
2300-2350	3560, 4405 & 7140/7180 (E Asia), W 7570 (W Europe), 9345, 9975 & 11535 (E Asia), W 12015, S 13760 & S 15245 (W Europe)

PYONGYANG BROADCASTING STATION

0000-0050	3560, 7140, 9345 & 9730 (E Asia)
0000-0925	6248 (E Asia)
0000-1800	6398 (E Asia)
0000-1900	3320 (E Asia)
0200-0630	3250 (E Asia)
0700-0750	4405, 7140 & 9345 (E Asia)
0900-0950	3560, 9975 & 11735 (E Asia), 13760 & 15245 (E Europe)
1000-1050 & 1200-1250	4405, 7140 & 9345 (E Asia)
1300-1350	W 6285, 9325 & S 12015 (Europe)
1500-1900	6248 (E Asia)
1500-2030	3250 (E Asia)
2100-2400	3320, 6248 & 6398 (E Asia)

KOREA (REPUBLIC)—Korean

KBS WORLD RADIO

0300-0400	11810 (S America)
0700-0800	*9870* (Europe)
0900-1000	15210 (Mideast)
0900-1100	7275 (E Asia), 9570 (SE Asia)
1200-1300	7275 (E Asia)
1400-1500	*9650* (N America)
1600-1800	7275 (Europe), 9730 (Mideast & Africa)
1700-1900	9515 (Europe)

KUWAIT—Arabic

RADIO KUWAIT

0200-0500	6055 (Mideast & W Asia)
0200-0530	11675 (W North Am)
0200-1305	15495 (N Africa)
0400-0740	15505 (E Europe & W Asia)
0800-0925	15110 (S Asia)
0900-1305	6055 (Mideast & W Asia)
1015-1740	15505 (W Africa & C Africa)
1200-1505	17885 (E Asia & Australasia)
1315-1600	15110 (S Asia)
1315-1605	13620/11990 (Europe & E North Am)
1615-1800	11990 (Europe & E North Am)

1730-2130	9880 (N Africa)
1745-2130	15505 (Europe & E North Am)
1800-2400	15495 (W Africa & C Africa)
1815-2400	9855 (Europe & E North Am)

LITHUANIA—Lithuanian

RADIO VILNIUS

0000-0030 ←	9875 (E North Am)
0000-0030	[S] 11690 (E North Am)
0900-0930 ←	9710 (W Europe)
2300-2330	[W] 7325 (E North Am)

MEXICO—Spanish

RADIO EDUCACION

0000-1200 ←	6185

RADIO MIL

24 Hr	6010

MOROCCO

RADIO MEDI UN—(Europe & N Africa)
Arabic, French

0500-0400	9575

RTV MAROCAINE—(N Africa & Mideast)
Arabic

0900-2200	15345/15340

NETHERLANDS—Dutch

RADIO NEDERLAND WERELDOMROEP

0300-0400	[S] *6190* (N America)
0400-0500	[S] *5975* (W North Am), [W] *5975* (C America), [W] *6165* (N America)
0500-0600	[S] *6015* (S Europe), *6165* (W North Am)
0600-0700 ←	*6120* (S Europe)
0600-0700	[W] *3955* (W Europe), [W] *7305* (Europe), [S] *9625* (Australasia), [S] *11655* (S Europe), [S] *11935* (Europe)
0600-0900 ←	9895 (S Europe)
0600-1100 ←	5955 (W Europe)
0700-0800	6035 (W Europe), [S] Su *11655* (S Europe)
0700-0900	[W] *6120* (S Europe)
0800-0900 ←	*11935* (S Europe & Atlantic)
0800-0900	[S] *6035* (Europe), [W] *6035* (W Europe), [W] *12065* (Australasia)
0900-1000	[W] *6035* (Europe), [S] *9795* & [W] *12065* (Australasia)
0900-1100 ←	*6120* (S Europe)
0900-1600 ←	Su 9895 (S Europe)
0930-1015	M-Sa *6020* (C America)
1100-1200	[S] *21560* (SE Asia)
1100-1600 ←	Su 5955 (W Europe)
1200-1300	[W] *9670* (SE Asia), [W] *12065* (E Asia), [S] *17740* (SE Asia)
1200-1600	[S] *7235* (W Europe)
1300-1400	*5910* (E Asia & SE Asia), [W] *9390*, [S] *9655*, [W] *12065* & [S] *12085* (SE Asia), [W] *17580* & [S] *17585* (S Asia & SE Asia)
1500-1700	[S] *13700* (S Europe & N Africa)
1600-1700 ←	9895 (S Europe)
1600-1700	[W] *6110*, [W] *9750* & [S] *9895* (S Europe), [W] *11655* (E Africa), *13740/13840* & [S] *15335* (Mideast)
1600-1800 ←	5955 (W Europe)
1700-1800	[W] *6010* (S Europe & Atlantic), *6020* (S Africa), [S] *9895* (C Africa), [W] *9895* (E Africa)
2000-2200	[S] *6040* (W Europe), [S] *6125* (S Europe)
2100-2200	[W] *11655* (W Africa & C Africa), [W] *15315* (S America), *17810* (W Africa), [W] *17895* (S America)
2100-2300	[W] *6040* (W Europe), [S] *17605* (S America)
2200-2300	[W] *11730* (Atlantic & W Europe), [W] *15315* & [S] *15540* (S America)
2300-2400	[W] *6165* (E North Am), [W] *9520* & [S] *9525* (C America & S America), [S] *11970* (E North Am)

OMAN—Arabic

RADIO SULTANATE OF OMAN

0000-0200	9760 (Europe & Mideast)
0200-0300	15355 (E Africa)
0200-0400	[S] 6085/6000 & [W] 6085/7175 (Mideast)

0400-0600	9515 (Mideast), 17590 (E Africa)
0600-0800	17630/17660 (Europe & Mideast)
0600-1400	13640 (Mideast)
0800-1000	17630 (Europe & Mideast)
1400-1800	15375 (E Africa)
1500-2200	15140 (Europe & Mideast)
1800-2000	6190 & 15355 (E Africa)
2000-2200	6085 (E Africa), 13640 (Europe & Mideast)
2200-2400	15355 (Europe & Mideast)
2300-2400	9760 (Europe & Mideast)

POLAND—Polish

POLISH RADIO EXTERNAL SERVICE

1030-1100	S *11915* (W Europe), S *11995* (E Europe)
1130-1200	W *7285* (E Europe), W *9445* (W Europe)
1530-1630	S *9670* (E Europe)
1630-1730	W *6140* (C Asia)
2100-2200	S *5975* (E Europe), S *7135* (W Europe)
2200-2300	W *6050* (E Europe), W *9660* (W Europe)

ROMANIA—Romanian

RADIO ROMANIA

0700-0800	S Su 9700, S Su 11970, S Su 15260 & S Su 17720 (Mideast)
0800-0900	S Su 9700, W Su 11730, S Su 11970 & W Su 15370 (Mideast), W Su 15430 (W Asia), S Su 15450 (N Africa & Mideast), W Su 17775 (W Asia)
0900-1000	S Su 11830 (W Europe), S Su 11875 (N Africa & Mideast), S Su 11925 (N Africa), S Su 15250 (W Europe), W Su 15380 (N Africa & Mideast), W Su 15430 (Mideast), W Su 17745 (N Africa & Mideast), W Su 17775 (Mideast)
1000-1100 ⬅	Su 15380 (N Africa)
1000-1100	S Su 11830 & W Su 15260 (W Europe), W Su 17780 (N Africa), W Su 17825 (W Europe)

RADIO ROMANIA INTERNATIONAL

0000-0200	S 9525 & S 11960 (E North Am)
0100-0300	W 5910 & W 9640 (E North Am)
0500-0600	W 6055 & W 7220 (S Europe)
1200-1300	S 7155 & S 7165 (W Europe), S 11920 & S 15195 (S Europe)
1300-1400	W 15170 (S Europe)
1300-1500	W 11940 (S Europe)
1400-1500	S 9760 (W Europe), S 11965 (S Europe)
1600-1700	S 7205 & S 9690 (Mideast), W 9700 & W 11870 (S Europe)
1700-1800	W 7335 & W 9595 (Mideast), S 11865 (W Europe)
1700-1900	S 9625 (W Europe)
1800-1900	S 11945 (S Europe)
2000-2100	W 7125 & W 9565 (S Europe)

RUSSIA—Russian

VOICE OF RUSSIA

0100-0200	S *9860* (E North Am)
0100-0300	S 5900/6180 (S America), S 9880/5900 (E North Am), S 15425 (W North Am)
0200-0300	W *6155* (E North Am), W 6195 (S America), W *7350* & S *9515* (E North Am), S 12065 (W North Am)
0200-0400 ⬅	7260 (C America & S America)
0200-0400	W 7150 & W 7240/6250 (E North Am), W 12010 & W 12030 (W North Am)
0300-0400 ⬅	7330 (S America)
1200-1300	S 9640 (E Asia)
1200-1400	S 7165 (E Asia & SE Asia), S 9745 (S Asia), S 12030 (SE Asia & Australasia)
1200-1500	S 9555 (C Asia & S Asia), S 9875 (C Asia)

1300-1400	W 12025 (S Asia), S 15540 (Mideast), S 15660 (SE Asia)
1300-1500	W 6170 (E Asia), W 7260 (E Asia & SE Asia), W 9800 (SE Asia & Australasia), W *9885* (S Asia), W 11630/15460 (S Asia & SE Asia)
1300-1600	W 7135 (C Asia)
1300-1700	W 6185 (C Asia)
1400-1500	W 5940 (E Asia), W 5945 (W Asia & C Asia), W 7110 (S Asia), W 12055 (S Asia & SE Asia), S 13855 & S *15430* (Mideast)
1400-1700	S 11830 (Mideast)
1400-1800	S 9800 (C Asia)
1400-1900	S 9480/7285 (Europe)
1500-1600	W *9555* (Mideast), S 12055 (W Asia & S Asia), S 13650/7130 (Mideast & W Asia), S *13755* (Mideast)
1500-1700	W 6045 (Europe), S 9865 (C Asia)
1500-1900	W 5995 (C Asia)
1500-2200	W 7285 (Mideast & W Asia)
1600-1700	W 6005 (Mideast), W 7110 & W *9885* (S Asia)
1700-1800	S 11630/9480 (N Europe), S 13855 & S 15540 (Mideast)
1700-2100	S 12055/7165 (Mideast & W Asia)
1800-1900	W 5985 (Mideast), W 7290 (N Europe)
1900-2000	S 11630/9480 (N Europe)
1900-2100	W 5940 (Europe)
2000-2100	W 7230 (Europe & N Africa), W 7290 (N Europe), S 9795 (Europe)

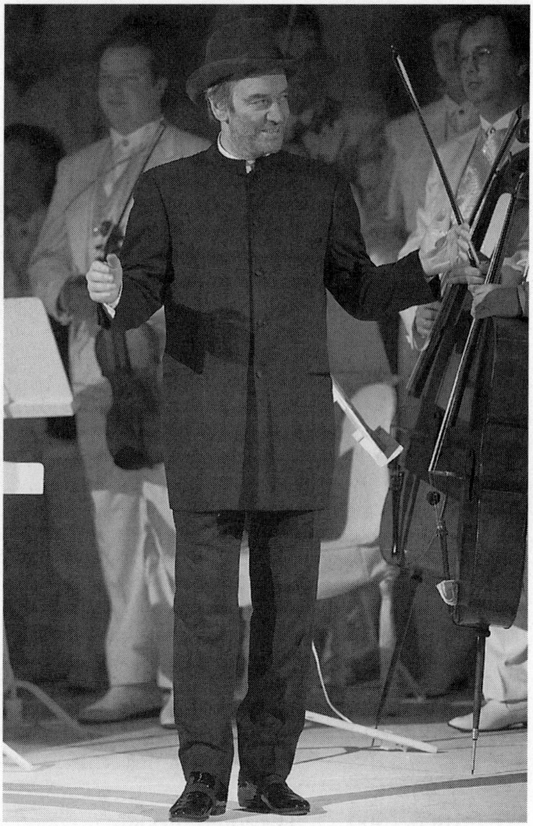

Russian conductor and musician Valery Gergiev is among the outstanding performers featured on the Voice of Russia. Shutterstock/Sergey Petrov

SAUDI ARABIA—Arabic

BROADCASTING SERVICE OF THE KINGDOM

0300-0600	9580 (Mideast & E Africa), 15170 (E Europe & W Asia)
0300-0800	17895 (C Asia & E Asia)
0300-0900	9675 (Mideast)
0600-0900	15380 (Mideast), 17730 (N Africa), 17740 (W Europe)
0600-1700	11855 (Mideast & E Africa)
0900-1200	11935 (Mideast), 17615 (S Asia & SE Asia), 17805 (N Africa), 21495 (E Asia & SE Asia), 21705 (W Europe)
0900-1600	9675 (Mideast)
1200-1400	15380 (Mideast), 21600 (SE Asia)
1200-1500	17895 & 21505 (N Africa), 21640 (W Europe)
1300-1600	21460 (E Africa)
1500-1800	13710 & 15225 (N Africa), 15435 (W Europe)
1600-1800	15205 (W Europe), 17560 (C Africa & W Africa)
1700-2200	9580 (Mideast & E Africa)
1800-2300	9555 (N Africa), 9870 (W Europe), 11715 (C Africa & W Africa), 11820 (W Europe), 11915 (N Africa)

World band can be enjoyed virtually anywhere. Lifelong DXer Lars Rydén plies his interest from this ca. 1912 apartment in Sweden.

L. Rydén

SERBIA—Serbian

INTERNATIONAL RADIO SERBIA

0000-0030	[S] Su *6190* (N America)
0030-0100	[W] *7115* (N America)
0100-0130	[W] Su *7115* (N America)
1000-1300	[S] 7200 (Europe)
1100-1400	[W] 7240 (Europe)
1330-1400	[S] 7200 (Europe)
1430-1500	[W] 7240 (Europe)
1930-2000	[S] 7200 (Europe)
2000-2030	[S] Sa 7200 (Europe)
2030-2100 ⇦	*6100* (W Europe)
2030-2100	[W] 7240 (Europe)
2100-2130 ⇦	Sa *6100* (W Europe)
2100-2130	[W] Sa 7240 (Europe)
2330-2400	[S] *6190* (N America)

SLOVAKIA—Slovak

RADIO SLOVAKIA INTERNATIONAL

0130-0200	[S] 5930 & [W] 7230 (N America), 9440 (S America)
0730-0800	[S] 9440, [S] 11650, [W] 13715 & [W] 15460 (Australasia)
1530-1600	[S] 5920 (W Europe)
1630-1700 ⇦	6055 (W Europe)
1630-1700	[W] 5915 (W Europe)
1900-1930	[S] 5920 & [S] 6055 (W Europe)
2000-2030	[W] 5915 & [W] 7345 (W Europe)

SWEDEN—Swedish

RADIO SWEDEN

0000-0030	*9490* (S America)
0030-0100	[W] *6100* (E North Am & C America)
0200-0230 ⇦	*6010* (E North Am)
0200-0230	*11550* (S Asia)
0300-0330 ⇦	*6010* (W North Am)
0300-0330	[S] *9490* (S America)
0400-0600	[S] M-F 6065 (Europe & N Africa)
0500-0600 ⇦	M-F 9490 (Mideast & E Africa)
0600-0700	[S] M-Sa 9490 (Europe & N Africa)
0600-0800	[W] M-F 6065 (Europe & N Africa)
0700-0800	[S] Sa/Su 9490 (Europe & N Africa)
0800-0900	[S] Su 9490 (Europe & N Africa)
1200-1215	[W] 7420 & [S] M-F 15735 (E Asia)
1215-1230	[W] Sa/Su 7420 (E Asia), [W] M-F 11550 (E Asia & Australasia), [S] 15735 (E Asia)
1300-1315	[W] 11675 (SE Asia & Australasia), [S] 15735 (SE Asia)

1315-1330	[W] M-F 7420 (E Asia), [W] Sa/Su 11675 (SE Asia & Australasia), [S] M-F 15735 (E Asia), [S] Sa/Su 15735 (SE Asia)
1400-1430	[W] 9400 (SE Asia), [W] 11540 (W Asia & S Asia), [S] 13820 (S Asia), [S] 15735 (E Asia)
1500-1530	[W] 9360 & [S] 11595 (Mideast)
1600-1630	[S] 7480 (E Europe & W Asia)
1645-1700 ←	6065 (Europe)
1645-1700	[W] 5865 (W Europe)
1700-1715 ←	M-Sa 6065 (Europe)
1700-1715	[W] M-Sa 5865 (W Europe)
1700-1730	[W] 7465 (Mideast), [W] 7475 (E Europe & W Asia), [S] 11555 (Mideast)
1800-1830 ←	6065 (Europe)
1800-1830	[W] 5865 (W Europe & N Africa), [S] 13710 (W Africa)
1900-1930 ←	6065 (Europe & N Africa)
1900-1930	[W] 5865 (W Europe & N Africa), [W] 7465 (W Europe & W Africa)
2000-2030 ←	6065 (Europe & N Africa)
2000-2030	[W] 5850 (W Europe & N Africa), [S] *7395* & [W] *9895* (E Africa)
2100-2130	[W] *7395* (C Africa)
2100-2230 ←	6065 (Europe & N Africa)

THAILAND—Thai

RADIO THAILAND

0100-0200	[W] 12095 & [S] 12120 (E North Am)
0230-0330	15275 (W North Am)
1000-1100	[W] 6185 & [S] 11870 (SE Asia)
1330-1400	[W] 7365 & [S] 11625 (E Asia)
1800-1900	[S] 9680 & [W] 11855 (Mideast)
2045-2115	[W] 9535 & [S] 9680 (Europe)

TUNISIA—Arabic

RTV TUNISIENNE

0200-0500 ←	9720 & 12005 (N Africa & Mideast)
0400-0630 ←	7275 (W Europe)
0400-0800 ←	7190 (N Africa)
1600-1900 ←	12005 (N Africa & Mideast)
1600-2100 ←	9720 (N Africa & Mideast)
1700-2110 ←	7225 (W Europe)
1700-2310 ←	7190 (N Africa)

TURKEY—Turkish

VOICE OF TURKEY

0100-0300	[S] 7260 (W Asia & C Asia)
0200-0400	[W] 7180 (C Asia)
0400-0700	[S] 6040 (Mideast), [S] 11980 (W Europe)
0500-0800	[W] 9700 (W Europe), [W] 9820 (Mideast)
0700-0900	[S] 11750 (Mideast)
0700-1300	[S] 13635 (Europe)
0800-1000	[W] 11925 (W Asia)
0800-1400 ←	11955 (Mideast)
0800-1400	[W] 15350 (W Europe)
0900-1300	[S] 15390 (Australasia)
1000-1400	[W] 15475 (Australasia)
1300-1530	[S] 11680 (W Europe)
1400-1630	[W] 5980 (W Europe)
1530-2100	[S] 5960 (Mideast), [S] 6120 (W Asia), [S] 9460 (Europe)
1630-2000	[W] 7190 (Australasia)
1630-2200	[W] 5980 (W Europe & E North Am), [W] 6120 (Mideast), [W] 6165 (W Asia)

VIETNAM—Vietnamese

VOICE OF VIETNAM

0000-0100	7285 (SE Asia)
0130-0230	*6175* (E North Am & C America)
0430-0530	*6175* (N America & C America)
1500-1600	7220 & 9550 (Mideast)
1700-1800	7280 & 9730 (Europe)
1730-1830	[S] *9725* (W Europe)
1830-1930	[W] *5955* (W Europe)
2030-2130	[W] *7370* & [S] *11840* (S Europe)

YEMEN—Arabic

REPUBLIC OF YEMEN RADIO—(Mideast)

0300-0650	9780
0300-1500	5950 & 6135
1700-1800 & 1900-2208	9780

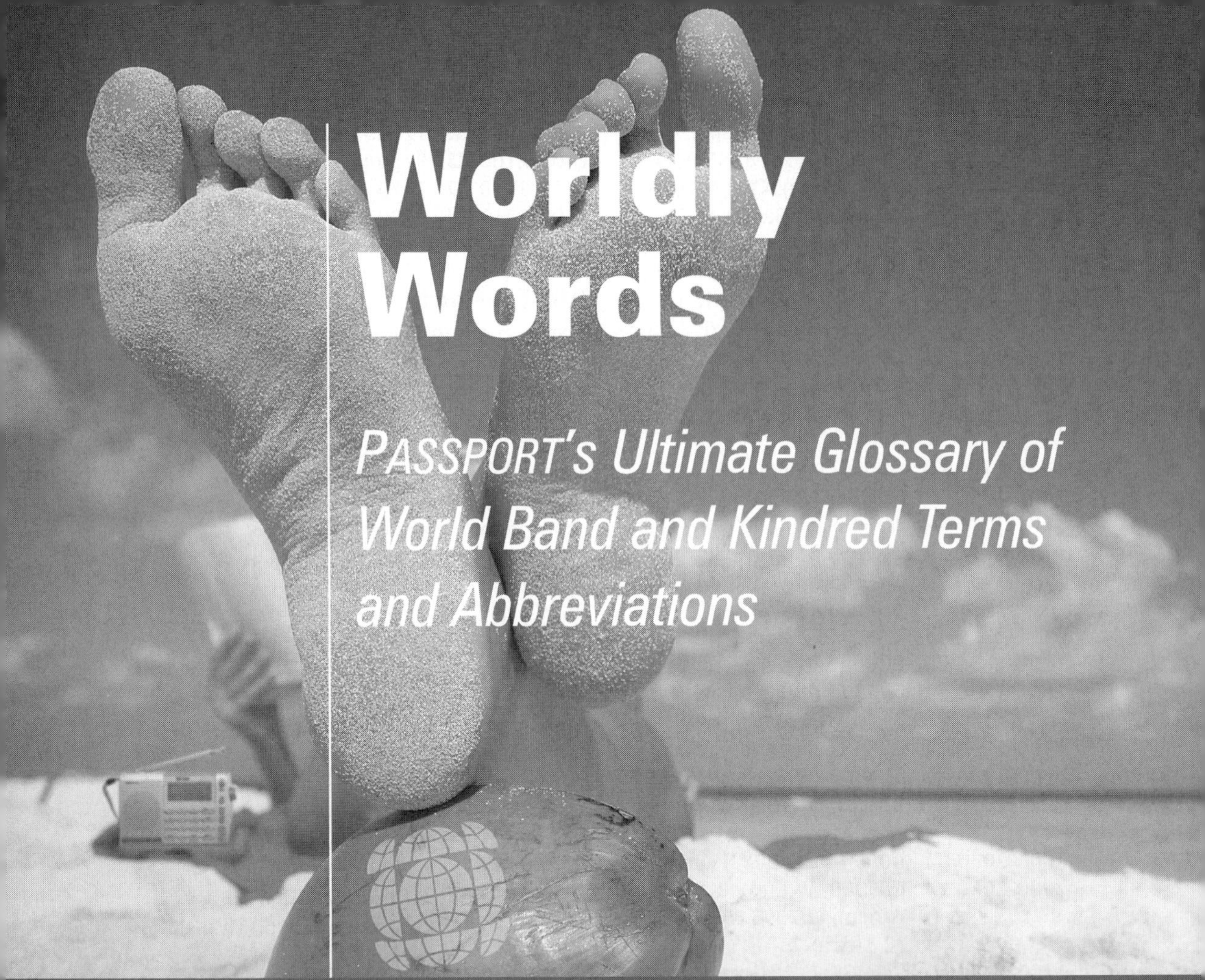

Worldly Words

Passport's Ultimate Glossary of World Band and Kindred Terms and Abbreviations

A variety of terms and abbreviations are used in world band parlance. Many are specialized and benefit from explanation; some are foreign words that need translation; while others are simply adaptations of everyday usage.

Here, then, is PASSPORT's A–Z guide to world band words and what they mean to your listening. For a thorough understanding of the specialized terms and lab tests used in evaluating world band radios, read the Radio Database International White Paper, *How to Interpret Receiver Lab Tests and Measurements*.

A

A. Summer schedule season for world band stations, typically valid from the last Sunday in March until the last Sunday in October. *See* S. *See* HFCC. *Cf.* B, W.
Absorption. Reduction in signal strength during bounces (refraction) off the earth's ionosphere (*see* Propagation) or the earth itself.
AC. Alternating ("household" or "mains") Current, 120V throughout North America, 100V in Japan and usually 220–240V elsewhere in the world.
AC Adaptor. Commonplace outboard device—"wall wart" or "pig in the anaconda"—that converts utility/mains current (*see* AC) to DC suitable for a given electronic or electrical device, such as a portable radio. AC input can be single-voltage, dual-voltage or automatic universal voltage; DC output needs to be of the correct voltage, center-tip polarity and minimum amperage to power the desired radio or other device. Finally, AC adaptors convert AC to DC using either a transformer or switching circuitry, but switching tends to cause RFI that can bother radio reception. Better AC adaptors 1) don't cause audible hum or buzzing in the companion radio, 2) tend to be regulated, and 3) are UL and/or CE approved for fire and other safety.
Active Antenna. An antenna that electronically amplifies signals. Active, or amplified, antennas are typically mounted indoors, but some weatherproofed models can also be erected outdoors. Active antennas take up relatively little space, but their amplification circuits may introduce certain problems that can result in unwanted sounds being heard (*see* Dynamic Range). *Cf.* Passive Antenna. *See* Feedline.
Adjacent-Channel Interference. *See* Interference.
Adjacent-Channel Rejection. *See* Selectivity.
AGC. *See* Automatic Gain Control.
AGC Threshold. The threshold at which the automatic gain control (AGC, *see*) chooses to act relates to both listening pleasure and audible sensitivity. If the threshold is too low, the AGC will tend to act on internal receiver noise and minor static, desensitizing the receiver. However, if the threshold is too high, variations in loudness will be uncomfortable to the ear, forcing the listener to manually twiddle with the volume control to do, in effect, what the AGC should be doing automatically. Measured in µV (microvolts).
Alt. Freq. Alternative frequency or channel. Frequency or channel which may be used in place of that which is regularly scheduled.
Amateur Radio. *See* Hams.
AM Band. The 520–1705 kHz radio broadcast band that lies within the 0.3–3.0 MHz (300–3,000 kHz) mediumwave (MW) or Medium Frequency (MF) portion of the radio spectrum. Outside North America it is usually called the mediumwave (MW) band. However, in parts of Latin America it is sometimes called, by the general public and a few stations, *onda larga*—longwave band *(see)*—strictly speaking, a misnomer. In the United States, travelers information stations (TIS) and other public information services are sometimes also found on 1710 kHz, making 1715 kHz the *de facto* upper limit of the American AM band. *See* X-Band.
AM Equivalent (AME). *See* Single Sideband (third paragraph).
AM Mode. *See* Mode.
Amplified Antenna. *See* Active Antenna.
Analog Frequency Readout. This type of received-frequency indication is used on radios having needle-and-dial or "slide-rule" tuning. This is much less accurate and handy than digital frequency readout. *See* Synthesizer. *Cf.* Digital Frequency Display.
Antenna. *See* Active Antenna, Feedline, Passive Antenna.
Antennae. The accepted spelling for feelers protruding from insects. In electronics, the preferred plural for "antenna" is "antennas."
Antenna Polarization. *See* Polarization.
Arrestor. *See* MOV.
ATS. Automatic Tuning System; also, Auto Tuning Scan. Allows a receiver, while scanning up or down frequencies, to enter active frequencies into presets automatically, like when setting up a VCR or DVD recorder.
Attenuator. A circuit, typically switched with one or more levels, to desensitize a receiver by reducing the strength of incoming signals. *See* RF Gain.
Audio Quality. At Passport, audio quality refers to what in computer testing is called "benchmark" quality. This means, primarily, freedom from distortion of a signal fed through a receiver's entire circuitry—*not* just the audio stage—from the antenna input through to the speaker terminals. A lesser characteristic of audio quality is the audio bandwidth needed for pleasant world band reception of music. Finally, with digitally synthesized receivers audio quality can be degraded by harshness. Also, *see* Enhanced Fidelity.
Automatic Gain Control (AGC). Smooths out fluctuations in signal strength brought about by fading *(see)*, a regular occurrence with world band signals, so a receiver's audio level tends to stay relatively constant. This is accomplished by AGC attack, then AGC hang, and finally AGC decay. Each of these three actions involved in smoothing a fade has a micro-time preset at the factory for optimum performance. Top-end receivers often provide for user control of at least the decay timing—a few rarified models also allow for user control over one or both of the other two actions. *See* AGC Threshold.
Auto Tuning Scan. *See* ATS.
Automatic Tuning System. *See* ATS.
AV. A Voz—Portuguese for "The Voice." In Passport, this term is also used to represent "The Voice of."

B

B. Winter schedule season for world band stations, typically valid from the last Sunday in October until the last Sunday in March. *See* W. *See* HFCC. *Cf.* A, S.
Balun. BALanced-to-UNbalanced device to match the two. Typically, a balun is placed between an unbalanced antenna feedline and a balanced antenna input, or *vice versa*.
Bands, Shortwave Broadcasting. *See* World Band Segments.
Bandwidth. A key variable that determines selectivity *(see)*, bandwidth is the amount of radio signal, at –6 dB (–3 dB with *i.a.* professional gear), a radio's circuitry will let pass, and thus be heard. With world band channel spacing standardized at 5 kHz, the best single bandwidths are usually in the vicinity of 3 to 6 kHz. Better radios offer two or more selectable bandwidths: at least one of 5 to 9 kHz or so for when a station is in the clear, and one or more others between 2 to 6 kHz for when a station is hemmed in by other signals next to it; with synchronous selectable sideband (*see* Synchronous Detector), these bandwidths can safely be at the upper ends of these ranges to provide enhanced fidelity. Proper selectivity is a key determinant of the aural quality of what you hear.

Radio France Internationale's rotatable *curtain antenna* is among the most versatile and effective available. George Woodard

Most receivers use discrete filters to create bandwidths, but some newer models incorporate dozens of software-defined bandwidths.

Bandscanning. Hunting around for stations by continuously tuning up and/or down a given world band segment *(see)*, such as in concert with PASSPORT's Blue Pages.

Baud. Measurement of the speed by which radioteletype *(see)*, radiofax *(see)* and other digital data are transmitted. Baud is properly written entirely in lower case, and thus is abbreviated as b (baud), kb (kilobaud) or Mb (Megabaud). Baud rate standards are usually set by the international CCITT regulatory body.

BC. Broadcaster, Broadcasters, Broadcasting, Broadcasting Company, Broadcasting Corporation.

BCB (Broadcast Band). *See* AM Band.

Beverage Antenna. *See* Longwire Antenna.

BFO (beat-frequency oscillator). Carrier generated within a receiver. *Inter alia*, this replaces a received signal's full or vestigial transmitted carrier when a receiver is in the single-sideband mode *(see)* or synchronous selectable sideband mode *(see)*.

Birdie. A silent spurious signal, similar to a station's open carrier, created by circuit interaction within a receiver. The fewer and weaker the birdies within a receiver's tuning range, the better, although in reality birdies rarely degrade reception.

Blocking. The ability of a receiver to avoid being desensitized by powerful adjacent signals or signals from other nearby frequencies. Measured in dB (decibels) at 100 kHz signal spacing.

BNC (British Naval Connector, Bayonet Nut Connector, Bayonet Neill Concelman). Reliable-performance, quick-connect/disconnect coaxial cable connector as defined by the IEC 169-8 standard. One of the three most common low-impedance (around 75 ohm) coax fittings used *i.a.* to connect world band and kindred outboard antenna lead-ins *(see)* to a receiver (typically tabletop or professional).

Boat Anchor. Radio slang for a classic or vintage tube-type communications receiver. These large, heavy biceps builders—Jackie Gleason called them "real radios"—were manufactured mainly from before World War II through the mid-1970s, although a few continued to be available up to a decade later. The definitive reference for collectors of elder receivers is *Shortwave Receivers Past & Present* by Universal Radio.

BPL. Broadband over Power Lines. Emerging technology to allow Internet and other digital communication via AC (mains) power grids. Thus far it has seen only limited use, offering throughput faster than that of dial-up but slower than that of broadband. A major side effect is noise *(see)* radiation, which seriously disrupts traditional and DRM *(see)* world band radio reception. From the perspective of enhanced government oversight this is a positive tradeoff, as it blots out relatively unfettered world band information and replaces it with controllable Internet links. Nevertheless, to date BPL tests have met with, at best, underwhelming success.

Broadcast. A radio or television transmission meant for the general public. *Cf.* Utility Stations, Hams.

BS. Broadcasting Station, Broadcasting Service.

Buzz. Noise typically generated by digital electronic circuitry. *See* Noise.

C

Can. Metal container for reel of tape or film. It continues to be used today in the expression, "It's in the can," meaning that a shooting, recording, manuscript or other task has been completed. *See* Cans.

Cans. Vintage slang for "headphones."

Carrier. *See* Mode.

Cd. Ciudad—Spanish for "City."

Cellular Telephone Bands. In the United States, the cellular telephone bands are 824–849 and 869–894 MHz. Years ago, when analog cell transmissions were the norm, a powerful senator was overheard engaged in an awkward conversation. Shortly thereafter, receivers which could tune cellular frequencies were made illegal in the United States. As a practical matter, eavesdropping on these bands yields nothing intelligible because of the encrypted nature of digital cellular transmissions that by now have replaced analog. Receivers tuning these "forbidden" ranges are readily acquired in Canada and nearly every other part of the world except North Korea and the United States.

Channel. An everyday term to indicate where a station is supposed to be located on the dial. World band channels are standardized at 5 kHz spacing. Stations operating outside this norm are "off-channel" (for these, PASSPORT provides resolution to better than 1 kHz to aid in station identification).

CINCH/AV. *See* RCA.

Chuffing, Chugging. The sound made by some synthesized tuning systems when the tuning knob is turned. Called "chugging" or "chuffing," as it is suggestive of the rhythmic "chuff, chuff" sound of steam locomotives or "chugalug" gulping of beverages.

Cl. Club, Clube.

Co-Channel Interference. *See* Interference.

CODEC (Compression, Decompression). A given proprietary or industry standard—there are many—that takes a native file or signal and converts (compresses) it into a smaller file or narrower signal without undue loss of quality.

Conversion. *See* IF.

Coordinated Universal Time. *See* UTC, World Time.

Cult. Cultura, Cultural.

Curtain Antennas. Often used for long-distance world band transmitting, these consist of horizontal dipole arrays interconnected and typically strung between a pair of masts or towers that are usually fixed, but which sometimes can be rotated. Curtains produce excellent forward gain, reasonable directivity and a low takeoff angle that is desirable for successful long-distance broadcasts. *See* Polarization.

CW. Continuous wave, or telegraph-type ("Morse code," etc.) communication by telegraph key that opens and closes an unmodulated signal to create variations of long and short bursts that on a radio with a BFO *(see)* sound like dih-dah "beeps." Used mainly by hams *(see)*, occasionally by utility stations *(see)*.

D

DAB. Digital audio broadcasting, typically referring to a digital system, not compatible with analog receivers, used for domestic broadcasting in Europe and various other parts of the world. *Cf.* Digital Radio Mondiale, HD Radio.
dBm. Logarithmic unit of power in decibels above the reference level of 1 milliwatt. An increase of 10 dBm represents a tenfold increase in power.
dB. *see* Decibel.
dBm. Logarithmic unit of power in decibels (dB) above the reference level of one milliwatt (mW). An increase of 10 dBm represents a tenfold increase in power.
DC. Direct current, such as emanates from batteries. *Cf.* AC.
DC-to-Daylight. Hyperbolic slang for an exceptionally wide frequency tuning range. For example, some wideband receivers will tune from under 10 kHz to over 3 GHz *(see)*. However, in the United States it is illegal to sell new radios to the public that tune the cellular telephone bands *(see)*.
Decibel (dB). Logarithmic measurement of the ratio between two quantities; *e.g.,* signal-to-noise ratio.
Default. The setting at which a control of a digitally operated electronic device, including many world band radios, normally operates, and to which it will eventually return (e.g., when the radio is next switched on).
Digital Frequency Display, Digital Frequency Readout. Indicates that a receiver displays the tuned frequency digitally, usually in kilohertz *(see)*. Because this is so much handier than an analog (slide rule) frequency readout, all models included in Passport Reports have digital frequency readout. Most models with digital frequency display are synthesizer *(see)* tuned, which allows for handy tuning aids, but some low-cost models are analog tuned with digital frequency counters.
Digital Radio Mondiale (DRM). International organization (www.drm.org) seeking to convert world band and other transmissions from traditional analog mode to DRM digital mode. DRM is now in limited regular use for international broadcasts, plus domestic-service tests are being considered within the shortwave spectrum. DRM transmissions cannot be received on traditional analog receivers. Also, DRM transmissions—unlike the conventional analog variety—are easily jammed and disrupted by interference. *See* Mode, Interference. *Cf.* DAB, HD Radio.
Digital Signal Processing (DSP). Where digital circuitry and software are used to perform radio circuit functions traditionally done using analog circuits. Used on certain world band receivers; also, available as an add-on accessory for audio processing only. *See* Software Defined Radio.
Dipole. Center fed, usually passive *(see)*, antenna with two or more lengths of wire or other metal on either side of the feeder wire or cable. A simple dipole is half a wavelength, with limited effectiveness beyond a relatively narrow slice of frequencies as defined by doubling its half-wavelength. However, dipoles equipped with traps have a much broader range of covered frequencies. *See* Trap Dipole Antenna.
Distortion. *See* Overall Distortion.
Domestic Service. *See* DS.
Double Conversion a/k/a **Dual Conversion.** *See* IF.
DRM. *See* Digital Radio Mondiale.
DS. Domestic Service—Broadcasting intended primarily for audiences in the broadcaster's home country. However, some domestic programs are beamed on world band to expatriates and other kinfolk abroad, as well as to interested foreigners. *Cf.* ES.
DSP. *See* Digital Signal Processing.
Dual Conversion a/k/a/ **Double Conversion.** *See* IF.
DX, DXers, DXing. From an old telegraph abbreviation for distance (D) unknown (X); thus, to DX is to communicate over a great distance. DXers are those who specialize in finding distant or exotic stations that are considered to be rare catches. Few world band listeners are considered to be regular DXers, but many others seek out DX stations every now and then—usually by bandscanning, which is facilitated by Passport's Blue Pages.
DXpedition. Typically, a gathering of DXers who camp out in a remote location favorable to catching the toughest of stations. These DX bases are usually far away from electrically noisy AC power and cable TV lines.
Dynamic Range. The ability of, *i.a.*, a receiver or active antenna *(see)* to handle weak signals in the presence of strong competing signals within or near the same world band segment (*see* World Band Spectrum). Devices with inferior dynamic range sometimes "overload," especially with external antennas, causing a mishmash of false signals up and down—and even beyond—the segment being received. Dynamic range is closely related to the third-order intercept point, or IP3. Where possible, Passport measures dynamic range and IP3 at the traditional 20 kHz and more challenging 5 kHz signal-separation, or signal spacing, points.

E

Earliest Heard (or Latest Heard). See key at the bottom of each Blue Page. If the Passport monitoring team cannot establish the definite sign-on (or sign-off) time of a station, the earliest (or latest) time that the station could be traced is indicated by a left-facing or right-facing "arrowhead flag." This means that the station almost certainly operates beyond the time shown by that "flag." It also means that, unless you live relatively close to the station, you're unlikely to be able to hear it beyond that "flagged" time.
ECSS (Exalted-Carrier Selectable Sideband). Manual tuning of a conventional AM-mode signal, using a receiver's single-sideband circuitry to zero-beat *(see)* the receiver's BFO with the transmitted signal's carrier. The better-sounding of the signal's sidebands is then selected by the listener. As ECSS is manual, there is a degree, however slight, of phase mismatch between the fade-prone transmitted carrier and the stable synthetic replacement carrier generated within the receiver. *Cf.* Synchronous Selectable Sideband, Synchronous Detector.
Ed, Educ. Educational, Educação, Educadora.
Electrical Noise. *See* Noise.
Elevation Panel, Elevation Rod. Plastic panel or metal rod which flips out from a radio's back or bottom panel to place the radio at a comfortable operating angle. Also known as tilt panel and tilt rod.
Elevation Tab. Plastic tab, typically affixed to a portable radio's carrying strap, which when inserted into the radio's back panel places the radio at a comfortable operating angle.
Em. Emissora, Emisora, Emissor, Emetteur—in effect, "station" in various languages.

Enhanced Fidelity. Radios with good audio performance and certain types of high-tech circuitry that can improve the fidelity of world band signals. Among newer fidelity-enhancing techniques is synchronous detection (*see* Synchronous Detector), especially when coupled with selectable sideband (*see* Synchronous Selectable Sideband). Another technological means to improve fidelity is digital world band transmission (*see* Digital Radio Mondiale).
EP. Emissor Provincial—Portuguese for "Provincial Station."
ER. Emissor Regional—Portuguese for "Regional Station."
Ergonomics. How user-friendly and comfortable—intuitive—a set is to operate, especially hour after hour.
ES. External Service—Broadcasting intended primarily for audiences abroad. *Cf.* DS.
Exalted-Carrier Selectable Sideband. *See* ECSS.
External Service. *See* ES.

F

F. Friday.
Fading. Signals which scatter off the ionosphere (*see* Propagation) are subject to some degree of phase mismatch as the scattered bits of signal arrive at a receiver at minutely varying times. This causes fading, where signal strength varies anywhere from a few times per minute to many times per second, the latter being known as "flutter fading" and often caused by disruption of the earth's geomagnetic field (*see* Great Circle Path). "Selective fading" is a special type that is audible on shortwave and mediumwave AM when a fade momentarily sweeps across a signal's three components (lower sideband, carrier, upper sideband), selectively attenuating the carrier more than the sidebands; with the carrier thus attenuated, the result is "selective-fading distortion." *See* Automatic Gain Control, Propagation, Synchronous Detection, Synchronous Selectable Sideband.
Fax. *See* Radiofax.
Feeder, Shortwave. A utility *(see)* shortwave transmission from the broadcaster's home country to a shortwave or other relay site or local placement facility *(see)* some distance away. Although these specialized transmissions carry world band programs, they are not intended to be received by the general public. Many world band radios can process these quasi-broadcasts anyway. Shortwave feeders operate in lower sideband (LSB), upper sideband (USB) or independent sideband (termed ISL if heard on the lower side, ISU if heard on the upper side) modes. Feeders are now exclusively via satellites and Internet audio, but a few stations keep shortwave feeders in reserve should their satellite/Internet feeders fail. *See* Single Sideband, Utility Stations, NBFM.
Feedline. The wire or cable that runs between an antenna's receiving element(s) and a receiver. For sophisticated antennas, twin-lead ribbon feedlines are unusually efficient, and can reject much nearby electrical noise via phasing. However, coaxial cable feedlines are generally superior in high-local-electrical-noise environments. *See* Balun.
First IF Rejection. A relatively uncommon source of false signals occurs when powerful transmitters operate on the same frequency as a receiver's first intermediate frequency (IF). The ability of receiving circuitry to avoid such transmitters' causing reception problems is called "IF rejection."
Flutter Fading. *See* Fading.
FM. The FM broadcast band is now standardized at 87.5–108 MHz worldwide except in Japan (76–90 MHz) and parts of Eastern Europe (66–74 MHz). Also, for communications there is a special narrow-FM mode (*see* NBFM).
Frequency. The standard term to indicate where a station is located within the radio spectrum—regardless of whether it is "on-channel" or "off-channel" (*see* Channel). Below 30 MHz this is customarily expressed in kilohertz (kHz, *see*), but some receivers display in Megahertz (MHz, *see*) and require that a decimal be entered when keypads are used. The two measurements differ only in the placement of a decimal; e.g., 5970 kHz is the same as 5.97 MHz. Either is equally valid, but to minimize confusion PASSPORT and most stations designate frequencies only in kHz. *Cf.* Meters.
Frequency Synthesizer. *See* Synthesizer, Frequency.
Front-End Selectivity. The ability of the initial stage of receiving circuitry to admit only limited frequency ranges into succeeding stages of circuitry. Good front-end selectivity keeps signals from other, powerful bands or segments from being superimposed upon the frequency range you're tuning. For example, a receiver with good front-end selectivity will receive only shortwave signals at full strength within the range 3200–3400 kHz. However, a receiver with mediocre front-end selectivity might allow powerful local mediumwave AM stations from 520–1700 kHz to be heard "ghosting in" between 3200 and 3400 kHz, along with the desired shortwave signals. Obviously, mediumwave AM signals don't belong on shortwave. Receivers with inadequate front-end selectivity can benefit from the addition of a preselector *(see)* or a high-pass filter *(see)*.

G

GHz. Gigahertz, equivalent to 1,000 MHz *(see)*.
GMT. Greenwich Mean Time. *See* World Time.
Great Circle Path. The shortest route a signal takes to arrive at a receiving location, following the circumference of the earth. Normal printed maps are too distorted for this purpose, but an ideal solution is to take a globe and run a string from a station's transmitter site (*see* PASSPORT's Blue Pages) to your location. Among other things, the closer a signal's path is to the geomagnetic North Pole, the greater the chance of its being disrupted by flutter fading (*see* Fading) during geomagnetic propagational disturbances (*see* Propagation). An Internet search can turn up several software programs, such as gc.kls2.com, to generate great circle maps centered at your location, but for most a globe and string are more visually intuitive.
GUI. Graphical user interface for operating PCs and related hardware.

H

Hams. Government-licensed amateur radio hobbyists who *transmit* to each other by radio, often by voice using single sideband *(see)*, within special amateur bands. Many of these bands are within the shortwave spectrum *(see)*. This spectrum is also used by world band radio, but world band radio and ham radio, which laymen sometimes confuse with each other, are two very separate entities. The easiest way is to think of hams is as making something like phone calls, whereas world band stations are like long-distance versions of ordinary mediumwave AM stations.
Harmonic, Harmonic Radiation, Harmonic Signal. Usually, an unwanted weak spurious repeat of a signal in multiple(s) of the fundamental, or "real," frequency.

Thus, the third harmonic of a mediumwave AM station on 1120 kHz might be heard faintly on 4480 kHz within the world band spectrum. Stations almost always try to minimize harmonic radiation, as it wastes energy and spectrum space. However, in the past there were rare cases where stations amplified a harmonic signal so they could operate inexpensively on a second frequency. Also, *see* Subharmonic.

Hash. Electrical buzzing noise. *See* Noise.

HD Radio. Digital broadcasting system that is receivable with limited fidelity on traditional analog radios, and with full fidelity on HD receivers. Used primarily on AM/FM in the United States. *Cf.* DAB, Digital Radio Mondiale.

Hertz. *See* Hz.

Heterodyne. A whistle equal in pitch to the separation between two carriers. Thus, two world band stations 5 kHz apart will generate a 5000 Hz whistle unless receiver circuitry (e.g., *see* Notch Filter) keeps this from being audible.

High Fidelity. *See* Enhanced Fidelity.

High-Pass Filter. A filter which lets frequencies pass unattenuated only if they are above a designated frequency. For world band receivers and antennas, 2 MHz or thereabouts is the norm for high-pass filters, as this keeps out mediumwave AM and longwave signals.

HF (High Frequency). Shortwave. *See* Shortwave Spectrum.

HFCC (High Frequency Co-ordination Conference). Founded in 1990 and headquartered in Prague, the HFCC (www.hfcc.org) helps coordinate frequency usage by dozens of broadcasting organizations from numerous countries. These represent a solid majority of the global output for international shortwave broadcasting. Coordination meetings take place twice yearly: once for the "A" (summer) schedule season from the last Sunday in March until the last Sunday in October, another for "B" (winter), and these gatherings have been a great help in preventing frequency conflicts.

Hz. Hertz, a unit of frequency measurement formerly known as cycles per second (c/s). A thousand Hertz is equivalent to 1 kHz *(see)*. Also, *see* Frequency, Meters, MHz.

I

IBS. International Broadcasting Services, Ltd., publishers of *i.a.* PASSPORT TO WORLD BAND RADIO.

IF (Intermediate Frequency). Virtually all world band receivers use the "superheterodyne" principle, where tuned radio frequencies are converted to an intermediate frequency (IF) to facilitate reception, then amplified and detected to produce audio. In nearly all world band portables and many tabletop models, this IF is either 455 kHz or 450 kHz. If this is not complemented by an additional and higher intermediate frequency (making it double conversion a/k/a dual conversion), it is called single conversion. The "images" resulting from single conversion readily appear at twice the IF; i.e., 910 kHz (2 x 455 kHz) or 900 kHz (2 x 450 kHz) away from the fundamental frequency. *See* Image.

IF Shift. *See* Passband Offset.

Image. A common type of unwanted signal found on low-cost "single conversion" (single IF) radios where a strong signal appears at reduced strength, usually on a frequency 910 kHz or 900 kHz lower down (or higher up, although this type of circuit design is uncommon). For example, on a receiver with a single 455 kHz IF the BBC on 5875 kHz might repeat at lower strength on 4965 kHz, its "image frequency" (5875 kHz minus 2 x 455 kHz). Double-conversion (dual IF) receivers have relatively little problem with images, but the additional IF's circuitry adds to manufacturing cost. *See* IF, Spurious-Signal Rejection.

Impedance. Opposition, expressed in ohms, to the flow of alternating current. Components work best when impedance is comparable from one to another; so, for example, a receiver with a 75-ohm antenna socket will work best with antennas having a similar feedline impedance. Antenna tuning units can resolve this, albeit at the cost of added operational complexity.

Independent Sideband. *See* Single Sideband.

Interference. Sounds from other signals, notably on the same frequency ("co-channel interference"), or on an adjacent or other nearby channel(s) ("adjacent-channel interference"), that disturb the station you are trying to hear; DRM *(see)* signals cause interference over a wider frequency range than do conventional analog signals. Worthy radios reduce interference by having good selectivity *(see)* and synchronous selectable sideband (*see* Synchronous Detector). Nearby television sets and cable television wiring may also generate a special type of radio interference called TVI, a "growl," typically from a television horizontal oscillator, heard every 15 kHz or so. Sometimes referred to as QRM, a term based on Morse-code shorthand.

Intermediate Frequency. *See* IF.

International Reply Coupon (IRC). Sold by selected post offices in various parts of the world, IRCs amount to official international "scrip" that may be exchanged for postage in most countries of the world. Because they amount to an international form of postage repayment, over many decades they have been handy for listeners trying to encourage foreign stations to write back. However, IRCs are very costly for the amount in stamps that is provided in return. Too, an increasing number of countries are not forthcoming about "cashing in" IRCs, which are fast fading from use and now have a finite period when they can be redeemed. Specifics on this and related issues are provided in the Addresses PLUS section of this PASSPORT.

International Telecommunication Union (ITU). The regulatory body, headquartered in Geneva, for all international telecommunications, including world band radio. Sometimes incorrectly referred to as the "International Telecommunications Union." In recent years, the ITU has become increasingly ineffective as a regulatory body for world band radio, with much of its former role having been taken up by the HFCC *(see)*.

Internet Radio. *See* Web radio.

Inverted-L Antenna. *See* Passive Antenna.

Ionosphere. *See* Propagation.

IP3. Third-order intercept point. *See* Dynamic Range.

IRC. *See* International Reply Coupon.

Irr. Irregular operation or hours of operation; i.e., schedule tends to be unpredictable.

ISB. Independent sideband. *See* Single Sideband.

ISL. Independent sideband, lower. *See* Feeder.

ISO. International Organization for Standardization.

ISU. Independent sideband, upper. *See* Feeder.

ITU. *See* International Telecommunication Union.

J

Jack. Counterintuitive, perhaps, but a *female* connector.

Jamming. Deliberate interference to a transmission with the intent of discouraging reception. However, analog shortwave broadcasts, when properly transmitted, are uniquely resistant to jamming. This ability to avoid

The Wellbrook ALA 1530 *loop antenna* produces unusually noise-free reception. J.R. Sherwood

"gatekeeping" is a major reason why world band radio continues to be the workhorse for international news broadcasting. There's less jamming now than during the Cold War, but in China superpower transmitters and rotatable curtain antennas from France are increasingly being used to disrupt world band broadcasts. Jamming also takes place in Cuba and parts of the Middle East and Africa. For details, see the Blue Pages.

Japanese FM. *See* FM.

K

Keypad. On a world band radio, like with a cell phone, a keypad can be used to control many variables. Radio keypads are used primarily to enter a station's frequency for reception, and the best keypads have real keys (not a membrane) in standard telephone format of 3x4 with "zero" under the "8" key. Many keypads are also used for station presets, but this means you have to remember code numbers for stations (e.g., BBC 5975 kHz is "07"); handier radios have separate keys for presets, while some others use displayed "pages" to access presets, which increasingly can be tagged alphanumerically.

kHz. Kilohertz, the most common unit of frequency for measuring where a station is located on the world band dial if it is below 30,000 kHz. Formerly known as "kilocycles per second," or kc/s. 1,000 kilohertz equals one Megahertz. *See* Frequency. *Cf.* MHz, Meters.

kilohertz. *See* kHz. The "k" in "kilo" is not properly capitalized, although the computer modem industry got it wrong years back and most modem and kindred organizations have as yet to correct the error.

kilowatt. *See* kW.

kW. A kilowatt(s), the most common unit of measurement for transmitter power (*see* Power).

L

LCD. Liquid-crystal display. LCDs, if properly designed, are fairly easily seen in bright light, but require illumination under darker conditions. LCDs—still typically gray-on-gray monochrome on world band radios—also tend to have mediocre contrast. Sometimes can be read from only a certain angle, but the plus is that they consume nearly no battery power.

Lead-in. Wire, twinlead or coaxial cable between an antenna's capture element (the "antenna" itself that catches signals from the air) and a receiver.

LED. Light-emitting diode. LEDs have a long life and are very easily read in the dark or in normal room light, but consume more power than LCDs and are hard to read in bright ambient light.

Lightning Arrestor. *See* MOV.

Line Output. Fixed-level audio output typically used to feed a recorder or outboard audio amplifier-speaker system.

Local Placement. *See* Placement facility.

Location. Physical location. In the case of a radio station, the transmitter location, which is cited in PASSPORT's Blue Pages, may be different from that of the studio location. Transmitter location is useful as a guide to reception quality. For example, if you're in eastern North America and wish to listen to the Voice of Russia, a transmitter located in St. Petersburg will almost certainly provide better reception than, say, one located in Siberia.

Longwave (LW) Band. The 148.5–283.5 kHz portion of the low-frequency (LF) radio spectrum used for domestic broadcasting in Europe, the Near East, North Africa, Russia and Mongolia. As a practical matter, these longwave signals, which have nothing to do with world band or other shortwave signals, are not readily audible in other parts of the world.

Longwire Antenna. A passive antenna *(see)* that is at least one wavelength at the lowest desired reception frequency. A variant is the Beverage antenna, preferably one-and-a-half to two wavelengths at the lowest desired reception frequency, mounted not far from the ground and with a terminating resistor at the far end.

Loop Antenna. Round (like a hula hoop) or square-ish antenna often used for reception of longwave, mediumwave AM and even shortwave signals. These can be highly directive below around 2 MHz, and can even show some directivity up to 5 MHz or 6 MHz. For this reason, most such antennas can be rotated and even tilted manually—or by an antenna rotor. "Barefoot" loops tend to have low gain, and thus need electrical amplification in order to reach their potential. When properly mounted, top-caliber amplified loops can produce superior signal-to-noise ratios that help with weak-signal (DX) reception.

☞ Strictly speaking, ferrite-rod antennas, found inside nearly every mediumwave AM radio as well as some specialty outboard antennas, are not loops. However, in everyday parlance these tiny antennas are often referred to as "loops" or "loopsticks."

Low-Pass Filter. A filter which lets frequencies pass unattenuated only if they are below a designated frequency. For world band receivers and antennas, 30 MHz or thereabouts is the norm for low-pass filters, as this keeps out VHF/UHF signals.

LSB. Lower Sideband. *See* Mode, Single Sideband, Feeder.

LV. La Voix, La Voz—French and Spanish for "The Voice." In PASSPORT, this term is also used to represent "The Voice of."

LW. *See* Longwave (LW) Band.

M

M. Monday.

Mains. *See* AC.

Manual Selectable Sideband. *See* ECSS.

Mediumwave Band, Mediumwave AM Band, Mediumwave Spectrum. *See* AM Band.

Megahertz. *See* MHz.
Memory, Memories. *See* Preset.
Meters (Wavelength). An elder unit of measurement used *i.a.* for individual world band segments of the shortwave spectrum. The frequency range covered by a given meters designation—also known as "wavelength"—can be gleaned from the following formula: *frequency (kHz) = 299,792 divided by meters.* Thus, 49 meters comes out to a frequency of 6118 kHz—well within the range of frequencies included in that segment (*see* World Band Spectrum). Inversely, wavelength in meters can be derived from the following: *wavelength (meters) = 299,792 divided by frequency (kHz).*
☞ The figure 299,792 is based on the speed of light (299,792,458 m/s) as agreed upon by the International Committee on Weights and Measurements in 1983. However, in practice this is rounded to 300,000. Thus, in everyday practice the two formulas are: *frequency (kHz) = 300,000 divided by meters; wavelength (meters) = 300,000 divided by frequency (kHz).*
MHz. Megahertz, a common unit of frequency *(see)* to measure where a station is located on the dial, especially above 30 MHz, although in the purest sense all measurements above 3 MHz are supposed to be in MHz. In earlier days of radio this was known as "Megacycles per second," or Mc/s. One Megahertz equals 1,000 kilohertz. *See* Frequency. *Cf.* kHz, Meters.
Mini-Plug (male), Mini-Jack (female). Low-impedance (around 50–75 ohm) 1/8-inch (3 mm) connector, usually for lightweight headphones or earpieces. These may be stereo or mono.
Mode. Method of transmission of radio signals. World band radio broadcasts are almost always in the analog AM (amplitude modulation) mode, the same that's used in the mediumwave AM band *(see)*. The AM mode consists of three components: two "sidebands," plus one "carrier" that resides between the two sidebands. Each sideband contains the same programming as the other, and the carrier carries no programming, so a few stations have experimented with the single-sideband (SSB, *see*) mode. SSB contains only one sideband, either the lower sideband (LSB) or upper sideband (USB), and a reduced carrier. It requires special radio circuitry to be demodulated, or made intelligible, which is the main reason SSB has not been adopted as a world band standard. However, efforts are continuing to implement digital-mode world band transmissions (*see* Digital Radio Mondiale).
☞ There are yet other modes used on shortwave, but not for world band. These include CW (Morse-type code, *see*), radiofax *(see)* and RTTY (radioteletype, *see*) used by utility *(see)* and ham *(see)* stations. A variant FM mode, narrow-band FM (NBFM, *see*), is also used by utility and ham operations; however, it is not for music nor is it within the FM broadcast bands (*see* FM).
Modulation. The sounds—music, voices and so on—contained within a radio signal.
MOV. Often used in power-line and antenna surge arrestors (a/k/a lightning arrestors) to shunt static and line-power surges to ground. MOVs perform well and are inexpensive, but tend to lose effectiveness with use; costlier alternatives are thus sometimes worth considering. On rare occasion they also appear to have been implicated in starting fires, so a UL or other recognized certification is helpful. For both these reasons MOV-based arrestors should be replaced at least once every decade that they are in service. *See* Surge Arrestor.
MW. Mediumwave AM band; *see* AM Band. Also, Megawatt, which equals 1,000 kW; *cf.* kilowatt; *see* Power.

N

N. New, Nueva, Nuevo, Nouvelle, Nacional, National, Nationale.
Nac. Nacional. Spanish and Portuguese for "National."
Narrow-band FM. *See* NBFM, Mode.
Nat, Natl, Nat'l. National, Nationale.
NB. *See* Noise Blanker.
NBFM. Narrow-band FM, used within the shortwave spectrum by some "utility" stations, including (between 25–30 MHz) point-to-point domestic broadcast station remote links. *See* Mode.
NTSC (National Television Standards Committee). Traditional analog TV/video format with 525 lines per frame. This broadcast standard saw long use in United States and various other countries. But as of February 17, 2009, in the United States it is being replaced by digital HDTV. This means that multiband radios which currently include "TV audio" will no longer be able to perform this function and channel 6 audio will no longer be heard at the low end of the FM band. Similar limitations apply to such other legacy standards as PAL and SECAM.
Noise. Static, buzzes, pops and the like caused by the earth's atmosphere (typically lightning), and to a lesser extent by galactic noise. Also, electrical noise emanating from such man-made sources as electric blankets, fish-tank heaters, heating pads, electrical and gasoline motors, light dimmers, flickering light bulbs, non-incandescent lights, computers and computer peripherals, office machines, electric fences, electric utility wiring—especially with BPL *(see)*—and related components. Sometimes referred to as QRN, a term based on Morse-code shorthand.
Noise Blanker. Receiver circuit, often found on costly tabletop and professional models, that reduces the impact of pulse-type electrical noises (nearby light dimmers, etc.) or certain unusual types of pulse transmissions. In practice, these circuits use long-established designs which act only on pulses which are greater in strength than the received signal, although designs without this limitation exist on paper.
Noise Floor. *See* Sensitivity.
Notch Filter, Tunable. A feature found on some tabletop and professional receivers for reducing or rejecting annoying heterodyne *(see)* interference—the whistles, howls and squeals for which shortwave has traditionally been notorious. Some notch filters operate within the IF *(see)* stage, whereas others operate as audio filters. IF notch filters tend to respond exceptionally well where there is fading, whereas audio filters usually have more capacity to attack higher-pitched heterodynes. However, audio notch filters can be and increasingly are automatic, thanks to a concept pioneered by the U.K.'s David Tong.

O

Other. Programs are in a language other than one of the world's primary languages.
Overall Distortion. Nothing makes listening quite so tiring as distortion. PASSPORT and Sherwood Engineering have devised techniques to measure overall cumulative distortion from signal input through audio output—not just distortion within the audio stage. This level of distortion is thus equal to what is heard by the ear.
Overloading. *See* Dynamic Range.

P

Passband Offset. Continuously variable control that can be user-adjusted such that only the best-sounding

slice of a given sideband is heard when the receiver is in either the single-sideband mode *(see)* or the synchronous selectable sideband mode *(see)*. This allows for a finer degree of control over adjacent-channel interference and tonal response than does a simple LSB or USB switch associated with a fixed BFO *(see)*. Also known as Passband Tuning, Passband Shift and IF Shift. The same nomenclature is sometimes used to describe variable-bandwidth circuitry.
Passband Shift. *See* Passband Offset.
Passband Tuning. *See* Passband Offset.
Passive Antenna. Not electronically amplified. Typically, such antennas are mounted outdoors, although the "tape-measure" type that comes as an accessory with some portables is usually strung indoors. For world band reception, virtually all outboard models for consumers are made from wire, rather than rods or tubular elements. The two most common designs are the inverted-L (so-called "longwire") and trapped dipole (mounted either horizontally or as a "sloper"). These antennas are reviewed at length, along with construction and erection instructions, in the Radio Database International White Paper, *Passport Evaluation of Popular Outdoor Antennas (Unamplified)*. *See* Feedline. *Cf.* Active Antennas.
PBS. In China, People's Broadcasting Station.
Phase Cancellation. In relation to synchronous selectable sideband *(see)*, two identical wave patterns (lower and upper sidebands) are brought together 180 degrees out of phase so as to cancel out the unwanted sideband. This is a less costly way of sideband attenuation than through the use of discrete IF filtering.
Phase Noise. Synthesizers and other circuits can create a "rushing" noise that is usually noticed only when the receiver is tuned alongside the edge of a powerful broadcast or other carrier. In effect, the signal becomes "modulated" by the noise. Phase noise is a useful measurement if you tune weak signals alongside powerful signals. Measured in dBc (decibels below carrier).
Phone Plug (male), Phone Connector (male), Phone Jack (female). Low-impedance (around 50–75 ohm) 1/4-inch (6 mm) connector, usually for full-sized headphones. These may be mono or stereo.
Phono Plug (male), Phono Connector (male), Phono Jack (female). *See RCA.*
Pirate. Illegal radio station operated mainly for personal gratification by enthusiast(s) with little if any political purpose other than to defy radio laws. Programs typically consist of music, satire or comments relevant to pirate colleagues.
Placement Facility. Typically a local FM or mediumwave AM station which leases airtime for one or more programs or program segments from an international broadcaster. These programs are usually supplied by satellite feed, although some placement facilities pick up programs via regular world band radio.
PLL (Phase-Locked Loop). With world band receivers, a PLL circuit means that the radio can be tuned digitally, often using a number of handy tuning techniques, such as a keypad *(see)* and station presets *(see)*.
Plug. Male connector.
Polarization. Radio and other over-the-air signals tend to be either horizontally or vertically polarized. Unsurprisingly, stations which transmit using vertical antennas produce vertically polarized signals, and so on. Long-haul world band transmissions are almost always horizontally polarized (*see* Curtain Antennas), so most outdoor receiving antennas are also horizontal. However, the scattering effects of the ionosphere turn the single horizontal transmitted signal, like a bread slicer, into numerous bits (*see* Fading). Some continue on as horizontal while others morph into vertical, but most fall somewhere in between. As a result, the angle of receiving antenna elements tends to be noncritical for reception of long-distance shortwave signals.
Power. Transmitter power *before* antenna gain, expressed in kilowatts (kW). The present range of world band powers is virtually always 0.01 to 1,000 kW.
Power Lock. *See* Travel Power Lock.
PR. People's Republic.
Preamplifier. An inboard or outboard broadband amplifier to increase the strength of signals fed into a receiver's circuitry. Active antennas *(see)* incorporate a preamplifier or an amplified preselector *(see)*.
Preselector. A circuit—outboard as an accessory, or inboard as part of the receiver—that effectively limits the range of frequencies which can enter a receiver's circuitry or the circuitry of an active antenna *(see)* at full strength; that is, which improves front-end selectivity *(see)*. For example, a preselector may let in the range 15000–16000 kHz unattenuated, thus helping ensure that your receiver or active antenna will not encounter problems within that range caused by signals from, say, 5730–6250 kHz or local mediumwave AM signals (520–1705 kHz). This range usually can be varied, manually or automatically, according to the frequency to which the receiver is being tuned. A preselector may be passive (unamplified) or active (amplified).
Preset. Allows you to select a station pre-stored in a radio's memory. The handiest presets require only one push of a button, as on a traditional car radio.
Propagation. World band signals travel, like a basketball, up and down from the station to your radio. The "floor" below is the earth's surface, whereas the "player's hand" on high is the *ionosphere*, a gaseous layer that envelops the planet. While the earth's surface remains pretty much the same from day to day, the ionosphere—nature's own passive "satellite"—varies in how it propagates radio signals, depending on how much sunlight hits the "bounce points."

Thus, some world band segments do well mainly by day, whereas others are best by night. During winter there's less sunlight, so the "night bands" become unusually active, whereas the "day bands" become correspondingly less useful (*see* World Band Spectrum). Day-to-day changes in the sun's weather also cause short-term changes in world band radio reception; this explains why some days you can hear rare signals.

Additionally, the 11-year sunspot cycle has a long term effect on propagation, with sunspot maximum greatly enhancing reception on higher world band segments. The last maximum was in late 2000 with the next forecast to be around 2012 or 2013.

These bounce, or refraction, points are not absolutely efficient. Some loss comes about from absorption *(see)*, and signal scattering brings about fading *(see)*. Too, some bounce points for a signal may be in sunlight (favoring higher frequencies), whereas others aren't (favoring lower frequencies), thus compromising propagation efficiency.

Propagation, like the weather, varies considerably, which adds to the intrigue of world band radio. The accepted standard for propagation prediction is WWV (and sometimes WWVH) on 2500, 5000, 10000, 15000 and 20000 kHz. An explanation of prediction measurements is at www.boulder.nist.gov/timefreq/stations/iform.html#geo.
PS. Provincial Station, Pangsong.
Pto. Puerto, Porto.

Q

QRM. *See* Interference.
QRN. *See* Noise.
QSL. *See* Verification.

R

R. Radio, Radiodiffusion, Radiodifusora, Radiodifusão, Radiophonikos, Radiostantsiya, Radyo, Radyosu, and so forth.
Radiofax, Radio Facsimile. Like ordinary telefax (facsimile by telephone lines), but by radio.
Radioteletype (RTTY). Characters, but not illustrations, transmitted by radio. *See* Baud.
RCA Plug (male), RCA Connector (male), RCA Jack (female). Low-impedance (around 50–75 ohm) coaxial cable connector. Simple, inexpensive and ubiquitous in audio systems, but flawed because 1) it is prone to discontinuity from everyday atmospheric corrosion; 2) male and female connectors must fit exactly but often don't; and 3) the positive ("hot") lead connects before the ground/negative lead. Sometimes also used as an antenna connector. Also known, instead of "RCA," as "phono" and CINCH/AV.
RDI®. Radio Database International®, a registered trademark of International Broadcasting Services, Ltd.
Receiver. Synonym for "radio," but sometimes—especially when called a "communications receiver"—implying a radio with superior tough-signal or utility-signal performance.
Reception Report. *See* Verification.
Reduced Carrier. *See* Single Sideband.
Reg. Regional.
Relay. A retransmission facility, often highlighted in "Worldwide Broadcasts in English" and "Voices from Home" in PASSPORT's WorldScan® section. Relay facilities are generally considered to be located outside the broadcaster's country, but are not local placement facilities *(see)*. Being closer to the target audience, they usually provide superior reception. *See* Feeder.
Rep. Republic, République, República.
RF Gain. A variable control to reduce the gain of a receiver's earliest amplification, in the RF stage. However, modern receivers often function better without an RF stage, in which case an RF gain control usually acts simply as a variable attenuator *(see)*.
RN. *See* R and N.
RS. Radio Station, Radiostantsiya, Radiostudiya, Radiophonikos Stathmos.
RT, RTV. Radiodiffusion Télévision, Radio Télévision, and so forth.
RTTY. *See* Radioteletype.

S

S Transmission aired summer (midyear) only, typically from the last Sunday in March until the last Sunday in October; *see* "HFCC." *Cf.* **W**
S. San, Santa, Santo, São, Saint, Sainte. Also, South.
Sa. Saturday.
SASE. Self-addressed, stamped envelope. *See* introduction to Addresses PLUS in this PASSPORT.
Scan, Scanning. Circuitry within a radio that allows it to bandscan or memory scan automatically.
SDR. *See* Software Defined Radio.
Season, Schedule Season. *See* HFCC.
Segments. *See* Shortwave Spectrum.
Selectivity. The ability of a radio to reject interference *(see)* from signals on adjacent channels. Thus, also known as adjacent-channel rejection, a key variable in radio quality. *See* Bandwidth, Shape Factor, Ultimate Rejection, Synchronous Detector and Synchronous Selectable Sideband.
Sensitivity. The ability of a radio to receive weak signals; thus, also known somewhat redundantly as weak-signal sensitivity. Of special importance if you are listening during the day or tuning domestic tropical band broadcasts—or if you are located in such parts of the world as Western North America, Hawaii or Australasia, where signals tend to be relatively weak. Measured in microvolts (µV), or in dBm as the noise floor.
Shape Factor. Skirt selectivity helps reduce interference and increase audio fidelity. It is important if you will be tuning stations that are weaker than adjacent-channel signals. Skirt selectivity is measured by the shape factor, the ratio between the bandwidth at –6 dB (adjacent signal at about the same strength as the received station) and –60 dB (adjacent signal relatively much stronger), although with some professional receivers and in certain labs –3 dB is used in lieu of –6 dB and/or –66 dB in lieu of –60 dB. A good shape factor provides the best defense against adjacent powerful signals' muscling their way in to disturb reception of the desired signal.
SHF. Super high frequency, 3–30 GHz.
Shortwave Spectrum. The shortwave spectrum—also known as the High Frequency (HF) spectrum—is that portion of the radio spectrum from 3 MHz through 30 MHz (3,000–30,000 kHz). The shortwave spectrum is occupied not only by world band radio (*see* World Band Segments), but also hams *(see)* and utility stations *(see)*. World band radio additionally occupies the 2.3–2.5 MHz portion of the 0.3–3.0 MHz mediumwave spectrum (*see* AM Band).
Sideband. *See* Mode.
Signal Polarization. *See* Polarization.
Signal Separation, Signal Separation Points. *See* Dynamic Range.
Signal Spacing. *See* Dynamic Range.
Signal-to-Noise Ratio. A common form of noise comes from a radio's (and/or active antenna's) electronic circuitry and often sounds like hissing or buzzing. Depending upon its antenna's location, a receiver may also pick up and reproduce noise *(see)* from nearby electrical and electronic sources, such as power and cable TV lines, light dimmers and digital electronic products. A third type of noise, galactic, is rarely a problem, and even then can be heard only above 20 MHz. Thus, a key part of enjoyable radio reception is to have a worthy signal-to-noise ratio; that is, where the received radio signal is strong enough relative to the various noises that it drowns out those noises.
SINAD. Ratio of signal-plus-noise-plus-distortion to noise-plus-distortion.
Single Conversion. *See* IF, Image.
Single Sideband, Independent Sideband. Spectrum- and power-conserving modes of transmission commonly used by utility stations *(see)* and hams *(see)*. Single-sideband transmitted signals usually consist of one full sideband (lower sideband, LSB; or, more typically, upper sideband, USB) and a reduced or suppressed carrier, but no second sideband. Very few broadcasters (e.g., the popular American AFRTS) use, or are expected ever to use, the single-sideband mode. Many world band radios are already capable of demodulating single-sideband transmissions, and some can even process independent-sideband signals.

Independent-sideband (ISB) signals are like single-sideband signals, but with both sidebands. Content is usually different in the two sidebands—for stereo, as in the original Kahn AM-stereo system where the left channel can be LSB, right channel USB. More typically, entirely different programming may be carried by each sideband, such as was formerly done with shortwave feeds to relay facilities that would retransmit two different programs. *See* Feeder, Mode.

Certain world band broadcasters and time-standard stations emit single-sideband transmissions which have virtually no carrier reduction, or a minimum of reduction; say, 3 or 6 dB. These "AM equivalent" (AME) signals can be listened to, with slightly added distortion, on ordinary radios not equipped to demodulate pure single sideband signals. Properly designed synchronous detectors *(see)* help reduce distortion with AME transmissions. A former variety of AME signal, called "compatible AM," included a minor FM component to help improve reception fidelity. This concept was experimented with decades ago by inventor Leonard Kahn and the VOA. However, it didn't take off, as it was not found to offer meaningful improvement over ordinary AME transmission.

Site. *See* Location.

Skirt Selectivity. *See* Shape Factor.

Skyhook. Outdoor antenna, typically wire.

Slew Controls, Slewing Controls. Up/down controls, usually buttons, to tune a radio. On many radios with synthesized tuning, slewing is used in lieu of tuning by knob. Better is when slew controls are complemented by a genuine tuning knob, which is more versatile for bandscanning.

Sloper Antenna. *See* Passive Antenna.

Socket. Female connector.

Software Defined Radio (SDR). Software-defined radio receivers use computer-type software and processing to perform circuit activities traditionally handled by discrete electronic components. Over the longer haul this technology will almost certainly result in higher performance receivers at a lower cost than has heretofore been possible. *See* Digital Signal Processing.

Solar Cycle. Synonym for "sunspot cycle." *See* Propagation.

SPR. Spurious (false) extra signal from a transmitter actually operating on another frequency. One such type is harmonic *(see)*.

Spur. *See* SPR.

Spurious Signal. *See* SPR.

Spurious-Signal Rejection. The ability of a radio receiver to avoid producing false signals, such as images *(see)* and birdies *(see)*, that might otherwise interfere with the clarity of the station you're trying to hear.

Squelch. A circuit which mutes a receiver until the received signal's strength exceeds a specified threshold, which is usually user-adjustable.

SSB. *See* Single Sideband.

St, Sta, Sto. Abbreviations for words that mean "Saint."

Stability. The ability of a receiver to rest exactly the tuned frequency without drifting.

Static. *See* Noise.

Static Arrestor. *See* Surge Arrestor.

Su. Sunday.

Subharmonic. A harmonic heard at 1.5 or 0.5 times the operating frequency. This anomaly is caused by the way signals are generated within vintage-model transmitters, and thus cannot take place with modern transmitters. For example, the subharmonic of a station on 3360 kHz might be heard faintly on 5040 or 1680 kHz. Also, *see* Harmonic.

Sunspot Cycle. *See* Propagation.

Superheterodyne. *See* IF.

Surge Arrestor. Protective device to eliminate the harmful impact of voltage spikes, which enter electronic equipment via AC (mains) power lines, telephone lines and radio/TV antennas. *See* MOV, although some premium arrestors—notably Zero-Surge and Brick Wall—use non-MOV technologies.

SW. *See* Shortwave Spectrum.

SWL. Shortwave listener. The overwhelming preponderance of shortwave listening is to world band stations, but some radio enthusiasts also enjoy eavesdropping on utility stations *(see)* and hams *(see)*.

Synchronous Detector, Synchronous Detection. Some world band radios are equipped with this advanced circuit that greatly reduces fading distortion; unlike ECSS *(see)* it automatically steers clear of received *vs.* internally generated carrier phase mismatch. Better synchronous detectors also allow for synchronous selectable sideband *(see)*; that is, the ability to select the less-interfered of the two sidebands of a world band or other AM-mode signal. *See* Mode, Phase Cancellation.

Synchronous Selectable Sideband. Derived from synchronous detection *(see)* circuitry, this function greatly reduces the impact of adjacent-channel interference *(see)* on listening. Desirable when implemented properly.

Synthesizer, Frequency. Better world band receivers utilize a digital frequency synthesizer to tune signals. Among other things, such synthesizers allow for pushbutton tuning and station presets, and display the exact frequency digitally—pluses that make tuning to the world considerably easier. Almost a "must" feature. *See* Analog Frequency Readout, Digital Frequency Display.

T

Target. The part of the world where a transmission is beamed, a/k/a target zone.

Th. Thursday.

THD. Total harmonic distortion.

Third Order Intercept Point. *See* Dynamic Range.

Tilt Panel, Tilt Rod. *See* Elevation Panel, Elevation Rod.

Travel Power Lock. Control which disables the on/off control to prevent a radio from switching on accidentally. Better locks deactivate illumination, as well.

Transmitter Power. *See* Power.

Trap Dipole Antenna, Trapped Dipole Antenna. Dipole *(see)* antenna with several coil "traps" that allow for optimum reception on several world band or other segments or bands. *See* Passive Antenna.

Tropical Band Segments. *See* World Band Segments.

Tu. Tuesday.

Twinlead, Twin Lead. Ribbon wire or "zip cord" *(see)* typically used as an antenna lead-in *(see)*. Impedance may be high (300 ohms) or low (around 50–75 ohms).

U

UHF. Ultra High Frequency, 300 MHz through 3 GHz.

UHF Connector. One of the three most common coax fittings (a/k/a PL-259, SO-239) used *i.a.* to connect world band and kindred outboard antenna lead-ins *(see)* to a receiver (typically tabletop or professional). Robust, but because it screws on it takes more time to connect/disconnect than most alternatives. Impedance varies, but typically is low (50–75 ohms).

Ultimate Rejection, Ultimate Selectivity. The point at which a receiver is no longer able to reject adjacent-channel interference. Ultimate rejection is important if

you listen to signals that are markedly weaker than are adjacent signals. *See* Selectivity.
Universal Day. *See* World Time.
Universal Time. *See* World Time.
URL. Universal Resource Locator; i.e., the Internet address for a given webpage.
USB. Upper Sideband. *See* Mode, Single Sideband, Feeder.
UTC. Coordinated Universal Time. The occasional variation "Universal Time Coordinated" is not correct, although for everyday use it's okay to refer simply to "Universal Time." *See* World Time.
Utility Stations. Most signals within the shortwave spectrum are not world band stations. Rather, they are utility stations—radio telephones, ships at sea, aircraft, ionospheric sounders, over-the-horizon radar and the like—that transmit strange sounds (growls, gurgles, dih-dah sounds, etc.). Although these can be picked up on many receivers, they are rarely intended to be utilized by the general public. *Cf.* Broadcast, Feeders, Hams and Mode.

V

v. Variable frequency; i.e., one that is unstable or drifting because of a transmitter malfunction or, less often, to avoid jamming or other interference.
Variable-Rate Incremental Slewing (VRIS). Slewing button or other on/off bandscanning control where the tuning rate increases the longer the control is held down or otherwise kept on.
Variable-Rate Incremental Tuning (VRIT). Tuning knob or similar bandscanning control where the tuning rate increases the faster the control is turned. So, the faster the control is turned, the faster the *rate* in which frequencies zip by.
Verification. A "QSL" card or letter from a station verifying that a listener indeed heard that particular station. In order to stand a chance of qualifying for a verification card or letter, you should respond with a reception report shortly after having heard the transmission. You need to provide the station heard with, at a minimum, the following information in a three-number "SIO" code, in which "SIO 555" is best and "SIO 111" is worst:

- **S**ignal strength, with 5 being of excellent quality, comparable to that of a local mediumwave AM station, and 1 being inaudible or at least so weak as to be virtually unintelligible, 2 (faint, but somewhat intelligible), 3 (moderate strength) and 4 (good strength) represent the signal-strength levels usually encountered with world band stations.
- **I**nterference from other stations, with 5 indicating no interference whatsoever, and 1 indicating such extreme interference that the desired signal is virtually drowned out. Ratings of 2 (heavy interference), 3 (moderate interference) and 4 (slight interference) represent the differing degrees of interference more typically encountered with world band signals. If possible, indicate the names of the interfering station(s) and the channel(s) they are on. Otherwise, at least describe what the interference sounds like.
- **O**verall quality of the signal, with 5 being best, 1 worst.

In addition to providing SIO findings, you should indicate which programs you've heard, as well as comments on how you liked or disliked those programs. Refer to the Addresses PLUS section of this edition for information on where and to whom your report should be sent, and whether return postage should be included.

Expanded versions of the SIO reporting code are the SINPO and SINFO codes, where "N" refers to atmospheric noise, "F" to fading and "P" to propagation conditions on the same 1–5 scale. As atmospheric noise is rarely audible below 20 MHz and propagation conditions are highly subjective, SIO tends to provide more accurate feedback. Fading, however, is not hard for an experienced monitor to rate, but the SIFO code has never caught on.

Few stations wish to receive unsolicited recordings of their transmissions. However, a few stations' websites actively seek MP3, RealAudio or other Internet-sent files or mailed CD recordings of certain transmissions.
VHF. Very high frequency spectrum, 30–300 MHz, which starts just above the shortwave spectrum *(see)* and ends at the UHF spectrum. *See* FM, which operates within the VHF spectrum. Somewhat confusingly, in German VHF is known as UKW (Ultra Short Wave), which is different from UHF (Ultra High Frequency).
VHF Connector. *See* UHF Connector.
Vo. Voice of.
VRIS. *See* Variable-Rate Incremental Slewing.
VRIT. *See* Variable-Rate Incremental Tuning.

W

W Transmission aired winter only, typically from the last Sunday in October until the last Sunday in March; *see* HFCC. *Cf.* **S**
W. Wednesday.
Wavelength. *See* Meters.
Weak-Signal Sensitivity. *See* Sensitivity.
Webcasting. *See* Web Radio.
Web Radio, Webcasts, Web Simulcasts. Broadcasts aired over the Internet. These thousands of stations worldwide include simulcast FM, mediumwave AM and world band stations, as well as Internet-only stations. Although webcasting was originally unfettered, it has increasingly been subjected to official gatekeeping (censorship), as well as uniquely steep copyright and union royalties and rules that have hobbled web simulcasting by AM/FM stations in the United States and certain other countries. This PASSPORT's "Addresses PLUS" lists URL information for all world band stations which webcast live or on-demand.
World Band Radio. Broadcasts (news, music, sports and the like) transmitted within and just below the shortwave spectrum *(see)*. Virtually all are found within 14 discrete world band segments *(see)*. These broadcasting stations are similar to regular mediumwave AM band and FM band broadcasters, except that world band stations can be heard over enormous distances. As a result, they often carry programs created especially for audiences abroad. Traditional analog world band transmissions—with properly located, configured and operated facilities—are also uniquely difficult to "jam" (*see* Jamming), making world band the most effective vehicle for outflanking official censorship. Some world band stations have regular audiences in the tens of millions, and even over 100 million, including many who listen for extended periods. Although world band lacks the glamour of new broadcasting technologies, making it an easy target for tech-hungry officials, over half a billion worldwide are believed to listen.
World Band Segments. Fourteen slices—13 within the 3–30 MHz shortwave spectrum *(see)*, one in the upper reaches of the 0.3–3 MHz mediumwave spectrum (*see* AM Band)—that are used almost exclusively for world band broadcasts. Those below 5.1 MHz are called "Tropical Band Segments" or simply "Tropical Bands." *See* "Best Times and Frequencies" sidebar elsewhere within this PASSPORT.

World Band Spectrum. *See* World Band Segments.
World Day. *See* World Time.
World Time. Also known as Coordinated Universal Time (UTC), Greenwich Mean Time (GMT), Zulu time (Z) and "military time." With over 150 countries on world band radio, if each announced its own local time you would need a calculator to figure it all out. To get around this, a single international time—World Time—is used. The differences between World Time and local time are detailed in the Addresses PLUS and Setting Your World Time Clock sections of this edition. World Time can also be determined simply by listening to time announcements given on the hour by world band stations—or minute by minute by WWV in the United States on 2500, 5000, 10000, 15000 and 20000 kHz; WWVH in Hawaii on 2500, 5000, 10000 and 15000 kHz; and CHU in Canada on 3330, 7335 and 14670 kHz. A 24-hour clock format is used, so "1800 World Time" means 6:00 PM World Time. If you're in, say, North America, Eastern Time is five hours behind World Time winters and four hours behind World Time summers, so 1800 World Time would be 1:00 PM EST or 2:00 PM EDT. The easiest solution is to use a 24-hour digital clock set to World Time. Many radios already have these built in, and World Time clocks and watches are also available as accessories. World Time also applies to the days of the week. So if it's 9:00 PM (21:00) Wednesday in New York during the winter, it's 0200 *Thursday* World Time.
WS. World Service.

X

X-Band. The mediumwave AM band segment from 1605–1705 kHz in the Western Hemisphere, Australia and certain other areas. In the United States, travelers information stations (TIS) and other public information services are sometimes also found on 1710 kHz. *See* AM Band.

Y

Yagi. Pioneering directional beam antenna invented by Japanese engineer Hidetsugu Yagi. Pickup elements are usually of aluminum tubing and include one or more of each of these three elements: dipole, slightly longer reflector and slightly shorter director. Size, cost and erection challenges make yagis impractical for nighttime world band listening. However, they are commonly used for VHF/UHF reception, as well as amateur radio shortwave transceiving down to 14 MHz/20 meters and occasionally 7 MHz/40 meters.

Z

Zero beat. When tuning a world band or other AM-mode signal in the single-sideband mode, there is a whistle, or "beat," whose pitch is the result of the difference in frequency between the receiver's internally generated carrier (BFO, or beat-frequency oscillator) and the station's transmitted carrier. By tuning carefully, the listener can reduce the difference between these two carriers to the point where the whistle is deeper and deeper, to the point where it no longer audible. This silent sweet spot is known as "zero beat." *See* ECSS.
Zip Cord. Conventional twin-lead wire used to connect ordinary household appliances and lights to mains/wall-socket AC outlets. Sometimes used as low-cost antenna twinlead *(see)*.
Zulu Time. *See* World Time.

DIRECTORY OF ADS—2009

Amazon.com IFC–1, 8–9, 20–21, 38–39
Bay Bloor Radio 20–21
Cabela's 8–9
C. Crane Company 33, 47
Committee to Preserve Radio Verifications 309
Cumbre DX 257
Durham Radio 8–9
Future Shop 8–9, 38–39
Grundig/Etón IFC–1, 8–9, 20–21, 28–29, 38–39, 52–53
IBS Japan 281
Icom America 5
Kromer 38–39
Monitoring Times/Grove Enterprises 43
Passport 2010 221
Popular Communications IBC
RadioShack (U.S.) IFC–1, 8–9, 20–21, 38–39
Radioworld 8–9
RDI White Papers 193, 359
Sherwood Engineering Inc. 233, 291
The Source IFC–1, 8–9, 20–21, 38–39
Universal Radio 17, 52–53, 199, 213

Jock Elliott, Advertising Manager
IBS, Ltd.
Box 300
Penn's Park, PA 18943 USA
Voice: +1 (215) 598 9018
Fax: +1 (215) 598 3794
Email: mktg@passband.com

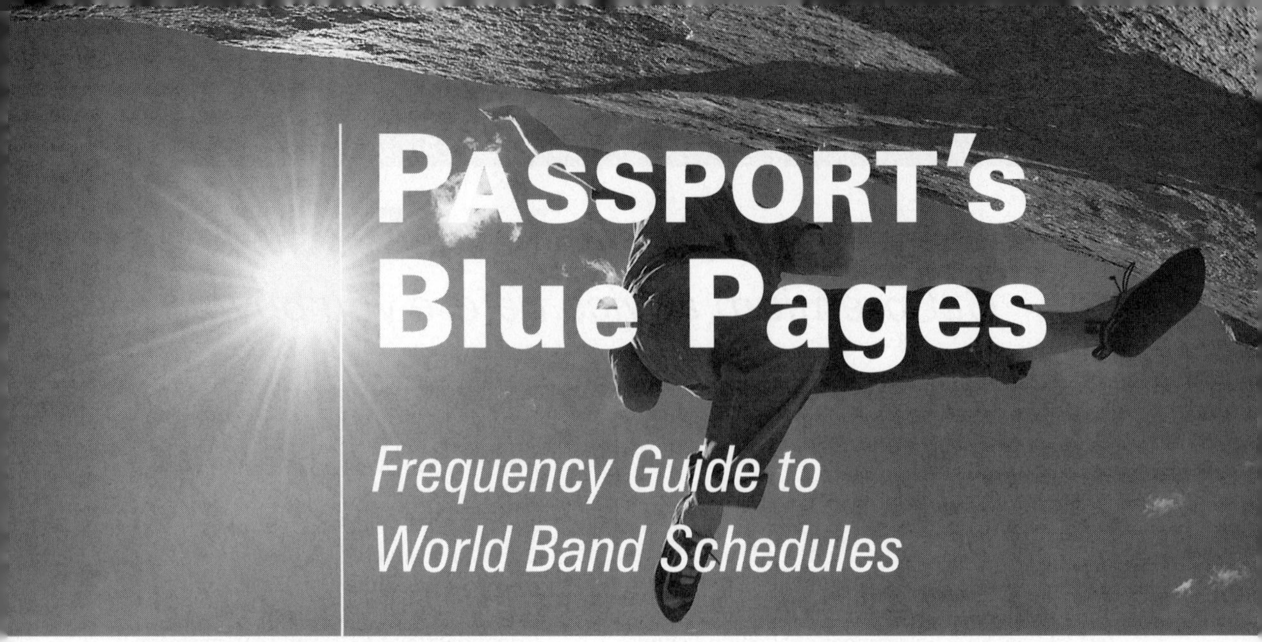

PASSPORT's Blue Pages

Frequency Guide to World Band Schedules

If you scan the world band airwaves, you'll even find stations that aren't aimed your way. That's because shortwave signals are scattered by the heavens, allowing broadcasts not targeted to your area to be heard.

Blue Pages Identify Stations

Yet, bandscanning can be frustrating if you don't have a "map"—PASSPORT's Blue Pages. Let's say you've stumbled across something Asian-sounding on 7410 kHz at 2035 World Time. The Blue Pages show All India Radio beamed to Western Europe, with 250 kW of power from Delhi. These suggest this is probably what you're hearing, even if you're not in Europe. You can also see that English from India will begin on that same channel in about ten minutes.

Signals targeted your way usually come in best, but those aimed elsewhere may also be heard—especially when they're beamed to nearby regions.

Schedules for Entire Year

Times and days of the week are in World Time, explained in "Setting Your World Time Clock" and "Worldly Words"; for local times in each country, see "Addresses PLUS." Midyear, some stations are an hour earlier (⇦) or later (⇨) because of Daylight Saving/Summer Time. Frequencies used only seasonally are labeled **S** for summer (midyear) and **W** for winter. Stations may also extend hours of transmission, or air special programs, for national holidays, emergencies or sports events.

To be as useful as possible over the months to come, PASSPORT's schedules consist not just of observed activity, but also that which we have creatively opined will take place during the forthcoming year. This predictive material is based on decades of experience and is original from us. Although inherently not as exact as real-time data, over the years it has been of tangible value to PASSPORT readers.

Guide to Blue Pages Format

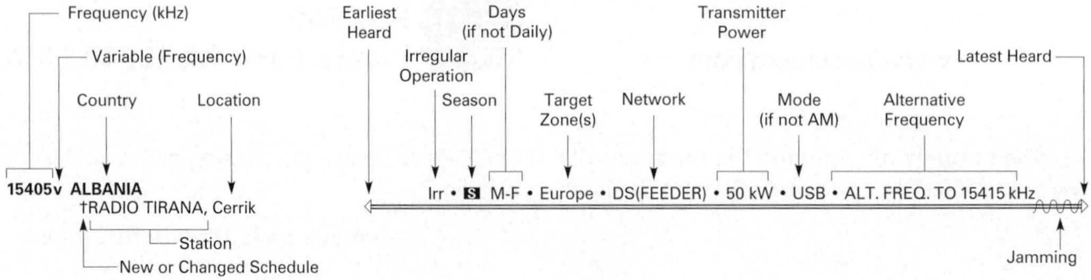

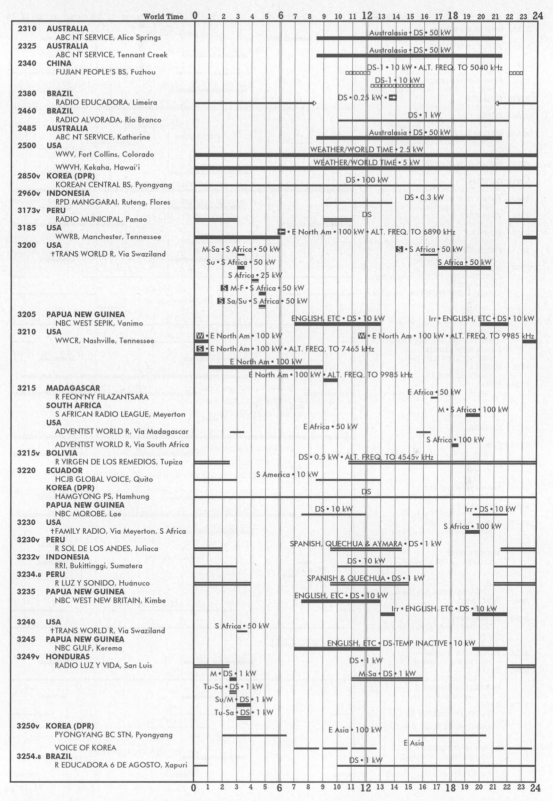

kHz	Country / Station	Details (World Time 0–24)
2310	**AUSTRALIA** ABC NT SERVICE, Alice Springs	Australasia • DS • 50 kW
2325	**AUSTRALIA** ABC NT SERVICE, Tennant Creek	Australasia • DS • 50 kW
2340	**CHINA** FUJIAN PEOPLE'S BS, Fuzhou	DS-1 • 10 kW • ALT. FREQ. TO 5040 kHz
		DS-1 • 10 kW
2380	**BRAZIL** RADIO EDUCADORA, Limeira	DS • 0.25 kW • ➡
2460	**BRAZIL** RADIO ALVORADA, Rio Branco	DS • 1 kW
2485	**AUSTRALIA** ABC NT SERVICE, Katherine	Australasia • DS • 50 kW
2500	**USA** WWV, Fort Collins, Colorado	WEATHER/WORLD TIME • 2.5 kW
	WWVH, Kekaha, Hawai'i	WEATHER/WORLD TIME • 5 kW
2850v	**KOREA (DPR)** KOREAN CENTRAL BS, Pyongyang	DS • 100 kW
2960v	**INDONESIA** RPD MANGGARAI, Ruteng, Flores	DS • 0.3 kW
3173v	**PERU** RADIO MUNICIPAL, Panao	DS
3185	**USA** WWRB, Manchester, Tennessee	⬅ • E North Am • 100 kW • ALT. FREQ. TO 6890 kHz
3200	**USA** †TRANS WORLD R, Via Swaziland	M-Sa • S Africa • 50 kW
		S • S Africa • 50 kW
		Su • S Africa • 50 kW
		S Africa • 50 kW
		S Africa • 25 kW
		S M-F • S Africa • 50 kW
		S Sa/Su • S Africa • 50 kW
3205	**PAPUA NEW GUINEA** NBC WEST SEPIK, Vanimo	ENGLISH, ETC • DS • 10 kW
		Irr • ENGLISH, ETC • DS • 10 kW
3210	**USA** WWCR, Nashville, Tennessee	W • E North Am • 100 kW
		W • E North Am • 100 kW • ALT. FREQ. TO 9985 kHz
		S • E North Am • 100 kW • ALT. FREQ. TO 7465 kHz
		E North Am • 100 kW
		E North Am • 100 kW • ALT. FREQ. TO 9985 kHz
3215	**MADAGASCAR** R FEON'NY FILAZANTSARA	E Africa • 50 kW
	SOUTH AFRICA S AFRICAN RADIO LEAGUE, Meyerton	M • S Africa • 100 kW
	USA ADVENTIST WORLD R, Via Madagascar	E Africa • 50 kW
	ADVENTIST WORLD R, Via South Africa	S Africa • 100 kW
3215v	**BOLIVIA** R VIRGEN DE LOS REMEDIOS, Tupiza	DS • 0.5 kW • ALT. FREQ. TO 4545v kHz
3220	**ECUADOR** HCJB GLOBAL VOICE, Quito	S America • 10 kW
	KOREA (DPR) HAMGYONG PS, Hamhung	DS
	PAPUA NEW GUINEA NBC MOROBE, Lae	DS • 10 kW
		Irr • DS • 10 kW
3230	**USA** †FAMILY RADIO, Via Meyerton, S Africa	S Africa • 100 kW
3230v	**PERU** R SOL DE LOS ANDES, Juliaca	SPANISH, QUECHUA & AYMARA • DS • 1 kW
3232v	**INDONESIA** RRI, Bukittinggi, Sumatera	DS • 10 kW
3234.8	**PERU** R LUZ Y SONIDO, Huánuco	SPANISH & QUECHUA • DS • 1 kW
3235	**PAPUA NEW GUINEA** NBC WEST NEW BRITAIN, Kimbe	ENGLISH, ETC • DS • 10 kW
		Irr • ENGLISH, ETC • DS • 10 kW
3240	**USA** †TRANS WORLD R, Via Swaziland	S Africa • 50 kW
3245	**PAPUA NEW GUINEA** NBC GULF, Kerema	ENGLISH, ETC • DS-TEMP INACTIVE • 10 kW
3249v	**HONDURAS** RADIO LUZ Y VIDA, San Luis	DS • 1 kW
		M • DS • 1 kW
		M-Sa • DS • 1 kW
		Tu-Su • DS • 1 kW
		Su/M • DS • 1 kW
		Tu-Sa • DS • 1 kW
3250v	**KOREA (DPR)** PYONGYANG BC STN, Pyongyang	E Asia • 100 kW
	VOICE OF KOREA	E Asia
3254.8	**BRAZIL** R EDUCADORA 6 DE AGOSTO, Xapuri	DS • 1 kW

SEASONAL S OR W   1-HR TIMESHIFT MIDYEAR ⬅ OR ➡   JAMMING / OR /\   EARLIEST HEARD ◁   LATEST HEARD ▷   NEW FOR 2009 †

kHz	Country / Station	Schedule (World Time 0–24)
3255	**UNITED KINGDOM** BBC, Via Meyerton, South Africa	S Africa • 100 kW
3260	**PAPUA NEW GUINEA** NBC MADANG, Madang	ENGLISH, ETC • DS • 10 kW; Irr • ENGLISH, ETC • DS • 10 kW
3266v	**INDONESIA** RRI, Gorontalo, Gorontalo	Irr • DS-TEMP INACTIVE • 10 kW
3275	**PAPUA NEW GUINEA** NBC SOUTHERN HIGHLANDS, Mendi	ENGLISH, ETC • DS • 10 kW; Irr • ENGLISH, ETC • DS • 10 kW
3279v	**ECUADOR** LA VOZ DEL NAPO, Tena	SPANISH, ETC • DS-LOCAL, R MARIA • 2.5 kW
3280	**CHINA** VOICE OF PUJIANG, Shanghai	E Asia • 50 kW
3288v	**MADAGASCAR** RTV MALAGASY, Antananarivo	DS-1 • 30 kW; Sa • DS-1 • 30 kW
3290	**PAPUA NEW GUINEA** †NBC CENTRAL, Boroko	Irr • ENGLISH, ETC • DS • 10 kW; Irr • DS • 10 kW
3291v	**GUYANA** VOICE OF GUYANA, Georgetown	DS-TEMP INACTIVE • 5 kW
3305	**PAPUA NEW GUINEA** NBC WESTERN, Daru	Irr • ENGLISH, ETC • DS • 10 kW; ENGLISH, ETC • DS • 10 kW
3306	**ZIMBABWE** ZIMBABWE BC CORP, Gweru	ENGLISH, ETC • DS-RADIO ZIMBABWE • 50/100 kW • ALT. FREQ. TO 6045 kHz
3310	**BOLIVIA** RADIO MOSOJ CHASKI, Cochabamba	Tu-Su • DS • 10 kW; DS • 10 kW; M-Sa • DS • 10 kW
3315	**PAPUA NEW GUINEA** NBC MANUS, Lorengau	ENGLISH, ETC • DS • 10 kW; Irr • ENGLISH, ETC • DS • 10 kW
3320	**KOREA (DPR)** PYONGYANG BC STN, Pyongyang	E Asia
	SOUTH AFRICA †RADIO SONDERGRENSE, Meyerton	S Africa • DS • 100 kW; S • S Africa • DS • 100 kW
3325	**BRAZIL** RADIO MUNDIAL, São Paulo	DS • 2.5 kW
	INDONESIA RRI, Palangkaráya, Kalimantan	DS • 10 kW
	PAPUA NEW GUINEA NBC BOUGANVILLE, Buka	ENGLISH, ETC • DS • 10 kW; Irr • ENGLISH, ETC • DS • 10 kW
3326	**NIGERIA** RADIO NIGERIA, Lagos	DS-1 • 50 kW
3329.5	**PERU** ONDAS DEL HUALLAGA, Huánuco	SPANISH & QUECHUA • DS • 0.5 kW • ALT. FREQ. TO 3330.4 kHz; Irr • DS • 0.5 kW • ALT. FREQ. TO 3330.4 kHz; Su • SPANISH & QUECHUA • DS • 0.5 kW • ALT. FREQ. TO 3330.4 kHz
3330	**CANADA** CHU, Ottawa	WORLD TIME • 3 kW • USB
3330.4	**PERU** ONDAS DEL HUALLAGA, Huánuco	SPANISH & QUECHUA • DS • 0.5 kW • ALT. FREQ. TO 3329.5 kHz; Irr • DS • 0.5 kW • ALT. FREQ. TO 3329.5 kHz; Su • SPANISH & QUECHUA • DS • 0.5 kW • ALT. FREQ. TO 3329.5 kHz
3335	**PAPUA NEW GUINEA** †NBC EAST SEPIK, Wewak	ENGLISH, ETC • DS • 10 kW; Irr • ENGLISH, ETC • DS • 10 kW
3340	**HONDURAS** †HRMI-R MISIONES INTL, Tegucigalpa	Irr • SPANISH, ETC • DS • 0.15/2.5 kW • USB
3345	**PAPUA NEW GUINEA** NBC NORTHERN, Popondetta	ENGLISH, ETC • DS • 10 kW; ENGLISH, ETC • DS-TEMP INACTIVE • 10 kW
	SOUTH AFRICA †CHANNEL AFRICA, Meyerton	S Africa • 100 kW; S • S Africa • 100 kW
	USA ADVENTIST WORLD R, Via South Africa	S Africa • 100 kW
3345v	**INDONESIA** RRI, Ternate, Maluku	DS • 10 kW
3350	**KOREA (DPR)** SOUTH PYONGYANG PS, Pyŏngsong	DS
	SPAIN R EXTERIOR ESPANA, Via Costa Rica	C America • 100 kW
3355	**PAPUA NEW GUINEA** NBC SIMBU, Kundiawa	Irr • ENGLISH, ETC • DS • 10 kW; ENGLISH, ETC • DS • 10 kW
3365	**BRAZIL** RADIO CULTURA, Araraquara	DS • 1 kW
	PAPUA NEW GUINEA NBC MILNE BAY, Alotau	ENGLISH, ETC • DS • 10 kW; Irr • ENGLISH, ETC • DS • 10 kW
3375	**BRAZIL** RADIO EDUCADORA, Guajará Mirim	DS • 5 kW
	RADIO MUNICIPAL, S Gab Cachoeira	DS • 5 kW; M-Sa • DS • 5 kW
	PAPUA NEW GUINEA NBC WESTERN HIGHLANDS, Mt Hagen	Irr • ENGLISH, ETC • DS • 10 kW
	PERU RADIO SAN ANTONIO, Callalli	DS • 1 kW

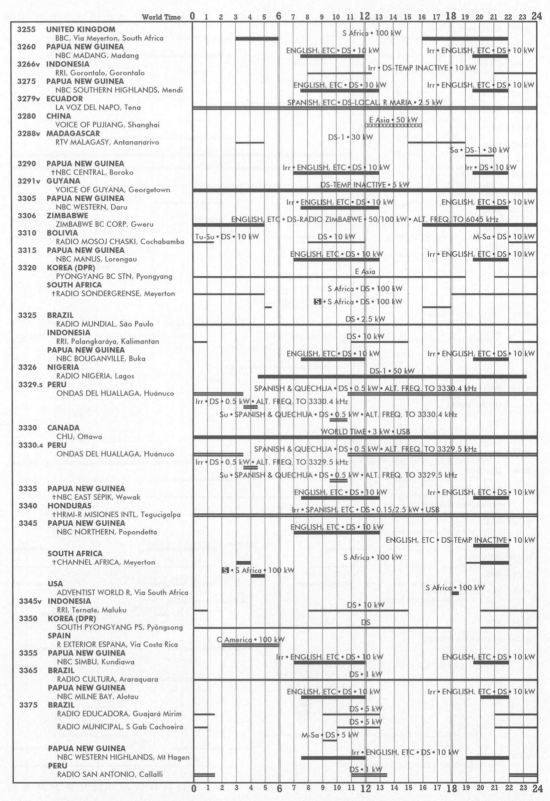

ENGLISH ▬ ARABIC ▭ CHINESE ▯▯▯ FRENCH ═ GERMAN ═ RUSSIAN ═ SPANISH ═ OTHER —

World Time 0 1 2 3 4 5 6 7 8 9 10 11 12 13 14 15 16 17 18 19 20 21 22 23 24

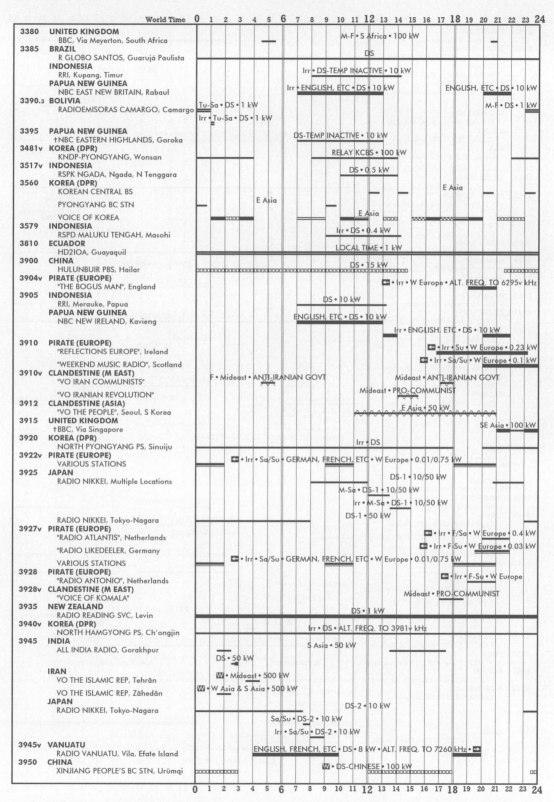

kHz	Country / Station	Schedule
3380	**UNITED KINGDOM**	
	BBC, Via Meyerton, South Africa	M-F • S Africa • 100 kW
3385	**BRAZIL**	
	R GLOBO SANTOS, Guarujá Paulista	DS
	INDONESIA	
	RRI, Kupang, Timur	Irr • DS-TEMP INACTIVE • 10 kW
	PAPUA NEW GUINEA	
	NBC EAST NEW BRITAIN, Rabaul	Irr • ENGLISH, ETC • DS • 10 kW; ENGLISH, ETC • DS • 10 kW
3390.3	**BOLIVIA**	
	RADIOEMISORAS CAMARGO, Camargo	Tu-Sa • DS • 1 kW; M-F • DS • 1 kW; Irr • Tu-Sa • DS • 1 kW
3395	**PAPUA NEW GUINEA**	
	†NBC EASTERN HIGHLANDS, Goroka	DS-TEMP INACTIVE • 10 kW
3481v	**KOREA (DPR)**	
	KNDP-PYONGYANG, Wonsan	RELAY KCBS • 100 kW
3517v	**INDONESIA**	
	RSPK NGADA, Ngada, N Tenggara	DS • 0.5 kW
3560	**KOREA (DPR)**	
	KOREAN CENTRAL BS	E Asia
	PYONGYANG BC STN	E Asia
	VOICE OF KOREA	E Asia
3579	**INDONESIA**	
	RSPD MALUKU TENGAH, Masohi	Irr • DS • 0.4 kW
3810	**ECUADOR**	
	HD2IOA, Guayaquil	LOCAL TIME • 1 kW
3900	**CHINA**	
	HULUNBUIR PBS, Hailar	DS • 15 kW
3904v	**PIRATE (EUROPE)**	
	"THE BOGUS MAN", England	Irr • W Europe • ALT. FREQ. TO 6295v kHz
3905	**INDONESIA**	
	RRI, Merauke, Papua	DS • 10 kW
	PAPUA NEW GUINEA	
	NBC NEW IRELAND, Kavieng	ENGLISH, ETC • DS • 10 kW; Irr • ENGLISH, ETC • DS • 10 kW
3910	**PIRATE (EUROPE)**	
	"REFLECTIONS EUROPE", Ireland	Irr • Su • W Europe • 0.23 kW
	"WEEKEND MUSIC RADIO", Scotland	Irr • Sa/Su • W Europe • 0.1 kW
3910v	**CLANDESTINE (M EAST)**	
	"VO IRAN COMMUNISTS"	F • Mideast • ANTI-IRANIAN GOVT; Mideast • ANTI-IRANIAN GOVT
	"VO IRANIAN REVOLUTION"	Mideast • PRO-COMMUNIST
3912	**CLANDESTINE (ASIA)**	
	"VO THE PEOPLE", Seoul, S Korea	E Asia • 50 kW
3915	**UNITED KINGDOM**	
	†BBC, Via Singapore	SE Asia • 100 kW
3920	**KOREA (DPR)**	
	NORTH PYONGYANG PS, Sinuiju	Irr • DS
3922v	**PIRATE (EUROPE)**	
	VARIOUS STATIONS	Irr • Sa/Su • GERMAN, FRENCH, ETC • W Europe • 0.01/0.75 kW
3925	**JAPAN**	
	RADIO NIKKEI, Multiple Locations	DS-1 • 10/50 kW; M-Sa • DS-1 • 10/50 kW; Irr • M-Sa • DS-1 • 10/50 kW
	RADIO NIKKEI, Tokyo-Nagara	DS-1 • 50 kW
3927v	**PIRATE (EUROPE)**	
	"RADIO ATLANTIS", Netherlands	Irr • F/Sa • W Europe • 0.4 kW
	"RADIO LIKEDEELER, Germany	Irr • F-Su • W Europe • 0.03 kW
	VARIOUS STATIONS	Irr • Sa/Su • GERMAN, FRENCH, ETC • W Europe • 0.01/0.75 kW
3928	**PIRATE (EUROPE)**	
	"RADIO ANTONIO", Netherlands	Irr • F-Su • W Europe
3928v	**CLANDESTINE (M EAST)**	
	"VOICE OF KOMALA"	Mideast • PRO-COMMUNIST
3935	**NEW ZEALAND**	
	RADIO READING SVC, Levin	DS • 1 kW
3940v	**KOREA (DPR)**	
	NORTH HAMGYONG PS, Ch'ongjin	Irr • DS • ALT. FREQ. TO 3981v kHz
3945	**INDIA**	
	ALL INDIA RADIO, Gorakhpur	S Asia • 50 kW; DS • 50 kW
	IRAN	
	VO THE ISLAMIC REP, Tehrān	W • Mideast • 500 kW
	VO THE ISLAMIC REP, Zāhedān	W • W Asia & S Asia • 500 kW
	JAPAN	
	RADIO NIKKEI, Tokyo-Nagara	DS-2 • 10 kW; Sa/Su • DS-2 • 10 kW; Irr • Sa/Su • DS-2 • 10 kW
3945v	**VANUATU**	
	RADIO VANUATU, Vila, Efate Island	ENGLISH, FRENCH, ETC • DS • 8 kW • ALT. FREQ. TO 7260 kHz
3950	**CHINA**	
	XINJIANG PEOPLE'S BC STN, Urümqi	W • DS-CHINESE • 100 kW

0 1 2 3 4 5 6 7 8 9 10 11 12 13 14 15 16 17 18 19 20 21 22 23 24

SEASONAL S OR W · 1-HR TIMESHIFT MIDYEAR ⇦ OR ⇨ · JAMMING / OR /\ · EARLIEST HEARD ◁ · LATEST HEARD ▷ · NEW FOR 2009 †

World Time 0 1 2 3 4 5 6 7 8 9 10 11 12 13 14 15 16 17 18 19 20 21 22 23 24

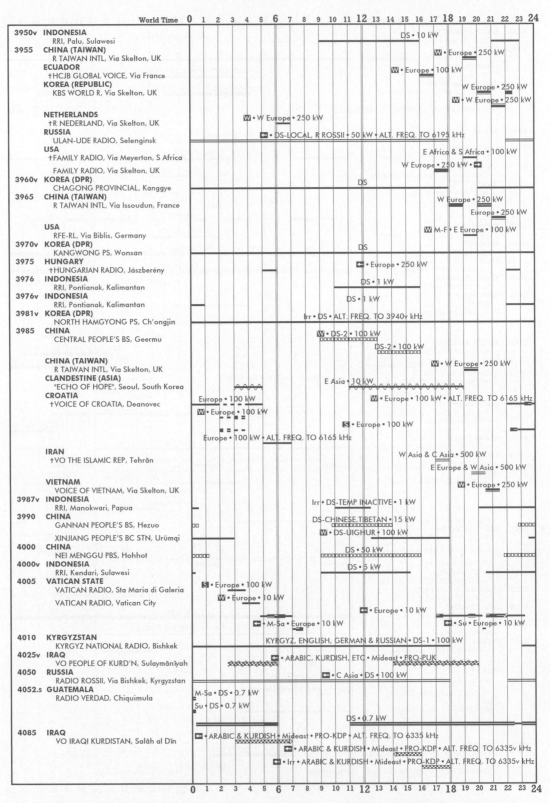

Frequency	Country / Station	Schedule notes
3950v	**INDONESIA** RRI, Palu, Sulawesi	DS • 10 kW
3955	**CHINA (TAIWAN)** R TAIWAN INTL, Via Skelton, UK	W • Europe • 250 kW
	ECUADOR †HCJB GLOBAL VOICE, Via France	W • Europe • 100 kW
	KOREA (REPUBLIC) KBS WORLD R, Via Skelton, UK	W Europe • 250 kW
		W • W Europe • 250 kW
	NETHERLANDS †R NEDERLAND, Via Skelton, UK	W • W Europe • 250 kW
	RUSSIA ULAN-UDE RADIO, Selenginsk	← • DS-LOCAL, R ROSSII • 50 kW • ALT. FREQ. TO 6195 kHz
	USA †FAMILY RADIO, Via Meyerton, S Africa	E Africa & S Africa • 100 kW
	FAMILY RADIO, Via Skelton, UK	W Europe • 250 kW • →
3960v	**KOREA (DPR)** CHAGONG PROVINCIAL, Kanggye	DS
3965	**CHINA (TAIWAN)** R TAIWAN INTL, Via Issoudun, France	W Europe • 250 kW
		Europe • 250 kW
	USA RFE-RL, Via Biblis, Germany	W M-F • E Europe • 100 kW
3970v	**KOREA (DPR)** KANGWONG PS, Wonsan	DS
3975	**HUNGARY** †HUNGARIAN RADIO, Jászberény	← • Europe • 250 kW
3976	**INDONESIA** RRI, Pontianak, Kalimantan	DS • 1 kW
3976v	**INDONESIA** RRI, Pontianak, Kalimantan	DS • 1 kW
3981v	**KOREA (DPR)** NORTH HAMGYONG PS, Ch'ongjin	Irr • DS • ALT. FREQ. TO 3940v kHz
3985	**CHINA** CENTRAL PEOPLE'S BS, Geermu	W • DS-2 • 100 kW
		DS-2 • 100 kW
	CHINA (TAIWAN) R TAIWAN INTL, Via Skelton, UK	W • W Europe • 250 kW
	CLANDESTINE (ASIA) "ECHO OF HOPE", Seoul, South Korea	E Asia • 10 kW
	CROATIA †VOICE OF CROATIA, Deanovec	W • Europe • 100 kW • ALT. FREQ. TO 6165 kHz
		Europe • 100 kW
		W • Europe • 100 kW
		S • Europe • 100 kW
		Europe • 100 kW • ALT. FREQ. TO 6165 kHz
	IRAN †VO THE ISLAMIC REP, Tehrān	W Asia & C Asia • 500 kW
		E Europe & W Asia • 500 kW
	VIETNAM VOICE OF VIETNAM, Via Skelton, UK	W • Europe • 250 kW
3987v	**INDONESIA** RRI, Manokwari, Papua	Irr • DS-TEMP INACTIVE • 1 kW
3990	**CHINA** GANNAN PEOPLE'S BS, Hezuo	DS-CHINESE, TIBETAN • 15 kW
	XINJIANG PEOPLE'S BC STN, Urümqi	W • DS-UIGHUR • 100 kW
4000	**CHINA** NEI MENGGU PBS, Hohhot	DS • 50 kW
4000v	**INDONESIA** RRI, Kendari, Sulawesi	DS • 5 kW
4005	**VATICAN STATE** VATICAN RADIO, Sta Maria di Galeria	S • Europe • 100 kW
		W • Europe • 10 kW
	VATICAN RADIO, Vatican City	← • Europe • 10 kW
		← • M-Sa • Europe • 10 kW
		← • Su • Europe • 10 kW
4010	**KYRGYZSTAN** KYRGYZ NATIONAL RADIO, Bishkek	KYRGYZ, ENGLISH, GERMAN & RUSSIAN • DS-1 • 100 kW
4025v	**IRAQ** VO PEOPLE OF KURD'N, Sulaymānīyah	← • ARABIC, KURDISH, ETC • Mideast • PRO-PUK
4050	**RUSSIA** RADIO ROSSII, Via Bishkek, Kyrgyzstan	← • C Asia • DS • 100 kW
4052.5	**GUATEMALA** RADIO VERDAD, Chiquimula	M-Sa • DS • 0.7 kW
		Su • DS • 0.7 kW
		DS • 0.7 kW
4085	**IRAQ** VO IRAQI KURDISTAN, Salāh al Dīn	← • ARABIC & KURDISH • Mideast • PRO-KDP • ALT. FREQ. TO 6335 kHz
		← • ARABIC & KURDISH • Mideast • PRO-KDP • ALT. FREQ. TO 6335v kHz
		← • Irr • ARABIC & KURDISH • Mideast • PRO-KDP • ALT. FREQ. TO 6335v kHz

0 1 2 3 4 5 6 7 8 9 10 11 12 13 14 15 16 17 18 19 20 21 22 23 24

ENGLISH ▬ ARABIC ▭ CHINESE ▫▫▫ FRENCH ═ GERMAN ▬ RUSSIAN ═ SPANISH ═ OTHER —

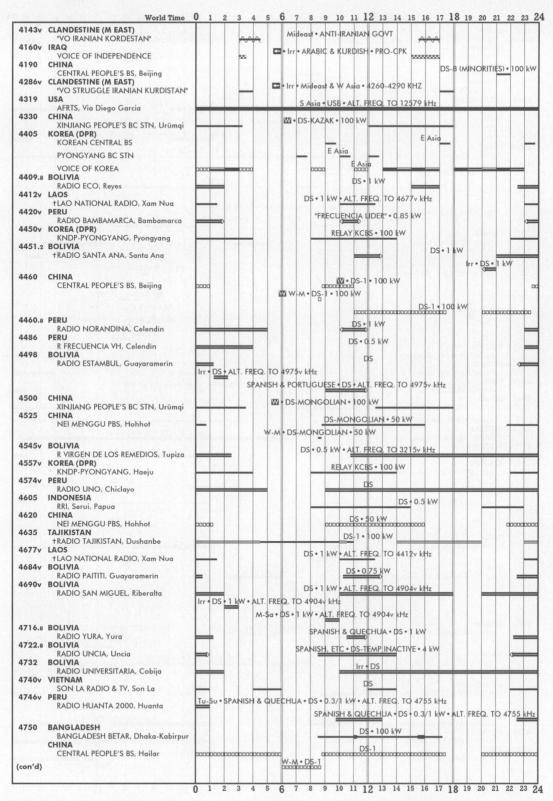

World Time 0 1 2 3 4 5 6 7 8 9 10 11 12 13 14 15 16 17 18 19 20 21 22 23 24

Freq.	Country / Station	Notes
4143v	**CLANDESTINE (M EAST)** "VO IRANIAN KORDESTAN"	Mideast • ANTI-IRANIAN GOVT
4160v	**IRAQ** VOICE OF INDEPENDENCE	Irr • ARABIC & KURDISH • PRO-CPK
4190	**CHINA** CENTRAL PEOPLE'S BS, Beijing	DS-8 (MINORITIES) • 100 kW
4286v	**CLANDESTINE (M EAST)** "VO STRUGGLE IRANIAN KURDISTAN"	Irr • Mideast & W Asia • 4260-4290 KHZ
4319	**USA** AFRTS, Via Diego Garcia	S Asia • USB • ALT. FREQ. TO 12579 kHz
4330	**CHINA** XINJIANG PEOPLE'S BC STN, Urümqi	W • DS-KAZAK • 100 kW
4405	**KOREA (DPR)** KOREAN CENTRAL BS	E Asia
	PYONGYANG BC STN	E Asia
	VOICE OF KOREA	E Asia
4409.8	**BOLIVIA** RADIO ECO, Reyes	DS • 1 kW
4412v	**LAOS** †LAO NATIONAL RADIO, Xam Nua	DS • 1 kW • ALT. FREQ. TO 4677v kHz
4420v	**PERU** RADIO BAMBAMARCA, Bambamarca	"FRECUENCIA LIDER" • 0.85 kW
4450v	**KOREA (DPR)** KNDP-PYONGYANG, Pyongyang	RELAY KCBS • 100 kW
4451.2	**BOLIVIA** †RADIO SANTA ANA, Santa Ana	DS • 1 kW; Irr • DS • 1 kW
4460	**CHINA** CENTRAL PEOPLE'S BS, Beijing	W • DS-1 • 100 kW; W W-M • DS-1 • 100 kW; DS-1 • 100 kW
4460.8	**PERU** RADIO NORANDINA, Celendín	DS • 1 kW
4486	**PERU** R FRECUENCIA VH, Celendín	DS • 0.5 kW
4498	**BOLIVIA** RADIO ESTAMBUL, Guayaramerín	DS; Irr • DS • ALT. FREQ. TO 4975v kHz; SPANISH & PORTUGUESE • DS • ALT. FREQ. TO 4975v kHz
4500	**CHINA** XINJIANG PEOPLE'S BC STN, Urümqi	W • DS-MONGOLIAN • 100 kW
4525	**CHINA** NEI MENGGU PBS, Hohhot	DS-MONGOLIAN • 50 kW; W-M • DS-MONGOLIAN • 50 kW
4545v	**BOLIVIA** R VIRGEN DE LOS REMEDIOS, Tupiza	DS • 0.5 kW • ALT. FREQ. TO 3215v kHz
4557v	**KOREA (DPR)** KNDP-PYONGYANG, Haeju	RELAY KCBS • 100 kW
4574v	**PERU** RADIO UNO, Chiclayo	DS
4605	**INDONESIA** RRI, Serui, Papua	DS • 0.5 kW
4620	**CHINA** NEI MENGGU PBS, Hohhot	DS • 50 kW
4635	**TAJIKISTAN** †RADIO TAJIKISTAN, Dushanbe	DS-1 • 100 kW
4677v	**LAOS** †LAO NATIONAL RADIO, Xam Nua	DS • 1 kW • ALT. FREQ. TO 4412v kHz
4684v	**BOLIVIA** RADIO PAITITI, Guayaramerín	DS • 0.75 kW
4690v	**BOLIVIA** RADIO SAN MIGUEL, Riberalta	DS • 1 kW • ALT. FREQ. TO 4904v kHz; Irr • DS • 1 kW • ALT. FREQ. TO 4904v kHz; M-Sa • DS • 1 kW • ALT. FREQ. TO 4904v kHz
4716.8	**BOLIVIA** RADIO YURA, Yura	SPANISH & QUECHUA • DS • 1 kW
4722.8	**BOLIVIA** RADIO UNCIA, Uncía	SPANISH, ETC • DS-TEMP INACTIVE • 4 kW
4732	**BOLIVIA** RADIO UNIVERSITARIA, Cobija	Irr • DS
4740v	**VIETNAM** SON LA RADIO & TV, Son La	DS
4746v	**PERU** RADIO HUANTA 2000, Huanta	Tu-Su • SPANISH & QUECHUA • DS • 0.3/1 kW • ALT. FREQ. TO 4755 kHz; SPANISH & QUECHUA • DS • 0.3/1 kW • ALT. FREQ. TO 4755 kHz
4750	**BANGLADESH** BANGLADESH BETAR, Dhaka-Kabirpur	DS • 100 kW
	CHINA CENTRAL PEOPLE'S BS, Hailar	DS-1; W-M • DS-1

(con'd)

World Time 0 1 2 3 4 5 6 7 8 9 10 11 12 13 14 15 16 17 18 19 20 21 22 23 24

kHz	Country / Station	Schedule notes
4750 (con'd)	**CHINA** QINGHAI PEOPLE'S BS, Xining	DS • 50 kW
	INDONESIA RRI, Makassar, Sulawesi	DS-TEMP INACTIVE • 50 kW
	SUDAN RADIO PEACE	ENGLISH, ETC • DS • 1 kW
	UGANDA DUNAMIS SHORTWAVE, Mukono	1 kW
4755	**MICRONESIA** PMA RADIO STN, Ninseitamw, Pohnpei	M-F • Pacific • 1 kW
	PERU RADIO HUANTA 2000, Huanta	Tu-Su • SPANISH & QUECHUA • DS • 0.3/1 kW • ALT. FREQ. TO 4746v kHz; SPANISH & QUECHUA • DS • 0.3/1 kW • ALT. FREQ. TO 4746v kHz
4755v	**BRAZIL** R IMACULADA CONCEICAO, C Grande	DS • 10 kW
4760	**INDIA** ALL INDIA RADIO, Leh	S • DS • 50 kW; ENGLISH, ETC • DS • 50 kW; DS • 50 kW; ENGLISH, ETC • DS • 10 kW; Irr • DS • 50 kW
	ALL INDIA RADIO, Port Blair	ENGLISH, ETC • DS • 8.5 kW; Irr • DS • 8.5 kW; DS • 8.5 kW
	LIBERIA RADIO ELWA, Monrovia	DS • 1 kW; Irr • DS • 1 kW
	USA †TRANS WORLD R, Via Swaziland	S Sa • S Africa • 50 kW; S Su-F • S Africa • 50 kW; S • S Africa • 50 kW; S M-F • S Africa • 50 kW; S Sa/Su • S Africa • 50 kW; W • S Africa • 50 kW
4761.7	**BOLIVIA** RADIO GUANAY, Guanay	Irr • DS
4763.2	**BOLIVIA** RADIO CHICHA, Tocla	DS
4764v	**PERU** RADIO CHINCHEROS, Chincheros	SPANISH & QUECHUA • DS • 1 kW
4765	**BRAZIL** RADIO INTEGRACAO, Cruzeiro do Sul	DS-TEMP INACTIVE • 10 kW
	RADIO RURAL, Santarém	DS • 5 kW
4770	**NIGERIA** RADIO NIGERIA, Kaduna	ENGLISH, ETC • DS-2 • 50 kW
4770v	**ECUADOR** CENTINELA DEL SUR, Loja	DS • 2 kW
4775	**BRAZIL** RADIO CONGONHAS, Congonhas	M-Sa • DS • 1 kW • ➡; DS • 1 kW • ➡
	INDIA ALL INDIA RADIO, Imphal	DS • 50 kW; ENGLISH, ETC • DS • 50 kW; Irr • DS • 50 kW
	PERU RADIO TARMA, Tarma	DS • 1 kW; Tu-Su • DS • 1 kW
	USA †TRANS WORLD R, Via Swaziland	S Africa • 50 kW; S Africa • 25/50 kW; M-F • S Africa • 25/50 kW; Sa/Su • S Africa • 25/50 kW
4777	**GABON** RTV GABONAISE, Moyabi	DS-"RADIO GABON" • 250 kW; DS-"RADIO GABON" • 250 kW; Irr • DS-"RADIO GABON" • 250 kW
4780	**DJIBOUTI** RADIO DJIBOUTI, Djibouti	ARABIC, ETC • DS • 100 kW; Irr • ARABIC, ETC • DS-RAMADAN • 100 kW
	GUATEMALA R CULTURAL COATAN, San Sebastián	SPANISH, ETC • DS; Irr • DS
4781	**BOLIVIA** RADIO TACANA, Tumupasa	Irr • SPANISH, ETC • DS; SPANISH, ETC • DS
4781v	**ECUADOR** RADIO ORIENTAL, Tena	Irr • DS • 1 kW
4783v	**MALI** RTV DU MALI, Bamako	FRENCH, ETC • DS-TEMP INACTIVE • 100 kW; Sa • DS-TEMP INACTIVE • 100 kW
(con'd)		

World Time 0 1 2 3 4 5 6 7 8 9 10 11 12 13 14 15 16 17 18 19 20 21 22 23 24

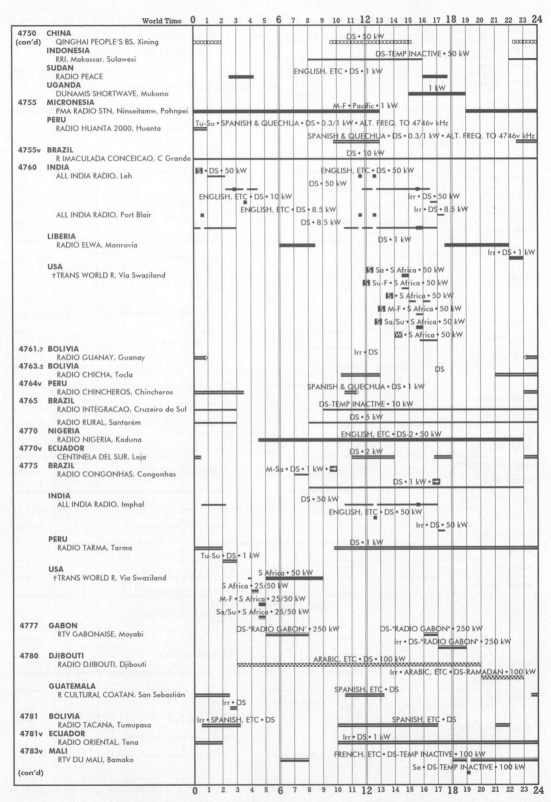

ENGLISH ▬ ARABIC ▩ CHINESE ▫▫▫ FRENCH ═ GERMAN ═ RUSSIAN ═ SPANISH ═ OTHER —

World Time 0–24

Frequency	Country	Station	Schedule
4783v (con'd)	MALI	RTV DU MALI, Bamako	Su-F • FRENCH, ETC • DS-TEMP INACTIVE • 100 kW
4785	BRAZIL	RADIO BRASIL, Campinas	DS • 1 kW
		RADIO CAIARI, Porto Velho	DS • 10 kW
	CHINA	NEI MENGGU PBS, Hohhot	DS-MONGOLIAN • 50 kW; W-M • DS-MONGOLIAN • 50 kW
4788v	BOLIVIA	RADIO BALLIVIAN, San Borja	Irr • Tu-Su • DS • 1 kW; Irr • DS • 1 kW; Irr • M-Sa • DS • 1 kW
4789v	INDONESIA	RRI, Fak Fak, Papua	DS • 1 kW
4790	INDIA	ALL INDIA RADIO, Chennai	SE Asia • 100 kW
	PERU	RADIO ATLANTIDA, Iquitos	DS • 1/3 kW; Su • DS • 1/3 kW
	SAUDI ARABIA	BS OF THE KINGDOM, Jiddah	Irr • 0.5 X 9580 KHZ • SPR
4790v	PAKISTAN (AZAD K)	AZAD KASHMIR RADIO, Via Islamabad	S Asia • 100 kW
		AZAD KASHMIR RADIO, Via Rawalpindi	S Asia • 10 kW
4790.2	PERU	RADIO VISION, Chiclayo	DS • 0.5 kW; Irr • DS • 0.5 kW
4795	KYRGYZSTAN	KYRGYZ NATIONAL RADIO, Bishkek	KYRGYZ, ENGLISH, GERMAN & RUSSIAN • DS-1 • 15 kW
4796.4	BOLIVIA	RADIO MALLKU, Uyuni	Tu-Su • DS • 1 kW; SPANISH & QUECHUA • DS • 1 kW; M-Sa • DS • 1 kW
4799.8	GUATEMALA	R BUENAS NUEVAS, San Sebastián	SPANISH, ETC • DS • 1 kW
4800	CHINA	CENTRAL PEOPLE'S BS, Geermu	DS-1 • 100 kW; W-M • DS-1 • 100 kW
	INDIA	ALL INDIA RADIO, Hyderabad	Irr • DS • 50 kW; DS • 50 kW; ENGLISH, ETC • DS • 50 kW
	LESOTHO	RADIO LESOTHO, Maseru	DS-TEMP INACTIVE • 100 kW
4805	BRAZIL	R DIF DO AMAZONAS, Manaus	DS • 5/10 kW
4810	ARMENIA	PUBLIC RADIO OF ARMENIA, Yerevan	⬅ • E Europe, Mideast & W Asia • DS • 100 kW
		VOICE OF ARMENIA, Yerevan	⬅ • E Europe, Mideast & W Asia • 100 kW
	INDIA	ALL INDIA RADIO, Bhopal	ENGLISH, ETC • DS • 50 kW; DS • 50 kW
4810v	MEXICO	R TRANSCONTINENTAL, México City	⬅ • Irr • 2.5/5 kW; ⬅ • Irr • M-Sa • 2.5/5 kW
4815	BRAZIL	RADIO DIFUSORA, Londrina	DS • 10 kW • ➡; Irr • DS • 10 kW • ➡
	ECUADOR	RADIO BUEN PASTOR, Saraguro	SPANISH, ETC • DS • 1 kW; DS • 1 kW
4819.2	HONDURAS	LA VOZ EVANGELICA, Tegucigalpa	DS-TEMP INACTIVE • 2/5 kW; M • DS-TEMP INACTIVE • 2/5 kW; Tu-Su • DS-TEMP INACTIVE • 2/5 kW
4820	CHINA	XIZANG PBS, Lhasa	DS • 100 kW; W-M • DS • 100 kW
	INDIA	ALL INDIA RADIO, Kolkata	DS • 50 kW; ENGLISH, ETC • DS • 50 kW
4824.4	PERU	LA VOZ DE LA SELVA, Iquitos	Tu-Su • DS • 10 kW; M-F • DS • 10 kW; Tu-Sa • DS • 10 kW; M-Sa • DS • 10 kW; DS • 10 kW
4825	BRAZIL	R CANCAO NOVA, Cachoeira Paulista	DS • 10 kW
		RADIO EDUCADORA, Bragança	DS • 5 kW
4826v	PERU	RADIO SICUANI, Sicuani	DS • 0.35/1 kW

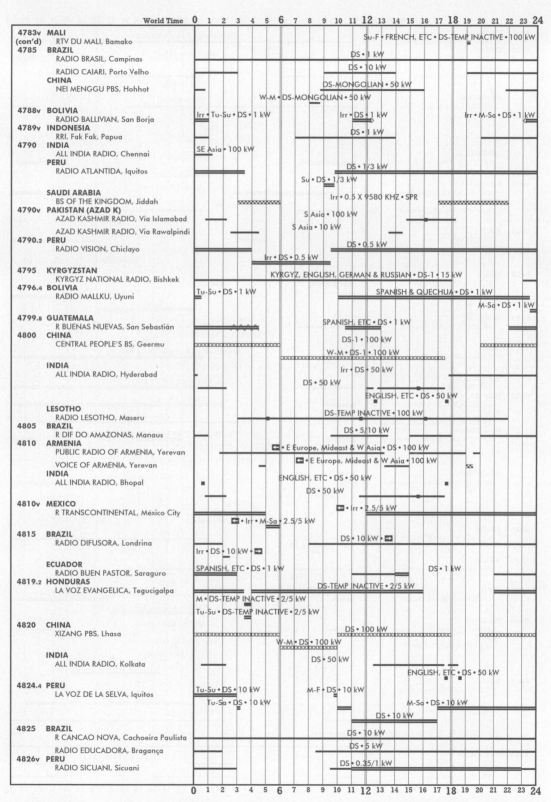

World Time 0 1 2 3 4 5 6 7 8 9 10 11 12 13 14 15 16 17 18 19 20 21 22 23 24

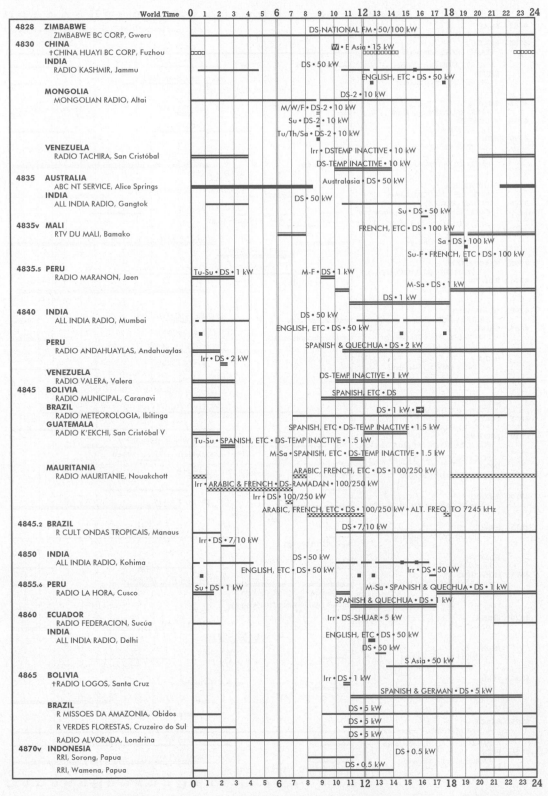

kHz	Country	Station	Schedule
4828	ZIMBABWE	ZIMBABWE BC CORP, Gweru	DS-NATIONAL FM • 50/100 kW
4830	CHINA	†CHINA HUAYI BC CORP, Fuzhou	W • E Asia • 15 kW
	INDIA	RADIO KASHMIR, Jammu	DS • 50 kW ENGLISH, ETC • DS • 50 kW
	MONGOLIA	MONGOLIAN RADIO, Altai	DS-2 • 10 kW M/W/F • DS-2 • 10 kW Su • DS-2 • 10 kW Tu/Th/Sa • DS-2 • 10 kW
	VENEZUELA	RADIO TACHIRA, San Cristóbal	Irr • DSTEMP INACTIVE • 10 kW DS-TEMP INACTIVE • 10 kW
4835	AUSTRALIA	ABC NT SERVICE, Alice Springs	Australasia • DS • 50 kW
	INDIA	ALL INDIA RADIO, Gangtok	DS • 50 kW Su • DS • 50 kW
4835v	MALI	RTV DU MALI, Bamako	FRENCH, ETC • DS • 100 kW Sa • DS • 100 kW Su-F • FRENCH, ETC • DS • 100 kW
4835.5	PERU	RADIO MARANON, Jaen	Tu-Su • DS • 1 kW M-F • DS • 1 kW M-Sa • DS • 1 kW DS • 1 kW
4840	INDIA	ALL INDIA RADIO, Mumbai	DS • 50 kW ENGLISH, ETC • DS • 50 kW
	PERU	RADIO ANDAHUAYLAS, Andahuaylas	SPANISH & QUECHUA • DS • 2 kW Irr • DS • 2 kW
	VENEZUELA	RADIO VALERA, Valera	DS-TEMP INACTIVE • 1 kW
4845	BOLIVIA	RADIO MUNICIPAL, Caranavi	SPANISH, ETC • DS
	BRAZIL	RADIO METEOROLOGIA, Ibitinga	DS • 1 kW •
	GUATEMALA	RADIO K'EKCHI, San Cristóbal V	SPANISH, ETC • DS-TEMP INACTIVE • 1.5 kW Tu-Su • SPANISH, ETC • DS-TEMP INACTIVE • 1.5 kW M-Sa • SPANISH, ETC • DS-TEMP INACTIVE • 1.5 kW
	MAURITANIA	RADIO MAURITANIE, Nouakchott	ARABIC, FRENCH, ETC • DS • 100/250 kW Irr • ARABIC & FRENCH • DS-RAMADAN • 100/250 kW Irr • DS • 100/250 kW ARABIC, FRENCH, ETC • DS • 100/250 kW • ALT. FREQ. TO 7245 kHz
4845.2	BRAZIL	R CULT ONDAS TROPICAIS, Manaus	DS • 7/10 kW Irr • DS • 7/10 kW
4850	INDIA	ALL INDIA RADIO, Kohima	DS • 50 kW ENGLISH, ETC • DS • 50 kW Irr • DS • 50 kW
4855.6	PERU	RADIO LA HORA, Cusco	Su • DS • 1 kW M-Sa • SPANISH & QUECHUA • DS • 1 kW SPANISH & QUECHUA • DS • 1 kW
4860	ECUADOR	RADIO FEDERACION, Sucúa	Irr • DS-SHUAR • 5 kW
	INDIA	ALL INDIA RADIO, Delhi	ENGLISH, ETC • DS • 50 kW DS • 50 kW S Asia • 50 kW
4865	BOLIVIA	†RADIO LOGOS, Santa Cruz	Irr • DS • 1 kW SPANISH & GERMAN • DS • 5 kW
	BRAZIL	R MISSOES DA AMAZONIA, Obidos	DS • 5 kW
		R VERDES FLORESTAS, Cruzeiro do Sul	DS • 5 kW
		RADIO ALVORADA, Londrina	DS • 5 kW
4870v	INDONESIA	RRI, Sorong, Papua	DS • 0.5 kW
		RRI, Wamena, Papua	DS • 0.5 kW

0 1 2 3 4 5 6 7 8 9 10 11 12 13 14 15 16 17 18 19 20 21 22 23 24

ENGLISH ARABIC CHINESE FRENCH GERMAN RUSSIAN SPANISH OTHER

World Time 0 1 2 3 4 5 6 7 8 9 10 11 12 13 14 15 16 17 18 19 20 21 22 23 24

kHz	Country / Station	Schedule notes
4876v	**BRAZIL**	
	R DIFUSORA RORAIMA, Boa Vista	Irr • PORTUGUESE & SPANISH • DS • 10 kW
4880	**CLANDESTINE (AFRICA)**	
	"SW RADIO AFRICA", Via S Africa	S Africa • 100 kW
	INDIA	
	ALL INDIA RADIO, Lucknow	ENGLISH, ETC • DS • 50 kW Irr • DS • 50 kW DS • 50 kW
4880.8	**PERU**	
	RADIO COMAS, Lima	DS-TEMP INACTIVE • 5 kW
4885	**BRAZIL**	
	R CLUBE DO PARA, Belém	DS • 2 kW
	R DIF ACREANA, Rio Branco	DS • 5 kW
	VOZ CORACAO IMACULADO, Anápolis	DS-TEMP INACTIVE • 0.25/1 kW • ➡
4886.8	**PERU**	
	R VIRGEN DEL CARMEN, Huancavelica	SPANISH & QUECHUA • DS • 1 kW
4890	**PAPUA NEW GUINEA**	
	NBC, Port Moresby	DS-TEMP INACTIVE • 100 kW • ALT. FREQ. TO 9675 kHz ENGLISH, ETC • DS-TEMP INACTIVE • 100 kW ENGLISH, ETC • DS-TEMP INACTIVE • 100 kW • ALT. FREQ. TO 9675 kHz
4890v	**PERU**	
	RADIO MACEDONIA, Arequipa	DS-TEMP INACTIVE • 1 kW
4890.3	**PERU**	
	RADIO CHOTA, Chota	DS • 1 kW Irr • DS • 1 kW
4895	**BRAZIL**	
	R GLOBO MANAUS, Manaus	DS • 5 kW
	RADIO NOVO TEMPO, Campo Grande	DS • 5 kW
	INDIA	
	ALL INDIA RADIO, Kurseong	DS • 20 kW ENGLISH, ETC • DS • 20 kW
	MONGOLIA	
	MONGOLIAN RADIO, Murun	DS-2 • 10 kW M/W/F • DS-2 • 10 kW Su • DS-2 • 10 kW Tu/Th/Sa • DS-2 • 10 kW
4899v	**ECUADOR**	
	LA VOZ DE SAQUISILI, Saquisilí	Irr • DS • 1 kW
4900	**CHINA**	
	†VO THE STRAIT-PLA, Fuzhou	E Asia • AMOY CHANNEL • 50 kW
4904v	**BOLIVIA**	
	RADIO SAN MIGUEL, Riberalta	DS • 1 kW • ALT. FREQ. TO 4690v kHz Irr • DS • 1 kW • ALT. FREQ. TO 4690v kHz M-Sa • DS • 1 kW • ALT. FREQ. TO 4690v kHz
4905	**BRAZIL**	
	RADIO ANHANGUERA, Araguaína	DS • 1 kW
	CHINA	
	XIZANG PBS, Lhasa	DS-TIBETAN • 100 kW W-M • DS-TIBETAN • 100 kW DS • 100 kW W-M • DS • 100 kW
4905v	**BRAZIL**	
	RADIO RELOGIO, Rio de Janeiro	Irr • DS • 2.5 kW • ➡
4909.3	**ECUADOR**	
	RADIO CHASKIS, Otavalo	SPANISH, ETC • DS
4910	**AUSTRALIA**	
	ABC NT SERVICE, Tennant Creek	Australasia • DS • 50 kW
	INDIA	
	ALL INDIA RADIO, Jaipur	DS • 50 kW ENGLISH, ETC • DS • 50 kW
	ZAMBIA	
	RADIO ZAMBIA-ZNBC, Lusaka	ENGLISH, ETC • DS-1 • 100 kW • ALT. FREQ. TO 5915 kHz
4915	**BRAZIL**	
	R DIF DE MACAPA, Macapá	DS • 10 kW
	RADIO ANHANGUERA, Goiânia	DS • 10 kW • ➡
	GHANA	
	GHANA BC CORP, Accra	ENGLISH, ETC • DS-1 • 35/50 kW Sa/Su/Holidays • ENGLISH, ETC • DS-1 • 35/50 kW
	KENYA	
	KENYA BC CORP, Nairobi	M-F • DS-EASTERN SERVICE • 10 kW
4919	**ECUADOR**	
	RADIO QUITO, Quito	DS-TEMP INACTIVE • 5 kW
4920	**CHINA**	
	XIZANG PBS, Lhasa	DS-TIBETAN • 100 kW W-M • DS-TIBETAN • 100 kW DS • 100 kW W-M • DS • 100 kW
	INDIA	
(con'd)	ALL INDIA RADIO, Chennai	DS • 50 kW

World Time 0 1 2 3 4 5 6 7 8 9 10 11 12 13 14 15 16 17 18 19 20 21 22 23 24

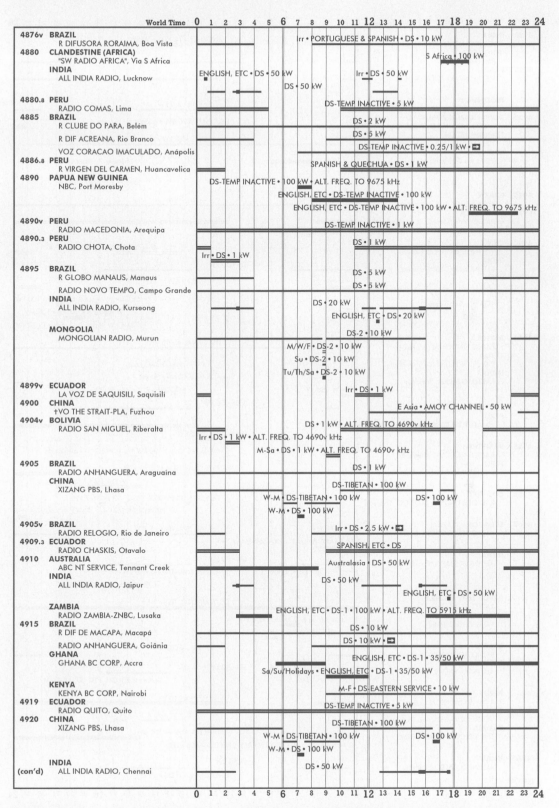

World Time 0 1 2 3 4 5 6 7 8 9 10 11 12 13 14 15 16 17 18 19 20 21 22 23 24

kHz	Country / Station	Schedule
4920 (con'd)	**INDIA** ALL INDIA RADIO, Chennai	ENGLISH, ETC • DS • 50 kW
	INDONESIA RRI, Biak, Papua	Irr • DS • 1 kW
4925	**BRAZIL** R EDUCACAO RURAL, Tefé	DS • 1 kW; Tu-Su • DS • 1 kW
	INDONESIA RRI, Jambi, Sumatera	Irr • DS • 2.5 kW
4930	**DOMINICAN REPUBLIC** RADIO BARAHONA, Barahona	DS-TEMP INACTIVE • 1 kW
	TURKMENISTAN TURKMEN RADIO, Ashgabat	DS-2 • 50 kW
	USA VOA, Via Botswana	S Africa • 100 kW; M-F • S Africa • 100 kW; Sa/Su • S Africa • 100 kW
4935	**BRAZIL** RADIO CAPIXABA, Vitória	DS • 1 kW
4939v	**VENEZUELA** RADIO AMAZONAS, Puerto Ayacucho	DS • 1 kW; Irr • DS • 1 kW
4940	**CHINA** †VO THE STRAIT-PLA, Fuzhou	E Asia • NEWS CHANNEL • 50 kW
	INDIA ALL INDIA RADIO, Guwahati	DS • 50 kW
	PERU RADIO SAN ANTONIO, Villa Atalaya	DS • 1 kW
	USA VOA, Via São Tomé	Sa/Su • W Africa & C Africa • 100 kW; W Africa & C Africa • 100 kW; M-F • W Africa & C Africa • 100 kW
4950	**ANGOLA** RADIO NACIONAL, Mulenvos	DS-CANAL A • 15 kW
	CHINA VOICE OF PUJIANG, Shanghai	E Asia
	INDIA RADIO KASHMIR, Srinagar	Irr • DS-RAMADAN • 50 kW; S • DS • 50 kW; ENGLISH, ETC • DS • 50 kW; DS • 50 kW
	PERU R MADRE DE DIOS, Puerto Maldonado	DS • 5 kW; M-Sa • DS • 5 kW
4955	**PAKISTAN** RADIO PAKISTAN, Islamabad	W Asia & C Asia • 100 kW • ALT. FREQ. TO 6065 kHz
	PERU R CULTURAL AMAUTA, Huanta	SPANISH & QUECHUA • DS • 1 kW; M-Sa • DS • 1 kW
4958	**BOLIVIA** RADIODIFUSORAS TROPICO, Trinidad	DS • 0.75/3 kW • ALT. FREQ. TO 6036.7 kHz; DS • 0.75/3 kW • ALT. FREQ. TO 6037.6 kHz
4960	**ECUADOR** RADIO FEDERACION, Sucúa	DS-SHUAR, SPANISH • 5 kW; Tu-Su • DS-SHUAR, SPANISH • 5 kW
	INDIA ALL INDIA RADIO, Ranchi	DS • 50 kW; Irr • DS • 50 kW; ENGLISH & HINDI • DS • 50 kW; ENGLISH, ETC • DS • 50 kW
	PAPUA NEW GUINEA RADIO ST GABRIEL, Vanimo	DS-TEMP INACTIVE • 1 kW
	USA VOA, Via São Tomé	W Africa & C Africa • 100 kW; S M-F • W Africa & C Africa • 100 kW
4965	**BRAZIL** RADIO ALVORADA, Parintins	DS • 5 kW
	INDIA ALL INDIA RADIO, Shimla	DS • 50 kW; Sa/Su • ENGLISH, ETC • DS • 50 kW
	PERU R SANTA MONICA, Cusco	DS-TEMP INACTIVE • 5 kW
	RUSSIA VOICE OF RUSSIA, Via Tajikistan	⇐ • W Asia & S Asia • 100 kW
	ZAMBIA THE VOICE-AFRICA, Lusaka	C Africa & S Africa • 100 kW; C Africa & S Africa • 100 kW • ALT. FREQ. TO 6065 kHz
4970 (con'd)	**INDIA** ALL INDIA RADIO, Shillong	DS • 50 kW; ENGLISH, ETC • DS • 50 kW

World Time 0 1 2 3 4 5 6 7 8 9 10 11 12 13 14 15 16 17 18 19 20 21 22 23 24

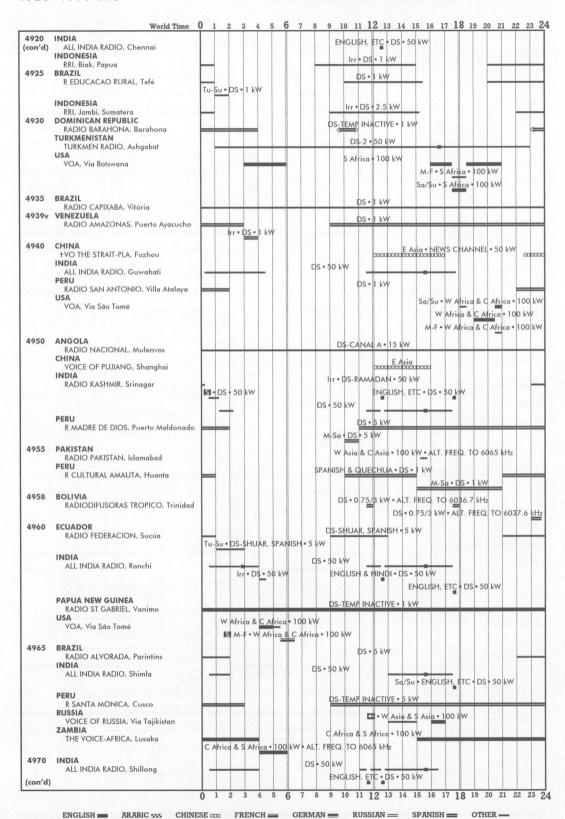

ENGLISH ▬ ARABIC ▭ CHINESE ▯▯▯ FRENCH ═ GERMAN ▬ RUSSIAN ═ SPANISH ═ OTHER —

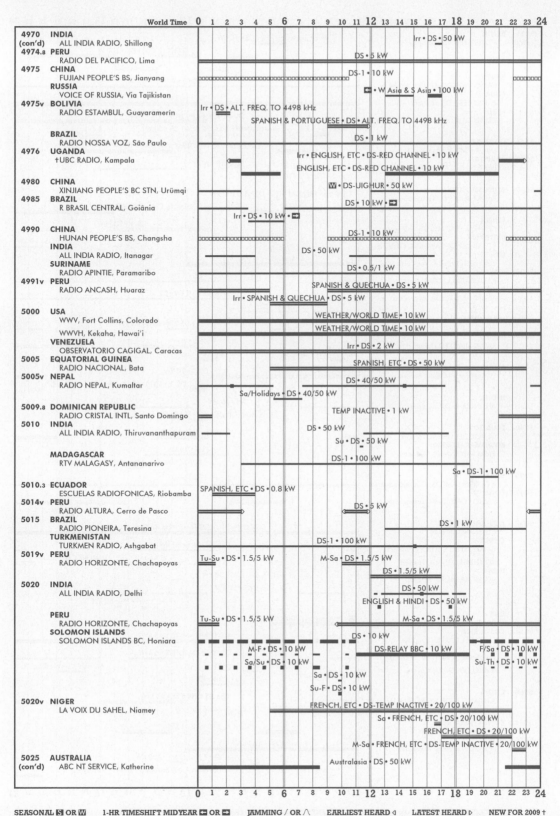

World Time 0 1 2 3 4 5 6 7 8 9 10 11 12 13 14 15 16 17 18 19 20 21 22 23 24

Frequency	Country / Station	Schedule
4970 (con'd)	**INDIA** ALL INDIA RADIO, Shillong	Irr • DS • 50 kW
4974.8	**PERU** RADIO DEL PACIFICO, Lima	DS • 5 kW
4975	**CHINA** FUJIAN PEOPLE'S BS, Jianyang	DS-1 • 10 kW
	RUSSIA VOICE OF RUSSIA, Via Tajikistan	• W Asia & S Asia • 100 kW
4975v	**BOLIVIA** RADIO ESTAMBUL, Guayaramerín	Irr • DS • ALT. FREQ. TO 4498 kHz
		SPANISH & PORTUGUESE • DS • ALT. FREQ. TO 4498 kHz
	BRAZIL RADIO NOSSA VOZ, São Paulo	DS • 1 kW
4976	**UGANDA** †UBC RADIO, Kampala	Irr • ENGLISH, ETC • DS-RED CHANNEL • 10 kW
		ENGLISH, ETC • DS-RED CHANNEL • 10 kW
4980	**CHINA** XINJIANG PEOPLE'S BC STN, Urümqi	W • DS-UIGHUR • 50 kW
4985	**BRAZIL** R BRASIL CENTRAL, Goiânia	DS • 10 kW •
		Irr • DS • 10 kW •
4990	**CHINA** HUNAN PEOPLE'S BS, Changsha	DS-1 • 10 kW
	INDIA ALL INDIA RADIO, Itanagar	DS • 50 kW
	SURINAME RADIO APINTIE, Paramaribo	DS • 0.5/1 kW
4991v	**PERU** RADIO ANCASH, Huaraz	SPANISH & QUECHUA • DS • 5 kW
		Irr • SPANISH & QUECHUA • DS • 5 kW
5000	**USA** WWV, Fort Collins, Colorado	WEATHER/WORLD TIME • 10 kW
	WWVH, Kekaha, Hawai'i	WEATHER/WORLD TIME • 10 kW
	VENEZUELA OBSERVATORIO CAGIGAL, Caracas	Irr • DS • 2 kW
5005	**EQUATORIAL GUINEA** RADIO NACIONAL, Bata	SPANISH, ETC • DS • 50 kW
5005v	**NEPAL** RADIO NEPAL, Kumaltar	DS • 40/50 kW
		Sa/Holidays • DS • 40/50 kW
5009.8	**DOMINICAN REPUBLIC** RADIO CRISTAL INTL, Santo Domingo	TEMP INACTIVE • 1 kW
5010	**INDIA** ALL INDIA RADIO, Thiruvananthapuram	DS • 50 kW
		Su • DS • 50 kW
	MADAGASCAR RTV MALAGASY, Antananarivo	DS-1 • 100 kW
		Sa • DS-1 • 100 kW
5010.3	**ECUADOR** ESCUELAS RADIOFONICAS, Riobamba	SPANISH, ETC • DS • 0.8 kW
5014v	**PERU** RADIO ALTURA, Cerro de Pasco	DS • 5 kW
5015	**BRAZIL** RADIO PIONEIRA, Teresina	DS • 1 kW
	TURKMENISTAN TURKMEN RADIO, Ashgabat	DS-1 • 100 kW
5019v	**PERU** RADIO HORIZONTE, Chachapoyas	Tu-Su • DS • 1.5/5 kW
		M-Sa • DS • 1.5/5 kW
		DS • 1.5/5 kW
5020	**INDIA** ALL INDIA RADIO, Delhi	DS • 50 kW
		ENGLISH & HINDI • DS • 50 kW
	PERU RADIO HORIZONTE, Chachapoyas	Tu-Su • DS • 1.5/5 kW
		M-Sa • DS • 1.5/5 kW
	SOLOMON ISLANDS SOLOMON ISLANDS BC, Honiara	DS • 10 kW
		M-F • DS • 10 kW
		DS-RELAY BBC • 10 kW
		F/Sa • DS • 10 kW
		Sa/Su • DS • 10 kW
		Su-Th • DS • 10 kW
		Sa • DS • 10 kW
		Su-F • DS • 10 kW
5020v	**NIGER** LA VOIX DU SAHEL, Niamey	FRENCH, ETC • DS-TEMP INACTIVE • 20/100 kW
		Sa • FRENCH, ETC • DS • 20/100 kW
		FRENCH, ETC • DS • 20/100 kW
		M-Sa • FRENCH, ETC • DS-TEMP INACTIVE • 20/100 kW
5025 (con'd)	**AUSTRALIA** ABC NT SERVICE, Katherine	Australasia • DS • 50 kW

0 1 2 3 4 5 6 7 8 9 10 11 12 13 14 15 16 17 18 19 20 21 22 23 24

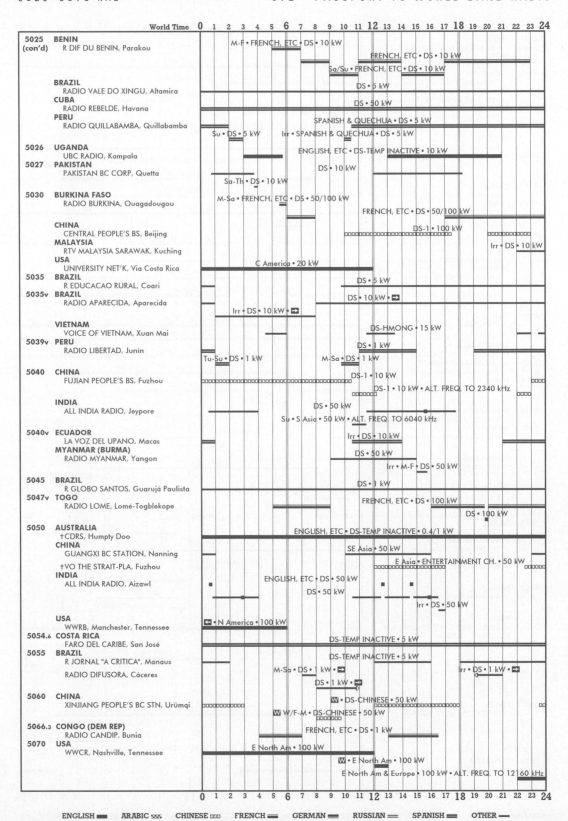

World Time 0 1 2 3 4 5 6 7 8 9 10 11 12 13 14 15 16 17 18 19 20 21 22 23 24

kHz	Country / Station	Schedule
5025 (con'd)	**BENIN** R DIF DU BENIN, Parakou	M-F • FRENCH, ETC • DS • 10 kW FRENCH, ETC • DS • 10 kW Sa/Su • FRENCH, ETC • DS • 10 kW
	BRAZIL RADIO VALE DO XINGU, Altamira	DS • 5 kW
	CUBA RADIO REBELDE, Havana	DS • 50 kW
	PERU RADIO QUILLABAMBA, Quillabamba	SPANISH & QUECHUA • DS • 5 kW Su • DS • 5 kW Irr • SPANISH & QUECHUA • DS • 5 kW
5026	**UGANDA** UBC RADIO, Kampala	ENGLISH, ETC • DS-TEMP INACTIVE • 10 kW
5027	**PAKISTAN** PAKISTAN BC CORP, Quetta	DS • 10 kW Sa-Th • DS • 10 kW
5030	**BURKINA FASO** RADIO BURKINA, Ouagadougou	M-Sa • FRENCH, ETC • DS • 50/100 kW FRENCH, ETC • DS • 50/100 kW
	CHINA CENTRAL PEOPLE'S BS, Beijing	DS-1 • 100 kW
	MALAYSIA RTV MALAYSIA SARAWAK, Kuching	Irr • DS • 10 kW
	USA UNIVERSITY NET'K, Via Costa Rica	C America • 20 kW
5035	**BRAZIL** R EDUCACAO RURAL, Coari	DS • 5 kW
5035v	**BRAZIL** RADIO APARECIDA, Aparecida	DS • 10 kW • ➡ Irr • DS • 10 kW • ➡
	VIETNAM VOICE OF VIETNAM, Xuan Mai	DS-HMONG • 15 kW
5039v	**PERU** RADIO LIBERTAD, Junín	DS • 1 kW Tu-Su • DS • 1 kW M-Sa • DS • 1 kW
5040	**CHINA** FUJIAN PEOPLE'S BS, Fuzhou	DS-1 • 10 kW DS-1 • 10 kW • ALT. FREQ. TO 2340 kHz
	INDIA ALL INDIA RADIO, Jeypore	DS • 50 kW Su • S Asia • 50 kW • ALT. FREQ. TO 6040 kHz
5040v	**ECUADOR** LA VOZ DEL UPANO, Macas	Irr • DS • 10 kW
	MYANMAR (BURMA) RADIO MYANMAR, Yangon	DS • 50 kW Irr • M-F • DS • 50 kW
5045	**BRAZIL** R GLOBO SANTOS, Guarujá Paulista	DS • 1 kW
5047v	**TOGO** RADIO LOME, Lomé-Togblekope	FRENCH, ETC • DS • 100 kW DS • 100 kW
5050	**AUSTRALIA** †CDRS, Humpty Doo	ENGLISH, ETC • DS-TEMP INACTIVE • 0.4/1 kW
	CHINA GUANGXI BC STATION, Nanning	SE Asia • 50 kW
	†VO THE STRAIT-PLA, Fuzhou	E Asia • ENTERTAINMENT CH. • 50 kW
	INDIA ALL INDIA RADIO, Aizawl	ENGLISH, ETC • DS • 50 kW DS • 50 kW Irr • DS • 50 kW
	USA WWRB, Manchester, Tennessee	⬅ • N America • 100 kW
5054.6	**COSTA RICA** FARO DEL CARIBE, San José	DS-TEMP INACTIVE • 5 kW
5055	**BRAZIL** R JORNAL "A CRITICA", Manaus	DS-TEMP INACTIVE • 5 kW
	RADIO DIFUSORA, Cáceres	M-Sa • DS • 1 kW • ➡ Irr • DS • 1 kW • ➡ DS • 1 kW • ➡
5060	**CHINA** XINJIANG PEOPLE'S BC STN, Urümqi	W • DS-CHINESE • 50 kW W W/F-M • DS-CHINESE • 50 kW
5066.3	**CONGO (DEM REP)** RADIO CANDIP, Bunia	FRENCH, ETC • DS • 1 kW
5070	**USA** WWCR, Nashville, Tennessee	E North Am • 100 kW W • E North Am • 100 kW E North Am & Europe • 100 kW • ALT. FREQ. TO 12160 kHz

0 1 2 3 4 5 6 7 8 9 10 11 12 13 14 15 16 17 18 19 20 21 22 23 24

ENGLISH ▬ ARABIC ▭ CHINESE ▫▫▫ FRENCH ═ GERMAN ═ RUSSIAN ═ SPANISH ═ OTHER ─

World Time 0 1 2 3 4 5 6 7 8 9 10 11 12 13 14 15 16 17 18 19 20 21 22 23 24

kHz	Country	Station	Schedule notes
5071v	PERU	ONDAS DEL SURORIENTE, Quillabamba	Irr • DS • 1 kW • ALT. FREQ. TO 5102v kHz
5075	CHINA	VOICE OF PUJIANG, Shanghai	E Asia • 50 kW • ALT. FREQ. TO 9705 kHz
5085	USA	WWRB, Manchester, Tennessee	E North Am • 100 kW; Sa/Su • E North Am • 100 kW; Pacific • 100 kW
5100	ERITREA	RADIO BANA, Asmara	DS; F • DS; Sa-Th • DS; Sa • DS; Su-F • DS
5101v	CLANDESTINE (ASIA)	"VO JAMMU & KASHMIR FREEDOM"	S Asia • ANTI-INDIAN GOVT
5102v	PERU	ONDAS DEL SURORIENTE, Quillabamba	Irr • DS • 1 kW • ALT. FREQ. TO 5071v kHz
5105	USA	WBCQ-"THE PLANET", Monticello,Maine	N America • 50 kW; M-F • N America • 50 kW; M/Sa • N America • 50 kW
5240	CHINA	XIZANG PBS, Lhasa	DS-TIBETAN • 100 kW; W-M • DS-TIBETAN • 100 kW; DS • 100 kW; W-M • DS • 100 kW
5300	PERU	RADIO SUPERIOR, Pardo M Naranjos	DS
5384.2	PERU	RADIO HUARMACA, Huarmaca	DS • 0.3 kW
5420	CHINA	CENTRAL PEOPLE'S BS, Beijing	DS-8 (MINORITIES) • 100 kW
5446.5	USA	AFRTS, Key West, Florida	C America • 8 kW • USB
5460v	PERU	LA VOZ DE BOLIVAR, Bolívar	DS
5470	LIBERIA	RADIO VERITAS, Monrovia	ENGLISH, ETC • DS • 6/10 kW; Irr • ENGLISH, ETC • DS • 6/10 kW
5470v	PERU	R SAN NICOLAS, Rodríguez Mendoza	Irr • DS
5486.6	PERU	REINA DE LA SELVA, Chachapoyas	DS • 0.06 kW; Irr • DS • 0.06 kW
5580.3	BOLIVIA	†RADIO SAN JOSE, San José Chiquitos	0.25 kW; Irr • 0.25 kW
5699.8	PERU	FREC SAN IGNACIO, San Ignacio	Irr • DS • 0.1 kW
5720	PIRATE (EUROPE)	"RADIO ORION", Netherlands	Irr • Sa/Su • W Europe • 0.08/0.4 kW • ALT. FREQ. TO 6300v kHz
5745	USA	†FAMILY RADIO, Okeechobee, Fl	W • C America • 100 kW; W • Europe • 100 kW; W • S America • 100 kW
		RADIO MARTI, Greenville, NC	W • C America • 250 kW
		WWRB, Manchester, Tennessee	N America • 100 kW
5750	USA	VOA, Via Kuwait	W • W Asia & S Asia • 250 kW
5755	USA	†KAIJ, Frisco, TX	W • W North Am • 100 kW; S • W North Am • TEMP INACTIVE • 100 kW • ALT. FREQ. TO 9480 kHz; N America • 100 kW
5765	USA	AFRTS, Via Guam	Pacific • USB • ALT. FREQ. TO 13362 kHz
		WWCR, Nashville, Tennessee	E North Am • 100 kW • ALT. FREQ. TO 7465 kHz; E North Am • 100 kW • ALT. FREQ. TO 5890 kHz
5770	MYANMAR (BURMA)	DEFENSE FORCES BC, Taunggyi	DS • 10 kW
5810	USA	R FREE ASIA, Via Tinian, N Marianas	W • E Asia • 250 kW
		†WEWN, Vandiver, Alabama	C America • 500 kW; W • C America • 500 kW; S • C America • 500 kW
5820	USA	FAMILY RADIO, Via Uzbekistan	W • Europe • 200 kW
		RFE-RL, Via Kuwait	W • W Asia & C Asia • 250 kW
5825	NETHERLANDS	†R NEDERLAND, Via Tajikistan	W • S Asia • 100 kW
5830	CZECH REPUBLIC	RADIO PRAGUE, Via Tajikistan	W • E Europe • 200 kW
(con'd)	NETHERLANDS	†R NEDERLAND, Via Tajikistan	S • S Asia • 100 kW

World Time 0 1 2 3 4 5 6 7 8 9 10 11 12 13 14 15 16 17 18 19 20 21 22 23 24

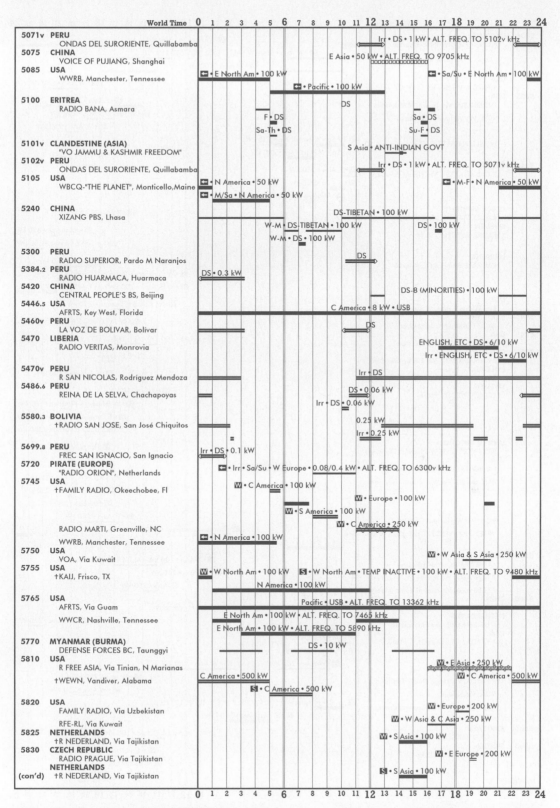

World Time 0 1 2 3 4 5 6 7 8 9 10 11 12 13 14 15 16 17 18 19 20 21 22 23 24

kHz	Country / Station	Schedule
5830 (con'd)	**UKRAINE** †RADIO UKRAINE INTL, Kharkiv	W • W Europe • 100 kW S • W Asia • 100 kW • ALT. FREQ. TO 7530 kHz W • W Asia • 100 kW
	USA †R FARDA, Via Kuwait	S • W Asia • 250 kW
5835	**USA** R FREE ASIA, Via Tinian, N Marianas	W • E Asia • 250 kW
	VOA, Via Iranawila, Sri Lanka	W • W Asia & S Asia • 250 kW W • W Asia • 250 kW
	WORLD HARVEST R, Cypress Creek, SC	W Tu-Sa • W North Am • 250 kW Tu-Sa • W North Am • 250 kW
5840	**CANADA** R CANADA INTL, Via Hörby, Sweden	W • E Asia • 350 kW W • S Asia • 350 kW ← • Mideast • 350 kW
	CZECH REPUBLIC †RADIO PRAGUE, Via Tajikistan	S • E Europe • 200 kW
	SWEDEN †RADIO SWEDEN, Hörby	W • E Europe • 350 kW W Sa/Su • E Europe • 350 kW
	UKRAINE †RADIO UKRAINE INTL, Kharkiv	W • W Europe • 100 kW S • W Europe • 100 kW • ALT. FREQ. TO 7490 kHz S • W Europe • 100 kW • ALT. FREQ. TO 7510 kHz
	USA RFE-RL, Via Tinian, N Marianas	W • W Asia & E Europe • 250 kW
5840v	**PAKISTAN** RADIO PAKISTAN, Islamabad	W • W Asia • 100 kW
5845	**USA** †FAMILY RADIO, Via Tajikistan	S • S Asia • 100 kW • ALT. FREQ. TO 5855 kHz
5850	**CANADA** †R CANADA INTL, Via Hörby, Sweden	W • E Europe • 350 kW
	POLAND POLISH RADIO, Via Jülich, Germany	W • E Europe • 100 kW
	SWEDEN †RADIO SWEDEN, Hörby	W • Asia • 350 kW W • W Europe & N Africa • 500 kW W • E Europe & W Asia • 350 kW S Sa/Su • E Europe • 350 kW
	UNITED KINGDOM BIBLE VOICE, Via Wertachtal, Germany	W Th • N Africa • 250 kW
	USA †FAMILY RADIO, Okeechobee, Fl	S • C America • 50 kW
	PAN AM BC, Via Wertachtal, Germany	W Sa/Su • N Africa • 250 kW W F-Su • N Africa • 250 kW
	†VOA	W • Europe • 250 kW
	VOA, Via Wertachtal, Germany	W • W Asia • 250 kW
	WORLD HARVEST R, Greenbush, Maine	W • Europe & Mideast • 250 kW Europe & Mideast • 250 kW
5855	**USA** †FAMILY RADIO, Via Tajikistan	S • S Asia • 100 kW • ALT. FREQ. TO 5845 kHz
	R FREE ASIA, Via Iranawila, Sri Lanka	W • SE Asia • 250 kW
	R FREE ASIA, Via Ulaanbaatar, Mongolia	SE Asia • 250 kW
5860	**CHINA** †VOICE OF JINLING, Nanjing	E Asia • 50 kW
	NETHERLANDS †R NEDERLAND, Via Philippines	W • SE Asia • 250 kW
	USA †R FARDA, Via Iranawila, Sri Lanka	W Asia • 250 kW W • W Asia • 250 kW
	†R FARDA, Via Kuwait	S • W Asia • 250 kW W • W Asia • 250 kW
	†R FARDA, Via Udon Thani, Thailand	S • W Asia • 250 kW
	VOA, Via Kuwait	S • W Asia • 250 kW
	WORLD HARVEST R, Cypress Creek, SC	S Tu-Sa • N America • 250 kW • ALT. FREQ. TO 9515 kHz W • E North Am • 250 kW
5860v	**PAKISTAN** RADIO PAKISTAN, Islamabad	W Asia & C Asia • 100 kW
5865	**SWEDEN** †RADIO SWEDEN, Hörby	W • W Europe • 500 kW W M-Sa • W Europe • 500 kW W • W Europe & N Africa • 500 kW

(con'd)

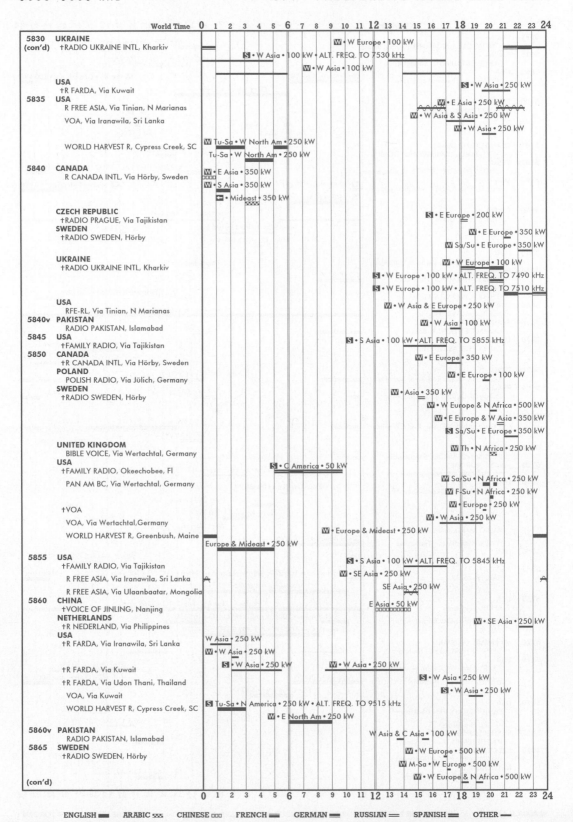

ENGLISH ARABIC CHINESE FRENCH GERMAN RUSSIAN SPANISH OTHER

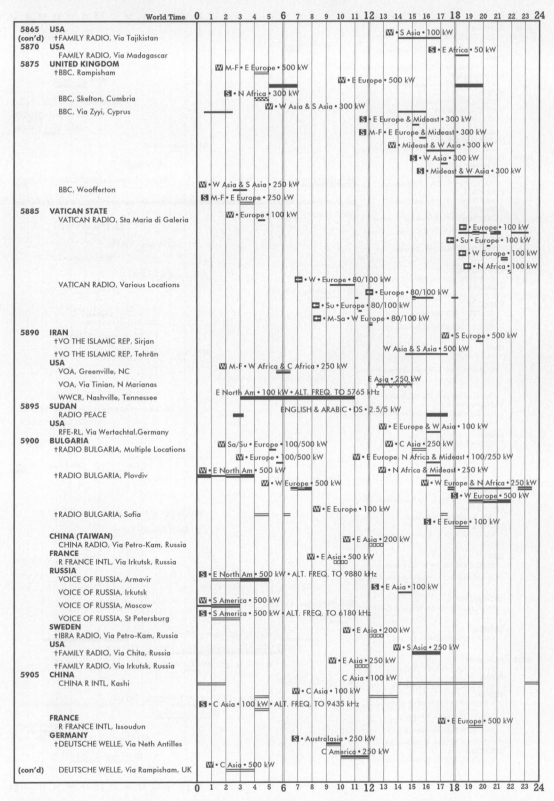

World Time 0 1 2 3 4 5 6 7 8 9 10 11 12 13 14 15 16 17 18 19 20 21 22 23 24

kHz	Country / Station	Schedule
5865 (con'd)	**USA** †FAMILY RADIO, Via Tajikistan	W • S Asia • 100 kW
5870	**USA** FAMILY RADIO, Via Madagascar	S • E Africa • 50 kW
5875	**UNITED KINGDOM** †BBC, Rampisham	W M-F • E Europe • 500 kW
		W • E Europe • 500 kW
	BBC, Skelton, Cumbria	S • N Africa • 300 kW
	BBC, Via Zyyi, Cyprus	W • W Asia & S Asia • 300 kW
		S • E Europe & Mideast • 300 kW
		S M-F • E Europe & Mideast • 300 kW
		W • Mideast & W Asia • 300 kW
		S • W Asia • 300 kW
		S • Mideast & W Asia • 300 kW
	BBC, Woofferton	W • W Asia & S Asia • 250 kW
		S M-F • E Europe • 250 kW
5885	**VATICAN STATE** VATICAN RADIO, Sta Maria di Galeria	W • Europe • 100 kW
		← • Europe • 100 kW
		← • Su • Europe • 100 kW
		← • W Europe • 100 kW
		← • N Africa • 100 kW
	VATICAN RADIO, Various Locations	← • W • Europe • 80/100 kW
		← • Europe • 80/100 kW
		← • Su • Europe • 80/100 kW
		← • M-Sa • W Europe • 80/100 kW
5890	**IRAN** †VO THE ISLAMIC REP, Sirjan	W • S Europe • 500 kW
	†VO THE ISLAMIC REP, Tehrān	W Asia & S Asia • 500 kW
	USA VOA, Greenville, NC	W M-F • W Africa & C Africa • 250 kW
	VOA, Via Tinian, N Marianas	E Asia • 250 kW
	WWCR, Nashville, Tennessee	E North Am • 100 kW • ALT. FREQ. TO 5765 kHz
5895	**SUDAN** RADIO PEACE	ENGLISH & ARABIC • DS • 2.5/5 kW
	USA RFE-RL, Via Wertachtal, Germany	W • E Europe & W Asia • 100 kW
5900	**BULGARIA** †RADIO BULGARIA, Multiple Locations	W Sa/Su • Europe • 100/500 kW
		W • C Asia • 250 kW
		W • Europe • 100/500 kW
		W • E Europe, N Africa & Mideast • 100/250 kW
	†RADIO BULGARIA, Plovdiv	W • E North Am • 500 kW
		W • N Africa & Mideast • 250 kW
		W • W Europe • 500 kW
		W • W Europe & N Africa • 250 kW
		S • W Europe • 500 kW
	†RADIO BULGARIA, Sofia	W • E Europe • 100 kW
		S • E Europe • 100 kW
	CHINA (TAIWAN) CHINA RADIO, Via Petro-Kam, Russia	W • E Asia • 200 kW
	FRANCE R FRANCE INTL, Via Irkutsk, Russia	W • E Asia • 500 kW
	RUSSIA VOICE OF RUSSIA, Armavir	S • E North Am • 500 kW • ALT. FREQ. TO 9880 kHz
	VOICE OF RUSSIA, Irkutsk	S • E Asia • 100 kW
	VOICE OF RUSSIA, Moscow	W • S America • 500 kW
	VOICE OF RUSSIA, St Petersburg	S • S America • 500 kW • ALT. FREQ. TO 6180 kHz
	SWEDEN †IBRA RADIO, Via Petro-Kam, Russia	W • E Asia • 200 kW
	USA †FAMILY RADIO, Via Chita, Russia	W • S Asia • 250 kW
	†FAMILY RADIO, Via Irkutsk, Russia	W • E Asia • 250 kW
5905	**CHINA** CHINA R INTL, Kashi	C Asia • 100 kW
		W • C Asia • 100 kW
		S • C Asia • 100 kW • ALT. FREQ. TO 9435 kHz
	FRANCE R FRANCE INTL, Issoudun	W • E Europe • 500 kW
	GERMANY †DEUTSCHE WELLE, Via Neth Antilles	S • Australasia • 250 kW
		C America • 250 kW
(con'd)	DEUTSCHE WELLE, Via Rampisham, UK	W • C Asia • 500 kW

0 1 2 3 4 5 6 7 8 9 10 11 12 13 14 15 16 17 18 19 20 21 22 23 24

SEASONAL S OR W 1-HR TIMESHIFT MIDYEAR ← OR → JAMMING / OR /\ EARLIEST HEARD ◁ LATEST HEARD ▷ NEW FOR 2009 †

World Time 0 1 2 3 4 5 6 7 8 9 10 11 12 13 14 15 16 17 18 19 20 21 22 23 24

kHz	Country / Station	Schedule
5905 (con'd)	**GERMANY**	
	DEUTSCHE WELLE, Via Sines, Portugal	W • Mideast • 250 kW
	DEUTSCHE WELLE, Via Woofferton, UK	W • W Africa • 250 kW
	IRAN	
	VO THE ISLAMIC REP, Tehrān	W • S Asia • 500 kW
	NETHERLANDS	
	R NEDERLAND, Via Madagascar	S • E Africa • 250 kW
	RUSSIA	
	RADIO ROSSII, Moscow	W • Europe • DS • 250 kW
	UNITED KINGDOM	
	†BBC, Multiple Locations	S • E Asia & SE Asia • 250 kW
	†BBC, Via A'Seela, Oman	S • E Asia • 250 kW
	VATICAN STATE	
	VATICAN RADIO, Via Novosibirsk, Russia	S • E Asia • 100 kW
5910	**CHINA**	
	CHINA R INTL, Beijing	SE Asia • 500 kW
	CLANDESTINE (AMER)	
	"RADIO REPUBLICA", Via Germany	S Tu-Sa • C America • ANTI-CASTRO • 100 kW; S M-F • C America • ANTI-CASTRO • 100 kW
	COLOMBIA	
	MARFIL ESTEREO, Puerto Lleras	DS • 2.5/5 kW
	GERMANY	
	DEUTSCHE WELLE, Various Locations	S • E Europe & W Asia • 250/500 kW
	†DEUTSCHE WELLE, Via Armavir, Russia	W • W Asia • 200 kW
	IRAN	
	†VO THE ISLAMIC REP, Tehrān	W • S Asia • 500 kW; S • S Europe • 500 kW
	NETHERLANDS	
	R NEDERLAND, Via Petro-K, Russia	E Asia & SE Asia • 250 kW
	ROMANIA	
	†R ROMANIA INTL, Bucharest	W • E North Am • 300 kW; S • E Europe • 300 kW
	RUSSIA	
	VOICE OF RUSSIA, Samara	W • S Asia • 100 kW
	VOICE OF RUSSIA, St Petersburg	W • Mideast • 200 kW; S • Europe • 200 kW
	USA	
	†FAMILY RADIO, Via Vladivostok, Russia	W • E Asia • 250 kW
	†TRANS WORLD R, Via Fontbonne, France	S • Europe • 100 kW; S M/Tu/Th/F • Europe • 100 kW
	†TRANS WORLD R, Via Jülich, Germany	S • S Europe • 100 kW
	VATICAN STATE	
	VATICAN RADIO, Sta Maria di Galeria	S • E Asia • 250 kW • ALT. FREQ. TO 9575 kHz; W • E Asia • 250 kW
5915	**CHINA**	
	CHINA R INTL, Beijing	W • E Asia • 150 kW
	CHINA R INTL, Hohhot	E Asia • 100 kW
	CHINA R INTL, Kashi	C Asia • 100 kW; W • C Asia • 100 kW; S Asia • 100 kW; S • S Asia • 100 kW
	GERMANY	
	†DEUTSCHE WELLE, Via Rampisham, UK	W • E Europe & W Asia • 500 kW
	PHILIPPINES	
	FEBC RADIO INTL, Bocaue	S M/W-Sa • SE Asia • 100 kW
	SLOVAKIA	
	R SLOVAKIA INTL, Rimavská Sobota	W • W Europe • 150 kW; W • E Europe & W Asia • 150 kW
	USA	
	†FAMILY RADIO, Via W'tal, Germany	S • N Africa • 250 kW
	†TRANS WORLD R, Via Fontbonne, France	W • Europe • 100 kW; W M/Tu/Th/F • Europe • 100 kW
	VATICAN STATE	
	VATICAN RADIO, Sta Maria di Galeria	W M/Th • S Asia • 250 kW; W • S Asia • 250 kW
	ZAMBIA	
	RADIO ZAMBIA-ZNBC, Lusaka	ENGLISH, ETC • DS-1 • 100 kW • ALT. FREQ. TO 4910 kHz; ENGLISH, ETC • DS-1 • 100 kW • ALT. FREQ. TO 7220 kHz
5920	**HUNGARY**	
	†HUNGARIAN RADIO, Jászberény	W • Europe • 250 kW • ALT. FREQ. TO 6025 kHz
	JAPAN	
	RADIO JAPAN, Via Skelton, UK	W • W Europe • 300 kW
	RUSSIA	
	KAMCHATKA RADIO, Petropavlovsk-K	S • E Asia • DS-LOCAL, R ROSSII • 100 kW
	VOICE OF RUSSIA, Irkutsk	W • E Asia • 100 kW
	VOICE OF RUSSIA, Samara	W • W Europe • 250 kW
	VOICE OF RUSSIA, St Petersburg	W • S Europe & N Africa • 200 kW
	SLOVAKIA	
	R SLOVAKIA INTL, Rimavská Sobota	S • W Europe • 150 kW; S • E Europe & W Asia • 150 kW
(con'd)		

World Time 0 1 2 3 4 5 6 7 8 9 10 11 12 13 14 15 16 17 18 19 20 21 22 23 24

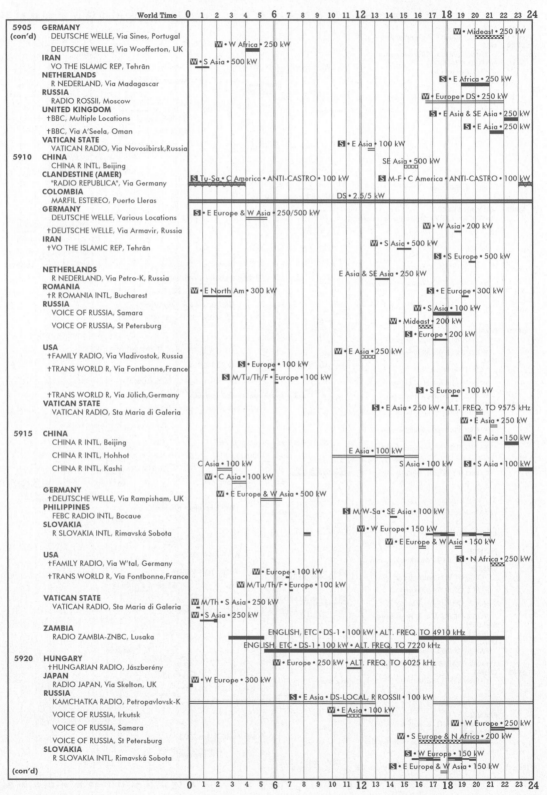

ENGLISH ▬ ARABIC ▨ CHINESE ▫▫▫ FRENCH ═ GERMAN ═ RUSSIAN ═ SPANISH ═ OTHER —

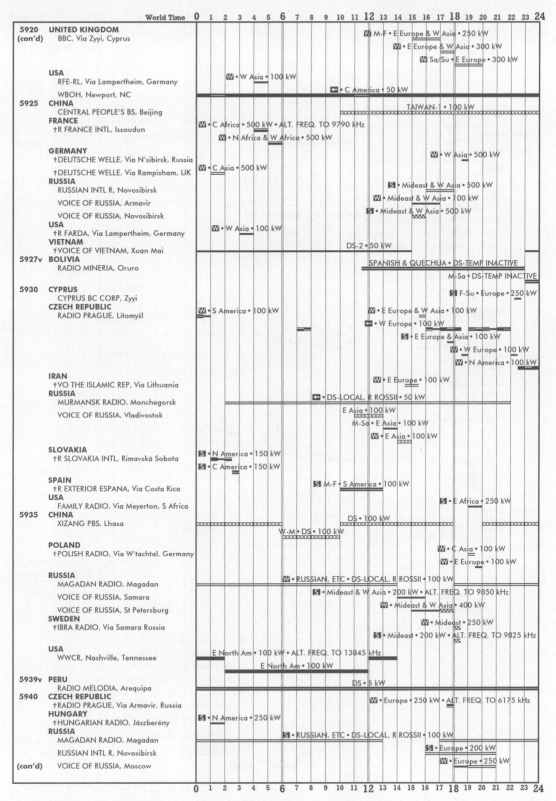

World Time 0 1 2 3 4 5 6 7 8 9 10 11 12 13 14 15 16 17 18 19 20 21 22 23 24

kHz	Country / Station	Schedule
5920 (con'd)	**UNITED KINGDOM** BBC, Via Zyyi, Cyprus	W M-F • E Europe & W Asia • 250 kW
		W • E Europe & W Asia • 300 kW
		W Sa/Su • E Europe • 300 kW
	USA RFE-RL, Via Lampertheim, Germany	W • W Asia • 100 kW
	WBOH, Newport, NC	← • C America • 50 kW
5925	**CHINA** CENTRAL PEOPLE'S BS, Beijing	TAIWAN-1 • 100 kW
	FRANCE †R FRANCE INTL, Issoudun	W • C Africa • 500 kW • ALT. FREQ. TO 9790 kHz
		W • N Africa & W Africa • 500 kW
	GERMANY †DEUTSCHE WELLE, Via N'sibirsk, Russia	W • W Asia • 500 kW
	†DEUTSCHE WELLE, Via Rampisham, UK	W • C Asia • 500 kW
	RUSSIA RUSSIAN INTL R, Novosibirsk	S • Mideast & W Asia • 500 kW
	VOICE OF RUSSIA, Armavir	W • Mideast & W Asia • 100 kW
	VOICE OF RUSSIA, Novosibirsk	S • Mideast & W Asia • 500 kW
	USA †R FARDA, Via Lampertheim, Germany	W • W Asia • 100 kW
	VIETNAM †VOICE OF VIETNAM, Xuan Mai	DS-2 • 50 kW
5927v	**BOLIVIA** RADIO MINERIA, Oruro	SPANISH & QUECHUA • DS-TEMP INACTIVE
		M-Sa • DS-TEMP INACTIVE
5930	**CYPRUS** CYPRUS BC CORP, Zyyi	S F-Su • Europe • 250 kW
	CZECH REPUBLIC RADIO PRAGUE, Litomyšl	W • S America • 100 kW
		W • E Europe & W Asia • 100 kW
		← • W Europe • 100 kW
		S • E Europe & Asia • 100 kW
		W • W Europe • 100 kW
		W • N America • 100 kW
	IRAN †VO THE ISLAMIC REP, Via Lithuania	W • E Europe • 100 kW
	RUSSIA MURMANSK RADIO, Monchegorsk	← • DS-LOCAL, R ROSSII • 50 kW
	VOICE OF RUSSIA, Vladivostok	E Asia • 100 kW
		M-Sa • E Asia • 100 kW
		W • E Asia • 100 kW
	SLOVAKIA †R SLOVAKIA INTL, Rimavská Sobota	S • N America • 150 kW
		S • C America • 150 kW
	SPAIN †R EXTERIOR ESPANA, Via Costa Rica	S M-F • S America • 100 kW
	USA FAMILY RADIO, Via Meyerton, S Africa	S • E Africa • 250 kW
5935	**CHINA** XIZANG PBS, Lhasa	DS • 100 kW
		W-M • DS • 100 kW
	POLAND †POLISH RADIO, Via W'tachtal, Germany	W • C Asia • 100 kW
		W • E Europe • 100 kW
	RUSSIA MAGADAN RADIO, Magadan	W • RUSSIAN, ETC • DS-LOCAL, R ROSSII • 100 kW
	VOICE OF RUSSIA, Samara	S • Mideast & W Asia • 200 kW • ALT. FREQ. TO 9850 kHz
	VOICE OF RUSSIA, St Petersburg	W • Mideast & W Asia • 400 kW
	SWEDEN †IBRA RADIO, Via Samara Russia	W • Mideast • 250 kW
		S • Mideast • 200 kW • ALT. FREQ. TO 9825 kHz
	USA WWCR, Nashville, Tennessee	E North Am • 100 kW • ALT. FREQ. TO 13845 kHz
		E North Am • 100 kW
5939v	**PERU** RADIO MELODIA, Arequipa	DS • 5 kW
5940	**CZECH REPUBLIC** †RADIO PRAGUE, Via Armavir, Russia	W • Europe • 250 kW • ALT. FREQ. TO 6175 kHz
	HUNGARY †HUNGARIAN RADIO, Jászberény	S • N America • 250 kW
	RUSSIA MAGADAN RADIO, Magadan	S • RUSSIAN, ETC • DS-LOCAL, R ROSSII • 100 kW
	RUSSIAN INTL R, Novosibirsk	S • Europe • 200 kW
(con'd)	VOICE OF RUSSIA, Moscow	W • Europe • 250 kW

World Time 0 1 2 3 4 5 6 7 8 9 10 11 12 13 14 15 16 17 18 19 20 21 22 23 24

kHz	Country / Station	Broadcast
5940 (con'd)	**RUSSIA**	
	VOICE OF RUSSIA, Novosibirsk	W • E Asia • 100 kW
	VOICE OF RUSSIA, St Petersburg	W • S Europe • 200 kW
	UNITED KINGDOM	
	BBC, Skelton, Cumbria	W • Mideast • 300 kW
	†BBC, Via Zyyi, Cyprus	W • W Asia • 250 kW
	FEBA RADIO, Via Armenia	W • S Asia • 100 kW
	FEBA RADIO, Via Dhabayya, UAE	W • S Asia • 100 kW
	VATICAN STATE	
	VATICAN RADIO, Various Locations	S • SE Asia • 500 kW • ALT. FREQ. TO 12055 kHz
5940v	**PERU**	
	RADIO BETHEL, Arequipa	DS • 1 kW • ALT. FREQ. TO 5950v kHz
5945	**BELGIUM**	
	R TRAUMLAND, Via Jülich, Germany	S Su • W Europe • 100 kW
	CHINA	
	CENTRAL PEOPLE'S BS, Beijing	DS-1 • 100 kW
		W • DS-1 • 100 kW
	GERMANY	
	†DEUTSCHE WELLE, Via Armavir, Russia	S • W Asia • 200 kW
	†DEUTSCHE WELLE, Via Rampisham, UK	S • N Africa & Mideast • 500 kW
	†DEUTSCHE WELLE, Via Sines, Portugal	W • W Africa & C Africa • 250 kW
	†DEUTSCHE WELLE, Via Woofferton, UK	S • N Africa & W Africa • 300 kW
		W • W Africa • 250 kW
	IRAN	
	†VO THE ISLAMIC REP, Sirjan	W • SE Asia • 500 kW
	VO THE ISLAMIC REP, Tehrān	C Asia • 500 kW
		W • S Europe • 500 kW
	RUSSIA	
	RUSSIAN INTL R, Novosibirsk	W • W Asia & C Asia • 500 kW
	RUSSIAN INTL R, Via Germany	S • Mideast • 125 kW
	VOICE OF RUSSIA, Armavir	W • S America • 500 kW
	VOICE OF RUSSIA, Novosibirsk	W • W Asia & C Asia • 500 kW
	SWITZERLAND	
	STIMME DES TROSTES, Via Germany	S Su • Europe • 250 kW
	UNITED KINGDOM	
	†BBC, Via Zyyi, Cyprus	W • W Asia • 250 kW
		W • Mideast & W Asia • 300 kW
	BIBLE VOICE, Via Nauen, Germany	Sa/Su • W Europe • 100 kW
		F-Su • W Europe • 100 kW
		F • W Europe • 100 kW
	BIBLE VOICE, Via Wertachtal, Germany	W F • Mideast • 125 kW
	USA	
	†FAMILY RADIO, Via W'tal, Germany	W • Mideast • 125 kW
	RFE-RL, Via Kuwait	S • W Asia & C Asia • 250 kW
	RFE-RL, Via Lampertheim, Germany	W • W Asia & C Asia • 100 kW
5950	**CANADA**	
	†R CANADA INTL, Via Vatican State	S • Mideast • 100 kW
	CHINA (TAIWAN)	
	R TAIWAN INTL, Via Okeechobee, USA	E North Am • 100 kW
		W North Am • 100 kW
	IRAN	
	VO THE ISLAMIC REP, Sirjan	W • W Africa & C Africa • 500 kW
		W • S Europe • 500 kW
	RUSSIA	
	VOICE OF RUSSIA, Kaliningrad	W • W Europe • 160 kW
	VOICE OF RUSSIA, Via Moldova	S • S Europe, N Africa & Mideast • 500 kW
	TURKEY	
	†VOICE OF TURKEY, Ankara-Çakirlar	W • S Europe • 250 kW
	UNITED KINGDOM	
	BIBLE VOICE, Via Khabarovsk, Russia	W M-F • E Asia & SE Asia • 100 kW
		W Sa/Su • E Asia & SE Asia • 100 kW
		W • E Asia & SE Asia • 100 kW
		W M • E Asia & SE Asia • 100 kW
		W Tu-Su • E Asia & SE Asia • 100 kW
		W Th • E Asia & SE Asia • 100 kW
		W Tu/W • E Asia & SE Asia • 100 kW
	USA	
	†FAMILY RADIO, Okeechobee, Fl	E North Am • 100 kW
		N America • 100 kW
		W • W North Am • 100 kW
		W • E North Am • 100 kW
		W North Am • 100 kW
(con'd)		

World Time 0 1 2 3 4 5 6 7 8 9 10 11 12 13 14 15 16 17 18 19 20 21 22 23 24

ENGLISH ARABIC CHINESE FRENCH GERMAN RUSSIAN SPANISH OTHER

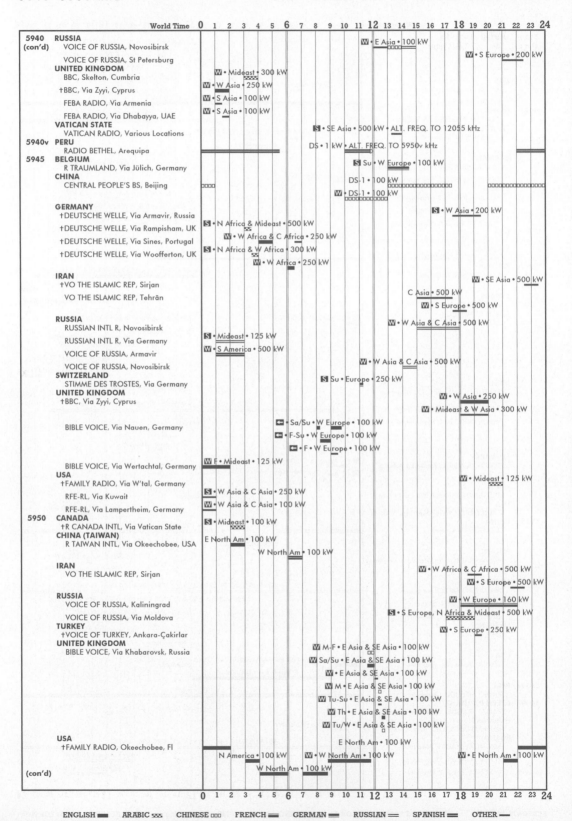

World Time 0 1 2 3 4 5 6 7 8 9 10 11 12 13 14 15 16 17 18 19 20 21 22 23 24

kHz	Country	Station	Schedule details
5950 (con'd)	USA	†FAMILY RADIO, Okeechobee, Fl	S • E North Am • 100 kW
	YEMEN	REP OF YEMEN RADIO, San'ā	Mideast • DS • 300 kW
5950v	PERU	RADIO BETHEL, Arequipa	DS • 1 kW • ALT. FREQ. TO 5940v kHz
5952.5	BOLIVIA	RADIO PIO DOCE, Llallagua-Siglo XX	SPANISH, ETC • DS • 1 kW; Tu-Su • SPANISH, ETC • DS • 1 kW; Irr • SPANISH, ETC • DS • 1 kW; Irr • M-F • SPANISH, ETC • DS • 1 kW
5955	BRAZIL	RADIO GAZETA, São Paulo	PORTUGUESE & SPANISH • DS • 10 kW
	CHINA	CHINA R INTL, Beijing	E Asia • 500 kW
		CHINA R INTL, Various Locations	E Asia • 500 kW
		CHINA R INTL, Xi'an	W • E Asia • 500 kW
	CLANDESTINE (ASIA)	"D'CRATIC VO BURMA", Via Germany	W • SE Asia • ANTI-MYANMAR GOVT • 125 kW
	GERMANY	†DEUTSCHE WELLE, Via Sri Lanka	S • SE Asia • 250 kW
	IRAN	VO THE ISLAMIC REP, Sirjan	W • C Asia • 500 kW; C Asia • 500 kW
	JAPAN	RADIO JAPAN, Tokyo-Yamata	E Asia • 300 kW
	NETHERLANDS	†R NEDERLAND, Various Locations	⇐ • W Europe • 250/500 kW; ⇐ • Su • W Europe • 250/500 kW
	ROMANIA	†R ROMANIA INTL, Bucharest	S • S Europe • 100 kW
	RUSSIA	VOICE OF RUSSIA, Vladivostok	W • E Asia • 500 kW
	UNITED KINGDOM	†BBC, Multiple Locations	W • E Asia & SE Asia • 250 kW
		BBC, Rampisham	W M-F • N Europe • 300 kW
		BBC, Via A'Seela, Oman	W • C Asia • 250 kW
		BBC, Via Zyyi, Cyprus	W Sa • E Europe & W Asia • 300 kW
	USA	RFE-RL, Via Biblis, Germany	W • W Asia & C Asia • 100 kW
		VOA, Via Philippines	SE Asia • 250 kW
		VOA, Via São Tomé	W M-F • W Africa • 100 kW; W • W Africa • 100 kW
	VIETNAM	VOICE OF VIETNAM, Via Austria	W • W Europe • 100 kW
5960	BELGIUM	R VLAANDEREN INTL, Via St P'burg, Rus	W • S Europe & N Africa • 400 kW
	CHILE	CVC-LA VOZ, Santiago	W • C America & S America • 100 kW
	CHINA	CHINA R INTL, Via Cerrik, Albania	W Europe • 150 kW
		CHINA R INTL, Via Sackville, Canada	S • E North Am • 250 kW; W • E North Am • 250 kW; W • N America • 250 kW
		XINJIANG PEOPLE'S BC STN, Urümqi	DS-CHINESE • 100 kW; W • DS-CHINESE • 100 kW; S • DS-CHINESE • 50 kW; W W/F-M • DS-CHINESE • 100 kW
	FRANCE	†R FRANCE INTL, Via French Guiana	W • C America • 250 kW
	JAPAN	RADIO JAPAN, Via Sackville, Can	E North Am & C America • 250 kW
		RADIO JAPAN, Via Skelton, UK	S • W Europe • 300 kW
	ROMANIA	†R ROMANIA INTL, Bucharest	W • E Europe • 100 kW
		†R ROMANIA INTL, Galbeni	W • C America • 300 kW
	TURKEY	VOICE OF TURKEY, Ankara-Emirler	S • Mideast • 500 kW; W • W Europe & E North Am • 500 kW
	UNITED KINGDOM	†BBC, Via Thailand	W • S Asia • 250 kW
	USA	†FAMILY RADIO, Via W'tal, Germany	W • N Africa • 500 kW
		RFE-RL, Via Iranawila, Sri Lanka	W • E Europe & W Asia • 250 kW
		RFE-RL, Via Lampertheim, Germany	W • E Europe & W Asia • 100 kW
		VOA, Greenville, NC	W Tu-Sa • C America • 250 kW
5964.7	BOLIVIA	RADIO NACIONAL, Huanuni	M-Sa • DS • 2 kW; M-F • DS • 2 kW; DS • 2 kW

World Time 0 1 2 3 4 5 6 7 8 9 10 11 12 13 14 15 16 17 18 19 20 21 22 23 24

SEASONAL S OR W 1-HR TIMESHIFT MIDYEAR ⇐ OR ⇒ JAMMING / OR /\ EARLIEST HEARD ◁ LATEST HEARD ▷ NEW FOR 2009 †

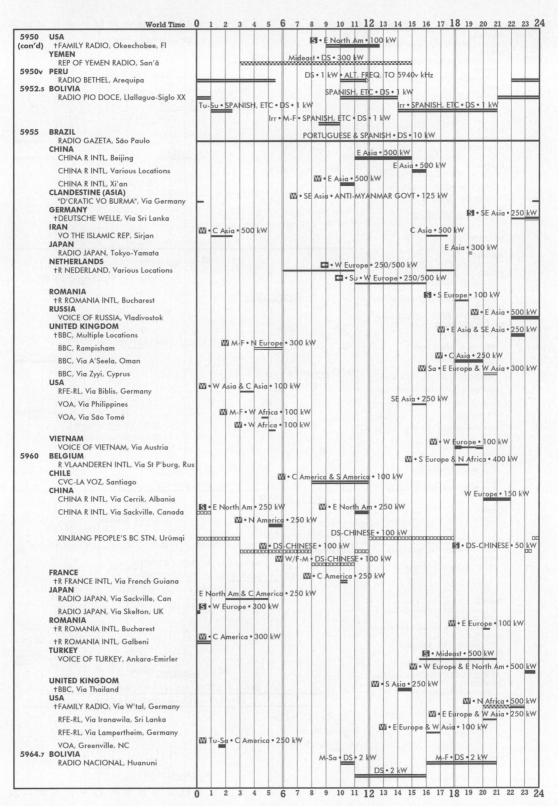

World Time 0–24

kHz	Country / Station	Schedule
5965	**BELGIUM**	
	R TRAUMLAND, Via Jülich, Germany	W Su • W Europe • 100 kW
	BRAZIL	
	RADIO TRANS MUNDIAL, Santa Maria	DS • 7.5 kW • ➡
	CANADA	
	†R CANADA INTL, Via Tokyo, Japan	W • E Asia • 300 kW
	CHINA	
	CHINA R INTL, Beijing	W • E Asia • 150 kW; E Asia • 500 kW
	CHINA R INTL, Xi'an	W • E Asia • 500 kW; E Asia • 500 kW
	CUBA	
	RADIO HABANA CUBA, Havana	C America • 100 kW
	ECUADOR	
	LA VOZ DEL UPANO, Macas	Irr • DS • 10 kW
	GERMANY	
	†DEUTSCHE WELLE, Via Armavir, Russia	S • W Asia • 200 kW
	†DEUTSCHE WELLE, Via Sri Lanka	W • S Asia • 250 kW
	MV BALTIC RADIO, Jülich	W Su • Europe • 1ST SUN OF MONTH • 100 kW
	INDIA	
	RADIO KASHMIR, Jammu	DS • 50 kW; ENGLISH & HINDI • DS • 50 kW
	MALAYSIA	
	RTV MALAYSIA, Kajang	KLASIK NASIONAL FM • 100 kW
	POLAND	
	†POLISH RADIO, Via W'tachtal, Germany	⬅ • Europe • 100 kW
	RUSSIA	
	VOICE OF RUSSIA, Irkutsk	S • E Europe • 250 kW
	SPAIN	
	R EXTERIOR ESPANA, Via Costa Rica	S America • 100 kW
	TURKEY	
	VOICE OF TURKEY, Ankara-Emirler	W • W Asia • 500 kW
	UNITED KINGDOM	
	BBC, Rampisham	W • C Asia • 500 kW; W • N Africa • 500 kW
	BBC, Via A'Seela, Oman	S • S Asia • 250 kW
	BBC, Via Thailand	E Asia • 250 kW
	USA	
	ADVENTIST WORLD R, Via Austria	W • S Asia • 300 kW
	ADVENTIST WORLD R, Via Germany	S • E Europe • 100 kW
	†FAMILY RADIO, Via Skelton, UK	W • Mideast • 300 kW
	†FAMILY RADIO, Via W'tal, Germany	S • N Africa & W Africa • 500 kW
	†TRANS WORLD R, Via W'tal, Germany	W M-F • W Asia • 100 kW; W Sa • E Europe • 100 kW
	†VOA	S • S Europe • 250 kW
5969.6	**CHINA**	
	GANNAN PEOPLE'S BS, Hezuo	DS-CHINESE,TIBETAN • 15 kW
5970	**BRAZIL**	
	RADIO ITATIAIA, Belo Horizonte	DS • 10 kW • ➡; Irr • DS • 10 kW • ➡
	CHINA	
	CHINA R INTL, Via Cerrik, Albania	Europe • 150 kW; W Europe • 150 kW
	CLANDESTINE (AMER)	
	"RADIO REPUBLICA", Via Germany	W Tu-Sa • C America • ANTI-CASTRO • 100 kW; W M-F • C America • ANTI-CASTRO • 100 kW
	ETHIOPIA	
	VO TIGRAY REVOL'N, Mek'ele	E Africa • 10 kW • ALT. FREQ. TO 5980 kHz; Sa/Su • E Africa • 10 kW • ALT. FREQ. TO 5980 kHz; M-F • E Africa • 10 kW • ALT. FREQ. TO 5980 kHz
	FRANCE	
	†R FRANCE INTL, Via French Guiana	S • C America • 250 kW
	NETHERLANDS	
	†R NEDERLAND, Via Issoudun, France	W M-F • N Africa • 500 kW
	ROMANIA	
	†R ROMANIA INTL, Bucharest	W • S Europe • 100 kW
	SPAIN	
	†R EXTERIOR ESPANA, Noblejas	W Sa/Su • Europe • 250 kW
	†R EXTERIOR ESPANA, Via Costa Rica	S M-F • C America • 100 kW
	UKRAINE	
	†UKRAINIAN RADIO, Kyiv	S • DS-1 • 100 kW • ALT. FREQ. TO 5980 kHz; W • DS-1 • 100 kW • ALT. FREQ. TO 6020 kHz
	UNITED KINGDOM	
	†BBC, Via A'Seela, Oman	S Asia & E Asia • 250 kW; E Asia • 250 kW; W • S Asia • 250 kW
	USA	
	†FAMILY RADIO, Via Nauen, Germany	W • E Europe & W Asia • 500 kW
(con'd)	†FAMILY RADIO, Via Samara, Russia	S • E Asia • 250 kW

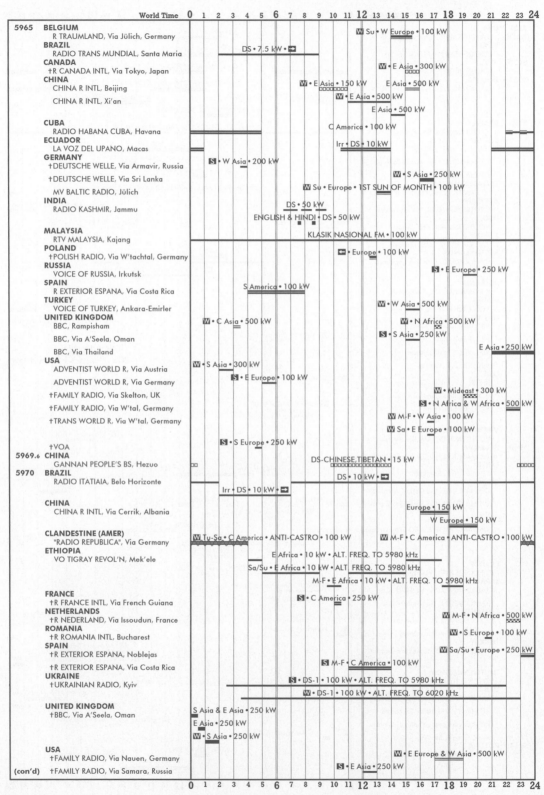

ENGLISH ▬ ARABIC ▭ CHINESE ▫▫▫ FRENCH ═ GERMAN ═ RUSSIAN ═ SPANISH ═ OTHER —

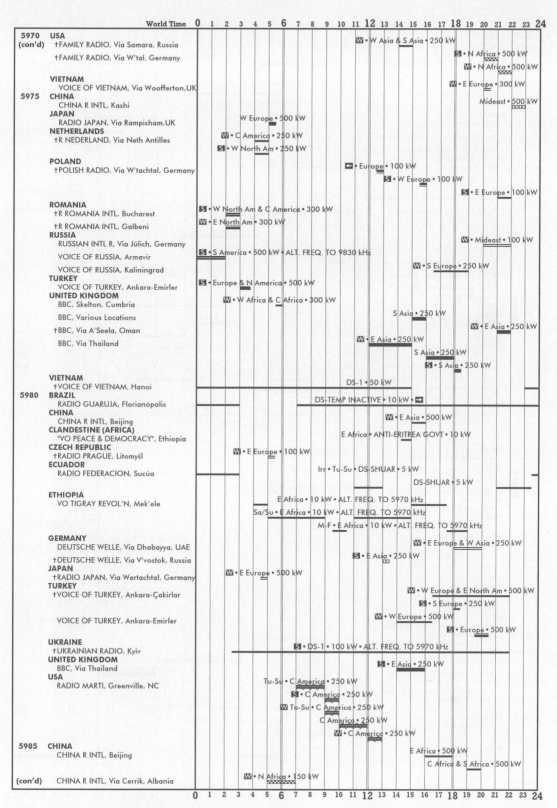

kHz	Country / Station	Schedule (World Time 0–24)
5970 (con'd)	**USA**	
	†FAMILY RADIO, Via Samara, Russia	W • W Asia & S Asia • 250 kW
	†FAMILY RADIO, Via W'tal, Germany	S • N Africa • 500 kW
		W • N Africa • 500 kW
	VIETNAM	
	VOICE OF VIETNAM, Via Woofferton, UK	W • E Europe • 300 kW
5975	**CHINA**	
	CHINA R INTL, Kashi	Mideast • 500 kW
	JAPAN	
	RADIO JAPAN, Via Rampisham, UK	W Europe • 500 kW
	NETHERLANDS	
	†R NEDERLAND, Via Neth Antilles	W • C America • 250 kW
		S • W North Am • 250 kW
	POLAND	
	†POLISH RADIO, Via W'tachtal, Germany	← • Europe • 100 kW
		S • W Europe • 100 kW
		S • E Europe • 100 kW
	ROMANIA	
	†R ROMANIA INTL, Bucharest	S • W North Am & C America • 300 kW
	†R ROMANIA INTL, Galbeni	W • E North Am • 300 kW
	RUSSIA	
	RUSSIAN INTL R, Via Jülich, Germany	W • Mideast • 100 kW
	VOICE OF RUSSIA, Armavir	S • S America • 500 kW • ALT. FREQ. TO 9830 kHz
	VOICE OF RUSSIA, Kaliningrad	W • S Europe • 250 kW
	TURKEY	
	VOICE OF TURKEY, Ankara-Emirler	S • Europe & N America • 500 kW
	UNITED KINGDOM	
	BBC, Skelton, Cumbria	W • W Africa & C Africa • 300 kW
	BBC, Various Locations	S Asia • 250 kW
	†BBC, Via A'Seela, Oman	W • E Asia • 250 kW
	BBC, Via Thailand	W • E Asia • 250 kW
		S Asia • 250 kW
		S • S Asia • 250 kW
	VIETNAM	
	†VOICE OF VIETNAM, Hanoi	DS-1 • 50 kW
5980	**BRAZIL**	
	RADIO GUARUJA, Florianópolis	DS-TEMP INACTIVE • 10 kW • →
	CHINA	
	CHINA R INTL, Beijing	W • E Asia • 500 kW
	CLANDESTINE (AFRICA)	
	"VO PEACE & DEMOCRACY", Ethiopia	E Africa • ANTI-ERITREA GOVT • 10 kW
	CZECH REPUBLIC	
	†RADIO PRAGUE, Litomyšl	W • E Europe • 100 kW
	ECUADOR	
	RADIO FEDERACION, Sucúa	Irr • Tu-Su • DS-SHUAR • 5 kW
		DS-SHUAR • 5 kW
	ETHIOPIA	
	VO TIGRAY REVOL'N, Mek'ele	E Africa • 10 kW • ALT. FREQ. TO 5970 kHz
		Sa/Su • E Africa • 10 kW • ALT. FREQ. TO 5970 kHz
		M-F • E Africa • 10 kW • ALT. FREQ. TO 5970 kHz
	GERMANY	
	DEUTSCHE WELLE, Via Dhabayya, UAE	W • E Europe & W Asia • 250 kW
	†DEUTSCHE WELLE, Via V'vostok, Russia	S • E Asia • 250 kW
	JAPAN	
	†RADIO JAPAN, Via Wertachtal, Germany	W • E Europe • 500 kW
	TURKEY	
	†VOICE OF TURKEY, Ankara-Çakirlar	W • W Europe & E North Am • 500 kW
		S • S Europe • 250 kW
	VOICE OF TURKEY, Ankara-Emirler	W • W Europe • 500 kW
		S • Europe • 500 kW
	UKRAINE	
	†UKRAINIAN RADIO, Kyiv	S • DS-1 • 100 kW • ALT. FREQ. TO 5970 kHz
	UNITED KINGDOM	
	BBC, Via Thailand	S • E Asia • 250 kW
	USA	
	RADIO MARTI, Greenville, NC	Tu-Su • C America • 250 kW
		S • C America • 250 kW
		W Tu-Su • C America • 250 kW
		C America • 250 kW
		W • C America • 250 kW
5985	**CHINA**	
	CHINA R INTL, Beijing	E Africa • 500 kW
		C Africa & S Africa • 500 kW
(con'd)	CHINA R INTL, Via Cerrik, Albania	W • N Africa • 150 kW

World Time 0 1 2 3 4 5 6 7 8 9 10 11 12 13 14 15 16 17 18 19 20 21 22 23 24

kHz	Country / Station	Schedule notes
5985 (con'd)	**CHINA**	
	CHINA R INTL, Xi'an	W • E Asia • 500 kW
	CONGO (REPUBLIC)	
	RTV CONGOLAISE, Brazzaville	FRENCH, ETC • DS • 50/100 kW
		DS • 50/100 kW
	INDIA	
	ALL INDIA RADIO, Ranchi	DS • 50 kW
		ENGLISH, ETC • DS • 50 kW
	RUSSIA	
	RUSSIAN INTL R, Moscow	W • Mideast • 250 kW
	RUSSIAN INTL R, Via Jülich, Germany	S • Mideast & W Asia • 100 kW
	VOICE OF RUSSIA, Moscow	W • Mideast • 250 kW
	UNITED KINGDOM	
	BBC, Rampisham	W • Mideast & W Asia • 500 kW
	BBC, Via Meyerton, South Africa	S • S Africa • 250 kW
	USA	
	ADVENTIST WORLD R, Via Agat, Guam	W • E Asia • 100 kW
	FAMILY RADIO, Okeechobee, Fl	C America • 50 kW
		N America • 100 kW
		S • N America • 100 kW
	SUDAN RADIO SVC, Via Kigali, Rwanda	M-F • C Africa • 250 kW
	VOA, Via Lampertheim, Germany	W • S Asia • 100 kW
	VOA, Via Udon Thani, Thailand	W • E Asia • 250 kW
	VOA, Via Woofferton, UK	W M-F • N Africa • 300 kW
5985v	**MYANMAR (BURMA)**	
	RADIO MYANMAR, Yangon	DS • 50 kW
5990	**BRAZIL**	
	RADIO SENADO, Brasília	DS • ➡
		M-F • DS • ➡
	CHINA	
	CHINA R INTL, Hohhot	E Asia • 100 kW
	CHINA R INTL, Via Havana, Cuba	C America • 250 kW
	QINGHAI PEOPLE'S BS, Xining	DS-TIBETAN • 50 kW
	CLANDESTINE (ASIA)	
	"VO JAMMU & KASHMIR FREEDOM"	S Asia • ANTI-INDIAN GOVT
	ETHIOPIA	
	RADIO ETHIOPIA, Gedja	DS • 100 kW
		Sa/Su • DS • 100 kW
		M-F • DS • 100 kW
	INDIA	
	ALL INDIA RADIO, Aligarh	S Asia • 250 kW
	IRAN	
	VO THE ISLAMIC REP, Tehrān	Mideast • 500 kW
	ITALY	
	†IRRS-SHORTWAVE, Via Slovakia	⬅ • M-Th • Europe, N Africa & Mideast • 150 kW
	PHILIPPINES	
	FEBC RADIO INTL, Bocaue	SE Asia • 100 kW
	TURKEY	
	†VOICE OF TURKEY, Ankara-Emirler	W • W Europe • 500 kW
	UNITED KINGDOM	
	BBC, Rampisham	W M-F • E Europe • 500 kW
		W • E Europe • 500 kW
		W Sa/Su • E Europe • 500 kW
		W Sa • E Europe • 500 kW
	BBC, Via Singapore	W • SE Asia • 250 kW
	BBC, Via Thailand	S Su-Th • SE Asia • 250 kW
	USA	
	R FREE ASIA, Via Tinian, N Marianas	W • E Asia • 250 kW
5990v	**CLANDESTINE (ASIA)**	
	"VO JAMMU & KASHMIR FREEDOM"	S Asia • ANTI-INDIAN GOVT
5995	**AUSTRALIA**	
	RADIO AUSTRALIA, Brandon	Pacific • 10 kW
	RADIO AUSTRALIA, Shepparton	Pacific & W North Am • 100 kW
	CANADA	
	R CANADA INTL, Via Vatican State	W • Mideast • 100 kW
	CHINA (TAIWAN)	
	FU HSING BC STATION, Taipei	E Asia • 10 kW
	FRANCE	
	R FRANCE INTL, Via French Guiana	W • C America • 250 kW • ALT. FREQ. TO 9800 kHz
		S • C America • 250 kW
	MALI	
	RTV DU MALI, Bamako	FRENCH, ETC • DS • 100 kW
		Sa • DS • 100 kW
		Su-F • FRENCH, ETC • DS • 100 kW
(con'd)		

World Time 0 1 2 3 4 5 6 7 8 9 10 11 12 13 14 15 16 17 18 19 20 21 22 23 24

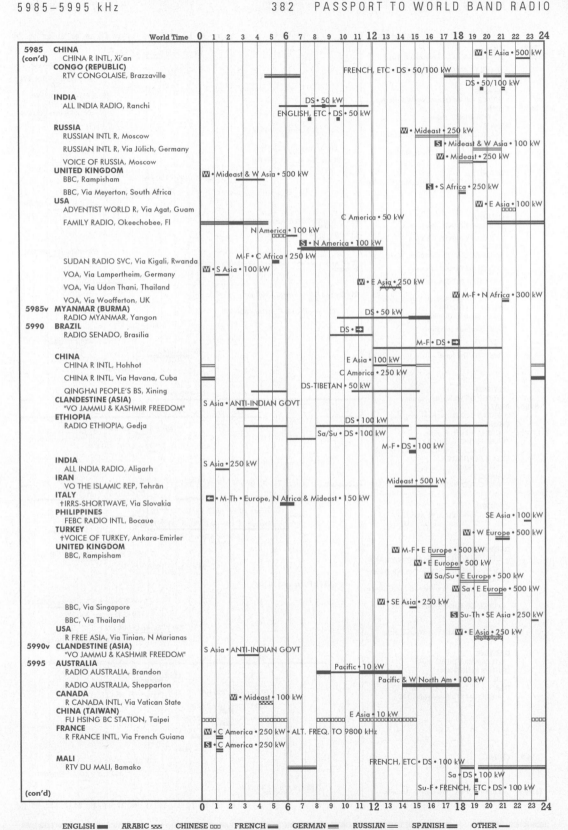

ENGLISH ARABIC CHINESE FRENCH GERMAN RUSSIAN SPANISH OTHER

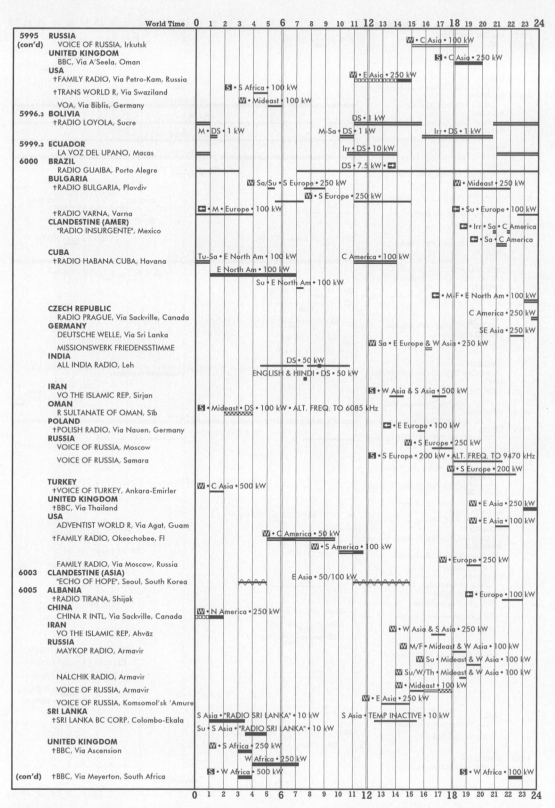

World Time 0 1 2 3 4 5 6 7 8 9 10 11 12 13 14 15 16 17 18 19 20 21 22 23 24

Frequency	Country / Station	Schedule
5995 (con'd)	**RUSSIA**	
	VOICE OF RUSSIA, Irkutsk	W • C Asia • 100 kW
	UNITED KINGDOM	
	BBC, Via A'Seela, Oman	S • C Asia • 250 kW
	USA	
	†FAMILY RADIO, Via Petro-Kam, Russia	W • E Asia • 250 kW
	†TRANS WORLD R, Via Swaziland	S • S Africa • 100 kW
	VOA, Via Biblis, Germany	W • Mideast • 100 kW
5996.3	**BOLIVIA**	
	†RADIO LOYOLA, Sucre	DS • 1 kW; M • DS • 1 kW; M-Sa • DS • 1 kW; Irr • DS • 1 kW
5999.3	**ECUADOR**	
	LA VOZ DEL UPANO, Macas	Irr • DS • 10 kW
6000	**BRAZIL**	
	RADIO GUAIBA, Porto Alegre	DS • 7.5 kW • ➡
	BULGARIA	
	†RADIO BULGARIA, Plovdiv	W Sa/Su • S Europe • 250 kW; W • Mideast • 250 kW; W • S Europe • 250 kW; ⬅ • M • Europe • 100 kW; ⬅ • Su • Europe • 100 kW
	†RADIO VARNA, Varna	
	CLANDESTINE (AMER)	
	"RADIO INSURGENTE", Mexico	⬅ • Irr • Sa • C America; ⬅ • Sa • C America
	CUBA	
	†RADIO HABANA CUBA, Havana	Tu-Sa • E North Am • 100 kW; C America • 100 kW; E North Am • 100 kW; Su • E North Am • 100 kW; ⬅ • M-F • E North Am • 100 kW
	CZECH REPUBLIC	
	RADIO PRAGUE, Via Sackville, Canada	C America • 250 kW
	GERMANY	
	DEUTSCHE WELLE, Via Sri Lanka	SE Asia • 250 kW
	MISSIONSWERK FRIEDENSSTIMME	W Sa • E Europe & W Asia • 250 kW
	INDIA	
	ALL INDIA RADIO, Leh	DS • 50 kW; ENGLISH & HINDI • DS • 50 kW
	IRAN	
	VO THE ISLAMIC REP, Sirjan	S • W Asia & S Asia • 500 kW
	OMAN	
	R SULTANATE OF OMAN, Sīb	S • Mideast • DS • 100 kW • ALT. FREQ. TO 6085 kHz
	POLAND	
	†POLISH RADIO, Via Nauen, Germany	⬅ • E Europe • 100 kW
	RUSSIA	
	VOICE OF RUSSIA, Moscow	W • S Europe • 250 kW
	VOICE OF RUSSIA, Samara	S • S Europe • 200 kW • ALT. FREQ. TO 9470 kHz; W • S Europe • 200 kW
	TURKEY	
	†VOICE OF TURKEY, Ankara-Emirler	W • C Asia • 500 kW
	UNITED KINGDOM	
	†BBC, Via Thailand	W • E Asia • 250 kW
	USA	
	ADVENTIST WORLD R, Via Agat, Guam	W • E Asia • 100 kW
	†FAMILY RADIO, Okeechobee, Fl	W • C America • 50 kW; W • S America • 100 kW
	FAMILY RADIO, Via Moscow, Russia	W • Europe • 250 kW
6003	**CLANDESTINE (ASIA)**	
	"ECHO OF HOPE", Seoul, South Korea	E Asia • 50/100 kW
6005	**ALBANIA**	
	†RADIO TIRANA, Shijak	⬅ • Europe • 100 kW
	CHINA	
	CHINA R INTL, Via Sackville, Canada	W • N America • 250 kW
	IRAN	
	VO THE ISLAMIC REP, Ahvāz	W • W Asia & S Asia • 250 kW
	RUSSIA	
	MAYKOP RADIO, Armavir	W M/F • Mideast & W Asia • 100 kW; W Su • Mideast & W Asia • 100 kW
	NALCHIK RADIO, Armavir	W Su/W/Th • Mideast & W Asia • 100 kW
	VOICE OF RUSSIA, Armavir	W • Mideast • 100 kW
	VOICE OF RUSSIA, Komsomol'sk 'Amure	W • E Asia • 250 kW
	SRI LANKA	
	†SRI LANKA BC CORP, Colombo-Ekala	S Asia • "RADIO SRI LANKA" • 10 kW; S Asia • TEMP INACTIVE • 10 kW; Su • S Asia • "RADIO SRI LANKA" • 10 kW
	UNITED KINGDOM	
	†BBC, Via Ascension	W • S Africa • 250 kW; W Africa • 250 kW
(con'd)	†BBC, Via Meyerton, South Africa	S • W Africa • 500 kW; S • W Africa • 100 kW

0 1 2 3 4 5 6 7 8 9 10 11 12 13 14 15 16 17 18 19 20 21 22 23 24

SEASONAL S OR W   1-HR TIMESHIFT MIDYEAR ⬅ OR ➡   JAMMING / OR ∧   EARLIEST HEARD ◁   LATEST HEARD ▷   NEW FOR 2009 †

World Time 0 1 2 3 4 5 6 7 8 9 10 11 12 13 14 15 16 17 18 19 20 21 22 23 24

kHz	Country	Station	Schedule
6005 (con'd)	UNITED KINGDOM	†BBC, Via Seychelles	W • E Africa • 250 kW; S • E Africa • 250 kW; E Africa • 250 kW; S Africa • 250 kW
	USA	†FAMILY RADIO, Via Komsomolsk, Russia	W • E Asia • 250 kW
6010	BAHRAIN	RADIO BAHRAIN, Abu Hayan	Mideast • DS
	BELARUS	BELARUSIAN R, Brest	⇐ • DS-1 • 5 kW
	BRAZIL	R INCONFIDENCIA, Belo Horizonte	DS • 5/10/25 kW
	CHILE	RADIO PARINACOTA, Putre	DS • 1 kW
	CHINA	CENTRAL PEOPLE'S BS, Xi'an	W • DS-2 • 100 kW; DS-8 (MINORITIES) • 100 kW; DS-2 • 100 kW
		CHINA R INTL, Beijing	W • Europe • 500 kW
		CHINA R INTL, Xi'an	W • SE Asia • 500 kW
	IRAN	VO THE ISLAMIC REP, Tehrān	W • W Asia & S Asia • 500 kW; W • Europe • 500 kW
	MEXICO	RADIO MIL, México City	DS • 1 kW
	NETHERLANDS	†R NEDERLAND, Via Wertachtal, Germany	W • S Europe & Atlantic • 250 kW
	SWEDEN	RADIO SWEDEN, Via Sackville, Canada	⇐ • E North Am • 250 kW; ⇐ • W North Am • 250 kW
	TURKEY	†VOICE OF TURKEY, Via Canada	W • W North Am • 250 kW
	UNITED KINGDOM	BIBLE VOICE, Via Dhabayya, UAE	F-Su • S Asia • 250 kW; M-Th • S Asia • 250 kW
	URUGUAY	EMISORA CIUDAD DE MONTEVIDEO	S America • DS-TEMP INACTIVE • 1.5/10 kW • ALT. FREQ. TO 9650 kHz
	USA	†FAMILY RADIO, Via W'tal, Germany	W • W Africa • 500 kW
		R FREE ASIA, Via Dhabayya, UAE	W • S Asia • 500 kW
6010v	COLOMBIA	LV DE TU CONCIENCIA, Puerto Lleras	DS • 5 kW
6015	CHINA	XINJIANG PEOPLE'S BC STN, Urümqi	DS-KAZAK • 100 kW; S • DS-KAZAK • 100 kW
	ECUADOR	†HCJB GLOBAL VOICE, Via France	S • Europe • 100 kW
	GERMANY	CHRISTLICHE WISSENSCHAFT, Jülich	S Su • Europe • 100 kW
	IRAN	VO THE ISLAMIC REP, Sirjan	W • W Asia & S Asia • 500 kW
	NETHERLANDS	†R NEDERLAND, Via Nauen, Germany	S • S Europe • 250 kW
	POLAND	POLISH RADIO, Via W'tachtal, Germany	W • W Europe • 100 kW
	ROMANIA	†R ROMANIA INTL, Bucharest	W • S Europe • 100 kW
		†R ROMANIA INTL, Galbeni	W • W Europe • 300 kW
	TANZANIA	VOICE OF TANZANIA, Dole, Zanzibar	DS • 50 kW
	UNITED KINGDOM	†BBC, Via A'Seela, Oman	S • S Asia • 250 kW
		BBC, Via Moosbrunn, Austria	W M-F • E Europe & Mideast • 100 kW
		BBC, Via Zyyi, Cyprus	Mideast • 250/300 kW; W • Mideast • 250/300 kW
		BIBLE VOICE, Via Jülich, Germany	⇐ • Sa/Su • E Europe • 100 kW; ⇐ • M-F • E Europe • 100 kW; ⇐ • Th • E Europe • 100 kW; ⇐ • Su • E Europe • 100 kW; ⇐ • Sa • E Europe • 100 kW
	USA	VOA, Via Iranawila, Sri Lanka	W • S Asia • 250 kW
		VOA, Via São Tomé	W M-F • W Africa & C Africa • 100 kW; W • W Africa & C Africa • 100 kW
6020	AUSTRALIA	RADIO AUSTRALIA, Shepparton	Pacific • 100 kW; Pacific & W North Am • 100 kW
(con'd)			

World Time 0 1 2 3 4 5 6 7 8 9 10 11 12 13 14 15 16 17 18 19 20 21 22 23 24

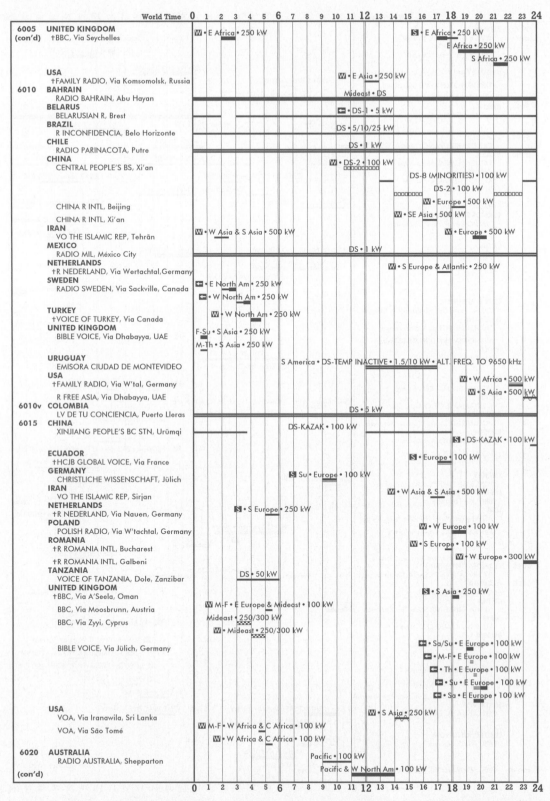

ENGLISH ▬ ARABIC ▭ CHINESE ▫▫▫ FRENCH ═ GERMAN ═ RUSSIAN ═ SPANISH ═ OTHER —

kHz	Country / Station	World Time 0–24
6020 (con'd)	**BRAZIL**	
	RADIO GAUCHA, Porto Alegre	DS • 10 kW • ➡
		Irr • DS • 10 kW • ➡
	CHINA	
	CHINA R INTL, Beijing	W • C Asia • 500 kW
	CHINA R INTL, Kashi	W • S Asia • 100 kW
	CHINA R INTL, Shijiazhuang	Europe • 500 kW
		W • Europe • 500 kW
	CHINA R INTL, Via Cerrik, Albania	N America • 300 kW
	CHINA R INTL, Via Sackville, Canada	S • W North Am • 250 kW
	INDIA	
	ALL INDIA RADIO, Shimla	DS • 50 kW
		ENGLISH, ETC • DS • 50 kW
		Su • DS • 50 kW
	NETHERLANDS	
	R NEDERLAND, Via Madagascar	S Africa • 250 kW
	R NEDERLAND, Via Neth Antilles	M-Sa • C America • 250 kW
	RUSSIA	
	VOICE OF RUSSIA, Samara	W • Mideast & W Asia • 250 kW
	SPAIN	
	R EXTERIOR ESPANA, Via Costa Rica	S • S America • 100 kW
	TURKEY	
	VOICE OF TURKEY, Ankara-Emirler	W • Europe & N America • 500 kW
	UKRAINE	
	†UKRAINIAN RADIO, Kyiv	W • DS-1 • 100 kW • ALT. FREQ. TO 5970 kHz
	UNITED KINGDOM	
	BBC, Via A'Seela, Oman	W • E Asia • 250 kW
	BIBLE VOICE, Via Dhabayya, UAE	W • S Asia • 250 kW
		W Sa • S Asia • 250 kW
	USA	
	FAMILY RADIO, Via Madagascar	E Africa • 50 kW
	†FAMILY RADIO, Via Samara, Russia	W • S Asia • 250 kW
	VATICAN STATE	
	VATICAN RADIO, Via Philippines	E Asia • 250 kW
	VIETNAM	
	†VOICE OF VIETNAM, Da Lai	DS • 50 kW
6020v	**PERU**	
	RADIO VICTORIA, Lima	SPANISH & PORTUGUESE • DS • 5 kW
6025	**ALGERIA**	
	R ALGERIENNE, Via Woofferton, UK	W • N Africa • DS • 300 kW
	BOLIVIA	
	RADIO ILLIMANI, La Paz	SPANISH, AYMARA & QUECHUA • DS • 10 kW
		Tu-Su • DS • 10 kW
	CANADA	
	R CANADA INTL, Via Vatican State	W • Mideast • 100 kW
	CHINA	
	CHINA R INTL, Xi'an	W • W Asia & C Asia • 250 kW
	DOMINICAN REPUBLIC	
	†R AMANECER INTL, Sto Domingo	DS-TEMP INACTIVE • 1/5 kW
	HUNGARY	
	†HUNGARIAN RADIO, Jászberény	S • Europe • 250 kW
		W • Europe • 250 kW • ALT. FREQ. TO 5920 kHz
		⬅ • Europe • 250 kW
	IRAN	
	†VO THE ISLAMIC REP, Mashhad	S • Mideast & N Africa • 500 kW
	†VO THE ISLAMIC REP, Tehrān	S • S Asia • 500 kW
	ROMANIA	
	†R ROMANIA INTL, Bucharest	W • E Europe • 300 kW
		W • S Europe • 100 kW
	USA	
	†TRANS WORLD R, Via Swaziland	W Sa • S Africa • 50 kW
		W Su-F • S Africa • 50 kW
		W • S Africa • 50 kW
		W M-F • S Africa • 50 kW
		W Sa/Su • S Africa • 50 kW
6030	**BRAZIL**	
	RADIO GLOBO, Rio de Janeiro	DS-TEMP INACTIVE • 10 kW • ➡
	CANADA	
	CFVP-CKMX, Calgary, Alberta	W North Am • DS • 0.1 kW
	CENTRAL AFRICAN REPUBLIC	
	RADIO ICDI, Baoli	FRENCH, ETC • C Africa • 1 kW
	CHINA	
	CENTRAL PEOPLE'S BS, Beijing	DS-1 • 50 kW
		W-M • DS-1 • 50 kW
	CLANDESTINE (ASIA)	
(con'd)	"MINGHUI RADIO", Via Taiwan	E Asia

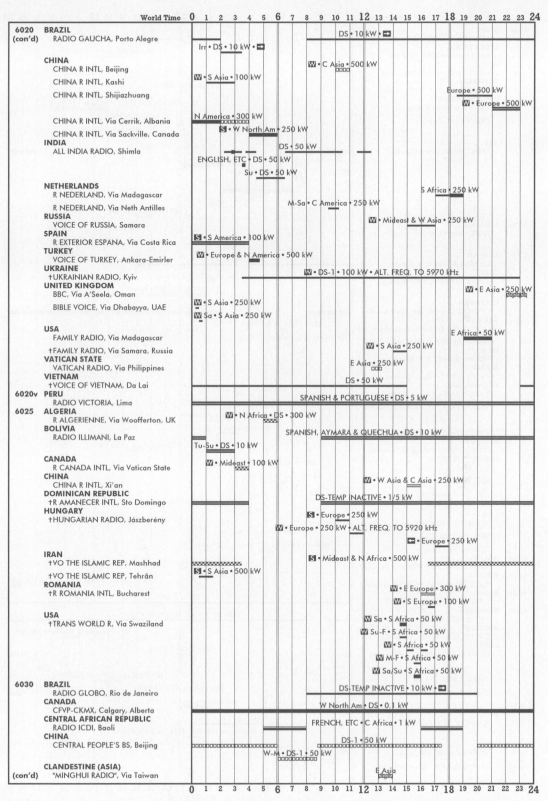

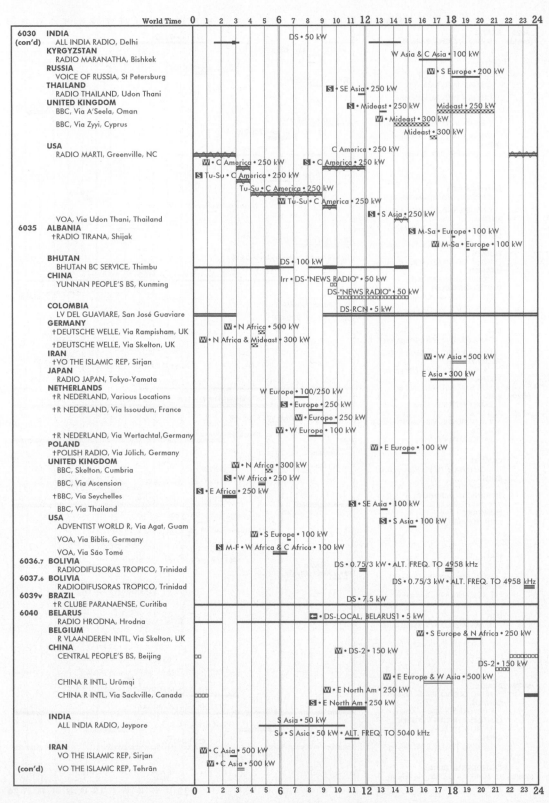

World Time 0 1 2 3 4 5 6 7 8 9 10 11 12 13 14 15 16 17 18 19 20 21 22 23 24

kHz	Country / Station	Schedule
6030 (con'd)	**INDIA**	
	ALL INDIA RADIO, Delhi	DS • 50 kW
	KYRGYZSTAN	
	RADIO MARANATHA, Bishkek	W Asia & C Asia • 100 kW
	RUSSIA	
	VOICE OF RUSSIA, St Petersburg	W • S Europe • 200 kW
	THAILAND	
	RADIO THAILAND, Udon Thani	S • SE Asia • 250 kW
	UNITED KINGDOM	
	BBC, Via A'Seela, Oman	S • Mideast • 250 kW; Mideast • 250 kW
	BBC, Via Zyyi, Cyprus	W • Mideast • 300 kW; Mideast • 300 kW
	USA	
	RADIO MARTI, Greenville, NC	C America • 250 kW; W • C America • 250 kW; S • C America • 250 kW; S Tu-Su • C America • 250 kW; Tu-Su • C America • 250 kW; W Tu-Su • C America • 250 kW
	VOA, Via Udon Thani, Thailand	S • S Asia • 250 kW
6035	**ALBANIA**	
	†RADIO TIRANA, Shijak	S M-Sa • Europe • 100 kW; W M-Sa • Europe • 100 kW
	BHUTAN	
	BHUTAN BC SERVICE, Thimbu	DS • 100 kW
	CHINA	
	YUNNAN PEOPLE'S BS, Kunming	Irr • DS-"NEWS RADIO" • 50 kW; DS-"NEWS RADIO" • 50 kW
	COLOMBIA	
	LV DEL GUAVIARE, San José Guaviare	DS-RCN • 5 kW
	GERMANY	
	†DEUTSCHE WELLE, Via Rampisham, UK	W • N Africa • 500 kW
	†DEUTSCHE WELLE, Via Skelton, UK	W • N Africa & Mideast • 300 kW
	IRAN	
	†VO THE ISLAMIC REP, Sirjan	W • W Asia • 500 kW
	JAPAN	
	RADIO JAPAN, Tokyo-Yamata	E Asia • 300 kW
	NETHERLANDS	
	†R NEDERLAND, Various Locations	W Europe • 100/250 kW
	†R NEDERLAND, Via Issoudun, France	S • Europe • 250 kW; W • Europe • 250 kW
	†R NEDERLAND, Via Wertachtal,Germany	W • W Europe • 100 kW
	POLAND	
	†POLISH RADIO, Via Jülich, Germany	W • E Europe • 100 kW
	UNITED KINGDOM	
	BBC, Skelton, Cumbria	W • N Africa • 300 kW
	BBC, Via Ascension	S • W Africa • 250 kW
	†BBC, Via Seychelles	S • E Africa • 250 kW
	BBC, Via Thailand	S • SE Asia • 100 kW
	USA	
	ADVENTIST WORLD R, Via Agat, Guam	S • S Asia • 100 kW
	VOA, Via Biblis, Germany	W • S Europe • 100 kW
	VOA, Via São Tomé	S M-F • W Africa & C Africa • 100 kW
6036.7	**BOLIVIA**	
	RADIODIFUSORAS TROPICO, Trinidad	DS • 0.75/3 kW • ALT. FREQ. TO 4958 kHz
6037.6	**BOLIVIA**	
	RADIODIFUSORAS TROPICO, Trinidad	DS • 0.75/3 kW • ALT. FREQ. TO 4958 kHz
6039v	**BRAZIL**	
	†R CLUBE PARANAENSE, Curitiba	DS • 7.5 kW
6040	**BELARUS**	
	RADIO HRODNA, Hrodna	← • DS-LOCAL, BELARUS1 • 5 kW
	BELGIUM	
	R VLAANDEREN INTL, Via Skelton, UK	W • S Europe & N Africa • 250 kW
	CHINA	
	CENTRAL PEOPLE'S BS, Beijing	W • DS-2 • 150 kW; DS-2 • 150 kW
	CHINA R INTL, Urümqi	W • E Europe & W Asia • 500 kW
	CHINA R INTL, Via Sackville, Canada	W • E North Am • 250 kW; S • E North Am • 250 kW
	INDIA	
	ALL INDIA RADIO, Jeypore	S Asia • 50 kW; Su • S Asia • 50 kW • ALT. FREQ. TO 5040 kHz
	IRAN	
	VO THE ISLAMIC REP, Sirjan	W • C Asia • 500 kW
(con'd)	VO THE ISLAMIC REP, Tehrān	W • C Asia • 500 kW

0 1 2 3 4 5 6 7 8 9 10 11 12 13 14 15 16 17 18 19 20 21 22 23 24

ENGLISH ARABIC CHINESE FRENCH GERMAN RUSSIAN SPANISH OTHER

World Time 0 1 2 3 4 5 6 7 8 9 10 11 12 13 14 15 16 17 18 19 20 21 22 23 24

kHz	Country / Station	Schedule
6040 (con'd)	**JAPAN**	
	†RADIO JAPAN, Via Netherlands Antilles	W • S America • 250 kW
	MOLDOVA	
	†RADIO PMR, Grigoriopol	S Su-Th • E North Am • 500 kW
	NETHERLANDS	
	†R NEDERLAND, Via Armavir, Russia	W • W Europe • 500 kW
	†R NEDERLAND, Via Moldova	S • W Europe • 500 kW
	R NEDERLAND, Via Petro-K, Russia	W • E Asia • 250 kW
	TURKEY	
	VOICE OF TURKEY, Ankara-Emirler	S • Mideast • 500 kW
	UNITED KINGDOM	
	†BBC, Via Thailand	W • SE Asia • 250 kW
	BIBLE VOICE, Via Dhabayya, UAE	W • S Asia • 250 kW
	USA	
	ADVENTIST WORLD R, Via Austria	W • W Asia • 300 kW
	GOSPEL FOR ASIA, Via Dhabayya, UAE	S Asia • 250 kW
	†TRANS WORLD R, Via Swaziland	E Africa • 100 kW
	VOA, Via Biblis, Germany	W • Mideast • 100 kW
	VOA, Via Dhabayya, UAE	S • W Asia • 500 kW
	VOA, Via Udon Thani, Thailand	W • E Asia • 500 kW
	VOA, Via Wertachtal, Germany	S • W Asia • 250 kW
	VATICAN STATE	
	VATICAN RADIO, Via Sackville, Canada	W • E North Am & C America • 100 kW • ALT. FREQ. TO 6100 kHz
6045	**CHINA**	
	NEI MENGGU PBS, Hohhot	DS • 50 kW
	CHINA (TAIWAN)	
	R TAIWAN INTL, Via Ramisham, UK	S • W Europe • 250 kW
	GERMANY	
	HAMBURGER LOKALRADIO, Jülich	Irr • Su • Europe • 100 kW
	MV BALTIC RADIO, Jülich	S Su • Europe • 1ST SUN OF MONTH • 100 kW
	INDIA	
	ALL INDIA RADIO, Delhi	S Asia • 100 kW
	JAPAN	
	SHIOKAZE, Tokyo-Yamata	E Asia • 100 kW
	KOREA (REPUBLIC)	
	KBS WORLD R, Via Sackville, Canada	W Europe • 250 kW
	MEXICO	
	RADIO UNIVERSIDAD, San Luis Potosí	DS • 0.25 kW
	RUSSIA	
	VOICE OF RUSSIA, Samara	W • Europe • 250 kW
	VOICE OF RUSSIA, St Petersburg	W • Europe • 200 kW
	VOICE OF RUSSIA, Vladivostok	S • E Asia & SE Asia • 250 kW
	USA	
	ADVENTIST WORLD R, Via Austria	W • N Africa • 300 kW
	ADVENTIST WORLD R, Via Germany	W • E Europe • 100 kW
	†FAMILY RADIO, Via Meyerton, S Africa	W • E Africa • 250 kW
		W • S Africa • 100 kW
	VOA, Via Udon Thani, Thailand	W • E Asia • 250 kW
	ZIMBABWE	
	ZIMBABWE BC CORP, Gweru	ENGLISH, ETC • DS-RADIO ZIMBABWE • 50/100 kW • ALT. FREQ. TO 3306 kHz
		ENGLISH, ETC • DS-RADIO ZIMBABWE • 50/100 kW
6047v	**PERU**	
	RADIO SANTA ROSA, Lima	Irr • DS • 3 kW
6049.6	**MALAYSIA**	
	RTV MALAYSIA, Kajang	DS-ASYIK FM • 50/100 kW
	VOICE OF MALAYSIA, Kajang	SE Asia • VOICE OF ISLAM • 50/100 kW
6050	**CHILE**	
	CVC-LA VOZ, Santiago	W • S America • 100 kW
	CHINA	
	XIZANG PBS, Lhasa	DS • 100 kW
		W-M • DS • 100 kW
	ECUADOR	
	†HCJB GLOBAL VOICE, Quito	S America • 50 kW
	GERMANY	
	DEUTSCHE WELLE, Via Sri Lanka	W • SE Asia • 250 kW
	POLAND	
	†POLISH RADIO, Via W'tachtal, Germany	S • E Europe • 100 kW
		W • E Europe • 250 kW
	ROMANIA	
	†R ROMANIA INTL, Galbeni	W • W Europe • 300 kW
	TURKEY	
	†VOICE OF TURKEY, Ankara-Emirler	S • S Europe • 500 kW
		W • W Europe • 500 kW
		W • N Africa & W Africa • 500 kW
(con'd)	**UNITED KINGDOM**	
	BBC, Via Meyerton, South Africa	S • C Africa & E Africa • 500 kW

World Time 0 1 2 3 4 5 6 7 8 9 10 11 12 13 14 15 16 17 18 19 20 21 22 23 24

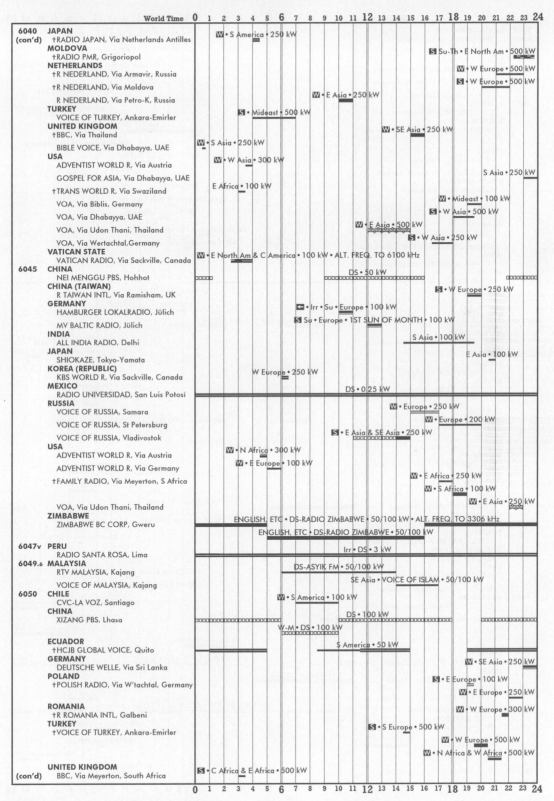

World Time 0 1 2 3 4 5 6 7 8 9 10 11 12 13 14 15 16 17 18 19 20 21 22 23 24

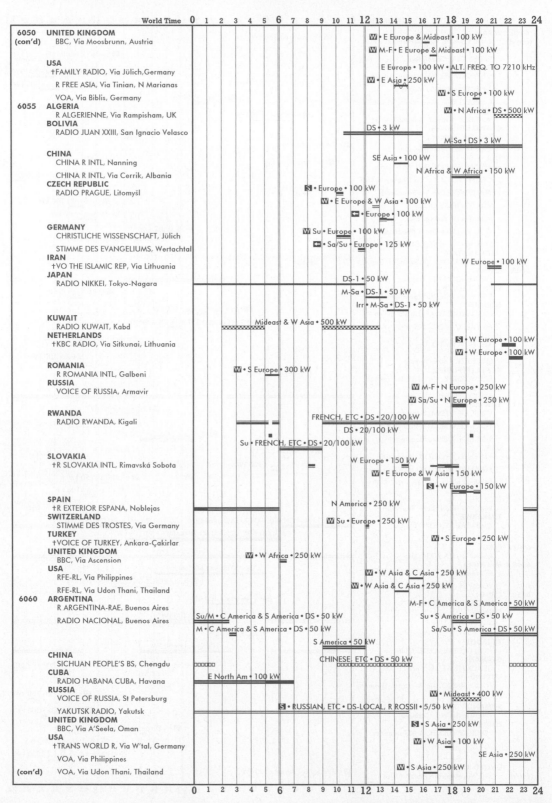

kHz	Country / Station	Schedule
6050 (con'd)	**UNITED KINGDOM** BBC, Via Moosbrunn, Austria	W • E Europe & Mideast • 100 kW
		W M-F • E Europe & Mideast • 100 kW
	USA †FAMILY RADIO, Via Jülich, Germany	E Europe • 100 kW • ALT. FREQ. TO 7210 kHz
	R FREE ASIA, Via Tinian, N Marianas	W • E Asia • 250 kW
	VOA, Via Biblis, Germany	W • S Europe • 100 kW
6055	**ALGERIA** R ALGERIENNE, Via Rampisham, UK	W • N Africa • DS • 500 kW
	BOLIVIA RADIO JUAN XXIII, San Ignacio Velasco	DS • 3 kW
		M-Sa • DS • 3 kW
	CHINA CHINA R INTL, Nanning	SE Asia • 100 kW
	CHINA R INTL, Via Cerrik, Albania	N Africa & W Africa • 150 kW
	CZECH REPUBLIC RADIO PRAGUE, Litomyšl	S • Europe • 100 kW
		W • E Europe & W Asia • 100 kW
		← • Europe • 100 kW
	GERMANY CHRISTLICHE WISSENSCHAFT, Jülich	W Su • Europe • 100 kW
	STIMME DES EVANGELIUMS, Wertachtal	← • Sa/Su • Europe • 125 kW
	IRAN †VO THE ISLAMIC REP, Via Lithuania	W Europe • 100 kW
	JAPAN RADIO NIKKEI, Tokyo-Nagara	DS-1 • 50 kW
		M-Sa • DS-1 • 50 kW
		Irr • M-Sa • DS-1 • 50 kW
	KUWAIT RADIO KUWAIT, Kabd	Mideast & W Asia • 500 kW
	NETHERLANDS †KBC RADIO, Via Sitkunai, Lithuania	S • W Europe • 100 kW
		W • W Europe • 100 kW
	ROMANIA R ROMANIA INTL, Galbeni	W • S Europe • 300 kW
	RUSSIA VOICE OF RUSSIA, Armavir	W M-F • N Europe • 250 kW
		W Sa/Su • N Europe • 250 kW
	RWANDA RADIO RWANDA, Kigali	FRENCH, ETC • DS • 20/100 kW
		DS • 20/100 kW
		Su • FRENCH, ETC • DS • 20/100 kW
	SLOVAKIA †R SLOVAKIA INTL, Rimavská Sobota	W Europe • 150 kW
		W • E Europe & W Asia • 150 kW
		S • W Europe • 150 kW
	SPAIN †R EXTERIOR ESPANA, Noblejas	N America • 250 kW
	SWITZERLAND STIMME DES TROSTES, Via Germany	W Su • Europe • 250 kW
	TURKEY †VOICE OF TURKEY, Ankara-Çakirlar	W • S Europe • 250 kW
	UNITED KINGDOM BBC, Via Ascension	W • W Africa • 250 kW
	USA RFE-RL, Via Philippines	W • W Asia & C Asia • 250 kW
	RFE-RL, Via Udon Thani, Thailand	W • W Asia & C Asia • 250 kW
6060	**ARGENTINA** R ARGENTINA-RAE, Buenos Aires	M-F • C America & S America • 50 kW
	RADIO NACIONAL, Buenos Aires	Su/M • C America & S America • DS • 50 kW
		Su • S America • DS • 50 kW
		M • C America & S America • DS • 50 kW
		Sa/Su • S America • DS • 50 kW
		S America • 50 kW
	CHINA SICHUAN PEOPLE'S BS, Chengdu	CHINESE, ETC • DS • 50 kW
	CUBA RADIO HABANA CUBA, Havana	E North Am • 100 kW
	RUSSIA VOICE OF RUSSIA, St Petersburg	W • Mideast • 400 kW
	YAKUTSK RADIO, Yakutsk	S • RUSSIAN, ETC • DS-LOCAL, R ROSSII • 5/50 kW
	UNITED KINGDOM BBC, Via A'Seela, Oman	S • S Asia • 250 kW
	USA †TRANS WORLD R, Via W'tal, Germany	W • W Asia • 100 kW
	VOA, Via Philippines	SE Asia • 250 kW
(con'd)	VOA, Via Udon Thani, Thailand	W • S Asia • 250 kW

0 1 2 3 4 5 6 7 8 9 10 11 12 13 14 15 16 17 18 19 20 21 22 23 24

ENGLISH ARABIC CHINESE FRENCH GERMAN RUSSIAN SPANISH OTHER

World Time 0 1 2 3 4 5 6 7 8 9 10 11 12 13 14 15 16 17 18 19 20 21 22 23 24

kHz	Country / Station	Schedule
6060 (con'd)	**USA**	
	VOA, Via Udon Thani, Thailand	S • E Asia • 250 kW
	VENEZUELA	
	RADIO NACIONAL, Via Havana, Cuba	C America • 100 kW
6060v	**BRAZIL**	
	RADIO TUPI, Curitiba	DS • 10 kW
6065	**CHINA**	
	CENTRAL PEOPLE'S BS, Beijing	DS-2 • 150 kW
	CHINA R INTL, Kashi	W • S Asia • 100 kW
	GERMANY	
	†DEUTSCHE WELLE, Via Wooffertοn, UK	S • N Africa & W Africa • 300 kW
	INDIA	
	ALL INDIA RADIO, Kohima	DS • 50 kW
	IRAN	
	VO THE ISLAMIC REP, Sirjan	W • Mideast & N Africa • 500 kW
	KOREA (REPUBLIC)	
	KBS WORLD R, In-Kimjae	E Asia • 250 kW
	PAKISTAN	
	PAKISTAN BC CORP, Islamabad	DS • 100 kW
	RADIO PAKISTAN, Islamabad	W Asia & C Asia • 100 kW • ALT. FREQ. TO 4955 kHz
	SWEDEN	
	†RADIO SWEDEN, Hörby	S M-F • Europe & N Africa • 500 kW
		W • E Europe • 500 kW
		W M-F • Europe & N Africa • 500 kW
		⇐ • Europe • 500 kW
		⇐ • M-Sa • Europe • 500 kW
		⇐ • Sa-Tu • E Europe • 350 kW
		⇐ • Europe & N Africa • 500 kW
		⇐ • E Europe • 350/500 kW
	TURKEY	
	VOICE OF TURKEY, Ankara-Emirler	W • W Asia & C Asia • 500 kW
	UNITED KINGDOM	
	BBC, Via A'Seela, Oman	S Asia • 250 kW
	BBC, Via Thailand	SE Asia • 250 kW
	ZAMBIA	
	THE VOICE-AFRICA, Lusaka	C Africa & S Africa • 100 kW • ALT. FREQ. TO 4965 kHz
		C Africa & S Africa • 100 kW
		C Africa & S Africa • 100 kW • ALT. FREQ. TO 9865 kHz
6070	**BELARUS**	
	BELARUSIAN R, Brest	⇐ • DS-1 • 5 kW
	CANADA	
	CFRX-CFRB, Mississauga, Ontario	E North Am • DS • 1 kW
	CHILE	
	CVC-LA VOZ, Santiago	S America • 100 kW
		S • S America • 100 kW
	CHINA	
	CHINA R INTL, Xi'an	W • W Asia & C Asia • 500 kW
	PHILIPPINES	
	FEBC RADIO INTL, Bocaue	W M/W-Sa • SE Asia • 100 kW
	ROMANIA	
	†R ROMANIA INTL, Bucharest	W • S America • 300 kW
	RUSSIA	
	VOICE OF RUSSIA, Novosibirsk	S • S Asia • 200 kW
	USA	
	†FAMILY RADIO, Via Armavir, Russia	W • S Asia • 250 kW
6070v	**INDONESIA**	
	RRI, Jayapura, Papua	DS-TEMP INACTIVE • 50 kW
	KOREA (DPR)	
	VOICE OF KOREA	E Asia
6075	**BOLIVIA**	
	†RADIO CAUSACHUN COCA, Lauca N	SPANISH, ETC • DS
	CANADA	
	R CANADA INTL, Sackville, NB	S • E North Am • 250 kW
	CHINA	
	CHINA R INTL, Kashi	S Asia • 100 kW
		W • S Asia • 100 kW
	YUSHU PEOPLE'S BS	DS-TIBETAN, CHINESE
	GERMANY	
	DEUTSCHE WELLE, Multiple Locations	Europe • 250/300/500 kW
	DEUTSCHE WELLE, Via Rampisham, UK	W • Mideast • 500 kW
	RUSSIA	
	KAMCHATKA RADIO, Petropavlovsk-K	W • E Asia • DS-LOCAL, R ROSSII • 100 kW
6080	**AUSTRALIA**	
	RADIO AUSTRALIA, Shepparton	SE Asia • 100 kW
		Pacific & E Asia • 100 kW
		F/Sa • Pacific • 100 kW
		Su-Th • Pacific • 100 kW
(con'd)	**BELARUS**	
	BELARUSIAN R, Minsk	⇐ • E Europe • DS-1, MINSK LOCAL • 100/150 kW

0 1 2 3 4 5 6 7 8 9 10 11 12 13 14 15 16 17 18 19 20 21 22 23 24

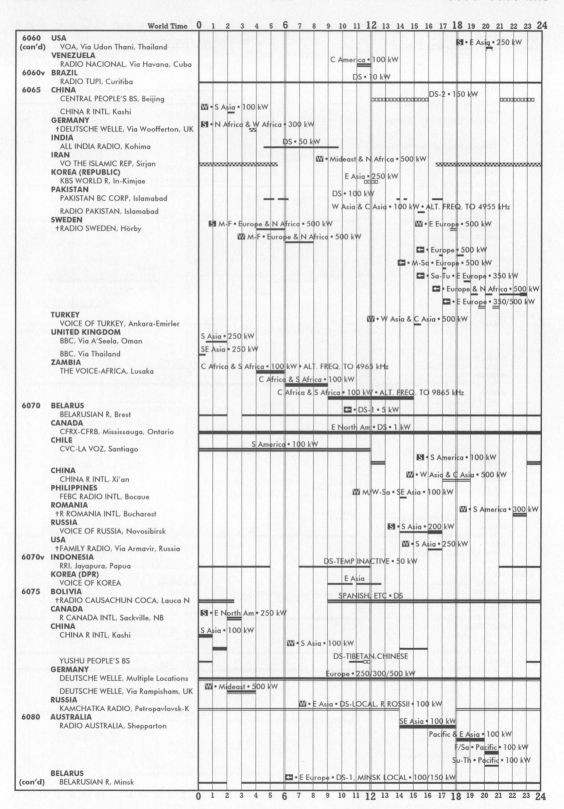

World Time 0 1 2 3 4 5 6 7 8 9 10 11 12 13 14 15 16 17 18 19 20 21 22 23 24

Frequency	Country / Station	Schedule
6080 (con'd)	**BOLIVIA** RADIO SAN GABRIEL, La Paz	DS • 5 kW • ALT. FREQ. TO 6085 kHz Tu-Su • DS • 5 kW • ALT. FREQ. TO 6085 kHz M-F • DS • 5 kW • ALT. FREQ. TO 6085 kHz M-Sa • DS • 5 kW • ALT. FREQ. TO 6085 kHz
	BRAZIL RADIO ANHANGUERA, Goiânia	DS • 10 kW • ➡
	RADIO MARUMBY, Curitiba	DS • 10 kW • ➡
	CHINA CENTRAL PEOPLE'S BS, Geermu	W • DS-1 • 100 kW DS-1 • 100 kW
	CHINA R INTL, Via Sackville, Canada	W • E North Am • 250 kW S • N America • 250 kW
	CHINA R INTL, Xi'an	W • C Asia & E Asia • 500 kW
	HULUNBUIR PBS, Hailar	DS-MONGOLIAN • 15 kW
	CZECH REPUBLIC †RADIO PRAGUE, Via Sackville, Canada	⬅ • Irr • W North Am • 250 kW
	ECUADOR HCJB GLOBAL VOICE, Quito	S America • 10 kW
	UNITED KINGDOM BBC, Via Singapore	SE Asia • 250 kW S Su-Th • SE Asia • 250 kW
	USA VOA, Via Botswana	W • C Africa & S Africa • 100 kW
	VOA, Via São Tomé	C Africa & S Africa • 100 kW S • C Africa & S Africa • 100 kW W Africa • 100 kW W • C Africa • 100 kW W • W Africa • 100 kW
6085	**BOLIVIA** RADIO SAN GABRIEL, La Paz	DS • 5 kW • ALT. FREQ. TO 6080 kHz Tu-Su • DS • 5 kW • ALT. FREQ. TO 6080 kHz M-F • DS • 5 kW • ALT. FREQ. TO 6080 kHz M-Sa • DS • 5 kW • ALT. FREQ. TO 6080 kHz
	CHINA (TAIWAN) R TAIWAN INTL, Tamsui	E Asia • 300 kW
	GERMANY BAYERISCHER RUNDFUNK, Ismaning	⬅ • DS • 100 kW
	INDIA ALL INDIA RADIO, Delhi	DS • 50 kW ENGLISH & HINDI • DS • 50 kW ENGLISH, ETC • DS • 50 kW Irr • DS • 50 kW
	ALL INDIA RADIO, Gangtok	DS • 10 kW
	JAPAN RADIO JAPAN, Tokyo-Yamata	W • E Asia • 300 kW
	OMAN R SULTANATE OF OMAN, Sīb	W • Mideast • DS • 100 kW • ALT. FREQ. TO 7175 kHz E Africa • DS • 100 kW S • Mideast • DS • 100 kW • ALT. FREQ. TO 6000 kHz
	PAKISTAN PAKISTAN BC CORP, Islamabad	DS • 100 kW
	RUSSIA KRASNOYARSK RADIO, Krasnoyarsk	⬅ • N Asia • DS-LOCAL, R ROSSII • 50 kW
	USA †FAMILY RADIO, Okeechobee, Fl	W • E North Am • 100 kW C America • 100 kW
6089v	**PERU** RADIO UNIVERSAL, Cusco	DS • 1.5 kW
6090	**ALGERIA** R ALGERIENNE, Via Rampisham, UK	W • N Africa • DS • 500 kW
	ANGUILLA CARIBBEAN BEACON	N America • 100 kW
	AUSTRALIA CVC, Darwin	S • SE Asia • 250 kW
	BRAZIL RADIO BANDEIRANTES, São Paulo	DS • 10 kW
	CHILE RADIO ESPERANZA, Temuco	DS • 10 kW • ➡ M-Sa • DS • 10 kW • ➡ Su • DS • 10 kW • ➡
	CHINA CENTRAL PEOPLE'S BS, Geermu	DS-2 • 100 kW W • DS-2 • 100 kW
	CHINA R INTL, Ürümqi	S • E Europe • 500 kW
	JAPAN †RADIO JAPAN, Tokyo-Yamata	E Asia • 300 kW
(con'd)	**LIBERIA** RADIO VERITAS, Monrovia	ENGLISH, ETC • DS • 6/10 kW

World Time 0 1 2 3 4 5 6 7 8 9 10 11 12 13 14 15 16 17 18 19 20 21 22 23 24

ENGLISH ▬ ARABIC ▒ CHINESE ▫▫▫ FRENCH ═ GERMAN ═ RUSSIAN ═ SPANISH ═ OTHER —

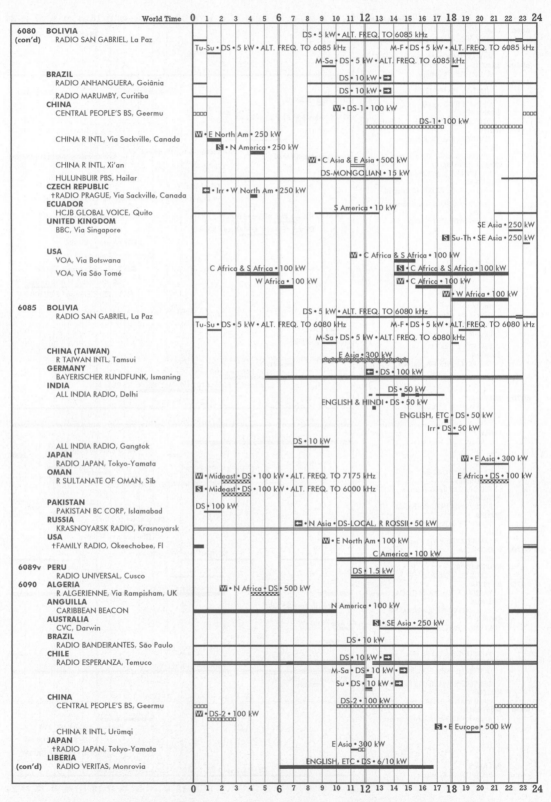

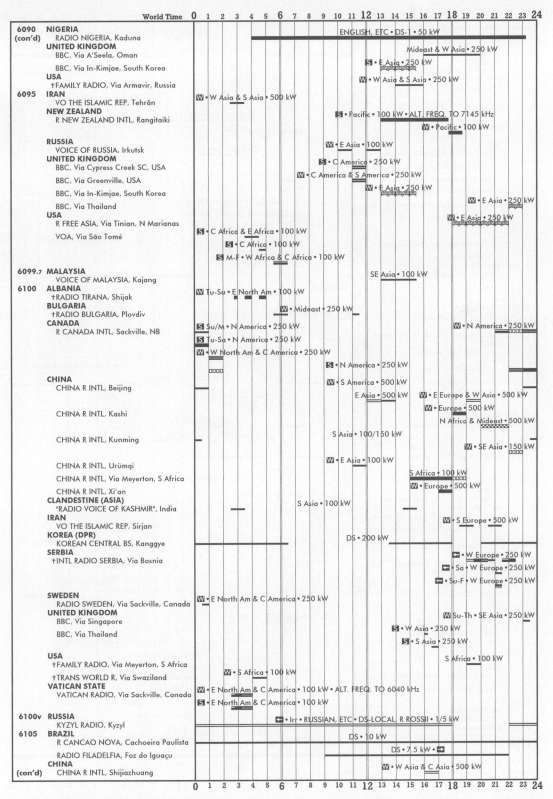

World Time 0 1 2 3 4 5 6 7 8 9 10 11 12 13 14 15 16 17 18 19 20 21 22 23 24

kHz	Country / Station	Schedule
6090 (con'd)	**NIGERIA**	
	RADIO NIGERIA, Kaduna	ENGLISH, ETC • DS-1 • 50 kW
	UNITED KINGDOM	
	BBC, Via A'Seela, Oman	Mideast & W Asia • 250 kW
	BBC, Via In-Kimjae, South Korea	S • E Asia • 250 kW
	USA	
	†FAMILY RADIO, Via Armavir, Russia	W • W Asia & S Asia • 250 kW
6095	**IRAN**	
	VO THE ISLAMIC REP, Tehrān	W • W Asia & S Asia • 500 kW
	NEW ZEALAND	
	R NEW ZEALAND INTL, Rangitaiki	S • Pacific • 100 kW • ALT. FREQ. TO 7145 kHz
		W • Pacific • 100 kW
	RUSSIA	
	VOICE OF RUSSIA, Irkutsk	W • E Asia • 100 kW
	UNITED KINGDOM	
	BBC, Via Cypress Creek SC, USA	S • C America • 250 kW
	BBC, Via Greenville, USA	W • C America & S America • 250 kW
	BBC, Via In-Kimjae, South Korea	W • E Asia • 250 kW
	BBC, Via Thailand	W • E Asia • 250 kW
	USA	
	R FREE ASIA, Via Tinian, N Marianas	W • E Asia • 250 kW
	VOA, Via São Tomé	S • C Africa & E Africa • 100 kW
		S • C Africa • 100 kW
		S M-F • W Africa & C Africa • 100 kW
6099.7	**MALAYSIA**	
	VOICE OF MALAYSIA, Kajang	SE Asia • 100 kW
6100	**ALBANIA**	
	†RADIO TIRANA, Shijak	W Tu-Su • E North Am • 100 kW
	BULGARIA	
	†RADIO BULGARIA, Plovdiv	W • Mideast • 250 kW
	CANADA	
	R CANADA INTL, Sackville, NB	S Su/M • N America • 250 kW
		W • N America • 250 kW
		S Tu-Sa • N America • 250 kW
		W • W North Am & C America • 250 kW
		S • N America • 250 kW
	CHINA	
	CHINA R INTL, Beijing	W • S America • 500 kW
		E Asia • 500 kW
		W • E Europe & W Asia • 500 kW
		W • Europe • 500 kW
	CHINA R INTL, Kashi	N Africa & Mideast • 500 kW
	CHINA R INTL, Kunming	S Asia • 100/150 kW
		W • SE Asia • 150 kW
	CHINA R INTL, Urümqi	W • E Asia • 100 kW
	CHINA R INTL, Via Meyerton, S Africa	S Africa • 100 kW
	CHINA R INTL, Xi'an	W • Europe • 500 kW
	CLANDESTINE (ASIA)	
	"RADIO VOICE OF KASHMIR", India	S Asia • 100 kW
	IRAN	
	VO THE ISLAMIC REP, Sirjan	W • S Europe • 500 kW
	KOREA (DPR)	
	KOREAN CENTRAL BS, Kanggye	DS • 200 kW
	SERBIA	
	†INTL RADIO SERBIA, Via Bosnia	⇦ • W Europe • 250 kW
		⇦ • Sa • W Europe • 250 kW
		⇦ • Su-F • W Europe • 250 kW
	SWEDEN	
	RADIO SWEDEN, Via Sackville, Canada	W • E North Am & C America • 250 kW
	UNITED KINGDOM	
	BBC, Via Singapore	W Su-Th • SE Asia • 250 kW
	BBC, Via Thailand	S • W Asia • 250 kW
		S • S Asia • 250 kW
	USA	
	†FAMILY RADIO, Via Meyerton, S Africa	S Africa • 100 kW
	†TRANS WORLD R, Via Swaziland	W • S Africa • 100 kW
	VATICAN STATE	
	VATICAN RADIO, Via Sackville, Canada	W • E North Am & C America • 100 kW • ALT. FREQ. TO 6040 kHz
		S • E North Am & C America • 100 kW
6100v	**RUSSIA**	
	KYZYL RADIO, Kyzyl	⇦ • Irr • RUSSIAN, ETC • DS-LOCAL, R ROSSII • 1/5 kW
6105	**BRAZIL**	
	R CANCAO NOVA, Cachoeira Paulista	DS • 10 kW
	RADIO FILADELFIA, Foz do Iguaçu	DS • 7.5 kW • ⇨
	CHINA	
(con'd)	CHINA R INTL, Shijiazhuang	W • W Asia & C Asia • 500 kW

0 1 2 3 4 5 6 7 8 9 10 11 12 13 14 15 16 17 18 19 20 21 22 23 24

World Time 0 1 2 3 4 5 6 7 8 9 10 11 12 13 14 15 16 17 18 19 20 21 22 23 24

Frequency	Country / Station	Schedule notes
6105 (con'd)	**CHINA (TAIWAN)** †R TAIWAN INTL, Kouhu	E Asia • 100 kW; E Asia • TAIWAN NETWORK • 100 kW
	COSTA RICA RADIO UNIVERSIDAD, San José	Irr • DS • 2 kW
	JORDAN RADIO JORDAN, Qasr el Kharana	[W] • Mideast, S Asia & Australasia • 500 kW
	ROMANIA †R ROMANIA INTL, Bucharest	[W] • S Europe • 100 kW; [S] • S Europe • 100 kW
	TANZANIA RADIO TANZANIA, Dar es Salaam	E Africa • DS-NATIONAL
	UNITED KINGDOM BBC, Via Ascension	[S] • W Africa • 250 kW
	USA FAMILY RADIO, Okeechobee, Fl	[W] • S America • 100 kW
	†FAMILY RADIO, Via Nauen, Germany	[W] • W Asia • 500 kW
	RFE-RL, Via Lampertheim, Germany	[S] • E Europe • 100 kW
	RFE-RL, Via Philippines	[W] • E Asia • 250 kW
	†TRANS WORLD R, Via W'tal, Germany	[←] • Su • W Europe • 100 kW; [←] • Su-F • W Europe • 100 kW; [←] • W Europe • 100 kW
	VOA, Via Lampertheim, Germany	[←] • E Europe • 100 kW
	VOA, Via São Tomé	[W] • W Africa & C Africa • 100 kW
6105v	**BOLIVIA** RADIO PANAMERICANA, La Paz	DS • 5 kW; Irr • DS • 5 kW; Irr • M-F • DS • 5 kW; M-F • DS • 5 kW
6110	**ALBANIA** RADIO TIRANA, Shijak	[W] • E North Am • 100 kW
	CANADA †R CANADA INTL, Via Tokyo, Japan	[S] • E Asia • 300 kW
	CHILE CVC-LA VOZ, Santiago	[S] • S America • 100 kW
	CHINA CHINA R INTL, Xi'an	W Asia & C Asia • 500 kW
	XIZANG PBS, Lhasa	DS-TIBETAN • 100 kW; W-M • DS-TIBETAN • 100 kW; DS • 100 kW; W-M • DS • 100 kW
	ETHIOPIA RADIO FANA, Addis Ababa	E Africa • DS • 10 kW; Sa/Su • E Africa • DS • 10 kW; M-F • E Africa • DS • 10 kW
	INDIA RADIO KASHMIR, Srinagar	DS • 50 kW; Su • DS • 50 kW; ENGLISH, ETC • DS • 50 kW
	JAPAN RADIO JAPAN, Via Sackville, Can	W North Am • 250 kW
	NETHERLANDS †KBC RADIO, Via Sitkunai, Lithuania	Su • E North Am • 100 kW
	†R NEDERLAND, Via Nauen, Germany	[W] • S Europe • 250 kW
	POLAND †POLISH RADIO, Via Jülich, Germany	[S] • W Europe • 100 kW
	ROMANIA †R ROMANIA INTL, Bucharest	[W] • S Europe • 100 kW
	UNITED KINGDOM BBC, Rampisham	[W] • N Africa • 500 kW
	†BBC, Skelton, Cumbria	[W] • N Africa • 300 kW; [W] • Mideast • 300 kW
	BBC, Various Locations	[W] • N Africa • 300/500 kW
	BBC, Via A'Seela, Oman	[W] • Mideast • 250 kW; [S] • W Asia & S Asia • 250 kW
	BBC, Via Thailand	[W] • SE Asia • 250 kW
	USA OVERCOMER MINISTRY, Via Germany	W Europe • 100 kW
	VOA, Via Philippines	[S] • E Asia • 250 kW; [W] • S Asia & SE Asia • 250 kW
	VATICAN STATE VATICAN RADIO, Via Samara, Russia	[W] • E Asia • 250 kW
6110v	**AZERBAIJAN** VOICE OF AZERBAIJAN, Baku	[←] • E Europe, Mideast & W Asia • 100 kW
6114.8	**PERU** RADIO UNION, Lima	DS • 10 kW
6115 (con'd)	**BELARUS** BELARUSIAN R, Minsk	[←] • Irr • E Europe • DS-1 • 50/100 kW

0 1 2 3 4 5 6 7 8 9 10 11 12 13 14 15 16 17 18 19 20 21 22 23 24

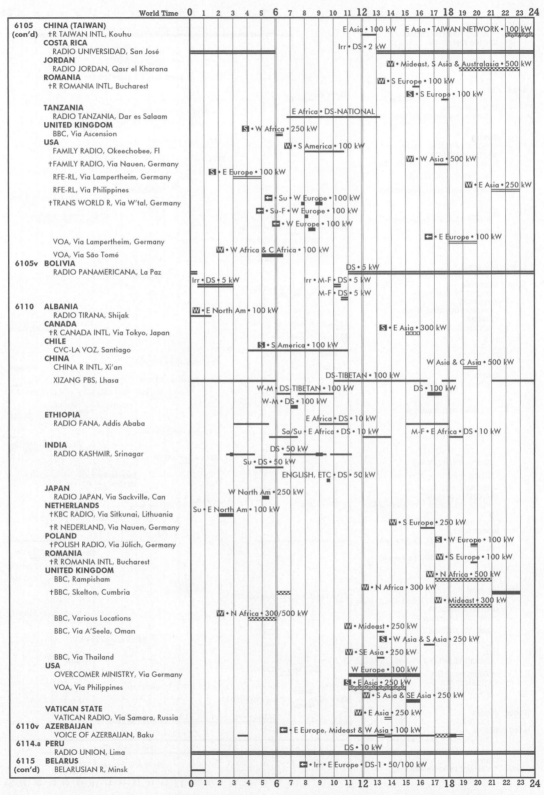

ENGLISH ARABIC CHINESE FRENCH GERMAN RUSSIAN SPANISH OTHER

World Time 0 1 2 3 4 5 6 7 8 9 10 11 12 13 14 15 16 17 18 19 20 21 22 23 24

kHz	Country / Station	Schedule
6115 (con'd)	**BELARUS**	
	BELARUSIAN R, Minsk	← • E Europe • DS-1, MINSK LOCAL • 50/100 kW
	CHINA	
	CHINA R INTL, Via Sackville, Canada	W • W North Am • 250 kW
	†VO THE STRAIT-PLA, Fuzhou	E Asia • AMOY CHANNEL • 50 kW
		Th-Tu • E Asia • AMOY CHANNEL • 50 kW
	GERMANY	
	DEUTSCHE WELLE, Via Rampisham, UK	W • C Asia • 500 kW
	IRAN	
	†VO THE ISLAMIC REP, Via Lithuania	W • W Europe • 100 kW
	JAPAN	
	RADIO NIKKEI, Tokyo-Nagara	DS-2 • 50 kW
		Sa/Su • DS-2 • 50 kW
		Irr • Sa/Su • DS-2 • 50 kW
	PHILIPPINES	
	RADIO VERITAS ASIA, Palauig	E Asia • 250 kW
	ROMANIA	
	†R ROMANIA INTL, Bucharest	W • W North Am • 300 kW
		W • E North Am • 300 kW
	UNITED KINGDOM	
	BBC, Via A'Seela, Oman	W • W Asia & S Asia • 250 kW
	USA	
	†FAMILY RADIO, Via Irkutsk, Russia	W • E Asia • 100 kW
	†FAMILY RADIO, Via Nauen, Germany	S • N Africa • 500 kW
	†R FARDA, Via Lampertheim, Germany	W • W Asia • 100 kW
6120	**CHINA**	
	XINJIANG PEOPLE'S BC STN, Urümqi	DS-UIGHUR • 50/100 kW
		S • DS-UIGHUR • 100 kW
	CHINA (TAIWAN)	
	†R TAIWAN INTL, Via Issoudun, France	W • E Europe • 500 kW
	IRAN	
	VO THE ISLAMIC REP, Tehrān	W • N America • 500 kW
	JAPAN	
	RADIO JAPAN, Via Sackville, Can	C America • 250 kW
		E North Am & C America • 250 kW
	NETHERLANDS	
	†R NEDERLAND, Via Issoudun, France	W • S Europe • 250 kW
	†R NEDERLAND, Via Nauen, Germany	← • S Europe • 500 kW
	†R NEDERLAND, Via Singapore	S • SE Asia • 250 kW
	†R NEDERLAND, Via Wertachtal,Germany	← • S Europe • 250 kW
	ROMANIA	
	†R ROMANIA INTL, Galbeni	W • W Europe • 300 kW
	SOUTH AFRICA	
	CHANNEL AFRICA, Meyerton	E Africa • 250 kW
	TURKEY	
	†VOICE OF TURKEY, Ankara-Çakirlar	W • Mideast • 250 kW
	†VOICE OF TURKEY, Ankara-Emirler	S • W Asia • 500 kW
	USA	
	†FAMILY RADIO, Via Nauen, Germany	W • S Europe • 250 kW
	†TRANS WORLD R, Via Swaziland	W • S Africa • 50 kW
		S Africa • 50 kW
	VOA, Via Iranawila, Sri Lanka	S • SE Asia • 250 kW
6120v	**BRAZIL**	
	RADIO GLOBO, São Paulo	DS • 7.5 kW • →
6125	**ALGERIA**	
	R ALGERIENNE, Via Woofferton, UK	W • N Africa • DS • 250 kW
	CHINA	
	CENTRAL PEOPLE'S BS, Shijiazhuang	DS-1 • 100 kW
		W • DS-1 • 100 kW
	NETHERLANDS	
	†R NEDERLAND, Via Nauen, Germany	S • S Europe • 250 kW
	SPAIN	
	†R EXTERIOR ESPANA, Noblejas	W • S America • 250 kW
		W Sa/Su • W Europe • 250 kW
	†R EXTERIOR ESPANA, Via Costa Rica	S • C America & S America • 100 kW
	UNITED KINGDOM	
	FEBA RADIO, Via Dhabayya, UAE	W • W Asia • 250 kW
		S F • Mideast • 250 kW
	URUGUAY	
	SODRE, Montevideo	DS • 0.2 kW
	USA	
	RFE-RL, Via Biblis, Germany	W M-F • E Europe • 100 kW
6130	**CHINA**	
	XIZANG PBS, Lhasa	DS-TIBETAN • 100 kW
		W-M • DS-TIBETAN • 100 kW
		DS • 100 kW
		W-M • DS • 100 kW
(con'd)		

World Time 0 1 2 3 4 5 6 7 8 9 10 11 12 13 14 15 16 17 18 19 20 21 22 23 24

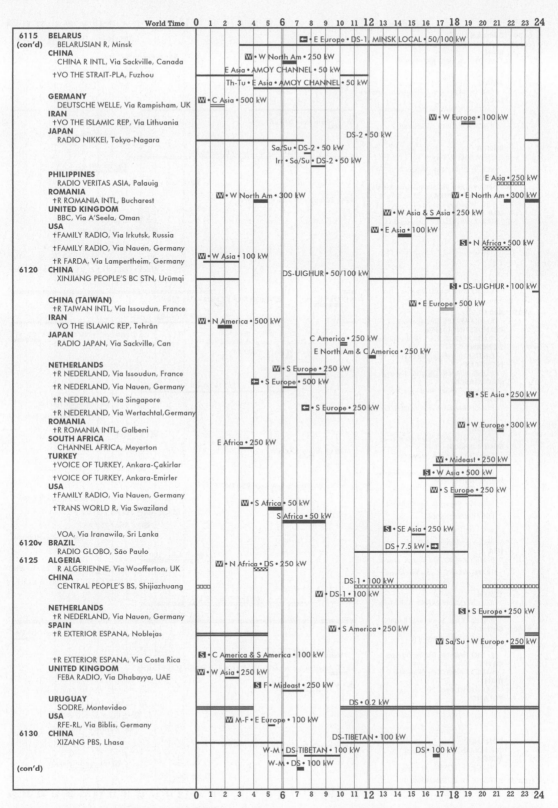

World Time 0 1 2 3 4 5 6 7 8 9 10 11 12 13 14 15 16 17 18 19 20 21 22 23 24

kHz	Country / Station	Schedule
6130 (con'd)	**GERMANY** DEUTSCHE WELLE, Via Skelton, UK	W • N Africa & W Africa • 250 kW
	IRAN †VO THE ISLAMIC REP, Tehrān	S • Mideast • 500 kW
		W • E Africa & C Africa • 500 kW
	JAPAN †RADIO JAPAN, Via Netherlands Antilles	W • W North Am & C America • 250 kW
	LAOS LAO NATIONAL RADIO, Vientiane	DS • 50 kW
	ROMANIA †R ROMANIA INTL, Bucharest	W • E North Am • 300 kW
		W • E Europe • 100 kW
		S • S Europe • 100 kW
	RUSSIA PERM RADIO, Perm	W • DS-LOCAL, R ROSSII • 5 kW
	VOICE OF RUSSIA, Moscow	W • Europe • 250 kW
	SWEDEN †IBRA RADIO, Via Novosibirsk, Russia	W • E Asia • 200 kW
	UNITED KINGDOM BBC, Woofferton	W • E Europe & W Asia • 250 kW
	USA †TRANS WORLD R, Via Swaziland	S Africa • 100 kW
		M-F • S Africa • 100 kW
		Sa/Su • S Africa • 100 kW
		M-F • S Africa • 100 kW • ALT. FREQ. TO 6135 kHz
		S Africa • 100 kW • ALT. FREQ. TO 6135 kHz
6134.8	**BOLIVIA** RADIO SANTA CRUZ, Santa Cruz	DS • 10 kW
		Irr • DS • 10 kW
		SPANISH & QUECHUA • DS • 10 kW
6135	**BRAZIL** RADIO APARECIDA, Aparecida	DS • 7.5 kW • ➡
	CLANDESTINE (AMER) "RADIO REPUBLICA", Via Rampisham,UK	C America • ANTI-CASTRO • 500 kW
	GERMANY DEUTSCHE WELLE, Via Skelton, UK	W • N Africa & W Africa • 300 kW
	HUNGARY †HUNGARIAN RADIO, Jászberény	W • N America • 250 kW
	MADAGASCAR RTV MALAGASY, Antananarivo	DS-1 • 30 kW
	POLAND †POLISH RADIO, Via W'tachtal, Germany	S • Europe • 100 kW
		W • E Europe • 100 kW
	ROMANIA †R ROMANIA INTL, Bucharest	S • S Europe • 100 kW
	SOUTH AFRICA †CHANNEL AFRICA, Meyerton	S • E Africa • 500 kW
	TURKEY VOICE OF TURKEY, Ankara-Emirler	W • E Europe & N Asia • 500 kW
	UNITED KINGDOM BBC, Via Ascension	W Africa & C Africa • 250 kW
	BBC, Via Meyerton, South Africa	M-F • S Africa • 250 kW
	BBC, Via Singapore	W • SE Asia • 250 kW
	BBC, Via Thailand	W • S Asia • 250 kW
	†BBC, Via Vladivostok, Russia	S • E Asia • 500 kW
	USA †FAMILY RADIO, Via Irkutsk, Russia	S • E Asia • 100 kW
	†TRANS WORLD R, Via Swaziland	M-F • S Africa • 100 kW • ALT. FREQ. TO 6130 kHz
		S Africa • 100 kW • ALT. FREQ. TO 6130 kHz
	YEMEN REP OF YEMEN RADIO, Al-Hiswah	Mideast • DS • 50 kW
6139.8	**COLOMBIA** RADIO LIDER, Santafé de Bogotá	Irr • DS • 5/20 kW
6140	**CHINA** CHINA R INTL, Kunming	SE Asia • 100 kW
	CUBA †RADIO HABANA CUBA, Havana	N America • 100 kW
	EGYPT †RADIO CAIRO, Kafr Silîm-Abis	S • C America & S America • 250 kW • ALT. FREQ. TO 9915 kHz
	IRAN VO THE ISLAMIC REP, Sirjan	W • W Asia & S Asia • 500 kW
	POLAND †POLISH RADIO, Via W'tachtal, Germany	W • C Asia • 100 kW
		W • E Europe • 100 kW
		S • E Europe • 100 kW
	ROMANIA †R ROMANIA INTL, Galbeni	W • W North Am & C America • 300 kW
	RUSSIA VOICE OF RUSSIA, Armavir	W • Mideast • 100 kW
(con'd)	VOICE OF RUSSIA, Chita	W • SE Asia • 500 kW

World Time 0 1 2 3 4 5 6 7 8 9 10 11 12 13 14 15 16 17 18 19 20 21 22 23 24

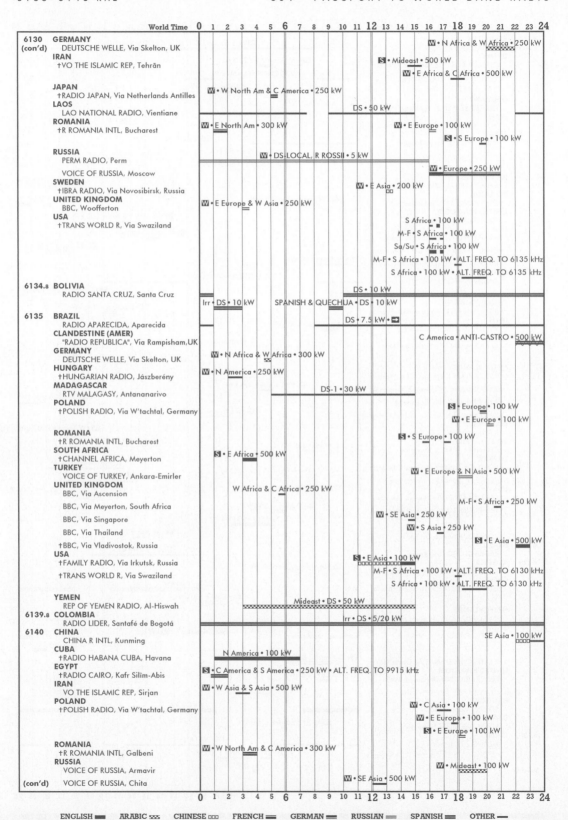

ENGLISH ▬ ARABIC ▭ CHINESE ▫▫▫ FRENCH ═ GERMAN ═ RUSSIAN ═ SPANISH ═ OTHER —

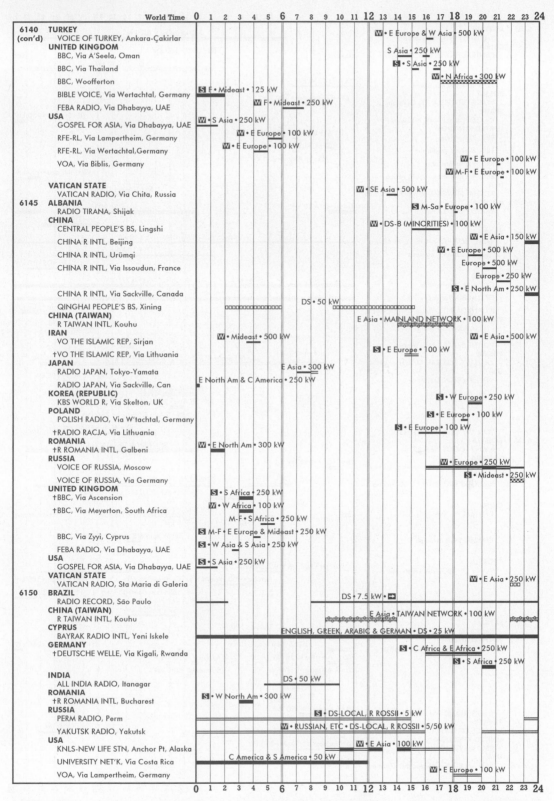

World Time 0 1 2 3 4 5 6 7 8 9 10 11 12 13 14 15 16 17 18 19 20 21 22 23 24

kHz	Country	Station	Schedule
6140 (con'd)	TURKEY	VOICE OF TURKEY, Ankara-Çakirlar	W • E Europe & W Asia • 500 kW
	UNITED KINGDOM	BBC, Via A'Seela, Oman	S Asia • 250 kW
		BBC, Via Thailand	S • S Asia • 250 kW
		BBC, Woofferton	W • N Africa • 300 kW
		BIBLE VOICE, Via Wertachtal, Germany	S F • Mideast • 125 kW
		FEBA RADIO, Via Dhabayya, UAE	W F • Mideast • 250 kW
	USA	GOSPEL FOR ASIA, Via Dhabayya, UAE	W • S Asia • 250 kW
		RFE-RL, Via Lampertheim, Germany	W • E Europe • 100 kW
		RFE-RL, Via Wertachtal, Germany	W • E Europe • 100 kW
		VOA, Via Biblis, Germany	W • E Europe • 100 kW
			W M-F • E Europe • 100 kW
	VATICAN STATE	VATICAN RADIO, Via Chita, Russia	W • SE Asia • 500 kW
6145	ALBANIA	RADIO TIRANA, Shijak	S M-Sa • Europe • 100 kW
	CHINA	CENTRAL PEOPLE'S BS, Lingshi	W • DS-B (MINORITIES) • 100 kW
		CHINA R INTL, Beijing	W • E Asia • 150 kW
		CHINA R INTL, Urümqi	W • E Europe • 500 kW
		CHINA R INTL, Via Issoudun, France	Europe • 500 kW
			Europe • 250 kW
			S • E North Am • 250 kW
		CHINA R INTL, Via Sackville, Canada	
		QINGHAI PEOPLE'S BS, Xining	DS • 50 kW
	CHINA (TAIWAN)	R TAIWAN INTL, Kouhu	E Asia • MAINLAND NETWORK • 100 kW
	IRAN	VO THE ISLAMIC REP, Sirjan	W • Mideast • 500 kW; W • E Asia • 500 kW
		†VO THE ISLAMIC REP, Via Lithuania	S • E Europe • 100 kW
	JAPAN	RADIO JAPAN, Tokyo-Yamata	E Asia • 300 kW
		RADIO JAPAN, Via Sackville, Can	E North Am & C America • 250 kW
	KOREA (REPUBLIC)	KBS WORLD R, Via Skelton, UK	S • W Europe • 250 kW
	POLAND	POLISH RADIO, Via W'tachtal, Germany	S • E Europe • 100 kW
		†RADIO RACJA, Via Lithuania	S • E Europe • 100 kW
	ROMANIA	†R ROMANIA INTL, Galbeni	W • E North Am • 300 kW
	RUSSIA	VOICE OF RUSSIA, Moscow	W • Europe • 250 kW
		VOICE OF RUSSIA, Via Germany	S • Mideast • 250 kW
	UNITED KINGDOM	†BBC, Via Ascension	S • S Africa • 250 kW
		†BBC, Via Meyerton, South Africa	W • W Africa • 100 kW
			M-F • S Africa • 250 kW
		BBC, Via Zyyi, Cyprus	S M-F • E Europe & Mideast • 250 kW
		FEBA RADIO, Via Dhabayya, UAE	S • W Asia & S Asia • 250 kW
	USA	GOSPEL FOR ASIA, Via Dhabayya, UAE	S • S Asia • 250 kW
	VATICAN STATE	VATICAN RADIO, Sta Maria di Galeria	W • E Asia • 250 kW
6150	BRAZIL	RADIO RECORD, São Paulo	DS • 7.5 kW • ➡
	CHINA (TAIWAN)	R TAIWAN INTL, Kouhu	E Asia • TAIWAN NETWORK • 100 kW
	CYPRUS	BAYRAK RADIO INTL, Yeni Iskele	ENGLISH, GREEK, ARABIC & GERMAN • DS • 25 kW
	GERMANY	†DEUTSCHE WELLE, Via Kigali, Rwanda	S • C Africa & E Africa • 250 kW
			S • S Africa • 250 kW
	INDIA	ALL INDIA RADIO, Itanagar	DS • 50 kW
	ROMANIA	†R ROMANIA INTL, Bucharest	S • W North Am • 300 kW
	RUSSIA	PERM RADIO, Perm	S • DS-LOCAL, R ROSSII • 5 kW
		YAKUTSK RADIO, Yakutsk	W • RUSSIAN, ETC • DS-LOCAL, R ROSSII • 5/50 kW
	USA	KNLS-NEW LIFE STN, Anchor Pt, Alaska	W • E Asia • 100 kW
		UNIVERSITY NET'K, Via Costa Rica	C America & S America • 50 kW
		VOA, Via Lampertheim, Germany	W • E Europe • 100 kW

0 1 2 3 4 5 6 7 8 9 10 11 12 13 14 15 16 17 18 19 20 21 22 23 24

World Time 0 1 2 3 4 5 6 7 8 9 10 11 12 13 14 15 16 17 18 19 20 21 22 23 24

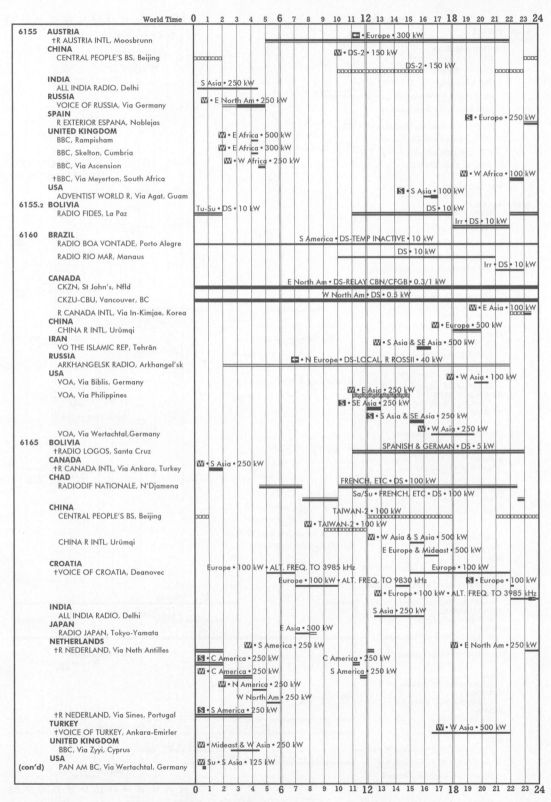

6155 AUSTRIA
- †R AUSTRIA INTL, Moosbrunn — Europe • 300 kW

CHINA
- CENTRAL PEOPLE'S BS, Beijing — W • DS-2 • 150 kW; DS-2 • 150 kW

INDIA
- ALL INDIA RADIO, Delhi — S Asia • 250 kW

RUSSIA
- VOICE OF RUSSIA, Via Germany — W • E North Am • 250 kW

SPAIN
- R EXTERIOR ESPANA, Noblejas — S • Europe • 250 kW

UNITED KINGDOM
- BBC, Rampisham — W • E Africa • 500 kW
- BBC, Skelton, Cumbria — W • E Africa • 300 kW
- BBC, Via Ascension — W • W Africa • 250 kW
- †BBC, Via Meyerton, South Africa — W • W Africa • 100 kW

USA
- ADVENTIST WORLD R, Via Agat, Guam — S • S Asia • 100 kW

6155.2 BOLIVIA
- RADIO FIDES, La Paz — Tu-Su • DS • 10 kW; DS • 10 kW; Irr • DS • 10 kW

6160 BRAZIL
- RADIO BOA VONTADE, Porto Alegre — S America • DS-TEMP INACTIVE • 10 kW
- RADIO RIO MAR, Manaus — DS • 10 kW; Irr • DS • 10 kW

CANADA
- CKZN, St John's, Nfld — E North Am • DS-RELAY CBN/CFGB • 0.3/1 kW
- CKZU-CBU, Vancouver, BC — W North Am • DS • 0.5 kW
- R CANADA INTL, Via In-Kimjae, Korea — W • E Asia • 100 kW

CHINA
- CHINA R INTL, Urümqi — W • Europe • 500 kW

IRAN
- VO THE ISLAMIC REP, Tehrān — W • S Asia & SE Asia • 500 kW

RUSSIA
- ARKHANGELSK RADIO, Arkhangel'sk — N Europe • DS-LOCAL, R ROSSII • 40 kW

USA
- VOA, Via Biblis, Germany — W • W Asia • 100 kW
- VOA, Via Philippines — W • E Asia • 250 kW; S • SE Asia • 250 kW; S • S Asia & SE Asia • 250 kW
- VOA, Via Wertachtal, Germany — W • W Asia • 250 kW

6165 BOLIVIA
- †RADIO LOGOS, Santa Cruz — SPANISH & GERMAN • DS • 5 kW

CANADA
- †R CANADA INTL, Via Ankara, Turkey — W • S Asia • 250 kW

CHAD
- RADIODIF NATIONALE, N'Djamena — FRENCH, ETC • DS • 100 kW; Sa/Su • FRENCH, ETC • DS • 100 kW

CHINA
- CENTRAL PEOPLE'S BS, Beijing — TAIWAN-2 • 100 kW; W • TAIWAN-2 • 100 kW
- CHINA R INTL, Urümqi — W • W Asia & S Asia • 500 kW; E Europe & Mideast • 500 kW

CROATIA
- †VOICE OF CROATIA, Deanovec — Europe • 100 kW • ALT. FREQ. TO 3985 kHz; Europe • 100 kW; Europe • 100 kW • ALT. FREQ. TO 9830 kHz; S • Europe • 100 kW; W • Europe • 100 kW • ALT. FREQ. TO 3985 kHz

INDIA
- ALL INDIA RADIO, Delhi — S Asia • 250 kW

JAPAN
- RADIO JAPAN, Tokyo-Yamata — E Asia • 300 kW

NETHERLANDS
- †R NEDERLAND, Via Neth Antilles — W • S America • 250 kW; W • E North Am • 250 kW; S • C America • 250 kW; C America • 250 kW; W • C America • 250 kW; S America • 250 kW; W • N America • 250 kW; W North Am • 250 kW
- †R NEDERLAND, Via Sines, Portugal — S • S America • 250 kW

TURKEY
- †VOICE OF TURKEY, Ankara-Emirler — W • W Asia • 500 kW

UNITED KINGDOM
- BBC, Via Zyyi, Cyprus — W • Mideast & W Asia • 250 kW

USA
- (con'd) PAN AM BC, Via Wertachtal, Germany — W Su • S Asia • 125 kW

0 1 2 3 4 5 6 7 8 9 10 11 12 13 14 15 16 17 18 19 20 21 22 23 24

ENGLISH ARABIC CHINESE FRENCH GERMAN RUSSIAN SPANISH OTHER

World Time 0 1 2 3 4 5 6 7 8 9 10 11 12 13 14 15 16 17 18 19 20 21 22 23 24

kHz	Country / Station	Schedule
6165 (con'd)	**ZAMBIA**	
	RADIO ZAMBIA-ZNBC, Lusaka	DS-2 • 100 kW; DS-2 • 100 kW • ALT. FREQ. TO 7235 kHz
6165v	**VIETNAM**	
	†VOICE OF VIETNAM, Xuan Mai	DS-HMONG • 50 kW
6170	**BRAZIL**	
	RADIO CULTURA, São Paulo	DS-RELAY FM 103.5 • 7.5 kW • ➡; DS-RELAY MW • 7.5 kW • ➡
	FRANCE	
	R FRANCE INTL, Issoudun	W • W Africa & C Africa • 250 kW • ALT. FREQ. TO 9805 kHz
	GERMANY	
	†DEUTSCHE WELLE, Via Sri Lanka	S • S Asia • 250 kW
	RUSSIA	
	VOICE OF RUSSIA, Irkutsk	W • S Europe • 250 kW
	VOICE OF RUSSIA, Khabarovsk	W • E Asia • 100 kW
	UNITED KINGDOM	
	BBC, Via In-Kimjae, South Korea	W • E Asia • 250 kW
	USA	
	VOA, Via Biblis, Germany	W M-F • E Europe • 100 kW
6173.8	**PERU**	
	RADIO TAWANTINSUYO, Cusco	SPANISH & QUECHUA • DS • 5 kW
6175	**CHINA**	
	CENTRAL PEOPLE'S BS, Beijing	DS-1 • 100 kW
	CHINA R INTL, Via Cerrik, Albania	W Europe • 150 kW
	CZECH REPUBLIC	
	†RADIO PRAGUE, Via Armavir, Russia	W • Europe • 250 kW • ALT. FREQ. TO 5940 kHz
	FRANCE	
	R FRANCE INTL, Issoudun	W Europe & Atlantic • 500 kW; W • W Africa • 500 kW
	IRAN	
	†VO THE ISLAMIC REP, Sirjan	W Asia & S Asia • 500 kW; W • W Asia & S Asia • 500 kW; S • S Asia • 500 kW
	VO THE ISLAMIC REP, Tehrān	C Asia • 500 kW; W • C Asia • 500 kW
	MALAYSIA	
	VOICE OF MALAYSIA, Kajang	SE Asia • VOICE OF ISLAM • 100 kW; SE Asia • 100 kW
	POLAND	
	POLISH RADIO, Via W'tachtal, Germany	S • E Europe • 100 kW
	ROMANIA	
	†R ROMANIA INTL, Bucharest	W • E Europe • 300 kW
	RUSSIA	
	VOICE OF RUSSIA, Armavir	S M-F • N Europe • 100 kW; W Sa/Su • N Europe • 100 kW; W • N Europe • 100 kW
	VOICE OF RUSSIA, Via Germany	W • Mideast • 125 kW
	TURKEY	
	VOICE OF TURKEY, Ankara-Emirler	W • Mideast • 500 kW
	UNITED KINGDOM	
	BBC, Via A'Seela, Oman	W • S Asia • 250 kW
	IBC TAMIL, Via Wertachtal, Germany	W • S Asia • 250 kW
	USA	
	FAMILY RADIO, Okeechobee, Fl	S • S America • 100 kW
	†FAMILY RADIO, Via W'tal, Germany	W • Mideast • 500 kW
	VIETNAM	
	VOICE OF VIETNAM, Via Canada	E North Am & C America • 250 kW; N America & C America • 250 kW
6180	**BRAZIL**	
	†R NACIONAL DA AMAZONIA, Brasília	DS • ALT. FREQ. TO 6185 kHz; W • DS • ALT. FREQ. TO 6185 kHz
	CHINA	
	CENTRAL PEOPLE'S BS, Lingshi	W • DS-1 • 100 kW; W • DS-8 (MINORITIES) • 100 kW
	CHINA R INTL, Beijing	W • W Asia & C Asia • 500 kW
	CUBA	
	†RADIO HABANA CUBA, Havana	C America • 100 kW; E North Am • 100 kW; Su • C America • 100 kW
	CYPRUS	
	CYPRUS BC CORP, Zyyi	W F-Su • Europe • 250 kW
	GERMANY	
	†DEUTSCHE WELLE, Via Dhabayya, UAE	S • C Asia • 250 kW
	DEUTSCHE WELLE, Via Kigali, Rwanda	C Africa & S Africa • 250 kW; W • C Africa & E Africa • 250 kW
	DEUTSCHE WELLE, Via Rampisham, UK	W • E Europe & W Asia • 500 kW
	DEUTSCHE WELLE, Via Sri Lanka	S • S Asia • 250 kW
	IRAN	
	†VO THE ISLAMIC REP, Sirjan	S • C Asia • 500 kW
(con'd)	VO THE ISLAMIC REP, Tehrān	W • Europe • 500 kW

World Time 0 1 2 3 4 5 6 7 8 9 10 11 12 13 14 15 16 17 18 19 20 21 22 23 24

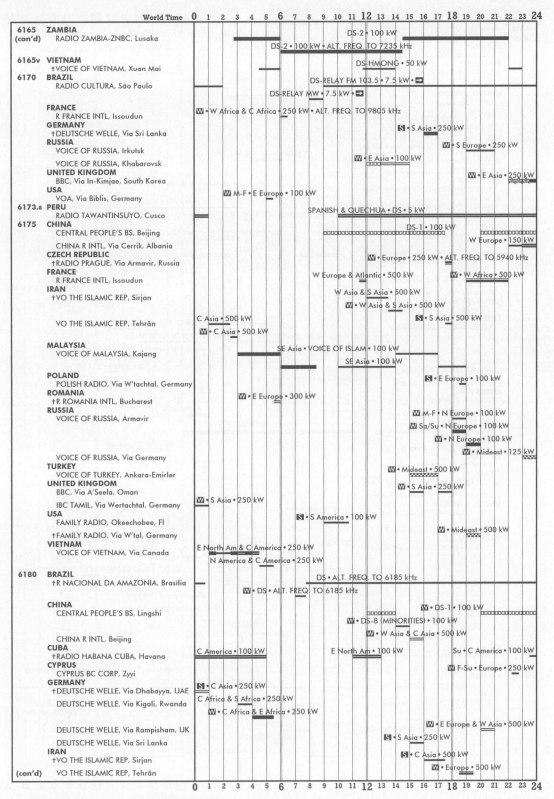

World Time 0 1 2 3 4 5 6 7 8 9 10 11 12 13 14 15 16 17 18 19 20 21 22 23 24

kHz	Country / Station	Schedule
6180 (con'd)	**IRAN**	
	†VO THE ISLAMIC REP, Via Lithuania	S • W Europe • 100 kW
	ROMANIA	
	†R ROMANIA INTL, Bucharest	W • S Europe • 100 kW
	RUSSIA	
	VOICE OF RUSSIA, Petropavlovsk-K	W • E Asia • 250 kW
	VOICE OF RUSSIA, St Petersburg	S • S America • 500 kW • ALT. FREQ. TO 5900 kHz
	UNITED KINGDOM	
	BBC, Rampisham	W • N Africa • 500 kW
	BBC, Via Zyyi, Cyprus	W • W Asia • 250 kW
	FEBA RADIO, Via Dhabayya, UAE	E Africa • 250 kW
	USA	
	†FAMILY RADIO, Via Meyerton, S Africa	S • S Africa • 100 kW
	†VOA	S • W Africa • 250 kW
	VOA, Via Udon Thani, Thailand	W • E Asia • 250 kW
	VENEZUELA	
	RADIO NACIONAL, Via Havana, Cuba	C America • 100 kW
6185	**BRAZIL**	
	†R NACIONAL DA AMAZONIA, Brasilia	DS • ALT. FREQ. TO 6180 kHz W • DS • ALT. FREQ. TO 6180 kHz
	CHILE	
	CVC-LA VOZ, Santiago	W • S America & C America • 100 kW
	CHINA	
	†CHINA HUAYI BC CORP, Fuzhou	E Asia • 15 kW Th-Tu • E Asia • 15 kW
	CHINA R INTL, Via Cerrik, Albania	N Africa • 150 kW
	CHINA R INTL, Xi'an	W • E Asia • 500 kW
	CHINA (TAIWAN)	
	R TAIWAN INTL, Via Skelton, UK	S • W Europe • 250 kW
	ETHIOPIA	
	VO TIGRAY REVOL'N, Mek'ele	E Africa • 10 kW • ALT. FREQ. TO 9650 kHz Sa/Su • E Africa • 10 kW • ALT. FREQ. TO 9650 kHz M-F • E Africa • 10 kW • ALT. FREQ. TO 9650 kHz
	IRAN	
	VO THE ISLAMIC REP, Sirjan	W • W Asia • 500 kW
	VO THE ISLAMIC REP, Tehrān	W • S Asia • 500 kW
	KOREA (DPR)	
	KOREAN CENTRAL BS	W • SE Asia
	VOICE OF KOREA	W • SE Asia
	MEXICO	
	RADIO EDUCACION, México City	← • DS • 5/10 kW
	RUSSIA	
	VOICE OF RUSSIA, Samara	W • C Asia • 200 kW
	THAILAND	
	RADIO THAILAND, Udon Thani	W • SE Asia • 250 kW
	TURKEY	
	VOICE OF TURKEY, Ankara-Çakirlar	W • S Europe • 250 kW
	VOICE OF TURKEY, Ankara-Emirler	W • S Europe • 500 kW
	UNITED KINGDOM	
	FEBA RADIO, Via Dhabayya, UAE	W • W Asia & S Asia • 250 kW
	USA	
	VOA, Via Udon Thani, Thailand	S • SE Asia • 250 kW
	VATICAN STATE	
	VATICAN RADIO, Sta Maria di Galeria	← • Mideast & W Asia • 250 kW ← • E Europe • 250 kW S • W Europe • 250 kW W • E Europe • 250 kW • ALT. FREQ. TO 9585 kHz S M-Sa • W Europe • 250 kW W M/W/Th • N Europe • 250 kW W • N Europe • 250 kW W • E Europe • 250 kW W M-Sa • E Europe • 250 kW W M-Sa • N Africa • 250 kW
6188	**PERU**	
	RADIO ORIENTE, Yurimaguas	M-Sa • DS • 1.5/5 kW DS • 1.5/5 kW
6190	**BELARUS**	
	RADIO MAHILIOU, Mahiliou	← • DS-LOCAL, BELARUS1 • 5 kW
	CHINA	
	CENTRAL PEOPLE'S BS, Geermu	DS-2 • 100 kW W • DS-2 • 100 kW
	CHINA R INTL, Via Sackville, Canada	W • W North Am • 250 kW W North Am • 250 kW
	XINJIANG PEOPLE'S BC STN, Urümqi	DS-MONGOLIAN • 100 kW S • DS-MONGOLIAN • 100 kW
(con'd)		

World Time 0 1 2 3 4 5 6 7 8 9 10 11 12 13 14 15 16 17 18 19 20 21 22 23 24

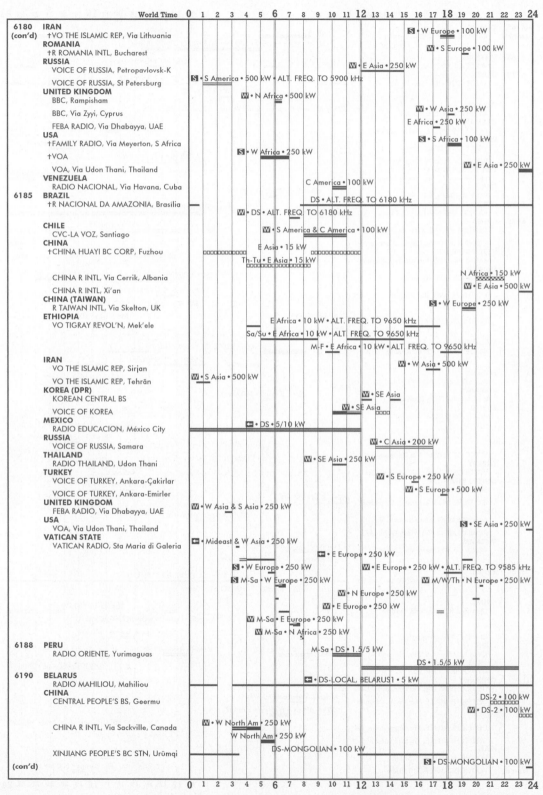

ENGLISH ARABIC CHINESE FRENCH GERMAN RUSSIAN SPANISH OTHER

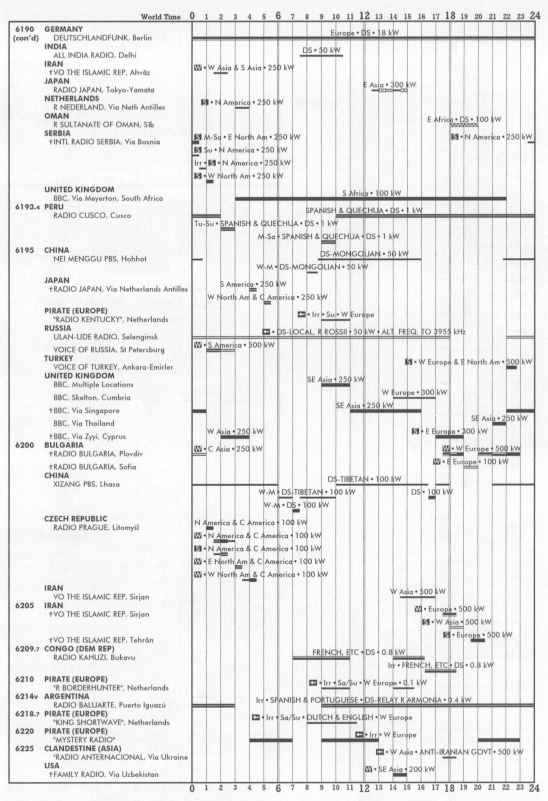

World Time 0 1 2 3 4 5 6 7 8 9 10 11 12 13 14 15 16 17 18 19 20 21 22 23 24

kHz	Country / Station	Schedule
6190 (con'd)	**GERMANY** DEUTSCHLANDFUNK, Berlin	Europe • DS • 18 kW
	INDIA ALL INDIA RADIO, Delhi	DS • 50 kW
	IRAN †VO THE ISLAMIC REP, Ahvāz	W • W Asia & S Asia • 250 kW
	JAPAN RADIO JAPAN, Tokyo-Yamata	E Asia • 300 kW
	NETHERLANDS R NEDERLAND, Via Neth Antilles	S • N America • 250 kW
	OMAN R SULTANATE OF OMAN, Sīb	E Africa • DS • 100 kW
	SERBIA †INTL RADIO SERBIA, Via Bosnia	S M-Sa • E North Am • 250 kW; S • N America • 250 kW
		S Su • N America • 250 kW
		Irr • S • N America • 250 kW
		S • W North Am • 250 kW
	UNITED KINGDOM BBC, Via Meyerton, South Africa	S Africa • 100 kW
6193.4	**PERU** RADIO CUSCO, Cusco	SPANISH & QUECHUA • DS • 1 kW
		Tu-Su • SPANISH & QUECHUA • DS • 1 kW
		M-Sa • SPANISH & QUECHUA • DS • 1 kW
6195	**CHINA** NEI MENGGU PBS, Hohhot	DS-MONGOLIAN • 50 kW
		W-M • DS-MONGOLIAN • 50 kW
	JAPAN †RADIO JAPAN, Via Netherlands Antilles	S America • 250 kW
		W North Am & C America • 250 kW
	PIRATE (EUROPE) "RADIO KENTUCKY", Netherlands	← • Irr • Su • W Europe
	RUSSIA ULAN-UDE RADIO, Selenginsk	← • DS-LOCAL, R ROSSII • 50 kW • ALT. FREQ. TO 3955 kHz
	VOICE OF RUSSIA, St Petersburg	W • S America • 500 kW
	TURKEY VOICE OF TURKEY, Ankara-Emirler	S • W Europe & E North Am • 500 kW
	UNITED KINGDOM BBC, Multiple Locations	SE Asia • 250 kW
	BBC, Skelton, Cumbria	W Europe • 300 kW
	†BBC, Via Singapore	SE Asia • 250 kW
	BBC, Via Thailand	SE Asia • 250 kW
	†BBC, Via Zyyi, Cyprus	W Asia • 250 kW; S • E Europe • 300 kW
6200	**BULGARIA** †RADIO BULGARIA, Plovdiv	W • C Asia • 250 kW; W • W Europe • 500 kW
	†RADIO BULGARIA, Sofia	W • E Europe • 100 kW
	CHINA XIZANG PBS, Lhasa	DS-TIBETAN • 100 kW
		W-M • DS-TIBETAN • 100 kW; DS • 100 kW
		W-M • DS • 100 kW
	CZECH REPUBLIC RADIO PRAGUE, Litomyšl	N America & C America • 100 kW
		W • N America & C America • 100 kW
		S • N America & C America • 100 kW
		W • E North Am & C America • 100 kW
		W • W North Am & C America • 100 kW
	IRAN VO THE ISLAMIC REP, Sirjan	W Asia • 500 kW
6205	**IRAN** †VO THE ISLAMIC REP, Sirjan	W • Europe • 500 kW
		S • W Asia • 500 kW
	†VO THE ISLAMIC REP, Tehrān	S • Europe • 500 kW
6209.7	**CONGO (DEM REP)** RADIO KAHUZI, Bukavu	FRENCH, ETC • DS • 0.8 kW
		Irr • FRENCH, ETC • DS • 0.8 kW
6210	**PIRATE (EUROPE)** "R BORDERHUNTER", Netherlands	← • Irr • Sa/Su • W Europe • 0.1 kW
6214v	**ARGENTINA** RADIO BALUARTE, Puerto Iguazú	Irr • SPANISH & PORTUGUESE • DS-RELAY R ARMONIA • 0.4 kW
6218.7	**PIRATE (EUROPE)** "KING SHORTWAVE", Netherlands	← • Irr • Sa/Su • DUTCH & ENGLISH • W Europe
6220	**PIRATE (EUROPE)** "MYSTERY RADIO"	← • Irr • W Europe
6225	**CLANDESTINE (ASIA)** "RADIO ANTERNACIONAL, Via Ukraine"	← • W Asia • ANTI-IRANIAN GOVT • 500 kW
	USA †FAMILY RADIO, Via Uzbekistan	W • SE Asia • 200 kW

0 1 2 3 4 5 6 7 8 9 10 11 12 13 14 15 16 17 18 19 20 21 22 23 24

SEASONAL S OR W   1-HR TIMESHIFT MIDYEAR ← OR →   JAMMING / OR /\   EARLIEST HEARD ◁   LATEST HEARD ▷   NEW FOR 2009 †

World Time 0 1 2 3 4 5 6 7 8 9 10 11 12 13 14 15 16 17 18 19 20 21 22 23 24

kHz	Country / Station	Schedule notes
6225v	**PAKISTAN** RADIO PAKISTAN, Islamabad	DS-NEWS CHANNEL • 100 kW; W • Mideast & N Africa • 100 kW
6230	**USA** †FAMILY RADIO, Via Taiwan	E Asia • 100 kW
6240	**MOLDOVA** †RADIO PMR, Grigoriopol	W M-F • E North Am • 500 kW; W Su-Th • E North Am • 500 kW
	RUSSIA VOICE OF RUSSIA, Via Moldova	W • E North Am • 500 kW
	USA †FAMILY RADIO, Via Moldova	W • Europe • 300 kW
	†FAMILY RADIO, Via Taiwan	E Asia • 100 kW
6245	**GERMANY** †DEUTSCHE WELLE, Via Moldova	W • W Asia & S Asia • 500 kW
6248v	**KOREA (DPR)** PYONGYANG BC STN, Pyongyang	E Asia • 100 kW
6249v	**EQUATORIAL GUINEA** RADIO NACIONAL, Malabo	SPANISH, ETC • DS • 10 kW
	PERU RADIO LA VOZ, Andahuaylas	SPANISH & QUECHUA • DS
6250	**RUSSIA** VOICE OF RUSSIA, Armavir	W • E North Am • 500 kW • ALT. FREQ. TO 7240 kHz
6250v	**PIRATE (EUROPE)** "RADIO LIKEDEELER, Germany	← • Irr • Su • GERMAN & ENGLISH • W Europe • ALT. FREQ. TO 6309v kHz
6255	**EGYPT** †RADIO CAIRO, Abu Za'bal	W • Europe • 250 kW
6260	**AUSTRALIA** CVC, Via Uzbekistan	W • S Asia • 100 kW
6264v	**PIRATE (EUROPE)** "RADIO PANDORA", England	← • Irr • Su • W Europe
6265	**PIRATE (EUROPE)** "PREMIER RADIO", Ireland	← • Irr • Su • W Europe • 0.04 kW; ← • Irr • Sa • W Europe • 0.04 kW
6265v	**PIRATE (EUROPE)** "RADIO ROB 007", Netherlands	← • Irr • Sa/Su • W Europe • ALT. FREQ. TO 6305v kHz
6270	**EGYPT** †RADIO CAIRO, Abu Za'bal	W Asia & S Asia • 250 kW
	PIRATE (EUROPE) "RADIO DEVALON", Germany	← • Irr • Su • W Europe
6270v	**PIRATE (EUROPE)** "RADIO SPACEMAN", Netherlands	← • Irr • DUTCH & ENGLISH • W Europe • 0.03 kW
6275v	**PIRATE (EUROPE)** "RADIO ALPENROOS", Netherlands	← • Irr • Sa/Su • W Europe • 0.04 kW
	"RADIO BLACKBIRD", Netherlands	← • Irr • Sa/Su • W Europe • 0.03 kW
6280	**CLANDESTINE (ASIA)** "SOUND OF HOPE", Via Taiwan	F/Sa • E Asia • 300 kW
	PIRATE (EUROPE) "RADIO MERLIN", England	← • Irr • Su • W Europe
	USA FAMILY RADIO, Via Taiwan	S Asia • 250 kW
6280v	**PIRATE (EUROPE)** "RADIO MAZDA", Netherlands	← • Irr • W Europe • ALT. FREQ. TO 6290 kHz
6285	**KOREA (DPR)** KOREAN CENTRAL BS	W • C America; W • Europe
	PYONGYANG BC STN	W • Europe
	VOICE OF KOREA	W • C America; W • Europe
6285v	**PIRATE (EUROPE)** "WNKR", England	← • Irr • W Europe
6290	**EGYPT** †EGYPTIAN RADIO, Kafr Silîm-Abis	← • Europe & E North Am • DS-GENERAL • 250 kW
	PIRATE (EUROPE) "RADIO MAZDA", Netherlands	← • Irr • W Europe • ALT. FREQ. TO 6280v kHz
6290v	**PIRATE (EUROPE)** "R BERMUDA DREIECK", Germany	← • Irr • ENGLISH & GERMAN • W Europe
	"R SCOTLAND INTL", Netherlands	← • Irr • Su • DUTCH & ENGLISH • W Europe • 0.25 kW
	"RADIO ATLANTIS", Netherlands	← • Irr • Su • W Europe • 0.4 kW
6295	**PIRATE (EUROPE)** "RADIO VICTORIA", Netherlands	← • Irr • Su • W Europe; ← • Irr • Sa • W Europe
6295v	**PIRATE (EUROPE)** "THE BOGUS MAN", England	← • Irr • W Europe • ALT. FREQ. TO 3904v kHz
6300	**WESTERN SAHARA** R NAC DE LA RASD, Rabuni, Algeria	DS • 20 kW; F • DS • 20 kW
6300v	**PIRATE (EUROPE)** "RADIO DOCTOR TIM", Germany	← • Irr • Su • W Europe • 0.04 kW; ← • Irr • Sa • W Europe • 0.04 kW
	"RADIO ORION", Netherlands	← • Irr • Sa/Su • W Europe • 0.08/0.4 kW • ALT. FREQ. TO 5720 kHz
6305v	**PIRATE (EUROPE)** "RADIO ROB 007", Netherlands	← • Irr • Sa/Su • W Europe • ALT. FREQ. TO 6265v kHz
	"RADIO SKYWIRE", Netherlands	← • Irr • Su • DUTCH & ENGLISH • W Europe
6306.3	**PIRATE (EUROPE)** VARIOUS STATIONS, Germany	← • Irr • Su • W Europe • 0.01/0.5 kW

World Time 0 1 2 3 4 5 6 7 8 9 10 11 12 13 14 15 16 17 18 19 20 21 22 23 24

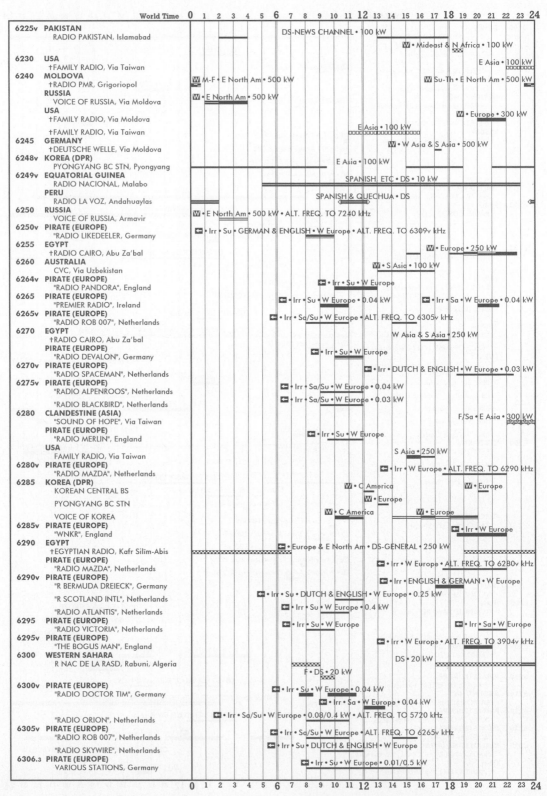

ENGLISH ARABIC CHINESE FRENCH GERMAN RUSSIAN SPANISH OTHER

World Time 0 1 2 3 4 5 6 7 8 9 10 11 12 13 14 15 16 17 18 19 20 21 22 23 24

Frequency	Country	Station	Schedule notes
6309v	PIRATE (EUROPE)	"RADIO LIKEDEELER, Germany	Irr • Su • GERMAN & ENGLISH • W Europe • ALT. FREQ. TO 6250v kHz
		"RADIO VALENCIA", Netherlands	Irr • W Europe
6310	PIRATE (EUROPE)	"RADIO ODYSSEY", Greece	Irr • Su/M • Europe • 1 kW; Irr • Sa/Su • Europe • 1 kW
6310v	PIRATE (EUROPE)	"RADIO BRANDARIS", Netherlands	Irr • Su • W Europe; Irr • Sa • W Europe
		"RADIO DELTA", Netherlands	Irr • Su • DUTCH, ENGLISH & GERMAN • W Europe • 0.1 kW
6311	PIRATE (EUROPE)	"RADIO UNDERGROUND", England	Irr • Su • W Europe • 0.02 kW
6311v	PIRATE (EUROPE)	"RADIO ALTREX", Netherlands	Irr • Sa/Su • W Europe
6335	IRAQ	VO IRAQI KURDISTAN, Salāh al Dīn	ARABIC & KURDISH • Mideast • PRO-KDP • ALT. FREQ. TO 4085 kHz
6335v	IRAQ	VO IRAQI KURDISTAN, Salāh al Dīn	ARABIC & KURDISH • Mideast • PRO-KDP • ALT. FREQ. TO 4085 kHz
			Irr • ARABIC & KURDISH • Mideast • PRO-KDP • ALT. FREQ. TO 4085 kHz
6348	CLANDESTINE (ASIA)	"ECHO OF HOPE", Seoul, South Korea	E Asia • 50 kW
		"SOUND OF HOPE", Via Taiwan	E Asia • 10 kW
6350	USA	AFRTS, Pearl Harbor, Hawai'i	Pacific • USB • ALT. FREQ. TO 10320 kHz
6375v	PIRATE (EUROPE)	"RADIO BRIGITTE", Belgium	Irr • Su • W Europe
6398v	KOREA (DPR)	PYONGYANG BC STN, Pyongyang	E Asia • 50 kW
6400v	PIRATE (EUROPE)	"WEEKEND MUSIC RADIO", Scotland	Irr • Su • W Europe • 0.1 kW
6479v	PERU	RADIO ALTURA, Huarmaca	DS
6520.3	PERU	R PAUCARTAMBO, Paucartambo (Cusco)	DS
6536.2	PERU	R DIF HUANCABAMBA, Huancabamba	DS • 0.8 kW; Irr • DS • 0.8 kW
6540v	PIRATE (EUROPE)	"RADIO HAMAMELIS", Germany	Irr • Su • W Europe
6585.4	BOLIVIA	RADIO NUEVA ESPERANZA, La Paz	SPANISH & AYMARA • DS
6600	CLANDESTINE (ASIA)	"VO THE PEOPLE", Seoul, S Korea	E Asia
6673	PERU	RADIO ANDINA, Huancabamba	DS
6785	PAKISTAN	RADIO PAKISTAN, Islamabad	Mideast & W Asia • 100 kW
6797.7	PERU	R ONDAS DEL RIO MAYO, N Cajamarca	DS • 1 kW
6819.5	PERU	LV DE LAS HUARINJAS, Huancabamba	DS • 1 kW
6850	EGYPT	†RADIO CAIRO, Abu Za'bal	W • E North Am • 250 kW
6860	EGYPT	†RADIO CAIRO, Abu Za'bal	ARABIC & ENGLISH • Australasia • 250 kW
			W Asia & S Asia • EEU/ME • 250 kW
		†RADIO CAIRO, Kafr Silîm-Abis	E Europe • 250 kW
6890	USA	FAMILY RADIO, Okeechobee, Fl	W • E North Am • 100 kW
		†KNLS-NEW LIFE STN, Anchor Pt, Alaska	S • E Asia • 100 kW; W • E Asia • 100 kW
		WWRB, Manchester, Tennessee	E North Am • 100 kW • ALT. FREQ. TO 3185 kHz
6895.3	PERU	R SAN MIGUEL, Pampa Alegre	DS • 0.25 kW
6915	USA	†FAMILY RADIO, Okeechobee, Fl	E North Am • 100 kW; W • Europe • 100 kW
		KNLS-NEW LIFE STN, Anchor Pt, Alaska	W • E Asia • 100 kW
6937	CHINA	YUNNAN PEOPLE'S BS, Kunming	DS-MINORITIES • 50 kW
6950	CHINA	CENTRAL PEOPLE'S BS, Shijiazhuang	DS-1 • 100 kW • ALT. FREQ. TO 7215 kHz
6955	PIRATE (N AMERICA)	VARIOUS STATIONS	Su • N America • 0.01/0.2 kW • USB; Sa • N America • 0.01/0.2 kW • USB
6957	PERU	RADIO LV DEL CAMPESINO, Huarmaca	DS; Irr • DS
6973v	ISRAEL	GALEI ZAHAL, Tel Aviv	Europe • DS • 10 kW
6985	USA	†FAMILY RADIO, Okeechobee, Fl	S • E North Am • 100 kW
7090	ERITREA	VO BROAD MASSES, Asmara	DS-1 • 100 kW • ALT. FREQ. TO 7100 kHz

World Time 0 1 2 3 4 5 6 7 8 9 10 11 12 13 14 15 16 17 18 19 20 21 22 23 24

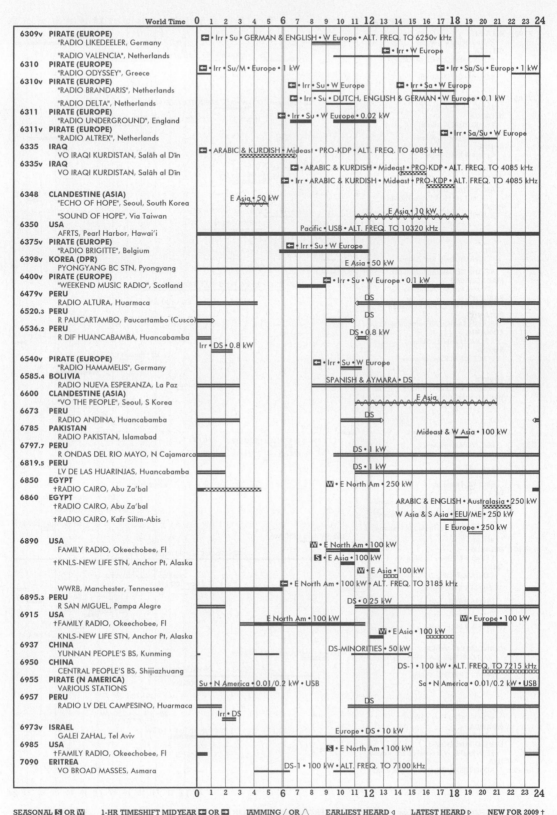

SEASONAL S OR W 1-HR TIMESHIFT MIDYEAR ⇐ OR ⇒ JAMMING / OR /\ EARLIEST HEARD ◁ LATEST HEARD ▷ NEW FOR 2009 †

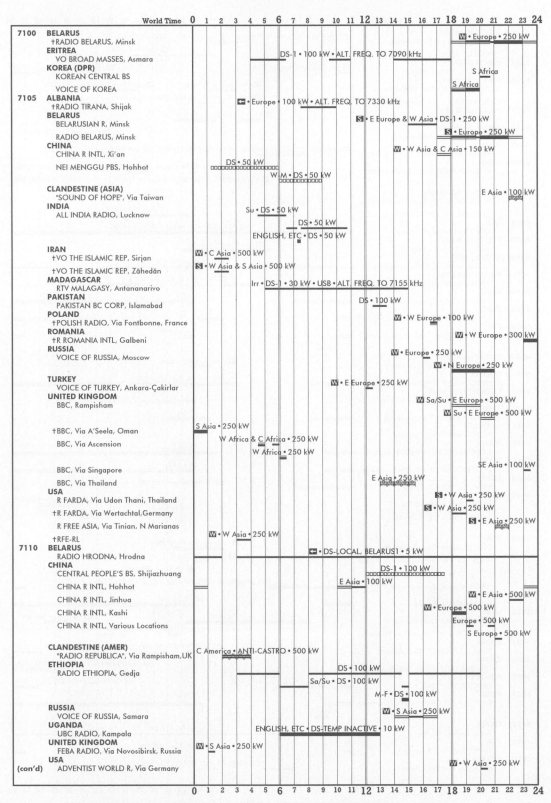

kHz	Country	Station	World Time 0–24
7100	BELARUS	†RADIO BELARUS, Minsk	W • Europe • 250 kW
	ERITREA	VO BROAD MASSES, Asmara	DS-1 • 100 kW • ALT. FREQ. TO 7090 kHz
	KOREA (DPR)	KOREAN CENTRAL BS	S Africa
		VOICE OF KOREA	S Africa
7105	ALBANIA	†RADIO TIRANA, Shijak	← • Europe • 100 kW • ALT. FREQ. TO 7330 kHz
	BELARUS	BELARUSIAN R, Minsk	S • E Europe & W Asia • DS-1 • 250 kW
		RADIO BELARUS, Minsk	S • Europe • 250 kW
	CHINA	CHINA R INTL, Xi'an	W • W Asia & C Asia • 150 kW
		NEI MENGGU PBS, Hohhot	DS • 50 kW; W-M • DS • 50 kW
	CLANDESTINE (ASIA)	"SOUND OF HOPE", Via Taiwan	E Asia • 100 kW
	INDIA	ALL INDIA RADIO, Lucknow	Su • DS • 50 kW; DS • 50 kW; ENGLISH, ETC • DS • 50 kW
	IRAN	†VO THE ISLAMIC REP, Sirjan	W • C Asia • 500 kW
		†VO THE ISLAMIC REP, Zāhedān	S • W Asia & S Asia • 500 kW
	MADAGASCAR	RTV MALAGASY, Antananarivo	Irr • DS-1 • 30 kW • USB • ALT. FREQ. TO 7155 kHz
	PAKISTAN	PAKISTAN BC CORP, Islamabad	DS • 100 kW
	POLAND	†POLISH RADIO, Via Fontbonne, France	W • W Europe • 100 kW
	ROMANIA	†R ROMANIA INTL, Galbeni	W • W Europe • 300 kW
	RUSSIA	VOICE OF RUSSIA, Moscow	W • Europe • 250 kW; W • N Europe • 250 kW
	TURKEY	VOICE OF TURKEY, Ankara-Çakirlar	W • E Europe • 250 kW
	UNITED KINGDOM	BBC, Rampisham	W Sa/Su • E Europe • 500 kW; W Su • E Europe • 500 kW
		†BBC, Via A'Seela, Oman	S Asia • 250 kW
		BBC, Via Ascension	W Africa & C Africa • 250 kW; W Africa • 250 kW
		BBC, Via Singapore	SE Asia • 100 kW
		BBC, Via Thailand	E Asia • 250 kW
	USA	R FARDA, Via Udon Thani, Thailand	S • W Asia • 250 kW
		†R FARDA, Via Wertachtal,Germany	S • W Asia • 250 kW
		R FREE ASIA, Via Tinian, N Marianas	S • E Asia • 250 kW
		†RFE-RL	W • W Asia • 250 kW
7110	BELARUS	RADIO HRODNA, Hrodna	← • DS-LOCAL, BELARUS1 • 5 kW
	CHINA	CENTRAL PEOPLE'S BS, Shijiazhuang	DS-1 • 100 kW
		CHINA R INTL, Hohhot	E Asia • 100 kW
		CHINA R INTL, Jinhua	W • E Asia • 500 kW
		CHINA R INTL, Kashi	W • Europe • 500 kW
		CHINA R INTL, Various Locations	Europe • 500 kW; S Europe • 500 kW
	CLANDESTINE (AMER)	"RADIO REPUBLICA", Via Rampisham,UK	C America • ANTI-CASTRO • 500 kW
	ETHIOPIA	RADIO ETHIOPIA, Gedja	DS • 100 kW; Sa/Su • DS • 100 kW; M-F • DS • 100 kW
	RUSSIA	VOICE OF RUSSIA, Samara	W • S Asia • 250 kW
	UGANDA	UBC RADIO, Kampala	ENGLISH, ETC • DS-TEMP INACTIVE • 10 kW
	UNITED KINGDOM	FEBA RADIO, Via Novosibirsk, Russia	W • S Asia • 250 kW
(con'd)	USA	ADVENTIST WORLD R, Via Germany	W • W Asia • 250 kW

ENGLISH ARABIC CHINESE FRENCH GERMAN RUSSIAN SPANISH OTHER

kHz	Country / Station	World Time 0–24
7110 (con'd)	**USA**	
	VOA, Via Udon Thani, Thailand	W • E Asia • 250 kW
7115	**CANADA**	
	R CANADA INTL, Via Tokyo, Japan	W • E Asia • 300 kW
	CHINA	
	CHINA R INTL, Various Locations	S Asia • 100/500 kW
	CHINA R INTL, Xi'an	E Asia • 500 kW
	CLANDESTINE (ASIA)	
	"DEGAR VOICE", Via Chita, Russia	Sa • SE Asia • 250 kW
	INDIA	
	ALL INDIA RADIO, Panaji	Mideast & W Asia • 250 kW
	ALL INDIA RADIO, Port Blair	DS • 8.5 kW
		Sa/Su • DS • 8.5 kW
		Su • DS • 8.5 kW
		ENGLISH, ETC • DS • 8.5 kW
	IRAN	
	†VO THE ISLAMIC REP, Sirjan	S • S Asia • 500 kW
		S • C Asia • 500 kW
	JAPAN	
	†RADIO JAPAN, Via Dhabayya, UAE	W • Mideast • 500 kW • ALT. FREQ. TO 7225 kHz
	RUSSIA	
	VOICE OF RUSSIA, Moscow	W • S Europe & N Africa • 250 kW
	SERBIA	
	†INTL RADIO SERBIA, Via Bosnia	W • N America • 250 kW
		W M-Sa • N America • 250 kW
		W Su • N America • 250 kW
		Irr • W • N America • 250 kW
		W • W North Am • 250 kW
	THAILAND	
	†RADIO THAILAND, Pathum Thani	W • SE Asia • 10 kW
	UNITED KINGDOM	
	BBC, Rampisham	W M-F • E Europe & W Asia • 500 kW
		W • E Europe & W Asia • 500 kW
	BBC, Via Zyyi, Cyprus	W • W Asia & S Asia • 300 kW
	USA	
	ADVENTIST WORLD R, Via Austria	S • S Asia • 300 kW
	†FAMILY RADIO, Via W'tal, Germany	S • N Africa & W Africa • 500 kW
	RFE-RL, Via Biblis, Germany	S • E Europe • 250 kW
	RFE-RL, Via Lampertheim, Germany	W • E Europe • 100 kW
		S • E Europe & W Asia • 100 kW
	†VOA	W • Mideast • 250 kW
		W • S Europe • 250 kW
	VOA, Via Lampertheim, Germany	S • Mideast • 100 kW
	VOA, Via Philippines	S • E Asia • 250 kW
	VOA, Via Udon Thani, Thailand	W • S Asia • 250 kW
7120	**CHINA**	
	CENTRAL PEOPLE'S BS, Beijing	DS-8 (MINORITIES) • 100 kW
		DS-8 (MINORITIES) • 50 kW
	CHINA R INTL, Beijing	Europe • 500 kW
	CHINA R INTL, Kashi	S Asia • 100 kW
	CHINA R INTL, Shijiazhuang	W • E Asia • 500 kW
	CHINA R INTL, Urümqi	W • Europe • 500 kW
	CHINA R INTL, Various Locations	Europe • 500 kW
	CHINA R INTL, Via Cerrik, Albania	W • N Africa • 150 kW
		W • E Europe & Mideast • 150 kW
	XINJIANG PEOPLE'S BC STN, Urümqi	W • DS-KYRGYZ • 50 kW
		W W/F-M • DS-KYRGYZ • 50 kW
	GERMANY	
	†DEUTSCHE WELLE, Via Sines, Portugal	W • S Asia • 250 kW
	INDIA	
	ALL INDIA RADIO, Jaipur	DS • 50 kW
		Su • DS • 50 kW
		ENGLISH, ETC • DS • 50 kW
	NETHERLANDS	
	R NEDERLAND, Via Madagascar	W • C Africa & S Africa • 250 kW
	ROMANIA	
	†R ROMANIA INTL, Galbeni	W • W Europe • 300 kW
	RUSSIA	
	RADIO ROSSII, Moscow	S • Europe • DS • 250 kW
	UNITED KINGDOM	
	†BBC, Via Meyerton, South Africa	S • W Africa • 250 kW
	USA	
	VOA, Via Philippines	W • SE Asia • 250 kW
	ZIMBABWE	
	RADIO V O P, Via Madagascar	S • ENGLISH, ETC • S Africa • 50 kW

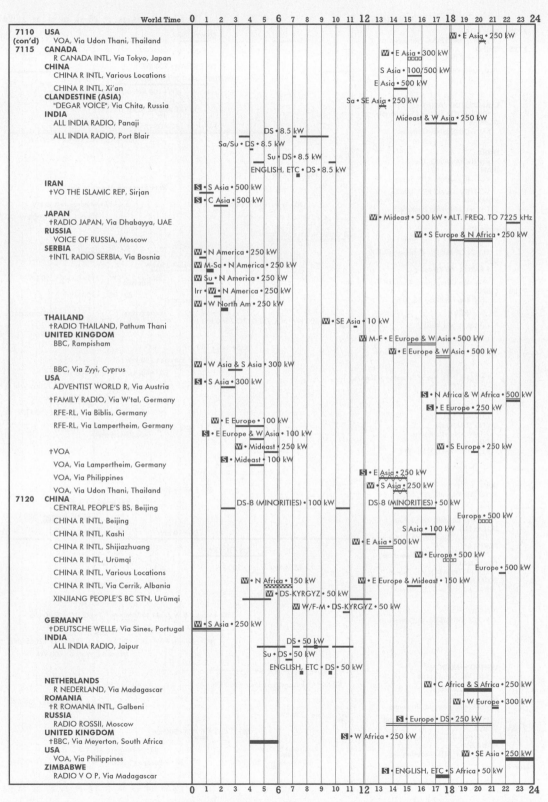

World Time 0 1 2 3 4 5 6 7 8 9 10 11 12 13 14 15 16 17 18 19 20 21 22 23 24

kHz	Country / Station	Schedule notes
7120v	**SOMALIA**	
	†RADIO HARGEYSA, Hargeysa	DS • 25 kW
7125	**CHINA**	
	CHINA R INTL, Kunming	W • SE Asia • 100 kW
	XIZANG PBS, Lhasa	DS-TIBETAN • 100 kW
		DS-TIBETAN • 100 kW • ALT. FREQ. TO 9490 kHz
		DS • 100 kW • ALT. FREQ. TO 9490 kHz
	CLANDESTINE (ASIA)	
	"DEGAR VOICE", Via Chita, Russia	Tu • SE Asia • 250 kW
	GUINEA	
	RTV GUINEENNE, Conakry	FRENCH, ETC • DS-"RADIO CONAKRY" • 50 kW
		DS-"RADIO CONAKRY" • 50 kW
	INDIA	
	ALL INDIA RADIO, Delhi	S Asia • 50/100 kW
	IRAN	
	VO THE ISLAMIC REP, Sirjan	W • C Asia • 500 kW
	VO THE ISLAMIC REP, Tehrān	W • E Europe & Mideast • 500 kW
	ROMANIA	
	†R ROMANIA INTL, Bucharest	S • W Europe • 300 kW
		W • W Europe • 300 kW
		W • S Europe • 300 kW
	RUSSIA	
	RUSSIAN INTL R, Via Moldova	← • E North Am • 500 kW
	VOICE OF RUSSIA, Petropavlovsk-K	W • SE Asia • 250 kW
	USA	
	R FARDA, Via Kuwait	S • W Asia • 250 kW
	VOA, Via Udon Thani, Thailand	S Asia • 250 kW
		S • E Asia • 250 kW
7130	**CHINA**	
	CENTRAL PEOPLE'S BS, Xi'an	W • DS-2 • 150 kW
		DS-2 • 150 kW
	†CHINA R INTL, Kashi	Europe • 500 kW • ALT. FREQ. TO 7350 kHz
		W Asia & S Asia • 100 kW
	CHINA R INTL, Various Locations	S Europe • 500 kW
	CHINA R INTL, Via Cerrik, Albania	E Europe • 150 kW
		S Europe & E Europe • 150 kW
	CHINA R INTL, Via St Petersburg, Russia	W • Mideast & W Asia • 400 kW
		S • Mideast & W Asia • 400 kW • ALT. FREQ. TO 12065 kHz
		Mideast & W Asia • 400 kW
	CHINA R INTL, Xi'an	W • C Africa & S Africa • 500 kW
	CHINA (TAIWAN)	
	R TAIWAN INTL, Kouhu	E Asia • MAINLAND NETWORK • 100 kW
	INDIA	
	ALL INDIA RADIO, Shillong	Irr • DS • 50 kW
		DS • 50 kW
		ENGLISH, ETC • DS • 50 kW
	IRAN	
	†VO THE ISLAMIC REP, Sirjan	W • E Asia • 500 kW
		S • W Asia & S Asia • 500 kW
		S • E Africa • 500 kW
	VO THE ISLAMIC REP, Tehrān	W • W Europe • 500 kW
	MALAYSIA	
	RTV MALAYSIA SARAWAK, Kuching	DS • 10 kW
	PAKISTAN	
	PAKISTAN BC CORP, Islamabad	DS • 100 kW
	PORTUGAL	
	†RDP INTERNATIONAL, Lisbon	W M-F • Europe • 300 kW
	ROMANIA	
	†R ROMANIA INTL, Bucharest	S • S Europe • 100 kW
		S Europe • 100 kW
	RUSSIA	
	VOICE OF RUSSIA, St Petersburg	S • Mideast & W Asia • 400 kW • ALT. FREQ. TO 13650 kHz
		W • Mideast & W Asia • 400 kW
		S • Mideast & W Asia • 400 kW • ALT. FREQ. TO 12065 kHz
		Mideast & W Asia • 400 kW
	UNITED KINGDOM	
	BBC, Via Zyyi, Cyprus	W • E Africa • 250 kW
	BBC, Woofferton	W M-F • E Europe & Mideast • 250 kW
	USA	
	VOA, Via Iranawila, Sri Lanka	S • SE Asia • 250 kW
	VOA, Via Udon Thani, Thailand	W • SE Asia • 250 kW
7135	**CHINA**	
	CHINA R INTL, Beijing	W • C Asia & E Asia • 500 kW
	FRANCE	
	R FRANCE INTL, Issoudun	C Africa • 500 kW
		W • N Europe • 500 kW
		W • W Africa • 500 kW
		S • E Europe • 500 kW • ALT. FREQ. TO 11670 kHz
(con'd)		

World Time 0 1 2 3 4 5 6 7 8 9 10 11 12 13 14 15 16 17 18 19 20 21 22 23 24

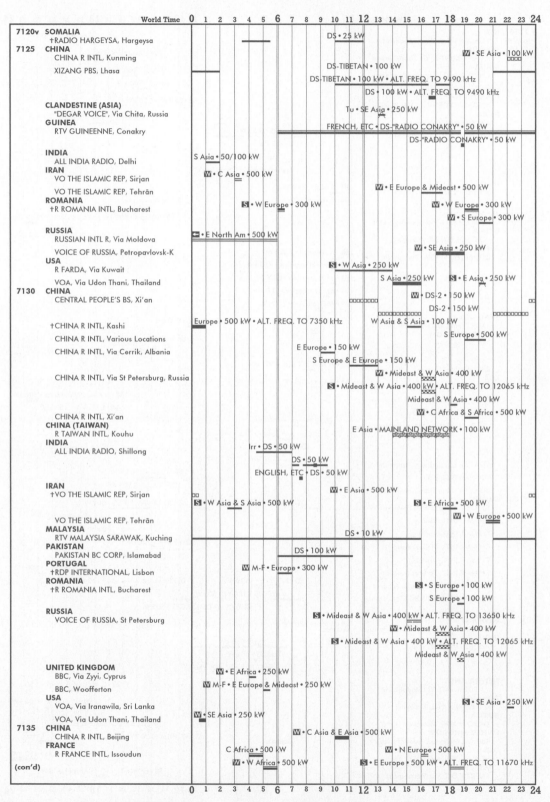

ENGLISH ▬ ARABIC ▭ CHINESE ▫▫▫ FRENCH ═ GERMAN ═ RUSSIAN ═ SPANISH ═ OTHER —

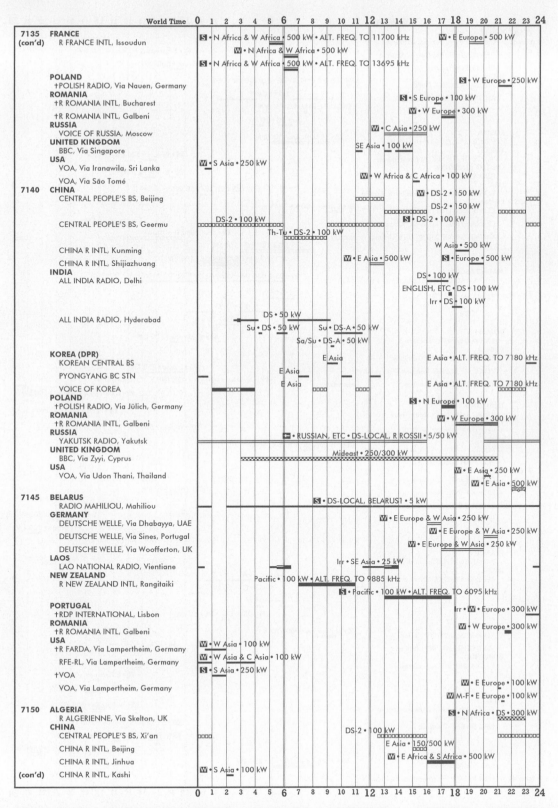

World Time 0 1 2 3 4 5 6 7 8 9 10 11 12 13 14 15 16 17 18 19 20 21 22 23 24

kHz	Country / Station	Schedule
7135 (con'd)	**FRANCE**	
	R FRANCE INTL, Issoudun	S • N Africa & W Africa • 500 kW • ALT. FREQ. TO 11700 kHz; W • E Europe • 500 kW
		W • N Africa & W Africa • 500 kW
		S • N Africa & W Africa • 500 kW • ALT. FREQ. TO 13695 kHz
	POLAND	
	†POLISH RADIO, Via Nauen, Germany	S • W Europe • 250 kW
	ROMANIA	
	†R ROMANIA INTL, Bucharest	S • S Europe • 100 kW
	†R ROMANIA INTL, Galbeni	W • W Europe • 300 kW
	RUSSIA	
	VOICE OF RUSSIA, Moscow	W • C Asia • 250 kW
	UNITED KINGDOM	
	BBC, Via Singapore	SE Asia • 100 kW
	USA	
	VOA, Via Iranawila, Sri Lanka	W • S Asia • 250 kW
	VOA, Via São Tomé	W • W Africa & C Africa • 100 kW
7140	**CHINA**	
	CENTRAL PEOPLE'S BS, Beijing	W • DS-2 • 150 kW
		DS-2 • 150 kW
	CENTRAL PEOPLE'S BS, Geermu	DS-2 • 100 kW; S • DS-2 • 100 kW
		Th-Tu • DS-2 • 100 kW
	CHINA R INTL, Kunming	W Asia • 500 kW
	CHINA R INTL, Shijiazhuang	W • E Asia • 500 kW; S • Europe • 500 kW
	INDIA	
	ALL INDIA RADIO, Delhi	DS • 100 kW
		ENGLISH, ETC • DS • 100 kW
		Irr • DS • 100 kW
	ALL INDIA RADIO, Hyderabad	DS • 50 kW
		Su • DS • 50 kW; Su • DS-A • 50 kW
		Sa/Su • DS-A • 50 kW
	KOREA (DPR)	
	KOREAN CENTRAL BS	E Asia; E Asia • ALT. FREQ. TO 7180 kHz
	PYONGYANG BC STN	E Asia
	VOICE OF KOREA	E Asia; E Asia • ALT. FREQ. TO 7180 kHz
	POLAND	
	†POLISH RADIO, Via Jülich, Germany	S • N Europe • 100 kW
	ROMANIA	
	†R ROMANIA INTL, Galbeni	W • W Europe • 300 kW
	RUSSIA	
	YAKUTSK RADIO, Yakutsk	⇐ • RUSSIAN, ETC • DS-LOCAL, R ROSSII • 5/50 kW
	UNITED KINGDOM	
	BBC, Via Zyyi, Cyprus	Mideast • 250/300 kW
	USA	
	VOA, Via Udon Thani, Thailand	W • E Asia • 250 kW
		W • E Asia • 500 kW
7145	**BELARUS**	
	RADIO MAHILIOU, Mahiliou	S • DS-LOCAL, BELARUS1 • 5 kW
	GERMANY	
	DEUTSCHE WELLE, Via Dhabayya, UAE	W • E Europe & W Asia • 250 kW
	DEUTSCHE WELLE, Via Sines, Portugal	W • E Europe & W Asia • 250 kW
	DEUTSCHE WELLE, Via Woofferton, UK	W • E Europe & W Asia • 250 kW
	LAOS	
	LAO NATIONAL RADIO, Vientiane	Irr • SE Asia • 25 kW
	NEW ZEALAND	
	R NEW ZEALAND INTL, Rangitaiki	Pacific • 100 kW • ALT. FREQ. TO 9885 kHz
		S • Pacific • 100 kW • ALT. FREQ. TO 6095 kHz
	PORTUGAL	
	†RDP INTERNATIONAL, Lisbon	Irr • W • Europe • 300 kW
	ROMANIA	
	†R ROMANIA INTL, Galbeni	W • W Europe • 300 kW
	USA	
	†R FARDA, Via Lampertheim, Germany	W • W Asia • 100 kW
	RFE-RL, Via Lampertheim, Germany	W • W Asia & C Asia • 100 kW
	†VOA	S • S Asia • 250 kW
	VOA, Via Lampertheim, Germany	W • E Europe • 100 kW
		W M-F • E Europe • 100 kW
7150	**ALGERIA**	
	R ALGERIENNE, Via Skelton, UK	S • N Africa • DS • 300 kW
	CHINA	
	CENTRAL PEOPLE'S BS, Xi'an	DS-2 • 100 kW
	CHINA R INTL, Beijing	E Asia • 150/500 kW
	CHINA R INTL, Jinhua	W • E Africa & S Africa • 500 kW
(con'd)	CHINA R INTL, Kashi	W • S Asia • 100 kW

0 1 2 3 4 5 6 7 8 9 10 11 12 13 14 15 16 17 18 19 20 21 22 23 24

SEASONAL S OR W 1-HR TIMESHIFT MIDYEAR ⇐ OR ⇒ JAMMING / OR ∧ EARLIEST HEARD ◁ LATEST HEARD ▷ NEW FOR 2009 †

World Time 0 1 2 3 4 5 6 7 8 9 10 11 12 13 14 15 16 17 18 19 20 21 22 23 24

kHz	Country / Station	Schedule
7150 (con'd)	**CHINA**	
	CHINA R INTL, Various Locations	Europe • 500 kW
	CHINA R INTL, Via Cerrik, Albania	S • E Europe & Mideast • 150 kW
	CHINA R INTL, Xi'an	W • E Asia • 500 kW
	INDIA	
	ALL INDIA RADIO, Delhi	ENGLISH & HINDI • DS • 50/100 kW
	ALL INDIA RADIO, Imphal	DS • 50 kW; ENGLISH, ETC • DS • 50 kW; Su • DS • 50 kW
	RUSSIA	
	VOICE OF RUSSIA, Armavir	W • E North Am • 500 kW
	TURKEY	
	†VOICE OF TURKEY, Ankara-Emirler	S • W Asia • 500 kW
	UNITED KINGDOM	
	FEBA RADIO, Via Novosibirsk, Russia	W • S Asia • 250 kW
	USA	
	FAMILY RADIO, Via Novosibirsk, Russia	W • E Asia • 250 kW
7155	**CHINA**	
	CHINA R INTL, Kashi	W • S Asia • 100 kW
	CHINA R INTL, Via Cerrik, Albania	Europe • 150 kW
	XINJIANG PEOPLE'S BC STN, Urümqi	S • DS-CHINESE • 100 kW; DS-CHINESE • 100 kW; W/F-M • DS-CHINESE • 100 kW
	MADAGASCAR	
	RTV MALAGASY, Antananarivo	Irr • DS-1 • 30 kW • USB • ALT. FREQ. TO 7105 kHz
	PAKISTAN	
	PAKISTAN BC CORP, Quetta	F • DS • 10 kW; DS • 10 kW; Sa-Th • DS • 10 kW
	ROMANIA	
	†R ROMANIA INTL, Bucharest	S • W Europe • 100 kW
	RUSSIA	
	RUSSIAN INTL R, Via Germany	S • Mideast • 100 kW
	VOICE OF RUSSIA, Komsomol'sk 'Amure	W • E Asia • 250 kW
	VOICE OF RUSSIA, Samara	S • S America • 500 kW • ALT. FREQ. TO 12010 kHz; W • S Europe & Mideast • 200 kW
	THAILAND	
	RADIO THAILAND, Udon Thani	S • N Europe • 250 kW
	TURKEY	
	†VOICE OF TURKEY, Ankara-Emirler	W • W Asia • 500 kW • ALT. FREQ. TO 7250 kHz
	USA	
	†RFE-RL	S • E Europe & W Asia • 250 kW
	VOA, Via Philippines	S • SE Asia • 50 kW
7160	**CHINA**	
	CHINA R INTL, Kunming	S Asia • 500 kW
	CHINA R INTL, Nanning	SE Asia • 500 kW
	CHINA R INTL, Urümqi	Mideast • 500 kW
	CHINA R INTL, Various Locations	E Asia • 500 kW; S Europe • 250/500 kW; S Asia • 100/500 kW; W Europe • 500 kW
	CHINA R INTL, Xi'an	W • E Africa • 500 kW
	FRANCE	
	R FRANCE INTL, Via South Africa	C Africa • 250 kW
	INDIA	
	ALL INDIA RADIO, Chennai	DS • 50 kW; Sa/Su • DS • 50 kW; Su • DS • 50 kW; ENGLISH, ETC • DS • 50 kW
	IRAN	
	VO THE ISLAMIC REP, Sirjan	W • N America • 500 kW
	†VO THE ISLAMIC REP, Tehrān	S • C Asia • 500 kW
	ROMANIA	
	†R ROMANIA INTL, Bucharest	W • S Europe • 100 kW; W • E Europe • 100 kW; S • W Europe • 300 kW
	TURKEY	
	VOICE OF TURKEY, Ankara-Emirler	W • W Europe • 500 kW
	UNITED KINGDOM	
	BBC, Skelton, Cumbria	W • E Europe & Mideast • 300 kW; W M-F • E Europe & Mideast • 300 kW
	BBC, Various Locations	W • E Asia • 250 kW
	†BBC, Via Ascension	S • W Africa & C Africa • 250 kW
(con'd)	FEBA RADIO, Via Meyerton, S Africa	W • C Africa • 100 kW

World Time 0 1 2 3 4 5 6 7 8 9 10 11 12 13 14 15 16 17 18 19 20 21 22 23 24

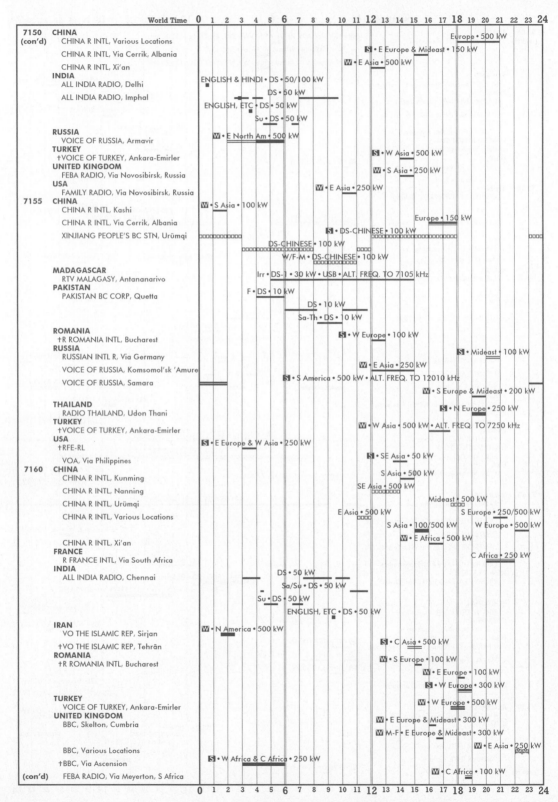

ENGLISH ARABIC CHINESE FRENCH GERMAN RUSSIAN SPANISH OTHER

World Time 0–24

kHz	Country / Station	Schedule details
7160 (con'd)	**USA**	
	GOSPEL FOR ASIA, Via Germany	W • S Asia • 250 kW
7165	**CHINA**	
	CHINA R INTL, Via Moscow, Russia	W • E Europe & Mideast • 200 kW • ALT. FREQ. TO 7175 kHz
	NEI MENGGU PBS, Hohhot	DS • 50 kW
		W-M • DS • 50 kW
	IRAN	
	†VO THE ISLAMIC REP, Tehrān	W • C Asia • 500 kW
		S • E Europe & Mideast • 500 kW
		W • S Europe • 500 kW
	ROMANIA	
	†R ROMANIA INTL, Bucharest	S • W Europe • 100 kW
	RUSSIA	
	VOICE OF RUSSIA, St Petersburg	S • Mideast & W Asia • 200 kW • ALT. FREQ. TO 12055 kHz
	VOICE OF RUSSIA, Vladivostok	S • E Asia & SE Asia • 500 kW
	UNITED KINGDOM	
	BBC, Various Locations	W • W Asia & S Asia • 250/300 kW
	BBC, Via Zyyi, Cyprus	W Asia & S Asia • 300 kW
		W • Mideast & W Asia • 300 kW
	BBC, Woofferton	S • W Africa & C Africa • 250 kW
	USA	
	†FAMILY RADIO, Via Petro-Kam, Russia	W • E Asia • 250 kW
	†RFE-RL	W • E Europe • 250 kW
7165v	**CLANDESTINE (AFRICA)**	
	"VO DEMOCRATIC ALLIANCE", Ethiopia	E Africa • ANTI-ERITREAN GOVT • 100 kW
	ETHIOPIA	
	RADIO ETHIOPIA, Gedja	E Africa • 100 kW
7170	**BELARUS**	
	BELARUSIAN R, Minsk	W • E Europe & W Asia • DS-1 • 150 kW
	CHINA	
	CHINA R INTL, Kashi	Europe • 500 kW
	CHINA R INTL, Via Bamako, Mali	W Africa • 100 kW
	CHINA R INTL, Via Moscow, Russia	W • N Europe • 250 kW
	CHINA R INTL, Xi'an	W • C Asia & E Asia • 500 kW
	XIZANG PBS, Lhasa	DS • 100 kW
		W-M • DS • 100 kW
	IRAN	
	VO THE ISLAMIC REP, Ahvāz	W • W Asia & C Asia • 250 kW
	†VO THE ISLAMIC REP, Tehrān	W • W Asia & S Asia • 500 kW
		S • W Africa & C Africa • 500 kW
	POLAND	
	POLISH RADIO, Via W'tachtal, Germany	W • E Europe • 100 kW
	ROMANIA	
	†R ROMANIA INTL, Bucharest	S • S Europe • 100 kW
	RUSSIA	
	VOICE OF RUSSIA, Moscow	W • S America • 500 kW
	TURKEY	
	†VOICE OF TURKEY, Ankara-Çakirlar	W • S Europe • 250 kW
	VOICE OF TURKEY, Ankara-Emirler	S • S Asia, SE Asia & Australasia • 500 kW
	UNITED KINGDOM	
	BBC, Via Thailand	W • S Asia • 250 kW
	USA	
	RFE-RL, Via Udon Thani, Thailand	S • W Asia & C Asia • 250 kW
	†TRANS WORLD R, Via W'tal, Germany	W M • E Europe • 100 kW
		W Tu-Su • E Europe • 100 kW
		W • E Europe • 100 kW
	VOA, Via Wertachtal,Germany	S • W Asia • 250 kW
7175	**CHINA**	
	CHINA R INTL, Via Cerrik, Albania	S • W Europe • 150 kW
	CHINA R INTL, Via Moscow, Russia	W • E Europe & Mideast • 200 kW • ALT. FREQ. TO 7165 kHz
		S • N Europe • 250 kW
	CHINA R INTL, Xi'an	W • E Africa • 150 kW
	ERITREA	
	VO BROAD MASSES, Asmara	ARABIC, ETC • DS-2 • 100 kW • ALT. FREQ. TO 7180 kHz
	IRAN	
	VO THE ISLAMIC REP, Ahvāz	S • W Asia & C Asia • 250 kW
	OMAN	
	R SULTANATE OF OMAN, Sīb	W • Mideast • DS • 100 kW • ALT. FREQ. TO 6085 kHz
	ROMANIA	
	†R ROMANIA INTL, Bucharest	W • W Europe • 300 kW
	RUSSIA	
	VOICE OF RUSSIA, Vladivostok	S • E Asia • 250 kW
	USA	
(con'd)	†FAMILY RADIO, Via Armavir, Russia	W • S Asia • 300 kW

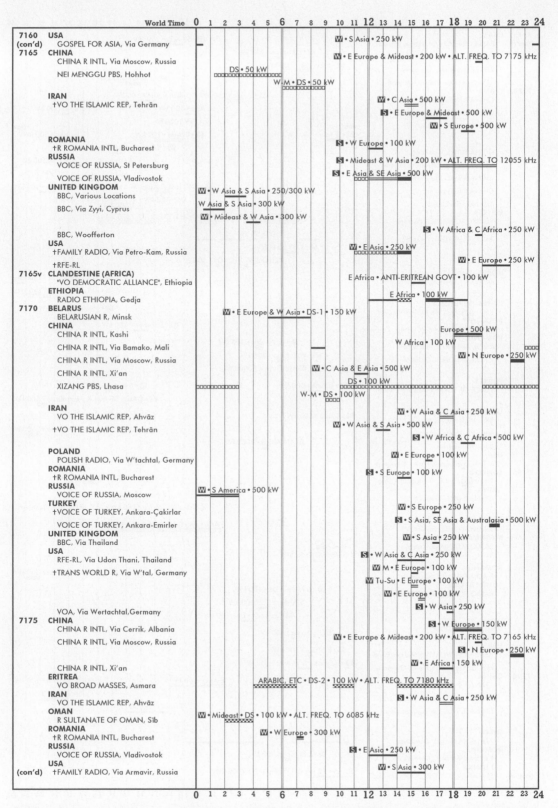

SEASONAL S OR W 1-HR TIMESHIFT MIDYEAR ⬅ OR ➡ JAMMING / OR /\ EARLIEST HEARD ◁ LATEST HEARD ▷ NEW FOR 2009 †

World Time 0–24

kHz	Country / Station	Schedule
7175 (con'd)	**USA**	
	†FAMILY RADIO, Via Irkutsk, Russia	W • SE Asia • 250 kW
	†RFE-RL	W • E Europe • 250 kW
	RFE-RL, Via Biblis, Germany	S • E Europe • 100 kW
	VOA, Via Udon Thani, Thailand	W • E Asia • 250 kW
7180	**CHINA**	
	CHINA R INTL, Beijing	W • E Asia • 150 kW; W • S Asia • 500 kW
	CHINA R INTL, Jinhua	SE Asia • 500 kW; S Europe • 500 kW
	CHINA R INTL, Kashi	S Asia • 100 kW; W • S Asia • 100 kW; S • C Asia • 100 kW; S Europe • 500 kW
	CHINA R INTL, Kunming	W • E Europe & Mideast • 500 kW
	CHINA R INTL, Various Locations	E Africa & S Africa • 150/500 kW
	CHINA R INTL, Via Cerrik, Albania	W • W Europe • 150 kW
	CHINA R INTL, Xi'an	W • W Asia & C Asia • 500 kW; W • E Asia • 500 kW
	XIZANG PBS, Lhasa	DS • 100 kW • ALT. FREQ. TO 7205 kHz
	ERITREA	
	VO BROAD MASSES, Asmara	ARABIC, ETC • DS-2 • 100 kW • ALT. FREQ. TO 7175 kHz
	INDIA	
	ALL INDIA RADIO, Bhopal	DS • 50 kW; Su • DS • 50 kW; ENGLISH, ETC • DS • 50 kW
	KOREA (DPR)	
	KOREAN CENTRAL BS	E Asia • ALT. FREQ. TO 7140 kHz
	VOICE OF KOREA	E Asia • ALT. FREQ. TO 7140 kHz
	KOREA (REPUBLIC)	
	KBS WORLD R, Via Rampisham, UK	W • N Africa • 500 kW
	POLAND	
	†POLISH RADIO, Via W'tachtal, Germany	← • E Europe • 100 kW
	ROMANIA	
	†R ROMANIA INTL, Bucharest	W • W Europe • 300 kW
	†R ROMANIA INTL, Galbeni	S • W Europe • 300 kW; W • W Europe • 300 kW
	TURKEY	
	†VOICE OF TURKEY, Ankara-Emirler	W • C Asia • 500 kW; W • S Europe • 500 kW; W • S Asia, SE Asia & Australasia • 500 kW
	UNITED KINGDOM	
	BBC, Via Armavir, Russia	S • S Asia • 500 kW
	BBC, Via Thailand	W • E Asia • 250 kW
	BBC, Woofferton	W • N Africa • 300 kW
	USA	
	RFE-RL, Via Lampertheim, Germany	S • E Europe & W Asia • 100 kW
7185	**CANADA**	
	R CANADA INTL, Via Kashi, China	W • E Africa • 100 kW
	CHINA	
	CHINA R INTL, Xi'an	E Africa & C Africa • 150 kW; E Africa & C Africa • 150 kW • ALT. FREQ. TO 11600 kHz
	CHINA (TAIWAN)	
	R TAIWAN INTL, Huwei	E Asia • TAIWAN NETWORK • 100 kW
	MYANMAR (BURMA)	
	RADIO MYANMAR, Yangon	DS • 50 kW; Sa/Su • DS • 50 kW
	ROMANIA	
	†R ROMANIA INTL, Galbeni	S • W Europe • 300 kW
	SOUTH AFRICA	
	RADIO SONDERGRENSE, Meyerton	W • S Africa • DS • 100 kW; S Africa • DS • 100 kW; S • S Africa • DS • 100 kW
	UNITED KINGDOM	
	BBC, Via Ascension	S • E Africa • 250 kW
	USA	
	ADVENTIST WORLD R, Via Germany	W • E Africa • 500 kW
	RFE-RL, Via Lampertheim, Germany	S • E Europe & W Asia • 100 kW
7190	**CHINA**	
	CHINA R INTL, Jinhua	E Asia • 500 kW; E Africa & S Africa • 500 kW
	CHINA R INTL, Kashi	Europe • 500 kW
	CHINA R INTL, Various Locations	E Asia • 150/500 kW; E Europe & W Asia • 500 kW
	INDIA	
	ALL INDIA RADIO, Guwahati	DS • 50 kW
	ROMANIA	
	†R ROMANIA INTL, Bucharest	S • E Europe • 300 kW; W • E Europe • 300 kW
(con'd)	**SRI LANKA**	
	†SRI LANKA BC CORP, Colombo-Ekala	S Asia • 10 kW • ALT. FREQ. TO 7300 kHz

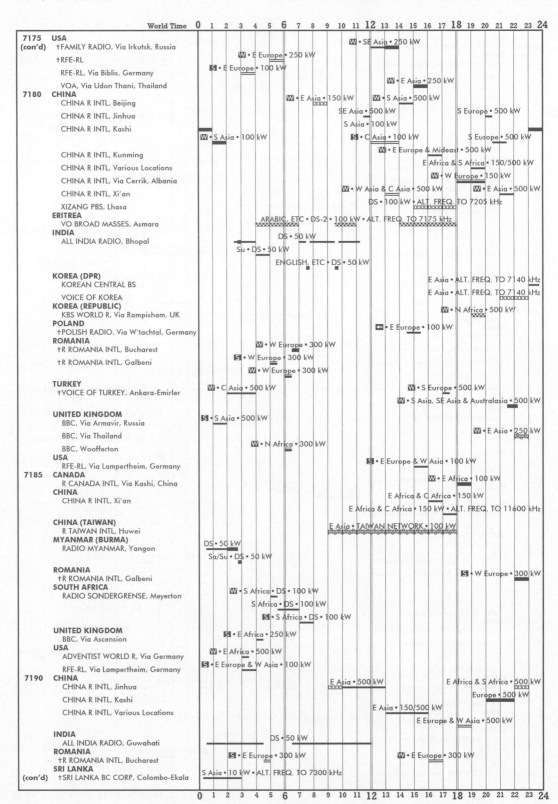

ENGLISH ▬ ARABIC ▒ CHINESE ▫▫▫ FRENCH ═ GERMAN ═ RUSSIAN ═ SPANISH ═ OTHER ▬

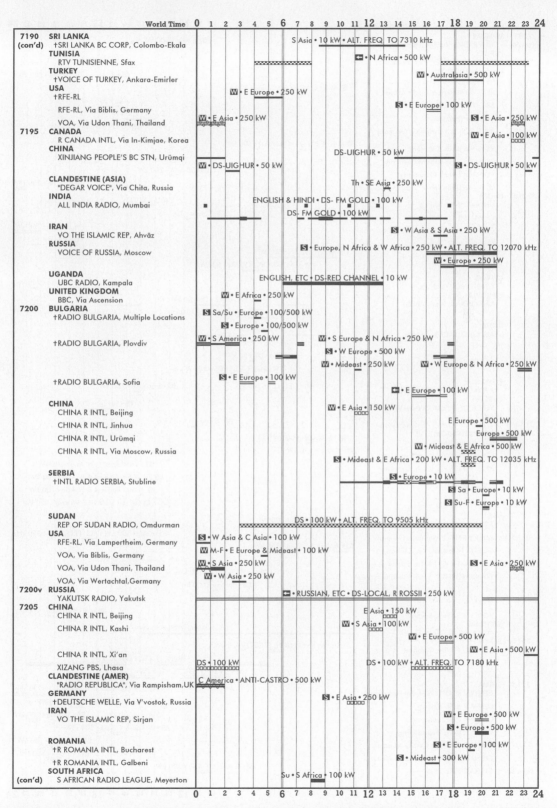

World Time 0 1 2 3 4 5 6 7 8 9 10 11 12 13 14 15 16 17 18 19 20 21 22 23 24

kHz	Country / Station	Schedule notes
7190 (con'd)	**SRI LANKA** †SRI LANKA BC CORP, Colombo-Ekala	S Asia • 10 kW • ALT. FREQ. TO 7310 kHz
	TUNISIA RTV TUNISIENNE, Sfax	⇐ • N Africa • 500 kW
	TURKEY †VOICE OF TURKEY, Ankara-Emirler	W • Australasia • 500 kW
	USA †RFE-RL	W • E Europe • 250 kW
	RFE-RL, Via Biblis, Germany	S • E Europe • 100 kW
	VOA, Via Udon Thani, Thailand	W • E Asia • 250 kW; S • E Asia • 250 kW
7195	**CANADA** R CANADA INTL, Via In-Kimjae, Korea	W • E Asia • 100 kW
	CHINA XINJIANG PEOPLE'S BC STN, Urümqi	DS-UIGHUR • 50 kW; W • DS-UIGHUR • 50 kW; S • DS-UIGHUR • 50 kW
	CLANDESTINE (ASIA) "DEGAR VOICE", Via Chita, Russia	Th • SE Asia • 250 kW
	INDIA ALL INDIA RADIO, Mumbai	ENGLISH & HINDI • DS- FM GOLD • 100 kW; DS- FM GOLD • 100 kW
	IRAN VO THE ISLAMIC REP, Ahvāz	S • W Asia & S Asia • 250 kW
	RUSSIA VOICE OF RUSSIA, Moscow	S • Europe, N Africa & W Africa • 250 kW • ALT. FREQ. TO 12070 kHz; W • Europe • 250 kW
	UGANDA UBC RADIO, Kampala	ENGLISH, ETC • DS-RED CHANNEL • 10 kW
	UNITED KINGDOM BBC, Via Ascension	W • E Africa • 250 kW
7200	**BULGARIA** †RADIO BULGARIA, Multiple Locations	S Sa/Su • Europe • 100/500 kW; S • Europe • 100/500 kW
	†RADIO BULGARIA, Plovdiv	W • S America • 250 kW; W • S Europe & N Africa • 250 kW; S • W Europe • 500 kW; W • Mideast • 250 kW; W • W Europe & N Africa • 250 kW
	†RADIO BULGARIA, Sofia	S • E Europe • 100 kW; ⇐ • E Europe • 100 kW
	CHINA CHINA R INTL, Beijing	W • E Asia • 150 kW
	CHINA R INTL, Jinhua	E Europe • 500 kW
	CHINA R INTL, Urümqi	Europe • 500 kW
	CHINA R INTL, Via Moscow, Russia	W • Mideast & E Africa • 500 kW; S • Mideast & E Africa • 200 kW • ALT. FREQ. TO 12035 kHz
	SERBIA †INTL RADIO SERBIA, Stubline	S • Europe • 10 kW; S Sa • Europe • 10 kW; S Su-F • Europe • 10 kW
	SUDAN REP OF SUDAN RADIO, Omdurman	DS • 100 kW • ALT. FREQ. TO 9505 kHz
	USA RFE-RL, Via Lampertheim, Germany	S • W Asia & C Asia • 100 kW
	VOA, Via Biblis, Germany	W M-F • E Europe & Mideast • 100 kW
	VOA, Via Udon Thani, Thailand	W • S Asia • 250 kW; S • E Asia • 250 kW
	VOA, Via Wertachtal,Germany	W • W Asia • 250 kW
7200v	**RUSSIA** YAKUTSK RADIO, Yakutsk	⇐ • RUSSIAN, ETC • DS-LOCAL, R ROSSII • 250 kW
7205	**CHINA** CHINA R INTL, Beijing	E Asia • 150 kW
	CHINA R INTL, Kashi	W • S Asia • 100 kW; W • E Europe • 500 kW
	CHINA R INTL, Xi'an	W • E Asia • 500 kW
	XIZANG PBS, Lhasa	DS • 100 kW; DS • 100 kW • ALT. FREQ. TO 7180 kHz
	CLANDESTINE (AMER) "RADIO REPUBLICA", Via Rampisham,UK	C America • ANTI-CASTRO • 500 kW
	GERMANY †DEUTSCHE WELLE, Via V'vostok, Russia	S • E Asia • 250 kW
	IRAN VO THE ISLAMIC REP, Sirjan	W • E Europe • 500 kW; S • Europe • 500 kW
	ROMANIA †R ROMANIA INTL, Bucharest	S • E Europe • 100 kW
	†R ROMANIA INTL, Galbeni	S • Mideast • 300 kW
(con'd)	**SOUTH AFRICA** S AFRICAN RADIO LEAGUE, Meyerton	Su • S Africa • 100 kW

0 1 2 3 4 5 6 7 8 9 10 11 12 13 14 15 16 17 18 19 20 21 22 23 24

SEASONAL S OR W 1-HR TIMESHIFT MIDYEAR ⇐ OR ⇒ JAMMING / OR /\ EARLIEST HEARD ◁ LATEST HEARD ▷ NEW FOR 2009 †

World Time 0 1 2 3 4 5 6 7 8 9 10 11 12 13 14 15 16 17 18 19 20 21 22 23 24

Freq	Country / Station	Schedule
7205 (con'd)	**SWEDEN**	
	IBRA RADIO, Via Petro-Kam, Russia	S • E Asia • 200 kW
	TURKEY	
	VOICE OF TURKEY, Ankara-Emirler	W • Europe • 500 kW
	UNITED KINGDOM	
	BBC, Rampisham	W • W Africa & C Africa • 500 kW
	BBC, Via Meyerton, South Africa	W M-F • C Africa & S Africa • 500 kW
	BBC, Via Singapore	S Asia • 250 kW
	BBC, Via Thailand	S Asia • 250 kW
	BIBLE VOICE, Via Nauen, Germany	W Su • W Europe • 125 kW
	USA	
	VOA, Via Biblis, Germany	S M-F • E Europe & Mideast • 100 kW
	VOA, Via Lampertheim, Germany	S • Mideast • 100 kW
	VOA, Via Tinian, N Marianas	W • SE Asia • 250 kW
	VOA, Via Udon Thani, Thailand	W • E Asia • 250 kW
7210	**CHINA**	
	CHINA R INTL, Beijing	E Asia • 150 kW
	CHINA R INTL, Urümqi	W • E Asia • 100 kW
	CHINA R INTL, Via Cerrik, Albania	W Europe • 150 kW
	CHINA R INTL, Xi'an	W • E Asia • 500 kW
	NEI MENGGU PBS, Hohhot	DS-MONGOLIAN • 50 kW
		W-M • DS-MONGOLIAN • 50 kW
	CYPRUS	
	CYPRUS BC CORP, Zyyi	F-Su • Europe • 250 kW
	ETHIOPIA	
	RADIO FANA, Addis Ababa	E Africa • DS • 10 kW
		Sa/Su • E Africa • DS • 10 kW
		M-F • E Africa • DS • 10 kW
	INDIA	
	ALL INDIA RADIO, Kolkata	DS • 50 kW
		Irr • ENGLISH, ETC • DS • 50 kW
		Su • DS • 50 kW
		ENGLISH, ETC • DS • 50 kW
	ROMANIA	
	†R ROMANIA INTL, Bucharest	W • E Europe • 300 kW
		S • E Europe • 100 kW
	RUSSIA	
	VOICE OF RUSSIA, St Petersburg	S • Europe • 200 kW
	TURKEY	
	†VOICE OF TURKEY, Ankara-Emirler	S • E Europe • 250 kW
	UNITED KINGDOM	
	BBC, Rampisham	S • E Africa • 500 kW
	BIBLE VOICE, Via Dhabayya, UAE	S • S Asia • 250 kW
	BIBLE VOICE, Via Jülich, Germany	W Sa • Mideast & W Asia • 100 kW
		W Su/W-F • Mideast & W Asia • 100 kW
		W W-Su • Mideast & W Asia • 100 kW
		W Sa/Su • Mideast & W Asia • 100 kW
	USA	
	ADVENTIST WORLD R, Via Austria	W • Mideast • 300 kW
	†FAMILY RADIO, Via Jülich, Germany	E Europe • 100 kW • ALT. FREQ. TO 6050 kHz
	GOSPEL FOR ASIA, Via Germany	W • W Asia & S Asia • 250 kW
	R FREE ASIA, Via Irkutsk, Russia	E Asia • 250 kW
	†TRANS WORLD R, Via Fontbonne, France	Sa • S Europe • 100 kW
		Europe • 100 kW
	†VOA	W M-F • E Europe • 250 kW
	VOA, Via Biblis, Germany	S M-F • S Europe • 100 kW
	VIETNAM	
	†VOICE OF VIETNAM, Da Lai	DS-1/MINORITIES • 50 kW
7210v	**BENIN**	
	R DIF DU BENIN, Cotonou	Irr • M-F • FRENCH, ETC • DS • 25 kW
		Irr • FRENCH, ETC • DS • 25 kW
		Irr • Sa/Su • FRENCH, ETC • DS • 25 kW
7215	**CHINA**	
	CENTRAL PEOPLE'S BS, Shijiazhuang	DS-1 • 100 kW • ALT. FREQ. TO 6950 kHz
	CHINA R INTL, Beijing	W • Europe • 500 kW
	CHINA R INTL, Kunming	S Asia • 500 kW
		S • SE Asia • 100 kW
	CHINA R INTL, Shijiazhuang	W • W Asia & C Asia • 500 kW
	CHINA R INTL, Via Cerrik, Albania	W • N Africa • 150 kW
	CHINA R INTL, Via Samara, Russia	W • Europe • 500 kW
(con'd)	CHINA R INTL, Xi'an	W • C Asia & E Asia • 500 kW

World Time 0 1 2 3 4 5 6 7 8 9 10 11 12 13 14 15 16 17 18 19 20 21 22 23 24

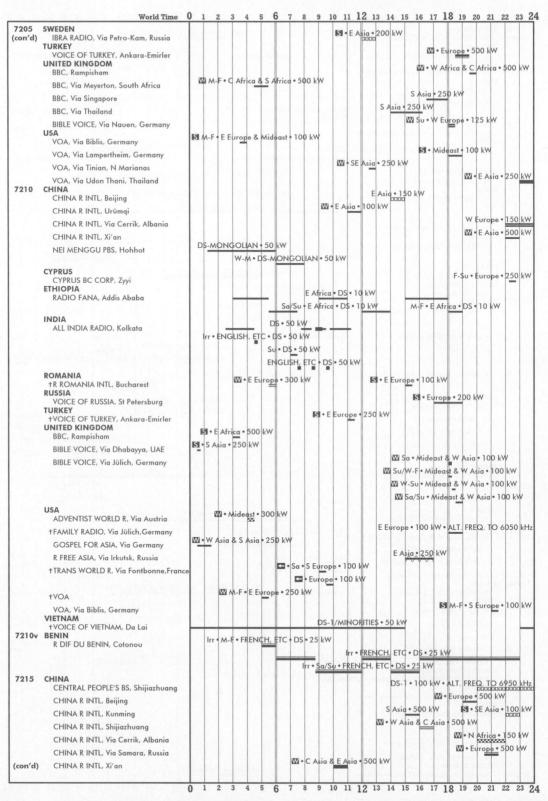

ENGLISH ▬ ARABIC ▭ CHINESE ▭ FRENCH ═ GERMAN ═ RUSSIAN ═ SPANISH ═ OTHER —

World Time 0 1 2 3 4 5 6 7 8 9 10 11 12 13 14 15 16 17 18 19 20 21 22 23 24

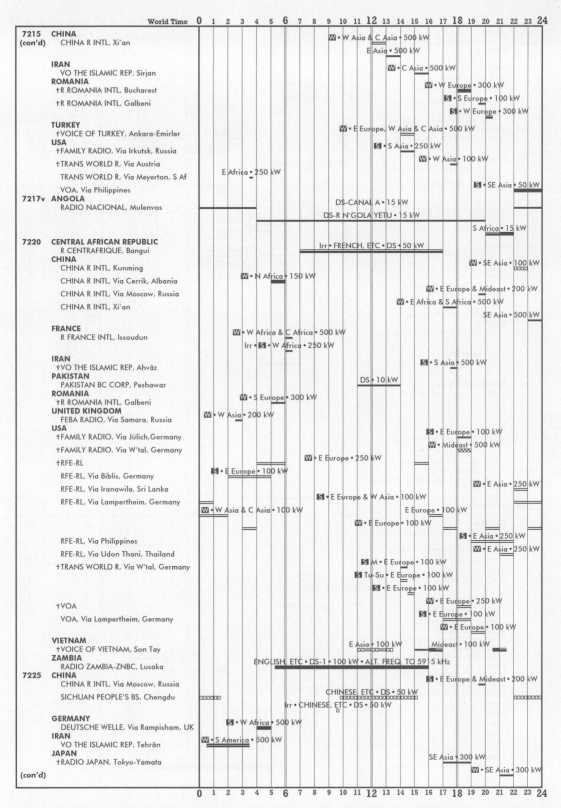

kHz	Country	Station	Schedule
7215 (con'd)	CHINA	CHINA R INTL, Xi'an	W • W Asia & C Asia • 500 kW; E Asia • 500 kW
	IRAN	VO THE ISLAMIC REP, Sirjan	W • C Asia • 500 kW
	ROMANIA	†R ROMANIA INTL, Bucharest	W • W Europe • 300 kW
		†R ROMANIA INTL, Galbeni	S • S Europe • 100 kW; S • W Europe • 300 kW
	TURKEY	†VOICE OF TURKEY, Ankara-Emirler	W • E Europe, W Asia & C Asia • 500 kW
	USA	†FAMILY RADIO, Via Irkutsk, Russia	S • S Asia • 250 kW
		†TRANS WORLD R, Via Austria	W • W Asia • 100 kW
		TRANS WORLD R, Via Meyerton, S Af	E Africa • 250 kW
		VOA, Via Philippines	S • SE Asia • 50 kW
7217v	ANGOLA	RADIO NACIONAL, Mulenvos	DS-CANAL A • 15 kW; DS-R N'GOLA YETU • 15 kW; S Africa • 15 kW
7220	CENTRAL AFRICAN REPUBLIC	R CENTRAFRIQUE, Bangui	Irr • FRENCH, ETC • DS • 50 kW
	CHINA	CHINA R INTL, Kunming	W • SE Asia • 100 kW
		CHINA R INTL, Via Cerrik, Albania	W • N Africa • 150 kW
		CHINA R INTL, Via Moscow, Russia	W • E Europe & Mideast • 200 kW
		CHINA R INTL, Xi'an	W • E Africa & S Africa • 500 kW; SE Asia • 500 kW
	FRANCE	R FRANCE INTL, Issoudun	W • W Africa & C Africa • 500 kW; Irr • S • W Africa • 250 kW
	IRAN	†VO THE ISLAMIC REP, Ahvāz	S • S Asia • 500 kW
	PAKISTAN	PAKISTAN BC CORP, Peshawar	DS • 10 kW
	ROMANIA	†R ROMANIA INTL, Galbeni	W • S Europe • 300 kW
	UNITED KINGDOM	FEBA RADIO, Via Samara, Russia	W • W Asia • 200 kW
	USA	†FAMILY RADIO, Via Jülich,Germany	S • E Europe • 100 kW
		†FAMILY RADIO, Via W'tal, Germany	W • Mideast • 500 kW
		†RFE-RL	W • E Europe • 250 kW
		RFE-RL, Via Biblis, Germany	S • E Europe • 100 kW
		RFE-RL, Via Iranawila, Sri Lanka	W • E Asia • 250 kW
		RFE-RL, Via Lampertheim, Germany	S • E Europe & W Asia • 100 kW; W • W Asia & C Asia • 100 kW; E Europe • 100 kW; W • E Europe • 100 kW
		RFE-RL, Via Philippines	S • E Asia • 250 kW
		RFE-RL, Via Udon Thani, Thailand	W • E Asia • 250 kW
		†TRANS WORLD R, Via W'tal, Germany	S M • E Europe • 100 kW; S Tu-Su • E Europe • 100 kW; S • E Europe • 100 kW
		†VOA	W • E Europe • 250 kW
		VOA, Via Lampertheim, Germany	S • E Europe • 100 kW; W • E Europe • 100 kW
	VIETNAM	†VOICE OF VIETNAM, Son Tay	E Asia • 100 kW; Mideast • 100 kW
	ZAMBIA	RADIO ZAMBIA-ZNBC, Lusaka	ENGLISH, ETC • DS-1 • 100 kW • ALT. FREQ. TO 5915 kHz
7225	CHINA	CHINA R INTL, Via Moscow, Russia	S • E Europe & Mideast • 200 kW
		SICHUAN PEOPLE'S BS, Chengdu	CHINESE, ETC • DS • 50 kW; Irr • CHINESE, ETC • DS • 50 kW
	GERMANY	DEUTSCHE WELLE, Via Rampisham, UK	S • W Africa • 500 kW
	IRAN	VO THE ISLAMIC REP, Tehrān	W • S America • 500 kW
	JAPAN	†RADIO JAPAN, Tokyo-Yamata	SE Asia • 300 kW; W • SE Asia • 300 kW
(con'd)			

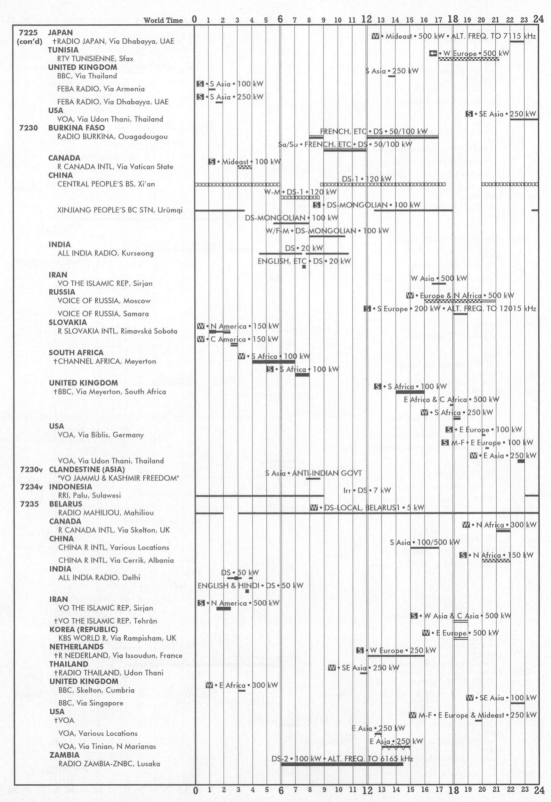

World Time 0 1 2 3 4 5 6 7 8 9 10 11 12 13 14 15 16 17 18 19 20 21 22 23 24

Frequency	Country / Station	Schedule
7225 (con'd)	**JAPAN**	
	†RADIO JAPAN, Via Dhabayya, UAE	W • Mideast • 500 kW • ALT. FREQ. TO 7115 kHz
	TUNISIA	
	RTV TUNISIENNE, Sfax	← • W Europe • 500 kW
	UNITED KINGDOM	
	BBC, Via Thailand	S Asia • 250 kW
	FEBA RADIO, Via Armenia	S • S Asia • 100 kW
	FEBA RADIO, Via Dhabayya, UAE	S • S Asia • 250 kW
	USA	
	VOA, Via Udon Thani, Thailand	S • SE Asia • 250 kW
7230	**BURKINA FASO**	
	RADIO BURKINA, Ouagadougou	FRENCH, ETC • DS • 50/100 kW
		Sa/Su • FRENCH, ETC • DS • 50/100 kW
	CANADA	
	R CANADA INTL, Via Vatican State	S • Mideast • 100 kW
	CHINA	
	CENTRAL PEOPLE'S BS, Xi'an	DS-1 • 120 kW
		W-M • DS-1 • 120 kW
	XINJIANG PEOPLE'S BC STN, Urümqi	S • DS-MONGOLIAN • 100 kW
		DS-MONGOLIAN • 100 kW
		W/F-M • DS-MONGOLIAN • 100 kW
	INDIA	
	ALL INDIA RADIO, Kurseong	DS • 20 kW
		ENGLISH, ETC • DS • 20 kW
	IRAN	
	VO THE ISLAMIC REP, Sirjan	W Asia • 500 kW
	RUSSIA	
	VOICE OF RUSSIA, Moscow	W • Europe & N Africa • 500 kW
	VOICE OF RUSSIA, Samara	S • S Europe • 200 kW • ALT. FREQ. TO 12015 kHz
	SLOVAKIA	
	R SLOVAKIA INTL, Rimavská Sobota	W • N America • 150 kW
		W • C America • 150 kW
	SOUTH AFRICA	
	†CHANNEL AFRICA, Meyerton	W • S Africa • 100 kW
		S • S Africa • 100 kW
	UNITED KINGDOM	
	†BBC, Via Meyerton, South Africa	S • S Africa • 100 kW
		E Africa & C Africa • 500 kW
		W • S Africa • 250 kW
	USA	
	VOA, Via Biblis, Germany	S • E Europe • 100 kW
		S M-F • E Europe • 100 kW
	VOA, Via Udon Thani, Thailand	W • E Asia • 250 kW
7230v	**CLANDESTINE (ASIA)**	
	"VO JAMMU & KASHMIR FREEDOM"	S Asia • ANTI-INDIAN GOVT
7234v	**INDONESIA**	
	RRI, Palu, Sulawesi	Irr • DS • 7 kW
7235	**BELARUS**	
	RADIO MAHILIOU, Mahiliou	W • DS-LOCAL, BELARUS1 • 5 kW
	CANADA	
	R CANADA INTL, Via Skelton, UK	W • N Africa • 300 kW
	CHINA	
	CHINA R INTL, Various Locations	S Asia • 100/500 kW
	CHINA R INTL, Via Cerrik, Albania	S • N Africa • 150 kW
	INDIA	
	ALL INDIA RADIO, Delhi	DS • 50 kW
		ENGLISH & HINDI • DS • 50 kW
	IRAN	
	VO THE ISLAMIC REP, Sirjan	S • N America • 500 kW
	†VO THE ISLAMIC REP, Tehrān	S • W Asia & C Asia • 500 kW
	KOREA (REPUBLIC)	
	KBS WORLD R, Via Rampisham, UK	W • E Europe • 500 kW
	NETHERLANDS	
	†R NEDERLAND, Via Issoudun, France	S • W Europe • 250 kW
	THAILAND	
	†RADIO THAILAND, Udon Thani	W • SE Asia • 250 kW
	UNITED KINGDOM	
	BBC, Skelton, Cumbria	W • E Africa • 300 kW
	BBC, Via Singapore	W • SE Asia • 100 kW
	USA	
	†VOA	W M-F • E Europe & Mideast • 250 kW
	VOA, Various Locations	E Asia • 250 kW
	VOA, Via Tinian, N Marianas	E Asia • 250 kW
	ZAMBIA	
	RADIO ZAMBIA-ZNBC, Lusaka	DS-2 • 100 kW • ALT. FREQ. TO 6165 kHz

0 1 2 3 4 5 6 7 8 9 10 11 12 13 14 15 16 17 18 19 20 21 22 23 24

ENGLISH ARABIC CHINESE FRENCH GERMAN RUSSIAN SPANISH OTHER

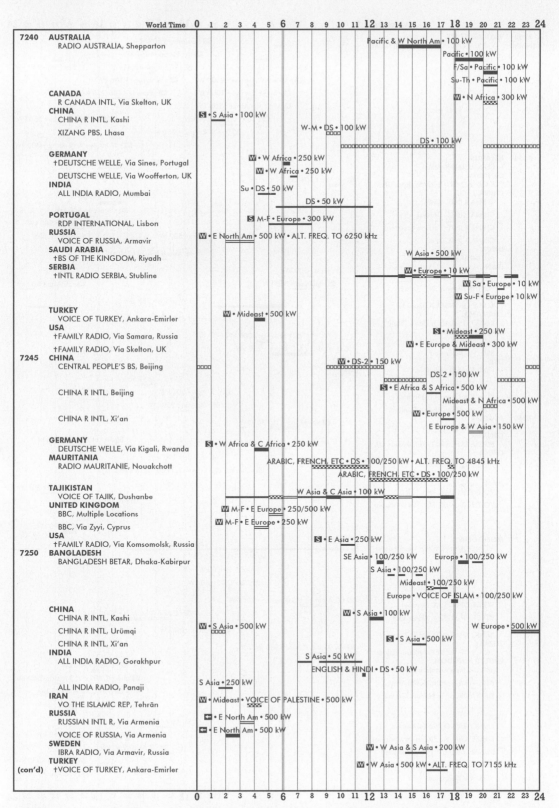

World Time 0 1 2 3 4 5 6 7 8 9 10 11 12 13 14 15 16 17 18 19 20 21 22 23 24

kHz	Country / Station	Service
7240	**AUSTRALIA** RADIO AUSTRALIA, Shepparton	Pacific & W North Am • 100 kW
		Pacific • 100 kW
		F/Sa • Pacific • 100 kW
		Su-Th • Pacific • 100 kW
	CANADA R CANADA INTL, Via Skelton, UK	W • N Africa • 300 kW
	CHINA CHINA R INTL, Kashi	S • S Asia • 100 kW
	XIZANG PBS, Lhasa	W-M • DS • 100 kW
		DS • 100 kW
	GERMANY †DEUTSCHE WELLE, Via Sines, Portugal	W • W Africa • 250 kW
	DEUTSCHE WELLE, Via Woofferton, UK	W • W Africa • 250 kW
	INDIA ALL INDIA RADIO, Mumbai	Su • DS • 50 kW
		DS • 50 kW
	PORTUGAL RDP INTERNATIONAL, Lisbon	S M-F • Europe • 300 kW
	RUSSIA VOICE OF RUSSIA, Armavir	W • E North Am • 500 kW • ALT. FREQ. TO 6250 kHz
	SAUDI ARABIA †BS OF THE KINGDOM, Riyadh	W Asia • 500 kW
	SERBIA †INTL RADIO SERBIA, Stubline	W • Europe • 10 kW
		W Sa • Europe • 10 kW
		W Su-F • Europe • 10 kW
	TURKEY VOICE OF TURKEY, Ankara-Emirler	W • Mideast • 500 kW
	USA †FAMILY RADIO, Via Samara, Russia	S • Mideast • 250 kW
	†FAMILY RADIO, Via Skelton, UK	W • E Europe & Mideast • 300 kW
7245	**CHINA** CENTRAL PEOPLE'S BS, Beijing	W • DS-2 • 150 kW
		DS-2 • 150 kW
	CHINA R INTL, Beijing	S • E Africa & S Africa • 500 kW
		Mideast & N Africa • 500 kW
	CHINA R INTL, Xi'an	W • Europe • 500 kW
		E Europe & W Asia • 150 kW
	GERMANY DEUTSCHE WELLE, Via Kigali, Rwanda	S • W Africa & C Africa • 250 kW
	MAURITANIA RADIO MAURITANIE, Nouakchott	ARABIC, FRENCH, ETC • DS • 100/250 kW • ALT. FREQ. TO 4845 kHz
		ARABIC, FRENCH, ETC • DS • 100/250 kW
	TAJIKISTAN VOICE OF TAJIK, Dushanbe	W Asia & C Asia • 100 kW
	UNITED KINGDOM BBC, Multiple Locations	W M-F • E Europe • 250/500 kW
	BBC, Via Zyyi, Cyprus	W M-F • E Europe • 250 kW
	USA †FAMILY RADIO, Via Komsomolsk, Russia	S • E Asia • 250 kW
7250	**BANGLADESH** BANGLADESH BETAR, Dhaka-Kabirpur	SE Asia • 100/250 kW
		Europe • 100/250 kW
		S Asia • 100/250 kW
		Mideast • 100/250 kW
		Europe • VOICE OF ISLAM • 100/250 kW
	CHINA CHINA R INTL, Kashi	W • S Asia • 100 kW
	CHINA R INTL, Urümqi	W • S Asia • 500 kW
		W Europe • 500 kW
	CHINA R INTL, Xi'an	S • S Asia • 500 kW
	INDIA ALL INDIA RADIO, Gorakhpur	S Asia • 50 kW
		ENGLISH & HINDI • DS • 50 kW
	ALL INDIA RADIO, Panaji	S Asia • 250 kW
	IRAN VO THE ISLAMIC REP, Tehrān	W • Mideast • VOICE OF PALESTINE • 500 kW
	RUSSIA RUSSIAN INTL R, Via Armenia	⬅ • E North Am • 500 kW
	VOICE OF RUSSIA, Via Armenia	⬅ • E North Am • 500 kW
	SWEDEN IBRA RADIO, Via Armavir, Russia	W • W Asia & S Asia • 200 kW
(con'd)	**TURKEY** †VOICE OF TURKEY, Ankara-Emirler	W • W Asia • 500 kW • ALT. FREQ. TO 7155 kHz

0 1 2 3 4 5 6 7 8 9 10 11 12 13 14 15 16 17 18 19 20 21 22 23 24

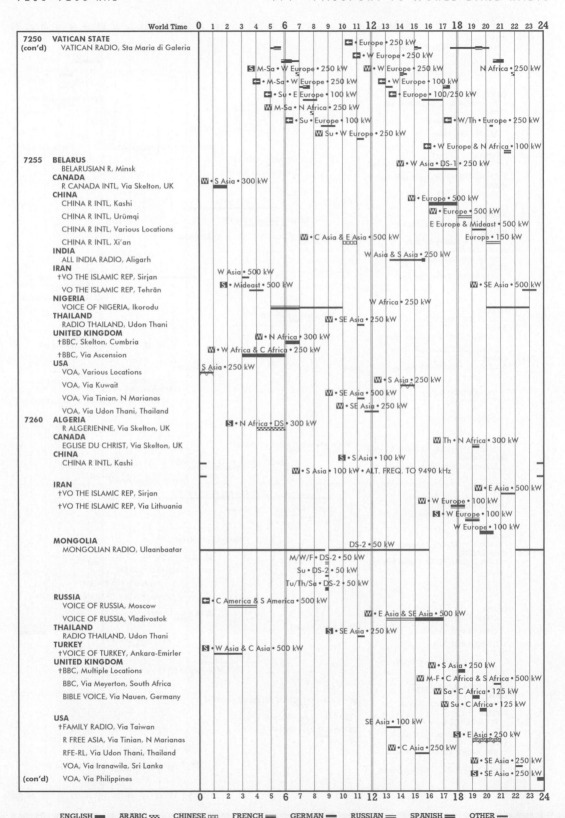

World Time 0 1 2 3 4 5 6 7 8 9 10 11 12 13 14 15 16 17 18 19 20 21 22 23 24

kHz	Country	Station	Schedule notes
7250 (con'd)	VATICAN STATE	VATICAN RADIO, Sta Maria di Galeria	[←] • Europe • 250 kW
			[←] • W Europe • 250 kW
			[S] M-Sa • W Europe • 250 kW
			[W] • W Europe • 250 kW
			N Africa • 250 kW
			[←] • M-Sa • W Europe • 250 kW
			[←] • W Europe • 100 kW
			[←] • Su • E Europe • 100 kW
			[←] • Europe • 100/250 kW
			[W] M-Sa • N Africa • 250 kW
			[←] • Su • Europe • 100 kW
			[←] • W/Th • Europe • 250 kW
			[W] Su • W Europe • 250 kW
			[←] • W Europe & N Africa • 100 kW
7255	BELARUS	BELARUSIAN R, Minsk	[W] • W Asia • DS-1 • 250 kW
	CANADA	R CANADA INTL, Via Skelton, UK	[W] • S Asia • 300 kW
	CHINA	CHINA R INTL, Kashi	[W] • Europe • 500 kW
		CHINA R INTL, Urümqi	[W] • Europe • 500 kW
		CHINA R INTL, Various Locations	E Europe & Mideast • 500 kW
		CHINA R INTL, Xi'an	[W] • C Asia & E Asia • 500 kW
			Europe • 150 kW
	INDIA	ALL INDIA RADIO, Aligarh	W Asia & S Asia • 250 kW
	IRAN	†VO THE ISLAMIC REP, Sirjan	W Asia • 500 kW
		VO THE ISLAMIC REP, Tehrān	[S] • Mideast • 500 kW
			[W] • SE Asia • 500 kW
	NIGERIA	VOICE OF NIGERIA, Ikorodu	W Africa • 250 kW
	THAILAND	RADIO THAILAND, Udon Thani	[W] • SE Asia • 250 kW
	UNITED KINGDOM	†BBC, Skelton, Cumbria	[W] • N Africa • 300 kW
		†BBC, Via Ascension	[W] • W Africa & C Africa • 250 kW
	USA	VOA, Various Locations	S Asia • 250 kW
		VOA, Via Kuwait	[W] • S Asia • 250 kW
		VOA, Via Tinian, N Marianas	[W] • SE Asia • 500 kW
		VOA, Via Udon Thani, Thailand	[W] • SE Asia • 250 kW
7260	ALGERIA	R ALGERIENNE, Via Skelton, UK	[S] • N Africa • DS • 300 kW
	CANADA	EGLISE DU CHRIST, Via Skelton, UK	[W] Th • N Africa • 300 kW
	CHINA	CHINA R INTL, Kashi	[S] • S Asia • 100 kW
			[W] • S Asia • 100 kW • ALT. FREQ. TO 9490 kHz
	IRAN	†VO THE ISLAMIC REP, Sirjan	[W] • E Asia • 500 kW
		†VO THE ISLAMIC REP, Via Lithuania	[W] • W Europe • 100 kW
			[S] • W Europe • 100 kW
			W Europe • 100 kW
	MONGOLIA	MONGOLIAN RADIO, Ulaanbaatar	DS-2 • 50 kW
			M/W/F • DS-2 • 50 kW
			Su • DS-2 • 50 kW
			Tu/Th/Sa • DS-2 • 50 kW
	RUSSIA	VOICE OF RUSSIA, Moscow	[←] • C America & S America • 500 kW
		VOICE OF RUSSIA, Vladivostok	[W] • E Asia & SE Asia • 500 kW
	THAILAND	RADIO THAILAND, Udon Thani	[S] • SE Asia • 250 kW
	TURKEY	†VOICE OF TURKEY, Ankara-Emirler	[S] • W Asia & C Asia • 500 kW
	UNITED KINGDOM	†BBC, Multiple Locations	[W] • S Asia • 250 kW
		BBC, Via Meyerton, South Africa	[W] M-F • C Africa & S Africa • 500 kW
		BIBLE VOICE, Via Nauen, Germany	[W] Sa • C Africa • 125 kW
			[W] Su • C Africa • 125 kW
	USA	†FAMILY RADIO, Via Taiwan	SE Asia • 100 kW
		R FREE ASIA, Via Tinian, N Marianas	[S] • E Asia • 250 kW
		RFE-RL, Via Udon Thani, Thailand	[W] • C Asia • 250 kW
		VOA, Via Iranawila, Sri Lanka	[W] • SE Asia • 250 kW
(con'd)		VOA, Via Philippines	[S] • SE Asia • 250 kW

0 1 2 3 4 5 6 7 8 9 10 11 12 13 14 15 16 17 18 19 20 21 22 23 24

ENGLISH ARABIC CHINESE FRENCH GERMAN RUSSIAN SPANISH OTHER

World Time 0 1 2 3 4 5 6 7 8 9 10 11 12 13 14 15 16 17 18 19 20 21 22 23 24

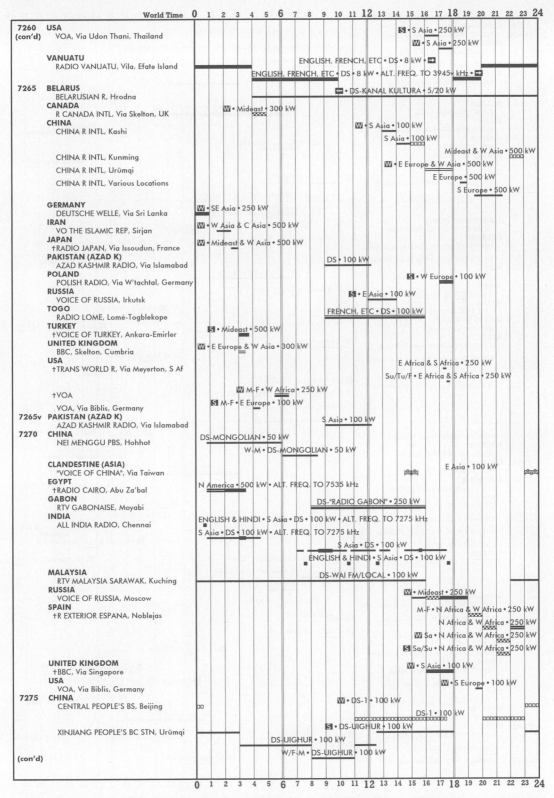

Freq.	Country / Station	Schedule
7260 (con'd)	**USA** VOA, Via Udon Thani, Thailand	[S] • S Asia • 250 kW; [W] • S Asia • 250 kW
	VANUATU RADIO VANUATU, Vila, Efate Island	ENGLISH, FRENCH, ETC • DS • 8 kW • ➡; ENGLISH, FRENCH, ETC • DS • 8 kW • ALT. FREQ. TO 3945v kHz • ➡
7265	**BELARUS** BELARUSIAN R, Hrodna	⬅ • DS-KANAL KULTURA • 5/20 kW
	CANADA R CANADA INTL, Via Skelton, UK	[W] • Mideast • 300 kW
	CHINA CHINA R INTL, Kashi	[W] • S Asia • 100 kW; S Asia • 100 kW
	CHINA R INTL, Kunming	Mideast & W Asia • 500 kW
	CHINA R INTL, Urümqi	[W] • E Europe & W Asia • 500 kW
	CHINA R INTL, Various Locations	E Europe • 500 kW; S Europe • 500 kW
	GERMANY DEUTSCHE WELLE, Via Sri Lanka	[W] • SE Asia • 250 kW
	IRAN VO THE ISLAMIC REP, Sirjan	[W] • W Asia & C Asia • 500 kW
	JAPAN †RADIO JAPAN, Via Issoudun, France	[W] • Mideast & W Asia • 500 kW
	PAKISTAN (AZAD K) AZAD KASHMIR RADIO, Via Islamabad	DS • 100 kW
	POLAND POLISH RADIO, Via W'tachtal, Germany	[S] • W Europe • 100 kW
	RUSSIA VOICE OF RUSSIA, Irkutsk	[S] • E Asia • 100 kW
	TOGO RADIO LOME, Lomé-Togblekope	FRENCH, ETC • DS • 100 kW
	TURKEY †VOICE OF TURKEY, Ankara-Emirler	[S] • Mideast • 500 kW
	UNITED KINGDOM BBC, Skelton, Cumbria	[W] • E Europe & W Asia • 300 kW
	USA †TRANS WORLD R, Via Meyerton, S Af	E Africa & S Africa • 250 kW; Su/Tu/F • E Africa & S Africa • 250 kW
	†VOA	[W] M-F • W Africa • 250 kW
	VOA, Via Biblis, Germany	[S] M-F • E Europe • 100 kW
7265v	**PAKISTAN (AZAD K)** AZAD KASHMIR RADIO, Via Islamabad	S Asia • 100 kW
7270	**CHINA** NEI MENGGU PBS, Hohhot	DS-MONGOLIAN • 50 kW; W-M • DS-MONGOLIAN • 50 kW
	CLANDESTINE (ASIA) "VOICE OF CHINA", Via Taiwan	E Asia • 100 kW
	EGYPT †RADIO CAIRO, Abu Za'bal	N America • 500 kW • ALT. FREQ. TO 7535 kHz
	GABON RTV GABONAISE, Moyabi	DS-"RADIO GABON" • 250 kW
	INDIA ALL INDIA RADIO, Chennai	ENGLISH & HINDI • S Asia • DS • 100 kW • ALT. FREQ. TO 7275 kHz; S Asia • DS • 100 kW • ALT. FREQ. TO 7275 kHz; S Asia • DS • 100 kW; ENGLISH & HINDI • S Asia • DS • 100 kW
	MALAYSIA RTV MALAYSIA SARAWAK, Kuching	DS-WAI FM/LOCAL • 100 kW
	RUSSIA VOICE OF RUSSIA, Moscow	[W] • Mideast • 250 kW
	SPAIN †R EXTERIOR ESPANA, Noblejas	M-F • N Africa & W Africa • 250 kW; N Africa & W Africa • 250 kW; [W] Sa • N Africa & W Africa • 250 kW; [S] Sa/Su • N Africa & W Africa • 250 kW
	UNITED KINGDOM †BBC, Via Singapore	[W] • S Asia • 100 kW
	USA VOA, Via Biblis, Germany	[W] • S Europe • 100 kW
7275	**CHINA** CENTRAL PEOPLE'S BS, Beijing	[W] • DS-1 • 100 kW; DS-1 • 100 kW
	XINJIANG PEOPLE'S BC STN, Urümqi	[S] • DS-UIGHUR • 100 kW; DS-UIGHUR • 100 kW; W/F-M • DS-UIGHUR • 100 kW
(con'd)		

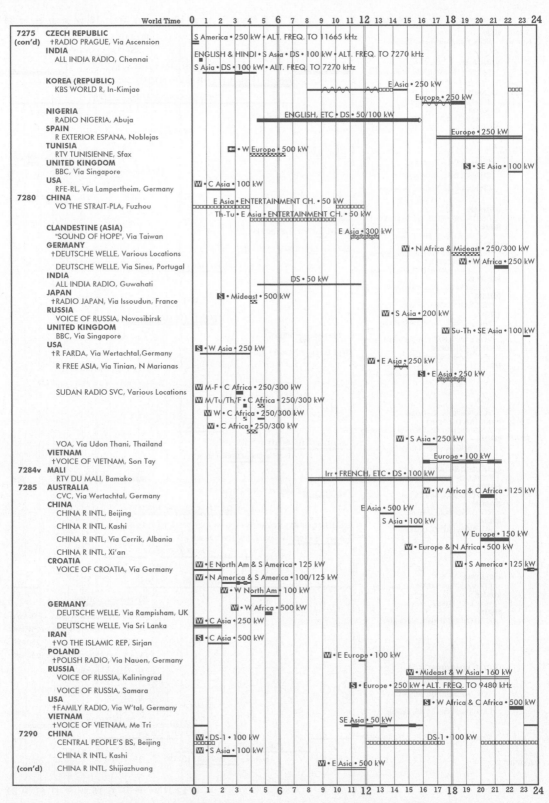

World Time 0 1 2 3 4 5 6 7 8 9 10 11 12 13 14 15 16 17 18 19 20 21 22 23 24

kHz	Country / Station	Schedule notes
7275 (con'd)	**CZECH REPUBLIC** †RADIO PRAGUE, Via Ascension	S America • 250 kW • ALT. FREQ. TO 11665 kHz
	INDIA ALL INDIA RADIO, Chennai	ENGLISH & HINDI • S Asia • DS • 100 kW • ALT. FREQ. TO 7270 kHz
		S Asia • DS • 100 kW • ALT. FREQ. TO 7270 kHz
	KOREA (REPUBLIC) KBS WORLD R, In-Kimjae	E Asia • 250 kW
		Europe • 250 kW
	NIGERIA RADIO NIGERIA, Abuja	ENGLISH, ETC • DS • 50/100 kW
	SPAIN R EXTERIOR ESPANA, Noblejas	Europe • 250 kW
	TUNISIA RTV TUNISIENNE, Sfax	W Europe • 500 kW
	UNITED KINGDOM BBC, Via Singapore	S • SE Asia • 100 kW
	USA RFE-RL, Via Lampertheim, Germany	W • C Asia • 100 kW
7280	**CHINA** VO THE STRAIT-PLA, Fuzhou	E Asia • ENTERTAINMENT CH. • 50 kW
		Th-Tu • E Asia • ENTERTAINMENT CH. • 50 kW
	CLANDESTINE (ASIA) "SOUND OF HOPE", Via Taiwan	E Asia • 300 kW
	GERMANY †DEUTSCHE WELLE, Various Locations	W • N Africa & Mideast • 250/300 kW
	DEUTSCHE WELLE, Via Sines, Portugal	W • W Africa • 250 kW
	INDIA ALL INDIA RADIO, Guwahati	DS • 50 kW
	JAPAN †RADIO JAPAN, Via Issoudun, France	S • Mideast • 500 kW
	RUSSIA VOICE OF RUSSIA, Novosibirsk	W • S Asia • 200 kW
	UNITED KINGDOM BBC, Via Singapore	W Su-Th • SE Asia • 100 kW
	USA †R FARDA, Via Wertachtal, Germany	S • W Asia • 250 kW
	R FREE ASIA, Via Tinian, N Marianas	W • E Asia • 250 kW
		S • E Asia • 250 kW
	SUDAN RADIO SVC, Various Locations	W M-F • C Africa • 250/300 kW
		W M/Tu/Th/F • C Africa • 250/300 kW
		W W • C Africa • 250/300 kW
		W • C Africa • 250/300 kW
	VOA, Via Udon Thani, Thailand	W • S Asia • 250 kW
	VIETNAM †VOICE OF VIETNAM, Son Tay	Europe • 100 kW
7284v	**MALI** RTV DU MALI, Bamako	Irr • FRENCH, ETC • DS • 100 kW
7285	**AUSTRALIA** CVC, Via Wertachtal, Germany	W • W Africa & C Africa • 125 kW
	CHINA CHINA R INTL, Beijing	E Asia • 500 kW
	CHINA R INTL, Kashi	S Asia • 100 kW
	CHINA R INTL, Via Cerrik, Albania	W Europe • 150 kW
	CHINA R INTL, Xi'an	W • Europe & N Africa • 500 kW
	CROATIA VOICE OF CROATIA, Via Germany	W • E North Am & S America • 125 kW
		W • S America • 125 kW
		W • N America & S America • 100/125 kW
		W • W North Am • 100 kW
	GERMANY DEUTSCHE WELLE, Via Rampisham, UK	W • W Africa • 500 kW
	DEUTSCHE WELLE, Via Sri Lanka	W • C Asia • 250 kW
	IRAN †VO THE ISLAMIC REP, Sirjan	S • C Asia • 500 kW
	POLAND †POLISH RADIO, Via Nauen, Germany	W • E Europe • 100 kW
	RUSSIA VOICE OF RUSSIA, Kaliningrad	W • Mideast & W Asia • 160 kW
	VOICE OF RUSSIA, Samara	S • Europe • 250 kW • ALT. FREQ. TO 9480 kHz
	USA †FAMILY RADIO, Via W'tal, Germany	S • W Africa & C Africa • 500 kW
	VIETNAM †VOICE OF VIETNAM, Me Tri	SE Asia • 50 kW
7290	**CHINA** CENTRAL PEOPLE'S BS, Beijing	W • DS-1 • 100 kW
		DS-1 • 100 kW
	CHINA R INTL, Kashi	W • S Asia • 100 kW
(con'd)	CHINA R INTL, Shijiazhuang	W • E Asia • 500 kW

0 1 2 3 4 5 6 7 8 9 10 11 12 13 14 15 16 17 18 19 20 21 22 23 24

ENGLISH ▬ ARABIC ▒ CHINESE ▭▭▭ FRENCH ═ GERMAN ═ RUSSIAN ═ SPANISH ═ OTHER —

World Time 0 1 2 3 4 5 6 7 8 9 10 11 12 13 14 15 16 17 18 19 20 21 22 23 24

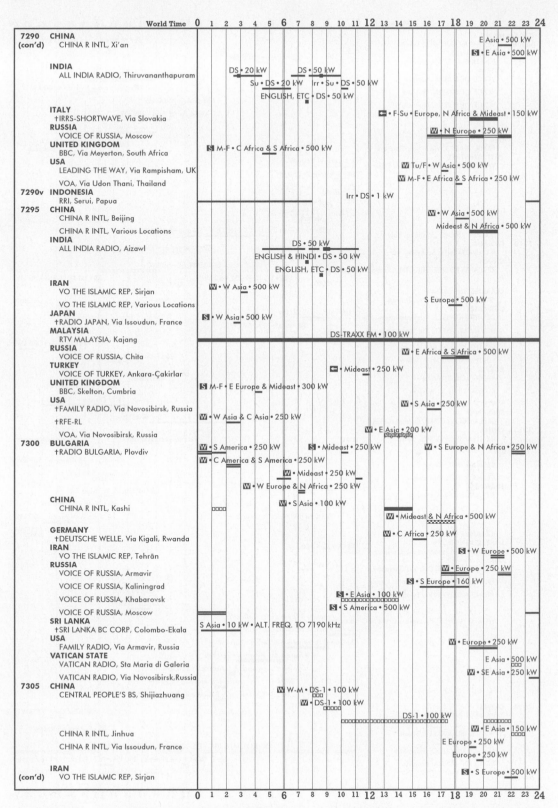

kHz	Country	Station	Schedule
7290 (con'd)	CHINA	CHINA R INTL, Xi'an	E Asia • 500 kW; S • E Asia • 500 kW
	INDIA	ALL INDIA RADIO, Thiruvananthapuram	DS • 20 kW; DS • 50 kW; Su • DS • 20 kW; Irr • Su • DS • 50 kW; ENGLISH, ETC • DS • 50 kW
	ITALY	†IRRS-SHORTWAVE, Via Slovakia	⇐ • F-Su • Europe, N Africa & Mideast • 150 kW
	RUSSIA	VOICE OF RUSSIA, Moscow	W • N Europe • 250 kW
	UNITED KINGDOM	BBC, Via Meyerton, South Africa	S M-F • C Africa & S Africa • 500 kW
	USA	LEADING THE WAY, Via Rampisham, UK	W Tu/F • W Asia • 500 kW
		VOA, Via Udon Thani, Thailand	W M-F • E Africa & S Africa • 250 kW
7290v	INDONESIA	RRI, Serui, Papua	Irr • DS • 1 kW
7295	CHINA	CHINA R INTL, Beijing	W • W Asia • 500 kW
		CHINA R INTL, Various Locations	Mideast & N Africa • 500 kW
	INDIA	ALL INDIA RADIO, Aizawl	DS • 50 kW; ENGLISH & HINDI • DS • 50 kW; ENGLISH, ETC • DS • 50 kW
	IRAN	VO THE ISLAMIC REP, Sirjan	W • W Asia • 500 kW
		VO THE ISLAMIC REP, Various Locations	S Europe • 500 kW
	JAPAN	†RADIO JAPAN, Via Issoudun, France	S • W Asia • 500 kW
	MALAYSIA	RTV MALAYSIA, Kajang	DS-TRAXX FM • 100 kW
	RUSSIA	VOICE OF RUSSIA, Chita	W • E Africa & S Africa • 500 kW
	TURKEY	VOICE OF TURKEY, Ankara-Çakirlar	⇐ • Mideast • 250 kW
	UNITED KINGDOM	BBC, Skelton, Cumbria	S M-F • E Europe & Mideast • 300 kW
	USA	†FAMILY RADIO, Via Novosibirsk, Russia	W • S Asia • 250 kW
		†RFE-RL	W • W Asia & C Asia • 250 kW
		VOA, Via Novosibirsk, Russia	W • E Asia • 200 kW
7300	BULGARIA	†RADIO BULGARIA, Plovdiv	W • S America • 250 kW; S • Mideast • 250 kW; W • S Europe & N Africa • 250 kW; W • C America & S America • 250 kW; W • Mideast • 250 kW; W • W Europe & N Africa • 250 kW
	CHINA	CHINA R INTL, Kashi	W • S Asia • 100 kW; W • Mideast & N Africa • 500 kW
	GERMANY	†DEUTSCHE WELLE, Via Kigali, Rwanda	W • C Africa • 250 kW
	IRAN	VO THE ISLAMIC REP, Tehrān	S • W Europe • 500 kW
	RUSSIA	VOICE OF RUSSIA, Armavir	W • Europe • 250 kW
		VOICE OF RUSSIA, Kaliningrad	S • S Europe • 160 kW
		VOICE OF RUSSIA, Khabarovsk	S • E Asia • 100 kW
		VOICE OF RUSSIA, Moscow	S • S America • 500 kW
	SRI LANKA	†SRI LANKA BC CORP, Colombo-Ekala	S Asia • 10 kW • ALT. FREQ. TO 7190 kHz
	USA	FAMILY RADIO, Via Armavir, Russia	W • Europe • 250 kW
	VATICAN STATE	VATICAN RADIO, Sta Maria di Galeria	E Asia • 500 kW
		VATICAN RADIO, Via Novosibirsk, Russia	W • SE Asia • 250 kW
7305	CHINA	CENTRAL PEOPLE'S BS, Shijiazhuang	W W-M • DS-1 • 100 kW; W • DS-1 • 100 kW; DS-1 • 100 kW
		CHINA R INTL, Jinhua	W • E Asia • 150 kW
		CHINA R INTL, Via Issoudun, France	E Europe • 250 kW; Europe • 250 kW
(con'd)	IRAN	VO THE ISLAMIC REP, Sirjan	S • S Europe • 500 kW

World Time 0 1 2 3 4 5 6 7 8 9 10 11 12 13 14 15 16 17 18 19 20 21 22 23 24

World Time 0 1 2 3 4 5 6 7 8 9 10 11 12 13 14 15 16 17 18 19 20 21 22 23 24

kHz	Country / Station	Schedule
7305 (con'd)	**IRAN**	
	VO THE ISLAMIC REP, Tehrān	W • W Asia & C Asia • 500 kW
	NETHERLANDS	
	R NEDERLAND, Via Moldova	W • Europe • 500 kW
	RUSSIA	
	VOICE OF RUSSIA, Armavir	S • Mideast & W Asia • 100 kW
	VOICE OF RUSSIA, Moscow	W • Mideast & E Africa • 100 kW
	VOICE OF RUSSIA, Novosibirsk	W • E Asia • 200 kW
		W M-Sa • E Asia • 200 kW
		W • S Asia • 500 kW
	USA	
	†FAMILY RADIO, Via W'tal, Germany	W • W Africa & C Africa • 500 kW
	VATICAN STATE	
	VATICAN RADIO, Sta Maria di Galeria	S America • 250 kW
		S • S America • 250 kW
		W • C America • 250 kW
		S • E North Am & C America • 250 kW
		E North Am • 125/250 kW
7306	**PIRATE (EUROPE)**	
	"RADIO EUROPE", Pioltello, Italy	← • Irr • F-Su • ITALIAN & ENGLISH • Europe • 0.6 kW • USB
7310	**CANADA**	
	R CANADA INTL, Sackville, NB	W • N America • 250 kW
	CHINA	
	XINJIANG PEOPLE'S BC STN, Urümqi	DS-CHINESE • 50 kW
		W • DS-CHINESE • 50 kW
		S • DS-CHINESE • 50 kW
	CLANDESTINE (ASIA)	
	"SOUND OF HOPE", Via Taiwan	E Asia • 300 kW
	GERMANY	
	DEUTSCHE WELLE, Via Rampisham, UK	S • Mideast • 500 kW
	DEUTSCHE WELLE, Via Sines, Portugal	S • W Africa • 250 kW
	IRAN	
	VO THE ISLAMIC REP, Sirjan	S • SE Asia • 500 kW
	VO THE ISLAMIC REP, Tehrān	W • E Europe & Mideast • 500 kW
	RUSSIA	
	RADIO ROSSII, Moscow	W • Europe • DS • 250 kW
	RUSSIAN INTL R, Moscow	W • Europe • 250 kW
	VOICE OF RUSSIA, Moscow	S • Europe • 250 kW
	SRI LANKA	
	†SRI LANKA BC CORP, Colombo-Ekala	S Asia • 10 kW • ALT. FREQ. TO 7190 kHz
7315	**CHINA**	
	CENTRAL PEOPLE'S BS, Xi'an	DS-2 • 120 kW
		W • DS-2 • 120 kW
	CHINA R INTL, Kashi	S America • 500 kW
	CHINA R INTL, Kunming	Mideast • 500 kW
	FRANCE	
	R FRANCE INTL, Issoudun	W • E Africa • 500 kW
		W M-F • W Africa & C Africa • 500 kW
		W Sa/Su • W Africa & C Africa • 500 kW
		W • Mideast & W Asia • 500 kW
		W • W Africa • 500 kW
		N Africa & W Africa • 500 kW
	R FRANCE INTL, Via Vladivostok	W • E Asia • 500 kW
	UNITED KINGDOM	
	IBC TAMIL, Via Wertachtal, Germany	S • S Asia • 250 kW
	USA	
	ADVENTIST WORLD R, Via Germany	W • E Africa • 250 kW
	†TRANS WORLD R, Via Samara, Russia	W • W Asia & S Asia • 250 kW
	†TRANS WORLD R, Via Swaziland	Su • S Africa • 50 kW
		S Africa • 50 kW
	WORLD HARVEST R, Cypress Creek, SC	M • C America & S America • 250 kW
		Su • C America & S America • 250 kW
		Sa/Su • C America & S America • 250 kW
		C America & S America • 250 kW
		M-Sa • C America & S America • 250 kW
		W M-Sa • C America & S America • 250 kW
		W Su • C America & S America • 250 kW
7320	**CHINA**	
	CHINA R INTL, Via Samara, Russia	S • Europe • 500 kW
	IRAN	
	VO THE ISLAMIC REP, Sirjan	W • Europe • 500 kW
	RUSSIA	
	MAGADAN RADIO, Magadan	← • RUSSIAN, ETC • DS-LOCAL, R ROSSII • 100 kW
	VOICE OF RUSSIA, Armavir	S M-F • N Europe • 250 kW • ALT. FREQ. TO 11675 kHz
		S Sa/Su • N Europe • 250 kW • ALT. FREQ. TO 11675 kHz
(con'd)		

World Time 0 1 2 3 4 5 6 7 8 9 10 11 12 13 14 15 16 17 18 19 20 21 22 23 24

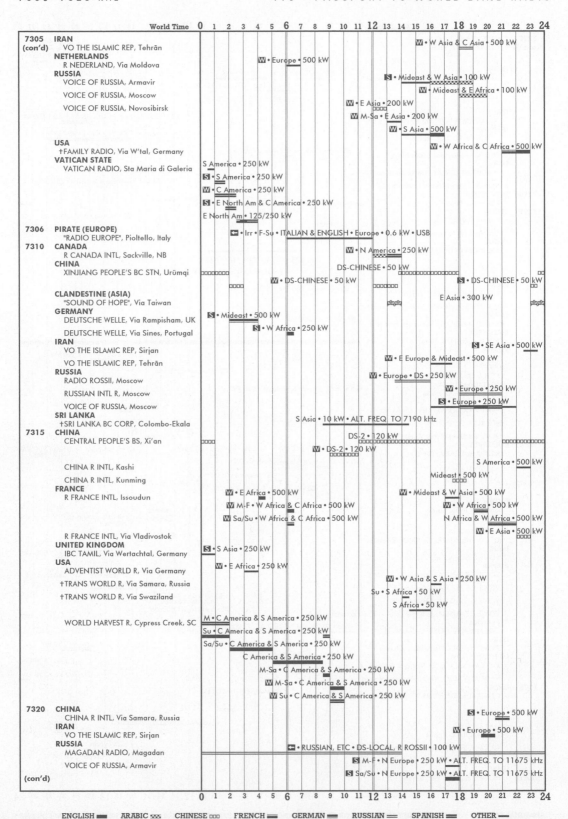

ENGLISH ARABIC CHINESE FRENCH GERMAN RUSSIAN SPANISH OTHER

World Time 0 1 2 3 4 5 6 7 8 9 10 11 12 13 14 15 16 17 18 19 20 21 22 23 24

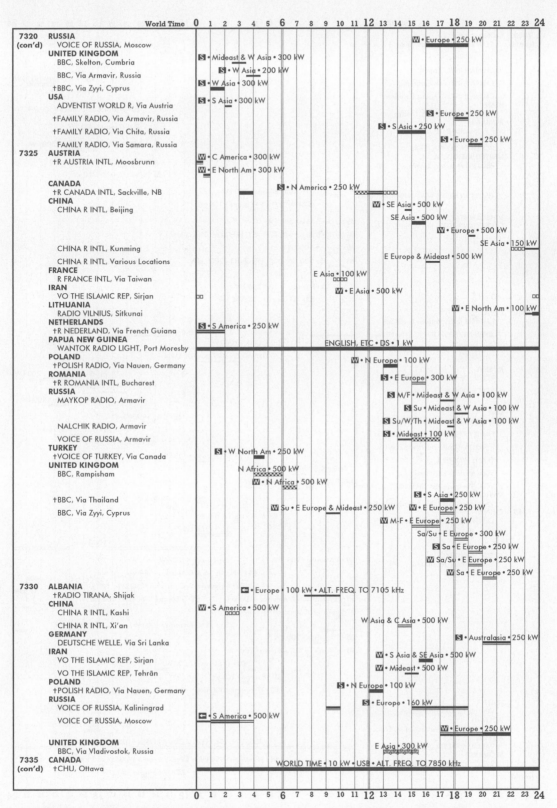

kHz	Country / Station	Schedule
7320 (con'd)	**RUSSIA**	
	VOICE OF RUSSIA, Moscow	W • Europe • 250 kW
	UNITED KINGDOM	
	BBC, Skelton, Cumbria	S • Mideast & W Asia • 300 kW
	BBC, Via Armavir, Russia	S • W Asia • 200 kW
	†BBC, Via Zyyi, Cyprus	S • W Asia • 300 kW
	USA	
	ADVENTIST WORLD R, Via Austria	S • S Asia • 300 kW
	†FAMILY RADIO, Via Armavir, Russia	S • Europe • 250 kW
	†FAMILY RADIO, Via Chita, Russia	S • S Asia • 250 kW
	FAMILY RADIO, Via Samara, Russia	S • Europe • 250 kW
7325	**AUSTRIA**	
	†R AUSTRIA INTL, Moosbrunn	W • C America • 300 kW
		W • E North Am • 300 kW
	CANADA	
	†R CANADA INTL, Sackville, NB	S • N America • 250 kW
	CHINA	
	CHINA R INTL, Beijing	W • SE Asia • 500 kW
		SE Asia • 500 kW
		W • Europe • 500 kW
	CHINA R INTL, Kunming	SE Asia • 150 kW
	CHINA R INTL, Various Locations	E Europe & Mideast • 500 kW
	FRANCE	
	R FRANCE INTL, Via Taiwan	E Asia • 100 kW
	IRAN	
	VO THE ISLAMIC REP, Sirjan	W • E Asia • 500 kW
	LITHUANIA	
	RADIO VILNIUS, Sitkunai	W • E North Am • 100 kW
	NETHERLANDS	
	†R NEDERLAND, Via French Guiana	S • S America • 250 kW
	PAPUA NEW GUINEA	
	WANTOK RADIO LIGHT, Port Moresby	ENGLISH, ETC • DS • 1 kW
	POLAND	
	†POLISH RADIO, Via Nauen, Germany	W • N Europe • 100 kW
	ROMANIA	
	†R ROMANIA INTL, Bucharest	S • E Europe • 300 kW
	RUSSIA	
	MAYKOP RADIO, Armavir	S M/F • Mideast & W Asia • 100 kW
		S Su • Mideast & W Asia • 100 kW
		S Su/W/Th • Mideast & W Asia • 100 kW
	NALCHIK RADIO, Armavir	S • Mideast • 100 kW
	VOICE OF RUSSIA, Armavir	
	TURKEY	
	†VOICE OF TURKEY, Via Canada	S • W North Am • 250 kW
	UNITED KINGDOM	
	BBC, Rampisham	N Africa • 500 kW
		W • N Africa • 500 kW
	†BBC, Via Thailand	S • S Asia • 250 kW
	BBC, Via Zyyi, Cyprus	W Su • E Europe & Mideast • 250 kW
		W • E Europe • 250 kW
		W M-F • E Europe • 250 kW
		Sa/Su • E Europe • 300 kW
		S Sa • E Europe • 250 kW
		W Sa/Su • E Europe • 250 kW
		W Sa • E Europe • 250 kW
7330	**ALBANIA**	
	†RADIO TIRANA, Shijak	⬅ • Europe • 100 kW • ALT. FREQ. TO 7105 kHz
	CHINA	
	CHINA R INTL, Kashi	W • S America • 500 kW
	CHINA R INTL, Xi'an	W Asia & C Asia • 500 kW
	GERMANY	
	DEUTSCHE WELLE, Via Sri Lanka	S • Australasia • 250 kW
	IRAN	
	VO THE ISLAMIC REP, Sirjan	W • S Asia & SE Asia • 500 kW
	VO THE ISLAMIC REP, Tehrān	W • Mideast • 500 kW
	POLAND	
	†POLISH RADIO, Via Nauen, Germany	S • N Europe • 100 kW
	RUSSIA	
	VOICE OF RUSSIA, Kaliningrad	S • Europe • 160 kW
	VOICE OF RUSSIA, Moscow	⬅ • S America • 500 kW
		W • Europe • 250 kW
	UNITED KINGDOM	
	BBC, Via Vladivostok, Russia	E Asia • 300 kW
7335 (con'd)	**CANADA**	
	†CHU, Ottawa	WORLD TIME • 10 kW • USB • ALT. FREQ. TO 7850 kHz

World Time 0 1 2 3 4 5 6 7 8 9 10 11 12 13 14 15 16 17 18 19 20 21 22 23 24

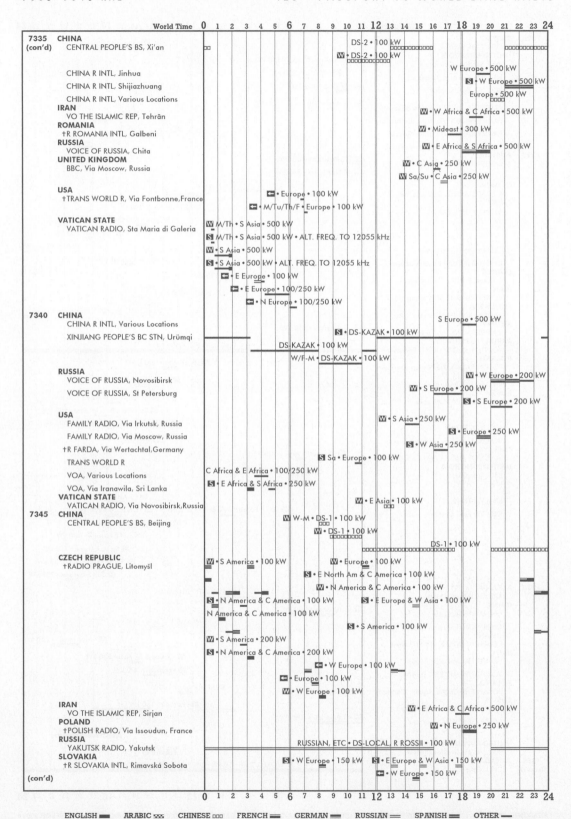

World Time 0 1 2 3 4 5 6 7 8 9 10 11 12 13 14 15 16 17 18 19 20 21 22 23 24

kHz	Country / Station	Schedule
7335 (con'd)	**CHINA**	
	CENTRAL PEOPLE'S BS, Xi'an	DS-2 • 100 kW
		[W] • DS-2 • 100 kW
	CHINA R INTL, Jinhua	W Europe • 500 kW
	CHINA R INTL, Shijiazhuang	[S] • W Europe • 500 kW
	CHINA R INTL, Various Locations	Europe • 500 kW
	IRAN	
	VO THE ISLAMIC REP, Tehrān	[W] • W Africa & C Africa • 500 kW
	ROMANIA	
	†R ROMANIA INTL, Galbeni	[W] • Mideast • 300 kW
	RUSSIA	
	VOICE OF RUSSIA, Chita	[W] • E Africa & S Africa • 500 kW
	UNITED KINGDOM	
	BBC, Via Moscow, Russia	[W] • C Asia • 250 kW
		[W] Sa/Su • C Asia • 250 kW
	USA	
	†TRANS WORLD R, Via Fontbonne,France	[←] • Europe • 100 kW
		[←] • M/Tu/Th/F • Europe • 100 kW
	VATICAN STATE	
	VATICAN RADIO, Sta Maria di Galeria	[W] M/Th • S Asia • 500 kW
		[S] M/Th • S Asia • 500 kW • ALT. FREQ. TO 12055 kHz
		[W] • S Asia • 500 kW
		[S] • S Asia • 500 kW • ALT. FREQ. TO 12055 kHz
		[←] • E Europe • 100 kW
		[←] • E Europe • 100/250 kW
		[←] • N Europe • 100/250 kW
7340	**CHINA**	
	CHINA R INTL, Various Locations	S Europe • 500 kW
	XINJIANG PEOPLE'S BC STN, Urümqi	[S] • DS-KAZAK • 100 kW
		DS-KAZAK • 100 kW
		W/F-M • DS-KAZAK • 100 kW
	RUSSIA	
	VOICE OF RUSSIA, Novosibirsk	[W] • W Europe • 200 kW
	VOICE OF RUSSIA, St Petersburg	[W] • S Europe • 200 kW
		[S] • S Europe • 200 kW
	USA	
	FAMILY RADIO, Via Irkutsk, Russia	[W] • S Asia • 250 kW
	FAMILY RADIO, Via Moscow, Russia	[S] • Europe • 250 kW
	†R FARDA, Via Wertachtal,Germany	[S] • W Asia • 250 kW
	TRANS WORLD R	[S] Sa • Europe • 100 kW
	VOA, Various Locations	C Africa & E Africa • 100/250 kW
	VOA, Via Iranawila, Sri Lanka	[S] • E Africa & S Africa • 250 kW
	VATICAN STATE	
	VATICAN RADIO, Via Novosibirsk,Russia	[W] • E Asia • 100 kW
7345	**CHINA**	
	CENTRAL PEOPLE'S BS, Beijing	[W] W-M • DS-1 • 100 kW
		[W] • DS-1 • 100 kW
		DS-1 • 100 kW
	CZECH REPUBLIC	
	†RADIO PRAGUE, Litomyšl	[W] • S America • 100 kW
		[W] • Europe • 100 kW
		[S] • E North Am & C America • 100 kW
		[W] • N America & C America • 100 kW
		[S] • N America & C America • 100 kW
		[S] • E Europe & W Asia • 100 kW
		N America & C America • 100 kW
		[S] • S America • 100 kW
		[W] • S America • 200 kW
		[S] • N America & C America • 200 kW
		[←] • W Europe • 100 kW
		[←] • Europe • 100 kW
		[W] • W Europe • 100 kW
	IRAN	
	VO THE ISLAMIC REP, Sirjan	[W] • E Africa & C Africa • 500 kW
	POLAND	
	†POLISH RADIO, Via Issoudun, France	[W] • N Europe • 250 kW
	RUSSIA	
	YAKUTSK RADIO, Yakutsk	RUSSIAN, ETC • DS-LOCAL/R ROSSII • 100 kW
	SLOVAKIA	
	†R SLOVAKIA INTL, Rimavská Sobota	[S] • W Europe • 150 kW
		[S] • E Europe & W Asia • 150 kW
		[←] • W Europe • 150 kW
(con'd)		

0 1 2 3 4 5 6 7 8 9 10 11 12 13 14 15 16 17 18 19 20 21 22 23 24

ENGLISH ARABIC CHINESE FRENCH GERMAN RUSSIAN SPANISH OTHER

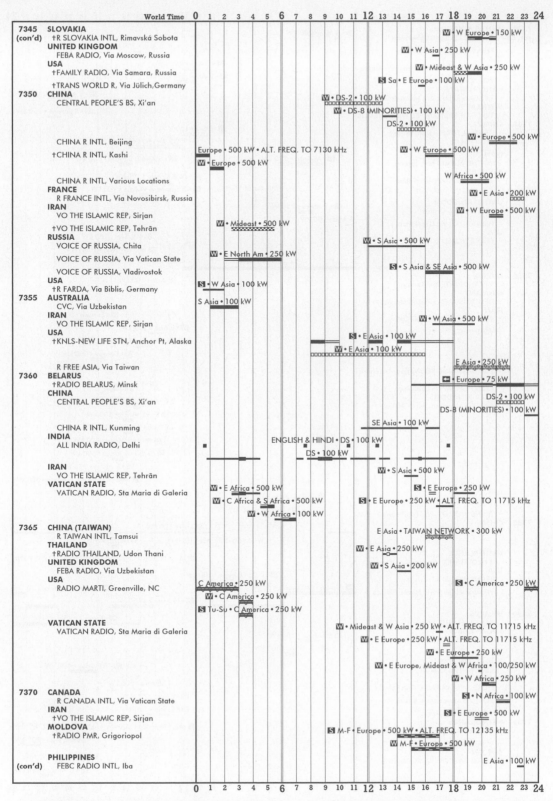

World Time 0 1 2 3 4 5 6 7 8 9 10 11 12 13 14 15 16 17 18 19 20 21 22 23 24

kHz	Country / Station	Schedule
7345 (con'd)	**SLOVAKIA**	
	†R SLOVAKIA INTL, Rimavská Sobota	W • W Europe • 150 kW
	UNITED KINGDOM	
	FEBA RADIO, Via Moscow, Russia	W • W Asia • 250 kW
	USA	
	†FAMILY RADIO, Via Samara, Russia	W • Mideast & W Asia • 250 kW
	†TRANS WORLD R, Via Jülich, Germany	S Sa • E Europe • 100 kW
7350	**CHINA**	
	CENTRAL PEOPLE'S BS, Xi'an	W • DS-2 • 100 kW W • DS-8 (MINORITIES) • 100 kW DS-2 • 100 kW
	CHINA R INTL, Beijing	W • Europe • 500 kW
	†CHINA R INTL, Kashi	Europe • 500 kW • ALT. FREQ. TO 7130 kHz W • W Europe • 500 kW W • Europe • 500 kW
	CHINA R INTL, Various Locations	W Africa • 500 kW
	FRANCE	
	R FRANCE INTL, Via Novosibirsk, Russia	W • E Asia • 200 kW
	IRAN	
	VO THE ISLAMIC REP, Sirjan	W • W Europe • 500 kW
	†VO THE ISLAMIC REP, Tehrān	W • Mideast • 500 kW
	RUSSIA	
	VOICE OF RUSSIA, Chita	W • S Asia • 500 kW
	VOICE OF RUSSIA, Via Vatican State	W • E North Am • 250 kW
	VOICE OF RUSSIA, Vladivostok	S • S Asia & SE Asia • 500 kW
	USA	
	†R FARDA, Via Biblis, Germany	S • W Asia • 100 kW
7355	**AUSTRALIA**	
	CVC, Via Uzbekistan	S Asia • 100 kW
	IRAN	
	VO THE ISLAMIC REP, Sirjan	W • W Asia • 500 kW
	USA	
	†KNLS-NEW LIFE STN, Anchor Pt, Alaska	S • E Asia • 100 kW W • E Asia • 100 kW
	R FREE ASIA, Via Taiwan	E Asia • 250 kW
7360	**BELARUS**	
	†RADIO BELARUS, Minsk	⬅ • Europe • 75 kW
	CHINA	
	CENTRAL PEOPLE'S BS, Xi'an	DS-2 • 100 kW DS-8 (MINORITIES) • 100 kW
	CHINA R INTL, Kunming	SE Asia • 100 kW
	INDIA	
	ALL INDIA RADIO, Delhi	ENGLISH & HINDI • DS • 100 kW DS • 100 kW
	IRAN	
	VO THE ISLAMIC REP, Tehrān	W • S Asia • 500 kW
	VATICAN STATE	
	VATICAN RADIO, Sta Maria di Galeria	W • E Africa • 500 kW S • E Europe • 250 kW W • C Africa & S Africa • 500 kW S • E Europe • 250 kW • ALT. FREQ. TO 11715 kHz W • W Africa • 100 kW
7365	**CHINA (TAIWAN)**	
	R TAIWAN INTL, Tamsui	E Asia • TAIWAN NETWORK • 300 kW
	THAILAND	
	†RADIO THAILAND, Udon Thani	W • E Asia • 250 kW
	UNITED KINGDOM	
	FEBA RADIO, Via Uzbekistan	W • S Asia • 200 kW
	USA	
	RADIO MARTI, Greenville, NC	C America • 250 kW S • C America • 250 kW W • C America • 250 kW S Tu-Su • C America • 250 kW
	VATICAN STATE	
	VATICAN RADIO, Sta Maria di Galeria	W • Mideast & W Asia • 250 kW • ALT. FREQ. TO 11715 kHz W • E Europe • 250 kW • ALT. FREQ. TO 11715 kHz W • E Europe • 250 kW W • E Europe, Mideast & W Africa • 100/250 kW W • W Africa • 250 kW
7370	**CANADA**	
	R CANADA INTL, Via Vatican State	S • N Africa • 100 kW
	IRAN	
	†VO THE ISLAMIC REP, Sirjan	S • E Europe • 500 kW
	MOLDOVA	
	†RADIO PMR, Grigoriopol	S M-F • Europe • 500 kW • ALT. FREQ. TO 12135 kHz W M-F • Europe • 500 kW
(con'd)	**PHILIPPINES**	
	FEBC RADIO INTL, Iba	E Asia • 100 kW

0 1 2 3 4 5 6 7 8 9 10 11 12 13 14 15 16 17 18 19 20 21 22 23 24

SEASONAL S OR W   1-HR TIMESHIFT MIDYEAR ⬅ OR ➡   JAMMING / OR /\   EARLIEST HEARD ◁   LATEST HEARD ▷   NEW FOR 2009 †

World Time 0 1 2 3 4 5 6 7 8 9 10 11 12 13 14 15 16 17 18 19 20 21 22 23 24

kHz	Country / Station	Schedule
7370 (con'd)	**UNITED KINGDOM**	
	BBC, Via Tashkent, Uzbekistan	W • S Asia • 200 kW
	FEBA RADIO, Via Uzbekistan	S Asia • 100 kW
	USA	
	†KNLS-NEW LIFE STN, Anchor Pt, Alaska	S • E Asia • 100 kW
	VOA, Greenville, NC	S • C America • 250 kW
	VATICAN STATE	
	VATICAN RADIO, Sta Maria di Galeria	⇐ • E Asia • 250/500 kW
	VIETNAM	
	†VOICE OF VIETNAM, Via Woofferton,UK	W • S Europe • 250 kW
7375	**CHINA**	
	CENTRAL PEOPLE'S BS, Beijing	W • DS-2 • 150 kW
		DS-2 • 150 kW
	IRAN	
	†VO THE ISLAMIC REP, Tehrān	S • Mideast • 500 kW
		S • S Asia & SE Asia • 500 kW
	PAKISTAN	
	RADIO PAKISTAN, Islamabad	W Asia & C Asia • 100 kW
		W • E Europe & W Asia • 100 kW
	UNITED KINGDOM	
	†BBC, Via Zyyi, Cyprus	W • E Africa • 250 kW
	FEBA RADIO, Via Uzbekistan	S Asia • 100 kW
	USA	
	TRANS WORLD R	W • W Asia • 100 kW
		W M-F • W Asia • 100 kW
	UNIVERSITY NET'K, Via Costa Rica	S America • 40 kW
7380	**FRANCE**	
	†R FRANCE INTL, Via Taiwan	SE Asia • 100 kW
	GERMANY	
	†DEUTSCHE WELLE, Via Madagascar	SE Asia • 250 kW
	IRAN	
	VO THE ISLAMIC REP, Sirjan	W • Europe • 500 kW
	†VO THE ISLAMIC REP, Tehrān	W • E Asia • 500 kW
		W • S Asia • 500 kW
		W • Europe • 500 kW
	†VO THE ISLAMIC REP, Various Locations	S Europe • 500 kW
	POLAND	
	†RADIO RACJA, Via Lithuania	W • E Europe • 100 kW
	UNITED KINGDOM	
	†BBC, Via Meyerton, South Africa	S • E Africa • 500 kW
		S Sa • E Africa • 500 kW
		S Su-F • E Africa • 500 kW
		S M-F • E Africa • 500 kW
		S Sa/Su • E Africa • 500 kW
		S • E Africa • 250 kW
		S M-F • C Africa & S Africa • 500 kW
	USA	
	TRANS WORLD R	S M-F • Europe • 100 kW
	TRANS WORLD R, Via Fontbonne,France	⇐ • Europe • 100 kW
7385	**CHINA**	
	XIZANG PBS, Lhasa	DS-TIBETAN • 100 kW
		W-M • DS-TIBETAN • 100 kW
		DS • 100 kW
	NETHERLANDS	
	†R NEDERLAND, Via Issoudun, France	W M-F • N Africa • 500 kW • ALT. FREQ. TO 7395 kHz
	USA	
	TRANS WORLD R	S Tu-Sa • Europe • 100 kW
	WRMI-R MIAMI INTL, Miami, Florida	⇐ • Tu-Sa • N America • 50 kW
		⇐ • M-F • N America • 50 kW
		⇐ • N America • 50 kW
7390	**BELARUS**	
	RADIO BELARUS, Minsk	⇐ • Europe • 75/150 kW
	SOUTH AFRICA	
	†CHANNEL AFRICA, Meyerton	W • E Africa • 500 kW
		S • C Africa • 500 kW
	UNITED KINGDOM	
	†BBC, Via Zyyi, Cyprus	W • E Europe • 300 kW
	USA	
	LITTLE SAIGON RADIO, Via Taiwan	SE Asia • 100 kW
	VOA, Via Novosibirsk, Russia	W • E Asia • 200 kW
	VOA, Via Philippines	W • E Asia • 250 kW
7395	**NETHERLANDS**	
	†R NEDERLAND, Via Issoudun, France	W M-F • N Africa • 500 kW • ALT. FREQ. TO 7385 kHz
	†R NEDERLAND, Via Philippines	S • SE Asia • 250 kW
	SWEDEN	
	†RADIO SWEDEN, Via Madagascar	S • E Africa • 250 kW
		W • C Africa • 250 kW
(con'd)		

World Time 0 1 2 3 4 5 6 7 8 9 10 11 12 13 14 15 16 17 18 19 20 21 22 23 24

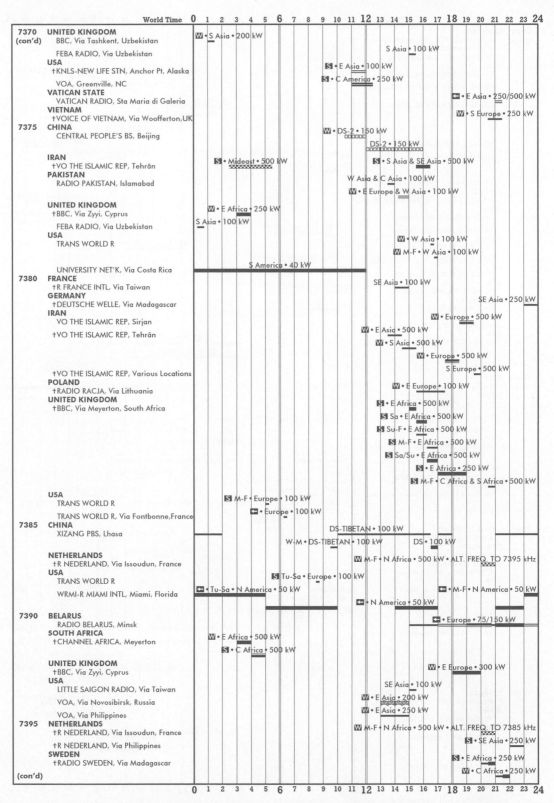

ENGLISH ▬ ARABIC ▩ CHINESE ▫▫▫ FRENCH ═ GERMAN ═ RUSSIAN ═ SPANISH ═ OTHER —

World Time 0 1 2 3 4 5 6 7 8 9 10 11 12 13 14 15 16 17 18 19 20 21 22 23 24

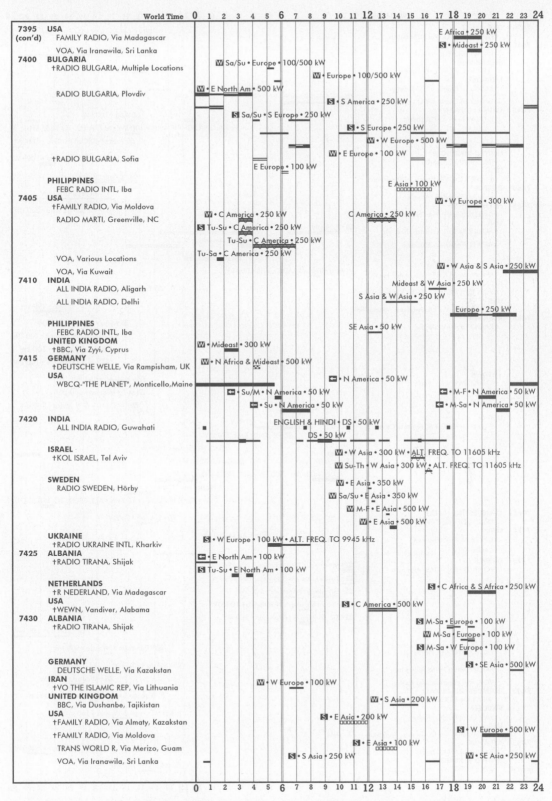

7395 (con'd) **USA**
FAMILY RADIO, Via Madagascar — E Africa • 250 kW
VOA, Via Iranawila, Sri Lanka — S • Mideast • 250 kW

7400 **BULGARIA**
†RADIO BULGARIA, Multiple Locations — W Sa/Su • Europe • 100/500 kW; W • Europe • 100/500 kW
RADIO BULGARIA, Plovdiv — W • E North Am • 500 kW; S • S America • 250 kW; S Sa/Su • S Europe • 250 kW; S • S Europe • 250 kW; W • W Europe • 500 kW; W • E Europe • 100 kW
†RADIO BULGARIA, Sofia — E Europe • 100 kW

PHILIPPINES
FEBC RADIO INTL, Iba — E Asia • 100 kW

7405 **USA**
†FAMILY RADIO, Via Moldova — W • W Europe • 300 kW
RADIO MARTI, Greenville, NC — W • C America • 250 kW; C America • 250 kW; S Tu-Su • C America • 250 kW; Tu-Su • C America • 250 kW; Tu-Sa • C America • 250 kW
VOA, Various Locations
VOA, Via Kuwait — W • W Asia & S Asia • 250 kW

7410 **INDIA**
ALL INDIA RADIO, Aligarh — Mideast & W Asia • 250 kW
ALL INDIA RADIO, Delhi — S Asia & W Asia • 250 kW; Europe • 250 kW

PHILIPPINES
FEBC RADIO INTL, Iba — SE Asia • 50 kW

UNITED KINGDOM
†BBC, Via Zyyi, Cyprus — W • Mideast • 300 kW

7415 **GERMANY**
†DEUTSCHE WELLE, Via Rampisham, UK — W • N Africa & Mideast • 500 kW

USA
WBCQ-"THE PLANET", Monticello, Maine — ⬅ • N America • 50 kW; ⬅ • Su/M • N America • 50 kW; ⬅ • Su • N America • 50 kW; ⬅ • M-F • N America • 50 kW; ⬅ • M-Sa • N America • 50 kW

7420 **INDIA**
ALL INDIA RADIO, Guwahati — ENGLISH & HINDI • DS • 50 kW; DS • 50 kW

ISRAEL
†KOL ISRAEL, Tel Aviv — W • W Asia • 300 kW • ALT. FREQ. TO 11605 kHz; W Su-Th • W Asia • 300 kW • ALT. FREQ. TO 11605 kHz

SWEDEN
RADIO SWEDEN, Hörby — W • E Asia • 350 kW; W Sa/Su • E Asia • 350 kW; W M-F • E Asia • 500 kW; W • E Asia • 500 kW

UKRAINE
†RADIO UKRAINE INTL, Kharkiv — S • W Europe • 100 kW • ALT. FREQ. TO 9945 kHz

7425 **ALBANIA**
†RADIO TIRANA, Shijak — ⬅ • E North Am • 100 kW; S Tu-Su • E North Am • 100 kW

NETHERLANDS
†R NEDERLAND, Via Madagascar — S • C Africa & S Africa • 250 kW

USA
†WEWN, Vandiver, Alabama — S • C America • 500 kW

7430 **ALBANIA**
†RADIO TIRANA, Shijak — S M-Sa • Europe • 100 kW; W M-Sa • Europe • 100 kW; S M-Sa • W Europe • 100 kW

GERMANY
DEUTSCHE WELLE, Via Kazakstan — S • SE Asia • 500 kW

IRAN
†VO THE ISLAMIC REP, Via Lithuania — W • W Europe • 100 kW

UNITED KINGDOM
BBC, Via Dushanbe, Tajikistan — W • S Asia • 200 kW

USA
†FAMILY RADIO, Via Almaty, Kazakstan — S • E Asia • 200 kW
†FAMILY RADIO, Via Moldova — S • W Europe • 500 kW
TRANS WORLD R, Via Merizo, Guam — S • E Asia • 100 kW
VOA, Via Iranawila, Sri Lanka — S • S Asia • 250 kW; W • SE Asia • 250 kW

World Time 0 1 2 3 4 5 6 7 8 9 10 11 12 13 14 15 16 17 18 19 20 21 22 23 24

World Time 0 1 2 3 4 5 6 7 8 9 10 11 12 13 14 15 16 17 18 19 20 21 22 23 24

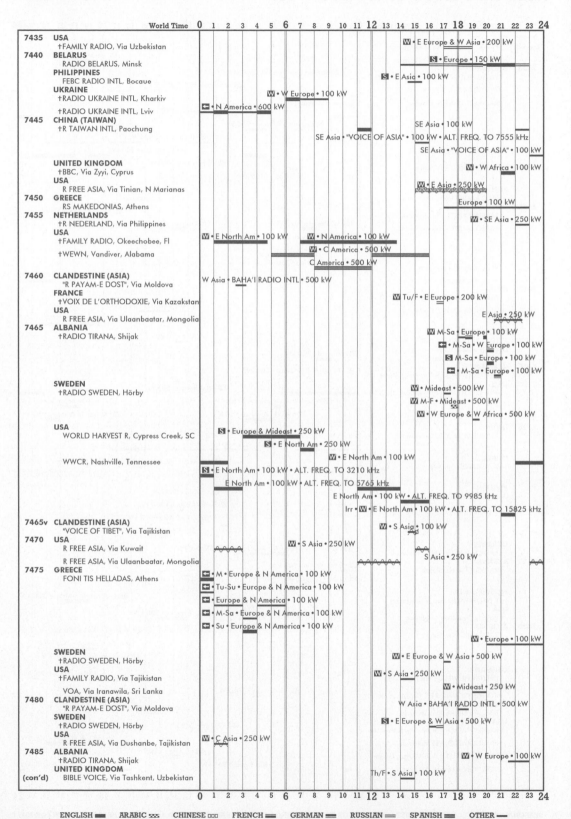

kHz	Country / Station	Schedule
7435	**USA**	
	†FAMILY RADIO, Via Uzbekistan	[W] • E Europe & W Asia • 200 kW
7440	**BELARUS**	
	RADIO BELARUS, Minsk	[S] • Europe • 150 kW
	PHILIPPINES	
	FEBC RADIO INTL, Bocaue	[S] • E Asia • 100 kW
	UKRAINE	
	†RADIO UKRAINE INTL, Kharkiv	[W] • W Europe • 100 kW
	†RADIO UKRAINE INTL, Lviv	← • N America • 600 kW
7445	**CHINA (TAIWAN)**	
	†R TAIWAN INTL, Paochung	SE Asia • 100 kW
		SE Asia • "VOICE OF ASIA" • 100 kW • ALT. FREQ. TO 7555 kHz
		SE Asia • "VOICE OF ASIA" • 100 kW
	UNITED KINGDOM	
	†BBC, Via Zyyi, Cyprus	[W] • W Africa • 100 kW
	USA	
	R FREE ASIA, Via Tinian, N Marianas	[W] • E Asia • 250 kW
7450	**GREECE**	
	RS MAKEDONIAS, Athens	Europe • 100 kW
7455	**NETHERLANDS**	
	†R NEDERLAND, Via Philippines	[W] • SE Asia • 250 kW
	USA	
	†FAMILY RADIO, Okeechobee, Fl	[W] • E North Am • 100 kW; [W] • N America • 100 kW
	†WEWN, Vandiver, Alabama	[W] • C America • 500 kW
		C America • 500 kW
7460	**CLANDESTINE (ASIA)**	
	"R PAYAM-E DOST", Via Moldova	W Asia • BAHA'I RADIO INTL • 500 kW
	FRANCE	
	†VOIX DE L'ORTHODOXIE, Via Kazakstan	[W] Tu/F • E Europe • 200 kW
	USA	
	R FREE ASIA, Via Ulaanbaatar, Mongolia	E Asia • 250 kW
7465	**ALBANIA**	
	†RADIO TIRANA, Shijak	[W] M-Sa • Europe • 100 kW
		← • M-Sa • W Europe • 100 kW
		[S] M-Sa • Europe • 100 kW
		← • M-Sa • Europe • 100 kW
	SWEDEN	
	†RADIO SWEDEN, Hörby	[W] • Mideast • 500 kW
		[W] M-F • Mideast • 500 kW
		[W] • W Europe & W Africa • 500 kW
	USA	
	WORLD HARVEST R, Cypress Creek, SC	[S] • Europe & Mideast • 250 kW
		[S] • E North Am • 250 kW
		[W] • E North Am • 100 kW
	WWCR, Nashville, Tennessee	[S] • E North Am • 100 kW • ALT. FREQ. TO 3210 kHz
		E North Am • 100 kW • ALT. FREQ. TO 5765 kHz
		E North Am • 100 kW • ALT. FREQ. TO 9985 kHz
		Irr • [W] • E North Am • 100 kW • ALT. FREQ. TO 15825 kHz
7465v	**CLANDESTINE (ASIA)**	
	"VOICE OF TIBET", Via Tajikistan	[W] • S Asia • 100 kW
7470	**USA**	
	R FREE ASIA, Via Kuwait	[W] • S Asia • 250 kW
	R FREE ASIA, Via Ulaanbaatar, Mongolia	S Asia • 250 kW
7475	**GREECE**	
	FONI TIS HELLADAS, Athens	← • M • Europe & N America • 100 kW
		← • Tu-Su • Europe & N America • 100 kW
		← • Europe & N America • 100 kW
		← • M-Sa • Europe & N America • 100 kW
		← • Su • Europe & N America • 100 kW
		[W] • Europe • 100 kW
	SWEDEN	
	†RADIO SWEDEN, Hörby	[W] • E Europe & W Asia • 500 kW
	USA	
	†FAMILY RADIO, Via Tajikistan	[W] • S Asia • 250 kW
	VOA, Via Iranawila, Sri Lanka	[W] • Mideast • 250 kW
7480	**CLANDESTINE (ASIA)**	
	"R PAYAM-E DOST", Via Moldova	W Asia • BAHA'I RADIO INTL • 500 kW
	SWEDEN	
	†RADIO SWEDEN, Hörby	[S] • E Europe & W Asia • 500 kW
	USA	
	R FREE ASIA, Via Dushanbe, Tajikistan	[W] • C Asia • 250 kW
7485	**ALBANIA**	
	†RADIO TIRANA, Shijak	[W] • W Europe • 100 kW
	UNITED KINGDOM	
(con'd)	BIBLE VOICE, Via Tashkent, Uzbekistan	Th/F • S Asia • 100 kW

0 1 2 3 4 5 6 7 8 9 10 11 12 13 14 15 16 17 18 19 20 21 22 23 24

ENGLISH ARABIC CHINESE FRENCH GERMAN RUSSIAN SPANISH OTHER

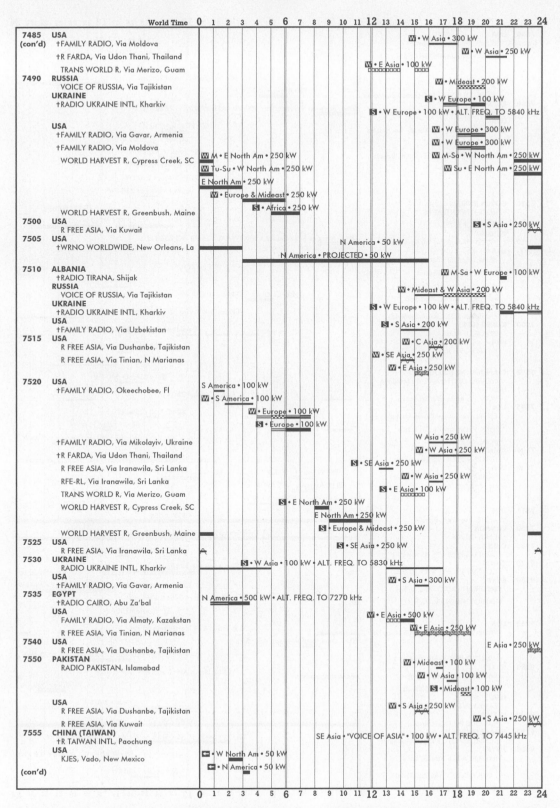

kHz	Country / Station	Schedule (World Time 0–24)
7485 (con'd)	**USA**	
	†FAMILY RADIO, Via Moldova	W • W Asia • 300 kW
	†R FARDA, Via Udon Thani, Thailand	W • W Asia • 250 kW
	TRANS WORLD R, Via Merizo, Guam	W • E Asia • 100 kW
7490	**RUSSIA**	
	VOICE OF RUSSIA, Via Tajikistan	W • Mideast • 200 kW
	UKRAINE	
	†RADIO UKRAINE INTL, Kharkiv	S • W Europe • 100 kW
		S • W Europe • 100 kW • ALT. FREQ. TO 5840 kHz
	USA	
	†FAMILY RADIO, Via Gavar, Armenia	W • W Europe • 300 kW
	†FAMILY RADIO, Via Moldova	W • W Europe • 300 kW
	WORLD HARVEST R, Cypress Creek, SC	W M • E North Am • 250 kW
		W Tu-Su • W North Am • 250 kW
		E North Am • 250 kW
		W • Europe & Mideast • 250 kW
		W M-Sa • W North Am • 250 kW
		W Su • E North Am • 250 kW
	WORLD HARVEST R, Greenbush, Maine	S • Africa • 250 kW
7500	**USA**	
	R FREE ASIA, Via Kuwait	S • S Asia • 250 kW
7505	**USA**	
	†WRNO WORLDWIDE, New Orleans, La	N America • 50 kW
		N America • PROJECTED • 50 kW
7510	**ALBANIA**	
	†RADIO TIRANA, Shijak	W M-Sa • W Europe • 100 kW
	RUSSIA	
	VOICE OF RUSSIA, Via Tajikistan	W • Mideast & W Asia • 200 kW
	UKRAINE	
	†RADIO UKRAINE INTL, Kharkiv	S • W Europe • 100 kW • ALT. FREQ. TO 5840 kHz
	USA	
	†FAMILY RADIO, Via Uzbekistan	S • S Asia • 200 kW
7515	**USA**	
	R FREE ASIA, Via Dushanbe, Tajikistan	W • C Asia • 200 kW
	R FREE ASIA, Via Tinian, N Marianas	W • SE Asia • 250 kW
		W • E Asia • 250 kW
7520	**USA**	
	†FAMILY RADIO, Okeechobee, Fl	S America • 100 kW
		W • S America • 100 kW
		W • Europe • 100 kW
		S • Europe • 100 kW
	†FAMILY RADIO, Via Mikolayiv, Ukraine	W Asia • 250 kW
	†R FARDA, Via Udon Thani, Thailand	W • W Asia • 250 kW
	R FREE ASIA, Via Iranawila, Sri Lanka	S • SE Asia • 250 kW
	RFE-RL, Via Iranawila, Sri Lanka	W • W Asia • 250 kW
	TRANS WORLD R, Via Merizo, Guam	S • E Asia • 100 kW
	WORLD HARVEST R, Cypress Creek, SC	S • E North Am • 250 kW
		E North Am • 250 kW
		S • Europe & Mideast • 250 kW
	WORLD HARVEST R, Greenbush, Maine	
7525	**USA**	
	R FREE ASIA, Via Iranawila, Sri Lanka	S • SE Asia • 250 kW
7530	**UKRAINE**	
	RADIO UKRAINE INTL, Kharkiv	S • W Asia • 100 kW • ALT. FREQ. TO 5830 kHz
	USA	
	†FAMILY RADIO, Via Gavar, Armenia	W • S Asia • 300 kW
7535	**EGYPT**	
	†RADIO CAIRO, Abu Za'bal	N America • 500 kW • ALT. FREQ. TO 7270 kHz
	USA	
	FAMILY RADIO, Via Almaty, Kazakstan	W • E Asia • 500 kW
	R FREE ASIA, Via Tinian, N Marianas	W • E Asia • 250 kW
7540	**USA**	
	R FREE ASIA, Via Dushanbe, Tajikistan	E Asia • 250 kW
7550	**PAKISTAN**	
	RADIO PAKISTAN, Islamabad	W • Mideast • 100 kW
		W • W Asia • 100 kW
		S • Mideast • 100 kW
	USA	
	R FREE ASIA, Via Dushanbe, Tajikistan	W • S Asia • 250 kW
	R FREE ASIA, Via Kuwait	W • S Asia • 250 kW
7555	**CHINA (TAIWAN)**	
	†R TAIWAN INTL, Paochung	SE Asia • "VOICE OF ASIA" • 100 kW • ALT. FREQ. TO 7445 kHz
	USA	
	KJES, Vado, New Mexico	⬅ • W North Am • 50 kW
		⬅ • N America • 50 kW
(con'd)		

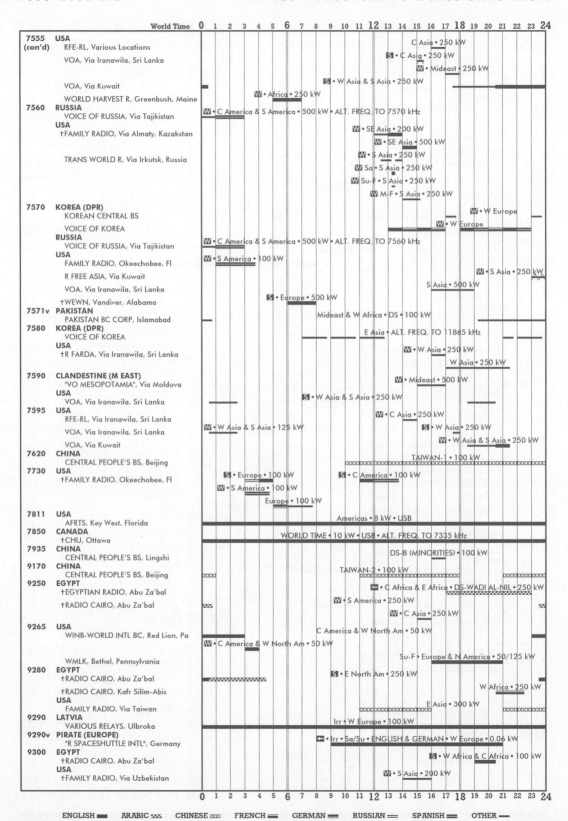

World Time 0 1 2 3 4 5 6 7 8 9 10 11 12 13 14 15 16 17 18 19 20 21 22 23 24

kHz	Country / Station	Schedule
7555 (con'd)	**USA**	
	RFE-RL, Various Locations	C Asia • 250 kW
	VOA, Via Iranawila, Sri Lanka	S • C Asia • 250 kW
		W • Mideast • 250 kW
	VOA, Via Kuwait	S • W Asia & S Asia • 250 kW
	WORLD HARVEST R, Greenbush, Maine	W • Africa • 250 kW
7560	**RUSSIA**	
	VOICE OF RUSSIA, Via Tajikistan	W • C America & S America • 500 kW • ALT. FREQ. TO 7570 kHz
	USA	
	†FAMILY RADIO, Via Almaty, Kazakstan	W • SE Asia • 200 kW
		W • SE Asia • 500 kW
	TRANS WORLD R, Via Irkutsk, Russia	W • S Asia • 250 kW
		W Sa • S Asia • 250 kW
		W Su-F • S Asia • 250 kW
		W M-F • S Asia • 250 kW
7570	**KOREA (DPR)**	
	KOREAN CENTRAL BS	W • W Europe
	VOICE OF KOREA	W • W Europe
	RUSSIA	
	VOICE OF RUSSIA, Via Tajikistan	W • C America & S America • 500 kW • ALT. FREQ. TO 7560 kHz
	USA	
	FAMILY RADIO, Okeechobee, Fl	W • S America • 100 kW
	R FREE ASIA, Via Kuwait	W • S Asia • 250 kW
	VOA, Via Iranawila, Sri Lanka	S Asia • 500 kW
	†WEWN, Vandiver, Alabama	S • Europe • 500 kW
7571v	**PAKISTAN**	
	PAKISTAN BC CORP, Islamabad	Mideast & W Africa • DS • 100 kW
7580	**KOREA (DPR)**	
	VOICE OF KOREA	E Asia • ALT. FREQ. TO 11865 kHz
	USA	
	†R FARDA, Via Iranawila, Sri Lanka	W • W Asia • 250 kW
		W Asia • 250 kW
7590	**CLANDESTINE (M EAST)**	
	"VO MESOPOTAMIA", Via Moldova	W • Mideast • 500 kW
	USA	
	VOA, Via Iranawila, Sri Lanka	S • W Asia & S Asia • 250 kW
7595	**USA**	
	RFE-RL, Via Iranawila, Sri Lanka	W • C Asia • 250 kW
	VOA, Via Iranawila, Sri Lanka	W • W Asia & S Asia • 125 kW
		S • W Asia • 250 kW
	VOA, Via Kuwait	W • W Asia & S Asia • 250 kW
7620	**CHINA**	
	CENTRAL PEOPLE'S BS, Beijing	TAIWAN-1 • 100 kW
7730	**USA**	
	†FAMILY RADIO, Okeechobee, Fl	S • Europe • 100 kW
		S • C America • 100 kW
		W • S America • 100 kW
		Europe • 100 kW
7811	**USA**	
	AFRTS, Key West, Florida	Americas • 8 kW • USB
7850	**CANADA**	
	†CHU, Ottawa	WORLD TIME • 10 kW • USB • ALT. FREQ. TO 7335 kHz
7935	**CHINA**	
	CENTRAL PEOPLE'S BS, Lingshi	DS-8 (MINORITIES) • 100 kW
9170	**CHINA**	
	CENTRAL PEOPLE'S BS, Beijing	TAIWAN-2 • 100 kW
9250	**EGYPT**	
	†EGYPTIAN RADIO, Abu Za'bal	← • C Africa & E Africa • DS-WADI AL-NIL • 250 kW
	†RADIO CAIRO, Abu Za'bal	W • S America • 250 kW
		W • C Asia • 250 kW
9265	**USA**	
	WINB-WORLD INTL BC, Red Lion, Pa	C America & W North Am • 50 kW
		W • C America & W North Am • 50 kW
	WMLK, Bethel, Pennsylvania	Su-F • Europe & N America • 50/125 kW
9280	**EGYPT**	
	†RADIO CAIRO, Abu Za'bal	S • E North Am • 250 kW
	†RADIO CAIRO, Kafr Silîm-Abis	W Africa • 250 kW
	USA	
	FAMILY RADIO, Via Taiwan	E Asia • 300 kW
9290	**LATVIA**	
	VARIOUS RELAYS, Ulbroka	Irr • W Europe • 100 kW
9290v	**PIRATE (EUROPE)**	
	"R SPACESHUTTLE INTL", Germany	← • Irr • Sa/Su • ENGLISH & GERMAN • W Europe • 0.06 kW
9300	**EGYPT**	
	†RADIO CAIRO, Abu Za'bal	S • W Africa & C Africa • 100 kW
	USA	
	†FAMILY RADIO, Via Uzbekistan	W • S Asia • 200 kW

0 1 2 3 4 5 6 7 8 9 10 11 12 13 14 15 16 17 18 19 20 21 22 23 24

ENGLISH ARABIC CHINESE FRENCH GERMAN RUSSIAN SPANISH OTHER

World Time 0 1 2 3 4 5 6 7 8 9 10 11 12 13 14 15 16 17 18 19 20 21 22 23 24

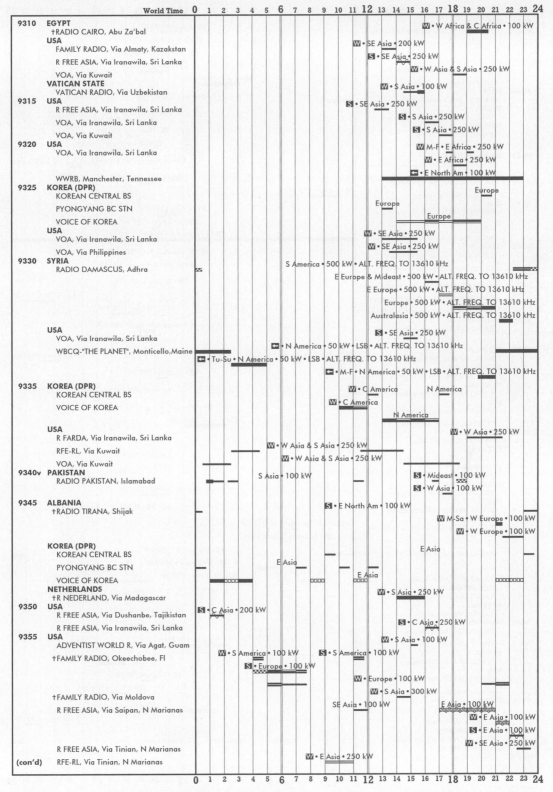

kHz	Country / Station	Schedule notes
9310	**EGYPT**	
	†RADIO CAIRO, Abu Za'bal	W • W Africa & C Africa • 100 kW
	USA	
	FAMILY RADIO, Via Almaty, Kazakstan	W • SE Asia • 200 kW
	R FREE ASIA, Via Iranawila, Sri Lanka	S • SE Asia • 250 kW
	VOA, Via Kuwait	W • W Asia & S Asia • 250 kW
	VATICAN STATE	
	VATICAN RADIO, Via Uzbekistan	W • S Asia • 100 kW
9315	**USA**	
	R FREE ASIA, Via Iranawila, Sri Lanka	S • SE Asia • 250 kW
	VOA, Via Iranawila, Sri Lanka	S • S Asia • 250 kW
	VOA, Via Kuwait	S • S Asia • 250 kW
9320	**USA**	
	VOA, Via Iranawila, Sri Lanka	W M-F • E Africa • 250 kW
		W • E Africa • 250 kW
	WWRB, Manchester, Tennessee	← • E North Am • 100 kW
9325	**KOREA (DPR)**	
	KOREAN CENTRAL BS	Europe
	PYONGYANG BC STN	Europe
	VOICE OF KOREA	Europe
	USA	
	VOA, Via Iranawila, Sri Lanka	W • SE Asia • 250 kW
	VOA, Via Philippines	W • SE Asia • 250 kW
9330	**SYRIA**	
	RADIO DAMASCUS, Adhra	S America • 500 kW • ALT. FREQ. TO 13610 kHz
		E Europe & Mideast • 500 kW • ALT. FREQ. TO 13610 kHz
		E Europe • 500 kW • ALT. FREQ. TO 13610 kHz
		Europe • 500 kW • ALT. FREQ. TO 13610 kHz
		Australasia • 500 kW • ALT. FREQ. TO 13610 kHz
	USA	
	VOA, Via Iranawila, Sri Lanka	S • SE Asia • 250 kW
	WBCQ-"THE PLANET", Monticello, Maine	← • N America • 50 kW • LSB • ALT. FREQ. TO 13610 kHz
		← • Tu-Su • N America • 50 kW • LSB • ALT. FREQ. TO 13610 kHz
		← • M-F • N America • 50 kW • LSB • ALT. FREQ. TO 13610 kHz
9335	**KOREA (DPR)**	
	KOREAN CENTRAL BS	W • C America; N America
	VOICE OF KOREA	W • C America
		N America
	USA	
	R FARDA, Via Iranawila, Sri Lanka	W • W Asia • 250 kW
	RFE-RL, Via Kuwait	W • W Asia & S Asia • 250 kW
	VOA, Via Kuwait	W • W Asia & S Asia • 250 kW
9340v	**PAKISTAN**	
	RADIO PAKISTAN, Islamabad	S Asia • 100 kW
		S • Mideast • 100 kW
		S • W Asia • 100 kW
9345	**ALBANIA**	
	†RADIO TIRANA, Shijak	S • E North Am • 100 kW
		W M-Sa • W Europe • 100 kW
		W • W Europe • 100 kW
	KOREA (DPR)	
	KOREAN CENTRAL BS	E Asia
	PYONGYANG BC STN	E Asia
	VOICE OF KOREA	E Asia
	NETHERLANDS	
	†R NEDERLAND, Via Madagascar	W • S Asia • 250 kW
9350	**USA**	
	R FREE ASIA, Via Dushanbe, Tajikistan	S • C Asia • 200 kW
	R FREE ASIA, Via Iranawila, Sri Lanka	S • C Asia • 250 kW
9355	**USA**	
	ADVENTIST WORLD R, Via Agat, Guam	W • S Asia • 100 kW
	†FAMILY RADIO, Okeechobee, Fl	W • S America • 100 kW; S • S America • 100 kW
		S • Europe • 100 kW
		W • Europe • 100 kW
		W • S Asia • 300 kW
	†FAMILY RADIO, Via Moldova	SE Asia • 100 kW
	R FREE ASIA, Via Saipan, N Marianas	E Asia • 100 kW
		W • E Asia • 100 kW
		S • E Asia • 100 kW
	R FREE ASIA, Via Tinian, N Marianas	W • SE Asia • 250 kW
(con'd)	RFE-RL, Via Tinian, N Marianas	W • E Asia • 250 kW

World Time 0 1 2 3 4 5 6 7 8 9 10 11 12 13 14 15 16 17 18 19 20 21 22 23 24

SEASONAL S OR W   1-HR TIMESHIFT MIDYEAR ← OR →   JAMMING / OR ∧   EARLIEST HEARD ◁   LATEST HEARD ▷   NEW FOR 2009 †

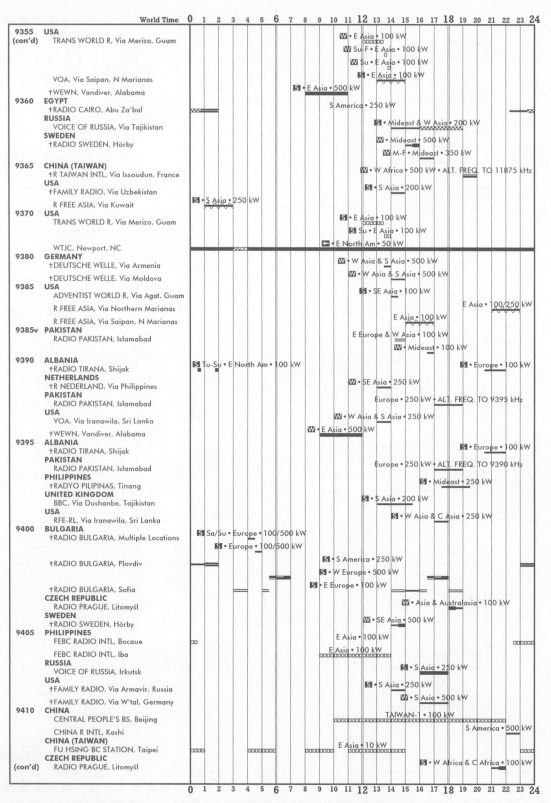

World Time 0 1 2 3 4 5 6 7 8 9 10 11 12 13 14 15 16 17 18 19 20 21 22 23 24

kHz	Country / Station	Schedule
9355 (con'd)	**USA**	
	TRANS WORLD R, Via Merizo, Guam	[W] • E Asia • 100 kW
		[W] Su-F • E Asia • 100 kW
		[W] Su • E Asia • 100 kW
	VOA, Via Saipan, N Marianas	[S] • E Asia • 100 kW
	†WEWN, Vandiver, Alabama	[S] • E Asia • 500 kW
9360	**EGYPT**	
	†RADIO CAIRO, Abu Za'bal	S America • 250 kW
	RUSSIA	
	VOICE OF RUSSIA, Via Tajikistan	[S] • Mideast & W Asia • 200 kW
	SWEDEN	
	†RADIO SWEDEN, Hörby	[W] • Mideast • 500 kW
		[W] M-F • Mideast • 350 kW
9365	**CHINA (TAIWAN)**	
	†R TAIWAN INTL, Via Issoudun, France	[W] • W Africa • 500 kW • ALT. FREQ. TO 11875 kHz
	USA	
	†FAMILY RADIO, Via Uzbekistan	[S] • S Asia • 200 kW
	R FREE ASIA, Via Kuwait	[S] • S Asia • 250 kW
9370	**USA**	
	TRANS WORLD R, Via Merizo, Guam	[S] • E Asia • 100 kW
		[S] Su • E Asia • 100 kW
	WTJC, Newport, NC	[←] • E North Am • 50 kW
9380	**GERMANY**	
	†DEUTSCHE WELLE, Via Armenia	[W] • W Asia & S Asia • 500 kW
	†DEUTSCHE WELLE, Via Moldova	[W] • W Asia & S Asia • 500 kW
9385	**USA**	
	ADVENTIST WORLD R, Via Agat, Guam	[S] • SE Asia • 100 kW
	R FREE ASIA, Via Northern Marianas	E Asia • 100/250 kW
	R FREE ASIA, Via Saipan, N Marianas	E Asia • 100 kW
9385v	**PAKISTAN**	
	RADIO PAKISTAN, Islamabad	E Europe & W Asia • 100 kW
		[W] • Mideast • 100 kW
9390	**ALBANIA**	
	†RADIO TIRANA, Shijak	[S] Tu-Su • E North Am • 100 kW
		[S] • Europe • 100 kW
	NETHERLANDS	
	†R NEDERLAND, Via Philippines	[W] • SE Asia • 250 kW
	PAKISTAN	
	RADIO PAKISTAN, Islamabad	Europe • 250 kW • ALT. FREQ. TO 9395 kHz
	USA	
	VOA, Via Iranawila, Sri Lanka	[W] • W Asia & S Asia • 250 kW
	†WEWN, Vandiver, Alabama	[W] • E Asia • 500 kW
9395	**ALBANIA**	
	†RADIO TIRANA, Shijak	[S] • Europe • 100 kW
	PAKISTAN	
	RADIO PAKISTAN, Islamabad	Europe • 250 kW • ALT. FREQ. TO 9390 kHz
	PHILIPPINES	
	†RADYO PILIPINAS, Tinang	[S] • Mideast • 250 kW
	UNITED KINGDOM	
	BBC, Via Dushanbe, Tajikistan	[S] • S Asia • 200 kW
	USA	
	RFE-RL, Via Iranawila, Sri Lanka	[S] • W Asia & C Asia • 250 kW
9400	**BULGARIA**	
	†RADIO BULGARIA, Multiple Locations	[S] Sa/Su • Europe • 100/500 kW
		[S] • Europe • 100/500 kW
	†RADIO BULGARIA, Plovdiv	[S] • S America • 250 kW
		[S] • W Europe • 500 kW
		[S] • E Europe • 100 kW
	†RADIO BULGARIA, Sofia	
	CZECH REPUBLIC	
	RADIO PRAGUE, Litomyšl	[W] • Asia & Australasia • 100 kW
	SWEDEN	
	†RADIO SWEDEN, Hörby	[W] • SE Asia • 500 kW
9405	**PHILIPPINES**	
	FEBC RADIO INTL, Bocaue	E Asia • 100 kW
	FEBC RADIO INTL, Iba	E Asia • 100 kW
	RUSSIA	
	VOICE OF RUSSIA, Irkutsk	[S] • S Asia • 250 kW
	USA	
	†FAMILY RADIO, Via Armavir, Russia	[S] • S Asia • 250 kW
	†FAMILY RADIO, Via W'tal, Germany	[W] • S Asia • 500 kW
9410	**CHINA**	
	CENTRAL PEOPLE'S BS, Beijing	TAIWAN-1 • 100 kW
	CHINA R INTL, Kashi	S America • 500 kW
	CHINA (TAIWAN)	
	FU HSING BC STATION, Taipei	E Asia • 10 kW
	CZECH REPUBLIC	
(con'd)	RADIO PRAGUE, Litomyšl	[S] • W Africa & C Africa • 100 kW

0 1 2 3 4 5 6 7 8 9 10 11 12 13 14 15 16 17 18 19 20 21 22 23 24

ENGLISH ▬ ARABIC ▭ CHINESE ▫▫▫ FRENCH ═ GERMAN ═ RUSSIAN ═ SPANISH ═ OTHER —

World Time 0 1 2 3 4 5 6 7 8 9 10 11 12 13 14 15 16 17 18 19 20 21 22 23 24

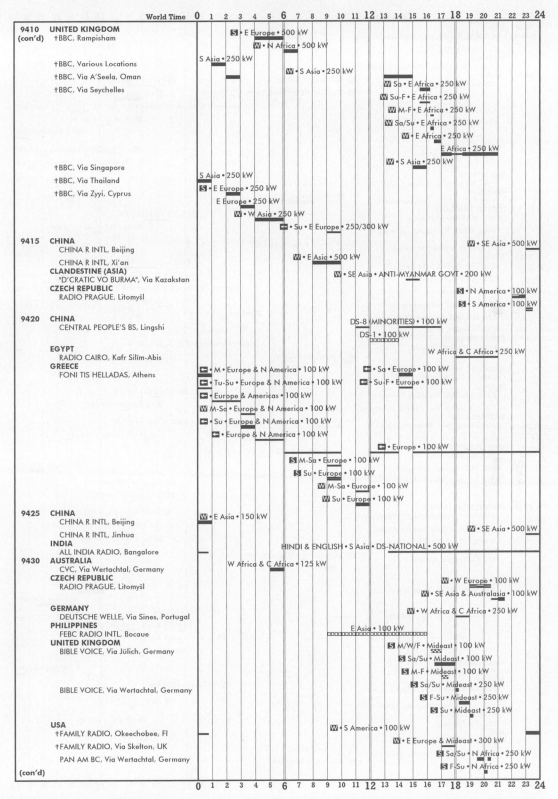

9410 (con'd) UNITED KINGDOM

†BBC, Rampisham
- S • E Europe • 500 kW
- W • N Africa • 500 kW

†BBC, Various Locations
- S Asia • 250 kW

†BBC, Via A'Seela, Oman
- W • S Asia • 250 kW

†BBC, Via Seychelles
- W Sa • E Africa • 250 kW
- W Su-F • E Africa • 250 kW
- W M-F • E Africa • 250 kW
- W Sa/Su • E Africa • 250 kW
- W • E Africa • 250 kW
- E Africa • 250 kW

†BBC, Via Singapore
- W • S Asia • 250 kW

†BBC, Via Thailand
- S Asia • 250 kW

†BBC, Via Zyyi, Cyprus
- S • E Europe • 250 kW
- E Europe • 250 kW
- W • W Asia • 250 kW
- ← • Su • E Europe • 250/300 kW

9415 CHINA

CHINA R INTL, Beijing
- W • SE Asia • 500 kW

CHINA R INTL, Xi'an
- W • E Asia • 500 kW

CLANDESTINE (ASIA)

"D'CRATIC VO BURMA", Via Kazakstan
- W • SE Asia • ANTI-MYANMAR GOVT • 200 kW

CZECH REPUBLIC

RADIO PRAGUE, Litomyšl
- S • N America • 100 kW
- S • S America • 100 kW

9420 CHINA

CENTRAL PEOPLE'S BS, Lingshi
- DS-8 (MINORITIES) • 100 kW
- DS-1 • 100 kW

EGYPT

RADIO CAIRO, Kafr Silîm-Abis
- W Africa & C Africa • 250 kW

GREECE

FONI TIS HELLADAS, Athens
- ← • M • Europe & N America • 100 kW
- ← • Sa • Europe • 100 kW
- ← • Tu-Su • Europe & N America • 100 kW
- ← • Su-F • Europe • 100 kW
- ← • Europe & Americas • 100 kW
- W M-Sa • Europe & N America • 100 kW
- ← • Su • Europe & N America • 100 kW
- ← • Europe & N America • 100 kW
- ← • Europe • 100 kW
- S M-Sa • Europe • 100 kW
- S Su • Europe • 100 kW
- W M-Sa • Europe • 100 kW
- W Su • Europe • 100 kW

9425 CHINA

CHINA R INTL, Beijing
- W • E Asia • 150 kW

CHINA R INTL, Jinhua
- W • SE Asia • 500 kW

INDIA

ALL INDIA RADIO, Bangalore
- HINDI & ENGLISH • S Asia • DS-NATIONAL • 500 kW

9430 AUSTRALIA

CVC, Via Wertachtal, Germany
- W Africa & C Africa • 125 kW

CZECH REPUBLIC

RADIO PRAGUE, Litomyšl
- W • W Europe • 100 kW
- W • SE Asia & Australasia • 100 kW

GERMANY

DEUTSCHE WELLE, Via Sines, Portugal
- W • W Africa & C Africa • 250 kW

PHILIPPINES

FEBC RADIO INTL, Bocaue
- E Asia • 100 kW

UNITED KINGDOM

BIBLE VOICE, Via Jülich, Germany
- S M/W/F • Mideast • 100 kW
- S Sa/Su • Mideast • 100 kW
- S M-F • Mideast • 100 kW

BIBLE VOICE, Via Wertachtal, Germany
- S Sa/Su • Mideast • 250 kW
- S F-Su • Mideast • 250 kW
- S Su • Mideast • 250 kW

USA

†FAMILY RADIO, Okeechobee, Fl
- W • S America • 100 kW

†FAMILY RADIO, Via Skelton, UK
- W • E Europe & Mideast • 300 kW

PAN AM BC, Via Wertachtal, Germany
- S Sa/Su • N Africa • 250 kW
- S F-Su • N Africa • 250 kW

(con'd)

World Time 0 1 2 3 4 5 6 7 8 9 10 11 12 13 14 15 16 17 18 19 20 21 22 23 24

World Time 0–24

kHz	Country / Station	Schedule
9430 (con'd)	**USA**	
	†R FARDA, Via Wertachtal, Germany	W • W Asia • 250 kW
	TRANS WORLD R	S M-F • N Europe • 100 kW
	VIETNAM	
	VOICE OF VIETNAM, Via Skelton, UK	S • Europe • 300 kW
9435	**CHINA**	
	CHINA R INTL, Kashi	W • S America • 500 kW; S • S Asia • 100 kW; S • C Asia • 100 kW • ALT. FREQ. TO 5905 kHz; W • Europe • 500 kW
	CHINA R INTL, Kunming	Mideast, W Africa & C Africa • 500 kW • ALT. FREQ. TO 9440 kHz
	CHINA R INTL, Urümqi	S • E Africa • 500 kW
	CHINA R INTL, Xi'an	W • E Asia • 500 kW
	CZECH REPUBLIC	
	RADIO PRAGUE, Litomyšl	W • W Europe & S America • 100 kW; W • W Africa & C Africa • 100 kW
	PHILIPPINES	
	FEBC RADIO INTL, Bocaue	SE Asia • 100 kW
	RUSSIA	
	VOICE OF RUSSIA, Petropavlovsk-K	S • W North Am • 250 kW
	UNITED KINGDOM	
	BBC, Via Armavir, Russia	W Su • S Asia • 300 kW
	BIBLE VOICE, Via Nauen, Germany	S Su • W Europe • 125 kW
	USA	
	GOSPEL FOR ASIA, Via Germany	S • W Asia & S Asia • 250 kW
9440	**CHINA**	
	CENTRAL PEOPLE'S BS, Beijing	W • DS-8 (MINORITIES) • 100 kW
	CHINA R INTL, Kunming	SE Asia • 150 kW; Mideast, W Africa & C Africa • 500 kW; Mideast, W Africa & C Africa • 500 kW • ALT. FREQ. TO 9435 kHz
	CHINA R INTL, Various Locations	SE Asia • 150/500 kW
	CHINA R INTL, Via Cerrik, Albania	S • E Europe • 150 kW
	CHINA R INTL, Xi'an	W • E Asia • 500 kW
	CZECH REPUBLIC	
	RADIO PRAGUE, Litomyšl	S • N America & C America • 100 kW; S • S America • 100 kW
	GERMANY	
	CHRISTLICHE WISSENSCHAFT, Jülich	S Sa • E Europe • 100 kW
	POLAND	
	†POLISH RADIO, Via Jülich, Germany	S • E Europe • 100 kW
	†POLISH RADIO, Via W'tachtal, Germany	W • E Europe • 100 kW
	SLOVAKIA	
	†R SLOVAKIA INTL, Rimavská Sobota	S America • 150 kW; S • E Europe & W Asia • 150 kW; S • Australasia • 150 kW; S • W Europe • 150 kW
	UNITED KINGDOM	
	BBC, Via Ascension	W • W Africa & C Africa • 250 kW
	†BBC, Via Vladivostok, Russia	S • E Asia • 500 kW
	USA	
	TRANS WORLD R	S • Europe • 100 kW; S Su • Europe • 100 kW
9445	**CLANDESTINE (AFRICA)**	
	"ANDENET LEDEMOCRACY", Via Russia	W Su/W/F • E Africa • 250 kW
	"DEJEN RADIO", Via Samara, Russia	W Sa • E Africa • ANTI-ETHIOPIA GOVT • 250 kW
	"R XORYIO OGADENIA", Samara,Russia	W Tu • E Africa • 250 kW
	CZECH REPUBLIC	
	RADIO PRAGUE, Litomyšl	S • Mideast & E Africa • 100 kW; S • E Europe • 100 kW
	INDIA	
	ALL INDIA RADIO, Bangalore	W Africa • 500 kW; Europe • 500 kW
	TRANS WORLD R, Via Uzbekistan	S • S Asia • 200 kW; S M-F • S Asia • 200 kW; S Sa/Su • S Asia • 200 kW; S M-Sa • S Asia • 200 kW
	PHILIPPINES	
	FEBC RADIO INTL, Iba	SE Asia • 50 kW
	POLAND	
	POLISH RADIO, Via W'tachtal, Germany	W • W Europe • 100 kW
	SLOVAKIA	
	R SLOVAKIA INTL, Rimavská Sobota	W • W Europe • 150 kW
	UNITED KINGDOM	
	BBC, Via Thailand	S • W Asia • 250 kW
	USA	
	ADVENTIST WORLD R, Via Austria	W • Mideast • 300 kW
	TRANS WORLD R, Via Nov'sibirsk,Russia	W • S Asia • 250 kW; W M-F • S Asia • 250 kW

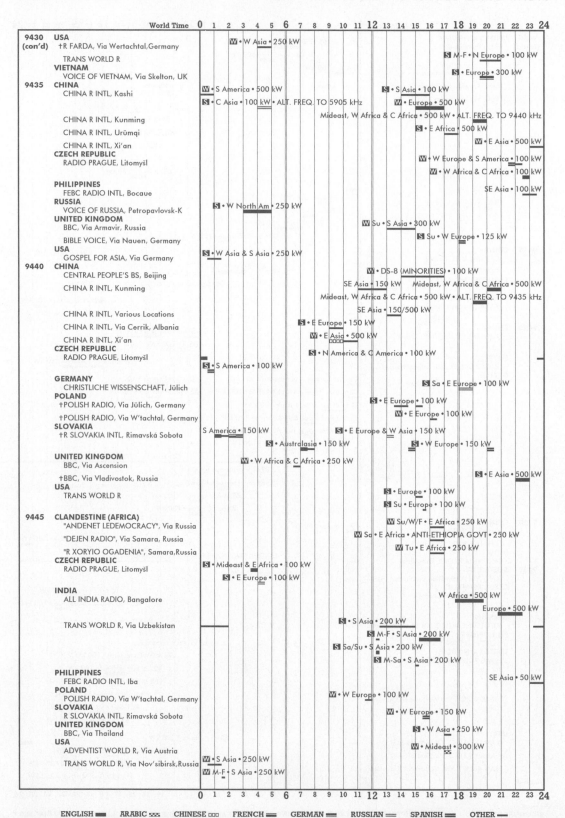

ENGLISH ARABIC CHINESE FRENCH GERMAN RUSSIAN SPANISH OTHER

World Time 0 1 2 3 4 5 6 7 8 9 10 11 12 13 14 15 16 17 18 19 20 21 22 23 24

kHz	Country / Station	Schedule
9450	**CHINA**	
	CHINA R INTL, Kashi	S • S Asia • 100 kW; W Africa & C Africa • 500 kW
		S Asia • 100 kW
		E Asia • 500 kW
	CHINA R INTL, Shijiazhuang	
	CHINA (TAIWAN)	
	CHINA RADIO, Via Petro-Kam, Russia	S • E Asia • 200 kW
	CZECH REPUBLIC	
	RADIO PRAGUE, Litomyšl	W • E Europe & W Asia • 100 kW
	NETHERLANDS	
	†R NEDERLAND, Via Sines, Portugal	S • C America • 250 kW
	POLAND	
	†POLISH RADIO, Via W'tachtal, Germany	W • W Europe • 100 kW
	UNITED KINGDOM	
	BBC, Via Zyyi, Cyprus	W M-F • E Europe & W Asia • 300 kW
	USA	
	†FAMILY RADIO, Via Irkutsk, Russia	E Asia • 250 kW • ALT. FREQ. TO 9460 kHz
	†FAMILY RADIO, Via Novosibirsk, Russia	W • SE Asia • 250 kW
9455	**ALGERIA**	
	R ALGERIENNE, Via Wooffferton, UK	W • N Africa • DS • 250 kW
	CHINA	
	CENTRAL PEOPLE'S BS, Lingshi	DS-8 (MINORITIES) • 100 kW; DS-1 • 100 kW
	PORTUGAL	
	†RDP INTERNATIONAL, Lisbon	W Tu-Sa • E North Am • 300 kW; W • Europe • 300 kW
		W Sa/Su • Europe • 300 kW
	USA	
	†FAMILY RADIO, Via Taiwan	SE Asia • 100 kW
	R FREE ASIA, Via Iranawila, Sri Lanka	S • SE Asia • 250 kW
	R FREE ASIA, Via Saipan, N Marianas	SE Asia • 100 kW; W • E Asia • 100 kW
		E Asia • 100 kW
		S • E Asia • 250 kW
	R FREE ASIA, Via Tinian, N Marianas	
	TRANS WORLD R, Via Merizo, Guam	S • S Asia • 100 kW
	†WEWN, Vandiver, Alabama	W • W Africa & C Africa • 500 kW
	WORLD HARVEST R, Greenbush, Maine	W • Africa • 250 kW
9460	**CHINA**	
	CHINA R INTL, Beijing	W • E Asia • 500 kW
	CHINA R INTL, Kashi	S Asia • 100 kW
		W • W Asia & S Asia • 500 kW
		SE Asia • 150 kW
	CHINA R INTL, Kunming	
		S • SE Asia • 150 kW
	CHINA R INTL, Urümqi	W • S Asia • 100 kW
	CHINA R INTL, Via Cerrik, Albania	W • E Europe • 150 kW
	PHILIPPINES	
	FEBC RADIO INTL, Bocaue	W • S Asia & C Asia • 100 kW
	SLOVAKIA	
	R SLOVAKIA INTL, Rimavská Sobota	W • W Europe & S America • 150 kW
	TURKEY	
	VOICE OF TURKEY, Ankara-Çakirlar	S • Europe • 500 kW
	UNITED KINGDOM	
	BIBLE VOICE, Via Jülich, Germany	W Su • Mideast • 100 kW
		W • Mideast • 100 kW
		W Th/Sa/Su • Mideast • 100 kW
		W Tu • Mideast • 100 kW
		W Tu/Sa/Su • Mideast • 100 kW
		W Sa/Su • Mideast • 100 kW
		W F-Su • Mideast • 100 kW
		W Sa • Mideast • 100 kW
	USA	
	†FAMILY RADIO, Via Irkutsk, Russia	E Asia • 250 kW • ALT. FREQ. TO 9450 kHz
	†R FARDA, Via Wertachtal,Germany	S • W Asia • 250 kW
9465	**NORTHERN MARIANA IS**	
	KFBS-FAR EAST BC, Saipan Island	W Asia & C Asia • 100 kW
		F • W Asia & C Asia • 100 kW
		Sa-Th • W Asia & C Asia • 100 kW
		Tu • W Asia & C Asia • 100 kW
		W-M • W Asia & C Asia • 100 kW
		Su-Tu/Th/F • W Asia & C Asia • 100 kW
		W/Sa • W Asia & C Asia • 100 kW
	USA	
	†FAMILY RADIO, Via Irkutsk, Russia	S • SE Asia • 250 kW
(con'd)	†FAMILY RADIO, Via Nauen, Germany	W • W Africa & C Africa • 500 kW

World Time 0 1 2 3 4 5 6 7 8 9 10 11 12 13 14 15 16 17 18 19 20 21 22 23 24

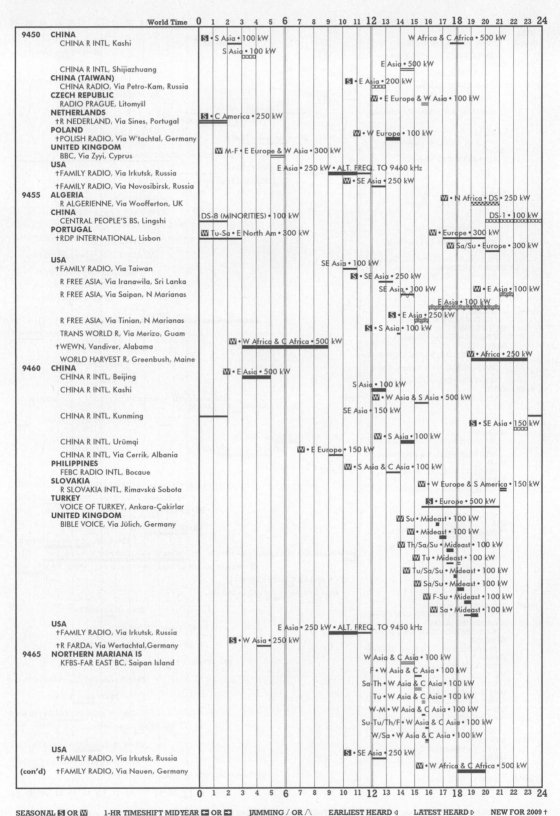

SEASONAL S OR W 1-HR TIMESHIFT MIDYEAR ⇐ OR ⇒ JAMMING / OR ∧ EARLIEST HEARD ◁ LATEST HEARD ▷ NEW FOR 2009 †

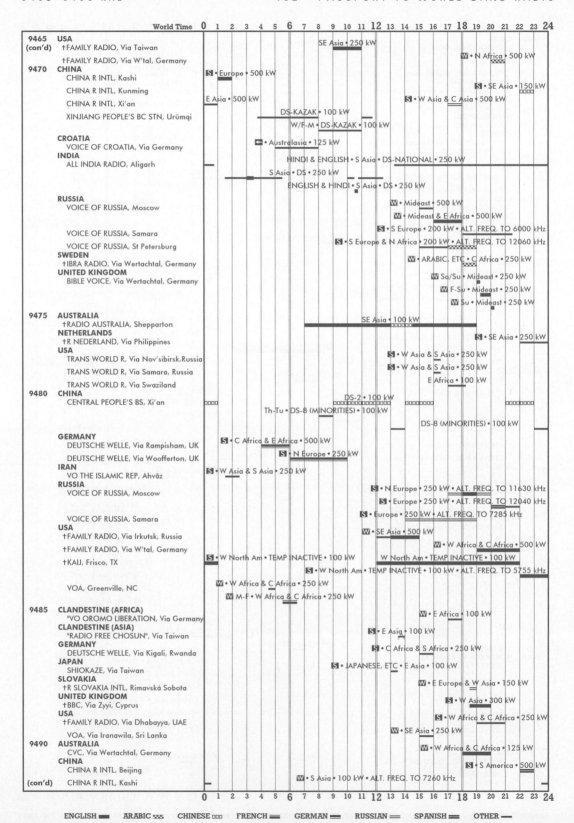

World Time 0 1 2 3 4 5 6 7 8 9 10 11 12 13 14 15 16 17 18 19 20 21 22 23 24

kHz	Country / Station	Schedule
9465 (con'd)	**USA**	
	†FAMILY RADIO, Via Taiwan	SE Asia • 250 kW
	†FAMILY RADIO, Via W'tal, Germany	W • N Africa • 500 kW
9470	**CHINA**	
	CHINA R INTL, Kashi	S • Europe • 500 kW
	CHINA R INTL, Kunming	S • SE Asia • 150 kW
	CHINA R INTL, Xi'an	E Asia • 500 kW; S • W Asia & C Asia • 500 kW
	XINJIANG PEOPLE'S BC STN, Urümqi	DS-KAZAK • 100 kW; W/F-M • DS-KAZAK • 100 kW
	CROATIA	
	VOICE OF CROATIA, Via Germany	• Australasia • 125 kW
	INDIA	
	ALL INDIA RADIO, Aligarh	HINDI & ENGLISH • S Asia • DS-NATIONAL • 250 kW; S Asia • DS • 250 kW; ENGLISH & HINDI • S Asia • DS • 250 kW
	RUSSIA	
	VOICE OF RUSSIA, Moscow	W • Mideast • 500 kW; W • Mideast & E Africa • 500 kW
	VOICE OF RUSSIA, Samara	S • S Europe • 200 kW • ALT. FREQ. TO 6000 kHz
	VOICE OF RUSSIA, St Petersburg	S • S Europe & N Africa • 200 kW • ALT. FREQ. TO 12060 kHz
	SWEDEN	
	†IBRA RADIO, Via Wertachtal, Germany	W • ARABIC, ETC • C Africa • 250 kW
	UNITED KINGDOM	
	BIBLE VOICE, Via Wertachtal, Germany	W Sa/Su • Mideast • 250 kW; W F-Su • Mideast • 250 kW; W Su • Mideast • 250 kW
9475	**AUSTRALIA**	
	†RADIO AUSTRALIA, Shepparton	SE Asia • 100 kW
	NETHERLANDS	
	†R NEDERLAND, Via Philippines	S • SE Asia • 250 kW
	USA	
	TRANS WORLD R, Via Nov'sibirsk,Russia	S • W Asia & S Asia • 250 kW
	TRANS WORLD R, Via Samara, Russia	S • W Asia & S Asia • 250 kW
	TRANS WORLD R, Via Swaziland	E Africa • 100 kW
9480	**CHINA**	
	CENTRAL PEOPLE'S BS, Xi'an	DS-2 • 100 kW; Th-Tu • DS-8 (MINORITIES) • 100 kW; DS-8 (MINORITIES) • 100 kW
	GERMANY	
	DEUTSCHE WELLE, Via Rampisham, UK	S • C Africa & E Africa • 500 kW
	DEUTSCHE WELLE, Via Woofferton, UK	S • N Europe • 250 kW
	IRAN	
	VO THE ISLAMIC REP, Ahvāz	S • W Asia & S Asia • 250 kW
	RUSSIA	
	VOICE OF RUSSIA, Moscow	S • N Europe • 250 kW • ALT. FREQ. TO 11630 kHz; S • Europe • 250 kW • ALT. FREQ. TO 12040 kHz
	VOICE OF RUSSIA, Samara	S • Europe • 250 kW • ALT. FREQ. TO 7285 kHz
	USA	
	†FAMILY RADIO, Via Irkutsk, Russia	W • SE Asia • 500 kW
	†FAMILY RADIO, Via W'tal, Germany	W • W Africa & C Africa • 500 kW
	†KAIJ, Frisco, TX	S • W North Am • TEMP INACTIVE • 100 kW; W North Am • TEMP INACTIVE • 100 kW; S • W North Am • TEMP INACTIVE • 100 kW • ALT. FREQ. TO 5755 kHz
	VOA, Greenville, NC	W • W Africa & C Africa • 250 kW; W M-F • W Africa & C Africa • 250 kW
9485	**CLANDESTINE (AFRICA)**	
	"VO OROMO LIBERATION, Via Germany	W • E Africa • 100 kW
	CLANDESTINE (ASIA)	
	"RADIO FREE CHOSUN", Via Taiwan	S • E Asia • 100 kW
	GERMANY	
	DEUTSCHE WELLE, Via Kigali, Rwanda	S • C Africa & S Africa • 250 kW
	JAPAN	
	SHIOKAZE, Via Taiwan	S • JAPANESE, ETC • E Asia • 100 kW
	SLOVAKIA	
	†R SLOVAKIA INTL, Rimavská Sobota	W • E Europe & W Asia • 150 kW
	UNITED KINGDOM	
	†BBC, Via Zyyi, Cyprus	S • W Asia • 300 kW
	USA	
	†FAMILY RADIO, Via Dhabayya, UAE	S • W Africa & C Africa • 250 kW
	VOA, Via Iranawila, Sri Lanka	W • SE Asia • 250 kW
9490	**AUSTRALIA**	
	CVC, Via Wertachtal, Germany	W • W Africa & C Africa • 125 kW
	CHINA	
	CHINA R INTL, Beijing	S • S America • 500 kW
(con'd)	CHINA R INTL, Kashi	W • S Asia • 100 kW • ALT. FREQ. TO 7260 kHz

0 1 2 3 4 5 6 7 8 9 10 11 12 13 14 15 16 17 18 19 20 21 22 23 24

ENGLISH ARABIC CHINESE FRENCH GERMAN RUSSIAN SPANISH OTHER

World Time 0 1 2 3 4 5 6 7 8 9 10 11 12 13 14 15 16 17 18 19 20 21 22 23 24

kHz	Country / Station	Schedule
9490 (con'd)	**CHINA**	
	CHINA R INTL, Kunming	S Asia • 150 kW
	CHINA R INTL, Various Locations	S Asia • 100/150 kW
	XIZANG PBS, Lhasa	DS-TIBETAN • 100 kW
		DS-TIBETAN • 100 kW • ALT. FREQ. TO 7125 kHz
		W-M • DS-TIBETAN • 100 kW
		DS • 100 kW • ALT. FREQ. TO 7125 kHz
		W-M • DS • 100 kW
	CLANDESTINE (ASIA)	
	"D'CRATIC VO BURMA", Via Germany	S • SE Asia • ANTI-MYANMAR GOVT • 125 kW
	"R FREE NORTH KOREA", Via Taiwan	S • E Asia • 100 kW • ALT. FREQ. TO 11750 kHz
	RUSSIA	
	VOICE OF RUSSIA, Irkutsk	S • E Asia • 100 kW
	SWEDEN	
	†RADIO SWEDEN, Hörby	← • M-F • Mideast & E Africa • 500 kW
		S M-Sa • Europe & N Africa • 500 kW
		S Sa/Su • Europe & N Africa • 500 kW
		S Su • Europe & N Africa • 500 kW
	RADIO SWEDEN, Via Sackville, Canada	S America • 250 kW
		S • S America • 250 kW
	USA	
	FAMILY RADIO, Via Moscow, Russia	S • Europe • 250 kW
	TRANS WORLD R	← • Tu-Sa • Europe • 100 kW
		← • Sa • Europe • 100 kW
	TRANS WORLD R, Via Jülich,Germany	S • S Europe • 100 kW
9494.8	**GEORGIA**	
	REP ABKHAZIA R, Sukhumi	← • Irr • M-Sa • RUSSIAN, ETC • DS • 5 kW
		← • Irr • M-Sa • RUSSIAN, ETC • DS
		← • RUSSIAN, ETC • DS • 5 kW
		← • Irr • DS • 5 kW
9495	**GERMANY**	
	†DEUTSCHE WELLE, Various Locations	N Africa & C Africa • 250 kW
	†DEUTSCHE WELLE, Via Sri Lanka	W • N Africa & Mideast • 250 kW
	DEUTSCHE WELLE, Via Woofferton, UK	W • W Asia & S Asia • 250 kW
	IRAN	
	VO THE ISLAMIC REP, Tehrān	S • N America • 250 kW
	UNITED KINGDOM	
	BBC, Via Thailand	W • C Asia • 250 kW
	USA	
	†FAMILY RADIO, Okeechobee, Fl	W • C America • 100 kW
	FAMILY RADIO, Via Uzbekistan	S • E Europe & W Asia • 200 kW
	†FAMILY RADIO, Via W'tal, Germany	S • Mideast • 500 kW
	TRANS WORLD R, Via Austria	W • E Europe • 100 kW
		W M • E Europe • 100 kW
		W Tu-Su • E Europe • 100 kW
		W M-F • E Europe • 100 kW
	VOA, Via Jülich,Germany	W • W Asia • 100 kW
	VOA, Via Wertachtal,Germany	W • W Asia • 250 kW
	WORLD HARVEST R, Cypress Creek, SC	S M-Sa • C America & S America • 250 kW
		S M-Sa • W North Am • 250 kW
		S Su • C America & S America • 250 kW
		C America • 250 kW
		W • C America • 250 kW
		W Sa/Su • W North Am • 250 kW
9500	**AUSTRALIA**	
	CVC, Via Uzbekistan	W • S Asia • 100 kW
	RADIO AUSTRALIA, Shepparton	SE Asia • 100 kW
	CHINA	
	CENTRAL PEOPLE'S BS, Shijiazhuang	DS-1 • 100 kW (jamming)
	CENTRAL PEOPLE'S BS, Xi'an	W-M • DS-1 • 100 kW (jamming)
	UNITED KINGDOM	
	FEBA RADIO, Via Novosibirsk, Russia	S • W Asia & S Asia • 250 kW
	USA	
	†FAMILY RADIO, Via Novosibirsk, Russia	S • S Asia • 250 kW
	†FAMILY RADIO, Via W'tal, Germany	W • N Africa • 500 kW
	TRANS WORLD R, Via Swaziland	S Africa & E Africa • 100 kW
		E Africa • 100 kW
9504v	**PERU**	
	RADIO TACNA, Tacna	DS-TEMP INACTIVE • 0.18 kW
9504.8	**BRAZIL**	
	RADIO RECORD, São Paulo	DS-TEMP INACTIVE • 7.5 kW • →
9505	**CHINA**	
	†VO THE STRAIT-PLA, Fuzhou	E Asia • NEWS CHANNEL • 50 kW (jamming)
(con'd)		Th-Tu • E Asia • NEWS CHANNEL • 50 kW (jamming)

World Time 0 1 2 3 4 5 6 7 8 9 10 11 12 13 14 15 16 17 18 19 20 21 22 23 24

SEASONAL S OR W 1-HR TIMESHIFT MIDYEAR ← OR → JAMMING / OR /\ EARLIEST HEARD ◁ LATEST HEARD ▷ NEW FOR 2009 †

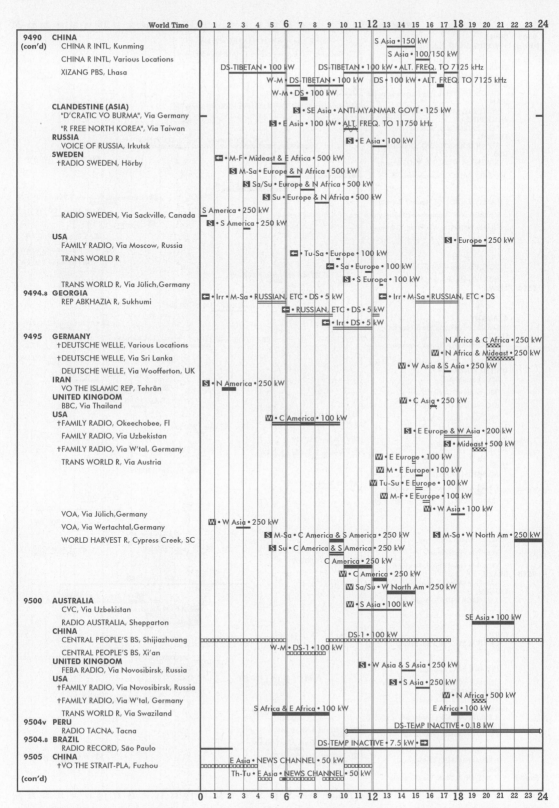

World Time 0 1 2 3 4 5 6 7 8 9 10 11 12 13 14 15 16 17 18 19 20 21 22 23 24

kHz	Country / Station	Schedule
9505 (con'd)	**CHINA**	
	†VO THE STRAIT-PLA, Fuzhou	Su • E Asia • NEWS CHANNEL • 50 kW
		Th-Sa/M/Tu • E Asia • NEWS CHANNEL • 50 kW
	CUBA	
	†RADIO HABANA CUBA, Havana	C America • 100 kW
	GERMANY	
	DEUTSCHE WELLE, Via Rampisham, UK	S • S Asia • 500 kW
	IRAN	
	†VO THE ISLAMIC REP, Tehrān	W • Mideast • VOICE OF PALESTINE • 500 kW
	PHILIPPINES	
	FEBC RADIO INTL, Bocaue	W • C Asia • 100 kW
	SUDAN	
	REP OF SUDAN RADIO, Omdurman	DS • 100 kW • ALT. FREQ. TO 7200 kHz
	USA	
	ADVENTIST WORLD R, Via Germany	W • N Africa • 100 kW
	†FAMILY RADIO, Okeechobee, Fl	N America • 100 kW
		S • C America • 100 kW
	†FAMILY RADIO, Via Nauen, Germany	S • E Europe & W Asia • 500 kW
	R FARDA, Via Lampertheim, Germany	S • W Asia • 100 kW
	†TRANS WORLD R, Via W'tal, Germany	S • W Asia • 100 kW
	†VOA	W • S Europe • 250 kW
		W M-F • S Europe • 250 kW
		S • SE Asia • 250 kW
	VOA, Via Iranawila, Sri Lanka	
	VOA, Via Woofferton, UK	W M-F • N Africa • 300 kW
9510	**CHINA**	
	XINJIANG PEOPLE'S BC STN, Urümqi	DS-MONGOLIAN • 100 kW
		W/F-M • DS-MONGOLIAN • 100 kW
	GERMANY	
	†DEUTSCHE WELLE, Via Sri Lanka	W • Australasia • 250 kW
	ITALY	
	†IRRS-SHORTWAVE, Via Slovakia	← • Su • Europe, N Africa & Mideast • 150 kW
	NETHERLANDS	
	†R NEDERLAND, Via Meyerton, S Africa	W M-F • N Africa • 500 kW
	UNITED KINGDOM	
	BBC, Rampisham	W • Mideast & W Asia • 500 kW
	BBC, Skelton, Cumbria	W • Mideast & W Asia • 300 kW
	BBC, Various Locations	S Asia • 250 kW
	BBC, Via A'Seela, Oman	W • S Asia • 250 kW
	BBC, Via Thailand	SE Asia • 250 kW
	BBC, Via Zyyi, Cyprus	W • S Asia • 250 kW
		W • W Asia & S Asia • 300 kW
	USA	
	ADVENTIST WORLD R, Via Agat, Guam	W • E Asia • 100 kW
	R FARDA, Via Wertachtal,Germany	S • W Asia • 250 kW
	TRANS WORLD R, Via Meyerton, S Af	W Africa • 500 kW
		Sa/Su • W Africa • 500 kW
		Su • W Africa • 500 kW
	VOA, Various Locations	S Asia • 250 kW
	VOA, Via Philippines	S • SE Asia • 250 kW; S • E Asia • 250 kW
	VOA, Via Udon Thani, Thailand	W • S Asia • 250 kW
9515	**BRAZIL**	
	RADIO MARUMBY, Curitiba	DS • 10 kW • →
	CANADA	
	R CANADA INTL, Sackville, NB	S • N America • 250 kW
		S M-F • N America • 250 kW
		S Sa/Su • N America • 250 kW
	CHINA	
	CENTRAL PEOPLE'S BS, Beijing	W • DS-2 • 100 kW
		DS-2 • 100 kW
	CHINA R INTL, Beijing	S • Europe • 500 kW
	CHINA R INTL, Via Cerrik, Albania	S • N Africa • 150 kW
	KOREA (REPUBLIC)	
	KBS WORLD R, In-Kimjae	Europe • 100 kW
	OMAN	
	R SULTANATE OF OMAN, Sīb	Mideast • DS • 100 kW
	ROMANIA	
	†R ROMANIA INTL, Bucharest	S • E North Am • 300 kW
		W • W North Am • 300 kW
	†R ROMANIA INTL, Galbeni	W • E North Am • 300 kW; S • W Europe • 300 kW
(con'd)	**RUSSIA**	
	VOICE OF RUSSIA, Via Germany	S • E North Am • 250 kW

World Time 0 1 2 3 4 5 6 7 8 9 10 11 12 13 14 15 16 17 18 19 20 21 22 23 24

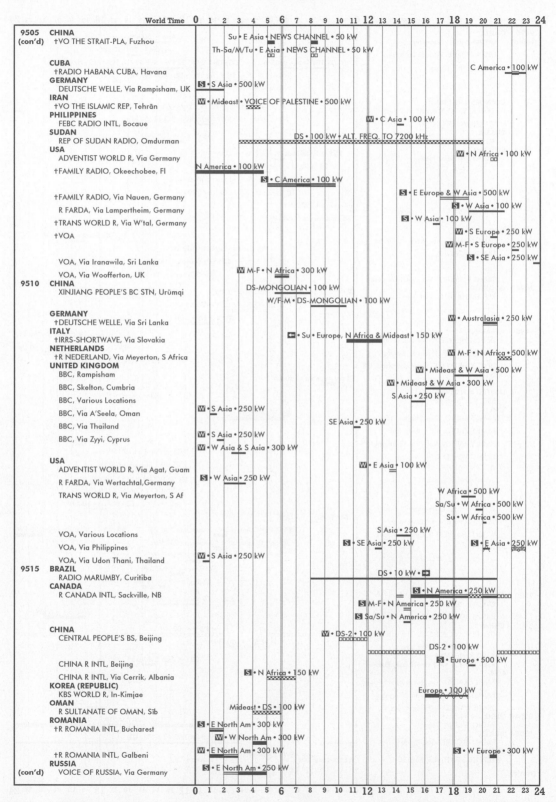

ENGLISH ARABIC CHINESE FRENCH GERMAN RUSSIAN SPANISH OTHER

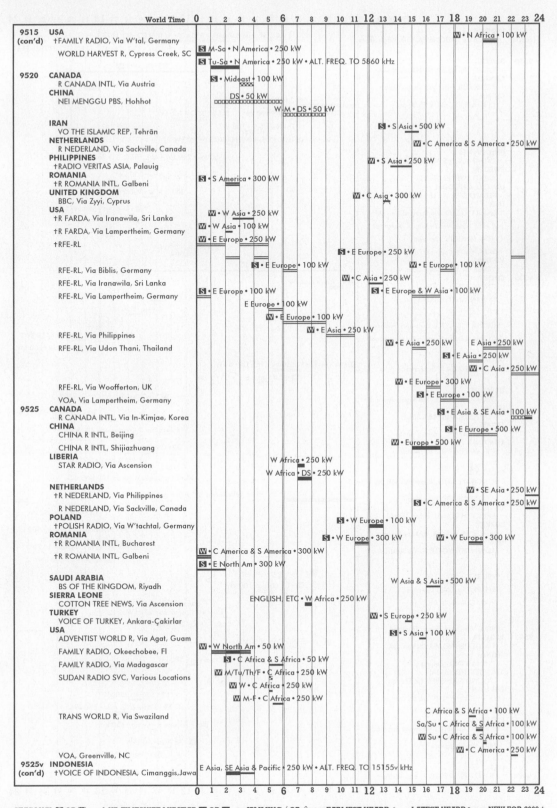

World Time 0 1 2 3 4 5 6 7 8 9 10 11 12 13 14 15 16 17 18 19 20 21 22 23 24

kHz	Country / Station	Schedule
9515 (con'd)	**USA**	
	†FAMILY RADIO, Via W'tal, Germany	W • N Africa • 100 kW
	WORLD HARVEST R, Cypress Creek, SC	S M-Sa • N America • 250 kW
		S Tu-Sa • N America • 250 kW • ALT. FREQ. TO 5860 kHz
9520	**CANADA**	
	R CANADA INTL, Via Austria	S • Mideast • 100 kW
	CHINA	
	NEI MENGGU PBS, Hohhot	DS • 50 kW
		W-M • DS • 50 kW
	IRAN	
	VO THE ISLAMIC REP, Tehrān	S • S Asia • 500 kW
	NETHERLANDS	
	R NEDERLAND, Via Sackville, Canada	W • C America & S America • 250 kW
	PHILIPPINES	
	†RADIO VERITAS ASIA, Palauig	W • S Asia • 250 kW
	ROMANIA	
	†R ROMANIA INTL, Galbeni	S • S America • 300 kW
	UNITED KINGDOM	
	BBC, Via Zyyi, Cyprus	W • C Asia • 300 kW
	USA	
	†R FARDA, Via Iranawila, Sri Lanka	W • W Asia • 250 kW
	†R FARDA, Via Lampertheim, Germany	W • W Asia • 100 kW
	†RFE-RL	W • E Europe • 250 kW
		S • E Europe • 250 kW
	RFE-RL, Via Biblis, Germany	S • E Europe • 100 kW
		W • E Europe • 100 kW
	RFE-RL, Via Iranawila, Sri Lanka	W • C Asia • 250 kW
	RFE-RL, Via Lampertheim, Germany	S • E Europe • 100 kW
		S • E Europe & W Asia • 100 kW
		E Europe • 100 kW
		W • E Europe • 100 kW
	RFE-RL, Via Philippines	W • E Asia • 250 kW
	RFE-RL, Via Udon Thani, Thailand	W • E Asia • 250 kW
		E Asia • 250 kW
		S • E Asia • 250 kW
		W • C Asia • 250 kW
	RFE-RL, Via Woofferton, UK	W • E Europe • 300 kW
	VOA, Via Lampertheim, Germany	S • E Europe • 100 kW
9525	**CANADA**	
	R CANADA INTL, Via In-Kimjae, Korea	S • E Asia & SE Asia • 100 kW
	CHINA	
	CHINA R INTL, Beijing	S • E Europe • 500 kW
	CHINA R INTL, Shijiazhuang	W • Europe • 500 kW
	LIBERIA	
	STAR RADIO, Via Ascension	W Africa • 250 kW
		W Africa • DS • 250 kW
	NETHERLANDS	
	†R NEDERLAND, Via Philippines	W • SE Asia • 250 kW
	R NEDERLAND, Via Sackville, Canada	S • C America & S America • 250 kW
	POLAND	
	†POLISH RADIO, Via W'tachtal, Germany	S • W Europe • 100 kW
	ROMANIA	
	†R ROMANIA INTL, Bucharest	S • W Europe • 300 kW
		W • W Europe • 300 kW
	†R ROMANIA INTL, Galbeni	W • C America & S America • 300 kW
		S • E North Am • 300 kW
	SAUDI ARABIA	
	BS OF THE KINGDOM, Riyadh	W Asia & S Asia • 500 kW
	SIERRA LEONE	
	COTTON TREE NEWS, Via Ascension	ENGLISH, ETC • W Africa • 250 kW
	TURKEY	
	VOICE OF TURKEY, Ankara-Çakirlar	W • S Europe • 250 kW
	USA	
	ADVENTIST WORLD R, Via Agat, Guam	S • S Asia • 100 kW
	FAMILY RADIO, Okeechobee, Fl	W • W North Am • 50 kW
	FAMILY RADIO, Via Madagascar	S • C Africa & S Africa • 50 kW
	SUDAN RADIO SVC, Various Locations	W M/Tu/Th/F • C Africa • 250 kW
		W W • C Africa • 250 kW
		W M-F • C Africa • 250 kW
	TRANS WORLD R, Via Swaziland	C Africa & S Africa • 100 kW
		Sa/Su • C Africa & S Africa • 100 kW
		W Su • C Africa & S Africa • 100 kW
	VOA, Greenville, NC	W • C America • 250 kW
9525v (con'd)	**INDONESIA**	
	†VOICE OF INDONESIA, Cimanggis, Jawa	E Asia, SE Asia & Pacific • 250 kW • ALT. FREQ. TO 15155v kHz

World Time 0 1 2 3 4 5 6 7 8 9 10 11 12 13 14 15 16 17 18 19 20 21 22 23 24

kHz	Country / Station	Schedule
9525v (con'd)	**INDONESIA** †VOICE OF INDONESIA, Cimanggis,Jawa	E Asia, SE Asia & Pacific • 250 kW • ALT. FREQ. TO 11785v kHz
		Europe • 250 kW • ALT. FREQ. TO 11785v kHz
9530	**BRAZIL** RADIO TRANS MUNDIAL, Santa Maria	DS • 10 kW • ➡
	CANADA R CANADA INTL, Via Kashi, China	S • E Africa • 100 kW
	CHINA CENTRAL PEOPLE'S BS, Xi'an	DS-2 • 100 kW
		DS-8 (MINORITIES) • 100 kW
		S • DS-2 • 100 kW
		Th-Tu • DS-2 • 100 kW
		Th-Tu • DS-8 (MINORITIES) • 100 kW
	PHILIPPINES †RADIO VERITAS ASIA, Palauig	S Asia • 250 kW • ALT. FREQ. TO 9665 kHz
	SWEDEN RADIO SWEDEN, Hörby	W • W Asia & C Asia • 350 kW
	UNITED KINGDOM FEBA RADIO, Via Uzbekistan	S • S Asia • 100 kW
	USA FAMILY RADIO, Via Rampisham, UK	W • Mideast • 500 kW
	R FREE ASIA, Via Tinian, N Marianas	S • E Asia • 250 kW
	VOA, Via Biblis, Germany	S • S Europe • 100 kW
	VOA, Via Philippines	W • E Asia • 250 kW
	VIETNAM †VOICE OF VIETNAM, Xuan Mai	DS-1 • 50 kW
9535	**CHINA** CHINA R INTL, Kashi	S • S Asia • 100 kW
	CHINA R INTL, Kunming	SE Asia • 100 kW • ALT. FREQ. TO 15135 kHz
		S Asia • 500 kW
	CHINA R INTL, Via Issoudun, France	E Europe • 500 kW
		S • C Africa & S Africa • 150 kW
	CHINA R INTL, Xi'an	S • E Asia • 500 kW
	GEORGIA REP ABKHAZIA R, Sukhumi	⬅ • Irr • M-Sa • RUSSIAN, ETC • DS • 5 kW
		⬅ • RUSSIAN, ETC • DS • 5 kW
	GERMANY DEUTSCHE WELLE, Via Kigali, Rwanda	W • C Africa & E Africa • 250 kW
	IRAN VO THE ISLAMIC REP, Sirjan	S • S Europe • 500 kW
	JAPAN RADIO JAPAN, Tokyo-Yamata	W North Am & C America • 300 kW
	ROMANIA †R ROMANIA INTL, Bucharest	W • C Asia • 300 kW
		S • W Europe • 300 kW
	SLOVAKIA †R SLOVAKIA INTL, Rimavská Sobota	S • E Europe & W Asia • 150 kW
	SPAIN R EXTERIOR ESPANA, Noblejas	N America & C America • 250 kW
	THAILAND RADIO THAILAND, Udon Thani	W • Europe • 250 kW
	TURKEY VOICE OF TURKEY, Ankara-Emirler	S • N Africa & W Africa • 500 kW
	USA ADVENTIST WORLD R, Via Austria	W • W Africa & C Africa • 300 kW
		W • C Africa • 300 kW
	†RFE-RL	W • E Europe • 250 kW
	RFE-RL, Via Biblis, Germany	W • E Europe • 100 kW
	VOA, Greenville, NC	C America • 250 kW
		W M-F • C America • 250 kW
		S • SE Asia • 250 kW
	VOA, Via Udon Thani, Thailand	
9540	**ALGERIA** R ALGERIENNE, Via Skelton, UK	S • N Africa • DS • 300 kW
	CHINA CHINA R INTL, Beijing	Australasia • 500 kW
	CLANDESTINE (ASIA) "SOUND OF HOPE", Via Taiwan	Sa/Su • E Asia • 100 kW
	GERMANY †DEUTSCHE WELLE, Via Sri Lanka	S • S Asia • 250 kW
		S • S Asia & SE Asia • 250 kW
	SLOVAKIA †R SLOVAKIA INTL, Rimavská Sobota	W • E Europe & W Asia • 150 kW
	UNITED KINGDOM BBC, Via Singapore	W • SE Asia • 100 kW
		W • S Asia • 100 kW
	USA	
(con'd)	ADVENTIST WORLD R, Via Austria	W • W Asia • 300 kW

World Time 0 1 2 3 4 5 6 7 8 9 10 11 12 13 14 15 16 17 18 19 20 21 22 23 24

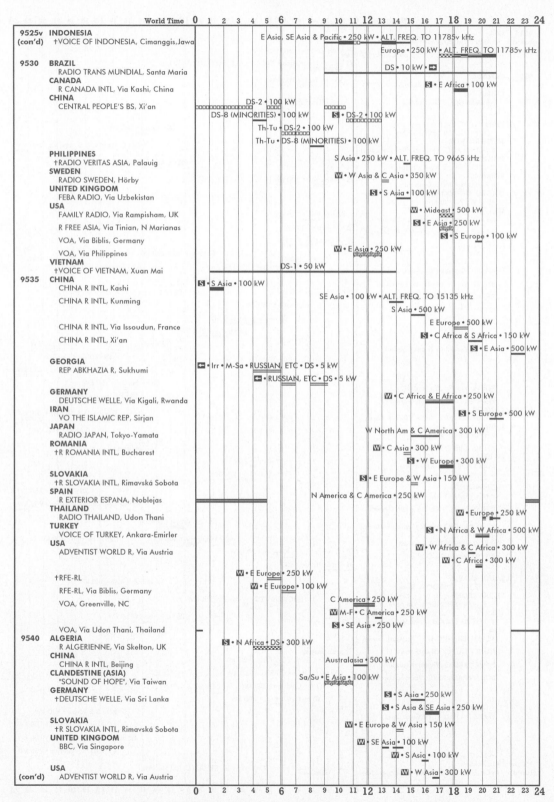

ENGLISH ▬ ARABIC ▭ CHINESE ▫▫▫ FRENCH ═ GERMAN ═ RUSSIAN ═ SPANISH ═ OTHER —

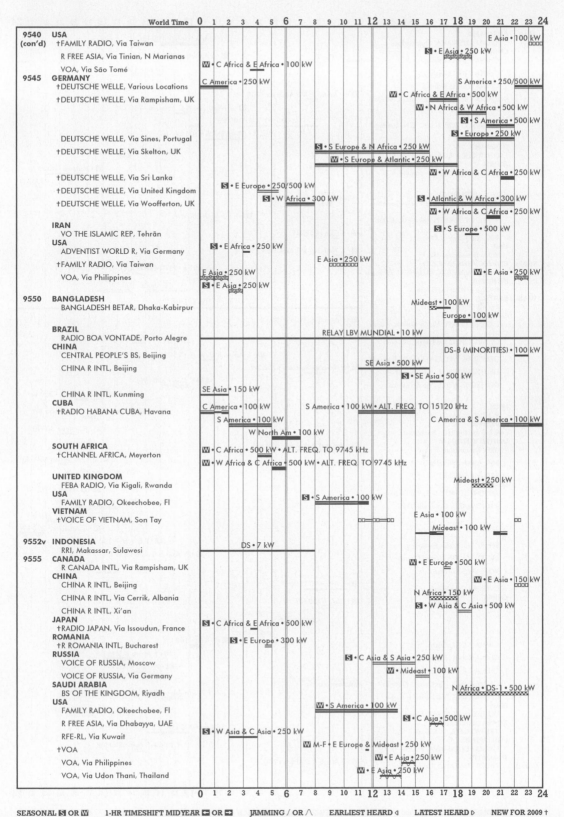

World Time 0 1 2 3 4 5 6 7 8 9 10 11 12 13 14 15 16 17 18 19 20 21 22 23 24

kHz	Country / Station	Target • Power
9540 (con'd)	**USA**	
	†FAMILY RADIO, Via Taiwan	E Asia • 100 kW
	R FREE ASIA, Via Tinian, N Marianas	S • E Asia • 250 kW
	VOA, Via São Tomé	W • C Africa & E Africa • 100 kW
9545	**GERMANY**	
	†DEUTSCHE WELLE, Various Locations	C America • 250 kW; S America • 250/500 kW
	†DEUTSCHE WELLE, Via Rampisham, UK	W • C Africa & E Africa • 500 kW
		W • N Africa & W Africa • 500 kW
		S • S America • 500 kW
	DEUTSCHE WELLE, Via Sines, Portugal	S • Europe • 250 kW
	†DEUTSCHE WELLE, Via Skelton, UK	S • S Europe & N Africa • 250 kW
		W • S Europe & Atlantic • 250 kW
	†DEUTSCHE WELLE, Via Sri Lanka	W • W Africa & C Africa • 250 kW
	†DEUTSCHE WELLE, Via United Kingdom	S • E Europe • 250/500 kW
	†DEUTSCHE WELLE, Via Woofferton, UK	S • W Africa • 300 kW; S • Atlantic & W Africa • 300 kW
		W • W Africa & C Africa • 250 kW
	IRAN	
	VO THE ISLAMIC REP, Tehrān	S • S Europe • 500 kW
	USA	
	ADVENTIST WORLD R, Via Germany	S • E Africa • 250 kW
	†FAMILY RADIO, Via Taiwan	E Asia • 250 kW
	VOA, Via Philippines	E Asia • 250 kW; W • E Asia • 250 kW
		S • E Asia • 250 kW
9550	**BANGLADESH**	
	BANGLADESH BETAR, Dhaka-Kabirpur	Mideast • 100 kW
		Europe • 100 kW
	BRAZIL	
	RADIO BOA VONTADE, Porto Alegre	RELAY LBV MUNDIAL • 10 kW
	CHINA	
	CENTRAL PEOPLE'S BS, Beijing	DS-8 (MINORITIES) • 100 kW
	CHINA R INTL, Beijing	SE Asia • 500 kW
		S • SE Asia • 500 kW
	CHINA R INTL, Kunming	SE Asia • 150 kW
	CUBA	
	†RADIO HABANA CUBA, Havana	C America • 100 kW; S America • 100 kW • ALT. FREQ. TO 15120 kHz
		S America • 100 kW; C America & S America • 100 kW
		W North Am • 100 kW
	SOUTH AFRICA	
	†CHANNEL AFRICA, Meyerton	W • C Africa • 500 kW • ALT. FREQ. TO 9745 kHz
		W • W Africa & C Africa • 500 kW • ALT. FREQ. TO 9745 kHz
	UNITED KINGDOM	
	FEBA RADIO, Via Kigali, Rwanda	Mideast • 250 kW
	USA	
	FAMILY RADIO, Okeechobee, Fl	S • S America • 100 kW
	VIETNAM	
	†VOICE OF VIETNAM, Son Tay	E Asia • 100 kW
		Mideast • 100 kW
9552v	**INDONESIA**	
	RRI, Makassar, Sulawesi	DS • 7 kW
9555	**CANADA**	
	R CANADA INTL, Via Rampisham, UK	W • E Europe • 500 kW
	CHINA	
	CHINA R INTL, Beijing	W • E Asia • 150 kW
	CHINA R INTL, Via Cerrik, Albania	N Africa • 150 kW
	CHINA R INTL, Xi'an	S • W Asia & C Asia • 500 kW
	JAPAN	
	†RADIO JAPAN, Via Issoudun, France	S • C Africa & E Africa • 500 kW
	ROMANIA	
	†R ROMANIA INTL, Bucharest	S • E Europe • 300 kW
	RUSSIA	
	VOICE OF RUSSIA, Moscow	S • C Asia & S Asia • 250 kW
	VOICE OF RUSSIA, Via Germany	W • Mideast • 100 kW
	SAUDI ARABIA	
	BS OF THE KINGDOM, Riyadh	N Africa • DS-1 • 500 kW
	USA	
	FAMILY RADIO, Okeechobee, Fl	W • S America • 100 kW
	R FREE ASIA, Via Dhabayya, UAE	S • C Asia • 500 kW
	RFE-RL, Via Kuwait	S • W Asia & C Asia • 250 kW
	†VOA	W M-F • E Europe & Mideast • 250 kW
	VOA, Via Philippines	W • E Asia • 250 kW
	VOA, Via Udon Thani, Thailand	W • E Asia • 250 kW

0 1 2 3 4 5 6 7 8 9 10 11 12 13 14 15 16 17 18 19 20 21 22 23 24

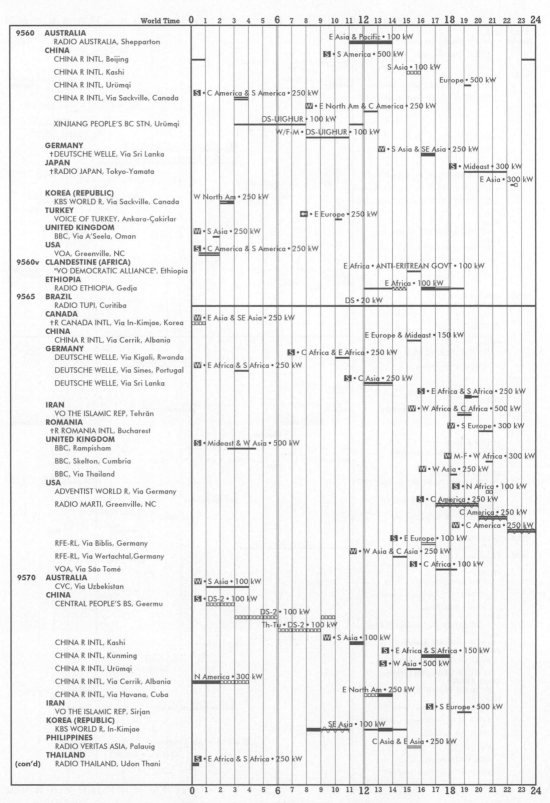

World Time 0 1 2 3 4 5 6 7 8 9 10 11 12 13 14 15 16 17 18 19 20 21 22 23 24

kHz	Country	Station	Schedule
9560	AUSTRALIA	RADIO AUSTRALIA, Shepparton	E Asia & Pacific • 100 kW
	CHINA	CHINA R INTL, Beijing	S • S America • 500 kW
		CHINA R INTL, Kashi	S Asia • 100 kW
		CHINA R INTL, Urümqi	Europe • 500 kW
		CHINA R INTL, Via Sackville, Canada	S • C America & S America • 250 kW
			W • E North Am & C America • 250 kW
		XINJIANG PEOPLE'S BC STN, Urümqi	DS-UIGHUR • 100 kW
			W/F-M • DS-UIGHUR • 100 kW
	GERMANY	†DEUTSCHE WELLE, Via Sri Lanka	W • S Asia & SE Asia • 250 kW
	JAPAN	†RADIO JAPAN, Tokyo-Yamata	S • Mideast • 300 kW
			E Asia • 300 kW
	KOREA (REPUBLIC)	KBS WORLD R, Via Sackville, Canada	W North Am • 250 kW
	TURKEY	VOICE OF TURKEY, Ankara-Çakirlar	• E Europe • 250 kW
	UNITED KINGDOM	BBC, Via A'Seela, Oman	W • S Asia • 250 kW
	USA	VOA, Greenville, NC	S • C America & S America • 250 kW
9560v	CLANDESTINE (AFRICA)	"VO DEMOCRATIC ALLIANCE", Ethiopia	E Africa • ANTI-ERITREAN GOVT • 100 kW
	ETHIOPIA	RADIO ETHIOPIA, Gedja	E Africa • 100 kW
9565	BRAZIL	RADIO TUPI, Curitiba	DS • 20 kW
	CANADA	†R CANADA INTL, Via In-Kimjae, Korea	W • E Asia & SE Asia • 250 kW
	CHINA	CHINA R INTL, Via Cerrik, Albania	E Europe & Mideast • 150 kW
	GERMANY	DEUTSCHE WELLE, Via Kigali, Rwanda	S • C Africa & E Africa • 250 kW
		DEUTSCHE WELLE, Via Sines, Portugal	W • E Africa & S Africa • 250 kW
		DEUTSCHE WELLE, Via Sri Lanka	S • C Asia • 250 kW
			S • E Africa & S Africa • 250 kW
	IRAN	VO THE ISLAMIC REP, Tehrān	W • W Africa & C Africa • 500 kW
	ROMANIA	†R ROMANIA INTL, Bucharest	W • S Europe • 300 kW
	UNITED KINGDOM	BBC, Rampisham	S • Mideast & W Asia • 500 kW
		BBC, Skelton, Cumbria	W M-F • W Africa • 300 kW
		BBC, Via Thailand	W • W Asia • 250 kW
	USA	ADVENTIST WORLD R, Via Germany	S • N Africa • 100 kW
		RADIO MARTI, Greenville, NC	S • C America • 250 kW
			C America • 250 kW
			W • C America • 250 kW
		RFE-RL, Via Biblis, Germany	S • E Europe • 100 kW
		RFE-RL, Via Wertachtal, Germany	W • W Asia & C Asia • 250 kW
		VOA, Via São Tomé	S • C Africa • 100 kW
9570	AUSTRALIA	CVC, Via Uzbekistan	W • S Asia • 100 kW
	CHINA	CENTRAL PEOPLE'S BS, Geermu	S • DS-2 • 100 kW
			DS-2 • 100 kW
			Th-Tu • DS-2 • 100 kW
		CHINA R INTL, Kashi	W • S Asia • 100 kW
		CHINA R INTL, Kunming	S • E Africa & S Africa • 150 kW
		CHINA R INTL, Urümqi	S • W Asia • 500 kW
		CHINA R INTL, Via Cerrik, Albania	N America • 300 kW
		CHINA R INTL, Via Havana, Cuba	E North Am • 250 kW
	IRAN	VO THE ISLAMIC REP, Sirjan	S • S Europe • 500 kW
	KOREA (REPUBLIC)	KBS WORLD R, In-Kimjae	SE Asia • 100 kW
	PHILIPPINES	RADIO VERITAS ASIA, Palauig	C Asia & E Asia • 250 kW
(con'd)	THAILAND	RADIO THAILAND, Udon Thani	S • E Africa & S Africa • 250 kW

0 1 2 3 4 5 6 7 8 9 10 11 12 13 14 15 16 17 18 19 20 21 22 23 24

ENGLISH ARABIC CHINESE FRENCH GERMAN RUSSIAN SPANISH OTHER

World Time 0–24

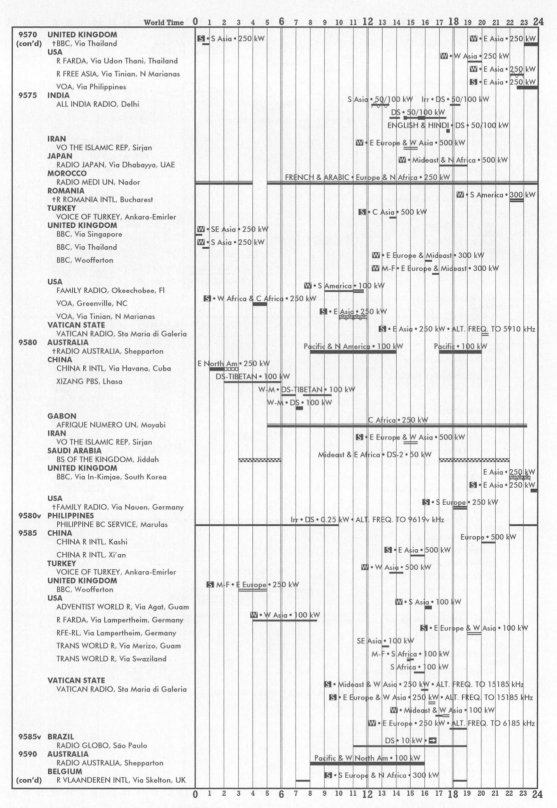

kHz	Country / Station	Schedule
9570 (con'd)	**UNITED KINGDOM** †BBC, Via Thailand	[S] • S Asia • 250 kW; [W] • E Asia • 250 kW
	USA R FARDA, Via Udon Thani, Thailand	[W] • W Asia • 250 kW
	R FREE ASIA, Via Tinian, N Marianas	[W] • E Asia • 250 kW
	VOA, Via Philippines	[S] • E Asia • 250 kW
9575	**INDIA** ALL INDIA RADIO, Delhi	S Asia • 50/100 kW; Irr • DS • 50/100 kW; DS • 50/100 kW; ENGLISH & HINDI • DS • 50/100 kW
	IRAN VO THE ISLAMIC REP, Sirjan	[W] • E Europe & W Asia • 500 kW
	JAPAN RADIO JAPAN, Via Dhabayya, UAE	[W] • Mideast & N Africa • 500 kW
	MOROCCO RADIO MEDI UN, Nador	FRENCH & ARABIC • Europe & N Africa • 250 kW
	ROMANIA †R ROMANIA INTL, Bucharest	[W] • S America • 300 kW
	TURKEY VOICE OF TURKEY, Ankara-Emirler	[S] • C Asia • 500 kW
	UNITED KINGDOM BBC, Via Singapore	[W] • SE Asia • 250 kW
	BBC, Via Thailand	[W] • S Asia • 250 kW
	BBC, Woofferton	[W] • E Europe & Mideast • 300 kW; [W] M-F • E Europe & Mideast • 300 kW
	USA FAMILY RADIO, Okeechobee, Fl	[W] • S America • 100 kW
	VOA, Greenville, NC	[S] • W Africa & C Africa • 250 kW
	VOA, Via Tinian, N Marianas	[S] • E Asia • 250 kW
	VATICAN STATE VATICAN RADIO, Sta Maria di Galeria	[S] • E Asia • 250 kW • ALT. FREQ. TO 5910 kHz
9580	**AUSTRALIA** †RADIO AUSTRALIA, Shepparton	Pacific & N America • 100 kW; Pacific • 100 kW
	CHINA CHINA R INTL, Via Havana, Cuba	E North Am • 250 kW
	XIZANG PBS, Lhasa	DS-TIBETAN • 100 kW; W-M • DS-TIBETAN • 100 kW; W-M • DS • 100 kW
	GABON AFRIQUE NUMERO UN, Moyabi	C Africa • 250 kW
	IRAN VO THE ISLAMIC REP, Sirjan	[S] • E Europe & W Asia • 500 kW
	SAUDI ARABIA BS OF THE KINGDOM, Jiddah	Mideast & E Africa • DS-2 • 50 kW
	UNITED KINGDOM BBC, Via In-Kimjae, South Korea	E Asia • 250 kW; [S] • E Asia • 250 kW
	USA †FAMILY RADIO, Via Nauen, Germany	[S] • S Europe • 250 kW
9580v	**PHILIPPINES** PHILIPPINE BC SERVICE, Marulas	Irr • DS • 0.25 kW • ALT. FREQ. TO 9619v kHz
9585	**CHINA** CHINA R INTL, Kashi	Europe • 500 kW
	CHINA R INTL, Xi'an	[S] • E Asia • 500 kW
	TURKEY VOICE OF TURKEY, Ankara-Emirler	[W] • W Asia • 500 kW
	UNITED KINGDOM BBC, Woofferton	[S] M-F • E Europe • 250 kW
	USA ADVENTIST WORLD R, Via Agat, Guam	[W] • S Asia • 100 kW
	R FARDA, Via Lampertheim, Germany	[W] • W Asia • 100 kW
	RFE-RL, Via Lampertheim, Germany	[S] • E Europe & W Asia • 100 kW
	TRANS WORLD R, Via Merizo, Guam	SE Asia • 100 kW
	TRANS WORLD R, Via Swaziland	M-F • S Africa • 100 kW; S Africa • 100 kW
	VATICAN STATE VATICAN RADIO, Sta Maria di Galeria	[S] • Mideast & W Asia • 250 kW • ALT. FREQ. TO 15185 kHz; [S] • E Europe & W Asia • 250 kW • ALT. FREQ. TO 15185 kHz; [W] • Mideast & W Asia • 100 kW; [W] • E Europe • 250 kW • ALT. FREQ. TO 6185 kHz
9585v	**BRAZIL** RADIO GLOBO, São Paulo	DS • 10 kW • ➡
9590	**AUSTRALIA** RADIO AUSTRALIA, Shepparton	Pacific & W North Am • 100 kW
(con'd)	**BELGIUM** R VLAANDEREN INTL, Via Skelton, UK	[S] • S Europe & N Africa • 300 kW

World Time 0 1 2 3 4 5 6 7 8 9 10 11 12 13 14 15 16 17 18 19 20 21 22 23 24

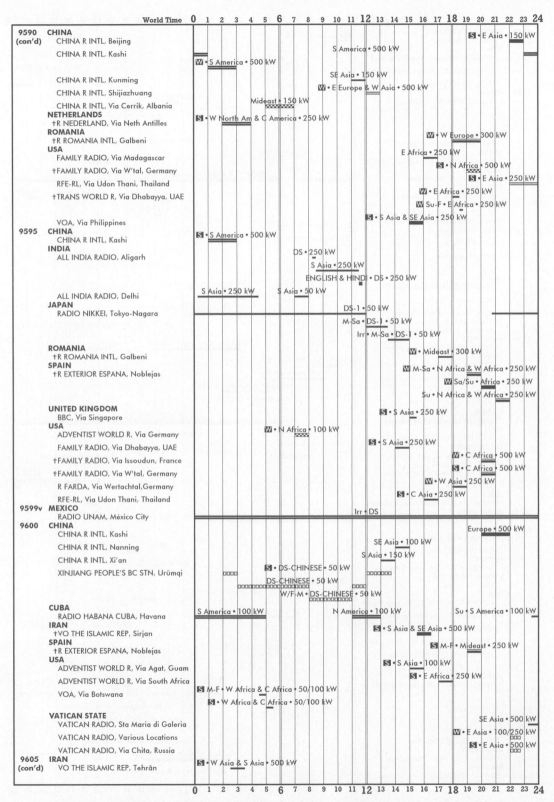

kHz	Country / Station	Schedule
9590 (con'd)	**CHINA**	
	CHINA R INTL, Beijing	S • E Asia • 150 kW
	CHINA R INTL, Kashi	S America • 500 kW
		W • S America • 500 kW
	CHINA R INTL, Kunming	SE Asia • 150 kW
	CHINA R INTL, Shijiazhuang	W • E Europe & W Asia • 500 kW
	CHINA R INTL, Via Cerrik, Albania	Mideast • 150 kW
	NETHERLANDS	
	†R NEDERLAND, Via Neth Antilles	S • W North Am & C America • 250 kW
	ROMANIA	
	†R ROMANIA INTL, Galbeni	W • W Europe • 300 kW
	USA	
	FAMILY RADIO, Via Madagascar	E Africa • 250 kW
	†FAMILY RADIO, Via W'tal, Germany	S • N Africa • 500 kW
	RFE-RL, Via Udon Thani, Thailand	S • E Asia • 250 kW
	†TRANS WORLD R, Via Dhabayya, UAE	W • E Africa • 250 kW
		W Su-F • E Africa • 250 kW
	VOA, Via Philippines	S • S Asia & SE Asia • 250 kW
9595	**CHINA**	
	CHINA R INTL, Kashi	S • S America • 500 kW
	INDIA	
	ALL INDIA RADIO, Aligarh	DS • 250 kW
		S Asia • 250 kW
		ENGLISH & HINDI • DS • 250 kW
	ALL INDIA RADIO, Delhi	S Asia • 250 kW
		S Asia • 50 kW
	JAPAN	
	RADIO NIKKEI, Tokyo-Nagara	DS-1 • 50 kW
		M-Sa • DS-1 • 50 kW
		Irr • M-Sa • DS-1 • 50 kW
	ROMANIA	
	†R ROMANIA INTL, Galbeni	W • Mideast • 300 kW
	SPAIN	
	†R EXTERIOR ESPANA, Noblejas	W M-Sa • N Africa & W Africa • 250 kW
		W Sa/Su • Africa • 250 kW
		Su • N Africa & W Africa • 250 kW
	UNITED KINGDOM	
	BBC, Via Singapore	S • S Asia • 250 kW
	USA	
	ADVENTIST WORLD R, Via Germany	W • N Africa • 100 kW
	FAMILY RADIO, Via Dhabayya, UAE	S • S Asia • 250 kW
	†FAMILY RADIO, Via Issoudun, France	W • C Africa • 500 kW
	†FAMILY RADIO, Via W'tal, Germany	S • C Africa • 500 kW
	R FARDA, Via Wertachtal, Germany	W • W Asia • 250 kW
	RFE-RL, Via Udon Thani, Thailand	S • C Asia • 250 kW
9599v	**MEXICO**	
	RADIO UNAM, México City	Irr • DS
9600	**CHINA**	
	CHINA R INTL, Kashi	Europe • 500 kW
	CHINA R INTL, Nanning	SE Asia • 100 kW
	CHINA R INTL, Xi'an	S Asia • 150 kW
	XINJIANG PEOPLE'S BC STN, Ürümqi	S • DS-CHINESE • 50 kW
		DS-CHINESE • 50 kW
		W/F-M • DS-CHINESE • 50 kW
	CUBA	
	RADIO HABANA CUBA, Havana	S America • 100 kW
		N America • 100 kW
		Su • S America • 100 kW
	IRAN	
	†VO THE ISLAMIC REP, Sirjan	S • S Asia & SE Asia • 500 kW
	SPAIN	
	†R EXTERIOR ESPANA, Noblejas	S M-F • Mideast • 250 kW
	USA	
	ADVENTIST WORLD R, Via Agat, Guam	S • S Asia • 100 kW
	ADVENTIST WORLD R, Via South Africa	S • E Africa • 250 kW
	VOA, Via Botswana	S M-F • W Africa & C Africa • 50/100 kW
		S • W Africa & C Africa • 50/100 kW
	VATICAN STATE	
	VATICAN RADIO, Sta Maria di Galeria	SE Asia • 500 kW
	VATICAN RADIO, Various Locations	W • E Asia • 100/250 kW
	VATICAN RADIO, Via Chita, Russia	S • E Asia • 500 kW
9605 (con'd)	**IRAN**	
	VO THE ISLAMIC REP, Tehrān	S • W Asia & S Asia • 500 kW

World Time 0 1 2 3 4 5 6 7 8 9 10 11 12 13 14 15 16 17 18 19 20 21 22 23 24

ENGLISH ARABIC CHINESE FRENCH GERMAN RUSSIAN SPANISH OTHER

World Time 0 1 2 3 4 5 6 7 8 9 10 11 12 13 14 15 16 17 18 19 20 21 22 23 24

kHz	Country / Station	Schedule
9605 (con'd)	**SPAIN** †R EXTERIOR ESPANA, Noblejas	W M-F • Mideast • 250 kW; W M-F • Africa • 250 kW
	TURKEY VOICE OF TURKEY, Ankara-Çakirlar	S • S Europe • 250 kW
	UNITED KINGDOM BBC, Various Locations	S Asia • 250 kW
	BBC, Via Singapore	E Asia • 250 kW
	†BBC, Via Thailand	W • E Asia • 250 kW; S Asia • 250 kW
	BIBLE VOICE, Via Dhabayya, UAE	S • S Asia • 250 kW
	BIBLE VOICE, Via Wertachtal, Germany	S Th • N Africa • 250 kW
	USA ADVENTIST WORLD R, Via Austria	W • N Africa • 300 kW
	†FAMILY RADIO, Okeechobee, Fl	S America • 100 kW; C America • 100 kW; S • C America • 100 kW
	RFE-RL, Via Biblis, Germany	W • E Europe • 100 kW
	VOA, Via Lampertheim, Germany	W • W Asia • 100 kW
9610	**CANADA** †R CANADA INTL, Sackville, NB	W • N America • 250 kW; W M-F • N America • 250 kW; W Sa/Su • N America • 250 kW
	CHINA CENTRAL PEOPLE'S BS, Beijing	DS-8 (MINORITIES) • 100 kW; Th-Tu • DS-8 (MINORITIES) • 100 kW
	CHINA R INTL, Kashi	S Asia • 100 kW
	CHINA R INTL, Kunming	SE Asia • 100 kW
	CHINA R INTL, Xi'an	S Asia • 150 kW
	CONGO (REPUBLIC) RTV CONGOLAISE, Brazzaville	FRENCH, ETC • DS • 50/100 kW
	IRAN VO THE ISLAMIC REP, Tehrān	S • Mideast • VOICE OF PALESTINE • 500 kW; S • Mideast • 500 kW
	ROMANIA †R ROMANIA INTL, Bucharest	W • E North Am • 300 kW
	†R ROMANIA INTL, Galbeni	W • W Europe • 300 kW
	TURKEY VOICE OF TURKEY, Ankara-Emirler	S • S Europe • 500 kW
	UNITED KINGDOM BBC, Rampisham	S • W Africa & C Africa • 500 kW
	BBC, Various Locations	E Africa • 250/500 kW
	BBC, Via Thailand	S • E Asia • 250 kW
	USA ADVENTIST WORLD R, Via Germany	W Su • S Europe • 100 kW
	ADVENTIST WORLD R, Via South Africa	S • E Africa • 250 kW
	†FAMILY RADIO, Via W'tal, Germany	S • W Africa & C Africa • 500 kW
	VATICAN STATE VATICAN RADIO, Sta Maria di Galeria	S America • 100 kW; C America • 100 kW
9615	**BRAZIL** RADIO CULTURA, São Paulo	DS • 7.5 kW • ➡
	CANADA †R CANADA INTL, Via Skelton, UK	W Sa/Su • E Europe • 300 kW
	CHINA CHINA R INTL, Urümqi	W • Europe • 500 kW
	NEW ZEALAND R NEW ZEALAND INTL, Rangitaiki	Pacific • 100 kW • ALT. FREQ. TO 15720 kHz
	PHILIPPINES †RADIO VERITAS ASIA, Palauig	E Asia • 250 kW; W • Mideast • 250 kW; W W/F/Su • Mideast • 250 kW
	RUSSIA VOICE OF RUSSIA, Samara	S • E Europe • 250 kW
	UNITED KINGDOM BBC, Via A'Seela, Oman	W • S Asia • 250 kW
	BBC, Via Singapore	S • C Asia • 100 kW
	USA ADVENTIST WORLD R, Via Agat, Guam	W • E Asia • 100 kW
	†FAMILY RADIO, Via Irkutsk, Russia	S • SE Asia • 500 kW
	FAMILY RADIO, Via Samara, Russia	S • Europe • 200 kW
	KNLS-NEW LIFE STN, Anchor Pt, Alaska	W • E Asia • 100 kW
	†RFE-RL	S • W Asia & C Asia • 250 kW

0 1 2 3 4 5 6 7 8 9 10 11 12 13 14 15 16 17 18 19 20 21 22 23 24

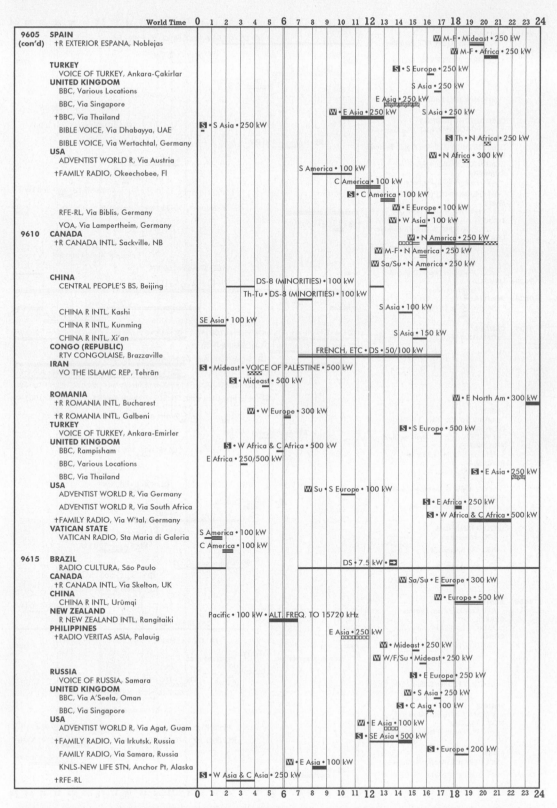

SEASONAL S OR W 1-HR TIMESHIFT MIDYEAR ⬅ OR ➡ JAMMING / OR /\ EARLIEST HEARD ◁ LATEST HEARD ▷ NEW FOR 2009 †

World Time 0 1 2 3 4 5 6 7 8 9 10 11 12 13 14 15 16 17 18 19 20 21 22 23 24

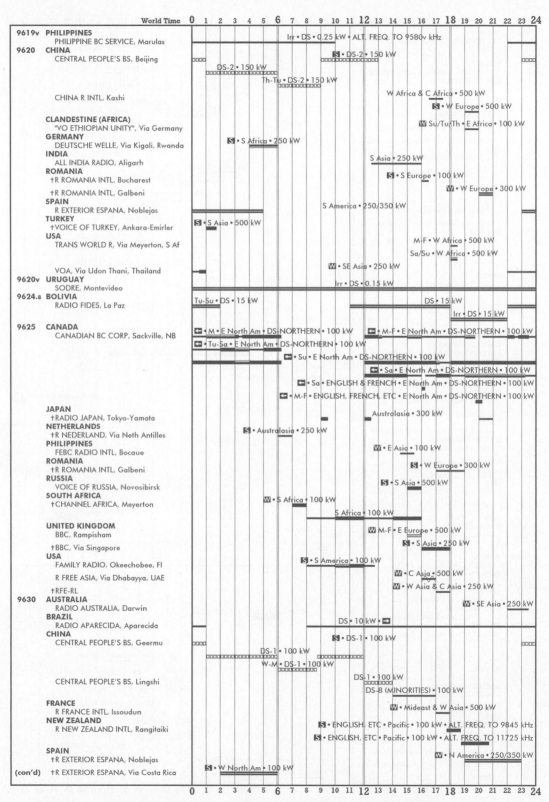

kHz	Country / Station	Schedule
9619v	**PHILIPPINES** PHILIPPINE BC SERVICE, Marulas	Irr • DS • 0.25 kW • ALT. FREQ. TO 9580v kHz
9620	**CHINA** CENTRAL PEOPLE'S BS, Beijing	S • DS-2 • 150 kW; DS-2 • 150 kW; Th-Tu • DS-2 • 150 kW
	CHINA R INTL, Kashi	W Africa & C Africa • 500 kW; S • W Europe • 500 kW
	CLANDESTINE (AFRICA) "VO ETHIOPIAN UNITY", Via Germany	W Su/Tu/Th • E Africa • 100 kW
	GERMANY DEUTSCHE WELLE, Via Kigali, Rwanda	S • S Africa • 250 kW
	INDIA ALL INDIA RADIO, Aligarh	S Asia • 250 kW
	ROMANIA †R ROMANIA INTL, Bucharest	S • S Europe • 100 kW
	†R ROMANIA INTL, Galbeni	W • W Europe • 300 kW
	SPAIN R EXTERIOR ESPANA, Noblejas	S America • 250/350 kW
	TURKEY †VOICE OF TURKEY, Ankara-Emirler	S • S Asia • 500 kW
	USA TRANS WORLD R, Via Meyerton, S Af	M-F • W Africa • 500 kW; Sa/Su • W Africa • 500 kW
	VOA, Via Udon Thani, Thailand	W • SE Asia • 250 kW
9620v	**URUGUAY** SODRE, Montevideo	Irr • DS • 0.15 kW
9624.8	**BOLIVIA** RADIO FIDES, La Paz	Tu-Su • DS • 15 kW; DS • 15 kW; Irr • DS • 15 kW
9625	**CANADA** CANADIAN BC CORP, Sackville, NB	← • M • E North Am • DS-NORTHERN • 100 kW; ← • M-F • E North Am • DS-NORTHERN • 100 kW; ← • Tu-Sa • E North Am • DS-NORTHERN • 100 kW; ← • Su • E North Am • DS-NORTHERN • 100 kW; ← • Sa • E North Am • DS-NORTHERN • 100 kW; ← • Sa • ENGLISH & FRENCH • E North Am • DS-NORTHERN • 100 kW; ← • M-F • ENGLISH, FRENCH, ETC • E North Am • DS-NORTHERN • 100 kW
	JAPAN †RADIO JAPAN, Tokyo-Yamata	Australasia • 300 kW
	NETHERLANDS †R NEDERLAND, Via Neth Antilles	S • Australasia • 250 kW
	PHILIPPINES FEBC RADIO INTL, Bocaue	W • E Asia • 100 kW
	ROMANIA †R ROMANIA INTL, Galbeni	S • W Europe • 300 kW
	RUSSIA VOICE OF RUSSIA, Novosibirsk	S • S Asia • 500 kW
	SOUTH AFRICA †CHANNEL AFRICA, Meyerton	W • S Africa • 100 kW; S Africa • 100 kW
	UNITED KINGDOM BBC, Rampisham	W M-F • E Europe • 500 kW
	†BBC, Via Singapore	S • S Asia • 250 kW
	USA FAMILY RADIO, Okeechobee, Fl	S • S America • 100 kW
	R FREE ASIA, Via Dhabayya, UAE	W • C Asia • 500 kW
	†RFE-RL	W • W Asia & C Asia • 250 kW
9630	**AUSTRALIA** RADIO AUSTRALIA, Darwin	W • SE Asia • 250 kW
	BRAZIL RADIO APARECIDA, Aparecida	DS • 10 kW • →
	CHINA CENTRAL PEOPLE'S BS, Geermu	S • DS-1 • 100 kW; DS-1 • 100 kW; W-M • DS-1 • 100 kW
	CENTRAL PEOPLE'S BS, Lingshi	DS-1 • 100 kW; DS-8 (MINORITIES) • 100 kW
	FRANCE R FRANCE INTL, Issoudun	W • Mideast & W Asia • 500 kW
	NEW ZEALAND R NEW ZEALAND INTL, Rangitaiki	S • ENGLISH, ETC • Pacific • 100 kW • ALT. FREQ. TO 9845 kHz; S • ENGLISH, ETC • Pacific • 100 kW • ALT. FREQ. TO 11725 kHz
	SPAIN †R EXTERIOR ESPANA, Noblejas	W • N America • 250/350 kW
(con'd)	†R EXTERIOR ESPANA, Via Costa Rica	S • W North Am • 100 kW

World Time 0 1 2 3 4 5 6 7 8 9 10 11 12 13 14 15 16 17 18 19 20 21 22 23 24

ENGLISH ARABIC CHINESE FRENCH GERMAN RUSSIAN SPANISH OTHER

World Time 0–24

kHz	Country	Station	Schedule
9630 (con'd)	UNITED KINGDOM	†BBC, Skelton, Cumbria	W • N Africa • 300 kW
9635	CANADA	R CANADA INTL, Via Xian, China	W • S Asia • 500 kW
	CHILE	CVC-LA VOZ, Santiago	W • S America • 100 kW
			S America • 100 kW
	CHINA	CHINA R INTL, Kashi	S Asia • 100 kW
			W • W Europe • 500 kW
	CLANDESTINE (ASIA)	"SOUND OF HOPE", Via Taiwan	E Asia • 100 kW
	INDIA	ALL INDIA RADIO, Aligarh	S Asia • 250 kW
	IRAN	VO THE ISLAMIC REP, Tehrān	W • E Asia • 500 kW
	MALI	RTV DU MALI, Bamako	FRENCH, ETC • DS • 100 kW
	ROMANIA	†R ROMANIA INTL, Bucharest	W • S America • 300 kW
	UNITED KINGDOM	BBC, Via Zyyi, Cyprus	S M-F • E Europe • 250 kW
			S • E Europe • 250 kW
			S Sa/Su • E Europe • 250 kW
			S Sa • E Europe • 250 kW
	USA	ADVENTIST WORLD R, Via Agat, Guam	W • E Asia • 100 kW
		†RFE-RL	S • E Europe • 250 kW
		TRANS WORLD R, Via Merizo, Guam	SE Asia • 100 kW
			Sa/Su • SE Asia • 100 kW
			S • S Asia • 100 kW
			S Sa/Su • S Asia • 100 kW
		†VOA	W • S Europe • 250 kW
		VOA, Via Lampertheim, Germany	W • W Asia & S Asia • 100 kW
	VATICAN STATE	VATICAN RADIO, Sta Maria di Galeria	W • Mideast • 100 kW
9639.8	VENEZUELA	ECOS DEL TORBES, San Cristóbal	DS-TEMP INACTIVE • 1 kW
9640	CANADA	R CANADA INTL, Sackville, NB	W • C America • 250 kW
	CHINA	CHINA R INTL, Kashi	W Europe • 500 kW
	KOREA (REPUBLIC)	KBS WORLD R, In-Kimjae	SE Asia • 100 kW
	POLAND	POLISH RADIO, Via French Guiana	W • W Europe • 250 kW
	ROMANIA	†R ROMANIA INTL, Bucharest	W • E North Am • 300 kW
			W • W Europe • 300 kW
	RUSSIA	VOICE OF RUSSIA, Novosibirsk	S • E Asia • 200 kW
	SAUDI ARABIA	†BS OF THE KINGDOM, Riyadh	C Asia • 500 kW
	USA	ADVENTIST WORLD R, Via Germany	W • N Africa • 100 kW
		GOSPEL FOR ASIA, Via Germany	S • S Asia • 250 kW
		PAN AM BC, Via Wertachtal, Germany	S Su • S Asia • 125 kW
9645	BRAZIL	RADIO BANDEIRANTES, São Paulo	DS • 10 kW
	CHINA	CENTRAL PEOPLE'S BS, Beijing	S • DS-1 • 100 kW
			DS-1 • 100 kW
			S • DS-8 (MINORITIES) • 100 kW
			W-M • DS-1 • 100 kW
			S W-M • DS-1 • 100 kW
		CHINA R INTL, Beijing	SE Asia • 500 kW
		CHINA R INTL, Kunming	W Africa • 500 kW
	CLANDESTINE (ASIA)	"R FREE NORTH KOREA", Via Taiwan	W • E Asia • 100 kW
	GERMANY	DEUTSCHE WELLE, Via Sri Lanka	S • W Asia & S Asia • 250 kW
	PHILIPPINES	RADIO VERITAS ASIA, Palauig	SE Asia • 250 kW
	ROMANIA	†R ROMANIA INTL, Bucharest	S • C America • 300 kW
			S • W North Am • 300 kW
	UNITED KINGDOM	BBC, Via Singapore	S • S Asia • 250 kW
(con'd)	USA	R FREE ASIA, Via Dhabayya, UAE	W • C Asia • 500 kW

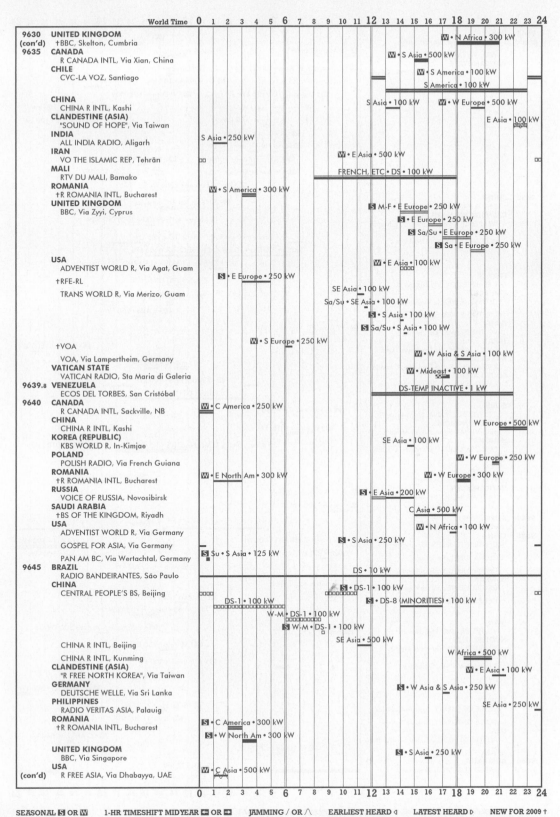

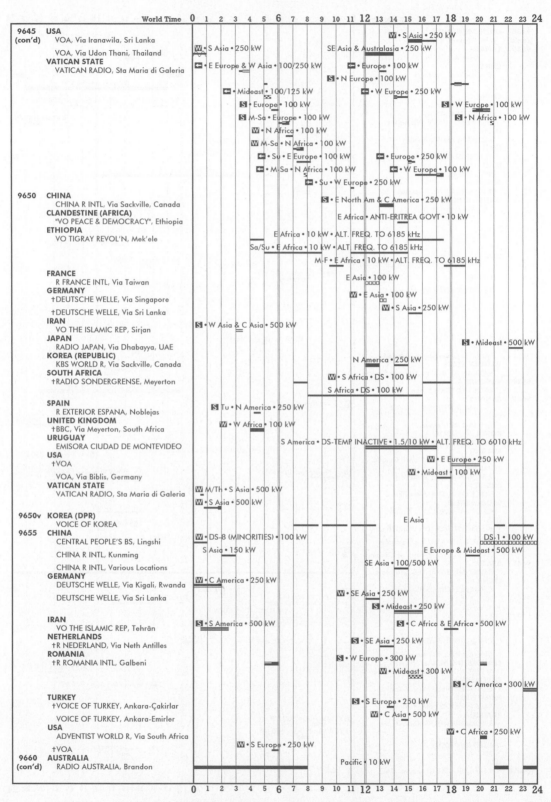

World Time 0 1 2 3 4 5 6 7 8 9 10 11 12 13 14 15 16 17 18 19 20 21 22 23 24

kHz	Country / Station	Schedule
9645 (con'd)	**USA**	
	VOA, Via Iranawila, Sri Lanka	W • S Asia • 250 kW
	VOA, Via Udon Thani, Thailand	W • S Asia • 250 kW; SE Asia & Australasia • 250 kW
	VATICAN STATE	
	VATICAN RADIO, Sta Maria di Galeria	← • E Europe & W Asia • 100/250 kW; ← • Europe • 100 kW
		S • N Europe • 100 kW
		← • Mideast • 100/125 kW; ← • W Europe • 250 kW
		S • Europe • 100 kW; S • W Europe • 100 kW
		S M-Sa • Europe • 100 kW; S • N Africa • 100 kW
		W • N Africa • 100 kW
		W M-Sa • N Africa • 100 kW
		← • Su • E Europe • 100 kW; ← • Europe • 250 kW
		← • M-Sa • N Africa • 100 kW; ← • W Europe • 100 kW
		← • Su • W Europe • 250 kW
9650	**CHINA**	
	CHINA R INTL, Via Sackville, Canada	S • E North Am & C America • 250 kW
	CLANDESTINE (AFRICA)	
	"VO PEACE & DEMOCRACY", Ethiopia	E Africa • ANTI-ERITREA GOVT • 10 kW
	ETHIOPIA	
	VO TIGRAY REVOL'N, Mek'ele	E Africa • 10 kW • ALT. FREQ. TO 6185 kHz
		Sa/Su • E Africa • 10 kW • ALT. FREQ. TO 6185 kHz
		M-F • E Africa • 10 kW • ALT. FREQ. TO 6185 kHz
	FRANCE	
	R FRANCE INTL, Via Taiwan	E Asia • 100 kW
	GERMANY	
	†DEUTSCHE WELLE, Via Singapore	W • E Asia • 100 kW
	†DEUTSCHE WELLE, Via Sri Lanka	W • S Asia • 250 kW
	IRAN	
	VO THE ISLAMIC REP, Sirjan	S • W Asia & C Asia • 500 kW
	JAPAN	
	RADIO JAPAN, Via Dhabayya, UAE	S • Mideast • 500 kW
	KOREA (REPUBLIC)	
	KBS WORLD R, Via Sackville, Canada	N America • 250 kW
	SOUTH AFRICA	
	†RADIO SONDERGRENSE, Meyerton	W • S Africa • DS • 100 kW
		S Africa • DS • 100 kW
	SPAIN	
	R EXTERIOR ESPANA, Noblejas	S Tu • N America • 250 kW
	UNITED KINGDOM	
	†BBC, Via Meyerton, South Africa	W • W Africa • 100 kW
	URUGUAY	
	EMISORA CIUDAD DE MONTEVIDEO	S America • DS-TEMP INACTIVE • 1.5/10 kW • ALT. FREQ. TO 6010 kHz
	USA	
	†VOA	W • E Europe • 250 kW
	VOA, Via Biblis, Germany	W • Mideast • 100 kW
	VATICAN STATE	
	VATICAN RADIO, Sta Maria di Galeria	W M/Th • S Asia • 500 kW
		W • S Asia • 500 kW
9650v	**KOREA (DPR)**	
	VOICE OF KOREA	E Asia
9655	**CHINA**	
	CENTRAL PEOPLE'S BS, Lingshi	W • DS-8 (MINORITIES) • 100 kW; DS-1 • 100 kW
	CHINA R INTL, Kunming	S Asia • 150 kW; E Europe & Mideast • 500 kW
	CHINA R INTL, Various Locations	SE Asia • 100/500 kW
	GERMANY	
	DEUTSCHE WELLE, Via Kigali, Rwanda	W • C America • 250 kW
	DEUTSCHE WELLE, Via Sri Lanka	W • SE Asia • 250 kW
		S • Mideast • 250 kW
	IRAN	
	VO THE ISLAMIC REP, Tehrān	S • S America • 500 kW; S • C Africa & E Africa • 500 kW
	NETHERLANDS	
	†R NEDERLAND, Via Neth Antilles	S • SE Asia • 250 kW
	ROMANIA	
	†R ROMANIA INTL, Galbeni	S • W Europe • 300 kW
		W • Mideast • 300 kW
		S • C America • 300 kW
	TURKEY	
	†VOICE OF TURKEY, Ankara-Çakirlar	S • S Europe • 250 kW
	VOICE OF TURKEY, Ankara-Emirler	W • C Asia • 500 kW
	USA	
	ADVENTIST WORLD R, Via South Africa	W • C Africa • 250 kW
	†VOA	W • S Europe • 250 kW
9660 (con'd)	**AUSTRALIA**	
	RADIO AUSTRALIA, Brandon	Pacific • 10 kW

0 1 2 3 4 5 6 7 8 9 10 11 12 13 14 15 16 17 18 19 20 21 22 23 24

ENGLISH ▬ ARABIC ▭ CHINESE ▫▫▫ FRENCH ▬ GERMAN ▬ RUSSIAN ═ SPANISH ═ OTHER —

World Time 0–24

Frequency	Country / Station	Schedule
9660 (con'd)	**CHINA (TAIWAN)** R TAIWAN INTL, Kouhu	E Asia • MAINLAND NETWORK • 100 kW
	IRAN VO THE ISLAMIC REP, Sirjan	W • W Asia & C Asia • 500 kW
	JAPAN RADIO JAPAN, Via Netherlands Antilles	S America • 300 kW
	POLAND POLISH RADIO, Via French Guiana	W • W Europe • 250 kW
	ROMANIA †R ROMANIA INTL, Bucharest	W • E Asia • 300 kW
	RUSSIA VOICE OF RUSSIA, Via Xi'an, China	SE Asia • 150 kW
	SWEDEN †IBRA RADIO, Via Jülich, Germany	W • E Africa • 100 kW
	UNITED KINGDOM BBC, Via Brandon, Australia	SE Asia • 10 kW
	USA FAMILY RADIO, Via Meyerton, S Africa	W • E Africa • 250 kW
	FAMILY RADIO, Via Skelton, UK	W • N Africa • 300 kW
	TRANS WORLD R, Via Jülich,Germany	S Sa • E Europe • 100 kW
	TRANS WORLD R, Via Meyerton, S Af	E Africa • 500 kW M-F • E Africa • 500 kW M-Sa • C Africa • 500 kW
	VATICAN STATE VATICAN RADIO, Sta Maria di Galeria	S • C Africa & E Africa • 500 kW C Africa & E Africa • 100/500 kW W • C Africa & E Africa • 100 kW S • C Africa & S Africa • 500 kW C Africa & S Africa • 500 kW W • C Africa & S Africa • 500 kW W • W Africa • 500 kW
9665	**BRAZIL** R VOZ MISSIONARIA, Florianópolis	DS • 10 kW
	CHINA CENTRAL PEOPLE'S BS, Beijing	TAIWAN-1 • 100 kW
	CHINA R INTL, Kashi	S • W Asia & S Asia • 500 kW
	CHINA R INTL, Kunming	SE Asia • 100 kW S • W Africa & C Africa • 500 kW
	CHINA R INTL, Various Locations	S Asia • 100/150 kW
	CHINA R INTL, Via Brasilia, Brazil	S America • 250 kW C America • 250 kW
	IRAN VO THE ISLAMIC REP, Tehrãn	S • Mideast • 500 kW
	PHILIPPINES †RADIO VERITAS ASIA, Palauig	S Asia • 250 kW • ALT. FREQ. TO 9530 kHz
	ROMANIA †R ROMANIA INTL, Bucharest	W • S America • 300 kW
	RUSSIA VOICE OF RUSSIA, Via Moldova	S • E North Am • 500 kW
	SPAIN †R EXTERIOR ESPANA, Noblejas	Sa/Su • Europe • 250 kW M/Th • Europe • 250 kW ← • M-F • Europe • 250 kW W M-F • Europe • 250 kW • ALT. FREQ. TO 9690 kHz S M-F • Europe • 250 kW W Sa/Su • Europe • 250 kW
	TURKEY †VOICE OF TURKEY, Ankara-Çakirlar	W • S Europe • 250 kW
9665v	**KOREA (DPR)** KOREAN CENTRAL BS, Pyongyang	DS • 200 kW
9670	**AUSTRALIA** CVC, Darwin	S • SE Asia • 250 kW
	CANADA R CANADA INTL, Via Skelton, UK	W • C Africa • 300 kW
	CHINA CHINA R INTL, Beijing	S • W Asia • 500 kW
	CHINA R INTL, Kunming	W • W Africa & C Africa • 500 kW
	JAPAN RADIO JAPAN, Tokyo-Yamata	W • Mideast • 300 kW
	NETHERLANDS †R NEDERLAND, Via Tinian	W • SE Asia • 100 kW
	PHILIPPINES RADIO VERITAS ASIA, Palauig	SE Asia • 250 kW
	POLAND †POLISH RADIO, Via Fontbonne, France	S • E Europe • 100 kW
(con'd)	**UNITED KINGDOM** †BBC, Skelton, Cumbria	S • N Africa • 300 kW

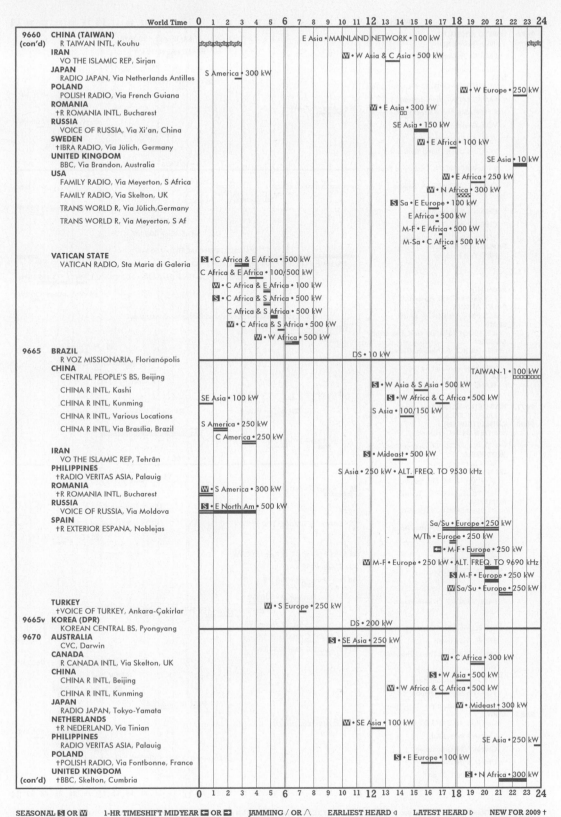

kHz	Country / Station (World Time 0–24)	Schedule notes
9670 (con'd)	**UNITED KINGDOM**	
	BBC, Via Singapore	S • SE Asia • 100 kW
	BBC, Via Thailand	S • SE Asia • 250 kW
	BBC, Wooferton	W • C Asia • 250 kW
	USA	
	ADVENTIST WORLD R, Via Agat, Guam	S • E Asia • 100 kW
	FAMILY RADIO, Via Germany	W • N Africa, W Africa & C Africa • 125 kW
	R FREE ASIA, Via Wertachtal, Germany	W • S Asia • 500 kW
	VOA, Greenville, NC	W • C America • 250 kW
	VOA, Via Philippines	S • C Asia • 250 kW
	VOA, Via Udon Thani, Thailand	S • Mideast • 250 kW
9675	**BRAZIL**	
	R CANCAO NOVA, Cachoeira Paulista	DS • 10 kW
	CHINA	
	CENTRAL PEOPLE'S BS, Beijing	DS-1 • 100 kW; W-M • DS-1 • 100 kW
	CHINA R INTL, Beijing	S • E Asia • 150 kW
	CHINA R INTL, Kunming	SE Asia • 100/150 kW
	CHINA R INTL, Shijiazhuang	S • E Asia • 500 kW
	PAPUA NEW GUINEA	
	NBC, Port Moresby	DS-TEMP INACTIVE • 100 kW; DS-TEMP INACTIVE • 100 kW • ALT. FREQ. TO 4890 kHz; ENGLISH, ETC • DS-TEMP INACTIVE • 100 kW • ALT. FREQ. TO 4890 kHz
	ROMANIA	
	†R ROMANIA INTL, Galbeni	S • W Europe • 300 kW
	SAUDI ARABIA	
	BS OF THE KINGDOM, Riyadh	Mideast • DS-1 • 500 kW
	SPAIN	
	†R EXTERIOR ESPANA, Via Costa Rica	W • W North Am • 100 kW
	SWEDEN	
	†IBRA RADIO, Via Nauen, Germany	S • W Africa • 100 kW
	UNITED KINGDOM	
	BBC, Skelton, Cumbria	W • N Africa • 300 kW
	USA	
	TRANS WORLD R, Via Meyerton, S Af	E Africa • 250 kW
	VOA, Via São Tomé	W • C Africa & S Africa • 100 kW
9677.7	**NAGORNO-KARABAKH**	
	RADIO VOICE OF JUSTICE, Stepanakert	← • W/Sa • W Asia; ← • Tu/F • W Asia
9680	**CHINA (TAIWAN)**	
	R TAIWAN INTL, Huwei	E Asia • TAIWAN NETWORK • 100 kW
	R TAIWAN INTL, Via Okeechobee, USA	N America • 100 kW
	INDONESIA	
	RRI, Cimanggis,Jawa	Irr • DS • 250 kW
	IRAN	
	†VO THE ISLAMIC REP, Sirjan	S • C Asia • 500 kW
	VO THE ISLAMIC REP, Tehrān	W • S America • 500 kW
	ROMANIA	
	†R ROMANIA INTL, Bucharest	S • W Europe • 300 kW
	THAILAND	
	RADIO THAILAND, Udon Thani	W • E Africa & S Africa • 250 kW; S • Mideast • 250 kW; S • Europe • 250 kW
	UNITED KINGDOM	
	BBC, Rampisham	S M-F • E Europe & W Asia • 500 kW
	BBC, Via Zyyi, Cyprus	S • C Asia • 250 kW; S M-F • E Europe • 250 kW
	USA	
	†FAMILY RADIO, Okeechobee, Fl	N America • 100 kW; W • S America • 100 kW
	RFE-RL, Via Biblis, Germany	W • W Asia • 100 kW
	RFE-RL, Via Kuwait	W • W Asia & C Asia • 125 kW
	RFE-RL, Via Udon Thani, Thailand	W • W Asia & C Asia • 250 kW
	†VOA	W M-F • W Africa • 250 kW
	VOA, Via Biblis, Germany	W • W Asia • 100 kW
	VOA, Via Jülich,Germany	W • W Asia • 100 kW
	VOA, Via Philippines	W • E Asia • 250 kW
9685	**CHINA**	
	†CENTRAL PEOPLE'S BS, Beijing	TAIWAN-1 • 100 kW
	CHINA R INTL, Kashi	S America • 500 kW
	CHINA R INTL, Kunming	W Africa & C Africa • 500 kW
	CHINA R INTL, Urümqi	E Europe & W Asia • 500 kW
(con'd)	CHINA R INTL, Xi'an	SE Asia • 500 kW

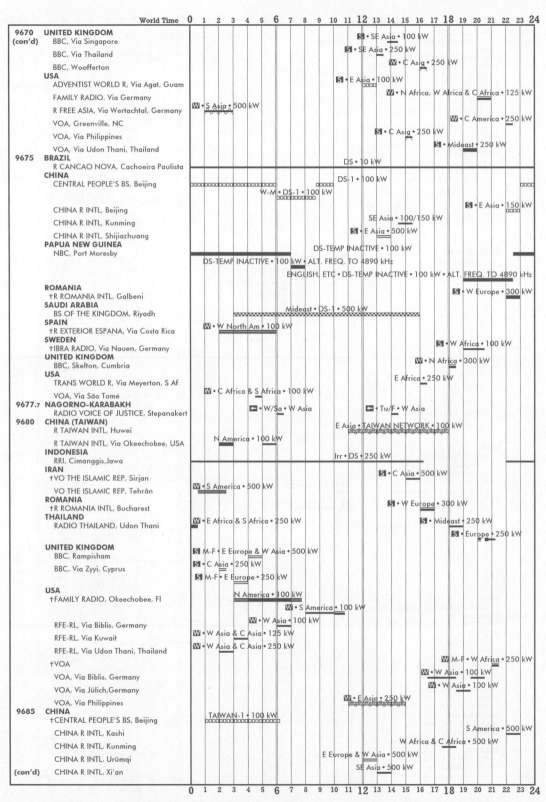

ENGLISH ▬ ARABIC ▒ CHINESE ▭ FRENCH ═ GERMAN ▬ RUSSIAN ═ SPANISH ═ OTHER —

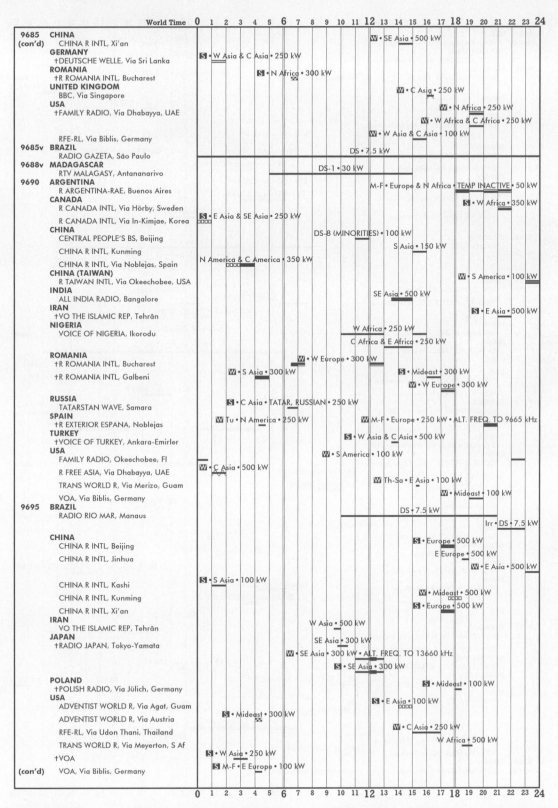

World Time 0 1 2 3 4 5 6 7 8 9 10 11 12 13 14 15 16 17 18 19 20 21 22 23 24

kHz	Country / Station	Schedule
9685 (con'd)	**CHINA**	
	CHINA R INTL, Xi'an	W • SE Asia • 500 kW
	GERMANY	
	†DEUTSCHE WELLE, Via Sri Lanka	S • W Asia & C Asia • 250 kW
	ROMANIA	
	†R ROMANIA INTL, Bucharest	S • N Africa • 300 kW
	UNITED KINGDOM	
	BBC, Via Singapore	W • C Asia • 250 kW
	USA	
	†FAMILY RADIO, Via Dhabayya, UAE	W • N Africa • 250 kW
		W • W Africa & C Africa • 250 kW
	RFE-RL, Via Biblis, Germany	W • W Asia & C Asia • 100 kW
9685v	**BRAZIL**	
	RADIO GAZETA, São Paulo	DS • 7.5 kW
9688v	**MADAGASCAR**	
	RTV MALAGASY, Antananarivo	DS-1 • 30 kW
9690	**ARGENTINA**	
	R ARGENTINA-RAE, Buenos Aires	M-F • Europe & N Africa • TEMP INACTIVE • 50 kW
	CANADA	
	R CANADA INTL, Via Hörby, Sweden	S • W Africa • 350 kW
	R CANADA INTL, Via In-Kimjae, Korea	S • E Asia & SE Asia • 250 kW
	CHINA	
	CENTRAL PEOPLE'S BS, Beijing	DS-8 (MINORITIES) • 100 kW
	CHINA R INTL, Kunming	S Asia • 150 kW
	CHINA R INTL, Via Noblejas, Spain	N America & C America • 350 kW
	CHINA (TAIWAN)	
	R TAIWAN INTL, Via Okeechobee, USA	W • S America • 100 kW
	INDIA	
	ALL INDIA RADIO, Bangalore	SE Asia • 500 kW
	IRAN	
	†VO THE ISLAMIC REP, Tehrān	S • E Asia • 500 kW
	NIGERIA	
	VOICE OF NIGERIA, Ikorodu	W Africa • 250 kW
		C Africa & E Africa • 250 kW
	ROMANIA	
	†R ROMANIA INTL, Bucharest	W • W Europe • 300 kW
	†R ROMANIA INTL, Galbeni	W • S Asia • 300 kW
		S • Mideast • 300 kW
		W • W Europe • 300 kW
	RUSSIA	
	TATARSTAN WAVE, Samara	S • C Asia • TATAR, RUSSIAN • 250 kW
	SPAIN	
	†R EXTERIOR ESPANA, Noblejas	W Tu • N America • 250 kW
		W M-F • Europe • 250 kW • ALT. FREQ. TO 9665 kHz
	TURKEY	
	†VOICE OF TURKEY, Ankara-Emirler	S • W Asia & C Asia • 500 kW
	USA	
	FAMILY RADIO, Okeechobee, Fl	W • S America • 100 kW
	R FREE ASIA, Via Dhabayya, UAE	W • C Asia • 500 kW
	TRANS WORLD R, Via Merizo, Guam	W Th-Sa • E Asia • 100 kW
	VOA, Via Biblis, Germany	W • Mideast • 100 kW
9695	**BRAZIL**	
	RADIO RIO MAR, Manaus	DS • 7.5 kW
		Irr • DS • 7.5 kW
	CHINA	
	CHINA R INTL, Beijing	S • Europe • 500 kW
	CHINA R INTL, Jinhua	E Europe • 500 kW
		W • E Asia • 500 kW
	CHINA R INTL, Kashi	S • S Asia • 100 kW
	CHINA R INTL, Kunming	W • Mideast • 500 kW
	CHINA R INTL, Xi'an	S • Europe • 500 kW
	IRAN	
	VO THE ISLAMIC REP, Tehrān	W Asia • 500 kW
	JAPAN	
	†RADIO JAPAN, Tokyo-Yamata	SE Asia • 300 kW
		W • SE Asia • 300 kW • ALT. FREQ. TO 13660 kHz
		S • SE Asia • 300 kW
	POLAND	
	†POLISH RADIO, Via Jülich, Germany	S • Mideast • 100 kW
	USA	
	ADVENTIST WORLD R, Via Agat, Guam	S • E Asia • 100 kW
	ADVENTIST WORLD R, Via Austria	S • Mideast • 300 kW
	RFE-RL, Via Udon Thani, Thailand	W • C Asia • 250 kW
	TRANS WORLD R, Via Meyerton, S Af	W Africa • 500 kW
	†VOA	S • W Asia • 250 kW
(con'd)	VOA, Via Biblis, Germany	S M-F • E Europe • 100 kW

0 1 2 3 4 5 6 7 8 9 10 11 12 13 14 15 16 17 18 19 20 21 22 23 24

SEASONAL S OR W 1-HR TIMESHIFT MIDYEAR ⇦ OR ⇨ JAMMING / OR /\ EARLIEST HEARD ◁ LATEST HEARD ▷ NEW FOR 2009 †

World Time 0 1 2 3 4 5 6 7 8 9 10 11 12 13 14 15 16 17 18 19 20 21 22 23 24

Frequency	Country / Station	Schedule
9695 (con'd)	**USA**	
	VOA, Via Lampertheim, Germany	W • S Asia • 100 kW
	VATICAN STATE	
	VATICAN RADIO, Sta Maria di Galeria	W • E Asia • 500 kW
9700	**BULGARIA**	
	RADIO BULGARIA, Plovdiv	S • E North Am • 500 kW; S • W Europe • 500 kW
	CHINA	
	CHINA R INTL, Kashi	W • Europe • 500 kW
	GERMANY	
	DEUTSCHE WELLE, Via Kigali, Rwanda	S • C Africa & S Africa • 250 kW; S • S Africa • 250 kW
	ROMANIA	
	†R ROMANIA INTL, Bucharest	S • Mideast • 300 kW; W • S Europe • 300 kW
	†RADIO ROMANIA, Bucharest	S Su • Mideast • 300 kW
	TURKEY	
	†VOICE OF TURKEY, Ankara-Çakirlar	S • S Europe • 250 kW
	VOICE OF TURKEY, Ankara-Emirler	W • W Europe • 500 kW
	USA	
	VOA, Via Udon Thani, Thailand	S • SE Asia • 250 kW; S • W Asia • 250 kW
9704v	**ETHIOPIA**	
	RADIO ETHIOPIA, Gedja	DS • 100 kW; Sa/Su • DS • 100 kW; M-F • DS • 100 kW
9705	**CHINA**	
	VOICE OF PUJIANG, Shanghai	E Asia • 50 kW • ALT. FREQ. TO 5075 kHz
	XINJIANG PEOPLE'S BC STN, Urümqi	DS-KYRGYZ • 50 kW; W/F-M • DS-KYRGYZ • 50 kW
	INDIA	
	ALL INDIA RADIO, Panaji	E Asia & SE Asia • 250 kW
	NIGER	
	LA VOIX DU SAHEL, Niamey	FRENCH, ETC • DS • 100 kW; M-Sa • FRENCH, ETC • DS • 100 kW
	USA	
	FAMILY RADIO, Via Jülich,Germany	S • Mideast • 100 kW
	VOA, Via Saipan, N Marianas	W • E Asia • 100 kW
9710	**ALGERIA**	
	R ALGERIENNE, Via Skelton, UK	S • N Africa • DS • 300 kW
	AUSTRALIA	
	†RADIO AUSTRALIA, Shepparton	Pacific • 100 kW; Pacific & W North Am • 100 kW
	CANADA	
	†R CANADA INTL, Via Woofferton, UK	W • Mideast • 300 kW
	CHINA	
	CENTRAL PEOPLE'S BS, Shijiazhuang	DS-1 • 100 kW
	CHINA R INTL, Kashi	S • S America • 500 kW; S America • 500 kW
	IRAN	
	VO THE ISLAMIC REP, Sirjan	W • S Asia • 500 kW
	VO THE ISLAMIC REP, Tehrān	W • S Europe • 500 kW
	JAPAN	
	RADIO JAPAN, Tokyo-Yamata	S America • 300 kW
	LITHUANIA	
	RADIO VILNIUS, Sitkunai	W Europe • 100 kW
	RUSSIA	
	VOICE OF RUSSIA, St Petersburg	S • Europe, N Africa & W Africa • 400 kW
	SPAIN	
	†R EXTERIOR ESPANA, Noblejas	Europe • 250/350 kW; W • Europe • 250/350 kW
	USA	
	VOA, Via São Tomé	S • W Africa & C Africa • 100 kW
9715	**GERMANY**	
	†DEUTSCHE WELLE, Various Locations	W Asia & C Asia • 250/500 kW
	DEUTSCHE WELLE, Via Dhabayya, UAE	W • W Asia & C Asia • 250 kW
	NETHERLANDS	
	R NEDERLAND, Via Neth Antilles	S • C America • 250 kW
	PORTUGAL	
	†RDP INTERNATIONAL, Lisbon	S Tu-Sa • E North Am • 300 kW; S M-F • E North Am • 300 kW
	USA	
	†FAMILY RADIO, Okeechobee, Fl	W • W North Am • 50 kW; S • W North Am • 50 kW; W North Am • 50 kW
	R FREE ASIA, Via Tinian, N Marianas	S • SE Asia • 250 kW
	VOA, Via Udon Thani, Thailand	S • SE Asia • 250 kW
9720 (con'd)	**CHINA**	
	CENTRAL PEOPLE'S BS, Xi'an	DS-2 • 150 kW

0 1 2 3 4 5 6 7 8 9 10 11 12 13 14 15 16 17 18 19 20 21 22 23 24

ENGLISH ARABIC CHINESE FRENCH GERMAN RUSSIAN SPANISH OTHER

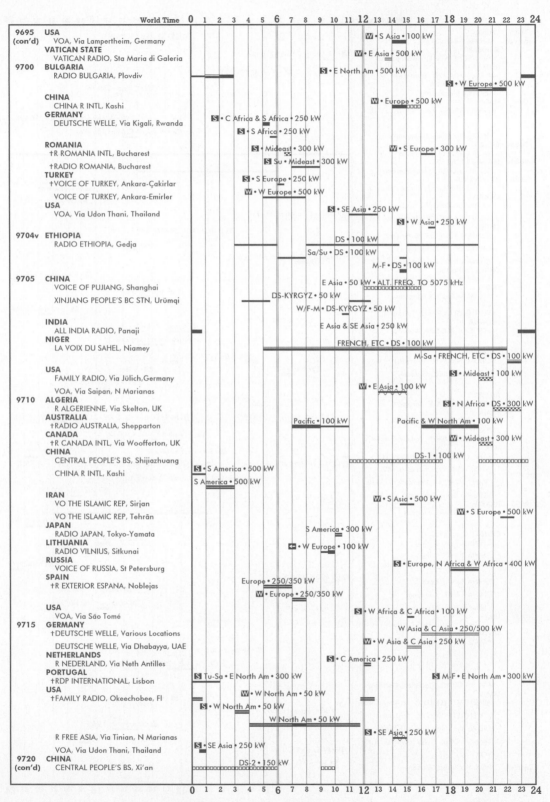

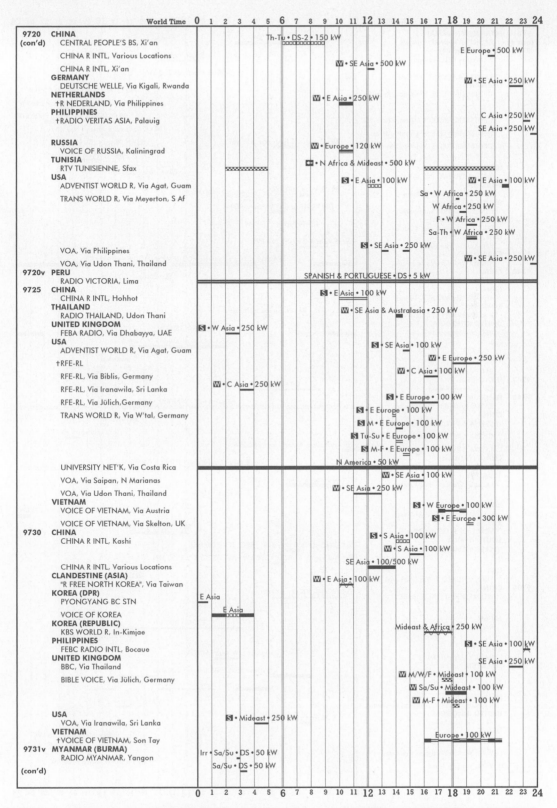

World Time 0 1 2 3 4 5 6 7 8 9 10 11 12 13 14 15 16 17 18 19 20 21 22 23 24

Frequency	Country / Station	Schedule
9720 (con'd)	**CHINA**	
	CENTRAL PEOPLE'S BS, Xi'an	Th-Tu • DS-2 • 150 kW
	CHINA R INTL, Various Locations	E Europe • 500 kW
	CHINA R INTL, Xi'an	W • SE Asia • 500 kW
	GERMANY	
	DEUTSCHE WELLE, Via Kigali, Rwanda	W • SE Asia • 250 kW
	NETHERLANDS	
	†R NEDERLAND, Via Philippines	W • E Asia • 250 kW
	PHILIPPINES	
	†RADIO VERITAS ASIA, Palauig	C Asia • 250 kW
		SE Asia • 250 kW
	RUSSIA	
	VOICE OF RUSSIA, Kaliningrad	W • Europe • 120 kW
	TUNISIA	
	RTV TUNISIENNE, Sfax	← • N Africa & Mideast • 500 kW
	USA	
	ADVENTIST WORLD R, Via Agat, Guam	S • E Asia • 100 kW
		W • E Asia • 100 kW
	TRANS WORLD R, Via Meyerton, S Af	Sa • W Africa • 250 kW
		W Africa • 250 kW
		F • W Africa • 250 kW
		Sa-Th • W Africa • 250 kW
	VOA, Via Philippines	S • SE Asia • 250 kW
	VOA, Via Udon Thani, Thailand	W • SE Asia • 250 kW
9720v	**PERU**	
	RADIO VICTORIA, Lima	SPANISH & PORTUGUESE • DS • 5 kW
9725	**CHINA**	
	CHINA R INTL, Hohhot	S • E Asia • 100 kW
	THAILAND	
	RADIO THAILAND, Udon Thani	W • SE Asia & Australasia • 250 kW
	UNITED KINGDOM	
	FEBA RADIO, Via Dhabayya, UAE	S • W Asia • 250 kW
	USA	
	ADVENTIST WORLD R, Via Agat, Guam	S • SE Asia • 100 kW
	†RFE-RL	W • E Europe • 250 kW
	RFE-RL, Via Biblis, Germany	W • C Asia • 100 kW
	RFE-RL, Via Iranawila, Sri Lanka	W • C Asia • 250 kW
	RFE-RL, Via Jülich, Germany	S • E Europe • 100 kW
	TRANS WORLD R, Via W'tal, Germany	S • E Europe • 100 kW
		S M • E Europe • 100 kW
		S Tu-Su • E Europe • 100 kW
		S M-F • E Europe • 100 kW
	UNIVERSITY NET'K, Via Costa Rica	N America • 50 kW
	VOA, Via Saipan, N Marianas	W • SE Asia • 100 kW
	VOA, Via Udon Thani, Thailand	W • SE Asia • 250 kW
	VIETNAM	
	VOICE OF VIETNAM, Via Austria	S • W Europe • 100 kW
	VOICE OF VIETNAM, Via Skelton, UK	S • E Europe • 300 kW
9730	**CHINA**	
	CHINA R INTL, Kashi	S • S Asia • 100 kW
		W • S Asia • 100 kW
	CHINA R INTL, Various Locations	SE Asia • 100/500 kW
	CLANDESTINE (ASIA)	
	"R FREE NORTH KOREA", Via Taiwan	W • E Asia • 100 kW
	KOREA (DPR)	
	PYONGYANG BC STN	E Asia
	VOICE OF KOREA	E Asia
	KOREA (REPUBLIC)	
	KBS WORLD R, In-Kimjae	Mideast & Africa • 250 kW
	PHILIPPINES	
	FEBC RADIO INTL, Bocaue	S • SE Asia • 100 kW
	UNITED KINGDOM	
	BBC, Via Thailand	SE Asia • 250 kW
	BIBLE VOICE, Via Jülich, Germany	W M/W/F • Mideast • 100 kW
		W Sa/Su • Mideast • 100 kW
		W M-F • Mideast • 100 kW
	USA	
	VOA, Via Iranawila, Sri Lanka	S • Mideast • 250 kW
	VIETNAM	
	†VOICE OF VIETNAM, Son Tay	Europe • 100 kW
9731v	**MYANMAR (BURMA)**	
	RADIO MYANMAR, Yangon	Irr • Sa/Su • DS • 50 kW
		Sa/Su • DS • 50 kW
(con'd)		

0 1 2 3 4 5 6 7 8 9 10 11 12 13 14 15 16 17 18 19 20 21 22 23 24

World Time 0–24

kHz	Country / Station	Schedule
9731v (con'd)	**MYANMAR (BURMA)** RADIO MYANMAR, Yangon	DS • 50 kW
9735	**CHINA (TAIWAN)** R TAIWAN INTL, Tainan	E Asia • 250 kW
	EGYPT †RADIO CAIRO, Kafr Silîm-Abis	S • S America • 250 kW
	GERMANY DEUTSCHE WELLE, Via Kigali, Rwanda	W • E Africa & S Africa • 250 kW
		W • C Africa, E Africa & S Africa • 250 kW
	DEUTSCHE WELLE, Via Rampisham, UK	S • C Africa & E Africa • 500 kW
	†DEUTSCHE WELLE, Via South Africa	S • C Africa & E Africa • 100 kW
	DEUTSCHE WELLE, Via Woofferton, UK	W • C Africa & E Africa • 300 kW
		W • N Africa • 250 kW
		S • N Africa • 250 kW
	IRAN VO THE ISLAMIC REP, Ahvāz	W • C Asia • 250 kW
	ROMANIA †R ROMANIA INTL, Galbeni	S • S Asia • 300 kW
	SOUTH AFRICA †CHANNEL AFRICA, Meyerton	S • W Africa & C Africa • 500 kW
	UNITED KINGDOM BBC, Via Moosbrunn, Austria	S • N Africa • 150 kW
	USA RFE-RL, Via Iranawila, Sri Lanka	W • W Asia & C Asia • 250 kW
9737	**PARAGUAY** RADIO NACIONAL, Asunción	SPANISH, ETC • S America • DS-TEMP INACTIVE • 40 kW • ➡
9740	**CHINA** CHINA R INTL, Kashi	W • Europe • 500 kW
	IRAN VO THE ISLAMIC REP, Tehrān	S • C Asia • 500 kW
		W • S Europe • 500 kW
	ROMANIA †R ROMANIA INTL, Bucharest	S • W Europe • 300 kW
	UNITED KINGDOM †BBC, Via Singapore	SE Asia • 250 kW
		SE Asia & Australasia • 250 kW
		W • S Asia • 250 kW
	BBC, Via Thailand	W • S Asia • 250 kW
9743.2	**INDONESIA** RRI, Sorong, Papua	DS • 10 kW
9745	**BAHRAIN** RADIO BAHRAIN, Abu Hayan	Mideast • DS-GENERAL • USB
	CHINA CHINA R INTL, Kunming	S • Mideast • 500 kW
	CHINA R INTL, Urümqi	Europe • 500 kW
	CHINA R INTL, Via Netherlands Antilles	W North Am & C America • 250 kW
	CHINA (TAIWAN) †VOICE OF HAN, Chingshui	E Asia • MAINLAND SERVICE • 100 kW
	ECUADOR †HCJB GLOBAL VOICE, Quito	W North Am & C America • 100 kW
		S America • 100 kW
	ROMANIA †R ROMANIA INTL, Bucharest	S • S America • 300 kW
	RUSSIA VOICE OF RUSSIA, Chita	S • S Asia • 500 kW
	SOUTH AFRICA †CHANNEL AFRICA, Meyerton	W • C Africa • 500 kW • ALT. FREQ. TO 9550 kHz
		W • W Africa & C Africa • 500 kW • ALT. FREQ. TO 9550 kHz
	USA TRANS WORLD R, Via Dhabayya, UAE	W F • E Africa • 250 kW
9750	**CHINA** NEI MENGGU PBS, Hohhot	DS-MONGOLIAN • 50 kW
		W-M • DS-MONGOLIAN • 50 kW
	JAPAN RADIO JAPAN, Tokyo-Yamata	E Asia • 300 kW
		W • N Europe • 300 kW
	KUWAIT RADIO KUWAIT, Kabd	Mideast & W Asia • 500 kW
	MALAYSIA VOICE OF MALAYSIA, Kajang	SE Asia • VOICE OF ISLAM • 100 kW
		SE Asia • 100 kW
	NETHERLANDS †R NEDERLAND, Via Nauen, Germany	W • S Europe • 250 kW
	UNITED KINGDOM BBC, Via Seychelles	E Africa • 250 kW
	USA †RFE-RL	S • E Europe • 250 kW
	VOA, Via Lampertheim, Germany	W • W Asia • 100 kW
	VOA, Via São Tomé	W Sa/Su • W Africa • 100 kW

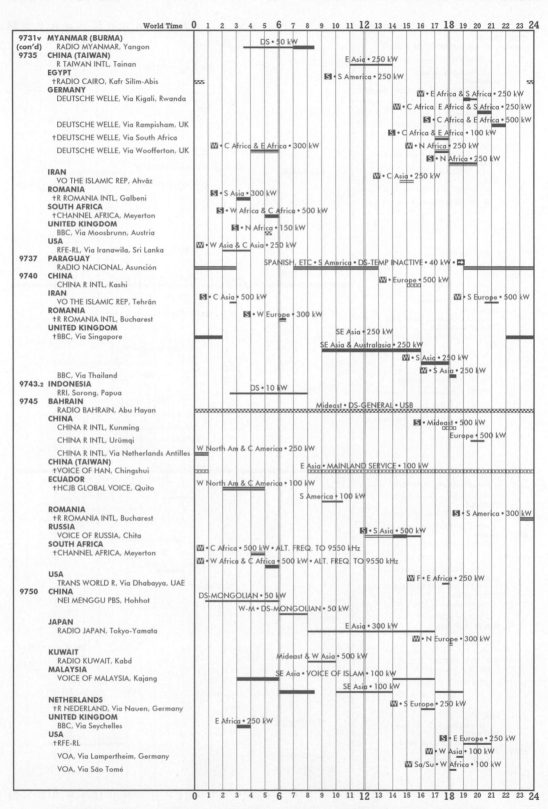

ENGLISH ARABIC CHINESE FRENCH GERMAN RUSSIAN SPANISH OTHER

World Time 0 1 2 3 4 5 6 7 8 9 10 11 12 13 14 15 16 17 18 19 20 21 22 23 24

kHz	Country / Station	Schedule
9755	**CANADA**	
	†R CANADA INTL, Sackville, NB	W • N America • 250 kW
		S • C America • 100 kW
		W Su/M • N America • 250 kW
		W Tu-Sa • N America • 250 kW
	CHINA	
	CENTRAL PEOPLE'S BS, Xi'an	DS-2 • 100 kW
	GERMANY	
	DEUTSCHE WELLE, Via Kigali, Rwanda	W • N Africa • 250 kW
		W • W Africa • 250 kW
	ROMANIA	
	†R ROMANIA INTL, Bucharest	W • E North Am • 300 kW
	†R ROMANIA INTL, Galbeni	S • S America • 300 kW
	TURKEY	
	†VOICE OF TURKEY, Ankara-Emirler	S • Mideast • 500 kW
	USA	
	FAMILY RADIO, Okeechobee, Fl	S • W North Am • 100 kW
	VOA, Via Udon Thani, Thailand	W • E Asia • 500 kW
	VATICAN STATE	
	VATICAN RADIO, Sta Maria di Galeria	W • E Africa • 500 kW
		S • C Africa & S Africa • 500 kW
		W Sa • W Africa • 100 kW
		S Sa • C Africa & S Africa • 500 kW
		W • W Africa • 100 kW
9760	**CHINA**	
	CHINA R INTL, Kunming	Australasia • 500 kW
		S • Australasia • 500 kW
	CLANDESTINE (ASIA)	
	"R FREE NORTH KOREA", Via Taiwan	S • E Asia • 100 kW
	CYPRUS	
	CYPRUS BC CORP, Zyyi	F-Su • Europe • 250 kW
	JAPAN	
	RADIO NIKKEI, Tokyo-Nagara	DS-2 • 50 kW
		Sa/Su • DS-2 • 50 kW
		Irr • Sa/Su • DS-2 • 50 kW
	OMAN	
	R SULTANATE OF OMAN, Thamarīt	Europe & Mideast • DS • 100 kW
	ROMANIA	
	†R ROMANIA INTL, Bucharest	S • E Europe • 300 kW
	†R ROMANIA INTL, Galbeni	S • W Europe • 300 kW
	SWITZERLAND	
	†RADIO REVEIL, Via Jülich, Germany	W Tu/Th • C Africa & S Africa • 100 kW
	TURKEY	
	VOICE OF TURKEY, Ankara-Emirler	S • W Asia • 500 kW
	UNITED KINGDOM	
	BBC, Via Zyyi, Cyprus	W • Mideast • 250 kW
	USA	
	RFE-RL, Via Kuwait	S • C Asia • 250 kW
	RFE-RL, Via Lampertheim, Germany	S • E Europe & W Asia • 100 kW
	VOA, Via Philippines	E Asia, S Asia & SE Asia • 250 kW
		W • E Asia, S Asia & SE Asia • 250 kW
		S • S Asia & SE Asia • 250 kW
9765	**ALGERIA**	
	R ALGERIENNE, Via Rampisham, UK	S • N Africa • DS • 500 kW
	CHINA	
	CHINA R INTL, Kashi	S • S Asia • 100 kW
	CHINA R INTL, Kunming	C Asia • 500 kW
		W • W Asia • 500 kW
	CHINA R INTL, Nanning	SE Asia • 100/500 kW
	CHINA R INTL, Shijiazhuang	S • E Europe & W Asia • 500 kW
	FRANCE	
	R FRANCE INTL, Issoudun	S M-F • W Africa & C Africa • 500 kW • ALT. FREQ. TO 11725 kHz
		S Sa/Su • W Africa & C Africa • 500 kW • ALT. FREQ. TO 11725 kHz
	ROMANIA	
	†R ROMANIA INTL, Galbeni	W • W North Am & C America • 300 kW
	RUSSIA	
	VOICE OF RUSSIA, Irkutsk	S • E Asia • 100 kW
	SPAIN	
	†R EXTERIOR ESPANA, Via Costa Rica	W • S America • 100 kW
		Su • C America • 100 kW
		Sa/Su • C America • 100 kW
		C America • 100 kW
		Irr • M-F • C America • 100 kW
		Irr • W Su • C America • 100 kW

(con'd)

World Time 0 1 2 3 4 5 6 7 8 9 10 11 12 13 14 15 16 17 18 19 20 21 22 23 24

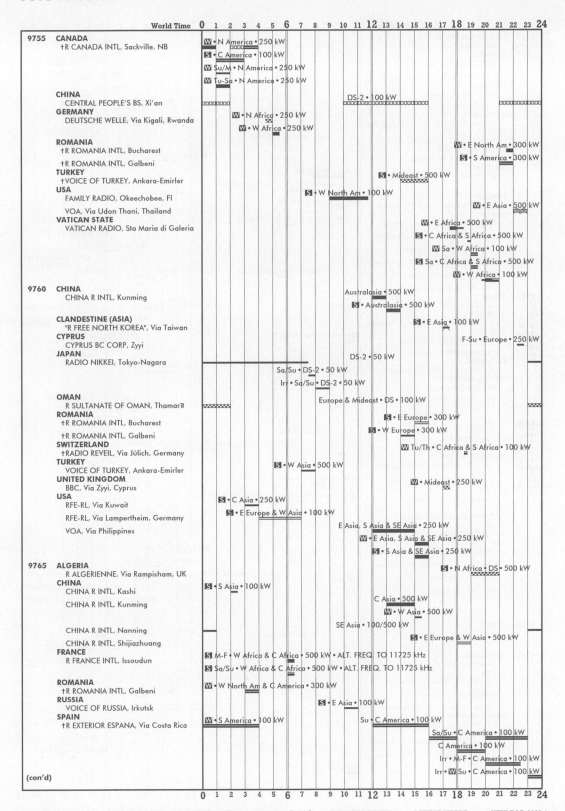

SEASONAL S OR W 1-HR TIMESHIFT MIDYEAR OR JAMMING / OR /\ EARLIEST HEARD ◁ LATEST HEARD ▷ NEW FOR 2009 †

kHz	Country / Station	World Time 0–24
9765 (con'd)	**UNITED KINGDOM**	
	BBC, Woofferton	W M-F • W Africa • 250 kW
9770	**CANADA**	
	R CANADA INTL, Sackville, NB	W • W Europe • 250 kW
	R CANADA INTL, Via Kashi, China	W • E Africa • 100 kW
	CHINA	
	CHINA R INTL, Kashi	W • Europe • 500 kW
	CHINA R INTL, Xi'an	W • E Africa & S Africa • 500 kW
	GERMANY	
	DEUTSCHE WELLE, Via Kigali, Rwanda	S • C Africa & E Africa • 250 kW
	JAPAN	
	†RADIO JAPAN, Via Issoudun, France	W • S Africa • 500 kW
	KOREA (REPUBLIC)	
	KBS WORLD R, In-Kimjae	SE Asia • 100 kW
	SRI LANKA	
	†SRI LANKA BC CORP, Colombo-Ekala	S Asia • "RADIO SRI LANKA" • 300 kW
		Su • S Asia • "RADIO SRI LANKA" • 300 kW
	TURKEY	
	†VOICE OF TURKEY, Ankara-Emirler	S • C America • 500 kW
	USA	
	ADVENTIST WORLD R, Via Austria	S • N Africa & E Africa • 300 kW; W • W Africa • 300 kW
	ADVENTIST WORLD R, Via Germany	S • W Asia • 250 kW
	†R FARDA, Via Biblis, Germany	S • W Asia • 100 kW
	R FREE ASIA, Via Tinian, N Marianas	S • E Asia • 250 kW
	RFE-RL, Via Biblis, Germany	W • W Asia • 100 kW; W • W Asia & C Asia • 100 kW
	VOA, Via Wertachtal,Germany	S • W Asia • 250 kW
9775	**CHINA**	
	CENTRAL PEOPLE'S BS, Beijing	DS-2 • 150 kW
	GERMANY	
	DEUTSCHE WELLE, Via Kigali, Rwanda	S • C America & S America • 250 kW
	ROMANIA	
	†R ROMANIA INTL, Bucharest	S • E North Am • 300 kW; S • W Europe • 300 kW
	†R ROMANIA INTL, Galbeni	S • W Europe • 300 kW
	SRI LANKA	
	SRI LANKA BC CORP, Colombo-Ekala	S Asia • TEMP INACTIVE • 100/200 kW
	UNITED KINGDOM	
	BBC, Rampisham	W • C Asia • 500 kW
	BIBLE VOICE, Via Wertachtal, Germany	S Sa • C Africa • 125 kW
		S Su • C Africa • 125 kW
9780	**CHINA**	
	QINGHAI PEOPLE'S BS, Xining	DS • 50 kW
	CHINA (TAIWAN)	
	R TAIWAN INTL, Kouhu	E Asia • TAIWAN NETWORK • 100 kW
	CLANDESTINE (ASIA)	
	VOICE OF WILDERNESS, Via Taiwan	E Asia • 100 kW
	ECUADOR	
	†HCJB GLOBAL VOICE, Quito	W North Am & C America • 100 kW
	FRANCE	
	R FRANCE INTL, Issoudun	W • E Africa • 500 kW • ALT. FREQ. TO 11995 kHz
	IRAN	
	VO THE ISLAMIC REP, Sirjan	S • W Asia • 500 kW
	JAPAN	
	FURUSATO NO KAZE, Via Taiwan	E Asia • 250 kW
	USA	
	†KNLS-NEW LIFE STN, Anchor Pt, Alaska	S • E Asia • 100 kW
	R FREE ASIA, Via Tinian, N Marianas	S • E Asia • 250 kW
	VOA, Via Philippines	S • SE Asia • 250 kW; W • E Asia • 250 kW
	VOA, Via São Tomé	W M-F • W Africa & C Africa • 250 kW
		W Sa/Su • W Africa & C Africa • 250 kW
		W M-F • C Africa • 250 kW
9780v	**YEMEN**	
	REP OF YEMEN RADIO, San'ā	Mideast • 50 kW
		Mideast • DS • 50 kW
9785	**AUSTRALIA**	
	RADIO AUSTRALIA, Darwin	S • SE Asia • 250 kW
	CHINA	
	CENTRAL PEOPLE'S BS, Beijing	DS-8 (MINORITIES) • 100 kW
	CHINA R INTL, Jinhua	W • S Asia • 500 kW
	CHINA R INTL, Various Locations	SE Asia • 150/500 kW
	CHINA (TAIWAN)	
	†R TAIWAN INTL, Via Issoudun, France	W • SE Asia • 500 kW • ALT. FREQ. TO 11995 kHz
	CLANDESTINE (ASIA)	
	"R FREE NORTH KOREA", Via Taiwan	S • E Asia • 100 kW
	"RADIO FREE CHOSUN", Via Taiwan	S • E Asia • 100 kW
(con'd)	**GERMANY**	
	DEUTSCHE WELLE, Via Sri Lanka	W • SE Asia • 250 kW

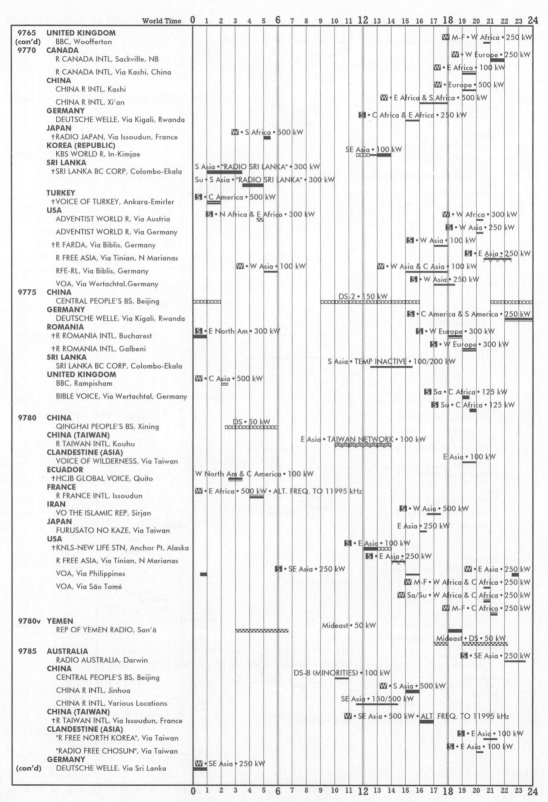

ENGLISH ARABIC CHINESE FRENCH GERMAN RUSSIAN SPANISH OTHER

World Time 0–24

kHz	Country	Station	Schedule / Target
9785 (con'd)	TURKEY	†VOICE OF TURKEY, Ankara-Emirler	W • W Asia & C Asia • 250 kW; S • W Europe • 500 kW
	USA	†R FARDA, Via Lampertheim, Germany	W • W Asia • 100 kW
		VOA, Via Lampertheim, Germany	W • Mideast • 100 kW
		VOA, Via Udon Thani, Thailand	S • S Asia • 250 kW
9790	BELGIUM	R VLAANDEREN INTL, Via Skelton, UK	W • S Europe & N Africa • 250 kW
	CHINA	CHINA R INTL, Via Havana, Cuba	W North Am • 250 kW
		CHINA R INTL, Via Sackville, Canada	S • W North Am • 250 kW
	FRANCE	†R FRANCE INTL, Issoudun	W • C Africa • 500 kW • ALT. FREQ. TO 5925 kHz; W • E Africa, C Africa & S Africa • 500 kW; S • C Africa & S Africa • 500 kW; W Africa, C Africa & S Africa • 500 kW; S • W Africa • 500 kW; W • W Africa • 500 kW; N Africa & W Africa • 500 kW; W • N Africa & W Africa • 500 kW
	GERMANY	DEUTSCHE WELLE, Via Dhabayya, UAE	S • E Africa & S Africa • 250 kW
	IRAN	†VO THE ISLAMIC REP, Sirjan	S • W Asia & C Asia • 500 kW; S • W Asia & S Asia • 500 kW
		†VO THE ISLAMIC REP, Tehrān	W • W Asia & S Asia • 500 kW
	POLAND	†POLISH RADIO, Via W'tachtal, Germany	W • E Europe • 100 kW
	ROMANIA	†R ROMANIA INTL, Bucharest	S • C Asia • 300 kW; S • E North Am • 300 kW
	SPAIN	†R EXTERIOR ESPANA, Noblejas	S Sa/Su • Africa • 250 kW
	TURKEY	†VOICE OF TURKEY, Ankara-Emirler	W • C America • 500 kW
	UNITED KINGDOM	BBC, Via Zyyi, Cyprus	W • W Asia & C Asia • 250 kW
	USA	ADVENTIST WORLD R, Via Germany	S Su • Europe • 100 kW
		FAMILY RADIO, Via Dhabayya, UAE	S • E Africa • 250 kW
		RFE-RL, Via Udon Thani, Thailand	S • C Asia • 250 kW
		VOA, Via Tinian, N Marianas	W • C Asia • 250 kW
9795	CHINA	CHINA R INTL, Urümqi	W • Europe • 500 kW; S • S Europe • 500 kW
	CLANDESTINE (ASIA)	"OPEN R FOR N KOREA", Via Taiwan	W • E Asia • 100 kW
		"R FREE NORTH KOREA", Via Taiwan	W • E Asia • 100 kW
		"RADIO FREE CHOSUN", Via Taiwan	W • E Asia • 100 kW
	JAPAN	†RADIO JAPAN, Via Sackville, Can	S America • 250 kW
	NETHERLANDS	R NEDERLAND, Via Khabarovsk, Russia	W • E Asia & SE Asia • 100 kW
		†R NEDERLAND, Via Saipan	S • Australasia • 100 kW
		R NEDERLAND, Via Singapore	SE Asia • 250 kW
	PHILIPPINES	FEBC RADIO INTL, Bocaue	SE Asia • 100 kW
	PORTUGAL	†RDP INTERNATIONAL, Lisbon	Irr • W M-F • Europe • 300 kW; Irr • W • Europe • 300 kW
	RUSSIA	RUSSIAN INTL R, Moscow	S • Europe • 200 kW
		VOICE OF RUSSIA, Moscow	S • Europe • 250 kW; S • Europe • 200 kW
	UNITED KINGDOM	BBC, Via Singapore	W • S Asia • 250 kW
	USA	†KNLS-NEW LIFE STN, Anchor Pt, Alaska	S • E Asia • 100 kW
		TRANS WORLD R, Via Fontbonne, France	← • Europe • 100 kW; W Sa • E Europe • 100 kW
9800	BULGARIA	†RADIO BULGARIA, Plovdiv	S • Mideast • 250 kW
	CHINA	CHINA R INTL, Jinhua	S • S Asia • 500 kW
		CHINA R INTL, Kashi	S America • 500 kW
		CHINA R INTL, Via Sackville, Canada	S • E North Am • 250 kW
(con'd)	FRANCE	R FRANCE INTL, Issoudun	W • E Europe • 500 kW • ALT. FREQ. TO 11670 kHz

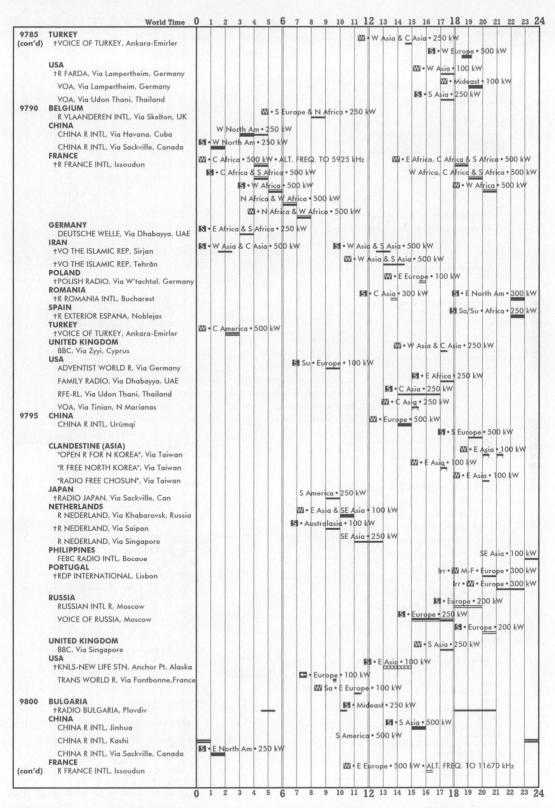

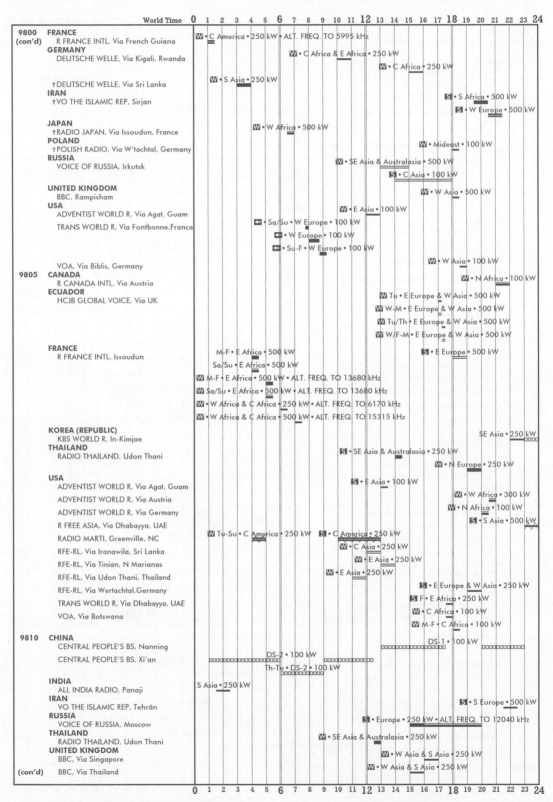

World Time 0 1 2 3 4 5 6 7 8 9 10 11 12 13 14 15 16 17 18 19 20 21 22 23 24

Freq.	Country / Station	Schedule
9800 (con'd)	**FRANCE**	
	R FRANCE INTL, Via French Guiana	W • C America • 250 kW • ALT. FREQ. TO 5995 kHz
	GERMANY	
	DEUTSCHE WELLE, Via Kigali, Rwanda	W • C Africa & E Africa • 250 kW
		W • C Africa • 250 kW
	†DEUTSCHE WELLE, Via Sri Lanka	W • S Asia • 250 kW
	IRAN	
	†VO THE ISLAMIC REP, Sirjan	S • S Africa • 500 kW
		S • W Europe • 500 kW
	JAPAN	
	†RADIO JAPAN, Via Issoudun, France	W • W Africa • 500 kW
	POLAND	
	†POLISH RADIO, Via W'tachtal, Germany	W • Mideast • 100 kW
	RUSSIA	
	VOICE OF RUSSIA, Irkutsk	W • SE Asia & Australasia • 500 kW
		S • C Asia • 100 kW
	UNITED KINGDOM	
	BBC, Rampisham	W • W Asia • 500 kW
	USA	
	ADVENTIST WORLD R, Via Agat, Guam	W • E Asia • 100 kW
	TRANS WORLD R, Via Fontbonne,France	← • Sa/Su • W Europe • 100 kW
		← • W Europe • 100 kW
		← • Su-F • W Europe • 100 kW
	VOA, Via Biblis, Germany	W • W Asia • 100 kW
9805	**CANADA**	
	R CANADA INTL, Via Austria	W • N Africa • 100 kW
	ECUADOR	
	HCJB GLOBAL VOICE, Via UK	W Tu • E Europe & W Asia • 500 kW
		W W-M • E Europe & W Asia • 500 kW
		W Tu/Th • E Europe & W Asia • 500 kW
		W W/F-M • E Europe & W Asia • 500 kW
	FRANCE	
	R FRANCE INTL, Issoudun	M-F • E Africa • 500 kW
		S • E Europe • 500 kW
		Sa/Su • E Africa • 500 kW
		W M-F • E Africa • 500 kW • ALT. FREQ. TO 13680 kHz
		W Sa/Su • E Africa • 500 kW • ALT. FREQ. TO 13680 kHz
		W • W Africa & C Africa • 250 kW • ALT. FREQ. TO 6170 kHz
		W • W Africa & C Africa • 500 kW • ALT. FREQ. TO 15315 kHz
	KOREA (REPUBLIC)	
	KBS WORLD R, In-Kimjae	SE Asia • 250 kW
	THAILAND	
	RADIO THAILAND, Udon Thani	S • SE Asia & Australasia • 250 kW
		W • N Europe • 250 kW
	USA	
	ADVENTIST WORLD R, Via Agat, Guam	S • E Asia • 100 kW
	ADVENTIST WORLD R, Via Austria	W • W Africa • 300 kW
	ADVENTIST WORLD R, Via Germany	W • N Africa • 100 kW
	R FREE ASIA, Via Dhabayya, UAE	S • S Asia • 500 kW
	RADIO MARTI, Greenville, NC	W Tu-Su • C America • 250 kW
		S • C America • 250 kW
	RFE-RL, Via Iranawila, Sri Lanka	W • C Asia • 250 kW
	RFE-RL, Via Tinian, N Marianas	W • E Asia • 250 kW
	RFE-RL, Via Udon Thani, Thailand	W • E Asia • 250 kW
	RFE-RL, Via Wertachtal,Germany	S • E Europe & W Asia • 250 kW
	TRANS WORLD R, Via Dhabayya, UAE	S F • E Africa • 250 kW
	VOA, Via Botswana	W • C Africa • 100 kW
		W M-F • C Africa • 100 kW
9810	**CHINA**	
	CENTRAL PEOPLE'S BS, Nanning	DS-1 • 100 kW
	CENTRAL PEOPLE'S BS, Xi'an	DS-2 • 100 kW
		Th-Tu • DS-2 • 100 kW
	INDIA	
	ALL INDIA RADIO, Panaji	S Asia • 250 kW
	IRAN	
	VO THE ISLAMIC REP, Tehrān	S • S Europe • 500 kW
	RUSSIA	
	VOICE OF RUSSIA, Moscow	S • Europe • 250 kW • ALT. FREQ. TO 12040 kHz
	THAILAND	
	RADIO THAILAND, Udon Thani	W • SE Asia & Australasia • 250 kW
	UNITED KINGDOM	
	BBC, Via Singapore	W • W Asia & S Asia • 250 kW
(con'd)	BBC, Via Thailand	W • W Asia & S Asia • 250 kW

0 1 2 3 4 5 6 7 8 9 10 11 12 13 14 15 16 17 18 19 20 21 22 23 24

ENGLISH ARABIC CHINESE FRENCH GERMAN RUSSIAN SPANISH OTHER

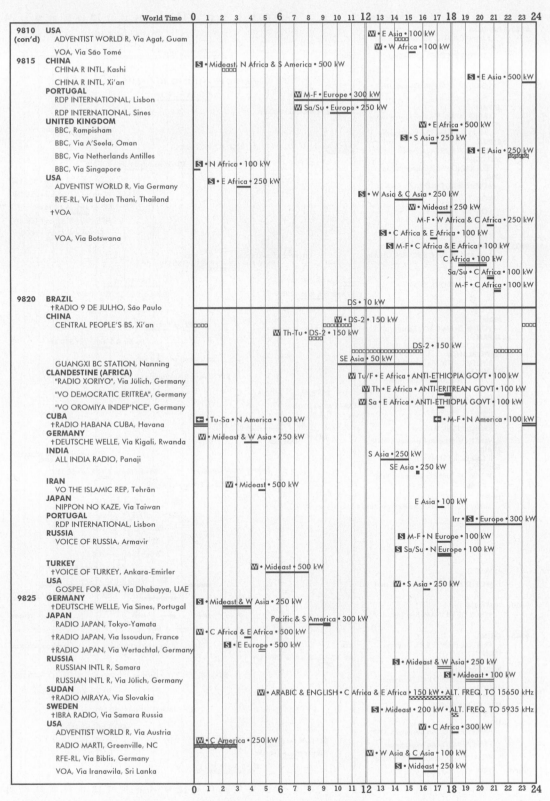

World Time 0 1 2 3 4 5 6 7 8 9 10 11 12 13 14 15 16 17 18 19 20 21 22 23 24

kHz	Country	Station	Schedule
9810 (con'd)	USA	ADVENTIST WORLD R, Via Agat, Guam	W • E Asia • 100 kW
		VOA, Via São Tomé	W • W Africa • 100 kW
9815	CHINA	CHINA R INTL, Kashi	S • Mideast, N Africa & S America • 500 kW
		CHINA R INTL, Xi'an	S • E Asia • 500 kW
	PORTUGAL	RDP INTERNATIONAL, Lisbon	W M-F • Europe • 300 kW
		RDP INTERNATIONAL, Sines	W Sa/Su • Europe • 250 kW
	UNITED KINGDOM	BBC, Rampisham	W • E Africa • 500 kW
		BBC, Via A'Seela, Oman	S • S Asia • 250 kW
		BBC, Via Netherlands Antilles	S • E Asia • 250 kW
		BBC, Via Singapore	S • N Africa • 100 kW
	USA	ADVENTIST WORLD R, Via Germany	S • E Africa • 250 kW
		RFE-RL, Via Udon Thani, Thailand	S • W Asia & C Asia • 250 kW
		†VOA	W • Mideast • 250 kW
			M-F • W Africa & C Africa • 250 kW
		VOA, Via Botswana	S • C Africa & E Africa • 100 kW
			S M-F • C Africa & E Africa • 100 kW
			C Africa • 100 kW
			Sa/Su • C Africa • 100 kW
			M-F • C Africa • 100 kW
9820	BRAZIL	†RADIO 9 DE JULHO, São Paulo	DS • 10 kW
	CHINA	CENTRAL PEOPLE'S BS, Xi'an	W • DS-2 • 150 kW
			W Th-Tu • DS-2 • 150 kW
			DS-2 • 150 kW
		GUANGXI BC STATION, Nanning	SE Asia • 50 kW
	CLANDESTINE (AFRICA)	"RADIO XORIYO", Via Jülich, Germany	W Tu/F • E Africa • ANTI-ETHIOPIA GOVT • 100 kW
		"VO DEMOCRATIC ERITREA", Germany	W Th • E Africa • ANTI-ERITREAN GOVT • 100 kW
		"VO OROMIYA INDEP'NCE", Germany	W Sa • E Africa • ANTI-ETHIOPIA GOVT • 100 kW
	CUBA	†RADIO HABANA CUBA, Havana	⬅ • Tu-Sa • N America • 100 kW; ⬅ • M-F • N America • 100 kW
	GERMANY	†DEUTSCHE WELLE, Via Kigali, Rwanda	W • Mideast & W Asia • 250 kW
	INDIA	ALL INDIA RADIO, Panaji	S Asia • 250 kW
			SE Asia • 250 kW
	IRAN	VO THE ISLAMIC REP, Tehrān	W • Mideast • 500 kW
	JAPAN	NIPPON NO KAZE, Via Taiwan	E Asia • 100 kW
	PORTUGAL	RDP INTERNATIONAL, Lisbon	Irr • S • Europe • 300 kW
	RUSSIA	VOICE OF RUSSIA, Armavir	S M-F • N Europe • 100 kW
			S Sa/Su • N Europe • 100 kW
	TURKEY	†VOICE OF TURKEY, Ankara-Emirler	W • Mideast • 500 kW
	USA	GOSPEL FOR ASIA, Via Dhabayya, UAE	W • S Asia • 250 kW
9825	GERMANY	†DEUTSCHE WELLE, Via Sines, Portugal	S • Mideast & W Asia • 250 kW
	JAPAN	RADIO JAPAN, Tokyo-Yamata	Pacific & S America • 300 kW
		†RADIO JAPAN, Via Issoudun, France	W • C Africa & E Africa • 500 kW
		†RADIO JAPAN, Via Wertachtal, Germany	S • E Europe • 500 kW
	RUSSIA	RUSSIAN INTL R, Samara	S • Mideast & W Asia • 250 kW
		RUSSIAN INTL R, Via Jülich, Germany	S • Mideast • 100 kW
	SUDAN	†RADIO MIRAYA, Via Slovakia	W • ARABIC & ENGLISH • C Africa & E Africa • 150 kW • ALT. FREQ. TO 15650 kHz
	SWEDEN	†IBRA RADIO, Via Samara Russia	S • Mideast • 200 kW • ALT. FREQ. TO 5935 kHz
	USA	ADVENTIST WORLD R, Via Austria	W • C Africa • 300 kW
		RADIO MARTI, Greenville, NC	W • C America • 250 kW
		RFE-RL, Via Biblis, Germany	W • W Asia & C Asia • 100 kW
		VOA, Via Iranawila, Sri Lanka	S • Mideast • 250 kW

0 1 2 3 4 5 6 7 8 9 10 11 12 13 14 15 16 17 18 19 20 21 22 23 24

World Time 0 1 2 3 4 5 6 7 8 9 10 11 12 13 14 15 16 17 18 19 20 21 22 23 24

kHz	Country / Station	Schedule / Notes
9830	**CANADA** †R CANADA INTL, Via Vatican State	W • E Europe • 250 kW
	CHINA CENTRAL PEOPLE'S BS, Beijing	DS-1 • 100 kW
		W-M • DS-1 • 100 kW
	CROATIA †VOICE OF CROATIA, Deanovec	Europe • 100 kW • ALT. FREQ. TO 6165 kHz
		Europe • 100 kW
	JAPAN †RADIO JAPAN, Via Issoudun, France	W • Mideast • 500 kW
	JORDAN RADIO JORDAN, Qasr el Kharana	← • W Europe • 500 kW
	RUSSIA VOICE OF RUSSIA, Armavir	S • S America • 500 kW • ALT. FREQ. TO 5975 kHz
	SWEDEN IBRA RADIO, Via Armavir, Russia	S • W Asia & S Asia • 200 kW
	USA ADVENTIST WORLD R, Via Austria	W • W Africa • 300 kW
	†VOA	S M-F • W Africa & C Africa • 250 kW
	VOA, Via São Tomé	S • W Africa • 100 kW
		S Sa/Su • W Africa • 100 kW
		S M-F • W Africa • 100 kW
9835	**CHINA** XINJIANG PEOPLE'S BC STN, Ürümqi	S • DS-CHINESE • 100 kW
		S W/F-M • DS-CHINESE • 100 kW
	INDIA ALL INDIA RADIO, Delhi	S Asia • 50/100 kW
		DS • 50 kW
		W Asia & S Asia • 250 kW
		ENGLISH, ETC • DS • 50 kW
		Irr • DS • 50 kW
	IRAN †VO THE ISLAMIC REP, Tehrān	W • Mideast • 500 kW
	JAPAN RADIO JAPAN, Tokyo-Yamata	Pacific & S America • 300 kW
	NETHERLANDS R NEDERLAND, Via Neth Antilles	W • C America • 250 kW
	THAILAND RADIO THAILAND, Udon Thani	S • SE Asia & Australasia • 250 kW
	UNITED KINGDOM BBC, Via Meyerton, South Africa	S • E Africa • 250 kW
	BBC, Via Thailand	S • S Asia • 250 kW
9840	**RUSSIA** RADIO ROSSII, Moscow	W • Europe • DS • 250 kW
	VOICE OF RUSSIA, Petropavlovsk-K	W • W North Am • 250 kW
	SPAIN †R EXTERIOR ESPANA, Noblejas	S Sa/Su • Europe • 250 kW
	TURKEY VOICE OF TURKEY, Ankara-Emirler	W • W Asia • 500 kW
		S • E Europe & N Asia • 500 kW
		← • S Europe • 500 kW
	USA SUDAN RADIO SVC, Via Moscow, Russia	W M-F • C Africa • 200 kW
		W M/Tu/Th/F • C Africa • 200 kW
		W W • C Africa • 200 kW
		W • C Africa • 200 kW
		W Sa • C Africa • 200 kW
	†VOA	S • S Europe • 250 kW
	WORLD HARVEST R, Cypress Creek, SC	W • E North Am • 250 kW
		E North Am • 250 kW
		S Su • E North Am • 250 kW
9840v	**VIETNAM** VOICE OF VIETNAM, Son Tay	SE Asia • 100 kW
		E Asia • 100 kW
9845	**CHINA** CENTRAL PEOPLE'S BS, Beijing	DS-1 • 100 kW
	IRAN VO THE ISLAMIC REP, Tehrān	S • W Asia & S Asia • 500 kW
	NEW ZEALAND R NEW ZEALAND INTL, Rangitaiki	S • ENGLISH, ETC • Pacific • 100 kW • ALT. FREQ. TO 9630 kHz
	SWEDEN †IBRA RADIO, Via Jülich, Germany	← • W Africa • 100 kW
	UNITED KINGDOM BBC, Via Zyyi, Cyprus	W • W Asia & S Asia • 250 kW
	USA FAMILY RADIO, Via Dhabayya, UAE	S • S Africa • 250 kW
	FAMILY RADIO, Via Madagascar	W • C Africa & S Africa • 50 kW
	RFE-RL, Via Lampertheim, Germany	S • W Asia • 100 kW
(con'd)	VOA, Via Philippines	W • E Asia • 250 kW

World Time 0 1 2 3 4 5 6 7 8 9 10 11 12 13 14 15 16 17 18 19 20 21 22 23 24

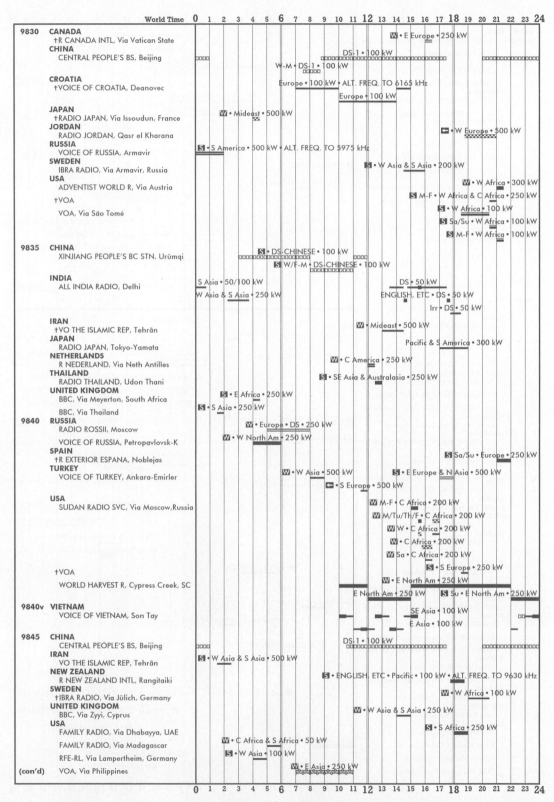

ENGLISH ▬ ARABIC ▭ CHINESE ▫▫▫ FRENCH ═ GERMAN ═ RUSSIAN ═ SPANISH ═ OTHER —

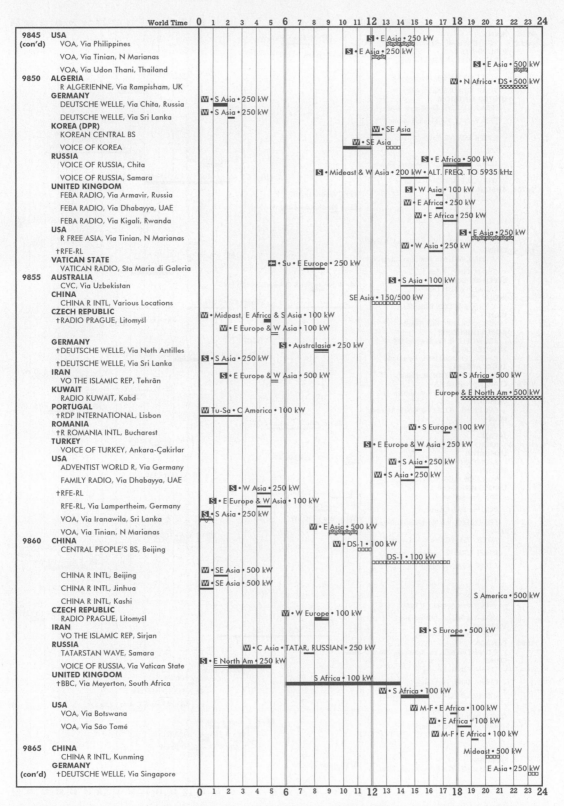

kHz	Country / Station	World Time 0–24
9845 (con'd)	**USA**	
	VOA, Via Philippines	S • E Asia • 250 kW
	VOA, Via Tinian, N Marianas	S • E Asia • 250 kW
	VOA, Via Udon Thani, Thailand	S • E Asia • 500 kW
9850	**ALGERIA**	
	R ALGERIENNE, Via Rampisham, UK	W • N Africa • DS • 500 kW
	GERMANY	
	DEUTSCHE WELLE, Via Chita, Russia	W • S Asia • 250 kW
	DEUTSCHE WELLE, Via Sri Lanka	W • S Asia • 250 kW
	KOREA (DPR)	
	KOREAN CENTRAL BS	W • SE Asia
	VOICE OF KOREA	W • SE Asia
	RUSSIA	
	VOICE OF RUSSIA, Chita	S • E Africa • 500 kW
	VOICE OF RUSSIA, Samara	S • Mideast & W Asia • 200 kW • ALT. FREQ. TO 5935 kHz
	UNITED KINGDOM	
	FEBA RADIO, Via Armavir, Russia	S • W Asia • 100 kW
	FEBA RADIO, Via Dhabayya, UAE	W • E Africa • 250 kW
	FEBA RADIO, Via Kigali, Rwanda	W • E Africa • 250 kW
	USA	
	R FREE ASIA, Via Tinian, N Marianas	S • E Asia • 250 kW
	†RFE-RL	W • W Asia • 250 kW
	VATICAN STATE	
	VATICAN RADIO, Sta Maria di Galeria	⇐ • Su • E Europe • 250 kW
9855	**AUSTRALIA**	
	CVC, Via Uzbekistan	S • S Asia • 100 kW
	CHINA	
	CHINA R INTL, Various Locations	SE Asia • 150/500 kW
	CZECH REPUBLIC	
	†RADIO PRAGUE, Litomyšl	W • Mideast, E Africa & S Asia • 100 kW
		W • E Europe & W Asia • 100 kW
	GERMANY	
	†DEUTSCHE WELLE, Via Neth Antilles	S • Australasia • 250 kW
	†DEUTSCHE WELLE, Via Sri Lanka	S • S Asia • 250 kW
		S • E Europe & W Asia • 500 kW
	IRAN	
	VO THE ISLAMIC REP, Tehrān	W • S Africa • 500 kW
	KUWAIT	
	RADIO KUWAIT, Kabd	Europe & E North Am • 500 kW
	PORTUGAL	
	†RDP INTERNATIONAL, Lisbon	W Tu-Sa • C America • 100 kW
	ROMANIA	
	†R ROMANIA INTL, Bucharest	W • S Europe • 100 kW
	TURKEY	
	VOICE OF TURKEY, Ankara-Çakirlar	S • E Europe & W Asia • 250 kW
	USA	
	ADVENTIST WORLD R, Via Germany	W • S Asia • 250 kW
	FAMILY RADIO, Via Dhabayya, UAE	W • S Asia • 250 kW
	†RFE-RL	S • W Asia • 250 kW
	RFE-RL, Via Lampertheim, Germany	S • E Europe & W Asia • 100 kW
	VOA, Via Iranawila, Sri Lanka	S • S Asia • 250 kW
	VOA, Via Tinian, N Marianas	W • E Asia • 500 kW
9860	**CHINA**	
	CENTRAL PEOPLE'S BS, Beijing	W • DS-1 • 100 kW
		DS-1 • 100 kW
	CHINA R INTL, Beijing	W • SE Asia • 500 kW
	CHINA R INTL, Jinhua	W • SE Asia • 500 kW
	CHINA R INTL, Kashi	S America • 500 kW
	CZECH REPUBLIC	
	RADIO PRAGUE, Litomyšl	W • W Europe • 100 kW
	IRAN	
	VO THE ISLAMIC REP, Sirjan	S • S Europe • 500 kW
	RUSSIA	
	TATARSTAN WAVE, Samara	W • C Asia • TATAR, RUSSIAN • 250 kW
	VOICE OF RUSSIA, Via Vatican State	S • E North Am • 250 kW
	UNITED KINGDOM	
	†BBC, Via Meyerton, South Africa	S Africa • 100 kW
		W • S Africa • 100 kW
	USA	
	VOA, Via Botswana	W M-F • E Africa • 100 kW
		W • E Africa • 100 kW
	VOA, Via São Tomé	W M-F • E Africa • 100 kW
9865	**CHINA**	
	CHINA R INTL, Kunming	Mideast • 500 kW
	GERMANY	
(con'd)	†DEUTSCHE WELLE, Via Singapore	E Asia • 250 kW

SEASONAL S OR W 1-HR TIMESHIFT MIDYEAR ⇐ OR ⇒ JAMMING / OR ∧ EARLIEST HEARD ◁ LATEST HEARD ▷ NEW FOR 2009 †

Frequency	Country	Station	World Time schedule (0–24)
9865 (con'd)	IRAN	VO THE ISLAMIC REP, Sirjan	[W] • W Asia • 500 kW
	PHILIPPINES	†RADIO VERITAS ASIA, Palauig	S Asia • 250 kW
	RUSSIA	VOICE OF RUSSIA, Novosibirsk	[W] • S Asia • 500 kW
		VOICE OF RUSSIA, Samara	[S] • C Asia • 250 kW
	UNITED KINGDOM	FEBA RADIO, Via Dhabayya, UAE	[S] • E Africa • 250 kW
		FEBA RADIO, Via Kigali, Rwanda	[S] • E Africa • 250 kW
	USA	R FREE ASIA, Via Tinian, N Marianas	[S] • E Asia • 250 kW
		†RFE-RL	[W] • E Europe • 250 kW
		TRANS WORLD R, Via Merizo, Guam	E Asia • 100 kW
	ZAMBIA	THE VOICE-AFRICA, Lusaka	C Africa & S Africa • 100 kW • ALT. FREQ. TO 6065 kHz
9870	AUSTRIA	†R AUSTRIA INTL, Moosbrunn	[S] • C America • 300 kW
			[S] • E North Am • 300 kW
			S America • 300 kW • →
	CANADA	R CANADA INTL, Via In-Kimjae, Korea	[S] • E Asia • 250 kW
	CHINA	CHINA R INTL, Via Santiago, Chile	[S] • S America • 100 kW
		CHINA R INTL, Xi'an	SE Asia • 500 kW
	CZECH REPUBLIC	RADIO PRAGUE, Litomyšl	[S] • W North Am & C America • 100 kW
	INDIA	ALL INDIA RADIO, Bangalore	S Asia • DS • 500 kW
	IRAN	VO THE ISLAMIC REP, Tehrān	[S] • E Europe & Mideast • 500 kW
	KOREA (REPUBLIC)	KBS WORLD R, Via Skelton, UK	Europe • 300 kW
	NEW ZEALAND	R NEW ZEALAND INTL, Rangitaiki	[W] • Pacific • 100 kW • ALT. FREQ. TO 13840 kHz
	SAUDI ARABIA	BS OF THE KINGDOM, Riyadh	W Europe • DS-1 • 500 kW
9875	CLANDESTINE (ASIA)	"RADIO SOLH", Via Rampisham, UK	[W] • W Asia & C Asia • 500 kW
	GERMANY	DEUTSCHE WELLE, Via Kigali, Rwanda	[S] • Australasia • 250 kW
	IRAN	VO THE ISLAMIC REP, Tehrān	[W] • W Asia & C Asia • 500 kW
	JAPAN	RADIO JAPAN, Tokyo-Yamata	[W] • S Asia • 300 kW
	LITHUANIA	RADIO VILNIUS, Sitkunai	← • E North Am • 100 kW
	RUSSIA	VOICE OF RUSSIA, Samara	[S] • C Asia • 250 kW
	UNITED KINGDOM	BBC, Rampisham	[S] • W Asia & S Asia • 500 kW
		BBC, Via Zyyi, Cyprus	[S] • W Asia & S Asia • 250 kW
		FEBA RADIO, Via Novosibirsk, Russia	[W] • S Asia • 250 kW
	USA	ADVENTIST WORLD R, Via Agat, Guam	[W] • E Asia • 100 kW
		R FREE ASIA, Various Locations	S Asia • 100/250 kW
		R FREE ASIA, Via Palau	[W] • E Asia • 80 kW
		†VOA	[S] • E Africa • 250 kW
			[S] M-F • E Africa • 250 kW
		VOA, Via Iranawila, Sri Lanka	[S] M-F • E Africa • 100 kW
		VOA, Via Saipan, N Marianas	[W] • E Asia • 100 kW
	VIETNAM	VOICE OF VIETNAM, Me Tri	DS-2 • 50 kW
9880	CANADA	R CANADA INTL, Via Kunming, China	[W] • SE Asia • 100 kW
	CHINA	CHINA R INTL, Beijing	[S] • E Asia • 500 kW
		CHINA R INTL, Kunming	SE Asia • 100 kW
		CHINA R INTL, Various Locations	SE Asia • 100/150 kW
		CHINA R INTL, Xi'an	[S] • W Asia & C Asia • 250 kW
	CZECH REPUBLIC	RADIO PRAGUE, Litomyšl	[S] • W Europe • 100 kW
			[S] • N Europe • 100 kW
			[W] • W Europe • 100 kW
	GERMANY (con'd)	†DEUTSCHE WELLE, Via Kigali, Rwanda	[W] • S Asia • 250 kW

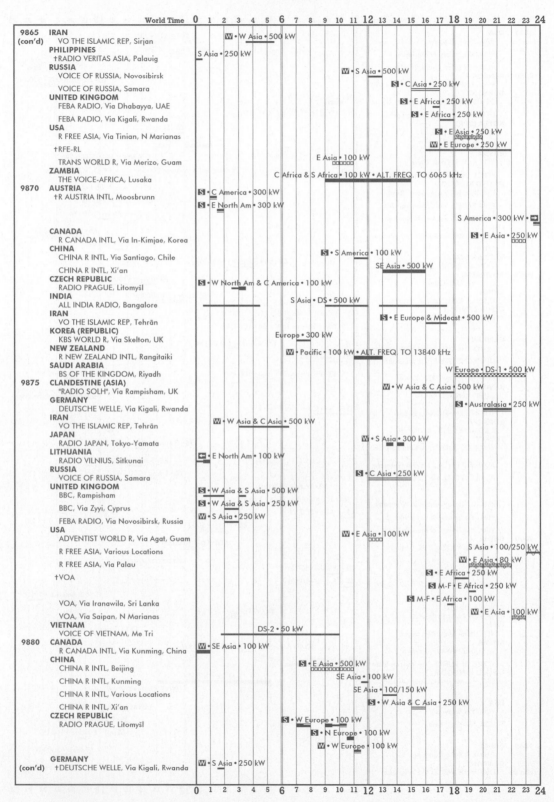

ENGLISH ARABIC CHINESE FRENCH GERMAN RUSSIAN SPANISH OTHER

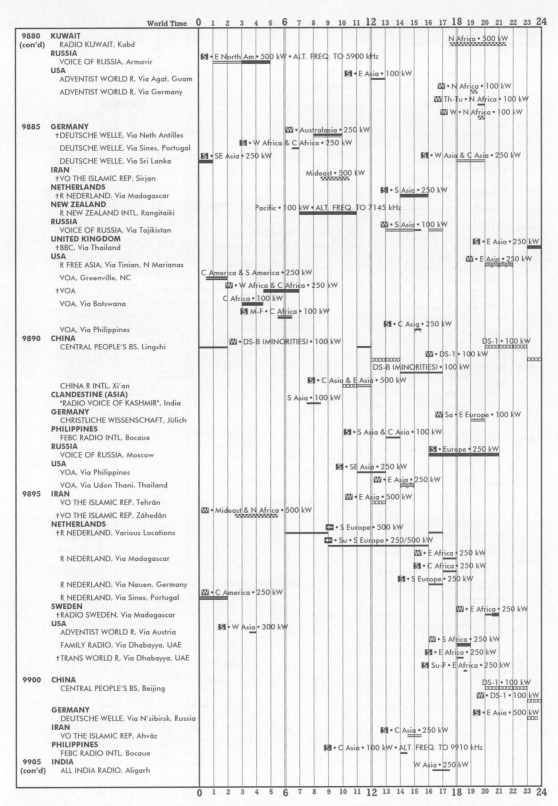

World Time 0 1 2 3 4 5 6 7 8 9 10 11 12 13 14 15 16 17 18 19 20 21 22 23 24

kHz	Country / Station	Schedule
9880 (con'd)	**KUWAIT**	
	RADIO KUWAIT, Kabd	N Africa • 500 kW
	RUSSIA	
	VOICE OF RUSSIA, Armavir	S • E North Am • 500 kW • ALT. FREQ. TO 5900 kHz
	USA	
	ADVENTIST WORLD R, Via Agat, Guam	S • E Asia • 100 kW
	ADVENTIST WORLD R, Via Germany	W • N Africa • 100 kW
		W Th-Tu • N Africa • 100 kW
		W W • N Africa • 100 kW
9885	**GERMANY**	
	†DEUTSCHE WELLE, Via Neth Antilles	W • Australasia • 250 kW
	DEUTSCHE WELLE, Via Sines, Portugal	S • W Africa & C Africa • 250 kW
	DEUTSCHE WELLE, Via Sri Lanka	S • SE Asia • 250 kW
		S • W Asia & C Asia • 250 kW
	IRAN	
	†VO THE ISLAMIC REP, Sirjan	Mideast • 500 kW
	NETHERLANDS	
	†R NEDERLAND, Via Madagascar	S • S Asia • 250 kW
	NEW ZEALAND	
	R NEW ZEALAND INTL, Rangitaiki	Pacific • 100 kW • ALT. FREQ. TO 7145 kHz
	RUSSIA	
	VOICE OF RUSSIA, Via Tajikistan	W • S Asia • 100 kW
	UNITED KINGDOM	
	†BBC, Via Thailand	S • E Asia • 250 kW
	USA	
	R FREE ASIA, Via Tinian, N Marianas	W • E Asia • 250 kW
	VOA, Greenville, NC	C America & S America • 250 kW
	†VOA	W • W Africa & C Africa • 250 kW
	VOA, Via Botswana	C Africa • 100 kW
		S M-F • C Africa • 100 kW
	VOA, Via Philippines	S • C Asia • 250 kW
9890	**CHINA**	
	CENTRAL PEOPLE'S BS, Lingshi	W • DS-8 (MINORITIES) • 100 kW
		DS-1 • 100 kW
		W • DS-1 • 100 kW
		DS-8 (MINORITIES) • 100 kW
	CHINA R INTL, Xi'an	S • C Asia & E Asia • 500 kW
	CLANDESTINE (ASIA)	
	"RADIO VOICE OF KASHMIR", India	S Asia • 100 kW
	GERMANY	
	CHRISTLICHE WISSENSCHAFT, Jülich	W Sa • E Europe • 100 kW
	PHILIPPINES	
	FEBC RADIO INTL, Bocaue	S • S Asia & C Asia • 100 kW
	RUSSIA	
	VOICE OF RUSSIA, Moscow	S • Europe • 250 kW
	USA	
	VOA, Via Philippines	S • SE Asia • 250 kW
	VOA, Via Udon Thani, Thailand	W • E Asia • 250 kW
9895	**IRAN**	
	VO THE ISLAMIC REP, Tehrān	W • E Asia • 500 kW
	†VO THE ISLAMIC REP, Zāhedān	W • Mideast & N Africa • 500 kW
	NETHERLANDS	
	†R NEDERLAND, Various Locations	S Europe • 500 kW
		Su • S Europe • 250/500 kW
	R NEDERLAND, Via Madagascar	W • E Africa • 250 kW
		S • C Africa • 250 kW
	R NEDERLAND, Via Nauen, Germany	S • S Europe • 250 kW
	R NEDERLAND, Via Sines, Portugal	W • C America • 250 kW
	SWEDEN	
	†RADIO SWEDEN, Via Madagascar	W • E Africa • 250 kW
	USA	
	ADVENTIST WORLD R, Via Austria	S • W Asia • 300 kW
	FAMILY RADIO, Via Dhabayya, UAE	W • S Africa • 250 kW
	†TRANS WORLD R, Via Dhabayya, UAE	S • E Africa • 250 kW
		S Su-F • E Africa • 250 kW
9900	**CHINA**	
	CENTRAL PEOPLE'S BS, Beijing	DS-1 • 100 kW
		W • DS-1 • 100 kW
	GERMANY	
	DEUTSCHE WELLE, Via N'sibirsk, Russia	S • E Asia • 500 kW
	IRAN	
	VO THE ISLAMIC REP, Ahvāz	S • C Asia • 250 kW
	PHILIPPINES	
	FEBC RADIO INTL, Bocaue	S • C Asia • 100 kW • ALT. FREQ. TO 9910 kHz
9905 (con'd)	**INDIA**	
	ALL INDIA RADIO, Aligarh	W Asia • 250 kW

0 1 2 3 4 5 6 7 8 9 10 11 12 13 14 15 16 17 18 19 20 21 22 23 24

SEASONAL S OR W   1-HR TIMESHIFT MIDYEAR ⇐ OR ⇒   JAMMING / OR /\   EARLIEST HEARD ◃   LATEST HEARD ▹   NEW FOR 2009 †

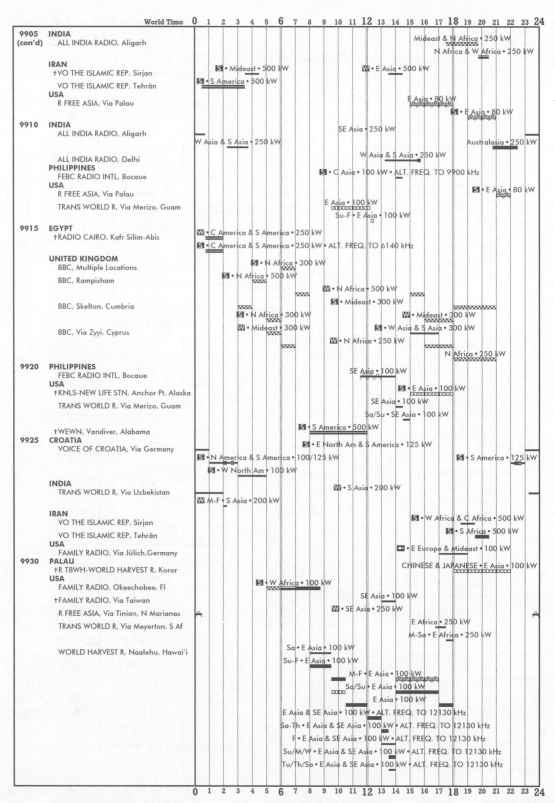

World Time 0 1 2 3 4 5 6 7 8 9 10 11 12 13 14 15 16 17 18 19 20 21 22 23 24

kHz	Country / Station	Schedule
9905 (con'd)	**INDIA** ALL INDIA RADIO, Aligarh	Mideast & N Africa • 250 kW N Africa & W Africa • 250 kW
	IRAN †VO THE ISLAMIC REP, Sirjan	S • Mideast • 500 kW W • E Asia • 500 kW
	VO THE ISLAMIC REP, Tehrān	S • S America • 500 kW
	USA R FREE ASIA, Via Palau	E Asia • 80 kW S • E Asia • 80 kW
9910	**INDIA** ALL INDIA RADIO, Aligarh	SE Asia • 250 kW W Asia & S Asia • 250 kW Australasia • 250 kW
	ALL INDIA RADIO, Delhi	W Asia & S Asia • 250 kW
	PHILIPPINES FEBC RADIO INTL, Bocaue	S • C Asia • 100 kW • ALT. FREQ. TO 9900 kHz
	USA R FREE ASIA, Via Palau	S • E Asia • 80 kW
	TRANS WORLD R, Via Merizo, Guam	E Asia • 100 kW Su-F • E Asia • 100 kW
9915	**EGYPT** †RADIO CAIRO, Kafr Silîm-Abis	W • C America & S America • 250 kW S • C America & S America • 250 kW • ALT. FREQ. TO 6140 kHz
	UNITED KINGDOM BBC, Multiple Locations	S • N Africa • 300 kW
	BBC, Rampisham	S • N Africa • 500 kW W • N Africa • 500 kW S • Mideast • 300 kW
	BBC, Skelton, Cumbria	S • N Africa • 300 kW W • Mideast • 300 kW W • Mideast • 300 kW
	BBC, Via Zyyi, Cyprus	S • W Asia & S Asia • 300 kW W • N Africa • 250 kW N Africa • 250 kW
9920	**PHILIPPINES** FEBC RADIO INTL, Bocaue	SE Asia • 100 kW
	USA †KNLS-NEW LIFE STN, Anchor Pt, Alaska	S • E Asia • 100 kW
	TRANS WORLD R, Via Merizo, Guam	SE Asia • 100 kW Sa/Su • SE Asia • 100 kW
	†WEWN, Vandiver, Alabama	S • S America • 500 kW
9925	**CROATIA** VOICE OF CROATIA, Via Germany	S • E North Am & S America • 125 kW S • N America & S America • 100/125 kW S • S America • 125 kW S • W North Am • 100 kW
	INDIA TRANS WORLD R, Via Uzbekistan	W • S Asia • 200 kW W M-F • S Asia • 200 kW
	IRAN VO THE ISLAMIC REP, Sirjan	S • W Africa & C Africa • 500 kW
	VO THE ISLAMIC REP, Tehrān	S • S Africa • 500 kW
	USA FAMILY RADIO, Via Jülich, Germany	⬅ • E Europe & Mideast • 100 kW
9930	**PALAU** †R T8WH-WORLD HARVEST R, Koror	CHINESE & JAPANESE • E Asia • 100 kW
	USA FAMILY RADIO, Okeechobee, Fl	S • W Africa • 100 kW
	†FAMILY RADIO, Via Taiwan	SE Asia • 100 kW
	R FREE ASIA, Via Tinian, N Marianas	W • SE Asia • 250 kW
	TRANS WORLD R, Via Meyerton, S Af	E Africa • 250 kW M-Sa • E Africa • 250 kW
	WORLD HARVEST R, Naalehu, Hawai'i	Sa • E Asia • 100 kW Su-F • E Asia • 100 kW M-F • E Asia • 100 kW Sa/Su • E Asia • 100 kW E Asia • 100 kW E Asia & SE Asia • 100 kW • ALT. FREQ. TO 12130 kHz Sa-Th • E Asia & SE Asia • 100 kW • ALT. FREQ. TO 12130 kHz F • E Asia & SE Asia • 100 kW • ALT. FREQ. TO 12130 kHz Su/M/W • E Asia & SE Asia • 100 kW • ALT. FREQ. TO 12130 kHz Tu/Th/Sa • E Asia & SE Asia • 100 kW • ALT. FREQ. TO 12130 kHz

0 1 2 3 4 5 6 7 8 9 10 11 12 13 14 15 16 17 18 19 20 21 22 23 24

ENGLISH ARABIC CHINESE FRENCH GERMAN RUSSIAN SPANISH OTHER

kHz	Country / Station	World Time schedule
9935	**GREECE** RS MAKEDONIAS, Athens	Europe • 100 kW
	IRAN VO THE ISLAMIC REP, Sirjan	S • Mideast & N Africa • 500 kW
9940	**IRAN** †VO THE ISLAMIC REP, Sirjan	S • Europe • 500 kW
	VO THE ISLAMIC REP, Tehrān	W Asia & C Asia • 500 kW
9945	**RUSSIA** VOICE OF RUSSIA, Via Tajikistan	← • C America & S America • 500 kW
	UKRAINE †RADIO UKRAINE INTL, Kharkiv	S • W Europe • 100 kW • ALT. FREQ. TO 7420 kHz
	USA TRANS WORLD R	S • Mideast & W Asia • 100 kW
		S M-F • Mideast & W Asia • 100 kW
9950	**CLANDESTINE (ASIA)** "RADIO FREE CHOSUN", Via Taiwan	W • E Asia • 100 kW
	FRANCE †VOIX DE L'ORTHODOXIE, Via Kazakstan	S Tu/F • E Europe • 200 kW
	INDIA ALL INDIA RADIO, Aligarh	E Asia • 250 kW
	ALL INDIA RADIO, Delhi	E Africa • 250 kW
		Europe • 250 kW
	JAPAN SHIOKAZE, Via Taiwan	W • JAPANESE, ETC • E Asia • 100 kW
	UKRAINE †RADIO UKRAINE INTL, Kharkiv	S • W Europe • 100 kW • ALT. FREQ. TO 11550 kHz
		W • W Europe • 100 kW
9955	**FRANCE** R FRANCE INTL, Via Taiwan	E Asia • 100 kW
	PALAU †R T8WH-WORLD HARVEST R, Koror	SE Asia • 100 kW
		E Asia • 100 kW
		CHINESE & ENGLISH • SE Asia • 100 kW
	USA WRMI-R MIAMI INTL, Miami, Florida	← • Su/M • SPANISH & ENGLISH • C America & S America • 50 kW
		← • Sa • C America • 50 kW
		← • Su-F • C America • 50 kW
		← • C America • 50 kW
		← • M-Sa • C America • 50 kW
		← • Su • C America • 50 kW
		← • M-F • C America • 50 kW
		← • M-F • SPANISH & ENGLISH • C America • 50 kW
		← • Sa/Su • C America • 50 kW
9955v	**USA** †FAMILY RADIO, Okeechobee, Fl	E Europe & W Asia • 250 kW
9960	**EGYPT** †EGYPTIAN RADIO, Abu Za'bal	S • E Africa • DS-VO THE ARABS • 100 kW
	USA †R FARDA, Via Udon Thani, Thailand	S • W Asia • 250 kW
	TRANS WORLD R	← • W Asia • 100 kW
		← • Su • W Asia • 100 kW
9965	**PALAU** †R T8WH-WORLD HARVEST R, Koror	E Asia • 100 kW
9970	**BELGIUM** RTBF INTERNATIONAL, Wavre	Su-F • S Europe • 250 kW
		S Europe • 250 kW
9975	**KOREA (DPR)** KOREAN CENTRAL BS	Mideast & N Africa
		E Asia
	PYONGYANG BC STN	E Asia
	VOICE OF KOREA	E Asia
		Mideast & N Africa
	USA KVOH, Rancho Simi, Ca	C America • 50 kW
	TRANS WORLD R, Via Merizo, Guam	SE Asia • 100 kW
		E Asia • 100 kW
		Sa/Su • E Asia • 100 kW
		M-F • S Asia • 100 kW
		M-Th • S Asia • 100 kW
	WWCR, Nashville, Tennessee	S • E North Am • 100 kW
		E North Am • 100 kW
9980 (con'd)	**USA** ADVENTIST WORLD R, Via Agat, Guam	Mideast • 100 kW

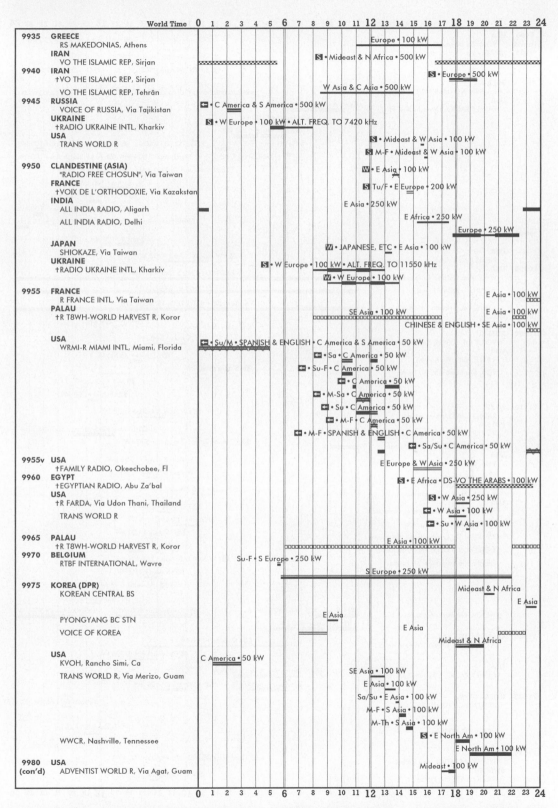

World Time 0 1 2 3 4 5 6 7 8 9 10 11 12 13 14 15 16 17 18 19 20 21 22 23 24

kHz	Country / Station	Schedule
9980 (con'd)	**USA**	
	VOA, Via Iranawila, Sri Lanka	W • Mideast & W Asia • 250 kW
9985	**ISRAEL**	
	†KOL ISRAEL, Tel Aviv	W • W Asia • 300 kW • ALT. FREQ. TO 13850 kHz
		W Su-Th • W Asia • 300 kW • ALT. FREQ. TO 13850 kHz
	PALAU	
	†R T8WH-WORLD HARVEST R, Koror	CHINESE, ETC • E Asia • 100 kW
	USA	
	FAMILY RADIO, Okeechobee, Fl	W • S America • 100 kW
		S • Europe • 100 kW
		W • W Africa • 100 kW
	WWCR, Nashville, Tennessee	E North Am • 100 kW • ALT. FREQ. TO 3210 kHz
		W M/W-F • E North Am • 100 kW
		W • ENGLISH & CHINESE • E North Am • 100 kW
		W Tu • E North Am • 100 kW
		E North Am • 100 kW • ALT. FREQ. TO 7465 kHz
		E North Am • 100 kW
		W • E North Am • 100 kW
		W Sa/Su • E North Am • 100 kW
		W • E North Am • 100 kW • ALT. FREQ. TO 3210 kHz
9990	**KOREA (DPR)**	
	VOICE OF KOREA	Mideast & N Africa
	USA	
	RFE-RL, Via Kuwait	W • W Asia & S Asia • 250 kW
10000	**USA**	
	WWV, Fort Collins, Colorado	WEATHER/WORLD TIME • 10 kW
	WWVH, Kekaha, Hawai'i	WEATHER/WORLD TIME • 10 kW
10320	**USA**	
	AFRTS, Pearl Harbor, Hawai'i	Pacific • USB • ALT. FREQ. TO 6350 kHz
10330	**INDIA**	
	ALL INDIA RADIO, Delhi	E Europe • 250 kW
11500	**RUSSIA**	
	VOICE OF RUSSIA, Via Tajikistan	S Asia • 500 kW
	USA	
	R FREE ASIA, Via Kuwait	W • S Asia • 250 kW
	VOA, Via Iranawila, Sri Lanka	W • S Asia • 250 kW
		S M-F • E Asia • 250 kW
		S • E Asia • 250 kW
11510	**EGYPT**	
	†RADIO CAIRO, Abu Za'bal	W • W Asia & C Asia • 100 kW
	RUSSIA	
	VOICE OF RUSSIA, Via Armenia	← • E Africa & S Africa • 500 kW
	VOICE OF RUSSIA, Via Tajikistan	S • C America & S America • 500 kW
	USA	
	VOA, Via Iranawila, Sri Lanka	W Asia & S Asia • 250 kW
	VOA, Via Kuwait	W Asia & S Asia • 250 kW
11520	**CHINA (TAIWAN)**	
	R TAIWAN INTL, Paochung	SE Asia • 100 kW
	USA	
	FAMILY RADIO, Via Almaty, Kazakstan	S • SE Asia • 200 kW
	FAMILY RADIO, Via Taiwan	SE Asia • 100 kW
	†R FARDA, Via Lampertheim, Germany	S • W Asia • 100 kW
	†R FARDA, Via Udon Thani, Thailand	S • W Asia • 250 kW
	RFE-RL, Via Iranawila, Sri Lanka	S • W Asia & C Asia • 250 kW
	VOA, Via Iranawila, Sri Lanka	S • S Asia • 250 kW
		S • Mideast & W Asia • 250 kW
		S • Mideast • 250 kW
	†WEWN, Vandiver, Alabama	W • W Asia & S Asia • 500 kW
		W • S America • 500 kW
		W • Mideast • 500 kW
		S • Mideast • 500 kW
11530	**CLANDESTINE (M EAST)**	
	"VO MESOPOTAMIA", Via Moldova	← • Mideast • 300 kW
		S • Mideast • 300/500 kW
	USA	
	FAMILY RADIO, Okeechobee, Fl	S • C Africa & S Africa • 100 kW
		W • Europe • 100 kW
		W • S America • 100 kW
11535	**KOREA (DPR)**	
	KOREAN CENTRAL BS	Mideast & N Africa
		E Asia
	VOICE OF KOREA	Mideast & N Africa
		E Asia
11540	**EGYPT**	
	†EGYPTIAN RADIO, Abu Za'bal	W • E Africa • DS-VO THE ARABS • 100 kW
	SWEDEN	
(con'd)	†RADIO SWEDEN, Hörby	W • W Asia & S Asia • 500 kW

0 1 2 3 4 5 6 7 8 9 10 11 12 13 14 15 16 17 18 19 20 21 22 23 24

ENGLISH ▬ ARABIC ▭ CHINESE ▫▫▫ FRENCH ═ GERMAN ═ RUSSIAN ═ SPANISH ═ OTHER —

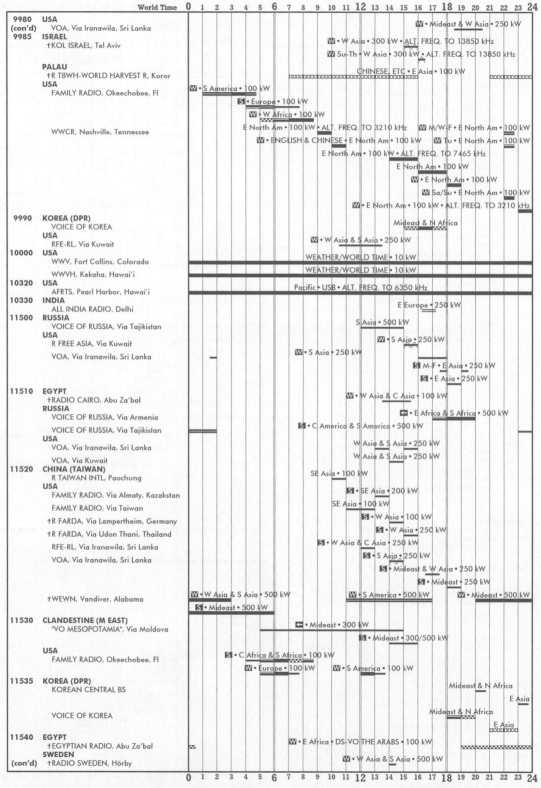

kHz	Country / Station	Schedule (World Time 0–24)
11540 (con'd)	**USA**	
	R FREE ASIA, Via Dushanbe, Tajikistan	[W] • S Asia • 200 kW
11540v	**PAKISTAN**	
	RADIO PAKISTAN, Islamabad	[S] • Mideast • 100 kW
		[S] • W Asia • 100 kW
		[S] • Mideast & N Africa • 100 kW
11545	**KOREA (DPR)**	
	VOICE OF KOREA	Mideast & N Africa
11550	**CHINA (TAIWAN)**	
	R TAIWAN INTL, Huwei	E Asia & S Asia • 100 kW
	†R TAIWAN INTL, Tainan	SE Asia • 250 kW
	EGYPT	
	†RADIO CAIRO, Kafr Silîm-Abis	[S] • Europe • 250 kW
	PAKISTAN	
	RADIO PAKISTAN, Islamabad	[S] • E Europe & W Asia • 100 kW
	SWEDEN	
	RADIO SWEDEN, Hörby	[W] M-F • E Asia & Australasia • 350 kW
	†RADIO SWEDEN, Via Madagascar	S Asia • 250 kW
	UKRAINE	
	†RADIO UKRAINE INTL, Kharkiv	[S] • W Europe • 100 kW • ALT. FREQ. TO 9950 kHz
	USA	
	FAMILY RADIO, Via Taiwan	SE Asia • 100 kW
	R FREE ASIA, Via Kuwait	[S] • S Asia • 250 kW
	RFE-RL, Via Kuwait	[S] • W Asia & S Asia • 250 kW
	†WEWN, Vandiver, Alabama	[S] • C America • 500 kW
		C America • 500 kW
11555	**SWEDEN**	
	†RADIO SWEDEN, Hörby	[S] • Mideast • 500 kW
		[S] M-F • Mideast • 500 kW
11560	**CLANDESTINE (ASIA)**	
	†"VOICE OF TIBET", Via Taiwan	M-F • E Asia • 100 kW
	USA	
	†FAMILY RADIO, Via Taiwan	SE Asia • 100 kW
		S Asia • 250 kW
	†WEWN, Vandiver, Alabama	[S] • E Asia • 500 kW
11565	**PAKISTAN**	
	RADIO PAKISTAN, Islamabad	S Asia • 250 kW
	USA	
	†FAMILY RADIO, Okeechobee, Fl	[W] • N America • 100 kW
		[S] • Europe • 100 kW
		[W] • Europe • 100 kW
	VOA, Via Kuwait	[S] • W Asia & S Asia • 250 kW
	WORLD HARVEST R, Naalehu, Hawai'i	Australasia • 100 kW
11570	**PAKISTAN**	
	RADIO PAKISTAN, Islamabad	Mideast • 250 kW
		E Asia • 250 kW
		Europe • 250 kW
		Mideast & N Africa • 250 kW
	USA	
	TRANS WORLD R, Via Merizo, Guam	[S] M-F • S Asia • 100 kW
		[S] M-Sa • S Asia • 100 kW
		[S] • E Asia • 100 kW
		[S] Th-Sa • E Asia • 100 kW
11580	**NORTHERN MARIANA IS**	
	KFBS-FAR EAST BC, Saipan Island	E Asia & C Asia • 100 kW
	USA	
	†FAMILY RADIO, Okeechobee, Fl	[S] • S America • 100 kW
		[W] • S America • 100 kW
		[W] • W Africa • 100 kW
		[S] • Europe • 100 kW
	R FREE ASIA, Via Ulaanbaatar, Mongolia	SE Asia • 250 kW
11585	**INDIA**	
	ALL INDIA RADIO, Delhi	S Asia • 250 kW
		Mideast & W Asia • 250 kW
11590	**SWEDEN**	
	†RADIO SWEDEN, Hörby	[S] M-F • Mideast • 500 kW
	USA	
	R FREE ASIA, Via Kuwait	[W] • S Asia • 250 kW
		S Asia • 250 kW
	VOA, Via Iranawila, Sri Lanka	[W] • C Asia • 250 kW
11595	**SWEDEN**	
	†RADIO SWEDEN, Hörby	[S] • Mideast • 500 kW
11600	**BULGARIA**	
	†RADIO BULGARIA, Plovdiv	[S] • C America • 250 kW
		[S] • W Europe & N Africa • 250 kW
		[S] • W Asia & C Asia • 250 kW
	RADIO BULGARIA, Sofia	[timeshift] • E Europe • 100 kW
	CHINA	
	CHINA R INTL, Xi'an	SE Asia • 150/500 kW
		E Africa & C Africa • 150 kW • ALT. FREQ. TO 7185 kHz
(con'd)		

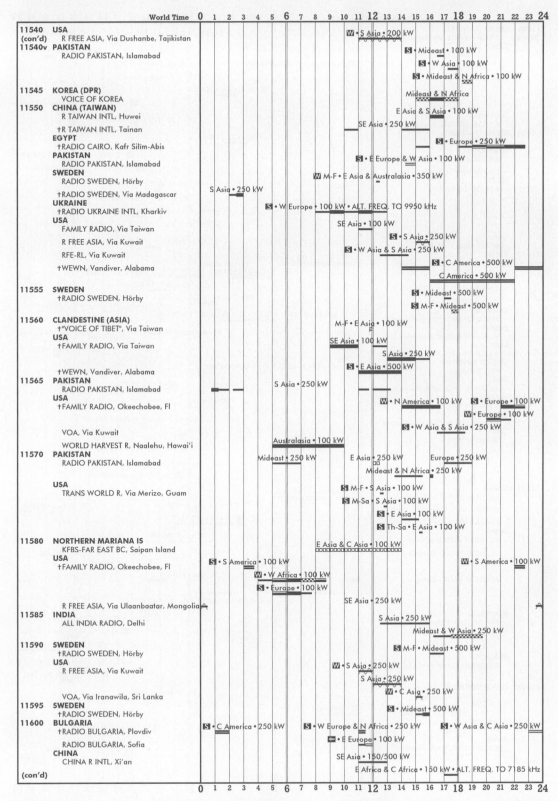

SEASONAL [S] OR [W] 1-HR TIMESHIFT MIDYEAR [timeshift] OR [timeshift] JAMMING / OR /\ EARLIEST HEARD ◁ LATEST HEARD ▷ NEW FOR 2009 †

World Time 0 1 2 3 4 5 6 7 8 9 10 11 12 13 14 15 16 17 18 19 20 21 22 23 24

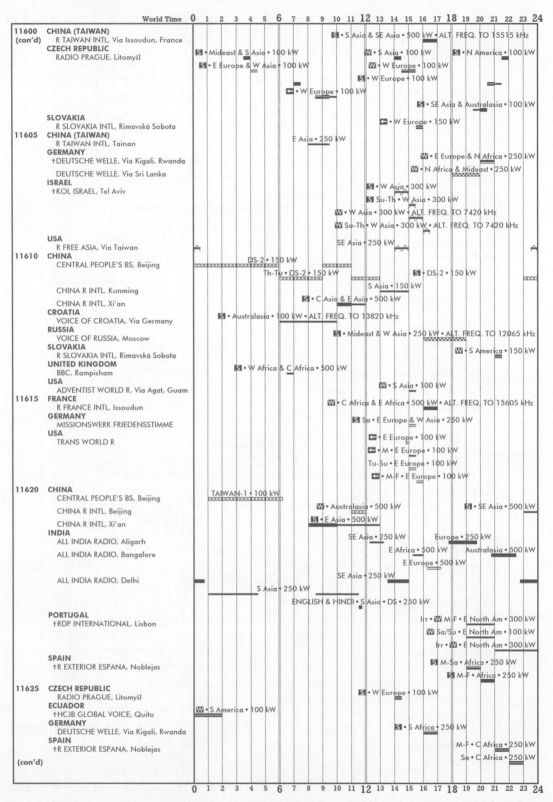

Frequency	Country / Station	Schedule
11600 (con'd)	**CHINA (TAIWAN)** R TAIWAN INTL, Via Issoudun, France	S • S Asia & SE Asia • 500 kW • ALT. FREQ. TO 15515 kHz
	CZECH REPUBLIC RADIO PRAGUE, Litomyšl	S • Mideast & S Asia • 100 kW; W • S Asia • 100 kW; S • N America • 100 kW
		S • E Europe & W Asia • 100 kW; W • W Europe • 100 kW
		S • W Europe • 100 kW
		← • W Europe • 100 kW
		S • SE Asia & Australasia • 100 kW
	SLOVAKIA R SLOVAKIA INTL, Rimavská Sobota	← • W Europe • 150 kW
11605	**CHINA (TAIWAN)** R TAIWAN INTL, Tainan	E Asia • 250 kW
	GERMANY †DEUTSCHE WELLE, Via Kigali, Rwanda	W • E Europe & N Africa • 250 kW
	DEUTSCHE WELLE, Via Sri Lanka	W • N Africa & Mideast • 250 kW
	ISRAEL †KOL ISRAEL, Tel Aviv	S • W Asia • 300 kW
		S Su-Th • W Asia • 300 kW
		W • W Asia • 300 kW • ALT. FREQ. TO 7420 kHz
		W Su-Th • W Asia • 300 kW • ALT. FREQ. TO 7420 kHz
	USA R FREE ASIA, Via Taiwan	SE Asia • 250 kW
11610	**CHINA** CENTRAL PEOPLE'S BS, Beijing	DS-2 • 150 kW
		Th-Tu • DS-2 • 150 kW; S • DS-2 • 150 kW
	CHINA R INTL, Kunming	S Asia • 150 kW
	CHINA R INTL, Xi'an	S • C Asia & E Asia • 500 kW
	CROATIA VOICE OF CROATIA, Via Germany	S • Australasia • 100 kW • ALT. FREQ. TO 13820 kHz
	RUSSIA VOICE OF RUSSIA, Moscow	S • Mideast & W Asia • 250 kW • ALT. FREQ. TO 12065 kHz
	SLOVAKIA R SLOVAKIA INTL, Rimavská Sobota	W • S America • 150 kW
	UNITED KINGDOM BBC, Rampisham	S • W Africa & C Africa • 500 kW
	USA ADVENTIST WORLD R, Via Agat, Guam	W • S Asia • 100 kW
11615	**FRANCE** R FRANCE INTL, Issoudun	W • C Africa & E Africa • 500 kW • ALT. FREQ. TO 15605 kHz
	GERMANY MISSIONSWERK FRIEDENSSTIMME	S Sa • E Europe & W Asia • 250 kW
	USA TRANS WORLD R	← • E Europe • 100 kW
		← • M • E Europe • 100 kW
		Tu-Su • E Europe • 100 kW
		← • M-F • E Europe • 100 kW
11620	**CHINA** CENTRAL PEOPLE'S BS, Beijing	TAIWAN-1 • 100 kW
	CHINA R INTL, Beijing	W • Australasia • 500 kW; S • SE Asia • 500 kW
	CHINA R INTL, Xi'an	S • E Asia • 500 kW
	INDIA ALL INDIA RADIO, Aligarh	SE Asia • 250 kW; Europe • 250 kW
	ALL INDIA RADIO, Bangalore	E Africa • 500 kW; Australasia • 500 kW
		E Europe • 500 kW
	ALL INDIA RADIO, Delhi	SE Asia • 250 kW
		S Asia • 250 kW
		ENGLISH & HINDI • S Asia • DS • 250 kW
	PORTUGAL †RDP INTERNATIONAL, Lisbon	Irr • W M-F • E North Am • 300 kW
		W Sa/Su • E North Am • 100 kW
		Irr • W • E North Am • 300 kW
	SPAIN †R EXTERIOR ESPANA, Noblejas	S M-Sa • Africa • 250 kW
		S M-F • Africa • 250 kW
11625	**CZECH REPUBLIC** RADIO PRAGUE, Litomyšl	S • W Europe • 100 kW
	ECUADOR †HCJB GLOBAL VOICE, Quito	W • S America • 100 kW
	GERMANY DEUTSCHE WELLE, Via Kigali, Rwanda	S • S Africa • 250 kW
	SPAIN †R EXTERIOR ESPANA, Noblejas	M-F • C Africa • 250 kW
(con'd)		Sa • C Africa • 250 kW

0 1 2 3 4 5 6 7 8 9 10 11 12 13 14 15 16 17 18 19 20 21 22 23 24

ENGLISH ▬ ARABIC ▭ CHINESE ▭ FRENCH ═ GERMAN ═ RUSSIAN ═ SPANISH ═ OTHER —

World Time 0 1 2 3 4 5 6 7 8 9 10 11 12 13 14 15 16 17 18 19 20 21 22 23 24

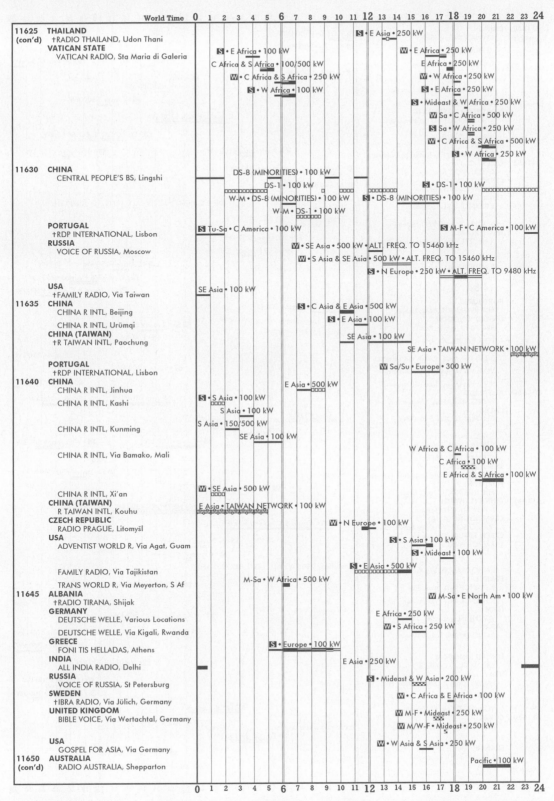

11625 (con'd) THAILAND
†RADIO THAILAND, Udon Thani — S • E Asia • 250 kW

VATICAN STATE
VATICAN RADIO, Sta Maria di Galeria — S • E Africa • 100 kW; W • E Africa • 250 kW; C Africa & S Africa • 100/500 kW; E Africa • 250 kW; W • C Africa & S Africa • 250 kW; W • W Africa • 250 kW; S • W Africa • 100 kW; S • E Africa • 250 kW; S • Mideast & W Africa • 250 kW; W Sa • C Africa • 500 kW; S Sa • W Africa • 250 kW; W • C Africa & S Africa • 500 kW; S • W Africa • 250 kW

11630 CHINA
CENTRAL PEOPLE'S BS, Lingshi — DS-8 (MINORITIES) • 100 kW; DS-1 • 100 kW; S • DS-1 • 100 kW; W-M • DS-8 (MINORITIES) • 100 kW; S • DS-8 (MINORITIES) • 100 kW; W-M • DS-1 • 100 kW

PORTUGAL
†RDP INTERNATIONAL, Lisbon — S Tu-Sa • C America • 100 kW; S M-F • C America • 100 kW

RUSSIA
VOICE OF RUSSIA, Moscow — W • SE Asia • 500 kW • ALT. FREQ. TO 15460 kHz; W • S Asia & SE Asia • 500 kW • ALT. FREQ. TO 15460 kHz; S • N Europe • 250 kW • ALT. FREQ. TO 9480 kHz

USA
†FAMILY RADIO, Via Taiwan — SE Asia • 100 kW

11635 CHINA
CHINA R INTL, Beijing — S • C Asia & E Asia • 500 kW
CHINA R INTL, Urümqi — S • E Asia • 100 kW

CHINA (TAIWAN)
†R TAIWAN INTL, Paochung — SE Asia • 100 kW; SE Asia • TAIWAN NETWORK • 100 kW

PORTUGAL
†RDP INTERNATIONAL, Lisbon — W Sa/Su • Europe • 300 kW

11640 CHINA
CHINA R INTL, Jinhua — E Asia • 500 kW
CHINA R INTL, Kashi — S • S Asia • 100 kW; S Asia • 100 kW; S Asia • 150/500 kW
CHINA R INTL, Kunming — SE Asia • 100 kW
CHINA R INTL, Via Bamako, Mali — W Africa & C Africa • 100 kW; C Africa • 100 kW; E Africa & S Africa • 100 kW
CHINA R INTL, Xi'an — W • SE Asia • 500 kW

CHINA (TAIWAN)
R TAIWAN INTL, Kouhu — E Asia • TAIWAN NETWORK • 100 kW

CZECH REPUBLIC
RADIO PRAGUE, Litomyšl — W • N Europe • 100 kW

USA
ADVENTIST WORLD R, Via Agat, Guam — S • S Asia • 100 kW; S • Mideast • 100 kW
FAMILY RADIO, Via Tajikistan — S • E Asia • 500 kW
TRANS WORLD R, Via Meyerton, S Af — M-Sa • W Africa • 500 kW

11645 ALBANIA
†RADIO TIRANA, Shijak — W M-Sa • E North Am • 100 kW

GERMANY
DEUTSCHE WELLE, Various Locations — E Africa • 250 kW
DEUTSCHE WELLE, Via Kigali, Rwanda — W • S Africa • 250 kW

GREECE
FONI TIS HELLADAS, Athens — S • Europe • 100 kW

INDIA
ALL INDIA RADIO, Delhi — E Asia • 250 kW

RUSSIA
VOICE OF RUSSIA, St Petersburg — S • Mideast & W Asia • 200 kW

SWEDEN
†IBRA RADIO, Via Jülich, Germany — W • C Africa & E Africa • 100 kW

UNITED KINGDOM
BIBLE VOICE, Via Wertachtal, Germany — W M-F • Mideast • 250 kW; W M/W-F • Mideast • 250 kW

USA
GOSPEL FOR ASIA, Via Germany — W • W Asia & S Asia • 250 kW

11650 (con'd) AUSTRALIA
RADIO AUSTRALIA, Shepparton — Pacific • 100 kW

0 1 2 3 4 5 6 7 8 9 10 11 12 13 14 15 16 17 18 19 20 21 22 23 24

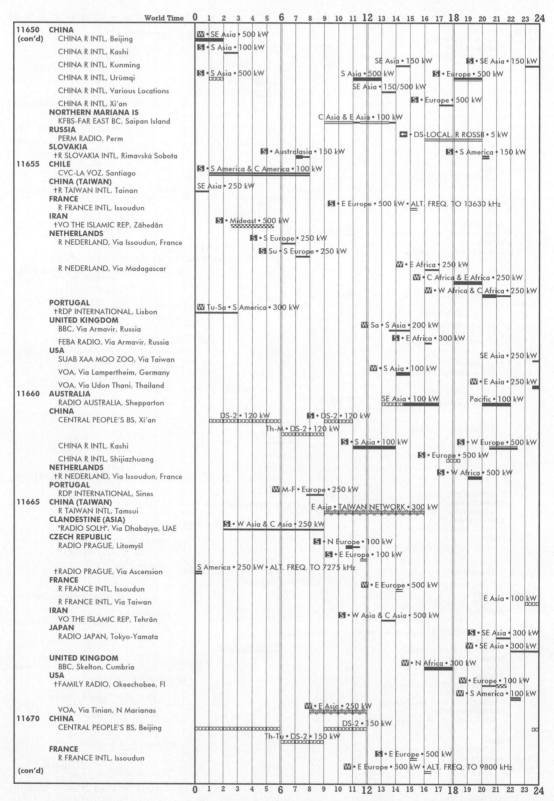

World Time 0 1 2 3 4 5 6 7 8 9 10 11 12 13 14 15 16 17 18 19 20 21 22 23 24

kHz	Country	Station	Schedule
11650 (con'd)	CHINA	CHINA R INTL, Beijing	W • SE Asia • 500 kW
		CHINA R INTL, Kashi	S • S Asia • 100 kW
		CHINA R INTL, Kunming	SE Asia • 150 kW; S • SE Asia • 150 kW
		CHINA R INTL, Urümqi	S • S Asia • 500 kW; S Asia • 500 kW; S • Europe • 500 kW
		CHINA R INTL, Various Locations	SE Asia • 150/500 kW
		CHINA R INTL, Xi'an	S • Europe • 500 kW
	NORTHERN MARIANA IS	KFBS-FAR EAST BC, Saipan Island	C Asia & E Asia • 100 kW
	RUSSIA	PERM RADIO, Perm	DS-LOCAL, R ROSSII • 5 kW
	SLOVAKIA	†R SLOVAKIA INTL, Rimavská Sobota	S • Australasia • 150 kW; S • S America • 150 kW
11655	CHILE	CVC-LA VOZ, Santiago	S • S America & C America • 100 kW
	CHINA (TAIWAN)	†R TAIWAN INTL, Tainan	SE Asia • 250 kW
	FRANCE	R FRANCE INTL, Issoudun	S • E Europe • 500 kW • ALT. FREQ. TO 13630 kHz
	IRAN	†VO THE ISLAMIC REP, Zāhedān	S • Mideast • 500 kW
	NETHERLANDS	R NEDERLAND, Via Issoudun, France	S • S Europe • 250 kW; S Su • S Europe • 250 kW
		R NEDERLAND, Via Madagascar	W • E Africa • 250 kW; W • C Africa & E Africa • 250 kW; W • W Africa & C Africa • 250 kW
	PORTUGAL	†RDP INTERNATIONAL, Lisbon	W Tu-Sa • S America • 300 kW
	UNITED KINGDOM	BBC, Via Armavir, Russia	W Sa • S Asia • 200 kW
		FEBA RADIO, Via Armavir, Russia	S • E Africa • 300 kW
	USA	SUAB XAA MOO ZOO, Via Taiwan	SE Asia • 250 kW
		VOA, Via Lampertheim, Germany	W • S Asia • 100 kW
		VOA, Via Udon Thani, Thailand	W • E Asia • 250 kW
11660	AUSTRALIA	RADIO AUSTRALIA, Shepparton	SE Asia • 100 kW; Pacific • 100 kW
	CHINA	CENTRAL PEOPLE'S BS, Xi'an	DS-2 • 120 kW; S • DS-2 • 120 kW; Th-M • DS-2 • 120 kW
		CHINA R INTL, Kashi	S • S Asia • 100 kW; S • W Europe • 500 kW
		CHINA R INTL, Shijiazhuang	S • Europe • 500 kW
	NETHERLANDS	†R NEDERLAND, Via Issoudun, France	S • W Africa • 500 kW
	PORTUGAL	RDP INTERNATIONAL, Sines	W M-F • Europe • 250 kW
11665	CHINA (TAIWAN)	R TAIWAN INTL, Tamsui	E Asia • TAIWAN NETWORK • 300 kW
	CLANDESTINE (ASIA)	"RADIO SOLH", Via Dhabayya, UAE	S • W Asia & C Asia • 250 kW
	CZECH REPUBLIC	RADIO PRAGUE, Litomyšl	S • N Europe • 100 kW; S • E Europe • 100 kW
		†RADIO PRAGUE, Via Ascension	S America • 250 kW • ALT. FREQ. TO 7275 kHz
	FRANCE	R FRANCE INTL, Issoudun	W • E Europe • 500 kW
		R FRANCE INTL, Via Taiwan	E Asia • 100 kW
	IRAN	VO THE ISLAMIC REP, Tehrān	S • W Asia & C Asia • 500 kW
	JAPAN	RADIO JAPAN, Tokyo-Yamata	S • SE Asia • 300 kW; W • SE Asia • 300 kW
	UNITED KINGDOM	BBC, Skelton, Cumbria	W • N Africa • 300 kW
	USA	†FAMILY RADIO, Okeechobee, Fl	W • Europe • 100 kW; W • S America • 100 kW
		VOA, Via Tinian, N Marianas	W • E Asia • 250 kW
11670	CHINA	CENTRAL PEOPLE'S BS, Beijing	DS-2 • 150 kW; Th-Tu • DS-2 • 150 kW
	FRANCE	R FRANCE INTL, Issoudun	S • E Europe • 500 kW; W • E Europe • 500 kW • ALT. FREQ. TO 9800 kHz
(con'd)			

0 1 2 3 4 5 6 7 8 9 10 11 12 13 14 15 16 17 18 19 20 21 22 23 24

ENGLISH ARABIC CHINESE FRENCH GERMAN RUSSIAN SPANISH OTHER

World Time 0 1 2 3 4 5 6 7 8 9 10 11 12 13 14 15 16 17 18 19 20 21 22 23 24

kHz	Country / Station	Schedule
11670 (con'd)	**FRANCE**	
	R FRANCE INTL, Issoudun	S • E Europe • 500 kW • ALT. FREQ. TO 7135 kHz
	GERMANY	
	†DEUTSCHE WELLE, Via Sines, Portugal	S • N Africa & Mideast • 250 kW
	IRAN	
	VO THE ISLAMIC REP, Tehrān	W • E Asia • 500 kW
	†VO THE ISLAMIC REP, Via Lithuania	S • W Europe • 100 kW
	USA	
	FAMILY RADIO, Okeechobee, Fl	S • C America • 100 kW
	R FREE ASIA, Via Tinian, N Marianas	S • SE Asia • 250 kW
	VENEZUELA	
	RADIO NACIONAL, Via Havana, Cuba	Su • C America • "ALO PRESIDENTE" • 100 kW
		C America • 100 kW
11675	**CANADA**	
	R CANADA INTL, Via Kunming, China	S • S Asia • 500 kW
	CHINA	
	CHINA R INTL, Kashi	S • S Asia • 100 kW
	CHINA R INTL, Kunming	S Asia • 500 kW
	CLANDESTINE (ASIA)	
	"RADIO SOLH", Via Dhabayya, UAE	W • W Asia & C Asia • 250 kW
		W Asia & C Asia • 250 kW
	FRANCE	
	R FRANCE INTL, Issoudun	W • W Asia & S Asia • 500 kW
	KUWAIT	
	RADIO KUWAIT, Kabd	W North Am • 500 kW
	POLAND	
	POLISH RADIO, Via W'tachtal, Germany	W • C Asia • 250 kW
	RUSSIA	
	VOICE OF RUSSIA, Armavir	S M-F • N Europe • 250 kW • ALT. FREQ. TO 7320 kHz
		S Sa/Su • N Europe • 250 kW • ALT. FREQ. TO 7320 kHz
	SWEDEN	
	†RADIO SWEDEN, Hörby	W • SE Asia & Australasia • 500 kW
		W Sa/Su • SE Asia & Australasia • 500 kW
	UNITED KINGDOM	
	FEBA RADIO, Via Dhabayya, UAE	W • S Asia • 250 kW
	USA	
	ADVENTIST WORLD R, Via Germany	W • S Asia • 250 kW
	†VOA	W • S Europe • 250 kW
	VOA, Various Locations	W M-F • E Africa • 250 kW
		W • E Africa • 50/100/250 kW
		W M-F • E Africa • 50/100/250 kW
	VOA, Via Botswana	W Sa • C Africa & E Africa • 100 kW
11680	**CHINA**	
	CHINA R INTL, Nanning	SE Asia • 100/500 kW
	CHINA R INTL	W • SE Asia
	CHINA R INTL, Xi'an	S • E Asia • 500 kW
	CUBA	
	†RADIO HABANA CUBA, Havana	S America • 100 kW
	NORTHERN MARIANA IS	
	KFBS-FAR EAST BC, Saipan Island	SE Asia • 100 kW
	SPAIN	
	R EXTERIOR ESPANA, Noblejas	S • S America • 250 kW
	TURKEY	
	†VOICE OF TURKEY, Ankara-Emirler	S • W Europe • 500 kW
	UNITED KINGDOM	
	BBC, Rampisham	S • N Africa • 500 kW
		W • N Africa • 500 kW
		S • N Africa • 300 kW
	BBC, Skelton, Cumbria	
	BBC, Via Zyyi, Cyprus	W • N Africa • 250 kW
	USA	
	R FREE ASIA, Via Iranawila, Sri Lanka	S • SE Asia • 250 kW
	VOA, Via Botswana	S M-F • W Africa & C Africa • 50/100 kW
		S • W Africa & C Africa • 50/100 kW
11680v	**KOREA (DPR)**	
	KOREAN CENTRAL BS, Pyongyang	DS • 100/200 kW
11685	**CHINA**	
	CENTRAL PEOPLE'S BS, Xi'an	DS-2 • 100 kW
		S • DS-2 • 100 kW
		DS-8 (MINORITIES) • 100 kW
		Th-Tu • DS-2 • 100 kW
		Th-Tu • DS-8 (MINORITIES) • 100 kW
		S • E Asia • 150 kW
	CHINA R INTL, Beijing	
	CHINA R INTL, Kashi	S • S Asia • 100 kW
	IRAN	
(con'd)	VO THE ISLAMIC REP, Tehrān	S • E Europe & Mideast • 500 kW

0 1 2 3 4 5 6 7 8 9 10 11 12 13 14 15 16 17 18 19 20 21 22 23 24

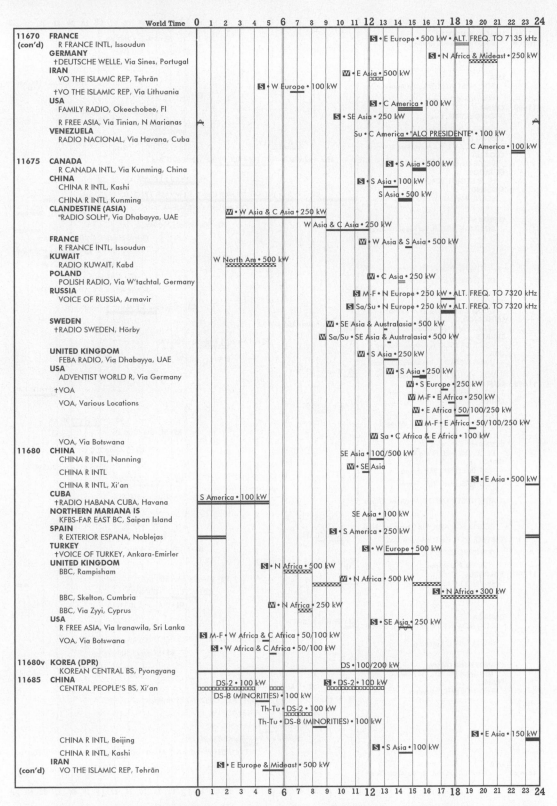

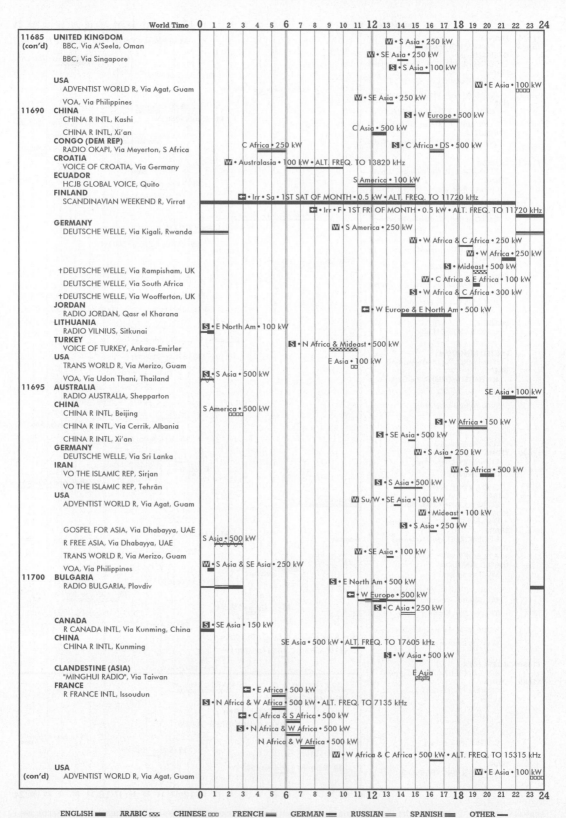

World Time 0 1 2 3 4 5 6 7 8 9 10 11 12 13 14 15 16 17 18 19 20 21 22 23 24

kHz	Country / Station	Schedule notes
11685 (con'd)	**UNITED KINGDOM**	
	BBC, Via A'Seela, Oman	W • S Asia • 250 kW
		W • SE Asia • 250 kW
	BBC, Via Singapore	S • S Asia • 100 kW
	USA	
	ADVENTIST WORLD R, Via Agat, Guam	W • E Asia • 100 kW
	VOA, Via Philippines	W • SE Asia • 250 kW
11690	**CHINA**	
	CHINA R INTL, Kashi	S • W Europe • 500 kW
	CHINA R INTL, Xi'an	C Asia • 500 kW
	CONGO (DEM REP)	
	RADIO OKAPI, Via Meyerton, S Africa	C Africa • 250 kW
		S • C Africa • DS • 500 kW
	CROATIA	
	VOICE OF CROATIA, Via Germany	W • Australasia • 100 kW • ALT. FREQ. TO 13820 kHz
	ECUADOR	
	HCJB GLOBAL VOICE, Quito	S America • 100 kW
	FINLAND	
	SCANDINAVIAN WEEKEND R, Virrat	⇐ • Irr • Sa • 1ST SAT OF MONTH • 0.5 kW • ALT. FREQ. TO 11720 kHz
		⇐ • Irr • F • 1ST FRI OF MONTH • 0.5 kW • ALT. FREQ. TO 11720 kHz
	GERMANY	
	DEUTSCHE WELLE, Via Kigali, Rwanda	W • S America • 250 kW
		W • W Africa & C Africa • 250 kW
		W • W Africa • 250 kW
	†DEUTSCHE WELLE, Via Rampisham, UK	S • Mideast • 500 kW
	DEUTSCHE WELLE, Via South Africa	W • C Africa & E Africa • 100 kW
	†DEUTSCHE WELLE, Via Woofferton, UK	S • W Africa & C Africa • 300 kW
	JORDAN	
	RADIO JORDAN, Qasr el Kharana	⇐ • W Europe & E North Am • 500 kW
	LITHUANIA	
	RADIO VILNIUS, Sitkunai	S • E North Am • 100 kW
	TURKEY	
	VOICE OF TURKEY, Ankara-Emirler	S • N Africa & Mideast • 500 kW
	USA	
	TRANS WORLD R, Via Merizo, Guam	E Asia • 100 kW
	VOA, Via Udon Thani, Thailand	S • S Asia • 500 kW
11695	**AUSTRALIA**	
	RADIO AUSTRALIA, Shepparton	SE Asia • 100 kW
	CHINA	
	CHINA R INTL, Beijing	S America • 500 kW
	CHINA R INTL, Via Cerrik, Albania	S • W Africa • 150 kW
	CHINA R INTL, Xi'an	S • SE Asia • 500 kW
	GERMANY	
	DEUTSCHE WELLE, Via Sri Lanka	W • S Asia • 250 kW
	IRAN	
	VO THE ISLAMIC REP, Sirjan	W • S Africa • 500 kW
	VO THE ISLAMIC REP, Tehrān	S • S Asia • 500 kW
	USA	
	ADVENTIST WORLD R, Via Agat, Guam	W Su/W • SE Asia • 100 kW
		W • Mideast • 100 kW
	GOSPEL FOR ASIA, Via Dhabayya, UAE	S • S Asia • 250 kW
	R FREE ASIA, Via Dhabayya, UAE	S Asia • 500 kW
	TRANS WORLD R, Via Merizo, Guam	W • SE Asia • 100 kW
	VOA, Via Philippines	W • S Asia & SE Asia • 250 kW
11700	**BULGARIA**	
	RADIO BULGARIA, Plovdiv	S • E North Am • 500 kW
		⇐ • W Europe • 500 kW
		S • C Asia • 250 kW
	CANADA	
	R CANADA INTL, Via Kunming, China	S • SE Asia • 150 kW
	CHINA	
	CHINA R INTL, Kunming	SE Asia • 500 kW • ALT. FREQ. TO 17605 kHz
		S • W Asia • 500 kW
	CLANDESTINE (ASIA)	
	"MINGHUI RADIO", Via Taiwan	E Asia
	FRANCE	
	R FRANCE INTL, Issoudun	⇐ • E Africa • 500 kW
		S • N Africa & W Africa • 500 kW • ALT. FREQ. TO 7135 kHz
		⇐ • C Africa & S Africa • 500 kW
		S • N Africa & W Africa • 500 kW
		N Africa & W Africa • 500 kW
		W • W Africa & C Africa • 500 kW • ALT. FREQ. TO 15315 kHz
(con'd)	**USA**	
	ADVENTIST WORLD R, Via Agat, Guam	W • E Asia • 100 kW

0 1 2 3 4 5 6 7 8 9 10 11 12 13 14 15 16 17 18 19 20 21 22 23 24

ENGLISH ARABIC CHINESE FRENCH GERMAN RUSSIAN SPANISH OTHER

World Time 0 1 2 3 4 5 6 7 8 9 10 11 12 13 14 15 16 17 18 19 20 21 22 23 24

kHz	Country / Station	Schedule
11700 (con'd)	**USA**	
	†FAMILY RADIO, Okeechobee, Fl	W • S America • 100 kW
	R FREE ASIA, Via Tinian, N Marianas	S • E Asia • 250 kW
	RFE-RL, Via Philippines	S • E Asia • 250 kW
11705	**AUSTRALIA**	
	CVC, Via Jülich, Germany	W • E Europe • 100 kW
	CHINA (TAIWAN)	
	†R TAIWAN INTL, Via Issoudun, France	S • E Europe • 500 kW
	CUBA	
	RADIO HABANA CUBA, Havana	S America • 100 kW
	FRANCE	
	R FRANCE INTL, Issoudun	W • C Africa & S Africa • 500 kW
		S • C Africa & S Africa • 500 kW
	IRAN	
	†VO THE ISLAMIC REP, Various Locations	Mideast • 500 kW
	JAPAN	
	†RADIO JAPAN, Tokyo-Yamata	SE Asia • 300 kW
	RADIO JAPAN, Via Sackville, Can	E North Am • 250 kW
	USA	
	R FREE ASIA, Via Irkutsk, Russia	S • E Asia • 250 kW
	R FREE ASIA, Via Tinian, N Marianas	S • S Asia • 250 kW
	†VOA	W • S Asia • 250 kW
	VOA, Various Locations	S Asia • 250 kW
	VOA, Via Philippines	W • E Asia • 250 kW
	VENEZUELA	
	RADIO NACIONAL, Via Havana, Cuba	C America • 100 kW
	ZIMBABWE	
	RADIO V O P, Via Madagascar	W • ENGLISH, ETC • S Africa • 50 kW
11710	**CHINA**	
	CENTRAL PEOPLE'S BS, Beijing	DS-1 • 100 kW
		W • DS-1 • 100 kW
	CHINA R INTL, Urümqi	W • C Asia • 500 kW
	CHINA R INTL, Via Cerrik, Albania	S • N Africa • 150 kW
	CHINA (TAIWAN)	
	R TAIWAN INTL, Huwei	E Asia • TAIWAN NETWORK • 300 kW
	INDIA	
	ALL INDIA RADIO, Delhi	DS • 50 kW
		ENGLISH & HINDI • DS • 50 kW
		SE Asia • 50 kW
	JAPAN	
	RADIO JAPAN, Via Skelton, UK	N Europe • 300 kW
	KOREA (DPR)	
	KOREAN CENTRAL BS	S • C America; N America
	VOICE OF KOREA	S • C America
		N America
	PHILIPPINES	
	†RADIO VERITAS ASIA, Palauig	S Asia • 250 kW
	ROMANIA	
	†R ROMANIA INTL, Bucharest	W • Mideast • 300 kW
	UNITED KINGDOM	
	BIBLE VOICE, Via Jülich, Germany	S Sa • Mideast & W Asia • 100 kW
		S Su/W-F • Mideast & W Asia • 100 kW
		S W-Su • Mideast & W Asia • 100 kW
		S Sa/Su • Mideast & W Asia • 100 kW
11710v	**ARGENTINA**	
	R ARGENTINA-RAE, Buenos Aires	Tu-Sa • Americas • 100 kW; M-F • E Asia • 100 kW; M-F • Europe & N Africa • 100 kW
		M-F • S America • 100 kW
	RADIO NACIONAL, Buenos Aires	M • S America • DS • 100 kW; Su • S America • DS • 100 kW
		Sa/Su • S America • DS • 100 kW
11715	**CHINA (TAIWAN)**	
	†R TAIWAN INTL, Tainan	SE Asia & Australasia • 250 kW
		SE Asia • 250 kW
	INDIA	
	ALL INDIA RADIO, Delhi	S Asia • 250 kW
	ALL INDIA RADIO, Panaji	Australasia • 250 kW
	JAPAN	
	RADIO JAPAN, Tokyo-Yamata	E Asia • 300 kW
	LEBANON	
	VOICE OF CHARITY, Via Vatican City	Mideast • 100 kW
	ROMANIA	
	†R ROMANIA INTL, Galbeni	S • W Europe • 300 kW
	SAUDI ARABIA	
	BS OF THE KINGDOM, Riyadh	C Africa & W Africa • DS-HOLY KORAN • 500 kW
(con'd)	**USA**	
	KJES, Vado, New Mexico	⬅ • E North Am • 50 kW

World Time 0 1 2 3 4 5 6 7 8 9 10 11 12 13 14 15 16 17 18 19 20 21 22 23 24

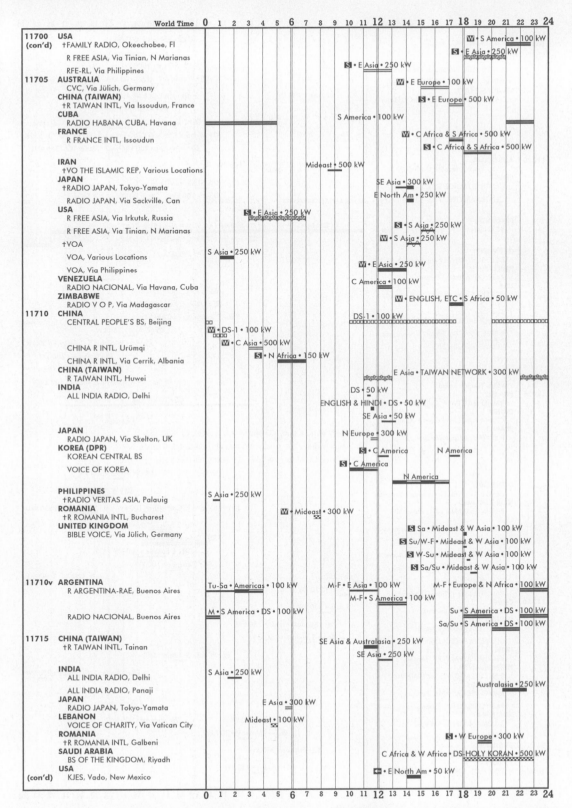

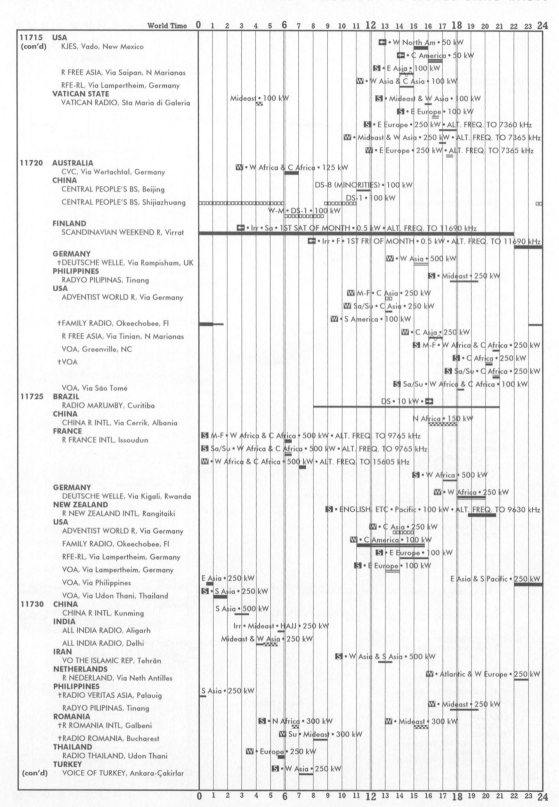

World Time 0 1 2 3 4 5 6 7 8 9 10 11 12 13 14 15 16 17 18 19 20 21 22 23 24

kHz	Country / Station	Schedule details
11715 (con'd)	**USA**	
	KJES, Vado, New Mexico	• W North Am • 50 kW
		• C America • 50 kW
	R FREE ASIA, Via Saipan, N Marianas	S • E Asia • 100 kW
	RFE-RL, Via Lampertheim, Germany	W • W Asia & C Asia • 100 kW
	VATICAN STATE	
	VATICAN RADIO, Sta Maria di Galeria	Mideast • 100 kW
		S • Mideast & W Asia • 100 kW
		S • E Europe • 100 kW
		S • E Europe • 250 kW • ALT. FREQ. TO 7360 kHz
		W • Mideast & W Asia • 250 kW • ALT. FREQ. TO 7365 kHz
		W • E Europe • 250 kW • ALT. FREQ. TO 7365 kHz
11720	**AUSTRALIA**	
	CVC, Via Wertachtal, Germany	W • W Africa & C Africa • 125 kW
	CHINA	
	CENTRAL PEOPLE'S BS, Beijing	DS-8 (MINORITIES) • 100 kW
	CENTRAL PEOPLE'S BS, Shijiazhuang	DS-1 • 100 kW
		W-M • DS-1 • 100 kW
	FINLAND	
	SCANDINAVIAN WEEKEND R, Virrat	• Irr • Sa • 1ST SAT OF MONTH • 0.5 kW • ALT. FREQ. TO 11690 kHz
		• Irr • F • 1ST FRI OF MONTH • 0.5 kW • ALT. FREQ. TO 11690 kHz
	GERMANY	
	†DEUTSCHE WELLE, Via Rampisham, UK	W • W Asia • 500 kW
	PHILIPPINES	
	RADYO PILIPINAS, Tinang	S • Mideast • 250 kW
	USA	
	ADVENTIST WORLD R, Via Germany	W M-F • C Asia • 250 kW
		W Sa/Su • C Asia • 250 kW
	†FAMILY RADIO, Okeechobee, Fl	W • S America • 100 kW
	R FREE ASIA, Via Tinian, N Marianas	W • C Asia • 250 kW
	VOA, Greenville, NC	S M-F • W Africa & C Africa • 250 kW
	†VOA	S • C Africa • 250 kW
		S Sa/Su • C Africa • 250 kW
	VOA, Via São Tomé	S Sa/Su • W Africa & C Africa • 100 kW
11725	**BRAZIL**	
	RADIO MARUMBY, Curitiba	DS • 10 kW •
	CHINA	
	CHINA R INTL, Via Cerrik, Albania	N Africa • 150 kW
	FRANCE	
	R FRANCE INTL, Issoudun	S M-F • W Africa & C Africa • 500 kW • ALT. FREQ. TO 9765 kHz
		S Sa/Su • W Africa & C Africa • 500 kW • ALT. FREQ. TO 9765 kHz
		W • W Africa & C Africa • 500 kW • ALT. FREQ. TO 15605 kHz
		S • W Africa • 500 kW
	GERMANY	
	DEUTSCHE WELLE, Via Kigali, Rwanda	W • W Africa • 250 kW
	NEW ZEALAND	
	R NEW ZEALAND INTL, Rangitaiki	S • ENGLISH, ETC • Pacific • 100 kW • ALT. FREQ. TO 9630 kHz
	USA	
	ADVENTIST WORLD R, Via Germany	W • C Asia • 250 kW
	FAMILY RADIO, Okeechobee, Fl	W • C America • 100 kW
	RFE-RL, Via Lampertheim, Germany	S • E Europe • 100 kW
	VOA, Via Lampertheim, Germany	S • E Europe • 100 kW
	VOA, Via Philippines	E Asia • 250 kW
		E Asia & S Pacific • 250 kW
	VOA, Via Udon Thani, Thailand	S • S Asia • 250 kW
11730	**CHINA**	
	CHINA R INTL, Kunming	S Asia • 500 kW
	INDIA	
	ALL INDIA RADIO, Aligarh	Irr • Mideast • HAJJ • 250 kW
	ALL INDIA RADIO, Delhi	Mideast & W Asia • 250 kW
	IRAN	
	VO THE ISLAMIC REP, Tehrān	S • W Asia & S Asia • 500 kW
	NETHERLANDS	
	R NEDERLAND, Via Neth Antilles	W • Atlantic & W Europe • 250 kW
	PHILIPPINES	
	†RADIO VERITAS ASIA, Palauig	S Asia • 250 kW
	RADYO PILIPINAS, Tinang	W • Mideast • 250 kW
	ROMANIA	
	†R ROMANIA INTL, Galbeni	S • N Africa • 300 kW
		W • Mideast • 300 kW
	†RADIO ROMANIA, Bucharest	W Su • Mideast • 300 kW
	THAILAND	
	RADIO THAILAND, Udon Thani	W • Europe • 250 kW
(con'd)	**TURKEY**	
	VOICE OF TURKEY, Ankara-Çakirlar	S • W Asia • 250 kW

0 1 2 3 4 5 6 7 8 9 10 11 12 13 14 15 16 17 18 19 20 21 22 23 24

ENGLISH ▬ ARABIC ▦ CHINESE ▫▫▫ FRENCH ═ GERMAN ═ RUSSIAN ═ SPANISH ═ OTHER —

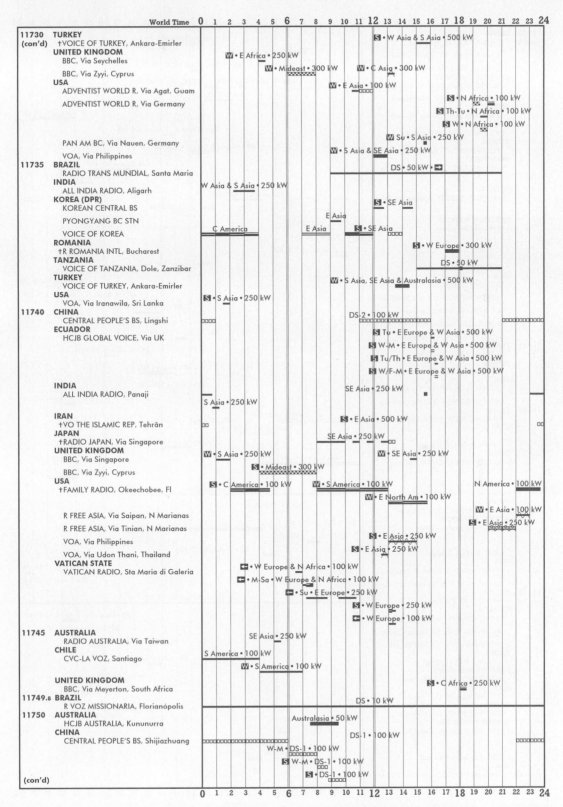

Frequency	Country	Station	Schedule (World Time 0–24)
11730 (con'd)	TURKEY	†VOICE OF TURKEY, Ankara-Emirler	S • W Asia & S Asia • 500 kW
	UNITED KINGDOM	BBC, Via Seychelles	W • E Africa • 250 kW
		BBC, Via Zyyi, Cyprus	W • Mideast • 300 kW; W • C Asia • 300 kW
	USA	ADVENTIST WORLD R, Via Agat, Guam	W • E Asia • 100 kW
		ADVENTIST WORLD R, Via Germany	S • N Africa • 100 kW; S Th-Tu • N Africa • 100 kW; S W • N Africa • 100 kW
		PAN AM BC, Via Nauen, Germany	W Su • S Asia • 250 kW
		VOA, Via Philippines	W • S Asia & SE Asia • 250 kW
11735	BRAZIL	RADIO TRANS MUNDIAL, Santa Maria	DS • 50 kW • ➡
	INDIA	ALL INDIA RADIO, Aligarh	W Asia & S Asia • 250 kW
	KOREA (DPR)	KOREAN CENTRAL BS	S • SE Asia
		PYONGYANG BC STN	E Asia
		VOICE OF KOREA	C America; E Asia; S • SE Asia
	ROMANIA	†R ROMANIA INTL, Bucharest	S • W Europe • 300 kW
	TANZANIA	VOICE OF TANZANIA, Dole, Zanzibar	DS • 50 kW
	TURKEY	VOICE OF TURKEY, Ankara-Emirler	W • S Asia, SE Asia & Australasia • 500 kW
	USA	VOA, Via Iranawila, Sri Lanka	S • S Asia • 250 kW
11740	CHINA	CENTRAL PEOPLE'S BS, Lingshi	DS-2 • 100 kW
	ECUADOR	HCJB GLOBAL VOICE, Via UK	S Tu • E Europe & W Asia • 500 kW; S W-M • E Europe & W Asia • 500 kW; S Tu/Th • E Europe & W Asia • 500 kW; S W/F-M • E Europe & W Asia • 500 kW
	INDIA	ALL INDIA RADIO, Panaji	SE Asia • 250 kW; S Asia • 250 kW
	IRAN	†VO THE ISLAMIC REP, Tehrān	S • E Asia • 500 kW
	JAPAN	†RADIO JAPAN, Via Singapore	SE Asia • 250 kW
	UNITED KINGDOM	BBC, Via Singapore	W • S Asia • 250 kW; W • SE Asia • 250 kW
		BBC, Via Zyyi, Cyprus	S • Mideast • 300 kW
	USA	†FAMILY RADIO, Okeechobee, Fl	S • C America • 100 kW; W • S America • 100 kW; N America • 100 kW; W • E North Am • 100 kW
		R FREE ASIA, Via Saipan, N Marianas	W • E Asia • 100 kW
		R FREE ASIA, Via Tinian, N Marianas	S • E Asia • 250 kW
		VOA, Via Philippines	S • E Asia • 250 kW
		VOA, Via Udon Thani, Thailand	S • E Asia • 250 kW
	VATICAN STATE	VATICAN RADIO, Sta Maria di Galeria	⬅ • W Europe & N Africa • 100 kW; ⬅ • M-Sa • W Europe & N Africa • 100 kW; ⬅ • Su • E Europe • 250 kW; S • W Europe • 250 kW; ⬅ • W Europe • 100 kW
11745	AUSTRALIA	RADIO AUSTRALIA, Via Taiwan	SE Asia • 250 kW
	CHILE	CVC-LA VOZ, Santiago	S America • 100 kW; W • S America • 100 kW
	UNITED KINGDOM	BBC, Via Meyerton, South Africa	S • C Africa • 250 kW
11749.8	BRAZIL	R VOZ MISSIONARIA, Florianópolis	DS • 10 kW
11750	AUSTRALIA	HCJB AUSTRALIA, Kununurra	Australasia • 50 kW
	CHINA	CENTRAL PEOPLE'S BS, Shijiazhuang	DS-1 • 100 kW; W-M • DS-1 • 100 kW; S W-M • DS-1 • 100 kW; S • DS-1 • 100 kW
(con'd)			

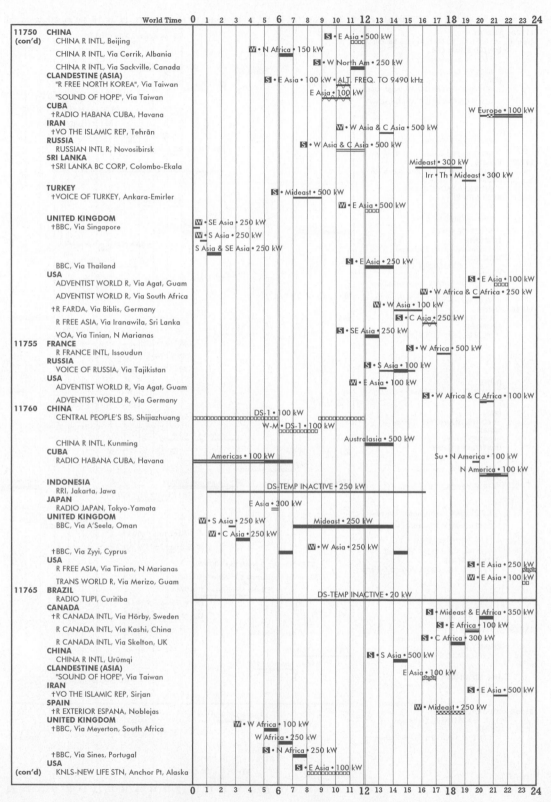

World Time 0 1 2 3 4 5 6 7 8 9 10 11 12 13 14 15 16 17 18 19 20 21 22 23 24

kHz	Country	Station	Schedule
11750 (con'd)	CHINA	CHINA R INTL, Beijing	S • E Asia • 500 kW
		CHINA R INTL, Via Cerrik, Albania	W • N Africa • 150 kW
		CHINA R INTL, Via Sackville, Canada	S • W North Am • 250 kW
	CLANDESTINE (ASIA)	"R FREE NORTH KOREA", Via Taiwan	S • E Asia • 100 kW • ALT. FREQ. TO 9490 kHz
		"SOUND OF HOPE", Via Taiwan	E Asia • 100 kW
	CUBA	†RADIO HABANA CUBA, Havana	W Europe • 100 kW
	IRAN	†VO THE ISLAMIC REP, Tehrān	W • W Asia & C Asia • 500 kW
	RUSSIA	RUSSIAN INTL R, Novosibirsk	S • W Asia & C Asia • 500 kW
	SRI LANKA	†SRI LANKA BC CORP, Colombo-Ekala	Mideast • 300 kW
			Irr • Th • Mideast • 300 kW
	TURKEY	†VOICE OF TURKEY, Ankara-Emirler	S • Mideast • 500 kW
			W • E Asia • 500 kW
	UNITED KINGDOM	†BBC, Via Singapore	W • SE Asia • 250 kW
			W • S Asia • 250 kW
			S Asia & SE Asia • 250 kW
		BBC, Via Thailand	S • E Asia • 250 kW
	USA	ADVENTIST WORLD R, Via Agat, Guam	S • E Asia • 100 kW
		ADVENTIST WORLD R, Via South Africa	W • W Africa & C Africa • 250 kW
		†R FARDA, Via Biblis, Germany	W • W Asia • 100 kW
		R FREE ASIA, Via Iranawila, Sri Lanka	S • C Asia • 250 kW
		VOA, Via Tinian, N Marianas	S • SE Asia • 250 kW
11755	FRANCE	R FRANCE INTL, Issoudun	S • W Africa • 500 kW
	RUSSIA	VOICE OF RUSSIA, Via Tajikistan	S • S Asia • 100 kW
	USA	ADVENTIST WORLD R, Via Agat, Guam	W • E Asia • 100 kW
		ADVENTIST WORLD R, Via Germany	S • W Africa & C Africa • 100 kW
11760	CHINA	CENTRAL PEOPLE'S BS, Shijiazhuang	DS-1 • 100 kW
			W-M • DS-1 • 100 kW
		CHINA R INTL, Kunming	Australasia • 500 kW
	CUBA	RADIO HABANA CUBA, Havana	Americas • 100 kW
			Su • N America • 100 kW
			N America • 100 kW
	INDONESIA	RRI, Jakarta, Jawa	DS-TEMP INACTIVE • 250 kW
	JAPAN	RADIO JAPAN, Tokyo-Yamata	E Asia • 300 kW
	UNITED KINGDOM	BBC, Via A'Seela, Oman	W • S Asia • 250 kW
			Mideast • 250 kW
			W • C Asia • 250 kW
		†BBC, Via Zyyi, Cyprus	W • W Asia • 250 kW
	USA	R FREE ASIA, Via Tinian, N Marianas	S • E Asia • 250 kW
		TRANS WORLD R, Via Merizo, Guam	W • E Asia • 100 kW
11765	BRAZIL	RADIO TUPI, Curitiba	DS-TEMP INACTIVE • 20 kW
	CANADA	†R CANADA INTL, Via Hörby, Sweden	S • Mideast & E Africa • 350 kW
		R CANADA INTL, Via Kashi, China	S • E Africa • 100 kW
		R CANADA INTL, Via Skelton, UK	S • C Africa • 300 kW
	CHINA	CHINA R INTL, Urümqi	S • S Asia • 500 kW
	CLANDESTINE (ASIA)	"SOUND OF HOPE", Via Taiwan	E Asia • 100 kW
	IRAN	†VO THE ISLAMIC REP, Sirjan	S • E Asia • 500 kW
	SPAIN	†R EXTERIOR ESPANA, Noblejas	W • Mideast • 250 kW
	UNITED KINGDOM	†BBC, Via Meyerton, South Africa	W • W Africa • 100 kW
			W Africa • 250 kW
		†BBC, Via Sines, Portugal	S • N Africa • 250 kW
(con'd)	USA	KNLS-NEW LIFE STN, Anchor Pt, Alaska	S • E Asia • 100 kW

0 1 2 3 4 5 6 7 8 9 10 11 12 13 14 15 16 17 18 19 20 21 22 23 24

ENGLISH ARABIC CHINESE FRENCH GERMAN RUSSIAN SPANISH OTHER

Frequency	Country / Station	Schedule (World Time 0–24)
11765 (con'd)	**USA**	
	R FREE ASIA, Via Tinian, N Marianas	S • E Asia • 250 kW
	TRANS WORLD R, Via Merizo, Guam	S • E Asia • 100 kW
	†VOA	W • W Asia & S Asia • 250 kW
	WORLD HARVEST R, Greenbush, Maine	S • Africa • 250 kW
11770	**AUSTRALIA**	
	CVC, Darwin	S • E Asia • 250 kW
	CHINA	
	CHINA R INTL, Beijing	SE Asia • 500 kW
	CHINA R INTL, Kashi	S Asia • 100 kW; W • Mideast • 100 kW
	XINJIANG PEOPLE'S BC STN, Urümqi	S • DS-CHINESE • 50 kW; DS-CHINESE • 50 kW; W/F-M • DS-CHINESE • 50 kW
	GERMANY	
	DEUTSCHE WELLE, Via Sri Lanka	S • SE Asia • 250 kW
	USA	
	ADVENTIST WORLD R, Via Agat, Guam	W • SE Asia • 100 kW
	FAMILY RADIO, Okeechobee, Fl	S • S America • 100 kW
11775	**ANGUILLA**	
	CARIBBEAN BEACON	N America • 100 kW
	CHINA	
	CHINA R INTL, Kashi	S • Europe • 500 kW
	CHINA R INTL, Via Cerrik, Albania	S • N Africa • 150 kW
	INDIA	
	ALL INDIA RADIO, Panaji	S Asia • 250 kW
	POLAND	
	†POLISH RADIO, Via Jülich, Germany	S • E Europe • 100 kW
	ROMANIA	
	†R ROMANIA INTL, Bucharest	S • W Europe • 300 kW
	USA	
	ADVENTIST WORLD R, Via Agat, Guam	S • E Asia • 100 kW
	R FREE ASIA, Via Tinian, N Marianas	W • E Asia • 250 kW
	RADIO MARTI, Greenville, NC	S • C America • 250 kW
	VOA, Greenville, NC	W M-F • W Africa & C Africa • 250 kW
	VOA, Via São Tomé	W • C Africa & S Africa • 100 kW; W Sa/Su • W Africa & C Africa • 100 kW
11780	**BRAZIL**	
	R NACIONAL DA AMAZONIA, Brasília	DS • ➡; Su • DS • ➡
	CHINA	
	CENTRAL PEOPLE'S BS, Beijing	DS-8 (MINORITIES) • 100 kW; Th-Tu • DS-8 (MINORITIES) • 100 kW
	CHINA R INTL, Jinhua	E Asia • 500 kW
	CHINA R INTL, Kunming	SE Asia • 100 kW
	GERMANY	
	DEUTSCHE WELLE, Via Kigali, Rwanda	S • E Europe & W Asia • 250 kW
	JAPAN	
	RADIO JAPAN, Via Rampisham, UK	W • N Europe • 500 kW
	RADIO JAPAN, Via Singapore	S • SE Asia • 250 kW
	USA	
	ADVENTIST WORLD R, Via Agat, Guam	S • E Asia • 100 kW
	ADVENTIST WORLD R, Via Germany	W • N Africa • 100 kW
	VOA, Via Udon Thani, Thailand	S • C Asia • 250 kW
11784v	**BRAZIL**	
	†RADIO GUAIBA, Porto Alegre	DS • 7.5 kW • ➡
11785	**CANADA**	
	R CANADA INTL, Via In-Kimjae, Korea	W • E Asia • 250 kW
	CHINA	
	CHINA R INTL, Via Cerrik, Albania	W • W Europe • 150 kW; S • W Europe • 150 kW
	TURKEY	
	†VOICE OF TURKEY, Ankara-Emirler	W • N Africa & W Africa • 500 kW
	USA	
	R FREE ASIA, Via Saipan, N Marianas	W • E Asia • 100 kW
	R FREE ASIA, Via Tinian, N Marianas	S • E Asia • 250 kW
	VOA, Via Udon Thani, Thailand	E Asia • 500 kW; W • E Asia • 500 kW
11785v	**INDONESIA**	
	†VOICE OF INDONESIA, Cimanggis, Jawa	E Asia, SE Asia & Pacific • 250 kW • ALT. FREQ. TO 9525v kHz; Europe • 250 kW • ALT. FREQ. TO 9525v kHz
11790 (con'd)	**CANADA**	
	R CANADA INTL, Via Madagascar	S • Mideast • 250 kW

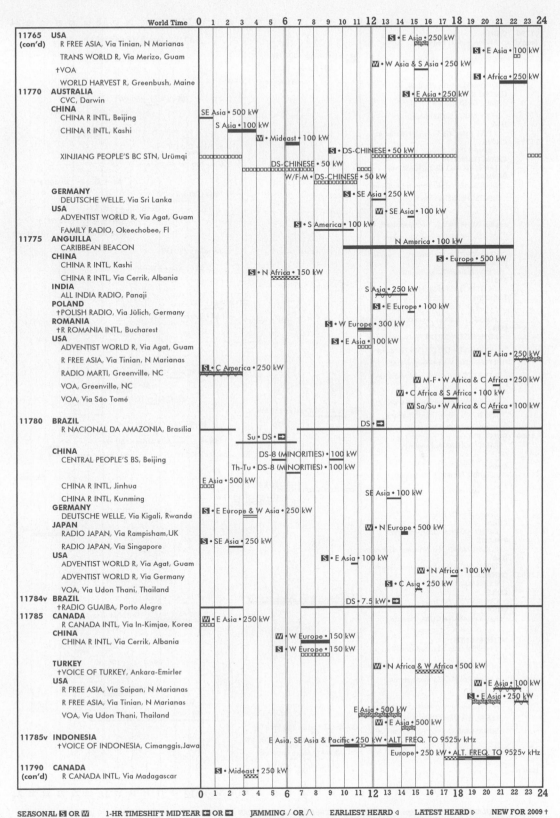

World Time 0 1 2 3 4 5 6 7 8 9 10 11 12 13 14 15 16 17 18 19 20 21 22 23 24

kHz	Country / Station	Broadcasts
11790 (con'd)	**CHINA**	
	CHINA R INTL, Beijing	S • E Europe & W Asia • 500 kW
	ROMANIA	
	†R ROMANIA INTL, Bucharest	S • E North Am • 300 kW
		S • E Asia • 300 kW
	†R ROMANIA INTL, Galbeni	S • Mideast • 300 kW
	UNITED KINGDOM	
	BBC, Via Singapore	S • S Asia • 250 kW
	FEBA RADIO, Rampisham	S • C Africa • 500 kW
	USA	
	R FREE ASIA, Via Tinian, N Marianas	W • E Asia • 250 kW
11795	**CHINA**	
	CHINA R INTL, Kashi	S Asia • 100 kW
	CHINA (TAIWAN)	
	TRANS WORLD BROADCASTING	E Asia • 100 kW
	GERMANY	
	†DEUTSCHE WELLE, Various Locations	S • E Africa • 250/500 kW
	†DEUTSCHE WELLE, Via Kigali, Rwanda	S • C Africa • 250 kW
		W • S Africa • 250 kW
	†DEUTSCHE WELLE, Via Rampisham, UK	S • S Africa • 500 kW
	DEUTSCHE WELLE, Via Sri Lanka	S • E Africa & S Africa • 250 kW
	KOREA (REPUBLIC)	
	KBS WORLD R, Via Sackville, Canada	S America • 250 kW
	ROMANIA	
	†R ROMANIA INTL, Bucharest	S • E Asia • 300 kW
	SPAIN	
	†R EXTERIOR ESPANA, Noblejas	Tu • S America • 250 kW
	TURKEY	
	†VOICE OF TURKEY, Ankara-Çakirlar	• W Asia • 500 kW
	VOICE OF TURKEY, Ankara-Emirler	S • C Asia • 500 kW
	USA	
	ADVENTIST WORLD R, Via Agat, Guam	W • Mideast • 100 kW
	ADVENTIST WORLD R, Via Germany	W • E Africa • 250 kW
	R FREE ASIA, Via Dhabayya, UAE	S • S Asia • 500 kW
	R FREE ASIA, Via Tinian, N Marianas	W • SE Asia • 250 kW
		S • E Asia • 250 kW
	RFE-RL, Via Lampertheim, Germany	W • C Asia • 100 kW
	RFE-RL, Via Udon Thani, Thailand	W • W Asia & C Asia • 250 kW
	TRANS WORLD R, Via Merizo, Guam	S • SE Asia • 100 kW
11800	**BULGARIA**	
	†RADIO BULGARIA, Plovdiv	S • S Europe & N Africa • 250 kW
		S • Mideast • 250 kW
		S • W Europe • 250 kW
	CHINA	
	CENTRAL PEOPLE'S BS, Beijing	S • DS-2 • 150 kW
		DS-2 • 150 kW
		Th-Tu • DS-2 • 150 kW
	CHINA R INTL, Kashi	S • S Asia • 100 kW
	CUBA	
	RADIO HABANA CUBA, Havana	C America • 100 kW
	POLAND	
	†POLISH RADIO, Via W'tachtal, Germany	S • E Europe • 100 kW
	USA	
	TRANS WORLD R, Via Merizo, Guam	M-Sa • S Asia • 100 kW
11805	**CANADA**	
	R CANADA INTL, Via Tokyo, Japan	S • E Asia • 300 kW
	CHILE	
	CVC-LA VOZ, Santiago	W • S America & C America • 100 kW
	CUBA	
	†RADIO HABANA CUBA, Havana	S America • 100 kW • ALT. FREQ. TO 15360 kHz
		Su • S America • 100 kW • ALT. FREQ. TO 15360 kHz
	NETHERLANDS	
	R NEDERLAND, Via Meyerton, S Africa	W • E Africa • 100 kW
	USA	
	ADVENTIST WORLD R, Via Agat, Guam	S • S Asia • 100 kW
	FAMILY RADIO, Via Madagascar	W • E Africa • 50 kW
	†RFE-RL	W • E Europe • 250 kW
	RFE-RL, Via Lampertheim, Germany	W • E Europe & W Asia • 100 kW
	RFE-RL, Via Udon Thani, Thailand	S • W Asia & S Asia • 250 kW
	SUDAN RADIO SVC, Via Skelton, UK	S M-F • C Africa • 300 kW
		S M/Tu/TH/F • C Africa • 300 kW
		S W • C Africa • 300 kW
		S • C Africa • 300 kW
(con'd)		

World Time 0 1 2 3 4 5 6 7 8 9 10 11 12 13 14 15 16 17 18 19 20 21 22 23 24

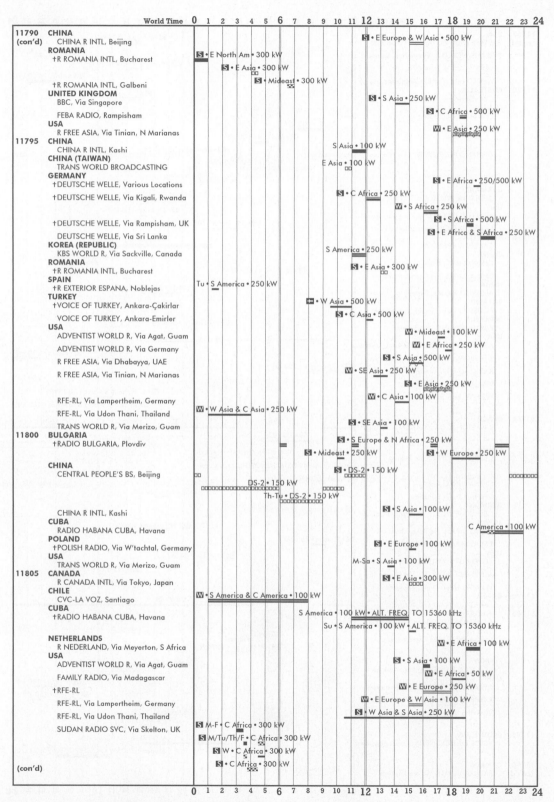

ENGLISH ARABIC CHINESE FRENCH GERMAN RUSSIAN SPANISH OTHER

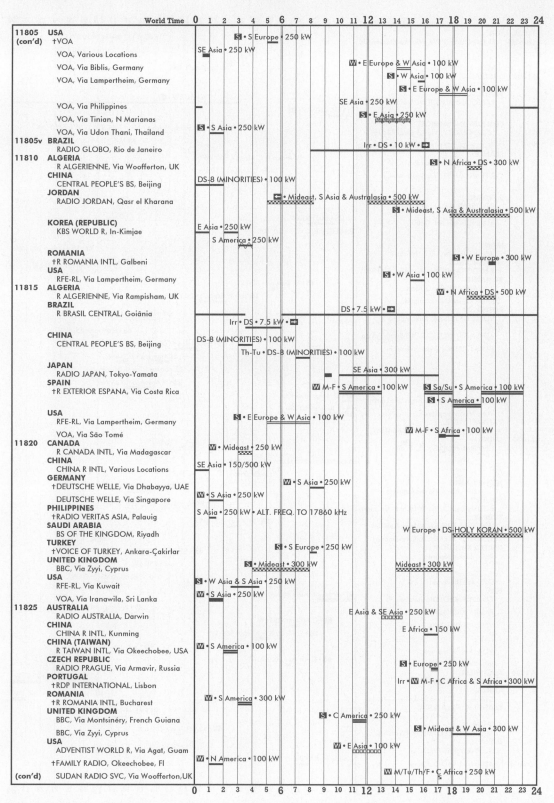

World Time 0 1 2 3 4 5 6 7 8 9 10 11 12 13 14 15 16 17 18 19 20 21 22 23 24

kHz	Country	Station	Schedule
11805 (con'd)	USA	†VOA	S • S Europe • 250 kW
		VOA, Various Locations	SE Asia • 250 kW
		VOA, Via Biblis, Germany	W • E Europe & W Asia • 100 kW
		VOA, Via Lampertheim, Germany	S • W Asia • 100 kW; S • E Europe & W Asia • 100 kW
		VOA, Via Philippines	SE Asia • 250 kW
		VOA, Via Tinian, N Marianas	S • E Asia • 250 kW
		VOA, Via Udon Thani, Thailand	S • S Asia • 250 kW
11805v	BRAZIL	RADIO GLOBO, Rio de Janeiro	Irr • DS • 10 kW • ⇨
11810	ALGERIA	R ALGERIENNE, Via Woofferton, UK	S • N Africa • DS • 300 kW
	CHINA	CENTRAL PEOPLE'S BS, Beijing	DS-8 (MINORITIES) • 100 kW
	JORDAN	RADIO JORDAN, Qasr el Kharana	⇦ • Mideast, S Asia & Australasia • 500 kW; S • Mideast, S Asia & Australasia • 500 kW
	KOREA (REPUBLIC)	KBS WORLD R, In-Kimjae	E Asia • 250 kW; S America • 250 kW
	ROMANIA	†R ROMANIA INTL, Galbeni	S • W Europe • 300 kW
	USA	RFE-RL, Via Lampertheim, Germany	S • W Asia • 100 kW
11815	ALGERIA	R ALGERIENNE, Via Rampisham, UK	W • N Africa • DS • 500 kW
	BRAZIL	R BRASIL CENTRAL, Goiânia	DS • 7.5 kW • ⇨; Irr • DS • 7.5 kW • ⇨
	CHINA	CENTRAL PEOPLE'S BS, Beijing	DS-8 (MINORITIES) • 100 kW; Th-Tu • DS-8 (MINORITIES) • 100 kW
	JAPAN	RADIO JAPAN, Tokyo-Yamata	SE Asia • 300 kW
	SPAIN	†R EXTERIOR ESPANA, Via Costa Rica	W M-F • S America • 100 kW; S Sa/Su • S America • 100 kW; S • S America • 100 kW
	USA	RFE-RL, Via Lampertheim, Germany	S • E Europe & W Asia • 100 kW
		VOA, Via São Tomé	W M-F • S Africa • 100 kW
11820	CANADA	R CANADA INTL, Via Madagascar	W • Mideast • 250 kW
	CHINA	CHINA R INTL, Various Locations	SE Asia • 150/500 kW
	GERMANY	†DEUTSCHE WELLE, Via Dhabayya, UAE	W • S Asia • 250 kW
		DEUTSCHE WELLE, Via Singapore	W • S Asia • 250 kW
	PHILIPPINES	†RADIO VERITAS ASIA, Palauig	S Asia • 250 kW • ALT. FREQ. TO 17860 kHz
	SAUDI ARABIA	BS OF THE KINGDOM, Riyadh	W Europe • DS-HOLY KORAN • 500 kW
	TURKEY	†VOICE OF TURKEY, Ankara-Çakirlar	S • S Europe • 250 kW
	UNITED KINGDOM	BBC, Via Zyyi, Cyprus	S • Mideast • 300 kW; Mideast • 300 kW
	USA	RFE-RL, Via Kuwait	S • W Asia & S Asia • 250 kW
		VOA, Via Iranawila, Sri Lanka	W • S Asia • 250 kW
11825	AUSTRALIA	RADIO AUSTRALIA, Darwin	E Asia & SE Asia • 250 kW
	CHINA	CHINA R INTL, Kunming	E Africa • 150 kW
	CHINA (TAIWAN)	R TAIWAN INTL, Via Okeechobee, USA	W • S America • 100 kW
	CZECH REPUBLIC	RADIO PRAGUE, Via Armavir, Russia	S • Europe • 250 kW
	PORTUGAL	†RDP INTERNATIONAL, Lisbon	Irr • W M-F • C Africa & S Africa • 300 kW
	ROMANIA	†R ROMANIA INTL, Bucharest	W • S America • 300 kW
	UNITED KINGDOM	BBC, Via Montsinéry, French Guiana	S • C America • 250 kW
		BBC, Via Zyyi, Cyprus	S • Mideast & W Asia • 300 kW
	USA	ADVENTIST WORLD R, Via Agat, Guam	W • E Asia • 100 kW
		†FAMILY RADIO, Okeechobee, Fl	W • N America • 100 kW
(con'd)		SUDAN RADIO SVC, Via Woofferton,UK	W M/Tu/Th/F • C Africa • 250 kW

0 1 2 3 4 5 6 7 8 9 10 11 12 13 14 15 16 17 18 19 20 21 22 23 24

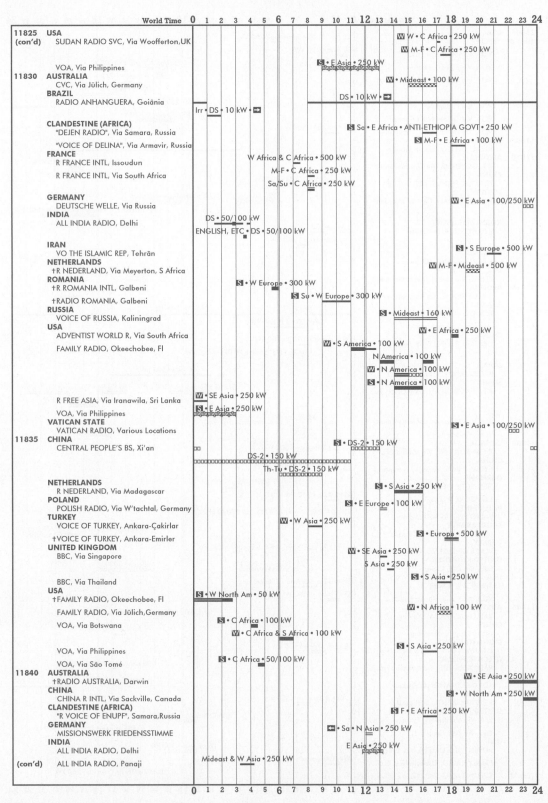

World Time 0 1 2 3 4 5 6 7 8 9 10 11 12 13 14 15 16 17 18 19 20 21 22 23 24

Frequency	Country / Station	Schedule
11825 (con'd)	**USA**	
	SUDAN RADIO SVC, Via Woofferton, UK	W • C Africa • 250 kW
		W M-F • C Africa • 250 kW
	VOA, Via Philippines	S • E Asia • 250 kW
11830	**AUSTRALIA**	
	CVC, Via Jülich, Germany	W • Mideast • 100 kW
	BRAZIL	
	RADIO ANHANGUERA, Goiânia	DS • 10 kW • ➡
		Irr • DS • 10 kW • ➡
	CLANDESTINE (AFRICA)	
	"DEJEN RADIO", Via Samara, Russia	S Sa • E Africa • ANTI-ETHIOPIA GOVT • 250 kW
	"VOICE OF DELINA", Via Armavir, Russia	S M-F • E Africa • 100 kW
	FRANCE	
	R FRANCE INTL, Issoudun	W Africa & C Africa • 500 kW
	R FRANCE INTL, Via South Africa	M-F • C Africa • 250 kW
		Sa/Su • C Africa • 250 kW
	GERMANY	
	DEUTSCHE WELLE, Via Russia	W • E Asia • 100/250 kW
	INDIA	
	ALL INDIA RADIO, Delhi	DS • 50/100 kW
		ENGLISH, ETC • DS • 50/100 kW
	IRAN	
	VO THE ISLAMIC REP, Tehrān	S • S Europe • 500 kW
	NETHERLANDS	
	†R NEDERLAND, Via Meyerton, S Africa	W M-F • Mideast • 500 kW
	ROMANIA	
	†R ROMANIA INTL, Galbeni	S • W Europe • 300 kW
	†RADIO ROMANIA, Galbeni	S Su • W Europe • 300 kW
	RUSSIA	
	VOICE OF RUSSIA, Kaliningrad	S • Mideast • 160 kW
	USA	
	ADVENTIST WORLD R, Via South Africa	W • E Africa • 250 kW
	FAMILY RADIO, Okeechobee, Fl	W • S America • 100 kW
		N America • 100 kW
		W • N America • 100 kW
		S • N America • 100 kW
	R FREE ASIA, Via Iranawila, Sri Lanka	W • SE Asia • 250 kW
	VOA, Via Philippines	S • E Asia • 250 kW
	VATICAN STATE	
	VATICAN RADIO, Various Locations	S • E Asia • 100/250 kW
11835	**CHINA**	
	CENTRAL PEOPLE'S BS, Xi'an	S • DS-2 • 150 kW
		DS-2 • 150 kW
		Th-Tu • DS-2 • 150 kW
	NETHERLANDS	
	R NEDERLAND, Via Madagascar	S • S Asia • 250 kW
	POLAND	
	POLISH RADIO, Via W'tachtal, Germany	S • E Europe • 100 kW
	TURKEY	
	VOICE OF TURKEY, Ankara-Çakirlar	W • W Asia • 250 kW
	†VOICE OF TURKEY, Ankara-Emirler	S • Europe • 500 kW
	UNITED KINGDOM	
	BBC, Via Singapore	W • SE Asia • 250 kW
		S Asia • 250 kW
	BBC, Via Thailand	S • S Asia • 250 kW
	USA	
	†FAMILY RADIO, Okeechobee, Fl	S • W North Am • 50 kW
	FAMILY RADIO, Via Jülich, Germany	W • N Africa • 100 kW
	VOA, Via Botswana	S • C Africa • 100 kW
		W • C Africa & S Africa • 100 kW
	VOA, Via Philippines	S • S Asia • 250 kW
	VOA, Via São Tomé	S • C Africa • 50/100 kW
11840	**AUSTRALIA**	
	†RADIO AUSTRALIA, Darwin	W • SE Asia • 250 kW
	CHINA	
	CHINA R INTL, Via Sackville, Canada	S • W North Am • 250 kW
	CLANDESTINE (AFRICA)	
	"R VOICE OF ENUPF", Samara, Russia	S F • E Africa • 250 kW
	GERMANY	
	MISSIONSWERK FRIEDENSSTIMME	⬅ • Sa • N Asia • 250 kW
	INDIA	
	ALL INDIA RADIO, Delhi	E Asia • 250 kW
(con'd)	ALL INDIA RADIO, Panaji	Mideast & W Asia • 250 kW

0 1 2 3 4 5 6 7 8 9 10 11 12 13 14 15 16 17 18 19 20 21 22 23 24

ENGLISH ARABIC CHINESE FRENCH GERMAN RUSSIAN SPANISH OTHER

World Time 0 1 2 3 4 5 6 7 8 9 10 11 12 13 14 15 16 17 18 19 20 21 22 23 24

kHz	Country / Station	Schedule
11840 (con'd)	**POLAND**	
	†POLISH RADIO, Via W'tachtal, Germany	W • E Europe • 100 kW
	RUSSIA	
	VOICE OF RUSSIA, Moscow	S • S Europe • 250 kW • ALT. FREQ. TO 12060 kHz
	USA	
	ADVENTIST WORLD R, Via Agat, Guam	W • SE Asia • 100 kW
	†R FARDA, Via Woofferton, UK	W • W Asia • 300 kW
	TRANS WORLD R, Via Merizo, Guam	M-Sa • Australasia & S Pacific • 100 kW
		M-F • Australasia & S Pacific • 100 kW
	VOA, Greenville, NC	W • C America • 250 kW
	†VOA	S • E Europe • 250 kW
		S M-F • E Europe • 250 kW
	VOA, Via Iranawila, Sri Lanka	W • SE Asia • 250 kW
	VOA, Via Lampertheim, Germany	W • C Asia • 100 kW
	VIETNAM	
	VOICE OF VIETNAM, Via Skelton, UK	S • S Europe • 300 kW
11845	**CANADA**	
	R CANADA INTL, Sackville, NB	W • N Africa • 250 kW
	R CANADA INTL, Via Skelton, UK	W • N Africa & W Africa • 500 kW
	CHINA	
	CENTRAL PEOPLE'S BS, Xi'an	S • DS-2 • 150 kW
		DS-2 • 150 kW
		Th-Tu • DS-2 • 150 kW
		S Th-Tu • DS-2 • 150 kW
	CHINA R INTL, Xi'an	W • SE Asia • 500 kW
	UNITED KINGDOM	
	BBC, Rampisham	S M-F • E Europe • 500 kW
		S Sa/Su • E Europe • 300 kW
		S Sa • E Europe • 500 kW
	BBC, Via Zyyi, Cyprus	S M-F • E Europe & W Asia • 250 kW
		S M-F • E Europe • 250 kW
		S • E Europe • 250 kW
		S Sa/Su • E Europe • 250 kW
	USA	
	ADVENTIST WORLD R, Via Agat, Guam	S • E Asia • 100 kW
	ADVENTIST WORLD R, Via South Africa	W • W Africa & C Africa • 250 kW
	RADIO MARTI, Greenville, NC	S • C America • 250 kW
11850	**CHINA (TAIWAN)**	
	R TAIWAN INTL, Via Issoudun, France	W • C Africa & S Africa • 500 kW
	INDIA	
	ALL INDIA RADIO, Delhi	S Asia • 50/100 kW
	PHILIPPINES	
	RADIO VERITAS ASIA, Palauig	SE Asia • 250 kW
	PORTUGAL	
	RDP INTERNATIONAL, Sines	S M-F • Europe • 250 kW
	UNITED KINGDOM	
	†BBC, Via Singapore	S • SE Asia • 250 kW
		S • S Asia • 250 kW
	USA	
	ADVENTIST WORLD R, Via Agat, Guam	S • E Asia • 100 kW
		SE Asia • 100 kW
	FAMILY RADIO, Via Armavir, Russia	S • S Asia • 300 kW
	FAMILY RADIO, Via Dhabayya, UAE	S • S Asia • 250 kW
	R FREE ASIA, Via Tinian, N Marianas	W • SE Asia • 250 kW
	VATICAN STATE	
	VATICAN RADIO, Sta Maria di Galeria	W Su/W • S Asia • 500 kW
		W • S Asia • 500 kW
11855	**BRAZIL**	
	RADIO APARECIDA, Aparecida	DS • 0.5/1 kW • ➡
	CHINA	
	CHINA R INTL, Via Cerrik, Albania	W • W Europe • 150 kW
	CHINA R INTL, Via Sackville, Canada	S • E North Am & C America • 250 kW
	CHINA (TAIWAN)	
	†R TAIWAN INTL, Via Okeechobee, USA	C America • 100 kW
	ROMANIA	
	†R ROMANIA INTL, Bucharest	S • C Asia • 300 kW
	THAILAND	
	RADIO THAILAND, Udon Thani	W • Mideast • 250 kW
	UNITED KINGDOM	
	BBC, Via A'Seela, Oman	S • C Asia • 250 kW
		S • W Asia • 250 kW
	BBC, Via Ascension	M-F • W Africa • 250 kW
(con'd)	BBC, Via Zyyi, Cyprus	S • W Asia • 250 kW

World Time 0 1 2 3 4 5 6 7 8 9 10 11 12 13 14 15 16 17 18 19 20 21 22 23 24

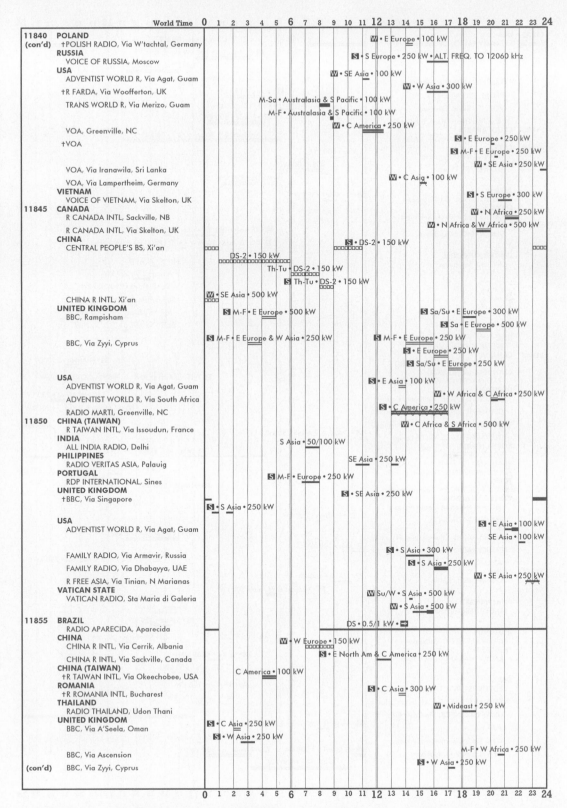

World Time 0–24

Frequency	Country / Station	Schedule labels
11855 (con'd)	**USA**	
	†FAMILY RADIO, Okeechobee, Fl	C America • 100 kW
		[S] • S America • 100 kW
		[W] • E North Am • 100 kW
	†FAMILY RADIO, Via Tajikistan	[S] • C Asia • 100 kW
	RFE-RL, Via Philippines	[S] • E Asia • 250 kW
	VOA, Via Biblis, Germany	[W] • Mideast • 100 kW
	VOA, Via Udon Thani, Thailand	[W] • E Asia • 500 kW
11855v	**SAUDI ARABIA**	
	BS OF THE KINGDOM, Jiddah	Mideast & E Africa • DS-2 • 50 kW
11860	**CHINA**	
	CHINA R INTL, Kunming	S Asia • 500 kW
	XIZANG PBS, Lhasa	DS • 100 kW
		W-M • DS • 100 kW
	JAPAN	
	RADIO JAPAN, Via Singapore	[W] • SE Asia • 250 kW
	LIBYA	
	†RADIO JAMAHIRIYA, Sabratha	C Africa • 500 kW
	PHILIPPINES	
	FEBC RADIO INTL, Bocaue	[S] • SE Asia • 100 kW • ALT. FREQ. TO 12095 kHz
		[S] Th • SE Asia • 100 kW • ALT. FREQ. TO 12095 kHz
	UNITED KINGDOM	
	†BBC, Via Seychelles	E Africa • 250 kW
		E Africa • 250/500 kW
		M-Sa • E Africa • 250/500 kW
		Su • E Africa • 250/500 kW
		M-F • E Africa • 250/500 kW
		Sa/Su • E Africa • 250/500 kW
	USA	
	RFE-RL, Via Philippines	[S] • E Asia • 250 kW
11865	**CANADA**	
	R CANADA INTL, Sackville, NB	[W] • N Africa • 250 kW
	CLANDESTINE (AFRICA)	
	"RADIO XORIYO", Via Jülich, Germany	[S] Tu/F • E Africa • ANTI-ETHIOPIA GOVT • 100 kW
	GERMANY	
	DEUTSCHE WELLE, Via Kigali, Rwanda	[S] • W Africa • 250 kW
	DEUTSCHE WELLE, Via Rampisham, UK	[S] • C Africa & S Africa • 250 kW
	DEUTSCHE WELLE, Via Sines, Portugal	S America • 250 kW
	DEUTSCHE WELLE, Via Sri Lanka	[S] • C Asia & E Asia • 250 kW
	KOREA (DPR)	
	VOICE OF KOREA	E Asia • ALT. FREQ. TO 7580 kHz
	ROMANIA	
	R ROMANIA INTL, Galbeni	[S] • W Europe • 250 kW
	TURKEY	
	†VOICE OF TURKEY, Ankara-Emirler	[W] • C Asia • 500 kW
	UNITED KINGDOM	
	BBC, Via Meyerton, South Africa	[W] • C Africa • 100 kW
	BBC, Via Seychelles	[W] • E Africa • 250 kW
	USA	
	FAMILY RADIO, Okeechobee, Fl	[S] • N America • 100 kW
	†FAMILY RADIO, Via Taiwan	SE Asia • 100 kW
	†VOA	[S] M-F • E Europe & Mideast • 250 kW
11870	**CHINA**	
	CHINA R INTL, Kashi	[S] • S Asia • 100 kW
		[S] • Mideast & W Asia • 500 kW
	PHILIPPINES	
	†RADIO VERITAS ASIA, Palauig	S Asia • 250 kW
		[S] • S Asia • 250 kW
	ROMANIA	
	†R ROMANIA INTL, Galbeni	[W] • S Europe • 300 kW
	THAILAND	
	RADIO THAILAND, Udon Thani	[S] • SE Asia • 250 kW
		SE Asia • 250 kW
	USA	
	ADVENTIST WORLD R, Via Agat, Guam	[W] • SE Asia • 100 kW
	†KNLS-NEW LIFE STN, Anchor Pt, Alaska	[S] • E Asia • 100 kW
	UNIVERSITY NET'K, Via Costa Rica	S America • 40 kW
	†VOA	[S] • Mideast & W Asia • 250 kW
	VOA, Via Lampertheim, Germany	[W] M-F • E Europe & Mideast • 100 kW
	†WEWN, Vandiver, Alabama	[S] • S America • 500 kW
		[W] • S America • 500 kW
		S America • 500 kW

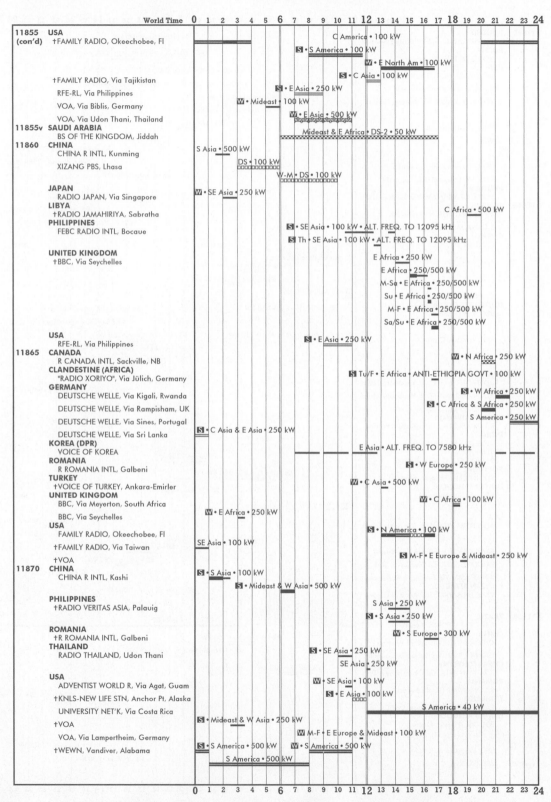

ENGLISH ARABIC CHINESE FRENCH GERMAN RUSSIAN SPANISH OTHER

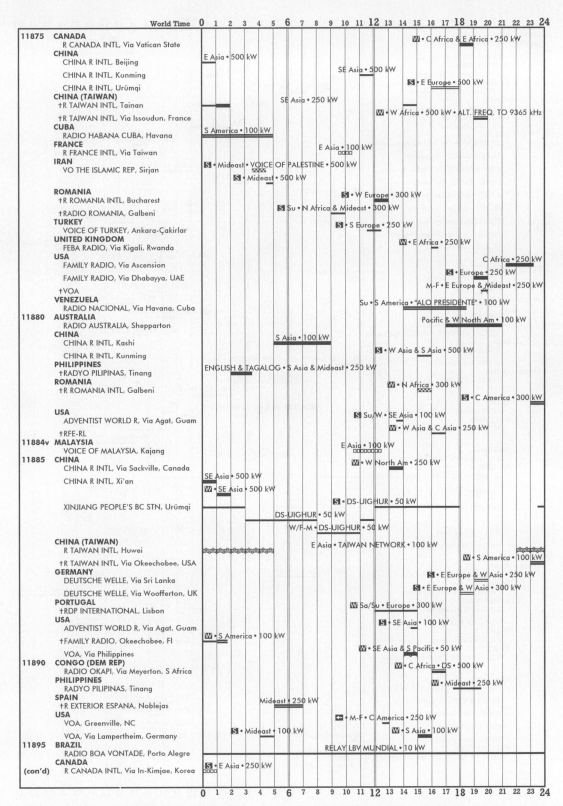

World Time 0 1 2 3 4 5 6 7 8 9 10 11 12 13 14 15 16 17 18 19 20 21 22 23 24

kHz	Country / Station	Schedule
11875	**CANADA**	
	R CANADA INTL, Via Vatican State	W • C Africa & E Africa • 250 kW
	CHINA	
	CHINA R INTL, Beijing	E Asia • 500 kW
	CHINA R INTL, Kunming	SE Asia • 500 kW
	CHINA R INTL, Urümqi	S • E Europe • 500 kW
	CHINA (TAIWAN)	
	†R TAIWAN INTL, Tainan	SE Asia • 250 kW
	†R TAIWAN INTL, Via Issoudun, France	W • W Africa • 500 kW • ALT. FREQ. TO 9365 kHz
	CUBA	
	RADIO HABANA CUBA, Havana	S America • 100 kW
	FRANCE	
	R FRANCE INTL, Via Taiwan	E Asia • 100 kW
	IRAN	
	VO THE ISLAMIC REP, Sirjan	S • Mideast • VOICE OF PALESTINE • 500 kW
		S • Mideast • 500 kW
	ROMANIA	
	†R ROMANIA INTL, Bucharest	S • W Europe • 300 kW
	†RADIO ROMANIA, Galbeni	S Su • N Africa & Mideast • 300 kW
	TURKEY	
	VOICE OF TURKEY, Ankara-Çakirlar	S • S Europe • 250 kW
	UNITED KINGDOM	
	FEBA RADIO, Via Kigali, Rwanda	W • E Africa • 250 kW
	USA	
	FAMILY RADIO, Via Ascension	C Africa • 250 kW
	FAMILY RADIO, Via Dhabayya, UAE	S • Europe • 250 kW
	†VOA	M-F • E Europe & Mideast • 250 kW
	VENEZUELA	
	RADIO NACIONAL, Via Havana, Cuba	Su • S America • "ALO PRESIDENTE" • 100 kW
11880	**AUSTRALIA**	
	RADIO AUSTRALIA, Shepparton	Pacific & W North Am • 100 kW
	CHINA	
	CHINA R INTL, Kashi	S Asia • 100 kW
	CHINA R INTL, Kunming	S • W Asia & S Asia • 500 kW
	PHILIPPINES	
	†RADYO PILIPINAS, Tinang	ENGLISH & TAGALOG • S Asia & Mideast • 250 kW
	ROMANIA	
	†R ROMANIA INTL, Galbeni	W • N Africa • 300 kW
		S • C America • 300 kW
	USA	
	ADVENTIST WORLD R, Via Agat, Guam	S Su/W • SE Asia • 100 kW
	†RFE-RL	W • W Asia & C Asia • 250 kW
11884v	**MALAYSIA**	
	VOICE OF MALAYSIA, Kajang	E Asia • 100 kW
11885	**CHINA**	
	CHINA R INTL, Via Sackville, Canada	W • W North Am • 250 kW
	CHINA R INTL, Xi'an	SE Asia • 500 kW
		W • SE Asia • 500 kW
	XINJIANG PEOPLE'S BC STN, Urümqi	S • DS-UIGHUR • 50 kW
		DS-UIGHUR • 50 kW
		W/F-M • DS-UIGHUR • 50 kW
	CHINA (TAIWAN)	
	R TAIWAN INTL, Huwei	E Asia • TAIWAN NETWORK • 100 kW
	†R TAIWAN INTL, Via Okeechobee, USA	W • S America • 100 kW
	GERMANY	
	DEUTSCHE WELLE, Via Sri Lanka	S • E Europe & W Asia • 250 kW
	DEUTSCHE WELLE, Via Woofferton, UK	S • E Europe & W Asia • 300 kW
	PORTUGAL	
	†RDP INTERNATIONAL, Lisbon	W Sa/Su • Europe • 300 kW
	USA	
	ADVENTIST WORLD R, Via Agat, Guam	S • SE Asia • 100 kW
	†FAMILY RADIO, Okeechobee, Fl	W • S America • 100 kW
	VOA, Via Philippines	W • SE Asia & S Pacific • 50 kW
11890	**CONGO (DEM REP)**	
	RADIO OKAPI, Via Meyerton, S Africa	W • C Africa • DS • 500 kW
	PHILIPPINES	
	RADYO PILIPINAS, Tinang	W • Mideast • 250 kW
	SPAIN	
	†R EXTERIOR ESPANA, Noblejas	Mideast • 250 kW
	USA	
	VOA, Greenville, NC	⬅ • M-F • C America • 250 kW
	VOA, Via Lampertheim, Germany	S • Mideast • 100 kW
		W • S Asia • 100 kW
11895	**BRAZIL**	
	RADIO BOA VONTADE, Porto Alegre	RELAY LBV MUNDIAL • 10 kW
	CANADA	
(con'd)	R CANADA INTL, Via In-Kimjae, Korea	S • E Asia • 250 kW

0 1 2 3 4 5 6 7 8 9 10 11 12 13 14 15 16 17 18 19 20 21 22 23 24

SEASONAL S OR W   1-HR TIMESHIFT MIDYEAR ⬅ OR ➡   JAMMING / OR ∧   EARLIEST HEARD ◁   LATEST HEARD ▷   NEW FOR 2009 †

World Time 0 1 2 3 4 5 6 7 8 9 10 11 12 13 14 15 16 17 18 19 20 21 22 23 24

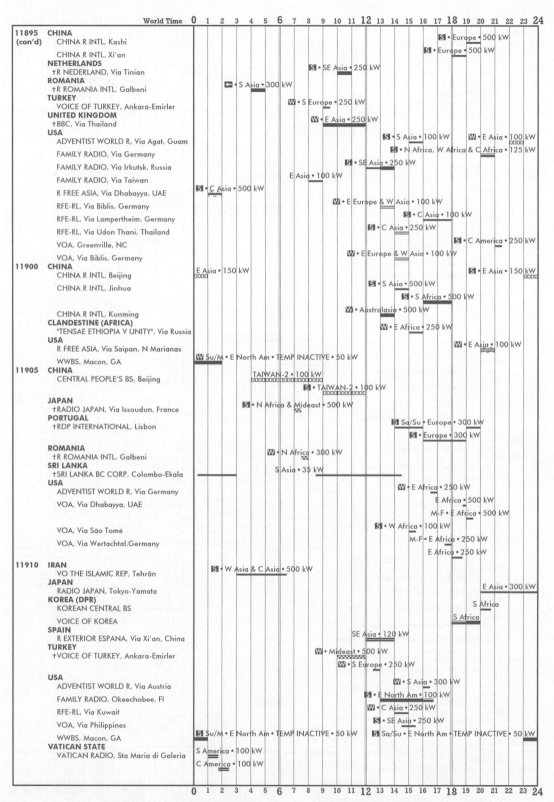

Frequency	Country / Station	Schedule
11895 (con'd)	**CHINA**	
	CHINA R INTL, Kashi	S • Europe • 500 kW
	CHINA R INTL, Xi'an	S • Europe • 500 kW
	NETHERLANDS	
	†R NEDERLAND, Via Tinian	S • SE Asia • 250 kW
	ROMANIA	
	†R ROMANIA INTL, Galbeni	← • S Asia • 300 kW
	TURKEY	
	VOICE OF TURKEY, Ankara-Emirler	W • S Europe • 250 kW
	UNITED KINGDOM	
	†BBC, Via Thailand	W • E Asia • 250 kW
	USA	
	ADVENTIST WORLD R, Via Agat, Guam	S • S Asia • 100 kW; W • E Asia • 100 kW
	FAMILY RADIO, Via Germany	S • N Africa, W Africa & C Africa • 125 kW
	FAMILY RADIO, Via Irkutsk, Russia	S • SE Asia • 250 kW
	FAMILY RADIO, Via Taiwan	E Asia • 100 kW
	R FREE ASIA, Via Dhabayya, UAE	S • C Asia • 500 kW
	RFE-RL, Via Biblis, Germany	W • E Europe & W Asia • 100 kW
	RFE-RL, Via Lampertheim, Germany	S • C Asia • 100 kW
	RFE-RL, Via Udon Thani, Thailand	S • C Asia • 250 kW
	VOA, Greenville, NC	S • C America • 250 kW
	VOA, Via Biblis, Germany	W • E Europe & W Asia • 100 kW
11900	**CHINA**	
	CHINA R INTL, Beijing	E Asia • 150 kW; S • E Asia • 150 kW
	CHINA R INTL, Jinhua	S • S Asia • 500 kW; S • S Africa • 500 kW
	CHINA R INTL, Kunming	W • Australasia • 500 kW
	CLANDESTINE (AFRICA)	
	"TENSAE ETHIOPIA V UNITY", Via Russia	W • E Africa • 250 kW
	USA	
	R FREE ASIA, Via Saipan, N Marianas	W • E Asia • 100 kW
	WWBS, Macon, GA	W Su/M • E North Am • TEMP INACTIVE • 50 kW
11905	**CHINA**	
	CENTRAL PEOPLE'S BS, Beijing	TAIWAN-2 • 100 kW; S • TAIWAN-2 • 100 kW
	JAPAN	
	†RADIO JAPAN, Via Issoudun, France	S • N Africa & Mideast • 500 kW
	PORTUGAL	
	†RDP INTERNATIONAL, Lisbon	S Sa/Su • Europe • 300 kW; S • Europe • 300 kW
	ROMANIA	
	†R ROMANIA INTL, Galbeni	W • N Africa • 300 kW
	SRI LANKA	
	†SRI LANKA BC CORP, Colombo-Ekala	S Asia • 35 kW
	USA	
	ADVENTIST WORLD R, Via Germany	W • E Africa • 250 kW
	VOA, Via Dhabayya, UAE	E Africa • 500 kW; M-F • E Africa • 500 kW
	VOA, Via São Tomé	S • W Africa • 100 kW; M-F • E Africa • 250 kW
	VOA, Via Wertachtal,Germany	E Africa • 250 kW
11910	**IRAN**	
	VO THE ISLAMIC REP, Tehrān	S • W Asia & C Asia • 500 kW
	JAPAN	
	RADIO JAPAN, Tokyo-Yamata	E Asia • 300 kW
	KOREA (DPR)	
	KOREAN CENTRAL BS	S Africa
	VOICE OF KOREA	S Africa
	SPAIN	
	R EXTERIOR ESPANA, Via Xi'an, China	SE Asia • 120 kW
	TURKEY	
	†VOICE OF TURKEY, Ankara-Emirler	W • Mideast • 500 kW; W • S Europe • 250 kW
	USA	
	ADVENTIST WORLD R, Via Austria	W • S Asia • 300 kW
	FAMILY RADIO, Okeechobee, Fl	S • E North Am • 100 kW
	RFE-RL, Via Kuwait	W • C Asia • 250 kW
	VOA, Via Philippines	S • SE Asia • 250 kW
	WWBS, Macon, GA	S Su/M • E North Am • TEMP INACTIVE • 50 kW; S Sa/Su • E North Am • TEMP INACTIVE • 50 kW
	VATICAN STATE	
	VATICAN RADIO, Sta Maria di Galeria	S America • 100 kW; C America • 100 kW

0 1 2 3 4 5 6 7 8 9 10 11 12 13 14 15 16 17 18 19 20 21 22 23 24

ENGLISH ARABIC CHINESE FRENCH GERMAN RUSSIAN SPANISH OTHER

kHz	Country / Station	Schedule (World Time 0–24)
11915	**BRAZIL**	
	RADIO GAUCHA, Porto Alegre	DS • 7.5 kW • ➡
		Irr • DS • 7.5 kW • ➡
	CHINA	
	CENTRAL PEOPLE'S BS, Xi'an	DS-2 • 100 kW
		Th-Tu • DS-2 • 100 kW
		S • DS-2 • 100 kW
	CHINA (TAIWAN)	
	†R TAIWAN INTL, Tainan	SE Asia • 250 kW
	GERMANY	
	DEUTSCHE WELLE, Via Kigali, Rwanda	S • C Asia • 250 kW
	DEUTSCHE WELLE, Via Sri Lanka	S • E Europe, W Asia & C Asia • 250 kW
	DEUTSCHE WELLE, Via Woofferton, UK	S • E Europe • 300 kW
	POLAND	
	POLISH RADIO, Via W'tachtal, Germany	S • W Europe • 100 kW
	RUSSIA	
	TATARSTAN WAVE, Samara	W • E Europe • TATAR, RUSSIAN • 250 kW
	SAUDI ARABIA	
	BS OF THE KINGDOM, Riyadh	N Africa • DS-HOLY KORAN • 500 kW
	SWEDEN	
	†IBRA RADIO, Via Jülich, Germany	S • C Africa & E Africa • 100 kW • ALT. FREQ. TO 11985 kHz
	UNITED KINGDOM	
	†BBC, Via A'Seela, Oman	W • S Asia • 250 kW
	†BBC, Via Singapore	W • S Asia • 250 kW
	BBC, Via Thailand	S • C Asia • 250 kW
	USA	
	ADVENTIST WORLD R, Via South Africa	W • E Africa • 250 kW
	VOA, Via São Tomé	W • C Africa & E Africa • 100 kW
11920	**CHINA**	
	CHINA R INTL, Via Cerrik, Albania	W Africa • 150 kW
	ECUADOR	
	†HCJB GLOBAL VOICE, Quito	S America • 100 kW
	NETHERLANDS	
	†R NEDERLAND, Via Singapore	S • SE Asia • 250 kW
	ROMANIA	
	†R ROMANIA INTL, Galbeni	S • S Europe • 300 kW
	SPAIN	
	†R EXTERIOR ESPANA, Noblejas	S Sa/Su • W Europe • 250 kW
	UNITED KINGDOM	
	BBC, Via Singapore	SE Asia • 250 kW
	†BBC, Via Thailand	S • SE Asia • 250 kW
		S • S Asia • 250 kW
	USA	
	WWRB, Manchester, Tennessee	⬅ • E North Am & Europe • 100 kW
11925	**BRAZIL**	
	RADIO BANDEIRANTES, São Paulo	DS • 10 kW
	CHINA	
	CENTRAL PEOPLE'S BS, Lingshi	W • DS-1 • 100 kW
		DS-1 • 100 kW
	GERMANY	
	DEUTSCHE WELLE, Via Kigali, Rwanda	W • N Africa & Mideast • 250 kW
	IRAN	
	VO THE ISLAMIC REP, Sirjan	W • Mideast • 500 kW
	VO THE ISLAMIC REP, Tehrān	S • C Asia • 500 kW
	PHILIPPINES	
	FEBC RADIO INTL, Bocaue	Sa/Su • SE Asia • 100 kW • ALT. FREQ. TO 12075 kHz
		Su-W • SE Asia • 100 kW
		SE Asia • 100 kW
	ROMANIA	
	†RADIO ROMANIA, Bucharest	S Su • N Africa • 300 kW
	RUSSIA	
	TATARSTAN WAVE, Samara	S • Europe • TATAR, RUSSIAN • 100 kW
	TURKEY	
	†VOICE OF TURKEY, Ankara-Emirler	W • W Asia • 500 kW
		S • W Europe • 500 kW
	UNITED KINGDOM	
	BBC, Via Zyyi, Cyprus	W • E Africa & Mideast • 250 kW
	USA	
	†RFE-RL	W • E Europe • 250 kW
	VOA, Greenville, NC	S M-F • C America • 250 kW
	†VOA	S • Mideast & W Asia • 250 kW
	VOA, Via Philippines	E Asia • 250 kW
		S • E Asia • 500 kW
	VOA, Via São Tomé	S Sa • C Africa & E Africa • 100 kW
11930	**BELARUS**	
	BELARUSIAN R, Minsk	S • E Europe & W Asia • DS-1 • 100 kW
	CHINA	
	CHINA R INTL, Via Sackville, Canada	S • W North Am • 250 kW
	USA	
	ADVENTIST WORLD R, Via Agat, Guam	S • SE Asia • 100 kW
(con'd)	RADIO MARTI, Greenville, NC	W • C America • 250 kW

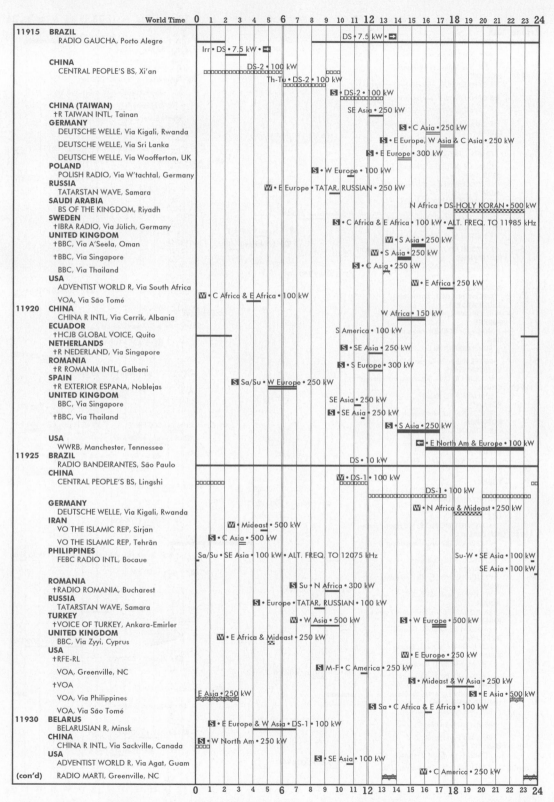

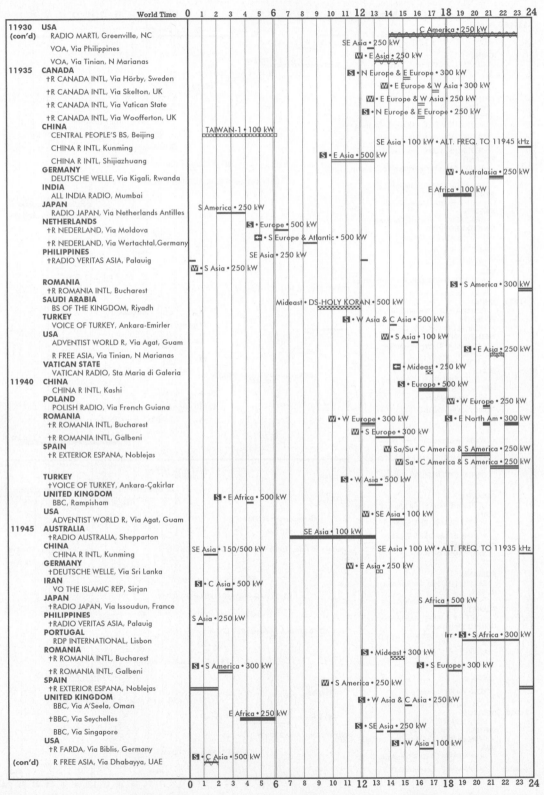

World Time 0 1 2 3 4 5 6 7 8 9 10 11 12 13 14 15 16 17 18 19 20 21 22 23 24

kHz	Country / Station	Schedule
11930 (con'd)	**USA**	
	RADIO MARTI, Greenville, NC	C America • 250 kW
	VOA, Via Philippines	SE Asia • 250 kW
	VOA, Via Tinian, N Marianas	W • E Asia • 250 kW
11935	**CANADA**	
	†R CANADA INTL, Via Hörby, Sweden	S • N Europe & E Europe • 300 kW
	†R CANADA INTL, Via Skelton, UK	W • E Europe & W Asia • 300 kW
	†R CANADA INTL, Via Vatican State	W • E Europe & W Asia • 250 kW
	†R CANADA INTL, Via Woofferton, UK	S • N Europe & E Europe • 250 kW
	CHINA	
	CENTRAL PEOPLE'S BS, Beijing	TAIWAN-1 • 100 kW
	CHINA R INTL, Kunming	SE Asia • 100 kW • ALT. FREQ. TO 11945 kHz
	CHINA R INTL, Shijiazhuang	S • E Asia • 500 kW
	GERMANY	
	DEUTSCHE WELLE, Via Kigali, Rwanda	W • Australasia • 250 kW
	INDIA	
	ALL INDIA RADIO, Mumbai	E Africa • 100 kW
	JAPAN	
	RADIO JAPAN, Via Netherlands Antilles	S America • 250 kW
	NETHERLANDS	
	†R NEDERLAND, Via Moldova	S • Europe • 500 kW
	†R NEDERLAND, Via Wertachtal, Germany	← • S Europe & Atlantic • 500 kW
	PHILIPPINES	
	†RADIO VERITAS ASIA, Palauig	SE Asia • 250 kW
		W • S Asia • 250 kW
	ROMANIA	
	†R ROMANIA INTL, Bucharest	S • S America • 300 kW
	SAUDI ARABIA	
	BS OF THE KINGDOM, Riyadh	Mideast • DS-HOLY KORAN • 500 kW
	TURKEY	
	VOICE OF TURKEY, Ankara-Emirler	S • W Asia & C Asia • 500 kW
	USA	
	ADVENTIST WORLD R, Via Agat, Guam	W • S Asia • 100 kW
	R FREE ASIA, Via Tinian, N Marianas	S • E Asia • 250 kW
	VATICAN STATE	
	VATICAN RADIO, Sta Maria di Galeria	← • Mideast • 250 kW
11940	**CHINA**	
	CHINA R INTL, Kashi	S • Europe • 500 kW
	POLAND	
	POLISH RADIO, Via French Guiana	W • W Europe • 250 kW
	ROMANIA	
	†R ROMANIA INTL, Bucharest	W • W Europe • 300 kW
		S • E North Am • 300 kW
	†R ROMANIA INTL, Galbeni	W • S Europe • 300 kW
	SPAIN	
	†R EXTERIOR ESPANA, Noblejas	W Sa/Su • C America & S America • 250 kW
		W Sa • C America & S America • 250 kW
	TURKEY	
	†VOICE OF TURKEY, Ankara-Çakirlar	S • W Asia • 500 kW
	UNITED KINGDOM	
	BBC, Rampisham	S • E Africa • 500 kW
	USA	
	ADVENTIST WORLD R, Via Agat, Guam	W • SE Asia • 100 kW
11945	**AUSTRALIA**	
	†RADIO AUSTRALIA, Shepparton	SE Asia • 100 kW
	CHINA	
	CHINA R INTL, Kunming	SE Asia • 150/500 kW
		SE Asia • 100 kW • ALT. FREQ. TO 11935 kHz
	GERMANY	
	†DEUTSCHE WELLE, Via Sri Lanka	W • E Asia • 250 kW
	IRAN	
	VO THE ISLAMIC REP, Sirjan	S • C Asia • 500 kW
	JAPAN	
	†RADIO JAPAN, Via Issoudun, France	S Africa • 500 kW
	PHILIPPINES	
	†RADIO VERITAS ASIA, Palauig	S Asia • 250 kW
	PORTUGAL	
	RDP INTERNATIONAL, Lisbon	Irr • S • S Africa • 300 kW
	ROMANIA	
	†R ROMANIA INTL, Bucharest	S • Mideast • 300 kW
	†R ROMANIA INTL, Galbeni	S • S America • 300 kW
		S • S Europe • 300 kW
	SPAIN	
	†R EXTERIOR ESPANA, Noblejas	W • S America • 250 kW
	UNITED KINGDOM	
	BBC, Via A'Seela, Oman	S • W Asia & C Asia • 250 kW
	†BBC, Via Seychelles	E Africa • 250 kW
	BBC, Via Singapore	S • SE Asia • 250 kW
	USA	
	†R FARDA, Via Biblis, Germany	S • W Asia • 100 kW
(con'd)	R FREE ASIA, Via Dhabayya, UAE	S • C Asia • 500 kW

0 1 2 3 4 5 6 7 8 9 10 11 12 13 14 15 16 17 18 19 20 21 22 23 24

ENGLISH ARABIC CHINESE FRENCH GERMAN RUSSIAN SPANISH OTHER

World Time 0 1 2 3 4 5 6 7 8 9 10 11 12 13 14 15 16 17 18 19 20 21 22 23 24

kHz	Country / Station	Schedule
11945 (con'd)	**USA** R FREE ASIA, Via Tinian, N Marianas	W • E Asia • 250 kW
11950	**CHINA** XIZANG PBS, Lhasa	DS • 100 kW; W-M • DS • 100 kW
	ROMANIA †R ROMANIA INTL, Bucharest	S • W Europe • 300 kW
	USA R FREE ASIA, Via Tinian, N Marianas	W • E Asia • 250 kW
11955	**AUSTRALIA** CVC, Darwin	S • SE Asia • 250 kW
	CHINA CHINA R INTL, Kunming	SE Asia • 500 kW
	IRAN †VO THE ISLAMIC REP, Sirjan	S • S Asia • 500 kW
	POLAND †POLISH RADIO, Via W'tachtal, Germany	S • E Europe • 100 kW
	TURKEY †VOICE OF TURKEY, Ankara-Çakirlar	⬅ • Mideast • 250 kW
	UNITED KINGDOM †BBC, Via A'Seela, Oman	S • S Asia • 250 kW
	BBC, Via Singapore	W • S Asia • 100 kW
	†BBC, Via Thailand	S • S Asia • 250 kW; S Asia • 250 kW; SE Asia • 250 kW
	USA ADVENTIST WORLD R, Via Austria	S • N Africa • 300 kW; S • W Africa & C Africa • 300 kW; S • W Africa • 300 kW
	ADVENTIST WORLD R, Via Germany	W • N Africa • 100 kW
	†TRANS WORLD R, Via Samara, Russia	S • W Asia & S Asia • 250 kW
11960	**CHINA** CENTRAL PEOPLE'S BS, Beijing	DS-1 • 100 kW; W-M • DS-1 • 100 kW
	CHINA R INTL, Xi'an	S • E Europe • 150 kW
	ECUADOR †HCJB GLOBAL VOICE, Quito	C America & W North Am • 100 kW
	JORDAN RADIO JORDAN, Qasr el Kharana	⬅ • E Europe • 500 kW
	MALI RTV DU MALI, Bamako	FRENCH, ETC • DS-TEMP INACTIVE • 100 kW
	PORTUGAL †RDP INTERNATIONAL, Lisbon	Irr • W M-F • W Africa & S America • 100 kW; Irr • W • W Africa & S America • 100 kW
	ROMANIA †R ROMANIA INTL, Bucharest	W • S America • 300 kW
	†R ROMANIA INTL, Galbeni	S • E North Am • 300 kW
	USA ADVENTIST WORLD R, Via Agat, Guam	W • E Asia • 100 kW
11965	**CHINA** CHINA R INTL, Kashi	S • Europe • 500 kW
	GERMANY DEUTSCHE WELLE, Via Kigali, Rwanda	S • W Africa & C Africa • 250 kW
	ROMANIA †R ROMANIA INTL, Galbeni	S • S Europe • 300 kW; S • S America • 300 kW
	UNITED KINGDOM BBC, Via Zyyi, Cyprus	S • W Asia & S Asia • 300 kW
	USA ADVENTIST WORLD R, Via Agat, Guam	W • SE Asia • 100 kW
	R FREE ASIA, Via Tinian, N Marianas	W • SE Asia • 250 kW
	VOA, Via Philippines	S • E Asia • 250 kW; W • SE Asia • 250 kW
	VOA, Via São Tomé	W Sa • C Africa & E Africa • 100 kW
	VOA, Via Udon Thani, Thailand	W • E Asia • 500 kW; E Asia • 500 kW
11970	**CHILE** CVC-LA VOZ, Santiago	W • C America & W North Am • 100 kW
	CHINA CHINA R INTL, Via Sackville, Canada	W • W North Am • 250 kW
	IRAN †VO THE ISLAMIC REP, Sirjan	S • E Asia • 500 kW
	JAPAN RADIO JAPAN, Tokyo-Yamata	S • N Europe • 300 kW
	†RADIO JAPAN, Via Issoudun, France	S • S Africa • 500 kW; S • W Africa • 500 kW
(con'd)	**NETHERLANDS** R NEDERLAND, Via Neth Antilles	S • E North Am • 250 kW

World Time 0 1 2 3 4 5 6 7 8 9 10 11 12 13 14 15 16 17 18 19 20 21 22 23 24

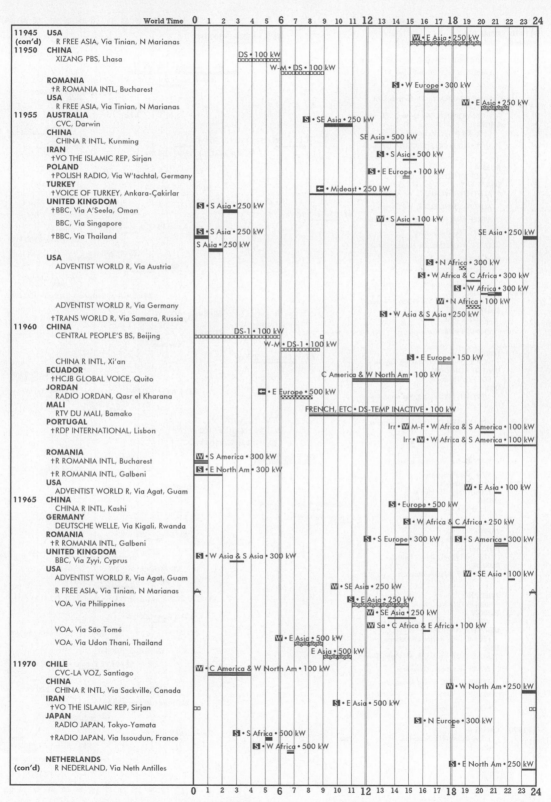

SEASONAL S OR W 1-HR TIMESHIFT MIDYEAR ⬅ OR ➡ JAMMING / OR /\ EARLIEST HEARD ◁ LATEST HEARD ▷ NEW FOR 2009 †

World Time 0 1 2 3 4 5 6 7 8 9 10 11 12 13 14 15 16 17 18 19 20 21 22 23 24

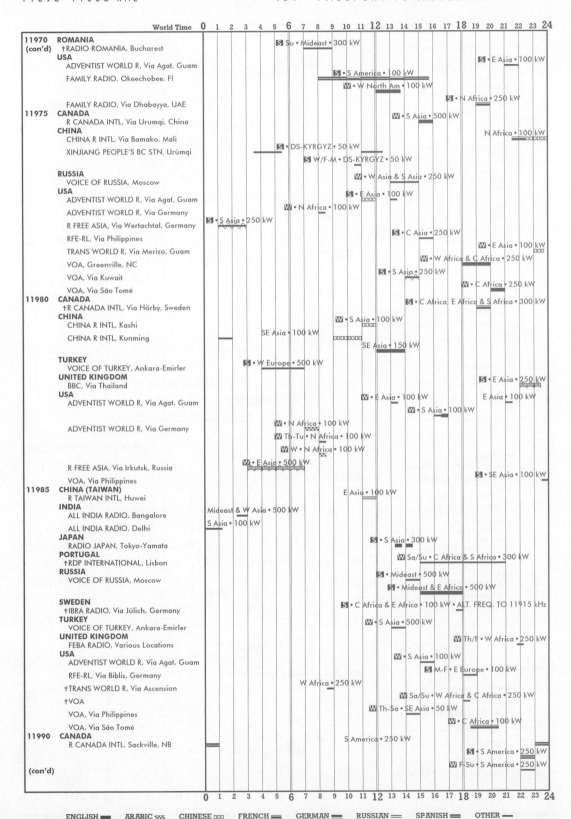

kHz	Country / Station	Schedule
11970 (con'd)	**ROMANIA**	
	†RADIO ROMANIA, Bucharest	S Su • Mideast • 300 kW
	USA	
	ADVENTIST WORLD R, Via Agat, Guam	S • E Asia • 100 kW
	FAMILY RADIO, Okeechobee, Fl	S • S America • 100 kW
		W • W North Am • 100 kW
	FAMILY RADIO, Via Dhabayya, UAE	S • N Africa • 250 kW
11975	**CANADA**	
	R CANADA INTL, Via Urumqi, China	W • S Asia • 500 kW
	CHINA	
	CHINA R INTL, Via Bamako, Mali	N Africa • 100 kW
	XINJIANG PEOPLE'S BC STN, Urümqi	S • DS-KYRGYZ • 50 kW
		S W/F-M • DS-KYRGYZ • 50 kW
	RUSSIA	
	VOICE OF RUSSIA, Moscow	W • W Asia & S Asia • 250 kW
	USA	
	ADVENTIST WORLD R, Via Agat, Guam	S • E Asia • 100 kW
	ADVENTIST WORLD R, Via Germany	W • N Africa • 100 kW
	R FREE ASIA, Via Wertachtal, Germany	S • S Asia • 250 kW
	RFE-RL, Via Philippines	S • C Asia • 250 kW
	TRANS WORLD R, Via Merizo, Guam	W • E Asia • 100 kW
	VOA, Greenville, NC	W • W Africa & C Africa • 250 kW
	VOA, Via Kuwait	S • S Asia • 250 kW
	VOA, Via São Tomé	W • C Africa • 250 kW
11980	**CANADA**	
	†R CANADA INTL, Via Hörby, Sweden	S • C Africa, E Africa & S Africa • 300 kW
	CHINA	
	CHINA R INTL, Kashi	W • S Asia • 100 kW
	CHINA R INTL, Kunming	SE Asia • 100 kW
		SE Asia • 150 kW
	TURKEY	
	VOICE OF TURKEY, Ankara-Emirler	S • W Europe • 500 kW
	UNITED KINGDOM	
	BBC, Via Thailand	S • E Asia • 250 kW
	USA	
	ADVENTIST WORLD R, Via Agat, Guam	W • E Asia • 100 kW
		E Asia • 100 kW
		W • S Asia • 100 kW
	ADVENTIST WORLD R, Via Germany	W • N Africa • 100 kW
		W Th-Tu • N Africa • 100 kW
		W W • N Africa • 100 kW
	R FREE ASIA, Via Irkutsk, Russia	W • E Asia • 500 kW
	VOA, Via Philippines	S • SE Asia • 100 kW
11985	**CHINA (TAIWAN)**	
	R TAIWAN INTL, Huwei	E Asia • 100 kW
	INDIA	
	ALL INDIA RADIO, Bangalore	Mideast & W Asia • 500 kW
	ALL INDIA RADIO, Delhi	S Asia • 100 kW
	JAPAN	
	RADIO JAPAN, Tokyo-Yamata	S • S Asia • 300 kW
	PORTUGAL	
	†RDP INTERNATIONAL, Lisbon	W Sa/Su • C Africa & S Africa • 300 kW
	RUSSIA	
	VOICE OF RUSSIA, Moscow	S • Mideast • 500 kW
		S • Mideast & E Africa • 500 kW
	SWEDEN	
	†IBRA RADIO, Via Jülich, Germany	S • C Africa & E Africa • 100 kW • ALT. FREQ. TO 11915 kHz
	TURKEY	
	VOICE OF TURKEY, Ankara-Emirler	W • S Asia • 500 kW
	UNITED KINGDOM	
	FEBA RADIO, Various Locations	W Th/F • W Africa • 250 kW
	USA	
	ADVENTIST WORLD R, Via Agat, Guam	W • S Asia • 100 kW
	RFE-RL, Via Biblis, Germany	S M-F • E Europe • 100 kW
	†TRANS WORLD R, Via Ascension	W Africa • 250 kW
	†VOA	W Sa/Su • W Africa & C Africa • 250 kW
	VOA, Via Philippines	W Th-Sa • SE Asia • 50 kW
	VOA, Via São Tomé	W • C Africa • 100 kW
11990	**CANADA**	
	R CANADA INTL, Sackville, NB	S America • 250 kW
		S • S America • 250 kW
		W F-Su • S America • 250 kW
(con'd)		

ENGLISH ▬ ARABIC ▭ CHINESE ▫▫▫ FRENCH ═ GERMAN ═ RUSSIAN ═ SPANISH ═ OTHER —

World Time 0 1 2 3 4 5 6 7 8 9 10 11 12 13 14 15 16 17 18 19 20 21 22 23 24

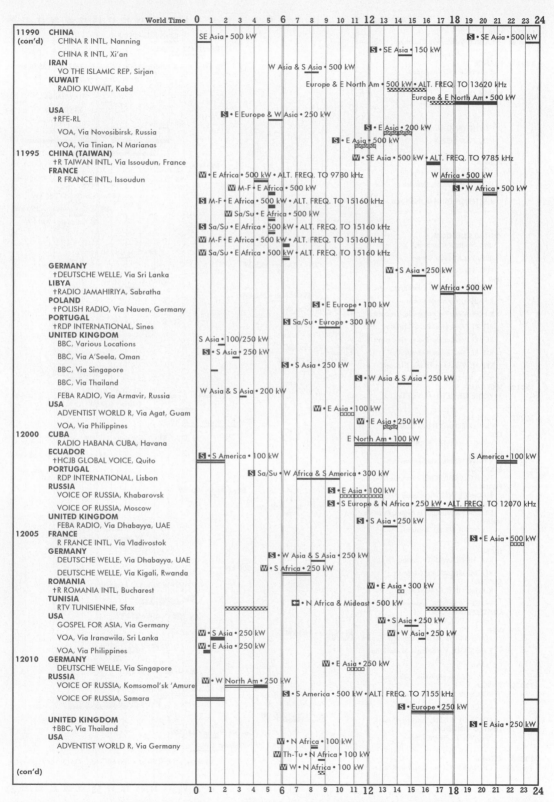

kHz	Country / Station	Schedule notes
11990 (con'd)	CHINA	
	CHINA R INTL, Nanning	SE Asia • 500 kW; S • SE Asia • 500 kW
	CHINA R INTL, Xi'an	S • SE Asia • 150 kW
	IRAN	
	VO THE ISLAMIC REP, Sirjan	W Asia & S Asia • 500 kW
	KUWAIT	
	RADIO KUWAIT, Kabd	Europe & E North Am • 500 kW • ALT. FREQ. TO 13620 kHz
		Europe & E North Am • 500 kW
	USA	
	†RFE-RL	S • E Europe & W Asia • 250 kW
	VOA, Via Novosibirsk, Russia	S • E Asia • 200 kW
	VOA, Via Tinian, N Marianas	S • E Asia • 500 kW
11995	CHINA (TAIWAN)	
	†R TAIWAN INTL, Via Issoudun, France	W • SE Asia • 500 kW • ALT. FREQ. TO 9785 kHz
	FRANCE	
	R FRANCE INTL, Issoudun	W • E Africa • 500 kW • ALT. FREQ. TO 9780 kHz; W Africa • 500 kW
		W M-F • E Africa • 500 kW; S • W Africa • 500 kW
		S M-F • E Africa • 500 kW • ALT. FREQ. TO 15160 kHz
		W Sa/Su • E Africa • 500 kW
		S Sa/Su • E Africa • 500 kW • ALT. FREQ. TO 15160 kHz
		W M-F • E Africa • 500 kW • ALT. FREQ. TO 15160 kHz
		W Sa/Su • E Africa • 500 kW • ALT. FREQ. TO 15160 kHz
	GERMANY	
	†DEUTSCHE WELLE, Via Sri Lanka	W • S Asia • 250 kW
	LIBYA	
	†RADIO JAMAHIRIYA, Sabratha	W Africa • 500 kW
	POLAND	
	†POLISH RADIO, Via Nauen, Germany	S • E Europe • 100 kW
	PORTUGAL	
	†RDP INTERNATIONAL, Sines	S Sa/Su • Europe • 300 kW
	UNITED KINGDOM	
	BBC, Various Locations	S Asia • 100/250 kW
	BBC, Via A'Seela, Oman	S • S Asia • 250 kW
	BBC, Via Singapore	S • S Asia • 250 kW
	BBC, Via Thailand	S • W Asia & S Asia • 250 kW
	FEBA RADIO, Via Armavir, Russia	W Asia & S Asia • 200 kW
	USA	
	ADVENTIST WORLD R, Via Agat, Guam	W • E Asia • 100 kW
	VOA, Via Philippines	W • E Asia • 250 kW
12000	CUBA	
	RADIO HABANA CUBA, Havana	E North Am • 100 kW
	ECUADOR	
	†HCJB GLOBAL VOICE, Quito	S • S America • 100 kW; S America • 100 kW
	PORTUGAL	
	RDP INTERNATIONAL, Lisbon	S Sa/Su • W Africa & S America • 300 kW
	RUSSIA	
	VOICE OF RUSSIA, Khabarovsk	S • E Asia • 100 kW
	VOICE OF RUSSIA, Moscow	S • S Europe & N Africa • 250 kW • ALT. FREQ. TO 12070 kHz
	UNITED KINGDOM	
	FEBA RADIO, Via Dhabayya, UAE	S • S Asia • 250 kW
12005	FRANCE	
	R FRANCE INTL, Via Vladivostok	S • E Asia • 500 kW
	GERMANY	
	DEUTSCHE WELLE, Via Dhabayya, UAE	S • W Asia & S Asia • 250 kW
	DEUTSCHE WELLE, Via Kigali, Rwanda	W • S Africa • 250 kW
	ROMANIA	
	†R ROMANIA INTL, Bucharest	W • E Asia • 300 kW
	TUNISIA	
	RTV TUNISIENNE, Sfax	⇐ • N Africa & Mideast • 500 kW
	USA	
	GOSPEL FOR ASIA, Via Germany	W • S Asia • 250 kW
	VOA, Via Iranawila, Sri Lanka	W • S Asia • 250 kW; W • W Asia • 250 kW
	VOA, Via Philippines	W • E Asia • 250 kW
12010	GERMANY	
	DEUTSCHE WELLE, Via Singapore	W • E Asia • 250 kW
	RUSSIA	
	VOICE OF RUSSIA, Komsomol'sk 'Amure	W • W North Am • 250 kW
	VOICE OF RUSSIA, Samara	S • S America • 500 kW • ALT. FREQ. TO 7155 kHz
		S • Europe • 250 kW
	UNITED KINGDOM	
	†BBC, Via Thailand	S • E Asia • 250 kW
	USA	
	ADVENTIST WORLD R, Via Germany	W • N Africa • 100 kW
		W Th-Tu • N Africa • 100 kW
		W W • N Africa • 100 kW
(con'd)		

0 1 2 3 4 5 6 7 8 9 10 11 12 13 14 15 16 17 18 19 20 21 22 23 24

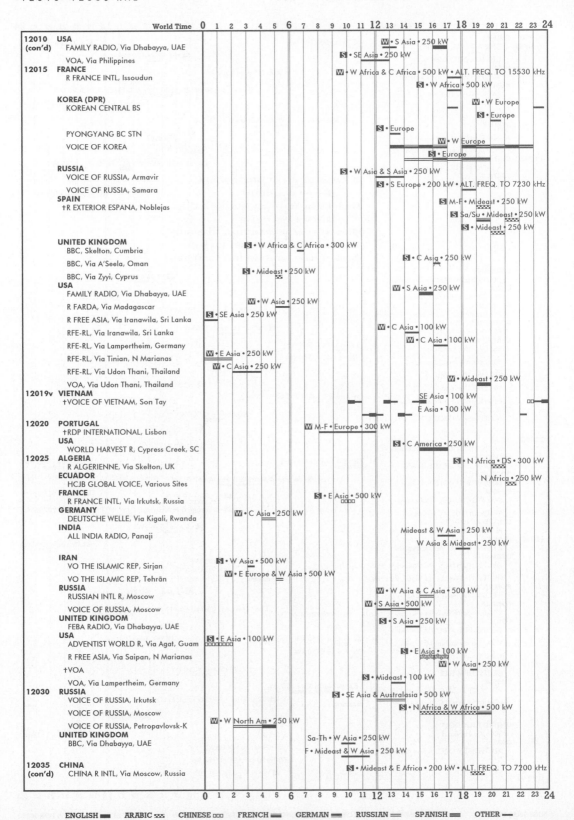

World Time 0 1 2 3 4 5 6 7 8 9 10 11 12 13 14 15 16 17 18 19 20 21 22 23 24

kHz	Country	Station	Schedule
12010 (con'd)	USA	FAMILY RADIO, Via Dhabayya, UAE	W • S Asia • 250 kW
		VOA, Via Philippines	S • SE Asia • 250 kW
12015	FRANCE	R FRANCE INTL, Issoudun	W • W Africa & C Africa • 500 kW • ALT. FREQ. TO 15530 kHz
			S • W Africa • 500 kW
	KOREA (DPR)	KOREAN CENTRAL BS	W • W Europe
			S • Europe
		PYONGYANG BC STN	S • Europe
		VOICE OF KOREA	W • W Europe
			S • Europe
	RUSSIA	VOICE OF RUSSIA, Armavir	S • W Asia & S Asia • 250 kW
		VOICE OF RUSSIA, Samara	S • S Europe • 200 kW • ALT. FREQ. TO 7230 kHz
	SPAIN	†R EXTERIOR ESPANA, Noblejas	S M-F • Mideast • 250 kW
			S Sa/Su • Mideast • 250 kW
			S • Mideast • 250 kW
	UNITED KINGDOM	BBC, Skelton, Cumbria	S • W Africa & C Africa • 300 kW
		BBC, Via A'Seela, Oman	S • C Asia • 250 kW
		BBC, Via Zyyi, Cyprus	S • Mideast • 250 kW
	USA	FAMILY RADIO, Via Dhabayya, UAE	W • S Asia • 250 kW
		R FARDA, Via Madagascar	W • W Asia • 250 kW
		R FREE ASIA, Via Iranawila, Sri Lanka	S • SE Asia • 250 kW
		RFE-RL, Via Iranawila, Sri Lanka	W • C Asia • 100 kW
		RFE-RL, Via Lampertheim, Germany	W • C Asia • 100 kW
		RFE-RL, Via Tinian, N Marianas	W • E Asia • 250 kW
		RFE-RL, Via Udon Thani, Thailand	W • C Asia • 250 kW
		VOA, Via Udon Thani, Thailand	W • Mideast • 250 kW
12019v	VIETNAM	†VOICE OF VIETNAM, Son Tay	SE Asia • 100 kW
			E Asia • 100 kW
12020	PORTUGAL	†RDP INTERNATIONAL, Lisbon	W M-F • Europe • 300 kW
	USA	WORLD HARVEST R, Cypress Creek, SC	S • C America • 250 kW
12025	ALGERIA	R ALGERIENNE, Via Skelton, UK	S • N Africa • DS • 300 kW
	ECUADOR	HCJB GLOBAL VOICE, Various Sites	N Africa • 250 kW
	FRANCE	R FRANCE INTL, Via Irkutsk, Russia	S • E Asia • 500 kW
	GERMANY	DEUTSCHE WELLE, Via Kigali, Rwanda	W • C Asia • 250 kW
	INDIA	ALL INDIA RADIO, Panaji	Mideast & W Asia • 250 kW
			W Asia & Mideast • 250 kW
	IRAN	VO THE ISLAMIC REP, Sirjan	S • W Asia • 500 kW
		VO THE ISLAMIC REP, Tehrān	W • E Europe & W Asia • 500 kW
	RUSSIA	RUSSIAN INTL R, Moscow	W • W Asia & C Asia • 500 kW
		VOICE OF RUSSIA, Moscow	W • S Asia • 500 kW
	UNITED KINGDOM	FEBA RADIO, Via Dhabayya, UAE	S • S Asia • 250 kW
	USA	ADVENTIST WORLD R, Via Agat, Guam	S • E Asia • 100 kW
		R FREE ASIA, Via Saipan, N Marianas	S • E Asia • 100 kW
		†VOA	W • W Asia • 250 kW
		VOA, Via Lampertheim, Germany	S • Mideast • 100 kW
12030	RUSSIA	VOICE OF RUSSIA, Irkutsk	S • SE Asia & Australasia • 500 kW
		VOICE OF RUSSIA, Moscow	S • N Africa & W Africa • 500 kW
		VOICE OF RUSSIA, Petropavlovsk-K	W • W North Am • 250 kW
	UNITED KINGDOM	BBC, Via Dhabayya, UAE	Sa-Th • W Asia • 250 kW
			F • Mideast & W Asia • 250 kW
12035 (con'd)	CHINA	CHINA R INTL, Via Moscow, Russia	S • Mideast & E Africa • 200 kW • ALT. FREQ. TO 7200 kHz

0 1 2 3 4 5 6 7 8 9 10 11 12 13 14 15 16 17 18 19 20 21 22 23 24

ENGLISH — ARABIC — CHINESE — FRENCH — GERMAN — RUSSIAN — SPANISH — OTHER —

World Time 0 1 2 3 4 5 6 7 8 9 10 11 12 13 14 15 16 17 18 19 20 21 22 23 24

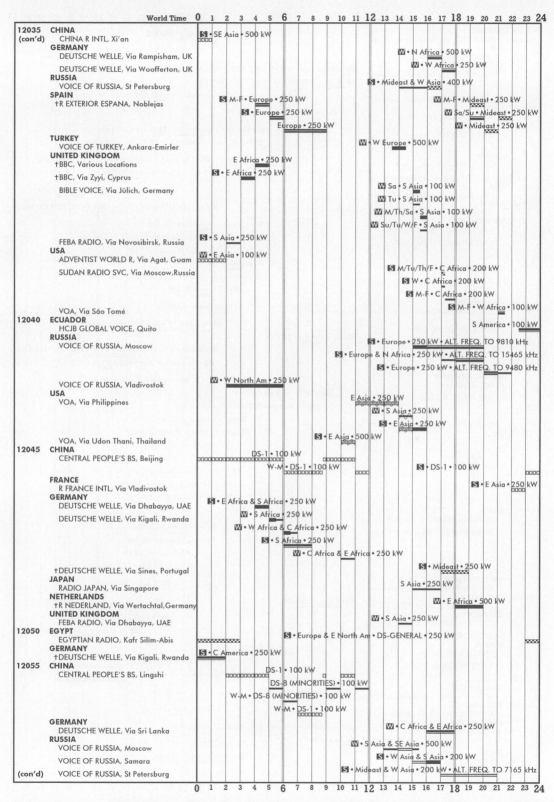

kHz	Country / Station	Schedule
12035 (con'd)	**CHINA**	
	CHINA R INTL, Xi'an	S • SE Asia • 500 kW
	GERMANY	
	DEUTSCHE WELLE, Via Rampisham, UK	W • N Africa • 500 kW
	DEUTSCHE WELLE, Via Woofferton, UK	W • W Africa • 250 kW
	RUSSIA	
	VOICE OF RUSSIA, St Petersburg	S • Mideast & W Asia • 400 kW
	SPAIN	
	†R EXTERIOR ESPANA, Noblejas	S M-F • Europe • 250 kW
		W M-F • Mideast • 250 kW
		S • Europe • 250 kW
		W Sa/Su • Mideast • 250 kW
		Europe • 250 kW
		W • Mideast • 250 kW
	TURKEY	
	VOICE OF TURKEY, Ankara-Emirler	W • W Europe • 500 kW
	UNITED KINGDOM	
	†BBC, Various Locations	E Africa • 250 kW
	†BBC, Via Zyyi, Cyprus	S • E Africa • 250 kW
	BIBLE VOICE, Via Jülich, Germany	W Sa • S Asia • 100 kW
		W Tu • S Asia • 100 kW
		W M/Th/Sa • S Asia • 100 kW
		W Su/Tu/W/F • S Asia • 100 kW
	FEBA RADIO, Via Novosibirsk, Russia	S • S Asia • 250 kW
	USA	
	ADVENTIST WORLD R, Via Agat, Guam	W • E Asia • 100 kW
	SUDAN RADIO SVC, Via Moscow,Russia	S M/Tu/Th/F • C Africa • 200 kW
		S W • C Africa • 200 kW
		S M-F • C Africa • 200 kW
	VOA, Via São Tomé	S M-F • W Africa • 100 kW
12040	**ECUADOR**	
	HCJB GLOBAL VOICE, Quito	S America • 100 kW
	RUSSIA	
	VOICE OF RUSSIA, Moscow	S • Europe • 250 kW • ALT. FREQ. TO 9810 kHz
		S • Europe & N Africa • 250 kW • ALT. FREQ. TO 15465 kHz
		S • Europe • 250 kW • ALT. FREQ. TO 9480 kHz
	VOICE OF RUSSIA, Vladivostok	W • W North Am • 250 kW
	USA	
	VOA, Via Philippines	E Asia • 250 kW
		W • S Asia • 250 kW
		S • E Asia • 250 kW
	VOA, Via Udon Thani, Thailand	S • E Asia • 500 kW
12045	**CHINA**	
	CENTRAL PEOPLE'S BS, Beijing	DS-1 • 100 kW
		W-M • DS-1 • 100 kW
		S • DS-1 • 100 kW
	FRANCE	
	R FRANCE INTL, Via Vladivostok	S • E Asia • 250 kW
	GERMANY	
	DEUTSCHE WELLE, Via Dhabayya, UAE	S • E Africa & S Africa • 250 kW
	DEUTSCHE WELLE, Via Kigali, Rwanda	W • S Africa • 250 kW
		W • W Africa & C Africa • 250 kW
		S • S Africa • 250 kW
		W • C Africa & E Africa • 250 kW
	†DEUTSCHE WELLE, Via Sines, Portugal	S • Mideast • 250 kW
	JAPAN	
	RADIO JAPAN, Via Singapore	S Asia • 250 kW
	NETHERLANDS	
	†R NEDERLAND, Via Wertachtal,Germany	W • E Africa • 500 kW
	UNITED KINGDOM	
	FEBA RADIO, Via Dhabayya, UAE	W • S Asia • 250 kW
12050	**EGYPT**	
	EGYPTIAN RADIO, Kafr Silîm-Abis	S • Europe & E North Am • DS-GENERAL • 250 kW
	GERMANY	
	†DEUTSCHE WELLE, Via Kigali, Rwanda	S • C America • 250 kW
12055	**CHINA**	
	CENTRAL PEOPLE'S BS, Lingshi	DS-1 • 100 kW
		DS-8 (MINORITIES) • 100 kW
		W-M • DS-8 (MINORITIES) • 100 kW
		W-M • DS-1 • 100 kW
	GERMANY	
	DEUTSCHE WELLE, Via Sri Lanka	W • C Africa & E Africa • 250 kW
	RUSSIA	
	VOICE OF RUSSIA, Moscow	W • S Asia & SE Asia • 500 kW
	VOICE OF RUSSIA, Samara	S • W Asia & S Asia • 200 kW
(con'd)	VOICE OF RUSSIA, St Petersburg	S • Mideast & W Asia • 200 kW • ALT. FREQ. TO 7165 kHz

0 1 2 3 4 5 6 7 8 9 10 11 12 13 14 15 16 17 18 19 20 21 22 23 24

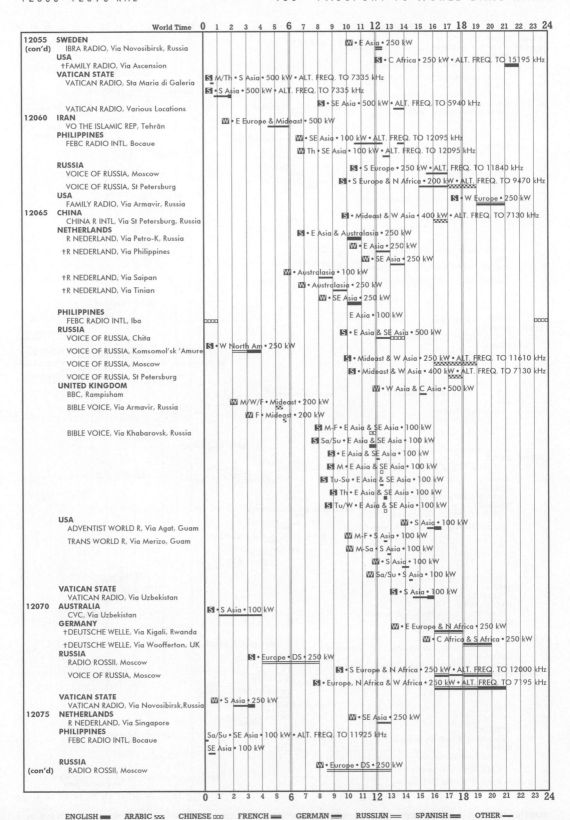

World Time 0 1 2 3 4 5 6 7 8 9 10 11 12 13 14 15 16 17 18 19 20 21 22 23 24

Frequency	Country / Station	Schedule
12055 (con'd)	**SWEDEN** IBRA RADIO, Via Novosibirsk, Russia	W • E Asia • 250 kW
	USA †FAMILY RADIO, Via Ascension	S • C Africa • 250 kW • ALT. FREQ. TO 15195 kHz
	VATICAN STATE VATICAN RADIO, Sta Maria di Galeria	S M/Th • S Asia • 500 kW • ALT. FREQ. TO 7335 kHz
		S • S Asia • 500 kW • ALT. FREQ. TO 7335 kHz
	VATICAN RADIO, Various Locations	S • SE Asia • 500 kW • ALT. FREQ. TO 5940 kHz
12060	**IRAN** VO THE ISLAMIC REP, Tehrān	W • E Europe & Mideast • 500 kW
	PHILIPPINES FEBC RADIO INTL, Bocaue	W • SE Asia • 100 kW • ALT. FREQ. TO 12095 kHz
		W Th • SE Asia • 100 kW • ALT. FREQ. TO 12095 kHz
	RUSSIA VOICE OF RUSSIA, Moscow	S • S Europe • 250 kW • ALT. FREQ. TO 11840 kHz
	VOICE OF RUSSIA, St Petersburg	S • S Europe & N Africa • 200 kW • ALT. FREQ. TO 9470 kHz
	USA FAMILY RADIO, Via Armavir, Russia	S • W Europe • 250 kW
12065	**CHINA** CHINA R INTL, Via St Petersburg, Russia	S • Mideast & W Asia • 400 kW • ALT. FREQ. TO 7130 kHz
	NETHERLANDS R NEDERLAND, Via Petro-K, Russia	S • E Asia & Australasia • 250 kW
	†R NEDERLAND, Via Philippines	W • E Asia • 250 kW
		W • SE Asia • 250 kW
	†R NEDERLAND, Via Saipan	W • Australasia • 100 kW
	†R NEDERLAND, Via Tinian	W • Australasia • 250 kW
		W • SE Asia • 250 kW
	PHILIPPINES FEBC RADIO INTL, Iba	E Asia • 100 kW
	RUSSIA VOICE OF RUSSIA, Chita	S • E Asia & SE Asia • 500 kW
	VOICE OF RUSSIA, Komsomol'sk 'Amure	S • W North Am • 250 kW
	VOICE OF RUSSIA, Moscow	S • Mideast & W Asia • 250 kW • ALT. FREQ. TO 11610 kHz
	VOICE OF RUSSIA, St Petersburg	S • Mideast & W Asia • 400 kW • ALT. FREQ. TO 7130 kHz
	UNITED KINGDOM BBC, Rampisham	W • W Asia & C Asia • 500 kW
	BIBLE VOICE, Via Armavir, Russia	W M/W/F • Mideast • 200 kW
		W F • Mideast • 200 kW
	BIBLE VOICE, Via Khabarovsk, Russia	S M-F • E Asia & SE Asia • 100 kW
		S Sa/Su • E Asia & SE Asia • 100 kW
		S • E Asia & SE Asia • 100 kW
		S M • E Asia & SE Asia • 100 kW
		S Tu-Su • E Asia & SE Asia • 100 kW
		S Th • E Asia & SE Asia • 100 kW
		S Tu/W • E Asia & SE Asia • 100 kW
	USA ADVENTIST WORLD R, Via Agat, Guam	W • S Asia • 100 kW
	TRANS WORLD R, Via Merizo, Guam	W M-F • S Asia • 100 kW
		W M-Sa • S Asia • 100 kW
		W • S Asia • 100 kW
		W Sa/Su • S Asia • 100 kW
	VATICAN STATE VATICAN RADIO, Via Uzbekistan	S • S Asia • 100 kW
12070	**AUSTRALIA** CVC, Via Uzbekistan	S • S Asia • 100 kW
	GERMANY †DEUTSCHE WELLE, Via Kigali, Rwanda	W • E Europe & N Africa • 250 kW
	†DEUTSCHE WELLE, Via Woofferton, UK	W • C Africa & S Africa • 250 kW
	RUSSIA RADIO ROSSII, Moscow	S • Europe • DS • 250 kW
	VOICE OF RUSSIA, Moscow	S • S Europe & N Africa • 250 kW • ALT. FREQ. TO 12000 kHz
		S • Europe, N Africa & W Africa • 250 kW • ALT. FREQ. TO 7195 kHz
	VATICAN STATE VATICAN RADIO, Via Novosibirsk, Russia	W • S Asia • 250 kW
12075	**NETHERLANDS** R NEDERLAND, Via Singapore	W • SE Asia • 250 kW
	PHILIPPINES FEBC RADIO INTL, Bocaue	Sa/Su • SE Asia • 100 kW • ALT. FREQ. TO 11925 kHz
		SE Asia • 100 kW
(con'd)	**RUSSIA** RADIO ROSSII, Moscow	W • Europe • DS • 250 kW

0 1 2 3 4 5 6 7 8 9 10 11 12 13 14 15 16 17 18 19 20 21 22 23 24

ENGLISH ARABIC CHINESE FRENCH GERMAN RUSSIAN SPANISH OTHER

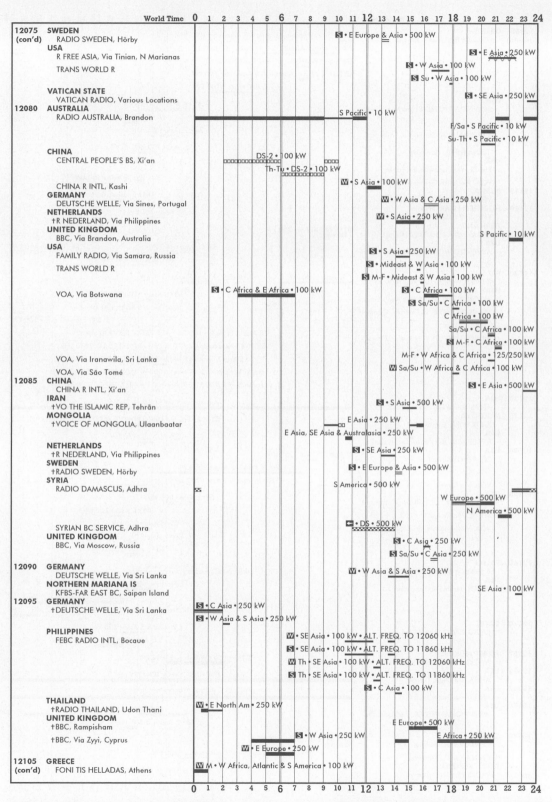

World Time 0 1 2 3 4 5 6 7 8 9 10 11 12 13 14 15 16 17 18 19 20 21 22 23 24

kHz	Country	Station	Schedule
12075 (con'd)	SWEDEN	RADIO SWEDEN, Hörby	S • E Europe & Asia • 500 kW
	USA	R FREE ASIA, Via Tinian, N Marianas	S • E Asia • 250 kW
		TRANS WORLD R	S • W Asia • 100 kW
			S Su • W Asia • 100 kW
	VATICAN STATE	VATICAN RADIO, Various Locations	S • SE Asia • 250 kW
12080	AUSTRALIA	RADIO AUSTRALIA, Brandon	S Pacific • 10 kW
			F/Sa • S Pacific • 10 kW
			Su-Th • S Pacific • 10 kW
	CHINA	CENTRAL PEOPLE'S BS, Xi'an	DS-2 • 100 kW
			Th-Tu • DS-2 • 100 kW
		CHINA R INTL, Kashi	W • S Asia • 100 kW
	GERMANY	DEUTSCHE WELLE, Via Sines, Portugal	W • W Asia & C Asia • 250 kW
	NETHERLANDS	†R NEDERLAND, Via Philippines	W • S Asia • 250 kW
	UNITED KINGDOM	BBC, Via Brandon, Australia	S Pacific • 10 kW
	USA	FAMILY RADIO, Via Samara, Russia	S • S Asia • 250 kW
		TRANS WORLD R	S • Mideast & W Asia • 100 kW
			S M-F • Mideast & W Asia • 100 kW
		VOA, Via Botswana	S • C Africa & E Africa • 100 kW
			S • C Africa • 100 kW
			S Sa/Su • C Africa • 100 kW
			C Africa • 100 kW
			Sa/Su • C Africa • 100 kW
			S M-F • C Africa • 100 kW
		VOA, Via Iranawila, Sri Lanka	M-F • W Africa & C Africa • 125/250 kW
		VOA, Via São Tomé	W Sa/Su • W Africa & C Africa • 100 kW
12085	CHINA	CHINA R INTL, Xi'an	S • E Asia • 500 kW
	IRAN	†VO THE ISLAMIC REP, Tehrān	S • S Asia • 500 kW
	MONGOLIA	†VOICE OF MONGOLIA, Ulaanbaatar	E Asia • 250 kW
			E Asia, SE Asia & Australasia • 250 kW
	NETHERLANDS	†R NEDERLAND, Via Philippines	S • SE Asia • 250 kW
	SWEDEN	†RADIO SWEDEN, Hörby	S • E Europe & Asia • 500 kW
	SYRIA	RADIO DAMASCUS, Adhra	S America • 500 kW
			W Europe • 500 kW
			N America • 500 kW
		SYRIAN BC SERVICE, Adhra	← • DS • 500 kW
	UNITED KINGDOM	BBC, Via Moscow, Russia	S • C Asia • 250 kW
			S Sa/Su • C Asia • 250 kW
12090	GERMANY	DEUTSCHE WELLE, Via Sri Lanka	W • W Asia & S Asia • 250 kW
	NORTHERN MARIANA IS	KFBS-FAR EAST BC, Saipan Island	SE Asia • 100 kW
12095	GERMANY	†DEUTSCHE WELLE, Via Sri Lanka	S • C Asia • 250 kW
			S • W Asia & S Asia • 250 kW
	PHILIPPINES	FEBC RADIO INTL, Bocaue	W • SE Asia • 100 kW • ALT. FREQ. TO 12060 kHz
			S • SE Asia • 100 kW • ALT. FREQ. TO 11860 kHz
			W Th • SE Asia • 100 kW • ALT. FREQ. TO 12060 kHz
			S Th • SE Asia • 100 kW • ALT. FREQ. TO 11860 kHz
			S • C Asia • 100 kW
	THAILAND	†RADIO THAILAND, Udon Thani	W • E North Am • 250 kW
	UNITED KINGDOM	†BBC, Rampisham	E Europe • 500 kW
		†BBC, Via Zyyi, Cyprus	S • W Asia • 250 kW
			E Africa • 250 kW
			W • E Europe • 250 kW
12105 (con'd)	GREECE	FONI TIS HELLADAS, Athens	W M • W Africa, Atlantic & S America • 100 kW

0 1 2 3 4 5 6 7 8 9 10 11 12 13 14 15 16 17 18 19 20 21 22 23 24

kHz	Country / Station	World Time 0–24
12105 (con'd)	**GREECE**	
	FONI TIS HELLADAS, Athens	W Tu-Su • W Africa, Atlantic & S America • 100 kW
		W • W Africa, Atlantic & S America • 100 kW
		W M-Sa • W Africa, Atlantic & S America • 100 kW
		W Su • W Africa, Atlantic & S America • 100 kW
		W • W Africa • 100 kW
	USA	
	ADVENTIST WORLD R, Via Agat, Guam	S • E Asia • 100 kW
		W • S Asia • 100 kW
	R FREE ASIA, Via Iranawila, Sri Lanka	W • SE Asia • 250 kW
12110	**CHINA**	
	CHINA R INTL, Kunming	SE Asia • 100 kW
	USA	
	RFE-RL, Via Iranawila, Sri Lanka	C Asia • 250 kW
	VOA, Via Jülich, Germany	W • W Asia • 100 kW
12115	**RUSSIA**	
	VOICE OF RUSSIA, Via Tajikistan	S • S Asia • 100 kW
12120	**NORTHERN MARIANA IS**	
	KFBS-FAR EAST BC, Saipan Island	SE Asia • 100 kW
	THAILAND	
	†RADIO THAILAND, Udon Thani	S • E North Am • 250 kW
	USA	
	ADVENTIST WORLD R, Via Agat, Guam	W • E Asia • 100 kW; S • E Asia • 100 kW
	VOA, Via Tinian, N Marianas	S • SE Asia • 250 kW
12130	**PALAU**	
	†R T8WH-WORLD HARVEST R, Koror	SE Asia • 100 kW; CHINESE, ETC • SE Asia • 100 kW
	USA	
	ADVENTIST WORLD R, Via Agat, Guam	S • S Asia • 100 kW
		E Asia • 100 kW
	†TRANS WORLD R, Via Merizo, Guam	← • F/Sa • E Asia • 100 kW
	WORLD HARVEST R, Naalehu, Hawai'i	E Asia & SE Asia • 100 kW • ALT. FREQ. TO 9930 kHz
		Sa-Th • E Asia & SE Asia • 100 kW • ALT. FREQ. TO 9930 kHz
		F • E Asia & SE Asia • 100 kW • ALT. FREQ. TO 9930 kHz
		Su/M/W • E Asia & SE Asia • 100 kW • ALT. FREQ. TO 9930 kHz
		Tu/Th/Sa • E Asia & SE Asia • 100 kW • ALT. FREQ. TO 9930 kHz
12133.5	**USA**	
	AFRTS, Key West, Florida	Americas • 8 kW • USB
12135	**MOLDOVA**	
	†RADIO PMR, Grigoriopol	S M-F • Europe • 500 kW • ALT. FREQ. TO 7370 kHz
	USA	
	R FREE ASIA, Via Iranawila, Sri Lanka	W • SE Asia • 250 kW
12140	**USA**	
	RFE-RL, Via Kuwait	W Asia & S Asia • 250 kW
		W • W Asia & S Asia • 250 kW
		S • W Asia & S Asia • 250 kW
	VOA, Via Kuwait	
12150	**USA**	
	FAMILY RADIO, Via Almaty, Kazakstan	W • E Asia • 500 kW
	RFE-RL, Via Kuwait	S • C Asia • 250 kW
	VOA, Via Iranawila, Sri Lanka	W • S Asia • 250 kW
		W • E Asia & SE Asia • 250 kW
		S • S Asia • 250 kW
12160	**PALAU**	
	†R T8WH-WORLD HARVEST R, Koror	CHINESE, ETC • SE Asia • 100 kW
	USA	
	WWCR, Nashville, Tennessee	Irr • E North Am & Europe • 100 kW
		E North Am & Europe • 100 kW
		E North Am & Europe • 100 kW • ALT. FREQ. TO 5070 kHz
12170	**EGYPT**	
	†RADIO CAIRO, Abu Za'bal	W Asia & S Asia • 250 kW
		C Africa & S Africa • 250 kW
12257	**PIRATE (EUROPE)**	
	"WREKIN RADIO INTL", England	← • Irr • Su • W Europe • 0.03 kW
12579	**USA**	
	AFRTS, Via Diego Garcia	S Asia • USB • ALT. FREQ. TO 4319 kHz
13362	**USA**	
	AFRTS, Via Guam	Pacific • USB • ALT. FREQ. TO 5765 kHz
13570	**USA**	
	WINB-WORLD INTL BC, Red Lion, Pa	C America & W North Am • 50 kW
		W • C America & W North Am • 50 kW
13580	**CHINA**	
	CHINA R INTL, Beijing	SE Asia • 500 kW
	CHINA R INTL, Kunming	Australasia • 500 kW
	CZECH REPUBLIC	
(con'd)	†RADIO PRAGUE, Litomyšl	S • W Europe • 100 kW

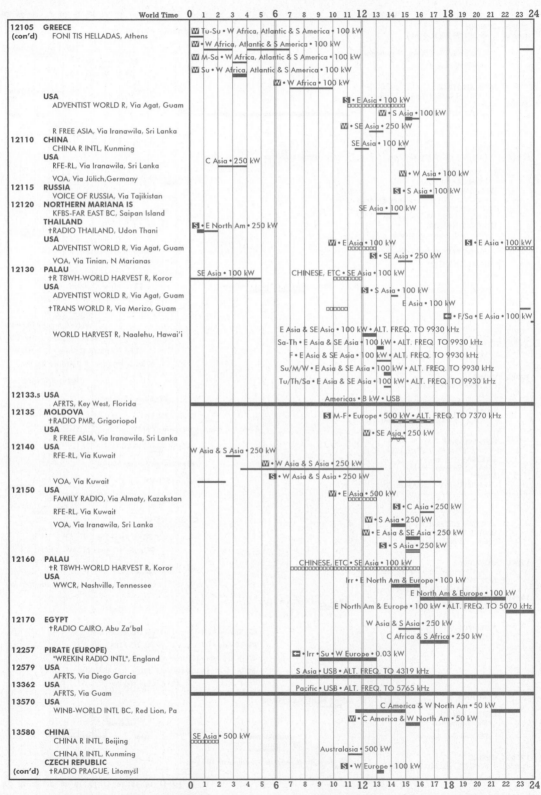

ENGLISH ▬ ARABIC ▭ CHINESE ▢▢▢ FRENCH ═ GERMAN ═ RUSSIAN ═ SPANISH ═ OTHER —

Frequency	Country / Station	Schedule (World Time 0–24)
13580 (con'd)	CZECH REPUBLIC — †RADIO PRAGUE, Litomyšl	S • C Africa & S Africa • 100 kW
		W • N America • 100 kW
		W • W Africa • 100 kW
		S • E Europe & W Asia • 100 kW
		⇐ • W Europe • 100 kW
		S • S Europe & N Africa • 100 kW
	EGYPT — †RADIO CAIRO, Abu Za'bal	S • C Asia • 250 kW
	UNITED KINGDOM — BIBLE VOICE, Via Wertachtal, Germany	S M-F • Mideast • 250 kW
		S M/W-F • Mideast • 250 kW
13590	CHINA — CHINA R INTL, Beijing	SE Asia • 500 kW
	GERMANY — †DEUTSCHE WELLE, Via Sines, Portugal	S • N Africa • 250 kW
	RUSSIA — VOICE OF RUSSIA, Novosibirsk	S • E Asia • 200 kW
		S M-Sa • E Asia • 200 kW
	UNITED KINGDOM — BIBLE VOICE, Via Jülich, Germany	S Su • Mideast • 100 kW
		S • Mideast • 100 kW
		S Th/Sa/Su • Mideast • 100 kW
		S Tu • Mideast • 100 kW
		S Tu/Sa/Su • Mideast • 100 kW
		S Sa/Su • Mideast • 100 kW
		S Su/F • Mideast • 100 kW
		S Tu/Sa • Mideast • 100 kW
		S Sa • Mideast • 100 kW
13600	ALBANIA — †RADIO TIRANA, Shijak	S M-Sa • E North Am • 100 kW
	BULGARIA — †RADIO BULGARIA, Plovdiv	⇐ • S Europe & N Africa • 250 kW
	RADIO BULGARIA, Sofia	⇐ • E Europe • 100 kW
	CHINA — CHINA R INTL, Kashi	S • S Asia • 100 kW
	CHINA R INTL, Kunming	S Asia • 150 kW
	CHINA R INTL, Xi'an	W Asia & C Asia • 500 kW
		S • W Asia & C Asia • 500 kW
	IRAN — †VO THE ISLAMIC REP, Sirjan	W • W Europe & N Africa • 500 kW
	USA — GOSPEL FOR ASIA, Via Germany	W • S Asia • 250 kW
	VOA, Via São Tomé	W • C Africa & S Africa • 100 kW
	VOA, Via Udon Thani, Thailand	S • SE Asia & Australasia • 250 kW
13605	INDIA — ALL INDIA RADIO, Aligarh	E Africa • 250 kW
	ALL INDIA RADIO, Bangalore	E Asia & SE Asia • 500 kW
		W Africa • 500 kW
13610	CHINA — CENTRAL PEOPLE'S BS, Nanning	DS-1 • 100 kW
		W-M • DS-1 • 100 kW
	CHINA R INTL, Kashi	S • S Asia • 100 kW
		Europe • 00 kW
	CHINA R INTL, Xi'an	W • E Asia • 500 kW
	SYRIA — RADIO DAMASCUS, Adhra	S America • 500 kW • ALT. FREQ. TO 9330 kHz
		E Europe & Mideast • 500 kW • ALT. FREQ. TO 9330 kHz
		E Europe • 500 kW • ALT. FREQ. TO 9330 kHz
		Europe • 500 kW • ALT. FREQ. TO 9330 kHz
		Australasia • 500 kW • ALT. FREQ. TO 9330 kHz
	UNITED KINGDOM — BBC, Skelton, Cumbria	S • E Europe & Mideast • 300 kW
		S M-F • E Europe & Mideast • 300 kW
	BBC, Via Zyyi, Cyprus	S • W Asia & S Asia • 300 kW
		S • W Asia • 300 kW
	USA — VOA, Via Tinian, N Marianas	S • E Asia • 250 kW
	WBCQ-"THE PLANET", Monticello, Maine	⇐ • N America • 50 kW • LSB • ALT. FREQ. TO 9330 kHz
(con'd)		⇐ • Tu-Su • N America • 50 kW • LSB • ALT. FREQ. TO 9330 kHz

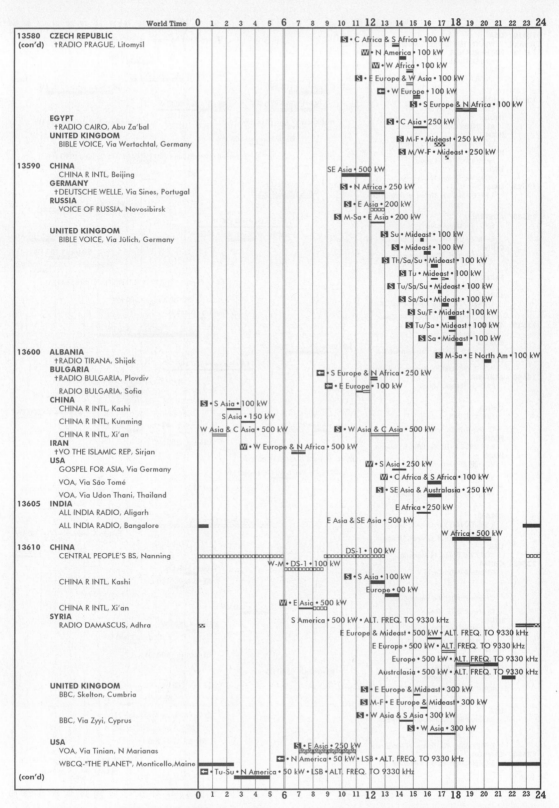

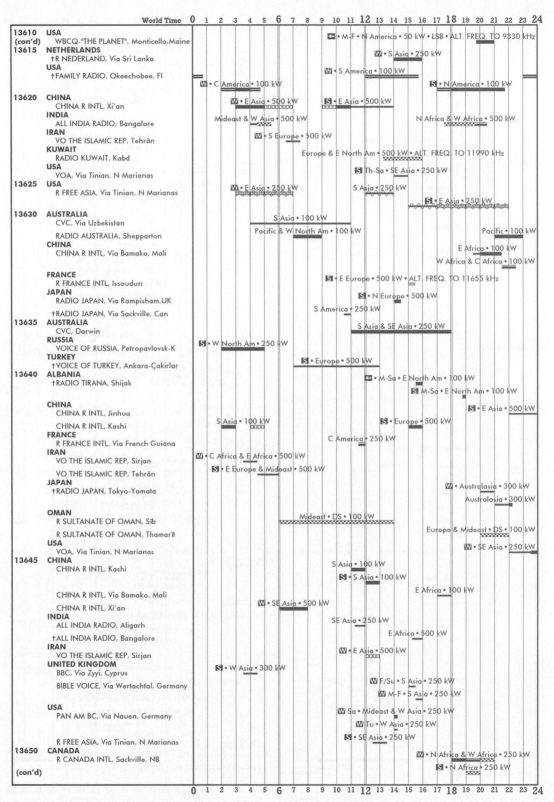

World Time 0 1 2 3 4 5 6 7 8 9 10 11 12 13 14 15 16 17 18 19 20 21 22 23 24

kHz	Country / Station	Schedule
13610 (con'd)	**USA**	
	WBCQ-"THE PLANET", Monticello, Maine	← • M-F • N America • 50 kW • LSB • ALT. FREQ. TO 9330 kHz
13615	**NETHERLANDS**	
	†R NEDERLAND, Via Sri Lanka	W • S Asia • 250 kW
	USA	
	†FAMILY RADIO, Okeechobee, Fl	W • S America • 100 kW
		W • C America • 100 kW; S • N America • 100 kW
13620	**CHINA**	
	CHINA R INTL, Xi'an	W • E Asia • 500 kW; S • E Asia • 500 kW
	INDIA	
	ALL INDIA RADIO, Bangalore	Mideast & W Asia • 500 kW; N Africa & W Africa • 500 kW
	IRAN	
	VO THE ISLAMIC REP, Tehrān	W • S Europe • 500 kW
	KUWAIT	
	RADIO KUWAIT, Kabd	Europe & E North Am • 500 kW • ALT. FREQ. TO 11990 kHz
	USA	
	VOA, Via Tinian, N Marianas	S Th-Sa • SE Asia • 250 kW
13625	**USA**	
	R FREE ASIA, Via Tinian, N Marianas	W • E Asia • 250 kW; S Asia • 250 kW
		S • E Asia • 250 kW
13630	**AUSTRALIA**	
	CVC, Via Uzbekistan	S Asia • 100 kW
	RADIO AUSTRALIA, Shepparton	Pacific & W North Am • 100 kW; Pacific • 100 kW
	CHINA	
	CHINA R INTL, Via Bamako, Mali	E Africa • 100 kW
		W Africa & C Africa • 100 kW
	FRANCE	
	R FRANCE INTL, Issoudun	S • E Europe • 500 kW • ALT. FREQ. TO 11655 kHz
	JAPAN	
	RADIO JAPAN, Via Rampisham, UK	S • N Europe • 500 kW
	†RADIO JAPAN, Via Sackville, Can	S America • 250 kW
13635	**AUSTRALIA**	
	CVC, Darwin	S Asia & SE Asia • 250 kW
	RUSSIA	
	VOICE OF RUSSIA, Petropavlovsk-K	S • W North Am • 250 kW
	TURKEY	
	†VOICE OF TURKEY, Ankara-Çakirlar	S • Europe • 500 kW
13640	**ALBANIA**	
	†RADIO TIRANA, Shijak	← • M-Sa • E North Am • 100 kW
		S M-Sa • E North Am • 100 kW
	CHINA	
	CHINA R INTL, Jinhua	S • E Asia • 500 kW
	CHINA R INTL, Kashi	S Asia • 100 kW; S • Europe • 500 kW
	FRANCE	
	R FRANCE INTL, Via French Guiana	C America • 250 kW
	IRAN	
	VO THE ISLAMIC REP, Sirjan	W • C Africa & E Africa • 500 kW
	VO THE ISLAMIC REP, Tehrān	S • E Europe & Mideast • 500 kW
	JAPAN	
	†RADIO JAPAN, Tokyo-Yamata	W • Australasia • 300 kW
		Australasia • 300 kW
	OMAN	
	R SULTANATE OF OMAN, Sīb	Mideast • DS • 100 kW
	R SULTANATE OF OMAN, Thamarīt	Europe & Mideast • DS • 100 kW
	USA	
	VOA, Via Tinian, N Marianas	W • SE Asia • 250 kW
13645	**CHINA**	
	CHINA R INTL, Kashi	S Asia • 100 kW
		S • S Asia • 100 kW
	CHINA R INTL, Via Bamako, Mali	E Africa • 100 kW
	CHINA R INTL, Xi'an	W • SE Asia • 500 kW
	INDIA	
	ALL INDIA RADIO, Aligarh	SE Asia • 250 kW
	†ALL INDIA RADIO, Bangalore	E Africa • 500 kW
	IRAN	
	VO THE ISLAMIC REP, Sirjan	W • E Asia • 500 kW
	UNITED KINGDOM	
	BBC, Via Zyyi, Cyprus	S • W Asia • 300 kW
	BIBLE VOICE, Via Wertachtal, Germany	W F/Su • S Asia • 250 kW
		W M-F • S Asia • 250 kW
	USA	
	PAN AM BC, Via Nauen, Germany	W Sa • Mideast & W Asia • 250 kW
		W Tu • W Asia • 250 kW
		S • SE Asia • 250 kW
	R FREE ASIA, Via Tinian, N Marianas	
13650	**CANADA**	
	R CANADA INTL, Sackville, NB	W • N Africa & W Africa • 250 kW
(con'd)		S • N Africa • 250 kW

0 1 2 3 4 5 6 7 8 9 10 11 12 13 14 15 16 17 18 19 20 21 22 23 24

ENGLISH ARABIC CHINESE FRENCH GERMAN RUSSIAN SPANISH OTHER

kHz	Country / Station	World Time (0–24)
13650 (con'd)	CANADA	
	†R CANADA INTL, Via Skelton, UK	S • N Africa & W Africa • 300 kW
	CHINA	
	CHINA R INTL, Urümqi	Mideast • 500 kW
	CHINA R INTL, Via Cerrik, Albania	S • W Europe • 150 kW
	CHINA R INTL, Via Havana, Cuba	S America • 250 kW
	GERMANY	
	†DEUTSCHE WELLE, Via Woofferton, UK	S • Mideast • 250 kW
	JAPAN	
	RADIO JAPAN, Tokyo-Yamata	SE Asia • 300 kW
	KOREA (DPR)	
	KOREAN CENTRAL BS	S • SE Asia
	VOICE OF KOREA	SE Asia; S • SE Asia
	RUSSIA	
	VOICE OF RUSSIA, St Petersburg	S • Mideast & W Asia • 400 kW • ALT. FREQ. TO 7130 kHz
	USA	
	VOA, Via Tinian, N Marianas	W • E Asia • 250 kW
	WORLD HARVEST R, Naalehu, Hawai'i	S M-Sa • E Asia • 100 kW; S Su • E Asia • 100 kW; S • E Asia • 100 kW
13655	CHINA	
	CHINA R INTL, Urümqi	S • E Europe • 500 kW
	CHINA R INTL, Xi'an	E Asia • 500 kW; W • E Asia • 500 kW
13660	CHINA	
	CHINA R INTL, Xi'an	S • SE Asia • 500 kW
	JAPAN	
	†RADIO JAPAN, Tokyo-Yamata	W • SE Asia • 300 kW • ALT. FREQ. TO 9695 kHz
	TURKEY	
	†VOICE OF TURKEY, Ankara-Emirler	S • E Europe & W Asia • 500 kW
	UNITED KINGDOM	
	BBC, Rampisham	S • N Africa • 500 kW; S • N Africa & Mideast • 500 kW
	BBC, Via A'Seela, Oman	Mideast • 250 kW; S • Mideast • 250 kW
	BBC, Via Zyyi, Cyprus	W • Mideast • 300 kW; Mideast • 250/300 kW
	USA	
	FAMILY RADIO, Via Germany	W • E Africa • 500 kW
	VOA, Via Udon Thani, Thailand	W Th-Sa • SE Asia • 250 kW
13665	CHINA	
	CHINA R INTL, Via Cerrik, Albania	W • W Europe • 150 kW
	RUSSIA	
	RADIO ROSSII, Moscow	S • Europe • DS • 250 kW
13670	CHINA	
	CHINA R INTL, Via Bamako, Mali	W Africa & C Africa • 100 kW
	†CHINA R INTL, Via Cerrik, Albania	W Africa • 150 kW • ALT. FREQ. TO 13760 kHz
	XINJIANG PEOPLE'S BC STN, Urümqi	S • DS-UIGHUR • 50 kW; DS-UIGHUR • 50 kW; W/F-M • DS-UIGHUR • 50 kW
	USA	
	R FREE ASIA, Via Tinian, N Marianas	S • E Asia • 250 kW; W • E Asia • 250 kW
	VOA, Via Iranawila, Sri Lanka	S M-F • E Africa • 250 kW
	VOA, Via São Tomé	S • E Africa • 100 kW
13675	AUSTRIA	
	†R AUSTRIA INTL, Via Sackville, Canada	W • W North Am • 250 kW
	CANADA	
	†R CANADA INTL, Sackville, NB	S • C America • 250 kW
	CHINA	
	CHINA R INTL, Via Sackville, Canada	W • W North Am • 250 kW
	FRANCE	
	R FRANCE INTL, Issoudun	S • W Africa & C Africa • 500 kW; W Africa • 500 kW; W • W Africa • 500 kW
	UNITED KINGDOM	
	†BBC, Rampisham	S • E Europe & W Asia • 500 kW
	USA	
	R FREE ASIA, Via Tinian, N Marianas	S • SE Asia • 250 kW; S • E Asia • 250 kW
13680	CHINA	
	CHINA R INTL, Kashi	S • Europe • 500 kW
(con'd)	CHINA R INTL, Xi'an	W • SE Asia • 500 kW

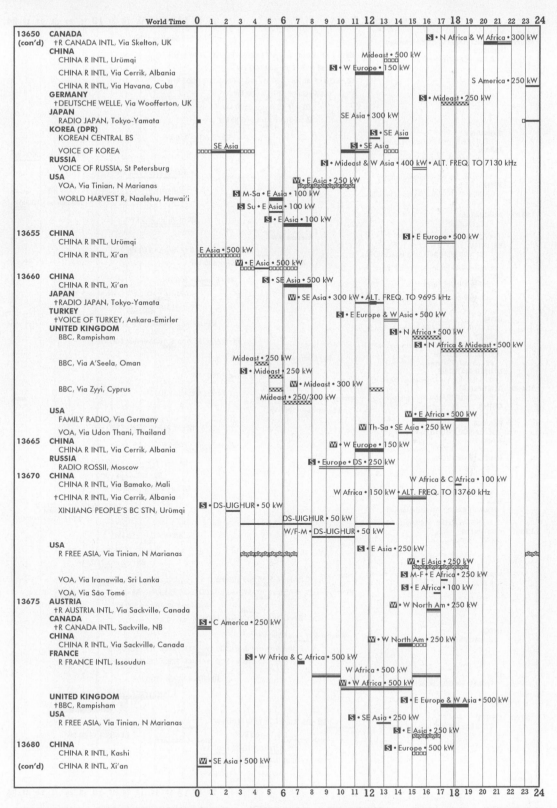

World Time 0 1 2 3 4 5 6 7 8 9 10 11 12 13 14 15 16 17 18 19 20 21 22 23 24

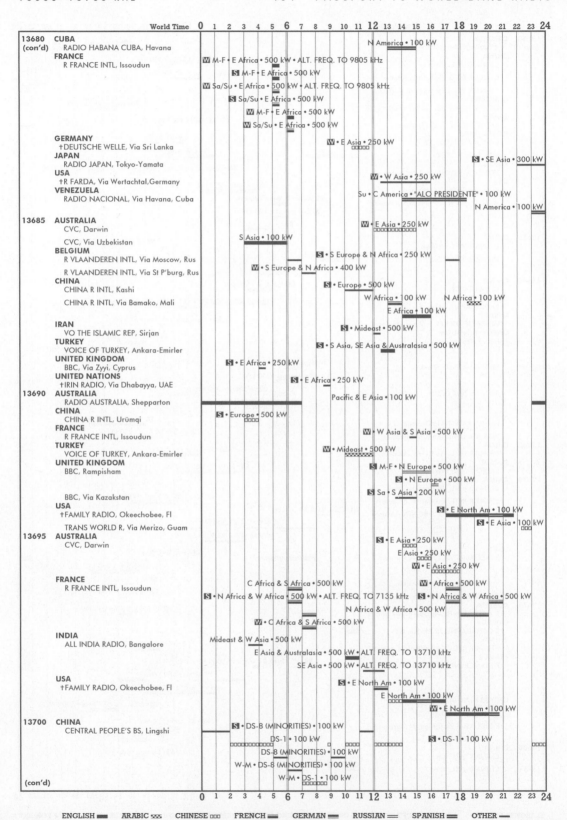

kHz	Country / Station	Schedule notes
13680 (con'd)	**CUBA** RADIO HABANA CUBA, Havana	N America • 100 kW
	FRANCE R FRANCE INTL, Issoudun	W M-F • E Africa • 500 kW • ALT. FREQ. TO 9805 kHz
		S M-F • E Africa • 500 kW
		W Sa/Su • E Africa • 500 kW • ALT. FREQ. TO 9805 kHz
		S Sa/Su • E Africa • 500 kW
		W M-F • E Africa • 500 kW
		W Sa/Su • E Africa • 500 kW
	GERMANY †DEUTSCHE WELLE, Via Sri Lanka	W • E Asia • 250 kW
	JAPAN RADIO JAPAN, Tokyo-Yamata	S • SE Asia • 300 kW
	USA †R FARDA, Via Wertachtal, Germany	W • W Asia • 250 kW
	VENEZUELA RADIO NACIONAL, Via Havana, Cuba	Su • C America • "ALO PRESIDENTE" • 100 kW
		N America • 100 kW
13685	**AUSTRALIA** CVC, Darwin	W • E Asia • 250 kW
	CVC, Via Uzbekistan	S Asia • 100 kW
	BELGIUM R VLAANDEREN INTL, Via Moscow, Rus	S • S Europe & N Africa • 250 kW
	R VLAANDEREN INTL, Via St P'burg, Rus	W • S Europe & N Africa • 400 kW
	CHINA CHINA R INTL, Kashi	S • Europe • 500 kW
	CHINA R INTL, Via Bamako, Mali	W Africa • 100 kW
		N Africa • 100 kW
		E Africa • 100 kW
	IRAN VO THE ISLAMIC REP, Sirjan	S • Mideast • 500 kW
	TURKEY VOICE OF TURKEY, Ankara-Emirler	S • S Asia, SE Asia & Australasia • 500 kW
	UNITED KINGDOM BBC, Via Zyyi, Cyprus	S • E Africa • 250 kW
	UNITED NATIONS †IRIN RADIO, Via Dhabayya, UAE	S • E Africa • 250 kW
13690	**AUSTRALIA** RADIO AUSTRALIA, Shepparton	Pacific & E Asia • 100 kW
	CHINA CHINA R INTL, Urümqi	S • Europe • 500 kW
	FRANCE R FRANCE INTL, Issoudun	W • W Asia & S Asia • 500 kW
	TURKEY VOICE OF TURKEY, Ankara-Emirler	W • Mideast • 500 kW
	UNITED KINGDOM BBC, Rampisham	S M-F • N Europe • 500 kW
		S • N Europe • 500 kW
	BBC, Via Kazakstan	S Sa • S Asia • 200 kW
	USA †FAMILY RADIO, Okeechobee, Fl	S • E North Am • 100 kW
	TRANS WORLD R, Via Merizo, Guam	S • E Asia • 100 kW
13695	**AUSTRALIA** CVC, Darwin	S • E Asia • 250 kW
		E Asia • 250 kW
		W • E Asia • 250 kW
	FRANCE R FRANCE INTL, Issoudun	C Africa & S Africa • 500 kW
		W • Africa • 500 kW
		S • N Africa & W Africa • 500 kW • ALT. FREQ. TO 7135 kHz
		S • N Africa & W Africa • 500 kW
		N Africa & W Africa • 500 kW
		W • C Africa & S Africa • 500 kW
	INDIA ALL INDIA RADIO, Bangalore	Mideast & W Asia • 500 kW
		E Asia & Australasia • 500 kW • ALT. FREQ. TO 13710 kHz
		SE Asia • 500 kW • ALT. FREQ. TO 13710 kHz
	USA †FAMILY RADIO, Okeechobee, Fl	S • E North Am • 100 kW
		E North Am • 100 kW
		W • E North Am • 100 kW
13700	**CHINA** CENTRAL PEOPLE'S BS, Lingshi	S • DS-8 (MINORITIES) • 100 kW
		DS-1 • 100 kW
		S • DS-1 • 100 kW
		DS-8 (MINORITIES) • 100 kW
		W-M • DS-8 (MINORITIES) • 100 kW
		W-M • DS-1 • 100 kW
(con'd)		

World Time 0 1 2 3 4 5 6 7 8 9 10 11 12 13 14 15 16 17 18 19 20 21 22 23 24

ENGLISH ARABIC CHINESE FRENCH GERMAN RUSSIAN SPANISH OTHER

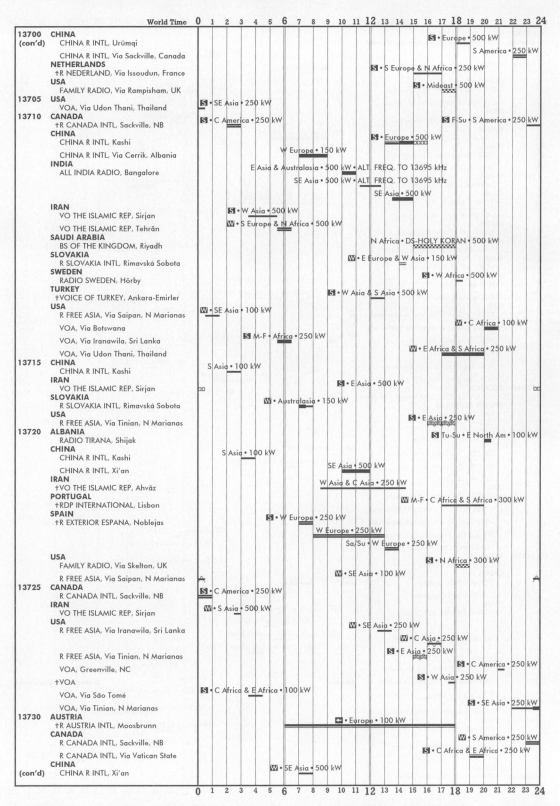

kHz	Country / Station	World Time 0–24
13700 (con'd)	**CHINA**	
	CHINA R INTL, Urümqi	S • Europe • 500 kW
	CHINA R INTL, Via Sackville, Canada	S America • 250 kW
	NETHERLANDS	
	†R NEDERLAND, Via Issoudun, France	S • S Europe & N Africa • 250 kW
	USA	
	FAMILY RADIO, Via Rampisham, UK	S • Mideast • 500 kW
13705	**USA**	
	VOA, Via Udon Thani, Thailand	S • SE Asia • 250 kW
13710	**CANADA**	
	†R CANADA INTL, Sackville, NB	S • C America • 250 kW
		S F-Su • S America • 250 kW
	CHINA	
	CHINA R INTL, Kashi	S • Europe • 500 kW
	CHINA R INTL, Via Cerrik, Albania	W Europe • 150 kW
	INDIA	
	ALL INDIA RADIO, Bangalore	E Asia & Australasia • 500 kW • ALT. FREQ. TO 13695 kHz
		SE Asia • 500 kW • ALT. FREQ. TO 13695 kHz
		SE Asia • 500 kW
	IRAN	
	VO THE ISLAMIC REP, Sirjan	S • W Asia • 500 kW
	VO THE ISLAMIC REP, Tehrān	W • S Europe & N Africa • 500 kW
	SAUDI ARABIA	
	BS OF THE KINGDOM, Riyadh	N Africa • DS-HOLY KORAN • 500 kW
	SLOVAKIA	
	R SLOVAKIA INTL, Rimavská Sobota	W • E Europe & W Asia • 150 kW
	SWEDEN	
	RADIO SWEDEN, Hörby	S • W Africa • 500 kW
	TURKEY	
	†VOICE OF TURKEY, Ankara-Emirler	S • W Asia & S Asia • 500 kW
	USA	
	R FREE ASIA, Via Saipan, N Marianas	W • SE Asia • 100 kW
	VOA, Via Botswana	W • C Africa • 100 kW
	VOA, Via Iranawila, Sri Lanka	S M-F • Africa • 250 kW
	VOA, Via Udon Thani, Thailand	W • E Africa & S Africa • 250 kW
13715	**CHINA**	
	CHINA R INTL, Kashi	S Asia • 100 kW
	IRAN	
	VO THE ISLAMIC REP, Sirjan	S • E Asia • 500 kW
	SLOVAKIA	
	R SLOVAKIA INTL, Rimavská Sobota	W • Australasia • 150 kW
	USA	
	R FREE ASIA, Via Tinian, N Marianas	S • E Asia • 250 kW
13720	**ALBANIA**	
	RADIO TIRANA, Shijak	S Tu-Su • E North Am • 100 kW
	CHINA	
	CHINA R INTL, Kashi	S Asia • 100 kW
	CHINA R INTL, Xi'an	SE Asia • 500 kW
	IRAN	
	†VO THE ISLAMIC REP, Ahvāz	W Asia & C Asia • 250 kW
	PORTUGAL	
	†RDP INTERNATIONAL, Lisbon	W M-F • C Africa & S Africa • 300 kW
	SPAIN	
	†R EXTERIOR ESPANA, Noblejas	S • W Europe • 250 kW
		W Europe • 250 kW
		Sa/Su • W Europe • 250 kW
	USA	
	FAMILY RADIO, Via Skelton, UK	S • N Africa • 300 kW
	R FREE ASIA, Via Saipan, N Marianas	W • SE Asia • 100 kW
13725	**CANADA**	
	R CANADA INTL, Sackville, NB	S • C America • 250 kW
	IRAN	
	VO THE ISLAMIC REP, Sirjan	W • S Asia • 500 kW
	USA	
	R FREE ASIA, Via Iranawila, Sri Lanka	W • SE Asia • 250 kW
		W • C Asia • 250 kW
	R FREE ASIA, Via Tinian, N Marianas	S • E Asia • 250 kW
	VOA, Greenville, NC	S • C America • 250 kW
	†VOA	S • W Asia • 250 kW
	VOA, Via São Tomé	S • C Africa & E Africa • 100 kW
	VOA, Via Tinian, N Marianas	S • SE Asia • 250 kW
13730	**AUSTRIA**	
	†R AUSTRIA INTL, Moosbrunn	← • Europe • 100 kW
	CANADA	
	R CANADA INTL, Sackville, NB	W • S America • 250 kW
	R CANADA INTL, Via Vatican State	S • C Africa & E Africa • 250 kW
	CHINA	
(con'd)	CHINA R INTL, Xi'an	W • SE Asia • 500 kW

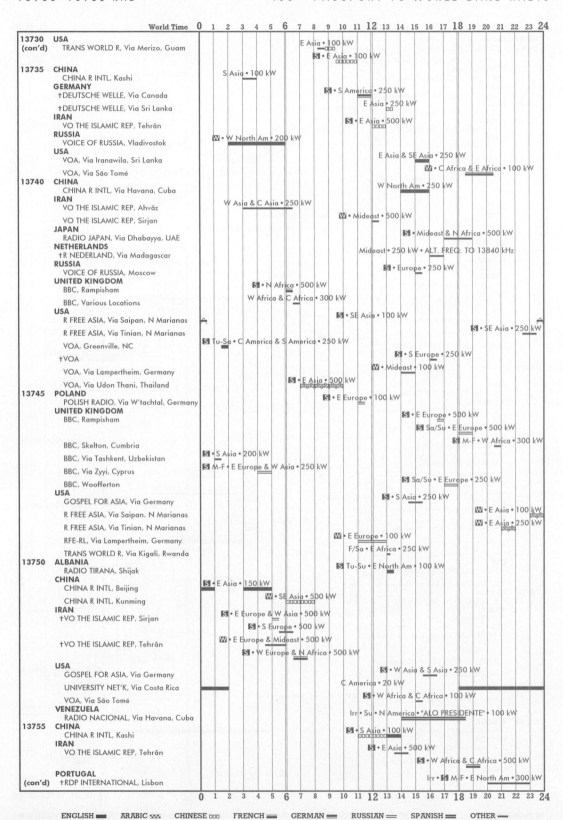

kHz	Country	Station	World Time (0–24)
13730 (con'd)	USA	TRANS WORLD R, Via Merizo, Guam	E Asia • 100 kW; [S] • E Asia • 100 kW
13735	CHINA	CHINA R INTL, Kashi	S Asia • 100 kW
	GERMANY	†DEUTSCHE WELLE, Via Canada	[S] • S America • 250 kW
		†DEUTSCHE WELLE, Via Sri Lanka	E Asia • 250 kW
	IRAN	VO THE ISLAMIC REP, Tehrān	[S] • E Asia • 500 kW
	RUSSIA	VOICE OF RUSSIA, Vladivostok	[W] • W North Am • 200 kW
	USA	VOA, Via Iranawila, Sri Lanka	E Asia & SE Asia • 250 kW
		VOA, Via São Tomé	[W] • C Africa & E Africa • 100 kW
13740	CHINA	CHINA R INTL, Via Havana, Cuba	W North Am • 250 kW
	IRAN	VO THE ISLAMIC REP, Ahvāz	W Asia & C Asia • 250 kW
		VO THE ISLAMIC REP, Sirjan	[W] • Mideast • 500 kW
	JAPAN	RADIO JAPAN, Via Dhabayya, UAE	[S] • Mideast & N Africa • 500 kW
	NETHERLANDS	†R NEDERLAND, Via Madagascar	Mideast • 250 kW • ALT. FREQ. TO 13840 kHz
	RUSSIA	VOICE OF RUSSIA, Moscow	[S] • Europe • 250 kW
	UNITED KINGDOM	BBC, Rampisham	[S] • N Africa • 500 kW
		BBC, Various Locations	W Africa & C Africa • 300 kW
	USA	R FREE ASIA, Via Saipan, N Marianas	[S] • SE Asia • 100 kW
		R FREE ASIA, Via Tinian, N Marianas	[S] • SE Asia • 250 kW
		VOA, Greenville, NC	[S] Tu-Sa • C America & S America • 250 kW
		†VOA	[S] • S Europe • 250 kW
		VOA, Via Lampertheim, Germany	[W] • Mideast • 100 kW
		VOA, Via Udon Thani, Thailand	[S] • E Asia • 500 kW
13745	POLAND	POLISH RADIO, Via W'tachtal, Germany	[S] • E Europe • 100 kW
	UNITED KINGDOM	BBC, Rampisham	[S] • E Europe • 500 kW; [S] Sa/Su • E Europe • 500 kW
		BBC, Skelton, Cumbria	[S] M-F • W Africa • 300 kW
		BBC, Via Tashkent, Uzbekistan	[S] • S Asia • 200 kW
		BBC, Via Zyyi, Cyprus	[S] M-F • E Europe & W Asia • 250 kW
		BBC, Woofferton	[S] Sa/Su • E Europe • 250 kW
	USA	GOSPEL FOR ASIA, Via Germany	[S] • S Asia • 250 kW
		R FREE ASIA, Via Saipan, N Marianas	[W] • E Asia • 100 kW
		R FREE ASIA, Via Tinian, N Marianas	[W] • E Asia • 250 kW
		RFE-RL, Via Lampertheim, Germany	[W] • E Europe • 100 kW
		TRANS WORLD R, Via Kigali, Rwanda	F/Sa • E Africa • 250 kW
13750	ALBANIA	RADIO TIRANA, Shijak	[S] Tu-Su • E North Am • 100 kW
	CHINA	CHINA R INTL, Beijing	[S] • E Asia • 150 kW
		CHINA R INTL, Kunming	[W] • SE Asia • 500 kW
	IRAN	†VO THE ISLAMIC REP, Sirjan	[S] • E Europe & W Asia • 500 kW; [S] • S Europe • 500 kW
		†VO THE ISLAMIC REP, Tehrān	[W] • E Europe & Mideast • 500 kW; [S] • W Europe & N Africa • 500 kW
	USA	GOSPEL FOR ASIA, Via Germany	[S] • W Asia & S Asia • 250 kW
		UNIVERSITY NET'K, Via Costa Rica	C America • 20 kW
		VOA, Via São Tomé	[S] • W Africa & C Africa • 100 kW
	VENEZUELA	RADIO NACIONAL, Via Havana, Cuba	Irr • Su • N America • "ALO PRESIDENTE" • 100 kW
13755	CHINA	CHINA R INTL, Kashi	[S] • S Asia • 100 kW
	IRAN	VO THE ISLAMIC REP, Tehrān	[S] • E Asia • 500 kW; [S] • W Africa & C Africa • 500 kW
(con'd)	PORTUGAL	†RDP INTERNATIONAL, Lisbon	Irr • [S] M-F • E North Am • 300 kW

ENGLISH ARABIC CHINESE FRENCH GERMAN RUSSIAN SPANISH OTHER

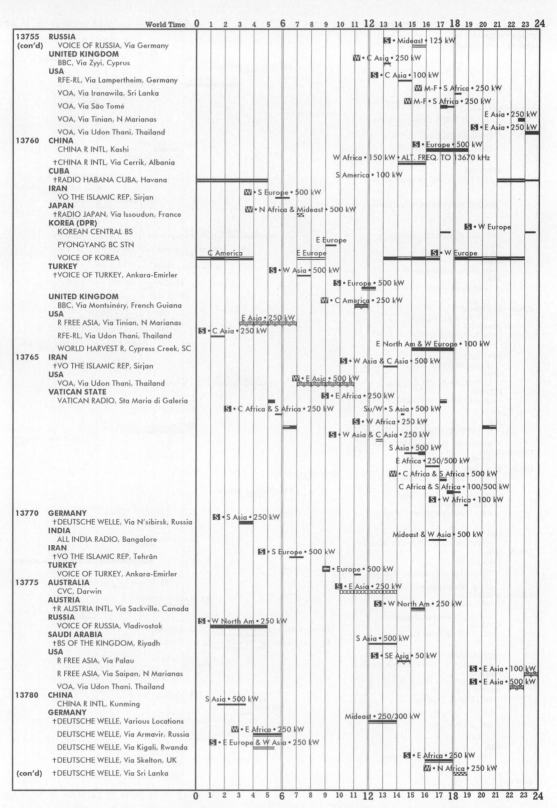

World Time 0 1 2 3 4 5 6 7 8 9 10 11 12 13 14 15 16 17 18 19 20 21 22 23 24

kHz	Country / Station	Schedule
13755 (con'd)	**RUSSIA**	
	VOICE OF RUSSIA, Via Germany	S • Mideast • 125 kW
	UNITED KINGDOM	
	BBC, Via Zyyi, Cyprus	W • C Asia • 250 kW
	USA	
	RFE-RL, Via Lampertheim, Germany	S • C Asia • 100 kW
	VOA, Via Iranawila, Sri Lanka	W M-F • S Africa • 250 kW
	VOA, Via São Tomé	W M-F • S Africa • 250 kW
	VOA, Via Tinian, N Marianas	E Asia • 250 kW
	VOA, Via Udon Thani, Thailand	S • E Asia • 250 kW
13760	**CHINA**	
	CHINA R INTL, Kashi	S • Europe • 500 kW
	†CHINA R INTL, Via Cerrik, Albania	W Africa • 150 kW • ALT. FREQ. TO 13670 kHz
	CUBA	
	†RADIO HABANA CUBA, Havana	S America • 100 kW
	IRAN	
	VO THE ISLAMIC REP, Sirjan	W • S Europe • 500 kW
	JAPAN	
	†RADIO JAPAN, Via Issoudun, France	W • N Africa & Mideast • 500 kW
	KOREA (DPR)	
	KOREAN CENTRAL BS	S • W Europe
	PYONGYANG BC STN	E Europe
	VOICE OF KOREA	C America; E Europe; S • W Europe
	TURKEY	
	†VOICE OF TURKEY, Ankara-Emirler	S • W Asia • 500 kW; S • Europe • 500 kW
	UNITED KINGDOM	
	BBC, Via Montsinéry, French Guiana	W • C America • 250 kW
	USA	
	R FREE ASIA, Via Tinian, N Marianas	E Asia • 250 kW
	RFE-RL, Via Udon Thani, Thailand	S • C Asia • 250 kW
	WORLD HARVEST R, Cypress Creek, SC	E North Am & W Europe • 100 kW
13765	**IRAN**	
	†VO THE ISLAMIC REP, Sirjan	S • W Asia & C Asia • 500 kW
	USA	
	VOA, Via Udon Thani, Thailand	W • E Asia • 500 kW
	VATICAN STATE	
	VATICAN RADIO, Sta Maria di Galeria	S • E Africa • 250 kW; S • C Africa & S Africa • 250 kW; Su/W • S Asia • 500 kW; S • W Africa • 250 kW; S • W Asia & C Asia • 250 kW; S Asia • 500 kW; E Africa • 250/500 kW; W • C Africa & S Africa • 500 kW; C Africa & S Africa • 100/500 kW; S • W Africa • 100 kW
13770	**GERMANY**	
	†DEUTSCHE WELLE, Via N'sibirsk, Russia	S • S Asia • 250 kW
	INDIA	
	ALL INDIA RADIO, Bangalore	Mideast & W Asia • 500 kW
	IRAN	
	†VO THE ISLAMIC REP, Tehrān	S • S Europe • 500 kW
	TURKEY	
	VOICE OF TURKEY, Ankara-Emirler	⇐ • Europe • 500 kW
13775	**AUSTRALIA**	
	CVC, Darwin	S • E Asia • 250 kW
	AUSTRIA	
	†R AUSTRIA INTL, Via Sackville, Canada	S • W North Am • 250 kW
	RUSSIA	
	VOICE OF RUSSIA, Vladivostok	S • W North Am • 250 kW
	SAUDI ARABIA	
	†BS OF THE KINGDOM, Riyadh	S Asia • 500 kW
	USA	
	R FREE ASIA, Via Palau	S • SE Asia • 50 kW
	R FREE ASIA, Via Saipan, N Marianas	S • E Asia • 100 kW
	VOA, Via Udon Thani, Thailand	S • E Asia • 500 kW
13780	**CHINA**	
	CHINA R INTL, Kunming	S Asia • 500 kW
	GERMANY	
	†DEUTSCHE WELLE, Various Locations	Mideast • 250/300 kW
	DEUTSCHE WELLE, Via Armavir, Russia	W • E Africa • 250 kW
	DEUTSCHE WELLE, Via Kigali, Rwanda	S • E Europe & W Asia • 250 kW
	†DEUTSCHE WELLE, Via Skelton, UK	S • E Africa • 250 kW
(con'd)	†DEUTSCHE WELLE, Via Sri Lanka	W • N Africa • 250 kW

0 1 2 3 4 5 6 7 8 9 10 11 12 13 14 15 16 17 18 19 20 21 22 23 24

Frequency	Country / Station	Schedule (World Time 0–24)
13780 (con'd)	**GERMANY**	
	†DEUTSCHE WELLE, Via Sri Lanka	W • E Africa & S Africa • 250 kW
		W • W Africa, C Africa & E Africa • 250 kW
	†DEUTSCHE WELLE, Via Woofferton, UK	S • Mideast • 300 kW
		Mideast • 300 kW
	USA	
	FAMILY RADIO, Via Rampisham, UK	S • Mideast • 500 kW
13785	**VATICAN STATE**	
	VATICAN RADIO, Various Locations	E Asia • 100/250 kW
13790	**CHINA**	
	CHINA R INTL, Kashi	S • Mideast & N Africa • 500 kW
	CHINA R INTL, Urümqi	Europe • 500 kW
		S • Europe • 500 kW
	GERMANY	
	DEUTSCHE WELLE, Via Kigali, Rwanda	W • Mideast • 250 kW
		W • N Africa & W Africa • 250 kW
	†DEUTSCHE WELLE, Via Sines, Portugal	W • C Africa & S Africa • 250 kW
		S • N Africa & Mideast • 250 kW
	IRAN	
	†VO THE ISLAMIC REP, Tehrān	Mideast • 500 kW
	USA	
	VOA, Greenville, NC	S • C America & S America • 250 kW
13795	**INDIA**	
	ALL INDIA RADIO, Aligarh	SE Asia • 250 kW
	USA	
	VOA, Via Botswana	S • C Africa • 100 kW
		S • C Africa & E Africa • 100 kW
13800	**AUSTRALIA**	
	CVC, Via Jülich, Germany	S • E Europe • 100 kW
	BULGARIA	
	†RADIO BULGARIA, Plovdiv	S • Mideast • 250 kW
		S • S Europe & N Africa • 250 kW
	GERMANY	
	DEUTSCHE WELLE, Via Rampisham, UK	S • W Asia • 500 kW
	IRAN	
	†VO THE ISLAMIC REP, Zāhedān	N Africa & Mideast • 500 kW
	POLAND	
	†POLISH RADIO, Via W'tachtal, Germany	S • C Asia • 100 kW
		S • C Asia • 250 kW
	USA	
	FAMILY RADIO, Okeechobee, Fl	S • S America • 100 kW
	R FREE ASIA, Via Tinian, N Marianas	W • E Asia • 250 kW
13805	**IRAN**	
	VO THE ISLAMIC REP, Sirjan	S • S Asia • 500 kW
13810	**GERMANY**	
	†DEUTSCHE WELLE, Via Dhabayya, UAE	W • S Asia • 250 kW
	IRAN	
	†VO THE ISLAMIC REP, Sirjan	S • S Europe • 500 kW
	UNITED KINGDOM	
	BIBLE VOICE, Via Nauen, Germany	E Africa • 100 kW
		Sa/Su • E Africa • 100 kW
	USA	
	OVERCOMER MINISTRY, Via Germany	Mideast • 100 kW
13815	**USA**	
	KAIJ, Frisco, TX	N America • 100 kW
	R FREE ASIA, Via Iranawila, Sri Lanka	W • SE Asia • 250 kW
	RFE-RL, Via Wertachtal,Germany	S • W Asia & C Asia • 250 kW
13820	**AUSTRALIA**	
	CVC, Via Uzbekistan	S • S Asia • 100 kW
	CVC, Via Wertachtal, Germany	S • W Africa & C Africa • 125 kW
	CROATIA	
	VOICE OF CROATIA, Via Germany	W • Australasia • 100 kW • ALT. FREQ. TO 11690 kHz
		S • Australasia • 100 kW • ALT. FREQ. TO 11610 kHz
	NETHERLANDS	
	R NEDERLAND, Via Khabarovsk, Russia	S • E Asia & SE Asia • 100 kW
	SWEDEN	
	†RADIO SWEDEN, Hörby	S • S Asia • 500 kW
	UNITED KINGDOM	
	†BBC, Skelton, Cumbria	S • N Africa • 300 kW
	†BBC, Via Sines, Portugal	S • N Africa • 250 kW
	BBC, Via Zyyi, Cyprus	W Sa-Th • W Asia • 300 kW
		W F • Mideast & W Asia • 300 kW
	USA	
	PAN AM BC, Via Jülich, Germany	W Su • S Asia • 100 kW
		W Su • Mideast & W Asia • 100 kW
		W Th • Mideast & W Asia • 100 kW
(con'd)		

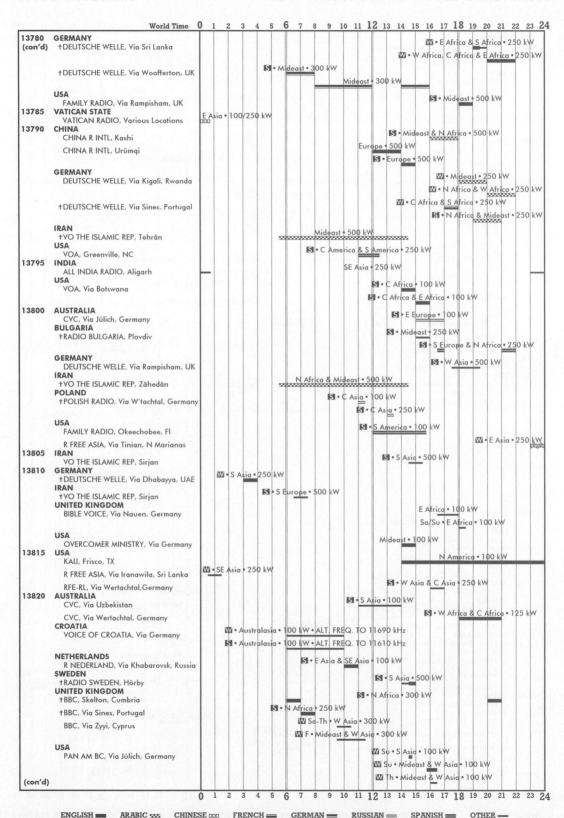

ENGLISH ARABIC CHINESE FRENCH GERMAN RUSSIAN SPANISH OTHER

World Time 0 1 2 3 4 5 6 7 8 9 10 11 12 13 14 15 16 17 18 19 20 21 22 23 24

Freq.	Country / Station	Schedule
13820 (con'd)	**USA**	
	R FREE ASIA, Via Iranawila, Sri Lanka	[S] • SE Asia • 250 kW
	RADIO MARTI, Greenville, NC	[S] • C America • 250 kW; [W] • C America • 250 kW; C America • 250 kW
13825	**USA**	
	R FREE ASIA, Via Dushanbe, Tajikistan	[S] • S Asia • 200 kW
13830	**AUSTRALIA**	
	CVC, Via Jülich, Germany	E Europe • 100 kW
	CLANDESTINE (AFRICA)	
	"VO DEMOCRATIC ERITREA", Germany	[S] Th • E Africa • ANTI-ERITREAN GOVT • 100 kW
	"VO OROMO LIBERATION, Via Germany	[S] • E Africa • 100 kW
	USA	
	R FREE ASIA, Via Dushanbe, Tajikistan	[S] • S Asia • 200 kW
13840	**GERMANY**	
	DEUTSCHE WELLE, Via Armavir, Russia	[S] • W Asia & S Asia • 250 kW
	DEUTSCHE WELLE, Via Sri Lanka	[S] • E Asia • 250 kW
	NETHERLANDS	
	†R NEDERLAND, Via Madagascar	Mideast • 250 kW • ALT. FREQ. TO 13740 kHz
	NEW ZEALAND	
	R NEW ZEALAND INTL, Rangitaiki	[W] • Pacific • 100 kW • ALT. FREQ. TO 9870 kHz
	PALAU	
	†R T8WH-WORLD HARVEST R, Koror	ENGLISH, ETC • SE Asia • 100 kW
	POLAND	
	†POLISH RADIO, Via W'tachtal, Germany	[←] • E Europe • 100 kW
	SWEDEN	
	IBRA RADIO, Via Wertachtal, Germany	[S] • ARABIC, ETC • C Africa • 250 kW
	UNITED KINGDOM	
	BIBLE VOICE, Via Wertachtal, Germany	[S] F/Su • S Asia • 250 kW; [S] M-F • S Asia • 250 kW
	USA	
	FAMILY RADIO, Via Jülich,Germany	[S] • N Africa • 100 kW
13845	**USA**	
	WWCR, Nashville, Tennessee	E North Am • 100 kW • ALT. FREQ. TO 5935 kHz; E North Am • 100 kW
13850	**CHINA**	
	CHINA R INTL, Beijing	[W] • SE Asia • 500 kW; SE Asia • 500 kW
	ISRAEL	
	†KOL ISRAEL, Tel Aviv	[S] • W Asia • 300 kW; [S] Su-Th • W Asia • 300 kW; [W] • W Asia • 300 kW • ALT. FREQ. TO 9985 kHz; [W] Su-Th • W Asia • 300 kW • ALT. FREQ. TO 9985 kHz
13855	**RUSSIA**	
	RUSSIAN INTL R, Moscow	[S] • Mideast • 200 kW
	VOICE OF RUSSIA, Moscow	[S] • Mideast • 200 kW
	UNITED KINGDOM	
	BBC, Via Zyyi, Cyprus	[S] • C Asia • 250 kW
13860	**CHINA**	
	CHINA R INTL, Shijiazhuang	[S] • E Europe • 500 kW
	USA	
	GOSPEL FOR ASIA, Via Germany	[S] • S Asia • 250 kW
13865	**USA**	
	R FREE ASIA, Via Iranawila, Sri Lanka	[W] • SE Asia • 250 kW; [S] • SE Asia • 250 kW
	R FREE ASIA, Via Tinian, N Marianas	[S] • E Asia • 250 kW
	VOA, Via Iranawila, Sri Lanka	[W] • E Africa • 250 kW
13870	**USA**	
	VOA, Various Locations	M-F • E Africa • 100 kW; E Africa • 250 kW
	VOA, Via Lampertheim, Germany	M-F • E Africa • 250 kW
14670	**CANADA**	
	CHU, Ottawa	WORLD TIME • 3 kW • USB
15000	**USA**	
	WWV, Fort Collins, Colorado	WEATHER/WORLD TIME • 10 kW
	WWVH, Kekaha, Hawai'i	WEATHER/WORLD TIME • 10 kW
15020	**INDIA**	
	ALL INDIA RADIO, Aligarh	E Asia • 250 kW
15040	**EGYPT**	
	†RADIO CAIRO, Abu Za'bal	[S] • W Asia & C Asia • 100 kW
15050	**INDIA**	
	ALL INDIA RADIO, Delhi	S Asia • 100/250 kW
15065	**PAKISTAN**	
	RADIO PAKISTAN, Islamabad	Mideast & N Africa • 250 kW • ALT. FREQ. TO 15100 kHz
15070	**PAKISTAN**	
	RADIO PAKISTAN, Islamabad	E Asia • 250 kW
15075	**INDIA**	
	ALL INDIA RADIO, Bangalore	Mideast & W Asia • 500 kW; Mideast & E Africa • 500 kW; E Africa • 500 kW
(con'd)		

World Time 0 1 2 3 4 5 6 7 8 9 10 11 12 13 14 15 16 17 18 19 20 21 22 23 24

kHz	Country / Station	Schedule (World Time 0–24)
15075 (con'd)	**INDIA** ALL INDIA RADIO, Delhi	E Africa • 250 kW
15080	**EGYPT** †RADIO CAIRO, Kafr Silîm-Abis	W Africa & C Africa • 250 kW
15085	**IRAN** VO THE ISLAMIC REP, Tehrān	Europe • 500 kW; S • Europe • 500 kW
15090	**USA** RFE-RL, Via Kuwait	S • W Asia & S Asia • 250 kW
	VOA, Via Kuwait	S • W Asia & S Asia • 250 kW
15100	**CHINA** CHINA R INTL, Jinhua	S • SE Asia • 500 kW
	KOREA (DPR) VOICE OF KOREA	SE Asia
	PAKISTAN RADIO PAKISTAN, Islamabad	URDU & ENGLISH • Europe • 250 kW • ALT. FREQ. TO 21465 kHz; Mideast & N Africa • 250 kW • ALT. FREQ. TO 15065 kHz
15105	**GERMANY** DEUTSCHE WELLE, Via Sri Lanka	S • SE Asia • 250 kW
	ROMANIA †R ROMANIA INTL, Bucharest	W • W Europe • 300 kW
	RUSSIA TATARSTAN WAVE, Samara	W • E Asia • TATAR, RUSSIAN • 160 kW
	UNITED KINGDOM BBC, Rampisham	S M-F • W Africa • 500 kW
	BBC, Via Ascension	W Africa & C Africa • 250 kW
	†BBC, Via Meyerton, South Africa	S • W Africa & C Africa • 500 kW; W • E Africa • 250 kW; W M-F • E Africa • 250 kW; W Sa/Su • E Africa • 250 kW
	USA VOA, Via Philippines	S Th-Sa • SE Asia • 250 kW
	VOA, Via Udon Thani, Thailand	S • S Asia • 250 kW
	WORLD HARVEST R, Cypress Creek, SC	W • C America • 250 kW
15110	**CHINA** CHINA R INTL, Kashi	S Asia • 100 kW
	CHINA R INTL, Urümqi	S • E Asia • 100 kW; Mideast • 500 kW
	KUWAIT RADIO KUWAIT, Kabd	S Asia • 500 kW
	NETHERLANDS †R NEDERLAND, Via Philippines	S • E Asia & SE Asia • 250 kW
	RUSSIA TATARSTAN WAVE, Samara	S • E Asia • TATAR, RUSSIAN • 250 kW
	SPAIN R EXTERIOR ESPANA, Noblejas	N America & C America • 250/350 kW
15115	**EGYPT** †EGYPTIAN RADIO, Abu Za'bal	S • W Africa • DS-GENERAL • 100 kW
	USA †FAMILY RADIO, Okeechobee, Fl	W • W Africa • 100 kW
15120	**CHINA** CHINA R INTL, Beijing	C Asia & E Asia • 500 kW
	CHINA R INTL, Via Havana, Cuba	S America • 250 kW
	CUBA †RADIO HABANA CUBA, Havana	S America • 100 kW • ALT. FREQ. TO 9550 kHz
	NIGERIA VOICE OF NIGERIA, Ikorodu	N Africa & Europe • 250 kW
	USA †RFE-RL	W • W Asia & C Asia • 250 kW
	RFE-RL, Via Lampertheim, Germany	W • W Asia & C Asia • 100 kW; W • E Europe & W Asia • 100 kW
	RFE-RL, Via Udon Thani, Thailand	S • W Asia & C Asia • 250 kW
15125	**CHINA** CHINA R INTL, Beijing	S • SE Asia • 500 kW
	CHINA R INTL, Via Bamako, Mali	C Africa • 100 kW; E Africa • 100 kW
	INDONESIA RRI, Cimanggis, Jawa	Irr • SE Asia • DS-TEMP INACTIVE • 250 kW
	SPAIN †R EXTERIOR ESPANA, Via Costa Rica	W Su • C America & S America • 100 kW; W Sa/Su • C America & S America • 100 kW; W • C America & S America • 100 kW; Irr • W M-F • C America & S America • 100 kW; Irr • W Su • C America & S America • 100 kW
15130 (con'd)	**CHINA** CHINA R INTL, Various Locations	E Asia • 150/500 kW

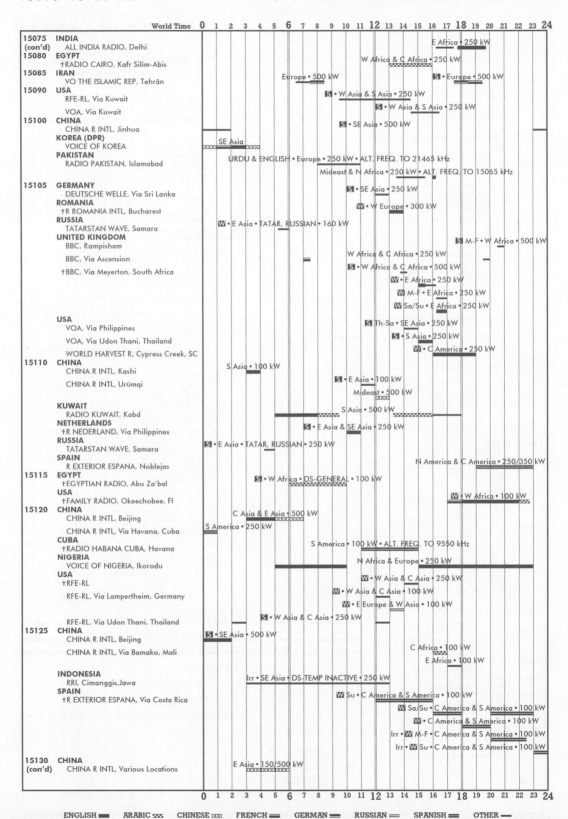

ENGLISH ARABIC CHINESE FRENCH GERMAN RUSSIAN SPANISH OTHER

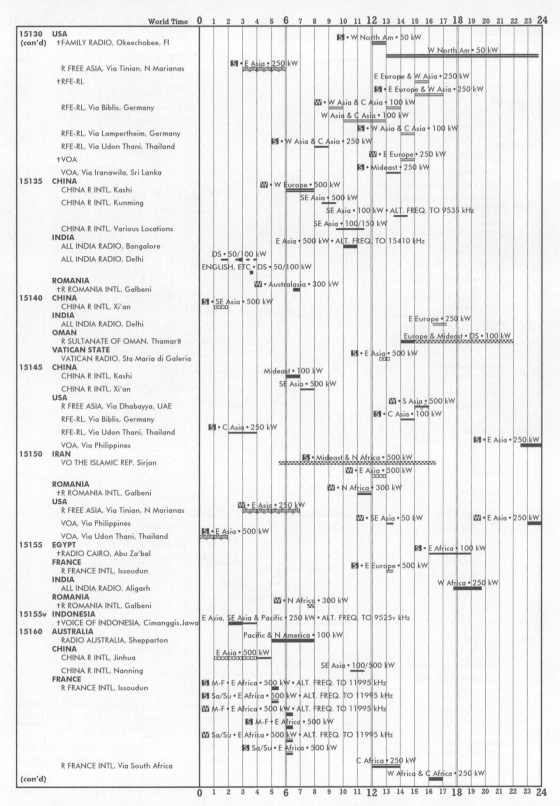

World Time 0 1 2 3 4 5 6 7 8 9 10 11 12 13 14 15 16 17 18 19 20 21 22 23 24

kHz	Country / Station	Schedule
15130 (con'd)	**USA**	
	†FAMILY RADIO, Okeechobee, Fl	S • W North Am • 50 kW
		W North Am • 50 kW
	R FREE ASIA, Via Tinian, N Marianas	S • E Asia • 250 kW
	†RFE-RL	E Europe & W Asia • 250 kW
		S • E Europe & W Asia • 250 kW
	RFE-RL, Via Biblis, Germany	W • W Asia & C Asia • 100 kW
		W Asia & C Asia • 100 kW
	RFE-RL, Via Lampertheim, Germany	S • W Asia & C Asia • 100 kW
	RFE-RL, Via Udon Thani, Thailand	S • W Asia & C Asia • 250 kW
	†VOA	W • E Europe • 250 kW
	VOA, Via Iranawila, Sri Lanka	S • Mideast • 250 kW
15135	**CHINA**	
	CHINA R INTL, Kashi	W • W Europe • 500 kW
	CHINA R INTL, Kunming	SE Asia • 500 kW
		SE Asia • 100 kW • ALT. FREQ. TO 9535 kHz
	CHINA R INTL, Various Locations	SE Asia • 100/150 kW
	INDIA	
	ALL INDIA RADIO, Bangalore	E Asia • 500 kW • ALT. FREQ. TO 15410 kHz
	ALL INDIA RADIO, Delhi	DS • 50/100 kW
		ENGLISH, ETC • DS • 50/100 kW
	ROMANIA	
	†R ROMANIA INTL, Galbeni	W • Australasia • 300 kW
15140	**CHINA**	
	CHINA R INTL, Xi'an	S • SE Asia • 500 kW
	INDIA	
	ALL INDIA RADIO, Delhi	E Europe • 250 kW
	OMAN	
	R SULTANATE OF OMAN, Thamarīt	Europe & Mideast • DS • 100 kW
	VATICAN STATE	
	VATICAN RADIO, Sta Maria di Galeria	S • E Asia • 500 kW
15145	**CHINA**	
	CHINA R INTL, Kashi	Mideast • 100 kW
	CHINA R INTL, Xi'an	SE Asia • 500 kW
	USA	
	R FREE ASIA, Via Dhabayya, UAE	W • S Asia • 500 kW
	RFE-RL, Via Biblis, Germany	S • C Asia • 100 kW
	RFE-RL, Via Udon Thani, Thailand	S • C Asia • 250 kW
	VOA, Via Philippines	S • E Asia • 250 kW
15150	**IRAN**	
	VO THE ISLAMIC REP, Sirjan	S • Mideast & N Africa • 500 kW
		W • E Asia • 500 kW
	ROMANIA	
	†R ROMANIA INTL, Galbeni	W • N Africa • 300 kW
	USA	
	R FREE ASIA, Via Tinian, N Marianas	W • E Asia • 250 kW
	VOA, Via Philippines	W • SE Asia • 50 kW
		W • E Asia • 250 kW
	VOA, Via Udon Thani, Thailand	S • E Asia • 500 kW
15155	**EGYPT**	
	†RADIO CAIRO, Abu Za'bal	S • E Africa • 100 kW
	FRANCE	
	R FRANCE INTL, Issoudun	S • E Europe • 500 kW
	INDIA	
	ALL INDIA RADIO, Aligarh	W Africa • 250 kW
	ROMANIA	
	†R ROMANIA INTL, Galbeni	W • N Africa • 300 kW
15155v	**INDONESIA**	
	†VOICE OF INDONESIA, Cimanggis, Jawa	E Asia, SE Asia & Pacific • 250 kW • ALT. FREQ. TO 9525v kHz
15160	**AUSTRALIA**	
	RADIO AUSTRALIA, Shepparton	Pacific & N America • 100 kW
	CHINA	
	CHINA R INTL, Jinhua	E Asia • 500 kW
	CHINA R INTL, Nanning	SE Asia • 100/500 kW
	FRANCE	
	R FRANCE INTL, Issoudun	S M-F • E Africa • 500 kW • ALT. FREQ. TO 11995 kHz
		S Sa/Su • E Africa • 500 kW • ALT. FREQ. TO 11995 kHz
		W M-F • E Africa • 500 kW • ALT. FREQ. TO 11995 kHz
		S M-F • E Africa • 500 kW
		W Sa/Su • E Africa • 500 kW • ALT. FREQ. TO 11995 kHz
		S Sa/Su • E Africa • 500 kW
	R FRANCE INTL, Via South Africa	C Africa • 250 kW
		W Africa & C Africa • 250 kW
(con'd)		

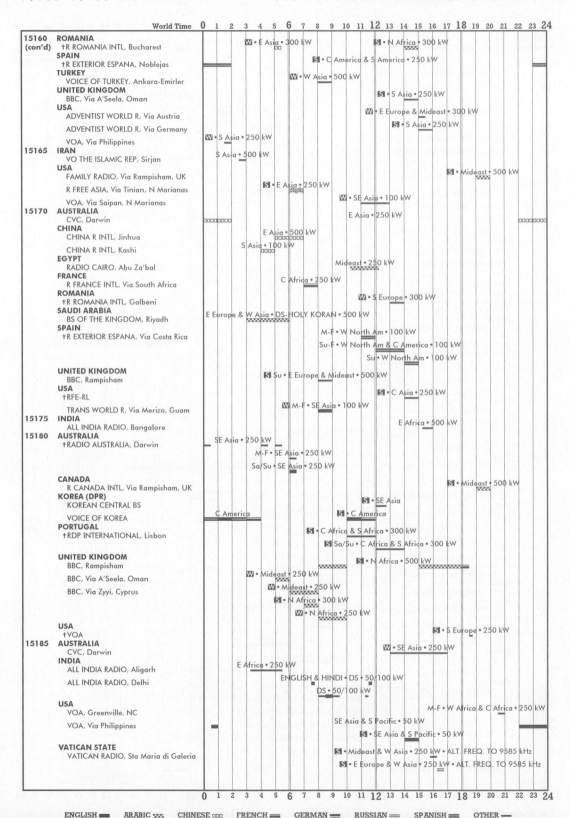

kHz	Country / Station	World Time 0–24: Details
15160 (con'd)	**ROMANIA**	
	†R ROMANIA INTL, Bucharest	W • E Asia • 300 kW; S • N Africa • 300 kW
	SPAIN	
	†R EXTERIOR ESPANA, Noblejas	S • C America & S America • 250 kW
	TURKEY	
	VOICE OF TURKEY, Ankara-Emirler	W • W Asia • 500 kW
	UNITED KINGDOM	
	BBC, Via A'Seela, Oman	S • S Asia • 250 kW
	USA	
	ADVENTIST WORLD R, Via Austria	W • E Europe & Mideast • 300 kW
	ADVENTIST WORLD R, Via Germany	S • S Asia • 250 kW
	VOA, Via Philippines	W • S Asia • 250 kW
15165	**IRAN**	
	VO THE ISLAMIC REP, Sirjan	S Asia • 500 kW
	USA	
	FAMILY RADIO, Via Rampisham, UK	S • Mideast • 500 kW
	R FREE ASIA, Via Tinian, N Marianas	S • E Asia • 250 kW
	VOA, Via Saipan, N Marianas	W • SE Asia • 100 kW
15170	**AUSTRALIA**	
	CVC, Darwin	E Asia • 250 kW
	CHINA	
	CHINA R INTL, Jinhua	E Asia • 500 kW
	CHINA R INTL, Kashi	S Asia • 100 kW
	EGYPT	
	RADIO CAIRO, Abu Za'bal	Mideast • 250 kW
	FRANCE	
	R FRANCE INTL, Via South Africa	C Africa • 250 kW
	ROMANIA	
	†R ROMANIA INTL, Galbeni	W • S Europe • 300 kW
	SAUDI ARABIA	
	BS OF THE KINGDOM, Riyadh	E Europe & W Asia • DS-HOLY KORAN • 500 kW
	SPAIN	
	†R EXTERIOR ESPANA, Via Costa Rica	M-F • W North Am • 100 kW; Su-F • W North Am & C America • 100 kW; Su • W North Am • 100 kW
	UNITED KINGDOM	
	BBC, Rampisham	S Su • E Europe & Mideast • 500 kW
	USA	
	†RFE-RL	S • C Asia • 250 kW
	TRANS WORLD R, Via Merizo, Guam	W M-F • SE Asia • 100 kW
15175	**INDIA**	
	ALL INDIA RADIO, Bangalore	E Africa • 500 kW
15180	**AUSTRALIA**	
	†RADIO AUSTRALIA, Darwin	SE Asia • 250 kW; M-F • SE Asia • 250 kW; Sa/Su • SE Asia • 250 kW
	CANADA	
	R CANADA INTL, Via Rampisham, UK	S • Mideast • 500 kW
	KOREA (DPR)	
	KOREAN CENTRAL BS	S • SE Asia
	VOICE OF KOREA	C America; S • C America
	PORTUGAL	
	†RDP INTERNATIONAL, Lisbon	S • C Africa & S Africa • 300 kW; S Sa/Su • C Africa & S Africa • 300 kW
	UNITED KINGDOM	
	BBC, Rampisham	S • N Africa • 500 kW
	BBC, Via A'Seela, Oman	W • Mideast • 250 kW
	BBC, Via Zyyi, Cyprus	W • Mideast • 250 kW; S • N Africa • 300 kW; W • N Africa • 250 kW
	USA	
	†VOA	S • S Europe • 250 kW
15185	**AUSTRALIA**	
	CVC, Darwin	W • SE Asia • 250 kW
	INDIA	
	ALL INDIA RADIO, Aligarh	E Africa • 250 kW
	ALL INDIA RADIO, Delhi	ENGLISH & HINDI • DS • 50/100 kW; DS • 50/100 kW
	USA	
	VOA, Greenville, NC	M-F • W Africa & C Africa • 250 kW
	VOA, Via Philippines	SE Asia & S Pacific • 50 kW; S • SE Asia & S Pacific • 50 kW
	VATICAN STATE	
	VATICAN RADIO, Sta Maria di Galeria	S • Mideast & W Asia • 250 kW • ALT. FREQ. TO 9585 kHz; S • E Europe & W Asia • 250 kW • ALT. FREQ. TO 9585 kHz

ENGLISH ▬ ARABIC ▦ CHINESE ▫▫▫ FRENCH ═ GERMAN ═ RUSSIAN ═ SPANISH ═ OTHER —

kHz	Country	Station	Schedule (World Time 0–24)
15190	BRAZIL	R INCONFIDENCIA, Belo Horizonte	DS-TEMP INACTIVE
	CHINA	CHINA R INTL, Kashi	S Asia • 100 kW
	CHINA (TAIWAN)	†R TAIWAN INTL, Via Okeechobee, USA	S • S America • 100 kW
	CUBA	RADIO HABANA CUBA, Havana	S America • 100 kW
	EQUATORIAL GUINEA	RADIO AFRICA, Bata	M-F • S Africa • 50 kW; M-F • ENGLISH & FRENCH • W Africa • 50 kW; Irr • M-F • S Africa • 50 kW; M-F • W Africa • 50 kW; Irr • M-F • W Africa • 50 kW
		RADIO EAST AFRICA, Bata	Sa/Su • E Africa • 50 kW; Su • E Africa • 50 kW
	IRAN	VO THE ISLAMIC REP, Tehrān	S • E Asia • 500 kW
	JAPAN	†RADIO JAPAN, Via Wertachtal, Germany	W Asia • 500 kW
	PHILIPPINES	RADYO PILIPINAS, Tinang	Mideast • 250 kW
	USA	†FAMILY RADIO, Okeechobee, Fl	S • S America • 100 kW
		VOA, Via Iranawila, Sri Lanka	W • E Asia • 250 kW
15195	JAPAN	RADIO JAPAN, Tokyo-Yamata	E Asia • 300 kW; SE Asia • 300 kW
	PORTUGAL	†RDP INTERNATIONAL, Lisbon	S • C Africa & S Africa • 300 kW; S Sa/Su • C Africa & S Africa • 300 kW
	ROMANIA	†R ROMANIA INTL, Galbeni	S • S Europe • 300 kW
	RUSSIA	VOICE OF RUSSIA, Chita	W • S Asia • 500 kW
	SPAIN	†R EXTERIOR ESPANA, Noblejas	W M-F • Europe • 250 kW
	USA	ADVENTIST WORLD R, Via Austria	S • S Asia • 300 kW
		†FAMILY RADIO, Via Ascension	C Africa • 250 kW; W • C Africa • 250 kW; S • C Africa • 250 kW • ALT. FREQ. TO 12055 kHz
		RFE-RL, Via Woofferton, UK	S • W Asia & C Asia • 250 kW
		VOA, Via Biblis, Germany	S • S Asia • 100 kW
15200	IRAN	VO THE ISLAMIC REP, Sirjan	SE Asia • 500 kW
	USA	TRANS WORLD R, Via Merizo, Guam	SE Asia • 100 kW
15205	GERMANY	†DEUTSCHE WELLE, Multiple Locations	S • C Africa, E Africa & S Africa • 250/500 kW
		†DEUTSCHE WELLE, Via Dhabayya, UAE	← • E Europe • 250 kW
		DEUTSCHE WELLE, Via Kigali, Rwanda	S • W Africa • 250 kW
	SAUDI ARABIA	BS OF THE KINGDOM, Riyadh	W Europe • DS-HOLY KORAN • 500 kW
	UNITED KINGDOM	BBC, Woofferton	S • W Asia & C Asia • 250 kW
		FEBA RADIO, Via Dhabayya, UAE	W • S Asia • 250 kW
	USA	ADVENTIST WORLD R, Via Germany	S • W Africa • 100 kW
		PAN AM BC, Via Nauen, Germany	S Sa • Mideast & W Asia • 250 kW; S Tu • W Asia • 250 kW; S Su • S Asia • 250 kW
		RFE-RL, Via Udon Thani, Thailand	S • W Asia & C Asia • 250 kW
		RFE-RL, Via Wertachtal,Germany	S • W Asia & C Asia • 250 kW
		SSIRI, Via Dhabayya, UAE	M-F • C Africa • 250 kW
		VOA, Via Iranawila, Sri Lanka	S • S Asia • 250 kW
		VOA, Via Lampertheim, Germany	S M-F • E Europe & Mideast • 100 kW; W • S Asia & C Asia • 100 kW
		VOA, Via Philippines	W • SE Asia • 50 kW; SE Asia • 50 kW
		VOA, Via Woofferton, UK	S • W Asia & C Asia • 250 kW
15210	CHINA	CHINA R INTL, Kashi	W • S Asia • 100 kW
		CHINA R INTL, Kunming	Australasia • 500 kW
	KOREA (REPUBLIC)	KBS WORLD R, In-Kimjae	Mideast • 250 kW
	USA	FAMILY RADIO, Okeechobee, Fl	W • S America • 100 kW

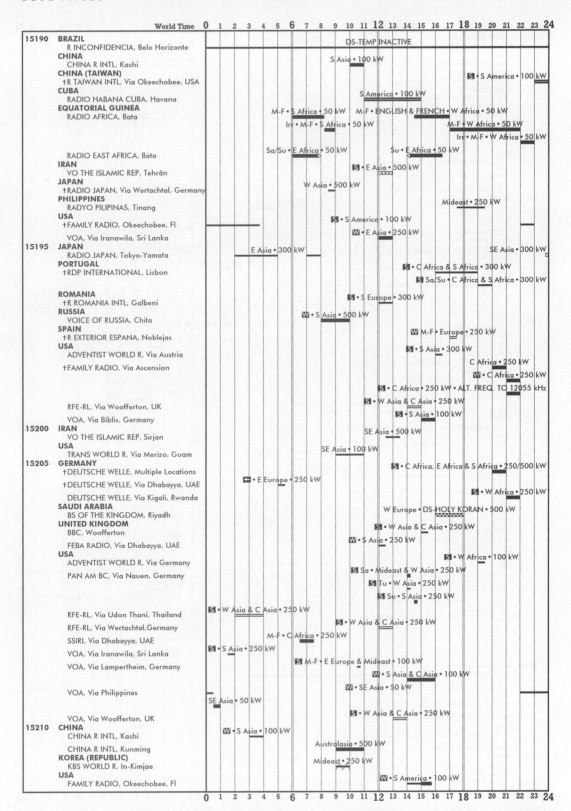

SEASONAL S OR W   1-HR TIMESHIFT MIDYEAR ← OR →   JAMMING / OR ∧   EARLIEST HEARD ◁   LATEST HEARD ▷   NEW FOR 2009 †

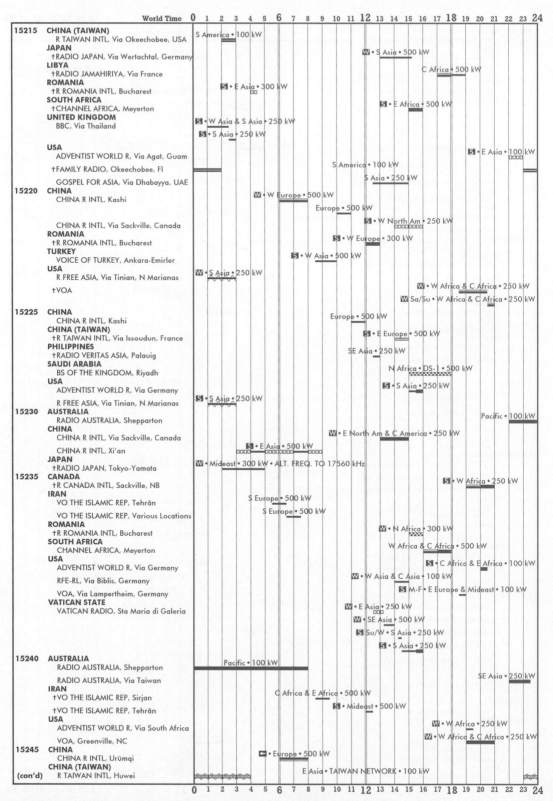

World Time 0 1 2 3 4 5 6 7 8 9 10 11 12 13 14 15 16 17 18 19 20 21 22 23 24

kHz	Country / Station	Schedule
15215	**CHINA (TAIWAN)**	
	R TAIWAN INTL, Via Okeechobee, USA	S America • 100 kW
	JAPAN	
	†RADIO JAPAN, Via Wertachtal, Germany	W • S Asia • 500 kW
	LIBYA	
	†RADIO JAMAHIRIYA, Via France	C Africa • 500 kW
	ROMANIA	
	†R ROMANIA INTL, Bucharest	S • E Asia • 300 kW
	SOUTH AFRICA	
	†CHANNEL AFRICA, Meyerton	S • E Africa • 500 kW
	UNITED KINGDOM	
	BBC, Via Thailand	S • W Asia & S Asia • 250 kW
		S • S Asia • 250 kW
	USA	
	ADVENTIST WORLD R, Via Agat, Guam	S • E Asia • 100 kW
	†FAMILY RADIO, Okeechobee, Fl	S America • 100 kW
	GOSPEL FOR ASIA, Via Dhabayya, UAE	S Asia • 250 kW
15220	**CHINA**	
	CHINA R INTL, Kashi	W • W Europe • 500 kW
		Europe • 500 kW
	CHINA R INTL, Via Sackville, Canada	S • W North Am • 250 kW
	ROMANIA	
	†R ROMANIA INTL, Bucharest	S • W Europe • 300 kW
	TURKEY	
	VOICE OF TURKEY, Ankara-Emirler	S • W Asia • 500 kW
	USA	
	R FREE ASIA, Via Tinian, N Marianas	W • S Asia • 250 kW
	†VOA	W • W Africa & C Africa • 250 kW
		W Sa/Su • W Africa & C Africa • 250 kW
15225	**CHINA**	
	CHINA R INTL, Kashi	Europe • 500 kW
	CHINA (TAIWAN)	
	†R TAIWAN INTL, Via Issoudun, France	S • E Europe • 500 kW
	PHILIPPINES	
	†RADIO VERITAS ASIA, Palauig	SE Asia • 250 kW
	SAUDI ARABIA	
	BS OF THE KINGDOM, Riyadh	N Africa • DS-1 • 500 kW
	USA	
	ADVENTIST WORLD R, Via Germany	S • S Asia • 250 kW
	R FREE ASIA, Via Tinian, N Marianas	S • S Asia • 250 kW
15230	**AUSTRALIA**	
	RADIO AUSTRALIA, Shepparton	Pacific • 100 kW
	CHINA	
	CHINA R INTL, Via Sackville, Canada	W • E North Am & C America • 250 kW
	CHINA R INTL, Xi'an	S • E Asia • 500 kW
	JAPAN	
	†RADIO JAPAN, Tokyo-Yamata	W • Mideast • 300 kW • ALT. FREQ. TO 17560 kHz
15235	**CANADA**	
	†R CANADA INTL, Sackville, NB	S • W Africa • 250 kW
	IRAN	
	VO THE ISLAMIC REP, Tehrān	S Europe • 500 kW
	VO THE ISLAMIC REP, Various Locations	S Europe • 500 kW
	ROMANIA	
	†R ROMANIA INTL, Bucharest	W • N Africa • 300 kW
	SOUTH AFRICA	
	CHANNEL AFRICA, Meyerton	W Africa & C Africa • 500 kW
	USA	
	ADVENTIST WORLD R, Via Germany	S • C Africa & E Africa • 100 kW
	RFE-RL, Via Biblis, Germany	W • W Asia & C Asia • 100 kW
	VOA, Via Lampertheim, Germany	S M-F • E Europe & Mideast • 100 kW
	VATICAN STATE	
	VATICAN RADIO, Sta Maria di Galeria	W • E Asia • 250 kW
		W • SE Asia • 500 kW
		S Su/W • S Asia • 250 kW
		S • S Asia • 250 kW
15240	**AUSTRALIA**	
	RADIO AUSTRALIA, Shepparton	Pacific • 100 kW
	RADIO AUSTRALIA, Via Taiwan	SE Asia • 250 kW
	IRAN	
	†VO THE ISLAMIC REP, Sirjan	C Africa & E Africa • 500 kW
	†VO THE ISLAMIC REP, Tehrān	S • Mideast • 500 kW
	USA	
	ADVENTIST WORLD R, Via South Africa	W • W Africa • 250 kW
	VOA, Greenville, NC	W • W Africa & C Africa • 250 kW
15245	**CHINA**	
	CHINA R INTL, Urümqi	• Europe • 500 kW
	CHINA (TAIWAN)	
(con'd)	R TAIWAN INTL, Huwei	E Asia • TAIWAN NETWORK • 100 kW

0 1 2 3 4 5 6 7 8 9 10 11 12 13 14 15 16 17 18 19 20 21 22 23 24

ENGLISH ARABIC CHINESE FRENCH GERMAN RUSSIAN SPANISH OTHER

World Time 0 1 2 3 4 5 6 7 8 9 10 11 12 13 14 15 16 17 18 19 20 21 22 23 24

kHz	Country / Station	Schedule
15245 (con'd)	**KOREA (DPR)**	
	KOREAN CENTRAL BS	S • W Europe
	PYONGYANG BC STN	E Europe
	VOICE OF KOREA	E Europe; S • W Europe
	UNITED KINGDOM	
	BBC, Via A'Seela, Oman	W • S Asia • 250 kW
	BBC, Woofferton	S M-F • E Europe & W Asia • 250 kW; S • E Europe & W Asia • 250 kW; S Sa/Su • E Europe & W Asia • 250 kW
15250	**AUSTRALIA**	
	CVC, Darwin	SE Asia • 250 kW; W • E Asia • 250 kW
	CHINA	
	CHINA R INTL, Kunming	SE Asia • 100 kW
	ROMANIA	
	†R ROMANIA INTL, Galbeni	S • W Europe • 300 kW
	†RADIO ROMANIA, Galbeni	S Su • W Europe • 300 kW
	SAUDI ARABIA	
	†BS OF THE KINGDOM, Riyadh	W Africa & C Africa • 500 kW
	USA	
	RFE-RL, Via Philippines	W • E Asia • 250 kW
	VOA, Via Philippines	S • E Asia • 250 kW
	WWRB, Manchester, Tennessee	• Africa • 100 kW
	VENEZUELA	
	RADIO NACIONAL, Via Havana, Cuba	C America • 100 kW
15255	**CZECH REPUBLIC**	
	RADIO PRAGUE, Litomyšl	W • W Europe • 100 kW
	ROMANIA	
	†R ROMANIA INTL, Bucharest	W • W Europe • 300 kW
	SOUTH AFRICA	
	CHANNEL AFRICA, Meyerton	W Africa & C Africa • 500 kW
	USA	
	ADVENTIST WORLD R, Via Agat, Guam	W • S Asia • 100 kW
	FAMILY RADIO, Okeechobee, Fl	S • S America • 100 kW
	R FARDA, Via Iranawila, Sri Lanka	S • W Asia • 250 kW
	†RFE-RL	S • W Asia & C Asia • 250 kW
15260	**CHINA**	
	CHINA R INTL, Via Sackville, Canada	S • W North Am • 250 kW
	CLANDESTINE (ASIA)	
	†"MOJ THEM RADIO", Via Taiwan	M/W/F • SE Asia • 100 kW
	INDIA	
	ALL INDIA RADIO, Delhi	DS • 50 kW; ENGLISH & HINDI • DS • 50 kW; S Asia • 50 kW
	IRAN	
	VO THE ISLAMIC REP, Sirjan	W Asia • 500 kW
	VO THE ISLAMIC REP, Tehrān	W • C Africa & E Africa • 500 kW
	ROMANIA	
	†RADIO ROMANIA, Galbeni	S Su • Mideast • 300 kW; W Su • W Europe • 300 kW
	USA	
	ADVENTIST WORLD R, Via Agat, Guam	W • E Asia • 100 kW; W • SE Asia • 100 kW
	ADVENTIST WORLD R, Via Germany	S • N Africa • 100 kW; S Th-Tu • N Africa • 100 kW; S • C Africa • 100 kW; S W • N Africa • 100 kW
	FAMILY RADIO, Via Meyerton, S Africa	S • S Africa • 250 kW
	†HAIV HMOOB RADIO, Via Taiwan	Tu • SE Asia • 100 kW
	†HMONG LAO RADIO, Via Taiwan	Th/Su • SE Asia • 100 kW
	†HMONG WORLD CHRIST R, Via Taiwan	Sa • SE Asia • 100 kW
15265	**CLANDESTINE (ASIA)**	
	"RADIO SOLH", Via Rampisham, UK	W • W Asia & C Asia • 500 kW
	FRANCE	
	†R FRANCE INTL, Via Taiwan	M-F • SE Asia • 250 kW; SE Asia • 250 kW
	IRAN	
	†VO THE ISLAMIC REP, Sirjan	S • C Africa & E Africa • 500 kW
	JAPAN	
	†RADIO JAPAN, Via Netherlands Antilles	S • S America • 250 kW
	USA	
	ADVENTIST WORLD R, Via Austria	S • Mideast • 300 kW
	VOA, Greenville, NC	W • S America • 250 kW; W M-F • C America • 250 kW
(con'd)		

World Time 0 1 2 3 4 5 6 7 8 9 10 11 12 13 14 15 16 17 18 19 20 21 22 23 24

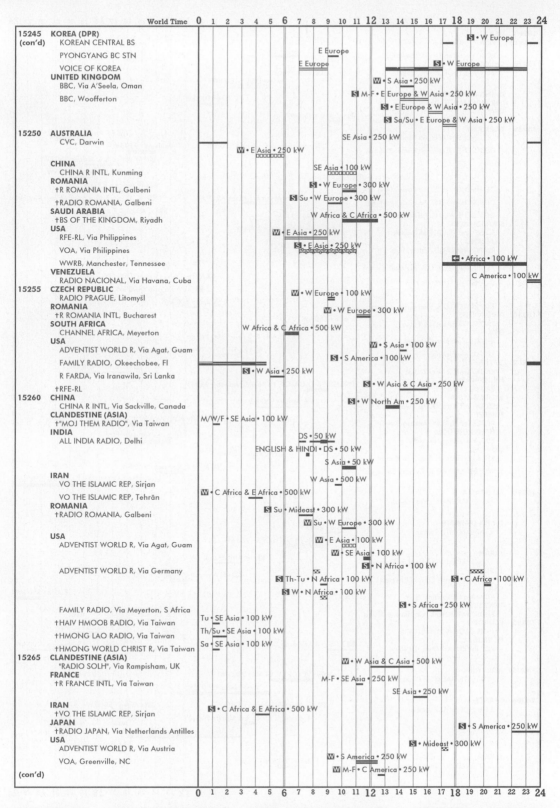

World Time 0 1 2 3 4 5 6 7 8 9 10 11 12 13 14 15 16 17 18 19 20 21 22 23 24

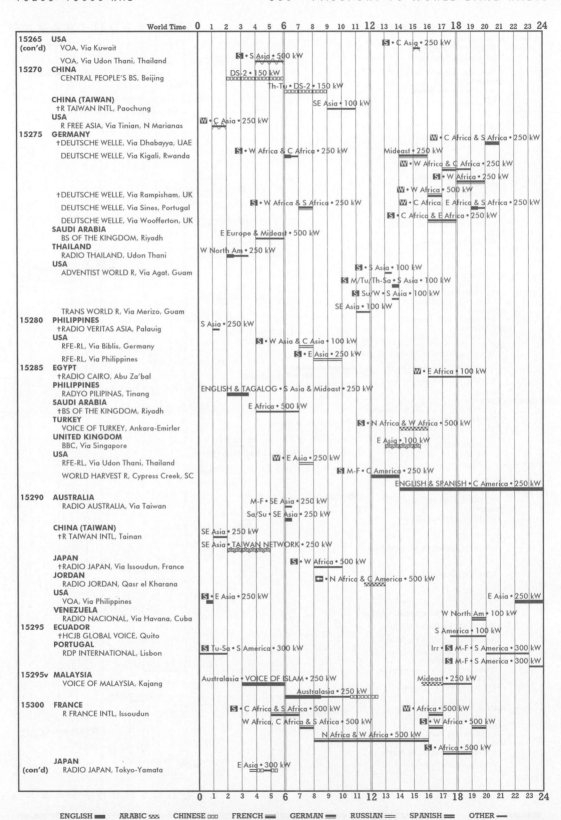

kHz	Country / Station	Schedule
15265 (con'd)	**USA** VOA, Via Kuwait	S • C Asia • 250 kW
	VOA, Via Udon Thani, Thailand	S • S Asia • 500 kW
15270	**CHINA** CENTRAL PEOPLE'S BS, Beijing	DS-2 • 150 kW
		Th-Tu • DS-2 • 150 kW
	CHINA (TAIWAN) †R TAIWAN INTL, Paochung	SE Asia • 100 kW
	USA R FREE ASIA, Via Tinian, N Marianas	W • C Asia • 250 kW
15275	**GERMANY** †DEUTSCHE WELLE, Via Dhabayya, UAE	W • C Africa & S Africa • 250 kW
	DEUTSCHE WELLE, Via Kigali, Rwanda	S • W Africa & C Africa • 250 kW
		Mideast • 250 kW
		W • W Africa & C Africa • 250 kW
		S • W Africa • 250 kW
	†DEUTSCHE WELLE, Via Rampisham, UK	W • W Africa • 500 kW
	DEUTSCHE WELLE, Via Sines, Portugal	S • W Africa & S Africa • 250 kW
		W • C Africa, E Africa & S Africa • 250 kW
	DEUTSCHE WELLE, Via Woofferton, UK	S • C Africa & E Africa • 250 kW
	SAUDI ARABIA BS OF THE KINGDOM, Riyadh	E Europe & Mideast • 500 kW
	THAILAND RADIO THAILAND, Udon Thani	W North Am • 250 kW
	USA ADVENTIST WORLD R, Via Agat, Guam	S • S Asia • 100 kW
		S M/Tu/Th-Sa • S Asia • 100 kW
		S Su/W • S Asia • 100 kW
	TRANS WORLD R, Via Merizo, Guam	SE Asia • 100 kW
15280	**PHILIPPINES** †RADIO VERITAS ASIA, Palauig	S Asia • 250 kW
	USA RFE-RL, Via Biblis, Germany	S • W Asia & C Asia • 100 kW
	RFE-RL, Via Philippines	S • E Asia • 250 kW
15285	**EGYPT** †RADIO CAIRO, Abu Za'bal	W • E Africa • 100 kW
	PHILIPPINES RADYO PILIPINAS, Tinang	ENGLISH & TAGALOG • S Asia & Mideast • 250 kW
	SAUDI ARABIA †BS OF THE KINGDOM, Riyadh	E Africa • 500 kW
	TURKEY VOICE OF TURKEY, Ankara-Emirler	S • N Africa & W Africa • 500 kW
	UNITED KINGDOM BBC, Via Singapore	E Asia • 100 kW
	USA RFE-RL, Via Udon Thani, Thailand	W • E Asia • 250 kW
	WORLD HARVEST R, Cypress Creek, SC	S M-F • C America • 250 kW
		ENGLISH & SPANISH • C America • 250 kW
15290	**AUSTRALIA** RADIO AUSTRALIA, Via Taiwan	M-F • SE Asia • 250 kW
		Sa/Su • SE Asia • 250 kW
	CHINA (TAIWAN) †R TAIWAN INTL, Tainan	SE Asia • 250 kW
		SE Asia • TAIWAN NETWORK • 250 kW
	JAPAN †RADIO JAPAN, Via Issoudun, France	S • W Africa • 500 kW
	JORDAN RADIO JORDAN, Qasr el Kharana	◄ • N Africa & C America • 500 kW
	USA VOA, Via Philippines	S • E Asia • 250 kW
		E Asia • 250 kW
	VENEZUELA RADIO NACIONAL, Via Havana, Cuba	W North Am • 100 kW
15295	**ECUADOR** †HCJB GLOBAL VOICE, Quito	S America • 100 kW
	PORTUGAL RDP INTERNATIONAL, Lisbon	S Tu-Sa • S America • 300 kW
		Irr • S M-F • S America • 300 kW
		S M-F • S America • 300 kW
15295v	**MALAYSIA** VOICE OF MALAYSIA, Kajang	Australasia • VOICE OF ISLAM • 250 kW
		Mideast • 250 kW
		Australasia • 250 kW
15300	**FRANCE** R FRANCE INTL, Issoudun	S • C Africa & S Africa • 500 kW
		W • Africa • 500 kW
		W Africa, C Africa & S Africa • 500 kW
		S • W Africa • 500 kW
		N Africa & W Africa • 500 kW
		S • Africa • 500 kW
	JAPAN (con'd) RADIO JAPAN, Tokyo-Yamata	E Asia • 300 kW

World Time 0 1 2 3 4 5 6 7 8 9 10 11 12 13 14 15 16 17 18 19 20 21 22 23 24

ENGLISH ▬ ARABIC ▬ CHINESE ▭ FRENCH ═ GERMAN ▬ RUSSIAN ═ SPANISH ═ OTHER —

kHz	Country / Station	World Time 0–24
15300 (con'd)	**USA**	
	ADVENTIST WORLD R, Via Agat, Guam	S • E Asia • 100 kW
15305	**CANADA**	
	R CANADA INTL, Sackville, NB	W F-Su • S America • 250 kW
15310	**UNITED KINGDOM**	
	†BBC, Various Locations	S Asia • 250 kW
	BBC, Via A'Seela, Oman	S Asia • 250 kW; S • S Asia • 250 kW
	†BBC, Via Thailand	S Asia • 250 kW
	USA	
	WORLD HARVEST R, Greenbush, Maine	S • Europe • 250 kW
15315	**FRANCE**	
	R FRANCE INTL, Issoudun	W • W Africa & C Africa • 500 kW • ALT. FREQ. TO 9805 kHz; S • W Africa & C Africa • 500 kW; W • W Africa & C Africa • 500 kW • ALT. FREQ. TO 11700 kHz
	NETHERLANDS	
	†R NEDERLAND, Via Neth Antilles	W • S America • 250 kW
	USA	
	ADVENTIST WORLD R, Via Austria	S • C Africa • 300 kW
15320	**CANADA**	
	†R CANADA INTL, Via Skelton, UK	S • N Africa & W Africa • 300 kW
	CHINA (TAIWAN)	
	†R TAIWAN INTL, Paochung	SE Asia • 100 kW
	IRAN	
	VO THE ISLAMIC REP, Sirjan	W • S Europe & N Africa • 500 kW
	USA	
	ADVENTIST WORLD R, Via Agat, Guam	S • SE Asia • 100 kW; SE Asia • 100 kW
	ADVENTIST WORLD R, Via Germany	S M-F • C Asia • 250 kW; S Sa/Su • C Asia • 250 kW; S • C Asia & E Asia • 250 kW
15325	**BRAZIL**	
	RADIO GAZETA, São Paulo	PORTUGUESE & SPANISH • DS • 1/10 kW
	CANADA	
	EGLISE DU CHRIST, Via Skelton, UK	S Th • N Africa • 300 kW
	R CANADA INTL, Via Rampisham, UK	S • E Europe & W Asia • 500 kW
	†R CANADA INTL, Via Woofferton, UK	S • E Europe & W Asia • 250 kW
	JAPAN	
	RADIO JAPAN, Tokyo-Yamata	S Asia • 300 kW
	SPAIN	
	†R EXTERIOR ESPANA, Noblejas	S M-F • Europe • 250 kW
	USA	
	SUDAN RADIO SVC, Various Locations	S M/Tu/Th/F • C Africa • 250/300 kW; S W • C Africa • 250/300 kW; S M-F • C Africa • 250/300 kW
15330	**CANADA**	
	†R CANADA INTL, Sackville, NB	S • N Africa • 250 kW
	PHILIPPINES	
	FEBC RADIO INTL, Bocaue	SE Asia • 100 kW • ALT. FREQ. TO 15355 kHz
	ROMANIA	
	†R ROMANIA INTL, Bucharest	W • Mideast • 300 kW
	UNITED KINGDOM	
	BBC, Via Zyyi, Cyprus	S • C Asia • 300 kW
	USA	
	RADIO MARTI, Greenville, NC	W • C America • 250 kW
15335	**AUSTRALIA**	
	CVC, Darwin	S Asia & SE Asia • 250 kW
	CHINA	
	CHINA R INTL, Kashi	W • E Europe & W Asia • 500 kW • ALT. FREQ. TO 15360 kHz
	NETHERLANDS	
	R NEDERLAND, Via Madagascar	S • Mideast • 250 kW
	†R NEDERLAND, Via Nauen, Germany	S • W Africa • 500 kW
	UNITED KINGDOM	
	BBC, Rampisham	S • E Europe & Mideast • 500 kW; S M-F • E Europe & Mideast • 500 kW
	†BBC, Via Singapore	SE Asia • 100 kW
15340	**CHINA**	
	CHINA R INTL, Xi'an	W • SE Asia • 500 kW
	FRANCE	
	R FRANCE INTL, Issoudun	S • W Asia & S Asia • 500 kW
	GERMANY	
	DEUTSCHE WELLE, Via Singapore	S • E Asia • 250 kW
	IRAN	
	VO THE ISLAMIC REP, Tehrān	S • C Africa & E Africa • 500 kW
	MOROCCO	
	RTV MAROCAINE, Nador	N Africa & Mideast • 250 kW • ALT. FREQ. TO 15345 kHz
	UNITED KINGDOM	
	†BBC, Via Singapore	S • SE Asia • 100 kW
	USA	
	FAMILY RADIO, Via Dhabayya, UAE	S • S Asia • 250 kW

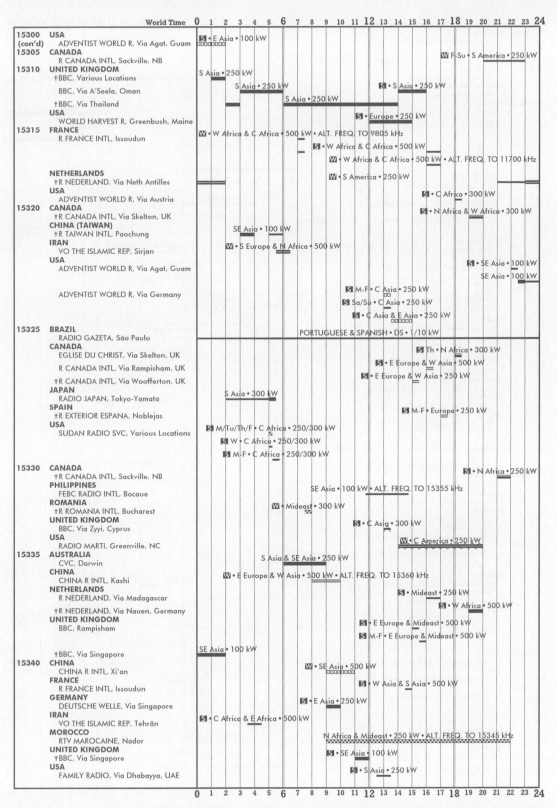

World Time 0 1 2 3 4 5 6 7 8 9 10 11 12 13 14 15 16 17 18 19 20 21 22 23 24

Frequency	Country / Station	Schedule
15345	**FRANCE** R FRANCE INTL, Issoudun	S • E Europe • 500 kW
	GERMANY DEUTSCHE WELLE, Via Singapore	S • S Asia • 100 kW
	MOROCCO RTV MAROCAINE, Nador	N Africa & Mideast • 250 kW • ALT. FREQ. TO 15340 kHz
	UNITED KINGDOM BBC, Via Thailand	W • W Asia & S Asia • 250 kW
15345v	**ARGENTINA** R ARGENTINA-RAE, Buenos Aires	M-F • Europe • 100 kW
	RADIO NACIONAL, Buenos Aires	Su/M • Americas • 100 kW; Su • Europe • 100 kW; M • Americas • 100 kW; Sa/Su • Europe • 100 kW
15350	**CHINA** CHINA R INTL, Kashi	S Asia • 100 kW; S Asia • 100/500 kW
	PHILIPPINES FEBC RADIO INTL, Bocaue	SE Asia • 100 kW
	TURKEY †VOICE OF TURKEY, Ankara-Emirler	W • W Europe • 500 kW
15355	**OMAN** R SULTANATE OF OMAN, Thamarīt	E Africa • DS • 100 kW; Europe & Mideast • DS • 100 kW
	PHILIPPINES FEBC RADIO INTL, Bocaue	SE Asia • 100 kW • ALT. FREQ. TO 15330 kHz
	USA FAMILY RADIO, Okeechobee, Fl	W • C America • 100 kW; W • S America • 100 kW
15360	**CHINA** CHINA R INTL, Kashi	W • E Europe & W Asia • 500 kW • ALT. FREQ. TO 15335 kHz; S • E Europe & W Asia • 500 kW
	CUBA †RADIO HABANA CUBA, Havana	S America • 100 kW • ALT. FREQ. TO 11805 kHz; Su • S America • 100 kW • ALT. FREQ. TO 11805 kHz
	GERMANY DEUTSCHE WELLE, Via Singapore	S • E Asia • 100 kW
	DEUTSCHE WELLE, Via Sri Lanka	S • E Asia • 250 kW
	KOREA (REPUBLIC) KBS WORLD R, Via Rampisham, UK	S • E Europe • 500 kW
	SOUTH AFRICA †CHANNEL AFRICA, Meyerton	S • E Africa • 250 kW
	UNITED KINGDOM †BBC, Via A'Seela, Oman	S • C Asia • 250 kW; C Asia • 250 kW
	†BBC, Via Thailand	E Asia • 250 kW
	USA ADVENTIST WORLD R, Via Austria	S • W Asia • 300 kW
15365	**AUSTRALIA** CVC, Darwin	W • SE Asia • 250 kW
	CANADA R CANADA INTL, Sackville, NB	W • W Africa & C Africa • 250 kW
	FRANCE R FRANCE INTL, Issoudun	S • C America • 500 kW • ALT. FREQ. TO 17800 kHz
	KOREA (REPUBLIC) KBS WORLD R, Via Rampisham, UK	S • N Africa • 500 kW
15370	**CHINA** CENTRAL PEOPLE'S BS, Shijiazhuang	DS-1 • 100 kW; W-M • DS-1 • 100 kW
	CUBA RADIO HABANA CUBA, Havana	E North Am • 100 kW
	ROMANIA †RADIO ROMANIA, Bucharest	W Su • Mideast • 300 kW
	USA ADVENTIST WORLD R, Via Agat, Guam	E Asia • 100 kW
	SIRIP, Via Dhabayya, UAE	Irr • W M/Tu/Th • E Africa • 250 kW
	†VOA	W • E Europe • 250 kW
15375	**OMAN** R SULTANATE OF OMAN, Sīb	E Africa • DS • 100 kW
	USA R FREE ASIA, Via Dhabayya, UAE	W • S Asia • 500 kW
15380	**CHINA** CENTRAL PEOPLE'S BS, Beijing	S • DS-1 • 100 kW; DS-1 • 100 kW; W-M • DS-1 • 100 kW
	PHILIPPINES FEBC RADIO INTL, Bocaue	SE Asia • 100 kW
	ROMANIA †R ROMANIA INTL, Bucharest	S • N Africa • 300 kW
(con'd)	†RADIO ROMANIA, Galbeni	W Su • N Africa & Mideast • 300 kW

World Time 0 1 2 3 4 5 6 7 8 9 10 11 12 13 14 15 16 17 18 19 20 21 22 23 24

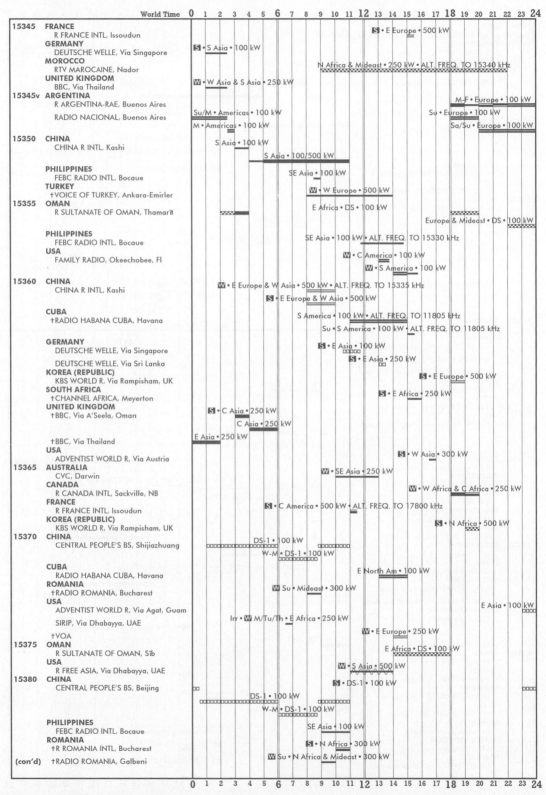

ENGLISH ARABIC CHINESE FRENCH GERMAN RUSSIAN SPANISH OTHER

kHz	Country / Station	World Time 0–24
15380 (con'd)	**ROMANIA**	
	†RADIO ROMANIA, Galbeni	Su • N Africa • 300 kW
	SAUDI ARABIA	
	BS OF THE KINGDOM, Riyadh	Mideast • DS-HOLY KORAN • 500 kW
	UNITED KINGDOM	
	BBC, Skelton, Cumbria	S • Mideast & W Asia • 300 kW
	BBC, Woofferton	S • Mideast & W Asia • 250 kW
	USA	
	†RFE-RL	S • E Europe • 250 kW
15385	**SPAIN**	
	†R EXTERIOR ESPANA, Noblejas	S M • N Africa & Mideast • 250 kW
		M-Sa • W Africa & C Africa • 250 kW
	USA	
	KJES, Vado, New Mexico	• Australasia • 50 kW
		• C America • 50 kW
	SIRIP, Via Dhabayya, UAE	Irr • W M/Tu/Th • E Africa • 250 kW
	VOA, Via Philippines	S • E Asia • 250 kW
15390	**CHINA**	
	CENTRAL PEOPLE'S BS, Lingshi	S • DS-8 (MINORITIES) • 100 kW
		DS-8 (MINORITIES) • 100 kW
		DS-1 • 100 kW
		W-M • DS-8 (MINORITIES) • 100 kW
		W-M • DS-1 • 100 kW
	IRAN	
	VO THE ISLAMIC REP, Tehrān	W • Mideast • 500 kW
	TURKEY	
	†VOICE OF TURKEY, Ankara-Emirler	S • Australasia • 500 kW
	USA	
	VOA, Greenville, NC	S M-F • C America • 250 kW
		S • C America • 250 kW
	†VOA	S • Mideast • 250 kW
	VOA, Via Kuwait	C Asia • 250 kW
15395	**JAPAN**	
	†RADIO JAPAN, Via Issoudun, France	W • W Africa • 500 kW
	USA	
	R FREE ASIA, Via Tinian, N Marianas	W • SE Asia • 250 kW
	VOA, Via Philippines	W • E Asia • 250 kW
15400	**AUSTRALIA**	
	†HCJB AUSTRALIA, Kununurra	E Asia • 100 kW
		M-F • E Asia • 100 kW
		Sa/Su • E Asia • 100 kW
	GERMANY	
	†DEUTSCHE WELLE, Via Sri Lanka	S • C Africa • 250 kW
	JAPAN	
	†RADIO JAPAN, Via Issoudun, France	S • W Africa • 500 kW
	UNITED KINGDOM	
	BBC, Skelton, Cumbria	S • N Africa • 300 kW
	BBC, Various Locations	E Africa • 250 kW
	†BBC, Via Ascension	W Africa • 250 kW
		Sa/Su • W Africa • 250 kW
	BBC, Via Seychelles	S Sa • E Africa • 250 kW
		S Sa/Su • E Africa • 250 kW
	USA	
	ADVENTIST WORLD R, Via Austria	S • S Asia • 300 kW
	FAMILY RADIO, Okeechobee, Fl	W • S America • 100 kW
15405	**AUSTRALIA**	
	†HCJB AUSTRALIA, Kununurra	SE Asia • 100 kW
	RUSSIA	
	VOICE OF RUSSIA, Novosibirsk	S • S Asia • 500 kW
	UNITED KINGDOM	
	BBC, Via Thailand	S Asia • 250 kW
15410	**CHILE**	
	CVC-LA VOZ, Santiago	W • S America • 100 kW
		S America • 100 kW
	GERMANY	
	DEUTSCHE WELLE, Via Kigali, Rwanda	W • W Africa & C Africa • 250 kW
		E Africa & S Africa • 250 kW
		W • C Africa & E Africa • 250 kW
		S • W Africa & C Africa • 250 kW
		W Africa & C Africa • 250 kW
	DEUTSCHE WELLE, Via South Africa	S • E Africa • 250 kW
(con'd)	**INDIA**	
	ALL INDIA RADIO, Bangalore	E Asia • 500 kW • ALT. FREQ. TO 15135 kHz

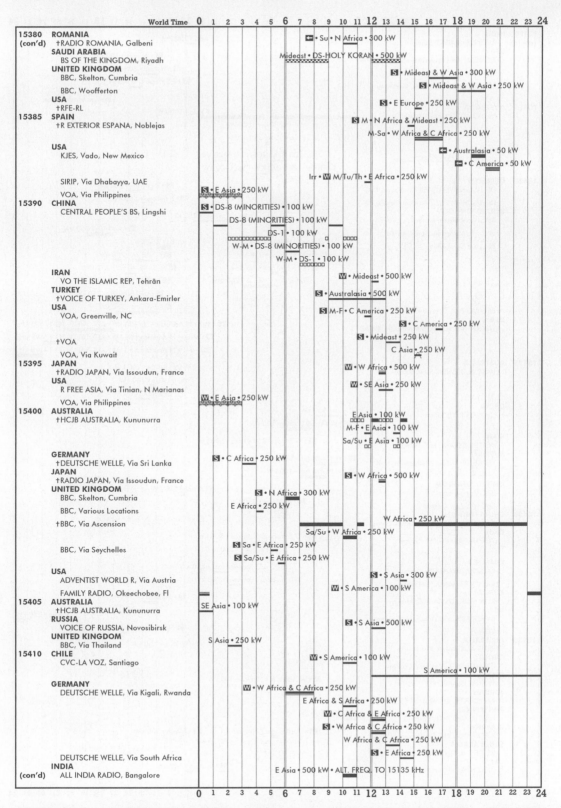

SEASONAL S OR W 1-HR TIMESHIFT MIDYEAR OR JAMMING / OR /\ EARLIEST HEARD ◁ LATEST HEARD ▷ NEW FOR 2009 †

World Time 0 1 2 3 4 5 6 7 8 9 10 11 12 13 14 15 16 17 18 19 20 21 22 23 24

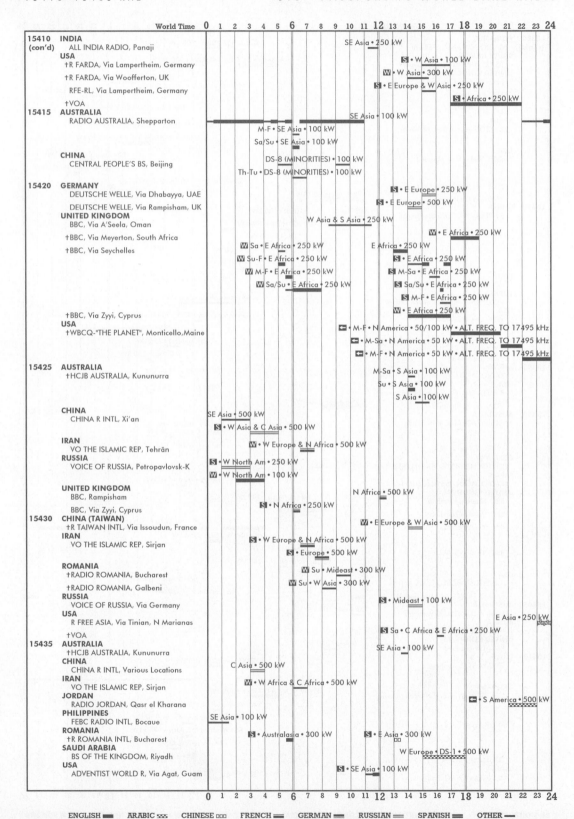

Frequency	Country / Station	Schedule
15410 (con'd)	**INDIA** ALL INDIA RADIO, Panaji	SE Asia • 250 kW
	USA †R FARDA, Via Lampertheim, Germany	S • W Asia • 100 kW
	†R FARDA, Via Woofferton, UK	W • W Asia • 300 kW
	RFE-RL, Via Lampertheim, Germany	S • E Europe & W Asia • 250 kW
	†VOA	S • Africa • 250 kW
15415	**AUSTRALIA** RADIO AUSTRALIA, Shepparton	SE Asia • 100 kW M-F • SE Asia • 100 kW Sa/Su • SE Asia • 100 kW
	CHINA CENTRAL PEOPLE'S BS, Beijing	DS-8 (MINORITIES) • 100 kW Th-Tu • DS-8 (MINORITIES) • 100 kW
15420	**GERMANY** DEUTSCHE WELLE, Via Dhabayya, UAE	S • E Europe • 250 kW
	DEUTSCHE WELLE, Via Rampisham, UK	S • E Europe • 500 kW
	UNITED KINGDOM BBC, Via A'Seela, Oman	W Asia & S Asia • 250 kW
	†BBC, Via Meyerton, South Africa	W • E Africa • 250 kW
	†BBC, Via Seychelles	W Sa • E Africa • 250 kW E Africa • 250 kW W Su-F • E Africa • 250 kW S • E Africa • 250 kW W M-F • E Africa • 250 kW S M-Sa • E Africa • 250 kW W Sa/Su • E Africa • 250 kW S Sa/Su • E Africa • 250 kW S M-F • E Africa • 250 kW
	†BBC, Via Zyyi, Cyprus	W • E Africa • 250 kW
	USA †WBCQ-"THE PLANET", Monticello, Maine	← • M-F • N America • 50/100 kW • ALT. FREQ. TO 17495 kHz ← • M-Sa • N America • 50 kW • ALT. FREQ. TO 17495 kHz ← • M-F • N America • 50 kW • ALT. FREQ. TO 17495 kHz
15425	**AUSTRALIA** †HCJB AUSTRALIA, Kununurra	M-Sa • S Asia • 100 kW Su • S Asia • 100 kW S Asia • 100 kW
	CHINA CHINA R INTL, Xi'an	SE Asia • 500 kW S • W Asia & C Asia • 500 kW
	IRAN VO THE ISLAMIC REP, Tehrān	W • W Europe & N Africa • 500 kW
	RUSSIA VOICE OF RUSSIA, Petropavlovsk-K	S • W North Am • 250 kW W • W North Am • 100 kW
	UNITED KINGDOM BBC, Rampisham	N Africa • 500 kW
	BBC, Via Zyyi, Cyprus	S • N Africa • 250 kW
15430	**CHINA (TAIWAN)** †R TAIWAN INTL, Via Issoudun, France	W • E Europe & W Asia • 500 kW
	IRAN VO THE ISLAMIC REP, Sirjan	S • W Europe & N Africa • 500 kW S • Europe • 500 kW
	ROMANIA †RADIO ROMANIA, Bucharest	W Su • Mideast • 300 kW
	†RADIO ROMANIA, Galbeni	W Su • W Asia • 300 kW
	RUSSIA VOICE OF RUSSIA, Via Germany	S • Mideast • 100 kW
	USA R FREE ASIA, Via Tinian, N Marianas	E Asia • 250 kW
	†VOA	S Sa • C Africa & E Africa • 250 kW
15435	**AUSTRALIA** †HCJB AUSTRALIA, Kununurra	SE Asia • 100 kW
	CHINA CHINA R INTL, Various Locations	C Asia • 500 kW
	IRAN VO THE ISLAMIC REP, Sirjan	W • W Africa & C Africa • 500 kW
	JORDAN RADIO JORDAN, Qasr el Kharana	← • S America • 500 kW
	PHILIPPINES FEBC RADIO INTL, Bocaue	SE Asia • 100 kW
	ROMANIA †R ROMANIA INTL, Bucharest	S • Australasia • 300 kW S • E Asia • 300 kW
	SAUDI ARABIA BS OF THE KINGDOM, Riyadh	W Europe • DS-1 • 500 kW
	USA ADVENTIST WORLD R, Via Agat, Guam	S • SE Asia • 100 kW

0 1 2 3 4 5 6 7 8 9 10 11 12 13 14 15 16 17 18 19 20 21 22 23 24

ENGLISH ARABIC CHINESE FRENCH GERMAN RUSSIAN SPANISH OTHER

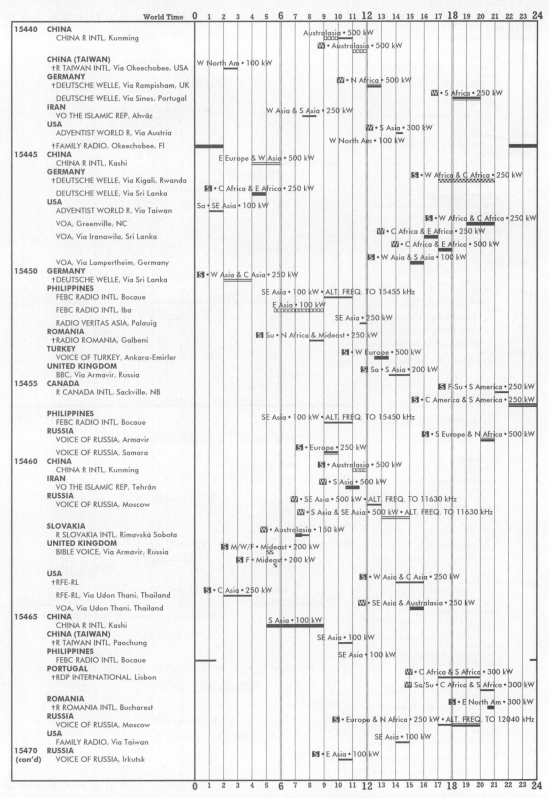

World Time 0 1 2 3 4 5 6 7 8 9 10 11 12 13 14 15 16 17 18 19 20 21 22 23 24

kHz	Country / Station	Schedule
15440	**CHINA**	
	CHINA R INTL, Kunming	Australasia • 500 kW
		W • Australasia • 500 kW
	CHINA (TAIWAN)	
	†R TAIWAN INTL, Via Okeechobee, USA	W North Am • 100 kW
	GERMANY	
	†DEUTSCHE WELLE, Via Rampisham, UK	W • N Africa • 500 kW
	DEUTSCHE WELLE, Via Sines, Portugal	W • S Africa • 250 kW
	IRAN	
	VO THE ISLAMIC REP, Ahvāz	W Asia & S Asia • 250 kW
	USA	
	ADVENTIST WORLD R, Via Austria	W • S Asia • 300 kW
	†FAMILY RADIO, Okeechobee, Fl	W North Am • 100 kW
15445	**CHINA**	
	CHINA R INTL, Kashi	E Europe & W Asia • 500 kW
	GERMANY	
	†DEUTSCHE WELLE, Via Kigali, Rwanda	S • W Africa & C Africa • 250 kW
	DEUTSCHE WELLE, Via Sri Lanka	S • C Africa & E Africa • 250 kW
	USA	
	ADVENTIST WORLD R, Via Taiwan	Sa • SE Asia • 100 kW
	VOA, Greenville, NC	S • W Africa & C Africa • 250 kW
	VOA, Via Iranawila, Sri Lanka	W • C Africa & E Africa • 250 kW
		W • C Africa & E Africa • 500 kW
	VOA, Via Lampertheim, Germany	S • W Asia & S Asia • 100 kW
15450	**GERMANY**	
	†DEUTSCHE WELLE, Via Sri Lanka	S • W Asia & C Asia • 250 kW
	PHILIPPINES	
	FEBC RADIO INTL, Bocaue	SE Asia • 100 kW • ALT. FREQ. TO 15455 kHz
	FEBC RADIO INTL, Iba	E Asia • 100 kW
	RADIO VERITAS ASIA, Palauig	SE Asia • 250 kW
	ROMANIA	
	†RADIO ROMANIA, Galbeni	S Su • N Africa & Mideast • 250 kW
	TURKEY	
	VOICE OF TURKEY, Ankara-Emirler	S • W Europe • 500 kW
	UNITED KINGDOM	
	BBC, Via Armavir, Russia	S Sa • S Asia • 200 kW
15455	**CANADA**	
	R CANADA INTL, Sackville, NB	S F-Su • S America • 250 kW
		S • C America & S America • 250 kW
	PHILIPPINES	
	FEBC RADIO INTL, Bocaue	SE Asia • 100 kW • ALT. FREQ. TO 15450 kHz
	RUSSIA	
	VOICE OF RUSSIA, Armavir	S • S Europe & N Africa • 500 kW
	VOICE OF RUSSIA, Samara	S • Europe • 250 kW
15460	**CHINA**	
	CHINA R INTL, Kunming	S • Australasia • 500 kW
	IRAN	
	VO THE ISLAMIC REP, Tehrān	W • S Asia • 500 kW
	RUSSIA	
	VOICE OF RUSSIA, Moscow	W • SE Asia • 500 kW • ALT. FREQ. TO 11630 kHz
		W • S Asia & SE Asia • 500 kW • ALT. FREQ. TO 11630 kHz
	SLOVAKIA	
	R SLOVAKIA INTL, Rimavská Sobota	W • Australasia • 150 kW
	UNITED KINGDOM	
	BIBLE VOICE, Via Armavir, Russia	S M/W/F • Mideast • 200 kW
		S F • Mideast • 200 kW
	USA	
	†RFE-RL	S • W Asia & C Asia • 250 kW
	RFE-RL, Via Udon Thani, Thailand	S • C Asia • 250 kW
	VOA, Via Udon Thani, Thailand	W • SE Asia & Australasia • 250 kW
15465	**CHINA**	
	CHINA R INTL, Kashi	S Asia • 100 kW
	CHINA (TAIWAN)	
	†R TAIWAN INTL, Paochung	SE Asia • 100 kW
	PHILIPPINES	
	FEBC RADIO INTL, Bocaue	SE Asia • 100 kW
	PORTUGAL	
	†RDP INTERNATIONAL, Lisbon	W • C Africa & S Africa • 300 kW
		W Sa/Su • C Africa & S Africa • 300 kW
	ROMANIA	
	†R ROMANIA INTL, Bucharest	S • E North Am • 300 kW
	RUSSIA	
	VOICE OF RUSSIA, Moscow	S • Europe & N Africa • 250 kW • ALT. FREQ. TO 12040 kHz
	USA	
	FAMILY RADIO, Via Taiwan	SE Asia • 100 kW
15470 (con'd)	**RUSSIA**	
	VOICE OF RUSSIA, Irkutsk	S • E Asia • 100 kW

0 1 2 3 4 5 6 7 8 9 10 11 12 13 14 15 16 17 18 19 20 21 22 23 24

SEASONAL S OR W 1-HR TIMESHIFT MIDYEAR ⇐ OR ⇒ JAMMING / OR ∧ EARLIEST HEARD ◁ LATEST HEARD ▷ NEW FOR 2009 †

World Time 0 1 2 3 4 5 6 7 8 9 10 11 12 13 14 15 16 17 18 19 20 21 22 23 24

kHz	Country	Station	Schedule
15470 (con'd)	USA	R FREE ASIA, Via Tinian, N Marianas	W • SE Asia • 250 kW
		RFE-RL, Via Udon Thani, Thailand	S • E Asia • 250 kW
15475	GABON	AFRIQUE NUMERO UN, Moyabi	W Africa & E North Am • 250 kW
	TURKEY	VOICE OF TURKEY, Ankara-Emirler	W • Australasia • 500 kW
	USA	†VOA	S • W Asia • 250 kW
		VOA, Via Lampertheim, Germany	S • W Asia & C Asia • 100 kW; S • W Asia • 100 kW
15476	ANTARCTICA	R NACIONAL-LRA36, Base Esperanza	M-F • 2/10 kW
15480	CHINA	CENTRAL PEOPLE'S BS, Beijing	DS-1 • 100 kW; W-M • DS-1 • 100 kW; S • DS-1 • 100 kW
	CLANDESTINE (ASIA)	"D'CRATIC VO BURMA", Via Armenia	S • SE Asia • ANTI-MYANMAR GOVT • 200 kW
15485	GERMANY	†DEUTSCHE WELLE, Via Sri Lanka	S • C Africa & S Africa • 250 kW
	PAKISTAN	RADIO PAKISTAN, Islamabad	SE Asia • 250 kW; E Africa • 100 kW
15490	USA	VOA, Via Iranawila, Sri Lanka	S • S Asia • 250 kW
		VOA, Via Lampertheim, Germany	S • S Asia • 100 kW
15495	KUWAIT	RADIO KUWAIT, Kabd	N Africa • 500 kW; W Africa & C Africa • 500 kW
	USA	ADVENTIST WORLD R, Via Germany	W • SE Asia • 250 kW
		LEADING THE WAY, Via Rampisham, UK	S Tu/F • W Asia • 500 kW
		R FREE ASIA, Via Tinian, N Marianas	S • E Asia • 250 kW
15500	CHINA	CENTRAL PEOPLE'S BS, Beijing	S • DS-2 • 150 kW; DS-2 • 150 kW; Th-Tu • DS-2 • 150 kW
	INTERNATIONAL WATERS	CMF RADIO ONE, Middle East	ENGLISH, ETC • Mideast • 0.25/0.5 kW
15505	CHINA	CHINA R INTL, Via Bamako, Mali	W Africa, C Africa & E Africa • 100 kW
	KUWAIT	RADIO KUWAIT, Kabd	E Europe & W Asia • 500 kW; W Africa & C Africa • 500 kW; Europe & E North Am • 500 kW
15510	PHILIPPINES	FEBC RADIO INTL, Bocaue	S • E Asia • 100 kW
		RADYO PILIPINAS, Tinang	S • ENGLISH & TAGALOG • S Asia & Mideast • 250 kW
	RUSSIA	VOICE OF RUSSIA, Samara	S • W Asia & S Asia • 250 kW
	UNITED KINGDOM	BBC, Via Irkutsk, Russia	W • S Asia • 250 kW
		BBC, Via Thailand	S • S Asia • 250 kW
	USA	ADVENTIST WORLD R, Via Agat, Guam	S • SE Asia • 100 kW; S • E Asia • 100 kW
		R FREE ASIA, Via Dhabayya, UAE	S • S Asia • 500 kW
		R FREE ASIA, Via Tinian, N Marianas	S • E Asia • 250 kW
15515	AUSTRALIA	CVC, Via Armenia	W • S Asia • 100 kW
		RADIO AUSTRALIA, Shepparton	Pacific & N America • 100 kW; Pacific • 100 kW
	CHINA (TAIWAN)	R TAIWAN INTL, Via Issoudun, France	S • S Asia & SE Asia • 500 kW • ALT. FREQ. TO 11600 kHz
	FRANCE	R FRANCE INTL, Via French Guiana	C America • 250 kW
	SWEDEN	†IBRA RADIO, Via Jülich, Germany	S • E Africa • 100 kW
	UNITED KINGDOM	BBC, Rampisham	S • W Africa & C Africa • 500 kW; S • Mideast • 500 kW
	USA	VOA, Via Udon Thani, Thailand	W • E Asia • 500 kW
15520	PHILIPPINES	RADIO VERITAS ASIA, Palauig	SE Asia • 250 kW
	POLAND	POLISH RADIO, Via W'tachtal, Germany	W • E Europe • 100 kW
	TURKEY	VOICE OF TURKEY, Ankara-Emirler	S • Mideast • 500 kW
	USA	ADVENTIST WORLD R, Via Agat, Guam	S • E Asia • 100 kW
(con'd)		FAMILY RADIO, Via Dhabayya, UAE	S Asia • 250 kW

World Time 0 1 2 3 4 5 6 7 8 9 10 11 12 13 14 15 16 17 18 19 20 21 22 23 24

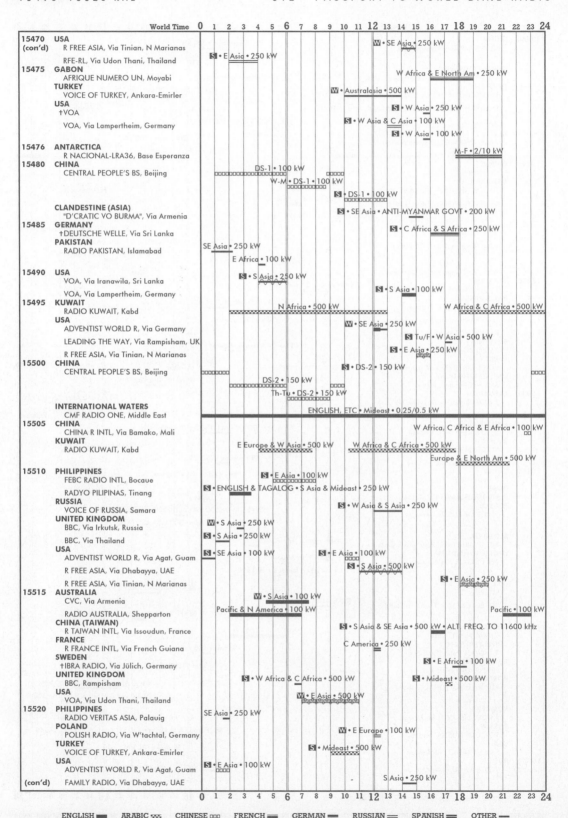

ENGLISH ARABIC CHINESE FRENCH GERMAN RUSSIAN SPANISH OTHER

WEDC — WCRW — WSBC

WEDC	WCRW	WSBC
1A - 7A	12N - 3P	7A - 9 30 A
9 30 A - 11A	6P - 8P	11A - 12N
4 30 P - 6P		3P - 4 30 P
8P - 9P		9P - 11P
11P - 12 MIDNITE		12 MIDNITE - 1A

CHICAGO, ILL

1240 KC

1KW

ERNIE LEGMAN

232-1009

SAT. DISH

Championship
at Morehead, Ky.
Final James Madison 79 Young

Third Place
at Morehead, Ky.
Final Florida Atlantic 82 Moreh

Four Points LAX Shootout

Championship
at Malibu, Calif.
Final Montana 61 Peppe

Third Place
at Malibu, Calif.
Final Cal St.-Fullerton 65 East

Hampton Inn Classic

First Round
at Bloomington, Ind.
Final Indiana 56 Belm
Final Cent. Michigan 57 Chic

Hilton Concord Thanksgiving Classic

Championship
at Moraga, Calif.
Final Chattanooga 84 Wash

Third Place
at Moraga, Calif.
Final St. Ma

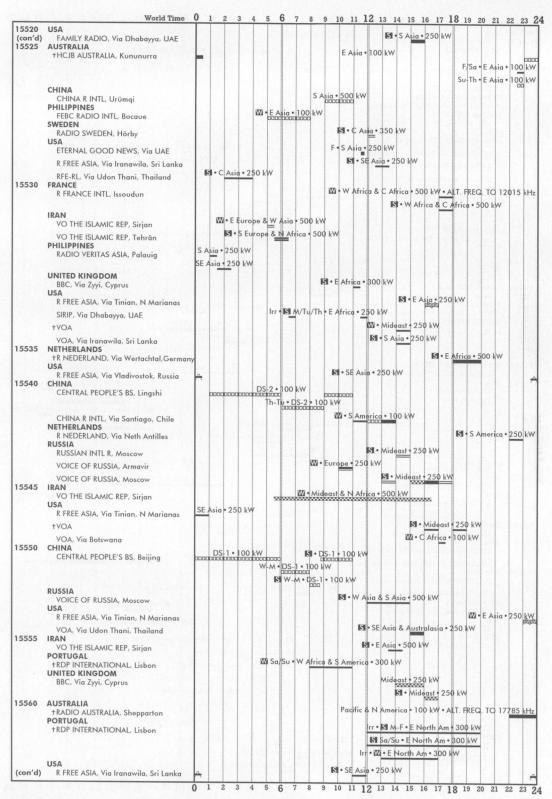

World Time 0 1 2 3 4 5 6 7 8 9 10 11 12 13 14 15 16 17 18 19 20 21 22 23 24

kHz	Country	Station	Schedule
15520 (con'd)	USA	FAMILY RADIO, Via Dhabayya, UAE	S • S Asia • 250 kW
15525	AUSTRALIA	†HCJB AUSTRALIA, Kununurra	E Asia • 100 kW; F/Sa • E Asia • 100 kW; Su-Th • E Asia • 100 kW
	CHINA	CHINA R INTL, Urümqi	S Asia • 500 kW
	PHILIPPINES	FEBC RADIO INTL, Bocaue	W • E Asia • 100 kW
	SWEDEN	RADIO SWEDEN, Hörby	S • C Asia • 350 kW
	USA	ETERNAL GOOD NEWS, Via UAE	F • S Asia • 250 kW
		R FREE ASIA, Via Iranawila, Sri Lanka	S • SE Asia • 250 kW
		RFE-RL, Via Udon Thani, Thailand	S • C Asia • 250 kW
15530	FRANCE	R FRANCE INTL, Issoudun	W • W Africa & C Africa • 500 kW • ALT. FREQ. TO 12015 kHz; S • W Africa & C Africa • 500 kW
	IRAN	VO THE ISLAMIC REP, Sirjan	W • E Europe & W Asia • 500 kW
		VO THE ISLAMIC REP, Tehrān	S • S Europe & N Africa • 500 kW
	PHILIPPINES	RADIO VERITAS ASIA, Palauig	S Asia • 250 kW; SE Asia • 250 kW
	UNITED KINGDOM	BBC, Via Zyyi, Cyprus	S • E Africa • 300 kW
	USA	R FREE ASIA, Via Tinian, N Marianas	S • E Asia • 250 kW
		SIRIP, Via Dhabayya, UAE	Irr • S • M/Tu/Th • E Africa • 250 kW
		†VOA	W • Mideast • 250 kW
		VOA, Via Iranawila, Sri Lanka	S • S Asia • 250 kW
15535	NETHERLANDS	†R NEDERLAND, Via Wertachtal,Germany	S • E Africa • 500 kW
	USA	R FREE ASIA, Via Vladivostok, Russia	S • SE Asia • 250 kW
15540	CHINA	CENTRAL PEOPLE'S BS, Lingshi	DS-2 • 100 kW; Th-Tu • DS-2 • 100 kW
		CHINA R INTL, Via Santiago, Chile	W • S America • 100 kW
	NETHERLANDS	R NEDERLAND, Via Neth Antilles	S • S America • 250 kW
	RUSSIA	RUSSIAN INTL R, Moscow	S • Mideast • 250 kW
		VOICE OF RUSSIA, Armavir	W • Europe • 250 kW
		VOICE OF RUSSIA, Moscow	S • Mideast • 250 kW
15545	IRAN	VO THE ISLAMIC REP, Sirjan	W • Mideast & N Africa • 500 kW
	USA	R FREE ASIA, Via Tinian, N Marianas	SE Asia • 250 kW
		†VOA	S • Mideast • 250 kW
		VOA, Via Botswana	W • C Africa • 100 kW
15550	CHINA	CENTRAL PEOPLE'S BS, Beijing	DS-1 • 100 kW; S • DS-1 • 100 kW; W-M • DS-1 • 100 kW; S W-M • DS-1 • 100 kW
	RUSSIA	VOICE OF RUSSIA, Moscow	S • W Asia & S Asia • 500 kW
	USA	R FREE ASIA, Via Tinian, N Marianas	W • E Asia • 250 kW
		VOA, Via Udon Thani, Thailand	S • SE Asia & Australasia • 250 kW
15555	IRAN	VO THE ISLAMIC REP, Sirjan	S • E Asia • 500 kW
	PORTUGAL	†RDP INTERNATIONAL, Lisbon	W Sa/Su • W Africa & S America • 300 kW
	UNITED KINGDOM	BBC, Via Zyyi, Cyprus	Mideast • 250 kW; S • Mideast • 250 kW
15560	AUSTRALIA	†RADIO AUSTRALIA, Shepparton	Pacific & N America • 100 kW • ALT. FREQ. TO 17785 kHz
	PORTUGAL	†RDP INTERNATIONAL, Lisbon	Irr • S M-F • E North Am • 300 kW; S Sa/Su • E North Am • 300 kW; Irr • W • E North Am • 300 kW
	USA (con'd)	R FREE ASIA, Via Iranawila, Sri Lanka	S • SE Asia • 250 kW

0 1 2 3 4 5 6 7 8 9 10 11 12 13 14 15 16 17 18 19 20 21 22 23 24

SEASONAL S OR W 1-HR TIMESHIFT MIDYEAR OR JAMMING / OR /\ EARLIEST HEARD ◁ LATEST HEARD ▷ NEW FOR 2009 †

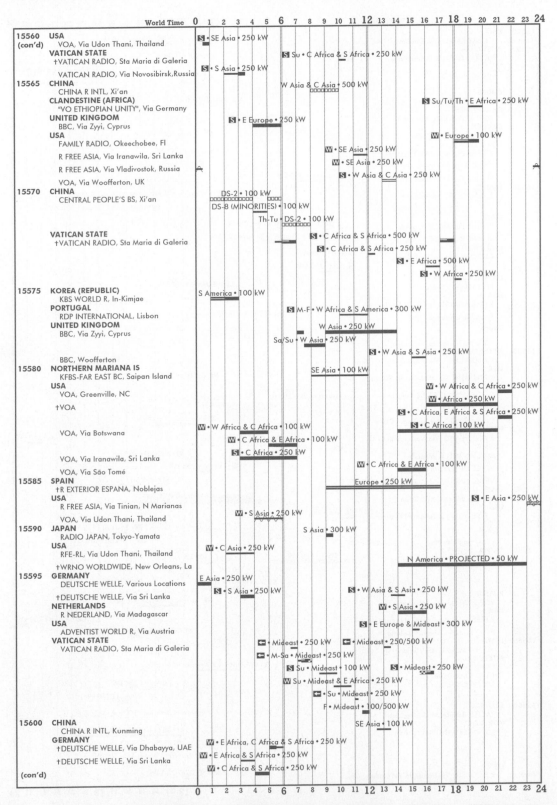

World Time 0 1 2 3 4 5 6 7 8 9 10 11 12 13 14 15 16 17 18 19 20 21 22 23 24

kHz	Country / Station	Schedule
15560 (con'd)	**USA**	
	VOA, Via Udon Thani, Thailand	S • SE Asia • 250 kW
	VATICAN STATE	
	†VATICAN RADIO, Sta Maria di Galeria	S Su • C Africa & S Africa • 250 kW
	VATICAN RADIO, Via Novosibirsk,Russia	S • S Asia • 250 kW
15565	**CHINA**	
	CHINA R INTL, Xi'an	W Asia & C Asia • 500 kW
	CLANDESTINE (AFRICA)	
	"VO ETHIOPIAN UNITY", Via Germany	S Su/Tu/Th • E Africa • 250 kW
	UNITED KINGDOM	
	BBC, Via Zyyi, Cyprus	S • E Europe • 250 kW
	USA	
	FAMILY RADIO, Okeechobee, Fl	W • Europe • 100 kW
	R FREE ASIA, Via Iranawila, Sri Lanka	W • SE Asia • 250 kW
	R FREE ASIA, Via Vladivostok, Russia	W • SE Asia • 250 kW
	VOA, Via Woofferton, UK	S • W Asia & C Asia • 250 kW
15570	**CHINA**	
	CENTRAL PEOPLE'S BS, Xi'an	DS-2 • 100 kW
		DS-8 (MINORITIES) • 100 kW
		Th-Tu • DS-2 • 100 kW
	VATICAN STATE	
	†VATICAN RADIO, Sta Maria di Galeria	S • C Africa & S Africa • 500 kW
		S • C Africa & S Africa • 250 kW
		S • E Africa • 500 kW
		S • W Africa • 250 kW
15575	**KOREA (REPUBLIC)**	
	KBS WORLD R, In-Kimjae	S America • 100 kW
	PORTUGAL	
	RDP INTERNATIONAL, Lisbon	S M-F • W Africa & S America • 300 kW
	UNITED KINGDOM	
	BBC, Via Zyyi, Cyprus	W Asia • 250 kW
		Sa/Su • W Asia • 250 kW
		S • W Asia & S Asia • 250 kW
	BBC, Woofferton	
15580	**NORTHERN MARIANA IS**	
	KFBS-FAR EAST BC, Saipan Island	SE Asia • 100 kW
	USA	
	VOA, Greenville, NC	W • W Africa & C Africa • 250 kW
		W • Africa • 250 kW
	†VOA	S • C Africa, E Africa & S Africa • 250 kW
		S • C Africa • 100 kW
		W • W Africa & C Africa • 100 kW
	VOA, Via Botswana	W • C Africa & E Africa • 100 kW
		S • C Africa • 250 kW
	VOA, Via Iranawila, Sri Lanka	
	VOA, Via São Tomé	W • C Africa & E Africa • 100 kW
15585	**SPAIN**	
	†R EXTERIOR ESPANA, Noblejas	Europe • 250 kW
	USA	
	R FREE ASIA, Via Tinian, N Marianas	S • E Asia • 250 kW
	VOA, Via Udon Thani, Thailand	W • S Asia • 250 kW
15590	**JAPAN**	
	RADIO JAPAN, Tokyo-Yamata	S Asia • 300 kW
	USA	
	RFE-RL, Via Udon Thani, Thailand	W • C Asia • 250 kW
	†WRNO WORLDWIDE, New Orleans, La	N America • PROJECTED • 50 kW
15595	**GERMANY**	
	DEUTSCHE WELLE, Various Locations	E Asia • 250 kW
		S • S Asia • 250 kW
	†DEUTSCHE WELLE, Via Sri Lanka	S • W Asia & S Asia • 250 kW
	NETHERLANDS	
	R NEDERLAND, Via Madagascar	W • S Asia • 250 kW
	USA	
	ADVENTIST WORLD R, Via Austria	S • E Europe & Mideast • 300 kW
	VATICAN STATE	
	VATICAN RADIO, Sta Maria di Galeria	← • Mideast • 250 kW
		← • Mideast • 250/500 kW
		← • M-Sa • Mideast • 250 kW
		S Su • Mideast • 100 kW
		S • Mideast • 250 kW
		W Su • Mideast & E Africa • 250 kW
		← • Su • Mideast • 250 kW
		F • Mideast • 100/500 kW
15600	**CHINA**	
	CHINA R INTL, Kunming	SE Asia • 100 kW
	GERMANY	
	†DEUTSCHE WELLE, Via Dhabayya, UAE	W • E Africa, C Africa & S Africa • 250 kW
		W • E Africa & S Africa • 250 kW
	†DEUTSCHE WELLE, Via Sri Lanka	W • C Africa & S Africa • 250 kW
(con'd)		

ENGLISH ARABIC CHINESE FRENCH GERMAN RUSSIAN SPANISH OTHER

World Time 0 1 2 3 4 5 6 7 8 9 10 11 12 13 14 15 16 17 18 19 20 21 22 23 24

Frequency	Country / Station	Schedule
15600 (con'd)	**IRAN** VO THE ISLAMIC REP, Tehrān	[S] • S Asia • 500 kW
	USA †FAMILY RADIO, Okeechobee, Fl	[S] • Europe • 100 kW
15605	**FRANCE** R FRANCE INTL, Issoudun	[W] • W Africa & C Africa • 500 kW • ALT. FREQ. TO 11725 kHz
		[W] • E Europe • 500 kW
		[W] • C Africa & E Africa • 500 kW • ALT. FREQ. TO 11615 kHz
		[S] • C Africa & S Africa • 500 kW
	GERMANY DEUTSCHE WELLE, Via Sri Lanka	[S] • C Africa & E Africa • 250 kW
		[S] • SE Asia & Australasia • 250 kW
	DEUTSCHE WELLE, Via Woofferton, UK	[S] • C Africa & S Africa • 250 kW
	RUSSIA VOICE OF RUSSIA, Moscow	[S] • S Asia • 500 kW
15610	**CHINA (TAIWAN)** †R TAIWAN INTL, Paochung	SE Asia • 100 kW
	GERMANY DEUTSCHE WELLE, Via Sri Lanka	[W] • SE Asia & Australasia • 250 kW
		[W] • S Asia & C Asia • 250 kW
	USA †WEWN, Vandiver, Alabama	[W] • Mideast • 500 kW
	WORLD HARVEST R, Naalehu, Hawai'i	[W] M-Sa • E Asia • 100 kW
		[W] Su • E Asia • 100 kW
		[W] • E Asia • 100 kW
15615	**USA** ADVENTIST WORLD R, Via Agat, Guam	[S] • E Asia • 100 kW
	RFE-RL, Via Iranawila, Sri Lanka	[S] • W Asia & S Asia • 250 kW
	RFE-RL, Via Kuwait	[S] • W Asia & S Asia • 250 kW
15620	**CHINA** CHINA R INTL, Kashi	[W] • S Europe • 500 kW
	GERMANY †DEUTSCHE WELLE, Via Kigali, Rwanda	[S] • W Asia & C Asia • 250 kW
	†DEUTSCHE WELLE, Via Rampisham, UK	[S] • W Africa • 500 kW
	†DEUTSCHE WELLE, Via Sines, Portugal	[W] • W Asia • 250 kW
		[S] • W Africa & C Africa • 250 kW
	†DEUTSCHE WELLE, Via Sri Lanka	[S] • Mideast • 250 kW
		[W] • E Africa • 250 kW
15625v	**PAKISTAN** RADIO PAKISTAN, Islamabad	S Asia • 100 kW
15630	**GREECE** FONI TIS HELLADAS, Athens	[W] • Europe • 100 kW
		[S] • W Europe, Atlantic & N America • 100 kW
		[S] • W Europe & Atlantic • 100 kW
		[S] Sa • W Europe & Atlantic • 100 kW
		[S] Su-F • W Europe & Atlantic • 100 kW
		[1-hr timeshift] • W Europe & Atlantic • 100 kW
15640	**AUSTRALIA** CVC, Via Wertachtal, Germany	[S] • W Africa & C Africa • 125 kW
		W Africa & C Africa • 125 kW
	GERMANY DEUTSCHE WELLE, Via Kigali, Rwanda	[W] • E Europe • 250 kW
	†DEUTSCHE WELLE, Via Rampisham, UK	[W] • Mideast & W Asia • 500 kW
		[S] • S Asia & SE Asia • 500 kW
		[S] • W Asia & S Asia • 500 kW
	†DEUTSCHE WELLE, Via Sines, Portugal	[W] • Mideast & W Asia • 250 kW
	†DEUTSCHE WELLE, Via Sri Lanka	[W] • C Asia & E Asia • 250 kW
		E Asia • 250 kW
		[W] • C Asia • 250 kW
		[W] • SE Asia • 250 kW
		[W] • W Asia & S Asia • 250 kW
	NETHERLANDS †R NEDERLAND, Via Madagascar	[S] • SE Asia • 250 kW
15645	**USA** †VOA	[W] • W Asia & S Asia • 250 kW
15650	**CLANDESTINE (AFRICA)** "VO OROMIYA INDEP'NCE", Germany	[S] Sa • E Africa • ANTI-ETHIOPIA GOVT • 100 kW
	GERMANY †DEUTSCHE WELLE, Via Kigali, Rwanda	[S] • E Africa • 250 kW
	†DEUTSCHE WELLE, Via Sri Lanka	[S] • Australasia • 250 kW
	GREECE FONI TIS HELLADAS, Athens	[S] • Mideast & Australasia • 100 kW
		[S] M-Sa • Mideast & Australasia • 100 kW
		[S] Su • Mideast & Australasia • 100 kW
(con'd)	**SUDAN** †RADIO MIRAYA, Via Slovakia	[W] • ARABIC & ENGLISH • C Africa & E Africa • 150 kW • ALT. FREQ. TO 9825 kHz

World Time 0 1 2 3 4 5 6 7 8 9 10 11 12 13 14 15 16 17 18 19 20 21 22 23 24

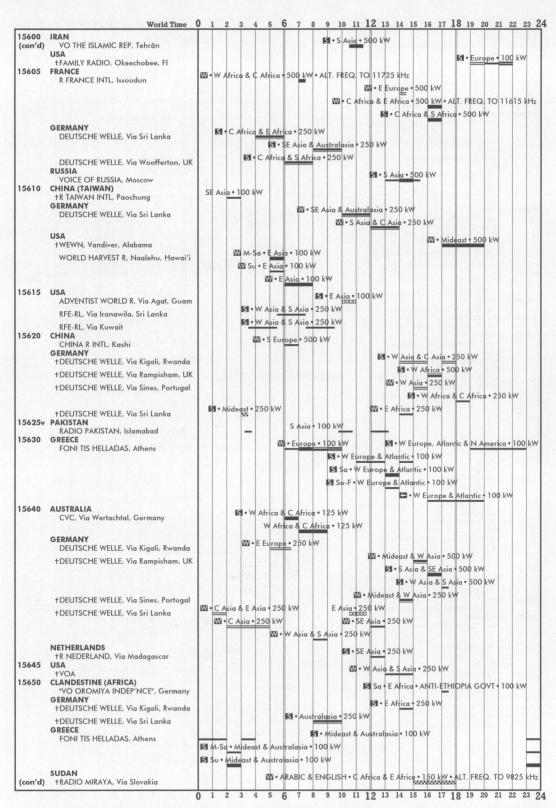

World Time 0 1 2 3 4 5 6 7 8 9 10 11 12 13 14 15 16 17 18 19 20 21 22 23 24

kHz	Country / Station	Schedule
15650 (con'd)	**SUDAN** †RADIO MIRAYA, Via Slovakia	S • ARABIC & ENGLISH • C Africa & E Africa • 150 kW
	USA PAN AM BC, Via Jülich, Germany	S Su • S Asia • 100 kW
		S Su • Mideast & W Asia • 100 kW
		S Th • Mideast & W Asia • 100 kW
15655v	**USA** †QUE HUONG R, Via Tajikistan	W-Sa • SE Asia • 100 kW • ALT. FREQ. TO 15680v kHz
15660	**CLANDESTINE (AFRICA)** "TENSAE ETHIOPIA V UNITY", Via Russia	S • E Africa • 250 kW
	LIBYA †RADIO JAMAHIRIYA, Sabratha	W Africa • 500 kW
	RUSSIA VOICE OF RUSSIA, Moscow	S • SE Asia • 250 kW
	USA ADVENTIST WORLD R, Via Agat, Guam	W • S Asia • 100 kW
		W M/Tu/Th-Sa • S Asia • 100 kW
		W Su/W • S Asia • 100 kW
15665	**CHINA** CHINA R INTL, Kashi	E Europe & W Asia • 500 kW
	CLANDESTINE (AFRICA) "VO BIAFRA INTL", Via WHRI, USA	F • W Africa • 250 kW
	USA R FREE ASIA, Via Tinian, N Marianas	W • E Asia • 250 kW
	VOA, Via Saipan, N Marianas	S • E Asia • 100 kW
	†WEWN, Vandiver, Alabama	S • W Africa & C Africa • 500 kW
	WORLD HARVEST R, Greenbush, Maine	W • Europe • 250 kW
		S • Africa • 250 kW
15670	**CHINA** CENTRAL PEOPLE'S BS, Beijing	DS-8 (MINORITIES) • 100 kW
15675	**SWITZERLAND** RADIO REVEIL, Via Jülich, Germany	S Tu/Th • C Africa • 100 kW
15680	**AUSTRALIA** CVC, Via Wertachtal, Germany	W • W Africa & C Africa • 125 kW
	FRANCE †R FRANCE INTL, Via Taiwan	M-F • SE Asia • 100 kW
	PALAU †R T8WH-WORLD HARVEST R, Koror	CHINESE, ETC • SE Asia • 100 kW
	UNITED KINGDOM BIBLE VOICE, Via Jülich, Germany	S Sa • S Asia • 100 kW
		S Tu • S Asia • 100 kW
		S M/Th/Sa • S Asia • 100 kW
		S Su/Tu/W/F • S Asia • 100 kW
15680v	**USA** †QUE HUONG R, Via Tajikistan	W-Sa • SE Asia • 100 kW • ALT. FREQ. TO 15655v kHz
15685	**USA** R FREE ASIA, Via Tinian, N Marianas	S • E Asia • 250 kW
15690	**CHINA (TAIWAN)** R TAIWAN INTL, Via Issoudun, France	S • C Africa & S Africa • 500 kW
	GERMANY †DEUTSCHE WELLE, Via Rampisham, UK	S • E Europe, W Asia & C Asia • 500 kW
	PORTUGAL RDP INTERNATIONAL, Lisbon	W M-F • Mideast & S Asia • 100 kW
	USA †R FARDA, Via Iranawila, Sri Lanka	W • W Asia • 250 kW
		W Asia • 250 kW
		S • W Asia • 250 kW
	†R FARDA, Via Lampertheim, Germany	W • W Asia • 100 kW
	R FARDA, Via Udon Thani, Thailand	W • W Asia • 250 kW
15695	**USA** †FAMILY RADIO, Okeechobee, Fl	S • Europe • 100 kW
15700	**BULGARIA** †RADIO BULGARIA, Plovdiv	← • W Europe • 500 kW
		← • S Africa • 500 kW
	CZECH REPUBLIC RADIO PRAGUE, Litomyšl	W • S Asia • 100 kW
	GERMANY DEUTSCHE WELLE, Via Rampisham, UK	S • E Europe, W Asia & C Asia • 500 kW
	USA R FREE ASIA, Via Tinian, N Marianas	W • SE Asia • 250 kW
15710	**CHINA** †CENTRAL PEOPLE'S BS, Beijing	TAIWAN-2 • 100 kW
	CZECH REPUBLIC RADIO PRAGUE, Litomyšl	S • W Europe • 100 kW
		W • W Africa & C Africa • 100 kW
		S • E Africa & Mideast • 100 kW
		W • C Africa • 100 kW
		S • S Asia • 100 kW
		S • E Europe & W Asia • 100 kW
(con'd)	**EGYPT** †EGYPTIAN RADIO, Abu Za'bal	W • W Africa • DS-GENERAL • 100 kW

World Time 0 1 2 3 4 5 6 7 8 9 10 11 12 13 14 15 16 17 18 19 20 21 22 23 24

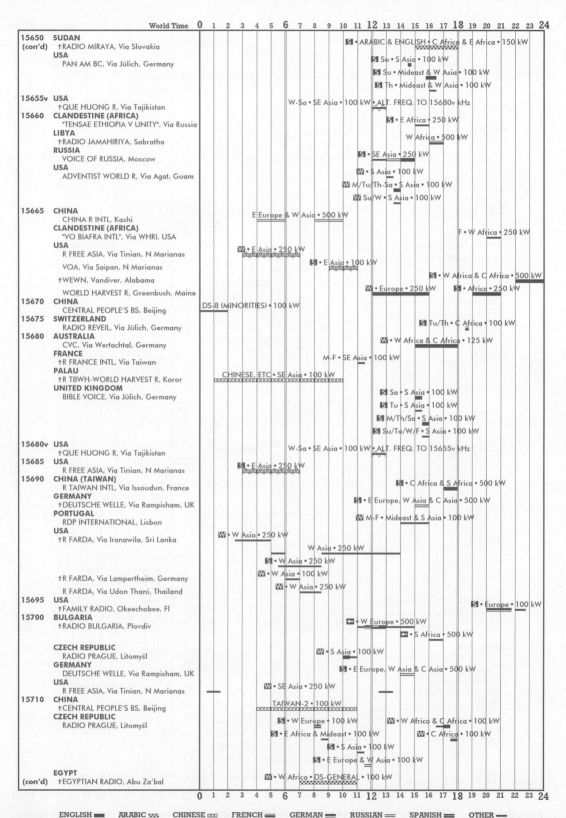

ENGLISH ARABIC CHINESE FRENCH GERMAN RUSSIAN SPANISH OTHER

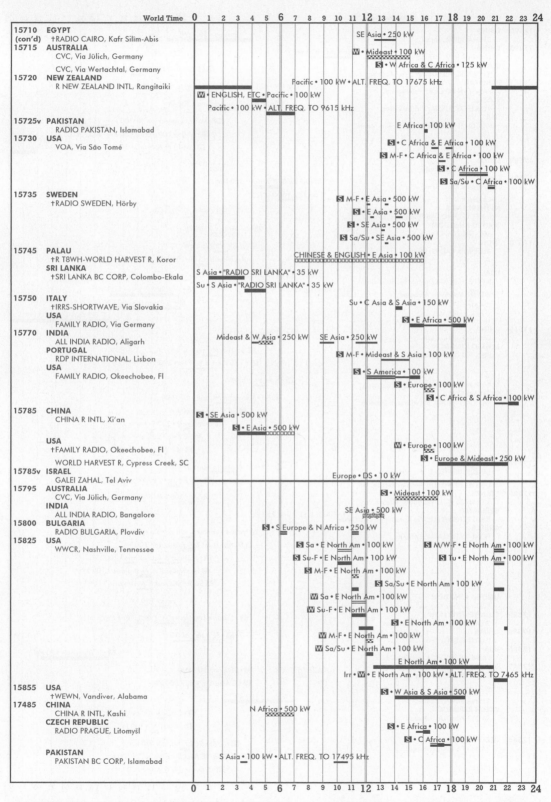

World Time 0 1 2 3 4 5 6 7 8 9 10 11 12 13 14 15 16 17 18 19 20 21 22 23 24

kHz	Country / Station	Schedule
15710 (con'd)	**EGYPT** †RADIO CAIRO, Kafr Silîm-Abis	SE Asia • 250 kW
15715	**AUSTRALIA** CVC, Via Jülich, Germany	W • Mideast • 100 kW
	CVC, Via Wertachtal, Germany	S • W Africa & C Africa • 125 kW
15720	**NEW ZEALAND** R NEW ZEALAND INTL, Rangitaiki	Pacific • 100 kW • ALT. FREQ. TO 17675 kHz W • ENGLISH, ETC • Pacific • 100 kW Pacific • 100 kW • ALT. FREQ. TO 9615 kHz
15725v	**PAKISTAN** RADIO PAKISTAN, Islamabad	E Africa • 100 kW
15730	**USA** VOA, Via São Tomé	S • C Africa & E Africa • 100 kW S M-F • C Africa & E Africa • 100 kW S • C Africa • 100 kW S Sa/Su • C Africa • 100 kW
15735	**SWEDEN** †RADIO SWEDEN, Hörby	S M-F • E Asia • 500 kW S • E Asia • 500 kW S • SE Asia • 500 kW S Sa/Su • SE Asia • 500 kW
15745	**PALAU** †R T8WH-WORLD HARVEST R, Koror	CHINESE & ENGLISH • E Asia • 100 kW
	SRI LANKA †SRI LANKA BC CORP, Colombo-Ekala	S Asia • "RADIO SRI LANKA" • 35 kW Su • S Asia • "RADIO SRI LANKA" • 35 kW
15750	**ITALY** †IRRS-SHORTWAVE, Via Slovakia	Su • C Asia & S Asia • 150 kW
	USA FAMILY RADIO, Via Germany	S • E Africa • 500 kW
15770	**INDIA** ALL INDIA RADIO, Aligarh	Mideast & W Asia • 250 kW SE Asia • 250 kW
	PORTUGAL RDP INTERNATIONAL, Lisbon	S M-F • Mideast & S Asia • 100 kW
	USA FAMILY RADIO, Okeechobee, Fl	S • S America • 100 kW S • Europe • 100 kW S • C Africa & S Africa • 100 kW
15785	**CHINA** CHINA R INTL, Xi'an	S • SE Asia • 500 kW S • E Asia • 500 kW
	USA †FAMILY RADIO, Okeechobee, Fl	W • Europe • 100 kW
	WORLD HARVEST R, Cypress Creek, SC	S • Europe & Mideast • 250 kW
15785v	**ISRAEL** GALEI ZAHAL, Tel Aviv	Europe • DS • 10 kW
15795	**AUSTRALIA** CVC, Via Jülich, Germany	S • Mideast • 100 kW
	INDIA ALL INDIA RADIO, Bangalore	SE Asia • 500 kW
15800	**BULGARIA** RADIO BULGARIA, Plovdiv	S • S Europe & N Africa • 250 kW
15825	**USA** WWCR, Nashville, Tennessee	S Sa • E North Am • 100 kW S M/W-F • E North Am • 100 kW S Su-F • E North Am • 100 kW S Tu • E North Am • 100 kW S M-F • E North Am • 100 kW S Sa/Su • E North Am • 100 kW W Sa • E North Am • 100 kW W Su-F • E North Am • 100 kW S • E North Am • 100 kW W M-F • E North Am • 100 kW W Sa/Su • E North Am • 100 kW E North Am • 100 kW Irr • W • E North Am • 100 kW • ALT. FREQ. TO 7465 kHz
15855	**USA** †WEWN, Vandiver, Alabama	S • W Asia & S Asia • 500 kW
17485	**CHINA** CHINA R INTL, Kashi	N Africa • 500 kW
	CZECH REPUBLIC RADIO PRAGUE, Litomyšl	S • E Africa • 100 kW S • C Africa • 100 kW
	PAKISTAN PAKISTAN BC CORP, Islamabad	S Asia • 100 kW • ALT. FREQ. TO 17495 kHz

0 1 2 3 4 5 6 7 8 9 10 11 12 13 14 15 16 17 18 19 20 21 22 23 24

World Time 0 1 2 3 4 5 6 7 8 9 10 11 12 13 14 15 16 17 18 19 20 21 22 23 24

kHz	Country / Station	Schedule details
17490	**CHINA**	
	CHINA R INTL, Kashi	Europe • 500 kW
17495	**CHINA**	
	CHINA R INTL, Beijing	SE Asia • 500 kW
	CLANDESTINE (ASIA)	
	"D'CRATIC VO BURMA", Via Madagascar	W • SE Asia • ANTI-MYANMAR GOVT • 50 kW
	PAKISTAN	
	PAKISTAN BC CORP, Islamabad	S Asia • 100 kW • ALT. FREQ. TO 17485 kHz
	RUSSIA	
	VOICE OF RUSSIA, Via Tajikistan	← • SE Asia & Australasia • 500 kW
	USA	
	†WBCQ-"THE PLANET", Monticello,Maine	← • M-F • N America • 50/100 kW • ALT. FREQ. TO 15420 kHz
		← • M-Sa • N America • 50 kW • ALT. FREQ. TO 15420 kHz
		← • M-F • N America • 50 kW • ALT. FREQ. TO 15420 kHz
17500	**CHINA**	
	CHINA R INTL, Kashi	S Asia • 100 kW
17505	**CHINA**	
	CHINA R INTL, Kashi	N Africa & W Africa • 500 kW
	CHINA R INTL, Xi'an	SE Asia • 500 kW
	NETHERLANDS	
	†R NEDERLAND, Via Dhabayya, UAE	W • SE Asia • 250 kW
	UNITED KINGDOM	
	BBC, Via Zyyi, Cyprus	S • N Africa • 250 kW
17510	**INDIA**	
	ALL INDIA RADIO, Delhi	SE Asia • 100/250 kW
		Australasia • 100/250 kW
	USA	
	R FREE ASIA, Via Dushanbe, Tajikistan	S • S Asia • 200 kW
	†WEWN, Vandiver, Alabama	W • S America • 500 kW
		W • W Asia & S Asia • 500 kW
		S • S America • 500 kW
		S America • 500 kW
17515	**CHINA**	
	CHINA R INTL, Kashi	S • S Europe • 500 kW
	UNITED KINGDOM	
	BBC, Via Zyyi, Cyprus	S Sa-Th • W Asia • 300 kW
		S F • Mideast & W Asia • 300 kW
	USA	
	R FREE ASIA, Via Dushanbe, Tajikistan	W • S Asia • 200 kW
	VATICAN STATE	
	VATICAN RADIO, Sta Maria di Galeria	S Su • Mideast & W Asia • 100 kW
		S Su • E Asia • 500 kW
		S F • Mideast • 250 kW
		S • E Asia • 250 kW
		S • SE Asia • 500 kW
17520	**GERMANY**	
	DEUTSCHE WELLE, Via Sri Lanka	W • SE Asia & Australasia • 250 kW
	†DEUTSCHE WELLE, Via Woofferton, UK	W • W Africa • 250 kW
17525	**FRANCE**	
	R FRANCE INTL, Via South Africa	C Africa • 500 kW
	GERMANY	
	DEUTSCHE WELLE, Via Komsomolsk,Rus	S • E Asia & SE Asia • 250 kW
	GREECE	
	FONI TIS HELLADAS, Athens	W M-Sa • Mideast & Australasia • 100 kW
		W Su • Mideast & Australasia • 100 kW
		W • Mideast & Australasia • 100 kW
		W Sa • Mideast & Australasia • 100 kW
		W Su-F • Mideast & Australasia • 100 kW
	UNITED KINGDOM	
	BBC, Via Zyyi, Cyprus	S • C Asia • 250 kW
17525v	**CLANDESTINE (ASIA)**	
	"VOICE OF TIBET", Via Tajikistan	S • S Asia • 100 kW • ALT. FREQ. TO 17565v kHz
17530	**CHINA**	
	CHINA R INTL, Xi'an	S • SE Asia • 500 kW
17535	**USA**	
	FAMILY RADIO, Okeechobee, Fl	W • N America • 100 kW
17540	**CHINA**	
	CHINA R INTL, Beijing	S Asia • 500 kW
		S • SE Asia • 500 kW
		S • C Asia & E Asia • 500 kW
	CHINA R INTL, Kashi	S Asia • 100 kW
	CZECH REPUBLIC	
	RADIO PRAGUE, Litomyšl	S • S Asia • 100 kW
		S • C Africa • 100 kW
17545	**CZECH REPUBLIC**	
	RADIO PRAGUE, Litomyšl	W • C Africa & E Africa • 100 kW
		W • S Asia, SE Asia & Australasia • 100 kW
		W • E Europe & W Asia • 100 kW
(con'd)		

World Time 0 1 2 3 4 5 6 7 8 9 10 11 12 13 14 15 16 17 18 19 20 21 22 23 24

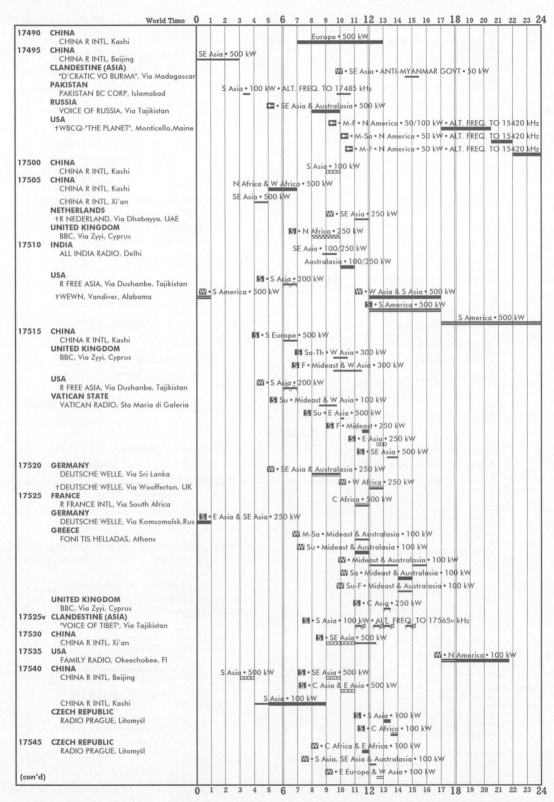

ENGLISH ▬ ARABIC ▭ CHINESE ▭ FRENCH ═ GERMAN ▬ RUSSIAN ═ SPANISH ═ OTHER —

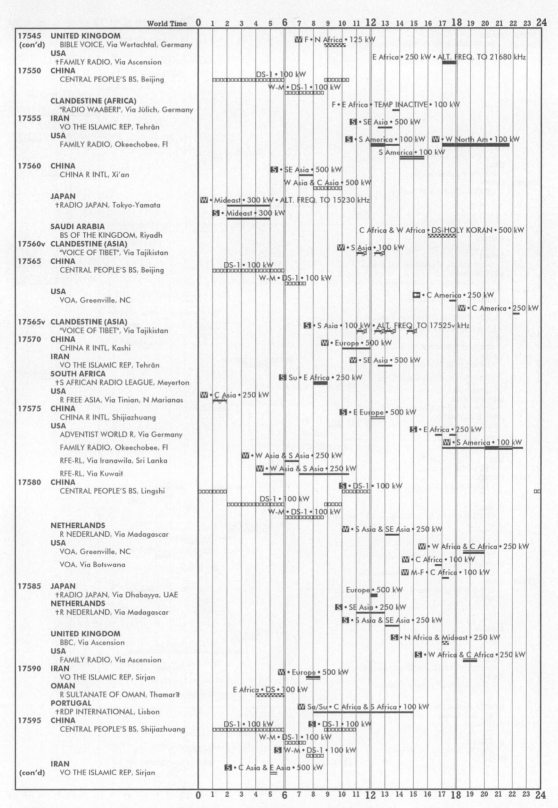

World Time 0 1 2 3 4 5 6 7 8 9 10 11 12 13 14 15 16 17 18 19 20 21 22 23 24

kHz	Country	Station	Schedule
17545 (con'd)	UNITED KINGDOM	BIBLE VOICE, Via Wertachtal, Germany	W F • N Africa • 125 kW
	USA	†FAMILY RADIO, Via Ascension	E Africa • 250 kW • ALT. FREQ. TO 21680 kHz
17550	CHINA	CENTRAL PEOPLE'S BS, Beijing	DS-1 • 100 kW; W-M • DS-1 • 100 kW
	CLANDESTINE (AFRICA)	"RADIO WAABERI", Via Jülich, Germany	F • E Africa • TEMP INACTIVE • 100 kW
17555	IRAN	VO THE ISLAMIC REP, Tehrān	S • SE Asia • 500 kW
	USA	FAMILY RADIO, Okeechobee, Fl	S • S America • 100 kW; W • W North Am • 100 kW; S America • 100 kW
17560	CHINA	CHINA R INTL, Xi'an	S • SE Asia • 500 kW; W Asia & C Asia • 500 kW
	JAPAN	†RADIO JAPAN, Tokyo-Yamata	W • Mideast • 300 kW • ALT. FREQ. TO 15230 kHz; S • Mideast • 300 kW
	SAUDI ARABIA	BS OF THE KINGDOM, Riyadh	C Africa & W Africa • DS-HOLY KORAN • 500 kW
17560v	CLANDESTINE (ASIA)	"VOICE OF TIBET", Via Tajikistan	W • S Asia • 100 kW
17565	CHINA	CENTRAL PEOPLE'S BS, Beijing	DS-1 • 100 kW; W-M • DS-1 • 100 kW
	USA	VOA, Greenville, NC	⬅ • C America • 250 kW; W • C America • 250 kW
17565v	CLANDESTINE (ASIA)	"VOICE OF TIBET", Via Tajikistan	S • S Asia • 100 kW • ALT. FREQ. TO 17525v kHz
17570	CHINA	CHINA R INTL, Kashi	W • Europe • 500 kW
	IRAN	VO THE ISLAMIC REP, Tehrān	W • SE Asia • 500 kW
	SOUTH AFRICA	†S AFRICAN RADIO LEAGUE, Meyerton	S Su • E Africa • 250 kW
	USA	R FREE ASIA, Via Tinian, N Marianas	W • C Asia • 250 kW
17575	CHINA	CHINA R INTL, Shijiazhuang	S • E Europe • 500 kW
	USA	ADVENTIST WORLD R, Via Germany	S • E Africa • 250 kW
		FAMILY RADIO, Okeechobee, Fl	W • S America • 100 kW
		RFE-RL, Via Iranawila, Sri Lanka	W • W Asia & S Asia • 250 kW
		RFE-RL, Via Kuwait	W • W Asia & S Asia • 250 kW
17580	CHINA	CENTRAL PEOPLE'S BS, Lingshi	S • DS-1 • 100 kW; DS-1 • 100 kW; W-M • DS-1 • 100 kW
	NETHERLANDS	R NEDERLAND, Via Madagascar	W • S Asia & SE Asia • 250 kW
	USA	VOA, Greenville, NC	W • W Africa & C Africa • 250 kW
		VOA, Via Botswana	W • C Africa • 100 kW; W M-F • C Africa • 100 kW
17585	JAPAN	†RADIO JAPAN, Via Dhabayya, UAE	Europe • 500 kW
	NETHERLANDS	†R NEDERLAND, Via Madagascar	S • SE Asia • 250 kW; S • S Asia & SE Asia • 250 kW
	UNITED KINGDOM	BBC, Via Ascension	S • N Africa & Mideast • 250 kW
	USA	FAMILY RADIO, Via Ascension	S • W Africa & C Africa • 250 kW
17590	IRAN	VO THE ISLAMIC REP, Sirjan	W • Europe • 500 kW
	OMAN	R SULTANATE OF OMAN, Thamarīt	E Africa • DS • 100 kW
	PORTUGAL	†RDP INTERNATIONAL, Lisbon	W Sa/Su • C Africa & S Africa • 100 kW
17595	CHINA	CENTRAL PEOPLE'S BS, Shijiazhuang	DS-1 • 100 kW; S • DS-1 • 100 kW; W-M • DS-1 • 100 kW; S W-M • DS-1 • 100 kW
(con'd)	IRAN	VO THE ISLAMIC REP, Sirjan	S • C Asia & E Asia • 500 kW

0 1 2 3 4 5 6 7 8 9 10 11 12 13 14 15 16 17 18 19 20 21 22 23 24

kHz	Country / Station	Schedule (World Time 0–24)
17595 (con'd)	**JAPAN** †RADIO JAPAN, Via Wertachtal, Germany	S • S Asia • 500 kW
	SPAIN †R EXTERIOR ESPANA, Noblejas	M-F • N America & C America • 250 kW
		M-F • S America • 250 kW
		Sa/Su • S America • 250 kW
		C America & S America • 250 kW
		M-F • C America & S America • 250 kW
		W Sa/Su • S America • 250 kW
		S Sa/Su • C America & S America • 250 kW
		Irr • W Su • S America • 250 kW
	UNITED KINGDOM BIBLE VOICE, Via Wertachtal, Germany	S F • N Africa • 125 kW
	USA †WEWN, Vandiver, Alabama	S • W Africa & C Africa • 500 kW
17605	**CHINA** CENTRAL PEOPLE'S BS, Beijing	S • DS-1 • 100 kW
		DS-1 • 100 kW
		W-M • DS-1 • 100 kW
	CHINA R INTL, Kunming	SE Asia • 500 kW • ALT. FREQ. TO 11700 kHz
	FRANCE R FRANCE INTL, Issoudun	S • E Africa • 500 kW
	JAPAN †RADIO JAPAN, Via Netherlands Antilles	W • S America • 250 kW
	NETHERLANDS †R NEDERLAND, Via Neth Antilles	S • S America • 250 kW
17610	**FRANCE** R FRANCE INTL, Issoudun	W • C America • 500 kW
	GERMANY †DEUTSCHE WELLE, Via Sines, Portugal	S • W Africa & C Africa • 250 kW
	DEUTSCHE WELLE, Via Woofferton, UK	S • C Africa & S Africa • 250 kW
	USA ADVENTIST WORLD R, Via Austria	E Africa • 300 kW
17615	**CHINA** CHINA R INTL, Kunming	S • SE Asia • 500 kW
	CHINA R INTL, Via Santiago, Chile	S • S America • 100 kW
	CHINA R INTL, Xi'an	S • W Asia & C Asia • 500 kW
	SAUDI ARABIA BS OF THE KINGDOM, Riyadh	S Asia & SE Asia • DS-HOLY KORAN • 500 kW
	UNITED KINGDOM †BBC, Via Singapore	SE Asia • 250 kW
	†BBC, Via Thailand	E Asia • 250 kW
		W • S Asia • 250 kW
	USA R FREE ASIA, Via Saipan, N Marianas	E Asia • 100 kW
17620	**FRANCE** R FRANCE INTL, Issoudun	W Africa • 500 kW
		W • W Africa • 500 kW
17625	**CHINA** CENTRAL PEOPLE'S BS, Beijing	DS-2 • 100 kW
		Th-Tu • DS-2 • 100 kW
		S • DS-2 • 100 kW
	CHINA R INTL, Via Santiago, Chile	S • S America • 100 kW
	CLANDESTINE (ASIA) "D'CRATIC VO BURMA", Via Madagascar	S • SE Asia • ANTI-MYANMAR GOVT • 50 kW
17630	**CHINA** CHINA R INTL, Via Bamako, Mali	C Africa • 100 kW
	FRANCE R FRANCE INTL, Via French Guiana	C America • 500 kW
		C America • 250 kW
	GABON AFRIQUE NUMERO UN, Moyabi	Irr • W Africa • 250 kW
		W Africa • 250 kW
	GERMANY DEUTSCHE WELLE, Via Rampisham, UK	W • S Asia & SE Asia • 500 kW
	OMAN R SULTANATE OF OMAN, Thamarīt	Europe & Mideast • DS • 100 kW • ALT. FREQ. TO 17660 kHz
		Europe & Mideast • DS • 100 kW
	UNITED KINGDOM BBC, Woofferton	S • C Asia • 300 kW
17635	**AUSTRALIA** CVC, Darwin	W • E Asia • 250 kW
	GERMANY DEUTSCHE WELLE, Via Sri Lanka	S • E Asia & SE Asia • 250 kW
(con'd)	**IRAN** VO THE ISLAMIC REP, Sirjan	S • S Asia • 500 kW
		S • E Asia • 500 kW

ENGLISH ▬ ARABIC ▨ CHINESE ▫▫▫ FRENCH ═ GERMAN ═ RUSSIAN ═ SPANISH ═ OTHER —

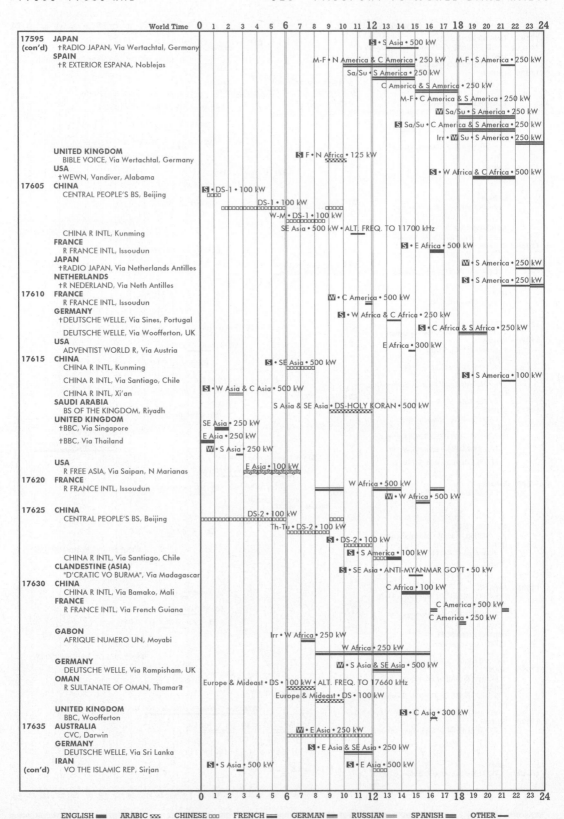

kHz	Country / Station	Target • Power (World Time 0–24)
17635 (con'd)	**RUSSIA**	
	VOICE OF RUSSIA, Komsomol'sk 'Amure	S • Australasia • 250 kW
	USA	
	ADVENTIST WORLD R, Via Agat, Guam	W • SE Asia • 100 kW
		W • E Asia • 100 kW
17640	**CHINA**	
	CHINA R INTL, Xi'an	W • W Asia & C Asia • 500 kW
		W • E Europe & W Asia • 500 kW
	UNITED KINGDOM	
	BBC, Via Meyerton, South Africa	W • E Africa • 500 kW
		W M-F • E Africa • 500 kW
		W Sa/Su • E Africa • 500 kW
	BBC, Via Seychelles	W • E Africa • 250 kW
	†BBC, Via Zyyi, Cyprus	E Africa • 250 kW
		S • E Africa • 250 kW
	USA	
	R FREE ASIA, Via Tinian, N Marianas	S • C Asia • 250 kW
	†VOA	W • E Africa • 250 kW
	WORLD HARVEST R, Greenbush, Maine	S • Africa • 250 kW
17645	**CHINA**	
	CHINA R INTL, Via Santiago, Chile	W • S America • 100 kW
	USA	
	ADVENTIST WORLD R, Via Agat, Guam	E Asia • 100 kW
	VOA, Via Philippines	W • E Asia • 250 kW
17650	**CHINA**	
	CHINA R INTL, Kashi	Europe • 500 kW
		S • Europe • 500 kW
	GERMANY	
	DEUTSCHE WELLE, Via Sri Lanka	S • C Africa & E Africa • 250 kW
	USA	
	†R FARDA, Via Udon Thani, Thailand	S • W Asia • 250 kW
	WORLD HARVEST R, Greenbush, Maine	W • Africa • 250 kW
17655	**IRAN**	
	VO THE ISLAMIC REP, Sirjan	S • C Asia & E Asia • 500 kW
	THAILAND	
	RADIO THAILAND, Udon Thani	S • Europe • 250 kW
	USA	
	RFE-RL, Via Iranawila, Sri Lanka	W • W Asia • 250 kW
	WORLD HARVEST R, Naalehu, Hawai'i	E Asia • 100 kW
		Sa • E Asia • 100 kW
		Su-F • E Asia • 100 kW
17660	**IRAN**	
	VO THE ISLAMIC REP, Tehrān	C Africa & E Africa • 500 kW
		S Asia • 500 kW
	OMAN	
	R SULTANATE OF OMAN, Thamarīt	Europe & Mideast • DS • 100 kW • ALT. FREQ. TO 17630 kHz
	SAUDI ARABIA	
	†BS OF THE KINGDOM, Riyadh	W Africa & C Africa • 500 kW
	USA	
	FAMILY RADIO, Via Ascension	W • W Africa & C Africa • 250 kW
	SUDAN RADIO SVC, Via Skelton, UK	S M-F • C Africa • 300 kW
		S M/Tu/Th/F • C Africa • 300 kW
		S W • C Africa • 300 kW
		S • C Africa • 300 kW
		S Sa • C Africa • 300 kW
17665	**RUSSIA**	
	VOICE OF RUSSIA, Komsomol'sk 'Amure	W • Australasia • 250 kW
	USA	
	TRANS WORLD R, Via Merizo, Guam	S M-F • SE Asia • 100 kW
17670	**CHINA**	
	CHINA R INTL, Kunming	Australasia • 500 kW
	INDIA	
	ALL INDIA RADIO, Delhi	E Africa • 250 kW
	IRAN	
	†VO THE ISLAMIC REP, Sirjan	S • E Asia • 500 kW
	USA	
	ADVENTIST WORLD R, Via Madagascar	SE Asia • 250 kW
	†R FARDA, Via Wertachtal, Germany	S • W Asia • 250 kW
	RFE-RL, Via Iranawila, Sri Lanka	S • W Asia & S Asia • 250 kW
	RFE-RL, Via Kuwait	S • W Asia & S Asia • 250 kW
17675	**NEW ZEALAND**	
	R NEW ZEALAND INTL, Rangitaiki	Pacific • 100 kW • ALT. FREQ. TO 15720 kHz
	USA	
	R FARDA, Via Iranawila, Sri Lanka	W • W Asia • 250 kW
	R FARDA, Via Wertachtal, Germany	W • W Asia • 250 kW

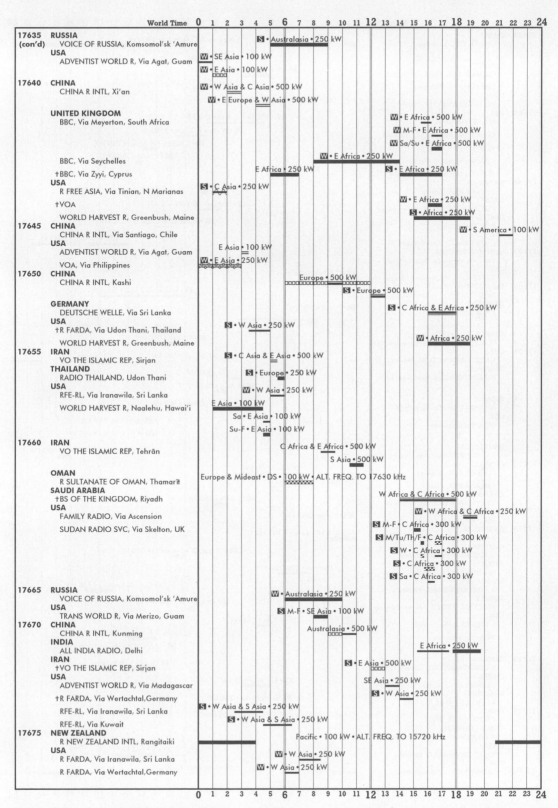

kHz	Country / Station	Schedule (World Time 0–24)
17680	**CHILE**	
	CVC-LA VOZ, Santiago	S America & C America • 100 kW
		W • S America & C America • 100 kW
	CHINA	
	CHINA R INTL, Kashi	S • W Europe • 500 kW
	CHINA R INTL, Kunming	SE Asia • 100/150 kW
	IRAN	
	VO THE ISLAMIC REP, Sirjan	W • C Asia & E Asia • 500 kW
17685	**USA**	
	RFE-RL, Via Kuwait	S • W Asia & S Asia • 250 kW
	RFE-RL, Via Udon Thani, Thailand	S • W Asia & S Asia • 250 kW
	†VOA	S • C Africa & S Africa • 250 kW
	VOA, Via Lampertheim, Germany	S • C Asia • 100 kW
	VOA, Via Udon Thani, Thailand	S • S Asia • 500 kW
17690	**CHINA**	
	CHINA R INTL, Jinhua	Australasia • 500 kW
	TURKEY	
	VOICE OF TURKEY, Ankara-Emirler	W • W Asia • 500 kW
	UNITED KINGDOM	
	BBC, Rampisham	W • W Africa & C Africa • 500 kW
	USA	
	†FAMILY RADIO, Okeechobee, Fl	W • W Africa • 100 kW
17695	**UNITED KINGDOM**	
	BBC, Via Meyerton, South Africa	C Africa • 500 kW
	USA	
	R FREE ASIA, Via Tinian, N Marianas	S • C Asia • 250 kW
17700	**CLANDESTINE (ASIA)**	
	"RADIO SOLH", Via Rampisham, UK	S • W Asia & C Asia • 500 kW
	GERMANY	
	DEUTSCHE WELLE, Via Sri Lanka	W • E Asia • 250 kW
		W • E Europe • 250 kW
	TURKEY	
	VOICE OF TURKEY, Ankara-Emirler	W • Europe • 500 kW
17705	**CUBA**	
	RADIO HABANA CUBA, Havana	S America • 100 kW
	GERMANY	
	DEUTSCHE WELLE, Via Sri Lanka	S • W Asia & S Asia • 250 kW
		S • E Asia • 250 kW
	INDIA	
	ALL INDIA RADIO, Bangalore	E Asia • 500 kW
	USA	
	VOA, Via Botswana	W • E Africa • 100 kW
		W M-F • E Africa • 100 kW
	VENEZUELA	
	RADIO NACIONAL, Via Havana, Cuba	S America • 100 kW
17710	**CHINA**	
	CHINA R INTL, Beijing	SE Asia • 500 kW
	CHINA R INTL, Xi'an	W Asia & C Asia • 500 kW
	GERMANY	
	DEUTSCHE WELLE, Via Sri Lanka	W • E Asia • 250 kW
	UNITED KINGDOM	
	BBC, Via Irkutsk, Russia	S • S Asia • 250 kW
17715	**AUSTRALIA**	
	RADIO AUSTRALIA, Shepparton	Pacific & N America • 100 kW
	AUSTRIA	
	†R AUSTRIA INTL, Moosbrunn	S • SE Asia & Australasia • 300 kW
	INDIA	
	ALL INDIA RADIO, Delhi	E Africa • 100/250 kW
	SPAIN	
	†R EXTERIOR ESPANA, Noblejas	S America • 250 kW
	TURKEY	
	VOICE OF TURKEY, Ankara-Emirler	S • E Asia • 500 kW
	USA	
	R FREE ASIA, Via Kuwait	W • S Asia • 250 kW
	VOA, Via Botswana	C Africa & E Africa • 100 kW
	VOA, Via São Tomé	W • C Africa & E Africa • 100 kW
17720	**CANADA**	
	R CANADA INTL, Via Urumqi, China	S • S Asia • 500 kW
	CHINA	
	CHINA R INTL, Kashi	← • Europe • 500 kW
	ROMANIA	
	†RADIO ROMANIA, Galbeni	S Su • Mideast • 300 kW
17725	**CHINA**	
	CHINA R INTL, Xi'an	C Asia • 500 kW • ALT. FREQ. TO 17730 kHz
	CHINA (TAIWAN)	
	†R TAIWAN INTL, Via Okeechobee, USA	S • S America • 100 kW
	LIBYA	
	†RADIO JAMAHIRIYA, Sabratha	C Africa • 500 kW
	USA	
(con'd)	†FAMILY RADIO, Okeechobee, Fl	S • S America • 100 kW

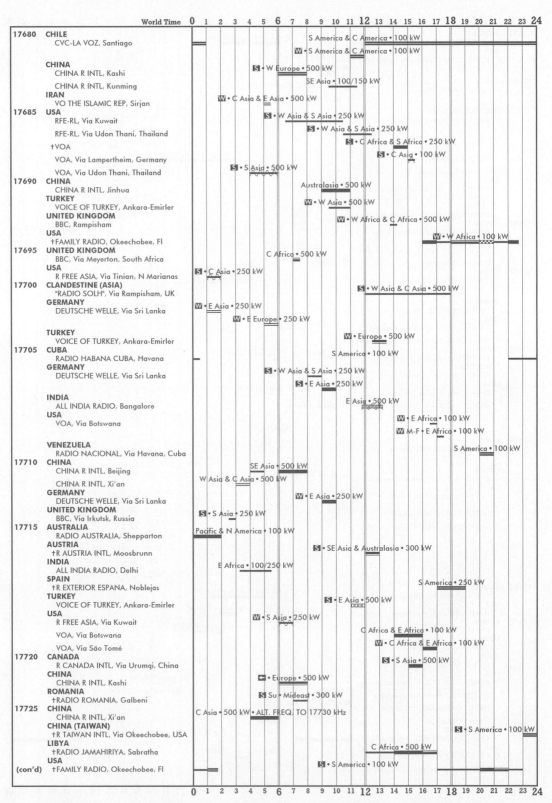

World Time 0 1 2 3 4 5 6 7 8 9 10 11 12 13 14 15 16 17 18 19 20 21 22 23 24

ENGLISH ARABIC CHINESE FRENCH GERMAN RUSSIAN SPANISH OTHER

kHz	Country / Station	World Time 0–24: Target • Power
17725 (con'd)	**USA**	
	†VOA	S Sa • C Africa & E Africa • 250 kW
17730	**CHINA**	
	CHINA R INTL, Xi'an	C Asia • 500 kW • ALT. FREQ. TO 17725 kHz
	SAUDI ARABIA	
	BS OF THE KINGDOM, Riyadh	N Africa • DS-1 • 500 kW
	USA	
	R FREE ASIA, Via Ulaanbaatar, Mongolia	S Asia • 250 kW
	RFE-RL, Via Lampertheim, Germany	S • W Asia & C Asia • 100 kW
	RFE-RL, Via Philippines	S • E Asia • 250 kW
	RFE-RL, Via Udon Thani, Thailand	W • E Asia • 250 kW
		S • E Asia • 250 kW
	†VOA	M-F • S Africa • 250 kW
	VOA, Various Locations	S Africa • 250 kW
	VOA, Via Botswana	S • C Africa & E Africa • 100 kW
	VOA, Via Lampertheim, Germany	S • W Asia & C Asia • 100 kW
17735	**CANADA**	
	†R CANADA INTL, Sackville, NB	S • W Africa • 500 kW
	CHINA	
	CHINA R INTL, Kunming	SE Asia • 100 kW
	CHINA R INTL, Via Sackville, Canada	W • W North Am • 250 kW
	JAPAN	
	†RADIO JAPAN, Via Issoudun, France	C Africa & E Africa • 500 kW
17740	**CHINA**	
	CHINA R INTL, Xi'an	SE Asia • 500 kW
	INDIA	
	ALL INDIA RADIO, Delhi	SE Asia • 100/250 kW
	NETHERLANDS	
	†R NEDERLAND, Via Madagascar	S • SE Asia • 250 kW
	SAUDI ARABIA	
	BS OF THE KINGDOM, Riyadh	W Europe • DS-1 • 250 kW
	USA	
	†VOA	W • W Asia & S Asia • 250 kW
	VOA, Via Iranawila, Sri Lanka	W • W Asia • 250 kW
		S M-F • E Europe & Mideast • 250 kW
17745	**PORTUGAL**	
	†RDP INTERNATIONAL, Lisbon	W M-F • C Africa & S Africa • 300 kW
	ROMANIA	
	†R ROMANIA INTL, Bucharest	W • W Europe • 300 kW
	†RADIO ROMANIA, Galbeni	W Su • N Africa & Mideast • 300 kW
	USA	
	†VOA	S • Mideast • 250 kW
17750	**AUSTRALIA**	
	†RADIO AUSTRALIA, Shepparton	SE Asia • 100 kW
	CHINA	
	CHINA R INTL, Kashi	S Asia • 100 kW
	USA	
	†FAMILY RADIO, Okeechobee, Fl	S • S America • 100 kW
		S • Europe • 100 kW
	†VOA	W • Mideast • 250 kW
	VENEZUELA	
	RADIO NACIONAL, Via Havana, Cuba	Irr • Su • N America • "ALO PRESIDENTE" • 100 kW
17755	**SPAIN**	
	†R EXTERIOR ESPANA, Noblejas	C Africa & S Africa • 250 kW
		Su • C Africa & S Africa • 250 kW
	USA	
	R FARDA, Via Biblis, Germany	S • W Asia • 100 kW
17760	**SAUDI ARABIA**	
	BS OF THE KINGDOM, Riyadh	E Africa • 500 kW
	UNITED KINGDOM	
	†BBC, Via Singapore	SE Asia • 100 kW
	†BBC, Via Thailand	S • E Asia • 250 kW
	USA	
	†FAMILY RADIO, Okeechobee, Fl	W • W North Am • 100 kW
		W • Europe • 100 kW
17765	**CANADA**	
	R CANADA INTL, Sackville, NB	W F-Su • S America • 250 kW
	USA	
	VOA, Via Philippines	S • E Asia • 250 kW
	VATICAN STATE	
	VATICAN RADIO, Sta Maria di Galeria	W Su • Mideast & W Asia • 250 kW
		W Su • SE Asia • 500 kW
		W F • Mideast • 250 kW
17770	**GERMANY**	
	DEUTSCHE WELLE, Via Ascension	W • S America • 250 kW
	PHILIPPINES	
(con'd)	RADYO PILIPINAS, Tinang	W • ENGLISH & TAGALOG • S Asia & Mideast • 250 kW

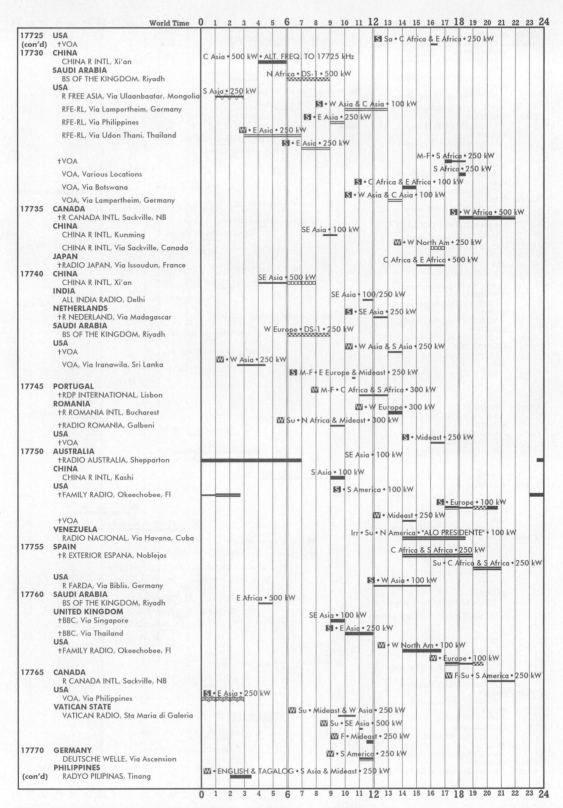

SEASONAL S OR W 1-HR TIMESHIFT MIDYEAR ⇦ OR ⇨ JAMMING / OR ⋀ EARLIEST HEARD ◃ LATEST HEARD ▹ NEW FOR 2009 †

World Time 0 1 2 3 4 5 6 7 8 9 10 11 12 13 14 15 16 17 18 19 20 21 22 23 24

kHz	Country / Station	Schedule
17770 (con'd)	**ROMANIA**	
	†R ROMANIA INTL, Bucharest	S • Australasia • 300 kW
	SOUTH AFRICA	
	†CHANNEL AFRICA, Meyerton	W • E Africa • 500 kW
	SPAIN	
	†R EXTERIOR ESPANA, Noblejas	Australasia • 250 kW
		W M • N Africa & Mideast • 250 kW
	USA	
	RFE-RL, Via Udon Thani, Thailand	S • W Asia & C Asia • 250 kW
	VOA, Via Udon Thani, Thailand	W • S Asia • 500 kW
17775	**AUSTRALIA**	
	RADIO AUSTRALIA, Darwin	SE Asia • 250 kW
	ROMANIA	
	†RADIO ROMANIA, Bucharest	W Su • Mideast • 300 kW
	†RADIO ROMANIA, Galbeni	W Su • W Asia • 300 kW
	SAUDI ARABIA	
	BS OF THE KINGDOM, Riyadh	W Africa & C Africa • 500 kW
	USA	
	KVOH, Rancho Simi, Ca	C America • 50 kW
17780	**IRAN**	
	VO THE ISLAMIC REP, Sirjan	W • C Asia & E Asia • 500 kW
	ROMANIA	
	†R ROMANIA INTL, Galbeni	W • Australasia • 300 kW
	†RADIO ROMANIA, Bucharest	W Su • N Africa • 300 kW
	UNITED KINGDOM	
	BBC, Via Ascension	W Africa • 250 kW
	USA	
	R FREE ASIA, Via Kuwait	S • S Asia • 250 kW
	VOA, Via Tinian, N Marianas	S • E Asia • 250 kW
17785	**AUSTRALIA**	
	†RADIO AUSTRALIA, Shepparton	Pacific & N America • 100 kW • ALT. FREQ. TO 15560 kHz
	IRAN	
	VO THE ISLAMIC REP, Sirjan	S • S Europe & N Africa • 500 kW
	ROMANIA	
	†R ROMANIA INTL, Bucharest	S • N Africa • 300 kW
	SAUDI ARABIA	
	BS OF THE KINGDOM, Riyadh	W Africa & C Africa • 500 kW
	USA	
	†VOA	W Sa • C Africa & E Africa • 250 kW
		S • C Africa • 250 kW
		S • W Africa & C Africa • 250 kW
17790	**CANADA**	
	†R CANADA INTL, Sackville, NB	W • W Africa & C Africa • 250 kW
	ROMANIA	
	†R ROMANIA INTL, Bucharest	W • N Africa • 300 kW
	UNITED KINGDOM	
	†BBC, Via A'Seela, Oman	S Asia • 250 kW
		S • S Asia • 250 kW
	BBC, Via Thailand	S Asia • 250 kW
17795	**AUSTRALIA**	
	RADIO AUSTRALIA, Shepparton	Pacific & W North Am • 100 kW
	UNITED KINGDOM	
	†BBC, Skelton, Cumbria	S • N Africa • 300 kW
	USA	
	†FAMILY RADIO, Okeechobee, Fl	S • W North Am • 100 kW
17800	**FRANCE**	
	R FRANCE INTL, Issoudun	S M-F • E Africa • 500 kW
		S Sa/Su • E Africa • 500 kW
		S • C America • 500 kW • ALT. FREQ. TO 15365 kHz
		S • E Africa • 500 kW • ALT. FREQ. TO 21620 kHz
	GERMANY	
	DEUTSCHE WELLE, Via Dhabayya, UAE	S • E Africa & S Africa • 250 kW
		W • C Africa & S Africa • 250 kW
	DEUTSCHE WELLE, Via Kigali, Rwanda	W • W Africa & C Africa • 250 kW
		W Africa & C Africa • 250 kW
	DEUTSCHE WELLE, Via Sines, Portugal	W • W Africa • 250 kW
	†DEUTSCHE WELLE, Via Singapore	W • S Asia • 250 kW
	DEUTSCHE WELLE, Via Sri Lanka	W • E Africa & S Africa • 250 kW
	INDIA	
	ALL INDIA RADIO, Bangalore	E Asia • 500 kW
17805	**FRANCE**	
	R FRANCE INTL, Issoudun	S • E Europe • 500 kW
	RUSSIA	
	VOICE OF RUSSIA, Irkutsk	W • Australasia • 250 kW
	SAUDI ARABIA	
	BS OF THE KINGDOM, Riyadh	N Africa • DS-1 • 500 kW
	USA	
	†FAMILY RADIO, Okeechobee, Fl	S • S America • 100 kW
17810 (con'd)	**CANADA**	
	R CANADA INTL, Via Skelton, UK	S • W Africa & C Africa • 300 kW

World Time 0 1 2 3 4 5 6 7 8 9 10 11 12 13 14 15 16 17 18 19 20 21 22 23 24

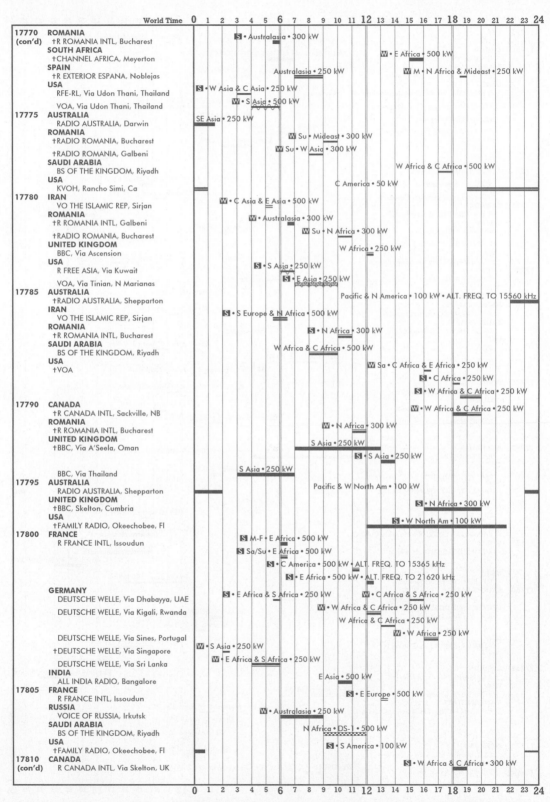

ENGLISH ARABIC CHINESE FRENCH GERMAN RUSSIAN SPANISH OTHER

kHz	Country / Station	Schedule (World Time 0–24)
17810 (con'd)	**EGYPT** RADIO CAIRO, Abu Za'bal	E Africa • 100 kW
	INDIA ALL INDIA RADIO, Panaji	SE Asia • 250 kW
	IRAN VO THE ISLAMIC REP, Sirjan	W Africa & C Africa • 500 kW
	JAPAN †RADIO JAPAN, Tokyo-Yamata	SE Asia • 300 kW
	NETHERLANDS R NEDERLAND, Via Neth Antilles	W Africa • 250 kW
	UNITED KINGDOM BBC, Via Ascension	[S] • W Africa & C Africa • 250 kW
17815	**BRAZIL** RADIO CULTURA, São Paulo	DS • 1 kW • [➡]
	USA RFE-RL, Via Iranawila, Sri Lanka	[S] • W Asia & S Asia • 250 kW
17820	**AUSTRALIA** CVC, Darwin	SE Asia • 250 kW
	GERMANY DEUTSCHE WELLE, Via Sri Lanka	[S] • E Asia • 250 kW
	SAUDI ARABIA †BS OF THE KINGDOM, Riyadh	S Asia • 500 kW
	USA VOA, Via Philippines	[S] • E Asia • 250 kW
17825	**PAKISTAN** RADIO PAKISTAN, Islamabad	E Africa • 100 kW
	PORTUGAL †RDP INTERNATIONAL, Lisbon	Irr • [W] M-F • E North Am • 300 kW
		[W] Sa/Su • E North Am • 100 kW
	ROMANIA †RADIO ROMANIA, Galbeni	[W] Su • W Europe • 300 kW
17830	**AUSTRALIA** CVC, Darwin	[S] • E Asia • 250 kW
	PHILIPPINES RADIO VERITAS ASIA, Palauig	E Asia • 250 kW
	UNITED KINGDOM BBC, Via Ascension	W Africa & C Africa • 250 kW
		Sa/Su • W Africa & C Africa • 250 kW
	†BBC, Via Meyerton, South Africa	[S] • W Africa • 500 kW
17835	**EGYPT** RADIO CAIRO, Abu Za'bal	S Asia & SE Asia • 250 kW
	PAKISTAN RADIO PAKISTAN, Islamabad	Mideast & W Africa • 250 kW
		URDU & ENGLISH • Europe • 250 kW
	USA R FREE ASIA, Via Saipan, N Marianas	[S] • SE Asia • 100 kW
17840	**GERMANY** †DEUTSCHE WELLE, Via Sines, Portugal	[S] • Mideast & W Asia • 250 kW
	USA †VOA	[S] • W Asia & S Asia • 250 kW
17845	**CHINA** CENTRAL PEOPLE'S BS, Shijiazhuang	[W] W-M • DS-1 • 100 kW
		[W] • DS-1 • 100 kW
	CHINA (TAIWAN) R TAIWAN INTL, Via Okeechobee, USA	[S] • S America • 100 kW
	GERMANY DEUTSCHE WELLE, Via Singapore	[S] • S Asia & SE Asia • 100 kW
	INDIA ALL INDIA RADIO, Delhi	Mideast & W Asia • 100/250 kW
		Irr • Mideast • HAJJ • 100/250 kW
	ROMANIA †R ROMANIA INTL, Galbeni	[W] • W Europe • 300 kW
	USA †FAMILY RADIO, Okeechobee, Fl	[S] • S America • 100 kW
		[S] • W Africa • 100 kW
	R FARDA, Via Iranawila, Sri Lanka	[S] • W Asia • 250 kW
	R FARDA, Via Lampertheim, Germany	[S] • W Asia • 100 kW
17850	**FRANCE** R FRANCE INTL, Issoudun	C Africa & S Africa • 500 kW
		[S] • C Africa & S Africa • 500 kW
		[S] • W Asia & S Asia • 500 kW
	SPAIN †R EXTERIOR ESPANA, Via Costa Rica	Su • W North Am • 100 kW
		Sa/Su • W North Am • 100 kW
		W North Am • 100 kW
		Irr • M-F • W North Am • 100 kW
		Irr • [W] Su • W North Am • 100 kW
(con'd)	**UNITED KINGDOM** BBC, Via Zyyi, Cyprus	E Africa • 250 kW

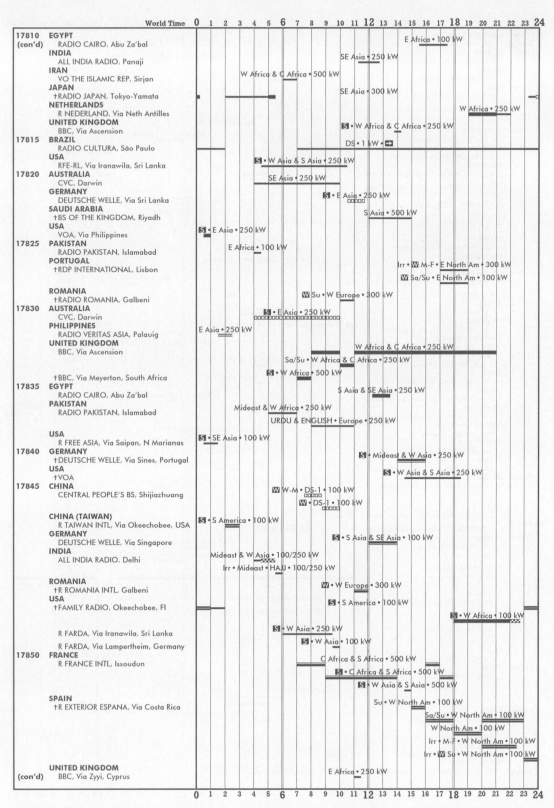

World Time 0 1 2 3 4 5 6 7 8 9 10 11 12 13 14 15 16 17 18 19 20 21 22 23 24

kHz	Country / Station	Service
17850 (con'd)	**UNITED KINGDOM**	
	BBC, Via Zyyi, Cyprus	W • E Africa • 250 kW
17855	**AUSTRIA**	
	†R AUSTRIA INTL, Moosbrunn	W • SE Asia & Australasia • 300 kW
	CHINA	
	CHINA R INTL, Beijing	C Asia • 500 kW
	USA	
	R FREE ASIA, Via Kuwait	S • S Asia • 250 kW
	VOA, Via Iranawila, Sri Lanka	S • W Asia • 250 kW
	VOA, Via Philippines	S • E Asia • 250 kW
17860	**AUSTRALIA**	
	CVC, Via Jülich, Germany	S • Mideast • 100 kW
	CANADA	
	R CANADA INTL, Sackville, NB	S F-Su • S America • 250 kW
	GERMANY	
	DEUTSCHE WELLE, Via Kigali, Rwanda	S • W Africa • 250 kW
	†DEUTSCHE WELLE, Via Sines, Portugal	S • C Africa & S Africa • 250 kW
	INDIA	
	ALL INDIA RADIO, Delhi	S Asia • 50/100 kW
		DS • 50/100 kW
		ENGLISH, ETC • DS • 50/100 kW
	JAPAN	
	RADIO JAPAN, Tokyo-Yamata	SE Asia • 300 kW
	PHILIPPINES	
	†RADIO VERITAS ASIA, Palauig	S Asia • 250 kW • ALT. FREQ. TO 11820 kHz
	SOUTH AFRICA	
	†CHANNEL AFRICA, Meyerton	W • E Africa • 250 kW
	†S AFRICAN RADIO LEAGUE, Meyerton	W Su • E Africa • 250 kW
17865	**CHINA**	
	CHINA R INTL, Kashi	S • W Europe • 500 kW
	GERMANY	
	†DEUTSCHE WELLE, Via Singapore	S • E Asia • 250 kW
	UNITED KINGDOM	
	BBC, Via Ascension	W • W Africa & C Africa • 250 kW
17870	**AUSTRIA**	
	†R AUSTRIA INTL, Moosbrunn	• Mideast • 100 kW
	IRAN	
	VO THE ISLAMIC REP, Sirjan	S • W Africa & C Africa • 500 kW
	JAPAN	
	†RADIO JAPAN, Via Issoudun, France	C Africa & E Africa • 500 kW
	ROMANIA	
	†R ROMANIA INTL, Bucharest	W • E Asia • 300 kW
	UNITED KINGDOM	
	BBC, Via Zyyi, Cyprus	W Asia & S Asia • 250/300 kW
17875	**INDIA**	
	ALL INDIA RADIO, Aligarh	SE Asia • 250 kW
	JAPAN	
	†RADIO JAPAN, Via Issoudun, France	W • W Africa • 500 kW
17880	**CHINA**	
	CHINA R INTL, Via Bamako, Mali	W Africa & C Africa • 100 kW
		N Africa • 100 kW
	USA	
	ADVENTIST WORLD R, Via Agat, Guam	W • E Asia • 100 kW
	R FREE ASIA, Via Saipan, N Marianas	E Asia • 100 kW
17885	**KUWAIT**	
	RADIO KUWAIT, Kabd	SE Asia • 500 kW
		E Asia & Australasia • 500 kW
	UNITED KINGDOM	
	BBC, Via Ascension	W Africa • 250 kW
		W Africa & C Africa • 250 kW
	BBC, Via Meyerton, South Africa	W Sa • E Africa • 250 kW
		W Sa/Su • E Africa • 250 kW
	BBC, Via Seychelles	E Africa • 250 kW
		S Sa • E Africa • 250 kW
	USA	
	†FAMILY RADIO, Okeechobee, Fl	S • W Africa • 100 kW
17890	**CHINA**	
	CENTRAL PEOPLE'S BS, Beijing	S • DS-1 • 100 kW
		DS-1 • 100 kW
		W-M • DS-1 • 100 kW
17895	**INDIA**	
	ALL INDIA RADIO, Aligarh	Australasia • 250 kW
	NETHERLANDS	
	R NEDERLAND, Via Neth Antilles	W • S America • 250 kW
	PAKISTAN	
	†RADIO PAKISTAN, Islamabad	SE Asia • 250 kW
	SAUDI ARABIA	
(con'd)	BS OF THE KINGDOM, Riyadh	C Asia & E Asia • DS-HOLY KORAN • 500 kW

World Time 0 1 2 3 4 5 6 7 8 9 10 11 12 13 14 15 16 17 18 19 20 21 22 23 24

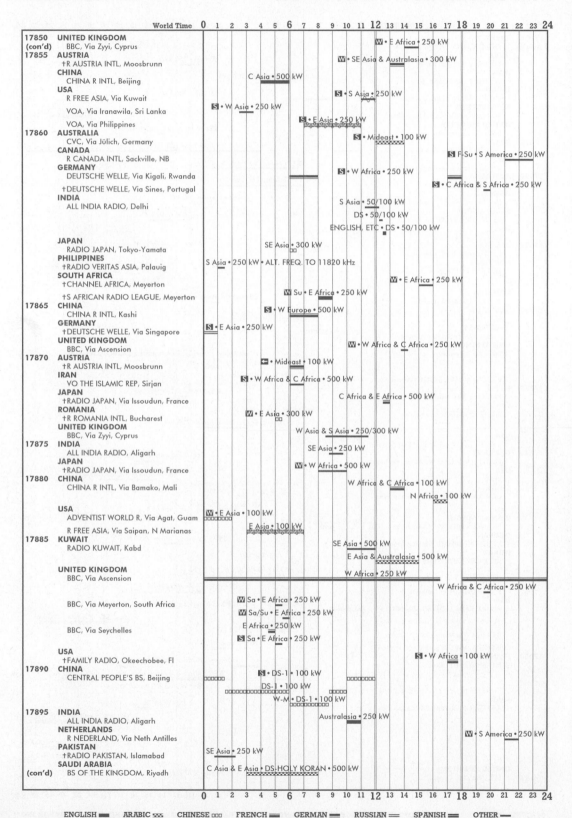

ENGLISH ARABIC CHINESE FRENCH GERMAN RUSSIAN SPANISH OTHER